SAP Transaction Codes – Volume Two

A Listing of Every SAP Transaction Code

By Stan X. Kubiyevski

First edition copyright 2017

ISBN: 978-1979771979

SAP Transaction Codes – Volume Two

In this series of books you will find a listing of every SAP transaction code in existence, based on SAP ECC6, ehp4

SAP Transaction Codes

Q000	Quality management
QA00	Quality inspection
QA01	Create Inspection Lot
QA01A	Create Inspection Lot
QA02	Change Inspection Lot
QA02A	Change Inspection Lot
QA03	Display inspection lot
QA05	Job planning: Periodic inspection
QA06	Job overview: Periodic inspection
QA07	Trigger for recurring inspection
QA07L	Deadline Monitoring Log
QA08	Collective Processing of Insp. Setup
QA09	No. range maintenance for insp.lots
QA10	Trigger automatic usage decision
QA10L	Log for Automatic Usage Decision
QA11	Record usage decision
QA12	Change usage decision with history
QA13	Display usage decision
QA14	Change UD without history
QA16	Collective UD for accepted lots
QA17	Job planning for auto usage decision
QA18	Job overview for auto usage decision
QA19	Automatic usage decision
QA22	Change inspection point quantities
QA23	Display insp.point quantities
QA32	Change data for inspection lot
QA32WP	QA32 -Call from Workplace/MiniApp
QA33	Display data for inspection lot
QA40	Auto. Usage Decision for Production
QA40L	Log for Automatic Usage Decision
QA41	Scheduling UD for Production Lots
QA42	Job planning: UD prod. insp.lots
QA51	Scheduling Source Inspections
QA52	Source inspections: Job overview
QAC1	Change insp. lot actual quantity
QAC2	Transfer stock to insp. lot
QAC3	Reset sample
QAER	Display archive objects
QAS1	Download Insp. Specs. (Obsolete)
QAS2	Download Basic Data (Obsolete)
QAS3	Upload Results (Obsolete)
QAS4	Upload UD (Obsolete)
QC01	Create certificate profile
QC02	Change certificate profile
QC03	Display certificate profile
QC06	Immediate delete of cert. profiles
QC11	Create cert. profile assignment
QC12	Change cert. profile assignment
QC13	Display cert. profile assignment

QC14	Create cert.prof.assign.w/copy model
QC15	Create cert. profile assignment
QC16	Change cert. profile assignment
QC17	Display cert. profile assignment
QC18	Create cert.prof.assign.w/copy model
QC20	Certificates for Deliveries
QC21	Quality certificate for the insp.lot
QC22	Quality Certificate for Batch
QC31	Archive display: Delivery item
QC32	Archive display: Inspection lot
QC40	Internet Certificate for Delivery
QC40A	Internet Certificate for Delivery
QC42	Batch certificate on WWW
QC51	Create certificate in procurement
QC52	Change certificate in procurement
QC53	Display certificate in procurement
QC55	Worklist: Certificates - Procurement
QCC0	QM: Direct Access to IMG
QCC1	Direct Access to IMG: Notification
QCC2	IMG Direct Access: QM Q-Notification
QCC3	IMG Direct Access: QM Q-Inspection
QCC4	IMG Direct Access: QM Q-Planning
QCC5	IMG Direct Selection: QM Bus. Add-In
QCCC	QM standard settings complete
QCCF	QM standard forms
QCCK	QM standard settings: Catalogs
QCCM	QM std. settings: Qual. notifs.
QCCN	QM standard number ranges
QCCP	QM std. settings: Quality planning
QCCS	QM sampling schemes
QCCT	QM standard texts
QCCU	QM standard settings: Environment
QCCW	QM std. settings: Quality inspection
QCCY	Transport QM tolerance key
QCCZ	QM std. settings: Qual. certificates
QCC_STABI	Copy Stability Study Customizing
QCC_STABI_NK	Copy Stability Study Number Ranges
QCE2	Edit Communication Support
QCE3	Display Communication Support
QCHECK	Check Query
QCMS	Certificate for Inspection Lot w. MS
QCYF	QM standard forms (general)
QCYT	QM standard texts (general)
QD21	Mark completed notifications
QD22	Archiving Notifications: Archive
QD24	Archiving Notifications: Delete
QD25	Archiving Notifications: Admin.
QD33	Delete quality level
QD34	Delete quality level planning
QD35	Delete job overview for Q-levels
QDA1	Edit sampling type
QDA3	Display sampling type
QDB1	Maintain allowed relationships
QDB3	Display allowed relationships

SAP Transaction Codes – Volume Two

QDH1	Q-level evaluation: Change data
QDH2	Q-level evaluation: Display data
QDL1	Create quality level
QDL2	Change quality level
QDL3	Display quality level
QDM1	Edit valuation mode
QDM3	Display valuation mode
QDP1	Create sampling scheme
QDP2	Change sampling scheme
QDP3	Display sampling scheme
QDR1	Create dynamic modification rule
QDR2	Change dynamic modification rule
QDR3	Display dynamic modification rule
QDR6	Disp. where-used list-dyn. mod. rule
QDR7	Replace dynamic mod. rule used
QDV1	Create sampling procedure
QDV2	Change sampling procedure
QDV3	Display sampling procedure
QDV6	Uses: Sampling procedures
QDV7	Replace sampling procedure used
QE00	Quality Planning
QE01	Record characteristic results
QE02	Change characteristic results
QE03	Display characteristic results
QE04	Record sample results
QE05	Change sample results
QE06	Display sample results
QE09	Indiv.display of charac.result
QE09WP	Call QE09 from Workplace
QE11	Record results for inspection point
QE12	Change results for inspection point
QE13	Display results for inspection point
QE14	Record results for delivery note
QE15	Change results for delivery note
QE16	Display results for delivery note
QE17	Record results for equipment
QE18	Change results for equipment
QE19	Display results for equipment
QE20	Record results for funct. location
QE21	Change results for funct. location
QE22	Display results for funct. location
QE23	Record results for phys. sample
QE24	Change results for phys. sample
QE25	Display results for phys. sample
QE29	No. Range Maint.: Conf. No. for Char
QE51	Results recording worklist
QE51N	Results Recording Worklist
QE52	Worklist: Results for phys. sample
QE53	Worklist: Record results for equip.
QE54	Worklist: Results for funct. loctns
QE71	Tabular res. recording for insp. pts
QE72	Tabular Results Rec. for Insp. Lots
QE73	Tabular res. recording for characs.
QEDS	Signature Process

SAP Transaction Codes – Volume Two

QEH1	Worklist for Mobile Results Rec.
QEI1	Displaying QM Interfaces Appl. Log
QEI2	Deleting QM Interfaces Appl. Log
QEW01	Results Recording on Web
QEW01V	Variant Maint.: Recording on Web
QF01	Record defect data
QF02	Change defect data
QF03	Display defect data
QF11	Record defects for inspection lot
QF21	Record defects for operation
QF31	Record defects for characteristic
QF4	Available queries
QF41_WD	Record Defects for Char./Insp. Point
QG09	Maint. num. range Q control charts
QGA1	Display quality score time line
QGA2	Display inspection results
QGA3	Print inspection results
QGA4	General QM Evaluations
QGC1	Qual. control charts for insp. lots
QGC2	Control charts for task list charac.
QGC3	Control charts for master insp. char
QGD1	Test Equipment Usage List
QGD2	Test Equipment Tracking
QGP1	Results history for task list charac
QGP2	Results History for Task List Charac
QI01	Create quality info. - purchasing
QI02	Change qual.information - purchasing
QI03	Display quality info. - purchasing
QI04	Job planning for QM procurement keys
QI05	Mass maintenance QM procurement keys
QI06	QM Releases: Mass maintenance
QI07	Incoming insp. and open pur. orders
QI08	Job overview of QM procurement keys
QISR	Internal Service Request
QISR1	Internal Service Request - Forms
QISRACTIVITY	ISR Activity
QISRCONF	ISR Wizard Initial Screen
QISRLIST	ISR Wizard: List of Scenarios
QISRSCENARIO	Customizing Szenario
QISRSCENARIO_OVS	ISR Scenario - Extended Search Help
QISRTRANSPORT	ISR Customizing Transport
QISRW	Internal Service Request on the Web
QISR_BCK	ISR: Popup for Editing in the Portal
QISR_PCR60	vc_scenario for Message type 60(PCR)
QISR_SM29	ISR Customizing: Table Transfer
QISR_SR12_START	Suggestion System
QI_DISPLAY_PLAN	Display Task List
QK01	Assign QM order to material
QK02	Display assigned QM orders
QK03	Maintain Specs for Order Type
QK04	Create QM order
QK05	Confirmed activities for insp. lot
QL11	Mat: Distribute Inspection Setup-ALE
QL21	Master Inspection Characs (ALE)

QL31	Distribute Inspection Methods (ALE)	
QL41	Distribute Code Groups (ALE)	
QM00	Quality Notifications	
QM01	Create quality notification	
QM02	Change quality notification	
QM03	Display quality notification	
QM10	Change list of quality notifications	
QM10WP	QM10 - Call from Workplace/MiniApp	
QM11	Display List of Qual. Notifications	
QM12	Change list of tasks	
QM13	Display list of tasks	
QM13WP	QM13 - Call from Workplace/MiniApp	
QM14	Change list of items	
QM15	Display list of items	
QM16	Change activity list	
QM17	Display activity list	
QM19	List of Q Notifications, Multi-Level	
QM50	Time line display Q notifications	
QMW1	Create quality notification (WWW)	
QM_FMEA	FMEA Cockpit	
QM_FMEAMONITOR	FMEA Monitor	
QM_FMEA_DISPLAY	Display FMEA	
QM_FMEA_RESIDENCE	FMEA: Determine Residence Duration	
QP01	Create	
QP02	Change	
QP03	Display	
QP05	Print inspection plan	
QP06	List: Missing/unusable insp. plans	
QP07	List: Missing/Unusable GR InspPlans	
QP08	Print task lists for material	
QP11	Create reference operation set	
QP12	Change reference operation set	
QP13	Display reference operation set	
QP48	Number Ranges for Physical Samples	
QP49	Number range for phys. samp. drawing	
QP60	Time-related development of plans	
QP61	Display change documents insp.plan	
QP62	Change documents ref.operation sets	
QPCP	Control Plan	
QPCP_NUM	Number Range for Control Plan	
QPIQS8	QM MiniApp Selection Variant	
QPIQS9	QM MiniApp Selection Variant	
QPNQ	Number ranges for inspection plans	
QPQA32	QM MiniApp Selection Variant	
QPQGC1	QM MiniApp Selection Variant	
QPQM10	QM MiniApp Selection Variant	
QPQM13	QM MiniApp Selection Variant	
QPR1	Create physical sample	
QPR2	Change Sample	
QPR3	Display physical sample	
QPR4	Confirm physical sample drawing	
QPR5	Manual inspection lots for physSamps	
QPR6	Create new phys.-samp. drawing w.ref	
QPR7	Storage Data Maintenance	

SAP Transaction Codes – Volume Two

QPV2	Maintain sample drawing procedure
QPV3	Display sample drawing procedure
QS21	Create master insp. characteristic
QS22	Create master insp. charac. version
QS23	Change master insp. charac. version
QS24	Display master insp. charac. version
QS25	Delete master insp. charac. version
QS26	Display characteristic use
QS27	Replace master insp. characteristic
QS28	Display insp. charac. list
QS29	Maintain characteristic number range
QS31	Create inspection method
QS32	Create inspection method version
QS33	Change inspection method version
QS34	Display inspection method version
QS35	Delete inspection method version
QS36	Display inspection method use
QS37	Central replacement of methods
QS38	Display inspection method list
QS39	Maintain method number range
QS41	Maintain catalog
QS42	Display catalog
QS43	Maintain catalog
QS44	Maintain catalog
QS45	Display catalog
QS46	Display code group use
QS47	Central replacement of code groups
QS48	Usage indicator - code groups
QS49	Display code groups and codes
QS4A	Display catalog
QS51	Edit Selected Sets
QS52	Display selected set index
QS53	Maintain individual selected set
QS54	Maintain selected set
QS55	Display selected set
QS58	Usage indicator - selected sets
QS59	Display selected sets
QS61	Maintain material specification
QS62	Display material specification
QS63	Maintain material spec: Planning
QS64	Display material spec: For key date
QS65	Activate material specification
QS66	Plan activation of material spec.
QS67	Job overview: Activate mat. spec.
QSFF	Customizing Template
QSR5	Archive inspection plans
QSR6	Delete routings
QST01	Create Stability Study
QST03	Display Stability History
QST04	Display Inspection Plans
QST05	Graphical Scheduling Overview
QST06	Scheduling Overview (StabilityStudy)
QST07	Change Testing Schedule Items
QST08	Display Testing Schedule Items

SAP Transaction Codes – Volume Two

QST09	Maintain Planning Building Block
QST10	Display Planning Module
QSUB	Define subsystems
QT00	Test Equipment Management
QT01	Test equipment management
QTSA	Product Allocations: Send Quantities
QTSP	Product Allocations:Send Customizing
QUERY_BP_FSBPBILDER	BP: Screen Customizing for Query
QV01	Create quality assurance agreement
QV02	Change quality assurance agreement
QV03	Display quality assurance agreement
QV04	Find Quality Assurance Agreement
QV11	Create technical delivery terms
QV12	Change technical delivery terms
QV13	Display technical delivery terms
QV14	Search technical terms of delivery
QV21	Create QA agreement (DocType Q03)
QV22	Change Q-agreement (doc. type Q03)
QV23	Display Q-agreement (doc. type Q03)
QV24	Find Q-agreement (doc. type Q03)
QV31	Create Q-spec. (doc.type Q04)
QV32	Change Q-specification (docType Q04)
QV33	Displ. Q-specification (docType Q04)
QV34	Find Q-specification (doc. type Q04)
QV51	Create control for QM in SD
QV52	Change control for QM in SD
QV53	Display control for QM in SD
QVM1	Inspection lots without completion
QVM2	Inspection lots with open quantities
QVM3	Lots without usage decision
QZ00	Quality Certificates
R2RMM126	Misc. Mass Update for Matl Master
R2RMM140	Monitor Changed Planned Prices
R2RMM142	Effect of recently changed price
R3A1	Customizing Events
RADKFCHK	Accessibility of Archive Files
RAEP1	Procedure for Single Records in MRA
RAEP1_VT_OLD	Procedure for Single Records in MRA
RAEP2	Procedure for Final Results: RA
RARCCOA1	Generate CO-OM Table Analysis
RARCCOA2	Analyze CO-OM Table Analysis
RARCCOA3	CO-OM Table Analysis: Periods
RARCCOA5	Simulation of CO line item summariz.
RARCCOAA	Table Analysis for CO_ALLO_ST
RARDB1	RDB: Archive Single Records
RARDB2	Delete Archived Single Records
RASRPDEL	Reorganization Single Records Proc.
RATRACE0N	Display Depreciation Calculation
RBDAPP01	Variante for RBDAPP01
RBDAUD01	Statistical Evaluations for AL
RBDCONCH	Variant for RBDCONCH
RBDCONCH_BCE	Consistency Check with WF Connection
RBDCPCLR	Variant for RBDCPCLR
RBDMANI2	Variant for RBDMANI2

SAP Transaction Codes – Volume Two

RBDMIDOC	Variant for RBDMIDOC
RBDMOIND	Variant for RBDMOIND
RBDSER01	Variant for RBDSER01
RBDSTATE	Variant for RBDSTATE
RBPCT	List of Customer Contacts
RBT_ENH_ACT	Update of Indirect Sales
RBT_ENH_CHECK	Check Variable Key
RBT_ENH_GEN	Generation of the Update
RBT_ENH_PLAN	Update of Indirect Planning Data
RBT_ENH_REBUILD	Reorganization of Infostructure S469
RBT_ENH_SIMULATE	Comparison of Info Structure S469
RBT_ENH_VB3	Comparison: Bill. Docs and Stats
RBT_ENH_VB7	Settlement Extended Rebate Agreement
RBT_ENH_VB8	List of Rebate Agreements
RC01_FICA	Comparison FI-FM for FI-CA Data
RCA00	Edit Generic Transaction
RCA01	Create Risk Object
RCA02	Change Risk Object
RCA03	Display Risk Object
RCA04	Copy Risk Object
RCA06	Delete Risk Object
RCC00	Configuration Menu for Risk Objects
RCC01	RO Control: Applications
RCC02	RO Control: Field Groups
RCC03	RO Control: Views
RCC04	RO Control: Sections
RCC05	RO Control: Screens
RCC06	RO Control: Screen Sequences
RCC07	RO Control: Events
RCC08	RO Control: Standard Functions
RCC09	RO Control: Additional Functions
RCC0G	RT Control: Tables
RCC10	RO Control: Search Help
RCC11	RO Control: Assign DB Screen
RCC12	RO Control: Modification Criteria
RCC15	RO Control: Application Transaction
RCC18	RO Control: Activities
RCC19	RO Control: Field Mod. per Act. Cat.
RCC20	Authorization Types
RCC23	RO Control: Data Sets
RCCFM	RT Control: GFORM Modification
RCCG2	Change trans. form
RCCG3	Display Transaction Form
RCCMREP01	Organization/Agent Time Report
RCCMREP02	Organization/Agent Call Vol. (DNIS)
RCCMREP03	Agent Activities
RCCMREP04	Agent Profile Report
RCCMREP05	Agent Profile Overview
RCCMREP06	PD Organization Profile - Detail
RCCMREP07	Document Flow Report
RCC_CUST	RCCF: Edit Destinations
RCC_LOG	RCCF: Log Display
RCC_PARAM	RCCF: Settings for Experts
RCC_SESSION	RCCF: Display Active Session

SAP Transaction Codes – Volume Two

RCC_VERSION	RCCF: Version Display
RCDEF	Definition of Risk Object
RCDEF_OLD	Definition of Risk Object
RCJCLMIG	Conversion report for free charact.
RCMPROACT2	Start RCMPROACT2
RCNPRECP	Activation of ECP Plan Versions
RCP02	Dummy Recipe Transaction for EH&S
RCP03	Dummy Recipe Transaction for EH&S
RCPOTPT	RMS-RCP: Recipe Output
RCP_NR	Maintain Number Ranges for Vers.
RCP_PPMIG	RMS-RCP: Process Parameter Migration
RDART_MERGE	Merge SAFT-PT files for Portugal
RDCA	Send Vendor Documents
RDCA_WIZ	Evaluate Vendor Document Interface
RDDDDATC_AUDIT_DISP	View
RDDPRCHK_AUDIT	Customer Tables without Log
RDDTDDAT_BCE	Check Table Logging
RDPT1	List of Redemption Schedule Sets
RDPT2	List of Redemption Schedules
RDPT3	Delete Redemption Schedule Sets
RDPT4	Delete Redemption Schedules
RDPT_FACTOR	Edit Drawing Factors
RE80	RE80: RE Navigator
REAJADJMCONTROL	Adjustment Control
REAJADJMCTRLRULE	Adjustment Control Rule
REAJADJMRULECTRLRULE	Adjustment Rule and Control Rule
REAJADJMVAR	Variables for Adjustment Control
REAJAHCN	Adjustments on Contracts
REAJAHRO	Adjustments on Rental Objects
REAJAT	Edit Adjustment Measure
REAJATAR	Archive Adjustment Measures
REAJATARE	Display Adjustment Measures
REAJATCHECK	Mass Check: Adjustment Measures
REAJATCOSTS	Costs Item Group for Rule
REAJATRP	Change Pers.Resp: Adjustment Measure
REAJBLREAS	Reasons for Adjustment Locks
REAJCEAEXPMC	Mass Change of Current Expenses
REAJCG	Edit Comparative Group of Apartments
REAJCG0001	CG: Applications
REAJCG0002	CG: Field Groups
REAJCG0003	CG: Views
REAJCG0004	CG: Sections
REAJCG0005	CG: Screens
REAJCG0006	CG: Screen Sequences
REAJCG0007	CG: Events
REAJCG0008	CG: CUA Standard Functions
REAJCG0009	CG: CUA Additional Functions
REAJCG0011	CG: Assignment Screen Fld->DB Field
REAJCG0012	CG: Field Modification Criteria
REAJCG0016	CG: Tables
REAJCG0017	CG: External Applications
REAJCG0018	CG: Activities
REAJCG0019	CG: Feldmod. per Activity (Control)
REAJCG0022	CG: Where-Used List: Structure

REAJCG0100	CG: Field Modification per Activity
REAJCG0102	CG: Authorization Types
REAJCG0103	CG: Field Groups for Authorization
REAJCG0104	CG: Screen Configuration
REAJCG0105	CG: Fld Mod. per Ext. Application
REAJCG0106	CG: Assignmt Object Part --> Memo ID
REAJCG0107	CG: Where-Used List: Views
REAJCGAR	Archive Comparative Groups
REAJCGARE	Display Comparative Groups
REAJCGCHECK	Mass Check: Comparative Apartments
REAJCGRP	Change Pers.Resp: Comp. Apartments
REAJCH	Continue Adjustment
REAJCHCEA	Continue with Adjustments - CEA
REAJCHECKINDX	Check Unmaintained Index Points
REAJCOSTSGRP	Costs Item Group
REAJCOSTSPOS	Costs Item
REAJEDIT	Process Adjustments Directly
REAJEPCRTD	WB: Calc. Formula - Expense Item
REAJINDX	Index Classes, Series and Points
REAJINDXCONV	Index - Rebasing
REAJMAXINC	Adjustment Rule Capping Provisions
REAJMETH	Adjustment Method
REAJMETHCOMB	Combinable Adjustment Method
REAJPR	Specify Adjustments
REAJPRCEA	Specify Adjustments - CEA
REAJPRTASK	Determine Adjustments - TASK
REAJREASON	Adjustment reasons
REAJREBASEINDEX	Rebasing of Index Points
REAJRLRAAMT	Value Table for Rep. List of Rents
REAJRLRAVC	Maintenance of Rep. List of Rents
REAJRLRAVCST	Structure Maint. for Fixt./Fittings
REAJRULE	Adjustment Rules
REAJRULECOMB	Combinable Adjustment Rules
REAJRULECOMP	Comp. Apartment Adjustment Rule
REAJRULECOND	Adjustment Rule and Condition Type
REAJRULEINDX	Index Adjustment Rule
REAJRULERLRA	Rep.List of Rents Adjustment Rule
REAJRULETASK	Adjustment Measure Adjustment Rule
REAJRV	Reverse Adjustments
REAJRVCEA	Reverse Adjustments - CEA
REAJSH	Display Adjustments
REAJSHCEA	Display Adjustments - CEA
REAT0001	AM: Applications
REAT0002	AM: Field Groups
REAT0003	AM: Views
REAT0004	AM: Sections
REAT0005	AM: Screens
REAT0006	AM: Screen Sequences
REAT0007	AM: Events
REAT0008	AM: CUA Standard Functions
REAT0009	AM: CUA Additional Functions
REAT0011	AM: Assignment Scrn Field->DB Field
REAT0012	AM: Field Modification Criteria
REAT0016	AM: Tables

REAT0017	AM: External Applications
REAT0018	AM: Activities
REAT0019	AM: Field Mod. per Activity (Contr)
REAT0022	AM: Where-Used List: Structure
REAT0100	AM: Field Modification per Activity
REAT0102	AM: Authorization Types
REAT0103	AM: Field Groups for Authorization
REAT0104	AM: Screen Configuration
REAT0105	AM: Field Modification per External
REAT0106	AM:Assignment Object Part --> MemoID
REAT0107	AM: Where-Used List: Views
REATFSVAR	Field Status Variant Adjust. Measure
REATFSVARFM	Field Modific. Field Status Variant
REATTYPE	Type of Adjustment Measure
REBDAO	Process Architectural Object
REBDAO0001	AO: Applications
REBDAO0002	AO: Field Groups
REBDAO0003	AO: Views
REBDAO0004	AO: Sections
REBDAO0005	AO: Screens
REBDAO0006	AO: Screen Sequences
REBDAO0007	AO: Events
REBDAO0008	AO: CUA Standard Functions
REBDAO0009	AO: CUA Additional Functions
REBDAO0010	AO: Matchcode
REBDAO0011	AO: Assgmt Screen Field->DB Field
REBDAO0012	AO: Field Modification Criteria
REBDAO0013	AO: Role Categories
REBDAO0014	AO: Role Category Groupings
REBDAO0016	AO: Tables
REBDAO0017	AO: External Applications
REBDAO0018	AO: Activities
REBDAO0019	AO:Fld Grouping per Activity(Contr.)
REBDAO0022	AO: Where-Used List: Structure
REBDAO0023	AO: Data Sets
REBDAO0100	AO: Field Modification per Activity
REBDAO0102	AO: Authorization Types
REBDAO0103	AO: Field Groups for Authorization
REBDAO0104	AO: Screen Configuration
REBDAO0105	AO: Field Grouping per Ext. Appl.
REBDAO0106	AO:Assignment Obj Part --> Notice ID
REBDAO0107	AO: Where-Used List: Views
REBDAOAR	Archive Architectural Objects
REBDAOARE	Display Architectural Objects
REBDAOCHECK	Mass Check: Architect. Objects
REBDAORP	Change Person Resp.: Arch. Objects
REBDBE	Process Business Entity
REBDBE0001	BE: Applications
REBDBE0002	BE: Field Groups
REBDBE0003	BE: Views
REBDBE0004	BE: Sections
REBDBE0005	BE: Screens
REBDBE0006	BE: Screen Sequences
REBDBE0007	BE: Events

REBDBE0008	BE: Standard GUI Functions
REBDBE0009	BE: Additional GUI Functions
REBDBE0011	BE: Assignment Screen Fld to DB Fld
REBDBE0012	BE: Field Modification Criteria
REBDBE0013	BE: Role Categories
REBDBE0014	BE: Role Category Groupings
REBDBE0016	BE: Tables
REBDBE0017	BE: External Applications
REBDBE0018	BE: Activities
REBDBE0019	BE: Fld Modif. per Activity(Control)
REBDBE0022	BE: Where-Used List: Structure
REBDBE0100	BE: Field Modification per Activity
REBDBE0102	BE: Authorization Types
REBDBE0103	BE: Field Groups for Authorization
REBDBE0104	BE: Screen Configuration
REBDBE0105	BE: Field Modif per External Applic.
REBDBE0106	BE: Assignment Object Part -> NoteID
REBDBE0107	BE: Where-Used List: Views
REBDBEAR	Archive Business Entities
REBDBEARE	Display Business Entities
REBDBU	Process Building
REBDBU0001	BU: Applications
REBDBU0002	BU: Field Groups
REBDBU0003	BU: Views
REBDBU0004	BU: Stages
REBDBU0005	BU: Screens
REBDBU0006	BU: Screen Sequences
REBDBU0007	BU: Events
REBDBU0008	BU: CUA Standard Functions
REBDBU0009	BU: CUA Additional Functions
REBDBU0011	BU: Assgmt Screen Field->DB Field
REBDBU0012	BU: Field Modification Criteria
REBDBU0013	BU: Role Categories
REBDBU0014	BU: Role Category Groupings
REBDBU0016	BU: Tables
REBDBU0017	BU: External Applications
REBDBU0018	BU: Activities
REBDBU0019	BU:Fld Grouping per Activity(Contr.)
REBDBU0022	BU: Where-Used List: Structure
REBDBU0100	BU: Field Modification per Activity
REBDBU0102	BU: Authorization Types
REBDBU0103	BU: Field Groups for Authorization
REBDBU0104	BU: Screen Configuration
REBDBU0105	BU: Fld Grouping Per External Appl.
REBDBU0106	BU:Assignment Obj Part --> Notice ID
REBDBU0107	BU: Where-Used List: Views
REBDBUAR	Archive Buildings
REBDBUARE	Display building
REBDCACHECK	Mass Check: Usage Objects
REBDCARP	Change Person Resp.: Usage Objects
REBDCOBJASSTYPE	Object Assignment Types
REBDCOBJASSUSED	Object Types for Obj. Assign. Types
REBDCOBJTYPEASS	Obj.Assignment Types per Object Type
REBDDEFPS	Definition of Pooled Space

REBDFIXFITCHAR	Fixt./Fittings Characteristics
REBDMSA	Maintain Measurement Types
REBDOCC	Occupancy Planning of Architecture
REBDOCCUSE	Occupancy Planning of Usage
REBDPR	Process Property
REBDPR0001	PR: Applications
REBDPR0002	PR: Field Groupings
REBDPR0003	PR: Views
REBDPR0004	PR: Stages
REBDPR0005	PR: Screens
REBDPR0006	PR: Screen sequences
REBDPR0007	PR: Events
REBDPR0008	PR: GUI Standard Functions
REBDPR0009	PR: GUI Additional Functions
REBDPR0011	PR:Assignment Screen Field->DB-Field
REBDPR0012	PR: Field Grouping Criteria
REBDPR0016	PR: Tables
REBDPR0017	PR: External Applications
REBDPR0018	PR: Activities
REBDPR0019	PR:Fld Grouping per Actvty (Control)
REBDPR0022	PR: Where-Used List: Structure
REBDPR0100	PR: Field Modification per Activity
REBDPR0102	PR: Authorization Types
REBDPR0103	PR: Field Groups for Authorization
REBDPR0104	PR: Screen Configuration
REBDPR0105	PR: Field Grouping Per Ext. Appl.
REBDPR0106	PR: Assign. Object Part --> NoticeID
REBDPR0107	PR: Where-Used List: Views
REBDPRAR	Archive Land
REBDPRARE	Display Properties
REBDRO	Process Rental Object
REBDRO0001	RO: Applications
REBDRO0002	RO: Field Groups
REBDRO0003	RO: Views
REBDRO0004	RO: Sections
REBDRO0005	RO: Screens
REBDRO0006	RO: Screen Sequences
REBDRO0007	RO: Events
REBDRO0008	RO: CUA Standard Functions
REBDRO0009	RO: CUA Additional Functions
REBDRO0011	RO: Assgmt Screen Field -> DB Field
REBDRO0012	RO: Field Modification Criteria
REBDRO0016	RO: Tables
REBDRO0017	RO: External Applications
REBDRO0018	RO: Activities
REBDRO0019	RO:Fld Grouping per Actvty (Control)
REBDRO0022	RO: Where-Used List: Structure
REBDRO0100	RO: Field Modification per Activity
REBDRO0102	RO: Authorization Types
REBDRO0103	RO: Field Groups for Authorization
REBDRO0104	RO: Screen Configuration
REBDRO0105	RO: Field Grouping per Ext. Appl.
REBDRO0106	RO: Assign. Object Part --> NoticeID
REBDRO0107	RO: Where-Used List: Views

SAP Transaction Codes – Volume Two

REBDROAR	Archive Rental Objects
REBDROARE	Display Rental Objects
REBDROCFAR	Archive Cash Flow of Rental Objects
REBDROCFARE	Display Cash Flow of Rental Objects
REBDRSRETURN	End Rental Spaces
REBDTIVBDMEASRO	Cust:Maint. Msrmnt Type per Usg Type
REBDTIVBDROFSTATUS	Cust: Maintain Field Grp per UsgType
REBDTIVBDROUSGREL	Cust: Maintain Usg Type per RO Type
REBFCR01	Generate Customizing Classes (TAB)
REBFCR03	Generate Table Buffer Classes
REBFCR04	Generate Update Modules
REBFCR05	Generate Business Object Types
REBFCR06	Generate Manager Object Types
REBFCR11	Template Classes for Generation
REBFCR12	Excluded Fields for Detailed Compar.
REBPZA	Applications
REBPZC	Role Types
REBPZD	Allowed Role Categories
REBPZE	BP grouping
REB_CONDTYPE	maintain rebate condition type
RECAAC	Allowed Object Types and Properties
RECAALVIMPORT	System Report ALV Variants
RECAALVTRANS	Transport RE ALV Variants
RECAARE	Archive Explorer
RECABDTSCR	Manager Subscreens in BDT
RECABT	Generate BDT Subscreen Containers
RECABUSOBJAPPLSTART	Start Business Object Display
RECACC	Check Customizing Settings
RECACDOBJREL	Change Doc. Objects per Object Type
RECACOLOR	Colors in the Application
RECACOLORTYPE	Types of Colors
RECACOPA	Parameters for Create with Template
RECACPROCESS	RE-FX: System Table Setting- Process
RECACPROCESSMODE	Processing Mode
RECACPROCESSSTEP	Process Step
RECACPROCESSTYPE	Process Type
RECACPROCSTEPABLE	Process Mode and Process Step
RECACUST	Display IMG for RE-FX
RECAGUICUST	System Settings: Interface
RECAIC	Icon Assignment
RECAICONFOR	Icon - Icon Area
RECAICONFORKEY	Icon Key for Icon Area
RECAKEY	Conversion of RE Key Fields
RECALA	Analyze Logs
RECALA_USER	Analyze Own Logs
RECALD	Delete Logs
RECALN	Number Range Maint: RECALOG
RECALP	Param. for Log Overview (Internal)
RECAPICCUST	System Settings: Background Graphic
RECARECURNO	Number Range Maintenance: RECARECUR
RECARG	Worklist: Update Objects
RECARS	Process Dates for All Objects
RECARSCN	Process Dates for Contracts
RECARSGEN	Generate Reminder Dates

SAP Transaction Codes – Volume Two

RECASHOWIMG   Display IMG
RECASTATOBJ   Possible Status Activ. per Obj.Type
RECATM   Manage Text Modules
RECATMCLIENTCOPY   Client Copy Text Modules
RECATRACE   Set Trace Options
RECAWBLIST   Overview Lists per Object Type
RECAWBNAVTOOL   Navigation Tools in Navigator
RECAWBREQTOOL   Tools for RE Workbench Requests
RECAWBTYPE   Object Types in the Workbench
RECAYA   Interface Implementation
RECAYB   Reasons for Registration
RECAYC   Object Statuses
RECAZA   Internal Performance Log
RECAZR   Retention Periods
RECDCA   Internal Calculation Rules
RECDCB   External Calculation Rules
RECDCC   Internal Distribution Rules
RECDCD   External Distribution Rules
RECDCE   Internal Condition Purpose
RECDCF   External Condition Purpose
RECDCG   Cash Flow Update for Contract
RECDCGOL   Cash Flow Update for Contract
RECDCGOLACT   Activate CF Update Contract w/o LD
RECDCH   Update Cash Flow for Rental Object
RECDCHGREAS   Maintenance - Change Reasons
RECDCOAJ   Adjustment Rules for Conditions
RECDCOND   Maintain Condition Types
RECDCONDGROUP   Maintain Condition Groups
RECDCONDGROUPCOND   Maintain Cond. Groups, Assignment
RECDCONDGROUPREL   Maint. - Condition Types -> Groups
RECDDC01   Derivation Tool:Maintain Transaction
RECDDC02   Derivation Tool: Rule Values
RECDDD   Due Date Correction Rule
RECDFIXPER   Maintenance - Fixed Periods
RECDFIXPERDATE   Maintenance- Periods of Fixed Period
RECDFLOWRELFLOW   Maintain Reference Flow Type
RECDFLOWTYPE   Maintain Flow Types
RECDFLOWTYPEREL   Maintain Flow Type Relationships
RECDZY   Maintenance-Conditions-View Cluster
RECDZZ   Test - Conditions
RECN   Process Contract
RECNAA   Contract Type Field Modification
RECNAB   Contract Type
RECNAD   ObjTypes Permitted For Contract Type
RECNAR   Archive Real Estate Contracts
RECNARE   Display Real Estate Contracts
RECNCFAR   Archive Cash Flow of Contracts
RECNCFARE   Display Cash Flow of Contracts
RECNCHECK   Mass Check: Contracts
RECNCUST   Display "Contract Types" RE-FX IMG
RECNDPMETHOD   Form of Security Deposit
RECNRP   Change Pers.Resp: Contracts
RECNZA   Notice Reasons
RECNZB   Reasons for Rejection

RECON1	Process Ext. Sec. Acct Statements
RECON2	Reconcile Ext. Sec. Acct Statements
RECON3	Delete Ext. Security Acct Statements
RECON4	Process Ext. Sec. Acct Statements
RECON5	Reconcile Ext. Sec. Acct Statements
RECON6	Delete Ext. Security Acct Statements
RECOPLACT02	RE: Planning -Change Activity Input
RECOPLACT03	RE: Planning - Display Activ. Input
RECOPLACTCOPY	Copy Actual->Plan for Real Estate
RECOPLCFCOPY	Copy Cash Flow to CO Planning
RECOPLCST02	RE: Planning - Change CElem/Act.Inp.
RECOPLCST03	RE: Planning -Display CElem/Act.Inp.
RECOPLCSTLAY01	Create Cost Element Planning Layout
RECOPLCSTLAY02	Change Cost Element Planning Layout
RECOPLCSTLAY03	Display Cost Element Planning Layout
RECOPLKYF02	RE: Planning - Change Stat.Key Fig.
RECOPLKYF03	RE: Planning -Display Stat.Key Fig.
RECOPLKYFLAY01	Create Stat. KF Planning Layout
RECOPLKYFLAY02	Change Stat. KF Planning Layout
RECOPLKYFLAY03	Display Stat. KF Planning Layout
RECOPLLAYIMP	RE: Import Planning Layout
RECOPLLAYTR	RE: Transport Planning Layouts
RECOPLPLANCOPY	Copy Plan->Plan for Real Estate
RECOPLPRM02	RE: Planning - Change Prim.CostElem
RECOPLPRM03	RE: Planning -Display Prim.CostElem
RECOPLREV02	RE: Planning - Change Revenue Elems
RECOPLREV03	RE: Planning -Display Revenue Elems
RECOPLSU	RE: Cost Element Planning for SU
RECOSESNG	CO Settlement of Real Estate Objects
RECOSEVAR	RE: CO Collective Settlement
RECOSEVAR_MAINT_CN	Variant Maint.Contracts f.CO Settlmt
RECOSEVAR_MAINT_OBJ	Variant Maint. Obj.for CO Settlement
RECOSTKFBD	Transfer Measmt to Stat. Key Figure
RECOSTKFSU	Transfer Measmt to Stat. Key Figure
RECPA100	General Corresp.(Arch.Obj.)
RECPA110	Master Data Summary(Arch.Obj.)
RECPA120	General Correspondence (BE)
RECPA130	Master Data Summary (BE)
RECPA140	General Letter (Land)
RECPA150	Master Data Summary (Land)
RECPA160	General Correspondence (Buildings)
RECPA170	Master Data Summary (Buildings)
RECPA180	General Correspondence (RO)
RECPA190	Master Data Summary (Rental Object)
RECPA200	General Letter (Parcel)
RECPA210	Master Data Summary (Parcel)
RECPA220	General Letter (Parcel Update)
RECPA230	Master Data Summary (Parcel Update)
RECPA240	General Letter (Land Register)
RECPA250	Master Data Summary (Land Register)
RECPA260	General Letter (Public Register)
RECPA270	Master Data Summ. (Public Register)
RECPA280	General Letter (Notice of Assessmt)
RECPA290	Master Data Summ.(Notice of Assessmt

SAP Transaction Codes – Volume Two

RECPA330	General Letter (RE Search Request)
RECPA340	Master Data Summary (RE Search Req.)
RECPA350	RE Search Request
RECPA360	General Letter (Contract Offer)
RECPA370	Master Data Summary (Contract Offer)
RECPA380	Contract Offer
RECPA390	Lease Abstract
RECPA400	General Correspondence
RECPA410	Master Data Summary
RECPA420	Contract Form
RECPA440	General Letter (Adjustment Measure)
RECPA460	Master Data Summary (Adj. Measure)
RECPA500	Contract Account Sheet
RECPA520	Invoice for Rent
RECPA550	Service Charge Settlement
RECPA560	COA Settlement
RECPA562	Annual Budget
RECPA564	Tenant Settlement
RECPA566	Statement of Reserve Fund
RECPA570	Sales-Based Settlement
RECPA580	Sales Report
RECPA590	Reminder of Missing Sales Reports
RECPA600	Adjustment
RECPA610	Approve Adjustment
RECPA620	Adjustment Approval Reminder
RECPA630	Notify About Adjustment
RECPA700	Notice/Confirmation of Notice
RECPDOC	Overview of Created Documents
RECPYA	Basic Settings and Doc. Templates
RECPYX	Supported Object Types
RECPZA	Basic Settings
RECPZE	Correspondence activities
RECPZF	Correspondence Applications
RECPZR	Output Documents
RECPZX	Supported Object Types
RECPZY	Supported Corresp.Applications
RECRWF	Customizing Workflow Recruitmnt Form
RECTHP01	IDE: Generation of FI Vendor Posting
RECTHP02	IDE: Generation of FI Vendor Posting
REDISND1	Create Electronic Bill
REDSLOADGEN	Generation of Program Loads
REDSRS01	Mass Syntax Check
REDSTAXBASEBUILD	Generate Tax Items to Be Distributed
REEXACCSTGNDAT	Electr. Account Statement: Test Data
REEXACCSTGNTXT	Electr. Acct Statement: Gen. File
REEXACRCARRYFORWARD	Balance Carry Fwd for RE Accruals
REEXACRPOSTTRANSFER	Transfer of ACE Documents
REEXACRPPRV	Reverse Contracts Accruals/Deferrals
REEXACRSHOW	Display Accrual Objects
REEXAI02	AIS: Autom. Generated RE Documents
REEXCNTYPE	Approval for Contract Type
REEXFB05	RE: Post with Clearing
REEXFB1D	RE: Customer Clearing
REEXF_26	RE: Incoming Payment Fast Entry

SAP Transaction Codes – Volume Two

REEXF_28   RE: Post Incoming Payment
REEXOUCOPY   Tables for Organizational Units
REEXOUCOPYEXCL   Tables to Be Excluded
REEXPL   Posting Log
REEXPOSTCC   Itemization for Settlement Units
REEXSET   Edit Sets
REEXSETGENBD   Generate Sets for Usage Objects
REEXSETGENCN   Generate Sets for Contracts
REEXSETGENSU   Generate Sets for SU
REEXZA   Document Type Determination
REEXZB   Tax Code Assignment
REEXZC   Replace Account Symbols
REEXZD   Assignment of Tax Transaction Key
REEXZE   RE Dunning Areas
REEXZF   Assign. User/Role Cat./DunningParam.
REFSITE   Reference site management
REGC0001   Applications
REGC0002   Field Groups
REGC0003   Views
REGC0004   Sections
REGC0005   Screens
REGC0006   Screen Sequences
REGC0007   Events
REGC0008   GUI Standard Functions
REGC0009   GUI Additional Functions
REGC0010   Matchcode
REGC0011   Assign Screen Field->DB Field
REGC0012   Field Grouping Criteria
REGC0013   Role Categories
REGC0014   Role Cat. Groupings
REGC0016   Tables
REGC0017   External Applications
REGC0018   Activities
REGC0019   Field Modifictn per Actvty (Control)
REGC0022   Where-Used List: Structure
REGC0023   Data Sets
REGC0100   GC: Field Modification per Activity
REGC0102   Authorization Types
REGC0103   Field groups for authorization
REGC0104   Screen configuration
REGC0105   Field Grouping per Ext. Application
REGC0106   Assign object part --> Note ID
REGC0107   Where-used list: Views
REISAJAT   Info System: Measure Overview
REISAJATCOSTS   Info System: Measure Costs
REISAJATCOSTSCEA   Info System: CEA Costs
REISAJATEXPENSE   Info System: CEA Current Expenses
REISAJATFINPLAN   Info System: CEA Financing Plan
REISAJATOBJ   Info System: Measure Objects/Meas.
REISAJATPRESTAGE   InfoSystem: CEA Prestage Adjustments
REISALIT   Accruals/Deferrals
REISAO   Info System: Architectural Objects
REISAOPO   Info System: Arch.Obj. - Cont.Occup.
REISBDOA   Info System: Object Assignment

SAP Transaction Codes – Volume Two

REISBE	Info System: Business Entities
REISBP	Info System: Objects for Partner
REISBPBD	Info System: Partner for Master Data
REISBU	Info System: Buildings
REISCDBD	Info System: Conditions for RO
REISCDCF	Info System: Cash Flow
REISCDCFOBJ	Info System: Object Cash Flow Contr.
REISCDCFVAC	Info System: Vacancy Cash Flow
REISCDCN	Info System:Conditions for Contracts
REISCDCNAJ	Info System: Cond./Adjustment Rule
REISCN	Info System: Contracts
REISCNBP	IS: Business Partners of Contracts
REISCNDP	Infosystem: Security Dep. Agreements
REISCNMS	Info System: Contract Measurements
REISCNNT	Infosystem: Notice on Contracts
REISCNNTRULE	Info System: Notice Rules
REISCNOA	Info System: Objects for Contracts
REISCNPE	Infosystem: Term of Contracts
REISCNRN	Infosystem: Renewal of Contracts
REISCNRNRULE	Info System: Renewal Rules
REISCOCSTACT	Costs/Revenue: Actuals Overview
REISCOCSTACTPLN	Costs/Revenue: Plan/Actual Comp.
REISCOCSTACTPRE	Costs/Rev: Comparison Actual PrevYr
REISCOCSTCMNT	Costs/Revenues: Commitment Overview
REISCOCSTPLN	Costs/Revenue: Plan Overview
REISCOLIBD	Actual Line Items - Master Data
REISCOLICN	Actual Line Items - Contracts
REISCOSKFACT	Stat. Key Figures: Actuals Overview
REISCOSKFACTPLN	Stat.Key Fig: Plan/Actual Comparison
REISCOSKFACTPRE	Stat.Key Fig: Compar. Actual PrevYr
REISCOSKFPLN	Stat. Key Figures: Plan Overview
REISITOR	Overview: Option Rates of RE Objects
REISITORCALC	Info System: Option Rate - Calcul.
REISJL	Info System: Joint Liability
REISLR	Info System: Land Registers
REISLRJL	Info System: Land Reg. - J.Liability
REISLRRG	InfoSystem: Land Reg. w/ RE Register
REISMMCAP	InfoSystem:Statement of Reserve Fund
REISMMCAPD	Info Syst: Reserve Fund Stmt Details
REISMSAO	InfoSystem: Measurements f.Arch. Obj
REISMSBD	Infosystem: Measurements - Mast.Data
REISMSCN	Infosystem: Measurements - Contracts
REISNA	Info System: Notices of Assessment
REISNAMF	Info System: Not. of Assessmt - Muni
REISNAVL	InfoSystem: Assessmt Not.-AnnualVal.
REISOF	Info System: Contract Offer
REISOFRES	Info System: Contract Offer
REISOO	Info System: Offered Object
REISPE	Info System: Other Public Registers
REISPL	Information System: Parcels
REISPLCS	Info System: Contaminated Parcels
REISPLDB	InfoSystem: Curtailmts and Benefits
REISPLDP	Info System: Parcels - Develop. Plan
REISPLER	Info System: Parcels - Easements

SAP Transaction Codes – Volume Two

REISPLLR	InfoSystem: Land Registers f. Parcel
REISPLMS	Info System: Parcels - Measurements
REISPLOBJ	Info System: Objects for Parcels
REISPLP	Info System: Predecessor Parcels
REISPLPF	Info System: Area Analysis
REISPLS	Info System: Successor Parcels
REISPLSL	Info System: Cad. Classifications
REISPLUS	Info System: Usages of Parcels
REISPO	Info System: Continuous Occupancy
REISPOCAP	Info System: Cont. Occupancy List
REISPR	Info System: Land
REISRADOCITEM	Item Overview
REISRC	Information System: Parcel Updates
REISREP	Reports of Info System
REISREPTREE	Info System Report Tree
REISRO	Info System: Rental Objects
REISROAS	Rental Objects -Assessment Contracts
REISROOC	Info System: Occupancy of ROs
REISRR	Info System: RE Search Request
REISRS	Information System: Reservations
REISRSOBJ	Info System: Reservation Object
REISRSSRV	Services for Reservation
REISSQMAIN	Start SAP Query
REITDS	Input Tax Distribution
REITDSOBJSHOW	Input Tax Distribution for Objects
REITDSRV	Reverse Input Tax Distribution
REITISTC	Overview of Correction Objects
REITORCALC	Option Rate Determin.: All Objects
REITORCALCDAILY	Option Rate Determin.: All Objects
REITORCALCSCS	Option Rate Determination for SCS
REITORSHOW	Option Rate Determ: Display Results
REITTC	Edit Correction Object
REITTC0001	TC: Applications
REITTC0002	TC: Field Groups
REITTC0003	TC: Views
REITTC0004	TC: Sections
REITTC0005	TC: Screens
REITTC0006	TC: Screen Sequences
REITTC0007	TC: Events
REITTC0008	TC: CUA Standard Functions
REITTC0009	TC: CUA Addit. Functions
REITTC0011	TC: Assgnmt Screen Field->DB Field
REITTC0012	TC: Field Modification Criteria
REITTC0016	TC: Tables
REITTC0017	TC: External Applications
REITTC0018	TC: Activities
REITTC0019	TC: Fld Mod. per Activity (Control)
REITTC0022	TC: Where-Used List: Structure
REITTC0100	TC: Fld Modification per Activity Cu
REITTC0102	TC: Authorization Types
REITTC0103	TC: Field Groups for Authorization
REITTC0104	TC: Screen Configuration
REITTC0105	TC: Fld Mod. per Ext. Application
REITTC0106	TC: Assignmt Object Part --> Memo ID

SAP Transaction Codes – Volume Two

REITTC0107	TC: Where-Used List: Views
REITTCAR	Archive Rental Objects
REITTCARE	Display Rental Objects
REITTCASSIGN	Assign Correction Objects
REITTCBASE	Overview of Input Tax Corr. Basis
REITTCCALC	Execute Input Tax Correction
REITTCCALCRV	Reverse Input Tax Correction
REITTCCALCSHOW	Overview of Input Tax Correction
REITTCCUST	Input Tax Correction IMG
REITTCID	Number Range Maint. Correction Obj.
REITTCNO	Number Range Maintenance: REITTC
REITTCPOST	InpTaxCorr: Manual Posting
REITXR	Display Planned Retirements
REITZA	Maintain Option Rate Methods
RELINVDOC	Call transaction MRBR from Portal
RELMJL	Process Joint Liability
RELMJLAR	Archive Joint Liabilities
RELMJLARE	Display Joint Liabilities
RELMJLCHECK	Mass Check: Joint Liabilities
RELMJLRP	Change Pers.Resp: Joint Liabilities
RELML00001	L0: Applications
RELML00002	L0: Field Groups
RELML00003	L0: Views
RELML00004	L0: Sections
RELML00005	L0: Screens
RELML00006	L0: Screen Sequences
RELML00007	L0: Events
RELML00008	L0: CUA Standard Functions
RELML00009	L0: CUA Additional Functions
RELML00011	L0: Assignment Scrn Fld->DB Field
RELML00012	L0: Field Modification Criteria
RELML00016	L0: Tables
RELML00017	L0: External Applications
RELML00018	L0: Activities
RELML00019	L0: Field Mod. per Activity (Control
RELML00100	L0: Field Modifcation per Activity
RELML00104	L0: Screen Configuration
RELML00105	L0: Field Mod. per Ext. Application
RELML00106	L0: Assignmt Object Part --> Memo ID
RELML10001	L1: Applications
RELML10002	L1: Field Groups
RELML10003	L1: Views
RELML10004	L1: Sections
RELML10005	L1: Screens
RELML10006	L1: Screen Sequences
RELML10007	L1: Events
RELML10008	L1: CUA Standard Functions
RELML10009	L1: CUA Additional Functions
RELML10011	L1: Assignment Screen Fld->DB Field
RELML10012	L1: Field Modification Criteria
RELML10016	L1: Tables
RELML10017	L1: External Applications
RELML10018	L1: Activities
RELML10019	L1: Field Mod. per Activity (Control

RELML10100	L1: Field Modification per Activity
RELML10104	L1: Screen Configuration
RELML10105	L1: Field Mod. per External Applic.
RELML10106	L1: Assignmt Object Part --> Memo ID
RELML20001	L2: Applications
RELML20002	L2: Field Groups
RELML20003	L2: Views
RELML20004	L2: Sections
RELML20005	L2: Screens
RELML20006	L2: Screen Sequences
RELML20007	L2: Events
RELML20008	L2: CUA Standard Functions
RELML20009	L2: CUA Additional Functions
RELML20011	L2: Assignmt Screen Fld->DB-Field
RELML20012	L2: Field Modification Criteria
RELML20016	L2: Tables
RELML20017	L2: External Applications
RELML20018	L2: Activities
RELML20019	L2: Field Mod. per Activity (Control
RELML20100	L2: Field Modification per Activity
RELML20104	L2: Screen Configuration
RELML20105	L2: Field Mod. per Ext. Application
RELML20106	L2: Assignmt Object Part --> Memo ID
RELML30001	L3: Applications
RELML30002	L3: Field Groups
RELML30003	L3: Views
RELML30004	L3: Sections
RELML30005	L3: Screens
RELML30006	L3: Screen Sequences
RELML30007	L3: Events
RELML30008	L3: CUA Standard Functions
RELML30009	L3: CUA Additional Functions
RELML30011	L3: Assignment Screen Fld->DB Field
RELML30012	L3: Field Modification Criteria
RELML30016	L3: Tables
RELML30017	L3: Extrnal Applications
RELML30018	L3: Activities
RELML30019	L3: Field Mod. per Activity(Control)
RELML30100	L3: Field Modification per Activity
RELML30104	L3: Screen Configuration
RELML30105	L3: Field Mod. per Ext.Application
RELML30106	L3: Assignment Obj. Part --> Memo ID
RELML40001	L4: Applications
RELML40002	L4: Field Groups
RELML40003	L4: Views
RELML40004	L4: Sections
RELML40005	L4: Screens
RELML40006	L4: Screen Sequences
RELML40007	L4: Events
RELML40008	L4: CUA Standard Functions
RELML40009	L4: CUA Additional Functions
RELML40011	L4: Assignmt Screen Field->DB Field
RELML40012	L4: Field Modification Criteria
RELML40016	L4: Tables

RELML40017	L4: External Applications
RELML40018	L4: Activities
RELML40019	L4: Field Mod. per Activity (Control
RELML40100	L4: Field Modification per Activity
RELML40104	L4: Screen Configuration
RELML40105	L4: Field Mod. per External Applic.
RELML40106	L4: Assignmt Object Part --> Memo ID
RELML50001	L5: Applications
RELML50002	L5: Field Groups
RELML50003	L5: Views
RELML50004	L5: Sections
RELML50005	L5: Screens
RELML50006	L5: Screen Sequences
RELML50007	L5: Events
RELML50008	L5: CUA Standard Functions
RELML50009	L5: CUA Additional Functions
RELML50011	L5: Assignment Screen Fld->DB Field
RELML50012	L5: Field Modification Criteria
RELML50016	L5: Tables
RELML50017	L5: External Applications
RELML50018	L5: Activities
RELML50019	L5: Field Mod. per Activity (Control
RELML50100	L5: Field Modification per Activity
RELML50104	L5: Screen Configuration
RELML50105	L5: Field Mod. per Ext. Application
RELML50106	L5: Assgnmt Object Part --> Memo ID
RELMLR	Process Land Register
RELMLRAR	Archive Land Registers
RELMLRARE	Display Land Registers
RELMLRCHECK	Mass Check: Land Registers
RELMLRRP	Change Resp. Person: Land Registers
RELMNA	Process Notice of Assessment
RELMNAAR	Archive Notices of Assessment
RELMNAARE	Display Notices of Assessment
RELMNACHECK	Mass Check: Notices of Assessment
RELMNARP	Change Pers.Resp: Notice of Assmt
RELMPE	Process Other Public Register
RELMPEAR	Archive Other Public Registers
RELMPEARE	Display Other Public Registers
RELMPECHECK	Mass Check: Public Registers
RELMPECSNO	Number Range Maintenance: RELMPECS
RELMPEPSNO	Number Range Maintenance: RELMPEPS
RELMPERP	Change Pers.Resp: Public Registers
RELMPL	Process Parcel of Land
RELMPLAR	Archive Parcels
RELMPLARE	Display Parcels
RELMPLCHECK	Mass Check: Parcels
RELMPLRP	Change Pers.Resp: Parcels
RELMRC	Process Parcel Update
RELMRCAR	Archive Parcel Updates
RELMRCARE	Display Parcel Updates
RELMRCCHECK	Mass Check: Parcel Updates
RELMRCRP	Change Resp. Person: Parcel Updates
REMIACCRUALGC	Migration of Accrual-General Contr.

SAP Transaction Codes – Volume Two

REMIACCRUALLOEXE   Migration LO Accruals - Update Run
REMIACCRUALLOSIM   Migration LO Accruals - Simulation
REMIBP   Migr. Class.RE-> RE-FX: IMG BP Conv.
REMICL   Migration from Classic RE to RE-FX
REMICLBATCH   Migration from Classic RE to RE-FX
REMICLCUST   Migration Classic RE to RE-FX (Cust)
REMICLCUSTAPPL   Migration Classic RE to RE-FX (Cust)
REMICLTRREQ   Transport Customizing/Decision
REMIC_TIVMISET   Basic Settings
REMIC_VIMIMAPCNNR   Contract Numbers
REMIREFXCUST   Display IMG for RE-FX
REMIZA   Activate Flexible RE Management
REMMBAMN   Compare Reference CoCd and Mandates
REMMBAPLANT   Compare Reference Plant - Mandates
REMMBUDGET   Create Annual Budget
REMMCCSET   Company-Code-Dependent Settings
REMMHB   Number Range Maint. for House Banks
REMMHBACC   House-Bank-Dependent Settings
REMMMN   Edit Mandate
REMMMN1   Edit COA Mandate
REMMMN2   Edit Object Mandate
REMMMNCHECK   Mass Check: Mandates
REMMMNID   Number Range Maintenance - Mandates
REMMMNRP   Change Pers. Responsible: Mandates
REMMMNSET   Settings Dependent on Mandate Type
REMMOBJADOPT   Transfer Objects to COA
REMN0001   MN: Applications
REMN0002   MN: Field Groups
REMN0003   MN: Views
REMN0004   MN: Sections
REMN0005   MN: Screens
REMN0006   MN: Screen Sequences
REMN0007   MN: Events
REMN0008   MN: CUA Standard Functions
REMN0009   MN: CUA Additional Functions
REMN0011   MN: Assignmt Screen Field->DB Fld
REMN0012   MN: Field Modification Criteria
REMN0016   MN: Tables
REMN0017   MN: External Applications
REMN0018   MN: Activities
REMN0019   MN: Field Mod. per Activity (Control
REMN0022   MN: Where-Used List: Structure
REMN0100   MN: Fld Modific. per Acktivity Custo
REMN0102   MN: Authorization Types
REMN0103   MN: Field Groups for Authorization
REMN0104   MN: Screen Configuration
REMN0105   MN: Field Mod. per External Applic.
REMN0106   MN: Assignmt Object Part --> Memo ID
REMN0107   MN: Where-Used List: Views
REORCOST   Costs of Reservation/Cont.Occupancy
REORCOSTPOSTPO   Posting of Continuous Occupancy
REORCOSTPOSTPORV   Reversal of Cont. Occupancy
REORCOSTPOSTRS   Posting of Reservations
REORCOSTPOSTRSRV   Reversal of Reservations

SAP Transaction Codes – Volume Two

REORMP	Move Planning
REORMP0001	MP: Applications
REORMP0002	MP: Field Groups
REORMP0003	MP: Views
REORMP0004	MP: Sections
REORMP0005	MP: Screens
REORMP0006	MP: Screen Sequences
REORMP0007	MP: Events
REORMP0008	MP: CUA Standard Functions
REORMP0009	MP: CUA Additional Functions
REORMP0011	MP: Assignment Screen Field->DB Fld
REORMP0012	MP: Field Modification Criteria
REORMP0016	MP: Tables
REORMP0017	MP: External Applications
REORMP0018	MP: Activities
REORMP0019	MP: Field Mod. per Activity (Cont.)
REORMP0022	MP: Where-Used List: Structure
REORMP0100	MP: Field Modification per Activity
REORMP0102	MP: Authorization Types
REORMP0103	MP: Field Groups for Authorization
REORMP0104	MP: Screen Configuration
REORMP0105	MP: Fld Mod. per Ext. Application
REORMP0106	MP: Assgnmt Object Part --> Memo ID
REORMPID	Number Range Maintenance: REORMP
REOROF	Edit Contract Offer
REOROF0001	OF: Applications
REOROF0002	OF: Field Groups
REOROF0003	OF: Views
REOROF0004	OF: Sections
REOROF0005	OF: Screens
REOROF0006	OF: Screen Sequences
REOROF0007	OF: Events
REOROF0008	OF: CUA Standard Functions
REOROF0009	OF: CUA Additional Functions
REOROF0011	OF: Assignment Screen Fld->DB Field
REOROF0012	OF: Field Modification Criteria
REOROF0016	OF: Tables
REOROF0017	OF: External Applications
REOROF0018	OF: Activities
REOROF0019	OF: Field Mod. per Activity (Contr.)
REOROF0022	OF: Where-Used List: Structure
REOROF0100	OF: Field Modification per Activity
REOROF0102	OF: Authorization Types
REOROF0103	OF: Field Groups for Authorization
REOROF0104	OF: Screen Configuration
REOROF0105	OF: Field Mod. per Ext. Application
REOROF0106	OF: Assignmt Object Part --> MemoID
REOROF0107	OF: Where-Used List: Views
REOROFAR	Archive Contract Offers
REOROFARE	Display Contract Offers
REOROFCHECK	Mass Check: Contract Offers
REOROFID	Number Range Maintenance: REOROF
REOROFRP	Change Pers. Resp: Contract Offers
REOROO	Edit Offered Object

REOROO0001	OO: Applications
REOROO0002	OO: Field Groups
REOROO0003	OO: Views
REOROO0004	OO: Sections
REOROO0005	OO: Screens
REOROO0006	OO: Screen Sequences
REOROO0007	OO: Events
REOROO0008	OO: CUA Standard Functions
REOROO0009	OO: CUA Additional Functions
REOROO0011	OO: Assignment Screen Fld->DB Field
REOROO0012	OO: Field Modification Criteria
REOROO0016	OO: Tables
REOROO0017	OO: External Applications
REOROO0018	OO: Activities
REOROO0019	OO: Field Mod. per Activity (Control
REOROO0022	OO: Where-Used List: Structure
REOROO0100	OO: Field Modification per Activity
REOROO0102	OO: Authorization Types
REOROO0103	OO: Field Groups for Authorization
REOROO0104	OO: Screen Configuration
REOROO0105	OO: Field Mod. per Ext. Application
REOROO0106	OO: Assignment Obj. Part--> Memo ID
REOROO0107	OO: Where-Used List: Views
REOROOAR	Archive Offered Objects
REOROOARE	Display Offered Objects
REOROOCHECK	Mass Check: Offered Objects
REOROOCREATE	Creation of Offered Objects
REOROOID	Number Range Maintenance: REOROO
REOROORP	Change Pers. Resp: Offered Objects
REORPDRES1	Reservation Price: Derivation Rule
REORPDRES2	Reservation Price: Derivation
REORPDSRV1	Service Price: Derivation Rule
REORPDSRV2	Price of Service: Derivation
REORPOMULTI	Continuous Occupancy Mass Processing
REORRR	Edit RE Search Request
REORRR0001	RR: Applications
REORRR0002	RR: Field Groups
REORRR0003	RR: Views
REORRR0004	RR: Sections
REORRR0005	RR: Screens
REORRR0006	RR: Screen Sequences
REORRR0007	RR: Events
REORRR0008	RR: CUA Standard Functions
REORRR0009	RR: CUA Additional Functions
REORRR0011	RR: Assignment Screen Fld->DB Field
REORRR0012	RR: Field Modification Criteria
REORRR0016	RR: Tables
REORRR0017	RR: External Applications
REORRR0018	RR: Activities
REORRR0019	RR: Field Mod. per Activity (Control
REORRR0022	RR: Where-Used List: Structure
REORRR0100	RR: Field Modification per Activity
REORRR0102	RR: Authorization Types
REORRR0103	RR: Field Groups for Authorization

SAP Transaction Codes – Volume Two

REORRR0104	RR: Screen Configuration
REORRR0105	RR: Field Mod. per Ext. Application
REORRR0106	RR: Assignmt Object Part --> MemoID
REORRR0107	RR: Where-Used List: Views
REORRRAR	Archive RE Search Requests
REORRRARE	Display RE Search Requests
REORRRCHECK	Mass Check: RE Search Requests
REORRRFE	RE Search Request - Ad Hoc Search
REORRRID	Number Range Maintenance: REORRR
REORRRRP	Change Pers.Resp: RE Search Requests
REORRS	Edit Reservation
REORRSIDINT	Number Range Maintenance: REORRS
REORRSOBJCOST	Change Account Determination Data
REORRSOBJCREATEUPD	Generate/Update Reservation Objects
REORRSPOST	Posting of Reservation
REORRSREC	Edit Recurring Reservation
REORSRVPROV	Services for Reservation
REORSRVRECV	Services for Reservation
REOR_HM_TRANSFER	Distribution of Arch. Objects
REPAST	I18N:repast transaction
REPORTING_AGENT	Scheduler Test Call
REPP1	CO-OM-IS User Settings: Customizing
RERAALCN	Accrual/Deferral: Contracts
RERAALCNRV	Accrual/Deferral: Reverse Contracts
RERAALCNRVIU	Accrual: Cont. Reverse Incept./Updt.
RERAALCN_PD	Accr/Deferral: Contracts PstgDate
RERADOCAR	Archive RE Documents
RERADOCARE	Display RE Documents
RERAINVNO	Number Range Maint: RERAINV
RERAIV	Create Invoices
RERAIVRV	Reverse Invoices
RERALA	Analyze Logs
RERAOP	One-Time Posting
RERAOPRV	Reversal of One-Time Posting
RERAOPSUTP	One-Time Posting: Transfer for SU
RERAOPSUTPRV	Reverse Transfer Posting for SU
RERAOP_MAIN	One-Time Posting
RERAOP_SC1100	One-Time Posting - Insurance
RERAPL	General Real Estate Posting Log
RERAPP	Periodic Posting: Contracts
RERAPPRV	Reverse Contract Postings
RERAVP	Per. Posting: Rental Obj.(Vacancies)
RERAVPRV	Reverse Vacancy Postings
RERAZA	Account determination values
RERAZB	Account Symbols
RERAZC	Account Determination
RERAZD	Posting Transactions
RERAZE	Tax groups
RERAZF	Tax Types
RERAZG	Accounting Systems
RERAZH	Default Values Tax Grp / Tax Type
RERAZI	Line Item Texts
RERFVICUP8	Check Prog Customizing Bank Statemnt
RESCA	Import A-tape

RESCAJ	Specify Adjustments for SCS
RESCAJAA	Adjustment of Assessments
RESCAJCO	Adjustment for COA Settlement
RESCAJTN	Adjustment for Tenant Settlement
RESCBC	Posting of Settlement
RESCBCAL	Posting of Accrual/Deferral
RESCBCCO	Posting of COA Settlement
RESCBCTN	Posting of Tenant Settlement
RESCCC	Generate Cost Collector
RESCCH	Continue a Service Charge Settlement
RESCCHAA	Continue Assessment Adjustment
RESCCHAL	Continuation of Accrual/Deferral
RESCCHCO	Continue COA Settlement
RESCCHTN	Continue Tenant Settlement
RESCD	Import D-tape
RESCDC	Distribution Overview
RESCDCO	Import D-Tape for COA
RESCD_BY_EVALGRP	Import D-Tape by Evaluation Group
RESCFIX	Store a Simulated SC Settlement
RESCFIXAL	Storing of Accrual/Deferral
RESCFIXCO	Store a COA Settlement
RESCFIXTN	Store a Tenant Settlement
RESCGC	Cost Overview
RESCIS	Report for Service Charge Settlement
RESCISAA	Report on Assessment Adjustment
RESCISAL	Evaluation of Accrual/Deferral
RESCISCO	Report on COA Settlement
RESCISMULTI	Report on Multiple Settlements
RESCISMULTIRO	Report on Multiple Settlements
RESCISTN	Report on Tenant Settlement
RESCML	Create M/L-Tape
RESCMLCO	Create M/L-Tape for COA
RESCMOAL	Change of Accrual/Deferral Results
RESCMOBEAL	Change of Accrual/Deferral Results
RESCMPRO	Display Meters for Rental Objects
RESCMPSU	Meters for Settlement Units
RESCPG	Process Participation Group
RESCPG0001	PG: Applications
RESCPG0002	PG: Field Groups
RESCPG0003	PG: Views
RESCPG0004	PG: Sections
RESCPG0005	PG: Screens
RESCPG0006	PG: Screen Sequences
RESCPG0007	PG: Events
RESCPG0008	PG: CUA Standard Functions
RESCPG0009	PG: CUA Additional Functions
RESCPG0011	PG: Assignment Screen Fld->DB-Field
RESCPG0012	PG: Field Modification Criteria
RESCPG0013	PG: Role Categories
RESCPG0014	PG: Role Category Grouping
RESCPG0016	PG: Tables
RESCPG0017	PG: External Applications
RESCPG0018	PG: Activities
RESCPG0019	PG: Fld Mod. per Activity (Control)

RESCPG0022	PG: Where-Used List: Structure
RESCPG0100	PG: Field Modification per Activity
RESCPG0102	PG: Authorization Types
RESCPG0103	PG: Field Groups for Authorization
RESCPG0104	PG: Screen Configuration
RESCPG0105	PG: Fld Modif. per External Applic.
RESCPG0106	PG: Assignment ObjectPart --> MemoID
RESCPG0107	PG: Where-Used List: Views
RESCPGAR	Archive Participation Groups
RESCPGARE	Display Participation Groups
RESCPGCHECK	Mass Check: Participation Groups
RESCPGRO	Rental Objects for Particip.Groups
RESCPGRP	Change Pers.Resp: Particip. Groups
RESCROSU	Settlement Units for Rental Objects
RESCRV	Reversal of Service Chg Settlement
RESCRVAA	Reversal of Assessment Adjustment
RESCRVAL	Reversal of Accrual/Deferral
RESCRVCO	Reversal of COA Settlement
RESCRVTN	Reversal of Tenant Settlement
RESCSE	Service Charge Settlement
RESCSEAA	Assessment Adjustment
RESCSEAL	Accrual/Deferral
RESCSEAR	Archive SC Settlements
RESCSEARE	Display SC Settlements
RESCSECO	COA Settlement
RESCSESTATUS	Current Settlement Periods per SU
RESCSESTATUSPER	Settlement Periods of SU
RESCSETASK	Service Charge Settlement
RESCSETN	Tenant Settlement
RESCSP	Settlement Participation
RESCSU	Edit Settlement Unit
RESCSU0001	SU: Applications
RESCSU0002	SU: Field Groups
RESCSU0003	SU: Views
RESCSU0004	SU: Sections
RESCSU0005	SU: Screens
RESCSU0006	SU: Screen Sequences
RESCSU0007	SU: Events
RESCSU0008	SU: CUA Standard Functions
RESCSU0009	SU: CUA Additional Functions
RESCSU0011	SU: Assignment Screen Fld->DB Field
RESCSU0012	SU: Field Modification Criteria
RESCSU0013	SU: Role Categories
RESCSU0014	SU: Role Category Groupings
RESCSU0016	SU: Tables
RESCSU0017	SU: Non-SAP Applications
RESCSU0018	SU: Activities
RESCSU0019	SU: Field Mod. per Activity (Control
RESCSU0022	SU: Where-Used List: Structure
RESCSU0100	SU: Field Modification per Activity
RESCSU0102	SU: Authorization Types
RESCSU0103	SU: Field Grops for Authorization
RESCSU0104	SU: Screen Configuration
RESCSU0105	SU: Field Mod. per Non-SAP Applic.

RESCSU0106	SU: Assigment Obj.Part --> Memo ID
RESCSU0107	SU: Where-Used List: Views
RESCSUAR	Archive Settlement Units
RESCSUARE	Display Settlement Units
RESCSUBYBE	Collective Creation of SUs
RESCSUCHECK	Mass Check: Settlement Units
RESCSURO	Rental Objects for Settlement Units
RESCSURP	Change Pers.Resp: Settlement Unit
RESCSUSHAREOUT	Allocation Rules of Settlement Unit
RESCZD	Settlement Parameters
RESCZE	Settlement and Settlement Steps
RESCZF	Settlement Types
RESCZG	Settlement Methods
RESCZH	Char. of Service Charge Settlmt Keys
RESCZI	Characteristics-Settlement Companies
RESCZJ	Settlement Participation
RESCZK	Purpose
RESCZL	Which Step Is Dependent on Which
RESCZM	Possible Settlement Steps
RESRBC	Posting of Settlement
RESRBCSINGLE	Posting of Settlement
RESRCL	Display Results of Calculation
RESRIS	Report on Sales-Based Settlement
RESRISSINGLE	Report on Sales-Based Settlement
RESRMO	Change Results
RESRMOSINGLE	Change Results
RESRRP	Collective Entry of Sales Reports
RESRRV	Reversal of Sales-Based Settlement
RESRRVERR	Reversal for Incorrect Settlement
RESRRVSINGLE	Reversal of Sales-Based Settlement
RESRSE	Sales-Based Rent Settlement
RESRSECORRECT	Adjustment of Sales-Based Settlement
RESRSESINGLE	Sales-Based Rent Settlement
RESRSETASK	Sales-Based Settlement
RETAIL_ACTIVATE	Retail Ledger: Activation
RETAIL_BLOCK	Retail Ledger: Block Company Codes
RETAIL_GB01	Retail Ledger: Post Document
RETAIL_GCU1	Retail Ledger: Transfer Data from FI
RETAIL_GCU3	Retail Ledger: Transfer CO Act. Data
RETAIL_GCU6	Retail Ledger: Transfer CO Plan Data
RETAIL_GVTR	Balance C/F Retail Ledger
RETAIL_ITEMS	Line Items Retail Ledger
RETAIL_SUBPOST	Retail Ledger: Allow Subsequent Post
RETAIL_TOTALS	Retail Ledger:Display Totals Records
RETAIL_VERSIONS	Retail Ledger: Block Company Codes
RETMZA	Groups of Term Categories
RETMZB	Term Categories
RETMZE	Notice Rules - Period Regulations
RETMZF	Notice Rules - Deadline Regulations
RETMZG	Notice Procedures
REWBMODESTART	RE80: Start New Mode
REXCAJLOCCH01	Location for Adj.Rule and Off.Lang.
REXCAJMGRCH01	Maintain Pass On Rates for Mrtg Rate
REXCAJMICNCH01	LO Migration: Adj. Data - Swiss Law

REXCAJMIROCH01   RO Migration: Adj. Data - Swiss Law
REXCAJRULECH01   Adjustment Rule per Swiss Law
REXCCL   Read Fuel Level
REXCCPCHA400   CH Law: Graduated Rent
REXCFC   Determine Consumption
REXCFCMIFSCH   Migration: Fuel Level
REXCFFS   Enter Mass Process. of Ending Level
REXCFL   Overview of Fuel Screen
REXCFOB   Enter Mass Process. of Initial Level
REXCFR   Reverse Consumption
REXCFT   Mass Processing of Fuel Additions
REXCITICI   ICI Cockpit
REXCITIRE   IRE Cockpit
REXCJPCOSTDISTR   RFREXCJPSCSCONSCOSTDISTR
REXCJPFORMS179   RFREXCJPFORMS179
REXCJPFUP   Fixed Unit Price Maintenance
REXCJPPAYMENTREP   Payment Charge Report
REXCMS   Main Rent Statement
REXCMSCE   Number Range Maintenance: REXCMSCE
REXCOTSHOW   Log for VAT Calculation
REXCPTIMI   IMI Cockpit
REXCRAESRASS   Assignment POR Vendor Inv./Cash Flow
REXCRAESRPARAM   Read ISR Payments Parameter
REXCSCCHCR   Reverse Measurement Documents
REXCSCCHCT   Create Tape
REXCSCCHET   Process Imported Tape
REXCSCCHIT   Import Tape
REXCSCCHTAPE   Tape Management
RE_HR_SYNC_PERSON   For Report HR_SYNC_PERSON
RE_MASS   Rental Unit Mass Change
RE_RHAKTI00   Change Object Status
RE_RHALEACU   HR: ALE Auto Customizing HR-RW/LO
RE_RHALEBAPIPROOF   HR: Import BAPI Data Online
RE_RHALECLEANRELA   HR: Clean Relationships
RE_RHALECPS   HR: Display ALE Change Pointers
RE_RHALEHRMDORIGINIT   HR: Initialize Orig.Sys. - Plan.Data
RE_RHALEHRMDORIGXPER   HR: Maintain HRMDORIGIN (Experts)
RE_RHALEORGMOVE   HR: Transfer Planning Data
RE_RHALEORIGINIT_APP   HR: Initialize Appl. Original System
RE_RHALEORIGINIT_EMP   HR: Initialize EE Original System
RE_RHALEORIGLIST   HR: Orig.System List - Planning Data
RE_RHALEORIGLIST_APP   HR: Original System List for Appl.
RE_RHALEORIGLIST_EMP   HR: Original System List for EEs
RE_RHALERELAX   HR: Expert Relationship Cleanup
RE_RHALESERCHECK   HR: Check Registration
RE_RHALESMD   HR: Evaluate ALE Change Pointers
RE_RHALE_HRMDRGIN   HR: Maintain HRMDRGIN
RE_RHALE_HRMDRGOUT   HR: Maintain HRMDRGOUT
RE_RHALE_RGIN2IDOC   HR: Adjust HRMDRGIN to IDoc
RE_RHAUTH00   Authorized Objects
RE_RHBEGDA0   Change start date
RE_RHCHECK1   Check Database Consistency
RE_RHCHECKV   Check Relationships
RE_RHCHEXOB   Reconcile Infotypes Ext. Objects

RE_RHCOPL00	Copy Plan Version W/O Comparison
RE_RHCOPLPT	Reconcile Plan Versions (Partly)
RE_RHCOPY00	Copy Object
RE_RHCOPY10	Copy Objects Using Selection List
RE_RHCOPYSTRUCT	Copy structures
RE_RHDBST00	PD Database Statistics
RE_RHDBST10	Database Statistics: No. of Objects
RE_RHDBST20	Database Statistics: No. of Notes
RE_RHDBST30	Database Statistics: Infotype
RE_RHDBST40	Database Statistics: Infotypes
RE_RHDESC10	Display Infotypes of an Object
RE_RHEXIST0	Existing Objects
RE_RHGRENZ0	Delimit Objects
RE_RHGRENZ1	Set New End Date
RE_RHGRENZ2	Delimit Infotypes
RE_RHGRENZ4	Set new end date for infotypes
RE_RHINFAW0	Infotype Reporting
RE_RHMOVE30	Manual Transport Link
RE_RHNAVIG0	Structure Navigation Instrument
RE_RHPNPSUB	Start PA Reporting via PD
RE_RHREFDOC0	Reference Document Reporting
RE_RHREPL20	Replace User With Person
RE_RHRHAZ00	Display PD Database Records
RE_RHRHDC00	Delete HR Database Records via List
RE_RHRHDL00	Delete PD Database Records
RE_RHSOLO	Planned labor costs
RE_RHTRANS0	Translate Language-Dependent Records
RE_RHU_INF_BPD_ACT	Activation Infotypes for Budget Per.
RE_RHU_INF_BPD_UPD	Update Infotypes for Budget Period
RE_RHVOPOS1	Obsolete positions
RE_RHVSTA00	Database Statistics: No. of Objects
RE_RHVSTA10	Database Statistics: No. of Notes
RE_RHVSTA20	Database Statistics: Infotype
RE_RHVSTA30	Database Statistics: Infotypes
RE_RHXDESC0	Job Description
RE_RHXDESC1	Position Description
RE_RHXEXI00	Existing Organizational Units
RE_RHXEXI01	Existing Work Centers
RE_RHXEXI02	Existing Jobs
RE_RHXEXI03	Existing Positions
RE_RHXEXI04	Existing Tasks
RE_RHXFILLPOS	Time period of unoccupied positions
RE_RHXHFMT0	Authorities and Resources
RE_RHXIAW00	Work Centers with Restrictions
RE_RHXIAW01	Single Work Centers with Restriction
RE_RHXIAW02	Work Centers with Health Exams
RE_RHXIAW03	Single Work Centers with Health Exam
RE_RHXIAW04	Character of Tasks
RE_RHXIAW05	Character of Individual Tasks
RE_RHXSBES0	Staff assignments
RE_RHXSOLO0	Planned Labor Costs
RE_RHXSSREF	Instructor Information
RE_RHXSSTL1	Attendees (Organizational Unit)
RE_RHXSSTL2	Attendees (Persons)

SAP Transaction Codes – Volume Two

RE_RHXSSTLN	Attendees (Users)
RE_RHXSTAB0	Staff Functions for Org. Units
RE_RHXSTAB1	Staff Functions for Positions
RE_RHXSTEL0	Job Index
RE_RHXSTR00	Organizational Plan (Org.Units Only)
RE_RHXSTR01	Org. Structure with Positions
RE_RHXSTR02	Org. Structure with Persons
RE_RHXSTR03	Org. Structure with Work Centers
RE_RHXSTR04	Reporting Structure with Persons
RE_RHXSTR05	Reporting Structure Without Persons
RE_RHXSTR06	Work Centers per Org. Unit
RE_RHXSTR07	Activity Profile Without Persons
RE_RHXSTR08	Activity Profile with Persons
RE_RHXTASKC	Task Description
RE_RHXTASKS	Task Description Position
RE_SEARCH	RE: REsearch RE Market Place
RF01	C FI Maintain Table TBKSP
RFACTS1_BL	FACTS 1: Trial Balance
RFACTS1_FILE_SEND	FACTS 1: Send File to Treasury
RFACTS1_TR	FACTS 1: Transaction Register
RFACTS2_BL	FACTS 2: Trial Balance
RFACTS2_EDGRP	FACTS 2: Customize Edits 2,3,5 & 11.
RFACTS2_EDINV	FACTS 2: Customize Edit 6.
RFACTS2_EDITS	FACTS 2: Edits
RFACTS2_EDSGL	FACTS 2: Customize Edits 4,7 & 12
RFACTS2_EXTRACT	FACTS 2: Data Extract
RFACTS2_FADT	Specify G/L Accounts for Extraction
RFACTS2_FILE_SEND	FACTS 2: Send File to Treasury
RFACTS2_FOOTNOTE	FACTS 2: Footnote Maintenance
RFACTS2_MAF	FACTS 2: Maintain MAF File
RFACTS2_PREDA	FACTS 2: Customize Pre-Edit A
RFACTS2_PREDC	FACTS 2: Customize Pre-Edit C
RFACTS2_TR	FACTS 2: Transaction Register
RFACTS2_UPLMAF	FACTS 2: Upload MAF File
RFAF	Store order follow-on documents
RFAUDI06_BCE	RFAUDI06_BCE
RFAUDI20_BCE	Where-Used List: Authorization Obj.
RFCASH_HU_AVP	RFCASH_HU_AVP
RFC_T_SCMA_RFC	Call Transaction in Satellite
RFEULIST	EU Sales and Purchase List
RFFMFG_AGINGBYFUND	Aging Report by Fund
RFFM_DOC_CHAIN	Document Chain Display
RFIDATAFS	Annual Financial Statement
RFIDITCVLCODE	Annual Tax Return: Customers/Vendors
RFIDMX29	Monthly VAT Return for Vendors
RFIDPL19	Exchange Difference Valuation (PL)
RFKKO1	Display Documents from Requests
RFKKO2	Display Documents from Standing Req.
RFKKO2H	Reconcile Docs from Standing Request
RFKRADEC	Declining balance Depreciation (KR)
RFKRASL	Straight Line Depreciation Korea
RFKRASUP	Asset Accounting detail Report
RFKRAUP	Si Bu In Amount update
RFKRIBG	Goods Mvmt. between Bus. Places

SAP Transaction Codes – Volume Two

RFKRIBP	Inter bus place tax invoice printing
RFKRIBR	Inter bus. place tax invoice reprint
RFKRINV	Print Tax Invoices (South Korea)
RFKRMIG	Migration of Tax Invoices- Korea
RFKRREP	Reprint/Cancel Tax Invoices (Korea)
RFKRSUM	VAT Summary Report (South Korea)
RFKRTIM	VAT Time Stamp Report for Korea
RFKRWCT	Withholding Tax Certificates
RFKRWDL	Withholding Tax on Business Income
RFKRWDT	Detail Information on Total Tax
RFMCAO4	Display Docs from General Requests
RFMFGRCN_RP1	Reconciliation Analysis Report
RFMFGRCN_RP2	Batch Reconciliation Check
RFM_DEBT_RESCHEDULE	Reschedule debt into installments
RFPM_MIGR	Migration 4.0 to 5.0
RFREXCJP_PAYMENTREPO	Payment Charge Report
RFSCD_COV	FSCD: Cluster Builder - Disp. Func.
RFTBPROT_BCE_AISFIBU	AIS Financial Accounting
RFTBPROT_BCE_AIS_BIL	AIS Financial Statements
RFTBPROT_BCE_AIS_FIN	AIS Finances
RFTBPROT_BCE_AUDIT	Standard Variant
RFTBUH06_BPUM_DEVCL	Maintain Development Classes
RFTREY30_SINGLE_XFER	Send Planning Data to Central System
RFTREY40_SINGLE_XFER	Retrieve Planning Data
RFTS6510	Load TR-CM Payment Advices from File
RFTS6510CS	Create Structure for External Advcs
RFUMSV52	Analysis of Deferred Tax Accounts
RFUMSV53	Deferred Tax Toolbox
RFVATRTNMX	VAT Return (Mexico)
RFVOBJ01CS	Structure for Object Transfer
RFVPAR	Display Initialization Date
RFVSIC01CS	Structure for Collateral Transfer
RG_SAC_CALCPL	Half-Year Closing-Retained earnings
RG_SAC_CENTRAL	Closing - Centralization
RISV	Setup: Retail Info System - Versions
RJB1	External Data Transfer Workbench
RJKREBOOKING	Transfer Post Add.Payments/Refunds
RKABSHOW	Display CO Document
RKACGRID	CO Table Display
RKACSHOW	Display CO Cost Segments
RKARSHOW	Display Follow-On Documents
RKE_KA03	Start KA03
RKE_KS03	Start KS03
RKE_VD03	Start VD03
RKLNT	Counterparty Risk of Netting Group
RKLSI	Overview of Collateral Provision
RKPSANALYSE	RKPSANALYSE
RL00	Returnable packaging accounts
RL01	Create returnable packaging account
RL02	Change returnable packaging account
RL03	Display returnable packaging account
RL04	Archive Returnable Packaging Accts
RL05	Read Ret. Pcking Accts from Archive
RL06A	RP Accounts With Sub-Relationshps

SAP Transaction Codes – Volume Two

RL06L	RP Accounts by RP Matl and Location
RL06M	RP Accounts by Material
RL06R	RP Accounts by Relationship
RL06X	RP Accounts by Locn and Exchge Part.
RL07	Purchase Order for Ret. Packaging
RL11	RP Account Posting Entry
RL12	Reprocess RP Account Postings
RL14	List of account postings
RL15	Archive Account Postings
RL16	Read Account Postings from Archive
RL17A	RP account postings for account
RL17D	Account Postings for Ref. Document
RL17L	RP Account Postings by Location
RL17M	RP Account Postings by Material
RL17P	All RP account postings
RL17X	Account postings by exchange partner
RL23	Document Display for Ledger 3A
RL24	Matching via statements
RL24I	Statement Overview (Inbd) and Matchg
RL24O	Statement Overview (Outbound)
RL34	Acct balances per RtnPck/acct holder
RL42	Change External Partner Descriptions
RL43	Display ext. partner descriptions
RL52	Returnable packaging acct matching
RL53	ReturnPack acct matching (display)
RL61	Create Account Statement
RL62	Change account statement
RL63	Display account statement
RL64	Archive Accounts Statements
RL65	Read Account Statements from Archive
RL71	Create RP Account Statements
RL71F	Issue Account Statement Messages
RL71I	Create Initial Statements
RL72D	Delete Last Statement per Account
RL73	Display Statement Log
RL73D	Delete Statement Logs
RL73I	Display Internet Matching Logs
RL74	Archive Transmissions
RL75	Read Transmissions from Archive
RL84	Archive Matching Groups
RL85	Read Matching Groups from Archive
RLC1	Create Condition Records
RLC2	Change Condition Records
RLC3	Display Condition Records
RLMFW_CUST	Settings for Release Management
RLMFW_NUM	Number Ranges for Release Management
RLMFW_OOCU	Processor in Release Management
RLMFW_ORDER	Edit Release Order
RM00	Position of Risk Objects
RM01	Position of Risk Objects
RM02	RM: Position Groups
RM10	RM: Views
RM10D	RM: Views
RM11	RM: Portfolio Hierarchies

SAP Transaction Codes – Volume Two

RM11D	RM: Portfolio Hierarchies (Display)
RMBDS1	Archiving of Report Data
RMBDS2	Delete Archived Report Data
RMBDS3	Report Data: Overview of Archive
RMBDSA	Overview of Report Data
RMBDSB	Create Report Data
RMBDSN	BDS: Number Range for Runs
RMBK1	BCA: Derivation Strategy
RMBK2	BCA: Rule Entries
RMCM	Link Between Cash Mgmt and Risk Mgmt
RMD01	FO: Derivation Strategy
RMD02	Financial Object: Rule Entries
RMDR1	Gen.Transaction: Derivation Strategy
RMDR2	Gen. Transaction: Rule Entries
RMFD	Financial Object Data
RMFZ1	Derivation of RM Part for Facilities
RMHWCAL	Calibration of the Hull-White Model
RMIBKKA	BCA Account: FO Integr. act./inact.
RMIFGDT	Gen.Trans.: Act/Deact FO Integration
RMIJBVT	Var. Trans.: FO Integr. act./inact.
RMIKLFZ	Facility: Activate/Deactivate FO Int
RMMDG	Market Data Generator
RMMDGSBP	Forex Swap Basis Points Generator
RMPSACTIVATEWF	Activation of Process Routes
RMPSDISPOSALFINALIZE	Finish Disposal
RMPSDISPOSALOFFER	Create List of Providers
RMPSE_SOA_DOC	Customizing for DocTypes for ESOA
RMPSE_SOA_REC	Customizing for RecTypes for ESOA
RMPSP_GEN_ATTRIBUTE	Generating of Attributes
RMPSP_PART_CLOSE	Close Parts
RMPSP_RECTYPE	Create Disposal Document Type
RMPSRETDURPW	Maintain Res. Time of Temp. Objects
RMPSSTORDUR	Define Storage Duration in Stor.Cat
RMPSSTORPLACE	Define Storage Location
RMPS_ACL_STATUS	Status Maintenance Dstb Lists in ACL
RMPS_AUDIT	Log
RMPS_AUDIT_CUST	Help for Log Customizing
RMPS_AUDIT_REORG	Log Reorganization
RMPS_CUSTOMIZING	Customizing Public Sector RecordsMgt
RMPS_DIPT_NRRANGE	Nummer Range Maintenance: RMPSDIPTID
RMPS_DOCNR	Nummer Range Maintenance: RMPSDOCNR
RMPS_DP_REP	TNA: Disposal Reporting
RMPS_EVENTTYPES	TNA: Event Types for Disposal
RMPS_EXPDEST	TNA: Maintain Export Destinations
RMPS_EXPORT	Export in Case Management
RMPS_IMPORT_KC	Import Key Word Catalog
RMPS_LIST_ATTRIBUTES	List Attributes for Document Class
RMPS_MAINT_PATH	Maintain Process Route
RMPS_MAINT_PATH_CASE	Maintain Process Route Case
RMPS_MAINT_PATH_POST	Maintain P. Route Incoming Post Item
RMPS_MT_STORAGE_P	Check and Define Retention Periods
RMPS_POST_HISTORY	Call Incoming Post Book
RMPS_POST_PROCESS	TNA: Object Postprocessing Disposal
RMPS_PRO_DISPOSAL	TNA: Start Disposal Process

SAP Transaction Codes – Volume Two

RMPS_PRO_TRANS   TNA: Disposal Transactions
RMPS_PUTAWAY_DELETE   Delete Temporary Objects
RMPS_RATING_LIST   Load Valuation Directory
RMPS_RECORD_LIST   Records Directory
RMPS_RECTYPE   TNA: Declare Record Types
RMPS_RECTYPEC   TNA: Record Types Customizing
RMPS_RULEBASE   TNA: Disposal Schedules
RMPS_SECL   Convert Authorization Levels
RMPS_SET_SUBSTITUTE   Maintain Substitute (Administration)
RMPS_UNRESERVE   Deletion Report for Reservations
RMRB   Dataset Management
RMRBA1   Dataset Archiving
RMRBA2   Delete Archived Dataset
RMSL02   Change Label Set
RMSL03   Display Label Set
RMSL_NR   Number Range for Label Set
RMSTAT   Mass Status Change
RMS_EQR_NR   Maintain Number Ranges for Equip.Req
RMS_GLOB   Global Recipe Customizing
RMS_POB_NR   Maintain No. Ranges for Process Mgmt
RMTABLEINFO   RM Data Analysis Report
RMV0   Single Value Analysis: VAR
RMVARS   Display Shifts during VaR Evaluation
RMVC   Correlations between Exchange Rates
RMVT1   Variable Trans: Derivation Strategy
RMVT2   Variable Transaction: Rule Entries
RMW99   Area Menu
RMWB   Start Workbench
RMWBCUST   Workbench Settings
RMXM_BOM_CMP   Compare Bills of Material
RMXTPLAN02   Change Trial Planning
RMXTPLAN03   Display Trial Planning
RMXT_IMG01   Transf. Characteristics frm Client 0
RM_01   Initialize view
RM_02   Regenerate View
RM_97   Display of DB Logs
RM_98   Diagnosis of BP Admin. Tables
RM_99   Deactivate Financial Objects
ROE1   Number Range for ROE Evaluation Run
ROEMPROACT2   Start ROEMPROACT2
ROLE_CMP   Compare Roles
RO_DEF   Define Reimbursable Orders
RP09_LOAN_INIT   Loans: Initialization (IT3,VIEKN)
RP3214GAPI0_PS   Gap Analisys
RPA0   Info.Sys. Rec.Ledger: Presettings
RPA1   Info. Sys. Rec.Ldgr: Report Currency
RPAM   Info. Sys. Rec.Ldgr: Report Currency
RPAN   Info.Sys. Rec.Ledger: Presettings
RPB0   Info.Sys. Proc.: Presettings
RPBN   Info.Sys. Proc.: Presettings
RPC0   Info. System CCtrs: Presettings
RPC1   Info. System CCtrs: Presettings
RPC2   Info. System CCtrs: Presettings
RPCN   Info. System CCtrs: Presettings

SAP Transaction Codes – Volume Two

RPDK	Workflow for Danish Payroll
RPKFDEF	Reporting Key Figures definition
RPLM_MT_REPORTING	Report-Launchpad Maint. Technician
RPLM_PSS_REPORTING	Report LaunchPad PSS
RPLM_QI_REPORTING	Support LaunchPad- Quality Inspector
RPLSVED0	Detailed Display Report RPLSVED0
RPMTIME01	HR Time/Rate info for employees
RPO0	Info. System Orders: Presettings
RPON	Info. System Orders: Presettings
RPP0	Proj. Info System: Default Settings
RPPN	Proj. Info System: Default Settings
RPRTPROACT	Start RPRTPROACT
RPU_T5D83_TO_T5D8S	Start Report RPU_T5D83_TO_T5D8S
RPX0	CO-OM Information System: Settings
RPXN	CO-OM Information System: Settings
RRC1	Create Currency Conversion Type
RRC2	Edit Currency Conversion Type
RRC3	Display Currency Translation Type
RRMB	Upload Screens from BEx Browser
RRMX	Start the Business Explorer Analyzer
RRMXP	Initial Trans. for Excel wth Params
RRMX_CUST	Initial Trans. for Excel wth Params
RRV_FILL	Fill Bucket
RS00	Start menu
RS09	Transport Browser for BI Objects
RS12	Overview of master data locks
RS50	Old SM50
RSA0	Content Settings Maintenance
RSA1	Modeling - DW Workbench
RSA10	Realtime Test Interface Srce System
RSA11	DW Workbench: InfoProvider Tree
RSA12	DW Workbench: InfoSource Tree
RSA13	DW Workbench: Source System Tree
RSA14	DW Workbench: InfoObject Tree
RSA15	DW Workbench: DataSource Tree
RSA16	DW Workbench: Favorites Tree
RSA17	DW Workbench: General Search
RSA18	DW Workbench: Open Hub Destination
RSA1GM	GM Demo in AWB: Test Purposes Only
RSA1OLD	BW Administrator Workbench (old)
RSA2	SAPI DataSource Repository
RSA2OLD	SAPI DataSource (Old GUI)
RSA3	Extractor Checker
RSA5	Install Business Content
RSA6	Maintain DataSources
RSA7	BW Delta Queue Monitor
RSA8	DataSource Repository
RSA9	Transfer Application Components
RSABAPSC	Statistical Prog. Anal. for Search
RSABAUTH	Transfer of Authorization Groups
RSABTPGP	Authorization Groups
RSADMIN	RSADMIN maintenance
RSADRTC70TOADR11	Conversion of table TC70 in ADR11
RSAFT_XML	RSAFT_PT:XML Generation for Portugal

SAP Transaction Codes – Volume Two

RSANWB   Analysis Process Designer
RSANWB_EXEC   Execute Analysis Process
RSANWB_MONITOR   Monitor for Analysis Run
RSANWB_START_ALL   Model the Analysis Process
RSAN_VERI   Analysis Process: Test Monitor
RSAN_WB_TST   Analysis Process - Display Data
RSAP_AUDIT_PREVIEW   Preview for System Measurement in BI
RSARCH_ADMIN   BW Archive Administration
RSARFCEX   Variant for RSARFCEX
RSASSIBTCH   Schedule Assistant in Background
RSATTR   Attribute/Hierarchy Realignment Run
RSAUDITC_BCE   Display Locked Transactions
RSAUDITM_BCE_IMPO   Import Overview
RSAUDITM_BCE_SYSO   System Overview
RSAUDITM_BCE_TPLGA   Transport Monitor ALOG
RSAUDITM_BCE_TPLGS   Transport Monitor SLOG
RSAU_SELECT_EVENTS   Display Audit Events (Batch Proc.)
RSAWB   DW Workbench (Last View)
RSAWBSETTINGSDEL   Delete user settings of the AWB
RSB2   Data Marts Generation Center
RSBATCH   Management of RSBATCH/SEARCHLOGS
RSBBS   Maintaining BW Sender-Receiver
RSBBS_WEB   Transaction for the RRI in the Web
RSBEB   Business Explorer Browser
RSBMO2   Open Hub Monitor
RSBO   Open Hub Maintenance
RSBOH1   Open Hub Maintenance
RSBOH2   Open Hub Maintenance
RSBOH3   Open Hub Maintenance
RSBO_EXTRACT   Auth. - Check Open Hub Extraction
RSBROWSER   BW Browser
RSBWREMOTE   Create Warehouse User
RSB_GUI_START   Editing an Open Hub Destination
RSCATTAWB   CATT Admin. Workbench
RSCONCHA   Channel conversion
RSCONFAV   Favorites Conversion
RSCRMDEBUG   Set Debug Options
RSCRMISQ   Register Infosets for Target Groups
RSCRMMDX   Edit MDX
RSCRMMON   Monitor Query Extracts
RSCRMSCEN   Register Closed-Loop Scenarios
RSCRM_BAPI   Generation of Query Extracts
RSCRM_REPORT   BW Queries with ODBO (to 2nd 0B)
RSCRM_REPORT_OLD   BW Queries with ODBO (to 2nd 0B)
RSCRT   BW Monitor (Near)-Real-Time Loading
RSCR_MAINT_PUBLISH   Maint. of Publishing Variables CR/CE
RSCR_MAINT_URL   Maint. of URL Variables for CR/CE
RSCSAUTH   Maintain/Restore Authorization Group
RSCUR   Start: Currency Translation Type
RSCUSTA   Maintain BW Settings
RSCUSTA2   ODS Settings
RSCUSTV1   BW Customizing - View 1
RSCUSTV10   BW Customizing - View 10
RSCUSTV11   BW Customizing - View 11

SAP Transaction Codes – Volume Two

RSCUSTV12	Microsoft Analysis Services
RSCUSTV13	RRI Settings for Web Reporting
RSCUSTV14	OLAP: Cache Parameters
RSCUSTV15	BW Customizing - View 11
RSCUSTV16	BW Reporting
RSCUSTV17	Settings: Currency Translation
RSCUSTV18	DB Connect Settings
RSCUSTV19	InfoSet Settings
RSCUSTV2	BW Customizing - View 2
RSCUSTV21	BW Customizing - View 21
RSCUSTV23	Analysis Authorization System
RSCUSTV24	Quantity Conversion: Buffer Setting
RSCUSTV25	Database Interface/Performance
RSCUSTV26	Database Interface/Perf. (ORA)
RSCUSTV27	Set Standard Web Templates
RSCUSTV28	Determine Settings for Web Templates
RSCUSTV29	Settings for Web Template
RSCUSTV3	BW Customizing - View 3
RSCUSTV30	Load Distribution for Analys. Proc.
RSCUSTV4	BW Customizing - View 4
RSCUSTV5	BW Customizing - View 5
RSCUSTV6	BW Customizing - View 6
RSCUSTV7	BW Customizing - View 7
RSCUSTV8	BW Customizing - View 8
RSCUSTV9	BW Customizing - View 9
RSD1	Characteristic maintenance
RSD2	Maintenance of key figures
RSD3	Maintenance of units
RSD4	Maintenance of time characteristics
RSD5	Internal: Maint. of Techn. Chars
RSDANLCON	Set Up Near-Line Connections
RSDAP	Edit Data Archiving Process
RSDAS_BROWSE	Browser for Data Access Services
RSDBC	DB connect
RSDB_ADD_ID_2_CRM	Create External ID for CRM-GP
RSDB_INIT	Initial Download of D&B Data
RSDCUBE	Start: InfoCube editing
RSDCUBED	Start: InfoCube editing
RSDCUBEM	Start: InfoCube editing
RSDDAGGRCHECK	Maintenance of Aggregate Check
RSDDBIAMON	BI Accelerator Maintenance Monitor
RSDDBIAMON2	BI Accelerator Maintenance Monitor
RSDDBIAMON3	BI Accelerator Maintenance Monitor
RSDDSTAT	Maintain the BW Statistics Settings
RSDDTPS	Start Explorer Maintenance
RSDDV	Maintaining Aggregates/BIA Index
RSDEMO02	Testtransaction Table Control
RSDIOBC	Start: InfoObject catalog editing
RSDIOBCD	Start: InfoObject catalog editing
RSDIOBCM	Start: InfoObject catalog editing
RSDIPROP	Maintain InfoProvider Properties
RSDL	DB Connect - Test Program
RSDMCUS	Data Mining Customising
RSDMD	Master Data Maintenance w.Prev. Sel.

SAP Transaction Codes – Volume Two

RSDMD_TEST   Master Data Test
RSDMPRO   Initial Screen: MultiProvider Proc.
RSDMPROD   Initial Screen: MultiProvider Proc.
RSDMPROM   Initial Screen: MultiProvider Proc.
RSDMWB   Datamining Workbench
RSDMWB_OLD   Data Mining Workbench
RSDMWB_OO   Datamining Workbench
RSDODS   Initial Screen: ODS Object Processng
RSDODSD   Initial Screen: ODS Proces. (Deliv.)
RSDPMDDBSETUP   Creates a MOLAP Database in MSAS
RSDPMOLAPDS   MOLAP DataSource creation
RSDPRFCDSETUP   Create MOLAP Rfc Tests
RSDS   DataSource
RSDSD   DataSource Documentation
RSDTA   Administration of the Data Targets
RSDTP   DTP Maintenance
RSDV   Validity Slice Maintenance
RSECADMIN   Manage Analysis Authorizations
RSECAUTH   Maintenance of Analysis Auth.
RSECPROT   Maintenance of Analysis Auth.
RSEDIT   Old editor
RSEIDOC2   IDoc List
RSEIDOCA   Active IDoc Monitoring with Workflow
RSEIDOCM   Variant for RSEIDOCA
RSENQ   Display of Lock Log
RSEOUT00   Variant for RSEOUT00
RSESH_TLOGO_MAINT   Start of Object Maintenance
RSFC   Analytic Engine - Demo Content
RSFH   Test Transaction Data Extractors
RSFLAT   Flat MDX
RSGWLST   Accessible Gateways
RSH1   Edit hierarchy initial screen
RSH3   Simulate hierarchies
RSHIER   Hierarchy maintenance w/o AdmWB
RSHIERSIM   Simulate hierarchies
RSICUBE   Maintain/Change InfoCubes (Internal)
RSIMG   BW IMG
RSIMPCUR   Load Exchange Rates from File
RSINFO00_BCE_AUD_MOD   Customer Exits
RSINPUT   Manual Data Entry
RSIR_DELTATRACK   Delta Tracking KPRO
RSISET   Maintain InfoSets
RSISW   Service Designer
RSKC   Maintaining the Permittd Extra Chars
RSLDAPSYNC_USER   LDAP Synchronization of Users
RSLGMP   Maintain RSLOGSYSMAP
RSM37   Job List with Program Variant
RSMD   Extractor Checker
RSMDCNVEXIT   Conversn to Consistent Intern. Vals
RSMDEXITON   Activate Conversion Routine
RSMIPROACT2   Start RSMIPROACT2
RSMO   Data Load Monitor Start
RSMON   Administration - DW Workbench
RSMONCOLOR   Traffic light color in the Monitor

RSMONITOR	Generic Monitor
RSMONITOR_DB	D&B Integration
RSMONMAIL	Mail Addresses for Monitor Assistant
RSMRT	Metadata Remodelling Toolbox
RSMT_CHECK	Check Customizing
RSMT_VARIANT	Create Event Variant
RSNPGTEST	Test Network Plan Control
RSNPGTEST2	Test Network Plan Control
RSNSPACE	BW Namespace Maintenance
RSO2	Oltp Metadata Repository
RSO3	Set Up Deltas for Master Data
RSOBI1	SOBI Design Time (DataSource)
RSOCONTENT	Administration of a Content System
RSODADMIN	Administration Metadata Search
RSODADMIN_DOC	Document Administration
RSODMIGRATION	Migration of Documen. into Portal KM
RSODSO_BRKPNT	DataStore-Specific Breakpoints
RSODSO_RUNTIME	Runtime Measurements
RSODSO_SETTINGS	Maintenance of Runtime Param. DS Obj
RSODSO_SHOWLOG	Logs for DataStore Object
RSOR	BW Metadata Repository
RSORBCT	BI Business Content Transfer
RSORMDR	BW Metadata Repository
RSOS_SEARCH	BI Metadata Search
RSPC	Process Chain Maintenance
RSPC1	Process Chain Display
RSPC1_NOLOG	Process Chain Maintenance
RSPC2	Process Chain via Process
RSPCM	Monitor daily process chains
RSPCP	Process Log
RSPC_RESTART	Restart Process Chain Run
RSPFPAR	Display profile parameter
RSPFPAR_AUTH	Authorization All
RSPFPAR_CALLSYSTEM	Call System
RSPFPAR_GATEWAY	SAP Gateway
RSPFPAR_LOGIN	Logon Rules
RSPFPAR_PROFGEN	Profile Generator
RSPFPAR_RFC	Remote Function Call
RSPFPAR_SAPSTAR	Hardcoded SAP*
RSPFPAR_SNC	SNC
RSPFPAR_SPOOL	Spool Parameters
RSPFPAR_STATISTICS	Workload Statistics
RSPFPAR_SYSLOG	Syslog Parameters
RSPFPAR_TABLEREC	Table Recording
RSPFPAR_TABLESTAT	Table Access Statistics
RSPLAN	Modeling BI Integrated Planning
RSPLF1	Start: Function Type Editing
RSPLSA	BI Planning: Starter Settings
RSPLSE	BI Planning: Lock Management
RSPO0055	Installation Check: Spool
RSPOR_CUST01	NetWeaver Customizing - Step 1
RSPOR_CUST02	NetWeaver Customizing - Step 2
RSPOR_CUST03	NetWeaver Customizing - Step 3
RSPOR_CUST04	NetWeaver Customizing - Step 4

RSPOR_CUST05	NetWeaver Customizing - Step 5
RSPOR_CUST06	NetWeaver Customizing - Step 6
RSPOR_CUST07	NetWeaver Customizing - Step 7
RSPOR_CUST08	NetWeaver Customizing - Step 8
RSPOR_CUST09	NetWeaver Customizing - Step 9
RSPOR_CUST10	NetWeaver Customizing - Step 10
RSPOR_CUST11	NetWeaver Customizing - Step 11
RSPOR_CUST12	NetWeaver Customizing - Step 12
RSPOR_CUST13	NetWeaver Customizing - Step 13
RSPRECADMIN	BW Excel Workbook Precalc Admin
RSPROXY	SOBI Design Time (ESI Business Obj.)
RSPSADEL_PATTERN	Maintain Src System Pattern Assignm.
RSQ02	Maintain InfoSets
RSQ10	SAP Query: Role Administration
RSRAJ	Starts a Reporting Agent Job
RSRAM	Reporting Agent Monitor
RSRAPS	Manages Page Store
RSRCACHE	OLAP: Cache Monitor
RSRCATTTRACE	Catt transaction for trace tool
RSRDA	Real-Time Data Acquisition Monitor
RSRD_ADMIN	Broadcasting Administration
RSRD_LOG	Broadcaster Application Log
RSRD_REPLAY	Restart Broadcasting for Log Number
RSRD_START	Start Broadcaster for Test Purposes
RSRD_TEST	Test Producer/Converter/Distributor
RSREP	BW Administrator Workbench
RSREQARCH	Req. Archive Administration Dialog
RSRFCCHK	RFC destinations with logon data
RSRFCSTX	RFC statistics
RSRFCTRC	RFC Trace
RSRHIERARCHYVIRT	Maintain Virtual Time Hierarchies
RSRQ	Data Load Monitor for a Request
RSRR	BW RRI on the Web
RSRR_WEB	Report-Report Interface in Web
RSRSDEST	System Overview Output
RSRT	Start of the report monitor
RSRT1	Start of the Report Monitor
RSRT2	Start of the Report Monitor
RSRTQ	Query Definition
RSRTRACE	Set trace configuration
RSRTRACETEST	Trace tool configuration
RSRV	Analysis and Repair of BW Objects
RSRVALT	Analysis of the BW objects
RSSCD100	Display Change Documents
RSSCD100_PFCG	Change Documents for Role Admin.
RSSCD100_PFCG_USER	For Role Assignment
RSSCD150	Display Change Documents
RSSCM_APPL	Application settings SCM4.0 and BW
RSSD	Access for scheduler
RSSDK	DB Connect
RSSE	Selection start InfoCube
RSSEM_RFC_MDF	Maint. Callback Destinations in MDF
RSSGPCLA	Maintain program class
RSSG_BROWSER	Simple Data Browser

SAP Transaction Codes – Volume Two

RSSM   Authorizations for Reporting
RSSMQ   Start Query with User
RSSMTRACE   Reporting Log Authorization
RSSNCSRV   SNC Status of Application Server
RSSTARTMON   Starting the monitor in parall.proc.
RSSTAT10   Performance Analysis: Workload Anal.
RSSTAT20   Performance Analysis: Single Stats
RSSWOUSR   List of Internet users
RST22   Old Short-Dump Overview
RSTBHIST   Table history
RSTCIMP   Importance of BW Object
RSTCO_ADMIN   Technical BW Content
RSTC_CUST_BIAC   Customizing to call BI Admin Cockpit
RSTG_BUPA   Target Group Sel. Business Partners
RSTG_CUST   Target Group Selection Customers
RSTG_DB   Target Group Selection D&B
RSTHJTMAINT   Maintenance THJT
RSTMSAMO   TMS: Alert Viewer
RSTMSCON_VERBOSE   Verbose
RSTMSDIC   TMS: Display Configuration
RSTPRFC   Create Destination for After-Import
RSTRANGUI   Transformations
RSTT   RS Trace Tool Monitor
RSU0   Update rules overview
RSU01   User Maint. BI Analysis Auth.
RSU1   Create update rules
RSU1I   Create update rules
RSU1O   Create Update Rules
RSU2   Change update rules
RSU2I   Change update rules
RSU2O   Change Update Rules
RSU3   Display update rules
RSU3I   Display update rules
RSU3O   Display Update Rules
RSU6   Delete update rules
RSU6I   Delete update rules
RSU6O   Delete update rules
RSU7   Data Extraction: Maintain Parameters
RSUDO   Execution as Other User
RSUDU   Execution as Other User
RSUOM   UOM: BW
RSUSR000   Currently Active Users
RSUSR002_AUDIT_ABAP   Users with ABAP Authorization
RSUSR002_AUDIT_CTS   Users who can use CTS
RSUSR002_AUDIT_OSCL   Users who can call OS commands
RSUSR002_AUDIT_RFC   Users who can execute RFC functions
RSUSR002_AUDIT_UAP   Update Accounting Periods
RSUSR002_AUDIT_UCA   Update Chart of Accounts
RSUSR002_AUDIT_UCC   Update Company Codes
RSUSR003   Check standard user passwords
RSUSR007   List Users
RSUSR200   List of Users per Login Date
RSUSR200_INITPASS   Users with Initial Password
RSUSR200_PWDCHG180   Unchanged for 180 Days

SAP Transaction Codes – Volume Two

RSUSR200_UNUSED30   Not Logged On for 30 Days
RSUSR_SYS_LIC   Cross-System Information Report
RSWBO004   Set System Change Option
RSWBO040   Search for Objects in Requests/Tasks
RSWBO040_AUDIT_PA   Requests with PA tables
RSWBO040_AUDIT_USR   Requests with USR tables
RSWBO050   Analyze Objects in Orders/Tasks
RSWBOSSR   RSWBOSSR
RSWELOGD   Delete Event Trace
RSWEWWDHMSHOW   Display Background Job SWWERRE
RSWEWWDHSHOW   Display Work Item Deadline Monitorng
RSWWCLEAR   Execute Work Item Clearing Work
RSWWCOND   Execute Work Item Rule Monitoring
RSWWCOND_MON   Monitoring - Rule Monitoring
RSWWDHEX   ExecuteWorkItemDeadlineMonitoring
RSWWERRE   Start RSWWERRE
RSZC   Copying Queries between InfoCubes
RSZDELETE   Deletion of query objects
RSZRESTORE   Call report COMPONENT_RESTORE
RSZT   Get Test Component
RSZTABLES   Call ANALYZE_RSZ_TABLES
RSZV   Call up of view V_RSZGLOBV
RSZVERSION   Set frontend version
RS_AWB_REMOTE   Remote AWB Staging
RS_BA_PCK_CLEANUP   Deletion of Selected Packages
RS_CONV_ACTIVATE   Activate InfoObject Conversion
RS_DS_CHECK   Check consistency request
RS_FRONTEND_INIT   Initialization of the BW Front End
RS_ISTD_REMOTE   Maintain InfoSource
RS_LOGSYS_CHECK   Source System Tool
RS_PERS_ACTIVATE   Activation of BEx Personalization
RS_PERS_BOD_ACTIVATE   Activate BEx Open Pers.
RS_PERS_BOD_DEACTIVA   Deactivate Pers. for BEx Open
RS_PERS_VAR_ACTIVATE   Activate Variable Pers.
RS_PERS_VAR_DEACTIVA   Deactivate Pers. for Variables
RS_PERS_WTE_ACTIVATE   Activate Web Template Pers.
RS_PERS_WTE_DEACTIVA   Deactivate Pers. for Web Templates
RTAXMCHECK   Tax Material Check for MLAN Table
RTBSTD   Position Management for Gen.Trans.
RTDE   Retail Ledger: Del. Transaction Data
RTGDI   Direct input for routings
RTHCOC   Create Retail Object Assignment
RTHCOD   Display Retail Object Assignment
RTHCOM   Change Retail Object Assignment
RTKB   Maintain Number Range: KB_NRRANGE
RTOHC01   Realtime customizing
RTOHC02   Acti Realtime Overh for Business Tra
RTOHC03   Activate Work Date = Document Date
RTOHC04   Special Valuation Date Settings
RTOHC_REPOST   Repost Realtime Overhead
RTOHC_UPGRADE   Realtime Overhead Upgrade Postings
RTPB01   RPUS Cntrl: Application Transactions
RTPB02   RPUS Cntrl: Tables
RTPB03   RPUS Cntrl: Activities

RTPB04	RPUS struct: Applications
RTPB05	RPUS Struct Scr Layout: Field Groups
RTPB06	RPUS Struct Scr Layout: Views
RTPB07	RPUS Struct Scr Layout: Sections
RTPB08	RPUS Struct Scr Layout: Screens
RTPB09	RPUS Struct: Screen Sequence
RTPB10	RPUS Struct: Events
RTPB11	RPUS GUI: Standard Functions
RTPB12	RPUS GUI: Additional Functions
RTPB13	RPUS GUI: Assignm scrn fld -> DB fld
RTPB14	RPUS Field Mod: Criteria
RTPB15	RPUS Field Mod: Activity Category
RTPB16	Create data set for retirement plan
RTPB17	Retirement types
RTPB18	RPUS Authorization types
RTPB19	RPUS Field groups for authorization
RTP_US_C1	Create a retirement plan
RTP_US_CUST	Maintain defaults
RTP_US_D1	Display a retirement plan
RTP_US_DEFAULT	Maintain defaults retirement plan
RTP_US_M1	Change a retirement plan
RTP_US_PLAN_NO	Transaction code for number range
RTP_US_R1	Retirement plan year-end report
RTP_US_R2	Retirement plan age limit report
RTP_US_R3	Retirement plan contribution limit
RTP_US_R4	Retirement plan distribution limit
RTP_US_R5	Calculate fair market value
RTP_US_R6	Check consistency fair market value
RTP_US_R7	Application log for FMV updates
RTREAS_OFFSET_FILE	Create Treasury Offset File
RTREAS_OFFSET_UPDATE	Treasury Offset Update Report
RTTE_SET_3XTAXDET	Enable 3.x TTE Tax Determination
RTTREE_MIGRATION	Report tree migration
RUNSCHED	Scheduler Test Call
RVND	Create Payment Requests Online
RWBE	Stock Overview
RWBILL	Billing
RWDEL	Delete Billing Data
RWPOS_PARA	POS Sales IDOC Enqueue Control
RWPRINT	Print Billing Data
RWUF_CHECK	Check Customizing
RZ01	Job Scheduling Monitor
RZ03	Presentation, Control SAP Instances
RZ04	Maintain SAP Instances
RZ10	Maintain Profile Parameters
RZ11	Profile Parameter Maintenance
RZ12	Maintain RFC Server Group Assignment
RZ15	Read XMI log
RZ20	CCMS Monitoring
RZ21	CCMS Monitoring Arch. Customizing
RZ23	Central perfomance history reports
RZ23N	Central Performance History
RZ25	Start Tools for a TID
RZ26	Start Methods for an Alert

RZ27   Start RZ20 for a Monitor
RZ27_SECURITY   MiniApp CCMS Alerts Security
RZ28   Start Alert Viewer for Monitor
RZ29   Remote Login for WebAdmin Monitoring
RZ30   Remote Execution of Transactions
RZ70   SLD Administration
RZAL_ALERT_PROXY   Alerts: IMC Data Proxy for Alerts
RZAL_MONITOR_PROXY   Alerts: IMC Data Proxy for Monitor
RZAL_MTE_DATA_PROXY   Alerts: IMC Data Proxy for MTEs
RZPT   Residence Time Maintenance Tool
S-32
S-33   Display table
S00   Short Message
S000   System Menu
S001
S002   Menu Administration
S1MD   System Menu
S2KDT   Spec2000 IDoc Display Tool
S2KEVENTS   SPEC2000: Activate Event Linkage
S2L   Supply-to-Production Table
SA01   Number range maintenance: ADRNR
SA02   Academic Title (Bus. Addr. Services)
SA03   Titles (Business Address Services)
SA04   Name Prefixes (Bus. Addr. Services)
SA05   Name Suffix (Bus. Address Services)
SA06   Address or personal data source
SA07   Address Groups (Bus. Addr. Services)
SA08   Person Groups (Bus. Addr. Services)
SA09   Internat. versions address admin.
SA10   Address admin. communication type
SA11   Number range maintenance: ADRV
SA12   Number Range Maintenance: ADRVP
SA13   Name format rules
SA14   Pager Services (Bus. Addr. Services)
SA15   Address screen variants
SA15V   Version-Specific Address Masks
SA16   Transport zones
SA17   Index pools for duplicate check
SA18   Reasons for Nondelivery (BAS)
SA19   Titles (Business Address Services)
SA20   Conversion of Street Sections
SA21   Customizing Regional Structure (BAS)
SA22   Deactivate Specific Corrections
SA23   Address Version Regional Structure
SA24   Limit for Duplicate List
SA38   ABAP Reporting
SA38PARAMETER   Schedule PFCG_TIME_DEPENDENCY
SA39   SA38 for Parameter Transaction
SAAB   Checkpoints that Can Be Activated
SABRE   SABRE Bypass
SABRE_PNR   Display a Sabre PNR
SABRE_VPNR   SABRE Bypass VPNR
SACC2   Set accessibility
SACCRESULTS   Check Results for Accessibility

SAP Transaction Codes – Volume Two

SACCSEL	ACC: Select relevant objects
SAD0	(Obsolete) Address Management Call
SADC	(Obsolete) Communication Types
SADJ	Customizing Transfer Assistant
SADP	Contact person addr.maint. init.scr.
SADQ	Private address maint. initial scrn
SADR	Address maint. - Group required!
SADV	(Obsolete) Intern. Address Versions
SAINT	Add-On Installation Tool
SAKB0	Transfer of Released Data
SAKB01	Process Exceptions
SAKB1	Overview: Frozen Objects
SAKB2	Usage Overview
SAKB2OLD	Usage Overview
SAKB3	Compatibility Text
SAKB4	Create Usage Explanations
SAKB5	Check Table Enhancements
SALE	Display ALE Customizing
SALE_CUA	Display ALE Customizing for CUA
SALRT01	Maintain RFC Dest. for Alert Server
SALRT02	Maintain Events for Alert Framework
SALRT1	Maintain RFC Dest. for Alert Server
SAMT	ABAP Program Set Processing
SAPBWNEWS	PRINT SAP BW NEWS
SAPCALENDAR_NAVI	Testtransaction Calendar Control
SAPCOLUMN_TREE	Testtransaktion für Column Tree
SAPRDEMOVIEWING	Testtransaction HTML Control
SAPSIMPLE_TREE	Testtransaktion für Simple Tree
SAPTERM	SAPterm: SAP Dictionary
SAPTEXTEDIT_TEST_2	Test for Textedit Control
SAPTOOLBAR_DEMO1	Test Transaction: Toolbar Control
SAP_GENERATE	SAP_GENERATE
SARA	Archive Administration
SARE	Archive Explorer
SARFC	Server Resources for Asynchr. RFC
SARI	Archive Information System
SARJ	Archive Retrieval Configurator
SARP	Reporting (Tree Structure): Execute
SARPN	Display Report Trees
SART	Display Report Tree
SARTN	Display Report Trees
SAR_DA_STAT_ANALYSIS	Analysis of DA Statistics
SAR_FLAG_SESSIONS	To be archived or invalid status set
SAR_OBJ_IND_CUS	Cross-Archiving-Obj. Customizing
SAR_SHOW_MONITOR	Data Archiving Monitor
SAR_SYNC_HOME_PATH	Synchronization of Home Paths
SASAPFLAVOR	Maintain Flavor
SASAPIMG	Call Up Project IMG
SASAPROLE	Maintain Roles for ASAP
SASAPSUBJECT	Maintain Subject for ASAP
SAT	ABAP Trace
SATTR	Maintain Characteristics
SAUNIT_CLIENT_SETUP	ABAP Unit Configuration
SB01	Application Components

SAP Transaction Codes – Volume Two

SBAC	Edit Application Components
SBACH02	Edit SAP Application Hierarchy
SBACH03	Display SAP Application Hierarchy
SBACH04	Edit Component Structures
SBACH05	Extend Application Hierarchy
SBAL_TEST_REPORT	Application Log: Internal Test
SBCA	Routing Server Administration
SBCS_ADDR	BCS: Where-Used List for Addresses
SBCS_ADRDUP	BCS: Delete Duplicate Addresses
SBCS_ADRVP	BCS: Delete Addresses
SBCS_DFRE	BCS: Delete from Dark Folder
SBCS_DLI	BCS: Consistency of Distr. Lists
SBCS_EXTCOM	BCS: Consistency of Distr. Lists
SBCS_FOLID	BCS: Delete SOFM Without Folder ID
SBCS_IFREC	BCS: Delete BCST_CAM/BCST_BOR
SBCS_MIME	BCS: Set MIME Repository
SBCS_MIMEDEL	BCS: Delete MIME Documents
SBCS_NUM	BCS: Consistency of Number Ranges
SBCS_PRIV	BCS: Delete from Private Folders
SBCS_PRRP	BCS: Repair SAP Office Profile
SBCS_QUEUE	BCS: Delete from Queue
SBCS_REORG	BCS: Reorganization
SBCS_RESTORE	BCS: Restore from Backup
SBCS_SOC3	BCS: Consistency of SOC3 and SOOD
SBCS_USCO	BCS: User Consistency
SBCS_USFD	BCS: Create Private Root Folders
SBDS1	Displaying Open Bar Codes
SBDS2	Open Internal Bar Codes
SBDS3	Open External Bar Codes
SBDS4	Open Bar Codes with Keep Flag
SBDS5	Internal Bar Codes with Keep Flag
SBDS6	External Bar Codes with Keep Flag
SBDS7	Compare Open Bar Codes
SBDSV1	Maintenance View for BDS_LOCL
SBDSV2	Maintenance View for BDS_LOCL
SBDSV3	Maintenance View for BDS_LOCL
SBEA	BEAC corporate flight system
SBGRFCCONF	bgRFC Configuration
SBGRFCHIST	Display Unit History
SBGRFCMON	bgRFC Monitor
SBGRFCPERFMON	bgRFC Performance Monitor
SBI1	Maintain enhanced InfoSource
SBI2	Maintain enhanced master data str.
SBI3	Maintain append for InfoSource
SBI4	Maintain append for master data
SBI5	Delete InfoObjects
SBIT	BAPI Test Environment
SBIW	BIW in IMG for OLTP
SBIZCLOG	Business Content: Application Log
SBIZCT	BizContent Framework Test
SBIZCTC	BizContent Configuration Test
SBIZCTO	BizContent Framework Test
SBIZC_CFGT	Display Configuration Templates
SBMA	BOR Migration Assistant

SAP Transaction Codes – Volume Two

SBPT   Administration Process Technology
SBPT_WB   Wizard Builder
SBPT_WIZARD_BUILDER   Wizard Builder
SBRAC   Catalog of Routing Attributes
SBRNFICHT   SBRN Transction Test Environment
SBRREORG   Routing Server Reorganization
SBRT   BCOM RBR: Test Interface
SBRT2   Routing Test
SBRT3   RBR Test Server - Configuration
SBTA   Test background processing
SBWP   SAP Business Workplace
SBWP_GP   SAP Business Workplace for GP
SC2_IDE   C2 Server IDE
SC2_IDE_APP_SYS   Configuration Object
SC38   Start Report (Remote)
SCA1   Cannot be executed directly
SCA2   Cannot be executed directly
SCA3   Cannot be executed directly
SCA4_D   Cannot be executed directly
SCA4_U   Cannot be executed directly
SCA5_D   Cannot be executed directly
SCA5_U   Cannot be executed directly
SCA6_D   Cannot be executed directly
SCA6_U   Cannot be executed directly
SCAL   Factory Calendar with GUI
SCAL_TCONVC   Customizing: Techn. Calendar Conv.
SCASE   Case Management
SCASEPS   Electronic Desk
SCASEPSCUSTOMIZING   Customizing Electronic Desk
SCASE_ARCHIVE   SCMG : Case Archiving
SCASE_CUSTOMIZING   Customizing Case Management
SCASE_NUMBERRANGE   Number Range Maintenance: SCMGCASEID
SCAT   Computer Aided Test Tool
SCC1   Client Copy - Special Selections
SCC3   Client Copy Log
SCC4   Client Administration
SCC5   Delete Client
SCC7   Post-Client Import Methods
SCC8   Client Export
SCC9   Remote Client Copy
SCCL   Local Client Copy
SCDN   Change Documents: Number Ranges
SCDO   Display Change Document Objects
SCDT_MAPPING   Edit Synchronization Objects
SCEM   CATT - EM
SCFB   Role Manager: Start of a Function
SCHAR   Classification browser
SCHED_ANALYZE_ACT   Activate Scheduling Analysis
SCHED_ANALYZE_DISP   Display Scheduling Analysis
SCI   ABAP Code Inspector
SCID   Code Inspector for Specified Object
SCII   Code Inspector: Inspection
SCLAS   Classification browser
SCLS   Classification Tool-Set

SAP Transaction Codes – Volume Two

SCLS_TRANSP_CLASSI   Transport Classifications
SCMA   Schedule Manager: Scheduler
SCMACUS   Maintain Task Lists
SCMAN   Change Management Server
SCMAPROG_CUST   Schedule Manager: Register Programs
SCMATP   SchedMan: Task List Maintenance
SCMATRANS_CUST   SchedMan: Register Transactions
SCMA_PROG_CUST   SCMA: Registrat. of Cust. Programs
SCMC   SAP Central Monitoring Console
SCMGVIEWGEN   View Generator
SCMO   Schedule Manager: Monitor
SCMP   View/Table Comparison
SCMSCA   Caches
SCMSHO   Locations of Hosts
SCMSIP   Locations of IP Subnets
SCMSLP   Location Path for Caching
SCMSMO   Knowledge Provider Monitor
SCMSPL   Additional Locations for CS Alias
SCMSPLD   Cache Preload
SCMSPX   Content Server Aliases
SCON   SAPconnect - Administration
SCOOLTOOL   Administration of ESF Tools
SCOT   SAPconnect - Administration
SCOV   ABAP Coverage Analyzer
SCP   Display and Maintain Code Page
SCPE_PQ1   Maintain Price Quotations for CPE
SCPE_PQ2   Maintain Price Quotations for CPE
SCPE_PQ3   Display Price Quotations for CPE
SCPE_PQ_SIM   Define Price Quotation f. Simulation
SCPE_TCURR_SIM   Define Exchange Rates for Simulation
SCPI   Production Optimization Interface
SCPM   CATT - EM
SCPMIG   Character Conversion
SCPR20   Activate BC Sets
SCPR20PR   BC Set Activation Logs
SCPR3   Display and maintain BC Sets
SCPRAT   Change BC Set Value Attributes
SCPRCOP   Copy Several BC Sets
SCPRIP   Delete Several BC Sets
SCPRSETUP   BC Sets: Central Settings
SCPRUPP   Use of BC Sets in IMG
SCRE   Role Manager: Start of a Report
SCRK   Number range maintenance: CSCR_KEYN
SCRM   CRM-Relevant IMG in PlugIn of R/3
SCSM   Maintenance Dialog for CCMSYSAS
SCTS_RESNAME   Naming Conventions in ABAP Workbench
SCTS_RSWBO004   System Change Option
SCTS_TRANS_PATH_EDIT   Navigation IMG -> Trans.Route Editor
SCU0   Customizing Cross-System Viewer
SCU3   Table History
SCU3ARCH1   Create Database Log Archives
SCUA   Central User Administration
SCUC   CUA: Synchronize company addresses
SCUG   Transfer Users

SAP Transaction Codes – Volume Two

SCUL	Central User Administration Log
SCUM	Central User Administration
SCUSSEQUENCE	Call Sequence for Hierarchies
SCWB	Correction Workbench
SD11	Data Modeler
SDBE	Explain an SQL statement
SDCAS_MCQ	Call MC/Q From Address Selection
SDCC	Service Data Control Center
SDCCN	Service Data Control Center
SDD1	Duplicate Sales Documents in Period
SDHB	Test Online Help
SDME_MDB	DME: Maintenance Dialog Builder
SDME_MDB_NEW	DME: Maintenance Dialog Builder
SDME_MOB	DME: Maintenance Object Builder
SDME_START	DME: Maintenance Transaction Call
SDMO	Dynamic Menu (old)
SDO1	Orders within time period
SDOCU	Maintain Documentation Structure
SDOK_QUEUE01	Test Transaction for KPRO Queueing
SDPI	Number Range Maint.: SD_PICKING
SDPV	Generate product proposal
SDQ1	Expiring Quotations
SDQ2	Expired Quotations
SDQ3	Completed Quotations
SDV	Document Viewer
SDV1	Expiring Contracts
SDV2	Expired Contracts
SDV3	Completed Contracts
SDVK	Purchase Analysis Sales Documents
SDW0	ABAP Development WB Initial Screen
SDW0_OLD	ABAP Development WB Initial Screen
SDWB	Service Definition Work Bench
SE01	Transport Organizer (Extended)
SE03	Transport Organizer Tools
SE06	Set Up Transport Organizer
SE07	CTS Status Display
SE09	Transport Organizer
SE10	Transport Organizer
SE11	ABAP Dictionary Maintenance
SE11_OLD	ABAP Dictionary Maintenance
SE12	ABAP Dictionary Display
SE12_OLD	ABAP Dictionary Display
SE13	Maintain Technical Settings (Tables)
SE14	Utilities for Dictionary Tables
SE15	ABAP/4 Repository Information System
SE16	Data Browser
SE16N	General Table Display
SE16RFCDESSECU	Data Browser RFCDESSECU
SE16T000	Data Browser T000
SE16TXCOMSECU	Data Browser TXCOMSECU
SE16USR40	Data Browser USR40
SE16USRACL	Data Browser USRACL
SE16USRACLEXT	Data Browser USRACLEXT
SE16V_T599R	Data Browser V_T599R

SE16W3TREES	Data Browser W3TREES
SE16WWWFUNC	Data Browser WWWFUNC
SE16WWWREPS	Data Browser WWWREPS
SE16_ANEA	Data Browser ANEA
SE16_ANEK	Data Browser ANEK
SE16_ANEP	Data Browser ANEP
SE16_ANLA	Data Browser ANLA
SE16_ANLC	Data Browser ANLC
SE16_ANLP	Data Browser ANLP
SE16_ANLZ	Data Browser ANLZ
SE16_BKPF	Data Browser BKPF
SE16_BSEG	Data Browser BSEG
SE16_BSEG_ADD	Data Browser BSEG_ADD
SE16_BSID	Data Browser BSID
SE16_BSIK	Data Browser BSIK
SE16_BSIS	Data Browser BSIS
SE16_ECMCA	Data Browser Journal Entries
SE16_ECMCT	Data Browser Totals Records
SE16_KNA1	Data Browser KNA1
SE16_KNB1	Data Browser KNB1
SE16_LFA1	Data Browser LFA1
SE16_LFB1	Data Browser LFB1
SE16_MARA	Data Browser MARA
SE16_MARC	Data Browser MARC
SE16_RFCDESSECU	Data Browser RFCDESSECU
SE16_SKA1	Data Browser SKA1
SE16_SKB1	Data Browser SKB1
SE16_T000	Data Browser T000
SE16_T807R	Data Browser T807R
SE16_TCJ_CHECK_STACK	Data Browser TCJ_CHECK_STACKS
SE16_TCJ_CPD	Data Browser TCJ_CPD
SE16_TCJ_C_JOURNALS	Data Browser TCJ_C_JOURNALS
SE16_TCJ_DOCUMENTS	Data Browser TCJ_DOCUMENTS
SE16_TCJ_POSITIONS	Data Browser TCJ_POSITIONS
SE16_TCJ_WTAX_ITEMS	Data Browser TCJ_WTAX_ITEMS
SE16_TXCOMSECU	Data Browser TXCOMSECU
SE16_USR40	Data Browser USR40
SE16_USRACL	Data Browser USRACL
SE16_USRACLEXT	Data Browser USRACLEXT
SE16_V_T599R	Data Browser V_T599R
SE16_W3TREES	Data Browser W3TREES
SE16_WWWFUNC	Data Browser WWWFUNC
SE16_WWWREPS	Data Browser WWWREPS
SE17	General Table Display
SE18	Business Add-Ins: Definitions
SE19	Business Add-Ins: Implementations
SE20	Enhancements
SE21	Package Builder
SE24	Class Builder
SE29	Application Packets
SE30	ABAP Objects Runtime Analysis
SE32	ABAP Text Element Maintenance
SE32_OLD	ABAP Text Element Maintenance
SE32_WB99	ABAP Text Element Maintenance

SAP Transaction Codes – Volume Two

SE33	Context Builder
SE35	ABAP/4 Dialog Modules
SE36	Logical Database Builder
SE37	ABAP Function Modules
SE38	ABAP Editor
SE38L	SE38 with RCIFIMAX
SE38M	Define Variant for RAPOKZFX
SE38N	SE38 with Default RDELALOG
SE38P	Delete ALE Change Pointers
SE38Q	Init. Data Transfer In Transit Qty
SE39	Splitscreen Editor: (New)
SE39O	Splitscreen Editor: Program Compare
SE40	MP: Standards Maint. and Translation
SE41	Menu Painter
SE43	Maintain Area Menu
SE43N	Maintain Area Menu
SE51	Screen Painter
SE54	Generate table view
SE55	Internal table view maintenance call
SE56	Internal table view display call
SE57	Internal table view deletion call
SE58	Web Dynpro Converter
SE61	SAP Documentation
SE61D	Display of SAPScript Text
SE61_03	Display SE61 Documents in Modal View
SE62	Industry Utilities
SE63	Translation: Initial Screen
SE63_OTR	Translation - OTR
SE64	Terminology
SE71	SAPscript form
SE72	SAPscript Styles
SE73	SAPscript Font Maintenance
SE74	SAPscript format conversion
SE75	SAPscript Settings
SE75TTDTGC	SAPscript: Change standard symbols
SE75TTDTGD	SAPscript: Display standard symbols
SE76	SAPscript: Form Translation
SE77	SAPscript Styles Translation
SE78	Administration of Form Graphics
SE80	Object Navigator
SE80_ENH	Object Navigator
SE81	Application Hierarchy
SE82	Application Hierarchy
SE83	Reuse Library
SE83_START	Start Reuse Library
SE84	Repository Information System
SE85	ABAP/4 Repository Information System
SE89	Maintain Trees in Information System
SE8I	Lists in Repository Infosystem
SE90	Process Model Information System
SE91	Message Maintenance
SE92	New SysLog Msg Maintenance as of 46A
SE92N	Maintain System Log Messages
SE93	Maintain Transaction Codes

SAP Transaction Codes – Volume Two

SE94   Customer enhancement simulation
SE95   Modification Browser
SE95_UTIL   Modification Browser Utilities
SE97   Maint. transaction call authorizatn
SEARCH_SAP_MENU   Find in SAP Menu
SEARCH_USER_MENU   Find in User Menu
SECATT   Extended Computer Aided Test Tool
SECATT_HIST   eCATT User History
SECATT_UTIL   eCATT Utilities
SECOCO   Control Composer
SECR   Audit Information System
SECSTORE   Administration of Secure Storage
SEEF_MIGWB   Migration Workbench
SELVIEW   Selection view maintenance
SEM_BEX   Business Explorer Analyzer
SEM_CHAR_HIER   OLTP Metadata Repository
SEM_CHAR_TEXT   OLTP Metadata Repository
SEM_NAV   Business Explorer Navigator
SEND_BUHI_IDOC   Send Group Hierarchy Directly
SENG   Administration of External Indexes
SENGEXPLORER   Explorer Index Administration
SENH   Display Enhancement Information
SEPA   EPS Server: Administration
SEPM_DG   EPM: Data Generator
SEPS   SAP Electronic Parcel Service
SERP   Reporting: Change Tree Structure
SESF_GCP_TEST   Starts Test Environment
SESS   Session Manager Menu Tree Display
SESSION_MANAGER   Session Manager Menu Tree Display
SESS_START_OBJECT   Start an Object
SES_ADMIN   Search Engine Service: Admin
SETB   Direct Input for BUSAB
SEU_DEPTYPE   Maintain dependency types
SEU_INT   Object Browser
SEU_INT_ENH   Object Navigator
SF01   Client-Specific File Names
SF07   File Name Analysis
SFAC   Field selection maintenance
SFACBOM   BOM header field selection
SFACCOM   Component assignment field selection
SFACITM   BOM item field selection
SFACMBM   Mat. BOM assignment field selection
SFACMK   Field sel. insp. characteristics
SFACMTK   Mat. task list assignment field sel.
SFACMW   Field sel. insp. charac. values
SFACOPR   Field selection operations
SFACPRT   Field selection PRT
SFACSEQ   Field selection sequence
SFACTSK   Task list header field selection
SFAW   Field Selection Maintenance
SFCMT   IMG: Structured Facts Capture
SFGDT_TOOL   Tool for Risk Objects
SFP   Form Builder
SFP_ZCI_UPDATE   Interactive Forms: ZCI Update

SAP Transaction Codes – Volume Two

SFSQB	Fast Search Query Builder
SFSSETUP	Fast Search Initial Setup
SFT1	Maintain Public Holidays
SFT2	Maintain Public Holiday Calendar
SFT3	Maintain Factory Calendar
SFTRACE	SAP Smart Forms: Trace
SFW1	Switch
SFW2	Switch
SFW3	Switch
SFW5	Switch Framework Customizing
SFW_BROWSER	Switch Framework Browser
SG10	Workflow Overview
SG11	Start Workflow
SG12	Send Object with Memo
SG1C	Sent Documents
SG1E	Private Memo
SG1H	Display Relationships
SG1I	Attachment List
SG1J	Create Memo for Object
SG1K	Subscribe To Object
SGEN	SAP Load Generator
SGOS	Customizing Generic Object Services
SGOSHI	Object History
SGOSM	Definition of Generic Services
SGOSTEST	Test Tool Generic Object Services
SGOSTEST2	Test Service Components
SGOS_OBJ_DISP	Default Method of Object
SGR_OLDWORKFLOW_CUST	Store GR: Workflow Customizing
SGR_WORKFLOW_CUST	Store GR: Workflow Customizing
SH01	Online help: F1 Help server
SH02	Online help: Link tracing
SH03	Call extended help
SHD0	Transaction and Screen Variants
SHD0_MANDT	Client Dependent Tr. Variants
SHD1	Internal: Variant transaction call
SHDB	Batch Input Transaction Recorder
SHDG	Global Fields: Change and Display
SHDI	Transaction Variant Image Archive
SHDS	Internal: Save transaction variant
SHD_CHECK	Test Screen Variants and GuiXT
SHD_SWITCH	Activate Standard Variant User
SHI0	Structure buffer: Node type maint.
SHI1	Structure buffer: Link type maint.
SHI2	Structure buffer: Struc. type maint.
SHI3	Structure maintenance
SHMA	Shared Objects: Management
SHMM	Shared Objects Monitor
SHN0	IMG Shift Note
SHN1	Create Shift Note
SHN1_	Create Shift Note
SHN2	Change Shift Note
SHN2_	Change Shift Note
SHN3	Display Shift Note
SHN3_	Display Shift Note

SHN4	List Shift Notes	
SHN4_	List Shift Notes	
SHOW_REPORT_R1	Display Source for Report R_TAB...	
SHOW_REPORT_R2	Display Source for Report R_ALV...	
SHOW_REPORT_R3	Display Source for Report R_ALV...	
SHOW_REPORT_R4	Display Source for Report R_QUE...	
SHOW_REPORT_R5	Display Source for Report R_ALV_...	
SHOW_REPORT_R6	Display Source for Report R_ALV_...	
SHOW_REPORT_SOURCE	Call ABAP Code Display from Docu.	
SHP_DELIC	MiniApp: Incomplete Shipment	
SHR0	IMG Shift Report	
SHR1	Create Shift Report	
SHR2	Change Shift Report	
SHR3	Display Shift Report	
SHR4	List Shift Reports	
SHR4_	List Shift Reports	
SHXC	Maintain HOTPACKEXC	
SHXC1	Special Approvals Procedure	
SI00	SAP Knowledge Warehouse	
SI00_DOCU	SAP Knowledge Warehouse	
SI00_OLD	SAP Knowledge Warehouse	
SI00_TRAIN	SAP Knowledge Warehouse	
SI21	Migration of extended help	
SI22	Create Command Files	
SI23	Init. screen of cust. maint. interf.	
SI23_1	Maintain standard release	
SI23_2	Maintain enhancement	
SI23_3	Maintain enhancement chain	
SI23_4	Lock/unlock releases	
SI23_6	Edit templates	
SI24	Initial Screen of IMG (KW)	
SI24_1	Customizing System (KW)	
SI24_10	RSIWB_EXPORT_MAIL_SERVICES	
SI24_11	KW: Customizing Transport	
SI24_12	KW: Customizing Workflow	
SI24_13	KW: Customizing Authorizations	
SI24_14	KW Customizing	
SI24_2	Customizing Server (KW)	
SI24_3	Customizing Assignments (KW)	
SI24_4	Customizing Export Variants (KW)	
SI24_5	Define Initial Structure (Custom.)	
SI24_6	Automat. Instantiation of Info Obj.	
SI24_7	Set export_range in iwbsetting	
SI24_8	Support R/3 Link Maintenance (Cust)	
SI24_9	Document Management Areas (View)	
SI24_CSCONFIG	Autoconfiguration Content Server	
SI24_EXTENSION	Maintain Enhancement Rel./String	
SI24_WF1	KW WF - Authorization Procedure	
SI24_WF2	KW Customizing - WF Copy Editing	
SI80	Knowledge Warehouse	
SI80_BF_ADMIN	Admin Functions for BF Assignments	
SI81	Management	
SI85	Knowledge Warehouse (General)	
SI86	Management	

SAP Transaction Codes – Volume Two

SI88   HTML Export
SI88_FOLDER_LIST   Create Folder/Structure List
SI88_PREANALYSIS   Preanalyze Structure-Based Exports
SI89   Analyze HTML Export Logs
SI90   Knowledge Warehouse: Training
SIAC1   Display Web Objects (Old Format)
SIAC_ICON_UPLOAD   ITS: Upload ICONS for WebGUI
SIAC_PUBLISH_ALL_INT   Publish All ITS Services
SIAC_REGENERATE_TEMP   Regenerate IAC Templates
SIAT   System Menu
SIBU   Industry Maintenance
SICF   HTTP Service Hierarchy Maintenance
SICFRECORDER   ICF: Display Recorded Objects
SICFREC_SHOW   Display ICFRECORDER Entry
SICF_INST   Activate Service During Installation
SICK   Installation Check
SIC_MA   Maintain SWP authorities for vendors
SIC_MD   Maintain JIT Authorities for vendors
SIC_NORM_CASCO_CFG_M   Maintain Configuration of CASECON
SIC_NORM_CASCO_CFG_S   Maintain Configuration of CASECON
SIC_NORM_FORMC_CFG_M   Maintain Configuration of FORMCTY
SIC_NORM_FORMC_CFG_S   DISPLAY Configuration of FORMCTY
SIC_NORM_QUACO_CFG_M   Maintain Configuration of QUACON
SIC_NORM_QUACO_CFG_S   Show Configuration of QUACON
SIC_NORM_REGEX_CFG_M   Maintain Configuration of REGEX
SIC_NORM_REGEX_CFG_S   Display Configuration of REGEX
SIC_NORM_TOKEN_CFG_M   Maintain Configuration of TOKENIZE
SIC_NORM_TOKEN_CFG_S   Display Configuration of TOKENIZE
SIDELTA   Delta delivery of content
SIGNA   Register Signature Application
SIGNO   Register Signature Object
SIGS   IGS Administration
SII0   Change management
SII00   Display management
SII1   Change documentation
SII10   Display documentation
SII2   Change training
SII20   Display training
SII3   Change HTML-Based Documents
SII30   Display HTML-Based Documents
SII4   XML Training Transaction
SII40   Display XML Documents
SII5   XML Documents Transaction
SIIALL   Change all areas
SIIALL0   Display all areas
SIMGH   IMG Structure Maintenance
SIMG_SPORT   IMG Business / Functional Packages
SIN1   SAPBPT: Inbox
SINA   SAPBPT: Maintain Standard Config.
SISH   System Menu
SISTATE   Maintenance of Hierarchy Status
SISTATE2   Functions for Areas On/Off
SISU   IS-U main menu
SIT0   Translate management

SAP Transaction Codes – Volume Two

SIT00	KW: Documentation Development
SIT1	Translate documentation
SIT10	KW: Documentation Development
SIT2	Translate training
SIT20	KW: Documentation Development
SIT3	Translate HTML-Based Documents
SIT4	Translate XML Training
SIT5	Translate XML Documentation
SITALL	Translate all areas
SITSPMON	Monitor for Internal ITS
SITSQ_ALV	Test Program: ALV Grid
SITSQ_ALV_COMBO	Test Program: ALV Grid
SITSQ_LISTE	Report List Test Program
SITSQ_TOOLBAR	Toolbar Control Test
SI_SEL	KW: Structure Editor Link
SKEP	KEPlicator
SKNF	Maintain Configuration Groups
SKNF_SINGLE	Maintain Configuration Groups
SKPR02	Maintain Document Areas
SKPR03	Display Document Areas
SKPR04	Maintaining Physical Document Class
SKPR06	Index Activation of Document Area
SKPR07	Monitoring for KPRO Retrieval
SKPR08	Category for Document Class
SKPR09	Test Content Repositories
SKPR12	Maintain MIME Content-Types
SKPR13	File Name Extensions
SKPR14	Web Server for Document Areas
SKPR15	Web Servers for Document Classes
SKPRM01	Copy Model Entities
SKPRM03	Copy Class Links
SKPRM04	Copy Instance Table Set
SKPRMC1	Customizing Entity Attributes
SKPRMIC	Invalidate Model Layer Caches
SKPR_INDEXING1	Maintenance Transact. Kpro Indexing
SKPR_MULINDEXING	Multiple Indexing
SKWFIVC	Invalidate all SKWF Caches
SKWR01	Taxonomy Tree Management
SKWR02	Restore Index
SKWR03	Classify Documents
SKWS	CM: Status Management
SL02	PAW - Main Menu
SL100	Change Participant Data
SL101	Create Excel sheet for event results
SL102	Results by tests and locations
SL104	PAW - Deleting Results
SL12	PAW - Survey result answer details
SL13	PAW - Maintain Dynamic Scenarios
SL31	PAW - Test type definitions
SL32	PAW - Location Definitions
SL37	Software Logistic Check (SM37)
SL60	PAW - Test Results Overview
SL601	PAW - Test Results Overview
SL61	PAW - Test Results Transfer to HR

SAP Transaction Codes – Volume Two

SL62	PAW - Lookup Definition Tree
SL63	PAW - Location Test-Catalog
SL64	PAW - Statistical Evaluations
SL65	PAW - Export Test Results
SL66	PAW - Download Certification Details
SL67	PAW - Download Test-Catalog for Loc.
SL69	PAW - Qualification Transfer Log.
SL70	PAW - Person Results Overview
SL71	PAW - Initial Data Generator
SL72	PAW - Enjoy Desktop
SL73	PAW - Batch Qualification Generation
SL74	PAW - Batch Q.- Generation Protocol
SL75	PAW - Item Results Overview
SL76	PAW - Test Structure Display
SL77	PAW - Show comments for test items
SL79	PAW - Location Profile Maintenance
SL80	PAW - Item Statistics
SL90	PAW - Cert Printing Information
SL91	PAW - Maintain location profile
SL92	PAW - Maintain test type profil
SL93	PAW - Maintain Settings
SL94	PAW - Maintain test IO profile
SL95	PAW - Maintain User Profiles
SL96	PAW - Release Control Settings
SL99	PAW - Display authorization profiles
SLAT	Additional Translation Tools
SLAW	License Administration Workbench
SLDAPICUST	SLD API Customizing
SLDB	Logical Databases (Tree Structure)
SLDCHECK	Test SLD Connection
SLDHTMLGUI	Start SLD GUI in Browser
SLDQMON	LDQ Monitor
SLG0	Application Log: Object Maintenance
SLG1	Application Log: Display Logs
SLG2	Application Log: Delete logs
SLGN	Applic.log: Number range maintenance
SLGT	Register in Central Object Directory
SLG_ISU	Log Display for Parallel Mass Run
SLIB	Reuse Library
SLIBN	Maintain Reuse Library
SLIBP	Maintain Reuse Product
SLIB_START	Maintain Reuse Library
SLICENSE	Administer SAP Licenses
SLIN	ABAP: Extended Program Check
SLIS	FI-SL Spec.Purpose Ledg. Info.System
SLLS	Translation Statistics
SLLT	Translation Performance Statistics
SLOG	Overview of Static Extract Creation
SLPP	Proposal Pool
SLW3	Worklist Scheduler
SLW4	Translation: Application Hierarchy
SLWA	Translation Environment Admin.
SLWB	Translation Environment Scheduler
SLXT	Translation Transport

SAP Transaction Codes – Volume Two

SM01	Lock Transactions
SM02	System Messages
SM04	User List
SM12	Display and Delete Locks
SM12OLD	Old sm12
SM13	Administrate Update Records
SM14	Update Program Administration
SM18	Reorganize Security Audit Log
SM19	Security Audit Configuration
SM20	Analysis of Security Audit Log
SM20N	Analysis of Security Audit Log
SM20_OLD	Security Audit Log Evaluation (Old)
SM21	Online System Log Analysis
SM21_E2E	Syslog Analysis Using E2E
SM28	Installation Check
SM29	Model Transfer for Tables
SM30	Call View Maintenance
SM30VSNCSYSACL	Call of SM30 for Table VSNCSYSACL
SM30V_BRG	Call of SM30 for View V_BRG
SM30V_DDAT	Call of SM30 for View V_DDAT
SM30_CUS_COUNT	Maintain Table CUS_COUNT
SM30_CUS_INDU	Maintain Table CUS_INDU
SM30_CUS_SYST	Maintain Table CUS_SYST
SM30_PRGN_CUST	Maintain Table SSM_CUST
SM30_SSM_CUST	Maintain Table SSM_CUST
SM30_SSM_RFC	Maintain Table SSM_RFC
SM30_SSM_VAR	Maintain Table SSM_VAR
SM30_STXSFREPL	Smart Styles: Replace Font
SM30_TVARV	Call SM30 for Table TVARV
SM30_VAL_AKH	Maintain Table VAL_AKH
SM30_VSNCSYSACL	Call Up SM30 for Table VSNCSYSACL
SM30_V_001_COS	Cost of sales accounting status
SM30_V_BRG	Call SM30 for View V_BRG
SM30_V_DDAT	Call SM30 for View V_DDAT
SM30_V_FAGL_T881	Callup of SM30 for View V_FAGL_T881
SM30_V_FAGL_T882G	Callup of SM30 for View V_FAGL_T882G
SM30_V_T001A	Callup of SM30 for View V_T001A
SM30_V_T585A	Call Up SM30 for Table V_T585A
SM30_V_T585B	Call SM30 for Table V_T585B
SM30_V_T585C	Call SM30 for Table V_T585C
SM30_V_T599R	Call Up SM30 for Table V_T599R
SM30_V_TKA05	Cost Center Categories
SM31	Call View Maintenance Like SM30
SM31_OLD	Old Table Maintenance
SM32	Maintain Table Parameter ID TAB
SM33	Display Table Parameter ID TAB
SM34	Viewcluster maintenance call
SM34_VC_FAGLLDGRPMAP	Call SM34 for View VC_FAGL_LDGRPMAP
SM35	Batch Input Monitoring
SM35P	Batch Input: Log Monitoring
SM36	Schedule Background Job
SM36WIZ	Job definition wizard
SM37	Overview of job selection
SM37B	Simple version of job selection

SAP Transaction Codes – Volume Two

SM37BAK	Old SM37 backup
SM37C	Flexible version of job selection
SM38	Queue Maintenance Transaction
SM39	Job Analysis
SM49	Execute external OS commands
SM50	Work Process Overview
SM51	List of SAP Systems
SM52	Virtual Machine Overview
SM53	VMC Monitoring and Administration
SM54	TXCOM Maintenance
SM55	THOST Maintenance
SM56	Number Range Buffer
SM58	Asynchronous RFC Error Log
SM580	Transaction for Drag & Relate
SM59	RFC Destinations (Display/Maintain)
SM59_OLD	RFC Destinations (Display/Maintain)
SM5A	RFC Chain Analysis
SM5B	Maintenance of DPTIMETAB
SM61	Backgroup control objects monitor
SM61B	New control object management
SM61BAK	Old SM61
SM62	Event History and Background Events
SM63	Display/Maintain Operating Mode Sets
SM64	Manage Background Processing Events
SM65	Background Processing Analysis Tool
SM66	Systemwide Work Process Overview
SM69	Maintain External OS Commands
SMAP01	Maintain Solution Map objects
SMARTFORMS	SAP Smart Forms
SMARTFORM_CODE	SAP Smart Forms: Target Coding
SMARTFORM_TRACE	SAP Smart Forms: Trace
SMARTSTYLES	SAP Smart Styles
SMCL	CSL: Monitor
SMCX	Matchcode OCX
SMED	IS-H*MED area menu (consolidated)
SMEN	Session Manager Menu Tree Display
SMET	Display frequency of function calls
SMETDELBUFF	Del. Measurement data in shared bfr
SMETDELPROG	Delete programs in shared buffer
SMGW	Gateway Monitor
SMICM	ICM Monitor
SMICM_SOS	ICM Monitor
SMI_AGREEMENTS	Maintain SMI Agreements
SMI_APPLICATION_LOG	Application log for SMI messages
SMI_MESS	Maintain Customizable Error Messages
SMI_PROFILE_A	Activate planning Profile
SMI_PROFILE_C	Maintain SMI planning Profile
SMI_PROFILE_D	Delete SMI planning Profile
SMI_PROFILE_S	Display SMI planning Profile
SMLG	Maint.Assign. Logon Grp to Instance
SMLT	Language Management
SMLT_EX	Language Export
SMME	Output control Message Block Table
SMMS	Message Server Monitor

SAP Transaction Codes – Volume Two

SMOD	SAP Enhancement Management
SMOMO	Mobile Engine
SMQ1	qRFC Monitor (Outbound Queue)
SMQ2	qRFC Monitor (Inbound Queue)
SMQ3	qRFC Monitor (Saved E-Queue)
SMQA	tRFC/qRFC: Confirm. status & data
SMQE	qRFC Administration
SMQR	Registration of Inbound Queues
SMQS	Registration of Destinations
SMT	Customizing Transformation Workbench
SMT1	Trusted Systems (Display <-> Maint.)
SMT2	Trusting systems (Display <->Maint.)
SMTHACTION	Execute Specific Actions in ABAP
SMTR_START_HISTORY	Call object history
SMT_C	Client-Dependent Transformations
SMT_OLD	Customizing Transformation Workbench
SMT_START_APPL	Maintain mappings
SMT_START_CONTEXT	Maintain mappings' contexts
SMT_START_EXTENSION	Maintain mappings' extensions
SMW0	SAP Web Repository
SMX	Display Own Jobs
SMXX	Display Own Jobs
SMY1	Maintenance of nodes for MyObjects
SN00	IS-H: System Menu Hospital
SNC0	SNC Access Control List: Systems
SNC1	Generate SNC name for user
SNC2	Export SNC name of user
SNC3	User initial control list 3.1-4.0
SNC4	Check canonical SNC names
SNL1	Display NLS (character set, lang.)
SNL2	Set NLS (character set, language...)
SNL3	Develop NLS (character set, lang...)
SNLB	IS-H*MED: SAP R/3
SNLS	Display NLS (character set, lang.)
SNOTE	Note Assistant
SNRO	Number Range Objects
SNUM	Number Range Driver
SO00	SAPoffice: Short Message
SO01	SAPoffice: Inbox
SO01X	SAPoffice: Inbox
SO02	SAPoffice: Outbox
SO02X	SAPoffice: Outbox
SO03	SAPoffice: Private Folders
SO03X	SAPoffice: Private Folders
SO04	SAPoffice: Shared Folders
SO04X	SAPoffice: Shared Folders
SO05	SAPoffice: Private Trash
SO05X	SAPoffice: Private Trash
SO06	SAPoffice: Substitution on/off
SO07	SAPoffice: Resubmission
SO07X	SAPoffice: Resubmission
SO10	SAPscript: Standard Texts
SO12	SAPoffice: User Master
SO13	SAPoffice: Substitute

SO15	SAPoffice: Distribution Lists
SO16	SAPoffice: Profile
SO17	SAPoffice: Delete Shared Trash
SO18	SAPoffice: Shared Trash
SO19	SAPoffice: Default Documents
SO20	SAPoffice: Private Default Document
SO21	Maintain PC Work Directory
SO22	SAPoffice: Delete PC Temp. Files
SO23	SAPoffice: Distribution Lists
SO24	SAPoffice: Maintenance of default PC
SO28	Maintain SOGR
SO2_MIME_REPOSITORY	Mime Repository
SO2_TAG_BROWSER	Tag Library
SO30	Business Workplace: Reorg.
SO31	Reorganization (daily)
SO36	Create Automatic Forwarding
SO38	SAPoffice: Synchr. of Folder Auths.
SO40	SAPoffice: Cust. Layout Set MAIL
SO41	SAPoffice: Cust. Layout Set TELEFAX
SO42	SAPoffice: Cust.Layout Set TELEFAX_K
SO43	SAPoffice: Cust.Layout Set TELEFAX_M
SO44	SAPoffice: Cust. Layout Set TELEX
SO50	Rules for inbound distribution
SO52	Deletes Address from User Master
SO55	User consistency check
SO70	Hypertext: Display/Maint. Structure
SO71	Test plan management
SO72	Maintain Hypertext Module
SO73	Import graphic into SAPfind
SO81	SAPfind: Free Text Indexing (Test)
SO82	SAPfind: Free Text Retrieval Batch
SO85	SAPfind: txt_seq_search
SO86	SAPfind: Txt_seq_search_1
SO90	SAPfind: shell folders service prog.
SO91	SAPfind SO: SAPoffice Marketing Info
SO95	Pregenerated Search Queries - Selec.
SO99	Put Information System
SOA	SAP ArchiveLink
SOA0	ArchiveLink Workflow document types
SOAACT	Actual Calculation of Provisions
SOAAD	ACE Account Assignment
SOAADCONT01	Acct Determntn: Mntn Entries Area 01
SOAADCONT02	Acct Determntn: Mntn Entries Area 02
SOAADMETA01	Acct Determntn: Define Rule Area 01
SOAADMETA02	Acct Determntn: Define Rule Area 02
SOAADMETASGL	Acct Detrmn: Def 1-Step Set of Rules
SOAAD_MAIN	Acct Determination: Maintain Entries
SOAAD_META	ACE Account Assignment
SOAARCHPREP	Preparation of the Archiving Run
SOACARRYFORWARD	Balance Carryforward
SOAD	SAPoffice: External Addresses
SOADATADEL	Deletion of Data in the Accrl Engine
SOADSITEMS	Reporting Accrual Objects SOA
SOADSPARAMS	Reporting ACE Object Parameters SOA

SAP Transaction Codes – Volume Two

SOAFCHART	Simulation: Separation Rates
SOAFIRECON	Accrual Engine / FI Reconciliation
SOAFISCYEAR	Open/Lock Fiscal Years in ACE
SOAFVERS	Versions for Separation Rates
SOAHRCON	Set Up Connection to HR System
SOAHRFI	Assignmnt Award <-> Method
SOAHRTRANS	Data Transfer from HR System
SOAIACE	Assignment Award <-> Index
SOAICHART	Simulation: Performance of Indexes
SOAIMG	IMG for Stock Option Accounting
SOAIVAL	Definition of Index Values
SOAIVERS	Versions for Performance of Indexes
SOAMANAGER	SOA Manager
SOAPPLOG	Display Periodic Posting Runs
SOAPSDOCITEMS	Display Line Items in the Acc Engine
SOAPSITEMS	Display Total Values in the Acc.Eng.
SOAREVERS	Reversal of Provisions Postings
SOASCHART	Simulation: Stock Price Performance
SOASIM	Simulation of Provisions
SOASVERS	Versions for Perfmce of Stock Prices
SOATRANSFER	Transferral of ACE Docs to Accnting
SOATREE01	Create allocations
SOATREE03	Displaying Grants
SOA_ACEPS_APPLLOG	Number Range Maintenance: ACEAPPLLOG
SOBJ	Maintenance Object Attributes
SOBL_MODEL	Model Data Object Relationships
SOBN01	Personal data
SOBT	Maintenance Object Attributes
SOCP	SAPoffice: External Addresses
SODIS	BCS: Disclosures Communication
SODS	SAPoffice: LDAP Browser
SOEX	Express Message
SOFF	SAPoffice: Area Menu
SOFR	Mapping of telex recipients
SOHI	Object History
SOIN	BCS: Inbound Send Requests (SMTP)
SOJ2	SAP Objects: Display Methods
SOJ3	SAP Objects: Display Return Values
SOL	Solutions: Check Solution Paths
SOLE	OLE Applications
SOLMAP	Maintain Solution Maps
SOLPA	Solution Paths
SOPE	Exclude Document Classes
SOSB	Send Request Overview (Users)
SOSG	Send Request Overview (Groups)
SOST	SAPconnect Send Requests
SOSV	SAPconnect Send Requests
SOTD	SAPoffice: Maintain Object Types
SOTG	Maintain object type groups
SOTR	Test transaction for API1 (received)
SOTR_EDIT	Editor for OTR Texts
SOY1	SAPoffice: Mass Maint. Users
SOY2	SAPoffice: Collect Statistics Data
SOY3	SAPoffice: Statistics Evaluation

SAP Transaction Codes – Volume Two

SOY4	SAPoffice: Access Overview
SOY5	SAPoffice: Inbox Overview
SOY6	SAPoffice: Document overview
SOY7	SAPoffice: Folder overview
SOY8	SAPoffice: Mass Archiving
SOY9	SAPoffice: Inbox Reorganization
SOYA	SAPoffice: Change Folder Owner
SP00	Spool and related areas
SP01	Output Controller
SP01O	Spool Controller
SP02	Display Spool Requests
SP02O	Display Output Requests
SP11	TemSe directory
SP12	TemSe Administration
SP1T	Output Control (Test)
SPACKAGE	Package Builder
SPAD	Spool Administration
SPAK	Package Builder
SPAM	Support Package Manager
SPAR	Determine Storage Parameters
SPAT	Spool Administration (Test)
SPAU	Display Modified DE Objects
SPAU_ENH	Object Navigator
SPBM	Monitoring parallel background tasks
SPBT	Test: Parallel background tasks
SPDD	Display Modified DDIC Objects
SPEC01	Specification system: Edit template
SPEC02	Specification system: Edit datasheet
SPERS_DIALOG	Edit Personalization
SPERS_MAINT	Personalization object processing
SPERS_REUSE_DEMO	Personalization Test Transaction
SPERS_TEST	Test personalization objects
SPFPAR	Display Profile Parameters
SPH1	Create and maintain telephony server
SPH2	Maintain outgoing number change
SPH3	Maintain incoming number change
SPH4	Activ./deactiv. telephony in system
SPH5	Define Address Data Areas
SPH6	Language-dependent server descrip.
SPH7	Language-dep. addr. data area texts
SPHA	Telephony administration
SPHB	SAPphone: System Administration
SPHD	SAPphone: Own telephone number
SPHS	SAPphone: Interface for Telephone
SPHSREMOTE	Start Softphone remote
SPHT	SAPphone Test Environment
SPHW	Initiate Call in Web Applications
SPIA	PMI Administration
SPIAPPLOG	Call Application Log
SPIC01	Process Information Repository
SPID	Display Process Repository
SPIG	Maintain Process Groups
SPIM	Process Monitoring: Meta Data
SPIO	Process Monitoring Overview

SAP Transaction Codes – Volume Two

SPIP   PMI: Self-Monitoring Logs
SPIS   Start User Interface for Monitoring
SPI_ALE01   ALE monitoring
SPI_BOR01   BOR Monitoring
SPI_TRFC01   tRFC Monitoring
SPL_GENERATE_DDIC   Generate additional fields
SPO0   Data for Drag&Relate
SPO1   Generic Transaction Starter
SPO4   Drag&Relate Metadata: Object View
SPO4_DISP   Drag&Relate Metadata (Display Only)
SPO5   Drag&Relate: Initial Screen
SPOV   Spool Request Overview
SPPFC   PPF: Initial Screen in Customizing
SPPFCADM   PPF: Administration
SPPFCONCREATE1   Edit Schedule Conditions
SPPFCONCREATE2   Edit Start Conditions
SPPFCONS   PPF: Check Consistency
SPPFCONSISTENCY   PPF: Consistency in Customizing
SPPFCWIZARD   PPF: Actions Definition Using Wizard
SPPFDEMO   PPF: Demo application
SPPFDET   PPF: Condition definition
SPPFDETCRM   PPF: Action Profile with Conditions
SPPFP   Process Actions
SPPF_PRPR   Print Profile Maintenance
SPRM   Current Customizing
SPRO   Customizing - Edit Project
SPROJECT   Project management
SPROJECT_ADMIN   Project Management
SPROXSET   Proxy Generation: Settings
SPROXY   Enterprise Repository Browser
SPROXY_START   Display Proxy Editor
SPRO_ADMIN   Customizing - Project Management
SPTP   Text elem. maint. for print formats
SPUMG   Unicode Preconversion
SPWSE_DTEL_EXIT_REG   Exit technology
SPWSE_DTEL_MAP   call program SPWSE_DTELmap
SQ00   SAP Query: Start queries
SQ00_DEL_PROT   SAP Query: Delete log data
SQ01   SAP Query: Maintain queries
SQ02   SAP Query: Maintain InfoSet
SQ03   SAP Query: Maintain user groups
SQ07   SAP Query: Language comparison
SQ09   SAP Query: Maintain additional func.
SQ10   SAP Query: Role Administration
SQ11   SAP Query: Web reporting (Admin)
SQADB01   Maintain Questions for QADB
SQADB01B   Maint. Questions for QADB Industries
SQADOKU   Maintain Documents for Review
SQASUBJECT   Maintain Subject Areas for Review
SQATOPIC   Maintain Topics for Review
SQBWPROP   BW Settings for Classic InfoSets
SQCIT   Maintain CI Templates
SQDEMO_ADHOC   Starts InfoSet Query for Ad Hoc rep.
SQF   Support Query Framework

SAP Transaction Codes – Volume Two

SQLR   SQL Trace Interpreter
SQVI   QuickViewer
SQ_DEMO_ADHOC   Demo: Start InfoSet Query (Ad Hoc)
SQ_DEMO_DEV   Demo: Start InfoSet Query (Dev.)
SQ_DEMO_DEVELOP   Startet InfoSet Query wth InfoSet
SQ_LEGEND   Sequence Sched.: Select Graphic Elmt
SQ_REPORT_INFOSET   Maintenance of Report Infosets
SR10   Create City
SR11   Change city
SR12   Display city
SR13   Area-Dependent Help
SR20   Create street
SR21   Change street
SR22   Display street
SR30   Create postal code
SR31   Change postal code
SR32   Display postal code
SRCN   Delete Country-Specific Reports
SRDEBUG   Activate Remote Debugging
SREFH00   Change SAP Reference Structure
SREFH04   Edit item in SAP Reference Structure
SREL_MODEL   ModelDataForBORObjectRelationships
SREP   Maintain report definition
SREPO   Repository Comparison
SRET   Report Selection
SRET06   Dummy Transaction
SRET07   Monitoring for Indexing: Non-KPRO
SREV   Review Authoring Environment
SREV01   Review Authoring Environment
SREVIEW   Review Questions Auth. Environment
SRIP   Import of Training Indexes
SRM01   Number Range Maintenance: INFREQUEST
SRM02   Number Range Maintenance: STH_EXPECT
SRM03   Number Range Maintenance: SRM_CONT
SRMBROWSER   Records Browser
SRMCALLMON   Monitor for Call Handler
SRMCMCREATE   Create Content Models
SRMCMEDIT   Edit Content Models
SRMCUSTOMIZING   Customizing Records Management
SRMCUSTSRV   SRM: Maintain Custom Services
SRMEXPORT   Starts Selection Report SRM_EXPORT
SRMMODELER   Records Modeler
SRMO   SAP Retrieval - Monitor
SRMO1   Call of IMS Monitoring
SRMORGTYP   BC-SRV-RM : Type Maint. Organizer
SRMPCR   POID Content Repository
SRMPCR_CLNT   POID Content Repository (Client)
SRMPLANER   Records (File) Planner
SRMPROTOVIEW   Records Management Log Viewer
SRMRECORDSCREATE   Create Personnel Records
SRMREFRULE   Generation Rules for Record Numbers
SRMREGEDIT   SRM Registry Maintenance
SRMREGEDITC   Maintain SRM Registry (Cust. View)
SRMSTART   Records Management

SAP Transaction Codes – Volume Two

SRMVIEWGEN   View Generator
SRM_APPL_LOG   Application Log Settings
SRM_DISP_NO   Number Range Maintenance: SRMDPDPID
SRM_DOCFINDER   SRM: Maintain DocFinder Settings
SRM_DOC_TEMPLATE   SRM: Maintain Status Network
SRM_KC_ADMIN   Administration Keyword Catalog
SRM_KC_EDIT   Maintain Keyword Catalog
SRM_PROFIL   SRM: Maintain Status Profile
SRM_PROP_PERSPUBLISH   Generate Attribute Properties
SRM_RECTEST1   Test BO RECORD Methods
SRM_RECTEST2   Test BO RECORD Dialog Methods
SRM_STATUS   SRM: Maintain Status
SRM_STATUS_NET   SRM: Maintain Status Network
SRM_WFPATH_NO   Number Range Maintenance: SRMWFPATH
SRM_WF_PATH_MAINT   Maintain Process Route
SRN1   Number range maintenance: ADRCITY
SRN2   Number range maintenance: ADRSTREET
SRN3   Number range maintenance: ADRPSTCODE
SROLE   Export User Roles to XML doc.
SRSE   Test Search for the IMS
SRS_GM_SH   Retail Store: Display MDE Data
SRT0   Repository Switch: PUTTB Handling
SRTERROR_E2E   WS related Runtime Errors - E2E
SRTIDOC   Inbound SOAP: Register Service
SRTLOG_E2E   SRT Error Log E2E
SRTM   Run Time Monitor Initial Screen
SRTUTIL   Tracing Utilities for Web Service
SRTUTIL_E2E   SRT Trace Analysis E2E
SRTV   Text Retrieval: Customizing
SRTV_COMPILE   Find Report: Index Generation
SRT_ADRMAP   Path Prefix in ICF for WSDs
SRT_CHANGE   Report Tree Maintenance
SRT_DISPLAY   Display Report Trees
SRT_LOG   SRT Error Log
SRT_TOOLS   SOA Runtime Tools
SRT_UTIL   Tracing Utilities for Web Service
SRZL
SSAA   System Administration Assistant
SSAA_TOP   System Administration Assistant
SSC   SAP Appointment Calendar (internal)
SSC0   SAP Appointment Calendar (Employee)
SSC0X   SAP Appointment Calendar (Employee)
SSC1   SAP (own) Appointment Calendar
SSC1X   SAP (own) Appointment Calendar
SSCA   Appointment Calendar: Auth. Maint.
SSCA1   Appointment calendar: Administration
SSCV   Appoint. diary: VisualBasic frontend
SSFA   SSF: Set Application Parameters
SSFI   IAC: Test: Browser Digital Signature
SSFIDEMO_DIGSIG   Digital Signature Demo (ITS)
SSFVA   Administration of Key Versions
SSM1   Transaction is Old
SSM2   Set Initial Area Menu
SSO2   Workplace Single Sign-On Admin.

SAP Transaction Codes – Volume Two

SSO2D	Workplace: Single Sign-On Display
SSO8	Display Workplace Application Server
SSO9	Maintain Workplace Applic. Server
SSPC	SAP DEFAULT Specifications
SST0	Project Analysis in Customizing
SST7	Complex Analysis
SSTDEMO1	Simple Transformations Demo: Flights
SSTDEMO2	XSLT and ST Demo: Flights
SSUC	Structure graphic: copy settings
SSUD	Structure graphic: delete settings
SSUO	Structure Graphic: Central Settings
ST01	System Trace
ST02	Setups/Tune Buffers
ST03	Workload and Performance Statistics
ST03G	Global Workload Statistics
ST03N	Workload and Performance Statistics
ST04	DB Performance Monitor
ST04M	Multi DB connection
ST04OLD	old DB Performance Monitor
ST04RFC	SAP Remote DB Monitor for SQL Server
ST04_MSS	St04 for MS SQL Server
ST05	Performance Analysis
ST05ACC	Barrier-Free Performance Trace
ST05SAVE	Old ST05
ST05_E2E	Performance Trace anzeigen
ST06	Operating System Monitor
ST06N	Operating System Monitor
ST07	Application monitor
ST10	Table Call Statistics
ST11	Display Developer Traces
ST12	Single transaction analysis
ST13	Analysis&Monitoring tool collection
ST14	Application Analysis
ST20	Screen Trace
ST20LC	Layout Check
ST22	ABAP dump analysis
ST22OLD	Old Dump Analysis
ST22_E2E	ABAP Dumpanalyse E2E
ST30	Global Perf. Analysis: Execute
ST33	Glob. Perf. Analysis: Display Data
ST34	Glob. Perf. Analysis: Log IDs
ST35	Glob. Perf. Analysis: Assign CATTs
ST36	Glob. Perf. Analysis: Delete Data
ST37	Global Perf. Analysis: Eval. Schema
ST62	Create Industry Short Texts
STAD	Statistics display for all systems
STARTING_URLS	SMTR_NAVIGATION_SEND_MESSAGE
START_20C_TRANSFORM	Convert Set Types and Attributes
START_40_TRANSFORM	Set Types Conversion
START_AGR_GENERATOR	Adjust all SAP roles
START_BSP	Start a BSP Application
START_REPORT	Starts report
STATTRACE	Global Statistics & Traces
STAV_TABR	Settle - Status Management

STCTRL_COPY   Copy Table Control User Settings
STCU   Assign Secondary Screens
STCUP   Table control variants upgrade
STDA   Debugger display/control (server)
STDC   Debugger output/control
STDR   Object Directory Consistency Check
STDU   Debugger display/control (user)
STEMPLATE   Customizing templates
STEMPMERGE   Mix templates
STEP10   Export STEP Data
STEP20   Import STEP Data
STERM   SAPterm Terminology Maintenance
STERM_EXTERNAL   Transaction STERM: External Callup
STERM_KEYWORDS   Maintain Index Entries
STERM_REMOTE   Transaction STERM: RFC Callup
STFB   CATT function module test
STFO   Plan Service Connection
STGTC   Konfiguration der Antwortzeit
STI1   Change Documents Payment Details
STI2   Change Docs Correspondence
STI3   Chg. Docs Transaction Authoriz.
STKONTEXTTRACE   Switch On Context Trace
STMS   Transport Management System
STMS_ALERT   TMS Alert Monitor
STMS_DOM   TMS System Overview
STMS_FSYS   Maintain TMS System Lists
STMS_IMPORT   TMS Import Queue
STMS_INBOX   TMS Worklist
STMS_MONI   TMS Import Monitor
STMS_PATH   TMS Transport Routes
STMS_QA   TMS Quality Assurance
STMS_QUEUES   TMS Import Overview
STMS_TCRI   Display/Maintain Table TMSTCRI
STMS_TRACK   TMS Import Tracking
STRANS   Start Transformation Tool
STRANSLDEPTH   Classify Translation Depth
STRUST   Trust Manager
STRUSTSSO2   Trust Manager for Logon Ticket
STSEC   Maintain events deadline segment
STSEC_DLV   Maintain events deadline segment
STSEC_TRA   Maintain events deadline segment
STSN   Customizing Number Ranges TimeStream
STSSC   Maintain deadline procedures
STSSC_DLV   Maintain shipping deadline procedure
STSSC_TRA   Maintain transportation dline proc.
STSTC   Maintain times in time segment
STSTC_DLV   Maintain times in time segment
STSTC_TRA   Maintain times in time segment
STTO   Test Organization
STUN   Menu Performance Monitor
STVARV   Selection variable maint. (TVARV)
STVARVC   Maintain TVARVC in Client '000'
STWBM   Test Repository
STWB_1   Test Catalog Management

SAP Transaction Codes – Volume Two

STWB_2	Test Plan Management
STWB_INFO	Test Workbench Information System
STWB_SET	Central Test Workbench settings
STWB_TC	Test Case Management
STWB_WORK	Tester worklist
STYLE_GUIDE	Style Guide Transaction
STZAC	Maintain time zone act. in client
STZAD	Disp.time zone activat.in client
STZBC	Maintain time zones in Basis Cust.
STZBD	Display time zones (Basis Cust.)
STZEC	Time zone mapping in ext. systems
STZED	Time zone mapping in ext. systems
STZGC	Time zones: Maintain geo.data
STZGD	Time zone cust.: Disp.geo.data
SU0	Maintain Own Fixed User Values
SU01	User Maintenance
SU01D	User Display
SU01_NAV	User maint. to include in navigation
SU02	Maintain Authorization Profiles
SU03	Maintain Authorizations
SU05_OLD	Maintain Internet Users
SU1	Maintain Own User Address
SU10	User Mass Maintenance
SU12	Mass Changes to User Master Records
SU2	Maintain Own User Parameters
SU20	Maintain Authorization Fields
SU21	Maintain Authorization Objects
SU21_OLD	Maintain Authorization Objects
SU22	Auth. Object Usage in Transactions
SU22_OLD	Auth. Object Usage in Transactions
SU24	Auth. Obj. Check Under Transactions
SU24_CHECK	Switch Off Authorizations: Test
SU24_OLD	Auth. Obj. Check Under Transactions
SU25	Upgrade Tool for Profile Generator
SU25_OLD	Upgrade Tool for Profile Generator
SU26	Upgrade Tool for Profile Generator
SU3	Maintain Users Own Data
SU50	Own data
SU51	Maintain Own User Address
SU52	Maintain Own User Parameters
SU53	Evaluate Authorization Check
SU55	Call the Session Manager menus
SU56	Analyze User Buffer
SU80	Archive user change documents
SU81	Archive user password change doc.
SU82	Archive profile documents
SU83	Archive authorization docs.
SU84	Read Archived User Change Documents
SU85	Read Archived Password Change Doc.
SU86	Read Profile Change Documents
SU87	Read Authorization Change Documents
SU96	Table maint.: Change SUKRIA
SU97	Table maint.: Display SUKRIA
SU98	Call Report RSUSR008

SAP Transaction Codes – Volume Two

SU99   Call report RSUSR008
SUB%   Internal call: Submit via commnd fld
SUCH   Translatability CHECKs
SUCOMP   User company address maintenance
SUCU   Table authorizations: Customizing
SUDDIREG   Maintain UDDI Registries
SUGR   Maintain User Groups
SUGRD   Display user groups
SUGRD_NAV   Display User Groups
SUGR_NAV   Maintain User Groups
SUIM   User Information System
SUIM_OLD   Call AUTH Reporting Tree (Info Sys.)
SUMG   Unicode Postconversion
SUPC   Role Profiles
SUPN   Number range maint.: PROF_VARIS
SUPO   Maintain org. levels
SUPO_PREPARE   Maintain Organizational Levels
SUPRES   Supplemental Reserves
SURAD   Survey Administration
SURAP   Survey: register application
SURF4   Survey: F4 Help assignment
SURFI   Survey: set application field
SURL_LAUNCHPAD_TEST   LaunchPad Generation: Test
SURL_PERS_ADMIN   Personalization for URL Gen. Admin.
SURL_PERS_USER   Personalization for URL Gen. User
SURL_SINGLE_GEN_TEST   LaunchPad & URL Generation: Test
SURQC   Survey: Question catalog
SURSETUP   Survey: Basic Settings
SURST   Survey: build questionnaire struct.
SURSY   Assignment: application - system
SURTRANS   Survey: Transport Link
SURVEY   Survey Cockpit
SURVEY_FORMS   Survey Forms
SUUM   Global User Manager
SUUMD   Display User Administration
SU_REFUSERVARIABLE   Maintain reference user variables
SU_VCUSRVARCOM_CHAN   Maintain View Cluster VCUSRVARCOM
SU_VCUSRVARCOM_DISP   Display View Cluster VCUSRVARCOM
SU_VCUSRVAR_CHANGE   Maintain View Cluster VCUSRVAR
SU_VCUSRVAR_DISP   Display View Cluster VCUSRVAR
SVGM   SAP R/3 Procedure Model
SVGS   View for activity in Procedure Model
SW10   Delivery Verification
SWB3   Maintain Start Conditions
SWB4   Display Start Conditions
SWB_COND   Maintain Workflow Start Conditions
SWB_COND_DISPLAY   Display Workflow Start Conditions
SWB_PROCUREMENT   Maintain B2B Start Conditions
SWDA   Alphanumeric Workflow Builder
SWDB   Create workflow
SWDC   Workflow Definition: Administration
SWDC_DEFINITION   Workflow Builder Administration
SWDC_INTERNAL   Workflow Definition: Administration
SWDC_RUNTIME   Maintain Administrator for Runtime

SAP Transaction Codes – Volume Two

SWDD   Workflow Builder
SWDD_CONFIG   Workflow Configuration
SWDI   Workflow Builder (Selection)
SWDM   Business Workflow Explorer
SWDN   Number Range Maint.: SWD_WDID
SWDP   Show Graphical Workflow Log
SWDS   Workflow Builder (Selection)
SWE2   Display/Maint. Event Type Linkages
SWE3   Display Instance Linkages
SWE4   Status Change Event Trace
SWE5   Checks for Event Linkages
SWEAD   Event Queue Administration
SWEC   Event Linkage for Change Documents
SWED   Assignment chng.doc./WF object type
SWEHR1   Linkage: Object Type to HR Infotype
SWEHR2   Event - Infotype Operation (SAP)
SWEHR3   Event-Infotype Operation (Customer)
SWEINST   Display Instance Linkages
SWEL   Display Event Trace
SWELS   Switch Event Trace On/Off
SWEM   Configure Event Trace
SWEQADM   Event Queue Administration
SWEQADM_1   Maintain Event Queue Administrator
SWEQBROWSER   Event Queue Browser
SWEQDEL   Delete Event Queue
SWETYPV   Display/Maint. Event Type Linkages
SWE_CD_TST   Test Environ. for Change Documents
SWE_SET_DELEGATION   Create Delegation in BOR
SWF3   Workflow Wizard Explorer
SWF4   Workflow Wizard Repository
SWFC   Automatic Workflow Customizing
SWFMOD_TRANSPORT   Transport workflow Modeler objects
SWFPOWLOBJ   Object
SWFPOWLWI   Display/Execute Work Item
SWFSLSA   Maintain Deadline Monitoring
SWFSLSC   Schedule Deadline-Monitoring Job
SWFSLSDLEX_SHOW   Job Selection for SWFSLSDLEX
SWFSLST   Display Deadline-Monitoring Trace
SWFVISU   Workflow Visualization Metadata
SWFVMD1   Workflow: Visualization Metadata
SWF_ADM_SUSPEND   Restart Suspended Workflows
SWF_ADM_SWWWIDH   Restart Suspended Deadlines
SWF_APPL_DISPLAY   Workflow: Application Log
SWF_AUTO   Automatic Workflow Customizing
SWF_BAM   BAM: Administration
SWF_BAM_TRC   Tracing for BAM
SWF_CCMS_CONFIG   CCMS: Configuration
SWF_CNT_MAINTENANCE   Diagnosis and Container Comparison
SWF_CRL1   Correlation Editor
SWF_DEBUG   Edit Workflow Breakpoints
SWF_GMP   Administrator Overview
SWF_GP   Guided Procedures
SWF_INB_ADM   Administration Inbound Processing
SWF_INB_CONF   Configuration Inbound Processing

SWF_INB_MON	Monitoring Inbound Processing
SWF_LOG_ADM	Administration for Log Profiles
SWF_OBJ_EXEC	Execute Object Method
SWF_OBJ_EXEC_BO	Execute Object Method (SWOOBJID)
SWF_OBJ_EXEC_CL	Execute Object Method (SIBFLPORB)
SWF_RESTART_CANCEL	Restart Suspended Cancel
SWF_RESTART_SUSPEND	Restart Suspended Callbacks
SWF_RFC_DEST	Configure RFC Destination
SWF_TRC	Workflow Trace: Display
SWF_TRC_ALL	Workflow Trace: Display All Comp.
SWF_TRC_DEMO	Workflow Trace: Display DEMO-K.
SWF_TRC_SEL	Workflow Trace: Display with Selectn
SWF_WAPI_TEST	Automatic Test of SAP_WAPI
SWF_XI_ADM_BPE	XI: Start/Stop BPE
SWF_XI_ADM_BPE_DISP	XI: Display BPE Status
SWF_XI_ARCHIV	Display Archived Processes
SWF_XI_CUSTOMIZING	Automatic BPM Customizing
SWF_XI_DISPATCH_SHOW	Display Message Dispatcher
SWF_XI_DISPCLR_SHOW	Display Message Dispatcher Cleanup
SWF_XI_PBUILDER	Process Builder
SWF_XI_SWI1	Process Selection
SWF_XI_SWI14	Processes for One Message Type
SWF_XI_SWI2_DEAD	Processes with Missed Deadline
SWF_XI_SWI2_DIAG	Diagnosis Processes with Errors
SWF_XI_SWI6	Processes for a Message
SWF_XI_SWPC	Continue Process After System Crash
SWF_XI_SWPR	Continue Process Following Error
SWF_XI_SWU2	RFC Monitor
SWF_XMP1	XML Object Type Builder
SWH_ADM1	Work Item Upgrade: Definition GUID
SWH_PROCESS_INFO	Demo for Process Info System
SWI1	Selection report for workflows
SWI11	Where-Used List for Tasks
SWI13	Task Profile
SWI14	Workflows for Object Type
SWI1_COND	Check Conditions for Work Items
SWI1_RULE	Execute Rules for Work Items
SWI2_ADM1	Work Items Without Agents
SWI2_ADM2	Work Items with Deleted Users
SWI2_DEAD	Work Items with Monitored Deadlines
SWI2_DIAG	Diagnosis of Workflows with Errors
SWI2_DURA	Work Items by Processing Duration
SWI2_FREQ	Work Items per Task
SWI3	Workflow Outbox
SWI30	Unlock Workflows
SWI5	Workload Analysis
SWI5N	Workload Analysis
SWI6	Workflows for Object
SWIA	WI Administration Report
SWIE	Unlock Work Item
SWJ1	Browser for Schedule Conditions
SWK1	Start Work Item Execution/Display
SWK2	Execute Object Method (SWOOBJID)
SWK3	Execute object method (SIBFLPORB)

SAP Transaction Codes – Volume Two

SWL1   Settings for dynamic columns
SWLC   Check Tasks for Agents
SWLD   Workbench for Workflow 4.0
SWLD_INPLACE1   Demo Embedded Inbox
SWLD_INPLACE2   Demo Embedded Inbox (Professional)
SWLO   Display work items for objects
SWLP   Copy a Plan Version
SWLV   Maintain Work Item Views
SWNADMIN   Administration of Notifications
SWNCONFIG   Configuration Notifications
SWNNOTIFDEL   Delete Notifications
SWNNOTIFDEL_DELETE   Deallocate 'SWNNOTIFDEL'
SWNNOTIFDEL_DISPLAY   Display 'SWNNOTIFDEL'
SWNNOTIFDEL_INSERT   Background Job 'SWNNOTIFDEL'
SWNWIEX   WF Notification: Edit Work Item
SWO1   Business Object Builder
SWO2   BOR Browser
SWO3   Business Object Builder
SWO4   Business Object Repository
SWO6   Customizing Object Types
SWO_ASYNC   Asynchronous Method Call in BOR
SWPA   Runtime System Customizing
SWPC   WFM: Continue Workflow
SWPR   WFM: Restart Workflow
SWP_CHANGE_MAXNODES   Change Maximum Number of Nodes
SWRK   Administrtation using work areas
SWRP   Dummy for IAC Workflow Status
SWR_WEBSERVER   Web Server Customizing
SWT0   Configure workflow trace
SWTFILTER   Administration: Trace Activation
SWTREORG   Reorganization Trace for Requests
SWTREQ   Analyze Workflow Trace for Requests
SWU0   Simulate event
SWU1   User RFC Monitor
SWU10   Delete Workflow Trace Files
SWU2   Workflow RFC Monitor
SWU3   Automatic Workflow Customizing
SWU3_OLD   Consistency check: Customizing
SWU4   Consistency Test for Standard Task
SWU5   Consistency Test for Customer Task
SWU6   Consistency Test for Workflow Task
SWU7   Consistency Test for Workflow Templ.
SWU8   Workflow Trace: On/Off
SWU9   Display Workflow Trace
SWUA   Start Verification Workflow
SWUB   Maintain Workflow RFC Destination
SWUC   Customizing decision task
SWUC_01   SAP Task Customizing
SWUD   Workflow Diagnosis
SWUE   Trigger an event
SWUG   Generate Workflow Start Transaction
SWUI   Start Workflow
SWUI_BENCHMARK   Start Performance Workflows
SWUI_DEMO   Start Demo Workflows

SAP Transaction Codes – Volume Two

SWUI_SINGLE   Start Workflow (Parameter)
SWUI_START   Start Workflow (Task Group)
SWUI_VERIFY   Start Test Workflows
SWUI_WFUNIT   Start Unit Workflows
SWUK   Mapping form type - mail address
SWUL   Customizing: Process Administrator
SWUN   Number Range Maintenance: FORMABSENC
SWUOCHECK   Test Report for Workflow Documents
SWUO_DEL   Deletion Report for Workflow Docs
SWUP   Switch SAPforms Trace On/Off
SWUR   Send mails for work items
SWUS   Test Workflow
SWUS_WITH_REFERENCE   Workflow: Start with Reference
SWUT   Namespace for Form Transactions
SWUU   SAPforms: Diagnosis
SWUV   Send E-Mail Notifications
SWUW   Number Range Maint.: SWW_WIID
SWUX   SAPforms Administration
SWUY   Workflow-Message Linkage
SWU_CONT_PERSISTENCE   Administrate Container Persistence
SWU_EWBTE   Wizard for Event Linkage (BTE)
SWU_EWCD   Wizard for Event Linkage (Chg. Doc.)
SWU_EWLIS   Wizard for Event Linkage (LIS)
SWU_OBUF   Runtime Buffer PD Org
SWWA   Maintain WI Deadline Monitoring
SWWB   Schedule WI Deadline Monitoring
SWWCLEAR_DELETE   Unschedule Workflow Clearing Tasks
SWWCLEAR_INSERT   Workflow: Background Job 'SWWCLEAR'
SWWCOND_DELETE   Unschedule Work Item Rule Monitoring
SWWCOND_INSERT   Workflow: Background Job 'SWWCOND'
SWWD   Maintain Work Item Error Monitoring
SWWDHEX_DEBUG   Work Item - Deadline Monitoring
SWWDHEX_DELETE   UnscheduleWorkItemDeadlineMonitoring
SWWERRE_APPL_LOG   Application Log for SWWERRE
SWWERRE_DEBUG   Work Item - Error Monitoring (Debug)
SWWERRE_DELETE   Unschedule WorkItem Error Monitoring
SWWERRE_INSERT   Workflow: Batch Job 'SWWERRE'
SWWH   WIM: Delete Work Item History
SWWL   WIM: Delete Work Item
SWWL_DEP   Delete Dependent Table Entries
SWWL_TOPLEVEL   Delete Top Level Work Item
SWW_ARCHIV   Display Workflows from Archive
SWW_DISPSWWCLEAR   Show Background Job for Clearing
SWW_DISPSWWCOND   Display: Background Job for Pre/Post
SWW_SARA   Archive Work Items
SWXF   DEMO: Create Notification of Absence
SWXFTB   DEMO: Notif. of Absence Toolbox
SWXML   XML Document Selection
SW_WW10   IAC Product Catalog for SAP Store
SXDA   Data Transfer Workbench
SXDA_TOOLS   DX Workbench: tools
SXDB   Data Transfer Workbench
SXIDEMO   XI Demo: Start of Application
SXIDEMO1   XI Demo: Start of Application (ABAP)

SXIDEMO2	XI Demo: Display Flight Data
SXIDEMO3	XI Demo: Generate Flight Data
SXIDEMO4	XI Demo: Send Booking Statistics
SXIPATT1	SAI_DEMO_PATTERNS
SXI_CACHE	XI Directory Cache
SXI_MAPPING_TEST	Test Environment for AII
SXI_MONITOR	XI: Message Monitoring
SXI_READ_ARCHIVE	Read from Archive (Using Archive)
SXI_READ_ARCHIVE_ID	Read from Archive (Using ID)
SXI_SHOW_MESSAGE	Displays an XI Message
SXI_STAT	Processing Statistics
SXI_SUPPORT	Test Environment for AII
SXMB_ADM	Integration Engine - Administration
SXMB_ADMIN	Integration Engine - All Functions
SXMB_ADM_BPE	Process Engine - Administration
SXMB_IFR	Start Integration Builder
SXMB_ITFACTION	Interf. for Archv. and Ret. Periods
SXMB_MONI	Integration Engine - Monitoring
SXMB_MONI_BPE	Process Engine - Monitoring
SXMSALRT	XI Alert Configuration
SXMSFILTER	Message Filter Maintenance
SXMSIF	Sender/Receiver Definitions
SXMSJOBS	Schedule Message Processing
SXMSJOBSCHEDULER	Scheduler for Message Processing
SXMSQUEUE	Conf. Queue Prioritization Filter
SXMS_ADMI_ARCH	Schedule Archiving Job
SXMS_ADMI_DEL	Schedule Delete Jobs
SXMS_ADMI_IND	Configuration XI Message Indexing
SXMS_BCM	Package Configuration Types
SXMS_BCONF	Package Configuration
SXMS_CONF_PP	Configure Principal Propagation
SXMS_CONF_SWITCH	Configure Delete Procedure
SXMS_IECONF	Integration Engine Configuration
SXMS_MONI_DB	Analysis of Persistence Layer
SXMS_MONI_IND	Monitoring XI Message Indexing
SXMS_MONI_JOB	Job overview
SXMS_PIPEL	Display Pipeline Definitions
SXMS_QREG	XI Queue Registration
SXMS_SAMON	Monitor for S/A Communication
SXMS_TRC	XMS: Trace Display
SXMS_TRC_CONF	Trace Configuration
SXMS_TRC_SEL	XMS: Trace Display with Selection
SXMS_TSTOOL	Settings for Error Analysis
SXSLT	XSLT Tester
SXSLTDEMO1	XSLT Demo: "Flights & Connections"
SYNT	Display Syntax Trace Output
SYSADM_CALL_DOCU	Documentation on Task
SYSADM_CALL_TA	Execute Task
SYSADM_TASK	System Administration: Task List
SYST	
SZGEOCD_COSTOMZVERIF	Verify Customizing (Analysis)
SZGEOCD_GEOCD2CLS	Register Geocoder in System
SZGEOCD_GEOCDRLFLD	Relevant Address Fields for Geocoder
SZGEOCD_GEOCODERS	Assign Geocoding Tools to Countries

SAP Transaction Codes – Volume Two

SZGEOCD_GEOT005	Maintain Geodata for Countries
SZGEOCD_GEOT005S	Maintain Geodata for Country/Region
SZGEOCD_MASS	Mass Assignment: Geocoder to Country
SZGEOCD_TEST	Geocoding Test Program
S_A4C_68001101	IMG Activity: PRODUCT_SET
S_ABA_72000001	IMG activity: _SAPA_NOTE_LANGUAGES
S_ABA_72000002	IMG activity: _CABP_TB019
S_ABA_72000003	IMG activity: _CABP_TB032
S_ABA_72000004	IMG activity: _CABP_TB025
S_ABA_72000005	IMG activity: _CABP_KCLL
S_ABA_72000006	IMG activity: _CABP_KC7R
S_ABA_72000007	IMG activity: _CABP_KCLJ
S_ABA_72000008	IMG activity: _CABP_KCLP
S_ABA_72000009	IMG activity: _CABP_TB023
S_ABA_72000010	IMG activity: _CABP_TB035
S_ABA_72000011	IMG activity: _CABP_TSAD2
S_ABA_72000012	IMG activity: _CABP_TSAD5
S_ABA_72000013	IMG activity: _CABP_TSAD4
S_ABA_72000014	IMG activity: _CABP_NAMEFORMAT
S_ABA_72000015	IMG activity: _CABP_TB027
S_ABA_72000016	IMG activity: _CABP_TB028
S_ABA_72000017	IMG activity: _CABP_GPB_TB914
S_ABA_72000018	IMG activity: _CABP_GPB_TB916
S_ABA_72000019	IMG activity: _CABP_GPB_TB930
S_ABA_72000020	IMG activity: _CABP_GPB_KCLL
S_ABA_72000021	IMG activity: _CABP_GPB_KC7R
S_ABA_72000022	IMG activity: _CABP_GPB_KCLJ
S_ABA_72000023	IMG activity: _CABP_GPB_KCLP
S_ABA_72000024	IMG activity: _CABP_GPB_TB912
S_ABA_72000025	IMG activity: _CABP_GPB_BUB9
S_ABA_72000026	IMG Activity: _CABP_GPB_V_TB905
S_ABA_72000027	IMG Activity: _CABP_GPB_V_TB905_RF
S_ABA_72000028	IMG Activity: _CABP_GPB_BUBP
S_ABA_72000029	IMG Activity: _CABP_GPB_BUBQ
S_ABA_72000030	IMG Activity: _CABP_GPB_V_TB105
S_ABA_72000031	IMG Activity: _CABP_GPB_TB910
S_ABA_72000032	IMG Activity: _CABP_BUCN
S_ABA_72000033	IMG Activity: _CABP_SU03
S_ABA_72000035	IMG Activity: _CABP_TB009
S_ABA_72000037	IMG Activity: _CABP_V_TSAD3
S_ABA_72000038	IMG Activity: _CABP_V_TB030
S_ABA_72000039	IMG Activity: _CABP_BUCF
S_ABA_72000040	IMG Activity: _CABP_V_TB001
S_ABA_72000041	IMG Activity: _CABP_V_TB004
S_ABA_72000042	IMG Activity: _CABP_BUCG
S_ABA_72000043	IMG Activity: _CABP_BUCH
S_ABA_72000044	IMG Activity: _CABP_V_TB004_01
S_ABA_72000045	IMG Activity: _CABP_TB029
S_ABA_72000046	IMG Activity: _CABP_TB034
S_ABA_72000047	IMG Activity: CABP_V_TB005
S_ABA_72000048	IMG Activity: _CABP_TCC1
S_ABA_72000049	IMG Activity: _CABP_TB033
S_ABA_72000051	IMG Activity: SIMG_CGJB01JBLC21
S_ABA_72000052	IMG Activity: SIMG_CGJB01JBLC19

SAP Transaction Codes – Volume Two

S_ABA_72000053	IMG Activity: SIMG_CGJB01JBLC12
S_ABA_72000054	IMG Activity: SIMG_CGJB01JBLC20
S_ABA_72000055	IMG Activity: SIMG_CGJB01JBLC24
S_ABA_72000056	IMG Activity: SIMG_CGJB01JBLC23
S_ABA_72000057	IMG Activity: SIMG_CGJB01JBLC16
S_ABA_72000058	IMG Activity: SIMG_CGJB01JBLC17
S_ABA_72000059	IMG Activity: SIMG_CGJB01JBLC11
S_ABA_72000060	IMG Activity: _USEREXITFDU
S_ABA_72000061	IMG Activity: SIMG_CFJB01SF07
S_ABA_72000062	IMG Activity: SIMG_CFJB01SF01
S_ABA_72000063	IMG Activity: SIMG_CFJB01FILE
S_ABA_72000064	IMG Activity: SIMG_CFJB01JB88
S_ABA_72000065	IMG Activity: SIMG_CFJB01JBLK
S_ABA_72000066	IMG Activity: SIMG_CFJB01JBLC
S_ABA_72000067	IMG Activity: SIMG_CFJB01JB18
S_ABA_72000068	IMG Activity: SIMG_CGJB01JBLC26
S_ABA_72000069	IMG Activity: SIMG_CGJB01JBLC8
S_ABA_72000070	IMG Activity: SIMG_CGJB01JBLC7
S_ABA_72000071	IMG Activity: SIMG_CGJB01JBLC6
S_ABA_72000072	IMG Activity: SIMG_CGJB01JBLC5
S_ABA_72000073	IMG Activity: SIMG_CGJB01JBLC13
S_ABA_72000074	IMG Activity: SIMG_CGJB01JBLC3
S_ABA_72000075	IMG Activity: SIMG_CGJB01JBLC22
S_ABA_72000076	IMG Activity: SIMG_CGJB01JBLC15
S_ABA_72000077	IMG Activity: SIMG_CGJB01JBLC18
S_ABA_72000078	IMG Activity: SIMG_CGJB01JBLC28
S_ABA_72000079	IMG Activity: SIMG_CGJB01JBLC10
S_ABA_72000080	IMG Activity: SIMG_CGJB01JBLC4
S_ABA_72000081	IMG Activity: SIMG_CGJB01JBLC27
S_ABA_72000082	IMG Activity: SIMG_CGJB01JBLC14
S_ABA_72000083	IMG Activity: SIMG_CGJB01JBLC2
S_ABA_72000157	Alert Customizing
S_ABA_72000162	IMG-Aktivität: COM_PRD_POST_FILTER
S_ABA_72000164	BDT Analyzer
S_ABA_72000309	Application Processes
S_ABA_72000310	Mapping Processes
S_ABA_72000311	Resolution Strategy
S_ABA_72000327	S_ABA_72000327
S_ABA_72000328	S_ABA_72000328
S_ABA_72000329	S_ABA_72000329
S_ABA_72000330	S_ABA_72000330
S_ABA_72000331	S_ABA_72000331
S_ABA_72000332	S_ABA_72000332
S_ABA_72000333	S_ABA_72000333
S_ABA_72000334	S_ABA_72000334
S_ABA_72000335	S_ABA_72000335
S_ABA_72000336	S_ABA_72000336
S_ABA_72000337	S_ABA_72000337
S_ABV_91000203	IMG Activity: BON_ENH_BADI_SETTLE
S_ABV_91000204	IMG Activity: RBT_ENH_BADI_IND
S_ABV_91000205	IMG Activity: RBT_ENH_CSEQ_CHECK
S_ABW_26000005	IMG Activity: RMPS_INIT_PATH
S_AC0_52000011	Application log: Standard log displa
S_AC0_52000012	J_1BLB56

SAP Transaction Codes – Volume Two

S_AC0_52000026	W/Tax Report for Italy: Modello
S_AC0_52000103	Purchase Ledger (Venezuela)
S_AC0_52000104	Sales Ledger (Venezuela)
S_AC0_52000143	Complete Settlement Requests
S_AC0_52000169	Complete Vendor Billing Documents
S_AC0_52000170	Complete Expenses Settlements
S_AC0_52000171	J_1AFR1547
S_AC0_52000172	Reopen Settlement Requests
S_AC0_52000174	Reopen Vendor Billing Documents
S_AC0_52000175	Reopen Expenses Settlements
S_AC0_52000396	Create Acquisition Tax Accruals
S_AC0_52000397	Reverse Acquisition Tax Accruals
S_AC0_52000496	AIS Reconciliation: Entry View
S_AC0_52000497	AIS Reconciliation -> Logs
S_AC0_52000498	Actual/Actual Comparison for Year
S_AC0_52000500	Audit Information System (AIS)
S_AC0_52000501	Totals and Balances
S_AC0_52000502	Audit
S_AC0_52000509	Audit Interactive List
S_AC0_52000517	IMG Activity: OHPSUSPROP04
S_AC0_52000518	IMG Activity: OHPSUSEEOC003
S_AC0_52000519	IMG Activity: OHPSUSEEOC002
S_AC0_52000520	IMG Activity: OHPSUSSBP003
S_AC0_52000521	IMG Activity: OHPSUSSBP004
S_AC0_52000522	IMG Activity: OHPSUSSBP005
S_AC0_52000528	Audit Private Folder
S_AC0_52000644	Deferred Tax Transfer
S_AC0_52000735	Report P4
S_AC0_52000751	Individual card of the account of pa
S_AC0_52000779	Deferred Tax Certificates (Mexico)
S_AC0_52000886	Program RCPE_SD_IMG
S_AC0_52000887	Receivables: Profit Center
S_AC0_52000888	Payables: Profit Center
S_AC0_52000889	Program RCPE_SD_IMG
S_ACR_23000230	RFIDITSR00
S_ACR_23000430	IMG Activity
S_ACR_23000490	Form SZV-K
S_ACR_23000548	Group and batch payment items
S_ACR_23000549	Reset Admin Data
S_AEC_66000279	BDT: Transport of Control Tables
S_AEN_10000032	Enhanced RemunLists from RemunList
S_AEN_10000033	Determine Relvnt Remuneration Lists
S_AEN_10000034	Simulation RemunLists frm RemunList
S_AEN_10000037	Posting List Creation Dispatcher
S_AEN_10000038	Customer Sttlmnt Creation Dispatcher
S_AEN_10000039	Doc. Index Reconstruction for AB Doc
S_AEN_10000042	Delete Doc. Index Data f. AB Doc.
S_AEN_10000050	Automatic AB Document Adjustment
S_AEN_10000060	Enhncd RemunLists frm Predecessor
S_AEN_10000065	Preceding Docs f. Remuneration Lists
S_AEN_10000066	Simulation RemunLists frm Predcessor
S_AEN_10000074	Dispatcher Sttlmnt Rqst List Crtn
S_AEN_10000075	Mass Release Dispatcher
S_AEN_10000083	Dispatcher Enhanced Remuneration Lst

SAP Transaction Codes – Volume Two

S_AEN_10000973	Analysis of Financing Link
S_AEN_10000984	Conditions of Insurance
S_AEN_10000987	Issue Volumes
S_AEN_10000988	Issue Charges
S_AEN_10000989	Issue Hedge
S_AEN_10000990	Issue Position
S_AEN_10001020	ABS MBS Positions
S_AEN_10001027	Conditions of Insurance
S_AHR_61008728	IMG-Aktivität: SIMG_OHAQ446
S_AHR_61008729	IMG-Aktivität: OHAHK_DV001
S_AHR_61008730	IMG Activity: OHAJRI042
S_AHR_61008731	IMG Activity: SIMG_OHAF432
S_AHR_61008732	IMG Activity: OHANAR02
S_AHR_61008733	IMG-Aktivität: OHAGRI061
S_AHR_61008734	IMG-Aktivität: OHAK0913
S_AHR_61008735	IMG-Aktivität: OHAQRI015
S_AHR_61008736	IMG-Aktivität: OHAHK_RI053
S_AHR_61008737	IMG Activity: OHAJRI031
S_AHR_61008738	IMG Activity: SIMG_OHAF426
S_AHR_61008739	IMG Activity: OHANAR03
S_AHR_61008740	IMG-Aktivität: OHAGRI062
S_AHR_61008741	IMG-Aktivität: OHAHK_CU010
S_AHR_61008742	IMG-Aktivität: OHAK0903
S_AHR_61008743	IMG-Aktivität: OHAQRI042
S_AHR_61008744	IMG Activity: OHAJRI051
S_AHR_61008745	IMG Activity: OHANAR04
S_AHR_61008746	IMG-Aktivität: OHAGRI063
S_AHR_61008747	IMG Activity: SIMG_OHAF428
S_AHR_61008748	IMG-Aktivität: OHAQRI031
S_AHR_61008749	IMG-Aktivität: OHAKDEC01
S_AHR_61008750	IMG Activity: OHAJAU427
S_AHR_61008751	IMG-Aktivität: OHAHK_KF001
S_AHR_61008752	IMG Activity: OHANBNI02
S_AHR_61008753	IMG Activity: OHAF0352
S_AHR_61008754	IMG-Aktivität: OHAQRI051
S_AHR_61008755	IMG-Aktivität: SIMG_OHAG426
S_AHR_61008756	IMG-Aktivität: OHAKUM105
S_AHR_61008757	IMG-Aktivität: OHAHK_KF002
S_AHR_61008758	IMG Activity: OHAJAU424
S_AHR_61008759	IMG Activity: OHANBNI03
S_AHR_61008760	IMG Activity: OHAF0021
S_AHR_61008761	IMG-Aktivität: OHAKUM104
S_AHR_61008762	IMG-Aktivität: OHAQEOM141
S_AHR_61008763	IMG Activity: OHANBNI04
S_AHR_61008764	IMG-Aktivität: SIMG_OHAG417
S_AHR_61008765	IMG-Aktivität: OHAHK_KL000
S_AHR_61008766	IMG Activity: OHAJAU430
S_AHR_61008767	IMG Activity: SIMG_OHAF527
S_AHR_61008768	IMG-Aktivität: OHAKTI120
S_AHR_61008769	IMG-Aktivität: OHAQEOM143
S_AHR_61008770	IMG Activity: OHANBN06
S_AHR_61008771	IMG-Aktivität: OHAHK_RI070
S_AHR_61008772	IMG Activity: SIMG_OHAJ470
S_AHR_61008773	IMG Activity: SIMG_OHAF528

S_AHR_61008774	IMG-Aktivität: OHAKTI322
S_AHR_61008775	IMG-Aktivität: SIMG_OHAG413
S_AHR_61008776	IMG Activity: OHANSP04
S_AHR_61008777	IMG-Aktivität: OHAQEOM145
S_AHR_61008778	IMG-Aktivität: OHAHK_SL001
S_AHR_61008779	IMG Activity: SIMG_OHAJ615
S_AHR_61008780	IMG Activity: SIMG_OHAF529
S_AHR_61008781	IMG-Aktivität: OHAKTI321
S_AHR_61008782	IMG-Aktivität: SIMG_OHAG480
S_AHR_61008783	IMG Activity: OHANWW04
S_AHR_61008784	IMG-Aktivität: OHAQEOM147
S_AHR_61008785	IMG Activity: OHAJWL000
S_AHR_61008786	IMG Activity: OHANWW05
S_AHR_61008787	IMG Activity: SIMG_OHAF409
S_AHR_61008788	IMG-Aktivität: SIMG_OHAG414
S_AHR_61008789	IMG Activity: OHAJTX210
S_AHR_61008790	IMG Activity: OHANWW06
S_AHR_61008791	IMG Activity: SIMG_OHAF407
S_AHR_61008792	IMG Activity: OHAJRI052
S_AHR_61008793	IMG-Aktivität: SIMG_OHAG814
S_AHR_61008794	IMG Activity: OHAF0030
S_AHR_61008795	IMG Activity: OHANSP07
S_AHR_61008796	IMG-Aktivität: OHAHK_SL002
S_AHR_61008797	IMG-Aktivität: OHAKTI325
S_AHR_61008798	IMG Activity: OHAJRI070
S_AHR_61008799	IMG-Aktivität: OHAQEOM149
S_AHR_61008800	IMG-Aktivität: SIMG_OHAG415
S_AHR_61008801	IMG Activity: OHANSP06
S_AHR_61008802	IMG Activity: OHAF0029
S_AHR_61008803	IMG Activity: OHAJRI071
S_AHR_61008804	IMG Activity: OHANSP02
S_AHR_61008805	IMG-Aktivität: SIMG_OHAG418
S_AHR_61008806	IMG Activity: OHAF0023
S_AHR_61008807	IMG Activity: OHAJRI080
S_AHR_61008808	IMG Activity: OHANSP05
S_AHR_61008809	IMG Activity: SIMG_OHAF525
S_AHR_61008810	IMG-Aktivität: SIMG_OHAG410
S_AHR_61008811	IMG Activity: OHAJRI081
S_AHR_61008812	IMG Activity: OHANSP03
S_AHR_61008813	IMG Activity: OHTF0122
S_AHR_61008814	IMG-Aktivität: OHAKTI310
S_AHR_61008815	IMG-Aktivität: OHAHK_SL003
S_AHR_61008816	IMG Activity: OHANBN07
S_AHR_61008817	IMG Activity: SIMG_OHAF402
S_AHR_61008818	IMG-Aktivität: OHAQEOM151
S_AHR_61008819	IMG-Aktivität: SIMG_OHAG408
S_AHR_61008820	IMG Activity: OHAJRI090
S_AHR_61008821	IMG-Aktivität: OHAK0911
S_AHR_61008822	IMG Activity: OHANL_MZ001
S_AHR_61008823	IMG-Aktivität: OHAHK_AVXT00
S_AHR_61008824	IMG Activity: SIMG_OHTX028
S_AHR_61008825	IMG-Aktivität: SIMG_OHAG527
S_AHR_61008826	IMG Activity: SIMG_OHAF403
S_AHR_61008827	IMG Activity: OHAJUM002

S_AHR_61008828	IMG-Aktivität: OHAQUM002
S_AHR_61008829	IMG-Aktivität: OHAKTI210
S_AHR_61008830	IMG-Aktivität: OHAHK_AVP15
S_AHR_61008831	IMG Activity: OHAJUM003
S_AHR_61008832	IMG Activity: OHANL_483
S_AHR_61008833	IMG-Aktivität: OHAQPYC002
S_AHR_61008834	IMG-Aktivität: SIMG_OHAG528
S_AHR_61008835	IMG-Aktivität: OHAKTI130
S_AHR_61008836	IMG Activity: SIMG_OHTX027
S_AHR_61008837	IMG Activity: SIMG_OHAF405
S_AHR_61008838	IMG-Aktivität: OHAHK_RI080
S_AHR_61008839	IMG-Aktivität: OHAQPYC003
S_AHR_61008840	IMG-Aktivität: SIMG_OHAG529
S_AHR_61008841	IMG Activity: OHAJRI056
S_AHR_61008842	IMG-Aktivität: OHACACSP200
S_AHR_61008843	IMG Activity: SIMG_OHTX803
S_AHR_61008844	IMG-Aktivität: OHAHK_BW21
S_AHR_61008845	IMG Activity: SIMG_OHAF406
S_AHR_61008846	IMG Activity: SIMG_OHANL_416
S_AHR_61008847	IMG-Aktivität: OHAQRI071
S_AHR_61008848	IMG-Aktivität: SIMG_OHAG409
S_AHR_61008849	IMG-Aktivität: OHACAAB200
S_AHR_61008850	IMG Activity: SIMG_OHTX805
S_AHR_61008851	IMG Activity: OHAJRI053
S_AHR_61008852	IMG-Aktivität: OHAHK_BW22
S_AHR_61008853	IMG Activity: SIMG_OHANL_515
S_AHR_61008854	IMG-Aktivität: OHAKAB010
S_AHR_61008855	IMG Activity: OHAJRI054
S_AHR_61008856	IMG Activity: OHTX5006
S_AHR_61008857	IMG-Aktivität: OHAQRI080
S_AHR_61008858	IMG-Aktivität: SIMG_OHAG407
S_AHR_61008859	IMG Activity: SIMG_OHAF408
S_AHR_61008860	IMG-Aktivität: OHAHK_RI071
S_AHR_61008861	IMG-Aktivität: OHAKAB012
S_AHR_61008862	IMG Activity: SIMG_OHANL_506
S_AHR_61008863	IMG Activity: OHAJRI055
S_AHR_61008864	IMG Activity: OHTX5001
S_AHR_61008865	IMG-Aktivität: OHAQRI081
S_AHR_61008866	IMG Activity: OHAF0362
S_AHR_61008867	IMG-Aktivität: SIMG_OHAG482
S_AHR_61008868	IMG-Aktivität: OHAKAB009
S_AHR_61008869	IMG Activity: SIMG_OHANL_507
S_AHR_61008875	IMG Activity: OHAJRI061
S_AHR_61008876	IMG-Aktivität: OHAQRI090
S_AHR_61008877	IMG-Aktivität: OHAHK_PART
S_AHR_61008878	IMG-Aktivität: SIMG_OHAG419
S_AHR_61008879	IMG Activity: SIMG_OHAF482
S_AHR_61008880	IMG Activity: SIMG_OHT0506
S_AHR_61008881	IMG Activity: SIMG_OHANL_518
S_AHR_61008882	IMG-Aktivität: OHAKAV001
S_AHR_61008883	IMG Activity: OHAJRI062
S_AHR_61008884	IMG-Aktivität: OHAQEOM201
S_AHR_61008885	IMG-Aktivität: SIMG_OHAG471
S_AHR_61008886	IMG Activity: OHTX3000

S_AHR_61008887	IMG Activity: SIMG_OHAF418
S_AHR_61008888	IMG-Aktivität: OHAHK_OCRP01
S_AHR_61008889	IMG Activity: SIMG_OHANL_530
S_AHR_61008890	IMG-Aktivität: OHAKAVBAS
S_AHR_61008891	IMG Activity: OHAJRI063
S_AHR_61008892	IMG-Aktivität: OHAQEOM203
S_AHR_61008893	IMG-Aktivität: SIMG_OHAG435
S_AHR_61008894	IMG-Aktivität: OHAHK_OCPM01
S_AHR_61008895	IMG Activity: OHANL_DT004
S_AHR_61008896	IMG Activity: OHTF0126
S_AHR_61008897	IMG Activity: SIMG_OHAF419
S_AHR_61008898	IMG-Aktivität: OHACACSP150
S_AHR_61008899	IMG-Aktivität: OHAQEOM205
S_AHR_61008900	IMG Activity: OHAJAU429
S_AHR_61008901	IMG Activity: OHANJW001
S_AHR_61008902	IMG-Aktivität: SIMG_OHAG422
S_AHR_61008903	IMG-Aktivität: OHAHK_OCPM001
S_AHR_61008904	IMG Activity: OHTY033
S_AHR_61008905	IMG-Aktivität: OHAQEOM211
S_AHR_61008906	IMG-Aktivität: OHAKBW005
S_AHR_61008907	IMG Activity: OHANL_0902
S_AHR_61008908	IMG Activity: OHAJLG409
S_AHR_61008909	IMG Activity: SIMG_OHAF483
S_AHR_61008910	IMG-Aktivität: SIMG_OHAG423
S_AHR_61008911	IMG Activity: OHTY055
S_AHR_61008912	IMG-Aktivität: OHAHK_OCV001
S_AHR_61008913	IMG Activity: OHANL_0911
S_AHR_61008914	IMG Activity: OHAJLG407
S_AHR_61008915	IMG-Aktivität: SIMG_OHAG425
S_AHR_61008916	IMG-Aktivität: OHAQEOM115
S_AHR_61008917	IMG-Aktivität: OHAKBW006
S_AHR_61008918	IMG-Aktivität: OHAHK_OCMCP1
S_AHR_61008919	IMG Activity: OHANL_0912
S_AHR_61008920	IMG Activity: OHTX5004
S_AHR_61008921	IMG Activity: SIMG_OHAF484
S_AHR_61008922	IMG Activity: OHAJLG482
S_AHR_61008923	IMG-Aktivität: OHAKBW019
S_AHR_61008924	IMG-Aktivität: SIMG_OHAG437
S_AHR_61008925	IMG-Aktivität: SIMG_OHAQ681
S_AHR_61008926	IMG-Aktivität: OHAHK_RI062
S_AHR_61008927	IMG Activity: OHANL_0913
S_AHR_61008928	IMG Activity: SIMG_OHT017
S_AHR_61008929	IMG Activity: OHAJLG410
S_AHR_61008930	IMG Activity: OHAFEDTINTERNET
S_AHR_61008931	IMG-Aktivität: OHAHK_RI063
S_AHR_61008932	IMG-Aktivität: SIMG_OHAG432
S_AHR_61008933	IMG Activity: OHIX0700
S_AHR_61008934	IMG Activity: OHANL_0903
S_AHR_61008935	IMG-Aktivität: OHAKBW004
S_AHR_61008936	IMG-Aktivität: SIMG_OHAQ483
S_AHR_61008937	IMG Activity: OHAF0022
S_AHR_61008938	IMG-Aktivität: SIMG_OHAG464
S_AHR_61008939	IMG Activity: OHTY054
S_AHR_61008940	IMG Activity: OHAJLG417

S_AHR_61008941	IMG-Aktivität: OHAHK_OCR001
S_AHR_61008942	IMG Activity: OHANL_DT002
S_AHR_61008943	IMG-Aktivität: SIMG_OHAQ484
S_AHR_61008944	IMG-Aktivität: OHACACSP250
S_AHR_61008945	IMG-Aktivität: OHAHK_TI330
S_AHR_61008946	IMG Activity: SIMG_OHAF431
S_AHR_61008947	IMG-Aktivität: SIMG_OHAG483
S_AHR_61008948	IMG Activity: SIMG_OHTX806
S_AHR_61008949	IMG Activity: OHAJLG413
S_AHR_61008950	IMG-Aktivität: SIMG_OHAHK_465
S_AHR_61008951	IMG Activity: OHANL_DT003
S_AHR_61008952	IMG-Aktivität: OHACACSP300
S_AHR_61008953	IMG-Aktivität: OHAAUEDTINTERNET
S_AHR_61008954	IMG Activity: SIMG_OHAF415
S_AHR_61008955	IMG-Aktivität: SIMG_OHAHK_454
S_AHR_61008956	IMG-Aktivität: SIMG_OHAG484
S_AHR_61008957	IMG Activity: OHTY017
S_AHR_61008958	IMG-Aktivität: SIMG_OHAQ457
S_AHR_61008959	IMG-Aktivität: SIMG_OHAHK_455
S_AHR_61008960	IMG Activity: OHANWW03
S_AHR_61008961	IMG-Aktivität: OHACACSP350
S_AHR_61008962	IMG Activity: OHAJLG414
S_AHR_61008963	IMG-Aktivität: OHAGEDTINTERNET
S_AHR_61008964	IMG Activity: OHTY034
S_AHR_61008965	IMG Activity: SIMG_OHAF410
S_AHR_61008966	IMG-Aktivität: SIMG_OHAHK_466
S_AHR_61008967	IMG Activity: OHAN9031
S_AHR_61008968	IMG-Aktivität: OHAKBW21
S_AHR_61008969	IMG-Aktivität: SIMG_OHAQ451
S_AHR_61008970	IMG-Aktivität: SIMG_OHAHK_456
S_AHR_61008971	IMG Activity: SIMG_OHAJ530
S_AHR_61008972	IMG-Aktivität: SIMG_OHAHK_520
S_AHR_61008973	IMG Activity: OHAF0028
S_AHR_61008974	IMG Activity: OHTY0559
S_AHR_61008975	IMG-Aktivität: OHAKBW22
S_AHR_61008976	IMG Activity: OHAN9033
S_AHR_61008977	IMG Activity: SIMG_OHR0078
S_AHR_61008978	IMG-Aktivität: SIMG_OHAG431
S_AHR_61008979	IMG Activity: OHAJLG416
S_AHR_61008980	IMG-Aktivität: SIMG_OHAHK_519
S_AHR_61008981	IMG-Aktivität: SIMG_OHAQ463
S_AHR_61008982	IMG-Aktivität: SIMG_OHAHK_421
S_AHR_61008983	IMG Activity: SIMG_OHR0010
S_AHR_61008984	IMG Activity: OHTY032
S_AHR_61008985	IMG Activity: OHAN9032
S_AHR_61008986	IMG-Aktivität: OHAKAB003
S_AHR_61008987	IMG Activity: SIMG_OHAF417
S_AHR_61008988	IMG Activity: OHAJLG402
S_AHR_61008989	IMG-Aktivität: SIMG_OHAG457
S_AHR_61008990	IMG-Aktivität: SIMG_OHAHK_517
S_AHR_61008991	IMG-Aktivität: SIMG_OHAQ464
S_AHR_61008992	IMG Activity: SIMG_OHR0016
S_AHR_61008993	IMG-Aktivität: SIMG_OHAHK_481
S_AHR_61008994	IMG Activity: SIMG_OHAF413

S_AHR_61008995	IMG-Aktivität: OHAKAB002
S_AHR_61008996	IMG Activity: SIMG_OHT045
S_AHR_61008997	IMG Activity: OHAN9002
S_AHR_61008998	IMG-Aktivität: SIMG_OHAG451
S_AHR_61008999	IMG Activity: OHAJLG403
S_AHR_61009000	IMG-Aktivität: SIMG_OHAQ471
S_AHR_61009001	IMG-Aktivität: SIMG_OHAHK_401
S_AHR_61009002	IMG Activity: SIMG_OHR0015
S_AHR_61009003	IMG-Aktivität: SIMG_OHAHK_439
S_AHR_61009004	IMG Activity: SIMG_OHT044
S_AHR_61009005	IMG Activity: SIMG_OHAF480
S_AHR_61009006	IMG-Aktivität: OHAKBO010
S_AHR_61009007	IMG Activity: OHAJLG405
S_AHR_61009008	IMG Activity: SIMG_OHR2000
S_AHR_61009009	IMG-Aktivität: SIMG_OHAG463
S_AHR_61009010	IMG-Aktivität: SIMG_OHAQ431
S_AHR_61009011	IMG Activity: OHAN9009
S_AHR_61009012	IMG-Aktivität: SIMG_OHAHK_450
S_AHR_61009013	IMG Activity: OHTY026
S_AHR_61009014	IMG-Aktivität: OHAGSL003
S_AHR_61009015	IMG Activity: SIMG_OHR_T702N_E
S_AHR_61009016	IMG-Aktivität: SIMG_OHAHK_524
S_AHR_61009017	IMG Activity: OHAN9012
S_AHR_61009018	IMG Activity: OHAJLG406
S_AHR_61009019	IMG Activity: SIMG_OHAF414
S_AHR_61009020	IMG-Aktivität: OHAKPART
S_AHR_61009021	IMG-Aktivität: SIMG_OHAHK_453
S_AHR_61009022	IMG-Aktivität: SIMG_OHAQ410
S_AHR_61009023	IMG-Aktivität: OHAGJW000
S_AHR_61009024	IMG Activity: OHTX2011
S_AHR_61009025	IMG Activity: OHAJLG408
S_AHR_61009026	IMG Activity: OHAN9003
S_AHR_61009027	IMG-Aktivität: SIMG_OHAHK_523
S_AHR_61009028	IMG-Aktivität: SIMG_OHAHK_522
S_AHR_61009029	IMG Activity: SIMG_OHAF814
S_AHR_61009030	IMG-Aktivität: OHAGAB001
S_AHR_61009031	IMG Activity: OHAJLG415
S_AHR_61009032	IMG Activity: SIMG_OHT040
S_AHR_61009033	IMG-Aktivität: OHAKKF001
S_AHR_61009034	IMG Activity: OHAN9004
S_AHR_61009035	IMG-Aktivität: SIMG_OHAQ417
S_AHR_61009036	IMG-Aktivität: SIMG_OHAHK_521
S_AHR_61009037	IMG-Aktivität: SIMG_OHAHK_516
S_AHR_61009038	IMG-Aktivität: OHAGAB002
S_AHR_61009039	IMG Activity: SIMG_OHT047
S_AHR_61009040	IMG Activity: SIMG_OHAJ471
S_AHR_61009041	IMG Activity: OHAN9035
S_AHR_61009042	IMG-Aktivität: OHAKAB011
S_AHR_61009043	IMG-Aktivität: SIMG_OHAHK_612
S_AHR_61009044	IMG Activity: OHAF0464
S_AHR_61009045	IMG-Aktivität: SIMG_OHAQ413
S_AHR_61009046	IMG-Aktivität: OHAGAB003
S_AHR_61009047	IMG-Aktivität: SIMG_OHAHK_613
S_AHR_61009048	IMG Activity: SIMG_OHT0301

S_AHR_61009049	IMG-Aktivität: OHAKAVX017
S_AHR_61009050	IMG Activity: OHANZI14
S_AHR_61009051	IMG Activity: OHAJAU431
S_AHR_61009052	IMG Activity: OHAFRI063
S_AHR_61009053	IMG-Aktivität: SIMG_OHAQ480
S_AHR_61009054	IMG-Aktivität: SIMG_OHAHK_614
S_AHR_61009055	IMG-Aktivität: OHAKAV018
S_AHR_61009056	IMG Activity: SIMG_OHT046
S_AHR_61009057	IMG-Aktivität: OHAGAB005
S_AHR_61009058	IMG Activity: OHAF0292
S_AHR_61009059	IMG-Aktivität: SIMG_OHAHK_841
S_AHR_61009060	IMG Activity: OHAJAU422
S_AHR_61009061	IMG Activity: OHANZI12
S_AHR_61009062	IMG Activity: OHTY057
S_AHR_61009063	IMG-Aktivität: SIMG_OHAQ414
S_AHR_61009064	IMG-Aktivität: SIMG_OHAHK_842
S_AHR_61009065	IMG Activity: OHAJAU423
S_AHR_61009066	IMG-Aktivität: OHAKAV511A
S_AHR_61009067	IMG-Aktivität: OHAGAB011
S_AHR_61009068	IMG Activity: OHANZI16
S_AHR_61009069	IMG Activity: OHAF0294
S_AHR_61009070	IMG-Aktivität: SIMG_OHAHK_843
S_AHR_61009071	IMG Activity: SIMG_OHT0304
S_AHR_61009072	IMG-Aktivität: OHAKAV511B
S_AHR_61009073	IMG Activity: OHAJAU425
S_AHR_61009074	IMG Activity: OHANZI17
S_AHR_61009075	IMG-Aktivität: OHAGSL002
S_AHR_61009076	IMG-Aktivität: SIMG_OHAHK_844
S_AHR_61009077	IMG-Aktivität: SIMG_OHAQ814
S_AHR_61009078	IMG Activity: OHAFRI062
S_AHR_61009079	IMG Activity: OHTX5000
S_AHR_61009080	IMG-Aktivität: OHAHK_RI011
S_AHR_61009081	IMG Activity: OHAJAU426
S_AHR_61009082	IMG-Aktivität: OHAGBW21
S_AHR_61009083	IMG-Aktivität: OHAKAV511C
S_AHR_61009084	IMG-Aktivität: OHAHK_RI012
S_AHR_61009085	IMG Activity: SIMG_OHT032
S_AHR_61009086	IMG Activity: OHAFRI061
S_AHR_61009087	IMG Activity: OHAN9059
S_AHR_61009088	IMG-Aktivität: SIMG_OHAQ415
S_AHR_61009089	IMG-Aktivität: SIMG_OHAHK_514
S_AHR_61009090	IMG-Aktivität: OHAGBW22
S_AHR_61009091	IMG Activity: OHAJAU428
S_AHR_61009092	IMG-Aktivität: SIMG_OHAHK_513
S_AHR_61009093	IMG-Aktivität: OHAKAVXT00
S_AHR_61009094	IMG Activity: OHAFPART
S_AHR_61009095	IMG Activity: SIMG_OHT020
S_AHR_61009096	IMG-Aktivität: OHAGPART
S_AHR_61009097	IMG Activity: OHAN9014
S_AHR_61009098	IMG-Aktivität: SIMG_OHAQ418
S_AHR_61009099	IMG-Aktivität: SIMG_OHAHK_512
S_AHR_61009100	IMG Activity: OHAJLG418
S_AHR_61009101	IMG-Aktivität: OHAKAVP15
S_AHR_61009102	IMG-Aktivität: SIMG_OHAHK_510

S_AHR_61009103	IMG Activity: OHAN9050
S_AHR_61009104	IMG Activity: OHAF0202
S_AHR_61009105	IMG-Aktivität: OHAGKF001
S_AHR_61009106	IMG Activity: SIMG_OHT019
S_AHR_61009107	IMG Activity: OHAJLG419
S_AHR_61009108	IMG-Aktivität: SIMG_OHAHK_509
S_AHR_61009109	IMG-Aktivität: SIMG_OHAQ419
S_AHR_61009110	IMG-Aktivität: OHAKUM103
S_AHR_61009111	IMG-Aktivität: SIMG_OHAHK_508
S_AHR_61009112	IMG Activity: OHAN9051
S_AHR_61009113	IMG Activity: OHAF0212
S_AHR_61009114	IMG Activity: OHTF0124
S_AHR_61009115	IMG-Aktivität: OHAGKF002
S_AHR_61009116	IMG Activity: OHAJEDTINTERNET
S_AHR_61009117	IMG-Aktivität: SIMG_OHAHK_502
S_AHR_61009118	IMG-Aktivität: OHAK1048
S_AHR_61009119	IMG-Aktivität: SIMG_OHAQ438
S_AHR_61009120	IMG Activity: OHAFAV511A
S_AHR_61009121	IMG-Aktivität: OHAGKL000
S_AHR_61009122	IMG-Aktivität: SIMG_OHAHK_501
S_AHR_61009123	IMG Activity: OHTX5008
S_AHR_61009124	IMG Activity: SIMG_OHAJ457
S_AHR_61009125	IMG-Aktivität: OHAK1041
S_AHR_61009126	IMG-Aktivität: SIMG_OHAHK_611
S_AHR_61009127	IMG-Aktivität: SIMG_OHAQ461
S_AHR_61009128	IMG Activity: OHAFAV511B
S_AHR_61009129	IMG Activity: OHTY027
S_AHR_61009130	IMG Activity: OHAN9023
S_AHR_61009131	IMG-Aktivität: OHAGSL001
S_AHR_61009132	IMG Activity: SIMG_OHAJ451
S_AHR_61009133	IMG-Aktivität: OHAK1044
S_AHR_61009134	IMG Activity: OHAFAV511C
S_AHR_61009135	IMG Activity: OHTY028
S_AHR_61009136	IMG-Aktivität: OHAK1045
S_AHR_61009137	IMG-Aktivität: SIMG_OHAQ429
S_AHR_61009138	IMG-Aktivität: OHAGFT009
S_AHR_61009139	IMG Activity: OHAN9025
S_AHR_61009140	IMG Activity: SIMG_OHAJ463
S_AHR_61009141	IMG-Aktivität: OHAKUM022
S_AHR_61009142	IMG Activity: SIMG_OHT200
S_AHR_61009143	IMG-Aktivität: SIMG_OHAQ427
S_AHR_61009144	IMG Activity: OHAFAVXT00
S_AHR_61009145	IMG Activity: SIMG_OHAJ464
S_AHR_61009146	IMG-Aktivität: OHAGFT010
S_AHR_61009147	IMG Activity: OHAN9026
S_AHR_61009148	IMG-Aktivität: OHAKPRID105
S_AHR_61009149	IMG Activity: SIMG_OHT201
S_AHR_61009150	IMG Activity: OHAFAVP15
S_AHR_61009151	IMG-Aktivität: SIMG_OHAQ424
S_AHR_61009152	IMG Activity: OHAJAB009
S_AHR_61009153	IMG Activity: OHAN9028
S_AHR_61009154	IMG-Aktivität: OHAGAB105
S_AHR_61009155	IMG-Aktivität: OHAK1043
S_AHR_61009156	IMG Activity: OHTY029

S_AHR_61009157	IMG Activity: SIMG_OHR0077
S_AHR_61009158	IMG Activity: OHAFRI070
S_AHR_61009159	IMG-Aktivität: OHAGAB106
S_AHR_61009160	IMG Activity: OHAJAB012
S_AHR_61009161	IMG-Aktivität: OHAKR1025
S_AHR_61009162	IMG-Aktivität: SIMG_OHAQ467
S_AHR_61009163	IMG Activity: OHTY035
S_AHR_61009164	IMG Activity: OHAN9029
S_AHR_61009165	IMG Activity: SIMG_OHR0013
S_AHR_61009166	IMG-Aktivität: OHIG0151
S_AHR_61009167	IMG Activity: OHAFBW21
S_AHR_61009168	IMG Activity: OHTX0304
S_AHR_61009169	IMG Activity: OHAJAB010
S_AHR_61009170	IMG-Aktivität: SIMG_OHAQ470
S_AHR_61009171	IMG-Aktivität: OHAKR1027
S_AHR_61009172	IMG Activity: OHAJSP003
S_AHR_61009173	IMG Activity: OHTX0303
S_AHR_61009174	IMG-Aktivität: OHIG0155
S_AHR_61009175	IMG Activity: SIMG_OHR0019
S_AHR_61009176	IMG Activity: OHAN9030
S_AHR_61009177	IMG Activity: OHAFBW22
S_AHR_61009178	IMG-Aktivität: SIMG_OHAQ665
S_AHR_61009179	IMG-Aktivität: OHAKTXEI010
S_AHR_61009180	IMG-Aktivität: OHIG0156
S_AHR_61009181	IMG Activity: OHAJTI110
S_AHR_61009182	IMG Activity: OHTY042
S_AHR_61009183	IMG Activity: SIMG_OHR0018
S_AHR_61009184	IMG Activity: OHAFAB004
S_AHR_61009185	IMG-Aktivität: SIMG_OHAQ447
S_AHR_61009186	IMG Activity: OHAN9001
S_AHR_61009187	IMG-Aktivität: OHAKR1028
S_AHR_61009188	IMG-Aktivität: OHAGFT007
S_AHR_61009189	IMG Activity: OHAJTI120
S_AHR_61009190	IMG Activity: SIMG_OHR0079
S_AHR_61009191	IMG Activity: OHIX0664
S_AHR_61009192	IMG Activity: OHAFAB005
S_AHR_61009193	IMG Activity: OHANWW02
S_AHR_61009194	IMG-Aktivität: SIMG_OHAQ435
S_AHR_61009195	IMG-Aktivität: OHAKUM006
S_AHR_61009196	IMG-Aktivität: OHAGAB009
S_AHR_61009197	IMG Activity: SIMG_OHR0070
S_AHR_61009198	IMG Activity: OHIX0669
S_AHR_61009199	IMG Activity: OHAJAB004
S_AHR_61009200	IMG Activity: OHAFRI054
S_AHR_61009201	IMG-Aktivität: OHAGAB012
S_AHR_61009202	IMG-Aktivität: SIMG_OHAQ422
S_AHR_61009203	IMG Activity: OHAJSP006
S_AHR_61009204	IMG Activity: OHAN9021
S_AHR_61009205	IMG-Aktivität: OHAKUM023
S_AHR_61009206	IMG Activity: OHTX0307
S_AHR_61009207	IMG Activity: SIMG_OHR0069
S_AHR_61009208	IMG Activity: OHAFAB009
S_AHR_61009209	IMG-Aktivität: OHAGAB010
S_AHR_61009210	IMG-Aktivität: OHAK1040A

S_AHR_61009211	IMG Activity: OHAJSP005
S_AHR_61009212	IMG Activity: SIMG_OHR0290
S_AHR_61009213	IMG Activity: OHAN9008
S_AHR_61009214	IMG Activity: OHAFAB011
S_AHR_61009215	IMG-Aktivität: SIMG_OHAQ423
S_AHR_61009216	IMG Activity: OHTX5005
S_AHR_61009217	IMG Activity: OHAFAB012
S_AHR_61009218	IMG-Aktivität: OHAGFT002
S_AHR_61009219	IMG Activity: SIMG_OHR0068
S_AHR_61009220	IMG-Aktivität: OHAK1046
S_AHR_61009221	IMG Activity: OHAN9005
S_AHR_61009222	IMG Activity: OHTX0306
S_AHR_61009223	IMG Activity: OHAJAB005
S_AHR_61009224	IMG-Aktivität: SIMG_OHAQ425
S_AHR_61009225	IMG-Aktivität: OHAK10502
S_AHR_61009226	IMG Activity: OHAJSP004
S_AHR_61009227	IMG Activity: OHAF0300
S_AHR_61009228	IMG-Aktivität: OHAGFT003
S_AHR_61009229	IMG Activity: OHAN9015
S_AHR_61009230	IMG Activity: OHIX0672
S_AHR_61009231	IMG-Aktivität: OHAKM010
S_AHR_61009232	IMG-Aktivität: SIMG_OHAQ437
S_AHR_61009233	IMG Activity: OHAFAB010
S_AHR_61009234	IMG-Aktivität: OHAGFT005
S_AHR_61009235	IMG Activity: OHAN9016
S_AHR_61009236	IMG Activity: OHTX0305
S_AHR_61009237	IMG Activity: OHAJAB011
S_AHR_61009238	IMG-Aktivität: OHACABEN005
S_AHR_61009239	IMG-Aktivität: SIMG_OHAQ432
S_AHR_61009240	IMG Activity: OHAFKL000
S_AHR_61009241	IMG-Aktivität: OHAGFT006
S_AHR_61009242	IMG Activity: OHIX0661
S_AHR_61009243	IMG Activity: OHAN9017
S_AHR_61009244	IMG Activity: OHAJKK002
S_AHR_61009245	IMG-Aktivität: OHACABEN001
S_AHR_61009246	IMG Activity: OHAF0222
S_AHR_61009247	IMG-Aktivität: SIMG_OHAQ426
S_AHR_61009248	IMG-Aktivität: OHAGT104
S_AHR_61009249	IMG Activity: OHAN9018
S_AHR_61009250	IMG Activity: OHIX0653
S_AHR_61009251	IMG Activity: OHAJTI321
S_AHR_61009252	IMG Activity: OHAF0224
S_AHR_61009253	IMG-Aktivität: OHACABEN004
S_AHR_61009254	IMG Activity: OHAJTI322
S_AHR_61009255	IMG-Aktivität: SIMG_OHAQ428
S_AHR_61009256	IMG Activity: OHIX0655
S_AHR_61009257	IMG Activity: OHAN9019
S_AHR_61009258	IMG-Aktivität: OHAGT101
S_AHR_61009259	IMG Activity: OHAF0332
S_AHR_61009260	IMG-Aktivität: OHACABEN002
S_AHR_61009261	IMG-Aktivität: SIMG_OHAQ459
S_AHR_61009262	IMG Activity: OHAJKK001
S_AHR_61009263	IMG-Aktivität: OHAGUM022
S_AHR_61009264	IMG Activity: OHAN9020

S_AHR_61009265	IMG Activity: OHIX0656
S_AHR_61009266	IMG-Aktivität: OHACABEN003
S_AHR_61009267	IMG Activity: OHAFRI055
S_AHR_61009268	IMG Activity: OHAJTI323
S_AHR_61009269	IMG-Aktivität: OHAGUM023
S_AHR_61009270	IMG-Aktivität: OHAQSUP00102
S_AHR_61009271	IMG Activity: SIMG_OHANL_525
S_AHR_61009272	IMG Activity: OHTY044
S_AHR_61009273	IMG Activity: OHAFAB001
S_AHR_61009274	IMG Activity: OHANL_601
S_AHR_61009275	IMG Activity: OHAJTI324
S_AHR_61009276	IMG-Aktivität: OHAGUM101
S_AHR_61009277	IMG-Aktivität: OHAQTI322
S_AHR_61009278	IMG-Aktivität: OHAKUM008
S_AHR_61009279	IMG Activity: OHIX0646
S_AHR_61009280	IMG Activity: OHAFAB002
S_AHR_61009281	IMG Activity: OHAJTI130
S_AHR_61009282	IMG-Aktivität: OHAGUM102
S_AHR_61009283	IMG-Aktivität: OHAQSL002
S_AHR_61009284	IMG-Aktivität: OHAK10501
S_AHR_61009285	IMG Activity: OHIX0660
S_AHR_61009286	IMG Activity: SIMG_OHANL_615
S_AHR_61009287	IMG Activity: OHAJTI210
S_AHR_61009288	IMG Activity: OHAF0232
S_AHR_61009289	IMG-Aktivität: OHAQTI321
S_AHR_61009290	IMG Activity: OHAN9205
S_AHR_61009291	IMG Activity: OHIX0662
S_AHR_61009292	IMG-Aktivität: OHAGUM103
S_AHR_61009293	IMG-Aktivität: OHAKTX014
S_AHR_61009294	IMG Activity: OHAJSP002
S_AHR_61009295	IMG Activity: OHAFUM010B
S_AHR_61009296	IMG Activity: OHAN9212
S_AHR_61009297	IMG-Aktivität: OHAQTI325
S_AHR_61009298	IMG-Aktivität: OHAGUM010
S_AHR_61009299	IMG Activity: OHAJTI310
S_AHR_61009300	IMG Activity: OHIX0663
S_AHR_61009301	IMG-Aktivität: OHAKTX011
S_AHR_61009302	IMG Activity: OHAFUM013
S_AHR_61009303	IMG-Aktivität: OHAGUM012
S_AHR_61009304	IMG-Aktivität: OHAQTI310
S_AHR_61009305	IMG-Aktivität: OHAKTX005
S_AHR_61009306	IMG Activity: OHANL_RI015
S_AHR_61009307	IMG Activity: OHAFUM010
S_AHR_61009308	IMG Activity: OHIX0668
S_AHR_61009309	IMG Activity: OHAJSP001
S_AHR_61009310	IMG-Aktivität: OHAGUM014
S_AHR_61009311	IMG-Aktivität: OHAQTI210
S_AHR_61009312	IMG Activity: OHANL_RI042
S_AHR_61009313	IMG Activity: OHAFUM003
S_AHR_61009314	IMG-Aktivität: OHAKUM013
S_AHR_61009315	IMG Activity: OHIX0666
S_AHR_61009316	IMG-Aktivität: OHAGUM006
S_AHR_61009317	IMG-Aktivität: OHAQSL003
S_AHR_61009318	IMG-Aktivität: OHAK1012

S_AHR_61009319	IMG Activity: OHAJTI325
S_AHR_61009320	IMG Activity: OHANL_RI031
S_AHR_61009321	IMG-Aktivität: OHAQTI323
S_AHR_61009322	IMG-Aktivität: OHAGUM008
S_AHR_61009323	IMG Activity: SIMG_OHT22A
S_AHR_61009324	IMG Activity: OHAFUM002
S_AHR_61009325	IMG Activity: OHANL_RI051
S_AHR_61009326	IMG-Aktivität: OHAKR1026
S_AHR_61009327	IMG Activity: OHAJAB003
S_AHR_61009328	IMG-Aktivität: OHAGUM009
S_AHR_61009329	IMG-Aktivität: OHAQKF002
S_AHR_61009330	IMG Activity: OHAFUM022
S_AHR_61009331	IMG Activity: SIMG_OHANL_470
S_AHR_61009332	IMG-Aktivität: OHAKTXEI020
S_AHR_61009333	IMG Activity: OHAFUM023
S_AHR_61009334	IMG-Aktivität: OHAQPPADJ
S_AHR_61009335	IMG-Aktivität: OHAGUM013
S_AHR_61009336	IMG Activity: SIMG_OHR0038
S_AHR_61009337	IMG Activity: OHAJKF001
S_AHR_61009338	IMG Activity: OHAFUM101
S_AHR_61009339	IMG-Aktivität: OHACATXEI015
S_AHR_61009340	IMG Activity: SIMG_OHANL_428
S_AHR_61009341	IMG Activity: SIMG_OHTX822
S_AHR_61009342	IMG-Aktivität: OHAGUM015
S_AHR_61009343	IMG Activity: SIMG_OHR0073
S_AHR_61009344	IMG-Aktivität: OHAQKL000
S_AHR_61009345	IMG Activity: OHAJJW912
S_AHR_61009346	IMG Activity: SIMG_OHANL_459
S_AHR_61009347	IMG Activity: SIMG_OHTX821
S_AHR_61009348	IMG-Aktivität: OHAGAVX017
S_AHR_61009349	IMG-Aktivität: OHIK1012
S_AHR_61009350	IMG Activity: OHAF0526
S_AHR_61009351	IMG Activity: SIMG_OHR0072
S_AHR_61009352	IMG-Aktivität: OHAQTI361
S_AHR_61009353	IMG Activity: OHAJOV002
S_AHR_61009354	IMG-Aktivität: OHIK1013
S_AHR_61009355	IMG-Aktivität: OHAGAVX018
S_AHR_61009356	IMG Activity: SIMG_OHANL_438
S_AHR_61009357	IMG Activity: SIMG_OHR0291
S_AHR_61009358	IMG Activity: OHAJJW913
S_AHR_61009359	IMG-Aktivität: OHAQSL001
S_AHR_61009360	IMG Activity: SIMG_OHTX820
S_AHR_61009361	IMG Activity: OHAF0524
S_AHR_61009362	IMG Activity: OHAJOV001
S_AHR_61009363	IMG Activity: SIMG_OHANL_461
S_AHR_61009364	IMG-Aktivität: OHAGAV511A
S_AHR_61009365	IMG-Aktivität: OHAQTI340
S_AHR_61009366	IMG Activity: OHAFAD002
S_AHR_61009367	IMG Activity: SIMG_OHR0071
S_AHR_61009368	IMG Activity: OHTY038
S_AHR_61009369	IMG-Aktivität: OHAKALL110
S_AHR_61009370	IMG-Aktivität: OHAQTI324
S_AHR_61009371	IMG Activity: SIMG_OHR2001
S_AHR_61009372	IMG Activity: SIMG_OHANL_429

S_AHR_61009373	IMG Activity: OHAJNT006
S_AHR_61009375	IMG-Aktivität: OHAK1016
S_AHR_61009376	IMG-Aktivität: OHAGAV511B
S_AHR_61009377	IMG Activity: OHAF0522
S_AHR_61009378	IMG-Aktivität: OHAQTI130
S_AHR_61009379	IMG Activity: SIMG_OHR0080
S_AHR_61009380	IMG Activity: SIMG_OHANL_427
S_AHR_61009381	IMG Activity: SIMG_OHTX825
S_AHR_61009382	IMG Activity: OHAJKL000
S_AHR_61009383	IMG Activity: OHAFUM012
S_AHR_61009384	IMG-Aktivität: OHAGAV511C
S_AHR_61009385	IMG-Aktivität: OHAK10171
S_AHR_61009386	IMG Activity: SIMG_OHR_FORM_FXTXT
S_AHR_61009387	IMG-Aktivität: OHAQUM102
S_AHR_61009388	IMG-Aktivität: OHAK1015
S_AHR_61009389	IMG Activity: OHAFUM014
S_AHR_61009390	IMG Activity: OHAJSL001
S_AHR_61009391	IMG Activity: SIMG_OHANL_424
S_AHR_61009392	IMG Activity: SIMG_OHR_TRVFO
S_AHR_61009393	IMG-Aktivität: OHAGAVXT00
S_AHR_61009394	IMG Activity: SIMG_OHTX824
S_AHR_61009395	IMG-Aktivität: OHAQCUM005
S_AHR_61009396	IMG-Aktivität: OHAKUM102
S_AHR_61009397	IMG Activity: OHAJSL002
S_AHR_61009398	IMG Activity: SIMG_OHR_V_T706FORM
S_AHR_61009399	IMG Activity: SIMG_OHANL_467
S_AHR_61009400	IMG Activity: SIMG_OHTX823
S_AHR_61009401	IMG Activity: OHAFUM006
S_AHR_61009402	IMG-Aktivität: OHAKALL120
S_AHR_61009403	IMG-Aktivität: OHAGAVP15
S_AHR_61009404	IMG-Aktivität: OHAQCUM006
S_AHR_61009405	IMG Activity: OHAJKF002
S_AHR_61009406	IMG Activity: OHANL_RI052
S_AHR_61009407	IMG Activity: SIMG_OHR_FORM_FRTXT
S_AHR_61009408	IMG Activity: OHTY036
S_AHR_61009409	IMG-Aktivität: OHAQJW000
S_AHR_61009410	IMG-Aktivität: OHAKR1024
S_AHR_61009411	IMG Activity: OHAFUM008
S_AHR_61009412	IMG-Aktivität: OHAGAVBAS
S_AHR_61009413	IMG Activity: SIMG_OHR0063
S_AHR_61009414	IMG Activity: OHAJJW902
S_AHR_61009415	IMG-Aktivität: OHAQUM101
S_AHR_61009416	IMG Activity: SIMG_OHT22B
S_AHR_61009417	IMG Activity: OHANL_RI080
S_AHR_61009418	IMG Activity: OHAFBW005
S_AHR_61009419	IMG-Aktivität: OHAGUM104
S_AHR_61009420	IMG Activity: OHAJJW911
S_AHR_61009421	IMG Activity: OHANL_RI081
S_AHR_61009422	IMG-Aktivität: OHAGUM105
S_AHR_61009423	IMG Activity: OHAF0282
S_AHR_61009424	IMG Activity: OHAJBW006B
S_AHR_61009425	IMG Activity: OHANL_RI090
S_AHR_61009426	IMG-Aktivität: OHAGBW004
S_AHR_61009427	IMG Activity: OHAF0284

S_AHR_61009428	IMG Activity: OHANL_UM002
S_AHR_61009429	IMG Activity: OHAJAB001
S_AHR_61009430	IMG-Aktivität: OHAKUM101
S_AHR_61009431	IMG Activity: OHAFRI071
S_AHR_61009432	IMG-Aktivität: OHAGBW005
S_AHR_61009433	IMG Activity: SIMG_OHR_T702N_A
S_AHR_61009434	IMG Activity: OHANL_UM003
S_AHR_61009435	IMG Activity: OHAJBW006
S_AHR_61009436	IMG Activity: OHAFAV001
S_AHR_61009437	IMG Activity: OHANUM05
S_AHR_61009438	IMG-Aktivität: OHAGBW006
S_AHR_61009439	IMG Activity: OHAJBW005
S_AHR_61009440	IMG Activity: OHAFAVBAS
S_AHR_61009441	IMG Activity: OHANL_PAY002
S_AHR_61009442	IMG-Aktivität: OHAGBW019
S_AHR_61009443	IMG-Aktivität: OHAQUM105
S_AHR_61009444	IMG-Aktivität: OHACAR1029
S_AHR_61009445	IMG Activity: SIMG_OHT022
S_AHR_61009446	IMG Activity: SIMG_OHR_FORM_BLKHD
S_AHR_61009447	IMG Activity: OHAJBW004
S_AHR_61009448	IMG Activity: OHANL_PAY003
S_AHR_61009449	IMG-Aktivität: OHAGAV001
S_AHR_61009450	IMG Activity: OHAFAVX017
S_AHR_61009451	IMG-Aktivität: OHAQUM104
S_AHR_61009452	IMG Activity: OHAJAB002
S_AHR_61009453	IMG Activity: OHANL_RI071
S_AHR_61009454	IMG Activity: OHAFAVX018
S_AHR_61009455	IMG-Aktivität: OHAKUM014
S_AHR_61009456	IMG-Aktivität: OHIG0157
S_AHR_61009457	IMG Activity: SIMG_OHR_FORM_FLDS
S_AHR_61009458	IMG-Aktivität: OHAQUM103
S_AHR_61009459	IMG Activity: SIMG_OHTX807
S_AHR_61009460	IMG Activity: OHAFUM102
S_AHR_61009461	IMG Activity: OHANL_RI056
S_AHR_61009462	IMG Activity: OHAJNT005
S_AHR_61009463	IMG-Aktivität: OHAGTI340
S_AHR_61009464	IMG Activity: SIMG_OHR_FORM_BCKGR
S_AHR_61009465	IMG-Aktivität: OHAQTI120
S_AHR_61009466	IMG-Aktivität: OHIK1014
S_AHR_61009467	IMG Activity: OHIX0667
S_AHR_61009468	IMG Activity: OHAJJW903
S_AHR_61009469	IMG Activity: OHAFUM103
S_AHR_61009470	IMG Activity: OHANL_RI053
S_AHR_61009471	IMG-Aktivität: OHAQTI110
S_AHR_61009472	IMG Activity: SIMG_OHR_FORM_BLKAT
S_AHR_61009473	IMG-Aktivität: OHAGP100
S_AHR_61009474	IMG Activity: SIMG_OHTX815
S_AHR_61009475	IMG Activity: OHANL_RI054
S_AHR_61009476	IMG Activity: OHAFUM104
S_AHR_61009477	IMG-Aktivität: OHAK1013
S_AHR_61009478	IMG-Aktivität: OHAQCUM003
S_AHR_61009479	IMG Activity: SIMG_OHR_FORM_COPY
S_AHR_61009480	IMG-Aktivität: OHAGBP007
S_AHR_61009481	IMG Activity: OHAJNT004

S_AHR_61009482	IMG Activity: OHAFUM105
S_AHR_61009483	IMG Activity: OHTY040
S_AHR_61009484	IMG Activity: OHANL_RI055
S_AHR_61009485	IMG Activity: OHPKAW000
S_AHR_61009486	IMG-Aktivität: OHIK1011
S_AHR_61009487	IMG Activity: SIMG_OHR_FORM_BLKND
S_AHR_61009488	IMG-Aktivität: OHAQDEC01
S_AHR_61009489	IMG-Aktivität: OHAGAB112
S_AHR_61009490	IMG Activity: OHANL_RI061
S_AHR_61009491	IMG Activity: OHAJNT003
S_AHR_61009492	IMG-Aktivität: OHAKUM012
S_AHR_61009493	IMG Activity: OHAFRI090
S_AHR_61009494	IMG Activity: OHPKWF082
S_AHR_61009495	IMG Activity: OHTY041
S_AHR_61009496	IMG Activity: SIMG_OHR_T702N_B
S_AHR_61009497	IMG-Aktivität: OHAQCUM001
S_AHR_61009498	IMG-Aktivität: OHACAREPEEA005
S_AHR_61009499	IMG Activity: OHANL_RI062
S_AHR_61009500	IMG-Aktivität: OHAGTI361
S_AHR_61009501	IMG-Aktivität: OHACAREPEEA010
S_AHR_61009502	IMG Activity: SIMG_OHT0451
S_AHR_61009503	IMG Activity: OHAFRI081
S_AHR_61009504	IMG-Aktivität: OHAGBP008
S_AHR_61009505	IMG-Aktivität: OHAQ_PM_CREATE
S_AHR_61009506	IMG Activity: OHAJNT002
S_AHR_61009507	IMG-Aktivität: OHAKDT004
S_AHR_61009508	IMG Activity: OHANL_RI063
S_AHR_61009509	IMG Activity: OHPKWF081
S_AHR_61009510	IMG-Aktivität: OHAKDT008
S_AHR_61009511	IMG Activity: SIMG_OHR0059
S_AHR_61009512	IMG Activity: OHAFRI080
S_AHR_61009513	IMG Activity: OHAJBW019
S_AHR_61009514	IMG Activity: SIMG_OHTX817
S_AHR_61009515	IMG-Aktivität: OHAGTI363
S_AHR_61009516	IMG-Aktivität: OHAQCUM004
S_AHR_61009517	IMG Activity: OHANL_RI070
S_AHR_61009518	IMG-Aktivität: SIMG_OHAK612
S_AHR_61009519	IMG Activity: SIMG_OHR0058
S_AHR_61009520	IMG-Aktivität: SIMG_OHAK611
S_AHR_61009521	IMG Activity: SIMG_OHTX809
S_AHR_61009522	IMG-Aktivität: OHAGAB111
S_AHR_61009523	IMG Activity: OHPKWF062
S_AHR_61009524	IMG Activity: OHAJUM012
S_AHR_61009525	IMG Activity: OHAF0262
S_AHR_61009526	IMG-Aktivität: SIMG_OHAK481
S_AHR_61009527	IMG Activity: SIMG_OHANL_426
S_AHR_61009528	IMG-Aktivität: OHAQBW004
S_AHR_61009529	IMG-Aktivität: OHAKAL01
S_AHR_61009530	IMG-Aktivität: OHAGTI362
S_AHR_61009531	IMG Activity: OHAJBN0001
S_AHR_61009532	IMG Activity: SIMG_OHR0064
S_AHR_61009533	IMG Activity: OHTY039
S_AHR_61009534	IMG Activity: OHPKWF061
S_AHR_61009535	IMG Activity: SIMG_OHANL_407

S_AHR_61009536	IMG Activity: OHAFRI053
S_AHR_61009537	IMG-Aktivität: OHAQBW005
S_AHR_61009538	IMG-Aktivität: SIMG_OHAK401
S_AHR_61009539	IMG Activity: SIMG_OHR_T702N_N
S_AHR_61009540	IMG-Aktivität: SIMG_OHAK524
S_AHR_61009541	IMG Activity: SIMG_OHTX808
S_AHR_61009542	IMG Activity: OHAJUM014J
S_AHR_61009543	IMG-Aktivität: OHAGBP005
S_AHR_61009544	IMG-Aktivität: SIMG_OHAK523
S_AHR_61009545	IMG Activity: OHPKWF060
S_AHR_61009546	IMG Activity: SIMG_OHANL_482
S_AHR_61009547	IMG-Aktivität: OHAQBW006
S_AHR_61009548	IMG Activity: OHAF0804
S_AHR_61009549	IMG Activity: OHAJUM013
S_AHR_61009550	IMG-Aktivität: SIMG_OHAK613
S_AHR_61009551	IMG Activity: OHPKWF040
S_AHR_61009552	IMG Activity: SIMG_OHT0400
S_AHR_61009553	IMG-Aktivität: OHAGAB110
S_AHR_61009554	IMG-Aktivität: OHAKRI012
S_AHR_61009555	IMG Activity: OHAF0806
S_AHR_61009556	IMG Activity: OHAJUM006
S_AHR_61009557	IMG Activity: SIMG_OHANL_410
S_AHR_61009558	IMG-Aktivität: OHAKRI011
S_AHR_61009559	IMG Activity: OHPKAW120
S_AHR_61009560	IMG-Aktivität: OHAQBW019
S_AHR_61009561	IMG Activity: SIMG_OHT0300
S_AHR_61009562	IMG-Aktivität: SIMG_OHAK844
S_AHR_61009563	IMG-Aktivität: OHAGTI323
S_AHR_61009564	IMG-Aktivität: OHAQAB002
S_AHR_61009565	IMG-Aktivität: SIMG_OHAK843
S_AHR_61009566	IMG Activity: OHAF0814
S_AHR_61009567	IMG Activity: OHAJAA001
S_AHR_61009568	IMG Activity: SIMG_OHANL_417
S_AHR_61009569	IMG Activity: SIMG_OHT088
S_AHR_61009570	IMG Activity: OHPKAW110
S_AHR_61009571	IMG-Aktivität: SIMG_OHAK842
S_AHR_61009572	IMG-Aktivität: OHAQAV001
S_AHR_61009573	IMG-Aktivität: SIMG_OHAK841
S_AHR_61009574	IMG-Aktivität: OHAGTI324
S_AHR_61009575	IMG Activity: OHAF0816
S_AHR_61009576	IMG Activity: OHAJUM022
S_AHR_61009577	IMG-Aktivität: SIMG_OHAK614
S_AHR_61009578	IMG Activity: SIMG_OHT0509
S_AHR_61009579	IMG Activity: SIMG_OHANL_413
S_AHR_61009580	IMG-Aktivität: OHAG0102
S_AHR_61009581	IMG Activity: OHPKAW065
S_AHR_61009582	IMG-Aktivität: OHAQAVBAS
S_AHR_61009583	IMG-Aktivität: SIMG_OHAK522
S_AHR_61009584	IMG-Aktivität: OHAG0101
S_AHR_61009585	IMG-Aktivität: SIMG_OHAK512
S_AHR_61009586	IMG Activity: OHPKAW060
S_AHR_61009587	IMG Activity: OHAJAA002
S_AHR_61009588	IMG Activity: OHAF0818
S_AHR_61009589	IMG Activity: SIMG_OHANL_480

S_AHR_61009590	IMG-Aktivität: OHAKR0007
S_AHR_61009591	IMG Activity: SIMG_OHT049
S_AHR_61009592	IMG-Aktivität: OHAQAB003
S_AHR_61009593	IMG-Aktivität: OHAGBP001
S_AHR_61009594	IMG-Aktivität: SIMG_OHAK510
S_AHR_61009595	IMG Activity: OHPKAW050
S_AHR_61009596	IMG Activity: OHAJFA000
S_AHR_61009597	IMG-Aktivität: OHAQAB200
S_AHR_61009598	IMG Activity: OHAF0812
S_AHR_61009599	IMG Activity: OHTY011
S_AHR_61009600	IMG-Aktivität: OHAGAB113
S_AHR_61009601	IMG-Aktivität: SIMG_OHAK509
S_AHR_61009602	IMG Activity: SIMG_OHANL_414
S_AHR_61009603	IMG Activity: OHPKAW020
S_AHR_61009604	IMG Activity: OHAJMA000
S_AHR_61009605	IMG-Aktivität: OHAGBP002
S_AHR_61009606	IMG-Aktivität: OHAQAB010
S_AHR_61009607	IMG Activity SIMG_OHAK508
S_AHR_61009608	IMG Activity: OHAF0810
S_AHR_61009609	IMG Activity: SIMG_OHT090
S_AHR_61009610	IMG Activity: OHPKAW010
S_AHR_61009611	IMG Activity SIMG_OHAK502
S_AHR_61009612	IMG Activity: SIMG_OHANL_814
S_AHR_61009613	IMG Activity: OHAJOCR001
S_AHR_61009614	IMG Activity: OHAF0802
S_AHR_61009615	IMG Activity SIMG_OHAK501
S_AHR_61009616	IMG Activity: SIMG_OHT0404
S_AHR_61009617	IMG Activity SIMG_OHAK513
S_AHR_61009618	IMG-Aktivität: OHAGBP003
S_AHR_61009619	IMG-Aktivität: OHAQAB012
S_AHR_61009620	IMG Activity: OHAJBN1131
S_AHR_61009621	IMG Activity: SIMG_OHANL_409
S_AHR_61009622	IMG Activity: OHPKWF003
S_AHR_61009623	IMG Activity SIMG_OHAK521
S_AHR_61009624	IMG Activity: OHAF0009
S_AHR_61009625	IMG Activity: SIMG_OHT0403
S_AHR_61009626	IMG-Aktivität: OHAGTI364
S_AHR_61009627	IMG Activity OHAKTI330
S_AHR_61009628	IMG Activity: OHPKWF002
S_AHR_61009629	IMG Activity: OHAJBN1132
S_AHR_61009630	IMG Activity: SIMG_OHANL_402
S_AHR_61009631	IMG-Aktivität: OHAQAB009
S_AHR_61009632	IMG Activity SIMG_OHAK520
S_AHR_61009633	IMG Activity: SIMG_OHT0402
S_AHR_61009634	IMG-Aktivität: OHAGTI321
S_AHR_61009635	IMG Activity SIMG_OHAK519
S_AHR_61009636	IMG Activity: OHPKWF001
S_AHR_61009637	IMG Activity: OHAF0005
S_AHR_61009638	IMG Activity: SIMG_OHANL_403
S_AHR_61009639	IMG Activity SIMG_OHAK517
S_AHR_61009640	IMG Activity: OHAJUM008A
S_AHR_61009641	IMG-Aktivität: OHAQAB011
S_AHR_61009642	IMG-Aktivität: OHAGTI210
S_AHR_61009643	IMG Activity SIMG_OHAK516

S_AHR_61009644	IMG Activity: OHPKAI120
S_AHR_61009645	IMG Activity: OHAJBN1133
S_AHR_61009646	IMG Activity SIMG_OHAK514
S_AHR_61009647	IMG Activity: OHTX0559
S_AHR_61009648	IMG-Aktivität: OHAQAB005
S_AHR_61009649	IMG Activity: OHAF0006
S_AHR_61009650	IMG-Aktivität: OHAGAB108
S_AHR_61009651	IMG Activity: SIMG_OHANL_405
S_AHR_61009652	IMG Activity: OHPKAI100
S_AHR_61009653	IMG Activity: OHAJBN1110
S_AHR_61009654	IMG-Aktivität: OHAQAB004
S_AHR_61009655	IMG Activity: OHTF0112
S_AHR_61009656	IMG-Aktivität: OHAGTI130
S_AHR_61009657	IMG Activity: OHAF0007
S_AHR_61009658	IMG Activity: OHPKAI110
S_AHR_61009659	IMG Activity: SIMG_OHANL_406
S_AHR_61009660	IMG Activity: OHAJBN1200
S_AHR_61009661	IMG-Aktivität: OHAQAVX017
S_AHR_61009662	IMG Activity: OHTF0110
S_AHR_61009663	IMG Activity: OHAJUM010B
S_AHR_61009664	IMG Activity: OHPKAI010
S_AHR_61009665	IMG-Aktivität: OHAGTI120
S_AHR_61009666	IMG-Aktivität: OHAQBW21
S_AHR_61009667	IMG Activity: OHTF0102
S_AHR_61009668	IMG Activity: SIMG_OHANL_408
S_AHR_61009669	IMG Activity: OHAF0001
S_AHR_61009670	IMG Activity: OHAJUM009
S_AHR_61009671	IMG Activity: OHPKWF032
S_AHR_61009672	IMG Activity: SIMG_OHANL_527
S_AHR_61009673	IMG-Aktivität: OHAGTI310
S_AHR_61009674	IMG-Aktivität: OHAQBW22
S_AHR_61009675	IMG Activity: OHAF0008
S_AHR_61009676	IMG Activity: OHTF0106
S_AHR_61009677	IMG Activity: OHPKWF031
S_AHR_61009678	IMG Activity: SIMG_OHANL_528
S_AHR_61009679	IMG Activity: OHAFRI015
S_AHR_61009680	IMG Activity: OHAJBN1120
S_AHR_61009681	IMG-Aktivität: OHAGAB107
S_AHR_61009682	IMG Activity: OHTF0105
S_AHR_61009683	IMG-Aktivität: OHAQTI364
S_AHR_61009684	IMG Activity: OHPKWF030
S_AHR_61009685	IMG Activity: OHAJBN2110
S_AHR_61009686	IMG Activity: SIMG_OHANL_529
S_AHR_61009687	IMG-Aktivität: OHAGAB104
S_AHR_61009688	IMG-Aktivität: OHAQTI362
S_AHR_61009689	IMG Activity: SIMG_OHT085
S_AHR_61009690	IMG Activity: OHPKWF023
S_AHR_61009691	IMG Activity: OHAF0104
S_AHR_61009692	IMG Activity: SIMG_OHANL_415
S_AHR_61009693	IMG Activity: OHAJTI362
S_AHR_61009694	IMG Activity: OHAF0106
S_AHR_61009695	IMG Activity: OHPKWF022
S_AHR_61009696	IMG-Aktivität: OHAGTI325
S_AHR_61009697	IMG Activity: SIMG_OHT020B

S_AHR_61009698	IMG-Aktivität: OHAQTI363
S_AHR_61009699	IMG Activity: OHAJTI363
S_AHR_61009700	IMG Activity: SIMG_OHANL_464
S_AHR_61009701	IMG-Aktivität: OHAQPART
S_AHR_61009702	IMG Activity: OHAF0108
S_AHR_61009703	IMG-Aktivität: OHAG0104
S_AHR_61009704	IMG Activity: OHPKWF021
S_AHR_61009705	IMG Activity: SIMG_OHT084
S_AHR_61009706	IMG Activity: OHAJTI361
S_AHR_61009707	IMG-Aktivität: OHAQKF001
S_AHR_61009708	IMG Activity: OHPKWF020
S_AHR_61009709	IMG Activity: OHAF0604
S_AHR_61009710	IMG Activity: SIMG_OHANL_471
S_AHR_61009711	IMG-Aktivität: OHIGA208
S_AHR_61009712	IMG Activity: OHAJUM104
S_AHR_61009713	IMG Activity: OHTY013
S_AHR_61009714	IMG-Aktivität: OHAQTI370
S_AHR_61009715	IMG Activity: OHPKAW150
S_AHR_61009716	IMG Activity: OHAF0606
S_AHR_61009717	IMG Activity: SIMG_OHANL_435
S_AHR_61009718	IMG Activity: OHTY014
S_AHR_61009719	IMG Activity: OHAJBN2132
S_AHR_61009720	IMG-Aktivität: OHAGTI110
S_AHR_61009721	IMG Activity: OHAF0608
S_AHR_61009722	IMG Activity: OHPKAO210
S_AHR_61009723	IMG-Aktivität: OHAQAV018
S_AHR_61009724	IMG Activity: SIMG_OHR0056
S_AHR_61009725	IMG Activity: OHAJUM105
S_AHR_61009726	IMG-Aktivität: OHAGTI370
S_AHR_61009727	IMG Activity: SIMG_OHANL_422
S_AHR_61009728	IMG-Aktivität: OHAQAV511A
S_AHR_61009729	IMG Activity: OHTX0401
S_AHR_61009730	IMG-Aktivität: OHAGTI322
S_AHR_61009731	IMG Activity: OHAF0610
S_AHR_61009732	IMG Activity: OHPKAO200
S_AHR_61009733	IMG Activity: OHAJBN2133
S_AHR_61009734	IMG Activity: SIMG_OHR_T702N_K
S_AHR_61009735	IMG Activity: SIMG_OHANL_423
S_AHR_61009736	IMG-Aktivität: SIMG_OHAG841
S_AHR_61009737	IMG Activity: OHTY007
S_AHR_61009738	IMG-Aktivität: OHAQAV511B
S_AHR_61009739	IMG-Aktivität: SIMG_OHAG842
S_AHR_61009740	IMG Activity: OHAJTI340
S_AHR_61009741	IMG Activity: OHPKAO150
S_AHR_61009742	IMG Activity: OHAF0102
S_AHR_61009743	IMG Activity: SIMG_OHANL_425
S_AHR_61009744	IMG Activity: SIMG_OHR0074
S_AHR_61009745	IMG-Aktivität: OHAQAV511C
S_AHR_61009746	IMG-Aktivität: SIMG_OHAG843
S_AHR_61009747	IMG Activity: OHPKAO140
S_AHR_61009748	IMG Activity: OHAJBN2200
S_AHR_61009749	IMG Activity: SIMG_OHT0306
S_AHR_61009750	IMG-Aktivität: SIMG_OHAG844
S_AHR_61009751	IMG Activity: OHAF0808

S_AHR_61009752	IMG Activity: SIMG_OHR0011
S_AHR_61009753	IMG Activity: OHAJUM023
S_AHR_61009754	IMG-Aktivität: OHAGRI011
S_AHR_61009755	IMG Activity: SIMG_OHT0410
S_AHR_61009756	IMG Activity: OHPKAO130
S_AHR_61009757	IMG Activity: SIMG_OHANL_437
S_AHR_61009758	IMG-Aktivität: OHAGRI012
S_AHR_61009759	IMG-Aktivität: OHAQAVXT00
S_AHR_61009760	IMG Activity: OHAF0820
S_AHR_61009761	IMG Activity: SIMG_OHR0240
S_AHR_61009762	IMG-Aktivität: SIMG_OHAG516
S_AHR_61009763	IMG Activity: OHTY009
S_AHR_61009764	IMG Activity: OHAJBN2120
S_AHR_61009765	IMG Activity: OHPKAO120
S_AHR_61009766	IMG-Aktivität: SIMG_OHAG517
S_AHR_61009767	IMG Activity: SIMG_OHR0061
S_AHR_61009768	IMG Activity: SIMG_OHANL_432
S_AHR_61009769	IMG-Aktivität: SIMG_OHAG519
S_AHR_61009770	IMG Activity: OHTY004
S_AHR_61009771	IMG Activity: OHPKAO110
S_AHR_61009772	IMG-Aktivität: OHAQAB001
S_AHR_61009773	IMG-Aktivität: SIMG_OHAG520
S_AHR_61009774	IMG Activity: OHAF0824
S_AHR_61009775	IMG Activity: SIMG_OHR0060
S_AHR_61009776	IMG-Aktivität: SIMG_OHAG521
S_AHR_61009777	IMG Activity: OHAJBN2131
S_AHR_61009778	IMG Activity: SIMG_OHR0047
S_AHR_61009779	IMG Activity: SIMG_OHANL_463
S_AHR_61009780	IMG-Aktivität: SIMG_OHAG522
S_AHR_61009781	IMG Activity: OHPKTR115
S_AHR_61009782	IMG-Aktivität: OHAQAVP15
S_AHR_61009783	IMG Activity: OHTY003
S_AHR_61009784	IMG Activity: OHAJTI370
S_AHR_61009785	IMG Activity: OHAF0822
S_AHR_61009786	IMG-Aktivität: SIMG_OHAG523
S_AHR_61009787	IMG Activity: OHPKTR112
S_AHR_61009788	IMG-Aktivität: SIMG_OHAG524
S_AHR_61009789	IMG Activity: OHAF0819
S_AHR_61009790	IMG-Aktivität: OHAQSUP008
S_AHR_61009791	IMG Activity: OHTY008
S_AHR_61009792	IMG-Aktivität: SIMG_OHAG514
S_AHR_61009793	IMG Activity: SIMG_OHR0032
S_AHR_61009794	IMG Activity: OHAJTI364
S_AHR_61009795	IMG Activity: SIMG_OHANL_418
S_AHR_61009796	IMG-Aktivität: OHAGAB109
S_AHR_61009797	IMG Activity: OHPKTR111
S_AHR_61009798	IMG Activity: SIMG_OHAJ439
S_AHR_61009799	IMG-Aktivität: OHAQWTM00004
S_AHR_61009800	IMG-Aktivität: SIMG_OHAG501
S_AHR_61009801	IMG Activity: SIMG_OHR0101
S_AHR_61009802	IMG Activity: SIMG_OHAJ516
S_AHR_61009803	IMG Activity: OHAF0384
S_AHR_61009804	IMG Activity: OHTX0403
S_AHR_61009805	IMG Activity: SIMG_OHAJ517

S_AHR_61009806	IMG-Aktivität: SIMG_OHAG502
S_AHR_61009807	IMG-Aktivität: SIMG_OHAG508
S_AHR_61009808	IMG Activity: OHPKTR015
S_AHR_61009809	IMG Activity: SIMG_OHR0034
S_AHR_61009810	IMG Activity: SIMG_OHAJ450
S_AHR_61009811	IMG Activity: SIMG_OHANL_419
S_AHR_61009812	IMG-Aktivität: OHAQUM010
S_AHR_61009813	IMG-Aktivität: SIMG_OHAG509
S_AHR_61009814	IMG Activity: SIMG_OHAJ514
S_AHR_61009815	IMG Activity: OHAF0382
S_AHR_61009816	IMG Activity: OHTX0402
S_AHR_61009817	IMG Activity: OHPKTR010
S_AHR_61009818	IMG-Aktivität: SIMG_OHAG510
S_AHR_61009819	IMG Activity: SIMG_OHAJ513
S_AHR_61009820	IMG-Aktivität: SIMG_OHAG512
S_AHR_61009821	IMG-Aktivität: OHAQTAX013
S_AHR_61009822	IMG Activity: SIMG_OHR0067
S_AHR_61009823	IMG Activity: SIMG_OHAJ453
S_AHR_61009824	IMG Activity: OHAF0002
S_AHR_61009825	IMG Activity: SIMG_OHANL_483
S_AHR_61009826	IMG-Aktivität: SIMG_OHAG513
S_AHR_61009827	IMG Activity: OHPKBE020
S_AHR_61009828	IMG Activity: SIMG_OHT0215
S_AHR_61009829	IMG Activity: OHAJLG481
S_AHR_61009830	IMG-Aktivität: SIMG_OHAG466
S_AHR_61009831	IMG-Aktivität: OHAQUM015
S_AHR_61009832	IMG Activity: OHAJDAB001
S_AHR_61009833	IMG Activity: SIMG_OHR_V_T702G
S_AHR_61009834	IMG Activity: SIMG_OHANL_484
S_AHR_61009835	IMG Activity: OHPKBE010
S_AHR_61009836	IMG-Aktivität: SIMG_OHAG456
S_AHR_61009837	IMG Activity: OHAF0242
S_AHR_61009838	IMG Activity: OHAJLG401
S_AHR_61009839	IMG Activity: SIMG_OHT096
S_AHR_61009840	IMG Activity: SIMG_OHAJ524
S_AHR_61009841	IMG-Aktivität: OHAGTI330
S_AHR_61009842	IMG Activity: OHPKOR003
S_AHR_61009843	IMG Activity: SIMG_OHR0050
S_AHR_61009844	IMG Activity: SIMG_OHAJ523
S_AHR_61009845	IMG-Aktivität: SIMG_OHAG421
S_AHR_61009846	IMG-Aktivität: OHAQUM013
S_AHR_61009847	IMG Activity: OHAFRI051
S_AHR_61009848	IMG-Aktivität: SIMG_OHAG611
S_AHR_61009849	IMG Activity: SIMG_OHAJ522
S_AHR_61009850	IMG Activity: OHANL_EDTINTERNET
S_AHR_61009851	IMG Activity: OHTY006
S_AHR_61009852	IMG Activity: SIMG_OHR0002
S_AHR_61009853	IMG-Aktivität: SIMG_OHAG612
S_AHR_61009854	IMG Activity: SIMG_OHAJ521
S_AHR_61009855	IMG Activity: OHPKOR002
S_AHR_61009856	IMG-Aktivität: OHAQTAX007
S_AHR_61009857	IMG Activity: SIMG_OHAJ520
S_AHR_61009858	IMG Activity: SIMG_OHANL_431
S_AHR_61009859	IMG-Aktivität: SIMG_OHAG613

S_AHR_61009860	IMG Activity: OHAFTI310
S_AHR_61009861	IMG Activity: OHTX2012
S_AHR_61009862	IMG Activity: SIMG_OHAJ519
S_AHR_61009863	IMG Activity: SIMG_OHR1080
S_AHR_61009864	IMG-Aktivität: OHAQWTM00003
S_AHR_61009865	IMG-Aktivität: SIMG_OHAG614
S_AHR_61009866	IMG Activity: OHPKOR001
S_AHR_61009867	IMG Activity: SIMG_OHAJ512
S_AHR_61009868	IMG-Aktivität: SIMG_OHAG455
S_AHR_61009869	IMG Activity: SIMG_OHR0048
S_AHR_61009870	IMG Activity: SIMG_OHANL_457
S_AHR_61009871	IMG Activity: OHAJLJ841
S_AHR_61009872	IMG Activity: SIMG_OHT092
S_AHR_61009873	IMG Activity: OHAFTI325
S_AHR_61009875	IMG Activity: OHPKOR000
S_AHR_61009876	IMG-Aktivität: OHAQTAX009
S_AHR_61009877	IMG Activity: OHAJLJ842
S_AHR_61009878	IMG-Aktivität: SIMG_OHAG401
S_AHR_61009879	IMG Activity: SIMG_OHT094
S_AHR_61009880	IMG Activity: OHPKAW430
S_AHR_61009881	IMG Activity: OHAJLJ843
S_AHR_61009882	IMG Activity: SIMG_OHANL_451
S_AHR_61009883	IMG Activity: SIMG_OHR0033
S_AHR_61009884	IMG-Aktivität: SIMG_OHAG481
S_AHR_61009885	IMG Activity: OHAFTI321
S_AHR_61009886	IMG Activity: OHAJLJ844
S_AHR_61009887	IMG-Aktivität: OHAQWTM00102
S_AHR_61009888	IMG Activity: OHPKAW140
S_AHR_61009889	IMG-Aktivität: OHAGAL01
S_AHR_61009890	IMG Activity: SIMG_OHR0031
S_AHR_61009891	IMG Activity: OHAJAU421
S_AHR_61009892	IMG Activity: SIMG_OHT0102
S_AHR_61009893	IMG-Aktivität: OHAQTAX010
S_AHR_61009894	IMG-Aktivität: SIMG_OHAG439
S_AHR_61009895	IMG Activity: OHANL_TI370
S_AHR_61009896	IMG Activity: SIMG_OHAJ614
S_AHR_61009897	IMG Activity: OHAFTI322
S_AHR_61009898	IMG Activity: SIMG_OHR0026
S_AHR_61009899	IMG Activity: SIMG_OHAJ501
S_AHR_61009900	IMG-Aktivität: OHAQWTM00103
S_AHR_61009901	IMG-Aktivität: SIMG_OHAG450
S_AHR_61009902	IMG Activity: OHPKAW130
S_AHR_61009903	IMG Activity: SIMG_OHT0101
S_AHR_61009904	IMG Activity: SIMG_OHAJ502
S_AHR_61009905	IMG Activity: OHANL_AB001
S_AHR_61009906	IMG Activity: SIMG_OHR0003
S_AHR_61009907	IMG-Aktivität: SIMG_OHAG453
S_AHR_61009908	IMG Activity: OHPKAO040
S_AHR_61009909	IMG-Aktivität: SIMG_OHAG465
S_AHR_61009910	IMG Activity: SIMG_OHAJ611
S_AHR_61009911	IMG Activity: OHAFTI323
S_AHR_61009912	IMG Activity: SIMG_OHT0100
S_AHR_61009913	IMG Activity: OHANL_AB002
S_AHR_61009914	IMG Activity: SIMG_OHR_T702N_L

S_AHR_61009915	IMG-Aktivität: OHAQTAX012
S_AHR_61009916	IMG Activity: SIMG_OHAJ612
S_AHR_61009917	IMG-Aktivität: SIMG_OHAG454
S_AHR_61009918	IMG Activity: OHPKAO030
S_AHR_61009919	IMG Activity: SIMG_OHT0217
S_AHR_61009920	IMG Activity: OHAFAB200
S_AHR_61009921	IMG Activity: SIMG_OHAJ613
S_AHR_61009922	IMG-Aktivität: OHAQWTM00105
S_AHR_61009923	IMG Activity: SIMG_OHR0036
S_AHR_61009924	IMG Activity: OHANL_AB003
S_AHR_61009925	IMG Activity: OHAJTI330
S_AHR_61009926	IMG Activity: OHPKAO020
S_AHR_61009927	IMG Activity: OHTY010
S_AHR_61009928	IMG Activity: OHAFAB100
S_AHR_61009929	IMG Activity: OHAJRI011
S_AHR_61009930	IMG Activity: OHANL_AB004
S_AHR_61009931	IMG Activity: SIMG_OHR0062
S_AHR_61009932	IMG Activity: OHAJRI012
S_AHR_61009933	IMG Activity: SIMG_OHAJ454
S_AHR_61009934	IMG Activity: OHTF0104
S_AHR_61009935	IMG Activity: SIMG_OHR0046
S_AHR_61009936	IMG Activity: SIMG_OHAJ465
S_AHR_61009937	IMG-Aktivität: OHAQUM006
S_AHR_61009938	IMG Activity: OHPKAO010
S_AHR_61009939	IMG Activity: OHANL_AB005
S_AHR_61009940	IMG Activity: OHAFRI056
S_AHR_61009941	IMG Activity: SIMG_OHAJ455
S_AHR_61009942	IMG Activity: SIMG_OHT058
S_AHR_61009943	IMG Activity: OHANL_AB011
S_AHR_61009944	IMG-Aktivität: OHAQTAX00301
S_AHR_61009945	IMG Activity: OHAFRI052
S_AHR_61009946	IMG Activity: SIMG_OHR0021
S_AHR_61009947	IMG Activity: SIMG_OHAJ508
S_AHR_61009948	IMG Activity: OHPKAO000
S_AHR_61009949	IMG Activity: SIMG_OHAJ509
S_AHR_61009950	IMG Activity: SIMG_OHAJ510
S_AHR_61009951	IMG Activity: OHANL_AB009
S_AHR_61009952	IMG Activity: OHAFTI110
S_AHR_61009953	IMG Activity: SIMG_OHAJ456
S_AHR_61009954	IMG Activity: SIMG_OHT0610
S_AHR_61009955	IMG Activity: SIMG_OHR0500
S_AHR_61009956	IMG-Aktivität: OHAQTAX00302
S_AHR_61009957	IMG Activity: SIMG_OHAJ466
S_AHR_61009958	IMG Activity: OHANL_TI322
S_AHR_61009959	IMG Activity: OHAFTI120
S_AHR_61009960	IMG Activity: OHPKOR005
S_AHR_61009961	IMG Activity: OHAFTI130
S_AHR_61009962	IMG Activity: SIMG_OHR0029
S_AHR_61009963	IMG Activity: OHANL_TI323
S_AHR_61009964	IMG Activity: SIMG_OHT0612
S_AHR_61009965	IMG-Aktivität: OHAQUM012
S_AHR_61009966	IMG Activity: OHANL_TI324
S_AHR_61009967	IMG Activity: OHPKOR004
S_AHR_61009968	IMG Activity: SIMG_OHT0611

S_AHR_61009969	IMG Activity: OHAFTI340
S_AHR_61009970	IMG Activity: SIMG_OHR0028
S_AHR_61009971	IMG Activity: OHPKKA030
S_AHR_61009972	IMG-Aktivität: OHAQTAX004
S_AHR_61009973	IMG Activity: OHANL_TI340
S_AHR_61009974	IMG Activity: SIMG_OHT057
S_AHR_61009975	IMG Activity: OHAFTI361
S_AHR_61009976	IMG Activity: SIMG_OHR0027
S_AHR_61009977	IMG Activity: OHPKKA020
S_AHR_61009978	IMG-Aktivität: OHAQUM014
S_AHR_61009979	IMG Activity: OHANL_TI361
S_AHR_61009980	IMG Activity: OHAFTI363
S_AHR_61009981	IMG-Aktivität: OHAQTAX005
S_AHR_61009982	IMG Activity: OHL059
S_AHR_61009983	IMG Activity: OHAFTI362
S_AHR_61009984	IMG Activity: OHANL_TI363
S_AHR_61009985	IMG Activity: OHTY020
S_AHR_61009986	IMG Activity: SIMG_OHR_T706B1_C
S_AHR_61009987	IMG Activity: OHPKVS042
S_AHR_61009988	IMG-Aktivität: OHAQTAX00201
S_AHR_61009989	IMG Activity: OHPKVS050
S_AHR_61009990	IMG Activity: SIMG_OHR0262
S_AHR_61009991	IMG Activity: OHANL_TI362
S_AHR_61009992	IMG Activity: OHL058
S_AHR_61009993	IMG Activity: OHAFTI364
S_AHR_61009994	IMG Activity: SIMG_OHT0116
S_AHR_61009995	IMG-Aktivität: OHAQTAX00202
S_AHR_61009996	IMG Activity: OHPKKA010
S_AHR_61009997	IMG Activity: OHL022
S_AHR_61009998	IMG Activity: SIMG_OHR0052
S_AHR_61009999	IMG Activity: OHANL_TI364
S_AHR_61010000	IMG-Aktivität: OHAQUM010B
S_AHR_61010001	IMG Activity: SIMG_OHT048
S_AHR_61010002	IMG Activity: OHAFTI370
S_AHR_61010003	IMG Activity: SIMG_OHR0045
S_AHR_61010004	IMG Activity: OHPKKA005
S_AHR_61010005	IMG Activity: OHANL_AB012
S_AHR_61010006	IMG-Aktivität: OHAQUM008
S_AHR_61010007	IMG Activity: OHL057
S_AHR_61010008	IMG Activity: SIMG_OHT0307
S_AHR_61010009	IMG Activity: SIMG_OHR0030
S_AHR_61010010	IMG Activity: OHAFRI042
S_AHR_61010011	IMG-Aktivität: OHAQTAX006
S_AHR_61010012	IMG Activity: OHANL_AVBAS
S_AHR_61010013	IMG Activity: OHPKVS060
S_AHR_61010014	IMG Activity: OHL026
S_AHR_61010015	IMG Activity: SIMG_OHT060
S_AHR_61010016	IMG Activity: SIMG_OHR_T706F1
S_AHR_61010017	IMG Activity: OHAFTI324
S_AHR_61010018	IMG-Aktivität: OHAQTAX00204
S_AHR_61010019	IMG Activity: OHANL_AVX017
S_AHR_61010020	IMG Activity: OHPKST020
S_AHR_61010021	IMG Activity: OHL051
S_AHR_61010022	IMG Activity: SIMG_OHR_T702N_M

S_AHR_61010023	IMG Activity: OHAFRI031
S_AHR_61010024	IMG Activity: OHTY021
S_AHR_61010025	IMG-Aktivität: OHAQTAX00205
S_AHR_61010026	IMG Activity: OHAFAL01
S_AHR_61010027	IMG Activity: OHANL_AVX018
S_AHR_61010028	IMG Activity: OHAFRI011
S_AHR_61010029	IMG Activity: OHL062
S_AHR_61010030	IMG Activity: SIMG_OHR_T702N_C
S_AHR_61010031	IMG Activity: OHPKST015
S_AHR_61010032	IMG Activity: SIMG_OHT053
S_AHR_61010033	IMG-Aktivität: OHAQDD1065
S_AHR_61010034	IMG Activity: OHAFRI012
S_AHR_61010035	IMG Activity: OHANL_AV511A
S_AHR_61010036	IMG Activity: OHAFTI330
S_AHR_61010037	IMG Activity: OHPKVS020
S_AHR_61010038	IMG Activity: OHL020
S_AHR_61010039	IMG Activity: SIMG_OHR_T702N_D
S_AHR_61010040	IMG Activity: SIMG_OHAF455
S_AHR_61010041	IMG-Aktivität: OHAQSUP00101
S_AHR_61010042	IMG Activity: SIMG_OHAF454
S_AHR_61010043	IMG Activity: OHANL_AV511B
S_AHR_61010044	IMG Activity: SIMG_OHT052
S_AHR_61010045	IMG Activity: OHPKST010
S_AHR_61010046	IMG Activity: OHL019
S_AHR_61010047	IMG Activity: SIMG_OHR_IAC_003
S_AHR_61010048	IMG Activity: SIMG_OHAF465
S_AHR_61010049	IMG-Aktivität: OHAQDD1062
S_AHR_61010050	IMG Activity: OHANL_AV511C
S_AHR_61010051	IMG Activity: SIMG_OHT0302
S_AHR_61010052	IMG Activity: SIMG_OHAF453
S_AHR_61010053	IMG-Aktivität: OHAQSUP00103
S_AHR_61010054	IMG Activity: OHPKVS030
S_AHR_61010055	IMG Activity: SIMG_OHR_V_706U_B
S_AHR_61010056	IMG Activity: SIMG_OHAF450
S_AHR_61010057	IMG Activity: OHL024
S_AHR_61010058	IMG Activity: OHANAVXT00
S_AHR_61010059	IMG Activity: SIMG_OHT051
S_AHR_61010060	IMG-Aktivität: OHAQUM022
S_AHR_61010061	IMG Activity: OHTY025
S_AHR_61010062	IMG Activity: SIMG_OHR0053
S_AHR_61010063	IMG Activity: OHL018
S_AHR_61010064	IMG Activity: OHPKST000
S_AHR_61010065	IMG-Aktivität: OHAQSUP010
S_AHR_61010066	IMG Activity: SIMG_OHT035
S_AHR_61010067	IMG Activity: OHPKVS320
S_AHR_61010068	IMG Activity: SIMG_OHR_T702N_G
S_AHR_61010069	IMG-Aktivität: OHAQDE1049
S_AHR_61010070	IMG Activity: OHL021
S_AHR_61010071	IMG-Aktivität: OHAQUM023
S_AHR_61010072	IMG Activity: OHTY023
S_AHR_61010073	IMG Activity: SIMG_OHR0300
S_AHR_61010074	IMG Activity: OHPKVS110
S_AHR_61010075	IMG Activity: OHL017
S_AHR_61010076	IMG-Aktivität: OHAQDE1040B

S_AHR_61010077	IMG Activity: SIMG_OHT0118
S_AHR_61010078	IMG Activity: SIMG_OHR_T702N_J
S_AHR_61010079	IMG Activity: OHPKVS105
S_AHR_61010080	IMG Activity: OHL016
S_AHR_61010081	IMG-Aktivität: OHAQDE1048
S_AHR_61010082	IMG Activity: SIMG_OHT0115
S_AHR_61010083	IMG Activity: SIMG_OHR1070
S_AHR_61010084	IMG Activity: OHPKVS321
S_AHR_61010085	IMG Activity: OHL010
S_AHR_61010086	IMG-Aktivität: OHAQDE1041
S_AHR_61010087	IMG Activity: SIMG_OHR1060
S_AHR_61010088	IMG Activity: OHTY024
S_AHR_61010089	IMG Activity: OHPKVS080
S_AHR_61010090	IMG Activity: OHL009
S_AHR_61010091	IMG-Aktivität: OHAQDE1044
S_AHR_61010092	IMG Activity: SIMG_OHR_T702N_I
S_AHR_61010093	IMG Activity: OHPKVS310
S_AHR_61010094	IMG Activity: SIMG_OHT0211
S_AHR_61010095	IMG Activity: SIMG_OHAF439
S_AHR_61010096	IMG Activity: OHL044
S_AHR_61010097	IMG Activity: OHPKVS330
S_AHR_61010098	IMG Activity: SIMG_OHT0212
S_AHR_61010099	IMG Activity: SIMG_OHR0410
S_AHR_61010100	IMG-Aktivität: OHAQDE1046
S_AHR_61010101	IMG Activity: OHPKKA000
S_AHR_61010102	IMG Activity: SIMG_OHR0261
S_AHR_61010103	IMG-Aktivität: OHAQSUP011
S_AHR_61010104	IMG Activity: OHL043
S_AHR_61010105	IMG Activity: SIMG_OHT0508
S_AHR_61010106	IMG-Aktivität: OHAQTAX008
S_AHR_61010107	IMG Activity: OHPKVS210
S_AHR_61010108	IMG Activity: SIMG_OHR_T702N_H
S_AHR_61010109	IMG Activity: OHL052
S_AHR_61010110	IMG Activity: SIMG_OHT075
S_AHR_61010111	IMG-Aktivität: OHAQSUP002
S_AHR_61010112	IMG Activity: OHPKVS044
S_AHR_61010113	IMG Activity: OHL090
S_AHR_61010114	IMG Activity: SIMG_OHR_IAC_002
S_AHR_61010115	IMG Activity: SIMG_OHT0507
S_AHR_61010116	IMG-Aktivität: OHAQWTM00001
S_AHR_61010117	IMG Activity: OHPKVS350
S_AHR_61010118	IMG Activity: OHL011
S_AHR_61010119	IMG Activity: SIMG_OHR0263
S_AHR_61010120	IMG Activity: OHTY015
S_AHR_61010121	IMG-Aktivität: OHAQWTM00101
S_AHR_61010122	IMG Activity: OHPKVS045
S_AHR_61010123	IMG Activity: OHL013
S_AHR_61010124	IMG Activity: SIMG_OHR_T702N_F
S_AHR_61010125	IMG Activity: OHPKVS340
S_AHR_61010126	IMG Activity: OHTY016
S_AHR_61010127	IMG-Aktivität: OHAQWTM00002
S_AHR_61010128	IMG Activity: SIMG_OHR_IAC_005
S_AHR_61010129	IMG Activity: OHL027
S_AHR_61010130	IMG Activity: SIMG_OHR_IAC_004

S_AHR_61010131	IMG Activity: OHPKVS010
S_AHR_61010132	IMG Activity: SIMG_OHR0400
S_AHR_61010133	IMG Activity: SIMG_OHT080
S_AHR_61010134	IMG-Aktivität: OHAQSUP009
S_AHR_61010135	IMG Activity: SIMG_OHAF481
S_AHR_61010136	IMG Activity: OHANAVP15
S_AHR_61010137	IMG Activity: OHL002
S_AHR_61010138	IMG Activity: OHPKKO000
S_AHR_61010139	IMG-Aktivität: OHAQDD1061
S_AHR_61010140	IMG Activity: OHL015
S_AHR_61010141	IMG Activity: SIMG_OHT079
S_AHR_61010142	IMG Activity: OHPKVS000
S_AHR_61010143	IMG Activity: SIMG_OHAF401
S_AHR_61010144	IMG-Aktivität: SIMG_OHAQ501
S_AHR_61010145	IMG Activity: SIMG_OHAF421
S_AHR_61010146	IMG Activity: OHANL_AB010
S_AHR_61010147	IMG Activity: OHL006
S_AHR_61010148	IMG-Aktivität: OHAQLVE00003
S_AHR_61010149	IMG Activity: SIMG_OHT076
S_AHR_61010150	IMG Activity: SIMG_OHAF661
S_AHR_61010151	IMG Activity: OHPKST150
S_AHR_61010152	IMG-Aktivität: OHAQTRM00001
S_AHR_61010153	IMG Activity: SIMG_OHAF662
S_AHR_61010154	IMG-Aktivität: OHAQTAX00203
S_AHR_61010155	IMG-Aktivität: OHAQADV00002
S_AHR_61010156	IMG Activity: OHANAB001
S_AHR_61010157	IMG Activity: SIMG_OHAF663
S_AHR_61010158	IMG Activity: OHPKST140
S_AHR_61010159	IMG Activity: SIMG_OHT0309
S_AHR_61010160	IMG-Aktivität: OHAQLVE00102
S_AHR_61010161	IMG-Aktivität: OHAQDT009
S_AHR_61010162	IMG Activity: OHANWE011
S_AHR_61010163	IMG Activity: SIMG_OHAF664
S_AHR_61010164	IMG-Aktivität: SIMG_OHAQ502
S_AHR_61010165	IMG Activity: SIMG_OHAF441
S_AHR_61010166	IMG Activity: SIMG_OHT067
S_AHR_61010167	IMG Activity: OHPKST130
S_AHR_61010168	IMG Activity: SIMG_OHAF456
S_AHR_61010169	IMG-Aktivität: SIMG_OHAQ481
S_AHR_61010170	IMG Activity: OHANBW004
S_AHR_61010171	IMG-Aktivität: OHAQAL01
S_AHR_61010172	IMG Activity: SIMG_OHAF466
S_AHR_61010173	IMG-Aktivität: SIMG_OHAQ401
S_AHR_61010174	IMG Activity: SIMG_OHAF514
S_AHR_61010175	IMG Activity: SIMG_OHT063
S_AHR_61010176	IMG Activity: OHPKST120
S_AHR_61010177	IMG Activity: OHANL_BW005
S_AHR_61010178	IMG-Aktivität: SIMG_OHAQ524
S_AHR_61010179	IMG Activity: SIMG_OHAF513
S_AHR_61010180	IMG Activity: SIMG_OHAF512
S_AHR_61010181	IMG-Aktivität: SIMG_OHAQ523
S_AHR_61010182	IMG Activity: OHPK00010
S_AHR_61010183	IMG Activity: SIMG_OHT064
S_AHR_61010184	IMG-Aktivität: SIMG_OHAQ661

S_AHR_61010185	IMG Activity: OHANBW01
S_AHR_61010186	IMG Activity: SIMG_OHAF510
S_AHR_61010187	IMG-Aktivität: SIMG_OHAQ662
S_AHR_61010188	IMG Activity: SIMG_OHAF509
S_AHR_61010189	IMG Activity: SIMG_OHT0210
S_AHR_61010190	IMG Activity: OHPKKO040
S_AHR_61010191	IMG-Aktivität: SIMG_OHAQ663
S_AHR_61010192	IMG Activity: OHANL_BW019
S_AHR_61010193	IMG Activity: SIMG_OHAF508
S_AHR_61010194	IMG-Aktivität: SIMG_OHAQ439
S_AHR_61010195	IMG Activity: OHPKKO030
S_AHR_61010196	IMG Activity: SIMG_OHAF502
S_AHR_61010197	IMG-Aktivität: SIMG_OHAQ465
S_AHR_61010198	IMG Activity: OHANL_AV001
S_AHR_61010199	IMG Activity: SIMG_OHT065
S_AHR_61010200	IMG-Aktivität: SIMG_OHAQ454
S_AHR_61010201	IMG Activity: SIMG_OHAF501
S_AHR_61010202	IMG-Aktivität: SIMG_OHAQ455
S_AHR_61010203	IMG Activity: OHANL_UM013
S_AHR_61010204	IMG Activity: OHPKKO020
S_AHR_61010205	IMG-Aktivität: SIMG_OHAQ466
S_AHR_61010206	IMG Activity: SIMG_CMMENUOH40OU46
S_AHR_61010207	IMG Activity: SIMG_OHAF524
S_AHR_61010208	IMG-Aktivität: SIMG_OHAQ456
S_AHR_61010209	IMG Activity: OHAXMZ001
S_AHR_61010210	IMG Activity: SIMG_OHAF523
S_AHR_61010211	IMG Activity: OHTY019
S_AHR_61010212	IMG Activity: OHANL_UM010
S_AHR_61010213	IMG Activity: OHPKKA001
S_AHR_61010214	IMG-Aktivität: SIMG_OHAQ453
S_AHR_61010215	IMG Activity: SIMG_OHAF522
S_AHR_61010216	IMG-Aktivität: SIMG_OHAQ421
S_AHR_61010217	IMG Activity: SIMG_CMMENUOH40OU45
S_AHR_61010218	IMG Activity: OHAX483
S_AHR_61010219	IMG Activity: OHPKKO010
S_AHR_61010220	IMG-Aktivität: SIMG_OHAQ450
S_AHR_61010221	IMG Activity : SIMG_OHAF521
S_AHR_61010222	IMG Activity: OHANUM02
S_AHR_61010223	IMG Activity: SIMG_OHT071
S_AHR_61010224	IMG-Aktivität: SIMG_OHAQ514
S_AHR_61010225	IMG Activity: SIMG_CMMENUOH40OU48
S_AHR_61010226	IMG Activity : SIMG_OHAF520
S_AHR_61010227	IMG Activity: OHPKVS070
S_AHR_61010228	IMG Activity: SIMG_OHAX416
S_AHR_61010229	IMG-Aktivität: SIMG_OHAQ513
S_AHR_61010230	IMG Activity: OHANUI01
S_AHR_61010231	IMG Activity : SIMG_OHAF519
S_AHR_61010232	IMG Activity: SIMG_OHT070
S_AHR_61010233	IMG-Aktivität: OHAQRI011
S_AHR_61010234	IMG-Aktivität: OHAQRI012
S_AHR_61010235	IMG Activity: SIMG_CMMENUOH40UO71
S_AHR_61010236	IMG Activity: OHPKST050
S_AHR_61010237	IMG Activity : SIMG_OHAF517
S_AHR_61010238	IMG Activity: SIMG_OHAX515

S_AHR_61010239	IMG Activity: OHIN0350
S_AHR_61010240	IMG-Aktivität: SIMG_OHAQ512
S_AHR_61010241	IMG Activity : SIMG_OHAF516
S_AHR_61010242	IMG Activity: SIMG_OHT72
S_AHR_61010243	IMG-Aktivität: SIMG_OHAQ510
S_AHR_61010244	IMG Activity: SIMG_CMMENUOH40OU73
S_AHR_61010245	IMG Activity: OHPKST100
S_AHR_61010246	IMG Activity: OHANUI04
S_AHR_61010247	IMG Activity: SIMG_OHAX506
S_AHR_61010248	IMG-Aktivität: SIMG_OHAQ509
S_AHR_61010249	IMG Activity: SIMG_OHT069
S_AHR_61010250	IMG-Aktivität: SIMG_OHAQ508
S_AHR_61010251	IMG Activity: OHPKST035
S_AHR_61010252	IMG Activity: SIMG_CMMENUOH40OU44
S_AHR_61010253	IMG Activity: OHANUM010
S_AHR_61010254	IMG Activity: SIMG_OHAX507
S_AHR_61010255	IMG-Aktivität: SIMG_OHAQ516
S_AHR_61010256	IMG-Aktivität: SIMG_OHAQ664
S_AHR_61010257	IMG Activity: OHIX0649
S_AHR_61010258	IMG Activity: OHPKST110
S_AHR_61010259	IMG Activity: OHANUI02
S_AHR_61010260	IMG Activity: SIMG_CMMENUOH40OU47
S_AHR_61010261	IMG Activity: SIMG_OHAX518
S_AHR_61010262	IMG-Aktivität: SIMG_OHAQ522
S_AHR_61010263	IMG-Aktivität: OHAQTI330
S_AHR_61010264	IMG Activity: OHTX3220
S_AHR_61010265	IMG Activity: OHPKST105
S_AHR_61010266	IMG Activity: OHANUM061
S_AHR_61010267	IMG Activity: SIMG_OHAX530
S_AHR_61010268	IMG Activity: SIMG_CMMENUOH40OU3G
S_AHR_61010269	IMG-Aktivität: SIMG_OHAQ441
S_AHR_61010270	IMG-Aktivität: SIMG_OHAQ521
S_AHR_61010271	IMG Activity: OHAXDT004
S_AHR_61010272	IMG Activity: OHANUM062
S_AHR_61010273	IMG Activity: OHID2003
S_AHR_61010274	IMG Activity: OHPKST030
S_AHR_61010275	IMG Activity: SIMG_CMMENUOH40OU3C
S_AHR_61010276	IMG-Aktivität: SIMG_OHAQ520
S_AHR_61010277	IMG Activity: OHANUM063
S_AHR_61010278	IMG Activity: OHAXJW000
S_AHR_61010279	IMG-Aktivität: SIMG_OHAQ519
S_AHR_61010280	IMG Activity: OHID2005
S_AHR_61010281	IMG Activity: SIMG_CMMENUOH40OU55
S_AHR_61010282	IMG-Aktivität: SIMG_OHAQ517
S_AHR_61010283	IMG Activity: OHANL_UM012
S_AHR_61010284	IMG Activity: OHAX0902
S_AHR_61010285	IMG Activity: OHID2004
S_AHR_61010286	IMG Activity: SIMG_CMMENUOH40OU5A
S_AHR_61010287	IMG Activity : OHANL_UM014
S_AHR_61010288	IMG Activity: OHAX0911
S_AHR_61010289	IMG Activity: OHID2002
S_AHR_61010290	IMG Activity: SIMG_CMMENUOH40OU4B
S_AHR_61010291	IMG Activity: OHANL_UM006
S_AHR_61010292	IMG Activity: OHID2010

S_AHR_61010293	IMG Activity: OHAX0912
S_AHR_61010294	IMG Activity: SIMG_CMMENUOH40OU4A
S_AHR_61010295	IMG Activity: OHANL_UM008
S_AHR_61010296	IMG Activity: OHID2009
S_AHR_61010297	IMG Activity: OHAX0913
S_AHR_61010298	IMG Activity: OHBX1031
S_AHR_61010299	IMG Activity: OHANUM010B
S_AHR_61010300	IMG Activity: OHID2011
S_AHR_61010301	IMG Activity: OHAX0903
S_AHR_61010302	IMG Activity: OHBX1047
S_AHR_61010303	IMG Activity: OHANUI03
S_AHR_61010304	IMG Activity: OHID2008
S_AHR_61010305	IMG Activity: OHBX1048
S_AHR_61010306	IMG Activity: OHAXDT002
S_AHR_61010307	IMG Activity: OHANL_UM105
S_AHR_61010308	IMG Activity: OHID2007
S_AHR_61010309	IMG Activity: OHAXDT003
S_AHR_61010310	IMG Activity: SIMG_CFMENUOH40OU13
S_AHR_61010311	IMG Activity: OHANL_TI110
S_AHR_61010312	IMG Activity: COPY_OHTX5209
S_AHR_61010313	IMG Activity: OHANL_TI120
S_AHR_61010314	IMG Activity: SIMG_OHAX409
S_AHR_61010315	IMG Activity: SIMG_CFMENUOH40OU14
S_AHR_61010316	IMG Activity: OHTG2000
S_AHR_61010317	IMG Activity: OHANL_TI130
S_AHR_61010318	IMG Activity: OHBXIAC001
S_AHR_61010319	IMG Activity: SIMG_OHAX407
S_AHR_61010320	IMG Activity: OHIX2000
S_AHR_61010321	IMG Activity: OHANTI210
S_AHR_61010322	IMG Activity: OHBXIAC002
S_AHR_61010323	IMG Activity: SIMG_OHAX482
S_AHR_61010324	IMG Activity: OHIX0186
S_AHR_61010325	IMG Activity: OHANL_TI310
S_AHR_61010326	IMG Activity: OHBX1045
S_AHR_61010327	IMG Activity: SIMG_OHAX410
S_AHR_61010328	IMG Activity: OHIX0192
S_AHR_61010329	IMG Activity: OHANL_TI325
S_AHR_61010330	IMG Activity: OHBX1041
S_AHR_61010331	IMG Activity: OHIX0185
S_AHR_61010332	IMG Activity: SIMG_OHAX417
S_AHR_61010333	IMG Activity: OHANL_TI321
S_AHR_61010334	IMG Activity: OHBX0002
S_AHR_61010335	IMG Activity: OHIX0189
S_AHR_61010336	IMG Activity: OHIN0431
S_AHR_61010337	IMG Activity: SIMG_OHAX413
S_AHR_61010338	IMG Activity: OHBX1042
S_AHR_61010339	IMG Activity: OHIX0191
S_AHR_61010340	IMG Activity: OHANUM011
S_AHR_61010341	IMG Activity: SIMG_OHAX480
S_AHR_61010342	IMG Activity: OHBX1043
S_AHR_61010343	IMG Activity: OHANUM09
S_AHR_61010344	IMG Activity: OHIU02162
S_AHR_61010345	IMG Activity: OHBX0639
S_AHR_61010346	IMG Activity: SIMG_OHAX414

S_AHR_61010347	IMG Activity: OHANUM03
S_AHR_61010348	IMG Activity: OHIX0190
S_AHR_61010349	IMG Activity: OHBX1044
S_AHR_61010350	IMG Activity: SIMG_OHAX529
S_AHR_61010351	IMG Activity: OHANUM04
S_AHR_61010352	IMG Activity: SIMG_CMMENUOH40OU5T
S_AHR_61010353	IMG Activity: SIMG_OHAX525
S_AHR_61010354	IMG Activity: SIMG_OHT0600
S_AHR_61010355	IMG Activity: SIMG_OHBMATCH2
S_AHR_61010356	IMG Activity: OHANL_UM022
S_AHR_61010357	IMG Activity: SIMG_OHAX402
S_AHR_61010358	IMG Activity: OHIX0229
S_AHR_61010359	IMG Activity: OHANL_UM023
S_AHR_61010360	IMG Activity: SIMG_OHAX403
S_AHR_61010361	IMG Activity: SIMG_CMMENUOH40OU4E
S_AHR_61010362	IMG Activity: OHANL_UM104
S_AHR_61010363	IMG Activity: OHIX0227
S_AHR_61010364	IMG Activity: SIMG_CFMENUOH40OU12
S_AHR_61010365	IMG Activity: SIMG_OHAX405
S_AHR_61010366	IMG Activity: OHAN9011
S_AHR_61010367	IMG Activity: OHTX0165
S_AHR_61010368	IMG Activity: OHBX1101
S_AHR_61010369	IMG Activity: SIMG_OHAX406
S_AHR_61010370	IMG Activity: OHAN9010
S_AHR_61010371	IMG Activity: SIMG_OHT421
S_AHR_61010372	IMG Activity: OHBX1102
S_AHR_61010373	IMG Activity: SIMG_OHAX408
S_AHR_61010375	IMG Activity: OHANL_KL000
S_AHR_61010376	IMG Activity: OHTX0192
S_AHR_61010377	IMG Activity: SIMG_CMMENUOH40OU21
S_AHR_61010378	IMG Activity: SIMG_OHAX527
S_AHR_61010379	IMG Activity: OHANL_SL001
S_AHR_61010380	IMG Activity: OHIX0233
S_AHR_61010381	IMG Activity: SIMG_CMMENUOH40OU22
S_AHR_61010382	IMG Activity: SIMG_OHAX528
S_AHR_61010383	IMG Activity: OHANL_SL002
S_AHR_61010384	IMG Activity: SIMG_CMMENUOH40OU23
S_AHR_61010385	IMG Activity: SIMG_OHT0109
S_AHR_61010386	IMG Activity: OHIX0702
S_AHR_61010387	IMG Activity: OHANL_SL003
S_AHR_61010388	IMG Activity: OHAXOCPM001
S_AHR_61010389	IMG Activity: SIMG_CMMENUOH40OU25
S_AHR_61010390	IMG Activity: OHIX0230
S_AHR_61010391	IMG Activity: OHIX0703
S_AHR_61010392	IMG Activity: OHAX1016
S_AHR_61010393	IMG Activity: OHANZI02
S_AHR_61010394	IMG Activity: SIMG_CMMENUOH40OU5C
S_AHR_61010395	IMG Activity: OHIX1671
S_AHR_61010396	IMG Activity: SIMG_OHT420
S_AHR_61010397	IMG Activity: OHAXR1024
S_AHR_61010398	IMG Activity: OHANZI01
S_AHR_61010399	IMG Activity: SIMG_CMMENUOH40OU5S
S_AHR_61010400	IMG Activity: OHIX0228
S_AHR_61010401	IMG Activity: OHAXR1026

S_AHR_61010402	IMG Activity: OHIX1672
S_AHR_61010403	IMG Activity: OHANKF02
S_AHR_61010404	IMG Activity: OHTX0188
S_AHR_61010405	IMG Activity: SIMG_CMMENUOH40OU4G
S_AHR_61010406	IMG Activity: OHAXR1025
S_AHR_61010407	IMG Activity: OHIX1673
S_AHR_61010408	IMG Activity: OHAN9091
S_AHR_61010409	IMG Activity: OHBX1046
S_AHR_61010410	IMG Activity: OHTX3209
S_AHR_61010411	IMG Activity: OHAXR1027
S_AHR_61010412	IMG Activity: OHAN9092
S_AHR_61010413	IMG Activity: OHIXP0402_02
S_AHR_61010414	IMG Activity: SIMG_CMMENUOH40OU3D
S_AHR_61010415	IMG Activity: OHIX2021
S_AHR_61010416	IMG Activity: OHAN9007
S_AHR_61010417	IMG Activity: OHAXR1021
S_AHR_61010418	IMG Activity: OHIXP0402_03
S_AHR_61010419	IMG Activity: SIMG_CMMENUOH40OU3E
S_AHR_61010420	IMG Activity: OHIX0224
S_AHR_61010421	IMG Activity: OHANL_IW061
S_AHR_61010422	IMG Activity: OHAXDE1040B
S_AHR_61010423	IMG Activity: OHIXP0402_01
S_AHR_61010424	IMG Activity: SIMG_CMMENUOH40OU3F
S_AHR_61010425	IMG Activity: OHIX0225
S_AHR_61010426	IMG Activity: OHANL_IW082
S_AHR_61010427	IMG Activity:: OHIXP0402_04
S_AHR_61010428	IMG Activity: OHAXOCRP01
S_AHR_61010429	IMG Activity: SIMG_OHBINT01
S_AHR_61010430	IMG Activity: OHTX3215
S_AHR_61010431	IMG Activity: SIMG_CFMENUOHP0OOAD
S_AHR_61010432	IMG Activity: OHAN90513
S_AHR_61010434	IMG Activity: SIMG_CFMENUOH40OU11
S_AHR_61010435	IMG Activity: OHTX0187
S_AHR_61010436	IMG Activity: OHANUM08
S_AHR_61010437	IMG Activity: SIMG_CFMENUOHP0OOPB
S_AHR_61010438	IMG Activity: OHAXOCR001
S_AHR_61010439	IMG Activity: OHTX0194
S_AHR_61010440	IMG Activity: OHAXOCV001
S_AHR_61010441	IMG Activity: SIMG_CFMENUOHP0OODB
S_AHR_61010442	IMG Activity: OHANL_DV001
S_AHR_61010443	IMG Activity: OHTX0193
S_AHR_61010444	IMG Activity: OHAXOCA001
S_AHR_61010445	IMG Activity: OHANL_IW037
S_AHR_61010446	IMG Activity: SIMG_CFMENUOHP0OOTG
S_AHR_61010447	IMG Activity: OHTX3200
S_AHR_61010448	IMG Activity: OHAXOCA002
S_AHR_61010449	IMG Activity: OHAN90631
S_AHR_61010450	IMG Activity: SIMG_CFMENUOHP0OODS
S_AHR_61010451	IMG Activity: OHTX1000
S_AHR_61010452	IMG Activity: OHAN90641
S_AHR_61010453	IMG Activity: OHAXOCAP001
S_AHR_61010454	IMG Activity: OHIX0701
S_AHR_61010455	IMG Activity: OHIX0139
S_AHR_61010456	IMG Activity: OHAN90514

S_AHR_61010457	IMG Activity: OHAXOCPM01
S_AHR_61010458	IMG Activity: OHIX0137
S_AHR_61010459	IMG Activity: OHANL_IW063
S_AHR_61010460	IMG Activity: OHAXOCMCP1
S_AHR_61010461	IMG Activity: OHIX0136
S_AHR_61010462	IMG Activity: OHAXBEN005
S_AHR_61010463	IMG Activity: OHAN90512
S_AHR_61010464	IMG Activity: OHIX1004
S_AHR_61010465	IMG Activity: OHANL_IW065
S_AHR_61010466	IMG Activity: OHAXDV001
S_AHR_61010467	IMG Activity: OHTX0201
S_AHR_61010468	IMG Activity: OHANL_KF002
S_AHR_61010469	IMG Activity: OHAXDL031
S_AHR_61010470	IMG Activity: OHIX0147
S_AHR_61010471	IMG Activity: OHANL_PART
S_AHR_61010472	IMG Activity: OHIX0144
S_AHR_61010473	IMG Activity: OHAXDL032
S_AHR_61010474	IMG Activity: OHANZI03
S_AHR_61010475	IMG Activity: OHIX0143
S_AHR_61010476	IMG Activity: OHANL_BW21
S_AHR_61010477	IMG Activity: OHAXDL034
S_AHR_61010478	IMG Activity: OHIX0142
S_AHR_61010479	IMG Activity: OHAXDL021
S_AHR_61010480	IMG Activity: OHANL_BW22
S_AHR_61010481	IMG Activity: OHIX0140
S_AHR_61010482	IMG Activity: OHANZI04
S_AHR_61010483	IMG Activity: OHAXDL022
S_AHR_61010484	IMG Activity: OHIX0134
S_AHR_61010485	IMG Activity: OHAXDL023
S_AHR_61010486	IMG Activity: OHANZI06
S_AHR_61010487	IMG Activity: OHIX0141
S_AHR_61010488	IMG Activity: OHAXBEN004
S_AHR_61010489	IMG Activity: OHANBW020
S_AHR_61010490	IMG Activity: OHT3300PTSP01
S_AHR_61010491	IMG Activity: OHAXDE1048
S_AHR_61010492	IMG Activity: OHANZI05
S_AHR_61010493	IMG Activity: OHIX1007
S_AHR_61010494	IMG Activity: OHAXDE1041
S_AHR_61010495	IMG Activity: OHANZI09
S_AHR_61010496	IMG Activity: OHT3300PTEV01
S_AHR_61010497	IMG Activity: OHAXDE1044
S_AHR_61010498	IMG Activity: OHT3300PTEV02
S_AHR_61010499	IMG Activity: OHANKF01
S_AHR_61010500	IMG Activity: OHAXDE1043
S_AHR_61010501	IMG Activity: OHTX0210
S_AHR_61010502	IMG Activity: OHANZI10
S_AHR_61010503	IMG Activity: OHAXDE1046
S_AHR_61010504	IMG Activity: OHANZI07
S_AHR_61010505	IMG Activity: OHIX0131
S_AHR_61010506	IMG Activity: OHAXBEN001
S_AHR_61010507	IMG Activity: OHANZI11
S_AHR_61010508	IMG Activity: OHIX0132
S_AHR_61010509	IMG Activity: SIMG_OHANL_513
S_AHR_61010510	IMG Activity: OHAXBEN002

S_AHR_61010511	IMG Activity: SIMG_OHANL_514
S_AHR_61010512	IMG Activity: OHIX0130
S_AHR_61010513	IMG Activity: OHANL_RI011
S_AHR_61010514	IMG Activity: OHAXBEN003
S_AHR_61010515	IMG Activity: SIMG_OHANL_516
S_AHR_61010516	IMG Activity: OHIX1003
S_AHR_61010517	IMG Activity: OHAXFOPJ203
S_AHR_61010518	IMG Activity: SIMG_OHANL_517
S_AHR_61010519	IMG Activity: OHAXFOPJ204
S_AHR_61010520	IMG Activity: OHANL_RI012
S_AHR_61010521	IMG Activity: OHIX0193
S_AHR_61010522	IMG Activity: OHAXRI011
S_AHR_61010523	IMG Activity: SIMG_OHANL_512
S_AHR_61010524	IMG Activity: OHAXRI012
S_AHR_61010525	IMG Activity: OHANL_DT009
S_AHR_61010526	IMG Activity: OHTX3110
S_AHR_61010527	IMG Activity: OHANL_AL01
S_AHR_61010528	IMG Activity: SIMG_OHANL_501
S_AHR_61010529	IMG Activity: OHAXRI015
S_AHR_61010530	IMG Activity: OHIX1000
S_AHR_61010531	IMG Activity: SIMG_OHANL_502
S_AHR_61010532	IMG Activity: SIMG_OHANL_508
S_AHR_61010533	IMG Activity: OHAXRI042
S_AHR_61010534	IMG Activity: OHTX3300
S_AHR_61010535	IMG Activity: SIMG_OHANL_509
S_AHR_61010536	IMG Activity: SIMG_OHANL_510
S_AHR_61010537	IMG Activity: OHAXRI031
S_AHR_61010538	IMG Activity: OHIX2020
S_AHR_61010539	IMG Activity: SIMG_OHANL_456
S_AHR_61010540	IMG Activity: OHANL_IW035
S_AHR_61010541	IMG Activity: OHAXRI051
S_AHR_61010542	IMG Activity: SIMG_OHANL_421
S_AHR_61010543	IMG Activity: OHIX0165
S_AHR_61010544	IMG Activity: OHAXFOPJ202
S_AHR_61010545	IMG Activity: OHANL_TI330
S_AHR_61010546	IMG Activity: OHAXFO006
S_AHR_61010547	IMG Activity: OHTX3109
S_AHR_61010548	IMG Activity: OHANL_IW069
S_AHR_61010549	IMG Activity: OHAXFO008
S_AHR_61010550	IMG Activity: SIMG_OHANL_481
S_AHR_61010551	IMG Activity: OHAXFORS001
S_AHR_61010552	IMG Activity: OHIX0188
S_AHR_61010553	IMG Activity: SIMG_OHANL_401
S_AHR_61010554	IMG Activity: OHAXFORS002
S_AHR_61010555	IMG Activity: SIMG_OHANL_466
S_AHR_61010556	IMG Activity: OHIX0187
S_AHR_61010557	IMG Activity: OHAXEDTINTERNET
S_AHR_61010558	IMG Activity: SIMG_OHANL_439
S_AHR_61010559	IMG Activity: OHAXFOPA002
S_AHR_61010560	IMG Activity: SIMG_OHANL_450
S_AHR_61010561	IMG Activity: OHIX0194
S_AHR_61010562	IMG Activity: OHAXFOPJ100
S_AHR_61010563	IMG Activity: SIMG_OHANL_453
S_AHR_61010564	IMG Activity: OHAXFOPJ201

S_AHR_61010565	IMG Activity: OHANL_IW041
S_AHR_61010566	IMG Activity: OHIN0185
S_AHR_61010567	IMG Activity: OHIX0148
S_AHR_61010568	IMG Activity: SIMG_OHT0113
S_AHR_61010569	IMG Activity: OHTX0148
S_AHR_61010570	IMG Activity: OHTX0147
S_AHR_61010571	IMG Activity: OHIX0145
S_AHR_61010572	IMG Activity: OHIX0183
S_AHR_61010573	IMG Activity: OHIX1183
S_AHR_61010574	IMG Activity: SIMG_OHT0112
S_AHR_61010575	IMG Activity: OHIX1005
S_AHR_61010576	IMG Activity: OHIX0149
S_AHR_61010577	IMG Activity: OHIX0234
S_AHR_61010578	IMG Activity: OHIX0161
S_AHR_61010579	IMG Activity: OHTY050
S_AHR_61010580	IMG Activity: OHTX213
S_AHR_61010581	IMG Activity: OHTY052
S_AHR_61010582	IMG Activity: OHTY053
S_AHR_61010583	IMG Activity: OHIX0166
S_AHR_61010584	IMG Activity: OHIX0171
S_AHR_61010585	IMG Activity: OHIW0002
S_AHR_61010586	IMG Activity: OHIX0162
S_AHR_61010587	IMG Activity: OHTY049
S_AHR_61010588	IMG Activity: OHIXQUOTACOMP04
S_AHR_61010589	IMG Activity: OHIXQUOTACOMP03
S_AHR_61010590	IMG Activity: OHIXQUOTACOMP01
S_AHR_61010591	IMG Activity: OHIXQUOTACOMP00
S_AHR_61010592	IMG Activity: SIMG_OHANL_465
S_AHR_61010593	IMG Activity: OHIXQUOTACOMP10
S_AHR_61010594	IMG Activity: OHAXRI071
S_AHR_61010595	IMG Activity: OHAXQUOTACOMP01
S_AHR_61010596	IMG Activity: OHIXQUOTACOMP08
S_AHR_61010597	IMG Activity: OHIXQUOTACOMP07
S_AHR_61010598	IMG Activity: OHIXQUOTACOMP06
S_AHR_61010599	IMG Activity: OHIXQUOTACOMP05
S_AHR_61010600	IMG Activity: OHIX0184
S_AHR_61010601	IMG Activity: OHTX3206
S_AHR_61010602	IMG Activity: OHTX3210
S_AHR_61010603	IMG Activity: OHTX3207
S_AHR_61010604	IMG Activity: OHTX3205
S_AHR_61010605	IMG Activity: OHIX0650
S_AHR_61010606	IMG Activity: OHTY045
S_AHR_61010607	IMG Activity: SIMG_OHANL_454
S_AHR_61010608	IMG Activity: SIMG_OHANL_455
S_AHR_61010609	IMG Activity: SIMG_OHANL_611
S_AHR_61010610	IMG Activity: OHIX0645
S_AHR_61010611	IMG Activity: OHAXRI080
S_AHR_61010612	IMG Activity: SIMG_OHANL_523
S_AHR_61010613	IMG Activity: SIMG_OHANL_522
S_AHR_61010614	IMG Activity: OHAN9210
S_AHR_61010615	IMG Activity: OHAXRI081
S_AHR_61010616	IMG Activity: OHIX0680
S_AHR_61010617	IMG Activity: OHAN9211
S_AHR_61010618	IMG Activity: SIMG_OHANL_521

S_AHR_61010619	IMG Activity: SIMG_OHANL_520
S_AHR_61010620	IMG Activity: OHAXRI090
S_AHR_61010621	IMG Activity: OHTY047
S_AHR_61010622	IMG Activity: SIMG_OHANL_519
S_AHR_61010623	IMG Activity: SIMG_OHANL_844
S_AHR_61010624	IMG Activity: OHAXUM002
S_AHR_61010625	IMG Activity: SIMG_OHANL_612
S_AHR_61010626	IMG Activity: OHTX3211
S_AHR_61010627	IMG Activity: SIMG_OHANL_613
S_AHR_61010628	IMG Activity: SIMG_OHANL_614
S_AHR_61010629	IMG Activity: OHAXPAY002
S_AHR_61010630	IMG Activity: SIMG_OHANL_524
S_AHR_61010631	IMG Activity: OHTX3212
S_AHR_61010632	IMG Activity: SIMG_OHANL_841
S_AHR_61010633	IMG Activity: SIMG_OHANL_842
S_AHR_61010634	IMG Activity: OHAXPAY003
S_AHR_61010635	IMG Activity: SIMG_OHANL_843
S_AHR_61010636	IMG Activity: OHTY048
S_AHR_61010637	IMG Activity: OHAXPU1200
S_AHR_61010638	IMG Activity: OHIW5150
S_AHR_61010639	IMG Activity: OHIX0181
S_AHR_61010640	IMG Activity: OHAXRI070
S_AHR_61010641	IMG Activity: OHIW6150
S_AHR_61010643	IMG Activity: OHIX0182
S_AHR_61010644	IMG Activity: OHAXRI052
S_AHR_61010645	IMG Activity: OHIPT_SS100
S_AHR_61010646	IMG Activity: OHTX3204
S_AHR_61010647	IMG Activity: OHAXRI056
S_AHR_61010648	IMG Activity: OHIPT_SS200
S_AHR_61010649	IMG Activity: OHAXRI053
S_AHR_61010650	IMG Activity: OHTX3203
S_AHR_61010651	IMG Activity: OHIPT_SS300
S_AHR_61010652	IMG Activity: OHAXRI054
S_AHR_61010653	IMG Activity: OHTX3202
S_AHR_61010654	IMG Activity: OHAXRI055
S_AHR_61010655	IMG Activity: OHIJ0039
S_AHR_61010656	IMG Activity: OHTX3208
S_AHR_61010657	IMG Activity: OHAXRI061
S_AHR_61010658	IMG Activity: OHIJ0015
S_AHR_61010659	IMG Activity: OHTX3201
S_AHR_61010660	IMG Activity: OHAXRI062
S_AHR_61010661	IMG Activity: OHIJ0124
S_AHR_61010662	IMG Activity: OHTX5002
S_AHR_61010663	IMG Activity: OHAXRI063
S_AHR_61010664	IMG Activity: OHIJ0126
S_AHR_61010665	IMG Activity: OHTX204
S_AHR_61010666	IMG Activity: OHIJ0127
S_AHR_61010667	IMG Activity: SIMG_OHAX451
S_AHR_61010668	IMG Activity: SIMGOHT091
S_AHR_61010669	IMG Activity: SIMG_OHAX463
S_AHR_61010670	IMG Activity: OHIJ0116
S_AHR_61010671	IMG Activity: SIMG_OHAX464
S_AHR_61010672	IMG Activity: SIMG_OHT0105
S_AHR_61010673	IMG Activity: OHIW4150

S_AHR_61010674	IMG Activity: SIMG_OHAX471
S_AHR_61010675	IMG Activity: OHIW3150
S_AHR_61010676	IMG Activity: SIMG_OHT0106
S_AHR_61010677	IMG Activity: SIMG_OHAX435
S_AHR_61010678	IMG Activity: OHIW2150
S_AHR_61010679	IMG Activity: SIMGOHT090
S_AHR_61010680	IMG Activity: SIMG_OHAX422
S_AHR_61010681	IMG Activity: OHIJ0016
S_AHR_61010682	IMG Activity: SIMG_OHAX423
S_AHR_61010683	IMG Activity: SIMGOHT096
S_AHR_61010684	IMG Activity: OHIN0403
S_AHR_61010685	IMG Activity: SIMG_OHAX425
S_AHR_61010686	IMG Activity: SIMGOHT095
S_AHR_61010687	IMG Activity: SIMG_OHAX457
S_AHR_61010688	IMG Activity: OHIMPENSEMPF
S_AHR_61010689	IMG Activity: SIMGOHT094
S_AHR_61010690	IMG Activity: OHIMAMPINST
S_AHR_61010691	IMG Activity: SIMG_OHAX814
S_AHR_61010692	IMG Activity: OHIMPENSINST
S_AHR_61010693	IMG Activity: SIMGOHT093
S_AHR_61010694	IMG Activity: SIMG_OHAX415
S_AHR_61010695	IMG Activity: SIMGOHT092
S_AHR_61010696	IMG Activity: OHIMPENSTYP
S_AHR_61010697	IMG Activity: OHTX5003
S_AHR_61010698	IMG Activity: SIMG_OHAX418
S_AHR_61010699	IMG Activity: OHIMATPKD
S_AHR_61010700	IMG Activity: SIMG_OHAX419
S_AHR_61010701	IMG Activity: SIMG_OHT0108
S_AHR_61010702	IMG Activity: OHIMEDUCCODES
S_AHR_61010703	IMG Activity: OHIX0236
S_AHR_61010704	IMG Activity: OHIJ0021
S_AHR_61010705	IMG Activity: SIMG_OHAX483
S_AHR_61010706	IMG Activity: OHIX0235
S_AHR_61010707	IMG Activity: OHIJ0001
S_AHR_61010708	IMG Activity: SIMG_OHAX484
S_AHR_61010709	IMG Activity: OHIJ0048
S_AHR_61010710	IMG Activity: OHID0234
S_AHR_61010711	IMG Activity: OHIW1151
S_AHR_61010712	IMG Activity: OHIX0177
S_AHR_61010713	IMG Activity: SIMG_OHAX431
S_AHR_61010714	IMG Activity: OHIN0402
S_AHR_61010715	IMG Activity: OHIX0221
S_AHR_61010716	IMG Activity: SIMG_OHAX424
S_AHR_61010717	IMG Activity: OHIN0400
S_AHR_61010718	IMG Activity: OHIX0179
S_AHR_61010719	IMG Activity: SIMG_OHAX467
S_AHR_61010720	IMG Activity: OHIN0401
S_AHR_61010721	IMG Activity: SIMG_OHAX470
S_AHR_61010722	IMG Activity: OHIX1177
S_AHR_61010723	IMG Activity: OHIA0381
S_AHR_61010724	IMG Activity: SIMG_OHT0107
S_AHR_61010725	IMG Activity: OHAX601
S_AHR_61010726	IMG Activity: OHIA0382
S_AHR_61010727	IMG Activity: OHIX0178

S_AHR_61010728	IMG Activity: SIMG_OHAX615
S_AHR_61010729	IMG Activity: OHIA0383
S_AHR_61010730	IMG Activity: OHAXFO003
S_AHR_61010731	IMG Activity: OHAXFO004
S_AHR_61010732	IMG Activity: SIMG_OHT0601
S_AHR_61010733	IMG Activity: OHAXFO005
S_AHR_61010734	IMG Activity: OHIA0384
S_AHR_61010735	IMG Activity: OHTX203
S_AHR_61010736	IMG Activity: SIMG_OHAX427
S_AHR_61010737	IMG Activity: OHIJ0009
S_AHR_61010738	IMG Activity: OHTX215
S_AHR_61010739	IMG Activity: SIMG_OHAX437
S_AHR_61010740	IMG Activity: OHIJ0010
S_AHR_61010741	IMG Activity: SIMG_OHAX432
S_AHR_61010742	IMG Activity: OHTX216
S_AHR_61010743	IMG Activity: OHIJ0036
S_AHR_61010744	IMG Activity: SIMG_OHAX426
S_AHR_61010745	IMG Activity: OHTX5007
S_AHR_61010746	IMG Activity: OHIF03622
S_AHR_61010747	IMG Activity: SIMG_OHAX428
S_AHR_61010748	IMG Activity: OHIF03631
S_AHR_61010749	IMG Activity: OHTX0217
S_AHR_61010750	IMG Activity: SIMG_OHAX459
S_AHR_61010751	IMG Activity: OHIF03633
S_AHR_61010752	IMG Activity: OHTX0218
S_AHR_61010753	IMG Activity: SIMG_OHAX438
S_AHR_61010754	IMG Activity: OHIF03632
S_AHR_61010755	IMG Activity: SIMG_OHT5217
S_AHR_61010756	IMG Activity: SIMG_OHAX461
S_AHR_61010757	IMG Activity: OHIF03592
S_AHR_61010758	IMG Activity: SIMG_OHAX429
S_AHR_61010759	IMG Activity: OHTX206
S_AHR_61010760	IMG Activity: OHAXAV001
S_AHR_61010761	IMG Activity: OHICA365
S_AHR_61010762	IMG Activity: SIMGOHT097
S_AHR_61010763	IMG Activity: OHIA0380
S_AHR_61010764	IMG Activity: OHAXAB004
S_AHR_61010765	IMG Activity: OHIHK_SL010
S_AHR_61010766	IMG Activity: OHIW0001
S_AHR_61010767	IMG Activity: OHIJ0082
S_AHR_61010768	IMG Activity: OHAXKF002
S_AHR_61010769	IMG Activity: OHT3300PTRC01
S_AHR_61010770	IMG Activity: SIMG_OHTX818
S_AHR_61010771	IMG Activity: OHIJ0012
S_AHR_61010772	IMG Activity: OHAXTI210
S_AHR_61010773	IMG Activity: SIMG_OHT098
S_AHR_61010774	IMG Activity: OHIJ0020
S_AHR_61010775	IMG Activity: OHAXKL000
S_AHR_61010776	IMG Activity: SIMG_OHT22C
S_AHR_61010777	IMG Activity: SIMG_OHTX827
S_AHR_61010778	IMG Activity: OHIJ0013
S_AHR_61010779	IMG Activity: OHAXBW019
S_AHR_61010780	IMG Activity: SIMG_OHT422
S_AHR_61010781	IMG Activity: SIMG_OHT0613

S_AHR_61010782	IMG Activity: OHIJ0007
S_AHR_61010783	IMG Activity: OHAXAVX018
S_AHR_61010784	IMG Activity: SIMG_OHTX826
S_AHR_61010785	IMG Activity: OHIJ0004
S_AHR_61010786	IMG Activity: OHAXAVX017
S_AHR_61010787	IMG Activity: SIMG_OHT056
S_AHR_61010788	IMG Activity: SIMG_OHTX800
S_AHR_61010789	IMG Activity: OHIJ0121
S_AHR_61010790	IMG Activity: SIMG_OHTX810
S_AHR_61010791	IMG Activity: OHAXPART
S_AHR_61010792	IMG Activity: OHIJ0123
S_AHR_61010793	IMG Activity: OHTY056
S_AHR_61010794	IMG Activity: OHTX212
S_AHR_61010795	IMG Activity: OHIJ0037
S_AHR_61010796	IMG Activity: OHAXKF001
S_AHR_61010797	IMG Activity: OHAXTI310
S_AHR_61010798	IMG Activity: OHIJ0005
S_AHR_61010799	IMG Activity: OHAXAVBAS
S_AHR_61010800	IMG Activity: OHIJ0043
S_AHR_61010801	IMG Activity: OHAXSL003
S_AHR_61010802	IMG Activity: OHIJ0006
S_AHR_61010803	IMG Activity: OHAXBW005
S_AHR_61010804	IMG Activity: OHIJ0044
S_AHR_61010805	IMG Activity: OHIJ0045
S_AHR_61010806	IMG Activity: OHAXBW004
S_AHR_61010807	IMG Activity: OHIJ0019
S_AHR_61010808	IMG Activity: OHAXAB005
S_AHR_61010809	IMG Activity: OHIJ0130
S_AHR_61010810	IMG Activity: OHAXX_PM_CREATE
S_AHR_61010811	IMG Activity: OHIJ0083
S_AHR_61010812	IMG Activity: OHAXIW063
S_AHR_61010813	IMG Activity: OHIJ0084
S_AHR_61010814	IMG Activity: OHAXTI130
S_AHR_61010815	IMG Activity: OHAXTI120
S_AHR_61010816	IMG Activity: OHIJ0026
S_AHR_61010817	IMG Activity: OHAXSL001
S_AHR_61010818	IMG Activity: OHIJ0085
S_AHR_61010819	IMG Activity: OHAXTI110
S_AHR_61010820	IMG Activity: OHIJ0040
S_AHR_61010821	IMG Activity: OHAXBW006
S_AHR_61010822	IMG Activity: OHIJ0075
S_AHR_61010823	IMG Activity: OHAXSL002
S_AHR_61010824	IMG Activity: OHIA0434
S_AHR_61010825	IMG Activity: OHIA0435
S_AHR_61010826	IMG Activity: OHAXTI325
S_AHR_61010827	IMG Activity: OHIA0436
S_AHR_61010828	IMG Activity: OHAXBW22
S_AHR_61010829	IMG Activity: OHAXTI362
S_AHR_61010830	IMG Activity: OHIA0437
S_AHR_61010831	IMG Activity: OHAXTI363
S_AHR_61010832	IMG Activity: OHIA0438
S_AHR_61010833	IMG Activity: OHAXTI361
S_AHR_61010835	IMG Activity: OHAXAB001
S_AHR_61010836	IMG Activity: OHIJ0129

S_AHR_61010837	IMG Activity: OHAXAVP15
S_AHR_61010838	IMG Activity: OHIJ0076
S_AHR_61010839	IMG Activity: OHAXTI370
S_AHR_61010840	IMG Activity: OHIJ0068
S_AHR_61010841	IMG Activity: OHAX_AV_2W
S_AHR_61010842	IMG Activity: OHIJ0069
S_AHR_61010843	IMG Activity: OHIJ0070
S_AHR_61010844	IMG Activity: OHAX_AV_ABCR
S_AHR_61010845	IMG Activity: OHIJ0071
S_AHR_61010846	IMG Activity: OHAX_AV_P
S_AHR_61010847	IMG Activity: OHIJ0072
S_AHR_61010848	IMG Activity: OHAXTI364
S_AHR_61010849	IMG Activity: OHAXBW21
S_AHR_61010850	IMG Activity: OHIW2149
S_AHR_61010851	IMG Activity: OHAXTI324
S_AHR_61010852	IMG Activity: OHIW1149
S_AHR_61010853	IMG Activity: SAPCOH04
S_AHR_61010854	IMG Activity: SAPCOH06
S_AHR_61010855	IMG Activity: OHAXTI323
S_AHR_61010856	IMG Activity: OHIJ0077
S_AHR_61010857	IMG Activity: SAPCOH03
S_AHR_61010858	IMG Activity: SAPCOH05
S_AHR_61010859	IMG Activity: OHAXAV511A
S_AHR_61010860	IMG Activity: SAPCOH02
S_AHR_61010861	IMG Activity: OHIJ0078
S_AHR_61010862	IMG Activity: SAPCOH01
S_AHR_61010863	IMG Activity: OHAXTI322
S_AHR_61010864	IMG Activity: OHIJ0079
S_AHR_61010865	IMG Activity: OHAXTI321
S_AHR_61010866	IMG Activity: OHIJ0081
S_AHR_61010867	IMG Activity: OHAXAB003
S_AHR_61010868	IMG Activity: OHIPT_IC005
S_AHR_61010869	IMG Activity: OHAXAVXT00
S_AHR_61010870	IMG Activity: OHIPT_IC100
S_AHR_61010871	IMG Activity: OHAXTI340
S_AHR_61010872	IMG Activity: OHIJ0066
S_AHR_61010873	IMG Activity: OHAXAV511C
S_AHR_61010874	IMG Activity: OHIMDKBOL
S_AHR_61010876	IMG Activity: OHAXAB002
S_AHR_61010877	IMG Activity: OHAXAL01
S_AHR_61010878	IMG Activity: OHIMDKPOS
S_AHR_61010879	IMG Activity: OHAXAV511B
S_AHR_61010880	IMG Activity: OHIMSTATFIELDS
S_AHR_61010882	IMG Activity: OHIMSTATVALUES
S_AHR_61010884	IMG Activity: OHIE0411
S_AHR_61010886	IMG Activity: OHIE0412
S_AHR_61010887	IMG Activity: OHAXSZ050
S_AHR_61010888	IMG Activity: OHIE0413
S_AHR_61010889	IMG Activity: OHAXUM006B
S_AHR_61010890	IMG Activity: OHIMDAWPCODES
S_AHR_61010891	IMG Activity: OHAXUM008
S_AHR_61010892	IMG Activity: OHIMDAPROP
S_AHR_61010894	IMG Activity: OHIMDKC23
S_AHR_61010896	IMG Activity: OHIMDKLON

S_AHR_61010898	IMG Activity: OHIMDKFTE
S_AHR_61010900	IMG Activity: OHIMDKSTA
S_AHR_61010901	IMG Activity: OHAXUM010B
S_AHR_61010902	IMG Activity: OHIMDKJUB
S_AHR_61010904	IMG Activity: OHIE0415
S_AHR_61010905	IMG Activity: OHAXUM012
S_AHR_61010906	IMG Activity: OHIN1003
S_AHR_61010908	IMG Activity: OHAXQUOTACOMP00
S_AHR_61010909	IMG Activity: OHIN1002
S_AHR_61010911	IMG Activity: OHIN1006
S_AHR_61010912	IMG Activity: OHAXAB200
S_AHR_61010913	IMG Activity: OHIN0425
S_AHR_61010915	IMG Activity: OHIN0429
S_AHR_61010916	IMG Activity: OHAXUM006
S_AHR_61010917	IMG Activity: OHIN0430
S_AHR_61010918	IMG Activity: OHAXUM014
S_AHR_61010919	IMG Activity: OHIN0428
S_AHR_61010921	IMG Activity: OHIE0414
S_AHR_61010923	IMG Activity: OHIB0408
S_AHR_61010925	IMG Activity: OHIB0409
S_AHR_61010927	IMG Activity: OHIB0410
S_AHR_61010928	IMG Activity: OHAXAB011
S_AHR_61010929	IMG Activity: OHIB0411
S_AHR_61010930	IMG Activity: OHAXUM105
S_AHR_61010931	IMG Activity: OHIN1004
S_AHR_61010932	IMG Activity: OHAXUM104
S_AHR_61010933	IMG Activity: OHIN0427
S_AHR_61010934	IMG Activity: OHAXIW037
S_AHR_61010935	IMG Activity: OHIF0428
S_AHR_61010936	IMG Activity: OHAXAB009
S_AHR_61010937	IMG Activity: OHIJ0091
S_AHR_61010938	IMG Activity: OHAXUM101
S_AHR_61010939	IMG Activity: OHAXUM103
S_AHR_61010940	IMG Activity: OHIMX111
S_AHR_61010941	IMG Activity: OHAXUM102
S_AHR_61010942	IMG Activity: OHIMX121
S_AHR_61010943	IMG Activity: OHIMX122
S_AHR_61010944	IMG Activity: OHAXIW065
S_AHR_61010945	IMG Activity: OHIMX123
S_AHR_61010946	IMG Activity: OHAXIW061
S_AHR_61010947	IMG Activity: OHIMX302
S_AHR_61010948	IMG Activity: OHAXIW082
S_AHR_61010949	IMG Activity: OHIMX301
S_AHR_61010951	IMG Activity: OHAXUM010
S_AHR_61010952	IMG Activity: OHIX0330
S_AHR_61010954	IMG Activity: OHIX0331
S_AHR_61010955	IMG Activity: OHAXUM013
S_AHR_61010956	IMG Activity: OHIX0331C
S_AHR_61010957	IMG Activity: OHIX0331D
S_AHR_61010959	IMG Activity: OHIX0331E
S_AHR_61010960	IMG Activity: OHAXAB010
S_AHR_61010961	IMG Activity: OHAXUM022
S_AHR_61010962	IMG Activity: OHIX0331F
S_AHR_61010963	IMG Activity: OHIJ0090

S_AHR_61010964	IMG Activity: OHIMX311
S_AHR_61010965	IMG Activity: OHIE0343
S_AHR_61010966	IMG Activity: OHIE0344
S_AHR_61010967	IMG Activity: OHIE0348
S_AHR_61010968	IMG Activity: OHIE0345
S_AHR_61010969	IMG Activity: OHIE0346
S_AHR_61010970	IMG Activity: OHIE0347
S_AHR_61010971	IMG Activity: OHIE0349
S_AHR_61010972	IMG Activity: OHIMX320
S_AHR_61010973	IMG Activity: OHIE0340
S_AHR_61010974	IMG Activity: OHIE0416
S_AHR_61010975	IMG Activity: OHIE0418
S_AHR_61010976	IMG Activity: OHIE0417
S_AHR_61010977	IMG Activity: OHIE0341
S_AHR_61010978	IMG Activity: OHIE0342
S_AHR_61010979	IMG Activity: OHIX0293D
S_AHR_61010980	IMG Activity: OHIX0293F
S_AHR_61010981	IMG Activity: OHIX0293G
S_AHR_61010982	IMG Activity: OHIX0293E
S_AHR_61010983	IMG Activity: OHIX0322
S_AHR_61010984	IMG Activity: OHIC0322
S_AHR_61010985	IMG Activity: OHIX0323
S_AHR_61010986	IMG Activity: OHIE0318
S_AHR_61010987	IMG Activity: OHIE0319
S_AHR_61010988	IMG Activity: OHIE0320
S_AHR_61010989	IMG Activity: OHIX0293
S_AHR_61010990	IMG Activity: OHIX0293B
S_AHR_61010991	IMG Activity: OHIX0293A
S_AHR_61010992	IMG Activity: OHIX0293C
S_AHR_61010993	IMG Activity: OHIXP3701
S_AHR_61010994	IMG Activity: OHIX0294C
S_AHR_61010995	IMG Activity: OHIX0294D
S_AHR_61010996	IMG Activity: OHIX0294F
S_AHR_61010997	IMG Activity: OHIX0294G
S_AHR_61010998	IMG Activity: OHIX0294E
S_AHR_61010999	IMG Activity: OHIE0328
S_AHR_61011000	IMG Activity: OHIE0329
S_AHR_61011001	IMG Activity: OHIXP3702
S_AHR_61011002	IMG Activity: OHIX0325
S_AHR_61011003	IMG Activity: OHIE0579
S_AHR_61011004	IMG Activity: OHAXAB012
S_AHR_61011005	IMG Activity: OHIE0326
S_AHR_61011006	IMG Activity: OHAXUM023
S_AHR_61011007	IMG Activity: OHIX0294
S_AHR_61011008	IMG Activity: SIMG_OHAX454
S_AHR_61011009	IMG Activity: SIMG_OHAX455
S_AHR_61011010	IMG Activity: OHIX0294B
S_AHR_61011011	IMG Activity: OHAX_AV_1
S_AHR_61011012	IMG Activity: SIMG_OHAX401
S_AHR_61011013	IMG Activity: OHIX0294A
S_AHR_61011014	IMG Activity: SIMG_OHAX465
S_AHR_61011015	IMG Activity: SIMG_OHAX453
S_AHR_61011016	IMG Activity: OHIB0340
S_AHR_61011017	IMG Activity: OHAXDT009

S_AHR_61011018	IMG Activity: SIMG_OHAX466
S_AHR_61011019	IMG Activity: OHAXIW041
S_AHR_61011020	IMG Activity: OHIB0341
S_AHR_61011021	IMG Activity: SIMG_OHAX439
S_AHR_61011022	IMG Activity: SIMG_OHAX421
S_AHR_61011023	IMG Activity: OHIB0342
S_AHR_61011024	IMG Activity: SIMG_OHAX450
S_AHR_61011025	IMG Activity: SIMG_OHAX481
S_AHR_61011026	IMG Activity: OHAXIW035
S_AHR_61011027	IMG Activity: OHIB0343
S_AHR_61011028	IMG Activity: OHAXIW069
S_AHR_61011029	IMG Activity: SIMG_OHAX456
S_AHR_61011030	IMG Activity: OHIB0344
S_AHR_61011031	IMG Activity: OHAXTI330
S_AHR_61011032	IMG Activity: SIMG_OHAX516
S_AHR_61011033	IMG Activity: OHIB0345
S_AHR_61011034	IMG Activity: SIMG_OHAX614
S_AHR_61011035	IMG Activity: SIMG_OHAX514
S_AHR_61011036	IMG Activity: OHIB0348
S_AHR_61011037	IMG Activity: SIMG_OHAX513
S_AHR_61011038	IMG Activity: SIMG_OHAX512
S_AHR_61011039	IMG Activity: SIMG_OHAX613
S_AHR_61011040	IMG Activity: OHIN1010
S_AHR_61011041	IMG Activity: SIMG_OHAX510
S_AHR_61011042	IMG Activity: SIMG_OHAX520
S_AHR_61011043	IMG Activity: OHIN1011
S_AHR_61011044	IMG Activity: SIMG_OHAX841
S_AHR_61011045	IMG Activity: SIMG_OHAX842
S_AHR_61011046	IMG Activity: OHIN1099
S_AHR_61011047	IMG Activity: SIMG_OHAX843
S_AHR_61011048	IMG Activity: SIMG_OHAX844
S_AHR_61011049	IMG Activity: SIMG_OHAX519
S_AHR_61011050	IMG Activity: OHIN0355
S_AHR_61011051	IMG Activity: SIMG_OHAX517
S_AHR_61011052	IMG Activity: OHAXFO002
S_AHR_61011053	IMG Activity: OHIN0356
S_AHR_61011054	IMG Activity: SIMG_OHAX509
S_AHR_61011055	IMG Activity: SIMG_OHAX612
S_AHR_61011056	IMG Activity: OHIN0357
S_AHR_61011057	IMG Activity: SIMG_OHAX502
S_AHR_61011058	IMG Activity: SIMG_OHAX501
S_AHR_61011059	IMG Activity: SIMG_OHAX611
S_AHR_61011060	IMG Activity: OHIB0349
S_AHR_61011061	IMG Activity: SIMG_OHAX521
S_AHR_61011062	IMG Activity: SIMG_OHAX522
S_AHR_61011063	IMG Activity: SIMG_OHAX523
S_AHR_61011064	IMG Activity: OHIB0347
S_AHR_61011065	IMG Activity: SIMG_OHAX524
S_AHR_61011066	IMG Activity: OHAXFORS010
S_AHR_61011067	IMG Activity: OHIF03601
S_AHR_61011068	IMG Activity: SIMG_OHAX508
S_AHR_61011069	IMG Activity: OHAXFORS030
S_AHR_61011070	IMG Activity: OHIF03602
S_AHR_61011071	IMG Activity: OHAXFORS031

S_AHR_61011072	IMG Activity: OHAXFORS040
S_AHR_61011073	IMG Activity: OHIF0361
S_AHR_61011074	IMG Activity: OHAXFORS050
S_AHR_61011075	IMG Activity: OHAXFORS060
S_AHR_61011076	IMG Activity: OHIF03621
S_AHR_61011077	IMG Activity: OHAXFORS070
S_AHR_61011078	IMG Activity: OHIF0422
S_AHR_61011079	IMG Activity: OHIF0424
S_AHR_61011080	IMG Activity: OHIF0426
S_AHR_61011081	IMG Activity: OHIF0366
S_AHR_61011082	IMG Activity: OHIF0402
S_AHR_61011083	IMG Activity: OHIF0404
S_AHR_61011084	IMG Activity: OHIF0408
S_AHR_61011085	IMG Activity: OHIF0406
S_AHR_61011086	IMG Activity: OHIF0410
S_AHR_61011087	IMG Activity: OHIF03591
S_AHR_61011088	IMG Activity: OHIEGC11B
S_AHR_61011089	IMG Activity: OHIEGC11C
S_AHR_61011090	IMG Activity: OHIEGC11F
S_AHR_61011091	IMG Activity: OHIEGC11G
S_AHR_61011092	IMG Activity: OHIEGC11D
S_AHR_61011093	IMG Activity: OHIEGC11E
S_AHR_61011094	IMG Activity: OHIEGCD
S_AHR_61011095	IMG Activity: OHIEGCA
S_AHR_61011096	IMG Activity: OHIEGCB
S_AHR_61011097	IMG Activity: OHIEGCC
S_AHR_61011098	IMG Activity: OHIEGC1A
S_AHR_61011099	IMG Activity: OHIEGC1B
S_AHR_61011100	IMG Activity: OHIEGC1C
S_AHR_61011101	IMG Activity: OHIEGC11A
S_AHR_61011102	IMG Activity: OHIEGCE
S_AHR_61011103	IMG Activity: OHINSV01
S_AHR_61011104	IMG Activity: OHINSV02
S_AHR_61011105	IMG Activity: OHINSV03
S_AHR_61011106	IMG Activity: OHINSV04
S_AHR_61011107	IMG Activity: OHIN0351
S_AHR_61011108	IMG Activity: OHIN0352
S_AHR_61011109	IMG Activity: OHIN0354
S_AHR_61011110	IMG Activity: OHIN1001
S_AHR_61011111	IMG Activity: OHINSV1G
S_AHR_61011112	IMG Activity: OHINSV1A
S_AHR_61011113	IMG Activity: OHINSV1B
S_AHR_61011114	IMG Activity: OHINSV1C
S_AHR_61011115	IMG Activity: OHINSV1D
S_AHR_61011116	IMG Activity: OHINSV1E
S_AHR_61011117	IMG Activity: OHIC0535
S_AHR_61011118	IMG Activity: OHIC0545
S_AHR_61011119	IMG Activity: OHIC0547
S_AHR_61011120	IMG Activity: OHIC0532
S_AHR_61011121	IMG Activity: OHIC0540
S_AHR_61011122	IMG Activity: OHIC0517
S_AHR_61011123	IMG Activity: OHIC0550
S_AHR_61011126	IMG Activity: OHIX0581
S_AHR_61011128	IMG Activity: OHIE0578

S_AHR_61011129	IMG Activity: OHIC0510
S_AHR_61011130	IMG Activity: OHIC0530
S_AHR_61011131	IMG Activity: OHIC0560
S_AHR_61011132	IMG Activity: OHIJ0093
S_AHR_61011133	IMG Activity: OHIJ0088
S_AHR_61011134	IMG Activity: OHIX0610
S_AHR_61011135	IMG Activity: OHIX0611
S_AHR_61011136	IMG Activity: OHIX0612
S_AHR_61011137	IMG Activity: OHIX0613
S_AHR_61011138	IMG Activity: OHIX0615
S_AHR_61011139	IMG Activity: OHIC0511
S_AHR_61011140	IMG Activity: OHIC0515
S_AHR_61011141	IMG Activity: OHIX0606
S_AHR_61011142	IMG Activity: OHIX0607
S_AHR_61011143	IMG Activity: OHIX0608
S_AHR_61011144	IMG Activity: OHIX0609
S_AHR_61011145	IMG Activity: OHIJ0092
S_AHR_61011146	IMG Activity: OHIJ0108
S_AHR_61011147	IMG Activity: OHIJ0109
S_AHR_61011148	IMG Activity: OHIJ0132
S_AHR_61011149	IMG Activity: OHIJ0133
S_AHR_61011150	IMG Activity: OHIJ0111
S_AHR_61011151	IMG Activity: OHIJ0112
S_AHR_61011152	IMG Activity: OHIJ0114
S_AHR_61011153	IMG Activity: OHIJ0098
S_AHR_61011154	IMG Activity: OHIJ0099
S_AHR_61011155	IMG Activity: OHIJ0102
S_AHR_61011156	IMG Activity: OHIJ0103
S_AHR_61011157	IMG Activity: OHIJ0104
S_AHR_61011158	IMG Activity: OHIJ0105
S_AHR_61011159	IMG Activity: OHIJ0107
S_AHR_61011160	IMG Activity: OHIJ0115
S_AHR_61011161	IMG Activity: OHIXLGART003
S_AHR_61011162	IMG Activity: OHIX0569
S_AHR_61011163	IMG Activity: OHIX0571
S_AHR_61011164	IMG Activity: OHIX0572
S_AHR_61011165	IMG Activity: OHIX0574
S_AHR_61011166	IMG Activity: OHIX0575
S_AHR_61011168	IMG Activity: OHIX_COMPCAR_000
S_AHR_61011169	IMG Activity: OHIX_COMPCAR_001
S_AHR_61011170	IMG Activity: OHIX_COMPCAR_111
S_AHR_61011171	IMG Activity: OHIX_COMPCAR_112
S_AHR_61011172	IMG Activity: OHIX_COMPCAR_120
S_AHR_61011173	IMG Activity: OHIX_COMPCAR_200
S_AHR_61011174	IMG Activity: OHIX_COMPCAR_300
S_AHR_61011175	IMG Activity: OHIX0017
S_AHR_61011176	IMG Activity: OHIX0018
S_AHR_61011177	IMG Activity: OHIXWFAC
S_AHR_61011178	IMG Activity: OHIX0036
S_AHR_61011179	IMG Activity: OHIX0037
S_AHR_61011180	IMG Activity: SIMGOHISXDA
S_AHR_61011181	IMG Activity: OHIX0004
S_AHR_61011182	IMG Activity: OHIX0007
S_AHR_61011183	IMG Activity: OHIX0031

S_AHR_61011184	IMG Activity: OHIX0032
S_AHR_61011185	IMG Activity: OHIX0009
S_AHR_61011186	IMG Activity: OHIX0012
S_AHR_61011187	IMG Activity: OHIX0005
S_AHR_61011188	IMG Activity: HRRSM_EXT_COM
S_AHR_61011189	IMG Activity: OHIX0691
S_AHR_61011190	IMG Activity: OHIURSX02
S_AHR_61011191	IMG Activity: OHIURSX03
S_AHR_61011192	IMG Activity: OHIURSX04
S_AHR_61011193	IMG Activity: OHIURSX05
S_AHR_61011194	IMG Activity: OHIURSX06
S_AHR_61011195	IMG Activity: OHIXIAC001
S_AHR_61011196	IMG Activity: HRRSM_EXT_ACT_MAINT
S_AHR_61011197	IMG Activity: HRRSM_NUMRANGEDEFINE
S_AHR_61011198	IMG Activity: OHIX0770
S_AHR_61011199	IMG Activity: OHIX0687
S_AHR_61011200	IMG Activity: OHIX0688
S_AHR_61011201	IMG Activity: OHIX0689
S_AHR_61011202	IMG Activity: OHIX0690
S_AHR_61011203	IMG Activity: OHIX06233
S_AHR_61011204	IMG Activity: OHIX06232
S_AHR_61011205	IMG Activity: OHIX06234
S_AHR_61011206	IMG Activity: OHIX0626
S_AHR_61011207	IMG Activity: OHIX0627
S_AHR_61011208	IMG Activity: OHIX0621
S_AHR_61011209	IMG Activity: OHIX0631
S_AHR_61011210	IMG Activity: OHIX0617
S_AHR_61011211	IMG Activity: OHIX0618
S_AHR_61011212	IMG Activity: OHIX0400
S_AHR_61011213	IMG Activity: OHIX0625
S_AHR_61011214	IMG Activity: OHIX0628
S_AHR_61011215	IMG Activity: OHIX06231
S_AHR_61011216	IMG Activity: OHIX0623
S_AHR_61011217	IMG Activity: OHIX0630
S_AHR_61011218	IMG Activity: OHIX0682
S_AHR_61011219	IMG Activity: OHIX0683
S_AHR_61011220	IMG Activity: OHIX0635
S_AHR_61011221	IMG Activity: OHIX0636
S_AHR_61011222	IMG Activity: OHIX0639
S_AHR_61011223	IMG Activity: OHIX0684
S_AHR_61011224	IMG Activity: OHIX0003
S_AHR_61011225	IMG Activity: OHIX0647
S_AHR_61011226	IMG Activity: OHIX0629
S_AHR_61011227	IMG Activity: OHIPT_MD105
S_AHR_61011228	IMG Activity: OHIX0632
S_AHR_61011229	IMG Activity: OHIMX330
S_AHR_61011230	IMG Activity: OHIX0634
S_AHR_61011231	IMG Activity: OHIX0681
S_AHR_61011232	IMG Activity: OHIJ0097
S_AHR_61011233	IMG Activity: OHIF03642
S_AHR_61011234	IMG Activity: OHIF03645
S_AHR_61011235	IMG Activity: OHIX0651
S_AHR_61011236	IMG Activity: OHIX0473
S_AHR_61011237	IMG Activity: OHIX0474

S_AHR_61011238	IMG Activity: OHIX0475
S_AHR_61011239	IMG Activity: OHIX0476
S_AHR_61011240	IMG Activity: OHIMOFKFEAT
S_AHR_61011241	IMG Activity: OHIMSHOFEAT
S_AHR_61011242	IMG Activity: OHIA0455
S_AHR_61011243	IMG Activity: OHIJ0028
S_AHR_61011244	IMG Activity: OHIF03644
S_AHR_61011245	IMG Activity: OHIF03641
S_AHR_61011246	IMG Activity: OHIF03643
S_AHR_61011247	IMG Activity: OHIX0477
S_AHR_61011248	IMG Activity: OHIJ0034
S_AHR_61011249	IMG Activity: OHIJ0035
S_AHR_61011250	IMG Activity: OHIJ0024
S_AHR_61011251	IMG Activity: OHIJ0061
S_AHR_61011252	IMG Activity: OHIJ0062
S_AHR_61011253	IMG Activity: OHIJ0063
S_AHR_61011254	IMG Activity: OHIC0480
S_AHR_61011255	IMG Activity: OHIJ0030
S_AHR_61011256	IMG Activity: OHIJ0049
S_AHR_61011257	IMG Activity: OHIJ0032
S_AHR_61011258	IMG Activity: OHIJ0052
S_AHR_61011259	IMG Activity: OHIJ0033
S_AHR_61011260	IMG Activity: OHIJ0050
S_AHR_61011261	IMG Activity: OHIJ0023
S_AHR_61011262	IMG Activity: OHIZAAGE04
S_AHR_61011263	IMG Activity: OHIW8149
S_AHR_61011264	IMG Activity: OHIW7149
S_AHR_61011265	IMG Activity: OHIARIG004
S_AHR_61011266	IMG Activity: OHIARIG005
S_AHR_61011267	IMG Activity: OHIARIG007
S_AHR_61011268	IMG Activity: OHIARIG008
S_AHR_61011269	IMG Activity: OHIW4149
S_AHR_61011270	IMG Activity: OHIW5149
S_AHR_61011271	IMG Activity: OHIW6149
S_AHR_61011272	IMG Activity: OHIZAAGE02
S_AHR_61011273	IMG Activity: OHIZAAGE05
S_AHR_61011274	IMG Activity: OHIZAAGE03
S_AHR_61011275	IMG Activity: OHIZAAGE06
S_AHR_61011276	IMG Activity: OHIARIG009
S_AHR_61011277	IMG Activity: OHIARIG019
S_AHR_61011278	IMG Activity: OHIARIG020
S_AHR_61011279	IMG Activity: OHIARIG021
S_AHR_61011280	IMG Activity: OHIARIG022
S_AHR_61011281	IMG Activity: OHIMVACCODES2
S_AHR_61011282	IMG Activity: OHIMABMFEAT
S_AHR_61011283	IMG Activity: OHIMTPRFEAT
S_AHR_61011284	IMG Activity: OHIARIG010
S_AHR_61011285	IMG Activity: OHIARIG011
S_AHR_61011286	IMG Activity: OHIARIG012
S_AHR_61011287	IMG Activity: OHIARIG014
S_AHR_61011288	IMG Activity: OHIARIG015
S_AHR_61011289	IMG Activity: OHIARIG017
S_AHR_61011290	IMG Activity: OHIARIG018
S_AHR_61011291	IMG Activity: OHIA6703

S_AHR_61011292	IMG Activity: OHIA6704
S_AHR_61011293	IMG Activity: OHIA6705
S_AHR_61011294	IMG Activity: OHIA6711
S_AHR_61011295	IMG Activity: OHIMGARREC
S_AHR_61011296	IMG Activity: OHIU0313
S_AHR_61011297	IMG Activity: OHIX0324
S_AHR_61011298	IMG Activity: OHIA6601
S_AHR_61011299	IMG Activity: OHIA6602
S_AHR_61011300	IMG Activity: OHIA6611
S_AHR_61011301	IMG Activity: OHIA6701
S_AHR_61011302	IMG Activity: OHIA6706
S_AHR_61011303	IMG Activity: OHIA6707
S_AHR_61011304	IMG Activity: OHIA6702
S_AHR_61011305	IMG Activity: OHIX0325A
S_AHR_61011306	IMG Activity: OHIRAW014
S_AHR_61011307	IMG Activity: OHIRAW015
S_AHR_61011308	IMG Activity: OHIRAW016
S_AHR_61011309	IMG Activity: OHIRAW001
S_AHR_61011310	IMG Activity: OHIRAW020
S_AHR_61011311	IMG Activity: OHIJ0095
S_AHR_61011312	IMG Activity: OHIJ0096
S_AHR_61011313	IMG Activity: OHIX0327
S_AHR_61011314	IMG Activity: OHIX0328
S_AHR_61011315	IMG Activity: OHIX0329
S_AHR_61011316	IMG Activity: OHIRAW011
S_AHR_61011317	IMG Activity: OHIRAW012
S_AHR_61011318	IMG Activity: OHIRAW017
S_AHR_61011319	IMG Activity: OHIRAW013
S_AHR_61011320	IMG Activity: OHICPK008
S_AHR_61011321	IMG Activity: OHICPK009
S_AHR_61011322	IMG Activity: OHICR490
S_AHR_61011323	IMG Activity: OHIC0484
S_AHR_61011324	IMG Activity: OHIC0485
S_AHR_61011325	IMG Activity: OHIC0486
S_AHR_61011326	IMG Activity: OHIC0488
S_AHR_61011327	IMG Activity: OHIC0481
S_AHR_61011328	IMG Activity: OHIC0482
S_AHR_61011329	IMG Activity: OHICPK002
S_AHR_61011330	IMG Activity: OHICPK004
S_AHR_61011331	IMG Activity: OHICPK005
S_AHR_61011332	IMG Activity: OHICPK006
S_AHR_61011333	IMG Activity: OHICPK007
S_AHR_61011334	IMG Activity: OHIC0489
S_AHR_61011335	IMG Activity: OHIJ0086
S_AHR_61011336	IMG Activity: OHIA6002
S_AHR_61011337	IMG Activity: OHIA6103
S_AHR_61011338	IMG Activity: OHIA6501
S_AHR_61011339	IMG Activity: OHIA6502
S_AHR_61011340	IMG Activity: OHIA6503
S_AHR_61011341	IMG Activity: OHIA6600
S_AHR_61011342	IMG Activity: OHIA0492
S_AHR_61011343	IMG Activity: OHIN0494
S_AHR_61011344	IMG Activity: OHIN0495
S_AHR_61011345	IMG Activity: OHIN0496

S_AHR_61011346	IMG Activity: OHIX0497
S_AHR_61011347	IMG Activity: OHIX0498
S_AHR_61011348	IMG Activity: OHIX0499
S_AHR_61011349	IMG Activity: OHID0072
S_AHR_61011350	IMG Activity: OHID0621
S_AHR_61011351	IMG Activity: OHID0622
S_AHR_61011352	IMG Activity: OHID0623
S_AHR_61011353	IMG Activity: OHIHKV_T7HK03
S_AHR_61011354	IMG Activity: OHIW8004
S_AHR_61011355	IMG Activity: OHIU02571
S_AHR_61011356	IMG Activity: OHIU02572
S_AHR_61011357	IMG Activity: OHIU02573
S_AHR_61011358	IMG Activity: OHIRRT001
S_AHR_61011359	IMG Activity: OHID0074
S_AHR_61011360	IMG Activity: OHID0620
S_AHR_61011361	IMG Activity: OHIX0263
S_AHR_61011362	IMG Activity: OHIX0264
S_AHR_61011363	IMG Activity: OHIW8001
S_AHR_61011364	IMG Activity: OHIX0265
S_AHR_61011365	IMG Activity: OHIXU510F
S_AHR_61011366	IMG Activity: OHIXALCUR
S_AHR_61011367	IMG Activity: OHIW8003
S_AHR_61011368	IMG Activity: OHIW8002
S_AHR_61011369	IMG Activity: OHIX0260
S_AHR_61011370	IMG Activity: OHIX0261
S_AHR_61011371	IMG Activity: OHIX0280
S_AHR_61011372	IMG Activity: OHIX0262
S_AHR_61011373	IMG Activity: OHIX0241
S_AHR_61011374	IMG Activity: OHIX0243
S_AHR_61011376	IMG Activity: OHIBR_CO001
S_AHR_61011377	IMG Activity: OHIBR_CO002
S_AHR_61011378	IMG Activity: OHIU00772
S_AHR_61011379	IMG Activity: OHIB0239
S_AHR_61011380	IMG Activity: OHIBR_FI008
S_AHR_61011381	IMG Activity: OHIBR_FI009
S_AHR_61011382	IMG Activity: OHIK00772
S_AHR_61011383	IMG Activity: OHIX0239
S_AHR_61011384	IMG Activity: OHIX0240
S_AHR_61011385	IMG Activity: OHIK00771
S_AHR_61011386	IMG Activity: OHIN0076
S_AHR_61011387	IMG Activity: OHIX0252
S_AHR_61011388	IMG Activity: OHIX0254
S_AHR_61011389	IMG Activity: OHIPT_DA100
S_AHR_61011390	IMG Activity: OHIX0256
S_AHR_61011391	IMG Activity: OHIPT_DA10A
S_AHR_61011392	IMG Activity: OHIB0240
S_AHR_61011393	IMG Activity: OHIU00771
S_AHR_61011394	IMG Activity: OHIX0246
S_AHR_61011395	IMG Activity: OHIX0248
S_AHR_61011396	IMG Activity: OHIN1007
S_AHR_61011397	IMG Activity: OHIX0247
S_AHR_61011398	IMG Activity: OHIX0266
S_AHR_61011399	IMG Activity: OHIX0279
S_AHR_61011400	IMG Activity: OHIX0277

S_AHR_61011401	IMG Activity: OHIX0282
S_AHR_61011402	IMG Activity: OHIIT_VI010
S_AHR_61011403	IMG Activity: OHIMX303
S_AHR_61011404	IMG Activity: OHIPT_PC000
S_AHR_61011405	IMG Activity: OHIX0273
S_AHR_61011406	IMG Activity: OHIX0274
S_AHR_61011407	IMG Activity: OHIX0275
S_AHR_61011408	IMG Activity: OHIMX304
S_AHR_61011409	IMG Activity: OHIX0276
S_AHR_61011410	IMG Activity: OHIX0278
S_AHR_61011411	IMG Activity: OHAIT_SCA50
S_AHR_61011412	IMG Activity: OHAIT_SCA60
S_AHR_61011413	IMG Activity: OHIB0067
S_AHR_61011414	IMG Activity: OHIG0066
S_AHR_61011415	IMG Activity: OHAIT_SCA70
S_AHR_61011416	IMG Activity: OHAIT_SCA80
S_AHR_61011417	IMG Activity: OHAIT_SCA10
S_AHR_61011418	IMG Activity: OHAIT_SCA20
S_AHR_61011419	IMG Activity: OHIU536B
S_AHR_61011420	IMG Activity: OHIU0068
S_AHR_61011421	IMG Activity: OHAIT_SCA30
S_AHR_61011422	IMG Activity: OHAIT_SCA40
S_AHR_61011423	IMG Activity: OHIX0249
S_AHR_61011424	IMG Activity: OHIU0676
S_AHR_61011425	IMG Activity: OHIX0250
S_AHR_61011426	IMG Activity: OHIX0251
S_AHR_61011427	IMG Activity: OHIX0068
S_AHR_61011428	IMG Activity: OHIX0268A
S_AHR_61011429	IMG Activity: OHIX510N
S_AHR_61011430	IMG Activity: OHIX0167
S_AHR_61011431	IMG Activity: OHIX0267
S_AHR_61011432	IMG Activity: OHIX0070
S_AHR_61011433	IMG Activity: OHIX0069
S_AHR_61011434	IMG Activity: OHIX0281
S_AHR_61011435	IMG Activity: OHIX0624
S_AHR_61011436	IMG Activity: OHIX0026
S_AHR_61011437	IMG Activity: OHIX0271
S_AHR_61011438	IMG Activity: OHIX0271B
S_AHR_61011439	IMG Activity: OHIX0271A
S_AHR_61011440	IMG Activity: OHIX0272
S_AHR_61011441	IMG Activity: OHIX0268B
S_AHR_61011442	IMG Activity: OHIX0268C
S_AHR_61011443	IMG Activity: OHIX0268F
S_AHR_61011444	IMG Activity: OHIX0268G
S_AHR_61011445	IMG Activity: OHIX0268H
S_AHR_61011446	IMG Activity: OHIX0268I
S_AHR_61011447	IMG Activity: OHIBR_FI024
S_AHR_61011448	IMG Activity: OHIC0123
S_AHR_61011449	IMG Activity: OHIC0128
S_AHR_61011450	IMG Activity: OHIC0124
S_AHR_61011451	IMG Activity: OHIC0125
S_AHR_61011452	IMG Activity: OHIC0127
S_AHR_61011453	IMG Activity: OHIC0129
S_AHR_61011454	IMG Activity: OHIX0109

S_AHR_61011455	IMG Activity: OHIX0093
S_AHR_61011456	IMG Activity: OHIC0114
S_AHR_61011457	IMG Activity: OHIC0116
S_AHR_61011458	IMG Activity: OHIC0117
S_AHR_61011459	IMG Activity: OHIA0087
S_AHR_61011460	IMG Activity: OHIXEXPAT003
S_AHR_61011461	IMG Activity: OHIA0091
S_AHR_61011462	IMG Activity: OHIXEXPAT005
S_AHR_61011463	IMG Activity: OHIA0085
S_AHR_61011464	IMG Activity: OHIXEXPAT006
S_AHR_61011465	IMG Activity: SAPCOHU5UCD
S_AHR_61011466	IMG Activity: OHIC0126
S_AHR_61011467	IMG Activity: OHIA0089
S_AHR_61011468	IMG Activity: OHIA0090
S_AHR_61011469	IMG Activity: OHIA0088
S_AHR_61011470	IMG Activity: OHIXEXPAT001
S_AHR_61011471	IMG Activity: OHIXEXPAT002
S_AHR_61011472	IMG Activity: OHID0099
S_AHR_61011473	IMG Activity: OHIX0099
S_AHR_61011474	IMG Activity: OHIX0106
S_AHR_61011475	IMG Activity: OHIX0107
S_AHR_61011476	IMG Activity: OHIK5K13
S_AHR_61011477	IMG Activity: OHIR5R13
S_AHR_61011478	IMG Activity: OHIX0102
S_AHR_61011479	IMG Activity: OHIX0102B
S_AHR_61011480	IMG Activity: OHIX0103
S_AHR_61011481	IMG Activity: OHIX0101
S_AHR_61011482	IMG Activity: OHIX0113
S_AHR_61011483	IMG Activity: OHID0100
S_AHR_61011484	IMG Activity: OHIU01074
S_AHR_61011485	IMG Activity: OHIU01073
S_AHR_61011486	IMG Activity: OHIUS1080
S_AHR_61011487	IMG Activity: OHIX0094
S_AHR_61011488	IMG Activity: OHIX0008
S_AHR_61011489	IMG Activity: OHIX0108
S_AHR_61011490	IMG Activity: OHIX0105
S_AHR_61011491	IMG Activity: OHIU5U13
S_AHR_61011492	IMG Activity: OHIX0096
S_AHR_61011493	IMG Activity: OHIU01071
S_AHR_61011494	IMG Activity: OHIX0095
S_AHR_61011495	IMG Activity: OHIU01072
S_AHR_61011496	IMG Activity: OHIA0084
S_AHR_61011497	IMG Activity: OHIMVACCODES
S_AHR_61011498	IMG Activity: OHIRN0604
S_AHR_61011499	IMG Activity: OHIMAGRUPPE
S_AHR_61011500	IMG Activity: OHIRID001
S_AHR_61011501	IMG Activity: OHIAROR001
S_AHR_61011502	IMG Activity: OHIAROR002
S_AHR_61011503	IMG Activity: OHIRID002
S_AHR_61011504	IMG Activity: OHIMPBSFIRMA
S_AHR_61011505	IMG Activity: OHIMTAXWPCODE
S_AHR_61011506	IMG Activity: OHIMDAWPCODE
S_AHR_61011507	IMG Activity: OHIMDSWPCODES
S_AHR_61011508	IMG Activity: OHIMPERSTEIL

S_AHR_61011509	IMG Activity: OHIBR_FI004
S_AHR_61011510	IMG Activity: OHIBR_FI005
S_AHR_61011511	IMG Activity: OHIBR_FI026
S_AHR_61011512	IMG Activity: OHIN1771
S_AHR_61011513	IMG Activity: OHIBR_FI006
S_AHR_61011514	IMG Activity: OHIBR_FI007
S_AHR_61011515	IMG Activity: OHIAROR003
S_AHR_61011516	IMG Activity: OHIAROR006
S_AHR_61011517	IMG Activity: OHIRAP003
S_AHR_61011518	IMG Activity: OHIRAP002
S_AHR_61011519	IMG Activity: OHIUSWC1024
S_AHR_61011520	IMG Activity: OHIUSWC1030
S_AHR_61011521	IMG Activity: OHIA0080
S_AHR_61011522	IMG Activity: OHIUSWC1050
S_AHR_61011523	IMG Activity: OHIUSWC1060
S_AHR_61011524	IMG Activity: OHIA0079
S_AHR_61011525	IMG Activity: SAPCOHU5U0P
S_AHR_61011526	IMG Activity: OHIA0083
S_AHR_61011527	IMG Activity: OHIUSWC1010
S_AHR_61011528	IMG Activity: OHIA0082
S_AHR_61011529	IMG Activity: OHIRAN001
S_AHR_61011530	IMG Activity: OHIUSWC1022
S_AHR_61011531	IMG Activity: OHIJ0002
S_AHR_61011532	IMG Activity: OHIPT_PC005
S_AHR_61011533	IMG Activity: OHIPT_PC010
S_AHR_61011534	IMG Activity: OHIMX340
S_AHR_61011535	IMG Activity: OHIIDID010
S_AHR_61011536	IMG Activity: OHIMSEKEY
S_AHR_61011537	IMG Activity: OHIPT_ID005
S_AHR_61011538	IMG Activity: OHIUSWC2010
S_AHR_61011539	IMG Activity: OHIUSWC2020
S_AHR_61011540	IMG Activity: OHIUSWC2030
S_AHR_61011541	IMG Activity: SAPCOHK5K0P
S_AHR_61011542	IMG Activity: OHIK5K0Q
S_AHR_61011543	IMG Activity: SIMGOHIOC0267PT
S_AHR_61011544	IMG Activity: SIMGOHIOC0267ZU
S_AHR_61011545	IMG Activity: OHIX0289B
S_AHR_61011546	IMG Activity: OHIX0289
S_AHR_61011547	IMG Activity: OHIX0023
S_AHR_61011548	IMG Activity: OHIX0013
S_AHR_61011549	IMG Activity: SIMGOHIOC0267LT
S_AHR_61011550	IMG Activity: SIMGOHIOC0267IT
S_AHR_61011551	IMG Activity: SIMGOHIOC0267LE
S_AHR_61011552	IMG Activity: SIMGOHIOC0267MK
S_AHR_61011553	IMG Activity: OHIPT_VA010
S_AHR_61011554	IMG Activity: OHIC0602
S_AHR_61011555	IMG Activity: OHIPT_VA031
S_AHR_61011556	IMG Activity: OHIPT_VA032
S_AHR_61011557	IMG Activity: OHIPT_VA020
S_AHR_61011558	IMG Activity: OHIXCUR00
S_AHR_61011559	IMG Activity: OHIX0287A
S_AHR_61011560	IMG Activity: OHIX0287C
S_AHR_61011561	IMG Activity: OHIX0287D
S_AHR_61011562	IMG Activity: OHIX0289D

S_AHR_61011563	IMG Activity: OHIX0011
S_AHR_61011564	IMG Activity: OHIX0035
S_AHR_61011565	IMG Activity: OHIX0287
S_AHR_61011566	IMG Activity: OHIX0287B
S_AHR_61011567	IMG Activity: OHIX0289G
S_AHR_61011568	IMG Activity: OHIX0289F
S_AHR_61011569	IMG Activity: OHIX0287F
S_AHR_61011570	IMG Activity: OHIX0289A
S_AHR_61011571	IMG Activity: OHIC0051
S_AHR_61011572	IMG Activity: SIMGOHIOC0267LK
S_AHR_61011573	IMG Activity: SIMGOHIOC0267LG
S_AHR_61011574	IMG Activity: OHIC0047
S_AHR_61011575	IMG Activity: OHIC0052
S_AHR_61011576	IMG Activity: OHIX0289C
S_AHR_61011577	IMG Activity: OHIX0287G
S_AHR_61011578	IMG Activity: OHIX0287E
S_AHR_61011579	IMG Activity: OHIX0292
S_AHR_61011580	IMG Activity: OHIX0288
S_AHR_61011581	IMG Activity: OHIX0288B
S_AHR_61011582	IMG Activity: OHIE0028
S_AHR_61011583	IMG Activity: OHIX0288A
S_AHR_61011584	IMG Activity: OHIX0288C
S_AHR_61011585	IMG Activity: OHIPT_CA110
S_AHR_61011586	IMG Activity: OHIPT_CA120
S_AHR_61011587	IMG Activity: OHIXT77S0
S_AHR_61011588	IMG Activity: OHIF0002
S_AHR_61011589	IMG Activity: OHIX0020
S_AHR_61011590	IMG Activity: OHIX0288E
S_AHR_61011591	IMG Activity: OHIPT_TI0021
S_AHR_61011592	IMG Activity: OHIX0305
S_AHR_61011593	IMG Activity: OHIX0021
S_AHR_61011594	IMG Activity: OHIX0306
S_AHR_61011595	IMG Activity: OHIX0288D
S_AHR_61011596	IMG Activity: OHIX0025
S_AHR_61011597	IMG Activity: OHIX0288F
S_AHR_61011598	IMG Activity: OHIX0024
S_AHR_61011599	IMG Activity: OHIX0288G
S_AHR_61011600	IMG Activity: OHIPT_VA120
S_AHR_61011601	IMG Activity: OHIPT_VA130
S_AHR_61011602	IMG Activity: OHIPT_VA140
S_AHR_61011603	IMG Activity: OHIC0601
S_AHR_61011604	IMG Activity: OHIPT_VA033
S_AHR_61011605	IMG Activity: OHIPT_VA040
S_AHR_61011606	IMG Activity: OHIU0604
S_AHR_61011607	IMG Activity: OHIPT_VA110
S_AHR_61011608	IMG Activity: OHIX0242
S_AHR_61011609	IMG Activity: OHIPT_CA010
S_AHR_61011610	IMG Activity: OHIPT_CA032
S_AHR_61011611	IMG Activity: OHIPT_CA033
S_AHR_61011612	IMG Activity: OHIPT_CA040
S_AHR_61011613	IMG Activity: OHIF0003
S_AHR_61011614	IMG Activity: OHICAIT80100
S_AHR_61011615	IMG Activity: OHIPT_CA020
S_AHR_61011616	IMG Activity: OHIZA_IT010

S_AHR_61011617	IMG Activity: OHIPT_CA031
S_AHR_61011618	IMG Activity: OHIBR_DE003
S_AHR_61011619	IMG Activity: OHIBR_DE002
S_AHR_61011620	IMG Activity: OHIPT_LA1A2
S_AHR_61011621	IMG Activity: OHIB0045
S_AHR_61011622	IMG Activity: OHIX0291D
S_AHR_61011623	IMG Activity: OHIX0291E
S_AHR_61011624	IMG Activity: OHIPT_LA105
S_AHR_61011625	IMG Activity: OHIX0291G
S_AHR_61011626	IMG Activity: OHIPT_LA110
S_AHR_61011627	IMG Activity: OHIX0291F
S_AHR_61011628	IMG Activity: OHIHKV_T7HK01
S_AHR_61011629	IMG Activity: OHIBR_VT002
S_AHR_61011630	IMG Activity: OHIX0291C
S_AHR_61011631	IMG Activity: OHID0043
S_AHR_61011632	IMG Activity: OHIN1012
S_AHR_61011633	IMG Activity: OHIPT_LA1A4
S_AHR_61011634	IMG Activity: OHIPT_LA1A6
S_AHR_61011635	IMG Activity: OHIPT_LA130
S_AHR_61011636	IMG Activity: OHIJ0134
S_AHR_61011637	IMG Activity: OHIBR_VT001
S_AHR_61011638	IMG Activity: OHIBR_DE004
S_AHR_61011639	IMG Activity: OHIX0281A
S_AHR_61011640	IMG Activity: OHIU0063
S_AHR_61011641	IMG Activity: OHIJ0058
S_AHR_61011642	IMG Activity: OHIX0061
S_AHR_61011643	IMG Activity: OHIPT_SE105
S_AHR_61011644	IMG Activity: OHAIT_SCA90
S_AHR_61011645	IMG Activity: OHIK0065
S_AHR_61011646	IMG Activity: OHIE0280
S_AHR_61011647	IMG Activity: OHIE0281
S_AHR_61011648	IMG Activity: OHIE0064
S_AHR_61011649	IMG Activity: OHIPT_SE1A4
S_AHR_61011650	IMG Activity: OHIPT_SE1A6
S_AHR_61011651	IMG Activity: OHIPT_SE130
S_AHR_61011652	IMG Activity: OHIPT_SE005
S_AHR_61011653	IMG Activity: OHIX0310
S_AHR_61011654	IMG Activity: OHIPT_SE110
S_AHR_61011655	IMG Activity: OHIX0671
S_AHR_61011656	IMG Activity: OHIPT_SE1A2
S_AHR_61011657	IMG Activity: OHIBR_DE008
S_AHR_61011658	IMG Activity: OHIX0670
S_AHR_61011659	IMG Activity: OHIX0291B
S_AHR_61011660	IMG Activity: OHIA0039
S_AHR_61011661	IMG Activity: OHIX0291
S_AHR_61011662	IMG Activity: OHIX0002
S_AHR_61011663	IMG Activity: OHIX0286J
S_AHR_61011664	IMG Activity: OHIA0041
S_AHR_61011665	IMG Activity: OHIX0286G
S_AHR_61011666	IMG Activity: OHIX0286E
S_AHR_61011667	IMG Activity: OHIX0290
S_AHR_61011668	IMG Activity: OHIA0040
S_AHR_61011669	IMG Activity: OHIX0010
S_AHR_61011670	IMG Activity: OHID0036

S_AHR_61011671	IMG Activity: OHIB0036
S_AHR_61011672	IMG Activity: OHIX0289E
S_AHR_61011673	IMG Activity: OHIX0280E
S_AHR_61011674	IMG Activity: OHIX0286K
S_AHR_61011675	IMG Activity: OHIX0286L
S_AHR_61011676	IMG Activity: OHIX0286M
S_AHR_61011677	IMG Activity: OHIA0037
S_AHR_61011678	IMG Activity: OHIX0001
S_AHR_61011679	IMG Activity: OHIX0286F
S_AHR_61011680	IMG Activity: OHIX0006
S_AHR_61011681	IMG Activity: OHIX0286C
S_AHR_61011682	IMG Activity: OHIX0286
S_AHR_61011683	IMG Activity: OHIX0286B
S_AHR_61011684	IMG Activity: OHIX0286A
S_AHR_61011685	IMG Activity: OHIA0042
S_AHR_61011686	IMG Activity: OHIX0280W
S_AHR_61011687	IMG Activity: OHIX0286D
S_AHR_61011688	IMG Activity: OHIX0291A
S_AHR_61011689	IMG Activity: OHIXLGART001
S_AHR_61011690	IMG Activity: OHIXLGART002
S_AHR_61011691	IMG Activity: OHIX0016
S_AHR_61011692	IMG Activity: SIMGOHIOC_NKI_001
S_AHR_61011693	IMG Activity: OHIX0401
S_AHR_61011694	IMG Activity: OHIA6001
S_AHR_61011766	IMG Activity: OHIX0015
S_AHR_61011783	IMG Activity: OHSXX_210
S_AHR_61011784	IMG Activity: OHSXX_135
S_AHR_61011787	IMG Activity: OHSXX_020
S_AHR_61011788	IMG Activity: OHSXX_245
S_AHR_61011789	IMG Activity: OHSXX_250
S_AHR_61011791	IMG Activity: OHSXX_055
S_AHR_61011792	IMG Activity: OHSXX_075
S_AHR_61011793	IMG Activity: OHSXX_080
S_AHR_61011794	IMG Activity: OHSXX_065
S_AHR_61011795	IMG Activity: OHSXX_050
S_AHR_61011796	IMG Activity: OHSXX_160
S_AHR_61011798	IMG Activity: OHSXX_085
S_AHR_61011823	IMG Activity: SIMG_OHP3OOCE1
S_AHR_61011824	IMG Activity: SIMG_OHP3OOUM
S_AHR_61011825	IMG Activity: SIMG_CFMENUOHP3OOKF
S_AHR_61011826	IMG Activity: SIMG_OHP3OOCA
S_AHR_61011827	IMG Activity: SIMG_OHP3OOCC
S_AHR_61011828	IMG Activity: SIMG_OHP3OOCE
S_AHR_61011829	IMG Activity: SIMG_OHP3OOIL
S_AHR_61011830	IMG Activity: SIMG_CFMENUOHP3OOIL
S_AHR_61011831	IMG Activity: SIMG_OHP3OOCC1
S_AHR_61011832	IMG Activity: SIMG_OHP3OOCE1
S_AHR_61011833	IMG Activity: SIMG_OHP3OOUM
S_AHR_61011834	IMG Activity: SIMG_CFMENUOHP3OOKF
S_AHR_61011835	IMG Activity: SIMG_OHP3OOCA
S_AHR_61011836	IMG Activity: SIMG_OHP3OOCC
S_AHR_61011837	IMG Activity: SIMG_OHP3OOCE
S_AHR_61011838	IMG Activity: SIMG_OHP3OOIL
S_AHR_61011839	IMG Activity: SIMG_CFMENUOHP3OOIL

S_AHR_61011840	IMG Activity: SIMG_OHP3OOCC1
S_AHR_61011841	IMG Activity: SIMG_CFMENUOHP3OOLC
S_AHR_61011842	IMG Activity: SIMG_OHP3OOFA
S_AHR_61011843	IMG Activity: SIMG_CFMENUOHP3OOAZ
S_AHR_61011844	IMG Activity: SIMG_CFMENUOHP3OOTM
S_AHR_61011845	IMG Activity: SIMG_CFMENUOHP3OOKB
S_AHR_61011846	IMG Activity: SIMG_OHP3OOMA
S_AHR_61011847	IMG Activity: SIMG_OHP3RFC
S_AHR_61011848	IMG Activity: SIMG_OHP3OOKB
S_AHR_61011849	IMG Activity: SIMG_OHP3OOSS
S_AHR_61011850	IMG Activity: SIMG_OHP3OOMP
S_AHR_61011851	IMG Activity: SIMG_OHP3MW
S_AHR_61011852	IMG Activity: SIMG_OHP3OOKA
S_AHR_61011853	IMG Activity: SIMG_OHP3OOZS
S_AHR_61011854	IMG Activity: SIMG_OHP3OOZW
S_AHR_61011855	IMG Activity: SIMG_OHP3777IBO
S_AHR_61011856	IMG Activity: SIMG_OHP3779X
S_AHR_61011857	IMG Activity: SIMG_OHP3OOWF
S_AHR_61011858	IMG Activity: SIMG_OHP3OOMG
S_AHR_61011859	IMG Activity: SIMG_OHP3OOSG
S_AHR_61011860	IMG Activity: SIMG_OHP3OOSR
S_AHR_61011861	IMG Activity: SIMG_OHP3OOSE
S_AHR_61011862	IMG Activity: SIMG_OHP3OOSD
S_AHR_61011863	IMG Activity: SIMG_CFMENUOHP3OOFA
S_AHR_61011864	IMG Activity: SIMG_OHP3_2530
S_AHR_61011865	IMG Activity: SIMG_OHP3_2520
S_AHR_61011866	IMG Activity: SIMG_OHP3_2510
S_AHR_61011867	IMG Activity: SIMG_CFMENUOHP3OOFO
S_AHR_61011868	IMG Activity: SIMG_CFMENUOHP3OOTA
S_AHR_61011869	IMG Activity: SIMG_CFMENUOHP3OOKU
S_AHR_61011870	IMG Activity: SIMG_CFMENUOHP3OOVM
S_AHR_61011871	IMG Activity: SIMG_CFMENUOHP3OOVI
S_AHR_61011872	IMG Activity: SIMG_CFMENUOHP3OOVS
S_AHR_61011873	IMG Activity: SIMG_CFMENUOHP3OOAA
S_AHR_61011874	IMG Activity: SIMG_OHP3CAR
S_AHR_61011875	IMG Activity: SIMG_CFMENUOHP3OOVD
S_AHR_61011876	IMG Activity: SIMG_OHP3OOOS
S_AHR_61011877	IMG Activity: SIMG_OHP3OOAW
S_AHR_61011878	IMG Activity: SIMG_CFMENUOHP3OO05
S_AHR_61011879	IMG Activity: SIMG_CFMENUOHP3OONB
S_AHR_61011880	IMG Activity: SIMG_OHP3CR
S_AHR_61011881	IMG Activity: SIMG_CFMENUOHP3OOEF
S_AHR_61011882	IMG Activity: SIMG_CFMENUOHP3OONA
S_AHR_61011883	IMG Activity: SIMG_CFMENUOHP3OOVC
S_AHR_61011884	IMG Activity: SIMG_OHP3OOBD
S_AHR_61011885	IMG Activity: SIMG_CFMENUOHP3OORA
S_AHR_61011886	IMG Activity: SIMG_CFMENUOHP3OORT
S_AHR_61011887	IMG Activity: SIMG_CFMENUOHP3OOC3
S_AHR_61011888	IMG Activity: SIMG_CFMENUOHP3OOET
S_AHR_61011889	IMG Activity: SIMG_CFMENUOHP3OOEG
S_AHR_61011890	IMG Activity: SIMG_CFMENUOHP3OOOU
S_AHR_61011891	IMG Activity: SIMG_CFMENUOHP3OOCP
S_AHR_61011892	IMG Activity: SIMG_OHP3OOPE
S_AHR_61011893	IMG Activity: SIMG_CFMENUOHP3OOER

S_AHR_61011894	IMG Activity: SIMG_OHP3OOEW
S_AHR_61011895	IMG Activity: SIMG_OHP3OOKR
S_AHR_61011896	IMG Activity: SIMG_OHP3OOEV
S_AHR_61011897	IMG Activity: SIMG_OHP3PPTV
S_AHR_61011898	IMG Activity: SIMG_OHP3OOVA
S_AHR_61011899	IMG Activity: SIMG_OHP3OOVW
S_AHR_61011900	IMG Activity: SIMG_CFMENUOHP3PVV0
S_AHR_61011901	IMG Activity: SIMG_CFMENUOHP3OORE
S_AHR_61011902	IMG Activity: SIMG_OHP3OOLA
S_AHR_61011903	IMG Activity: SIMG_OHP3NF
S_AHR_61011904	IMG Activity: SIMG_OHP3OOSF
S_AHR_61011905	IMG Activity: SIMG_OHP3OOLG
S_AHR_61011906	IMG Activity: SIMG_OHP3OOLE
S_AHR_61011907	IMG Activity: SIMG_OHP3OOMT
S_AHR_61011908	IMG Activity: SIMG_OHP3OY05
S_AHR_61011909	IMG Activity: SIMG_OHP3OOOD
S_AHR_61011910	IMG Activity: SIMG_OHP3UU
S_AHR_61011911	IMG Activity: SIMG_OHP3OOSB
S_AHR_61011912	IMG Activity: SIMG_OHP3OOSP
S_AHR_61011913	IMG Activity: SIMG_OHP3OOPR
S_AHR_61011914	IMG Activity: SIMG_OHP3OOAU
S_AHR_61011915	IMG Activity: SIMG_OHP3OOZI
S_AHR_61011916	IMG Activity: SIMG_OHP3OOFK
S_AHR_61011917	IMG Activity: SIMG_OHP3OOTT
S_AHR_61011918	IMG Activity: SIMG_OHP3OOOT
S_AHR_61011919	IMG Activity: SIMG_OHP3OORB
S_AHR_61011920	IMG Activity: SIMG_OHP3OONR
S_AHR_61011921	IMG Activity: SIMG_OHP3OONC
S_AHR_61011922	IMG Activity: SIMG_OHP3OOAP
S_AHR_61011923	IMG Activity: SIMG_OHP3OOPV
S_AHR_61011924	IMG Activity: SIMG_OHP3OOZR
S_AHR_61011925	IMG Activity: SIMG_OHP3OOVK
S_AHR_61011926	IMG Activity: SIMG_OHP3OO2S
S_AHR_61011927	IMG Activity: SIMG_OHP3OOSU
S_AHR_61011928	IMG Activity: SIMG_OHP3NI
S_AHR_61011929	IMG Activity: SIMG_OHP3CD
S_AHR_61011930	IMG Activity: SIMG_OHP3OOIT
S_AHR_61011931	IMG Activity: SIMG_OHP3OOGA
S_AHR_61011932	IMG Activity: SIMG_OHP3OOCR
S_AHR_61011933	IMG Activity: SIMG_OHP3TR
S_AHR_61011934	IMG Activity: SIMG_OHP3OOAD
S_AHR_61011935	IMG Activity: SIMG_OHP3OOPB
S_AHR_61011936	IMG Activity: SIMG_OHP3OODB
S_AHR_61011937	IMG Activity: SIMG_OHP3OOTG
S_AHR_61011938	IMG Activity: SIMG_OHP3OOCH
S_AHR_61011939	IMG Activity: SIMG_OHP3OG00
S_AHR_61011940	IMG Activity: SIMG_OHP3SXDA
S_AHR_61011941	IMG Activity: SIMG_OHP3OOBC
S_AHR_61011942	IMG Activity: SIMG_OHP3T770Q
S_AHR_61011943	IMG Activity: SIMG_OHP3SQ02
S_AHR_61011944	IMG Activity: SIMG_OHP3OOST
S_AHR_61011945	IMG Activity: SIMG_OHP3OOGT
S_AHR_61011946	IMG Activity: SIMG_OHP3OODS
S_AHR_61011947	IMG Activity: SIMG_OHP3MO

S_AHR_61011948	IMG Activity: SIMG_OHP3OOMS
S_AHR_61011976	IMG Activity: OHANSP02
S_AHR_61011977	IMG Activity: OHANSP05
S_AHR_61011978	IMG Activity: OHANSP03
S_AHR_61011979	IMG Activity: OHANSP04
S_AHR_61011980	IMG Activity: OHANAR01
S_AHR_61011981	IMG Activity: OHANAR02
S_AHR_61011982	IMG Activity: OHANAR03
S_AHR_61011983	IMG Activity: OHANAR04
S_AHR_61011984	IMG Activity: OHANBNI02
S_AHR_61011985	IMG Activity: OHAN9030
S_AHR_61011986	IMG Activity: OHAN9001
S_AHR_61011987	IMG Activity: OHANWW02
S_AHR_61011988	IMG Activity: OHANWW03
S_AHR_61011989	IMG Activity: OHANWW04
S_AHR_61011990	IMG Activity: OHANWW05
S_AHR_61011991	IMG Activity: OHANWW06
S_AHR_61011992	IMG Activity: OHANSP07
S_AHR_61011993	IMG Activity: OHANSP06
S_AHR_61011994	IMG Activity: OHANBNI03
S_AHR_61011995	IMG Activity: OHANL_DT002
S_AHR_61011996	IMG Activity: OHANL_DT003
S_AHR_61011997	IMG Activity: OHANL_DT004
S_AHR_61011998	IMG Activity: OHANL_MZ001
S_AHR_61011999	IMG Activity: OHANL_483
S_AHR_61012000	IMG Activity: SIMG_OHANL_416
S_AHR_61012001	IMG Activity: SIMG_OHANL_515
S_AHR_61012002	IMG Activity: SIMG_OHANL_506
S_AHR_61012003	IMG Activity: SIMG_OHANL_507
S_AHR_61012004	IMG Activity: OHANBNI04
S_AHR_61012005	IMG Activity: OHANBN06
S_AHR_61012006	IMG Activity: OHANBN07
S_AHR_61012007	IMG Activity: OHANJW001
S_AHR_61012008	IMG Activity: OHANL_0902
S_AHR_61012009	IMG Activity: OHANL_0911
S_AHR_61012010	IMG Activity: OHANL_0912
S_AHR_61012011	IMG Activity: OHANL_0913
S_AHR_61012012	IMG Activity: OHANL_0903
S_AHR_61012013	IMG Activity: OHAN9051
S_AHR_61012014	IMG Activity: OHAN9035
S_AHR_61012015	IMG Activity: OHAN9031
S_AHR_61012016	IMG Activity: OHAN9033
S_AHR_61012017	IMG Activity: OHAN9032
S_AHR_61012018	IMG Activity: OHAN9041
S_AHR_61012019	IMG Activity: OHAN9042
S_AHR_61012020	IMG Activity: OHAN9002
S_AHR_61012021	IMG Activity: OHAN9009
S_AHR_61012022	IMG Activity: OHANZI10
S_AHR_61012023	IMG Activity: OHANZI11
S_AHR_61012024	IMG Activity: OHANZI14
S_AHR_61012025	IMG Activity: OHANZI12
S_AHR_61012026	IMG Activity: OHANZI16
S_AHR_61012027	IMG Activity: OHANZI17
S_AHR_61012028	IMG Activity: OHAN9059

S_AHR_61012029	IMG Activity: OHAN9014
S_AHR_61012030	IMG Activity: OHAN9050
S_AHR_61012031	IMG Activity: OHAN9012
S_AHR_61012032	IMG Activity: OHAN9019
S_AHR_61012033	IMG Activity: OHAN9020
S_AHR_61012034	IMG Activity: OHAN9021
S_AHR_61012035	IMG Activity: OHAN9023
S_AHR_61012036	IMG Activity: OHAN9025
S_AHR_61012037	IMG Activity: OHAN9026
S_AHR_61012038	IMG Activity: OHAN9028
S_AHR_61012039	IMG Activity: OHAN9029
S_AHR_61012040	IMG Activity: OHAN9043
S_AHR_61012041	IMG Activity: OHAN9003
S_AHR_61012042	IMG Activity: OHAN9004
S_AHR_61012043	IMG Activity: OHAN9031
S_AHR_61012044	IMG Activity: OHAN9008
S_AHR_61012045	IMG Activity: OHAN9005
S_AHR_61012046	IMG Activity: OHAN9015
S_AHR_61012047	IMG Activity: OHAN9016
S_AHR_61012048	IMG Activity: OHAN9017
S_AHR_61012049	IMG Activity: OHAN9018
S_AHR_61012050	IMG Activity: SIMG_OHANL_518
S_AHR_61012051	IMG Activity: SIMG_OHANL_470
S_AHR_61012052	IMG Activity: OHANL_601
S_AHR_61012053	IMG Activity: SIMG_OHANL_615
S_AHR_61012054	IMG Activity: OHAN9205
S_AHR_61012055	IMG Activity: OHAN9211
S_AHR_61012056	IMG Activity: OHAN9212
S_AHR_61012057	IMG Activity: OHANL_RI015
S_AHR_61012058	IMG Activity: OHANL_RI042
S_AHR_61012059	IMG Activity: OHANL_RI031
S_AHR_61012060	IMG Activity: SIMG_OHANL_426
S_AHR_61012061	IMG Activity: SIMG_OHANL_428
S_AHR_61012062	IMG Activity: SIMG_OHANL_459
S_AHR_61012063	IMG Activity: SIMG_OHANL_438
S_AHR_61012064	IMG Activity: SIMG_OHANL_461
S_AHR_61012065	IMG Activity: SIMG_OHANL_429
S_AHR_61012066	IMG Activity: SIMG_OHANL_427
S_AHR_61012067	IMG Activity: SIMG_OHANL_424
S_AHR_61012068	IMG Activity: SIMG_OHANL_467
S_AHR_61012069	IMG Activity: OHANL_RI051
S_AHR_61012070	IMG Activity: OHANL_RI071
S_AHR_61012071	IMG Activity: OHANL_RI080
S_AHR_61012072	IMG Activity: OHANL_RI081
S_AHR_61012073	IMG Activity: OHANL_RI090
S_AHR_61012074	IMG Activity: OHANL_UM002
S_AHR_61012075	IMG Activity: OHANL_UM003
S_AHR_61012076	IMG Activity: OHANUM05
S_AHR_61012077	IMG Activity: OHANL_PAY002
S_AHR_61012078	IMG Activity: OHANL_PAY003
S_AHR_61012079	IMG Activity: OHANL_RI052
S_AHR_61012080	IMG Activity: OHANL_RI056
S_AHR_61012081	IMG Activity: OHANL_RI053
S_AHR_61012082	IMG Activity: OHANL_RI054

S_AHR_61012083	IMG Activity: OHANL_RI055
S_AHR_61012084	IMG Activity: OHANL_RI061
S_AHR_61012085	IMG Activity: OHANL_RI062
S_AHR_61012086	IMG Activity: OHANL_RI063
S_AHR_61012087	IMG Activity: OHANL_RI070
S_AHR_61012088	IMG Activity: SIMG_OHANL_529
S_AHR_61012089	IMG Activity: SIMG_OHANL_409
S_AHR_61012090	IMG Activity: SIMG_OHANL_407
S_AHR_61012091	IMG Activity: SIMG_OHANL_482
S_AHR_61012092	IMG Activity: SIMG_OHANL_410
S_AHR_61012093	IMG Activity: SIMG_OHANL_417
S_AHR_61012094	IMG Activity: SIMG_OHANL_413
S_AHR_61012095	IMG Activity: SIMG_OHANL_480
S_AHR_61012096	IMG Activity: SIMG_OHANL_414
S_AHR_61012097	IMG Activity: SIMG_OHANL_530
S_AHR_61012098	IMG Activity: SIMG_OHANL_525
S_AHR_61012099	IMG Activity: SIMG_OHANL_402
S_AHR_61012100	IMG Activity: SIMG_OHANL_403
S_AHR_61012101	IMG Activity: SIMG_OHANL_405
S_AHR_61012102	IMG Activity: SIMG_OHANL_406
S_AHR_61012103	IMG Activity: SIMG_OHANL_408
S_AHR_61012104	IMG Activity: SIMG_OHANL_527
S_AHR_61012105	IMG Activity: SIMG_OHANL_528
S_AHR_61012106	IMG Activity: SIMG_OHANL_814
S_AHR_61012107	IMG Activity: SIMG_OHANL_463
S_AHR_61012108	IMG Activity: SIMG_OHANL_464
S_AHR_61012109	IMG Activity: SIMG_OHANL_471
S_AHR_61012110	IMG Activity: SIMG_OHANL_435
S_AHR_61012111	IMG Activity: SIMG_OHANL_422
S_AHR_61012112	IMG Activity: SIMG_OHANL_423
S_AHR_61012113	IMG Activity: SIMG_OHANL_425
S_AHR_61012114	IMG Activity: SIMG_OHANL_437
S_AHR_61012115	IMG Activity: SIMG_OHANL_432
S_AHR_61012116	IMG Activity: SIMG_OHANL_415
S_AHR_61012117	IMG Activity: SIMG_OHANL_418
S_AHR_61012118	IMG Activity: SIMG_OHANL_419
S_AHR_61012119	IMG Activity: SIMG_OHANL_483
S_AHR_61012120	IMG Activity: SIMG_OHANL_484
S_AHR_61012121	IMG Activity: OHANL_EDTINTERNET
S_AHR_61012122	IMG Activity: SIMG_OHANL_431
S_AHR_61012123	IMG Activity: SIMG_OHANL_457
S_AHR_61012124	IMG Activity: SIMG_OHANL_451
S_AHR_61012125	IMG Activity: OHANL_TI361
S_AHR_61012126	IMG Activity: OHANL_TI363
S_AHR_61012127	IMG Activity: OHANL_TI362
S_AHR_61012128	IMG Activity: OHANL_TI364
S_AHR_61012129	IMG Activity: OHANL_TI370
S_AHR_61012130	IMG Activity: OHANL_AB001
S_AHR_61012131	IMG Activity: OHANL_AB002
S_AHR_61012132	IMG Activity: OHANL_AB003
S_AHR_61012133	IMG Activity: OHANTI210
S_AHR_61012134	IMG Activity: OHANL_TI310
S_AHR_61012135	IMG Activity: OHANL_TI325
S_AHR_61012136	IMG Activity: OHANL_TI321

S_AHR_61012137	IMG Activity: OHANL_TI322
S_AHR_61012138	IMG Activity: OHANL_TI323
S_AHR_61012139	IMG Activity: OHANL_TI324
S_AHR_61012140	IMG Activity: OHANL_TI340
S_AHR_61012141	IMG Activity: OHANL_AB004
S_AHR_61012142	IMG Activity: OHANL_BW005
S_AHR_61012143	IMG Activity: OHANBW01
S_AHR_61012144	IMG Activity: OHANL_BW019
S_AHR_61012145	IMG Activity: OHANL_AV001
S_AHR_61012146	IMG Activity: OHANL_AVBAS
S_AHR_61012147	IMG Activity: OHANL_AVX017
S_AHR_61012148	IMG Activity: OHANL_AVX018
S_AHR_61012149	IMG Activity: OHANL_AV511A
S_AHR_61012150	IMG Activity: OHANL_AB005
S_AHR_61012151	IMG Activity: OHANL_AB011
S_AHR_61012152	IMG Activity: OHANL_AB009
S_AHR_61012153	IMG Activity: OHANL_AB012
S_AHR_61012154	IMG Activity: OHANL_AB010
S_AHR_61012155	IMG Activity: OHANAB001
S_AHR_61012156	IMG Activity: OHANWE011
S_AHR_61012157	IMG Activity: OHANBW004
S_AHR_61012158	IMG Activity: OHANL_TI130
S_AHR_61012159	IMG Activity: OHANL_UM012
S_AHR_61012160	IMG Activity: OHANL_UM014
S_AHR_61012161	IMG Activity: OHANL_UM006
S_AHR_61012162	IMG Activity: OHANL_UM008
S_AHR_61012163	IMG Activity: OHANUM010B
S_AHR_61012164	IMG Activity: OHANL_UM013
S_AHR_61012165	IMG Activity: OHANL_UM010
S_AHR_61012166	IMG Activity: OHANUM02
S_AHR_61012167	IMG Activity: OHIN0497
S_AHR_61012168	IMG Activity: OHIN0498
S_AHR_61012169	IMG Activity: OHIN0499
S_AHR_61012170	IMG Activity: OHANDL022
S_AHR_61012171	IMG Activity: OHANDL021
S_AHR_61012172	IMG Activity: OHANUM061
S_AHR_61012173	IMG Activity: OHANUM062
S_AHR_61012174	IMG Activity: OHANUM063
S_AHR_61012175	IMG Activity: OHANUI01
S_AHR_61012176	IMG Activity: OHANUM03
S_AHR_61012177	IMG Activity: OHANUM04
S_AHR_61012178	IMG Activity: OHANL_UM022
S_AHR_61012179	IMG Activity: OHANL_UM023
S_AHR_61012180	IMG Activity: OHANL_UM104
S_AHR_61012181	IMG Activity: OHANL_UM105
S_AHR_61012182	IMG Activity: OHANL_TI110
S_AHR_61012183	IMG Activity: OHANL_TI120
S_AHR_61012184	IMG Activity: OHIN0350
S_AHR_61012185	IMG Activity: OHANUI04
S_AHR_61012186	IMG Activity: OHANUM010
S_AHR_61012187	IMG Activity: OHANUI02
S_AHR_61012188	IMG Activity: OHANUI03
S_AHR_61012189	IMG Activity: OHIN0431
S_AHR_61012190	IMG Activity: OHANUM011

S_AHR_61012191	IMG Activity: OHANUM09
S_AHR_61012192	IMG Activity: OHANL_AV511B
S_AHR_61012193	IMG Activity: OHAN9091
S_AHR_61012194	IMG Activity: OHAN90512
S_AHR_61012195	IMG Activity: OHAN90514
S_AHR_61012196	IMG Activity: OHANL_SL003
S_AHR_61012197	IMG Activity: OHAN9092
S_AHR_61012198	IMG Activity: OHAN90513
S_AHR_61012199	IMG Activity: OHANZI03
S_AHR_61012200	IMG Activity: OHANL_IW063
S_AHR_61012201	IMG Activity: OHANUM08
S_AHR_61012202	IMG Activity: OHANZI02
S_AHR_61012203	IMG Activity: OHANZI01
S_AHR_61012204	IMG Activity: OHANL_PART
S_AHR_61012205	IMG Activity: OHAN9011
S_AHR_61012206	IMG Activity: OHANL_KL000
S_AHR_61012207	IMG Activity: OHANL_KF002
S_AHR_61012208	IMG Activity: OHAN9010
S_AHR_61012209	IMG Activity: OHANKF02
S_AHR_61012210	IMG Activity: OHANKF01
S_AHR_61012211	IMG Activity: OHANL_SL002
S_AHR_61012212	IMG Activity: OHANL_SL001
S_AHR_61012213	IMG Activity: OHAN90641
S_AHR_61012214	IMG Activity: OHAN9007
S_AHR_61012215	IMG Activity: OHAN90631
S_AHR_61012216	IMG Activity: OHANZI07
S_AHR_61012217	IMG Activity: OHANL_BW21
S_AHR_61012218	IMG Activity: OHANL_BW22
S_AHR_61012219	IMG Activity: OHANBW020
S_AHR_61012220	IMG Activity: OHANZI06
S_AHR_61012221	IMG Activity: OHANL_AV511C
S_AHR_61012222	IMG Activity: OHANL_IW037
S_AHR_61012223	IMG Activity: OHANAVXT00
S_AHR_61012224	IMG Activity: OHANAVP15
S_AHR_61012225	IMG Activity: OHANZI09
S_AHR_61012226	IMG Activity: OHANZI05
S_AHR_61012227	IMG Activity: OHANZI04
S_AHR_61012228	IMG Activity: OHANL_IW065
S_AHR_61012229	IMG Activity: OHANL_IW061
S_AHR_61012230	IMG Activity: OHANL_IW082
S_AHR_61012231	IMG Activity: OHANL_DV001
S_AHR_61012249	IMG-Aktivität: OHAIE_0102
S_AHR_61012250	IMG-Aktivität: OHAIE_0101
S_AHR_61012251	IMG-Aktivität: OHAIE_0104
S_AHR_61012252	IMG-Aktivität: OHAIE_TI370
S_AHR_61012253	IMG-Aktivität: OHAIE_TI364
S_AHR_61012254	IMG-Aktivität: OHAIE_TI362
S_AHR_61012255	IMG-Aktivität: OHAIE_TI363
S_AHR_61012256	IMG-Aktivität: OHAIE_PEN
S_AHR_61012257	IMG-Aktivität: OHAIE_0112
S_AHR_61012258	IMG-Aktivität: OHAIE_0111
S_AHR_61012259	IMG-Aktivität: OHAIE_0113
S_AHR_61012260	IMG-Aktivität: OHAIE_ERA
S_AHR_61012261	IMG-Aktivität: OHAIE_BP005

S_AHR_61012262	IMG-Aktivität: OHAIEPEN3
S_AHR_61012263	IMG-Aktivität: OHAIE_PENP
S_AHR_61012264	IMG-Aktivität: OHAIE_TI310
S_AHR_61012265	IMG-Aktivität: OHAIE_TI210
S_AHR_61012266	IMG-Aktivität: OHAIE_TI130
S_AHR_61012267	IMG-Aktivität: OHAIE_TI120
S_AHR_61012268	IMG-Aktivität: OHAIE_TI110
S_AHR_61012269	IMG-Aktivität: OHAIE_AB010
S_AHR_61012270	IMG-Aktivität: OHAIE_AB012
S_AHR_61012271	IMG-Aktivität: OHAIE_TI325
S_AHR_61012272	IMG-Aktivität: OHAIE_TI361
S_AHR_61012273	IMG-Aktivität: OHAIE_TI340
S_AHR_61012274	IMG-Aktivität: OHAIE_PAY002
S_AHR_61012275	IMG-Aktivität: OHAIE_TI324
S_AHR_61012276	IMG-Aktivität: OHAIE_TI323
S_AHR_61012277	IMG-Aktivität: OHAIE_TI322
S_AHR_61012278	IMG-Aktivität: OHAIE_TI321
S_AHR_61012279	IMG-Aktivität: OHAIE_VHI
S_AHR_61012280	IMG-Aktivität: OHAIE_RI055
S_AHR_61012281	IMG-Aktivität: OHAIE_RI054
S_AHR_61012282	IMG-Aktivität: OHAIE_RI053
S_AHR_61012283	IMG-Aktivität: OHAIE_RI056
S_AHR_61012284	IMG-Aktivität: OHAIE_RI052
S_AHR_61012285	IMG-Aktivität: OHAIE_RI051
S_AHR_61012286	IMG-Aktivität: OHAIE_RI031
S_AHR_61012287	IMG-Aktivität: OHAIE_RI061
S_AHR_61012288	IMG-Aktivität: OHAIE_UM002
S_AHR_61012289	IMG-Aktivität: OHAIE_RI090
S_AHR_61012290	IMG-Aktivität: OHAIE_RI080
S_AHR_61012291	IMG-Aktivität: OHAIE_RI071
S_AHR_61012292	IMG-Aktivität: OHAIE_RI070
S_AHR_61012293	IMG-Aktivität: OHAIE_RI063
S_AHR_61012294	IMG-Aktivität: OHAIE_RI062
S_AHR_61012295	IMG-Aktivität: OHAIE_DT003
S_AHR_61012296	IMG-Aktivität: OHAIE_DT002
S_AHR_61012297	IMG-Aktivität: OHAIE_OFF110
S_AHR_61012298	IMG-Aktivität: OHAIE_DD100
S_AHR_61012299	IMG-Aktivität: OHAIE_LN100
S_AHR_61012300	IMG-Aktivität: OHAIE_NT100
S_AHR_61012301	IMG-Aktivität: OHAIE_CM100
S_AHR_61012302	IMG-Aktivität: OHAIE_DT004
S_AHR_61012303	IMG-Aktivität: OHAIE_RI042
S_AHR_61012304	IMG-Aktivität: OHAIE_RI015
S_AHR_61012305	IMG-Aktivität: OHAIE_UM003
S_AHR_61012306	IMG-Aktivität: SIMG_OHAIE_615
S_AHR_61012307	IMG-Aktivität: SIMG_OHAIE_457
S_AHR_61012308	IMG-Aktivität: SIMG_OHAIE_515
S_AHR_61012309	IMG-Aktivität: OHAIE_MZ001
S_AHR_61012310	IMG-Aktivität: OHAIE_AB009
S_AHR_61012311	IMG-Aktivität: OHAIE_AVP15
S_AHR_61012312	IMG-Aktivität: OHAIE_AVXT00
S_AHR_61012313	IMG-Aktivität: OHAIE_UM101
S_AHR_61012314	IMG-Aktivität: OHAIE_AV511C
S_AHR_61012315	IMG-Aktivität: OHAIE_AV511B

S_AHR_61012316	IMG-Aktivität: OHAIE_AV511A
S_AHR_61012317	IMG-Aktivität: OHAIE_PART
S_AHR_61012318	IMG-Aktivität: OHAIE_PAY003
S_AHR_61012319	IMG-Aktivität: OHAIE_BW22
S_AHR_61012320	IMG-Aktivität: OHAIE_BW21
S_AHR_61012321	IMG-Aktivität: OHAIE_UM022
S_AHR_61012322	IMG-Aktivität: OHAIE_UM023
S_AHR_61012323	IMG-Aktivität: OHAIE_BW019
S_AHR_61012324	IMG-Aktivität: OHAIE_BW006
S_AHR_61012325	IMG-Aktivität: OHAIE_BW005
S_AHR_61012326	IMG-Aktivität: OHAIE_BW004
S_AHR_61012327	IMG-Aktivität: OHAIE_UM104
S_AHR_61012328	IMG-Aktivität: OHAIE_UM105
S_AHR_61012329	IMG-Aktivität: OHAIE_AVX018
S_AHR_61012330	IMG-Aktivität: OHAIE_UM102
S_AHR_61012331	IMG-Aktivität: OHAIE_AVX017
S_AHR_61012332	IMG-Aktivität: OHAIE_AVBAS
S_AHR_61012333	IMG-Aktivität: OHAIE_AV001
S_AHR_61012334	IMG-Aktivität: OHAIE_UM103
S_AHR_61012335	IMG-Aktivität: OHAIE_UM013
S_AHR_61012336	IMG-Aktivität: OHAIE_UM014
S_AHR_61012337	IMG-Aktivität: OHAIE_DBC
S_AHR_61012338	IMG-Aktivität: OHAIE_UM006
S_AHR_61012339	IMG-Aktivität: OHAIE_GRSP
S_AHR_61012340	IMG-Aktivität: OHAIE_UM008
S_AHR_61012341	IMG-Aktivität: OHAIE_UM012
S_AHR_61012342	IMG-Aktivität: OHAIE_AB011
S_AHR_61012343	IMG-Aktivität: OHAIE_AB005
S_AHR_61012344	IMG-Aktivität: OHAIE_AB003
S_AHR_61012345	IMG-Aktivität: OHAIE_AB002
S_AHR_61012346	IMG-Aktivität: OHAIE_AB001
S_AHR_61012347	IMG-Aktivität: OHAIE_KF001
S_AHR_61012348	IMG-Aktivität: OHAIE_KL000
S_AHR_61012349	IMG-Aktivität: OHAIE_KF002
S_AHR_61012350	IMG-Aktivität: OHAIE_SL001
S_AHR_61012351	IMG-Aktivität: OHAIE_UM009
S_AHR_61012352	IMG-Aktivität: OHAIE_AVL
S_AHR_61012353	IMG-Aktivität: OHAIE_SL002
S_AHR_61012354	IMG-Aktivität: OHAIE_SL003
S_AHR_61012355	IMG-Aktivität: OHAIE_RI012
S_AHR_61012356	IMG-Aktivität: OHAIE_RI011
S_AHR_61012357	IMG-Aktivität: OHAIE_TI330
S_AHR_61012358	IMG-Aktivität: OHAIE_AL01
S_AHR_61012360	IMG-Aktivität: OHAIE_0101
S_AHR_61012361	IMG-Aktivität: OHAIE_0104
S_AHR_61012362	IMG-Aktivität: OHAIE_TI370
S_AHR_61012363	IMG-Aktivität: OHAIE_TI364
S_AHR_61012364	IMG-Aktivität: OHAIE_TI362
S_AHR_61012365	IMG-Aktivität: OHAIE_TI363
S_AHR_61012366	IMG-Aktivität: OHAIE_PEN
S_AHR_61012367	IMG-Aktivität: OHAIE_0112
S_AHR_61012368	IMG-Aktivität: OHAIE_0111
S_AHR_61012369	IMG-Aktivität: OHAIE_0113
S_AHR_61012373	IMG-Aktivität: OHAIE_PENP

S_AHR_61012374	IMG-Aktivität: OHAIE_TI310
S_AHR_61012375	IMG-Aktivität: OHAIE_TI210
S_AHR_61012376	IMG-Aktivität: OHAIE_TI130
S_AHR_61012377	IMG-Aktivität: OHAIE_TI120
S_AHR_61012378	IMG-Aktivität: OHAIE_TI110
S_AHR_61012379	IMG-Aktivität: OHAIE_AB010
S_AHR_61012380	IMG-Aktivität: OHAIE_AB012
S_AHR_61012381	IMG-Aktivität: OHAIE_TI325
S_AHR_61012382	IMG-Aktivität: OHAIE_TI361
S_AHR_61012383	IMG-Aktivität: OHAIE_TI340
S_AHR_61012384	IMG-Aktivität: OHAIE_PAY002
S_AHR_61012385	IMG-Aktivität: OHAIE_TI324
S_AHR_61012386	IMG-Aktivität: OHAIE_TI323
S_AHR_61012387	IMG-Aktivität: OHAIE_TI322
S_AHR_61012388	IMG-Aktivität: OHAIE_TI321
S_AHR_61012390	IMG-Aktivität: OHAIE_RI055
S_AHR_61012391	IMG-Aktivität: OHAIE_RI054
S_AHR_61012392	IMG-Aktivität: OHAIE_RI053
S_AHR_61012393	IMG-Aktivität: OHAIE_RI056
S_AHR_61012394	IMG-Aktivität: OHAIE_RI052
S_AHR_61012395	IMG-Aktivität: OHAIE_RI051
S_AHR_61012396	IMG-Aktivität: OHAIE_RI031
S_AHR_61012397	IMG-Aktivität: OHAIE_RI061
S_AHR_61012398	IMG-Aktivität: OHAIE_UM002
S_AHR_61012399	IMG-Aktivität: OHAIE_RI090
S_AHR_61012400	IMG-Aktivität: OHAIE_RI080
S_AHR_61012401	IMG-Aktivität: OHAIE_RI071
S_AHR_61012402	IMG-Aktivität: OHAIE_RI070
S_AHR_61012403	IMG-Aktivität: OHAIE_RI063
S_AHR_61012404	IMG-Aktivität: OHAIE_RI062
S_AHR_61012405	IMG-Aktivität: OHAIE_DT003
S_AHR_61012406	IMG-Aktivität: OHAIE_DT002
S_AHR_61012407	IMG-Aktivität: OHAIE_OFF110
S_AHR_61012409	IMG-Aktivität: OHAIE_LN100
S_AHR_61012412	IMG-Aktivität: OHAIE_DT004
S_AHR_61012413	IMG-Aktivität: OHAIE_RI042
S_AHR_61012414	IMG-Aktivität: OHAIE_RI015
S_AHR_61012415	IMG-Aktivität: OHAIE_UM003
S_AHR_61012416	IMG-Aktivität: SIMG_OHAIE_615
S_AHR_61012417	IMG-Aktivität: SIMG_OHAIE_457
S_AHR_61012418	IMG-Aktivität: SIMG_OHAIE_515
S_AHR_61012419	IMG-Aktivität: OHAIE_MZ001
S_AHR_61012420	IMG-Aktivität: OHAIE_AB009
S_AHR_61012421	IMG-Aktivität: OHAIE_AVP15
S_AHR_61012422	IMG-Aktivität: OHAIE_AVXT00
S_AHR_61012423	IMG-Aktivität: OHAIE_UM101
S_AHR_61012424	IMG-Aktivität: OHAIE_AV511C
S_AHR_61012425	IMG-Aktivität: OHAIE_AV511B
S_AHR_61012426	IMG-Aktivität: OHAIE_AV511A
S_AHR_61012427	IMG-Aktivität: OHAIE_PART
S_AHR_61012428	IMG-Aktivität: OHAIE_PAY003
S_AHR_61012429	IMG-Aktivität: OHAIE_BW22
S_AHR_61012430	IMG-Aktivität: OHAIE_BW21
S_AHR_61012431	IMG-Aktivität: OHAIE_UM022

S_AHR_61012432	IMG-Aktivität: OHAIE_UM023
S_AHR_61012434	IMG-Aktivität: OHAIE_BW006
S_AHR_61012436	IMG-Aktivität: OHAIE_BW004
S_AHR_61012437	IMG-Aktivität: OHAIE_UM104
S_AHR_61012438	IMG-Aktivität: OHAIE_UM105
S_AHR_61012439	IMG-Aktivität: OHAIE_AVX018
S_AHR_61012440	IMG-Aktivität: OHAIE_UM102
S_AHR_61012441	IMG-Aktivität: OHAIE_AVX017
S_AHR_61012442	IMG-Aktivität: OHAIE_AVBAS
S_AHR_61012443	IMG-Aktivität: OHAIE_AV001
S_AHR_61012444	IMG-Aktivität: OHAIE_UM103
S_AHR_61012445	IMG-Aktivität: OHAIE_UM013
S_AHR_61012446	IMG-Aktivität: OHAIE_UM014
S_AHR_61012447	IMG-Aktivität: OHAIE_DBC
S_AHR_61012448	IMG-Aktivität: OHAIE_UM006
S_AHR_61012450	IMG-Aktivität: OHAIE_UM008
S_AHR_61012451	IMG-Aktivität: OHAIE_UM012
S_AHR_61012452	IMG-Aktivität: OHAIE_AB011
S_AHR_61012453	IMG-Aktivität: OHAIE_AB005
S_AHR_61012454	IMG-Aktivität: OHAIE_AB003
S_AHR_61012455	IMG-Aktivität: OHAIE_AB002
S_AHR_61012456	IMG-Aktivität: OHAIE_AB001
S_AHR_61012457	IMG-Aktivität: OHAIE_KF001
S_AHR_61012458	IMG-Aktivität: OHAIE_KL000
S_AHR_61012459	IMG-Aktivität: OHAIE_KF002
S_AHR_61012460	IMG-Aktivität: OHAIE_SL001
S_AHR_61012461	IMG-Aktivität: OHAIE_UM009
S_AHR_61012462	IMG-Aktivität: OHAIE_AVL
S_AHR_61012463	IMG-Aktivität: OHAIE_SL002
S_AHR_61012464	IMG-Aktivität: OHAIE_SL003
S_AHR_61012465	IMG-Aktivität: OHAIE_RI012
S_AHR_61012466	IMG-Aktivität: OHAIE_RI011
S_AHR_61012467	IMG-Aktivität: OHAIE_TI330
S_AHR_61012468	IMG-Aktivität: OHAIE_AL01
S_AHR_61012471	IMG-Aktivität: OHAIEPEN
S_AHR_61012472	IMG-Aktivität: OHAIE_PRSIC
S_AHR_61012473	IMG-Aktivität: OHAIE_CUMPER
S_AHR_61012474	IMG-Aktivität: OHAIE_WTCUMS
S_AHR_61012475	IMG-Aktivität: OHAIE_CUMCAL
S_AHR_61012476	IMG-Aktivität: OHAIE_ERN1
S_AHR_61012477	IMG-Aktivität: OHAIE_ERN
S_AHR_61012478	IMG-Aktivität: OHAIEPEN2
S_AHR_61012479	IMG-Aktivität: OHAGUM003
S_AHR_61012480	IMG-Aktivität: OHAIEAHP
S_AHR_61012481	IMG-Aktivität: OHAIE_AHP2
S_AHR_61012482	IMG-Aktivität: OHAIE_AHP1
S_AHR_61012483	IMG-Aktivität: SIMG_OHAG665
S_AHR_61012484	IMG-Aktivität: OHAIE_AV_ABCR
S_AHR_61012485	IMG-Aktivität: OHAIE_AV_2W
S_AHR_61012486	IMG-Aktivität: OHAIE_AV_1
S_AHR_61012487	IMG-Aktivität: OHAIEAVB
S_AHR_61012488	IMG-Aktivität: OHAIEPRBA
S_AHR_61012489	IMG-Aktivität: OHAIECVBC
S_AHR_61012490	IMG-Aktivität: OHAIECVBB

S_AHR_61012491	IMG-Aktivität: OHAIE_AV_P
S_AHR_61012492	IMG-Aktivität: OHAIE_UM010
S_AHR_61012493	IMG-Aktivität: OHAIE_FT009
S_AHR_61012494	IMG-Aktivität: OHA_IEGRS
S_AHR_61012495	IMG-Aktivität: OHAIE_BTS
S_AHR_61012496	IMG-Aktivität: OHAIE_JW000
S_AHR_61012509	IMG
S_AHR_61012517	IMG Activity: OHADBAV380AA
S_AHR_61012518	IMG Activity: OHADBAV360BAA
S_AHR_61012519	IMG Activity: OHADBAV350BAA
S_AHR_61012520	IMG Activity: OHADBAV340BAA
S_AHR_61012521	IMG Activity: OHADBAV330BAA
S_AHR_61012522	IMG Activity: OHADBAV320BAA
S_AHR_61012523	IMG Activity: OHADBAV302B
S_AHR_61012524	IMG Activity: OHADBAV305B
S_AHR_61012525	IMG Activity: OHADBAV380AC
S_AHR_61012526	IMG Activity: OHADBAV730
S_AHR_61012527	IMG Activity: OHADBAV716
S_AHR_61012528	IMG Activity: OHADBAV714
S_AHR_61012529	IMG Activity: OHADBAV710
S_AHR_61012530	IMG Activity: OHADBAV750
S_AHR_61012531	IMG Activity: OHADBAV740
S_AHR_61012532	IMG Activity: OHADBAV450
S_AHR_61012533	IMG Activity: OHADBAV390A
S_AHR_61012534	IMG Activity: OHADBAV390AB
S_AHR_61012535	IMG Activity: OHADBAV395AB
S_AHR_61012536	IMG Activity: OHADBAV320AE
S_AHR_61012537	IMG Activity: OHADBAV395A
S_AHR_61012538	IMG Activity: OHADBAV210ABC
S_AHR_61012539	IMG Activity: OHADBAV310AD
S_AHR_61012540	IMG Activity: OHADBAV320ABA
S_AHR_61012541	IMG Activity: OHADBAV310ABA
S_AHR_61012543	IMG Activity: OHADBAV310B
S_AHR_61012544	IMG Activity: OHADBAV320AC
S_AHR_61012545	IMG Activity: OHADBAV310AC
S_AHR_61012546	IMG Activity: OHADBAV395A
S_AHR_61012547	IMG Activity: OHADBAV210ABC
S_AHR_61012548	IMG Activity: OHADBAV320ABA
S_AHR_61012549	IMG Activity: OHADBAV310ABA
S_AHR_61012550	IMG Activity: OHADBAV397AB
S_AHR_61012551	IMG Activity: OHADBAV350B
S_AHR_61012552	IMG Activity: OHADBAV840
S_AHR_61012553	IMG Activity: OHADBAV830
S_AHR_61012554	IMG Activity: OHADBAV650
S_AHR_61012555	IMG Activity: OHADBAV630
S_AHR_61012556	IMG Activity: OHADBAV620
S_AHR_61012557	IMG Activity: OHADBAV610
S_AHR_61012558	IMG Activity: OHADBAV608
S_AHR_61012559	IMG Activity: OHADBAV607
S_AHR_61012560	IMG Activity: OHADBAV340A
S_AHR_61012561	IMG Activity: OHADBAV355B
S_AHR_61012562	IMG Activity: OHADBAV375A
S_AHR_61012563	IMG Activity: OHADBAV1010D
S_AHR_61012564	IMG Activity: OHADBAV340B

S_AHR_61012565	IMG Activity: OHADBAV330B
S_AHR_61012566	IMG Activity: OHADBAV360A
S_AHR_61012567	IMG Activity: OHADBAV1010A
S_AHR_61012568	IMG Activity: OHADBAV315B
S_AHR_61012569	IMG Activity: OHADBAV350AE
S_AHR_61012570	IMG Activity: OHADBAV340AE
S_AHR_61012571	IMG Activity: OHADBAV330AE
S_AHR_61012572	IMG Activity: OHADBAV320AE
S_AHR_61012573	IMG Activity: OHADBAV310AE
S_AHR_61012574	IMG Activity: OHADBAV320AEA
S_AHR_61012575	IMG Activity: OHADBAV310AEA
S_AHR_61012576	IMG Activity: OHADBAV720
S_AHR_61012577	IMG Activity: OHADBAV360AE
S_AHR_61012578	IMG Activity: OHADBAV520
S_AHR_61012579	IMG Activity: OHADBAV510
S_AHR_61012580	IMG Activity: OHADBAV505
S_AHR_61012581	IMG Activity: OHADBAV020C
S_AHR_61012582	IMG Activity: OHADBAV010C
S_AHR_61012583	IMG Activity: OHADBAV030C
S_AHR_61012584	IMG Activity: OHADBAV040C
S_AHR_61012585	IMG Activity: OHADBAV370AE
S_AHR_61012586	IMG Activity: OHADBAV340AB
S_AHR_61012587	IMG Activity: OHADBAV311AB
S_AHR_61012588	IMG Activity: OHADBAV440
S_AHR_61012589	IMG Activity: OHADBAV310A
S_AHR_61012590	IMG Activity: OHADBAV420
S_AHR_61012591	IMG Activity: OHADBAV140
S_AHR_61012592	IMG Activity: OHADBAV120
S_AHR_61012593	IMG Activity: OHADBAV220A
S_AHR_61012594	IMG Activity: OHADBAV320A
S_AHR_61012595	IMG Activity: OHADBAV370AB
S_AHR_61012596	IMG Activity: OHADBAV335AB
S_AHR_61012597	IMG Activity: OHADBAV330AB
S_AHR_61012598	IMG Activity: OHADBAV330AA
S_AHR_61012599	IMG Activity: OHADBAV320AA
S_AHR_61012600	IMG Activity: OHADBAV310AA
S_AHR_61012601	IMG Activity: OHADBAV350A
S_AHR_61012602	IMG Activity: OHADBAV210A
S_AHR_61012603	IMG Activity: OHADBAV050A
S_AHR_61012604	IMG Activity: OHADBAV040A
S_AHR_61012605	IMG Activity: OHADBAV030A
S_AHR_61012606	IMG Activity: OHADBAV020A
S_AHR_61012607	IMG Activity: OHADBAV010A
S_AHR_61012608	IMG Activity: OHADBAV040
S_AHR_61012609	IMG Activity: OHADBAV030
S_AHR_61012610	IMG Activity: OHADBAV060A
S_AHR_61012611	IMG Activity: OHADBAV220
S_AHR_61012612	IMG Activity: OHADBAV210
S_AHR_61012613	IMG Activity: OHADBAV030B
S_AHR_61012614	IMG Activity: OHADBAV020B
S_AHR_61012615	IMG Activity: OHADBAV010B
S_AHR_61012616	IMG Activity: OHADBAV080A
S_AHR_61012617	IMG Activity: OHADBAV070A
S_AHR_61012618	IMG Activity: OHADBAV210ABC

S_AHR_61012619	IMG Activity: OHADBAV395A
S_AHR_61012620	IMG Activity: OHADBAV395A
S_AHR_61012621	IMG Activity: OHADBAV350AB
S_AHR_61012622	IMG Activity: OHADBAV310ABA
S_AHR_61012623	IMG Activity: OHADBAV360AB
S_AHR_61012624	IMG Activity: OHADBAV320ABA
S_AHR_61012625	IMG Activity: OHADBAV310ABA
S_AHR_61012626	IMG Activity: OHADBAV320AB
S_AHR_61012627	IMG Activity: OHADBAV310AD
S_AHR_61012628	IMG Activity: OHADBAV338AB
S_AHR_61012629	IMG Activity: OHADBAV370ABB
S_AHR_61012630	IMG Activity: OHADBAV310ABA
S_AHR_61012631	IMG Activity: OHADBAV395A
S_AHR_61012632	IMG Activity: OHADBAV320AD
S_AHR_61012633	IMG Activity: OHADBAV310AD
S_AHR_61012634	IMG Activity: OHADBAV320ABA
S_AHR_61012635	IMG Activity: OHADBAV320ABA
S_AHR_61012709	IMG Activity: SIMG_CFMENUOHP2OOB2
S_AHR_61012714	IMG
S_AHR_61012715	Customizing
S_AHR_61012735	IMG Activity: OHANSP02
S_AHR_61012736	IMG Activity: OHANSP05
S_AHR_61012737	IMG Activity: OHANSP03
S_AHR_61012738	IMG Activity: OHABNB001
S_AHR_61012739	IMG Activity: OHABPE010
S_AHR_61012740	IMG Activity: OHABPE011
S_AHR_61012741	IMG Activity: OHABPE002
S_AHR_61012742	IMG Activity: OHABPE003
S_AHR_61012743	IMG Activity: OHABPE004
S_AHR_61012744	IMG Activity: OHABPE005
S_AHR_61012745	IMG Activity: OHABE_DL023
S_AHR_61012746	IMG Activity: OHAB6002
S_AHR_61012747	IMG Activity: OHABE_DL031
S_AHR_61012748	IMG Activity: OHABE_DL032
S_AHR_61012749	IMG Activity: OHABE_DL034
S_AHR_61012750	IMG Activity: OHAB6001
S_AHR_61012751	IMG Activity: OHABE_DL021
S_AHR_61012752	IMG Activity: OHABE_DL022
S_AHR_61012753	IMG Activity: OHABBIL05
S_AHR_61012754	IMG Activity: OHABBIL01
S_AHR_61012755	IMG Activity: OHABBIL02
S_AHR_61012756	IMG Activity: OHABBIL03
S_AHR_61012757	IMG Activity: OHABBIL04
S_AHR_61012758	IMG Activity: OHABE_601
S_AHR_61012759	IMG Activity: OHABEL002
S_AHR_61012760	IMG Activity: OHABPE013
S_AHR_61012761	IMG Activity: OHABPE006
S_AHR_61012762	IMG Activity: OHABPE007
S_AHR_61012763	IMG Activity: OHABPE008
S_AHR_61012764	IMG Activity: OHABPE009
S_AHR_61012765	IMG Activity: SIMG_OHABE_615
S_AHR_61012766	IMG Activity: OHABPE012
S_AHR_61012767	IMG Activity: OHABPE014
S_AHR_61012768	IMG Activity: OHAB6003

S_AHR_61012769	IMG Activity: OHAB40055
S_AHR_61012770	IMG Activity: OHAB40056
S_AHR_61012771	IMG Activity: OHAB4006
S_AHR_61012772	IMG Activity: OHAB7001
S_AHR_61012773	IMG Activity: OHAB3001
S_AHR_61012774	IMG Activity: OHAB3002
S_AHR_61012775	IMG Activity: OHAB2001
S_AHR_61012776	IMG Activity: OHAB40054
S_AHR_61012777	IMG Activity: OHAB7003
S_AHR_61012778	IMG Activity: OHAB4002
S_AHR_61012779	IMG Activity: OHAB4003
S_AHR_61012780	IMG Activity: OHAB4004
S_AHR_61012781	IMG Activity: OHAB7002
S_AHR_61012782	IMG Activity: OHAB40051
S_AHR_61012783	IMG Activity: OHAB40053
S_AHR_61012784	IMG Activity: OHAB1002
S_AHR_61012785	IMG Activity: OHAB6004
S_AHR_61012786	IMG Activity: OHABPF001
S_AHR_61012787	IMG Activity: OHABPF002
S_AHR_61012788	IMG Activity: OHABPF003
S_AHR_61012789	IMG Activity: OHABPF005
S_AHR_61012790	IMG Activity: OHABPF004
S_AHR_61012791	IMG Activity: OHAB1001
S_AHR_61012792	IMG Activity: OHAB2002
S_AHR_61012793	IMG Activity: OHAB2003
S_AHR_61012794	IMG Activity: OHAB2005
S_AHR_61012795	IMG Activity: OHAB2006
S_AHR_61012796	IMG Activity: OHABNE000
S_AHR_61012797	IMG Activity: OHABNE001
S_AHR_61012798	IMG Activity: OHAB6005
S_AHR_61012799	IMG Activity: OHABEL006
S_AHR_61012800	IMG Activity: SIMG_OHABE_403
S_AHR_61012801	IMG Activity: SIMG_OHABE_405
S_AHR_61012802	IMG Activity: SIMG_OHABE_406
S_AHR_61012803	IMG Activity: SIMG_OHABE_408
S_AHR_61012804	IMG Activity: SIMG_OHABE_527
S_AHR_61012805	IMG Activity: SIMG_OHABE_528
S_AHR_61012806	IMG Activity: SIMG_OHABE_529
S_AHR_61012807	IMG Activity: SIMG_OHABE_402
S_AHR_61012808	IMG Activity: SIMG_OHABE_464
S_AHR_61012809	IMG Activity: SIMG_OHABE_463
S_AHR_61012810	IMG Activity: SIMG_OHABE_451
S_AHR_61012811	IMG Activity: SIMG_OHABE_530
S_AHR_61012812	IMG Activity: SIMG_OHABE_457
S_AHR_61012813	IMG Activity: SIMG_OHABE_431
S_AHR_61012814	IMG Activity: SIMG_OHABE_525
S_AHR_61012815	IMG Activity: SIMG_OHABE_413
S_AHR_61012816	IMG Activity: SIMG_OHABE_480
S_AHR_61012817	IMG Activity: SIMG_OHABE_414
S_AHR_61012818	IMG Activity: SIMG_OHABE_814
S_AHR_61012819	IMG Activity: SIMG_OHABE_415
S_AHR_61012820	IMG Activity: SIMG_OHABE_418
S_AHR_61012821	IMG Activity: SIMG_OHABE_419
S_AHR_61012822	IMG Activity: SIMG_OHABE_417

S_AHR_61012823	IMG Activity: SIMG_OHABE_409
S_AHR_61012824	IMG Activity: SIMG_OHABE_407
S_AHR_61012825	IMG Activity: OHABE_EDTINTERNET
S_AHR_61012826	IMG Activity: SIMG_OHABE_484
S_AHR_61012827	IMG Activity: SIMG_OHABE_482
S_AHR_61012828	IMG Activity: SIMG_OHABE_410
S_AHR_61012829	IMG Activity: SIMG_OHABE_483
S_AHR_61012830	IMG Activity: SIMG_OHABE_518
S_AHR_61012831	IMG Activity: SIMG_OHABE_467
S_AHR_61012832	IMG Activity: SIMG_OHABE_424
S_AHR_61012833	IMG Activity: OHABE_MZ001
S_AHR_61012834	IMG Activity: SIMG_OHABE_427
S_AHR_61012835	IMG Activity: SIMG_OHABE_429
S_AHR_61012836	IMG Activity: OHABE_483
S_AHR_61012837	IMG Activity: SIMG_OHABE_416
S_AHR_61012838	IMG Activity: OHABE_DT004
S_AHR_61012839	IMG Activity: OHABEL004
S_AHR_61012840	IMG Activity: OHABEL005
S_AHR_61012841	IMG Activity: OHABEL003
S_AHR_61012842	IMG Activity: OHABJW000
S_AHR_61012843	IMG Activity: SIMG_OHABE_470
S_AHR_61012844	IMG Activity: OHABE_DT002
S_AHR_61012845	IMG Activity: OHABE_DT003
S_AHR_61012846	IMG Activity: SIMG_OHABE_432
S_AHR_61012847	IMG Activity: SIMG_OHABE_437
S_AHR_61012848	IMG Activity: SIMG_OHABE_425
S_AHR_61012849	IMG Activity: SIMG_OHABE_423
S_AHR_61012850	IMG Activity: SIMG_OHABE_422
S_AHR_61012851	IMG Activity: SIMG_OHABE_435
S_AHR_61012852	IMG Activity: SIMG_OHABE_471
S_AHR_61012853	IMG Activity: SIMG_OHABE_426
S_AHR_61012854	IMG Activity: SIMG_OHABE_461
S_AHR_61012855	IMG Activity: SIMG_OHABE_515
S_AHR_61012856	IMG Activity: SIMG_OHABE_438
S_AHR_61012857	IMG Activity: SIMG_OHABE_459
S_AHR_61012858	IMG Activity: SIMG_OHABE_428
S_AHR_61012859	IMG Activity: SIMG_OHABE_506
S_AHR_61012860	IMG Activity: SIMG_OHABE_507
S_AHR_61012861	IMG Activity: OHABE_TI361
S_AHR_61012862	IMG Activity: OHABE_TI363
S_AHR_61012863	IMG Activity: OHABE_TI362
S_AHR_61012864	IMG Activity: OHABE_TI364
S_AHR_61012865	IMG Activity: OHABE_TI370
S_AHR_61012866	IMG Activity: OHABE_RI061
S_AHR_61012867	IMG Activity: OHABE_AB001
S_AHR_61012868	IMG Activity: OHABE_RI062
S_AHR_61012869	IMG Activity: OHABE_TI325
S_AHR_61012870	IMG Activity: OHABE_TI321
S_AHR_61012871	IMG Activity: OHABE_TI322
S_AHR_61012872	IMG Activity: OHABE_TI323
S_AHR_61012873	IMG Activity: OHABE_TI324
S_AHR_61012874	IMG Activity: OHABE_RI063
S_AHR_61012875	IMG Activity: OHABE_TI340
S_AHR_61012876	IMG Activity: OHABE_AB002

S_AHR_61012877	IMG Activity: OHABE_RI055
S_AHR_61012878	IMG Activity: OHABE_AB200
S_AHR_61012879	IMG Activity: OHABE_RI054
S_AHR_61012880	IMG Activity: OHABE_QUOTACOMP00
S_AHR_61012881	IMG Activity: OHABE_QUOTACOMP01
S_AHR_61012882	IMG Activity: OHABE_RI053
S_AHR_61012883	IMG Activity: OHABE_RI056
S_AHR_61012884	IMG Activity: OHABE_AB010
S_AHR_61012885	IMG Activity: OHABE_AB003
S_AHR_61012886	IMG Activity: OHABE_AB004
S_AHR_61012887	IMG Activity: OHABE_AB005
S_AHR_61012888	IMG Activity: OHABE_AB011
S_AHR_61012889	IMG Activity: OHABE_AB009
S_AHR_61012890	IMG Activity: OHABE_AB012
S_AHR_61012891	IMG Activity: OHABAB009
S_AHR_61012892	IMG Activity: OHABE_UM003
S_AHR_61012893	IMG Activity: OHABUM01
S_AHR_61012894	IMG Activity: OHABUM02
S_AHR_61012895	IMG Activity: OHABUM03
S_AHR_61012896	IMG Activity: OHABE_UM002
S_AHR_61012897	IMG Activity: OHABE_UM022
S_AHR_61012898	IMG Activity: OHABE_UM023
S_AHR_61012899	IMG Activity: OHABE_UM010
S_AHR_61012900	IMG Activity: OHABE_PAY003
S_AHR_61012901	IMG Activity: OHABE_PAY002
S_AHR_61012902	IMG Activity: OHABE_UM012
S_AHR_61012903	IMG Activity: OHABE_UM014
S_AHR_61012904	IMG Activity: OHABE_UM006
S_AHR_61012905	IMG Activity: OHABE_UM008
S_AHR_61012906	IMG Activity: OHABE_UM013
S_AHR_61012907	IMG Activity: OHABE_RI090
S_AHR_61012908	IMG Activity: OHABE_TI110
S_AHR_61012909	IMG Activity: OHABE_TI120
S_AHR_61012910	IMG Activity: OHABE_TI130
S_AHR_61012911	IMG Activity: OHABE_TI210
S_AHR_61012912	IMG Activity: OHABE_RI071
S_AHR_61012913	IMG Activity: OHABE_TI310
S_AHR_61012914	IMG Activity: OHABE_RI070
S_AHR_61012915	IMG Activity: OHABE_RI080
S_AHR_61012916	IMG Activity: OHABE_UM104
S_AHR_61012917	IMG Activity: OHABE_UM105
S_AHR_61012918	IMG Activity: OHABE_UM101
S_AHR_61012919	IMG Activity: OHABE_UM102
S_AHR_61012920	IMG Activity: OHABE_UM103
S_AHR_61012921	IMG Activity: OHABE_X_PM_CREATE
S_AHR_61012922	IMG Activity: OHABE_RI081
S_AHR_61012923	IMG Activity: OHABE_RI052
S_AHR_61012924	IMG Activity: OHABSL002
S_AHR_61012925	IMG Activity: OHABSL003
S_AHR_61012926	IMG Activity: OHABE_RI015
S_AHR_61012927	IMG Activity: OHABE_IW063
S_AHR_61012928	IMG Activity: OHABE_IW065
S_AHR_61012929	IMG Activity: OHABE_IW061
S_AHR_61012930	IMG Activity: OHABE_IW082

S_AHR_61012931	IMG Activity: OHABE_SL002
S_AHR_61012932	IMG Activity: OHABKF002
S_AHR_61012933	IMG Activity: OHABNB001
S_AHR_61012934	IMG Activity: OHABPE010
S_AHR_61012935	IMG Activity: OHABPE011
S_AHR_61012936	IMG Activity: OHABPE002
S_AHR_61012937	IMG Activity: OHABPE003
S_AHR_61012938	IMG Activity: OHABPE004
S_AHR_61012939	IMG Activity: OHABPE005
S_AHR_61012940	IMG Activity: OHABE_DL023
S_AHR_61012941	IMG Activity: OHAB6002
S_AHR_61012942	IMG Activity: OHABE_DL031
S_AHR_61012943	IMG Activity: OHABE_DL032
S_AHR_61012944	IMG Activity: OHABE_DL034
S_AHR_61012945	IMG Activity: OHAB6001
S_AHR_61012946	IMG Activity: OHABE_DL021
S_AHR_61012947	IMG Activity: OHABE_DL022
S_AHR_61012948	IMG Activity: OHABBIL05
S_AHR_61012949	IMG Activity: OHABBIL01
S_AHR_61012950	IMG Activity: OHABBIL02
S_AHR_61012951	IMG Activity: OHABBIL03
S_AHR_61012952	IMG Activity: OHABBIL04
S_AHR_61012953	IMG Activity: OHABE_601
S_AHR_61012954	IMG Activity: OHABEL002
S_AHR_61012955	IMG Activity: OHABPE013
S_AHR_61012956	IMG activity: OHAIFIN74
S_AHR_61012957	IMG Activity: OHABPE006
S_AHR_61012958	IMG activity: OHAIFIN72
S_AHR_61012959	IMG Activity: OHABPE007
S_AHR_61012960	IMG Activity: OHABPE008
S_AHR_61012961	IMG activity: OHAIFIN71
S_AHR_61012962	IMG Activity: OHABPE009
S_AHR_61012963	IMG activity: OHAIFIN70
S_AHR_61012964	IMG activity: OHAIT_ARE50
S_AHR_61012965	IMG Activity: SIMG_OHABE_615
S_AHR_61012966	IMG Activity: OHABPE012
S_AHR_61012967	IMG activity: OHAIT_ARE40
S_AHR_61012968	IMG Activity: OHABPE014
S_AHR_61012969	IMG activity: OHAIFIN05
S_AHR_61012970	IMG Activity: OHAB6003
S_AHR_61012971	IMG activity: OHAIT_FIP15
S_AHR_61012972	IMG Activity: OHAB40055
S_AHR_61012973	IMG activity: OHAIT_FIP10
S_AHR_61012974	IMG Activity: OHAB40056
S_AHR_61012975	IMG activity: OHAIT_FIP00
S_AHR_61012976	IMG Activity: OHAB4006
S_AHR_61012977	IMG activity: OHAIT_FIP05
S_AHR_61012978	IMG Activity: OHAB7001
S_AHR_61012979	IMG activity: OHAIFIN15
S_AHR_61012980	IMG Activity: OHAB3001
S_AHR_61012981	IMG activity: OHAIFIN10
S_AHR_61012982	IMG Activity: OHAB3002
S_AHR_61012983	IMG activity: OHAIT_ARE30
S_AHR_61012984	IMG Activity: OHAB2001

S_AHR_61012985	IMG activity: OHAITSE30
S_AHR_61012986	IMG Activity: OHAB40054
S_AHR_61012987	IMG activity: OHAITSE20
S_AHR_61012988	IMG Activity: OHAB7003
S_AHR_61012989	IMG activity: OHAITSE10
S_AHR_61012990	IMG Activity: OHAB4002
S_AHR_61012991	IMG activity: OHAIDTF50
S_AHR_61012992	IMG Activity: OHAB4003
S_AHR_61012993	IMG activity: OHAIDTF40
S_AHR_61012994	IMG Activity: OHAB4004
S_AHR_61012995	IMG activity: OHAIDTF45
S_AHR_61012996	IMG Activity: OHAB7002
S_AHR_61012997	IMG activity: OHAITSE50
S_AHR_61012998	IMG Activity: OHAB40051
S_AHR_61012999	IMG activity: OHAIT_ARE20
S_AHR_61013000	IMG Activity: OHAB40053
S_AHR_61013001	IMG activity: OHAIT_ARE10
S_AHR_61013002	IMG Activity: OHAB1002
S_AHR_61013003	IMG activity: OHAIT_TSE30
S_AHR_61013004	IMG Activity: OHAB6004
S_AHR_61013005	IMG activity: OHAIT_TSE20
S_AHR_61013006	IMG Activity: OHABPF001
S_AHR_61013007	IMG activity: OHAIT_TSE10
S_AHR_61013008	IMG Activity: OHABPF002
S_AHR_61013009	IMG Activity: OHABPF003
S_AHR_61013010	IMG activity: OHAIT_TSE00
S_AHR_61013011	IMG Activity: OHABPF005
S_AHR_61013012	IMG activity: SIMG_OHAIT_525
S_AHR_61013013	IMG Activity: OHABPF004
S_AHR_61013014	IMG activity: SIMG_OHAIT_530
S_AHR_61013015	IMG Activity: OHAB1001
S_AHR_61013016	IMG activity: SIMG_OHAIT_518
S_AHR_61013017	IMG Activity: OHAB2002
S_AHR_61013018	IMG activity: SIMG_OHAIT_507
S_AHR_61013019	IMG Activity: OHAB2003
S_AHR_61013020	IMG activity: SIMG_OHAIT_506
S_AHR_61013021	IMG Activity: OHAB2005
S_AHR_61013022	IMG activity: SIMG_OHAIT_515
S_AHR_61013023	IMG Activity: OHAB2006
S_AHR_61013024	IMG activity: SIMG_OHAIT_402
S_AHR_61013025	IMG Activity: OHABNE000
S_AHR_61013026	IMG activity: SIMG_OHAIT_528
S_AHR_61013027	IMG Activity: OHABNE001
S_AHR_61013028	IMG activity: SIMG_OHAIT_527
S_AHR_61013029	IMG Activity: OHAB6005
S_AHR_61013030	IMG activity: SIMG_OHAIT_408
S_AHR_61013031	IMG Activity: OHABEL006
S_AHR_61013032	IMG activity: SIMG_OHAIT_406
S_AHR_61013033	IMG Activity: SIMG_OHABE_403
S_AHR_61013034	IMG Activity: SIMG_OHABE_405
S_AHR_61013035	IMG activity: SIMG_OHAIT_405
S_AHR_61013036	IMG Activity: SIMG_OHABE_406
S_AHR_61013037	IMG activity: SIMG_OHAIT_403
S_AHR_61013038	IMG Activity: SIMG_OHABE_408

S_AHR_61013039	IMG activity: SIMG_OHAIT_416
S_AHR_61013040	IMG Activity: SIMG_OHABE_527
S_AHR_61013041	IMG activity: OHAIDT004
S_AHR_61013042	IMG Activity: SIMG_OHABE_528
S_AHR_61013043	IMG activity: OHAIDT003
S_AHR_61013044	IMG Activity: SIMG_OHABE_529
S_AHR_61013045	IMG activity: OHAIDT002
S_AHR_61013046	IMG Activity: SIMG_OHABE_402
S_AHR_61013047	IMG activity: OHAIT_ARR10
S_AHR_61013048	IMG Activity: SIMG_OHABE_464
S_AHR_61013049	IMG Activity: SIMG_OHABE_463
S_AHR_61013050	IMG activity: OHAIARR05
S_AHR_61013051	IMG Activity: SIMG_OHABE_451
S_AHR_61013052	IMG activity: OHAIT_FIP20
S_AHR_61013053	IMG Activity: SIMG_OHABE_530
S_AHR_61013054	IMG activity: OHAIT_0902
S_AHR_61013055	IMG Activity: SIMG_OHABE_457
S_AHR_61013056	IMG activity: OHAIT_483
S_AHR_61013057	IMG Activity: SIMG_OHABE_431
S_AHR_61013058	IMG activity: OHAIMZ001
S_AHR_61013059	IMG Activity: SIMG_OHABE_525
S_AHR_61013060	IMG activity: OHAIT_0903
S_AHR_61013061	IMG Activity: SIMG_OHABE_413
S_AHR_61013062	IMG activity: OHAIT_0913
S_AHR_61013063	IMG Activity: SIMG_OHABE_480
S_AHR_61013064	IMG activity: OHAIT_0912
S_AHR_61013065	IMG Activity: SIMG_OHABE_414
S_AHR_61013066	IMG activity: OHAIT_0911
S_AHR_61013067	IMG Activity: SIMG_OHABE_814
S_AHR_61013068	IMG activity: OHAIDTF35
S_AHR_61013069	IMG Activity: SIMG_OHABE_415
S_AHR_61013070	IMG activity: OHAIPRV09
S_AHR_61013071	IMG Activity: SIMG_OHABE_418
S_AHR_61013072	IMG Activity: SIMG_OHABE_419
S_AHR_61013073	IMG activity: OHAIPRV04
S_AHR_61013074	IMG Activity: SIMG_OHABE_417
S_AHR_61013075	IMG activity: OHAIPRV59
S_AHR_61013076	IMG Activity: SIMG_OHABE_409
S_AHR_61013077	IMG activity: OHAIPRV61
S_AHR_61013078	IMG Activity: SIMG_OHABE_407
S_AHR_61013079	IMG activity: OHAIPRV60
S_AHR_61013080	IMG Activity: OHABE_EDTINTERNET
S_AHR_61013081	IMG activity: OHAIPRV94
S_AHR_61013082	IMG Activity: SIMG_OHABE_484
S_AHR_61013083	IMG activity: OHAIPRV12
S_AHR_61013084	IMG Activity: SIMG_OHABE_482
S_AHR_61013085	IMG activity: OHAIPRV46
S_AHR_61013086	IMG Activity: SIMG_OHABE_410
S_AHR_61013087	IMG activity: OHAIPRV16
S_AHR_61013088	IMG Activity: SIMG_OHABE_483
S_AHR_61013089	IMG activity: OHAIPRV14
S_AHR_61013090	IMG Activity: SIMG_OHABE_518
S_AHR_61013091	IMG activity: OHAIPRV90
S_AHR_61013092	IMG Activity: SIMG_OHABE_467

S_AHR_61013093	IMG activity: OHAIPRV13
S_AHR_61013094	IMG Activity: SIMG_OHABE_424
S_AHR_61013095	IMG activity: OHAIPRV11
S_AHR_61013096	IMG Activity: OHABE_MZ001
S_AHR_61013097	IMG activity: OHAIPRV71
S_AHR_61013098	IMG Activity: SIMG_OHABE_427
S_AHR_61013099	IMG activity: OHAIT_SZ610
S_AHR_61013100	IMG Activity: SIMG_OHABE_429
S_AHR_61013101	IMG activity: OHAIT_SZ510
S_AHR_61013102	IMG Activity: OHABE_483
S_AHR_61013103	IMG activity: OHAIT_SZ410
S_AHR_61013104	IMG Activity: SIMG_OHABE_416
S_AHR_61013105	IMG activity: OHAIT_SZ310
S_AHR_61013106	IMG Activity: OHABE_DT004
S_AHR_61013107	IMG Activity: OHABEL004
S_AHR_61013108	IMG activity: OHAIT_SZ120
S_AHR_61013109	IMG Activity: OHABEL005
S_AHR_61013110	IMG activity: OHAIT_SZ110
S_AHR_61013111	IMG Activity: OHABEL003
S_AHR_61013112	IMG Activity: OHABJW000
S_AHR_61013113	IMG activity: OHAIPRV05
S_AHR_61013114	IMG Activity: SIMG_OHABE_470
S_AHR_61013115	IMG activity: OHAIPRV72
S_AHR_61013116	IMG Activity: OHABE_DT002
S_AHR_61013117	IMG activity: OHAIPRV70
S_AHR_61013118	IMG Activity: OHABE_DT003
S_AHR_61013119	IMG activity: OHAIPRV08
S_AHR_61013120	IMG Activity: SIMG_OHABE_432
S_AHR_61013121	IMG activity: OHAIT_PRV70
S_AHR_61013122	IMG Activity: SIMG_OHABE_437
S_AHR_61013123	IMG activity: OHAIPRV07
S_AHR_61013124	IMG Activity: SIMG_OHABE_425
S_AHR_61013125	IMG activity: OHAIPRV06
S_AHR_61013126	IMG Activity: SIMG_OHABE_423
S_AHR_61013127	IMG activity: OHAIDTF74
S_AHR_61013128	IMG Activity: SIMG_OHABE_422
S_AHR_61013129	IMG activity: OHAIDTF72
S_AHR_61013130	IMG Activity: SIMG_OHABE_435
S_AHR_61013131	IMG activity: OHAIDTF71
S_AHR_61013132	IMG Activity: SIMG_OHABE_471
S_AHR_61013133	IMG Activity: SIMG_OHABE_426
S_AHR_61013134	IMG activity: OHAIDTF70
S_AHR_61013135	IMG Activity: SIMG_OHABE_461
S_AHR_61013136	IMG activity: OHAITAS40
S_AHR_61013137	IMG Activity: SIMG_OHABE_515
S_AHR_61013138	IMG activity: OHAITAS35
S_AHR_61013139	IMG Activity: SIMG_OHABE_438
S_AHR_61013140	IMG activity: OHAIDTF01
S_AHR_61013141	IMG Activity: SIMG_OHABE_459
S_AHR_61013142	IMG activity: OHAIDTF30
S_AHR_61013143	IMG Activity: SIMG_OHABE_428
S_AHR_61013144	IMG Activity: SIMG_OHABE_506
S_AHR_61013145	IMG Activity: SIMG_OHABE_507
S_AHR_61013146	IMG Activity: OHABE_TI361

S_AHR_61013147	IMG Activity: OHABE_TI363
S_AHR_61013148	IMG Activity: OHABE_TI362
S_AHR_61013149	IMG Activity: OHABE_TI364
S_AHR_61013150	IMG Activity: OHABE_TI370
S_AHR_61013151	IMG Activity: OHABE_RI061
S_AHR_61013152	IMG Activity: OHABE_AB001
S_AHR_61013153	IMG Activity: OHABE_RI062
S_AHR_61013154	IMG Activity: OHABE_TI325
S_AHR_61013155	IMG Activity: OHABE_TI321
S_AHR_61013156	IMG Activity: OHABE_TI322
S_AHR_61013157	IMG Activity: OHABE_TI323
S_AHR_61013158	IMG Activity: OHABE_TI324
S_AHR_61013159	IMG Activity: OHABE_RI063
S_AHR_61013160	IMG Activity: OHABE_TI340
S_AHR_61013161	IMG Activity: OHABE_AB002
S_AHR_61013162	IMG Activity: OHABE_RI055
S_AHR_61013163	IMG Activity: OHABE_AB200
S_AHR_61013164	IMG Activity: OHABE_RI054
S_AHR_61013165	IMG Activity: OHABE_QUOTACOMP00
S_AHR_61013166	IMG Activity: OHABE_QUOTACOMP01
S_AHR_61013167	IMG Activity: OHABE_RI053
S_AHR_61013168	IMG Activity: OHABE_RI056
S_AHR_61013169	IMG Activity: OHABE_AB010
S_AHR_61013170	IMG Activity: OHABE_AB003
S_AHR_61013171	IMG Activity: OHABE_AB004
S_AHR_61013172	IMG Activity: OHABE_AB005
S_AHR_61013173	IMG Activity: OHABE_AB011
S_AHR_61013174	IMG Activity: OHABE_AB009
S_AHR_61013175	IMG Activity: OHABE_AB012
S_AHR_61013176	IMG Activity: OHABAB009
S_AHR_61013177	IMG Activity: OHABE_UM003
S_AHR_61013178	IMG Activity: OHABUM01
S_AHR_61013179	IMG Activity: OHABUM02
S_AHR_61013180	IMG Activity: OHABUM03
S_AHR_61013181	IMG Activity: OHABE_UM002
S_AHR_61013182	IMG Activity: OHABE_UM022
S_AHR_61013183	IMG Activity: OHABE_UM023
S_AHR_61013184	IMG Activity: OHABE_UM010
S_AHR_61013185	IMG Activity: OHABE_PAY003
S_AHR_61013186	IMG Activity: OHABE_PAY002
S_AHR_61013187	IMG Activity: OHABE_UM012
S_AHR_61013188	IMG Activity: OHABE_UM014
S_AHR_61013189	IMG Activity: OHABE_UM006
S_AHR_61013190	IMG Activity: OHABE_UM008
S_AHR_61013191	IMG Activity: OHABE_UM013
S_AHR_61013192	IMG Activity: OHABE_RI090
S_AHR_61013193	IMG Activity: OHABE_TI110
S_AHR_61013194	IMG Activity: OHABE_TI120
S_AHR_61013195	IMG Activity: OHABE_TI130
S_AHR_61013196	IMG Activity: OHABE_TI210
S_AHR_61013197	IMG Activity: OHABE_RI071
S_AHR_61013198	IMG Activity: OHABE_TI310
S_AHR_61013199	IMG Activity: OHABE_RI070
S_AHR_61013200	IMG Activity: OHABE_RI080

S_AHR_61013201	IMG Activity: OHABE_UM104
S_AHR_61013202	IMG Activity: OHABE_UM105
S_AHR_61013203	IMG Activity: OHABE_UM101
S_AHR_61013204	IMG Activity: OHABE_UM102
S_AHR_61013205	IMG Activity: OHABE_UM103
S_AHR_61013206	IMG activity: OHAIDTF25
S_AHR_61013207	IMG Activity: OHABE_X_PM_CREATE
S_AHR_61013208	IMG activity: OHAIDTF20
S_AHR_61013209	IMG Activity: OHABE_RI081
S_AHR_61013210	IMG activity: OHAIDTF15
S_AHR_61013211	IMG Activity: OHABE_RI052
S_AHR_61013212	IMG activity: OHAIDTF10
S_AHR_61013213	IMG Activity: OHABSL002
S_AHR_61013214	IMG activity: OHAIDTF00
S_AHR_61013215	IMG Activity: OHABSL003
S_AHR_61013216	IMG activity: OHAITAS30
S_AHR_61013217	IMG Activity: OHABE_RI015
S_AHR_61013218	IMG Activity: OHABE_IW063
S_AHR_61013219	IMG activity: OAHITAS74
S_AHR_61013220	IMG Activity: OHABE_IW065
S_AHR_61013221	IMG activity: OHAITAS71
S_AHR_61013222	IMG Activity: OHABE_IW061
S_AHR_61013223	IMG activity: OHAITAS72
S_AHR_61013224	IMG Activity: OHABE_IW082
S_AHR_61013225	IMG activity: OHAITAS70
S_AHR_61013226	IMG Activity: OHABE_SL002
S_AHR_61013227	IMG activity: OHAIPRV55
S_AHR_61013228	IMG Activity: OHABKF002
S_AHR_61013229	IMG activity: OHAIPRV50
S_AHR_61013230	IMG Activity: OHABBW022
S_AHR_61013231	IMG activity: OHAITAS00
S_AHR_61013232	IMG Activity: OHABBW010
S_AHR_61013233	IMG activity: OHAITAS25
S_AHR_61013234	IMG Activity: OHABE_KL000
S_AHR_61013235	IMG activity: OHAITAS20
S_AHR_61013236	IMG Activity: OHABKL000
S_AHR_61013237	IMG activity: OHAITAS95
S_AHR_61013238	IMG Activity: OHABE_RI042
S_AHR_61013239	IMG activity: OHAITAS10
S_AHR_61013240	IMG Activity: OHABSL001
S_AHR_61013241	IMG activity: OHAIT_TAS70
S_AHR_61013242	IMG Activity: OHAB0003
S_AHR_61013243	IMG activity: OHAITAS05
S_AHR_61013244	IMG Activity: OHAB0004
S_AHR_61013245	IMG activity: SIMG_OHAIT_529
S_AHR_61013246	IMG Activity: OHABSB000
S_AHR_61013247	IMG Activity: OHABSB001
S_AHR_61013248	IMG activity: OHAIT_DM120
S_AHR_61013249	IMG activity: OHAIT_DM080
S_AHR_61013250	IMG Activity: OHABBR000
S_AHR_61013251	IMG activity: OHAIT_DM070
S_AHR_61013252	IMG Activity: OHABE_DV001
S_AHR_61013253	IMG activity: OHAIT_DM010
S_AHR_61013254	IMG Activity: OHABCX006

S_AHR_61013255	IMG Activity: OHAB0002
S_AHR_61013256	IMG activity: OHAIT_DM020
S_AHR_61013257	IMG activity: OHAIT_DM060
S_AHR_61013258	IMG Activity: OHAB7009
S_AHR_61013259	IMG activity: OHAIT_DM130
S_AHR_61013260	IMG Activity: OHAB7008
S_AHR_61013261	IMG Activity: OHAB7007
S_AHR_61013262	IMG activity: OHAIT_DM024
S_AHR_61013263	IMG activity: OHAIT_DM040
S_AHR_61013264	IMG Activity: OHABE_IW037
S_AHR_61013265	IMG activity: OHAIT_DM021
S_AHR_61013266	IMG Activity: OHAB7006
S_AHR_61013267	IMG activity: OHAIT_DM100
S_AHR_61013268	IMG Activity: OHAB7005
S_AHR_61013269	IMG activity: OHAIT_DM090
S_AHR_61013270	IMG Activity: OHAB7004
S_AHR_61013271	IMG activity: OHAIT_DM140
S_AHR_61013272	IMG Activity: OHABKF001
S_AHR_61013273	IMG activity: OHAIT_DM030
S_AHR_61013274	IMG Activity: OHABE_AVX018
S_AHR_61013275	IMG activity: OHAIRI081
S_AHR_61013276	IMG Activity: OHABE_AVX017
S_AHR_61013277	IMG activity: OHAIRI080
S_AHR_61013278	IMG Activity: OHABE_BW22
S_AHR_61013279	IMG activity: OHAIRI071
S_AHR_61013280	IMG Activity: OHABE_AVBAS
S_AHR_61013281	IMG activity: OHAIRI070
S_AHR_61013282	IMG Activity: OHABE_AV001
S_AHR_61013283	IMG Activity: OHABE_AV511A
S_AHR_61013284	IMG activity: OHAIRI063
S_AHR_61013285	IMG activity: OHAIRI062
S_AHR_61013286	IMG Activity: OHABE_AV511C
S_AHR_61013287	IMG activity: OHAIRI090
S_AHR_61013288	IMG Activity: OHABAVXT00
S_AHR_61013289	IMG activity: OHAIT_DM045
S_AHR_61013290	IMG Activity: OHABE_AVP15
S_AHR_61013291	IMG Activity: OHABE_AV511B
S_AHR_61013292	IMG activity: OHAIT_DM005
S_AHR_61013293	IMG activity: OHAIPAY003
S_AHR_61013294	IMG Activity: OHABE_BW21
S_AHR_61013295	IMG activity: OHAIPAY002
S_AHR_61013296	IMG Activity: OHABE_RI051
S_AHR_61013297	IMG Activity: OHABBW009
S_AHR_61013298	IMG activity: OHAIUM003
S_AHR_61013299	IMG activity: OHAIUM002
S_AHR_61013300	IMG Activity: OHABE_RI031
S_AHR_61013301	IMG Activity: OHABE_BW005
S_AHR_61013302	IMG activity: OHAIT_CU020
S_AHR_61013303	IMG Activity: OHABE_PART
S_AHR_61013304	IMG activity: OHAIT_CU015
S_AHR_61013305	IMG Activity: OHABBW004
S_AHR_61013306	IMG activity: OHAIT_CU010
S_AHR_61013307	IMG activity: OHAIT_CU005
S_AHR_61013308	IMG Activity: OHABBW023

S_AHR_61013309	IMG Activity: OHABE_BW019
S_AHR_61013310	IMG activity: OHAIT_CU004
S_AHR_61013311	IMG Activity: OHABBW006
S_AHR_61013312	IMG activity: OHAIT_CU000
S_AHR_61013313	IMG Activity: OHABBW021
S_AHR_61013314	IMG activity: OHAIT_CU025
S_AHR_61013315	IMG Activity: SIMG_OHABE_454
S_AHR_61013316	IMG Activity: SIMG_OHABE_465
S_AHR_61013317	IMG activity: OHAIT_RET20
S_AHR_61013318	IMG Activity: SIMG_OHABE_519
S_AHR_61013319	IMG Activity: SIMG_OHABE_520
S_AHR_61013320	IMG Activity: OHABE_AL01
S_AHR_61013321	IMG Activity: SIMG_OHABE_456
S_AHR_61013322	IMG activity: OHAIT_RET10
S_AHR_61013323	IMG Activity: SIMG_OHABE_466
S_AHR_61013324	IMG Activity: SIMG_OHABE_455
S_AHR_61013325	IMG Activity: SIMG_OHABE_517
S_AHR_61013326	IMG Activity: SIMG_OHABE_523
S_AHR_61013327	IMG Activity: SIMG_OHABE_439
S_AHR_61013328	IMG Activity: SIMG_OHABE_524
S_AHR_61013329	IMG Activity: SIMG_OHABE_401
S_AHR_61013330	IMG Activity: SIMG_OHABE_481
S_AHR_61013331	IMG Activity: SIMG_OHABE_521
S_AHR_61013332	IMG Activity: SIMG_OHABE_453
S_AHR_61013333	IMG Activity: SIMG_OHABE_522
S_AHR_61013334	IMG Activity: OHABE_TI330
S_AHR_61013335	IMG Activity: SIMG_OHABE_450
S_AHR_61013336	IMG Activity: SIMG_OHABE_842
S_AHR_61013337	IMG Activity: SIMG_OHABE_843
S_AHR_61013338	IMG Activity: SIMG_OHABE_844
S_AHR_61013339	IMG Activity: SIMG_OHABE_501
S_AHR_61013340	IMG Activity: SIMG_OHABE_502
S_AHR_61013341	IMG Activity: SIMG_OHABE_508
S_AHR_61013342	IMG Activity: SIMG_OHABE_611
S_AHR_61013343	IMG Activity: SIMG_OHABE_612
S_AHR_61013344	IMG Activity: SIMG_OHABE_613
S_AHR_61013345	IMG Activity: SIMG_OHABE_614
S_AHR_61013346	IMG Activity: OHABE_DT009
S_AHR_61013347	IMG Activity: SIMG_OHABE_841
S_AHR_61013348	IMG Activity: SIMG_OHABE_513
S_AHR_61013349	IMG Activity: SIMG_OHABE_514
S_AHR_61013350	IMG Activity: OHABE_RI011
S_AHR_61013351	IMG Activity: OHABE_RI012
S_AHR_61013352	IMG Activity: SIMG_OHABE_421
S_AHR_61013353	IMG Activity: SIMG_OHABE_516
S_AHR_61013354	IMG Activity: SIMG_OHABE_509
S_AHR_61013355	IMG Activity: SIMG_OHABE_510
S_AHR_61013356	IMG Activity: OHABE_IW041
S_AHR_61013357	IMG Activity: SIMG_OHABE_512
S_AHR_61013358	IMG Activity: OHABE_IW035
S_AHR_61013359	IMG Activity: OHABE_IW069
S_AHR_61013360	IMG activity: OHAIT_NOR10
S_AHR_61013361	IMG activity: OHAIT_CU040
S_AHR_61013362	IMG activity: OHAIT_CU035

S_AHR_61013363	IMG activity: OHAIT_CU030
S_AHR_61013364	IMG activity: OHAIT_DM170
S_AHR_61013365	IMG activity: OHAIT_DM022
S_AHR_61013366	IMG activity: OHAIT_DM023
S_AHR_61013367	IMG activity: OHAIT_DM050
S_AHR_61013368	IMG activity: OHAIT_DM035
S_AHR_61013369	IMG activity: OHAIT_DM034
S_AHR_61013370	IMG activity: OHAIT_DM025
S_AHR_61013371	IMG activity: OHAIT_DM027
S_AHR_61013372	IMG Activity: OHABNB001
S_AHR_61013373	IMG Activity: OHABPE010
S_AHR_61013374	IMG Activity: OHABPE011
S_AHR_61013375	IMG Activity: OHABPE002
S_AHR_61013376	IMG Activity: OHABPE003
S_AHR_61013377	IMG Activity: OHABPE004
S_AHR_61013378	IMG Activity: OHABPE005
S_AHR_61013379	IMG Activity: OHABE_DL023
S_AHR_61013380	IMG Activity: OHAB6002
S_AHR_61013381	IMG Activity: OHABE_DL031
S_AHR_61013382	IMG Activity: OHABE_DL032
S_AHR_61013383	IMG Activity: OHABE_DL034
S_AHR_61013384	IMG Activity: OHAB6001
S_AHR_61013385	IMG Activity: OHABE_DL021
S_AHR_61013386	IMG Activity: OHABE_DL022
S_AHR_61013387	IMG Activity: OHABBIL05
S_AHR_61013388	IMG Activity: OHABBIL01
S_AHR_61013389	IMG Activity: OHABBIL02
S_AHR_61013390	IMG Activity: OHABBIL03
S_AHR_61013391	IMG Activity: OHABBIL04
S_AHR_61013392	IMG Activity: OHABE_601
S_AHR_61013393	IMG Activity: OHABEL002
S_AHR_61013394	IMG Activity: OHABPE013
S_AHR_61013395	IMG Activity: OHABPE006
S_AHR_61013396	IMG Activity: OHABPE007
S_AHR_61013397	IMG Activity: OHABPE008
S_AHR_61013398	IMG Activity: OHABPE009
S_AHR_61013399	IMG Activity: SIMG_OHABE_615
S_AHR_61013400	IMG Activity: OHABPE012
S_AHR_61013401	IMG Activity: OHABPE014
S_AHR_61013402	IMG Activity: OHAB6003
S_AHR_61013403	IMG Activity: OHAB40055
S_AHR_61013404	IMG Activity: OHAB40056
S_AHR_61013405	IMG Activity: OHAB4006
S_AHR_61013406	IMG Activity: OHAB7001
S_AHR_61013407	IMG Activity: OHAB3001
S_AHR_61013408	IMG Activity: OHAB3002
S_AHR_61013409	IMG Activity: OHAB2001
S_AHR_61013410	IMG Activity: OHAB40054
S_AHR_61013411	IMG Activity: OHAB7003
S_AHR_61013412	IMG Activity: OHAB4002
S_AHR_61013413	IMG Activity: OHAB4003
S_AHR_61013414	IMG Activity: OHAB4004
S_AHR_61013415	IMG Activity: OHAB7002
S_AHR_61013416	IMG Activity: OHAB40051

S_AHR_61013417	IMG Activity: OHAB40053
S_AHR_61013418	IMG Activity: OHAB1002
S_AHR_61013419	IMG Activity: OHAB6004
S_AHR_61013420	IMG Activity: OHABPF001
S_AHR_61013421	IMG Activity: OHABPF002
S_AHR_61013422	IMG Activity: OHABPF003
S_AHR_61013423	IMG activity: OHAIT_DM031
S_AHR_61013424	IMG Activity: OHABPF005
S_AHR_61013425	IMG activity: OHAIT_DM032
S_AHR_61013426	IMG Activity: OHABPF004
S_AHR_61013427	IMG activity: OHAIT_DM033
S_AHR_61013428	IMG Activity: OHAB1001
S_AHR_61013429	IMG activity: OHAIT_DM041
S_AHR_61013430	IMG Activity: OHAB2002
S_AHR_61013431	IMG activity: OHAIT_DM029
S_AHR_61013432	IMG Activity: OHAB2003
S_AHR_61013433	IMG activity: OHAIT_DM028
S_AHR_61013434	IMG Activity: OHAB2005
S_AHR_61013435	IMG activity: OHAIRI061
S_AHR_61013436	IMG Activity: OHAB2006
S_AHR_61013437	IMG Activity: OHABNE000
S_AHR_61013438	IMG activity: SIMG_OHAIT_464
S_AHR_61013439	IMG Activity: OHABNE001
S_AHR_61013440	IMG activity: SIMG_OHAIT_463
S_AHR_61013441	IMG Activity: OHAB6005
S_AHR_61013442	IMG Activity: OHABEL006
S_AHR_61013443	IMG activity: SIMG_OHAIT_451
S_AHR_61013444	IMG Activity: SIMG_OHABE_403
S_AHR_61013445	IMG activity: SIMG_OHAIT_457
S_AHR_61013446	IMG Activity: SIMG_OHABE_405
S_AHR_61013447	IMG activity: SIMG_OHAIT_431
S_AHR_61013448	IMG Activity: SIMG_OHABE_406
S_AHR_61013449	IMG activity: OHAITEDTINTERNET
S_AHR_61013450	IMG Activity: SIMG_OHABE_408
S_AHR_61013451	IMG activity: SIMG_OHAIT_471
S_AHR_61013452	IMG Activity: SIMG_OHABE_527
S_AHR_61013453	IMG Activity: SIMG_OHABE_528
S_AHR_61013454	IMG activity: SIMG_OHAIT_432
S_AHR_61013455	IMG Activity: SIMG_OHABE_529
S_AHR_61013456	IMG activity: SIMG_OHAIT_437
S_AHR_61013457	IMG Activity: SIMG_OHABE_402
S_AHR_61013458	IMG activity: SIMG_OHAIT_425
S_AHR_61013459	IMG Activity: SIMG_OHABE_464
S_AHR_61013460	IMG activity: SIMG_OHAIT_423
S_AHR_61013461	IMG Activity: SIMG_OHABE_463
S_AHR_61013462	IMG activity: SIMG_OHAIT_422
S_AHR_61013463	IMG Activity: SIMG_OHABE_451
S_AHR_61013464	IMG activity: SIMG_OHAIT_435
S_AHR_61013465	IMG Activity: SIMG_OHABE_530
S_AHR_61013466	IMG activity: SIMG_OHAIT_484
S_AHR_61013467	IMG Activity: SIMG_OHABE_457
S_AHR_61013468	IMG Activity: SIMG_OHABE_431
S_AHR_61013469	IMG activity: SIMG_OHAIT_413
S_AHR_61013470	IMG Activity: SIMG_OHABE_525

S_AHR_61013471	IMG activity: SIMG_OHAIT_417
S_AHR_61013472	IMG Activity: SIMG_OHABE_413
S_AHR_61013473	IMG activity: SIMG_OHAIT_410
S_AHR_61013474	IMG Activity: SIMG_OHABE_480
S_AHR_61013475	IMG activity: SIMG_OHAIT_482
S_AHR_61013476	IMG Activity: SIMG_OHABE_414
S_AHR_61013477	IMG Activity: SIMG_OHABE_814
S_AHR_61013478	IMG activity: SIMG_OHAIT_407
S_AHR_61013479	IMG Activity: SIMG_OHABE_415
S_AHR_61013480	IMG activity: SIMG_OHAIT_409
S_AHR_61013481	IMG Activity: SIMG_OHABE_418
S_AHR_61013482	IMG activity: SIMG_OHAIT_480
S_AHR_61013483	IMG Activity: SIMG_OHABE_419
S_AHR_61013484	IMG activity: SIMG_OHAIT_483
S_AHR_61013485	IMG Activity: SIMG_OHABE_417
S_AHR_61013486	IMG activity: SIMG_OHAIT_419
S_AHR_61013487	IMG Activity: SIMG_OHABE_409
S_AHR_61013488	IMG activity: SIMG_OHAIT_418
S_AHR_61013489	IMG Activity: SIMG_OHABE_407
S_AHR_61013490	IMG activity: SIMG_OHAIT_415
S_AHR_61013491	IMG Activity: OHABE_EDTINTERNET
S_AHR_61013492	IMG Activity: SIMG_OHABE_484
S_AHR_61013493	IMG activity: SIMG_OHAIT_814
S_AHR_61013494	IMG Activity: SIMG_OHABE_482
S_AHR_61013495	IMG activity: SIMG_OHAIT_414
S_AHR_61013496	IMG Activity: SIMG_OHABE_410
S_AHR_61013497	IMG activity: OHAIRI042
S_AHR_61013498	IMG Activity: SIMG_OHABE_483
S_AHR_61013499	IMG activity: OHAIRI015
S_AHR_61013500	IMG Activity: SIMG_OHABE_518
S_AHR_61013501	IMG activity: SIMG_OHAIT_446
S_AHR_61013502	IMG Activity: SIMG_OHABE_467
S_AHR_61013503	IMG activity: SIMG_OHAIT_445
S_AHR_61013504	IMG Activity: SIMG_OHABE_424
S_AHR_61013505	IMG Activity: OHABE_MZ001
S_AHR_61013506	IMG activity: SIMG_OHAIT_444
S_AHR_61013507	IMG Activity: SIMG_OHABE_427
S_AHR_61013508	IMG Activity: SIMG_OHABE_429
S_AHR_61013509	IMG Activity: OHABE_483
S_AHR_61013510	IMG Activity: SIMG_OHABE_416
S_AHR_61013511	IMG Activity: OHABE_DT004
S_AHR_61013512	IMG Activity: OHABEL004
S_AHR_61013513	IMG Activity: OHABEL005
S_AHR_61013514	IMG Activity: OHABEL003
S_AHR_61013515	IMG Activity: OHABJW000
S_AHR_61013516	IMG Activity: SIMG_OHABE_470
S_AHR_61013517	IMG Activity: OHABE_DT002
S_AHR_61013518	IMG Activity: OHABE_DT003
S_AHR_61013519	IMG Activity: SIMG_OHABE_432
S_AHR_61013520	IMG Activity: SIMG_OHABE_437
S_AHR_61013521	IMG Activity: SIMG_OHABE_425
S_AHR_61013522	IMG Activity: SIMG_OHABE_423
S_AHR_61013523	IMG Activity: SIMG_OHABE_422
S_AHR_61013524	IMG Activity: SIMG_OHABE_435

S_AHR_61013525	IMG Activity: SIMG_OHABE_471
S_AHR_61013526	IMG Activity: SIMG_OHABE_426
S_AHR_61013527	IMG Activity: SIMG_OHABE_461
S_AHR_61013528	IMG Activity: SIMG_OHABE_515
S_AHR_61013529	IMG Activity: SIMG_OHABE_438
S_AHR_61013530	IMG Activity: SIMG_OHABE_459
S_AHR_61013531	IMG Activity: SIMG_OHABE_428
S_AHR_61013532	IMG Activity: SIMG_OHABE_506
S_AHR_61013533	IMG Activity: SIMG_OHABE_507
S_AHR_61013534	IMG Activity: OHABE_TI361
S_AHR_61013535	IMG Activity: OHABE_TI363
S_AHR_61013536	IMG Activity: OHABE_TI362
S_AHR_61013537	IMG Activity: OHABE_TI364
S_AHR_61013538	IMG Activity: OHABE_TI370
S_AHR_61013539	IMG Activity: OHABE_RI061
S_AHR_61013540	IMG Activity: OHABE_AB001
S_AHR_61013541	IMG Activity: OHABE_RI062
S_AHR_61013542	IMG Activity: OHABE_TI325
S_AHR_61013543	IMG Activity: OHABE_TI321
S_AHR_61013544	IMG Activity: OHABE_TI322
S_AHR_61013545	IMG Activity: OHABE_TI323
S_AHR_61013546	IMG Activity: OHABE_TI324
S_AHR_61013547	IMG Activity: OHABE_RI063
S_AHR_61013548	IMG Activity: OHABE_TI340
S_AHR_61013549	IMG Activity: OHABE_AB002
S_AHR_61013550	IMG Activity: OHABE_RI055
S_AHR_61013551	IMG Activity: OHABE_AB200
S_AHR_61013552	IMG Activity: OHABE_RI054
S_AHR_61013553	IMG Activity: OHABE_QUOTACOMP00
S_AHR_61013554	IMG Activity: OHABE_QUOTACOMP01
S_AHR_61013555	IMG Activity: OHABE_RI053
S_AHR_61013556	IMG Activity: OHABE_RI056
S_AHR_61013557	IMG Activity: OHABE_AB010
S_AHR_61013558	IMG Activity: OHABE_AB003
S_AHR_61013559	IMG Activity: OHABE_AB004
S_AHR_61013560	IMG Activity: OHABE_AB005
S_AHR_61013561	IMG Activity: OHABE_AB011
S_AHR_61013562	IMG Activity: OHABE_AB009
S_AHR_61013563	IMG Activity: OHABE_AB012
S_AHR_61013564	IMG Activity: OHABAB009
S_AHR_61013565	IMG Activity: OHABE_UM003
S_AHR_61013566	IMG Activity: OHABUM01
S_AHR_61013567	IMG Activity: OHABUM02
S_AHR_61013568	IMG Activity: OHABUM03
S_AHR_61013569	IMG Activity: OHABE_UM002
S_AHR_61013570	IMG Activity: OHABE_UM022
S_AHR_61013571	IMG Activity: OHABE_UM023
S_AHR_61013572	IMG Activity: OHABE_UM010
S_AHR_61013573	IMG Activity: OHABE_PAY003
S_AHR_61013574	IMG Activity: OHABE_PAY002
S_AHR_61013575	IMG Activity: OHABE_UM012
S_AHR_61013576	IMG Activity: OHABE_UM014
S_AHR_61013577	IMG Activity: OHABE_UM006
S_AHR_61013578	IMG Activity: OHABE_UM008

S_AHR_61013579	IMG Activity: OHABE_UM013
S_AHR_61013580	IMG Activity: OHABE_RI090
S_AHR_61013581	IMG Activity: OHABE_TI110
S_AHR_61013582	IMG Activity: OHABE_TI120
S_AHR_61013583	IMG Activity: OHABE_TI130
S_AHR_61013584	IMG Activity: OHABE_TI210
S_AHR_61013585	IMG Activity: OHABE_RI071
S_AHR_61013586	IMG Activity: OHABE_TI310
S_AHR_61013587	IMG Activity: OHABE_RI070
S_AHR_61013588	IMG Activity: OHABE_RI080
S_AHR_61013589	IMG Activity: OHABE_UM104
S_AHR_61013590	IMG Activity: OHABE_UM105
S_AHR_61013591	IMG Activity: OHABE_UM101
S_AHR_61013592	IMG Activity: OHABE_UM102
S_AHR_61013593	IMG Activity: OHABE_UM103
S_AHR_61013594	IMG Activity: OHABE_X_PM_CREATE
S_AHR_61013595	IMG Activity: OHABE_RI081
S_AHR_61013596	IMG Activity: OHABE_RI052
S_AHR_61013597	IMG Activity: OHABSL002
S_AHR_61013598	IMG Activity: OHABSL003
S_AHR_61013599	IMG Activity: OHABE_RI015
S_AHR_61013600	IMG Activity: OHABE_IW063
S_AHR_61013601	IMG Activity: OHABE_IW065
S_AHR_61013602	IMG Activity: OHABE_IW061
S_AHR_61013603	IMG Activity: OHABE_IW082
S_AHR_61013604	IMG Activity: OHABE_SL002
S_AHR_61013605	IMG Activity: OHABKF002
S_AHR_61013606	IMG Activity: OHABBW022
S_AHR_61013607	IMG Activity: OHABBW010
S_AHR_61013608	IMG Activity: OHABE_KL000
S_AHR_61013609	IMG Activity: OHABKL000
S_AHR_61013610	IMG Activity: OHABE_RI042
S_AHR_61013611	IMG Activity: OHABSL001
S_AHR_61013612	IMG Activity: OHAB0003
S_AHR_61013613	IMG Activity: OHAB0004
S_AHR_61013614	IMG Activity: OHABSB000
S_AHR_61013615	IMG Activity: OHABSB001
S_AHR_61013616	IMG Activity: OHABBR000
S_AHR_61013617	IMG Activity: OHABE_DV001
S_AHR_61013618	IMG Activity: OHABCX006
S_AHR_61013619	IMG Activity: OHAB0002
S_AHR_61013620	IMG Activity: OHAB7009
S_AHR_61013621	IMG Activity: OHAB7008
S_AHR_61013622	IMG Activity: OHAB7007
S_AHR_61013623	IMG Activity: OHABE_IW037
S_AHR_61013624	IMG Activity: OHAB7006
S_AHR_61013625	IMG Activity: OHAB7005
S_AHR_61013626	IMG Activity: OHAB7004
S_AHR_61013627	IMG Activity: OHABKF001
S_AHR_61013628	IMG Activity: OHABE_AVX018
S_AHR_61013629	IMG Activity: OHABE_AVX017
S_AHR_61013630	IMG Activity: OHABE_BW22
S_AHR_61013631	IMG Activity: OHABE_AVBAS
S_AHR_61013632	IMG Activity: OHABE_AV001

S_AHR_61013633	IMG Activity: OHABE_AV511A
S_AHR_61013634	IMG Activity: OHABE_AV511C
S_AHR_61013635	IMG Activity: OHABAVXT00
S_AHR_61013636	IMG Activity: OHABE_AVP15
S_AHR_61013637	IMG Activity: OHABE_AV511B
S_AHR_61013638	IMG Activity: OHABE_BW21
S_AHR_61013639	IMG Activity: OHABE_RI051
S_AHR_61013640	IMG Activity: OHABBW009
S_AHR_61013641	IMG Activity: OHABE_RI031
S_AHR_61013642	IMG Activity: OHABE_BW005
S_AHR_61013643	IMG Activity: OHABE_PART
S_AHR_61013644	IMG Activity: OHABBW004
S_AHR_61013645	IMG Activity: OHABBW023
S_AHR_61013646	IMG Activity: OHABE_BW019
S_AHR_61013647	IMG Activity: OHABBW006
S_AHR_61013648	IMG Activity: OHABBW021
S_AHR_61013649	IMG Activity: SIMG_OHABE_454
S_AHR_61013650	IMG Activity: SIMG_OHABE_465
S_AHR_61013651	IMG Activity: SIMG_OHABE_519
S_AHR_61013652	IMG Activity: SIMG_OHABE_520
S_AHR_61013653	IMG Activity: OHABE_AL01
S_AHR_61013654	IMG Activity: SIMG_OHABE_456
S_AHR_61013655	IMG Activity: SIMG_OHABE_466
S_AHR_61013656	IMG Activity: SIMG_OHABE_455
S_AHR_61013657	IMG Activity: SIMG_OHABE_517
S_AHR_61013658	IMG Activity: SIMG_OHABE_523
S_AHR_61013659	IMG Activity: SIMG_OHABE_439
S_AHR_61013660	IMG Activity: SIMG_OHABE_524
S_AHR_61013661	IMG Activity: SIMG_OHABE_401
S_AHR_61013662	IMG Activity: SIMG_OHABE_481
S_AHR_61013663	IMG Activity: SIMG_OHABE_521
S_AHR_61013664	IMG Activity: SIMG_OHABE_453
S_AHR_61013665	IMG Activity: SIMG_OHABE_522
S_AHR_61013666	IMG Activity: OHABE_TI330
S_AHR_61013667	IMG Activity: SIMG_OHABE_450
S_AHR_61013668	IMG Activity: SIMG_OHABE_842
S_AHR_61013669	IMG Activity: SIMG_OHABE_843
S_AHR_61013670	IMG Activity: SIMG_OHABE_844
S_AHR_61013671	IMG Activity: SIMG_OHABE_501
S_AHR_61013672	IMG Activity: SIMG_OHABE_502
S_AHR_61013673	IMG Activity: SIMG_OHABE_508
S_AHR_61013674	IMG Activity: SIMG_OHABE_611
S_AHR_61013675	IMG Activity: SIMG_OHABE_612
S_AHR_61013676	IMG Activity: SIMG_OHABE_613
S_AHR_61013677	IMG Activity: SIMG_OHABE_614
S_AHR_61013678	IMG Activity: OHABE_DT009
S_AHR_61013679	IMG Activity: SIMG_OHABE_841
S_AHR_61013680	IMG Activity: SIMG_OHABE_513
S_AHR_61013681	IMG Activity: SIMG_OHABE_514
S_AHR_61013682	IMG Activity: OHABE_RI011
S_AHR_61013683	IMG Activity: OHABE_RI012
S_AHR_61013684	IMG Activity: SIMG_OHABE_421
S_AHR_61013685	IMG Activity: SIMG_OHABE_516
S_AHR_61013686	IMG Activity: SIMG_OHABE_509

S_AHR_61013687	IMG Activity: SIMG_OHABE_510
S_AHR_61013688	IMG Activity: OHABE_IW041
S_AHR_61013689	IMG Activity: SIMG_OHABE_512
S_AHR_61013690	IMG Activity: OHABE_IW035
S_AHR_61013691	IMG Activity: OHABE_IW069
S_AHR_61013692	IMG activity: OHAIFIN74
S_AHR_61013693	IMG activity: OHAIFIN72
S_AHR_61013694	IMG activity: OHAIFIN71
S_AHR_61013695	IMG activity: OHAIFIN70
S_AHR_61013696	IMG activity: OHAIT_ARE50
S_AHR_61013697	IMG activity: OHAIT_ARE40
S_AHR_61013698	IMG activity: OHAIFIN05
S_AHR_61013699	IMG activity: OHAIT_FIP15
S_AHR_61013700	IMG activity: OHAIT_FIP10
S_AHR_61013701	IMG activity: OHAIT_FIP00
S_AHR_61013702	IMG activity: OHAIT_FIP05
S_AHR_61013703	IMG activity: OHAIFIN15
S_AHR_61013704	IMG activity: OHAIFIN10
S_AHR_61013705	IMG activity: OHAIT_ARE30
S_AHR_61013706	IMG activity: OHAITSE30
S_AHR_61013707	IMG activity: OHAITSE20
S_AHR_61013708	IMG activity: OHAITSE10
S_AHR_61013709	IMG activity: OHAIDTF50
S_AHR_61013710	IMG activity: OHAIDTF40
S_AHR_61013711	IMG activity: OHAIDTF45
S_AHR_61013712	IMG activity: OHAITSE50
S_AHR_61013713	IMG activity: OHAIT_ARE20
S_AHR_61013714	IMG activity: OHAIT_ARE10
S_AHR_61013715	IMG activity: OHAIT_TSE30
S_AHR_61013716	IMG activity: OHAIT_TSE20
S_AHR_61013717	IMG activity: OHAIT_TSE10
S_AHR_61013718	IMG activity: OHAIT_TSE00
S_AHR_61013719	IMG activity: SIMG_OHAIT_525
S_AHR_61013720	IMG activity: SIMG_OHAIT_530
S_AHR_61013721	IMG activity: SIMG_OHAIT_518
S_AHR_61013722	IMG activity: SIMG_OHAIT_507
S_AHR_61013723	IMG activity: SIMG_OHAIT_506
S_AHR_61013724	IMG activity: SIMG_OHAIT_515
S_AHR_61013725	IMG activity: SIMG_OHAIT_402
S_AHR_61013726	IMG activity: SIMG_OHAIT_528
S_AHR_61013727	IMG activity: SIMG_OHAIT_527
S_AHR_61013728	IMG activity: SIMG_OHAIT_408
S_AHR_61013729	IMG activity: SIMG_OHAIT_406
S_AHR_61013730	IMG activity: SIMG_OHAIT_405
S_AHR_61013731	IMG activity: SIMG_OHAIT_403
S_AHR_61013732	IMG activity: SIMG_OHAIT_416
S_AHR_61013733	IMG activity: OHAIDT004
S_AHR_61013734	IMG activity: OHAIDT003
S_AHR_61013735	IMG activity: OHAIDT002
S_AHR_61013736	IMG activity: OHAIT_ARR10
S_AHR_61013737	IMG activity: OHAIARR05
S_AHR_61013738	IMG activity: OHAIT_FIP20
S_AHR_61013739	IMG activity: OHAIT_0902
S_AHR_61013740	IMG activity: OHAIT_483

S_AHR_61013741	IMG activity: OHAIMZ001
S_AHR_61013742	IMG activity: OHAIT_0903
S_AHR_61013743	IMG activity: OHAIT_0913
S_AHR_61013744	IMG activity: OHAIT_0912
S_AHR_61013745	IMG activity: OHAIT_0911
S_AHR_61013746	IMG activity: OHAIDTF35
S_AHR_61013747	IMG activity: OHAIPRV09
S_AHR_61013748	IMG activity: OHAIPRV04
S_AHR_61013749	IMG activity: OHAIPRV59
S_AHR_61013750	IMG activity: OHAIPRV61
S_AHR_61013751	IMG activity: OHAIPRV60
S_AHR_61013752	IMG activity: OHAIPRV94
S_AHR_61013753	IMG activity: OHAIPRV12
S_AHR_61013754	IMG activity: OHAIPRV46
S_AHR_61013755	IMG activity: OHAIPRV16
S_AHR_61013756	IMG activity: OHAIPRV14
S_AHR_61013757	IMG activity: OHAIPRV90
S_AHR_61013758	IMG activity: OHAIPRV13
S_AHR_61013759	IMG activity: OHAIPRV11
S_AHR_61013760	IMG activity: OHAIPRV71
S_AHR_61013761	IMG activity: OHAIT_SZ610
S_AHR_61013762	IMG activity: OHAIT_SZ510
S_AHR_61013763	IMG activity: OHAIT_SZ410
S_AHR_61013764	IMG activity: OHAIT_SZ310
S_AHR_61013765	IMG activity: OHAIT_SZ120
S_AHR_61013766	IMG activity: OHAIT_SZ110
S_AHR_61013767	IMG activity: OHAIPRV05
S_AHR_61013768	IMG activity: OHAIPRV72
S_AHR_61013769	IMG activity: OHAIPRV70
S_AHR_61013770	IMG activity: OHAIPRV08
S_AHR_61013771	IMG activity: OHAIT_PRV70
S_AHR_61013772	IMG activity: OHAIPRV07
S_AHR_61013773	IMG activity: OHAIPRV06
S_AHR_61013774	IMG activity: OHAIDTF74
S_AHR_61013775	IMG activity: OHAIDTF72
S_AHR_61013776	IMG activity: OHAIDTF71
S_AHR_61013777	IMG activity: OHAIDTF70
S_AHR_61013778	IMG activity: OHAITAS40
S_AHR_61013779	IMG activity: OHAITAS35
S_AHR_61013780	IMG activity: OHAIDTF01
S_AHR_61013781	IMG activity: OHAIDTF30
S_AHR_61013782	IMG activity: OHAIDTF25
S_AHR_61013783	IMG activity: OHAIDTF20
S_AHR_61013784	IMG activity: OHAIDTF15
S_AHR_61013785	IMG activity: OHAIDTF10
S_AHR_61013786	IMG activity: OHAIDTF00
S_AHR_61013787	IMG activity: OHAITAS30
S_AHR_61013788	IMG activity: OAHITAS74
S_AHR_61013789	IMG activity: OHAITAS71
S_AHR_61013790	IMG activity: OHAITAS72
S_AHR_61013791	IMG activity: OHAITAS70
S_AHR_61013792	IMG activity: OHAIPRV55
S_AHR_61013793	IMG activity: OHAIPRV50
S_AHR_61013794	IMG activity: OHAITAS00

S_AHR_61013795	IMG activity: OHAITAS25
S_AHR_61013796	IMG activity: OHAITAS20
S_AHR_61013797	IMG activity: OHAITAS95
S_AHR_61013798	IMG activity: OHAITAS10
S_AHR_61013799	IMG activity: OHAIT_TAS70
S_AHR_61013800	IMG activity: OHAITAS05
S_AHR_61013801	IMG activity: SIMG_OHAIT_529
S_AHR_61013802	IMG activity: OHAIT_DM120
S_AHR_61013803	IMG activity: OHAIT_DM080
S_AHR_61013804	IMG activity: OHAIT_DM070
S_AHR_61013805	IMG activity: OHAIT_DM010
S_AHR_61013806	IMG activity: OHAIT_DM020
S_AHR_61013807	IMG activity: OHAIT_DM060
S_AHR_61013808	IMG activity: OHAIT_DM130
S_AHR_61013809	IMG activity: OHAIT_DM024
S_AHR_61013810	IMG activity: OHAIT_DM040
S_AHR_61013811	IMG activity: OHAIT_DM021
S_AHR_61013812	IMG activity: OHAIT_DM100
S_AHR_61013813	IMG activity: OHAIT_DM090
S_AHR_61013814	IMG activity: OHAIT_DM140
S_AHR_61013815	IMG activity: OHAIT_DM030
S_AHR_61013816	IMG activity: OHAIRI081
S_AHR_61013817	IMG activity: OHAIRI080
S_AHR_61013818	IMG activity: OHAIRI071
S_AHR_61013819	IMG activity: OHAIRI070
S_AHR_61013820	IMG activity: OHAIRI063
S_AHR_61013821	IMG activity: OHAIRI062
S_AHR_61013822	IMG activity: OHAIRI090
S_AHR_61013823	IMG activity: OHAIT_DM045
S_AHR_61013824	IMG activity: OHAIT_DM005
S_AHR_61013825	IMG activity: OHAIPAY003
S_AHR_61013827	IMG activity: OHAIPAY002
S_AHR_61013828	IMG activity: OHAIUM003
S_AHR_61013829	IMG activity: OHAIUM002
S_AHR_61013830	IMG activity: OHAIT_CU020
S_AHR_61013831	IMG activity: OHAIT_CU015
S_AHR_61013832	IMG activity: OHAIT_CU010
S_AHR_61013833	IMG activity: OHAIT_CU005
S_AHR_61013834	IMG activity: OHAIT_CU004
S_AHR_61013835	IMG activity: OHAIT_CU000
S_AHR_61013836	IMG activity: OHAIT_CU025
S_AHR_61013837	IMG activity: OHAIT_RET20
S_AHR_61013838	IMG activity: OHAIT_RET10
S_AHR_61013840	IMG activity: OHAIT_NOR10
S_AHR_61013841	IMG activity: OHAIT_CU040
S_AHR_61013842	IMG activity: OHAIT_CU035
S_AHR_61013843	IMG activity: OHAIT_CU030
S_AHR_61013844	IMG activity: OHAIT_DM170
S_AHR_61013845	IMG activity: OHAIT_DM022
S_AHR_61013846	IMG activity: OHAIT_DM023
S_AHR_61013847	IMG activity: OHAIT_DM050
S_AHR_61013848	IMG activity: OHAIT_DM035
S_AHR_61013849	IMG activity: OHAIT_DM034
S_AHR_61013850	IMG activity: OHAIT_DM025

S_AHR_61013851	IMG activity: OHAIT_DM027
S_AHR_61013852	IMG activity: OHAIT_DM031
S_AHR_61013853	IMG activity: OHAIT_DM032
S_AHR_61013854	IMG activity: OHAIT_DM033
S_AHR_61013855	IMG activity: OHAIT_DM041
S_AHR_61013856	IMG activity: OHAIT_DM029
S_AHR_61013857	IMG activity: OHAIT_DM028
S_AHR_61013858	IMG activity: OHAIRI061
S_AHR_61013859	IMG activity: SIMG_OHAIT_464
S_AHR_61013860	IMG activity: SIMG_OHAIT_463
S_AHR_61013861	IMG activity: SIMG_OHAIT_451
S_AHR_61013862	IMG activity: SIMG_OHAIT_457
S_AHR_61013863	IMG activity: SIMG_OHAIT_431
S_AHR_61013864	IMG activity: OHAITEDTINTERNET
S_AHR_61013865	IMG activity: SIMG_OHAIT_471
S_AHR_61013866	IMG activity: SIMG_OHAIT_432
S_AHR_61013867	IMG activity: SIMG_OHAIT_437
S_AHR_61013868	IMG activity: SIMG_OHAIT_425
S_AHR_61013869	IMG activity: SIMG_OHAIT_423
S_AHR_61013870	IMG activity: SIMG_OHAIT_422
S_AHR_61013871	IMG activity: SIMG_OHAIT_435
S_AHR_61013872	IMG activity: SIMG_OHAIT_484
S_AHR_61013873	IMG activity: SIMG_OHAIT_413
S_AHR_61013874	IMG activity: SIMG_OHAIT_417
S_AHR_61013875	IMG activity: SIMG_OHAIT_410
S_AHR_61013876	IMG activity: SIMG_OHAIT_482
S_AHR_61013877	IMG activity: SIMG_OHAIT_407
S_AHR_61013878	IMG activity: SIMG_OHAIT_409
S_AHR_61013879	IMG activity: SIMG_OHAIT_480
S_AHR_61013880	IMG activity: SIMG_OHAIT_483
S_AHR_61013881	IMG activity: SIMG_OHAIT_419
S_AHR_61013882	IMG activity: SIMG_OHAIT_418
S_AHR_61013883	IMG activity: SIMG_OHAIT_415
S_AHR_61013884	IMG activity: SIMG_OHAIT_814
S_AHR_61013885	IMG activity: SIMG_OHAIT_414
S_AHR_61013886	IMG activity: OHAIRI042
S_AHR_61013887	IMG activity: OHAIRI015
S_AHR_61013888	IMG activity: SIMG_OHAIT_446
S_AHR_61013889	IMG activity: SIMG_OHAIT_445
S_AHR_61013890	IMG activity: SIMG_OHAIT_444
S_AHR_61013891	IMG activity: SIMG_OHAIT_443
S_AHR_61013892	IMG activity: OHAIRI031
S_AHR_61013893	IMG activity: OHAIRI055
S_AHR_61013894	IMG activity: OHAIRI054
S_AHR_61013895	IMG activity: OHAIRI053
S_AHR_61013896	IMG activity: OHAIRI056
S_AHR_61013897	IMG activity: OHAIRI052
S_AHR_61013898	IMG activity: OHAIRI051
S_AHR_61013899	IMG activity: SIMG_OHAIT_442
S_AHR_61013900	IMG activity: SIMG_OHAIT_429
S_AHR_61013901	IMG activity: SIMG_OHAIT_461
S_AHR_61013902	IMG activity: SIMG_OHAIT_438
S_AHR_61013903	IMG activity: SIMG_OHAIT_459
S_AHR_61013904	IMG activity: SIMG_OHAIT_428

S_AHR_61013905	IMG activity: SIMG_OHAIT_426
S_AHR_61013906	IMG activity: SIMG_OHAIT_427
S_AHR_61013907	IMG activity: SIMG_OHAIT_681
S_AHR_61013908	IMG activity: SIMG_OHAIT_447
S_AHR_61013909	IMG activity: SIMG_OHAIT_665
S_AHR_61013910	IMG activity: SIMG_OHAIT_470
S_AHR_61013911	IMG activity: SIMG_OHAIT_467
S_AHR_61013912	IMG activity: SIMG_OHAIT_424
S_AHR_61013913	IMG activity: OHAIACC44
S_AHR_61013914	IMG activity: OHAIACC41
S_AHR_61013915	IMG activity: OHAIACC42
S_AHR_61013916	IMG activity: OHAIAB002
S_AHR_61013917	IMG activity: OHAIAB003
S_AHR_61013918	IMG activity: OHAIT_MD014
S_AHR_61013919	IMG activity: OHAIACC15
S_AHR_61013920	IMG activity: OHAIACC05
S_AHR_61013921	IMG activity: OHAIAB001
S_AHR_61013922	IMG activity: OHAIACC10
S_AHR_61013923	IMG activity: OHAIBW006
S_AHR_61013924	IMG activity: OHAIBW019
S_AHR_61013925	IMG activity: OHAITFR10
S_AHR_61013926	IMG activity: OHAITFR50
S_AHR_61013927	IMG activity: OHAIAB011
S_AHR_61013928	IMG activity: OHAIACC40
S_AHR_61013929	IMG activity: OHAIBW004
S_AHR_61013930	IMG activity: OHAIAB004
S_AHR_61013931	IMG activity: OHAIAB005
S_AHR_61013932	IMG activity: OHAIBW005
S_AHR_61013933	IMG activity: OHAILCR05
S_AHR_61013934	IMG activity: OHAILCR44
S_AHR_61013935	IMG activity: OHAILCR41
S_AHR_61013936	IMG activity: OHAILCR42
S_AHR_61013937	IMG activity: OHAIT_MD009
S_AHR_61013938	IMG activity: OHAIKL000
S_AHR_61013939	IMG activity: OHAILCR30
S_AHR_61013940	IMG activity: OHAILCR20
S_AHR_61013941	IMG activity: OHAILCR10
S_AHR_61013942	IMG activity: OHAIT_APR61
S_AHR_61013943	IMG activity: OHAIT_MD011
S_AHR_61013944	IMG activity: OHAIT_MD012
S_AHR_61013945	IMG activity: OHAIT_MD013
S_AHR_61013946	IMG activity: OHAIACC25
S_AHR_61013947	IMG activity: OHAIACC20
S_AHR_61013948	IMG activity: OHAIAPR21
S_AHR_61013949	IMG activity: OHAIT_MD004
S_AHR_61013950	IMG activity: OHAIT_APR62
S_AHR_61013951	IMG activity: OHAIT_MD010
S_AHR_61013952	IMG activity: OHAILCR40
S_AHR_61013953	IMG activity: OHAIBAS10
S_AHR_61013954	IMG activity: OHAIAB200
S_AHR_61013955	IMG activity: OHAIAPR11
S_AHR_61013956	IMG activity: OHAIAPR10
S_AHR_61013957	IMG activity: OHAIAPR09
S_AHR_61013958	IMG activity: OHAIAB010

S_AHR_61013959	IMG activity: OHAIBW21
S_AHR_61013960	IMG activity: OHAIBW22
S_AHR_61013961	IMG activity: OHAIT_DEC01
S_AHR_61013962	IMG activity: OHAIAPR20
S_AHR_61013963	IMG activity: OHAIT_APR35
S_AHR_61013964	IMG activity: OHAIT_APR55
S_AHR_61013965	IMG activity: OHAIT_KF003
S_AHR_61013966	IMG activity: OHAIKF002
S_AHR_61013967	IMG activity: OHAIKF001
S_AHR_61013968	IMG activity: OHAIAPR08
S_AHR_61013969	IMG activity: OHAIAPR07
S_AHR_61013970	IMG activity: OHAIT_APR50
S_AHR_61013971	IMG activity: OHAIAPR05
S_AHR_61013972	IMG activity: OHAIT_APR40
S_AHR_61013973	IMG activity: OHAITFR20
S_AHR_61013974	IMG activity: OHAITFR00
S_AHR_61013975	IMG activity: OHAIAVBAS
S_AHR_61013976	IMG activity: OHAITFR74
S_AHR_61013977	IMG activity: OHAIAVX017
S_AHR_61013978	IMG activity: OHAIAB009
S_AHR_61013979	IMG activity: OHAITFR40
S_AHR_61013980	IMG activity: OHAIAV001
S_AHR_61013981	IMG activity: OHAITFR30
S_AHR_61013982	IMG activity: OHAITFR05
S_AHR_61013983	IMG activity: OHAIAV511C
S_AHR_61013984	IMG activity: OHAIAVXT00
S_AHR_61013985	IMG activity: OHAIAB012
S_AHR_61013986	IMG activity: OHAIAVP15
S_AHR_61013987	IMG activity: OHAITFR70
S_AHR_61013988	IMG activity: OHAIAVX018
S_AHR_61013989	IMG activity: OHAITFR71
S_AHR_61013990	IMG activity: OHAITFR73
S_AHR_61013991	IMG activity: OHAIAV511A
S_AHR_61013992	IMG activity: OHAIAV511B
S_AHR_61013993	IMG activity : OHAITI370
S_AHR_61013994	IMG activity: OHAIT_APR27
S_AHR_61013995	IMG activity: OHAIT_LIB10
S_AHR_61013996	IMG activity : OHAIT_LIB20
S_AHR_61013997	IMG activity: OHAIT_LIB30
S_AHR_61013998	IMG activity: OHAIUM010
S_AHR_61013999	IMG activity: OHAIUM013
S_AHR_61014000	IMG activity: OHAIT_SZ210
S_AHR_61014001	IMG activity: OHAIUM010B
S_AHR_61014002	IMG activity: OHAITI364
S_AHR_61014003	IMG activity: OHAIUM101
S_AHR_61014004	IMG activity: OHAITI340
S_AHR_61014005	IMG activity: OHAIUM023
S_AHR_61014006	IMG activity: OHAIAPR23
S_AHR_61014007	IMG activity: OHAIUM022
S_AHR_61014008	IMG activity: OHAIAPR24
S_AHR_61014009	IMG activity: OHAITI361
S_AHR_61014010	IMG activity: OHAITI363
S_AHR_61014011	IMG activity : OHAITI362
S_AHR_61014012	IMG activity: OHAIT_SZ221

S_AHR_61014013	IMG activity: OHAIUM012
S_AHR_61014014	IMG activity: OHAIT_SZ030
S_AHR_61014015	IMG activity: OHAIT_SZ040
S_AHR_61014016	IMG activity: OHAIAPR25
S_AHR_61014017	IMG activity: OHAIT_SZ050
S_AHR_61014018	IMG activity: OHAIT_SZ060
S_AHR_61014019	IMG activity: OHAIAPR26
S_AHR_61014020	IMG activity: OHAIT_SZ070
S_AHR_61014021	IMG activity: OHAIT_SZ080
S_AHR_61014022	IMG activity: OHAIT_SZ020
S_AHR_61014023	IMG activity : OHAIT_SZ222
S_AHR_61014024	IMG activity: OHAIT_SZ223
S_AHR_61014025	IMG activity: OHAIUM008
S_AHR_61014026	IMG activity: OHAIT_SZ224
S_AHR_61014027	IMG activity: OHAIUM006
S_AHR_61014028	IMG activity: OHAIT_SZ230
S_AHR_61014029	IMG activity: OHAIT_SZ240
S_AHR_61014030	IMG activity: OHAIT_SZ010
S_AHR_61014031	IMG activity : OHAIUM014
S_AHR_61014032	IMG activity: OHAIANF71
S_AHR_61014033	IMG activity: OHAIAPR22
S_AHR_61014034	IMG activity: OHAIANF73
S_AHR_61014035	IMG activity: OHAIANF72
S_AHR_61014036	IMG activity: OHAIANF75
S_AHR_61014037	IMG activity: OHAIANF05
S_AHR_61014038	IMG activity: OHAIANF10
S_AHR_61014039	IMG activity: OHAIANF60
S_AHR_61014040	IMG activity: OHAIANF30
S_AHR_61014041	IMG activity: OHAIT_MD003
S_AHR_61014042	IMG activity: OHAIT_MD008
S_AHR_61014043	IMG activity: OHAISL001
S_AHR_61014044	IMG activity: OHAISL002
S_AHR_61014045	IMG activity: OHAIT_MD007
S_AHR_61014046	IMG activity: OHAISL003
S_AHR_61014047	IMG activity: OHAIT_MD006
S_AHR_61014048	IMG activity: OHAIT_MD005
S_AHR_61014049	IMG activity: OHAIJW000
S_AHR_61014050	IMG activity: OHAIAPR19
S_AHR_61014051	IMG activity: OHAIANF40
S_AHR_61014052	IMG activity: OHAITI210
S_AHR_61014053	IMG activity: OHAITI310
S_AHR_61014054	IMG activity: OHAIUM103
S_AHR_61014055	IMG activity: OHAITI325
S_AHR_61014056	IMG activity: OHAITI321
S_AHR_61014057	IMG activity: OHAITI322
S_AHR_61014058	IMG activity: OHAITI323
S_AHR_61014059	IMG activity: OHAITI324
S_AHR_61014060	IMG activity: OHAIUM102
S_AHR_61014061	IMG activity: OHAIUM105
S_AHR_61014062	IMG activity: OHAIUM104
S_AHR_61014063	IMG activity: OHAITI110
S_AHR_61014064	IMG activity: OHAITI120
S_AHR_61014065	IMG activity: OHAIT_MD001
S_AHR_61014066	IMG activity: OHAITI130

S_AHR_61014067	IMG activity: OHAIT_MD002
S_AHR_61014068	IMG activity: OHAITI330
S_AHR_61014069	IMG activity: SIMG_OHAIT_481
S_AHR_61014070	IMG activity: SIMG_OHAIT_661
S_AHR_61014071	IMG activity: SIMG_OHAIT_662
S_AHR_61014073	IMG activity: SIMG_OHAIT_664
S_AHR_61014074	IMG activity: OHAIAL01
S_AHR_61014075	IMG activity: SIMG_OHAIT_401
S_AHR_61014076	IMG activity: SIMG_OHAIT_441
S_AHR_61014077	IMG activity: SIMG_OHAIT_524
S_AHR_61014078	IMG activity: SIMG_OHAIT_454
S_AHR_61014079	IMG activity: SIMG_OHAIT_455
S_AHR_61014080	IMG activity: SIMG_OHAIT_466
S_AHR_61014081	IMG activity: SIMG_OHAIT_456
S_AHR_61014082	IMG activity: SIMG_OHAIT_465
S_AHR_61014083	IMG activity: SIMG_OHAIT_421
S_AHR_61014084	IMG activity: SIMG_OHAIT_453
S_AHR_61014085	IMG activity: SIMG_OHAIT_450
S_AHR_61014086	IMG activity: SIMG_OHAIT_439
S_AHR_61014087	IMG activity: SIMG_OHAIT_514
S_AHR_61014088	IMG activity: SIMG_OHAIT_513
S_AHR_61014089	IMG activity: SIMG_OHAIT_512
S_AHR_61014090	IMG activity: SIMG_OHAIT_510
S_AHR_61014091	IMG activity: SIMG_OHAIT_509
S_AHR_61014092	IMG activity: SIMG_OHAIT_508
S_AHR_61014093	IMG activity: SIMG_OHAIT_502
S_AHR_61014094	IMG activity: SIMG_OHAIT_501
S_AHR_61014095	IMG activity: OHAIDT009
S_AHR_61014096	IMG activity: SIMG_OHAIT_523
S_AHR_61014097	IMG activity: SIMG_OHAIT_522
S_AHR_61014098	IMG activity: SIMG_OHAIT_521
S_AHR_61014099	IMG activity: SIMG_OHAIT_520
S_AHR_61014100	IMG activity: SIMG_OHAIT_519
S_AHR_61014101	IMG activity: OHAIRI011
S_AHR_61014102	IMG activity: OHAIRI012
S_AHR_61014103	IMG activity: SIMG_OHAIT_517
S_AHR_61014104	IMG activity: SIMG_OHAIT_516
S_AHR_61014105	IMG Activity: OHANSP02
S_AHR_61014106	IMG Activity: OHANSP05
S_AHR_61014107	IMG Activity: OHANSP03
S_AHR_61014108	IMG Activity: OHANSP04
S_AHR_61014109	IMG Activity: OHANAR01
S_AHR_61014110	IMG Activity: OHANAR02
S_AHR_61014111	IMG Activity: OHANAR03
S_AHR_61014112	IMG Activity: OHANAR04
S_AHR_61014113	IMG Activity: OHANBNI02
S_AHR_61014114	IMG Activity: OHAN9030
S_AHR_61014115	IMG Activity: OHAN9001
S_AHR_61014116	IMG Activity: OHANWW02
S_AHR_61014117	IMG Activity: OHANWW03
S_AHR_61014118	IMG Activity: OHANWW04
S_AHR_61014119	IMG Activity: OHANWW05
S_AHR_61014120	IMG Activity: OHANWW06
S_AHR_61014121	IMG Activity: OHANSP07

S_AHR_61014122	IMG Activity: OHANSP06
S_AHR_61014123	IMG Activity: OHANBNI03
S_AHR_61014124	IMG Activity: OHANL_DT002
S_AHR_61014125	IMG Activity: OHANL_DT003
S_AHR_61014126	IMG Activity: OHANL_DT004
S_AHR_61014127	IMG Activity: OHANL_MZ001
S_AHR_61014128	IMG Activity: OHANL_483
S_AHR_61014129	IMG Activity: SIMG_OHANL_416
S_AHR_61014130	IMG Activity: SIMG_OHANL_515
S_AHR_61014131	IMG Activity: SIMG_OHANL_506
S_AHR_61014132	IMG Activity: SIMG_OHANL_507
S_AHR_61014133	IMG Activity: OHANBNI04
S_AHR_61014134	IMG Activity: OHANBN06
S_AHR_61014135	IMG Activity: OHANBN07
S_AHR_61014136	IMG Activity: OHANJW001
S_AHR_61014137	IMG Activity: OHANL_0902
S_AHR_61014138	IMG Activity: OHANL_0911
S_AHR_61014139	IMG Activity: OHANL_0912
S_AHR_61014140	IMG Activity: OHANL_0913
S_AHR_61014141	IMG Activity: OHANL_0903
S_AHR_61014142	IMG Activity: OHAN9051
S_AHR_61014143	IMG Activity: OHAN9035
S_AHR_61014144	IMG Activity: OHAN9031
S_AHR_61014145	IMG Activity: OHAN9033
S_AHR_61014146	IMG Activity: OHAN9032
S_AHR_61014147	IMG Activity: OHAN9041
S_AHR_61014148	IMG Activity: OHAN9042
S_AHR_61014149	IMG Activity: OHAN9002
S_AHR_61014150	IMG Activity: OHAN9009
S_AHR_61014151	IMG Activity: OHANZI10
S_AHR_61014152	IMG Activity: OHANZI11
S_AHR_61014153	IMG Activity: OHANZI14
S_AHR_61014154	IMG Activity: OHANZI12
S_AHR_61014155	IMG Activity: OHANZI16
S_AHR_61014156	IMG Activity: OHANZI17
S_AHR_61014157	IMG Activity: OHAN9059
S_AHR_61014158	IMG Activity: OHAN9014
S_AHR_61014159	IMG Activity: OHAN9050
S_AHR_61014160	IMG Activity: OHAN9012
S_AHR_61014161	IMG Activity: OHAN9019
S_AHR_61014162	IMG Activity: OHAN9020
S_AHR_61014163	IMG Activity: OHAN9021
S_AHR_61014164	IMG Activity: OHAN9023
S_AHR_61014165	IMG Activity: OHAN9025
S_AHR_61014166	IMG Activity: OHAN9026
S_AHR_61014167	IMG Activity: OHAN9028
S_AHR_61014168	IMG Activity: OHAN9029
S_AHR_61014169	IMG Activity: OHAN9043
S_AHR_61014170	IMG Activity: OHAN9003
S_AHR_61014171	IMG Activity: OHAN9004
S_AHR_61014172	IMG Activity: OHAN9031
S_AHR_61014173	IMG Activity: OHAN9008
S_AHR_61014174	IMG Activity: OHAN9005
S_AHR_61014175	IMG Activity: OHAN9015

S_AHR_61014176	IMG Activity: OHAN9016
S_AHR_61014177	IMG Activity: OHAN9017
S_AHR_61014178	IMG Activity: OHAN9018
S_AHR_61014179	IMG Activity: SIMG_OHANL_518
S_AHR_61014180	IMG Activity: SIMG_OHANL_470
S_AHR_61014181	IMG Activity: OHANL_601
S_AHR_61014182	IMG Activity: SIMG_OHANL_615
S_AHR_61014183	IMG Activity: OHAN9205
S_AHR_61014184	IMG Activity: OHAN9211
S_AHR_61014185	IMG Activity: OHAN9212
S_AHR_61014186	IMG Activity: OHANL_RI015
S_AHR_61014187	IMG Activity: OHANL_RI042
S_AHR_61014188	IMG Activity: OHANL_RI031
S_AHR_61014189	IMG Activity: SIMG_OHANL_426
S_AHR_61014190	IMG Activity: SIMG_OHANL_428
S_AHR_61014191	IMG Activity: SIMG_OHANL_459
S_AHR_61014192	IMG Activity: SIMG_OHANL_438
S_AHR_61014193	IMG Activity: SIMG_OHANL_461
S_AHR_61014194	IMG Activity: SIMG_OHANL_429
S_AHR_61014195	IMG Activity: SIMG_OHANL_427
S_AHR_61014196	IMG Activity: SIMG_OHANL_424
S_AHR_61014197	IMG Activity: SIMG_OHANL_467
S_AHR_61014198	IMG Activity: OHANL_RI051
S_AHR_61014199	IMG Activity: OHANL_RI071
S_AHR_61014200	IMG Activity: OHANL_RI080
S_AHR_61014201	IMG Activity: OHANL_RI081
S_AHR_61014202	IMG Activity: OHANL_RI090
S_AHR_61014203	IMG Activity: OHANL_UM002
S_AHR_61014204	IMG Activity: OHANL_UM003
S_AHR_61014205	IMG Activity: OHANUM05
S_AHR_61014206	IMG Activity: OHANL_PAY002
S_AHR_61014207	IMG Activity: OHANL_PAY003
S_AHR_61014208	IMG Activity: OHANL_RI052
S_AHR_61014209	IMG Activity: OHANL_RI056
S_AHR_61014210	IMG Activity: OHANL_RI053
S_AHR_61014211	IMG Activity: OHANL_RI054
S_AHR_61014212	IMG Activity: OHANL_RI055
S_AHR_61014213	IMG Activity: OHANL_RI061
S_AHR_61014214	IMG Activity: OHANL_RI062
S_AHR_61014215	IMG Activity: OHANL_RI063
S_AHR_61014216	IMG Activity: OHANL_RI070
S_AHR_61014217	IMG Activity: SIMG_OHANL_529
S_AHR_61014218	IMG Activity: SIMG_OHANL_409
S_AHR_61014219	IMG Activity: SIMG_OHANL_407
S_AHR_61014220	IMG Activity: SIMG_OHANL_482
S_AHR_61014221	IMG Activity: SIMG_OHANL_410
S_AHR_61014222	IMG Activity: SIMG_OHANL_417
S_AHR_61014223	IMG Activity: SIMG_OHANL_413
S_AHR_61014224	IMG Activity: SIMG_OHANL_480
S_AHR_61014225	IMG Activity: SIMG_OHANL_414
S_AHR_61014226	IMG Activity: SIMG_OHANL_530
S_AHR_61014227	IMG Activity: SIMG_OHANL_525
S_AHR_61014228	IMG Activity: SIMG_OHANL_402
S_AHR_61014229	IMG Activity: SIMG_OHANL_403

S_AHR_61014230	IMG Activity: SIMG_OHANL_405
S_AHR_61014231	IMG Activity: SIMG_OHANL_406
S_AHR_61014232	IMG Activity: SIMG_OHANL_408
S_AHR_61014233	IMG Activity: SIMG_OHANL_527
S_AHR_61014234	IMG Activity: SIMG_OHANL_528
S_AHR_61014235	IMG Activity: SIMG_OHANL_814
S_AHR_61014236	IMG Activity: SIMG_OHANL_463
S_AHR_61014237	IMG Activity: SIMG_OHANL_464
S_AHR_61014238	IMG Activity: SIMG_OHANL_471
S_AHR_61014239	IMG Activity: SIMG_OHANL_435
S_AHR_61014240	IMG Activity: SIMG_OHANL_422
S_AHR_61014241	IMG Activity: SIMG_OHANL_423
S_AHR_61014242	IMG Activity: SIMG_OHANL_425
S_AHR_61014243	IMG Activity: SIMG_OHANL_437
S_AHR_61014244	IMG Activity: SIMG_OHANL_432
S_AHR_61014245	IMG Activity: SIMG_OHANL_415
S_AHR_61014246	IMG Activity: SIMG_OHANL_418
S_AHR_61014247	IMG Activity: SIMG_OHANL_419
S_AHR_61014248	IMG Activity: SIMG_OHANL_483
S_AHR_61014249	IMG Activity: SIMG_OHANL_484
S_AHR_61014250	IMG Activity: OHANL_EDTINTERNET
S_AHR_61014251	IMG Activity: SIMG_OHANL_431
S_AHR_61014252	IMG Activity: SIMG_OHANL_457
S_AHR_61014253	IMG Activity: SIMG_OHANL_451
S_AHR_61014254	IMG Activity: OHANL_TI361
S_AHR_61014255	IMG Activity: OHANL_TI363
S_AHR_61014256	IMG Activity: OHANL_TI362
S_AHR_61014257	IMG Activity: OHANL_TI364
S_AHR_61014258	IMG Activity: OHANL_TI370
S_AHR_61014259	IMG Activity: OHANL_AB001
S_AHR_61014260	IMG Activity: OHANL_AB002
S_AHR_61014261	IMG Activity: OHANL_AB003
S_AHR_61014262	IMG Activity: OHANTI210
S_AHR_61014263	IMG Activity: OHANL_TI310
S_AHR_61014264	IMG Activity: OHANL_TI325
S_AHR_61014265	IMG Activity: OHANL_TI321
S_AHR_61014266	IMG Activity: OHANL_TI322
S_AHR_61014267	IMG Activity: OHANL_TI323
S_AHR_61014268	IMG Activity: OHANL_TI324
S_AHR_61014269	IMG Activity: OHANL_TI340
S_AHR_61014270	IMG Activity: OHANL_AB004
S_AHR_61014271	IMG Activity: OHANL_BW005
S_AHR_61014272	IMG Activity: OHANBW01
S_AHR_61014273	IMG Activity: OHANL_BW019
S_AHR_61014274	IMG Activity: OHANL_AV001
S_AHR_61014275	IMG Activity: OHANL_AVBAS
S_AHR_61014276	IMG Activity: OHANL_AVX017
S_AHR_61014277	IMG Activity: OHANL_AVX018
S_AHR_61014278	IMG Activity: OHANL_AV511A
S_AHR_61014279	IMG Activity: OHANL_AB005
S_AHR_61014280	IMG Activity: OHANL_AB011
S_AHR_61014281	IMG Activity: OHANL_AB009
S_AHR_61014282	IMG Activity: OHANL_AB012
S_AHR_61014283	IMG Activity: OHANL_AB010

S_AHR_61014284	IMG Activity: OHANAB001
S_AHR_61014285	IMG Activity: OHANWE011
S_AHR_61014286	IMG Activity: OHANBW004
S_AHR_61014287	IMG Activity: OHANL_TI130
S_AHR_61014288	IMG Activity: OHANL_UM012
S_AHR_61014289	IMG Activity: OHANL_UM014
S_AHR_61014290	IMG Activity: OHANL_UM006
S_AHR_61014291	IMG Activity: OHANL_UM008
S_AHR_61014292	IMG Activity: OHANUM010B
S_AHR_61014293	IMG Activity: OHANL_UM013
S_AHR_61014294	IMG Activity: OHANL_UM010
S_AHR_61014295	IMG Activity: OHANUM02
S_AHR_61014296	IMG Activity: OHIN0497
S_AHR_61014297	IMG Activity: OHIN0498
S_AHR_61014298	IMG Activity: OHIN0499
S_AHR_61014299	IMG Activity: OHANDL022
S_AHR_61014300	IMG Activity: OHANDL021
S_AHR_61014301	IMG Activity: OHANUM061
S_AHR_61014302	IMG Activity: OHANUM062
S_AHR_61014303	IMG Activity: OHANUM063
S_AHR_61014304	IMG Activity: OHANUI01
S_AHR_61014305	IMG Activity: OHANUM03
S_AHR_61014306	IMG Activity: OHANUM04
S_AHR_61014307	IMG Activity: OHANL_UM022
S_AHR_61014308	IMG Activity: OHANL_UM023
S_AHR_61014309	IMG Activity: OHANL_UM104
S_AHR_61014310	IMG Activity: OHANL_UM105
S_AHR_61014311	IMG Activity: OHANL_TI110
S_AHR_61014312	IMG Activity: OHANL_TI120
S_AHR_61014313	IMG Activity: OHIN0350
S_AHR_61014314	IMG Activity: OHANUI04
S_AHR_61014315	IMG Activity: OHANUM010
S_AHR_61014316	IMG Activity: OHANUI02
S_AHR_61014317	IMG Activity: OHANUI03
S_AHR_61014318	IMG Activity: OHIN0431
S_AHR_61014319	IMG Activity: OHANUM011
S_AHR_61014320	IMG Activity: OHANUM09
S_AHR_61014321	IMG Activity: OHANL_AV511B
S_AHR_61014322	IMG Activity: OHAN9091
S_AHR_61014323	IMG Activity: OHAN90512
S_AHR_61014324	IMG Activity: OHAN90514
S_AHR_61014325	IMG Activity: OHANL_SL003
S_AHR_61014326	IMG Activity: OHAN9092
S_AHR_61014327	IMG Activity: OHAN90513
S_AHR_61014328	IMG Activity: OHANZI03
S_AHR_61014329	IMG Activity: OHANL_IW063
S_AHR_61014330	IMG Activity: OHANUM08
S_AHR_61014331	IMG Activity: OHANZI02
S_AHR_61014332	IMG Activity: OHANZI01
S_AHR_61014333	IMG Activity: OHANL_PART
S_AHR_61014334	IMG Activity: OHAN9011
S_AHR_61014335	IMG Activity: OHANL_KL000
S_AHR_61014336	IMG Activity: OHANL_KF002
S_AHR_61014337	IMG Activity: OHAN9010

S_AHR_61014338	IMG Activity: OHANKF02
S_AHR_61014339	IMG Activity: OHANKF01
S_AHR_61014340	IMG Activity: OHANL_SL002
S_AHR_61014341	IMG Activity: OHANL_SL001
S_AHR_61014342	IMG Activity: OHAN90641
S_AHR_61014343	IMG Activity: OHAN9007
S_AHR_61014344	IMG Activity: OHAN90631
S_AHR_61014345	IMG Activity: OHANZI07
S_AHR_61014346	IMG Activity: OHANL_BW21
S_AHR_61014347	IMG Activity: OHANL_BW22
S_AHR_61014348	IMG Activity: OHANBW020
S_AHR_61014349	IMG Activity: OHANZI06
S_AHR_61014350	IMG Activity: OHANL_AV511C
S_AHR_61014351	IMG Activity: OHANL_IW037
S_AHR_61014352	IMG Activity: OHANAVXT00
S_AHR_61014353	IMG Activity: OHANAVP15
S_AHR_61014354	IMG Activity: OHANZI09
S_AHR_61014355	IMG Activity: OHANZI05
S_AHR_61014356	IMG Activity: OHANZI04
S_AHR_61014357	IMG Activity: OHANL_IW065
S_AHR_61014358	IMG Activity: OHANL_IW061
S_AHR_61014359	IMG Activity: OHANL_IW082
S_AHR_61014360	IMG Activity: OHANL_DV001
S_AHR_61014361	IMG Activity: SIMG_OHANL_501
S_AHR_61014362	IMG Activity: OHANL_IW041
S_AHR_61014363	IMG Activity: SIMG_OHANL_421
S_AHR_61014364	IMG Activity: SIMG_OHANL_502
S_AHR_61014365	IMG Activity: SIMG_OHANL_509
S_AHR_61014366	IMG Activity: OHANL_AL01
S_AHR_61014367	IMG Activity: SIMG_OHANL_508
S_AHR_61014368	IMG Activity: OHANL_IW069
S_AHR_61014369	IMG Activity: OHANL_DT009
S_AHR_61014370	IMG Activity: OHANL_IW035
S_AHR_61014371	IMG Activity: SIMG_OHANL_453
S_AHR_61014372	IMG Activity: SIMG_OHANL_450
S_AHR_61014373	IMG Activity: SIMG_OHANL_439
S_AHR_61014374	IMG Activity: SIMG_OHANL_456
S_AHR_61014375	IMG Activity: SIMG_OHANL_466
S_AHR_61014376	IMG Activity: SIMG_OHANL_455
S_AHR_61014377	IMG Activity: SIMG_OHANL_454
S_AHR_61014378	IMG Activity: SIMG_OHANL_465
S_AHR_61014379	IMG Activity: SIMG_OHANL_510
S_AHR_61014380	IMG Activity: SIMG_OHANL_612
S_AHR_61014381	IMG Activity: SIMG_OHANL_613
S_AHR_61014382	IMG Activity: SIMG_OHANL_614
S_AHR_61014383	IMG Activity: SIMG_OHANL_521
S_AHR_61014384	IMG Activity: SIMG_OHANL_841
S_AHR_61014385	IMG Activity: SIMG_OHANL_842
S_AHR_61014386	IMG Activity: SIMG_OHANL_481
S_AHR_61014387	IMG Activity: SIMG_OHANL_401
S_AHR_61014388	IMG Activity: SIMG_OHANL_524
S_AHR_61014389	IMG Activity: SIMG_OHANL_523
S_AHR_61014390	IMG Activity: SIMG_OHANL_522
S_AHR_61014391	IMG Activity: SIMG_OHANL_611

S_AHR_61014392	IMG Activity: SIMG_OHANL_843
S_AHR_61014393	IMG Activity: SIMG_OHANL_514
S_AHR_61014394	IMG Activity: OHANL_RI011
S_AHR_61014395	IMG Activity: OHANL_RI012
S_AHR_61014396	IMG Activity: SIMG_OHANL_513
S_AHR_61014397	IMG Activity: SIMG_OHANL_512
S_AHR_61014398	IMG Activity: OHANL_TI330
S_AHR_61014399	IMG Activity: SIMG_OHANL_844
S_AHR_61014400	IMG Activity: SIMG_OHANL_520
S_AHR_61014401	IMG Activity: SIMG_OHANL_519
S_AHR_61014402	IMG Activity: OHAN9210
S_AHR_61014403	IMG Activity: SIMG_OHANL_517
S_AHR_61014404	IMG Activity: SIMG_OHANL_516
S_AHR_61014420	Customizing
S_AHR_61015471	Infotype Overview for Employee
S_AHR_61015472	address_list_of_employee
S_AHR_61015473	Employee w. Social & Employment Ins.
S_AHR_61015474	RPLDQAJ0
S_AHR_61015475	Job Assignment List (Japan)
S_AHR_61015476	RPLLRPJD
S_AHR_61015477	Change of Basic Pay List (Japan)
S_AHR_61015478	Residence Tax Entry Proof List (JP)
S_AHR_61015479	RPLTFIL0
S_AHR_61015480	Flexible Employee Data
S_AHR_61015482	Family Members
S_AHR_61015483	Birthday List
S_AHR_61015485	Vehicle - Search List
S_AHR_61015486	Employee List
S_AHR_61015487	Overview of Maternity Data
S_AHR_61015488	Education and Training
S_AHR_61015489	Telephone Directory
S_AHR_61015490	Powers of Attorney
S_AHR_61015491	Time spent in pay scale group/level
S_AHR_61015492	Defaults for Pay Scale Reclass.
S_AHR_61015493	Reference Personnel Numbers
S_AHR_61015495	HR Master Data Sheet
S_AHR_61015496	Seniority and Age
S_AHR_61015497	Headcount Development
S_AHR_61015498	Nationalities
S_AHR_61015499	Employee structure
S_AHR_61015500	Salary According to Seniority
S_AHR_61015501	Time-Related Statistical Evaluations
S_AHR_61015502	Assignment to Wage Level
S_AHR_61015504	New/Departing Employee
S_AHR_61015505	Logged Changes in Infotype Data
S_AHR_61015506	Log of Report Starts
S_AHR_61015507	Date Monitoring
S_AHR_61015508	Variable Applicant List
S_AHR_61015509	Applicants by Name
S_AHR_61015510	Applicants by action
S_AHR_61015511	Applicants' Education and Training
S_AHR_61015512	Applications
S_AHR_61015513	Applicant Statistics
S_AHR_61015514	Planned Activities for Personnel Off

SAP Transaction Codes – Volume Two

S_AHR_61015515	Vacancy Assignments
S_AHR_61015516	Vacancies
S_AHR_61015517	Job Advertisements
S_AHR_61015518	Evaluate Recruitment Instruments
S_AHR_61015519	Development plan history
S_AHR_61015520	Individual development plan
S_AHR_61015521	Display Development Plan Catalog
S_AHR_61015522	Persons "Developed" by Dev. Plan
S_AHR_61015523	Persons "Developed" by Dev.Plan Item
S_AHR_61015524	Evaluate Careers
S_AHR_61015525	Career planning
S_AHR_61015526	Succession Planning
S_AHR_61015527	Profile Matchup (Display Profile)
S_AHR_61015528	Find persons for selected qualif.
S_AHR_61015529	Find Objects for Qualifications
S_AHR_61015530	Find Objects for Requirements
S_AHR_61015531	Succession Overview
S_AHR_61015532	Profile Matchup: Positions/Holders
S_AHR_61015533	Profiles
S_AHR_61015534	Display Profile
S_AHR_61015535	Display Qualifications Catalog
S_AHR_61015536	Expired Qualifications
S_AHR_61015537	Display Appraisal
S_AHR_61015538	Display Appraisals Catalog
S_AHR_61015539	Attendance
S_AHR_61015540	Eligible Employees
S_AHR_61015541	Changes in Eligibility
S_AHR_61015542	Change in Benefits
S_AHR_61015543	Employee Demographics
S_AHR_61015544	Spending Account Premiums
S_AHR_61015545	Health Plan Premiums
S_AHR_61015546	Insurance Plan Premiums
S_AHR_61015547	Savings Plan Premiums
S_AHR_61015548	Vesting Percentages
S_AHR_61015549	Changes in Benefits Elections
S_AHR_61015550	Miscellaneous Premiums
S_AHR_61015551	Premium for stock purchase plans
S_AHR_61015552	Benefits Selection Analysis
S_AHR_61015553	Compa-Ratio Analysis
S_AHR_61015554	Salary Structure List
S_AHR_61015555	Assignment to Wage Level
S_AHR_61015556	Display Pay Scale Groups
S_AHR_61015557	Salary According to Seniority
S_AHR_61015558	Planned Labor Costs
S_AHR_61015559	Display an Existing Scenario Group
S_AHR_61015560	Plan Scenarios of Personnel Costs
S_AHR_61015561	Budget in FTE
S_AHR_61015562	Available Budget Per BS Element
S_AHR_61015563	Job chart
S_AHR_61015564	Financing from BS Element Budgets
S_AHR_61015565	Budget Year Comparison
S_AHR_61015566	Enhanced Budget in FTEs
S_AHR_61015567	RHPMSTOV
S_AHR_61015568	Job index

S_AHR_61015569	Business distribution plan
S_AHR_61015570	Different Service Type/Service Cat.
S_AHR_61015571	Report on teaching hours
S_AHR_61015572	Financing in Organizational Unit
S_AHR_61015573	Violations of earmarking
S_AHR_61015574	Display earmarkings
S_AHR_61015575	Display personal shift plan
S_AHR_61015576	Display attendance list
S_AHR_61015577	Undo Completed Target Plan
S_AHR_61015578	Personal Work Schedule
S_AHR_61015579	Daily Work Schedule
S_AHR_61015580	Attendance/Absence for Each Employee
S_AHR_61015581	Attendance/Absence for Each Employee
S_AHR_61015582	Attendance/Absence Data: Overview
S_AHR_61015583	Att./Absence Data: Calendar View
S_AHR_61015584	Attendance Check
S_AHR_61015585	Att./Absences: Graphical Overview
S_AHR_61015586	Att./Absences: Graphical Overview
S_AHR_61015587	Attendance/Absence for Each Employee
S_AHR_61015588	Attendance/Absence Data: Overview
S_AHR_61015589	Att./Absence Data: Calendar View
S_AHR_61015590	Att./Absences: Graphical Overview
S_AHR_61015591	Att./Absences: Graphical Overview
S_AHR_61015592	Time Leveling
S_AHR_61015593	Time Leveling
S_AHR_61015594	Time Statement Form
S_AHR_61015595	Time Statement Form
S_AHR_61015596	Time Statement Form
S_AHR_61015597	Cumulated Time Evaluation Results
S_AHR_61015598	Time Accounts
S_AHR_61015599	Display Absence Quota Information
S_AHR_61015600	Time Leveling
S_AHR_61015601	Time Leveling
S_AHR_61015602	Working Times of Time and Incentive
S_AHR_61015603	Reassignment Proposals for Wage Grps
S_AHR_61015604	Remuneration Statements
S_AHR_61015605	Remuneration Statements
S_AHR_61015606	Remuneration Statements
S_AHR_61015607	Payroll Accounts
S_AHR_61015608	Payments and Deductions
S_AHR_61015609	Bank Details
S_AHR_61015610	Payroll Journal --- International
S_AHR_61015611	Wage Type Statement
S_AHR_61015612	Wage Type Distribution
S_AHR_61015613	Posting to Accounting: Wage Type
S_AHR_61015614	Paydays on Holidays or Weekends
S_AHR_61015615	Payday Calendar
S_AHR_61015616	Book Law: Law 20,744 Art. 52
S_AHR_61015617	Form 649- Sworn Annual Declaration
S_AHR_61015618	Remuneration Statement: Argentina
S_AHR_61015619	Payments and Deductions
S_AHR_61015620	Bank Details
S_AHR_61015621	Payroll Account: Argentina
S_AHR_61015622	Payroll Journal: Argentina

S_AHR_61015623	Wage Type Statement
S_AHR_61015624	Wage Type Distribution
S_AHR_61015625	Posting to Accounting: Wage Type
S_AHR_61015626	Paydays on Holidays or Weekends
S_AHR_61015627	Payday Calendar
S_AHR_61015628	Remuneration Statements
S_AHR_61015629	Payroll accounts
S_AHR_61015630	Payments and Deductions
S_AHR_61015631	Bank Details
S_AHR_61015632	Absence Types Occuring in Personal C
S_AHR_61015633	Evaluation of Garnishment Results
S_AHR_61015634	Payroll journal (Austria)
S_AHR_61015635	Wage Type Statement
S_AHR_61015636	Wage Type Distribution
S_AHR_61015637	Posting to Accounting: Wage Type
S_AHR_61015638	Overview of Company Loans
S_AHR_61015639	Calc. Present Value for Company Loan
S_AHR_61015640	Account Statement for Company Loans
S_AHR_61015641	Economic Statistics for Central Off.
S_AHR_61015643	Sickness Certificates/Fees
S_AHR_61015644	RPCEDTQ0
S_AHR_61015645	Payroll Accounts
S_AHR_61015646	RPLDEDQ0
S_AHR_61015647	RPLDETQ1
S_AHR_61015648	RPLDMSQ0
S_AHR_61015649	RPLDMVQ0
S_AHR_61015650	RPLEXCQ1
S_AHR_61015651	RPLHISQ0
S_AHR_61015652	Payments and Deductions
S_AHR_61015653	Bank Details
S_AHR_61015654	RPLARRQ0
S_AHR_61015655	Superannuation Fund Report Australia
S_AHR_61015656	RPLGCTQ0
S_AHR_61015657	RPLRECQ0
S_AHR_61015658	RPLSUMQ0
S_AHR_61015659	Payroll Journal (AU)
S_AHR_61015660	Wage Type Statement
S_AHR_61015661	Wage Type Distribution
S_AHR_61015662	Posting to Accounting: Wage Type
S_AHR_61015663	Paydays on Holidays or Weekends
S_AHR_61015664	Payday Calendar
S_AHR_61015665	RPLLPVQ1
S_AHR_61015666	RPLLPVQ2
S_AHR_61015667	RPLLPVQ3
S_AHR_61015668	RPLLPVQ4
S_AHR_61015669	RPLLSLQ0
S_AHR_61015670	RPLLVPQ0
S_AHR_61015671	RPLVPYQ1
S_AHR_61015672	Bank Details
S_AHR_61015673	Payments and Deductions
S_AHR_61015674	Payroll Accounts
S_AHR_61015675	Remuneration Statements
S_AHR_61015676	Generate Personal Calendar: Belgium
S_AHR_61015677	Payroll Journal

S_AHR_61015678	Social Balance Declaration (Belgium)
S_AHR_61015679	Wage Type Statement
S_AHR_61015680	Wage Type Distribution
S_AHR_61015681	Posting to Accounting: Wage Type
S_AHR_61015682	Paydays on Holidays or Weekends
S_AHR_61015683	Payday Calendar
S_AHR_61015684	Payroll Accounting Program: Brazil
S_AHR_61015685	Remuneration Statements
S_AHR_61015686	Remuneration Statements
S_AHR_61015687	Payroll Accounts
S_AHR_61015689	Payroll Results Display: Cluster(BR)
S_AHR_61015690	HBRCDTA0
S_AHR_61015691	HBRDIRF0
S_AHR_61015692	HBRDARF0
S_AHR_61015693	HBRDEPD0
S_AHR_61015694	HBRGRPS0
S_AHR_61015695	HBRSALC0
S_AHR_61015696	HBRTERM0
S_AHR_61015697	HBRGRR00
S_AHR_61015698	HBRREMAG
S_AHR_61015699	HBRSEFIP
S_AHR_61015700	HBRCVTR0
S_AHR_61015701	HBRAVFE0
S_AHR_61015702	HBRCFER0
S_AHR_61015703	HBRETQCP
S_AHR_61015704	HBRAVPR0
S_AHR_61015705	HBRGRR00
S_AHR_61015706	HBRRECT0
S_AHR_61015707	HBRSEGDE
S_AHR_61015708	HBRCCED0
S_AHR_61015709	HBRRAIS0
S_AHR_61015710	HBRDIRF0
S_AHR_61015711	Remuneration Statements
S_AHR_61015712	Payments and Deductions
S_AHR_61015713	Bank Details
S_AHR_61015714	HBRFICHA
S_AHR_61015715	Payroll Results Display: Cluster(BR)
S_AHR_61015716	HBRCONTR
S_AHR_61015717	HBRDIRF0
S_AHR_61015718	HBRDEPD0
S_AHR_61015719	HBRTERM0
S_AHR_61015720	HBRETQCP
S_AHR_61015721	Wage Type Distribution
S_AHR_61015722	Posting to Accounting: Wage Type
S_AHR_61015723	Wage Type Statement(Read Cluster RX)
S_AHR_61015724	Paydays on Holidays or Weekends
S_AHR_61015725	Payday Calendar
S_AHR_61015726	HBRRAIS0
S_AHR_61015727	HBRDIRF0
S_AHR_61015728	HBRREMAG
S_AHR_61015729	HBRPISCA
S_AHR_61015730	HBRSEFIP
S_AHR_61015731	Display of TemSe files
S_AHR_61015732	HBRUTMS1

S_AHR_61015733	HBRUTMS2
S_AHR_61015734	HBRUTMS3
S_AHR_61015735	Subroutinas para o log da folha (Bra
S_AHR_61015736	Select Personnel Numbers for a
S_AHR_61015737	HBRCATT0
S_AHR_61015738	Display of TemSe files
S_AHR_61015739	HBRUTMS1
S_AHR_61015740	HBRUTMS2
S_AHR_61015741	HBRUTMS3
S_AHR_61015742	HBRVEXT0
S_AHR_61015743	HBRIAUT0
S_AHR_61015744	HBRIGUI0
S_AHR_61015745	HBRCMLI9
S_AHR_61015746	HBRCDTA0
S_AHR_61015747	Remuneration Statements
S_AHR_61015748	RPCPIEK0
S_AHR_61015749	RPCROEK0
S_AHR_61015750	RPUNTUK0
S_AHR_61015751	RPCCYRK0
S_AHR_61015752	RPCWCAK0
S_AHR_61015753	**Grievance Summary
S_AHR_61015754	Payroll Accounts
S_AHR_61015755	Payments and Deductions
S_AHR_61015756	Bank Details
S_AHR_61015757	Payroll Journal
S_AHR_61015758	RPSEEAKA
S_AHR_61015759	RPCROHK0
S_AHR_61015760	RPSCANK0
S_AHR_61015761	RPSCANK1
S_AHR_61015762	RPUKRMK0
S_AHR_61015763	Wage Type Statement
S_AHR_61015764	Wage Type Distribution
S_AHR_61015765	Posting to Accounting: Wage Type
S_AHR_61015766	Paydays on Holidays or Weekends
S_AHR_61015767	Payday Calendar
S_AHR_61015768	Remuneration Statements
S_AHR_61015769	Payroll Account
S_AHR_61015770	Payments and Deductions
S_AHR_61015771	Bank Details
S_AHR_61015772	HR-CH: AHV - Employee List with AHV
S_AHR_61015773	Payroll Journal (Switzerland)
S_AHR_61015774	Wage Type Statement
S_AHR_61015775	Wage Type Distribution
S_AHR_61015776	Posting to Accounting: Wage Type
S_AHR_61015777	Overview of Company Loans
S_AHR_61015778	Calc. Present Value for Company Loan
S_AHR_61015779	Account Statement for Company Loans
S_AHR_61015780	HR-CH: ASM - Wage and Salary Stats
S_AHR_61015781	HR-CH: BFS Quarterly Employment Stat
S_AHR_61015782	HR-CH: BFS statistics on Wage Level
S_AHR_61015783	HR-CH: Check Family-Related Bonuses
S_AHR_61015784	HR-CH: Subjectivity PDSDI/SAIA Revis
S_AHR_61015785	Infotype Overview for Employee
S_AHR_61015786	Remuneration Statements

SAP Transaction Codes – Volume Two

S_AHR_61015787	Payroll Accounts
S_AHR_61015788	Payments and Deductions
S_AHR_61015789	Bank Details
S_AHR_61015790	Evaluation of Garnishment Results
S_AHR_61015791	Monthly Net Income
S_AHR_61015792	Capital Formation Overview
S_AHR_61015793	Payroll journal
S_AHR_61015794	Severely Challenged Persons List
S_AHR_61015795	Wage Type Statement
S_AHR_61015796	Wage Type Distribution
S_AHR_61015797	Posting to Accounting: Wage Type
S_AHR_61015798	Overview of Company Loans
S_AHR_61015799	Calc. Present Value for Company Loan
S_AHR_61015800	Account Statement for Company Loans
S_AHR_61015801	Current and Annual Income Survey
S_AHR_61015802	Survey of Remuneration Struct. 1999
S_AHR_61015803	Income Statistics for Employers'
S_AHR_61015804	Income Statistics for Employers'
S_AHR_61015805	Survey on Labor Costs for 1996
S_AHR_61015806	Enhanced Std Pay Increase (Indirect
S_AHR_61015807	Pay Scale Reclassification by Age
S_AHR_61015810	Default List for Advancement of Case
S_AHR_61015811	Report to Represent Collective Agree
S_AHR_61015813	Standard Letter for Child Allowance
S_AHR_61015814	Check Child Allowance Data
S_AHR_61015815	Hospital statistics
S_AHR_61015816	Personnel statistics
S_AHR_61015817	Employment Statistics: Download TemS
S_AHR_61015818	College statistics
S_AHR_61015819	College statistics: Download TemSe
S_AHR_61015820	Full-time employee statistics
S_AHR_61015823	Pension Recipient Statistics
S_AHR_61015824	Child Allow. Stats (Civil Service)
S_AHR_61015825	Child Allow. Stats (Civ.Serv.Ger.)
S_AHR_61015826	Generate Queries (BEN) in Pension In
S_AHR_61015827	Eval. Info. in Pension Income Proc.
S_AHR_61015828	Sideline job evaluations
S_AHR_61015829	Payments and Deductions
S_AHR_61015830	Bank Details
S_AHR_61015831	Payroll account: Denmark
S_AHR_61015832	List for Infotype 72 (Tax DK) for Ye
S_AHR_61015833	Remuneration Statements (Denmark)
S_AHR_61015834	Wage Type Statement
S_AHR_61015835	Wage Type Distribution
S_AHR_61015836	Posting to Accounting: Wage Type
S_AHR_61015837	Paydays on Holidays or Weekends
S_AHR_61015838	Payday Calendar
S_AHR_61015839	Remuneration Statement
S_AHR_61015840	Payroll Accounts
S_AHR_61015841	Payments and Deductions
S_AHR_61015842	Bank Details
S_AHR_61015843	Monthly Overview of Payroll Results
S_AHR_61015844	Wage Type Distribution
S_AHR_61015845	Posting to Accounting: Wage Type

S_AHR_61015846	Wage Type Statement
S_AHR_61015847	Paydays on Holidays or Weekends
S_AHR_61015848	Payday Calendar
S_AHR_61015849	Overview of Company Loans
S_AHR_61015850	Calc. Present Value for Company Loan
S_AHR_61015851	Account Statement for Company Loans
S_AHR_61015852	Remuneration statements
S_AHR_61015853	Payroll accounts
S_AHR_61015854	Payments and Deductions
S_AHR_61015855	Bank Details
S_AHR_61015856	Payroll Journal
S_AHR_61015857	Wage Type Statement
S_AHR_61015858	Wage Type Distribution
S_AHR_61015859	Posting to Accounting: Wage Type
S_AHR_61015860	Paydays on Holidays or Weekends
S_AHR_61015861	Payday Calendar
S_AHR_61015862	Overview of Company Loans
S_AHR_61015863	Calc. Present Value for Company Loan
S_AHR_61015864	Account Statement for Company Loans
S_AHR_61015865	Indiv.Statement Current Profit Shar.
S_AHR_61015866	List of Current Profit Sharing
S_AHR_61015867	List of Paid Profit Sharing
S_AHR_61015868	Payments and Deductions
S_AHR_61015869	Bank Details
S_AHR_61015870	Remuneration statements
S_AHR_61015871	Payroll Accounts
S_AHR_61015872	Statutory Maternity Pay Record Sheet
S_AHR_61015873	Payroll Journal (GB)
S_AHR_61015874	Payroll Results Check Tool
S_AHR_61015875	Wage Type Statement
S_AHR_61015876	Wage Type Distribution
S_AHR_61015877	Posting to Accounting: Wage Type
S_AHR_61015878	Paydays on Holidays or Weekends
S_AHR_61015879	Payday Calendar
S_AHR_61015880	HHKCEDT0
S_AHR_61015881	Payments and Deductions
S_AHR_61015882	Bank Details
S_AHR_61015883	HHKCKTO0
S_AHR_61015884	HHKCLJN0
S_AHR_61015885	Wage Type Statement
S_AHR_61015886	Wage Type Distribution
S_AHR_61015887	Posting to Accounting: Wage Type
S_AHR_61015888	Paydays on Holidays or Weekends
S_AHR_61015889	Payday Calendar
S_AHR_61015890	HIDCANN0
S_AHR_61015891	HIDCEDT0
S_AHR_61015892	HIDCKTO0
S_AHR_61015893	Payments and Deductions
S_AHR_61015894	Bank Details
S_AHR_61015895	HIDCTAX1
S_AHR_61015896	HIDCJAM0
S_AHR_61015897	HIDCJAM1
S_AHR_61015898	HIDCLJN0
S_AHR_61015899	Cash Breakdown for Cash Payment Base

S_AHR_61015900	Cash Breakdown List (International)
S_AHR_61015901	Wage Type Statement
S_AHR_61015902	Wage Type Distribution
S_AHR_61015903	Posting to Accounting: Wage Type
S_AHR_61015904	Paydays on Holidays or Weekends
S_AHR_61015905	Payday Calendar
S_AHR_61015906	Payments and Deductions
S_AHR_61015907	Bank Details
S_AHR_61015908	HIECEDT0
S_AHR_61015909	HIECKTO0
S_AHR_61015910	Payroll Journal --- International
S_AHR_61015911	Wage Type Statement
S_AHR_61015912	Wage Type Distribution
S_AHR_61015913	Posting to Accounting: Wage Type
S_AHR_61015914	Paydays on Holidays or Weekends
S_AHR_61015915	Payday Calendar
S_AHR_61015916	Payments and Deductions
S_AHR_61015917	Bank Details
S_AHR_61015918	Remuneration Statements
S_AHR_61015919	RPCKTOI0
S_AHR_61015920	RPCCMEI0
S_AHR_61015921	RPCLJNI0
S_AHR_61015922	RPCRIEI0
S_AHR_61015923	Wage Type Distribution
S_AHR_61015924	Posting to Accounting: Wage Type
S_AHR_61015925	Paydays on Holidays or Weekends
S_AHR_61015926	Payday Calendar
S_AHR_61015927	Year-End-Adjustment Result List (JP)
S_AHR_61015928	Life/Accident Insurance Deduction Li
S_AHR_61015929	Life/Accident Insurance Deduction Li
S_AHR_61015930	List of Liable Amount for Fixed Labo
S_AHR_61015933	RPCSIBJ0
S_AHR_61015934	RPCSIGJ0
S_AHR_61015936	RPCSISJ0
S_AHR_61015939	RPCUNIJ0
S_AHR_61015940	Social Insurance Premium Check List
S_AHR_61015941	Payments and Deductions
S_AHR_61015942	Bank Details
S_AHR_61015943	Wage Ledger (Japan)
S_AHR_61015944	RPCLJNJ0
S_AHR_61015945	Payment Report (Total No. of Payment
S_AHR_61015946	Wage Type Statement
S_AHR_61015947	Wage Type Distribution
S_AHR_61015948	Posting to Accounting: Wage Type
S_AHR_61015949	Paydays on Holidays or Weekends
S_AHR_61015950	Payday Calendar
S_AHR_61015951	Overview of Company Loans
S_AHR_61015952	RPCLOHJ0
S_AHR_61015953	Life/Accident Insurance Deduction Li
S_AHR_61015954	Life/Accident Insurance Deduction Li
S_AHR_61015955	List of Liable Amount for Fixed Labo
S_AHR_61015958	Residence tax change - JAPAN
S_AHR_61015959	Remuneration Statements
S_AHR_61015960	Payments and Deductions

S_AHR_61015961	Bank Details
S_AHR_61015962	Payroll Journal x9 --- International
S_AHR_61015963	HPHCMLI9
S_AHR_61015964	Wage Type Statement
S_AHR_61015965	Wage Type Distribution
S_AHR_61015966	Posting to Accounting: Wage Type
S_AHR_61015967	Paydays on Holidays or Weekends
S_AHR_61015968	Payday Calendar
S_AHR_61015969	RPCANNL0
S_AHR_61015970	RPCEDTL0
S_AHR_61015971	RPCKTOL0
S_AHR_61015972	Payments and Deductions
S_AHR_61015973	Bank Details
S_AHR_61015974	RPCLJNL0
S_AHR_61015975	RPCMLIL9
S_AHR_61015976	Wage Type Statement
S_AHR_61015977	Wage Type Distribution
S_AHR_61015978	Posting to Accounting: Wage Type
S_AHR_61015979	Paydays on Holidays or Weekends
S_AHR_61015980	Payday Calendar
S_AHR_61015981	Mexican Payroll Program
S_AHR_61015982	Payments and Deductions
S_AHR_61015983	Bank Details
S_AHR_61015984	Remuneration Statement: Mexico
S_AHR_61015985	Payroll Accounts: Mexico
S_AHR_61015986	Payroll Journal: Mexico
S_AHR_61015987	Wage Type Statement
S_AHR_61015988	Wage Type Distribution
S_AHR_61015989	Posting to Accounting: Wage Type
S_AHR_61015990	Paydays on Holidays or Weekends
S_AHR_61015991	Payday Calendar
S_AHR_61015992	HMXCSDI0
S_AHR_61015993	HMXCSSI0
S_AHR_61015994	Generation of IMSS Notifications
S_AHR_61015995	Absence and Incapacity
S_AHR_61015996	HMXCDNT0
S_AHR_61015997	HMXTRTR0
S_AHR_61015998	IMSS and INFONAVIT Contrib. Calc.
S_AHR_61015999	HMXCRET0
S_AHR_61016000	HMXCCRE0
S_AHR_61016001	HMXCINO0
S_AHR_61016002	HMXCGRI0
S_AHR_61016003	HMXCRNS0
S_AHR_61016004	HMXCAJD0
S_AHR_61016005	HMXCNOM0
S_AHR_61016006	Income Tax Calculation
S_AHR_61016007	HMXCINF0
S_AHR_61016008	HMXCFNC0
S_AHR_61016009	INFONAVIT Deduction Release Record
S_AHR_61016010	Printout of Loan Results
S_AHR_61016011	HMXCIFA0
S_AHR_61016012	HMXCLFA0
S_AHR_61016013	HMXCSFA0
S_AHR_61016015	HMXCAGU0

S_AHR_61016016	HMXCFIC0
S_AHR_61016017	HMXCGRB0
S_AHR_61016018	HMXCGRH0
S_AHR_61016020	HMXTVAC0
S_AHR_61016021	HMXCDTA0
S_AHR_61016023	Display of TemSe files
S_AHR_61016024	Payroll Results (Cluster MX)
S_AHR_61016025	Remuneration Statements
S_AHR_61016026	Payroll Account (NL)
S_AHR_61016027	Payments and Deductions
S_AHR_61016028	Bank Details
S_AHR_61016029	Overview Master Data: Infotype 0060
S_AHR_61016030	Overview Infotype Premium Reduction
S_AHR_61016031	Overview premium reductions (NL)
S_AHR_61016032	Income Threshold Health Ins. Fund
S_AHR_61016033	Overview Infotype Special Provisions
S_AHR_61016034	CBS file
S_AHR_61016035	Report Wet SAMEN (Act)
S_AHR_61016036	Status register (cluster RN) (NL)
S_AHR_61016037	Wage Type Statement
S_AHR_61016038	Wage Type Distribution
S_AHR_61016039	Posting to Accounting: Wage Type
S_AHR_61016040	Paydays on Holidays or Weekends
S_AHR_61016041	Payday Calendar
S_AHR_61016042	Notifications of Sickness/Recovery
S_AHR_61016043	Analysis of Absences Due to Illness
S_AHR_61016044	Payments and Deductions
S_AHR_61016045	Bank Details
S_AHR_61016046	RPCFUNV0
S_AHR_61016047	Remuneration statements
S_AHR_61016048	RPCRBAV0
S_AHR_61016049	RPCRBTV0
S_AHR_61016050	RPCRFUV0
S_AHR_61016051	Wage Type Statement(Read Cluster RX)
S_AHR_61016052	Wage Type Distribution
S_AHR_61016053	Posting to Accounting: Wage Type
S_AHR_61016054	Paydays on Holidays or Weekends
S_AHR_61016055	Payday Calendar
S_AHR_61016056	HNZCEDT0
S_AHR_61016057	HNZLDET0
S_AHR_61016058	HNZLEXC0
S_AHR_61016059	HNZLSUM0
S_AHR_61016060	HNZLSUP0
S_AHR_61016061	Payments and Deductions
S_AHR_61016062	Bank Details
S_AHR_61016063	Payroll Journal - New Zealand
S_AHR_61016064	HNZCMLI9
S_AHR_61016065	HNZLREC0
S_AHR_61016066	Wage Type Statement
S_AHR_61016067	Wage Type Distribution
S_AHR_61016068	Posting to Accounting: Wage Type
S_AHR_61016069	Paydays on Holidays or Weekends
S_AHR_61016070	Payday Calendar
S_AHR_61016071	Payments and Deductions

S_AHR_61016072	Bank Details
S_AHR_61016073	RPCEDTP0
S_AHR_61016074	RPCKTOP0
S_AHR_61016075	RPCLJNP0
S_AHR_61016076	Wage Type Statement
S_AHR_61016077	Wage Type Distribution
S_AHR_61016078	Posting to Accounting: Wage Type
S_AHR_61016079	Paydays on Holidays or Weekends
S_AHR_61016080	Payday Calendar
S_AHR_61016081	Payments and Deductions
S_AHR_61016082	Bank Details
S_AHR_61016083	Remuneration Statements
S_AHR_61016084	Wage Type Statement
S_AHR_61016085	Wage Type Distribution
S_AHR_61016086	Posting to Accounting: Wage Type
S_AHR_61016087	Paydays on Holidays or Weekends
S_AHR_61016088	Payday Calendar
S_AHR_61016089	RPCEDTR0
S_AHR_61016090	RPCKTOR0
S_AHR_61016091	Payments and Deductions
S_AHR_61016092	Bank Details
S_AHR_61016093	RPCLJNR0
S_AHR_61016094	Cash Breakdown List (International)
S_AHR_61016095	Cash Breakdown for Cash Payment Base
S_AHR_61016096	Wage Type Statement
S_AHR_61016097	Wage Type Distribution
S_AHR_61016098	Posting to Accounting: Wage Type
S_AHR_61016099	Paydays on Holidays or Weekends
S_AHR_61016100	Payday Calendar
S_AHR_61016101	HTHCEDT0
S_AHR_61016102	HTHCKTO0
S_AHR_61016103	Payments and Deductions
S_AHR_61016104	Bank Details
S_AHR_61016105	HTHCTXF1
S_AHR_61016106	HTHCTX5B
S_AHR_61016107	HTHCTX1A
S_AHR_61016108	HTHCTX91
S_AHR_61016109	HTHCSSD1
S_AHR_61016110	HTHCSSS1
S_AHR_61016111	Payroll Journal - THAILAND
S_AHR_61016112	Wage Type Statement
S_AHR_61016113	Wage Type Distribution
S_AHR_61016114	Posting to Accounting: Wage Type
S_AHR_61016115	Paydays on Holidays or Weekends
S_AHR_61016116	Payday Calendar
S_AHR_61016117	HTWCEDT0
S_AHR_61016118	HTWCKTO0
S_AHR_61016119	Payments and Deductions
S_AHR_61016120	Bank Details
S_AHR_61016121	HTWCLJN0
S_AHR_61016122	Wage Type Statement
S_AHR_61016123	Wage Type Distribution
S_AHR_61016124	Posting to Accounting: Wage Type
S_AHR_61016125	Paydays on Holidays or Weekends

S_AHR_61016126	Payday Calendar
S_AHR_61016127	Remuneration Statements
S_AHR_61016128	Payroll Accounts
S_AHR_61016129	Employee history report
S_AHR_61016130	HR-NA: OSHA-200 Report
S_AHR_61016131	HR-NA: OSHA-101 Report
S_AHR_61016132	RPLHIPU0
S_AHR_61016133	Garnishment History
S_AHR_61016134	Listing of Customizing Tables
S_AHR_61016135	Garnishment Statistics
S_AHR_61016136	Display Notice Letters
S_AHR_61016137	Print Notice Letter
S_AHR_61016138	Display Answer Letters
S_AHR_61016139	Print Answer Letter
S_AHR_61016140	Benefits Dependents List
S_AHR_61016141	Grievance summary
S_AHR_61016142	Tax Infotype Summary
S_AHR_61016143	RPCTXUU0
S_AHR_61016144	Payments and Deductions
S_AHR_61016145	Bank Details
S_AHR_61016146	RPCGRNU0
S_AHR_61016147	RPCTXSU0
S_AHR_61016148	Workers' compensation report
S_AHR_61016149	Payroll Journal
S_AHR_61016150	New hire reporting
S_AHR_61016151	RPCCTXU1
S_AHR_61016152	EEO-1 report
S_AHR_61016153	AAP: Movement analysis report
S_AHR_61016154	AAP: Turnover analysis report
S_AHR_61016155	AAP: Workforce distribution report
S_AHR_61016156	VETS-100 Report
S_AHR_61016157	RPSBENU1
S_AHR_61016158	RPSBENU2
S_AHR_61016163	Display payroll posting document
S_AHR_61016164	Wage Type Statement
S_AHR_61016165	Wage Type Distribution
S_AHR_61016166	Posting to Accounting: Wage Type
S_AHR_61016168	Paydays on Holidays or Weekends
S_AHR_61016169	Payday Calendar
S_AHR_61016170	Payments and Deductions
S_AHR_61016171	Bank Details
S_AHR_61016172	HVECEDT0
S_AHR_61016173	Payroll accounts
S_AHR_61016174	HVECSVB0
S_AHR_61016175	Payroll Journal
S_AHR_61016176	Wage Type Statement
S_AHR_61016177	Wage Type Distribution
S_AHR_61016178	Posting to Accounting: Wage Type
S_AHR_61016179	Paydays on Holidays or Weekends
S_AHR_61016180	Payday Calendar
S_AHR_61016181	HVECPSR0
S_AHR_61016182	HVECADR0
S_AHR_61016183	HVECCCR0
S_AHR_61016184	HVECWHR0

S_AHR_61016185	HVECMIN0
S_AHR_61016186	HVECTRA1
S_AHR_61016187	HVECRAI0
S_AHR_61016188	HVECARC0
S_AHR_61016189	HVECRNR0
S_AHR_61016190	HVECSIE0
S_AHR_61016191	HVECSIE1
S_AHR_61016192	HVECIVS0
S_AHR_61016193	HVECSSR0
S_AHR_61016194	HVECINE0
S_AHR_61016195	HVECINR0
S_AHR_61016196	HVECLPH0
S_AHR_61016197	Overview of Company Loans
S_AHR_61016198	Calc. Present Value for Company Loan
S_AHR_61016199	Account Statement for Company Loans
S_AHR_61016200	Payments and Deductions
S_AHR_61016201	Bank Details
S_AHR_61016202	Remuneration Statements
S_AHR_61016203	Payroll Accounts
S_AHR_61016204	Payroll Journal
S_AHR_61016205	Wage Type Statement
S_AHR_61016206	Wage Type Distribution
S_AHR_61016207	Posting to Accounting: Wage Type
S_AHR_61016208	Paydays on Holidays or Weekends
S_AHR_61016209	Payday Calendar
S_AHR_61016210	Overview of Company Loans
S_AHR_61016211	Calc. Present Value for Company Loan
S_AHR_61016212	Account Statement for Company Loans
S_AHR_61016213	Attendance Statistics
S_AHR_61016214	Prebookings per attendee
S_AHR_61016215	Bookings per Attendee
S_AHR_61016216	Cancellations per attendee
S_AHR_61016217	Business Event Hierarchy
S_AHR_61016218	Business Event Brochure
S_AHR_61016219	Business Event Dates
S_AHR_61016220	Business Event Demand
S_AHR_61016221	Business Event Prices
S_AHR_61016222	Resource Reservation
S_AHR_61016223	Resources Not Yet Assigned
S_AHR_61016224	Resource Equipment
S_AHR_61016225	Available/Reserved Resources
S_AHR_61016226	Existing Organizational Units
S_AHR_61016227	Staff Functions for Org. Unit
S_AHR_61016228	Organizational Structure
S_AHR_61016229	Org. Structure with Positions
S_AHR_61016230	Org. Structure with Persons
S_AHR_61016231	Org. Structure with Work Centers
S_AHR_61016232	Existing Jobs
S_AHR_61016233	Job index
S_AHR_61016234	Job Description
S_AHR_61016235	Task Description for Jobs
S_AHR_61016236	Complete job description
S_AHR_61016237	Existing Positions
S_AHR_61016238	Staff assignments

S_AHR_61016239	Position Description
S_AHR_61016240	Task Description for Positions
S_AHR_61016241	Staff Functions for Positions
S_AHR_61016242	Authorities and Resources
S_AHR_61016243	Planned Labor Costs
S_AHR_61016244	Vacant/Obsolete Positions
S_AHR_61016245	Correct Vacancies
S_AHR_61016246	Complete Position Description
S_AHR_61016247	Report Structure Without Persons
S_AHR_61016248	Report Structure with Persons
S_AHR_61016249	Existing Work Centers
S_AHR_61016250	Work Centers per Organizational Unit
S_AHR_61016251	Authorities and Resources
S_AHR_61016252	Planned Labor Costs
S_AHR_61016253	Work Ctrs with Restrictions in Org.S
S_AHR_61016254	Single Work Centers w. Restrictions
S_AHR_61016255	Work Centers Requiring Health Exam.
S_AHR_61016256	Single Work Centers Req. Health Exam
S_AHR_61016257	Existing Tasks
S_AHR_61016258	Activity Profile for Positions Along
S_AHR_61016259	Activity Profile of Positions with P
S_AHR_61016260	Character of Tasks in Organizational
S_AHR_61016261	Character of Individual Tasks
S_AHR_61016262	Existing Objects
S_AHR_61016263	Structure Display/Maintenance
S_AHR_61016264	Structure Navigation Instrument
S_AHR_61016265	PD Graphics Interface
S_AHR_61016266	Display and Maintain Infotypes
S_AHR_61016267	Infotype Reporting
S_AHR_61016268	Start Payroll Report
S_AHR_61016269	General Trip Data/Trip Totals
S_AHR_61016270	Trip Receipts
S_AHR_61016271	Cost Assignment for Trip
S_AHR_61016272	Trip Framew.Data/Totals/Rcpts/Costs
S_AHR_61016273	Who is where? Search for Trip Dest.
S_AHR_61016274	Find documents using maximum rate
S_AHR_61016275	Travel Expense Reporting by Period
S_AHR_61016276	Income-Related Expenses Statement
S_AHR_61016277	Input Tax Recovery
S_AHR_61016278	Determination of Employees with Exce
S_AHR_61016279	Overview of Flights by Airlines
S_AHR_61016280	Overview of Flights by Airlines
S_AHR_61016281	Overview of Flights by Location
S_AHR_61016282	Ticket information for flights
S_AHR_61016283	Business Volume with Hotel Chains
S_AHR_61016284	Business volume with hotel chains
S_AHR_61016285	Business Volume by Hotel Location
S_AHR_61016286	Business Volume with Car Rental Cos
S_AHR_61016287	Business Volume by Rental Location
S_AHR_61016288	Overview of Planned Trips
S_AHR_61016289	Personal Work Schedule
S_AHR_61016290	Daily Work Schedule
S_AHR_61016291	Attendance/Absence for Each Employee
S_AHR_61016292	Attendance/Absence for Each Employee

SAP Transaction Codes – Volume Two

S_AHR_61016293	Att./Absence Data: Calendar View
S_AHR_61016294	Attendance Check
S_AHR_61016295	Att./Absences: Graphical Overview
S_AHR_61016296	Att./Absences: Graphical Overview
S_AHR_61016297	Attendance/Absence Data: Overview
S_AHR_61016298	Att./Absence Data: Calendar View
S_AHR_61016299	Leave Overview
S_AHR_61016300	Att./Absences: Graphical Overview
S_AHR_61016301	Att./Absences: Graphical Overview
S_AHR_61016302	Time Leveling
S_AHR_61016303	Time Leveling
S_AHR_61016304	Time Statement Form
S_AHR_61016305	Time Statement Form
S_AHR_61016306	Time Statement Form
S_AHR_61016307	Time Statement Form
S_AHR_61016308	Cumulated Time Evaluation Results
S_AHR_61016309	Time Accounts
S_AHR_61016310	Display Cluster PC: Personal Calen.
S_AHR_61016311	Display Cluster B1 of DB PCL1
S_AHR_61016312	Display Time Evaluation Results (Clu
S_AHR_61016313	Display Cluster L1 of Database PCL1
S_AHR_61016314	Display Cluster G1 of Database PCL1
S_AHR_61016315	Reorganization for Personal Calendar
S_AHR_61016316	Examine Table T554S
S_AHR_61016317	Revaluation of Attendance/Absence
S_AHR_61016318	Leave Accrual and Quota Deduction
S_AHR_61016319	Batch Input: Annual Leave
S_AHR_61016320	Leave Accrual
S_AHR_61016321	Generation of work schedules
S_AHR_61016322	Revaluate Daily Work Schedules
S_AHR_61016323	Revaluate Planned Working Time IT
S_AHR_61016324	Generate Personal Calendar
S_AHR_61016335	History and Total of Appraisal Pts
S_AHR_61016337	Change of Basic Pay List (Japan)
S_AHR_61016339	Social Insurance Premium Check List
S_AHR_61016341	Employee w. Social & Employment Ins.
S_AHR_61016342	List of Employees No Longer Qualif.
S_AHR_61016343	List of employees exempt from employ
S_AHR_61016344	List of Liable Amount for Fixed Labo
S_AHR_61016345	address_list_of_employee
S_AHR_61016346	Residence Tax Entry Proof List (JP)
S_AHR_61016353	Education and Training
S_AHR_61016354	Telephone Directory
S_AHR_61016355	Powers of Attorney
S_AHR_61016356	Time spent in pay scale group/level
S_AHR_61016357	Defaults for Pay Scale Reclass.
S_AHR_61016358	Reference Personnel Numbers
S_AHR_61016359	Severely challenged
S_AHR_61016360	HR Master Data Sheet
S_AHR_61016361	HR Master Data Sheet - Switzerland
S_AHR_61016362	Flexible Employee Data
S_AHR_61016364	Family Members
S_AHR_61016365	Birthday List
S_AHR_61016366	Birthdays

S_AHR_61016368	Vehicle - Search List
S_AHR_61016369	Employee List
S_AHR_61016370	Overview of Maternity Data
S_AHR_61016371	New/Departing Employee
S_AHR_61016372	Seniority and Age
S_AHR_61016373	Headcount Development
S_AHR_61016374	Nationalities
S_AHR_61016375	Employee structure
S_AHR_61016376	Salary According to Seniority
S_AHR_61016377	Time-Related Statistical Evaluations
S_AHR_61016378	Assignment to Wage Level
S_AHR_61016380	Logged Changes in Infotype Data
S_AHR_61016381	Log of Report Starts
S_AHR_61016382	Date Monitoring
S_AHR_61016383	Budget in FTE
S_AHR_61016384	Available Budget Per BS Element
S_AHR_61016385	Job chart
S_AHR_61016386	Financing from BS Element Budgets
S_AHR_61016387	Budget Year Comparison
S_AHR_61016388	Enhanced Budget in FTEs
S_AHR_61016389	Job index
S_AHR_61016390	Business distribution plan
S_AHR_61016391	Different Service Type/Service Cat.
S_AHR_61016392	Report on teaching hours
S_AHR_61016393	Financing in Organizational Unit
S_AHR_61016394	Infotype Reporting
S_AHR_61016395	Start Payroll Report
S_AHR_61016396	Violations of earmarking
S_AHR_61016397	RHPMZWSH
S_AHR_61016398	Payroll Simulation for FPM
S_AHR_61016399	Payroll Simulation for FPM
S_AHR_61016400	Validate Funding of Basic Pay
S_AHR_61016401	General Trip Data/Trip Totals
S_AHR_61016402	Trip Receipts
S_AHR_61016403	Trip Receipts Without Gen. Trip Data
S_AHR_61016404	Cost Assignment for Trip
S_AHR_61016405	Trip Framew.Data/Totals/Rcpts/Costs
S_AHR_61016406	Who is where? Search for Trip Dest.
S_AHR_61016407	Find documents using maximum rate
S_AHR_61016408	Travel Expense Reporting by Period
S_AHR_61016409	Income-Related Expenses Statement
S_AHR_61016410	Input Tax Recovery
S_AHR_61016411	Determination of Employees with Exce
S_AHR_61016412	IMG Activity: HRPTDW03B
S_AHR_61016413	IMG Activity: HRPTDW03A
S_AHR_61016414	IMG Activity: SIMGHRPTDW030
S_AHR_61016415	IMG Activity: HRPTDW02B
S_AHR_61016416	IMG Activity: HRPTDW02A
S_AHR_61016417	IMG Activity: HRPTDW01
S_AHR_61016420	AL0K028900
S_AHR_61016421	Process Model 37
S_AHR_61016422	AL0K028900
S_AHR_61016426	AL0K028900
S_AHR_61016427	AL0K028900

SAP Transaction Codes – Volume Two

S_AHR_61016429	AL0K028900
S_AHR_61016430	AL0K028900
S_AHR_61016447	AL0K028900
S_AHR_61016448	AL0K028900
S_AHR_61016476	Display Cluster PC: Personal Calen.
S_AHR_61016477	Display Cluster B1 of DB PCL1
S_AHR_61016478	Display Time Evaluation Results (Clu
S_AHR_61016479	Display Cluster L1 of Database PCL1
S_AHR_61016480	Display Cluster G1 of Database PCL1
S_AHR_61016481	Reorganization for Personal Calendar
S_AHR_61016482	Examine table T554S
S_AHR_61016483	Revaluation of Attendance/Absence
S_AHR_61016484	Leave Accrual and Quota Deduction
S_AHR_61016485	Batch Input: Annual Leave
S_AHR_61016486	Leave Accrual
S_AHR_61016487	Generation of Work Schedules
S_AHR_61016488	Revaluate Daily Work Schedules
S_AHR_61016489	Revaluate Planned Working Time IT
S_AHR_61016490	Generate Personal Calendar
S_AHR_61016491	Existing Organizational Units
S_AHR_61016492	Staff Functions for Org. Unit
S_AHR_61016493	Organizational Structure
S_AHR_61016494	Org. Structure with Positions
S_AHR_61016495	Org. Structure with Persons
S_AHR_61016496	Org. Structure with Work Centers
S_AHR_61016497	Existing Jobs
S_AHR_61016498	Job index
S_AHR_61016499	Job Description
S_AHR_61016500	Task Description for Jobs
S_AHR_61016501	Complete job description
S_AHR_61016502	Existing Positions
S_AHR_61016503	Staff assignments
S_AHR_61016504	Position Description
S_AHR_61016505	Task Description for Positions
S_AHR_61016506	Staff Functions for Positions
S_AHR_61016507	Authorities and Resources
S_AHR_61016508	Planned Labor Costs
S_AHR_61016509	Vacant/Obsolete Positions
S_AHR_61016510	Correct Vacancies
S_AHR_61016511	Complete Position Description
S_AHR_61016512	Report Structure Without Persons
S_AHR_61016513	Report Structure with Persons
S_AHR_61016514	Existing Work Centers
S_AHR_61016515	Work Centers per Organizational Unit
S_AHR_61016516	Authorities and Resources
S_AHR_61016517	Planned Labor Costs
S_AHR_61016518	Work Ctrs with Restrictions in Org.S
S_AHR_61016519	Single Work Centers w. Restrictions
S_AHR_61016520	Work Centers Requiring Health Exam.
S_AHR_61016521	Single Work Centers Req. Health Exam
S_AHR_61016522	Existing Tasks
S_AHR_61016523	Activity Profile for Positions Along
S_AHR_61016524	Activity Profile of Positions with P
S_AHR_61016525	Character of Tasks in Organizational

S_AHR_61016526	Character of Individual Tasks
S_AHR_61016527	Existing Objects
S_AHR_61016528	Structure Display/Maintenance
S_AHR_61016529	Structure Navigation Instrument
S_AHR_61016530	PD Graphics Interface
S_AHR_61016531	Display and Maintain Infotypes
S_AHR_61016532	Infotype Reporting
S_AHR_61016533	Start Payroll Report
S_AHR_61016565	IMG activity: BEN_00_BE_TOOL_09
S_AHR_61016668	IMG Activity: OHAES_OPTAA
S_AHR_61016669	IMG Activity: OHAES_TCNEG
S_AHR_61016670	IMG Activity: OHAEAN3B
S_AHR_61016671	AL0K028900
S_AHR_61016672	AL0K028900
S_AHR_61016673	AL0K028900
S_AHR_61016709	Normative instruction 68
S_AHR_61016720	Display facsimile TemSe files
S_AHR_61016797	IMG
S_AHR_61016798	IMG
S_AHR_61016799	IMG
S_AHR_61016800	IMG
S_AHR_61016802	IMG
S_AHR_61016886	S_AHR_61016886
S_AHR_61016887	S_AHR_61016887
S_AHR_61016888	S_AHR_61016888
S_AHR_61016889	S_AHR_61016889
S_AHR_61018613	Cost Assignment for Trip
S_AHR_61018652	Time Leveling
S_AHR_61018653	Time Leveling
S_AHR_61018654	Remuneration Statements
S_AHR_61018655	Remuneration Statements
S_AHR_61018656	Remuneration Statements
S_AHR_61018657	Att./Absences: Graphical Overview
S_AHR_61018658	Att./Absences: Graphical Overview
S_AHR_61018659	Attendance/Absence Data: Overview
S_AHR_61018660	Att./Absence Data: Calendar View
S_AHR_61018661	Display Temporary Assignment List
S_AHR_61018689	S_AHR_61018689
S_AHR_61018690	S_AHR_61018690
S_AHR_61018691	S_AHR_61018691
S_AHR_61018692	S_AHR_61018692
S_AHR_61018693	S_AHR_61018693
S_AHR_61018694	S_AHR_61018694
S_AHR_61018713	S_AHR_61018713
S_AHR_61018714	S_AHR_61018714
S_AHR_61018716	S_AHR_61018716
S_AHR_61018718	S_AHR_61018718
S_AHR_61018719	S_AHR_61018719
S_AHR_61018720	S_AHR_61018720
S_AHR_61018721	S_AHR_61018721
S_AHR_61018722	S_AHR_61018722
S_AHR_61018723	S_AHR_61018723
S_AHR_61018724	S_AHR_61018724
S_AHR_61018735	S_AHR_61018735

S_AHR_61018736	S_AHR_61018736
S_AHR_61018741	S_AHR_61018741
S_AHR_61018743	S_AHR_61018743
S_AHR_61018744	S_AHR_61018744
S_AHR_61018745	S_AHR_61018745
S_AHR_61018750	Welfare Fund (OS) List
S_AHR_61018751	Payroll Driver (USA)
S_AHR_61018752	Union Dues List
S_AHR_61018753	Certificate of Services
S_AHR_61018754	Display Cluster RU (USA Payroll Resu
S_AHR_61018755	Subsequent processed of off-cycle ac
S_AHR_61018756	Off-Cycle Batch Processes - Start Pr
S_AHR_61018757	Update Remittance Tables from TemSe
S_AHR_61018758	Create Third-Party Remittance Postin
S_AHR_61018759	Reconciliation of Transfers
S_AHR_61018760	EEA temse file handling.
S_AHR_61018774	Check Processing Classes
S_AHR_61018775	Acknowledgement Report for Third-Par
S_AHR_61018776	Undo Third-Party Remittance Steps
S_AHR_61018777	Taxability Models/Tax types by Tax A
S_AHR_61018778	Display tax authorities
S_AHR_61018779	Tax Authorites not included in a res
S_AHR_61018780	Client Transport Program for BTX* Ta
S_AHR_61018781	Delete/Insert tax table entries
S_AHR_61018782	Listing of tax amounts in tax interf
S_AHR_61018783	Canada Equal-Employement Act report
S_AHR_61018786	Payroll Driver (Canada)
S_AHR_61018788	Display Cluster RK (Payroll Results
S_AHR_61018789	Preliminary Program - Data Medium Ex
S_AHR_61018790	Canada bond savings
S_AHR_61018792	Garnishment Statistics (Canada)
S_AHR_61018793	Canadian garnishment: History
S_AHR_61018797	Planned Compensation for Jobs
S_AHR_61018798	Compare Actual Base Salaries
S_AHR_61018799	Compa-ratio Analysis
S_AHR_61018822	Planned Labor Costs
S_AHR_61018823	IMG
S_AHR_61018831	Obsolete positions
S_AHR_61018864	IMG activity: OHAWFORS060
S_AHR_61018869	Periods of unoccupied positions
S_AHR_61018872	List HR Objects in the TemSe
S_AHR_61018873	Business Survey - Canada
S_AHR_61018874	IDoc inbound processing via file
S_AHR_61019009	Payroll Monthly Report
S_AHR_61019036	Ad Hoc Query
S_AHR_61019041	Ad hoc query
S_AHR_61019047	AL0K028900
S_AHR_61019053	SAP Query
S_AHR_61019055	SAP Query
S_AHR_61019066	AL0K028900
S_AHR_61019205	Irish Pensions Contributions Report
S_AHR_61019216	Guide of Social Welfare
S_AHR_61019283	S_AHR_61019283
S_AHR_61019288	S_AHR_61019288

S_AHR_61019289	S_AHR_61019289
S_AHR_61019290	S_AHR_61019290
S_AHR_61019318	SAPLS_CUS_IMG_ACTIVITY
S_AHR_61019382	IMG activity: OHAIEOSP00100C
S_AHR_HRFPM_0001	FTE Limits
S_AHR_HRFPM_0002	Reconstruct Funds Precommitments
S_AL0_19000002	BAdI FAGL_COFI_LNITEM_SEL
S_AL0_19000008	IMG Activity: V_FAGL_AB_C
S_AL0_19000078	Consistency Check: Bill.Docs - FI
S_AL0_96000020	IMG Activity: CMMENUORFA_MITKO1
S_AL0_96000054	IMG Activity : OHAF0096
S_AL0_96000057	IMG activity: OHAPT_RS001
S_AL0_96000060	IMG activity: OHAPT_RI091
S_AL0_96000067	IMG Activity: OHAN9212B
S_AL0_96000068	IMG Activity: OHAN9212C
S_AL0_96000069	IMG Activity: OHAN9212A
S_AL0_96000099	IMG activity: J_1IREGSET
S_AL0_96000102	IMG activity: J_1IEXGRPS
S_AL0_96000103	IMG activity: J_1IWRKCUS
S_AL0_96000104	IMG activity: J_1ISRGRPS
S_AL0_96000105	IMG activity: J_1IEXCDEF
S_AL0_96000106	IMG activity: J_1ITRNACC
S_AL0_96000107	IMG activity: J_1IEXCACC
S_AL0_96000108	IMG activity: J_1IMINBAL
S_AL0_96000109	IMG activity: J_1IEX_SFAC
S_AL0_96000110	IMG activity: J_1IEX_CUST_ACT
S_AL0_96000111	IMG activity: J_1IEX_CUST_REF
S_AL0_96000112	IMG activity: J_1IREJMAS
S_AL0_96000113	IMG activity: J_1IMVMT
S_AL0_96000114	IMG activity: J_1ISUBATT
S_AL0_96000115	IMG activity: J_1IMVTGRP
S_AL0_96000116	IMG activity: J_1IEXCREF
S_AL0_96000117	IMG activity: J_1IUTILIZE
S_AL0_96000118	IMG activity: J_1IEXSRDET
S_AL0_96000119	IMG activity: J_1IJ1I9
S_AL0_96000120	IMG activity: J_1IVTTXID
S_AL0_96000121	IMG activity: J_1IMESG
S_AL0_96000122	IMG activity: J_1IVFRTYP
S_AL0_96000123	IMG activity: J_2ILAYCTR
S_AL0_96000154	IMG activity: J_1IEWTCALID
S_AL0_96000155	IMG activity: J_1IEWTDUEDATE
S_AL0_96000158	IMG activity: J_1IEWT_COMP
S_AL0_96000159	IMG activity: J_1IEWTSURC
S_AL0_96000160	IMG activity: J_1IEWT_SURC1
S_AL0_96000161	IMG activity: J_1IEWTDOCKEY
S_AL0_96000162	IMG activity: J_1IEWTHKONT
S_AL0_96000163	IMG activity: J_1IEWT_CUST
S_AL0_96000164	IMG activity: J_1IEWT_CUSTV
S_AL0_96000165	IMG activity: J_1IEWTNUMGR
S_AL0_96000166	IMG activity: J_1IEWTNUM
S_AL0_96000167	IMG activity: J_1IEWTNO
S_AL0_96000168	IMG activity: J_1IEWTPROVISACC
S_AL0_96000169	IMG activity: J_1IEWT_CERT
S_AL0_96000170	IMG activity: J_1IEWT_CERTNO

S_AL0_96000171	IMG activity: J_1ICERT
S_AL0_96000172	IMG activity: J_1IEWT_HEALTH_CHECK
S_AL0_96000173	IMG activity: J_1IEWT_MIGRATE
S_AL0_96000174	IMG activity: J_1ITDSSEC
S_AL0_96000175	IMG activity: J_1ITDSTXC
S_AL0_96000176	IMG activity: J_1ITDSDUE
S_AL0_96000182	IMG activity: J_1IEWTHKONT1
S_AL0_96000192	Create Customer Settlements
S_AL0_96000193	Customer Settlement (Header Info)
S_AL0_96000194	Customer Settlement (with Item Data)
S_AL0_96000195	Expenses Settlement (Header Data)
S_AL0_96000196	Expense Settlement (with Item Data)
S_AL0_96000197	Remuneration List from Cust. Settlmt
S_AL0_96000198	Settlement for Remuneration List
S_AL0_96000212	Mass Release of Customer Settlements
S_AL0_96000213	IMG Activity: OHANL_PS111
S_AL0_96000214	IMG Activity: OHANL_PS112
S_AL0_96000215	IMG Activity: OHANL_PS113
S_AL0_96000305	IMG Activity: CMP_00_LT_005
S_AL0_96000306	Mass Cancellation: Remuneration List
S_AL0_96000307	Mass Cancellation: Settlement Req.
S_AL0_96000308	Mass Cancellation: Customer Settlemt
S_AL0_96000309	Mass Cancellation of Posting Lists
S_AL0_96000324	Mass Pricing:Settlement Request List
S_AL0_96000325	Mass release payment documents
S_AL0_96000333	Remuneration List Expense Settlement
S_AL0_96000334	Release Expense Settlement Documents
S_AL0_96000335	Mass Release of Customer Settlement
S_AL0_96000336	Mass Cancellation: Expense Settlemt
S_AL0_96000380	IMG Activity: OHPSUSSICK03
S_AL0_96000381	IMG Activity: OHPSUSSICK21
S_AL0_96000385	Top Vendors Report
S_AL0_96000389	Top Customers Report
S_AL0_96000488	Sales Document
S_AL0_96000489	Delivery
S_AL0_96000490	Billing Document
S_AL0_96000491	Sales activity
S_AL0_96000492	Material Document
S_AL0_96000493	Purchase Order
S_AL0_96000495	Purchase Requisition
S_AL0_96000496	Logistics Invoice Verification
S_AL0_96000497	Accounting Document
S_AL0_96000502	HDA Increment Progression
S_AL0_96000597	IMG Activity: OHPSUSRIF003
S_AL0_96000598	IMG Activity: PAY_IN_TER_400
S_AL0_96000619	Audit Information System (AIS)
S_AL0_96000639	Resolution AFIP 615
S_AL0_96000640	Significant Trans. Cross Check CTTI
S_AL0_96000642	Daily Report for VAT
S_AL0_96000699	HR-NA: OSHA-301 Report
S_AL0_96000700	HR-NA: OSHA 300 & 300A Reports
S_AL0_96000702	Crryfwrd of Budget Hierarchy per F
S_AL0_96000703	Crryfwrd of Financing per FMAA
S_AL0_96000705	Validate Funding of Basic Pay

SAP Transaction Codes – Volume Two

S_AL0_96000706	RHPMSIM3
S_AL0_96000738	RFIDPTFO
S_AL0_96000745	IMG Activity: PAY_IN_TER_300
S_AL0_96000749	IMG activity: PAY_VE_TER_020
S_AL0_96000754	Maintain substitute tax percentage
S_AL0_96000771	Transfer of Payroll Already Posted
S_AL0_96000809	IMG Activity: J_1IN0002
S_AL0_96000810	IMG Activity: J_1IN0004
S_AL0_96000845	IMG Activity: OHPSUSNOA002
S_ALN_01000001	Program GMTEST_SCREENS
S_ALN_01000002	Post indirect costs (defined by spon
S_ALN_01000003	Annual Budget Vs. Commit./Actual Lin
S_ALN_01000079	Master Data Index for Grant
S_ALN_01000084	IMG-Activity: _ISPSFM_V_FMAVCBUDFI
S_ALN_01000095	Cust
S_ALN_01000128	IMG-Aktivität: SIMG_ISPSFM_V_T023G
S_ALN_01000159	Master data index for Sponsored Prog
S_ALN_01000160	Master data index for Sponsored Clas
S_ALN_01000161	Master Data Index for Grant Sponsors
S_ALN_01000167	IMG Activity: BEN_00_AD_ADJM_12
S_ALN_01000168	IMG Activity: BEN_00_AD_ADJM_13
S_ALN_01000170	Enhanced Remuneration Lists
S_ALN_01000171	Remuneration Lists From Posting List
S_ALN_01000172	Remuneration Lists From VBilling Doc
S_ALN_01000173	Remuneration List from Cust. Settlmt
S_ALN_01000174	Remun. Lists From Expense Settlement
S_ALN_01000175	Relevant Payment Documents
S_ALN_01000176	Customer Settlement Documents
S_ALN_01000177	Relevant Posting Lists
S_ALN_01000178	Expense Settlement Documents
S_ALN_01000179	Relevant Vendor Billing Documents
S_ALN_01000185	IMG Activity: _ISPSFM_N_FMKFDEF
S_ALN_01000203	IMG Activity: _ISPSFM_V_FMAVCLDGRA
S_ALN_01000204	IMG Activity: _ISPSFM_V_FMAVCL_ACT
S_ALN_01000213	IMG Activity: _ISPSFM_FMRULES
S_ALN_01000236	IMG Activity: V_TACE_ACCRU_SOA
S_ALN_01000276	Maintain File ID and Agency ID
S_ALN_01000277	Test
S_ALN_01000299	IMG Activity: MGE_00_PO_CGR
S_ALN_01000371	Simulation of Remuneration Lists
S_ALN_01000372	Simulation of Remuneration Lists
S_ALN_01000373	Simulation of Remuneration Lists
S_ALN_01000375	Simulation of Remuneration Lists
S_ALN_01000376	Simulation: Remu. List From Delivery
S_ALN_01000382	IMG Activity: _ISPSFM_N_V_FMBUDTYP
S_ALN_01000384	IMG Activity: _ISPSFM_N_GLPLC
S_ALN_01000385	IMG Activity: _ISPSFM_N_VC_TKA50_G
S_ALN_01000386	IMG Activity: _ISPSFM_N_V_FMLA
S_ALN_01000523	IMG Activity: SIMGH_LMON005
S_ALN_01000534	Grant Billing Reconciliation Report
S_ALN_01000598	PA: Settings
S_ALN_01000599	PA: Catalog for Appraisal Templates
S_ALN_01000630	IMG Activity: MGE_00_PO_SUM
S_ALN_01000840	IMG Activity: _ISPSFM_BUD_SM30

S_ALN_01000858	IMG Activity: _CFMENUOFTC_OFDM1
S_ALN_01000862	Account closure: Release
S_ALN_01001040	IMG Activity: SIMG_CFMENUOLPSPPE35
S_ALN_01001041	IMG Activity: SIMG_CFMENUOLPSPPDOK
S_ALN_01001049	SAPLS_CUS_IMG_ACTIVITY
S_ALN_01001054	SAPLS_CUS_IMG_ACTIVITY
S_ALN_01001055	SAPLS_CUS_IMG_ACTIVITY
S_ALN_01001085	S_ALN_01001088
S_ALN_01001086	S_ALN_01001088
S_ALN_01001088	S_ALN_01001088
S_ALN_01001098	Assignment Activation
S_ALN_01001106	IMG Activity: _ISPSFM_H_GRPNR
S_ALN_01001144	Overview - Positions
S_ALN_01001145	IAS - Classification
S_ALN_01001146	Structure Analysis
S_ALN_01001147	Rating Analysis
S_ALN_01001148	Country Analysis
S_ALN_01001149	Remaining Term Statistics
S_ALN_01001150	Share of Position (Based on EUR)
S_ALN_01001151	Overview - Accounting
S_ALN_01001152	TOP 5 - Positions
S_ALN_01001153	Currency analysis
S_ALN_01001154	Simulated Valuation
S_ALN_01001155	CFM Key Date Comparison
S_ALN_01001156	Asset History Sheet / HGB
S_ALN_01001157	Position Trend
S_ALN_01001158	Book Value Trend / P+L / OCI
S_ALN_01001159	Revenues
S_ALN_01001160	Sales Proceeds
S_ALN_01001161	Due Date Grid
S_ALN_01001230	IMG Activity: REFXCL_V_TIV35
S_ALN_01001257	IMG Activity: REFX_SNUMBDCN
S_ALN_01001279	Info System: Business Entities
S_ALN_01001286	Info System: Buildings
S_ALN_01001287	Info System: Land
S_ALN_01001288	Info System: Rental Objects
S_ALN_01001289	Info System: Contracts
S_ALN_01001290	Info System:Measurmts for MasterData
S_ALN_01001291	Info System:Measurements for Options
S_ALN_01001292	Info System: Conditions for ROs
S_ALN_01001293	Info System:Conditions for Contracts
S_ALN_01001335	Info System: Occupancy of ROs
S_ALN_01001336	Info System: Objects for Partner
S_ALN_01001337	Info System: Partner for Master Data
S_ALN_01001342	Exposure Overview Work Area
S_ALN_01001343	Exposure Overview for Person
S_ALN_01001344	Version Overview Work Areas
S_ALN_01001345	Version Overview Risk Assessments
S_ALN_01001346	Version Overview Inc./Acc. Log
S_ALN_01001347	Injury/Illness Log Entry Versions
S_ALN_01001359	Data Basis Employees
S_ALN_01001360	Databasis Positions
S_ALN_01001361	Data Basis Jobs
S_ALN_01001362	Data Basis Organizational Units

S_ALN_01001363	Ad Hoc Query Personnel Cost Planning
S_ALN_01001588	IMG Activity: HR_ECM_00_TC_E08
S_ALN_01001767	Property Tax Report (Japan)
S_ALN_01002146	IMG Activity: HR_ECM_00_TC_003
S_ALN_01002221	Check consistency of intercompany ma
S_ALN_01002396	Create Operational IDocs
S_ALN_01002397	Create Material Master Data IDocs
S_ALN_01002461	IMG Activity: V_TACE001_BUKRS_IPMO
S_ALN_01002462	IMG Activity: V_TACE_ACCR_IPMO
S_ALN_01002463	IMG Activity: V_TACE_COMB_IPMO
S_ALN_01002464	IMG Activity: V_TACE001_IPMO
S_ALN_01002465	IMG Activity: V_TACE_ACRTY_IPMO
S_ALN_01002517	Transfer IHC Financial Status to CM
S_ALN_13000100	IMG Activity: SIMG_BA-CA-V_TBKK8V
S_ALR_87000016	IMG Activity: SIMG_CFMENUOLI0OIYJ
S_ALR_87000017	IMG Activity: OLII_V_PMCOCKF
S_ALR_87000018	IMG Activity: SIMG_CFMENUOLMBBFCO
S_ALR_87000019	IMG Activity: OLIA_OITA
S_ALR_87000020	IMG Activity: SIMG_CFMENUOKCMKCR7
S_ALR_87000021	IMG Activity: OLII_TPMCKF
S_ALR_87000022	IMG Activity: OLIA_OITB
S_ALR_87000023	IMG Activity: SIMG_OLMA_OMEV
S_ALR_87000024	IMG Activity: SIMG_CFMENUOLI0IN20
S_ALR_87000025	IMG Activity: OKCM_TR_USER_EXIT
S_ALR_87000026	IMG Activity: SIMG_CFMENUOLMBBFMM
S_ALR_87000027	IMG Activity: SIMG_CFMENUOLIPOIL7
S_ALR_87000028	IMG Activity: SIMG_CFMENUOLIAOION
S_ALR_87000029	IMG Activity: OLIIOIAK
S_ALR_87000030	IMG Activity: SIMG_CFMENUOLI0OINI
S_ALR_87000031	IMG Activity: SIMG_OLMA_OMJI
S_ALR_87000032	IMG Activity: SIMG_CFMENUOLMBBEFIS
S_ALR_87000033	IMG Activity: SIMG_CFMENUOKCMOKCG
S_ALR_87000034	IMG Activity: SIMG_CFMENUOLIPOILB
S_ALR_87000035	IMG Activity: OLIIOIAW
S_ALR_87000036	IMG Activity: SIMG_OLMA_OMXL
S_ALR_87000037	IMG Activity: SIMG_CFMENUOLI0OINM
S_ALR_87000038	IMG Activity: SIMG_CFMENUOLIAOIOD
S_ALR_87000039	IMG Activity: SIMG_OLMB_NADU
S_ALR_87000040	IMG Activity: SIMG_CFMENUOKCMKCC1
S_ALR_87000041	IMG Activity: SIMG_CFMENUOLIPOILJ
S_ALR_87000042	IMG Activity: OLIA_V_T399X_QP
S_ALR_87000043	IMG Activity: OLI0V_T370N
S_ALR_87000044	IMG Activity: SIMG_CFMENUOLMBOMJ4
S_ALR_87000045	IMG Activity: SIMG_CFMENUOKCMOKCC
S_ALR_87000046	IMG Activity: OLIA_V_T350_IV
S_ALR_87000047	IMG Activity: SIMG_CFMENUOLIPOIWO
S_ALR_87000048	IMG Activity: OLI0_OIRC
S_ALR_87000049	IMG Activity: SIMG_CFMENUOLMBOMJ3
S_ALR_87000050	IMG Activity: OKCM_GRR2
S_ALR_87000051	IMG Activity: SIMG_CFMENUOLIAOIWU
S_ALR_87000052	IMG Activity: OLI0_OIUR
S_ALR_87000053	IMG Activity: OLIP_OIBD
S_ALR_87000054	IMG Activity: SIMG_CFMENUOLMBOMBO
S_ALR_87000055	IMG Activity: OKCM_OKX1_COMMENT

S_ALR_87000056	IMG Activity: SIMG_CFMENUOLIAOIWL
S_ALR_87000057	IMG Activity: OLI0_OIUQ
S_ALR_87000058	IMG Activity: SIMG_CFMENUOLMBBFRM
S_ALR_87000059	IMG Activity: SIMG_CFOKCMOKX5
S_ALR_87000060	IMG Activity: OLIP_OIBC
S_ALR_87000061	IMG Activity: SIMG_CFMENUOLIAOIOA
S_ALR_87000062	IMG Activity: SIMG_CFMENUOLI0OIXL
S_ALR_87000063	IMG Activity: SIMG_CFMENUOLMBBFREP
S_ALR_87000064	IMG Activity: OLIP_OIRT
S_ALR_87000065	IMG Activity: OLIAOIOL
S_ALR_87000066	IMG Activity: SIMG_CMMENUOKCMUB
S_ALR_87000067	IMG Activity: OLI0_V_T399U
S_ALR_87000068	IMG Activity: OLIP_OIRU
S_ALR_87000069	IMG Activity: SIMG_CFMENUOPP3OSP7
S_ALR_87000070	IMG Activity: OLIA_V_T350_RSORD
S_ALR_87000071	IMG Activity: SIMG_CFOKCMOKX1
S_ALR_87000072	IMG Activity: OLI0_OIML
S_ALR_87000073	IMG Activity: SIMG_CFMENUOLMBOSP7
S_ALR_87000074	IMG Activity: SIMG_CFMENUOLIPOIL1
S_ALR_87000075	IMG Activity: SIMG_CFMENUOLIAOIOS
S_ALR_87000076	IMG Activity: SIMG_OKCMOKX4
S_ALR_87000077	IMG Activity: SIMG_CFMENUOLMBBFWM
S_ALR_87000078	IMG Activity: SIMG_CFMENUOLI0OIAT
S_ALR_87000079	IMG Activity: SIMG_CFMENUOLIPOIL2
S_ALR_87000080	IMG Activity: OLIA_V_TPMIM
S_ALR_87000081	IMG Activity: OKCM_ACTIVITYGROUP
S_ALR_87000082	IMG Activity: SIMG_CFMENUOLMBLIEF
S_ALR_87000083	IMG Activity: SIMG_CFMENUOLIPOIL3
S_ALR_87000084	IMG Activity: SIMG_CFMENUOLI0OIAG
S_ALR_87000085	IMG Activity: OLIA_V_T350_IMZS
S_ALR_87000086	IMG Activity: SIMG_CFOKCMKEEU
S_ALR_87000087	IMG Activity: SIMG_CFMENUOLMBBFPK
S_ALR_87000088	IMG Activity: SIMG_CFMENUOLI0OIAA
S_ALR_87000089	IMG Activity: SIMG_CFMENUOLIPOIL4
S_ALR_87000090	IMG Activity: OLIAV_TPMP_A
S_ALR_87000091	IMG Activity: SIMG_CFMENUOKCMKCA1
S_ALR_87000092	IMG Activity: SIMG_CFMENUOLMBBFPU
S_ALR_87000093	IMG Activity: SIMG_CFMENUOLI0OIAI
S_ALR_87000094	IMG Activity: SIMG_CFMENUOLIPOIL5
S_ALR_87000095	IMG Activity: SIMG_CFMENUOLIPOIVA
S_ALR_87000096	IMG Activity: SIMG_CFMENUOLMBOMBU
S_ALR_87000097	IMG Activity: SIMG_CFMENUOLI0OIAB
S_ALR_87000098	IMG Activity: SIMG_CFMENUOKCMKCW1
S_ALR_87000099	IMG Activity: SIMG_CFMENUOLIPOIL0
S_ALR_87000100	IMG Activity: OLIA_V_T350_NOTDAT
S_ALR_87000101	IMG Activity: SIMG_CFMENUOLI0OIEA
S_ALR_87000102	IMG Activity: OKCM_OKCSL
S_ALR_87000103	IMG Activity: SIMG_CFMENUOLIPOIL6
S_ALR_87000104	IMG Activity: SIMG_CFMENUOLMBOMCF
S_ALR_87000105	IMG Activity: OLIA_V_T350_PZ
S_ALR_87000106	IMG Activity: SIMG_CFMENUOLI0OIWD
S_ALR_87000107	IMG Activity: SIMG_CFMENUOLIPYWY1
S_ALR_87000108	IMG Activity: OKCM_OKCSLA
S_ALR_87000109	IMG Activity: SIMG_CFMENUOLMBOMJL

S_ALR_87000110	IMG Activity: OLIAV_TPEXT_PM
S_ALR_87000111	IMG Activity: SIMG_CFMENUOLI0OIUC
S_ALR_87000112	IMG Activity: SIMG_CFMENUOLIPOP731
S_ALR_87000113	IMG Activity: OLIA_V_T350E
S_ALR_87000114	IMG Activity: SIMG_CFMENUOLMBOMB4
S_ALR_87000115	IMG Activity: OKCM_OKCSLU
S_ALR_87000116	IMG Activity: SIMG_CFMENUOLI0OIW1
S_ALR_87000117	IMG Activity: OLIAV_TCN41_PM
S_ALR_87000118	IMG Activity: SIMG_CFMENUOLMBOMB5
S_ALR_87000119	IMG Activity: SIMG_CFMENUOLIPOP801
S_ALR_87000120	IMG Activity: OKCM_OKCSLD
S_ALR_87000121	IMG Activity: OLI0_OIWQ
S_ALR_87000122	IMG Activity: OLIA_V_T350_HE
S_ALR_87000123	IMG Activity: SIMG_CFMENUOLIPOP471
S_ALR_87000124	IMG Activity: SIMG_CFMENUOLMBOMBR
S_ALR_87000125	IMG Activity: SIMG_CFMENUOLI0OIWE
S_ALR_87000126	IMG Activity: SIMG_CFOKCMSQ00
S_ALR_87000127	IMG Activity: OLIA_V_T350_BEZZT
S_ALR_87000128	IMG Activity: SIMG_CFMENUOLIPOP741
S_ALR_87000129	IMG Activity: SIMG_CFMENUOLMBOXK1
S_ALR_87000130	IMG Activity: SIMG_CFMENUOLI0OIES
S_ALR_87000131	IMG Activity: SIMG_CFEMNUOLIAOIWI
S_ALR_87000132	IMG Activity: OKCM_OKCE
S_ALR_87000133	IMG Activity: SIMG_CFMENUOLIPOP721
S_ALR_87000134	IMG Activity: J_1AASSIGN_BR_PLSL
S_ALR_87000135	IMG Activity: OLI0OIAD
S_ALR_87000136	IMG Activity: OLIA_OIW1
S_ALR_87000137	IMG Activity: SIMG_CFMENUOLIPOIZL1
S_ALR_87000138	IMG Activity: SIMG_CFMENUOLI0OIEV
S_ALR_87000139	IMG Activity: SIMG_CFMENUOLMBSE71
S_ALR_87000140	IMG Activity: OLIAOIYZ
S_ALR_87000141	IMG Activity: SIMG_CFMENUOKCMOKUP
S_ALR_87000142	IMG Activity: SIMG_CFMENUOLIPOIZM1
S_ALR_87000143	IMG Activity: SIMG_CFMENUOLI0OIEB
S_ALR_87000144	IMG Activity: OLIAOIYW
S_ALR_87000145	IMG Activity: SIMG_CMMENUOLMBNAKO
S_ALR_87000146	IMG Activity: SIMG_CFMENUOKCMOKUQ
S_ALR_87000147	IMG Activity: OLIAOIWK
S_ALR_87000148	IMG Activity: OLIA_OIUB
S_ALR_87000149	IMG Activity: SIMG_CFMENUOLMBM708
S_ALR_87000150	IMG Activity: SIMG_CFMENUOKCMOKCD
S_ALR_87000151	IMG Activity: OLIAOIRB
S_ALR_87000152	IMG Activity: OLIA_OIAL
S_ALR_87000153	IMG Activity: SIMG_CFMENUOLI0OIXK
S_ALR_87000154	IMG Activity: CFOKCMOKUY
S_ALR_87000155	IMG Activity: SIMG_CFMENUOLMBM706
S_ALR_87000156	IMG Activity: OLIP_OIRV
S_ALR_87000157	IMG Activity: SIMG_CFMENUOLIAOIDB
S_ALR_87000158	IMG Activity: SIMG_CFMENUOLI0OIXJ
S_ALR_87000159	IMG Activity: OKCM_KCF3
S_ALR_87000160	IMG Activity: OLIP_OIRW
S_ALR_87000161	IMG Activity: SIMG_CFMENUOLMBM710
S_ALR_87000162	IMG Activity: SIMG_CFMENUOLIAOIDC
S_ALR_87000163	IMG Activity: SIMG_CFMENUOLI0OIXI

S_ALR_87000164	IMG Activity: OLIP_OIRX
S_ALR_87000165	IMG Activity: SIMG_CFMENUOLIAOIZL2
S_ALR_87000166	IMG Activity: SIMG_CMMENUOLMBNAKT
S_ALR_87000167	IMG Activity: SIMG_CFMENUOLI0OIXH
S_ALR_87000168	IMG Activity: OKCM_KCV1
S_ALR_87000169	IMG Activity: OLIP_OIRY
S_ALR_87000170	IMG Activity: SIMG_CFMENUOLIAOIDD
S_ALR_87000171	IMG Activity: J_1ADEFINE_REL_MTYPE
S_ALR_87000172	IMG Activity: SIMG_CFMENUOLI0OIXG
S_ALR_87000173	IMG Activity: OKCM_KP34
S_ALR_87000174	IMG Activity: OLIP_OIRZ
S_ALR_87000175	IMG Activity: SIMG_CFMENUOLIAOIDE
S_ALR_87000176	IMG Activity: SIMG_CFMENUOLMBCMOD
S_ALR_87000177	IMG Activity: SIMG_CFMENUOLI0OIXF
S_ALR_87000178	IMG Activity: OLIP_OIR0
S_ALR_87000179	IMG Activity: OKCM_KCP7
S_ALR_87000180	IMG Activity: OLIAOIUI
S_ALR_87000181	IMG Activity: SIMG_CFMENUOLMBOMC9
S_ALR_87000182	IMG Activity: SIMG_CFMENUOLI0OIXE
S_ALR_87000183	IMG Activity: OLIP_OIS3
S_ALR_87000184	IMG Activity: SIMG_CFMENUOLIAOIXS
S_ALR_87000185	IMG Activity: OKCM_KCKB
S_ALR_87000186	IMG Activity: SIMG_CFMENUOLMBOMC8
S_ALR_87000187	IMG Activity: SIMG_CFMENUOLI0OIXD
S_ALR_87000188	IMG Activity: OLIP_OIS4
S_ALR_87000189	IMG Activity: SIMG_CFMENUOLIAOIXT
S_ALR_87000190	IMG Activity: SIMG_CFMENUOLIPOIW0
S_ALR_87000191	IMG Activity: SIMG_CFMENUOLMBOMC7
S_ALR_87000192	IMG Activity: OKCM_OKXR
S_ALR_87000193	IMG Activity: SIMG_CFMENUOLI0OIXC
S_ALR_87000194	IMG Activity: SIMG_CFMENUOLIPOIYL
S_ALR_87000195	IMG Activity: SIMG_CFMENUOLMBOMC4
S_ALR_87000196	IMG Activity: OKCM_KED0SAIS
S_ALR_87000197	IMG Activity: SIMG_CFMENUOLI0OICM
S_ALR_87000198	IMG Activity: SIMG_CFMENUOLIAOIXU
S_ALR_87000199	IMG Activity: SIMG_CFMENUOLIPOIYM
S_ALR_87000200	IMG Activity: SIMG_CFMENUOLMBOMJH
S_ALR_87000201	IMG Activity: OKCM_KED0UMW
S_ALR_87000202	IMG Activity: SIMG_CFMENUOLI0OICP
S_ALR_87000203	IMG Activity: SIMG_CFMENUOLIAOIXV
S_ALR_87000204	IMG Activity: SIMG_CFMENUOLIPOIY9
S_ALR_87000205	IMG Activity: SIMG_CMMENUOLMBOMC6
S_ALR_87000206	IMG Activity: SIMG_CFMENUOLI0OICX
S_ALR_87000207	IMG Activity: OKCM_KCPZ
S_ALR_87000208	IMG Activity: OLIA_OIYV
S_ALR_87000209	IMG Activity: SIMG_CFMENUOLIPOIWY
S_ALR_87000210	IMG Activity: SIMG_CFMENUOLI0OICK
S_ALR_87000212	IMG Activity: OKCM_KED0PROG
S_ALR_87000213	IMG Activity: SIMG_CFMENUOLIAOIXR
S_ALR_87000214	IMG Activity: SIMG_CFMENUOLIPOIWW
S_ALR_87000215	IMG Activity: SIMG_CFMENUOLI0OICL
S_ALR_87000216	IMG Activity: SIMG_CFMENUOLIAOIXM
S_ALR_87000217	IMG Activity: SIMG_CMMENUOLMBGWE08
S_ALR_87000218	IMG Activity: OKCM_KCPX

S_ALR_87000219	IMG Activity: OLIP_OIW5
S_ALR_87000220	IMG Activity: SIMG_CFMENUOLIAOIXN
S_ALR_87000221	IMG Activity: SIMG_CFMENUOLI0OICI
S_ALR_87000222	IMG Activity: OKCM_KCPV
S_ALR_87000223	IMG Activity: SIMG_CMMENUOLMBGWE09
S_ALR_87000224	IMG Activity: SIMG_CFMENUOLIAOIXO
S_ALR_87000225	IMG Activity: SIMG_CFMENUOLIPIP21
S_ALR_87000226	IMG Activity: SIMG_CFMENUOLI0OICG
S_ALR_87000227	IMG Activity: SIMG_CMMENUOLMBGWE07
S_ALR_87000228	IMG Activity: OKCM_OKX9
S_ALR_87000229	IMG Activity: SIMG_CFMENUOLIAOIXP
S_ALR_87000230	IMG Activity: SIMG_CFMENUOLIPOIBA
S_ALR_87000231	IMG Activity: SIMG_CFMENUOLI0OICF
S_ALR_87000232	IMG Activity: SIMG_CMMENUOLMBGWE06
S_ALR_87000233	IMG Activity: SIMG_CFMENUOKCMOKU0
S_ALR_87000234	IMG Activity: SIMG_CFMENUOLIPOIAB1
S_ALR_87000235	IMG Activity: SIMG_CFMENUOLIAOIXQ
S_ALR_87000236	IMG Activity: SIMG_CFMENUOLI0OICE
S_ALR_87000237	IMG Activity: SIMG_CMMENUOLMBGWE05
S_ALR_87000238	IMG Activity: OKCM_OKCDBC
S_ALR_87000239	IMG Activity: SIMG_CFMENUOLIPOIAI1
S_ALR_87000240	IMG Activity: OLIAOIAN
S_ALR_87000241	IMG Activity: OLI0_CMOD
S_ALR_87000242	IMG Activity: SIMG_CMMENUOLMBGWE04
S_ALR_87000243	IMG Activity: OKCM_OKCDBD
S_ALR_87000244	IMG Activity: SIMG_CFMENUOLIPOIAA1
S_ALR_87000245	IMG Activity: SIMG_CFMENUOLIAOIDI
S_ALR_87000246	IMG Activity: OLI0_IBIP
S_ALR_87000247	IMG Activity: SIMG_CMMENUOLMBGWE03
S_ALR_87000248	IMG Activity: SIMG_CFMENUOLIAOIO1
S_ALR_87000249	IMG Activity: SIMG_CFMENUOLIPOIVS
S_ALR_87000250	IMG Activity: OKCM_TKCUM
S_ALR_87000251	IMG Activity: SIMG_CFMENUOLI0OICA
S_ALR_87000252	IMG Activity: SIMG_CMMENUOLMBOMCG
S_ALR_87000253	IMG Activity: SIMG_CFMENUOLIAOIO2
S_ALR_87000254	IMG Activity: OLIP_V_T399W_I
S_ALR_87000255	IMG Activity: SIMG_CFMENUOLI0OICS
S_ALR_87000256	IMG Activity: SIMG_CFMENUOLMB001MB
S_ALR_87000257	IMG Activity: OKCM_OKX1_MASTER_HI
S_ALR_87000258	IMG Activity: SIMG_CFMENUOLIPIP20
S_ALR_87000259	IMG Activity: SIMG_CFMENUOLIAOIOP
S_ALR_87000260	IMG Activity: SIMG_CFMENUOLI0OICT
S_ALR_87000261	IMG Activity: SIMG_OLMB_001L_B
S_ALR_87000262	IMG Activity: SIMG_CFMENUOKCMOKX0
S_ALR_87000263	IMG Activity: SIMG_CFMENUOLIPOIZA
S_ALR_87000264	IMG Activity: SIMG_CFMENUOLI0OICQ
S_ALR_87000265	IMG Activity: SIMG_CFMENUOLIAOIMM
S_ALR_87000266	IMG Activity: SIMG_OLMB_V_156S_GR
S_ALR_87000267	IMG Activity: SIMG_CFMENUOKCMOKCL
S_ALR_87000268	IMG Activity: SIMG_CFMENUOLIPOIZ3
S_ALR_87000269	IMG Activity: SIMG_OLIA_V_TBMOT
S_ALR_87000270	IMG Activity: SIMG_CFMENUOLI0OICJ
S_ALR_87000271	IMG Activity: OLIP_V_PVBE
S_ALR_87000272	IMG Activity: OKCM_UPLOAD

S_ALR_87000274	IMG Activity: OLIA_OIKS
S_ALR_87000275	IMG Activity: SIMG_CFMENUOLI0OICO
S_ALR_87000276	IMG Activity: SIMG_CFMENUOLIPOIZV
S_ALR_87000277	IMG Activity: SIMG_CFMENUOLMBOMBG
S_ALR_87000278	IMG Activity: OKCM_RKCFILE0_EVENT
S_ALR_87000279	IMG Activity: SIMG_CFMENUOLI0OICN
S_ALR_87000280	IMG Activity: OLIAOIAP
S_ALR_87000281	IMG Activity: SIMG_CFMENUOLIPOIZD
S_ALR_87000282	IMG Activity: SIMG_CFMENUOLMBOMB9
S_ALR_87000283	IMG Activity: SIMG_CFOKCMKCF0
S_ALR_87000284	IMG Activity: OLI0OIRO
S_ALR_87000285	IMG Activity: OLIA_V_T418V
S_ALR_87000286	IMG Activity: SIMG_CFMENUOLIPOIZU
S_ALR_87000287	IMG Activity: SIMG_CFMENUOLMBOMBE
S_ALR_87000288	IMG Activity: SIMG_CFMENUOKCMOKCJ
S_ALR_87000289	IMG Activity: OLI0OIRN
S_ALR_87000290	IMG Activity: OLIA_V_TCOKO
S_ALR_87000291	IMG Activity: SIMG_CFMENUOLMBOMBV
S_ALR_87000292	IMG Activity: SIMG_CFMENUOLIPOIZ5
S_ALR_87000293	IMG Activity: SIMG_CFMENUOKCMOKCI
S_ALR_87000294	IMG Activity: OLI0OIRM
S_ALR_87000295	IMG Activity: SIMG_CFMENUOLMBSXDAR
S_ALR_87000296	IMG Activity: SIMG_CFMENUOLIPOIZ8
S_ALR_87000297	IMG Activity: OLIA_V_TCOKT_PM
S_ALR_87000298	IMG Activity: SIMG_CFMENUOKCMKCW2
S_ALR_87000299	IMG Activity: OLI0_OIYH
S_ALR_87000300	IMG Activity: SIMG_CMMENUOLMBOMB8
S_ALR_87000301	IMG Activity: OLIP_OP5A
S_ALR_87000302	IMG Activity: SIMG_CFMENUOLIAOIO8
S_ALR_87000303	IMG Activity: OKCM_KCA2
S_ALR_87000304	IMG Activity: SIMG_CFMENUOLI0OIS1
S_ALR_87000305	IMG Activity: SIMG_CFMENUOLMBOMBM
S_ALR_87000306	IMG Activity: OLIP_OP7B
S_ALR_87000307	IMG Activity: OLIAOIOM
S_ALR_87000308	IMG Activity: OKCM_KCA6
S_ALR_87000309	IMG Activity: SIMG_0KWM_KSES_IST
S_ALR_87000310	IMG Activity: OLI0_V_T377G
S_ALR_87000311	IMG Activity: SIMG_CFMENUOLMBSXDAB
S_ALR_87000312	IMG Activity: SIMG_CFMENUOLIAOIDG
S_ALR_87000313	IMG Activity: SIMG_CFMENUOLIPOIZ2
S_ALR_87000314	IMG Activity: CFOKCMOKXC
S_ALR_87000315	IMG Activity: SIMG_CFMENU0KWMXKA06
S_ALR_87000316	IMG Activity: SIMG_CMMENUOLMBOMB7
S_ALR_87000317	IMG Activity: SIMG_CFMENUOLI0OIS2
S_ALR_87000318	IMG Activity: SIMG_CFMENUOKCMKCRF
S_ALR_87000319	IMG Activity: SIMG_CFMENUOLIAOIOT
S_ALR_87000320	IMG Activity: SIMG_CFMENU0KWMKCAB
S_ALR_87000321	IMG Activity: SIMG_CFMENUOLI0OIW8
S_ALR_87000322	IMG Activity: SIMG_CFMENUOLMBOMBF
S_ALR_87000323	IMG Activity: SIMG_CFMENUOLIAOIOC
S_ALR_87000324	IMG Activity: SIMG_CFMENUOKCMOKUK
S_ALR_87000325	IMG Activity: SIMG_0KWMCPV1
S_ALR_87000326	IMG Activity: SIMG_CFMENUOLMBOMBQ
S_ALR_87000327	IMG Activity: SIMG_CFMENUOLI0OIWM

S_ALR_87000328	IMG Activity: SIMG_CFMENUOLIAOIOB
S_ALR_87000329	IMG Activity: SIMG_CFMENUOKCMOKUW
S_ALR_87000330	IMG Activity: SIMG_0KWMKCAV2
S_ALR_87000331	IMG Activity: SIMG_CFMENUOLI0OICD
S_ALR_87000332	IMG Activity: SIMG_CFMENUOLMBOMCD
S_ALR_87000333	IMG Activity: OLIAVOP21
S_ALR_87000334	IMG Activity: SIMG_CFMENU0KWMCPP1
S_ALR_87000335	IMG Activity: SIMG_CFMENUOKCMKCK0
S_ALR_87000336	IMG Activity: SIMG_CFMENUOLI0OICC
S_ALR_87000337	IMG Activity: SIMG_CFMENUOLMBOMCM
S_ALR_87000338	IMG Activity: SIMG_CFMENUOLIAOIO9
S_ALR_87000339	IMG Activity: SIMG_CFMENUOKCMOKTG
S_ALR_87000340	IMG Activity: SIMG_CFMENUORKSOKER1
S_ALR_87000341	IMG Activity: SIMG_CFMENUOLI0OICH
S_ALR_87000342	IMG Activity: SIMG_CFMENUOLMBOMBI
S_ALR_87000343	IMG Activity: SIMG_CFMENUOKCMKCC0
S_ALR_87000344	IMG Activity: SIMG_CFMENUOLI0OICB
S_ALR_87000345	IMG Activity: SIMG_CFMENUOLMBOMCJ
S_ALR_87000346	IMG Activity: SIMG_CFMENUORKSOKTZ1
S_ALR_87000347	IMG Activity: SIMG_CFMENUOKCMOKUI
S_ALR_87000348	IMG Activity: SIMG_CFMENUOLMBOMCH
S_ALR_87000349	IMG Activity: OLI0_OIRE
S_ALR_87000350	IMG Activity: SIMG_CFMENUORKSOKET1
S_ALR_87000351	IMG Activity: SIMG_CFMENUOKCMKCD0
S_ALR_87000352	IMG Activity: SIMG_OLMB_156_AB
S_ALR_87000353	IMG Activity: OLI0_OIRA
S_ALR_87000354	IMG Activity: SIMG_CFMENU0KWMCPC1
S_ALR_87000355	IMG Activity: OKCM_OKXU
S_ALR_87000356	IMG Activity: OLI0OIRR
S_ALR_87000357	IMG Activity: SIMG_CFMENUOLMBOMB3
S_ALR_87000358	IMG Activity: SIMG_CFMENU0KWMKCAM2
S_ALR_87000359	IMG Activity: OLI0OIRQ
S_ALR_87000360	IMG Activity: SIMG_CFMENUOKCMOKUH
S_ALR_87000361	IMG Activity: SIMG_CFMENUOLMBOMBC
S_ALR_87000362	IMG Activity: SIMG_CFMENU0KWMKVB0
S_ALR_87000363	IMG Activity: OLI0OIRP
S_ALR_87000364	IMG Activity: SIMG_CFMENUOLMBOMJA
S_ALR_87000365	IMG Activity: SIMG_CFMENUOKCMKCRU
S_ALR_87000366	IMG Activity: SIMG_CFMENU0KWMCPC7
S_ALR_87000367	IMG Activity: SIMG_CFMENUOLI0OISP
S_ALR_87000368	IMG Activity: SIMG_CFMENUOLMBOMJ9
S_ALR_87000369	IMG Activity: SIMG_CFMENU0KWMKCAM
S_ALR_87000370	IMG Activity: OKCM_KCC2
S_ALR_87000371	IMG Activity: SIMG_CFMENUOLMBOMJ8
S_ALR_87000372	IMG Activity: SIMG_CFMENU0KWMCPP7
S_ALR_87000373	IMG Activity: OKCM_OKXG
S_ALR_87000374	IMG Activity: OLI0_AD20
S_ALR_87000375	IMG Activity: SIMG_OLMB_158_OA
S_ALR_87000376	IMG Activity: SIMG_0KWM_KSES_PLAN
S_ALR_87000377	IMG Activity: SIMG_CFMENUOKCMOKCY
S_ALR_87000378	IMG Activity: SIMG_CFMENUOLI0OIR8
S_ALR_87000379	IMG Activity: SIMG_CFMENUOLMB001KL
S_ALR_87000380	IMG Activity: SIMG_CFMENU0KWMXKA07
S_ALR_87000381	IMG Activity: OLI0T370P

S_ALR_87000382	IMG Activity: CFOKCMOKXB
S_ALR_87000383	IMG Activity: SIMG_CFMENUOLMBOMJ5
S_ALR_87000384	IMG Activity: SIMG_CFMENUORKSOKET
S_ALR_87000385	IMG Activity: SIMG_CFMENUOLI0OIR7
S_ALR_87000386	IMG Activity: OKCM_GCT6
S_ALR_87000387	IMG Activity: SIMG_CFMENUOLMBOMBZ
S_ALR_87000388	IMG Activity: SIMG_CFMENU0KWMXKK02
S_ALR_87000389	IMG Activity: OLI0IK09
S_ALR_87000390	IMG Activity: SIMG_OLMB_OMJN
S_ALR_87000391	IMG Activity: OKCM_KCA5
S_ALR_87000392	IMG Activity: SIMG_CFMENUORKSKBC3
S_ALR_87000393	IMG Activity: SIMG_CFMENUOLI0OIST
S_ALR_87000394	IMG Activity: OKCM_KCT1
S_ALR_87000395	IMG Activity: OKCM_SF07
S_ALR_87000396	IMG Activity: SIMG_CFMENUOLMBOMC1
S_ALR_87000397	IMG Activity: SIMG_CFMENUORKSKBC2
S_ALR_87000398	IMG Activity: OLIA_OIAJ
S_ALR_87000399	IMG Activity: SIMG_CFMENUORKSOKER
S_ALR_87000400	IMG Activity: SIMG_CFMENUOLI0OIPT
S_ALR_87000401	IMG Activity: SIMG_CFMENUOLMBOMC2
S_ALR_87000402	IMG Activity: OKCM_SF01
S_ALR_87000403	IMG Activity: SIMG_CFMENUOLMBOMBT
S_ALR_87000404	IMG Activity: OLI0REFPLATZOIWR
S_ALR_87000405	IMG Activity: OKCM_FILE
S_ALR_87000406	IMG Activity: SIMG_CFMENUORKSOKTZ
S_ALR_87000407	IMG Activity: OKCM_KCDR
S_ALR_87000408	IMG Activity: SIMG_CFMENUOLI0OIPR
S_ALR_87000409	IMG Activity: SIMG_CFMENUORKSKA05
S_ALR_87000410	IMG Activity: SIMG_CFMENUOLMBOMBA
S_ALR_87000411	IMG Activity: OKCM_KCDV
S_ALR_87000412	IMG Activity: SIMG_0KWM_PARAM_RPXN
S_ALR_87000413	IMG Activity: OLI0_OIPV_IFLOALT
S_ALR_87000414	IMG Activity: SIMG_CFMENUOLMBOMCQ
S_ALR_87000415	IMG Activity: OLI0_OIPU_ITOBCUST
S_ALR_87000416	IMG Activity: SIMG_CFMENUOLMB159L
S_ALR_87000417	IMG Activity: OKCM_OKUE
S_ALR_87000418	IMG Activity: SIMG_CFMENU0KWMOKLB
S_ALR_87000419	IMG Activity: SIMG_CFMENUOLI0OIPK
S_ALR_87000420	IMG Activity: SIMG_CFMENU0KWMGR5G
S_ALR_87000421	IMG Activity: SIMG_CFMENUOLMBOMB2
S_ALR_87000422	IMG Activity: SIMG_CFMENUOKCMOKCP
S_ALR_87000423	IMG Activity: SIMG_CFMENUOLI0OIR6
S_ALR_87000424	IMG Activity: SIMG_CFMENU0KWMFGRP
S_ALR_87000425	IMG Activity: SIMG_CFMENUOLMBOMC0
S_ALR_87000426	IMG Activity: SIMG_CFMENUOKCMOKCA
S_ALR_87000427	IMG Activity: OLI0OIRF
S_ALR_87000428	IMG Activity: SIMG_CFMENU0KWMOPMI
S_ALR_87000429	IMG Activity: SIMG_CFMENUOKCMOKUO
S_ALR_87000430	IMG Activity: SIMG_CFMENUOLMBOMJ1
S_ALR_87000431	IMG Activity: SIMG_0KWM_SELEK_RPBN
S_ALR_87000432	IMG Activity: OLI0GM04
S_ALR_87000433	IMG Activity: OKCM_KCDU
S_ALR_87000434	IMG Activity: SIMG_CFMENUOLMBOMCC
S_ALR_87000435	IMG Activity: SIMG_CFMENU0KWMSU02

S_ALR_87000436	IMG Activity: OLI0GM03
S_ALR_87000437	IMG Activity: OKCM_KCVC
S_ALR_87000438	IMG Activity: SIMG_CFMENUOLMBOMCP
S_ALR_87000439	IMG Activity: SIMG_0KWM_EWZYK_CMOD
S_ALR_87000440	IMG Activity: OKCM_KCVA
S_ALR_87000441	IMG Activity: OLI0OIRL
S_ALR_87000442	IMG Activity: SIMG_CFMENUOLMBOMBJ
S_ALR_87000443	IMG Activity: SIMG_CFMENU0KWMSU03
S_ALR_87000444	IMG Activity: OLI0BG00
S_ALR_87000445	IMG Activity: OKCM_KCAN
S_ALR_87000446	IMG Activity: SIMG_CFMENUOLMBOMBW
S_ALR_87000447	IMG Activity: OLI0GM02
S_ALR_87000448	IMG Activity: SIMG_CFMENUORKSKR01
S_ALR_87000449	IMG Activity: OKCM_KCP4
S_ALR_87000450	IMG Activity: SIMG_CFMENUOLMBOMB6
S_ALR_87000451	IMG Activity: OLI0GM01
S_ALR_87000452	IMG Activity: SIMG_0KWM_EXTRA_GRE9
S_ALR_87000453	IMG Activity: OKCM_TKCCC
S_ALR_87000454	IMG Activity: SIMG_CFMENUOLMBOMJC
S_ALR_87000455	IMG Activity: OLI0IK19
S_ALR_87000456	IMG Activity: SIMG_CFMENU0KWMGR21
S_ALR_87000457	IMG Activity: SIMG_CFMENUOKCMKCS7
S_ALR_87000458	IMG Activity: SIMG_CFMENUOLMBOMCK
S_ALR_87000459	IMG Activity: SIMG_CFMENUOLI0OIR5
S_ALR_87000460	IMG Activity: SIMG_CFMENU0KWMKBH2
S_ALR_87000461	IMG Activity: SIMG_CFMENUOKCMOKCH
S_ALR_87000462	IMG Activity: SIMG_CFMENUOLMBOMB1
S_ALR_87000463	IMG Activity: SIMG_CFMENUOLI0OIR4
S_ALR_87000464	IMG Activity: SIMG_CFMENU0KWMCPH2
S_ALR_87000465	IMG Activity: OKCM_KCRH
S_ALR_87000466	IMG Activity: SIMG_CFMENUOLMBOMBK
S_ALR_87000467	IMG Activity: SIMG_CFMENUOLI0OIR3
S_ALR_87000468	IMG Activity: SIMG_CFMENUORKSOKV5
S_ALR_87000469	IMG Activity: SIMG_CFMENUOLMBOMCL
S_ALR_87000470	IMG Activity: SIMG_CFMENUOLI0OIR2
S_ALR_87000471	IMG Activity: SIMG_CFMENUOKCMOKUF
S_ALR_87000472	IMG Activity: SIMG_CFMENUORKSKAH21
S_ALR_87000473	IMG Activity: SIMG_CFMENUOLMBOMBN
S_ALR_87000474	IMG Activity: SIMG_CFMENUOLI0OIR1
S_ALR_87000475	IMG Activity: SIMG_CFMENUOKCMOKUD
S_ALR_87000476	IMG Activity: SIMG_CFMENUORKSOKVF
S_ALR_87000477	IMG Activity: SIMG_CFMENUOLMBOMJU
S_ALR_87000478	IMG Activity: OLI0_V_TPAER_PM
S_ALR_87000479	IMG Activity: SIMG_0KWM_INFO_KM3V
S_ALR_87000480	IMG Activity: SIMG_CFMENUOKCMOKCK
S_ALR_87000481	IMG Activity: SIMG_CFMENUOLMBOMBP
S_ALR_87000482	IMG Activity: SIMG_CFMENU0KWMGCRS2
S_ALR_87000483	IMG Activity: OLI0PARTNERSCHEMA
S_ALR_87000484	IMG Activity: SIMG_CFMENUOKCMKCK1
S_ALR_87000485	IMG Activity: SIMG_CFMENUOLMBOMC3
S_ALR_87000486	IMG Activity: SIMG_0KWM_EWEP_CMOD
S_ALR_87000487	IMG Activity: OLI0_OIRI
S_ALR_87000488	IMG Activity: SIMG_CFMENUOKCMOKUL
S_ALR_87000489	IMG Activity: SIMG_CFMENU0KWMOKWC

S_ALR_87000490	IMG Activity: OLI0_OIUP
S_ALR_87000491	IMG Activity: SIMG_CFMENUOLMBOMJ2
S_ALR_87000492	IMG Activity: OLI0_OIUO
S_ALR_87000493	IMG Activity: SIMG_CFMENU0KWMGCRS
S_ALR_87000494	IMG Activity: SIMG_CFMENUOLMBOMCN
S_ALR_87000495	IMG Activity: OKCM_KCCO
S_ALR_87000496	IMG Activity: OKCM_TR_WORK
S_ALR_87000497	IMG Activity: SIMG_CFMENU0KWM0KW9
S_ALR_87000498	IMG Activity: SIMG_CFMENUOLI0OIXB
S_ALR_87000499	IMG Activity: SIMG_CFMENUOLMBOMBH
S_ALR_87000500	IMG Activity: SIMG_CMMENUOKCM0010
S_ALR_87000501	IMG Activity: SIMG_CFMENU0KWMKCAB2
S_ALR_87000502	IMG Activity: OKCM_R2_DATATRANSFER
S_ALR_87000503	IMG Activity: SIMG_CFMENUOLI0OIXA
S_ALR_87000504	IMG Activity: SIMG_CFMENUOLMBOMBS
S_ALR_87000505	IMG Activity: OKCM_UNIT_CONC
S_ALR_87000506	IMG Activity: SIMG_CFMENU0KWMSBP
S_ALR_87000507	IMG Activity: SIMG_CFMENUOLI0OIX9
S_ALR_87000508	IMG Activity: J_1BIM_NF_TYPE
S_ALR_87000509	IMG Activity: SIMG_OKCMTRRESTART
S_ALR_87000510	IMG Activity: SIMG_CFMENUOLI0OIX8
S_ALR_87000511	IMG Activity: SIMG_CFMENU0KWMCP85
S_ALR_87000512	IMG Activity: SIMG_CFMENUOLMBOMJE
S_ALR_87000518	IMG Activity: OKCM_NET
S_ALR_87000519	IMG Activity: OKCM_USER
S_ALR_87000520	IMG Activity: SIMG_CFMENUOLI0OIX7
S_ALR_87000521	IMG Activity: SIMG_CFMENU0KWMKP34
S_ALR_87000522	IMG Activity: OKCM_R2_TR_PARAM
S_ALR_87000523	IMG Activity: SIMG_CFMENUOLMBOMJD
S_ALR_87000524	IMG Activity: OKCM_TR_PROGRAM
S_ALR_87000525	IMG Activity: SIMG_CFMENUOLI0OIEP
S_ALR_87000526	IMG Activity: OKCM_TR_EVENT
S_ALR_87000527	IMG Activity: SIMG_CFMENU0KWMOKEZ
S_ALR_87000528	IMG Activity: SIMG_CFMENUOLMBOMCO
S_ALR_87000529	IMG Activity: SIMG_CFMENUOLI0OIEZ
S_ALR_87000530	IMG Activity: OKCM_WEATTR
S_ALR_87000531	IMG Activity: SIMG_CFMENU0KWMOKEV2
S_ALR_87000532	IMG Activity: J_1BIM_TAX_POSTING
S_ALR_87000533	IMG Activity: OKCM_DISATTR
S_ALR_87000534	IMG Activity: SIMG_CFMENUOLI0OIEH
S_ALR_87000535	IMG Activity: OKCM_NAVATTR
S_ALR_87000536	IMG Activity: SIMG_CFMENUOLMBOMCR
S_ALR_87000537	IMG Activity: SIMG_CFMENU0KWMXCP01
S_ALR_87000538	IMG Activity: SIMG_CMMENUOLMBTIPN
S_ALR_87000539	IMG Activity: SIMG_CFMENUOLI0OIEN
S_ALR_87000540	IMG Activity: SIMG_CFMENUOLMBOSPA
S_ALR_87000541	IMG Activity: SIMG_CFMENU0KWMKP81
S_ALR_87000542	IMG Activity: OLI0V_T370T_A
S_ALR_87000543	IMG Activity: SIMG_0KWM_ERGP_0KW3
S_ALR_87000544	IMG Activity: SIMG_CFMENUOLI0OIET
S_ALR_87000545	IMG Activity: SIMG_CFMENU0KWMXKK01
S_ALR_87000546	IMG Activity: SIMG_CFMENUOLI0OIBA
S_ALR_87000547	IMG Activity: SIMG_CFMENU0KWMCPH3
S_ALR_87000548	IMG Activity: SIMG_CFMENUOLI0OIBS

S_ALR_87000549	IMG Activity: SIMG_CFMENU0KWMKBH3
S_ALR_87000550	IMG Activity: OLI0REFPLATZOIWP
S_ALR_87000551	IMG Activity: SIMG_CFMENU0KWMKBH4
S_ALR_87000552	IMG Activity: SIMG_CFMENUOLI0OIAW
S_ALR_87000553	IMG Activity: SIMG_0KWM_EWGP_CMOD
S_ALR_87000554	IMG Activity: OLI0OIAE
S_ALR_87000555	IMG Activity: SIMG_CFMENU0KWM0KWO
S_ALR_87000556	IMG Activity: SIMG_CFMENUOLI0OIUF
S_ALR_87000557	IMG Activity: SIMG_CFMENUOLI0OIW6
S_ALR_87000558	IMG Activity: SIMG_CFMENU0KWMCP65
S_ALR_87000559	IMG Activity: SIMG_CFMENUOLI0OIW7
S_ALR_87000560	IMG Activity: SIMG_CFMENU0KWMCP75
S_ALR_87000561	IMG Activity: OLI0_BS52
S_ALR_87000562	IMG Activity: SIMG_0KWM_STAM_KM3V
S_ALR_87000563	IMG Activity: SIMG_CFMENUOLI0OIX4
S_ALR_87000564	IMG Activity: SIMG_0KWMKTPF_ZUORDN
S_ALR_87000565	IMG Activity: SIMG_CFMENUOLI0OIX5
S_ALR_87000566	IMG Activity: SIMG_CFMENU0KWM0KW1
S_ALR_87000567	IMG Activity: SIMG_CFMENUOLI0OIX3
S_ALR_87000568	IMG Activity: SIMG_0KWMCPT2_SCHEMA
S_ALR_87000569	IMG Activity: SIMG_CFMENUOLI0OIX6
S_ALR_87000570	IMG Activity: SIMG_CFMENU0KWMOKKP
S_ALR_87000571	IMG Activity: SIMG_0KWMKCAV1
S_ALR_87000572	IMG Activity: SIMG_CFMENUOLI0OIX2
S_ALR_87000573	IMG Activity: SIMG_CFMENUOLMDOMIB
S_ALR_87000574	IMG Activity: OLI0_RISERNR9
S_ALR_87000575	IMG Activity: SIMG_CFMENUOLMDOMIR
S_ALR_87000576	IMG Activity: SIMG_0KWMCPV7
S_ALR_87000577	IMG Activity: SIMG_CFMENUOLSDVI62
S_ALR_87000578	IMG Activity: SIMG_CFMENUOLMDOMDD
S_ALR_87000579	IMG Activity: SIMG_0KWMCPT2_UMGEBG
S_ALR_87000580	IMG Activity: SIMG_CFMENUOLSD0VX1
S_ALR_87000581	IMG Activity: SIMG_CFMENU0KWMXCPH2
S_ALR_87000582	IMG Activity: SIMG_CFMENUOLMDOMDV
S_ALR_87000583	IMG Activity: SIMG_CFMENUOLSDVIM6
S_ALR_87000584	IMG Activity: SIMG_0KWM0KW2_EIG
S_ALR_87000585	IMG Activity: SIMG_CFMENUOLMDOPPH
S_ALR_87000586	IMG Activity: SIMG_CFMENUOLSDVI63
S_ALR_87000587	IMG Activity: SIMG_CFMENUOLMDOMD3
S_ALR_87000588	IMG Activity: SIMG_CFMENU0KWM0KWL
S_ALR_87000589	IMG Activity: SIMG_CFMENUOLSDVE80
S_ALR_87000590	IMG Activity: SIMG_CFMENUOLMDOMD5
S_ALR_87000591	IMG Activity: SIMG_CFMENU0KWMKSOP
S_ALR_87000592	IMG Activity: SIMG_CMMENUOLMCSETS
S_ALR_87000593	IMG Activity: SIMG_CFMENUOLSDVI30
S_ALR_87000594	IMG Activity: SIMG_CFMENUOLMDOMDJ
S_ALR_87000595	IMG Activity: SIMG_CFMENU0KWMXKK03
S_ALR_87000596	IMG Activity: SIMG_CMMENUOLMCVABL
S_ALR_87000597	IMG Activity: SIMG_CFMENUOLSDVI92
S_ALR_87000598	IMG Activity: SIMG_CFMENU0KWMKVB1
S_ALR_87000599	IMG Activity: FELDSTEUERUNGUMBUCHG
S_ALR_87000600	IMG Activity: SIMG_CFMENUOLMDOMDT
S_ALR_87000601	IMG Activity: OLIS_MC7F
S_ALR_87000602	IMG Activity: FELDSTEUERUNGVERTRAG

S_ALR_87000603	IMG Activity: SIMG_CFMENUOLSDVE64
S_ALR_87000604	IMG Activity: SIMG_CFMENUOLMDOMI5
S_ALR_87000605	IMG Activity: SIMG_CFMENU0KWMCPH4
S_ALR_87000606	IMG Activity: OLIS_MC60
S_ALR_87000607	IMG Activity: SIMG_0KWM_FREMD_PL
S_ALR_87000608	IMG Activity: SIMG_CFMENUOLMDOMDC
S_ALR_87000609	IMG Activity: SIMG_CFMENUOLSDVE65
S_ALR_87000610	IMG Activity: OLIS_MCNR
S_ALR_87000611	IMG Activity: SIMG_CFMENU0KWMXP_V
S_ALR_87000612	IMG Activity: SIMG_CFMENUOLMDOMIT
S_ALR_87000613	IMG Activity: SIMG_0KWM_FREMD_IST
S_ALR_87000614	IMG Activity: SIMG_CFMENUOLSDVE66
S_ALR_87000615	IMG Activity: SIMG_CFMENUOLMCMCRC
S_ALR_87000616	IMG Activity: SIMG_CFMENUOLMDOMDR
S_ALR_87000617	IMG Activity: SIMG_CFMENUOLSDVE71
S_ALR_87000618	IMG Activity: SIMG_CFMENUOLMCMCRT
S_ALR_87000619	IMG Activity: SIMG_CFMENUOLMDOMIM
S_ALR_87000620	IMG Activity: SIMG_CFMENUOLSDVE63
S_ALR_87000621	IMG Activity: SIMG_CFMENUOLMCMCRB
S_ALR_87000622	IMG Activity: SIMG_CFMENUOLMDOMIN
S_ALR_87000623	IMG Activity: SIMG_CFMENUOLMCMCRA
S_ALR_87000624	IMG Activity: SIMG_CFMENUOLSDUID
S_ALR_87000625	IMG Activity: SIMG_CFMENUOLMDOMDA
S_ALR_87000626	IMG Activity: SIMG_CMMENUOLMCLAY
S_ALR_87000627	IMG Activity: SIMG_CFMENUOLSDVE53
S_ALR_87000628	IMG Activity: W_DF_LT_0620
S_ALR_87000629	IMG Activity: OLIS_MC38
S_ALR_87000630	IMG Activity: SIMG_CFMENUOLSDVE62
S_ALR_87000631	IMG Activity: W_DF_LT_0621
S_ALR_87000632	IMG Activity: OLIS_MC70
S_ALR_87000633	IMG Activity: SIMG_CFMENUOLSDVE61
S_ALR_87000634	IMG Activity: W_DF_LT_0622
S_ALR_87000635	IMG Activity: OLIS_OPEB
S_ALR_87000636	IMG Activity: SIMG_CFMENUOLSDVE60
S_ALR_87000637	IMG Activity: SIMG_CMMENUOLMDOMI6
S_ALR_87000638	IMG Activity: OLIS_MC97
S_ALR_87000639	IMG Activity: SIMG_CFMENUOLSDGOTX
S_ALR_87000640	IMG Activity: SIMG_CFMENUOLMDOMDM
S_ALR_87000641	IMG Activity: OLIS_MC96
S_ALR_87000642	IMG Activity: SIMG_CFMENUOLSDVE51
S_ALR_87000643	IMG Activity: SIMG_CFMENUOLMDOMIQ
S_ALR_87000644	IMG Activity: OLIS_MP90
S_ALR_87000645	IMG Activity: SIMG_CFMENUOPP1OM0A
S_ALR_87000646	IMG Activity: SIMG_CFMENUOLSDREGI
S_ALR_87000647	IMG Activity: OLIS_OV7Z
S_ALR_87000648	IMG Activity: W_DF_LT_0611
S_ALR_87000649	IMG Activity: SIMG_CFMENUOLSDUNVO
S_ALR_87000650	IMG Activity: W_DF_LT_0355
S_ALR_87000651	IMG Activity: SIMG_CFMENUOLMDOPPC
S_ALR_87000652	IMG Activity: W_DF_LT_0350
S_ALR_87000653	IMG Activity: SIMG_CFMENUOLSDVE56
S_ALR_87000654	IMG Activity: SIMG_CFMENUOLMDOMIL
S_ALR_87000655	IMG Activity: W_DF_LT_0360
S_ALR_87000656	IMG Activity: SIMG_CFMENUOLSDVE57

S_ALR_87000657	IMG Activity: SIMG_CFMENUOLMDOMIO
S_ALR_87000658	IMG Activity: OLIS_MC7A
S_ALR_87000659	IMG Activity: SIMG_CFMENUOLSDVE59
S_ALR_87000660	IMG Activity: SIMG_CFMENUOLMDOMD2
S_ALR_87000661	IMG Activity: OLIS_PPIS_MCRG
S_ALR_87000662	IMG Activity: SIMG_CFMENUOLSDVE58
S_ALR_87000663	IMG Activity: SIMG_CFMENUOLMDOMDG
S_ALR_87000664	IMG Activity: SIMG_CFMENUOLISOQI1
S_ALR_87000665	IMG Activity: SIMG_CFMENUOLMDOMDK
S_ALR_87000666	IMG Activity: SIMG_CFMENUOLMEOMF9
S_ALR_87000667	IMG Activity: SIMG_CFMENUOLISOQI2
S_ALR_87000668	IMG Activity: W_DF_LT_0610
S_ALR_87000669	IMG Activity: SIMG_CFMENUOLISOQI3
S_ALR_87000670	IMG Activity: SIMG_CFMENUOLMEOMFC
S_ALR_87000671	IMG Activity: SIMG_CFMENUOPP1OWD1
S_ALR_87000672	IMG Activity: SIMG_CFMENUOLISOQI4
S_ALR_87000673	IMG Activity: SIMG_CFMENUOLMEOMF6
S_ALR_87000674	IMG Activity: SIMG_CFMENUOLMDOMD9
S_ALR_87000675	IMG Activity: OLIS_EKS_OMGO
S_ALR_87000676	IMG Activity: SIMG_CFMENUOLMDSML
S_ALR_87000677	IMG Activity: SIMG_CFMENUOLMEOME7
S_ALR_87000678	IMG Activity: OLIS_EKS_OLIB
S_ALR_87000679	IMG Activity: SIMG_CFMENUOLMDOMIP
S_ALR_87000680	IMG Activity: SIMG_CFMENUOLMEOMGO
S_ALR_87000681	IMG Activity: SIMG_CFMENUOLMCMCF9
S_ALR_87000682	IMG Activity: SIMG_CFMENUOLMDOMDU
S_ALR_87000683	IMG Activity: SIMG_CFMENUOLMEOMEG
S_ALR_87000684	IMG Activity: OLIAMELDSTATUSOIBS
S_ALR_87000685	IMG Activity: SIMG_CFMENUOLMCMCFA
S_ALR_87000686	IMG Activity: W_ZF_VK_0710
S_ALR_87000687	IMG Activity: SIMG_CFMENUOLIAOIOG
S_ALR_87000688	IMG Activity: SIMG_CFMENUOLMEOMFG
S_ALR_87000689	IMG Activity: SIMG_CFMENUOLMCOPJ5
S_ALR_87000690	IMG Activity: SIMG_CFMENUOPP1OM0E
S_ALR_87000691	IMG Activity: SIMG_CFMENUOLISOIAW
S_ALR_87000692	IMG Activity: SIMG_CFMENUOLIAOIDH
S_ALR_87000693	IMG Activity: SIMG_CFMENUOLMEOMFF
S_ALR_87000694	IMG Activity: SIMG_CFMENUOLMDOMDQ
S_ALR_87000695	IMG Activity: OLIAOIMD1
S_ALR_87000696	IMG Activity: SIMG_CFMENUOLMEOMFE
S_ALR_87000697	IMG Activity: SIMG_CMMENUOLISFOSI
S_ALR_87000698	IMG Activity: SIMG_CFMENUOLMDOMI8
S_ALR_87000699	IMG Activity: OLIAOIOV
S_ALR_87000700	IMG Activity: SIMG_CFMENUOLMEOMFD
S_ALR_87000701	IMG Activity: LIS_MC3V
S_ALR_87000702	IMG Activity: SIMG_CFMENUOLMDOPPZ
S_ALR_87000703	IMG Activity: OLIAOKKK
S_ALR_87000704	IMG Activity: SIMG_OLMEANFRAGESE71
S_ALR_87000705	IMG Activity: SIMG_CFMENUOLMDOMIG
S_ALR_87000706	IMG Activity: OLIA_V_CK05
S_ALR_87000707	IMG Activity: SIMG_CFMENUOLME0001
S_ALR_87000708	IMG Activity: SIMG_CFMENUOLMDOMI2
S_ALR_87000709	IMG Activity: SIMG_CFMENUOLIAOIOF
S_ALR_87000710	IMG Activity: SIMG_CFMENUOLISSASE

S_ALR_87000711	IMG Activity: SIMG_CFMENUOLMEOMH5
S_ALR_87000712	IMG Activity: SIMG_CFMENUOLMDOMI3
S_ALR_87000713	IMG Activity: SIMG_CFMENUOLIAOIO4
S_ALR_87000714	IMG Activity: SIMG_CFMENUOLMCOMO
S_ALR_87000715	IMG Activity: SIMG_CMMENUOLSDVI67
S_ALR_87000716	IMG Activity: SIMG_CFMENUOLMDOMD0
S_ALR_87000717	IMG Activity: SIMG_CFMENUOLIAOIO7
S_ALR_87000718	IMG Activity: SIMG_CFMENUOLMCGCRS
S_ALR_87000719	IMG Activity: SIMG_CFMENUOLMDOMDZ
S_ALR_87000720	IMG Activity: SIMG_CMMENUOLSDVI66
S_ALR_87000721	IMG Activity: SIMG_CFMENUOLISOIAK
S_ALR_87000722	IMG Activity: SIMG_CFMENUOLIAOIO6
S_ALR_87000723	IMG Activity: SIMG_CFMENUOLMDOPPI
S_ALR_87000724	IMG Activity: SIMG_CMMENUOLSDVI65
S_ALR_87000725	IMG Activity: OLIAOIOJ
S_ALR_87000726	IMG Activity: SIMG_CFMENUOLISOQN0
S_ALR_87000727	IMG Activity: SIMG_CFMENUOLMDOMDW
S_ALR_87000728	IMG Activity: SIMG_CFMENUOLIAOIO3
S_ALR_87000729	IMG Activity: SIMG_CFMENUOLMCMCH_
S_ALR_87000730	IMG Activity: SIMG_CFMENUOLSDVE78
S_ALR_87000731	IMG Activity: SIMG_CFMENUOLMDOMDY
S_ALR_87000732	IMG Activity: SIMG_CFMENUOLIAOIO5
S_ALR_87000733	IMG Activity: OLIS_GROBLAST_VLLV
S_ALR_87000734	IMG Activity: SIMG_CFMENUOLSDVE75
S_ALR_87000735	IMG Activity: SIMG_CFMENUOLMDOMI4
S_ALR_87000736	IMG Activity: SIMG_CFMENUOLIAOIOE
S_ALR_87000737	IMG Activity: SIMG_CFMENUOLMCMC30
S_ALR_87000738	IMG Activity: SIMG_CFMENUOLMDOMIA
S_ALR_87000739	IMG Activity: OLIAOPJL
S_ALR_87000740	IMG Activity: SIMG_CFMENUOLSDVE77
S_ALR_87000741	IMG Activity: OLIS_CUSTEX4
S_ALR_87000742	IMG Activity: SIMG_CFMENUOPP1OM0D
S_ALR_87000743	IMG Activity: OLIAV_441V
S_ALR_87000744	IMG Activity: SIMG_CFMENUOLMEOMH4
S_ALR_87000745	IMG Activity: OLIS_CUSTEX3
S_ALR_87000746	IMG Activity: SIMG_CFMENUOLMDOMI1
S_ALR_87000747	IMG Activity: SIMG_CFMENUOLIAOIOI
S_ALR_87000748	IMG Activity: SIMG_CFMENUOLMEOMQX
S_ALR_87000749	IMG Activity: OLIS_CUSTEX1
S_ALR_87000750	IMG Activity: SIMG_CFMENUOLMDOMDX
S_ALR_87000751	IMG Activity: OLIA_V_T350_PAGE
S_ALR_87000752	IMG Activity: SIMG_CFMENUOLMEOXK1
S_ALR_87000753	IMG Activity: OLIS_CUSTEX6
S_ALR_87000754	IMG Activity: SIMG_XXMENUOLMDU
S_ALR_87000755	IMG Activity: SIMG_CFMENUOLIAOIDJ
S_ALR_87000756	IMG Activity: SIMG_CFMENUOLMEOMG0
S_ALR_87000757	IMG Activity: OLIS_CUSTEX11
S_ALR_87000758	IMG Activity: OLIA_V_160_M_PM
S_ALR_87000759	IMG Activity: SIMG_CFMENUOLMEOME9
S_ALR_87000760	IMG Activity: OLIS_CUSTEX2
S_ALR_87000761	IMG Activity: OLIA_OOCU_WORKFLOW
S_ALR_87000762	IMG Activity: SIMG_CMMENUOLSDVI69
S_ALR_87000763	IMG Activity: OLIS_CUSTEX7
S_ALR_87000764	IMG Activity: SIMG_CFMENUOLIAOP722

S_ALR_87000765	IMG Activity: SIMG_CFMENUOLSDVI31
S_ALR_87000766	IMG Activity: LIS_CUSTEX_TIS
S_ALR_87000767	IMG Activity: OLIA_V_T399X_MB
S_ALR_87000768	IMG Activity: SIMG_CFMENUOLSDVE79
S_ALR_87000769	IMG Activity: OLIS_CUSTEX8
S_ALR_87000770	IMG Activity: OLIA_OIBY
S_ALR_87000771	IMG Activity: OLIS_CUSTEX5
S_ALR_87000772	IMG Activity: OLIA_V_T350W_K
S_ALR_87000773	IMG Activity: SIMG_CFMENUOLSDVE76
S_ALR_87000774	IMG Activity: OLIA_OIK1
S_ALR_87000775	IMG Activity: OLIS_OLPA_EXIT1
S_ALR_87000776	IMG Activity: SIMG_CFMENUOLSDVE49
S_ALR_87000777	IMG Activity: OLIA_OIK2
S_ALR_87000778	IMG Activity: OLIS_OLPA_EXIT7
S_ALR_87000779	IMG Activity: OLIS_OLPA_EXIT8
S_ALR_87000780	IMG Activity: OLIA_OICV_IMGDUMMY
S_ALR_87000781	IMG Activity: SIMG_CFMENUOLSDVE48
S_ALR_87000782	IMG Activity: OLIS_OLPA_EXIT9
S_ALR_87000783	IMG Activity: SIMG_CFMENUOLIAOIZM2
S_ALR_87000784	IMG Activity: SIMG_CFMENUOLSDVI54
S_ALR_87000785	IMG Activity: OLIS_CUSTEX9
S_ALR_87000786	IMG Activity: OLIA_ODP1
S_ALR_87000787	IMG Activity: SIMG_CFMENUOLSDVI89
S_ALR_87000788	IMG Activity: SIMG_CFMENUOLIAOIOR
S_ALR_87000789	IMG Activity: OLIS_CUSTEX10
S_ALR_87000790	IMG Activity: SIMG_CFMENUOLSDVI35
S_ALR_87000791	IMG Activity: OLIS_OLPA_EXIT2
S_ALR_87000792	IMG Activity: SIMG_CFMENUOLIAOKO71
S_ALR_87000793	IMG Activity: SIMG_CFMENUOLSDVI34
S_ALR_87000794	IMG Activity: OLIS_OLPA_EXIT3
S_ALR_87000795	IMG Activity: SIMG_CFMENUOLIAOKO61
S_ALR_87000796	IMG Activity: SIMG_CFMENUOLSDVI33
S_ALR_87000797	IMG Activity: OLIS_OLPA_EXIT4
S_ALR_87000798	IMG Activity: SIMG_CFMENUOLIAKEI11
S_ALR_87000799	IMG Activity: OLIS_OLPA_EXIT5
S_ALR_87000800	IMG Activity: OLIA_KEP9
S_ALR_87000801	IMG Activity: SIMG_CFMENUOLSDVI32
S_ALR_87000802	IMG Activity: OLIS_OLPA_EXIT6
S_ALR_87000803	IMG Activity: SIMG_CFMENUOLIAKO8N1
S_ALR_87000804	IMG Activity: SIMG_CFMENUOLSDVI37
S_ALR_87000805	IMG Activity: OLIA_ODP2
S_ALR_87000806	IMG Activity: OLIS_COPA1
S_ALR_87000807	IMG Activity: SIMG_CFMENUOLSDVI46
S_ALR_87000808	IMG Activity: OLIAOIRH
S_ALR_87000809	IMG Activity: OLIS_ALE
S_ALR_87000810	IMG Activity: SIMG_CFMENUOLSDVI48
S_ALR_87000811	IMG Activity: SIMG_CFMENUOLIAVOP2
S_ALR_87000812	IMG Activity: OLIS_MC8A
S_ALR_87000813	IMG Activity: SIMG_CFMENUOLSDVI50
S_ALR_87000814	IMG Activity: SIMG_CFMENUOLIAOIM6
S_ALR_87000815	IMG Activity: OLIS_MC7M
S_ALR_87000816	IMG Activity: SIMG_CFMENUOLSDVI47
S_ALR_87000817	IMG Activity: SIMG_CFMENUOLIAOIM9
S_ALR_87000818	IMG Activity: OLIS_MC80

S_ALR_87000819	IMG Activity: SIMG_CFMENUOLSDVI45
S_ALR_87000820	IMG Activity: OLIS_MP91
S_ALR_87000821	IMG Activity: OLIAOIRG
S_ALR_87000822	IMG Activity: OLIA_OIUK
S_ALR_87000823	IMG Activity: OLIS_ACTI
S_ALR_87000824	IMG Activity: SIMG_CFMENUOLSDVI61
S_ALR_87000825	IMG Activity: OLIS_COPYP
S_ALR_87000826	IMG Activity: SIMG_CFMENUOLSDVI36
S_ALR_87000827	IMG Activity: OLIA_ODP3
S_ALR_87000828	IMG Activity: OLIS_KEYF
S_ALR_87000829	IMG Activity: SIMG_CFMENUOLSDVI70
S_ALR_87000830	IMG Activity: OLIA_ODP4
S_ALR_87000831	IMG Activity: OLIS_TRAN
S_ALR_87000832	IMG Activity: OLIA_OIUN
S_ALR_87000833	IMG Activity: SIMG_CFMENUOLSDOVI95
S_ALR_87000834	IMG Activity: OLIS_MC79
S_ALR_87000835	IMG Activity: OLIAOKI0
S_ALR_87000836	IMG Activity: SIMG_CFMENUOLSDOVI76
S_ALR_87000837	IMG Activity: OLIS_KOPP1C
S_ALR_87000838	IMG Activity: OLIA_OIUL
S_ALR_87000839	IMG Activity: SIMG_CFMENUOLSDOVE3
S_ALR_87000840	IMG Activity: OLIS_KOPP1D
S_ALR_87000841	IMG Activity: OLIA_V_TRUG
S_ALR_87000842	IMG Activity: SIMG_CFMENUOLSDOVE2
S_ALR_87000843	IMG Activity: OLIS_KOPP2
S_ALR_87000844	IMG Activity: OLIA_CI31
S_ALR_87000845	IMG Activity: SIMG_CFMENUOLSDVX54
S_ALR_87000846	IMG Activity: OLIS_KOPP3
S_ALR_87000847	IMG Activity: OLIAOIZN
S_ALR_87000848	IMG Activity: SIMG_CFMENUOLMCOMO5
S_ALR_87000849	IMG Activity: SIMG_CFMENUOLSDVX58
S_ALR_87000850	IMG Activity: SIMG_CFMENUOLIAOIAB2
S_ALR_87000851	IMG Activity: SIMG_CFMENUOLMCMC0A
S_ALR_87000852	IMG Activity: SIMG_CFMENUOLSDVX56
S_ALR_87000853	IMG Activity: SIMG_CFMENUOLIAOIAI2
S_ALR_87000854	IMG Activity: SIMG_CFMENUOLMCMC0C
S_ALR_87000855	IMG Activity: SIMG_CFMENUOLSDVX52
S_ALR_87000856	IMG Activity: SIMG_CFMENUOLIAOIAA2
S_ALR_87000857	IMG Activity: OLIS_KOPP4B
S_ALR_87000858	IMG Activity: SIMG_CFMENUOLSDVX49
S_ALR_87000859	IMG Activity: OLIAOLPRBDE
S_ALR_87000860	IMG Activity: SIMG_CFMENUOLSDVX57
S_ALR_87000861	IMG Activity: SIMG_CFMENUOLSDVE50
S_ALR_87000862	IMG Activity: SIMG_CFMENUOLSDSTUBE
S_ALR_87000863	IMG Activity: OLIA_OIW3
S_ALR_87000864	IMG Activity: OLIS_KOPP1A
S_ALR_87000865	IMG Activity: SIMG_CFMENUOLSDOOVA7
S_ALR_87000866	IMG Activity: OLIS_KOPP1B
S_ALR_87000867	IMG Activity: OLIAOIYG
S_ALR_87000868	IMG Activity: SIMG_CFMENUOLSDOVX
S_ALR_87000869	IMG Activity: SIMG_CFMENUOLIAOIBA
S_ALR_87000870	IMG Activity: SIMG_CFMENUOLMCFORE
S_ALR_87000871	IMG Activity: SIMG_CFMENUOLSDVI52
S_ALR_87000872	IMG Activity: SIMG_CFMENUOLMCOMOG

S_ALR_87000873	IMG Activity: SIMG_CFMENUOLIAOIBS
S_ALR_87000874	IMG Activity: SIMG_CFMENUOLSDVX53
S_ALR_87000875	IMG Activity: SIMG_CFMENUOLMCMCS/
S_ALR_87000876	IMG Activity: OLIA_BS52
S_ALR_87000877	IMG Activity: SIMG_CFMENUOLSDVOTX
S_ALR_87000878	IMG Activity: SIMG_CFMENUOLMCMCSY
S_ALR_87000879	IMG Activity: OLIA_OPLI
S_ALR_87000880	IMG Activity: SIMG_CFMENUOLSDSE71
S_ALR_87000881	IMG Activity: SIMG_CFMENUOLMCMCSZ
S_ALR_87000882	IMG Activity: OLIA_OID6
S_ALR_87000883	IMG Activity: SIMG_CFMENUOLSDVI38
S_ALR_87000884	IMG Activity: OLIS_ALE36
S_ALR_87000885	IMG Activity: OLIA_OPKC
S_ALR_87000886	IMG Activity: OLIS_ALE33
S_ALR_87000887	IMG Activity: SIMG_CFMENUOLSDVI42
S_ALR_87000888	IMG Activity: SIMG_CFMENUOLIAOIDU
S_ALR_87000889	IMG Activity: OLIS010
S_ALR_87000890	IMG Activity: SIMG_CFMENUOLSDVI41
S_ALR_87000891	IMG Activity: SIMG_CFMENUOLIAOIDV
S_ALR_87000892	IMG Activity: SIMG_CFMENUOLIACO44
S_ALR_87000893	IMG Activity: SIMG_CFMENUOLSDVI40
S_ALR_87000894	IMG Activity: SIMG_CMMENUOLMCBED
S_ALR_87000895	IMG Activity: SIMG_CFMENUOLMCOVRI
S_ALR_87000896	IMG Activity: SIMG_CFMENUOLSDVI39
S_ALR_87000897	IMG Activity: SIMG_CFMENUOLIAOID5
S_ALR_87000898	IMG Activity: SIMG_CFMENUOLIAOID1
S_ALR_87000899	IMG Activity: SIMG_CFMENUOLMCOVRH
S_ALR_87000900	IMG Activity: SIMG_CFMENUOLSDVX51
S_ALR_87000901	IMG Activity: SIMG_CFMENUOLMCOVRN
S_ALR_87000902	IMG Activity: SIMG_CFMENUOLIAOID2
S_ALR_87000903	IMG Activity: SIMG_CFMENUOLSDVX50
S_ALR_87000904	IMG Activity: SIMG_CFMENUOLMCOVRF
S_ALR_87000905	IMG Activity: SIMG_CFMENUOLIAOID3
S_ALR_87000906	IMG Activity: SIMG_CMMENUOLSDVI28
S_ALR_87000907	IMG Activity: OLIA_OPKB
S_ALR_87000908	IMG Activity: SIMG_CFMENUOLMCOVRA
S_ALR_87000909	IMG Activity: SIMG_CMMENUOLSDVI56
S_ALR_87000910	IMG Activity: SIMG_CFMENUOLIAOID4
S_ALR_87000911	IMG Activity: SIMG_CMMENUOLSDVED1
S_ALR_87000912	IMG Activity: SIMG_CFMENUOLISAKTI
S_ALR_87000913	IMG Activity: OLIAOIMD
S_ALR_87000914	IMG Activity: SIMG_CFMENUOLSDV/83
S_ALR_87000915	IMG Activity: SIMG_CFMENUOLISMCST
S_ALR_87000916	IMG Activity: OLIAOIML
S_ALR_87000917	IMG Activity: SIMG_CFMENUOLMEWE20
S_ALR_87000918	IMG Activity: SIMG_CFMENUOLIAOIXZ
S_ALR_87000919	IMG Activity: SIMG_CMMENUOLMCFORM
S_ALR_87000920	IMG Activity: SIMG_CFMENUOLMEOMGK
S_ALR_87000921	IMG Activity: OLIAOIME
S_ALR_87000922	IMG Activity: SIMG_OLIS007
S_ALR_87000923	IMG Activity: OLIAOIMF
S_ALR_87000924	IMG Activity: SIMG_CFMENUOLMEOMEM
S_ALR_87000925	IMG Activity: SIMG_CFMENUOLISMCSS
S_ALR_87000926	IMG Activity: OLIAOIYP

S_ALR_87000927	IMG Activity: SIMG_CFMENUOLMEOMZ9
S_ALR_87000928	IMG Activity: SIMG_CMMENUOLMCINFP
S_ALR_87000929	IMG Activity: SIMG_CFMENUOLIAQS41
S_ALR_87000930	IMG Activity: SIMG_CMMENUOLMCFELD
S_ALR_87000931	IMG Activity: SIMG_CFMENUOLMEOMZ8
S_ALR_87000932	IMG Activity: SIMG_CFMENUOLIAQS49
S_ALR_87000933	IMG Activity: OLIS_KOMM3
S_ALR_87000934	IMG Activity: SIMG_CFMENUOLMEOMZ7
S_ALR_87000935	IMG Activity: OLIAOQN6
S_ALR_87000936	IMG Activity: OLIS_SE11
S_ALR_87000937	IMG Activity: SIMG_CFMENUOLIAOQN5
S_ALR_87000938	IMG Activity: SIMG_CFMENUOLMEOMZ6
S_ALR_87000939	IMG Activity: OLIS_WE30
S_ALR_87000940	IMG Activity: OLIA_OIMX
S_ALR_87000941	IMG Activity: SIMG_CFMENUOLMCAPP1
S_ALR_87000942	IMG Activity: SIMG_CFMENUOLMEOMHS
S_ALR_87000943	IMG Activity: OLIAOIM7
S_ALR_87000944	IMG Activity: SIMG_OLID
S_ALR_87000945	IMG Activity: SIMG_CFMENUOLMEOMFJ
S_ALR_87000946	IMG Activity: OLIAOIRS
S_ALR_87000947	IMG Activity: SIMG_CFMENUOLMEOMGY
S_ALR_87000948	IMG Activity: OLIS008
S_ALR_87000949	IMG Activity: SIMG_CFMENUOLIAOIMZ
S_ALR_87000950	IMG Activity: SIMG_CFMENUOLMEOMGX
S_ALR_87000951	IMG Activity: SIMG_CFMENUOLIAOIMW
S_ALR_87000952	IMG Activity: SIMG_OLIS006
S_ALR_87000953	IMG Activity: SIMG_CFMENUOLME8KEG
S_ALR_87000954	IMG Activity: SIMG_CFMENUOLIAOIXW
S_ALR_87000955	IMG Activity: OLIS_OLIQ
S_ALR_87000956	IMG Activity: SIMG_CFMENUOLMEOMRE
S_ALR_87000957	IMG Activity: SIMG_OLIS005
S_ALR_87000958	IMG Activity: SIMG_CFMENUOLMEOMZ5
S_ALR_87000959	IMG Activity: OLIS009
S_ALR_87000960	IMG Activity: W_ZF_ST_0332
S_ALR_87000961	IMG Activity: SIMG_OLIS003
S_ALR_87000962	IMG Activity: W_ZF_ST_0331
S_ALR_87000963	IMG Activity: SIMG_OLIS004
S_ALR_87000964	IMG Activity: W_ZF_ST_0324
S_ALR_87000965	IMG Activity: LIS_TIS
S_ALR_87000966	IMG Activity: W_ZF_ST_0323
S_ALR_87000967	IMG Activity: SIMG_CFMENUOLIS0VSU
S_ALR_87000968	IMG Activity: W_ZF_ST_0322
S_ALR_87000969	IMG Activity: SIMG_CFMENUOLMCOVCT
S_ALR_87000970	IMG Activity: W_ZF_ST_0311
S_ALR_87000971	IMG Activity: SIMG_CFMENUOLMCOVRM
S_ALR_87000972	IMG Activity: SIMG_CFMENUOLMEOMZ4
S_ALR_87000973	IMG Activity: SIMG_CFMENUOLMCOVCO
S_ALR_87000974	IMG Activity: SIMG_CFMENUOLMEOMZ3
S_ALR_87000975	IMG Activity: SIMG_CFMENUOLMCOVCU
S_ALR_87000976	IMG Activity: SIMG_CFMENUOLMEOMZ2
S_ALR_87000977	IMG Activity: SIMG_CFMENUOLMCOVRO
S_ALR_87000978	IMG Activity: SIMG_CFMENUOLMCOVRB
S_ALR_87000979	IMG Activity: SIMG_CFMENUOLMEOMZ1
S_ALR_87000980	IMG Activity: W_ZF_ST_0342

S_ALR_87000981	IMG Activity: SIMG_CFMENUOLMCOVRP
S_ALR_87000982	IMG Activity: SIMG_CFMENUOLIS0VSE
S_ALR_87000983	IMG Activity: W_ZF_ST_0341
S_ALR_87000984	IMG Activity: SIMG_CFMENUOLIS0VSF
S_ALR_87000985	IMG Activity: SIMG_CMMENUOLMEOMG7
S_ALR_87000986	IMG Activity: SIMG_CFMENUOLMCOVRK
S_ALR_87000987	IMG Activity: SIMG_OLME2OMFV
S_ALR_87000988	IMG Activity: SIMG_CFMENUOLIS0VST
S_ALR_87000989	IMG Activity: OLIAOQN2
S_ALR_87000990	IMG Activity: SIMG_OLME2ORKSOVA
S_ALR_87000991	IMG Activity: SIMG_CFMENUOLMCOVRL
S_ALR_87000992	IMG Activity: SIMG_CFMENUOLIAOIXY
S_ALR_87000993	IMG Activity: SIMG_OLMEOLISAKTI2
S_ALR_87000994	IMG Activity: SIMG_CFMENUOLIS0VSD
S_ALR_87000995	IMG Activity: OLIA_V_TQ85
S_ALR_87000996	IMG Activity: SIMG_OLMEOMQ3
S_ALR_87000997	IMG Activity: OLIS_REORG_METHOD
S_ALR_87000998	IMG Activity: OLIS_STRDANA_LIST
S_ALR_87000999	IMG Activity: SIMG_OLMEOMQ2
S_ALR_87001000	IMG Activity: OLIA_V_TQ07
S_ALR_87001001	IMG Activity: OLIS_ALE_EKS
S_ALR_87001002	IMG Activity: SIMG_CFMENUOLISTEIN
S_ALR_87001003	IMG Activity: SIMG_CFMENUOLIAOIXX
S_ALR_87001004	IMG Activity: SIMG_CFMENUOLMECMOD
S_ALR_87001005	IMG Activity: SIMG_OLIS001
S_ALR_87001006	IMG Activity: OLIAOIBS
S_ALR_87001007	IMG Activity: OLIS_KOPP4A
S_ALR_87001008	IMG Activity: SIMG_CFMENUOLMEOXW1
S_ALR_87001009	IMG Activity: OLIS_ALE_VIS
S_ALR_87001010	IMG Activity: SIMG_CFMENUOLIAOIMK
S_ALR_87001011	IMG Activity: SIMG_CFMENUOLMEOXW2
S_ALR_87001012	IMG Activity: OLIS_ALE35
S_ALR_87001024	IMG Activity: SIMG_CFMENUORKSOKER1
S_ALR_87001025	IMG Activity: SIMG_CFMENUORKSOKTZ1
S_ALR_87001026	IMG Activity: SIMG_CFMENUORKSOKET1
S_ALR_87001027	IMG Activity: SIMG_CFMENUORKSOKET
S_ALR_87001028	IMG Activity: SIMG_CFMENUORKSKBC3
S_ALR_87001029	IMG Activity: SIMG_CFMENUORKSKBC2
S_ALR_87001030	IMG Activity: SIMG_CFMENUORKSOKER
S_ALR_87001031	IMG Activity: SIMG_CFMENUORKSOKTZ
S_ALR_87001032	IMG Activity: SIMG_CFMENUORKSKA05
S_ALR_87001033	IMG Activity: SIMG_CFMENUORKSKR01
S_ALR_87001034	IMG Activity: SIMG_CFMENUORKSOKV5
S_ALR_87001035	IMG Activity: SIMG_CFMENUORKSKAH21
S_ALR_87001036	IMG Activity: SIMG_CFMENUORKSOKVF
S_ALR_87001037	IMG Activity: SIMG_CFMENUOLSDVI62
S_ALR_87001038	IMG Activity: SIMG_CFMENUOLSD0VX1
S_ALR_87001039	IMG Activity: SIMG_CFMENUOLSDVIM6
S_ALR_87001040	IMG Activity: SIMG_CFMENUOLSDVI63
S_ALR_87001041	IMG Activity: SIMG_CFMENUOLSDVE80
S_ALR_87001042	IMG Activity: SIMG_CFMENUOLSDVI30
S_ALR_87001043	IMG Activity: SIMG_CFMENUOLSDVI92
S_ALR_87001044	IMG Activity: SIMG_CFMENUOLSDVE64
S_ALR_87001045	IMG Activity: SIMG_CFMENUOLSDVE65

S_ALR_87001046	IMG Activity: SIMG_CFMENUOLSDVE66
S_ALR_87001047	IMG Activity: SIMG_CFMENUOLSDVE71
S_ALR_87001048	IMG Activity: SIMG_CFMENUOLSDVE63
S_ALR_87001049	IMG Activity: SIMG_CFMENUOLSDUID
S_ALR_87001050	IMG Activity: SIMG_CFMENUOLSDVE53
S_ALR_87001051	IMG Activity: SIMG_CFMENUOLSDVE62
S_ALR_87001052	IMG Activity: SIMG_CFMENUOLSDVE61
S_ALR_87001053	IMG Activity: SIMG_CFMENUOLSDVE60
S_ALR_87001054	IMG Activity: SIMG_CFMENUOLSDGOTX
S_ALR_87001055	IMG Activity: SIMG_CFMENUOLSDVE51
S_ALR_87001056	IMG Activity: SIMG_CFMENUOPP1OM0A
S_ALR_87001057	IMG Activity: SIMG_CFMENUOLSDREGI
S_ALR_87001058	IMG Activity: SIMG_CFMENUOLSDVE56
S_ALR_87001059	IMG Activity: SIMG_CFMENUOLSDVE57
S_ALR_87001060	IMG Activity: SIMG_CFMENUOLSDVE59
S_ALR_87001061	IMG Activity: SIMG_CFMENUOLSDVE58
S_ALR_87001062	IMG Activity: SIMG_CFMENUOPP1OWD1
S_ALR_87001063	IMG Activity: SIMG_CMMENUOLSDVI67
S_ALR_87001064	IMG Activity: SIMG_CMMENUOLSDVI66
S_ALR_87001065	IMG Activity: SIMG_CMMENUOLSDVI65
S_ALR_87001066	IMG Activity: SIMG_CFMENUOLSDVE78
S_ALR_87001067	IMG Activity: SIMG_CFMENUOLSDVE75
S_ALR_87001068	IMG Activity: SIMG_CFMENUOLSDVE77
S_ALR_87001069	IMG Activity: SIMG_CFMENUOPP1OM0D
S_ALR_87001070	IMG Activity: SIMG_CMMENUOLSDVI69
S_ALR_87001071	IMG Activity: SIMG_CFMENUOLSDVI31
S_ALR_87001072	IMG Activity: SIMG_CFMENUOLSDVE79
S_ALR_87001073	IMG Activity: SIMG_CFMENUOLSDVE76
S_ALR_87001074	IMG Activity: SIMG_CFMENUOLSDVE49
S_ALR_87001075	IMG Activity: SIMG_CFMENUOLSDVE48
S_ALR_87001076	IMG Activity: SIMG_CFMENUOLSDVI54
S_ALR_87001077	IMG Activity: SIMG_CFMENUOLSDVI89
S_ALR_87001078	IMG Activity: SIMG_CFMENUOLSDVI35
S_ALR_87001079	IMG Activity: SIMG_CFMENUOLSDVI34
S_ALR_87001080	IMG Activity: SIMG_CFMENUOLSDVI33
S_ALR_87001081	IMG Activity: SIMG_CFMENUOLSDVI32
S_ALR_87001082	IMG Activity: SIMG_CFMENUOLSDVI37
S_ALR_87001083	IMG Activity: SIMG_CFMENUOLSDVI46
S_ALR_87001084	IMG Activity: SIMG_CFMENUOLSDVI48
S_ALR_87001085	IMG Activity: SIMG_CFMENUOLSDVI50
S_ALR_87001086	IMG Activity: SIMG_CFMENUOLSDVI47
S_ALR_87001087	IMG Activity: SIMG_CFMENUOLSDVI45
S_ALR_87001088	IMG Activity: SIMG_CFMENUOLSDVI61
S_ALR_87001089	IMG Activity: SIMG_CFMENUOLSDVI36
S_ALR_87001090	IMG Activity: SIMG_CFMENUOLSDVI70
S_ALR_87001091	IMG Activity: SIMG_CFMENUOLSDOVI95
S_ALR_87001092	IMG Activity: SIMG_CFMENUOLSDOVI76
S_ALR_87001093	IMG Activity: SIMG_CFMENUOLSDOVE3
S_ALR_87001094	IMG Activity: SIMG_CFMENUOLSDOVE2
S_ALR_87001095	IMG Activity: SIMG_CFMENUOLSDVX54
S_ALR_87001096	IMG Activity: SIMG_CFMENUOLSDVX58
S_ALR_87001097	IMG Activity: SIMG_CFMENUOLSDVX56
S_ALR_87001098	IMG Activity: SIMG_CFMENUOLSDVX52
S_ALR_87001099	IMG Activity: SIMG_CFMENUOLSDVX49

S_ALR_87001100	IMG Activity: SIMG_CFMENUOLSDVX57
S_ALR_87001101	IMG Activity: SIMG_CFMENUOLSDVE50
S_ALR_87001102	IMG Activity: SIMG_CFMENUOLSDSTUBE
S_ALR_87001103	IMG Activity: SIMG_CFMENUOLSDOOVA7
S_ALR_87001104	IMG Activity: SIMG_CFMENUOLSDOVX
S_ALR_87001105	IMG Activity: SIMG_CFMENUOLSDVI52
S_ALR_87001106	IMG Activity: SIMG_CFMENUOLSDVX53
S_ALR_87001107	IMG Activity: SIMG_CFMENUOLSDVOTX
S_ALR_87001108	IMG Activity: SIMG_CFMENUOLSDSE71
S_ALR_87001109	IMG Activity: SIMG_CFMENUOLSDVI38
S_ALR_87001110	IMG Activity: SIMG_CFMENUOLSDVI42
S_ALR_87001111	IMG Activity: SIMG_CFMENUOLSDVI41
S_ALR_87001112	IMG Activity: SIMG_CFMENUOLSDVI40
S_ALR_87001113	IMG Activity: SIMG_CFMENUOLSDVI39
S_ALR_87001114	IMG Activity: SIMG_CFMENUOLSDVX51
S_ALR_87001115	IMG Activity: SIMG_CFMENUOLSDVX50
S_ALR_87001116	IMG Activity: SIMG_CMMENUOLSDVI28
S_ALR_87001117	IMG Activity: SIMG_CMMENUOLSDVI56
S_ALR_87001118	IMG Activity: SIMG_CMMENUOLSDVED1
S_ALR_87001119	IMG Activity: SIMG_CFMENUOLSDV/83
S_ALR_87001120	IMG Activity: OLIS_STRDANA_DATA
S_ALR_87001121	IMG Activity: SIMG_CFMENUOLIAOIR7
S_ALR_87001122	IMG Activity: SIMG_CFMENUOLMEOXW3
S_ALR_87001123	IMG Activity: OLIS_ALE_BCO
S_ALR_87001124	IMG Activity: OLIS_ALE34
S_ALR_87001125	IMG Activity: SIMG_CFMENUOLIAOIR8
S_ALR_87001126	IMG Activity: SIMG_CFMENUOLMEOMET
S_ALR_87001127	IMG Activity: OLIAOIYT
S_ALR_87001128	IMG Activity: SIMG_CFMENUOLMEOMEI
S_ALR_87001129	IMG Activity: OLIAOIYS
S_ALR_87001130	IMG Activity: SIMG_OLMEOMQ1
S_ALR_87001131	IMG Activity: OLIAOQN0
S_ALR_87001132	IMG Activity: SIMG_OLMEOMQ4
S_ALR_87001133	IMG Activity: SIMG_CFMENUOLIAOIR6
S_ALR_87001134	IMG Activity: SIMG_OLMEOBE8
S_ALR_87001135	IMG Activity: SIMG_CFMENUOLIAOIR1
S_ALR_87001136	IMG Activity: SIMG_CFMENUOLMEOMHK
S_ALR_87001137	IMG Activity: SIMG_CFMENUOLIAOIR2
S_ALR_87001138	IMG Activity: SIMG_CFMENUOLMEOMHT
S_ALR_87001139	IMG Activity: SIMG_CFMENUOLIAOIR3
S_ALR_87001140	IMG Activity: SIMG_CFMENUOLMEXOMFJ
S_ALR_87001141	IMG Activity: SIMG_CFMENUOLIAOIR4
S_ALR_87001142	IMG Activity: SIMG_CFMENUOLIAOIR5
S_ALR_87001143	IMG Activity: SIMG_CFMENUOLMEOMFL
S_ALR_87001144	IMG Activity: OLIA_V_TQSCR
S_ALR_87001145	IMG Activity: SIMG_OLME1OMFV
S_ALR_87001146	IMG Activity: OLIAOIYR
S_ALR_87001147	IMG Activity: SIMG_OLME1ORKSOVA
S_ALR_87001148	IMG Activity: SIMG_CFMENUOLIAOIMP
S_ALR_87001149	IMG Activity: SIMG_OLMEOLISAKTI1
S_ALR_87001150	IMG Activity: SIMG_CFMENUOLIAOIM8
S_ALR_87001151	IMG Activity: SIMG_OLME1OMY6
S_ALR_87001152	IMG Activity: SIMG_CFMENUOLIAOQN3
S_ALR_87001153	IMG Activity: SIMG_OLMEOMQ6

S_ALR_87001154	IMG Activity: OLIAOIYQ
S_ALR_87001155	IMG Activity: SIMG_OLME1OMQ5
S_ALR_87001156	IMG Activity: OLIAOQNA
S_ALR_87001157	IMG Activity: SIMGOLMEM/68
S_ALR_87001158	IMG Activity: SIMG_CFMENUOLIAOIM3
S_ALR_87001159	IMG Activity: SIMGOLMEM/36
S_ALR_87001160	IMG Activity: SIMG_CFMENUOLIAIW20
S_ALR_87001161	IMG Activity: OLIAOQN7
S_ALR_87001162	IMG Activity: SIMGOLMEM/32
S_ALR_87001163	IMG Activity: OLIA_V_TQ80_PAGE
S_ALR_87001164	IMG Activity: OLIA_RIAUFM00
S_ALR_87001165	IMG Activity: OLIAUEFAKTURA
S_ALR_87001166	IMG Activity: OLIA_INDX_FAKTURA
S_ALR_87001167	IMG Activity: SIMGOLMEM/40
S_ALR_87001168	IMG Activity: SIMGOLMEM/38
S_ALR_87001169	IMG Activity: SIMGOLMEOMTD
S_ALR_87001170	IMG Activity: SIMGOLMEOMTC
S_ALR_87001171	IMG Activity: SIMGOLMEOMTB
S_ALR_87001172	IMG Activity: SIMGOLMEOMTA
S_ALR_87001173	IMG Activity: SIMGOLMEVNE7
S_ALR_87001174	IMG Activity: SIMGOLMEM/42
S_ALR_87001175	IMG Activity: SIMGOLMEM/34
S_ALR_87001176	IMG Activity: SIMGOLMEVNE2
S_ALR_87001177	IMG Activity: SIMGOLMEM/64
S_ALR_87001178	IMG Activity: SIMGOLMEM/67
S_ALR_87001179	IMG Activity: SIMGOLMEM/61
S_ALR_87001180	IMG Activity: SIMGOLMEM/58
S_ALR_87001181	IMG Activity: SIMG_CFMENUOLMEEDI2
S_ALR_87001182	IMG Activity: SIMGOLMEM/30
S_ALR_87001183	IMG Activity: SIMGOLMEVNE4
S_ALR_87001184	IMG Activity: SIMGOLMEM/54
S_ALR_87001185	IMG Activity: SIMGOLMEM/52
S_ALR_87001186	IMG Activity: SIMGOLMEM/50
S_ALR_87001187	IMG Activity: SIMGOLMEM/48
S_ALR_87001188	IMG Activity: SIMG_CFMENUOLMEOMHF
S_ALR_87001189	IMG Activity: SIMG_CFMENUOLMEOMHE
S_ALR_87001190	IMG Activity: SIMG_CFMENUOLMEOMHD
S_ALR_87001191	IMG Activity: SIMG_CFMENUOLMESFT3
S_ALR_87001192	IMG Activity: SIMG_CFMENUOLMEVB(1
S_ALR_87001193	IMG Activity: SIMG_CFMENUOLMEOMKO
S_ALR_87001194	IMG Activity: SIMG_CMMENUOLMEABRE2
S_ALR_87001195	IMG Activity: SIMG_CMMENUOLMEABREC
S_ALR_87001196	IMG Activity: SIMG_CFMENUOLMEOVBA
S_ALR_87001197	IMG Activity: SIMG_CFMENUOLME_KONT
S_ALR_87001198	IMG Activity: SIMG_CFMENUOLMEKONDT
S_ALR_87001199	IMG Activity: SIMG_CFMENUOLMEOMHG
S_ALR_87001200	IMG Activity: SIMG_CFMENUOLMEOMKN
S_ALR_87001201	IMG Activity: SIMG_CFMENUOLMEOMGL
S_ALR_87001202	IMG Activity: SIMG_CFMENUOLMEOMGU
S_ALR_87001203	IMG Activity: SIMG_CFMENUOLMEOMGI
S_ALR_87001204	IMG Activity: SIMG_CFMENUOLMEOMGC
S_ALR_87001205	IMG Activity: SIMG_CFMENUOLMEOMGF
S_ALR_87001206	IMG Activity: SIMGOLMEVNE5
S_ALR_87001207	IMG Activity: SIMG_CFMENUOLMEOMKL

SAP Transaction Codes – Volume Two

S_ALR_87001208	IMG Activity: SIMG_CFMENUOLMEOMKM
S_ALR_87001209	IMG Activity: SIMG_CFMENUOLMEOMKK
S_ALR_87001210	IMG Activity: SIMG_CFMENUOLMEOMQL
S_ALR_87001211	IMG Activity: SIMG_CFMENUOLMEOMKD
S_ALR_87001212	IMG Activity: SIMG_CFMENUOLMEOMKH
S_ALR_87001213	IMG Activity: SIMG_CFMENUOLSDVE47
S_ALR_87001214	IMG Activity: SIMG_CMMENUOLMETORP
S_ALR_87001215	IMG Activity: W_ZF_ST_0125
S_ALR_87001216	IMG Activity: W_ZF_ST_0126
S_ALR_87001217	IMG Activity: W_ZF_ST_0127
S_ALR_87001218	IMG Activity: CATS0205
S_ALR_87001219	IMG Activity: CIC_CICAK
S_ALR_87001220	IMG Activity: SIMG_OLMEOM8R
S_ALR_87001221	IMG Activity: CATS0206
S_ALR_87001222	IMG Activity: SIMG_NOTPFLEGE
S_ALR_87001223	IMG Activity: CIC_EWFC0
S_ALR_87001224	IMG Activity: CATS0208
S_ALR_87001225	IMG Activity: W_DF_LT_0802
S_ALR_87001226	IMG Activity: CIC_V_CCMACTPROF
S_ALR_87001227	IMG Activity: CATS0401
S_ALR_87001228	IMG Activity: W_ZF_ST_0123
S_ALR_87001229	IMG Activity: CIC_V_CCMSCRPROF
S_ALR_87001230	IMG Activity: CATS0501
S_ALR_87001231	IMG Activity: SIMG_CMMENUOLMETORT
S_ALR_87001232	IMG Activity: CIC_V_CCMCSEARCH
S_ALR_87001233	IMG Activity: CATS0302
S_ALR_87001234	IMG Activity: CATS0303
S_ALR_87001235	IMG Activity: CIC_BDC_CICAG
S_ALR_87001236	IMG Activity: SIMG_CMMENUOLMETORZ
S_ALR_87001237	IMG Activity: CIC_CICAF
S_ALR_87001238	IMG Activity: CATS0301
S_ALR_87001239	IMG Activity: W_ZF_ST_0124
S_ALR_87001240	IMG Activity: CIC_CICAH
S_ALR_87001241	IMG Activity: CATS1001
S_ALR_87001242	IMG Activity: SIMG_OLMEOM7R
S_ALR_87001243	IMG Activity: CIC_CICAI
S_ALR_87001244	IMG Activity: CATS0201
S_ALR_87001245	IMG Activity: SIMG_OLMEOM2R
S_ALR_87001246	IMG Activity: CIC_CICAJ
S_ALR_87001247	IMG Activity: CATS0202
S_ALR_87001248	IMG Activity: CIC_V_CCMCCONT
S_ALR_87001249	IMG Activity: SIMG_OLMEOM1R
S_ALR_87001250	IMG Activity: CATS0203
S_ALR_87001251	IMG Activity: CIC_CICAL
S_ALR_87001252	IMG Activity: W_ZF_ST_0101
S_ALR_87001253	IMG Activity: CATS0204
S_ALR_87001254	IMG Activity: CIC_V_CICPROFMAST
S_ALR_87001255	IMG Activity: SIMG_CFMENUOLMEOME4
S_ALR_87001256	IMG Activity: CATS0207
S_ALR_87001257	IMG Activity: CIC_V_CCMAC
S_ALR_87001258	IMG Activity: CATS0101
S_ALR_87001259	IMG Activity: SIMG_CFMENUOLMEOMRP
S_ALR_87001260	IMG Activity: CIC_V_CCMADKEY
S_ALR_87001261	IMG Activity: SIMG_OLMEOM6R

S_ALR_87001262	IMG Activity: CIC_V_CCMCTIBKEY
S_ALR_87001263	IMG Activity: SIMG_OLMEOM5R
S_ALR_87001264	IMG Activity: CIC_V_CCMCBQUES
S_ALR_87001265	IMG Activity: SIMG_OLMEOM4R
S_ALR_87001266	IMG Activity: CIC_V_CCMCBQCLUST
S_ALR_87001267	IMG Activity: W_ZF_ST_0102
S_ALR_87001268	IMG Activity: CIC_V_CCMCLBC
S_ALR_87001269	IMG Activity: SIMG_OLMEOM3R
S_ALR_87001270	IMG Activity: CIC_V_CICPROF
S_ALR_87001271	IMG Activity: W_DF_LT_0803
S_ALR_87001272	IMG Activity: CIC_V_CICCCONF_CUST
S_ALR_87001273	IMG Activity: CIC_V_CCMCTIPROF
S_ALR_87001274	IMG Activity: W_ZE_EK_0240
S_ALR_87001275	IMG Activity: CIC_VCICTOOLBARCLUST
S_ALR_87001276	IMG Activity: W_ZE_EK_0210
S_ALR_87001277	IMG Activity: CIC_V_CICTOOLBAR
S_ALR_87001278	IMG Activity: W_ZE_EK_0212
S_ALR_87001279	IMG Activity: CIC_V_CICFHCASSN
S_ALR_87001280	IMG Activity: W_ZE_EK_0211
S_ALR_87001281	IMG Activity: CIC_V_CCMCCPROF
S_ALR_87001282	IMG Activity: W_ZF_ST_0113
S_ALR_87001283	IMG Activity: CIC_V_CCMCTIQUEUEA
S_ALR_87001284	IMG Activity: OLMEOMGS_3
S_ALR_87001285	IMG Activity: CIC_V_CCMCTIADMIN
S_ALR_87001286	IMG Activity: SIMG_CFMENUOLMEOMEF
S_ALR_87001287	IMG Activity: CIC_CICAE
S_ALR_87001288	IMG Activity: SIMG_CFMENUOLMEOMY6
S_ALR_87001289	IMG Activity: CIC_CICAD
S_ALR_87001290	IMG Activity: W_ZE_EK_0220
S_ALR_87001291	IMG Activity: CIC_V_CICCCONF
S_ALR_87001292	IMG Activity: W_ZE_EK_0250
S_ALR_87001293	IMG Activity: CIC_V_CICFSCASSN
S_ALR_87001294	IMG Activity: W_ZF_ST_0114
S_ALR_87001295	IMG Activity: W_DF_EK_0112
S_ALR_87001296	IMG Activity: W_ZF_ST_0121
S_ALR_87001297	IMG Activity: W_ZF_ST_0122
S_ALR_87001298	IMG Activity: W_DF_EK_0111
S_ALR_87001299	IMG Activity: W_DF_EK_0110
S_ALR_87001300	IMG Activity: W_ZF_ST_0115
S_ALR_87001301	IMG Activity: W_DF_LT_0820
S_ALR_87001302	IMG Activity: W_DF_LT_0810
S_ALR_87001303	IMG Activity: W_ZE_EK_0230
S_ALR_87001304	IMG Activity: OFRA_S_VERS
S_ALR_87001305	IMG Activity: SIMG_CFORFBT047I
S_ALR_87001306	IMG Activity: ORFA_S_VERM
S_ALR_87001307	IMG Activity: SIMG_CFMENUOLMEOMY7
S_ALR_87001308	IMG Activity: SIMG_CFORFBT047F
S_ALR_87001309	IMG Activity: ORFA_SONDER_KONTEN
S_ALR_87001310	IMG Activity: SIMG_CFORFBSE71MAHN
S_ALR_87001311	IMG Activity: SIMG_CFMENUOLMEOMEL
S_ALR_87001312	IMG Activity: SIMG_CFMENUORFAOAGL
S_ALR_87001313	IMG Activity: SIMG_CFMENUORFBOBAM
S_ALR_87001314	IMG Activity: SIMG_CFMENUOLMEOMEE
S_ALR_87001315	IMG Activity: SIMG_CFMENUORFAINF9

S_ALR_87001316	IMG Activity: SIMG_CFMENUORFBOBAL
S_ALR_87001317	IMG Activity: ORFA_VORSTEUER
S_ALR_87001318	IMG Activity: SIMG_CFMENUOLMEOMES
S_ALR_87001319	IMG Activity: SIMG_CFMENUORFAOAEA
S_ALR_87001320	IMG Activity: SIMG_CFMENUORFBOB42
S_ALR_87001321	IMG Activity: SIMG_CFMENUOLMEOMHP
S_ALR_87001322	IMG Activity: ORFA_S_FOERDER
S_ALR_87001323	IMG Activity: SIMG_CFMENUORFBOBAQ
S_ALR_87001324	IMG Activity: SIMG_CFMENUOLMEOMF1
S_ALR_87001325	IMG Activity: SIMG_CFMENUORFBOBL6
S_ALR_87001326	IMG Activity: ORFA_AS91
S_ALR_87001327	IMG Activity: OLMEOME6
S_ALR_87001328	IMG Activity: SIMG_CFORFBVT049E
S_ALR_87001329	IMG Activity: SIMG_CFMENUORFAOA13
S_ALR_87001330	IMG Activity: SIMG_CFMENUOLMEOMFY
S_ALR_87001331	IMG Activity: ORFA_S_ALTPAR
S_ALR_87001332	IMG Activity: SIMG_CFMENUOLMEOMEW
S_ALR_87001333	IMG Activity: SIMG_CFORFBFI12
S_ALR_87001334	IMG Activity: SIMG_CFMENUORFAALT9
S_ALR_87001335	IMG Activity: SIMG_CFMENUOLMEOMEB
S_ALR_87001336	IMG Activity: SIMG_CFORFBVT048Y
S_ALR_87001337	IMG Activity: SIMG_CFMENUORFAOABL
S_ALR_87001338	IMG Activity: SIMG_CFMENUOLMETEAP
S_ALR_87001339	IMG Activity: SIMG_CFORFBVT048X
S_ALR_87001340	IMG Activity: ORFA_S_VORSCHLAG
S_ALR_87001341	IMG Activity: SIMG_CFORFBVT048V
S_ALR_87001342	IMG Activity: SIMG_CFMENUORFAOAC1
S_ALR_87001343	IMG Activity: SIMG_CFMENUOLMEOMEQ
S_ALR_87001344	IMG Activity: ORFA_MIT_BEREICH
S_ALR_87001345	IMG Activity: SIMG_CFORFBCMODMAHN
S_ALR_87001346	IMG Activity: SIMG_CFMENUOLMEOME5
S_ALR_87001347	IMG Activity: ORFA_S_BEREICHT_TYP
S_ALR_87001348	IMG Activity: SIMG_ORFBT076A
S_ALR_87001349	IMG Activity: SIMG_CFMENUOLMEOMEP
S_ALR_87001350	IMG Activity: SIMG_CFMENUORFAOAK5
S_ALR_87001351	IMG Activity: SIMG_CFMENUOLMEOMHO
S_ALR_87001352	IMG Activity: SIMG_CFORFBOBCAZE
S_ALR_87001353	IMG Activity: SIMG_CFMENUORFAOAB1
S_ALR_87001354	IMG Activity: SIMG_CFMENUOLMEOMFT
S_ALR_87001355	IMG Activity: SIMG_CFMENUORFBOBAV
S_ALR_87001356	IMG Activity: SIMG_CFMENUORFAOAP1
S_ALR_87001357	IMG Activity: SIMG_CFMENUOLMEOMHL
S_ALR_87001358	IMG Activity: SIMG_CFMENUORFBOBL5
S_ALR_87001359	IMG Activity: SIMG_CFMENUORFAOASV
S_ALR_87001360	IMG Activity: SIMG_CFMENUOLMEOME8
S_ALR_87001361	IMG Activity: SIMG_CFORFBCHKEPZLZE
S_ALR_87001362	IMG Activity: SIMG_CFMENUORFAOABP
S_ALR_87001363	IMG Activity: SIMG_CFORFBCHKZAZLZE
S_ALR_87001364	IMG Activity: SIMG_CFOLMEOMGS_1
S_ALR_87001365	IMG Activity: SIMG_CFMENUORFAOAK1
S_ALR_87001366	IMG Activity: SIMG_CFORFBCMODDTA
S_ALR_87001367	IMG Activity: SIMG_CFMENUOLMEOMEA
S_ALR_87001368	IMG Activity: ORFA_HAUPT_KONT
S_ALR_87001369	IMG Activity: OLMEOMGQ

S_ALR_87001370	IMG Activity: ORFA_BESTANLKL
S_ALR_87001371	IMG Activity: SIMG_CFMENUORFBFBMP
S_ALR_87001372	IMG Activity: SIMG_CFMENUOLMEOMEY
S_ALR_87001373	IMG Activity: SIMG_CFMENUORFBOB18
S_ALR_87001374	IMG Activity: ORFA_S_KLASS_OBJ
S_ALR_87001375	IMG Activity: SIMG_CFMENUOLMETEFP
S_ALR_87001376	IMG Activity: SIMG_CFMENUORFBOB17
S_ALR_87001377	IMG Activity: ORFA_S_KLASS_KOP
S_ALR_87001378	IMG Activity: SIMG_CFMENUOLMEOMFV
S_ALR_87001379	IMG Activity: SIMG_CFMENUORFBOB61
S_ALR_87001380	IMG Activity: ORFA_S_USER
S_ALR_87001381	IMG Activity: W_OE_ZG_WL_0310
S_ALR_87001382	IMG Activity: SIMG_CFORFBTCCAA
S_ALR_87001383	IMG Activity: ORFA_S_MUSS
S_ALR_87001384	IMG Activity: SIMG_CFMENUOLMEOMF4
S_ALR_87001385	IMG Activity: ORFA_S_KLASSEN
S_ALR_87001386	IMG Activity: SIMG_CFORFBTCCFI
S_ALR_87001387	IMG Activity: SIMG_CFORFBCMODEDIAV
S_ALR_87001388	IMG Activity: SIMG_CFMENUOLMEOM9R
S_ALR_87001389	IMG Activity: SIMG_CFORFBOB09OP
S_ALR_87001390	IMG Activity: SIMG_CFMENUOLMEOMZB
S_ALR_87001391	IMG Activity: SIMG_CFORFBCHKKOBW
S_ALR_87001392	IMG Activity: SIMG_CFMENUOLMEOMGM
S_ALR_87001393	IMG Activity: SIMG_CFMENUORFBOBA8
S_ALR_87001394	IMG Activity: W_OE_EG_WL_0330
S_ALR_87001395	IMG Activity: SIMG_CFMENUORFBOB06
S_ALR_87001396	IMG Activity: SIMG_CFMENUORFBOB86
S_ALR_87001397	IMG Activity: SIMG_CFMENUORFBOBYK
S_ALR_87001398	IMG Activity: SIMG_CFMENUORFBOB73
S_ALR_87001399	IMG Activity: SIMG_CFMENUORFBOBA6
S_ALR_87001400	IMG Activity: SIMG_CFORFBCHKBLSW
S_ALR_87001401	IMG Activity: SIMG_CFMENUOLMEOMGN
S_ALR_87001402	IMG Activity: SIMG_CFMENUORFBOB92
S_ALR_87001403	IMG Activity: SIMG_CFMENUORFBOB91
S_ALR_87001404	IMG Activity: OLMEOMGS_2
S_ALR_87001405	IMG Activity: SIMG_CFORFBOB54
S_ALR_87001406	IMG Activity: SIMG_CFMENUOLMEOMHM
S_ALR_87001407	IMG Activity: SIMG_CFMENUORFBOBKF
S_ALR_87001408	IMG Activity: SIMG_CFMENUOLMEOMGR
S_ALR_87001409	IMG Activity: SIMG_CFORFBCHKKOBWZA
S_ALR_87001410	IMG Activity: SIMG_CFMENUOLMEOMEX
S_ALR_87001411	IMG Activity: SIMG_CFMENUORFBOBJ7
S_ALR_87001412	IMG Activity: SIMG_CFMENUOLMEOMFU
S_ALR_87001413	IMG Activity: SIMG_CFORFBOB40EANZ
S_ALR_87001414	IMG Activity: SIMG_CFMENUOLMEOMF2
S_ALR_87001415	IMG Activity: SIMG_CFMENUORFBOBXR
S_ALR_87001416	IMG Activity: SIMG_CFMENUOLMEOMEU
S_ALR_87001417	IMG Activity: SIMG_CFORFBCHKBLEANZ
S_ALR_87001418	IMG Activity: SIMG_CFMENUOLMEOMEC
S_ALR_87001419	IMG Activity: SIMG_CFMENUORFBOB74
S_ALR_87001420	IMG Activity: SIMG_CFORFBCHKBOPAGL
S_ALR_87001421	IMG Activity: SIMG_CFORFBOBXHOP
S_ALR_87001422	IMG Activity: SIMG_CFORFBOB00OP
S_ALR_87001423	IMG Activity: SIMG_CFMENUORFBOBYH

S_ALR_87001424	IMG Activity: SIMG_CFMENUORFBOBYN
S_ALR_87001425	IMG Activity: SIMG_CFORFBCHKBLBW
S_ALR_87001426	IMG Activity: SIMG_CFMENUORFBOBXD
S_ALR_87001427	IMG Activity: SIMG_CFMENUORFBOBYR
S_ALR_87001428	IMG Activity: SIMG_CFMENUOLMEOMEO
S_ALR_87001429	IMG Activity: SIMG_CFORFBCHKBLGANZ
S_ALR_87001430	IMG Activity: SIMG_CFMENUORFBOBXB
S_ALR_87001431	IMG Activity: SIMG_CFMENUOLMEOMRO
S_ALR_87001432	IMG Activity: SIMG_CFORFBOBCR
S_ALR_87001433	IMG Activity: SIMG_CFMENUOLMEOME1
S_ALR_87001434	IMG Activity: SIMG_CFMENUORFBOBCW
S_ALR_87001435	IMG Activity: SIMG_CFMENUOLMEOMPN
S_ALR_87001436	IMG Activity: SIMG_CFMENUORFBOBXL
S_ALR_87001437	IMG Activity: SIMG_CFMENUOLMEOMERA
S_ALR_87001438	IMG Activity: SIMG_CFMENUORFBOBBE
S_ALR_87001439	IMG Activity: SIMG_CFMENUORFBOB66
S_ALR_87001440	IMG Activity: SIMG_CFMENUOLMEOMER0
S_ALR_87001441	IMG Activity: SIMG_CFMENUORFBOBXH
S_ALR_87001442	IMG Activity: SIMG_CFMENUOLMEOMER9
S_ALR_87001443	IMG Activity: SIMG_CFMENUORFBOBXK
S_ALR_87001444	IMG Activity: SIMG_CFMENUOLMEOMEK
S_ALR_87001445	IMG Activity: SIMG_CFORFBOBCT
S_ALR_87001446	IMG Activity: SIMG_CFMENUOLSDXEIP
S_ALR_87001447	IMG Activity: SIMG_CFMENUORFBO7FA
S_ALR_87001448	IMG Activity: SIMG_CFMENUOLMEVDF1
S_ALR_87001449	IMG Activity: SIMG_CFMENUORFBO7F9
S_ALR_87001450	IMG Activity: SIMG_CFMENUOLMEOMG9
S_ALR_87001451	IMG Activity: SIMG_CFORFBOBCQ
S_ALR_87001452	IMG Activity: SIMG_CFMENUOLMEOMFQ
S_ALR_87001453	IMG Activity: SIMG_CFMENUORFBOBBC
S_ALR_87001454	IMG Activity: SIMG_CFMENUOLMEOMG8
S_ALR_87001455	IMG Activity: SIMG_CFMENUORFBOB27
S_ALR_87001456	IMG Activity: SIMG_CFORFBOBCS
S_ALR_87001457	IMG Activity: SIMG_CFMENUOLMEOMER2
S_ALR_87001458	IMG Activity: SIMG_CFORFBOB40RA
S_ALR_87001459	IMG Activity: SIMG_CFMENUOLMEOMER1
S_ALR_87001460	IMG Activity: SIMG_CFORFBOB70RA
S_ALR_87001461	IMG Activity: SIMG_CFMENUOLMEOAMP
S_ALR_87001462	IMG Activity: SIMG_CFMENUORFBOBB9
S_ALR_87001463	IMG Activity: SIMG_CFMENUOLMEOMQW
S_ALR_87001464	IMG Activity: SIMG_CFMENUORFBOBB8
S_ALR_87001465	IMG Activity: SIMG_CFMENUOLMEOMF0
S_ALR_87001466	IMG Activity: SIMG_CFORFBCHKBVRA
S_ALR_87001467	IMG Activity: SIMG_CFMENUOLMEOMER3
S_ALR_87001468	IMG Activity: SIMG_CFORFBCHKBLRA
S_ALR_87001469	IMG Activity: SIMG_CFORFBCHKEPZL
S_ALR_87001470	IMG Activity: SIMG_CFMENUOLMEOMER8
S_ALR_87001471	IMG Activity: SIMG_CFORFBOB00ZE
S_ALR_87001472	IMG Activity: SIMG_CFORFBOB09ZE
S_ALR_87001473	IMG Activity: SIMG_CFMENUOLMEOMER7
S_ALR_87001474	IMG Activity: SIMG_XXMENUORFBOBXL
S_ALR_87001475	IMG Activity: SIMG_CFMENUORFBOBXI
S_ALR_87001476	IMG Activity: SIMG_CFORFBCHKBLZE
S_ALR_87001477	IMG Activity: SIMG_CFMENUORFBOBKD

S_ALR_87001478	IMG Activity: SIMG_CFMENUOLMEOMER6
S_ALR_87001479	IMG Activity: SIMG_CFORFBCHKKOGA
S_ALR_87001480	IMG Activity: SIMG_CFORFBOBCU
S_ALR_87001481	IMG Activity: SIMG_CFMENUOLMEOMER5
S_ALR_87001482	IMG Activity: SIMG_CFORFBOB27ZVORE
S_ALR_87001483	IMG Activity: SIMG_CFORFBCHKEPZE
S_ALR_87001484	IMG Activity: SIMG_CFORFBCHKZAZE
S_ALR_87001485	IMG Activity: SIMG_CFMENUORFBOBAP
S_ALR_87001486	IMG Activity: SIMG_CFMENUORFBOB75
S_ALR_87001487	IMG Activity: SIMG_CFMENUORFBT042A
S_ALR_87001488	IMG Activity: SIMG_CFMENUORFBFBZP
S_ALR_87001489	IMG Activity: SIMG_CFORFBVCT015V
S_ALR_87001490	IMG Activity: SIMG_CFMENUORFBOB47
S_ALR_87001491	IMG Activity: SIMG_CFMENUOLMEOMER4
S_ALR_87001492	IMG Activity: SIMG_CFMENUORFBO7S2
S_ALR_87001493	IMG Activity: SIMG_CFMENUORFBO7S1
S_ALR_87001494	IMG Activity: SIMG_CFMENUOLSDVI43
S_ALR_87001495	IMG Activity: J_1A_BRA_ASSIGNMENT
S_ALR_87001496	IMG Activity: SIMG_CFMENUOLSDVI68
S_ALR_87001497	IMG Activity: J_1A_ASSIGNMENT_KEYS
S_ALR_87001498	IMG Activity: SIMG_CFMENUOLSDVI78
S_ALR_87001499	IMG Activity: SIMG_CFMENUORFBOBXC
S_ALR_87001500	IMG Activity: SIMG_CFMENUOLMEOME0
S_ALR_87001501	IMG Activity: SIMG_CFMENUORFBOB60
S_ALR_87001502	IMG Activity: SIMG_CFMENUORFBOBA3
S_ALR_87001503	IMG Activity: SIMG_CFMENUOLSDOMGT
S_ALR_87001504	IMG Activity: SIMG_CFMENUORFBOB57
S_ALR_87001505	IMG Activity: SIMG_CFMENUORFBOBA4
S_ALR_87001506	IMG Activity: SIMG_CFMENUORFBO7V6
S_ALR_87001507	IMG Activity: SIMG_CFMENUOLSDVI44
S_ALR_87001508	IMG Activity: SIMG_CFMENUORFBO7Z7
S_ALR_87001509	IMG Activity: SIMG_CFMENUOLSDOVE6
S_ALR_87001510	IMG Activity: SIMG_CFMENUORFBO7E1
S_ALR_87001511	IMG Activity: SIMG_CFMENUORFBOBKS
S_ALR_87001512	IMG Activity: SIMG_CFMENUOLSDOVE5
S_ALR_87001531	IMG Activity: SIMG_CFMENUOLMBOMJ5
S_ALR_87001532	IMG Activity: SIMG_CFMENUOLSDVI62
S_ALR_87001533	IMG Activity: SIMG_CFMENUOLSD0VX1
S_ALR_87001534	IMG Activity: SIMG_CFMENUOLSDVIM6
S_ALR_87001535	IMG Activity: SIMG_CFMENUOLSDVI63
S_ALR_87001536	IMG Activity: SIMG_CFMENUOLSDVE80
S_ALR_87001537	IMG Activity: SIMG_CFMENUOLSDVI30
S_ALR_87001538	IMG Activity: SIMG_CFMENUOLSDVI92
S_ALR_87001539	IMG Activity: SIMG_CFMENUOLSDVE64
S_ALR_87001540	IMG Activity: SIMG_CFMENUOLSDVE65
S_ALR_87001541	IMG Activity: SIMG_CFMENUOLSDVE66
S_ALR_87001542	IMG Activity: SIMG_CFMENUOLSDVE71
S_ALR_87001543	IMG Activity: SIMG_CFMENUOLSDVE63
S_ALR_87001544	IMG Activity: SIMG_CFMENUOLSDUID
S_ALR_87001545	IMG Activity: SIMG_CFMENUOLSDVE53
S_ALR_87001546	IMG Activity: SIMG_CFMENUOLSDVE62
S_ALR_87001547	IMG Activity: SIMG_CFMENUOLSDVE61
S_ALR_87001548	IMG Activity: SIMG_CFMENUOLSDVE60
S_ALR_87001549	IMG Activity: SIMG_CFMENUOLSDGOTX

S_ALR_87001550	IMG Activity: SIMG_CFMENUOLSDVE51
S_ALR_87001551	IMG Activity: SIMG_CFMENUOLSDREGI
S_ALR_87001552	IMG Activity: SIMG_CFMENUOLSDUNVO
S_ALR_87001553	IMG Activity: SIMG_CFMENUOLSDVE56
S_ALR_87001554	IMG Activity: SIMG_CFMENUOLSDVE57
S_ALR_87001555	IMG Activity: SIMG_CFMENUOLSDVE59
S_ALR_87001556	IMG Activity: SIMG_CFMENUOLSDVE58
S_ALR_87001557	IMG Activity: SIMG_CFMENUOLMEOMF9
S_ALR_87001558	IMG Activity: SIMG_CFMENUOLMEOMFC
S_ALR_87001559	IMG Activity: SIMG_CFMENUOLMEOMF6
S_ALR_87001560	IMG Activity: SIMG_CFMENUOLMEOME7
S_ALR_87001561	IMG Activity: SIMG_CFMENUOLMEOMGO
S_ALR_87001562	IMG Activity: SIMG_CFMENUOLMEOMEG
S_ALR_87001563	IMG Activity: SIMG_CFMENUOLMEOMFG
S_ALR_87001564	IMG Activity: SIMG_CFMENUOPP1OM0E
S_ALR_87001565	IMG Activity: SIMG_CFMENUOLMEOMFF
S_ALR_87001566	IMG Activity: SIMG_CFMENUOLMEOMFE
S_ALR_87001567	IMG Activity: SIMG_CFMENUOLMEOMFD
S_ALR_87001568	IMG Activity: SIMG_OLMEANFRAGESE71
S_ALR_87001569	IMG Activity: SIMG_CFMENUOLME0001
S_ALR_87001570	IMG Activity: SIMG_CFMENUOLMEOMH5
S_ALR_87001571	IMG Activity: SIMG_CMMENUOLSDVI67
S_ALR_87001572	IMG Activity: SIMG_CMMENUOLSDVI66
S_ALR_87001573	IMG Activity: SIMG_CMMENUOLSDVI65
S_ALR_87001574	IMG Activity: SIMG_CFMENUOLSDVE78
S_ALR_87001575	IMG Activity: SIMG_CFMENUOLSDVE75
S_ALR_87001576	IMG Activity: SIMG_CFMENUOLSDVE77
S_ALR_87001577	IMG Activity: SIMG_CFMENUOLMEOMH4
S_ALR_87001578	IMG Activity: SIMG_CFMENUOLMEOMQX
S_ALR_87001579	IMG Activity: SIMG_CFMENUOLMEOXK1
S_ALR_87001580	IMG Activity: SIMG_CFMENUOLMEOMG0
S_ALR_87001581	IMG Activity: SIMG_CFMENUOLMEOME9
S_ALR_87001582	IMG Activity: SIMG_CMMENUOLSDVI69
S_ALR_87001583	IMG Activity: SIMG_CFMENUOLSDVI31
S_ALR_87001584	IMG Activity: SIMG_CFMENUOLSDVE79
S_ALR_87001585	IMG Activity: SIMG_CFMENUOLSDVE76
S_ALR_87001586	IMG Activity: SIMG_CFMENUOLSDVE49
S_ALR_87001587	IMG Activity: SIMG_CFMENUOLSDVE48
S_ALR_87001588	IMG Activity: SIMG_CFMENUOLSDVI54
S_ALR_87001589	IMG Activity: SIMG_CFMENUOLSDVI89
S_ALR_87001590	IMG Activity: SIMG_CFMENUOLSDVI35
S_ALR_87001591	IMG Activity: SIMG_CFMENUOLSDVI34
S_ALR_87001592	IMG Activity: SIMG_CFMENUOLSDVI33
S_ALR_87001593	IMG Activity: SIMG_CFMENUOLSDVI32
S_ALR_87001594	IMG Activity: SIMG_CFMENUOLSDVI37
S_ALR_87001595	IMG Activity: OLIA_ODP2
S_ALR_87001596	IMG Activity: SIMG_CFMENUOLSDVI46
S_ALR_87001597	IMG Activity: SIMG_CFMENUOLSDVI48
S_ALR_87001598	IMG Activity: SIMG_CFMENUOLSDVI50
S_ALR_87001599	IMG Activity: SIMG_CFMENUOLSDVI47
S_ALR_87001600	IMG Activity: SIMG_CFMENUOLSDVI45
S_ALR_87001601	IMG Activity: SIMG_CFMENUOLSDVI61
S_ALR_87001602	IMG Activity: SIMG_CFMENUOLSDVI36
S_ALR_87001603	IMG Activity: OLIA_ODP3

S_ALR_87001604	IMG Activity: SIMG_CFMENUOLSDVI70
S_ALR_87001605	IMG Activity: OLIA_ODP4
S_ALR_87001606	IMG Activity: SIMG_CFMENUOLSDOVI95
S_ALR_87001607	IMG Activity: SIMG_CFMENUOLSDOVI76
S_ALR_87001608	IMG Activity: SIMG_CFMENUOLSDOVE3
S_ALR_87001609	IMG Activity: SIMG_CFMENUOLSDOVE2
S_ALR_87001610	IMG Activity: SIMG_CFMENUOLSDVX54
S_ALR_87001611	IMG Activity: SIMG_CFMENUOLSDVX58
S_ALR_87001612	IMG Activity: SIMG_CFMENUOLSDVX56
S_ALR_87001613	IMG Activity: SIMG_CFMENUOLSDVX52
S_ALR_87001614	IMG Activity: SIMG_CFMENUOLSDVX49
S_ALR_87001615	IMG Activity: SIMG_CFMENUOLSDVX57
S_ALR_87001616	IMG Activity: SIMG_CFMENUOLSDVE50
S_ALR_87001617	IMG Activity: SIMG_CFMENUOLSDSTUBE
S_ALR_87001618	IMG Activity: SIMG_CFMENUOLSDOOVA7
S_ALR_87001619	IMG Activity: SIMG_CFMENUOLSDOVX
S_ALR_87001620	IMG Activity: SIMG_CFMENUOLSDVI52
S_ALR_87001621	IMG Activity: SIMG_CFMENUOLSDVX53
S_ALR_87001622	IMG Activity: SIMG_CFMENUOLSDVOTX
S_ALR_87001623	IMG Activity: SIMG_CFMENUOLSDSE71
S_ALR_87001624	IMG Activity: SIMG_CFMENUOLSDVI38
S_ALR_87001625	IMG Activity: SIMG_CFMENUOLSDVI42
S_ALR_87001626	IMG Activity: SIMG_CFMENUOLSDVI41
S_ALR_87001627	IMG Activity: SIMG_CFMENUOLSDVI40
S_ALR_87001628	IMG Activity: SIMG_CFMENUOLSDVI39
S_ALR_87001629	IMG Activity: SIMG_CFMENUOLSDVX51
S_ALR_87001630	IMG Activity: SIMG_CFMENUOLSDVX50
S_ALR_87001631	IMG Activity: SIMG_CMMENUOLSDVI28
S_ALR_87001632	IMG Activity: SIMG_CMMENUOLSDVI56
S_ALR_87001633	IMG Activity: SIMG_CMMENUOLSDVED1
S_ALR_87001634	IMG Activity: SIMG_CFMENUOLSDV/83
S_ALR_87001635	IMG Activity: SIMG_CFMENUOLMEWE20
S_ALR_87001636	IMG Activity: SIMG_CFMENUOLMEOMGK
S_ALR_87001637	IMG Activity: SIMG_CFMENUOLMEOMEM
S_ALR_87001638	IMG Activity: SIMG_CFMENUOLMEOMZ9
S_ALR_87001639	IMG Activity: SIMG_CFMENUOLMEOMZ8
S_ALR_87001640	IMG Activity: SIMG_CFMENUOLMEOMZ7
S_ALR_87001641	IMG Activity: SIMG_CFMENUOLMEOMZ6
S_ALR_87001642	IMG Activity: SIMG_CFMENUOLMEOMHS
S_ALR_87001643	IMG Activity: SIMG_CFMENUOLMEOMFJ
S_ALR_87001644	IMG Activity: SIMG_CFMENUOLMEOMGY
S_ALR_87001645	IMG Activity: SIMG_CFMENUOLMEOMGX
S_ALR_87001646	IMG Activity: SIMG_CFMENUOLME8KEG
S_ALR_87001647	IMG Activity: SIMG_CFMENUOLMEOMRE
S_ALR_87001648	IMG Activity: SIMG_CFMENUOLMEOMZ5
S_ALR_87001649	IMG Activity: W_ZF_ST_0332
S_ALR_87001650	IMG Activity: W_ZF_ST_0311
S_ALR_87001651	IMG Activity: SIMGOLMEVNE2
S_ALR_87001652	IMG Activity: SIMGOLMEVNE4
S_ALR_87001653	IMG Activity: W_DF_LT_0820
S_ALR_87001654	IMG Activity: W_DF_LT_0810
S_ALR_87001655	IMG Activity: ORFA_SONDER_KONTEN
S_ALR_87001656	IMG Activity: SIMG_CFMENUORFAOAGL
S_ALR_87001657	IMG Activity: SIMG_CFMENUORFAINF9

S_ALR_87001658	IMG Activity: ORFA_VORSTEUER
S_ALR_87001659	IMG Activity: SIMG_CFMENUORFAOAEA
S_ALR_87001660	IMG Activity: ORFA_AS91
S_ALR_87001661	IMG Activity: SIMG_CFMENUORFAOA13
S_ALR_87001662	IMG Activity: SIMG_CFMENUORFAALT9
S_ALR_87001663	IMG Activity: SIMG_CFMENUORFAOABL
S_ALR_87001664	IMG Activity: ORFA_MIT_BEREICH
S_ALR_87001665	IMG Activity: SIMG_CFMENUORFAOAK5
S_ALR_87001666	IMG Activity: SIMG_CFMENUORFAOAB1
S_ALR_87001667	IMG Activity: SIMG_CFMENUORFAOAP1
S_ALR_87001668	IMG Activity: SIMG_CFMENUORFAOASV
S_ALR_87001669	IMG Activity: SIMG_CFMENUORFAOABP
S_ALR_87001670	IMG Activity: SIMG_CFMENUORFAOAK1
S_ALR_87001671	IMG Activity: ORFA_HAUPT_KONT
S_ALR_87001672	IMG Activity: ORFA_BESTANLKL
S_ALR_87001673	IMG Activity: ORFA_S_KLASSEN
S_ALR_87001674	IMG Activity: SIMG_CFMENUORFBOBKR
S_ALR_87001675	IMG Activity: SIMG_CFMENUOLSDOVE8
S_ALR_87001676	IMG Activity: SIMG_CFMENUORFBOBKT
S_ALR_87001677	IMG Activity: SIMG_CFMENUORFBOBK9
S_ALR_87001678	IMG Activity: SIMG_CFMENUOLSDOVE1
S_ALR_87001679	IMG Activity: SIMG_CFMENUORFBOB80
S_ALR_87001680	IMG Activity: SIMG_CFMENUOLSDXATR
S_ALR_87001681	IMG Activity: SIMG_CFORFBCHKKOAZ
S_ALR_87001682	IMG Activity: SIMG_CFMENUOLSDXAAM
S_ALR_87001683	IMG Activity: SIMG_CFORFBCHKBOPZE
S_ALR_87001684	IMG Activity: SIMG_CFMENUOLMEOMGJ
S_ALR_87001685	IMG Activity: SIMG_CFMENUORFBOBYM
S_ALR_87001686	IMG Activity: SIMG_CFMENUOLSDXAKK
S_ALR_87001687	IMG Activity: SIMG_ORFB_FDI1_2_3
S_ALR_87001688	IMG Activity: SIMG_CFMENUOLSDXDN1
S_ALR_87001689	IMG Activity: SIMG_XXMENUOLML1103
S_ALR_87001690	IMG Activity: SIMG_CFMENUOLSDGENE
S_ALR_87001691	IMG Activity: SIMG_ORFB_FDIZ
S_ALR_87001692	IMG Activity: SIMG_CFMENUOLMROBCD
S_ALR_87001693	IMG Activity: SIMG_XXMENUOLML1102
S_ALR_87001694	IMG Activity: SIMG_CFMENUOLSDOBXX
S_ALR_87001695	IMG Activity: SIMG_ORFB_FDIR
S_ALR_87001696	IMG Activity: COPA1
S_ALR_87001697	IMG Activity: SIMG_CFMENUOLMWOMW5W
S_ALR_87001698	IMG Activity: SIMG_CFMENUOLMROBCA
S_ALR_87001699	IMG Activity: SIMG_ORFB_FDIP
S_ALR_87001700	IMG Activity: SIMG_CFMENUOLSDOB49
S_ALR_87001701	IMG Activity: SIMG_OLMSRVML100
S_ALR_87001702	IMG Activity: SIMG_CFMENUOLPAALE
S_ALR_87001703	IMG Activity: SIMG_CFMENUOLMSOMSE
S_ALR_87001704	IMG Activity : SIMG_CFMENUCX01_CI18
S_ALR_87001705	IMG Activity: SIMG_CFMENUOLMROMRY
S_ALR_87001706	IMG Activity: SIMG_CFMENUOLSDOB31
S_ALR_87001707	IMG Activity: SIMG_CMMENUOLME0011
S_ALR_87001708	IMG Activity: SIMG_ORFB_FDI4_5_6
S_ALR_87001709	IMG Activity: SIMG_CFMENUOLSDXAEU
S_ALR_87001710	IMG Activity: SIMG_CFMENUOLPAMC8A
S_ALR_87001711	IMG Activity : SIMG_CFMENUCX01_3525

S_ALR_87001712	IMG Activity: SIMG_CFMENUOLMRM802
S_ALR_87001713	IMG Activity: SIMG_OLMEML99
S_ALR_87001714	IMG Activity: SIMG_CFMENUOLMSOMSG
S_ALR_87001715	IMG Activity: SIMG_CFMENUOLMSOMSZ
S_ALR_87001716	IMG Activity: SIMG_CFMENUOLMRM808
S_ALR_87001717	IMG-Aktivität: SIMG_CFMENUCX01_RC01
S_ALR_87001718	IMG Activity: SIMG_XXMENUOLML37
S_ALR_87001719	IMG Activity: SIMG_CFMENUOLPAMC8H
S_ALR_87001720	IMG Activity: SIMG_CFMENUOLMSOMFK
S_ALR_87001721	IMG Activity: SIMG_NOTIERUNGSART
S_ALR_87001722	IMG Activity: SIMG_CFORFBCMODINFDB
S_ALR_87001723	IMG Activity: SIMG_OLMEML89
S_ALR_87001724	IMG Activity: SIMG_CFMENUOLMWOMW8N
S_ALR_87001725	IMG Activity: W_WLFA_0011
S_ALR_87001726	IMG Activity: SIMG_CFMENUOLMSSXDA
S_ALR_87001727	(junk)
S_ALR_87001728	IMG Activity: OLPA_MC80
S_ALR_87001729	IMG Activity: SIMG_CFMENUOLMSOMSX
S_ALR_87001730	IMG Activity: SIMG_DATAPROVIDER
S_ALR_87001731	IMG Activity: SIMG_CFMENUORFBOBDF
S_ALR_87001732	IMG Activity: SIMG_CFMENUOLMLOMNU
S_ALR_87001733	IMG Activity: SIMG_CFMENUOLMEML60
S_ALR_87001734	IMG Activity: SIMG_CFMENUOLMSOMSM
S_ALR_87001735	IMG Activity: DRP4
S_ALR_87001736	IMG Activity: W_WLFA_0001
S_ALR_87001737	IMG Activity: SIMG_CFMENUOLMWOMW7N
S_ALR_87001738	(junk)
S_ALR_87001739	IMG Activity: SIMG_CFMENUOLMSOMSJ
S_ALR_87001740	IMG Activity: SIMG_CFMENUOLPAMP91
S_ALR_87001741	IMG Activity: SIMG_NOTIERUNGSDATEN
S_ALR_87001742	IMG Activity: SIMG_CFMENUORFBOBRK
S_ALR_87001743	IMG Activity: SIMG_CFFIBATPRQPB
S_ALR_87001744	IMG Activity: SIMG_EURO_RFEWUD0P
S_ALR_87001745	IMG Activity: SIMGOLMEOMQM
S_ALR_87001746	IMG Activity: SIMG_XXMENUOLML38
S_ALR_87001747	IMG Activity: SIMG_CFMENUOLMSOMIC
S_ALR_87001748	IMG Activity: W_WLFA_0015
S_ALR_87001749	IMG Activity: SIMG_CFMENUOLMWOMWV
S_ALR_87001750	(junk)
S_ALR_87001751	IMG Activity: SIMG_CFMENUOLSDOMSI
S_ALR_87001752	IMG Activity: SIMG_ORFB_FDIY
S_ALR_87001753	IMG Activity: SIMG_CFMENUOLPAACTI
S_ALR_87001754	IMG Activity: OLMEML94
S_ALR_87001755	IMG Activity: SIMG_CFFIBAT018V
S_ALR_87001756	IMG Activity: DRP5
S_ALR_87001757	IMG Activity: SIMG_XXMENUOLML35
S_ALR_87001758	IMG Activity: SIMG_CFMENUOLMSMMDE
S_ALR_87001759	IMG Activity: SIMG_CFMENUOLMWOMW6
S_ALR_87001760	IMG Activity: SIMG_EURO_NACHMONI
S_ALR_87001761	IMG Activity: SIMG_ORFB_FDIT
S_ALR_87001762	IMG Activity: SIMG_CFMENUOLMRKOND
S_ALR_87001763	IMG Activity: SIMG_CFMENUOLPACOPY
S_ALR_87001764	(junk)
S_ALR_87001765	IMG Activity: SIMG_CFMENUOLMEOMFI

S_ALR_87001766	IMG Activity: SIMG_CFMENUOLSDOB20
S_ALR_87001767	IMG Activity: SIMGOLMEML98
S_ALR_87001768	IMG Activity: SIMG_CFMENUOLMSMMPI
S_ALR_87001769	IMG Activity: SIMG_XXMENUOLML34
S_ALR_87001770	IMG Activity: SIMG_CFMENUOLMWOMW6W
S_ALR_87001771	IMG Activity: OLMK009
S_ALR_87001772	IMG Activity: SIMG_CFMENUOLPAKEYF
S_ALR_87001773	IMG Activity: SIMG_CFMENUOLMROMRF
S_ALR_87001774	IMG Activity: DRP_MC9V
S_ALR_87001775	IMG Activity: SIMG_ORFB_FDIV
S_ALR_87001776	IMG Activity: SIMG_CFMENUOLMSOMSD
S_ALR_87001777	IMG Activity: SIMG_ORFB_FDIX
S_ALR_87001778	IMG Activity: SIMG_CFFIBAF8BG
S_ALR_87001779	(junk)
S_ALR_87001780	IMG Activity: SIMG_CFMENUOLMWOMW5
S_ALR_87001781	IMG Activity: SIMG_XXMENUOLSDDT
S_ALR_87001782	IMG Activity: SIMG_CFMENUOLMEOMHR
S_ALR_87001783	IMG Activity: SIMG_CFMENUOLPATRAN
S_ALR_87001784	IMG Activity: SIMG_XXMENUOLML33
S_ALR_87001785	IMG Activity: SIMG_CFMENUOLMROMRG
S_ALR_87001786	IMG Activity: DRP6
S_ALR_87001787	IMG Activity: SIMG_ORFB_FDIQ
S_ALR_87001788	(junk)
S_ALR_87001789	IMG Activity: SIMG_EURO_HINTJOB02
S_ALR_87001790	IMG Activity: SIMG_CFMENUOLMLOMNZ
S_ALR_87001791	IMG Activity: SIMG_CFMENUOLMRMRO2
S_ALR_87001792	IMG Activity: OLPA_EXIT5
S_ALR_87001793	IMG Activity: SIMG_CFMENUOLMWOMX4Z
S_ALR_87001794	IMG Activity: SIMG_CFMENUOLMSOMT3
S_ALR_87001795	IMG Activity: OLPA_EXIT6
S_ALR_87001796	IMG Activity: SIMG_CFMENUOLMEOMCI
S_ALR_87001797	IMG Activity: DRP1
S_ALR_87001798	IMG Activity: SIMG_CFMENUOLMSDT
S_ALR_87001799	(junk)
S_ALR_87001800	IMG Activity: SIMG_XXMENUOLML1122
S_ALR_87001801	IMG Activity: OLPA_EXIT7
S_ALR_87001802	IMG Activity: SIMG_ORFB_FDIO
S_ALR_87001803	(junk)
S_ALR_87001804	IMG Activity: SIMG_CFMENUOLMROMRU
S_ALR_87001805	IMG Activity: SIMG_CFMENUOLMSOMSR
S_ALR_87001806	IMG Activity: SIMG_CFMENUOLMWOMWJ
S_ALR_87001807	IMG Activity: SIMGOLMEOMTE
S_ALR_87001808	IMG Activity: DRP2
S_ALR_87001809	IMG Activity: OLMK008
S_ALR_87001810	IMG Activity: SIMG_EURO_FREIGEBEN
S_ALR_87001811	IMG Activity: SIMG_XXMENUOLML1121
S_ALR_87001812	IMG Activity: SIMG_CFMENUOLSDVI96
S_ALR_87001813	(junk)
S_ALR_87001814	IMG Activity: SIMG_CFMENUOLPAOMI6
S_ALR_87001815	IMG Activity: SIMG_CFMENUORFBOBYU
S_ALR_87001816	IMG Activity: SIMG_CFMENUOLMSOMS9
S_ALR_87001817	IMG Activity: SIMG_CFMENUOLMROMR5
S_ALR_87001818	IMG Activity: SIMG_CFMENUOLMWOMWI
S_ALR_87001819	IMG Activity: SIMG_CFMENUOLSDOBD2

S_ALR_87001820	IMG Activity: SIMGOLMEM/77
S_ALR_87001821	IMG Activity: SIMG_XXMENUOLML1111
S_ALR_87001822	IMG Activity: DRP3
S_ALR_87001823	IMG Activity: SIMG_CFMENUOLPAOMDM
S_ALR_87001824	(junk)
S_ALR_87001825	IMG Activity: SIMG_XXMENUOLSDSL2
S_ALR_87001826	IMG Activity: SIMG_CFMENUORFBOBYT
S_ALR_87001827	IMG Activity: SIMG_CFMENUOLMSOMS3
S_ALR_87001828	IMG Activity: SIMG_CFMENUOLMROMR3
S_ALR_87001829	IMG Activity: SIMG_CFMENUOLMWOMW7R
S_ALR_87001830	IMG Activity: SIMG_CFMENUOLSDZAV
S_ALR_87001831	IMG Activity: SIMG_XXMENUOLML1110
S_ALR_87001832	IMG Activity: SIMG_EURO_RFFMRC04
S_ALR_87001833	IMG Activity: SIMGOLMEM/75
S_ALR_87001834	IMG Activity: SIMG_CFFIBAT042EA
S_ALR_87001835	IMG Activity: SIMG_CFMENUOLSDVI49
S_ALR_87001836	(junk)
S_ALR_87001837	IMG Activity: SIMG_CFORFBTFE19DK
S_ALR_87001838	IMG Activity: SIMG_CFMENUOLPAMC79
S_ALR_87001839	IMG Activity: SIMG_XXMENUOLSDS1A
S_ALR_87001840	IMG Activity: SIMG_CFMENUOLMSOMSA
S_ALR_87001841	IMG Activity: SIMG_CFMENUOLMRSE71
S_ALR_87001842	IMG Activity: SIMG_CFMENUOLMWOMW8R
S_ALR_87001843	IMG Activity: SIMG_XXMENUOLML1108
S_ALR_87001844	IMG Activity: SIMG_XXMENUOLSDS1B
S_ALR_87001845	IMG Activity: SIMGOLMEM/73
S_ALR_87001846	IMG Activity: SIMG_EURO_RBPEWU1M
S_ALR_87001847	IMG Activity: SIMG_CFMENUOLSDVI29
S_ALR_87001848	(junk)
S_ALR_87001849	IMG Activity: SIMG_CFMENUOLPAEXIT1
S_ALR_87001850	IMG Activity: SIMG_CFORFBTFE18DK
S_ALR_87001851	IMG Activity: SIMG_XXMENUOLSDS1C
S_ALR_87001852	IMG Activity: SIMG_CFMENUOLMSOMSH
S_ALR_87001853	IMG Activity: SIMG_CFMENUOLMROMRV
S_ALR_87001854	IMG Activity: SIMG_CFMENUOLMWOMWX
S_ALR_87001855	IMG Activity: SIMG_XXMENUOLSDS1D
S_ALR_87001856	IMG Activity: SIMG_XXMENUOLML1107
S_ALR_87001857	IMG Activity: SIMGOLMEM/72
S_ALR_87001858	IMG Activity: SIMG_XXMENUOLSDSK1
S_ALR_87001859	IMG Activity: SIMG_CFMENUOLPAEXIT2
S_ALR_87001860	IMG Activity: SIMG_CFFIBAT042Y
S_ALR_87001861	(junk)
S_ALR_87001862	IMG Activity: SIMG_CFORFBTFE05DK
S_ALR_87001863	IMG Activity: W_WLFA_0016
S_ALR_87001864	IMG Activity: SIMG_CFMENUOLMSOMSS
S_ALR_87001865	IMG Activity: SIMG_CFMENUOLMWOMWE
S_ALR_87001866	IMG Activity: SIMG_XXMENUOLML1106
S_ALR_87001867	IMG Activity: SIMG_CFMENUOLMEOMHQ
S_ALR_87001868	IMG Activity: EURO_FIAA_BETR
S_ALR_87001869	(junk)
S_ALR_87001870	IMG Activity: SIMG_CFORFBTFE02DK
S_ALR_87001871	IMG Activity: SIMG_XXMENUOLMKSKX
S_ALR_87001872	IMG Activity: SIMG_CFMENUOLPAEXIT3
S_ALR_87001873	IMG Activity: W_ZF_ST_0268

S_ALR_87001874	IMG Activity: SIMG_CFMENUOLSDXATD
S_ALR_87001875	IMG Activity: SIMG_CFMENUOLMRM806
S_ALR_87001876	IMG Activity: SIMG_CFMENUOLMWOMWT
S_ALR_87001877	IMG Activity: SIMG_CFFIBAF8BH
S_ALR_87001878	IMG Activity: SIMG_XXMENUOLML1105
S_ALR_87001879	(junk)
S_ALR_87001880	IMG Activity: SIMG_OLMELERFBLSE71
S_ALR_87001881	IMG Activity: W_ZF_ST_0230
S_ALR_87001882	IMG Activity: W_WLFA_0018
S_ALR_87001883	IMG Activity: SIMG_CFMENUOLPAEXIT4
S_ALR_87001884	IMG Activity: SIMG_CFORFBTFE01DK
S_ALR_87001885	IMG Activity: J_1A_MM_INF_CLS
S_ALR_87001886	IMG Activity: EURO_FIAA_NACH1
S_ALR_87001887	IMG Activity: SIMG_XXMENUOLML1104
S_ALR_87001888	(junk)
S_ALR_87001889	IMG Activity: W_ZF_ST_0240
S_ALR_87001890	IMG Activity: SIMG_CFMENUOLPAMC7A
S_ALR_87001891	IMG Activity: SIMG_CFMENUOLMEOMY9
S_ALR_87001892	IMG Activity: W_WLFA_0021
S_ALR_87001893	IMG Activity: SIMG_CFMENUORFBFY01
S_ALR_87001894	IMG Activity: J_1AMMINF_MOVEMENT
S_ALR_87001895	IMG Activity: SIMG_CFFIBATBKDC
S_ALR_87001896	IMG Activity: W_ZF_ST_0250
S_ALR_87001897	(junk)
S_ALR_87001898	IMG Activity: W_WLFA_0019
S_ALR_87001899	IMG Activity: SIMG_CFMENUORFBOBRD
S_ALR_87001900	IMG Activity: SIMG_CFMENUOLMWOMWK
S_ALR_87001901	IMG Activity: SIMG_CFMENUOLMEOXA3
S_ALR_87001902	IMG Activity: W_ZF_ST_0264
S_ALR_87001903	IMG Activity: OLMEOMGS_4
S_ALR_87001904	IMG Activity: W_WLFA_0010
S_ALR_87001905	IMG Activity: EURO_FIAA_NACH2
S_ALR_87001906	(junk)
S_ALR_87001907	IMG Activity: SIMG_CFMENUOLPAOV7Z
S_ALR_87001908	IMG Activity: SIMG_CFORFBSQ02A
S_ALR_87001909	IMG Activity: SIMG_CFFIBATBKFK
S_ALR_87001910	IMG Activity: SIMG_CFMENUOLMWOMWG
S_ALR_87001911	IMG Activity: SIMG_CFMENUOLMEOXA2
S_ALR_87001912	IMG Activity: W_ZF_VK_0107
S_ALR_87001913	IMG Activity: W_WLFA_0020
S_ALR_87001914	IMG Activity: SIMG_CFMENUOLPAMC38
S_ALR_87001915	IMG Activity: SIMG_CFMENUOLMEOMF7
S_ALR_87001916	(junk)
S_ALR_87001917	IMG Activity: SIMG_CFMENUORFBOBR20
S_ALR_87001918	IMG Activity: SIMG_CFMENUOLMWERWE
S_ALR_87001919	IMG Activity: SIMG_EURO_RFEWA014
S_ALR_87001920	IMG Activity: SIMG_CFMENUOLMEOXA1
S_ALR_87001921	IMG Activity: W_ZF_VK_0108
S_ALR_87001922	IMG Activity: SIMG_CFMENUOLMRM810
S_ALR_87001923	(junk)
S_ALR_87001924	IMG Activity: SIMG_CFMENUOLPAMCNR
S_ALR_87001925	IMG Activity: SIMG_CFMENUORFBOBR2
S_ALR_87001926	IMG Activity: W_DF_VK_0142
S_ALR_87001927	IMG Activity: SIMG_CFMENUOLMWOMWR

S_ALR_87001928	IMG Activity: SIMG_CFMENUOFTDOT56
S_ALR_87001929	IMG Activity: SIMG_CFMENUOLMRNAKO
S_ALR_87001930	IMG Activity: SIMG_EURO_RGCEUR50
S_ALR_87001931	(junk)
S_ALR_87001932	IMG Activity: SIMG_CFMENUOLPAMC60
S_ALR_87001933	IMG Activity: SIMG_CFMENUOLMEOMKC
S_ALR_87001934	IMG Activity: SIMG_CFORFBSXDAKD
S_ALR_87001935	IMG Activity: SIMG_CFMENUOLMWOMWL
S_ALR_87001936	IMG Activity: SIMG_CFMENUOLMEACNR
S_ALR_87001937	IMG Activity: W_ZF_ST_0220
S_ALR_87001938	(junk)
S_ALR_87001939	IMG Activity: W_WLFA_0012
S_ALR_87001940	IMG Activity: SIMG_CFFIBAF8BM
S_ALR_87001941	IMG Activity: SIMG_CFMENUOLPAMC7F
S_ALR_87001942	IMG Activity: SIMG_EURO_RAIPEWU1
S_ALR_87001943	IMG Activity: SIMG_CFMENUOLMEOMV1
S_ALR_87001944	IMG Activity: SIMG_CFMENUOLMWOMW4
S_ALR_87001945	IMG Activity: W_GE_0300
S_ALR_87001946	(junk)
S_ALR_87001947	IMG Activity: W_WLFA_0008
S_ALR_87001948	IMG Activity: OLPA_MC9V
S_ALR_87001949	IMG Activity: SIMG_CFMENUOLMEOMFW
S_ALR_87001950	IMG Activity: SIMG_CFMENUOLMWOMWP
S_ALR_87001951	IMG Activity: W_ZF_ST_0350
S_ALR_87001952	(junk)
S_ALR_87001953	IMG Activity: SIMG_CFMENUOLMEOMV2
S_ALR_87001954	IMG Activity: W_WLFA_0006
S_ALR_87001955	IMG Activity: SIMG_CFORFBSXDADB
S_ALR_87001956	IMG Activity: SIMG_CFMENUOLMWOMW3
S_ALR_87001957	IMG Activity: SIMG_CFMENUOFTDOT50
S_ALR_87001958	IMG Activity: SIMG_EURO_RKAABR02
S_ALR_87001959	IMG Activity: W_ZF_ST_0266
S_ALR_87001960	IMG Activity: W_WLFA_0007
S_ALR_87001961	(junk)
S_ALR_87001962	IMG Activity: OLMEML91
S_ALR_87001963	IMG Activity: SIMG_CFMENUOLMWOMW2
S_ALR_87001964	IMG Activity: SIMG_CFMENUOLMETELP
S_ALR_87001965	IMG Activity: SIMG_CFMENUORFBOB34
S_ALR_87001966	IMG Activity: W_WLFA_0009
S_ALR_87001967	IMG Activity: SIMG_EURO_RKACOR10
S_ALR_87001968	IMG Activity: W_ZF_ST_0267
S_ALR_87001969	(junk)
S_ALR_87001970	IMG Activity: SIMG_CFMENUOLMEOMYA
S_ALR_87001971	IMG Activity: SIMG_CFMENUOLMWOMWH
S_ALR_87001972	IMG Activity: W_WLFA_0017
S_ALR_87001973	IMG Activity: SIMG_CFMENUOLMEOMEN
S_ALR_87001974	IMG Activity: SIMG_CFMENUOLPAMC96
S_ALR_87001975	IMG Activity: SIMG_CFMENUOFTDOT45
S_ALR_87001976	IMG Activity: SIMG_CFMENUORFBOB51
S_ALR_87001977	(junk)
S_ALR_87001978	IMG Activity: OLMEML90
S_ALR_87001979	IMG Activity: W_ZF_ST_0210
S_ALR_87001980	IMG Activity: SIMG_CFMENUOLPAMP90
S_ALR_87001981	IMG Activity: W_WLFA_0013

S_ALR_87001982	IMG Activity: SIMG_CFMENUOLMWOMWA
S_ALR_87001983	IMG Activity: SIMG_CFMENUOLMEOMYB
S_ALR_87001984	(junk)
S_ALR_87001985	IMG Activity: SIMG_CFMENUORFBOB02
S_ALR_87001986	IMG Activity: W_WLFA_0004
S_ALR_87001987	IMG Activity: SIMG_EURO_RKACOR19
S_ALR_87001988	IMG Activity: SIMG_CFMENUOLPAMC97
S_ALR_87001989	IMG Activity: W_ZF_ST_0211
S_ALR_87001990	IMG Activity: W_DF_LT_0370
S_ALR_87001991	(junk)
S_ALR_87001992	IMG Activity: SIMG_CFMENUOLMEOMY8
S_ALR_87001993	IMG Activity: SIMG_CFMENUOLMEOMGP
S_ALR_87001994	IMG Activity: SIMG_CFMENUORFBOB01
S_ALR_87001995	IMG Activity: W_WLFA_0005
S_ALR_87001996	IMG Activity: SIMG_CFMENUOLPAOPEB
S_ALR_87001997	IMG Activity: W_ZF_ST_0212
S_ALR_87001998	(junk)
S_ALR_87001999	IMG Activity: SIMG_CFMENUORFBOB12
S_ALR_87002000	IMG Activity: SIMG_EURO_IMCHCK05
S_ALR_87002001	IMG Activity: SIMG_CFMENUOLMR169H
S_ALR_87002002	IMG Activity: SIMG_CFMENUOLMWOMWC
S_ALR_87002003	IMG Activity: SIMG_CFMENUOFTDOT54
S_ALR_87002004	IMG Activity: SIMG_CFMENUOLMEOMRP2
S_ALR_87002005	IMG Activity: SIMG_CFMENUOLPAMC70
S_ALR_87002006	IMG Activity: SIMG_CFMENUOLMSW4EO
S_ALR_87002007	(junk)
S_ALR_87002008	IMG Activity: SIMG_CFMENUOLMROMR7
S_ALR_87002009	IMG Activity: SIMG_CFMENUOLMWOMWM
S_ALR_87002010	IMG Activity: SIMG_CFMENUORFBOBT3
S_ALR_87002011	IMG Activity: SIMG_CFMENUOFTDFX78
S_ALR_87002012	IMG Activity: SIMG_CFMENUOLMSOMT2
S_ALR_87002031	IMG Activity: SIMG_CFMENUOLSDVI45
S_ALR_87002032	IMG Activity: W_ZF_ST_0331
S_ALR_87002033	IMG Activity: W_ZF_ST_0324
S_ALR_87002034	IMG Activity: W_ZF_ST_0323
S_ALR_87002035	IMG Activity: W_ZF_ST_0322
S_ALR_87002036	IMG Activity: SIMG_CFMENUOLMEOMZ4
S_ALR_87002037	IMG Activity: SIMG_CFMENUOLMEOMZ3
S_ALR_87002038	IMG Activity: SIMG_CFMENUOLMEOMZ2
S_ALR_87002039	IMG Activity: SIMG_CFMENUOLMEOMZ1
S_ALR_87002040	IMG Activity: W_ZF_ST_0342
S_ALR_87002041	IMG Activity: W_ZF_ST_0341
S_ALR_87002042	IMG Activity: SIMG_CMMENUOLMEOMG7
S_ALR_87002043	IMG Activity: SIMG_OLME2OMFV
S_ALR_87002044	IMG Activity: SIMG_OLME2ORKSOVA
S_ALR_87002045	IMG Activity: SIMG_OLMEOLISAKTI2
S_ALR_87002046	IMG Activity: SIMG_OLMEOMQ3
S_ALR_87002047	IMG Activity: SIMG_OLMEOMQ2
S_ALR_87002048	IMG Activity: SIMG_CFMENUOLMECMOD
S_ALR_87002049	IMG Activity: SIMG_CFMENUOLMEOXW1
S_ALR_87002050	IMG Activity: SIMG_CFMENUOLMEOXW2
S_ALR_87002051	IMG Activity: SIMG_CFMENUOLMEOXW3
S_ALR_87002052	IMG Activity: SIMG_CFMENUOLMEOMET
S_ALR_87002053	IMG Activity: SIMG_CFMENUOLMEOMEI

S_ALR_87002054	IMG Activity: SIMG_OLMEOMQ1
S_ALR_87002055	IMG Activity: SIMG_OLMEOMQ4
S_ALR_87002056	IMG Activity: SIMG_OLMEOBE8
S_ALR_87002057	IMG Activity: SIMG_CFMENUOLMEOMHK
S_ALR_87002058	IMG Activity: SIMG_CFMENUOLMEOMHT
S_ALR_87002059	IMG Activity: SIMG_CFMENUOLMEXOMFJ
S_ALR_87002060	IMG Activity: SIMG_CFMENUOLMEOMFL
S_ALR_87002061	IMG Activity: SIMG_OLME1OMFV
S_ALR_87002062	IMG Activity: SIMG_OLME1ORKSOVA
S_ALR_87002063	IMG Activity: SIMG_OLMEOLISAKTI1
S_ALR_87002064	IMG Activity: SIMG_OLME1OMY6
S_ALR_87002065	IMG Activity: SIMG_OLMEOMQ6
S_ALR_87002066	IMG Activity: SIMG_OLME1OMQ5
S_ALR_87002067	IMG Activity: SIMGOLMEM/68
S_ALR_87002068	IMG Activity: SIMGOLMEM/36
S_ALR_87002069	IMG Activity: SIMGOLMEM/32
S_ALR_87002070	IMG Activity: SIMGOLMEM/40
S_ALR_87002071	IMG Activity: SIMGOLMEM/38
S_ALR_87002072	IMG Activity: SIMGOLMEOMTD
S_ALR_87002073	IMG Activity: SIMGOLMEOMTC
S_ALR_87002074	IMG Activity: SIMGOLMEOMTB
S_ALR_87002075	IMG Activity: SIMGOLMEOMTA
S_ALR_87002076	IMG Activity: SIMGOLMEVNE7
S_ALR_87002077	IMG Activity: SIMGOLMEM/42
S_ALR_87002078	IMG Activity: SIMGOLMEM/34
S_ALR_87002079	IMG Activity: SIMGOLMEVNE2
S_ALR_87002080	IMG Activity: SIMGOLMEM/64
S_ALR_87002081	IMG Activity: SIMGOLMEM/67
S_ALR_87002082	IMG Activity: SIMGOLMEM/61
S_ALR_87002083	IMG Activity: SIMGOLMEM/58
S_ALR_87002084	IMG Activity: SIMG_CFMENUOLMEEDI2
S_ALR_87002085	IMG Activity: SIMGOLMEM/30
S_ALR_87002086	IMG Activity: SIMGOLMEVNE4
S_ALR_87002087	IMG Activity: SIMGOLMEM/54
S_ALR_87002088	IMG Activity: SIMGOLMEM/52
S_ALR_87002089	IMG Activity: SIMGOLMEM/50
S_ALR_87002090	IMG Activity: SIMGOLMEM/48
S_ALR_87002091	IMG Activity: SIMG_CFMENUOLMEOMHF
S_ALR_87002092	IMG Activity: SIMG_CFMENUOLMEOMHE
S_ALR_87002093	IMG Activity: SIMG_CFMENUOLMEOMHD
S_ALR_87002094	IMG Activity: SIMG_CFMENUOLMESFT3
S_ALR_87002095	IMG Activity: SIMG_CFMENUOLMEVB(1
S_ALR_87002096	IMG Activity: SIMG_CFMENUOLMEOMKO
S_ALR_87002097	IMG Activity: SIMG_CMMENUOLMEABRE2
S_ALR_87002098	IMG Activity: SIMG_CMMENUOLMEABREC
S_ALR_87002099	IMG Activity: SIMG_CFMENUOLMEOVBA
S_ALR_87002100	IMG Activity: SIMG_CFMENUOLME_KONT
S_ALR_87002101	IMG Activity: SIMG_CFMENUOLMEKONDT
S_ALR_87002102	IMG Activity: SIMG_CFMENUOLMEOMHG
S_ALR_87002103	IMG Activity: SIMG_CFMENUOLMEOMKN
S_ALR_87002104	IMG Activity: SIMG_CFMENUOLMEOMGL
S_ALR_87002105	IMG Activity: SIMG_CFMENUOLMEOMGU
S_ALR_87002106	IMG Activity: SIMG_CFMENUOLMEOMGI
S_ALR_87002107	IMG Activity: SIMG_CFMENUOLMEOMGC

S_ALR_87002108	IMG Activity: SIMG_CFMENUOLMEOMGF
S_ALR_87002109	IMG Activity: SIMGOLMEVNE5
S_ALR_87002110	IMG Activity: SIMG_CFMENUOLMEOMKL
S_ALR_87002111	IMG Activity: SIMG_CFMENUOLMEOMKM
S_ALR_87002112	IMG Activity: SIMG_CFMENUOLMEOMKK
S_ALR_87002113	IMG Activity: SIMG_CFMENUOLMEOMQL
S_ALR_87002114	IMG Activity: SIMG_CFMENUOLMEOMKD
S_ALR_87002115	IMG Activity: SIMG_CFMENUOLMEOMKH
S_ALR_87002116	IMG Activity: SIMG_CFMENUOLSDVE47
S_ALR_87002117	IMG Activity: SIMG_CMMENUOLMETORP
S_ALR_87002118	IMG Activity: W_ZF_ST_0125
S_ALR_87002119	IMG Activity: W_ZF_ST_0126
S_ALR_87002120	IMG Activity: W_ZF_ST_0127
S_ALR_87002121	IMG Activity: SIMG_OLMEOM8R
S_ALR_87002122	IMG Activity: W_DF_LT_0802
S_ALR_87002123	IMG Activity: W_ZF_ST_0123
S_ALR_87002124	IMG Activity: SIMG_CMMENUOLMETORT
S_ALR_87002125	IMG Activity: SIMG_CMMENUOLMETORZ
S_ALR_87002126	IMG Activity: W_ZF_ST_0124
S_ALR_87002127	IMG Activity: SIMG_OLMEOM7R
S_ALR_87002128	IMG Activity: SIMG_OLMEOM2R
S_ALR_87002129	IMG Activity: SIMG_OLMEOM1R
S_ALR_87002130	IMG Activity: W_ZF_ST_0101
S_ALR_87002131	IMG Activity: SIMG_CFMENUOLMEOME4
S_ALR_87002132	IMG Activity: SIMG_CFMENUOLMEOMRP
S_ALR_87002133	IMG Activity: SIMG_OLMEOM6R
S_ALR_87002134	IMG Activity: SIMG_OLMEOM5R
S_ALR_87002135	IMG Activity: SIMG_OLMEOM4R
S_ALR_87002136	IMG Activity: W_ZF_ST_0102
S_ALR_87002137	IMG Activity: SIMG_OLMEOM3R
S_ALR_87002138	IMG Activity: W_DF_LT_0803
S_ALR_87002139	IMG Activity: W_ZE_EK_0240
S_ALR_87002140	IMG Activity: W_ZE_EK_0210
S_ALR_87002141	IMG Activity: W_ZE_EK_0212
S_ALR_87002142	IMG Activity: W_ZE_EK_0211
S_ALR_87002143	IMG Activity: W_ZF_ST_0113
S_ALR_87002144	IMG Activity: OLMEOMGS_3
S_ALR_87002145	IMG Activity: SIMG_CFMENUOLMEOMEF
S_ALR_87002146	IMG Activity: SIMG_CFMENUOLMEOMY6
S_ALR_87002147	IMG Activity: W_ZE_EK_0220
S_ALR_87002148	IMG Activity: W_ZE_EK_0250
S_ALR_87002149	IMG Activity: W_ZF_ST_0114
S_ALR_87002150	IMG Activity: W_DF_EK_0112
S_ALR_87002152	IMG Activity: W_ZF_ST_0122
S_ALR_87002153	IMG Activity: W_DF_EK_0111
S_ALR_87002154	IMG Activity: W_DF_EK_0110
S_ALR_87002155	IMG Activity: W_ZF_ST_0115
S_ALR_87002156	IMG Activity: W_DF_LT_0820
S_ALR_87002157	IMG Activity: W_DF_LT_0810
S_ALR_87002158	IMG Activity: W_ZE_EK_0230
S_ALR_87002159	IMG Activity: SIMG_CFMENUOLMEOMY7
S_ALR_87002160	IMG Activity: SIMG_CFMENUOLMEOMEL
S_ALR_87002161	IMG Activity: SIMG_CFMENUOLMEOMEE
S_ALR_87002162	IMG Activity: SIMG_CFMENUOLMEOMES

S_ALR_87002163	IMG Activity: SIMG_CFMENUOLMEOMHP
S_ALR_87002164	IMG Activity: SIMG_CFMENUOLMEOMF1
S_ALR_87002165	IMG Activity: OLMEOME6
S_ALR_87002166	IMG Activity: SIMG_CFMENUOLMEOMFY
S_ALR_87002167	IMG Activity: SIMG_CFMENUOLMEOMEW
S_ALR_87002168	IMG Activity: SIMG_CFMENUOLMEOMEB
S_ALR_87002169	IMG Activity: SIMG_CFMENUOLMETEAP
S_ALR_87002170	IMG Activity: SIMG_CFMENUOLMEOMEQ
S_ALR_87002171	IMG Activity: SIMG_CFMENUOLMEOME5
S_ALR_87002172	IMG Activity: SIMG_CFMENUOLMEOMEP
S_ALR_87002173	IMG Activity: SIMG_CFMENUOLMEOMHO
S_ALR_87002174	IMG Activity: SIMG_CFMENUOLMEOMFT
S_ALR_87002175	IMG Activity: SIMG_CFMENUOLMEOMHL
S_ALR_87002176	IMG Activity: SIMG_CFMENUOLMEOME8
S_ALR_87002177	IMG Activity: SIMG_CFOLMEOMGS_1
S_ALR_87002178	IMG Activity: SIMG_CFMENUOLMEOMEA
S_ALR_87002179	IMG Activity: OLMEOMGQ
S_ALR_87002180	IMG Activity: SIMG_CFMENUOLMEOMEY
S_ALR_87002181	IMG Activity: SIMG_CFMENUOLMETEFP
S_ALR_87002182	IMG Activity: SIMG_CFMENUOLMEOMFV
S_ALR_87002183	IMG Activity: W_OE_ZG_WL_0310
S_ALR_87002184	IMG Activity: SIMG_CFMENUOLMEOMF4
S_ALR_87002185	IMG Activity: SIMG_CFMENUOLMEOM9R
S_ALR_87002186	IMG Activity: SIMG_CFMENUOLMEOMZB
S_ALR_87002187	IMG Activity: SIMG_CFMENUOLMEOMGM
S_ALR_87002188	IMG Activity: W_OE_EG_WL_0330
S_ALR_87002189	IMG Activity: SIMG_CFMENUOLMEOMGN
S_ALR_87002190	IMG Activity: OLMEOMGS_2
S_ALR_87002191	IMG Activity: SIMG_CFMENUOLMEOMHM
S_ALR_87002192	IMG Activity: SIMG_CFMENUOLMEOMGR
S_ALR_87002193	IMG Activity: SIMG_CFMENUOLMEOMEX
S_ALR_87002194	IMG Activity: SIMG_CFMENUOLMEOMFU
S_ALR_87002195	IMG Activity: SIMG_CFMENUOLMEOMF2
S_ALR_87002196	IMG Activity: SIMG_CFMENUOLMEOMEU
S_ALR_87002197	IMG Activity: SIMG_CFMENUOLMEOMEC
S_ALR_87002198	IMG Activity: SIMG_CFMENUOLMEOMEO
S_ALR_87002199	IMG Activity: SIMG_CFMENUOLMEOMRO
S_ALR_87002200	IMG Activity: SIMG_CFMENUOLMEOME1
S_ALR_87002201	IMG Activity: SIMG_CFMENUOLMEOMPN
S_ALR_87002202	IMG Activity: SIMG_CFMENUOLMEOMERA
S_ALR_87002203	IMG Activity: SIMG_CFMENUOLMEOMER0
S_ALR_87002204	IMG Activity: SIMG_CFMENUOLMEOMER9
S_ALR_87002205	IMG Activity: SIMG_CFMENUOLMEOMEK
S_ALR_87002206	IMG Activity: SIMG_CFMENUOLSDXEIP
S_ALR_87002207	IMG Activity: SIMG_CFMENUOLMEVDF1
S_ALR_87002208	IMG Activity: SIMG_CFMENUOLMEOMG9
S_ALR_87002209	IMG Activity: SIMG_CFMENUOLMEOMFQ
S_ALR_87002210	IMG Activity: SIMG_CFMENUOLMEOMG8
S_ALR_87002211	IMG Activity: SIMG_CFMENUOLMEOMER2
S_ALR_87002212	IMG Activity: SIMG_CFMENUOLMEOMER1
S_ALR_87002213	IMG Activity: SIMG_CFMENUOLMEOAMP
S_ALR_87002214	IMG Activity: SIMG_CFMENUOLMEOMQW
S_ALR_87002215	IMG Activity: SIMG_CFMENUOLMEOMF0
S_ALR_87002216	IMG Activity: SIMG_CFMENUOLMEOMER3

S_ALR_87002217	IMG Activity: SIMG_CFMENUOLMEOMER8
S_ALR_87002218	IMG Activity: SIMG_CFMENUOLMEOMER7
S_ALR_87002219	IMG Activity: SIMG_CFMENUOLMEOMER6
S_ALR_87002220	IMG Activity: SIMG_CFMENUOLMEOMER5
S_ALR_87002221	IMG Activity: SIMG_CFMENUOLMEOMER4
S_ALR_87002222	IMG Activity: SIMG_CFMENUOLSDVI43
S_ALR_87002223	IMG Activity: SIMG_CFMENUOLSDVI68
S_ALR_87002224	IMG Activity: SIMG_CFMENUOLSDVI78
S_ALR_87002225	IMG Activity: SIMG_CFMENUOLMEOME0
S_ALR_87002226	IMG Activity: SIMG_CFMENUOLSDOMGT
S_ALR_87002227	IMG Activity: SIMG_CFMENUOLSDVI44
S_ALR_87002228	IMG Activity: SIMG_CFMENUOLSDOVE6
S_ALR_87002229	IMG Activity: SIMG_CFMENUOLSDOVE5
S_ALR_87002230	IMG Activity: SIMG_CFMENUOLSDOVE8
S_ALR_87002231	IMG Activity: SIMG_CFMENUOLSDOVE1
S_ALR_87002232	IMG Activity: SIMG_CFMENUOLSDXATR
S_ALR_87002233	IMG Activity: SIMG_CFMENUOLSDXAAM
S_ALR_87002234	IMG Activity: SIMG_CFMENUOLMEOMGJ
S_ALR_87002235	IMG Activity: SIMG_CFMENUOLSDXAKK
S_ALR_87002236	IMG Activity: SIMG_CFMENUOLSDGENE
S_ALR_87002237	IMG Activity: SIMG_CFMENUOLSDXAEU
S_ALR_87002238	IMG Activity: SIMG_CFMENUOLMEOMFI
S_ALR_87002239	IMG Activity: SIMG_CFMENUOLSDVI96
S_ALR_87002240	IMG Activity: SIMG_CFMENUOLSDVI49
S_ALR_87002241	IMG Activity: SIMG_CFMENUOLSDVI29
S_ALR_87002242	IMG Activity: SIMG_CFMENUOLSDXATD
S_ALR_87002243	IMG Activity: OLMEOMGS_4
S_ALR_87002244	IMG Activity: SIMG_CFMENUOLMEOMF7
S_ALR_87002245	IMG Activity: SIMG_CFMENUOLMEOMKC
S_ALR_87002246	IMG Activity: SIMG_CFMENUOLMEOMFW
S_ALR_87002247	IMG Activity: SIMG_CFMENUOLMETELP
S_ALR_87002248	IMG Activity: SIMG_CFMENUOLMEOMEN
S_ALR_87002249	IMG Activity: SIMG_CFMENUOLMEOMGP
S_ALR_87002250	IMG Activity: SIMG_CFMENUOLMEOMRP2
S_ALR_87002251	IMG Activity: SIMG_EURO_RKEB090240
S_ALR_87002252	IMG Activity: SIMG_CFMENUOLMRSFAC1
S_ALR_87002253	IMG Activity: SIMG_CFMENUOLMWOMWD
S_ALR_87002254	(junk)
S_ALR_87002255	IMG Activity: SIMG_CFMENUOLMEOMUP
S_ALR_87002256	IMG Activity: SIMG_CFORFBT000CM
S_ALR_87002257	IMG Activity: SIMG_CFMENUOLMSOMSF
S_ALR_87002258	IMG Activity: SIMG_CFMENUOLMRSFAC2
S_ALR_87002259	IMG Activity: SIMG_CFMENUOLMWOMSK
S_ALR_87002260	IMG Activity: SIMG_CFORFBFYMN
S_ALR_87002261	IMG Activity: SIMG_CFMENUOFTDFX91
S_ALR_87002262	(junk)
S_ALR_87002263	IMG Activity: SIMG_EURO_RKACOFI2
S_ALR_87002264	IMG Activity: SIMG_CFMENUOLMSOMS5
S_ALR_87002265	IMG Activity: SIMG_CFMENUOLMWOMWN
S_ALR_87002266	IMG Activity: SIMG_CFMENUOLMROMRL
S_ALR_87002267	IMG Activity: SIMG_CFMENUOLMEOMFA
S_ALR_87002268	IMG Activity: SIMG_CFMENUOFTDFX92
S_ALR_87002269	IMG Activity: SIMG_EURO_BILABST
S_ALR_87002270	IMG Activity: SIMG_CFMENUORFBO7S3

S_ALR_87002271	(junk)
S_ALR_87002272	IMG Activity: SIMG_CFMENUOLMSOMSP
S_ALR_87002273	IMG Activity: SIMG_CFMENUOLMROMR2
S_ALR_87002274	IMG Activity: W_DF_LT_0331
S_ALR_87002275	(junk)
S_ALR_87002276	IMG Activity: SIMG_CFMENUOLMROMRW
S_ALR_87002277	IMG Activity: SIMG_CFMENUOFTDFX39
S_ALR_87002278	IMG Activity: SIMG_CFMENUOLMSOMS1
S_ALR_87002279	IMG Activity: W_DF_LT_0310
S_ALR_87002280	IMG Activity: W_ZF_ST_0112
S_ALR_87002281	IMG Activity: SIMG_CFMENUORFBO7V7
S_ALR_87002282	(junk)
S_ALR_87002283	IMG Activity: SIMG_EURO_LC1095
S_ALR_87002284	IMG Activity: SIMG_CFMENUOLMROMRMC
S_ALR_87002285	IMG Activity: W_DF_LT_0320
S_ALR_87002286	IMG Activity: SIMG_CFMENUOLMSOMS6
S_ALR_87002287	(junk)
S_ALR_87002288	IMG Activity: SIMG_CFMENUOFTDOT63
S_ALR_87002289	IMG Activity: SIMG_CFMENUOLMEOMFX
S_ALR_87002290	IMG Activity: SIMG_CFMENUORFBO7Z9
S_ALR_87002291	IMG Activity: SIMG_CFMENUOLMROMRJ
S_ALR_87002292	IMG Activity: SIMG_EURO_LC1030
S_ALR_87002293	IMG Activity: SIMG_CFMENUOLMSOMS7
S_ALR_87002294	IMG Activity: W_DF_LT_0330
S_ALR_87002295	IMG Activity: SIMG_CFMENUOLMSOMS8
S_ALR_87002296	(junk)
S_ALR_87002297	IMG Activity: SIMG_CMMENUORFF_2530
S_ALR_87002298	IMG Activity: SIMG_CFMENUOLMRERWE
S_ALR_87002299	IMG Activity: SIMG_CFMENUORFBOB39
S_ALR_87002300	IMG Activity: W_DF_LT_0340
S_ALR_87002301	IMG Activity: SIMG_CFMENUOFTDOT64
S_ALR_87002302	IMG Activity: SIMG_CFMENUOLMROMRM
S_ALR_87002303	IMG Activity: SIMG_CFMENUOLMETEKP
S_ALR_87002304	IMG Activity: SIMG_CMMENUORFF_2535
S_ALR_87002305	IMG Activity: SIMG_CFMENUOLMSOMT0
S_ALR_87002306	IMG Activity: SIMG_CFMENUOLMWOMWW
S_ALR_87002307	IMG Activity: SIMG_CFORFBAKOF
S_ALR_87002308	IMG Activity: SIMG_CFMENUOLMROMGJ
S_ALR_87002309	IMG Activity: SIMG_CFMENUOLMSOMSY
S_ALR_87002310	IMG Activity: SIMG_CFMENUORFBOB33
S_ALR_87002311	IMG Activity: SIMG_CMMENUORFF_2540
S_ALR_87002312	IMG Activity: SIMG_CFMENUOLMSOMS2
S_ALR_87002313	IMG Activity: SIMG_CFMENUOLMWOMW0
S_ALR_87002314	(junk)
S_ALR_87002315	IMG Activity: SIMG_CFMENUOLMROMR0
S_ALR_87002316	IMG Activity: SIMG_EURO_LC1060
S_ALR_87002317	IMG Activity: SIMG_CFMENUOFTDOT52
S_ALR_87002318	IMG Activity: SIMG_CMMENUORFF_3150
S_ALR_87002319	IMG Activity: SIMG_ORFB_FKI1_2_3
S_ALR_87002320	IMG Activity: SIMG_CFMENUORFCOC43
S_ALR_87002321	IMG Activity: SIMG_CFMENUOLMS134K
S_ALR_87002322	(junk)
S_ALR_87002323	IMG Activity: SIMG_EURO_LC1070
S_ALR_87002324	IMG Activity: SIMG_CFMENUOLMROMRC

S_ALR_87002325	IMG Activity: SIMG_CMMENUORFF_3140
S_ALR_87002326	IMG Activity: SIMG_CFMENUOLMWOMW9
S_ALR_87002327	IMG Activity: SIMG_CFOFTDCMODELKO
S_ALR_87002328	IMG Activity: SIMG_ORFB_FKIZ
S_ALR_87002329	IMG Activity: SIMG_CFMENUOLMEOMEZ
S_ALR_87002330	IMG Activity: SIMG_CFMENUOLMSMMNR
S_ALR_87002331	IMG Activity: SIMG_CFMENUORFCOC33
S_ALR_87002332	(junk)
S_ALR_87002333	IMG Activity: SIMG_CMMENUORFF_3210
S_ALR_87002334	IMG Activity: SIMG_EURO_LC1080
S_ALR_87002335	IMG Activity: SIMG_CFMENUOLMROMR4
S_ALR_87002336	IMG Activity: SIMG_CFMENUOLMWOMW1
S_ALR_87002337	IMG Activity: SIMG_ORFB_FKIR
S_ALR_87002338	IMG Activity: SIMG_CFMENUOLMSOMSL
S_ALR_87002339	IMG Activity: SIMG_CFMENUORFCGC25
S_ALR_87002340	IMG Activity: SIMG_CFFIBACMODELKO2
S_ALR_87002341	IMG Activity: SIMG_CFMENUOLMEOMRQ
S_ALR_87002342	(junk)
S_ALR_87002343	IMG Activity: SIMG_CMMENUORFF_3220
S_ALR_87002344	IMG Activity: SIMG_CFMENUOLMROMRB
S_ALR_87002345	IMG Activity: SIMG_EURO_LC1090
S_ALR_87002346	IMG Activity: SIMG_CFMENUOLMWOMX5
S_ALR_87002347	IMG Activity: SIMG_ORFB_FKIP
S_ALR_87002348	IMG Activity: SIMG_CFMENUOLMSOMS4
S_ALR_87002349	IMG Activity: SIMG_CFMENUORFCOC44
S_ALR_87002350	IMG Activity: SIMG_CMMENUORFF_3240
S_ALR_87002351	IMG Activity: SIMG_CFMENUOLMROMRJA
S_ALR_87002352	(junk)
S_ALR_87002353	IMG Activity: SIMG_CFMENUOLMWOMRN
S_ALR_87002354	IMG Activity: SIMG_CFMENUORFCOC41
S_ALR_87002355	IMG Activity: SIMG_CFMENUOLMSOMT4
S_ALR_87002356	IMG Activity: SIMG_CMMENUORFF_2210
S_ALR_87002357	IMG Activity: SIMG_ORFB_FKI4_5_6
S_ALR_87002358	IMG Activity: SIMG_CFMENUOLMROB56
S_ALR_87002359	IMG Activity: J_1BCODES
S_ALR_87002360	IMG Activity: SIMG_EURO_LC2150
S_ALR_87002361	IMG Activity: W_ZF_ST_0111
S_ALR_87002362	IMG Activity
S_ALR_87002363	IMG Activity: SIMG_CFMENUOLMWOMWB
S_ALR_87002364	IMG Activity: SIMG_CFMENUORFCGCRF
S_ALR_87002365	IMG Activity: SIMG_CMMENUORFF_2411
S_ALR_87002366	IMG Activity: J_1BWITH_HOLD_TRANS
S_ALR_87002367	IMG Activity: SIMG_CFMENUOLSDMATGR
S_ALR_87002368	IMG Activity: SIMG_CFORFBCMODINFKR
S_ALR_87002369	IMG Activity
S_ALR_87002370	IMG Activity: SIMG_CFMENUOLMWOMWO
S_ALR_87002371	IMG Activity: SIMG_CFMENUORFCOC47
S_ALR_87002372	IMG Activity: SIMG_CFMENUOFTDOBAY
S_ALR_87002373	IMG Activity: SIMG_CFMENUOLSDOVFVX
S_ALR_87002374	IMG Activity: SIMG_CMMENUORFF_2521
S_ALR_87002375	IMG Activity: SIMG_EURO_LC2140
S_ALR_87002376	IMG Activity: J_1BMAT_DOCU_LINES
S_ALR_87002377	IMG Activity: SIMG_OLMW_001K_EK
S_ALR_87002378	IMG Activity

S_ALR_87002379	IMG Activity: SIMG_CFMENUORFCOCBF
S_ALR_87002380	IMG Activity: SIMG_CFMENUOLMSW4ES
S_ALR_87002381	IMG Activity: SIMG_CMMENUORFF_2421
S_ALR_87002382	IMG Activity: SIMG_CFMENUOLMROMR9
S_ALR_87002383	IMG Activity: CFORFBT001CM
S_ALR_87002384	IMG Activity: SIMG_CFMENUOLMEOMED
S_ALR_87002385	IMG Activity: SIMG_OLMW_001K_EK2
S_ALR_87002386	IMG Activity: SIMG_CFMENUOLMSW4EN
S_ALR_87002387	IMG Activity
S_ALR_87002388	IMG Activity: SIMG_XXMENUOLML1019
S_ALR_87002389	IMG Activity: SIMG_FMMENUORFF_2522
S_ALR_87002390	IMG Activity: SIMG_CFMENUORFCOCBG
S_ALR_87002391	IMG Activity: SIMG_CFMENUOFTDOBAX
S_ALR_87002392	IMG Activity: SIMG_CFMENUOLMROMR6
S_ALR_87002393	IMG Activity: SIMG_CMMENUOLMWB
S_ALR_87002394	IMG Activity: SIMG_EURO_LC2160
S_ALR_87002395	IMG Activity: SIMG_ORFB_FKIY
S_ALR_87002396	IMG Activity: SIMG_CFMENUOLMEOMGB
S_ALR_87002397	IMG Activity: SIMG_CFMENUOLMSW4EM
S_ALR_87002398	IMG Activity
S_ALR_87002399	IMG Activity: SIMG_CFMENUORFCOC28
S_ALR_87002400	IMG Activity: SIMG_CFMENUORFF_2515
S_ALR_87002401	IMG Activity: SIMG_CFMENUOLMROMRZ
S_ALR_87002402	IMG Activity: SIMG_XXMENUOLML1041
S_ALR_87002403	IMG Activity: SIMG_CFMENUOFTDOBAV
S_ALR_87002404	IMG Activity: W_ZF_ST_0261
S_ALR_87002405	IMG Activity: SIMG_EURO_SL-GL_ABST
S_ALR_87002406	IMG Activity: SIMG_ORFB_FKIT
S_ALR_87002407	IMG Activity: SIMG_CFMENUOLMROMRH
S_ALR_87002408	IMG Activity
S_ALR_87002409	IMG Activity: SIMG_XXMENUOLML1040
S_ALR_87002410	IMG Activity: SIMG_CFMENUOLMEOMGZ
S_ALR_87002411	IMG Activity: SIMG_CMMENUORFF_2520
S_ALR_87002412	IMG Activity: SIMG_CFMENUORFCOC51
S_ALR_87002413	IMG Activity: SIMG_CFMENUORFBOBXG
S_ALR_87002414	IMG Activity: SIMG_CFMENUOLMSW4EQ
S_ALR_87002415	IMG Activity: SIMG_ORFB_FKIV
S_ALR_87002416	IMG Activity: SIMG_EURO_RFFMS002A
S_ALR_87002417	IMG Activity: SIMG_XXMENUOLML1039
S_ALR_87002418	IMG Activity
S_ALR_87002419	IMG Activity: SIMG_CFMENUOLMEOVTY
S_ALR_87002420	IMG Activity: SIMG_CFMENUOLMROMRI
S_ALR_87002421	IMG Activity: SIMG_CMMENUORFF_2525
S_ALR_87002422	IMG Activity: SIMG_CFMENUORFCOC29
S_ALR_87002423	IMG Activity: SIMG_CFMENUOLSDOVSV
S_ALR_87002424	IMG Activity: SIMG_XXMENUOLML1038
S_ALR_87002425	IMG Activity: SIMG_ORFB_FKIX
S_ALR_87002426	IMG Activity: SIMG_CFMENUOLMRM804
S_ALR_87002427	IMG Activity: SIMG_CMMENUORFF_3420
S_ALR_87002428	IMG Activity
S_ALR_87002429	IMG Activity: SIMG_CFMENUOLMSOMT6
S_ALR_87002430	IMG Activity: SIMG_CFMENUORFCPROD
S_ALR_87002431	IMG Activity: SIMG_CFORFBCMODBANK
S_ALR_87002432	IMG Activity: SIMG_XXMENUOLML1037

S_ALR_87002433	IMG Activity: SIMG_CFMENUOLMROMRA
S_ALR_87002434	IMG Activity: SIMG_CMMENUORFF_3606
S_ALR_87002435	IMG Activity: SIMG_ORFB_FKIQ
S_ALR_87002436	IMG Activity: SIMG_CFMENUOLSDOVSU
S_ALR_87002437	IMG Activity
S_ALR_87002438	IMG Activity: SIMG_CFMENUORFCOCBE
S_ALR_87002439	IMG Activity: SIMG_EURO_RBPEWU1P
S_ALR_87002440	IMG Activity: SIMG_CFMENUOLMEOME2
S_ALR_87002441	IMG Activity: SIMG_XXMENUOLML1036
S_ALR_87002442	IMG Activity: SIMG_CMMENUORFF_3610
S_ALR_87002443	IMG Activity: SIMG_CFMENUOLMROMR8
S_ALR_87002444	IMG Activity: SIMG_ORFB_FKIO
S_ALR_87002445	IMG Activity: SIMG_CFMENUORFCOC27
S_ALR_87002446	IMG Activity
S_ALR_87002447	IMG Activity: SIMG_XXMENUOLML1035
S_ALR_87002448	IMG Activity: SIMG_CFMENUORFF_4110
S_ALR_87002449	IMG Activity: SIMG_CFMENUOLMROMRK
S_ALR_87002450	IMG Activity: SIMG_CFMENUORFCOC42
S_ALR_87002451	IMG Activity: SIMG_XXMENUOLML1034
S_ALR_87002452	IMG Activity: SIMG_CFMENUOLMEOMSQ
S_ALR_87002453	IMG Activity
S_ALR_87002454	IMG Activity: SIMG_EURO_RCOPCA44B
S_ALR_87002455	IMG Activity: SIMG_CFMENUORFBOB46
S_ALR_87002456	IMG Activity: SIMG_CFMENUOLMROMRX
S_ALR_87002457	IMG Activity: SIMG_CFMENUORFF_4220
S_ALR_87002458	IMG Activity: SIMG_CFMENUORFCMEZU
S_ALR_87002459	IMG Activity
S_ALR_87002460	IMG Activity: SIMG_EURO_FINSTROM
S_ALR_87002461	IMG Activity: SIMG_CMMENUOLME0002
S_ALR_87002462	IMG Activity: SIMG_CFMENUORFF_4210
S_ALR_87002463	IMG Activity: SIMG_CFORFBV001NP2
S_ALR_87002464	IMG Activity: SIMG_CFMENUOLMROMRD
S_ALR_87002465	IMG Activity: SIMG_CFMENUORFCOC12
S_ALR_87002466	IMG Activity: SIMG_CFORFBOBR4DTUB
S_ALR_87002467	IMG Activity: J_1BNFITEM_TYPE
S_ALR_87002468	IMG Activity: SIMG_CFMENUORFF_4215
S_ALR_87002469	IMG Activity
S_ALR_87002470	IMG Activity: SIMG_CFMENUORFCOC59
S_ALR_87002471	IMG Activity: SIMG_CFMENUOLMLOMMB
S_ALR_87002472	IMG Activity: SIMG_CFORFBT041C
S_ALR_87002473	IMG Activity: SIMG_EURO_KONDITION1
S_ALR_87002474	IMG Activity: SIMG_CFMENUORFF_4310
S_ALR_87002475	IMG Activity
S_ALR_87002476	IMG Activity: SIMG_CFMENUOFTDOT61
S_ALR_87002477	IMG Activity: SIMG_CFMENUORFCOC16
S_ALR_87002478	IMG Activity: J_1BVALUE_TRANSFER
S_ALR_87002479	IMG Activity: SIMG_CFMENUOLMLOMLL
S_ALR_87002480	IMG Activity: CFORFBTHKON
S_ALR_87002481	IMG Activity: SIMG_CFMENUORFF_4320
S_ALR_87002482	IMG Activity: J_1BTEXT_KEYS
S_ALR_87002483	IMG Activity: SIMG_EURO_LC1050
S_ALR_87002484	IMG Activity
S_ALR_87002485	IMG Activity: SIMG_XXMENUOLML29
S_ALR_87002486	IMG Activity: SIMG_CFMENUORFCKUER

S_ALR_87002487	IMG Activity: SIMG_CFMENUOFTDOT58
S_ALR_87002488	IMG Activity: SIMG_CFMENUOLMRINDEX
S_ALR_87002489	IMG Activity: SIMG_CFMENUORFBOBL4
S_ALR_87002490	IMG Activity: SIMG_CMMENUORFF_3430
S_ALR_87002491	IMG Activity: SIMG_CFMENUORFCFZUO
S_ALR_87002492	IMG Activity: SIMG_CMMENUOLMRB
S_ALR_87002493	IMG Activity
S_ALR_87002494	IMG Activity: SIMG_CFMENUOLMLOMNK
S_ALR_87002495	IMG Activity: SIMG_EURO_LC1020
S_ALR_87002496	IMG Activity: SIMG_CMMENUORFF_3505
S_ALR_87002497	IMG Activity: SIMG_CFMENUORFBOBL3
S_ALR_87002498	IMG Activity
S_ALR_87002499	IMG Activity: SIMG_CFMENUOFTDOT43
S_ALR_87002500	IMG Activity: SIMG_CFMENUORFCFLOG
S_ALR_87002501	IMG Activity: SIMG_CFMENUOLMLOMLK
S_ALR_87002502	IMG Activity: SIMG_CMMENUORFF_3510
S_ALR_87002503	IMG Activity: SIMG_CFMENUORFBOBXS
S_ALR_87002504	IMG Activity
S_ALR_87002505	IMG Activity: SIMG_CFMENUORFCFSCH
S_ALR_87002506	IMG Activity: SIMG_CFMENUOFTDOBBY
S_ALR_87002507	IMG Activity: SIMG_EURO_LC2130
S_ALR_87002508	IMG Activity: SIMG_CMMENUORFF_3520
S_ALR_87002509	IMG Activity: SIMG_CFMENUOLMLOMLV
S_ALR_87002510	IMG Activity: SIMG_CFMENUORFBOB81
S_ALR_87002511	IMG Activity
S_ALR_87002512	IMG Activity: SIMG_CMMENUORFF_3525
S_ALR_87002531	IMG Activity: SIMG_CFMENUORFCDZUO
S_ALR_87002532	IMG Activity: SIMG_CFMENUOLMLOMLX
S_ALR_87002533	IMG Activity: SIMG_EURO_RAEWUC0B
S_ALR_87002534	IMG Activity: SIMG_CFFIBAOT74
S_ALR_87002535	IMG Activity: SIMG_XXMENUOLML0038
S_ALR_87002536	IMG Activity: SIMG_CFMENUORFBOBAC
S_ALR_87002537	IMG Activity: SIMG_EURO_BUPEZU
S_ALR_87002538	IMG Activity
S_ALR_87002539	IMG Activity: SIMG_CMMENUORFF_3530
S_ALR_87002540	IMG Activity: SIMG_CFFIBAOT73
S_ALR_87002541	IMG Activity: SIMG_CFMENUORFCGC31
S_ALR_87002542	IMG Activity: SIMG_XXMENUOLML0035
S_ALR_87002543	IMG Activity: SIMG_CFORFBT059ZZINS
S_ALR_87002544	IMG Activity: SIMG_EURO_SPERREN
S_ALR_87002545	IMG Activity: SIMG_CMMENUORFF_3604
S_ALR_87002546	IMG Activity: SIMG_CFMENUOFTDOT55
S_ALR_87002547	IMG Activity
S_ALR_87002548	IMG Activity: SIMG_CFMENUORFCBAWU
S_ALR_87002549	IMG Activity: SIMG_XXMENUOLML0034
S_ALR_87002550	IMG Activity: SIMG_CFMENUORFBOBAB
S_ALR_87002551	IMG Activity: SIMG_CFMENUORFCPBAG
S_ALR_87002552	IMG Activity: SIMG_CMMENUORFF_3605
S_ALR_87002553	IMG Activity
S_ALR_87002554	IMG Activity: SIMG_CFMENUOFTDOT57
S_ALR_87002555	IMG Activity: SIMG_XXMENUOLML0025
S_ALR_87002556	IMG Activity: SIMG_EURO_HINTJOB01
S_ALR_87002557	IMG Activity: SIMG_CFMENUORFBOBAA
S_ALR_87002558	IMG Activity: SIMG_CFMENUORFCOCBD

S_ALR_87002559	IMG Activity: SIMG_CFMENUORFF1412
S_ALR_87002560	IMG Activity
S_ALR_87002561	IMG Activity: SIMG_EURO_BUPEAKTAUF
S_ALR_87002562	IMG Activity: SIMG_XXMENUOLML0024
S_ALR_87002563	IMG Activity: SIMG_CFMENUOFTDOT51
S_ALR_87002564	IMG Activity: SIMG_CFMENUORFBOB82
S_ALR_87002565	IMG Activity: SIMG_CFMENUORFF_1418
S_ALR_87002566	IMG Activity: SIMG_CFMENUORFCPREG
S_ALR_87002567	IMG Activity
S_ALR_87002568	IMG Activity: SIMG_XXMENUOLML1028
S_ALR_87002569	IMG Activity: SIMG_CFMENUORFCOC36
S_ALR_87002570	IMG Activity: SIMG_EURO_BETRART01
S_ALR_87002571	IMG Activity: SIMG_CFMENUOLMLOMM0
S_ALR_87002572	IMG Activity: SIMG_CMMENUORFF_1411
S_ALR_87002573	IMG Activity: SIMG_CFORFBFBN1VZ
S_ALR_87002574	IMG Activity
S_ALR_87002575	IMG Activity: SIMG_CFMENUOFTDOT59
S_ALR_87002576	IMG Activity: SIMG_CFMENUORFCOC13
S_ALR_87002577	IMG Activity: SIMG_CFMENUOLMLOMNP
S_ALR_87002578	IMG Activity: SIMG_CMMENUORFF_1416
S_ALR_87002579	IMG Activity: SIMG_EURO_PARAMETER
S_ALR_87002580	IMG Activity: SIMG_CFORFBOBYNUMKK
S_ALR_87002581	IMG Activity
S_ALR_87002582	IMG Activity: SIMG_CFFIBAFIBD
S_ALR_87002583	IMG Activity: SIMG_CFMENUORFCONZU
S_ALR_87002584	IMG Activity: SIMG_CMMENUORFF_1414
S_ALR_87002585	IMG Activity: SIMG_CFMENUOLMLOMMP
S_ALR_87002586	IMG Activity: SIMG_EURO_SYSTEM02
S_ALR_87002587	IMG Activity: SIMG_XXMENUORFBOBXE
S_ALR_87002588	IMG Activity
S_ALR_87002589	IMG Activity: SIMG_CFFIBATBCH1
S_ALR_87002590	IMG Activity: SIMG_XXMENUOLML1008
S_ALR_87002591	IMG Activity: SIMG_CMMENUORFF_1413
S_ALR_87002592	IMG Activity: SIMG_CFMENUORFCOC09
S_ALR_87002593	IMG Activity: SIMG_CFORFBCHKBLAUW
S_ALR_87002594	IMG Activity
S_ALR_87002595	IMG Activity: SIMG_XXMENUOLML1007
S_ALR_87002596	IMG Activity: SIMG_CMMENUORFF_1415
S_ALR_87002597	IMG Activity: SIMG_EURO_START
S_ALR_87002598	IMG Activity: SIMG_CFMENUOFTDOT36
S_ALR_87002599	IMG Activity: SIMG_CFMENUORFCPTPF
S_ALR_87002600	IMG Activity: SIMG_CFORFBOBXSUMKD
S_ALR_87002601	IMG Activity
S_ALR_87002602	IMG Activity: SIMG_XXMENUOLML1005
S_ALR_87002603	IMG Activity: SIMG_CFMENUORFF_1417
S_ALR_87002604	IMG Activity: SIMG_EURO_MONITOR
S_ALR_87002605	IMG Activity: SIMG_CFMENUORFCOC07
S_ALR_87002606	IMG Activity
S_ALR_87002607	IMG Activity: SIMG_CFORFBOBYNUMKD
S_ALR_87002608	IMG Activity: SIMG_CFMENUOFTDOT26
S_ALR_87002609	IMG Activity: SIMG_XXMENUOLML0020
S_ALR_87002610	IMG Activity: SIMG_CFMENUORFF1201
S_ALR_87002611	IMG Activity: SIMG_EURO_EWUTFV02
S_ALR_87002612	IMG Activity: SIMG_CFMENUORFCSU02

S_ALR_87002613	IMG Activity
S_ALR_87002614	IMG Activity: SIMG_CFMENUORFBOB11
S_ALR_87002615	IMG Activity: SIMG_CFMENUOLMLOMMO
S_ALR_87002616	IMG Activity: SIMG_CFMENUORFBOBXE
S_ALR_87002617	IMG Activity: SIMG_CFMENUORFF1202
S_ALR_87002618	IMG Activity: SIMG_XXMENUOLML0030
S_ALR_87002619	IMG Activity: SIMG_CFMENUORFCSU03
S_ALR_87002620	IMG Activity
S_ALR_87002621	IMG Activity: SIMG_CFORFBCMODBKDT
S_ALR_87002622	IMG Activity: SIMG_CFORFBCHKBLUW
S_ALR_87002623	IMG Activity: SIMG_EURO_RKEB0902_4
S_ALR_87002624	IMG Activity: SIMG_CFMENUORFF1209
S_ALR_87002625	IMG Activity: SIMG_XXMENUOLML0029
S_ALR_87002626	IMG Activity: SIMG_CFMENUORFBOBBA
S_ALR_87002627	IMG Activity: SIMG_CFMENUORFCK3TE
S_ALR_87002628	IMG Activity: SIMG_XXMENUOLML1030
S_ALR_87002629	IMG Activity
S_ALR_87002630	IMG Activity: SIMG_CFMENUORFBOBXT
S_ALR_87002631	IMG Activity: SIMG_XXMENUOLML0039
S_ALR_87002632	IMG Activity: SIMG_EURO_BKPFKONV
S_ALR_87002633	IMG Activity: SIMG_CFMENUORFF1207
S_ALR_87002634	IMG Activity: SIMG_CFMENUORFBOBBK
S_ALR_87002635	IMG Activity: SIMG_CFMENUORFCOC49
S_ALR_87002636	IMG Activity
S_ALR_87002637	IMG Activity: SIMG_CFMENUORFBOBXY
S_ALR_87002638	IMG Activity: SIMG_XXMENUOLML0005
S_ALR_87002639	IMG Activity: SIMG_EURO_VORMONITOR
S_ALR_87002640	IMG Activity: SIMG_CFMENUORFF1208
S_ALR_87002641	IMG Activity
S_ALR_87002642	IMG Activity: SIMG_CFORFBCHKBLSHB
S_ALR_87002643	IMG Activity: SIMG_CFMENUORFCARCH
S_ALR_87002644	IMG Activity: SIMG_CFMENUORFBOBBL
S_ALR_87002645	IMG Activity: SIMG_CFMENUOLMLOMLR
S_ALR_87002646	IMG Activity: SIMG_CFMENUORFF1203
S_ALR_87002647	IMG Activity
S_ALR_87002648	IMG Activity: SIMG_CFMENUORFBOBKB
S_ALR_87002649	IMG Activity: SIMG_CFMENUORFCGC35
S_ALR_87002650	IMG Activity: SIMG_XXMENUOLML1003
S_ALR_87002651	IMG Activity: SIMG_CMMENUORFF_1421
S_ALR_87002652	IMG Activity
S_ALR_87002653	IMG Activity: SIMG_EURO_RESTARTTAB
S_ALR_87002654	IMG Activity: SIMG_CFMENUORFBOBR4
S_ALR_87002655	IMG Activity: SIMG_CFORFBCHKKOIU
S_ALR_87002656	IMG Activity: SIMG_CFMENUORFCOCDL
S_ALR_87002657	IMG Activity: SIMG_CMMENUORFF_1423
S_ALR_87002658	IMG Activity: SIMG_XXMENUOLML1024
S_ALR_87002659	IMG Activity
S_ALR_87002660	IMG Activity: SIMG_CFMENUORFCSKUE
S_ALR_87002661	IMG Activity: SIMG_CFORFBCHKBLIU
S_ALR_87002662	IMG Activity: SIMG_EURO_LAUFZEIT01
S_ALR_87002663	IMG Activity: SIMG_CMMENUORFF_1530
S_ALR_87002664	IMG Activity: SIMG_XXMENUOLML1016
S_ALR_87002665	IMG Activity
S_ALR_87002666	IMG Activity: SIMG_CFMENUORFBFI12

S_ALR_87002667	IMG Activity: SIMG_EURO_LAUFZEIT02
S_ALR_87002668	IMG Activity: SIMG_CFMENUORFCOC30
S_ALR_87002669	IMG Activity: SIMG_CFORFBOBXSUMKK
S_ALR_87002670	IMG Activity: SIMG_XXMENUOLML1023
S_ALR_87002671	IMG Activity: SIMG_CMMENUORFF_1520
S_ALR_87002672	IMG Activity
S_ALR_87002673	IMG Activity: SIMG_CFFIBATBCH0
S_ALR_87002674	IMG Activity: SIMG_XXMENUOLML1014
S_ALR_87002675	IMG Activity: SIMG_CMMENUORFF_1540
S_ALR_87002676	IMG Activity: SIMG_EURO_RESTARTPAK
S_ALR_87002677	IMG Activity: SIMG_CFMENUORFCPLUE
S_ALR_87002678	IMG Activity: SIMG_CFMENUORFBOB83
S_ALR_87002679	IMG Activity
S_ALR_87002680	IMG Activity: SIMG_XXMENUOLML1013
S_ALR_87002681	IMG Activity: SIMG_CMMENUORFF_1510
S_ALR_87002682	IMG Activity: SIMG_CFMENUOFTDOT60
S_ALR_87002683	IMG Activity: SIMG_CFMENUORFCPCUE
S_ALR_87002684	IMG Activity: SIMG_CFORFBOB46BEWT
S_ALR_87002685	IMG Activity: SIMG_CFMENUORFF0000
S_ALR_87002686	IMG Activity: SIMG_XXMENUOLML1117
S_ALR_87002687	IMG Activity
S_ALR_87002688	IMG Activity: SIMG_EURO_PARAMETERZ
S_ALR_87002689	IMG Activity: SIMG_CMMENUORFF_3310
S_ALR_87002690	IMG Activity: SIMG_CFMENUORFCOC15
S_ALR_87002691	IMG Activity: SIMG_CFMENUOFTDOT68
S_ALR_87002692	IMG Activity: SIMG_XXMENUOLML1116
S_ALR_87002693	IMG Activity: SIMG_ORFBT044G
S_ALR_87002694	IMG Activity
S_ALR_87002695	IMG Activity: SIMG_CMMENUORFF_2130
S_ALR_87002696	IMG Activity: SIMG_EURO_010
S_ALR_87002697	IMG Activity: SIMG_XXMENUOLML1002
S_ALR_87002698	IMG Activity: SIMG_CFMENUORFF2551
S_ALR_87002699	IMG Activity: SIMG_CFMENUORFCBAUE
S_ALR_87002700	IMG Activity: SIMG_CFORFBCMODFORD
S_ALR_87002701	IMG Activity
S_ALR_87002702	IMG Activity: SIMG_CFMENUOFTDOT65
S_ALR_87002703	IMG Activity: SIMG_CMMENUORFF_2110
S_ALR_87002704	IMG Activity: SIMG_XXMENUOLML2003
S_ALR_87002705	IMG Activity: SIMG_CMMENUORFF_2120
S_ALR_87002706	IMG Activity: SIMG_EURO_RFEWUS0P
S_ALR_87002707	IMG Activity: SIMG_XXMENUORFBOBXD
S_ALR_87002708	IMG Activity: SIMG_CFMENUORFCFGRW
S_ALR_87002709	IMG Activity
S_ALR_87002710	IMG Activity: SIMG_CFMENUORFF1206
S_ALR_87002711	IMG Activity: SIMG_XXMENUOLML0006
S_ALR_87002712	IMG Activity: SIMG_CFMENUOFTDOT66
S_ALR_87002713	IMG Activity: SIMG_CFMENUORFBOB04
S_ALR_87002714	IMG Activity: SIMG_CFMENUORFCMAZU
S_ALR_87002715	IMG Activity
S_ALR_87002716	IMG Activity: SIMG_EURO_RFEWUC0F
S_ALR_87002717	IMG Activity: SIMG_XXMENUOLML1033
S_ALR_87002718	IMG Activity: SIMG_CFMENUORFBOBA10
S_ALR_87002719	IMG Activity: SIMG_CFMENUORFCOC35
S_ALR_87002720	IMG Activity

SAP Transaction Codes – Volume Two

S_ALR_87002721	IMG Activity: SIMG_CFMENUORFBOB10
S_ALR_87002722	IMG Activity: SIMG_CFMENUOLMLOMLP
S_ALR_87002723	IMG Activity: SIMG_EURO_RFEWUC0O
S_ALR_87002724	IMG Activity: SIMG_CFMENUORFCOC26
S_ALR_87002725	IMG Activity: SIMG_CFMENUORFBOB590
S_ALR_87002726	IMG Activity
S_ALR_87002727	IMG Activity: SIMG_XXMENUOLML2001
S_ALR_87002728	IMG Activity: SIMG_CFMENUORFBOBBR
S_ALR_87002729	IMG Activity: SIMG_XXMENUOLML0018
S_ALR_87002730	IMG Activity: SIMG_EURO_EWUMMBEW
S_ALR_87002731	IMG Activity: SIMG_CFMENUORFCOCBI
S_ALR_87002732	IMG Activity: SIMG_CFMENUORFBOBBX
S_ALR_87002733	IMG Activity: SIMG_CFMENUCX01_RE16
S_ALR_87002734	IMG Activity: SIMG_XXMENUOLML15
S_ALR_87002735	IMG Activity: SIMG_CFMENUORFCKMZU
S_ALR_87002736	IMG Activity: SIMG_CFMENUOFTDOT49
S_ALR_87002737	IMG Activity: SIMG_CFMENUORFBOBBW
S_ALR_87002738	IMG Activity: SIMG_CFMENUCX01_RE17
S_ALR_87002739	IMG Activity: SIMG_XXMENUOLML1010
S_ALR_87002740	IMG Activity: SIMG_CFMENUORFCOCBK
S_ALR_87002741	IMG Activity: SIMG_EURO_EWUMMBST
S_ALR_87002742	IMG Activity: SIMG_CFMENUORFBOBBV
S_ALR_87002743	IMG Activity: SIMG_CFMENUOFTDOT53
S_ALR_87002744	IMG Activity: SIMG_CFMENUCX01_RE18
S_ALR_87002745	IMG Activity: SIMG_XXMENUOLML1021
S_ALR_87002746	IMG Activity: SIMG_CFMENUORFCERST
S_ALR_87002747	IMG Activity: SIMG_CFMENUCX01_RE19
S_ALR_87002748	IMG Activity: SIMG_CFMENUORFBOBBU
S_ALR_87002749	IMG Activity: SIMG_EURO_EWUMRTL
S_ALR_87002750	IMG Activity: SIMG_CFMENUORFBOBBB
S_ALR_87002751	IMG Activity: SIMG_CFMENUORFCOCBH
S_ALR_87002752	IMG Activity: SIMG_CFMENUOLMLOMM4
S_ALR_87002753	IMG Activity: SIMG_ORFBT044J
S_ALR_87002754	IMG Activity: SIMG_CFMENUCX01_RE05
S_ALR_87002755	IMG Activity: SIMG_CFMENUORFBOBBD
S_ALR_87002756	IMG Activity: SIMG_CFMENUORFCOCL6
S_ALR_87002757	IMG Activity: SIMG_EURO_EWUMFPST
S_ALR_87002758	IMG Activity: SIMG_CFMENUOLMLOMM3
S_ALR_87002759	IMG Activity: SIMG_ORFBT044I
S_ALR_87002760	IMG Activity: SIMG_CFMENUCX01_TR03
S_ALR_87002761	IMG Activity: SIMG_CFMENUORFCBUZU
S_ALR_87002762	IMG Activity: SIMG_CFMENUOLMLOMLU
S_ALR_87002763	IMG Activity: SIMG_CFMENUOFTDOT03
S_ALR_87002764	IMG Activity: SIMG_CFMENUCX01_TR05
S_ALR_87002765	IMG Activity: SIMG_ORFBOBB0
S_ALR_87002766	IMG Activity: SIMG_EURO_RAEWUS0B
S_ALR_87002767	IMG Activity: SIMG_CFMENUOLMLOMM7
S_ALR_87002768	IMG Activity: SIMG_CFMENUORFCOCA9
S_ALR_87002769	IMG Activity: SIMG_CFMENUCX01_TR04
S_ALR_87002770	IMG Activity: SIMG_CFMENUOFTDOT02
S_ALR_87002771	IMG Activity: SIMG_CFMENUOLMLOMM6
S_ALR_87002772	IMG Activity: SIMG_EURO_BETRART02
S_ALR_87002773	IMG Activity: SIMG_CFMENUORFCSOZU
S_ALR_87002774	IMG Activity: SIMG_CFMENUCX01_TC00

256

S_ALR_87002775	IMG Activity: SIMG_CFMENUOLMLOMM5
S_ALR_87002776	IMG Activity: SIMG_CFORFBCMODBKNR
S_ALR_87002777	IMG Activity: SIMG_CFORFBOBV4
S_ALR_87002778	IMG Activity: SIMG_CFMENUORFCOC01
S_ALR_87002779	IMG Activity: SIMG_EURO_BUPELFDAUF
S_ALR_87002780	IMG Activity: SIMG_CFMENUCX01_MD44
S_ALR_87002781	IMG Activity: SIMG_XXMENUOLML1004
S_ALR_87002782	IMG Activity: SIMG_CFMENUORFBOBV3
S_ALR_87002783	IMG Activity: SIMG_CFMENUORFCOC23
S_ALR_87002784	IMG Activity: SIMG_CFMENUOLMLOMLM
S_ALR_87002785	IMG Activity: SIMG_CFMENUCX01_DADE
S_ALR_87002786	IMG Activity: SIMG_CFMENUOFTDOT33
S_ALR_87002787	IMG Activity: SIMG_CFMENUORFBOBV9
S_ALR_87002788	IMG Activity: SIMG_CFMENUORFCGC27
S_ALR_87002789	IMG Activity: SIMG_XXMENUOLML1009
S_ALR_87002790	IMG Activity: SIMG_CFMENUCX01_DATR
S_ALR_87002791	IMG Activity: SIMG_CFMENUOFTDOT67
S_ALR_87002792	IMG Activity: SIMG_CFMENUORFBOBV1
S_ALR_87002793	IMG Activity: SIMG_XXMENUOLML1025
S_ALR_87002794	IMG Activity: SIMG_CFMENUORFCGC51
S_ALR_87002795	IMG Activity: SIMG_CFMENUCX01_3220
S_ALR_87002796	IMG Activity: SIMG_CFMENUORFBOB85
S_ALR_87002797	IMG Activity: SIMG_EURO_NACHALL
S_ALR_87002798	IMG Activity: SIMG_XXMENUOLML0016
S_ALR_87002799	IMG Activity: SIMG_CFMENUORFCDLOG
S_ALR_87002800	IMG Activity: SIMG_CFMENUCX01_3210
S_ALR_87002801	IMG Activity: SIMG_EURO_RFEWA009
S_ALR_87002802	IMG Activity: SIMG_CFORFBT033
S_ALR_87002803	IMG Activity: SIMG_CFMENUOLMLOMM9
S_ALR_87002804	IMG Activity: SIMG_CFMENUORFCOC08
S_ALR_87002805	IMG Activity: SIMG_CFMENUCX01_IN12
S_ALR_87002806	IMG Activity: SIMG_CFMENUORFBOB36
S_ALR_87002807	IMG Activity: SIMG_CFMENUOLMLOMLT
S_ALR_87002808	IMG Activity: SIMG_CFMENUORFCOCDC
S_ALR_87002809	IMG Activity: SIMG_EURO_RFEWUSHK
S_ALR_87002810	IMG Activity: SIMG_CFMENUCX01_IN13
S_ALR_87002811	IMG Activity: SIMG_CFMENUOLMLOMLS
S_ALR_87002812	IMG Activity: SIMG_CFMENUORFBOB35
S_ALR_87002813	IMG Activity: SIMG_EURO_CS2330
S_ALR_87002814	IMG Activity: SIMG_CFMENUCX01_IN14
S_ALR_87002815	IMG Activity: SIMG_CFMENUORFCOC04
S_ALR_87002816	IMG Activity: SIMG_CFMENUOLMLOMM8
S_ALR_87002817	IMG Activity: SIMG_CFMENUORFBFSSP
S_ALR_87002818	IMG Activity: SIMG_EURO_CS2340
S_ALR_87002819	IMG Activity: SIMG_CFMENUCX01_TR01
S_ALR_87002820	IMG Activity: SIMG_CFMENUOLMLOMLQ
S_ALR_87002821	IMG Activity: SIMG_CFMENUORFCOC83
S_ALR_87002822	IMG Activity: SIMG_CFMENUORFBFSAP
S_ALR_87002823	IMG Activity: SIMG_EURO_CS2390
S_ALR_87002824	IMG Activity: SIMG_XXMENUOLML0008
S_ALR_87002825	IMG Activity: SIMG_CFMENUCX01_TR02
S_ALR_87002826	IMG Activity: SIMG_CFMENUORFCOC81
S_ALR_87002827	IMG Activity: SIMG_CFORFBCHKKOSALD
S_ALR_87002828	IMG Activity: OHEUR105

S_ALR_87002829	IMG Activity: SIMG_CFMENUOLMLOMM1
S_ALR_87002830	IMG Activity: SIMG_CFMENUCX01_SPIT
S_ALR_87002831	IMG Activity: SIMG_CFMENUORFCGS01
S_ALR_87002832	IMG Activity: SIMG_CFMENUOLMLOML7
S_ALR_87002833	IMG Activity: SIMG_CFMENUORFBOB84
S_ALR_87002834	IMG Activity: OHEUR101
S_ALR_87002835	IMG Activity: SIMG_CFMENUCX01_SE00
S_ALR_87002836	IMG Activity: SIMG_CFMENUORFCOC05
S_ALR_87002837	IMG Activity: SIMG_XXMENUOLML1017
S_ALR_87002838	IMG Activity: SIMG_CFMENUORFBO7V2
S_ALR_87002839	IMG Activity: OHEUR211
S_ALR_87002840	IMG Activity: SIMG_CFMENUCX01_MD38
S_ALR_87002841	IMG Activity: SIMG_CFMENUORFCDEFA
S_ALR_87002842	IMG Activity: SIMG_XXMENUOLML1012
S_ALR_87002843	IMG Activity: SIMG_CFMENUORFBO7F2
S_ALR_87002844	IMG Activity: SIMG_CFMENUCX01_MD26
S_ALR_87002845	IMG Activity: OHEUR212
S_ALR_87002846	IMG Activity: SIMG_CFMENUORFCZU07
S_ALR_87002847	IMG Activity: SIMG_XXMENUOLML1000
S_ALR_87002848	IMG Activity: SIMG_CFMENUORFBO7F3
S_ALR_87002849	IMG Activity: SIMG_CFMENUCX01_DM01
S_ALR_87002850	IMG Activity: SIMG_CFMENUORFCZU06
S_ALR_87002851	IMG Activity: SIMG_CFMENUOLMLOML6
S_ALR_87002852	IMG Activity: OHEUR213
S_ALR_87002853	IMG Activity: SIMG_CFMENUORFBO7F8
S_ALR_87002854	IMG Activity: SIMG_CFMENUOLMLOML4
S_ALR_87002855	IMG Activity: SIMG_CFMENUCX01_CM02
S_ALR_87002856	IMG Activity: SIMG_CFMENUORFCZU08
S_ALR_87002857	IMG Activity: SIMG_CFMENUORFBO7F1
S_ALR_87002858	IMG Activity: SIMG_CFMENUCX01_1418
S_ALR_87002859	IMG Activity: SIMG_CFMENUOLMLOMLW
S_ALR_87002860	IMG Activity: OHEURDE221
S_ALR_87002861	IMG Activity: SIMG_CFMENUORFCZU05
S_ALR_87002862	IMG Activity: SIMG_CFMENUORFBO7V3
S_ALR_87002863	IMG Activity: SIMG_CFMENUOLMLOML1
S_ALR_87002864	IMG Activity: SIMG_CFMENUCX01_MD27
S_ALR_87002865	IMG Activity: SIMG_CFMENUORFCZU03
S_ALR_87002866	IMG Activity: SIMG_CFMENUORFBOBKE0
S_ALR_87002867	IMG Activity: SIMG_EURO_CS2250
S_ALR_87002868	IMG Activity: SIMG_CFMENUOLMLOML9
S_ALR_87002869	IMG Activity: SIMG_CFMENUCX01_MD41
S_ALR_87002870	IMG Activity: SIMG_CFMENUORFCZU02
S_ALR_87002871	IMG Activity: SIMG_CFMENUORFBOBKA0
S_ALR_87002872	IMG Activity: SIMG_CFMENUOLMLOMLZ
S_ALR_87002873	IMG Activity: SIMG_CFMENUCX01_MD28
S_ALR_87002874	IMG Activity: SIMG_EURO_CS2251B
S_ALR_87002875	IMG Activity: SIMG_CFMENUORFCZU01
S_ALR_87002876	IMG Activity: SIMG_CFMENUORFBOBAF0
S_ALR_87002877	IMG Activity: SIMG_CFMENUOLMLOMLY
S_ALR_87002878	IMG Activity: SIMG_CFMENUCX01_MD32
S_ALR_87002879	IMG Activity: SIMG_CFMENUOLMLOMNX
S_ALR_87002880	IMG Activity: SIMG_CFMENUCX01_MD30
S_ALR_87002881	IMG Activity: SIMG_CFORFBCHKKOKR
S_ALR_87002882	IMG Activity: SIMG_EURO_CS2252

S_ALR_87002883	IMG Activity: SIMG_CFMENUORFCGC17
S_ALR_87002884	IMG Activity: SIMG_CFMENUOLMLOMNQ
S_ALR_87002885	IMG Activity: SIMG_CFMENUORFBO7R1
S_ALR_87002886	IMG Activity: SIMG_EURO_CS2280
S_ALR_87002887	IMG Activity: SIMG_CFMENUORFCEBZT
S_ALR_87002888	IMG Activity: SIMG_CFMENUCX01_MD31
S_ALR_87002889	IMG Activity: SIMG_CFMENUOLMLOMLC
S_ALR_87002890	IMG Activity: SIMG_CFMENUOLMLOMLB
S_ALR_87002891	IMG Activity: SIMG_CFMENUORFCOC48
S_ALR_87002892	IMG Activity: SIMG_CFMENUCX01_MD42
S_ALR_87002893	IMG Activity: SIMG_EURO_CS2310
S_ALR_87002894	IMG Activity: SIMG_CFORFBOB55KROP
S_ALR_87002895	IMG Activity: SIMG_CFMENUOLMLOMLA
S_ALR_87002896	IMG Activity: SIMG_CFMENUCX01_ON04
S_ALR_87002897	IMG Activity: SIMG_CFMENUORFCGC12
S_ALR_87002898	IMG Activity: SIMG_CFMENUORFBO7F6
S_ALR_87002899	IMG Activity: SIMG_XXMENUOLML14
S_ALR_87002900	IMG Activity: SIMG_CFMENUCX01_ON05
S_ALR_87002901	IMG Activity: SIMG_CFMENUORFCOC37
S_ALR_87002902	IMG Activity: SIMG_CFMENUORFBO7F5
S_ALR_87002903	IMG Activity: SIMG_EURO_CS2319
S_ALR_87002904	IMG Activity: SIMG_XXMENUOLML1001
S_ALR_87002905	IMG Activity: SIMG_XXMENUOLML1018
S_ALR_87002906	IMG Activity: SIMG_CFMENUORFCLEDG
S_ALR_87002907	IMG Activity: SIMG_CFMENUCX01_OF04
S_ALR_87002908	IMG Activity: SIMG_EURO_CS2315
S_ALR_87002909	IMG Activity: SIMG_CFMENUOLMLOMLH
S_ALR_87002910	IMG Activity: SIMG_CFMENUORFCOC40
S_ALR_87002911	IMG Activity: SIMG_CFMENUCX01_OF01
S_ALR_87002912	IMG Activity: SIMG_CFMENUOLMLOMLG
S_ALR_87002913	IMG Activity: SIMG_EURO_CS2350
S_ALR_87002914	IMG Activity: SIMG_CFMENUCX01_OF02
S_ALR_87002915	IMG Activity: SIMG_CFMENUOLMLOMLF
S_ALR_87002916	IMG Activity: SIMG_CFMENUCX01_IT25
S_ALR_87002917	IMG Activity: SIMG_EURO_CS2320
S_ALR_87002918	IMG Activity: SIMG_CFMENUORFBO7F7
S_ALR_87002919	IMG Activity: SIMG_CFMENUOLMLOMLE
S_ALR_87002920	IMG Activity: SIMG_CFMENUORFCOC02
S_ALR_87002921	IMG Activity: SIMG_CFMENUCX01_FL01
S_ALR_87002922	IMG Activity: SIMG_XXMENUOLML2000
S_ALR_87002923	IMG Activity: OHEURDE222
S_ALR_87002924	IMG Activity: SIMG_CFMENUCX01_1412
S_ALR_87002925	IMG Activity: SIMG_CFMENUOLMLOMLJ
S_ALR_87002926	IMG Activity: SIMG_CFMENUCX01_ON01
S_ALR_87002927	IMG Activity: OHEUR254
S_ALR_87002928	IMG Activity: SIMG_XXMENUOLML09
S_ALR_87002929	IMG Activity: OHEUR255
S_ALR_87002930	IMG Activity: SIMG_CFMENUCX01_ON02
S_ALR_87002931	IMG Activity: SIMG_CFMENUOLMLOMLI
S_ALR_87002932	IMG Activity: SIMG_CFMENUORFCPFLE
S_ALR_87002933	IMG Activity: SIMG_CFMENUORFBO7Z4
S_ALR_87002934	IMG Activity: SIMG_XXMENUOLML08
S_ALR_87002935	IMG Activity: OHEUR256
S_ALR_87002936	IMG Activity: SIMG_CFMENUCX01_ON08

S_ALR_87002937	IMG Activity: SIMG_CFMENUORFCOC97
S_ALR_87002938	IMG Activity: SIMG_XXMENUOLML0017
S_ALR_87002939	IMG Activity: SIMG_CFMENUCX01_ON03
S_ALR_87002940	IMG Activity: SIMG_CFORFBOB55KREP
S_ALR_87002941	IMG Activity: OHEUR236
S_ALR_87002942	IMG Activity: SIMG_CFMENUORFCOCCT
S_ALR_87002944	IMG Activity: SIMG_CFMENUCX01_ON06
S_ALR_87002945	IMG Activity: OHEUR234
S_ALR_87002946	IMG Activity: SIMG_CFMENUOLMLOMM2
S_ALR_87002947	IMG Activity: SIMG_CFMENUORFBO7R2
S_ALR_87002948	IMG Activity: SIMG_CFMENUCX01_ON09
S_ALR_87002949	IMG Activity: SIMG_XXMENUOLML1026
S_ALR_87002950	IMG Activity: OHEUR241
S_ALR_87002951	IMG Activity: SIMG_XXMENUOLML0009
S_ALR_87002952	IMG Activity: SIMG_CFMENUCX01_MD04
S_ALR_87002953	IMG Activity: SIMG_CFMENUORFBOBKC0
S_ALR_87002954	IMG Activity: SIMG_CFMENUOLMLOML8
S_ALR_87002955	IMG Activity: SIMG_CFMENUORFCOC78
S_ALR_87002956	IMG Activity: OHEUR242
S_ALR_87002957	IMG Activity: SIMG_CFMENUORFBOBCB
S_ALR_87002958	IMG Activity: SIMG_CFMENUCX01_MD06
S_ALR_87002959	IMG Activity: SIMG_CFMENUOLMLOMLD
S_ALR_87002960	IMG Activity: SIMG_CFMENUORFCLOES
S_ALR_87002962	IMG Activity: SIMG_XXMENUOLML06
S_ALR_87002964	IMG Activity: SIMG_XXMENUOLML20
S_ALR_87002965	IMG Activity: SIMG_CFMENUCX01_MD25
S_ALR_87002966	IMG Activity: SIMG_CFORFBCHKQLRE
S_ALR_87002967	IMG Activity: SIMG_CFMENUORFCOC03
S_ALR_87002968	IMG Activity: SIMG_XXMENUOLML0004
S_ALR_87002969	IMG Activity: SIMG_XXMENUOLML19
S_ALR_87002970	IMG Activity: SIMG_CFMENUCX01_DI02
S_ALR_87002971	IMG Activity: SIMG_XXMENUOLML0001
S_ALR_87002972	IMG Activity: SIMG_CFMENUORFCFEST
S_ALR_87002973	IMG Activity: SIMG_CFMENUORFBOBXA
S_ALR_87002974	IMG Activity: OHEURDE223
S_ALR_87002975	IMG Activity: SIMG_XXMENUOLML0026
S_ALR_87002976	IMG Activity: SIMG_XXMENUOLML0037
S_ALR_87002977	IMG Activity: SIMG_CFMENUCX01_MD10
S_ALR_87002978	IMG Activity: SIMG_CFMENUORFCOC14
S_ALR_87002979	IMG Activity: OHEURAT222
S_ALR_87002980	IMG Activity: SIMG_CFMENUORFBOB16
S_ALR_87002981	IMG Activity: SIMG_XXMENUOLML17
S_ALR_87002982	IMG Activity: SIMG_XXMENUOLML0028
S_ALR_87002983	IMG Activity: OHEUR223
S_ALR_87002984	IMG Activity: SIMG_CFMENUORFCEIZU
S_ALR_87002985	IMG Activity: SIMG_CFMENUORFBO7E5
S_ALR_87002986	IMG Activity: SIMG_XXMENUOLML13
S_ALR_87002987	IMG Activity: SIMG_CFMENUCX01_MD11
S_ALR_87002988	IMG Activity: SIMG_XXMENUOLML0033
S_ALR_87002989	IMG Activity: SIMG_CFMENUORFCRZZU
S_ALR_87002990	IMG Activity: SIMG_XXMENUOLML0011
S_ALR_87002991	IMG Activity: SIMG_CFMENUCX01_MD35
S_ALR_87002992	IMG Activity: SIMG_CFMENUORFBOBXJ
S_ALR_87002993	IMG Activity: OHEUR231

S_ALR_87002994	IMG Activity: SIMG_XXMENUOLML0012
S_ALR_87002995	IMG Activity: SIMG_CFMENUORFCPBGA
S_ALR_87002996	IMG Activity: SIMG_CFMENUORFBOB49
S_ALR_87002997	IMG Activity: SIMG_CFMENUCX01_MD34
S_ALR_87002998	IMG Activity: OHEUR237
S_ALR_87002999	IMG Activity: SIMG_CFMENUORFCALOG
S_ALR_87003000	IMG Activity: SIMG_CFMENUCX01_GP00
S_ALR_87003001	IMG Activity: SIMG_CFORFBCMODEDI
S_ALR_87003002	IMG Activity: OHEUR232
S_ALR_87003003	IMG Activity: SIMG_CFMENUORFCRZSY
S_ALR_87003004	IMG Activity: SIMG_CFMENUCX01_MD01
S_ALR_87003005	IMG Activity: SIMG_CFMENUORFBOBCE
S_ALR_87003006	IMG Activity: SIMG_CFMENUCX01_CHIT
S_ALR_87003007	IMG Activity: SIMG_CFMENUORFCANSY
S_ALR_87003008	IMG Activity: OHEUR233
S_ALR_87003009	IMG Activity: SIMG_CFORFBOBCARE
S_ALR_87003010	IMG Activity: SIMG_CFMENUORFCANZU
S_ALR_87003011	IMG Activity: SIMG_CFMENUCX01_MD08
S_ALR_87003012	IMG Activity: OHEUR235
S_ALR_87003031	IMG Activity: SIMG_CFMENUORFBOBCD
S_ALR_87003032	IMG Activity: SIMG_CFMENUORFCAZUO
S_ALR_87003033	IMG Activity: SIMG_CFMENUCX01_MD02
S_ALR_87003034	IMG Activity: SIMG_CFMENUORFBOBCC
S_ALR_87003035	IMG Activity: OHEUR253
S_ALR_87003036	IMG Activity: SIMG_CFMENUCX01_DO08
S_ALR_87003037	IMG Activity: SIMG_CFMENUORFCEISY
S_ALR_87003038	IMG Activity: SIMG_CFORFBCHKBLRE
S_ALR_87003039	IMG Activity: SIMG_CFMENUCX01_MD46
S_ALR_87003040	IMG Activity: SIMG_CFMENUORFCAERH
S_ALR_87003041	IMG Activity: SIMG_EURO_CS2240
S_ALR_87003042	IMG Activity: SIMG_CFMENUORFBO7R3
S_ALR_87003043	IMG Activity: SIMG_CFMENUCX01_MD47
S_ALR_87003044	IMG Activity: SIMG_CFMENUORFCDPLA
S_ALR_87003045	IMG Activity: SIMG_CFMENUORFBO7F4
S_ALR_87003046	IMG Activity: SIMG_EURO_LC2251B
S_ALR_87003047	IMG Activity: SIMG_CFMENUCX01_MD20
S_ALR_87003048	IMG Activity: SIMG_CFMENUORFCABUE
S_ALR_87003049	IMG Activity: SIMG_CFMENUORFBO7S7
S_ALR_87003050	IMG Activity: SIMG_EURO_LC2252
S_ALR_87003051	IMG Activity: SIMG_CFMENUCX01_MD21
S_ALR_87003052	IMG Activity: SIMG_CFMENUCX01_MD22
S_ALR_87003053	IMG Activity: SIMG_EURO_LC2280
S_ALR_87003054	IMG Activity: SIMG_CFMENUCX01_MD45
S_ALR_87003055	IMG Activity: SIMG_EURO_LC2310
S_ALR_87003056	IMG Activity: SIMG_CFMENUCX01_MD23
S_ALR_87003057	IMG Activity: SIMG_EURO_LC2319
S_ALR_87003058	IMG Activity: SIMG_CFMENUORFCDBUE
S_ALR_87003059	IMG Activity: SIMG_CFMENUCX01_MD12
S_ALR_87003060	IMG Activity: SIMG_CFORFBOB55SLD2
S_ALR_87003061	IMG Activity: SIMG_EURO_LC2315
S_ALR_87003062	IMG Activity: SIMG_CFMENUCX01_MD14
S_ALR_87003063	IMG Activity: SIMG_EURO_LC2350
S_ALR_87003064	IMG Activity: SIMG_CFMENUORFCAVAL
S_ALR_87003065	IMG Activity: SIMG_CFMENUCX01_MD36

S_ALR_87003066	IMG Activity: SIMG_CFMENUORFBOBKG0
S_ALR_87003067	IMG Activity: SIMG_EURO_LC2320
S_ALR_87003068	IMG Activity: SIMG_CFMENUORFCDERH
S_ALR_87003069	IMG Activity: SIMG_CFMENUCX01_MD15
S_ALR_87003070	IMG Activity: SIMG_CFORFBOB70RE
S_ALR_87003071	IMG Activity: SIMG_CFMENUORFC0001
S_ALR_87003072	IMG Activity: SIMG_EURO_LC2330
S_ALR_87003073	IMG Activity: SIMG_CFMENUCX01_MD40
S_ALR_87003074	IMG Activity: SIMG_CFMENUORFBOB43
S_ALR_87003075	IMG Activity: SIMG_EURO_LC2170
S_ALR_87003076	IMG Activity: SIMG_CFMENUCX01_MD43
S_ALR_87003077	IMG Activity: SIMG_CFMENUORFBO7Z3
S_ALR_87003078	IMG Activity: SIMG_EURO_LC2270
S_ALR_87003079	IMG Activity: SIMG_CFMENUCX01_MD17
S_ALR_87003080	IMG Activity: SIMG_XXMENUORFBOBB9
S_ALR_87003081	IMG Activity: SIMG_EURO_LC2206
S_ALR_87003082	IMG Activity: SIMG_XXMENUORFBOBB8
S_ALR_87003083	IMG Activity: SIMG_EURO_LC2206B
S_ALR_87003084	IMG Activity: SIMG_CFORFBCHKBVRE
S_ALR_87003085	IMG Activity: SIMG_CFMENUCX01_VA02
S_ALR_87003086	IMG Activity: SIMG_EURO_LC2220
S_ALR_87003087	IMG Activity: J_1ATYPE_OF_ID5
S_ALR_87003088	IMG Activity: SIMG_CFMENUCX01_VA04
S_ALR_87003089	IMG Activity: J_1ALETTER_DOC_CLAS4
S_ALR_87003090	IMG Activity: SIMG_EURO_LC2210
S_ALR_87003091	IMG Activity: SIMG_CFMENUCX01_VA05
S_ALR_87003092	IMG Activity: SIMG_EURO_LC2230
S_ALR_87003093	IMG Activity: J_1AASSIGN_FISC_TYP2
S_ALR_87003094	IMG Activity: SIMG_EURO_LC2240
S_ALR_87003095	IMG Activity: SIMG_CFMENUCX01_7700
S_ALR_87003096	IMG Activity: J_1AFISCAL_TYPE1
S_ALR_87003097	IMG Activity: SIMG_CFMENUCX01_CF01
S_ALR_87003098	IMG Activity: SIMG_EURO_LC2250
S_ALR_87003099	IMG Activity: SIMG_CFORFBCHKKODB
S_ALR_87003100	IMG Activity: SIMG_EURO_LC2340
S_ALR_87003101	IMG Activity: SIMG_CFMENUORFBOBAF
S_ALR_87003102	IMG Activity: SIMG_CFMENUCX01_DO01
S_ALR_87003103	IMG Activity: SIMG_CFMENUORFBXKN1
S_ALR_87003104	IMG Activity: SIMG_EURO_CS1090
S_ALR_87003105	IMG Activity: SIMG_CFMENUCX01_PR00
S_ALR_87003106	IMG Activity: SIMG_ORFB_INDUSTYPKR
S_ALR_87003107	IMG Activity: SIMG_CFMENUCX01_7200
S_ALR_87003108	IMG Activity: SIMG_ORFB_BUSTYPEKRE
S_ALR_87003109	IMG Activity: SIMG_EURO_CS2150
S_ALR_87003110	IMG Activity: SIMG_CFMENUCX01_DO02
S_ALR_87003111	IMG Activity: SIMG_EURO_CS2140
S_ALR_87003112	IMG Activity: J_1AGI_DIST_TYPES4
S_ALR_87003113	IMG Activity: J_1AACTIVITY_GIT4
S_ALR_87003114	IMG Activity: SIMG_CFMENUCX01_DO03
S_ALR_87003115	IMG Activity: J_1AACTIVITY_SSWT4
S_ALR_87003116	IMG Activity: SIMG_EURO_CS2270
S_ALR_87003117	IMG Activity: SIMG_CFMENUCX01_PO03
S_ALR_87003118	IMG Activity: SIMG_CFMENUORFBOB23
S_ALR_87003119	IMG Activity: SIMG_EURO_CS2206

S_ALR_87003120	IMG Activity: SIMG_CFMENUCX01_PO05
S_ALR_87003121	IMG Activity: SIMG_CFMENUORFBOBKC
S_ALR_87003122	IMG Activity: SIMG_CFMENUCX01_1206
S_ALR_87003123	IMG Activity: SIMG_CFMENUORFBOB24
S_ALR_87003124	IMG Activity: SIMG_EURO_CS2206B
S_ALR_87003125	IMG Activity: SIMG_CFMENUCX01_KA06
S_ALR_87003126	IMG Activity: SIMG_CFMENUORFBOBD3
S_ALR_87003127	IMG Activity: SIMG_CFMENUCX01_DO04
S_ALR_87003128	IMG Activity: SIMG_EURO_CS2220
S_ALR_87003129	IMG Activity: SIMG_CFMENUORFBOBKG
S_ALR_87003130	IMG Activity: SIMG_CFMENUCX01_KA04
S_ALR_87003131	IMG Activity: SIMG_CFORFBOB55SLD1
S_ALR_87003132	IMG Activity: SIMG_EURO_CS2210
S_ALR_87003133	IMG Activity: SIMG_CFMENUCX01_CF02
S_ALR_87003134	IMG Activity: SIMG_CFMENUORFBOBKA
S_ALR_87003135	IMG Activity: SIMG_EURO_CS2230
S_ALR_87003136	IMG Activity: SIMG_CFMENUCX01_CF03
S_ALR_87003137	IMG Activity: SIMG_CFMENUORFBOB44K
S_ALR_87003138	IMG Activity: SIMG_EURO_LC2342
S_ALR_87003139	IMG Activity: SIMG_CFMENUCX01_7300
S_ALR_87003140	IMG Activity: SIMG_CFMENUORFBOB05K
S_ALR_87003141	IMG Activity: SIMG_EURO_LC2390
S_ALR_87003142	IMG Activity: SIMG_CFORFBCMODKR
S_ALR_87003143	IMG Activity: SIMG_CFMENUCX01_CM01
S_ALR_87003144	IMG Activity: SIMG_CFORFBOBA5KR
S_ALR_87003145	IMG Activity: SIMG_EURO_CS1020
S_ALR_87003146	IMG Activity: SIMG_CFMENUCX01_7100
S_ALR_87003147	IMG Activity: SIMG_CFMENUORFBOBKE
S_ALR_87003148	IMG Activity: SIMG_CFMENUCX01_DOTY
S_ALR_87003149	IMG Activity: SIMG_CFORFBOB55DBOP
S_ALR_87003150	IMG Activity: SIMG_EURO_CS2130
S_ALR_87003151	IMG Activity: SIMG_CFORFBOBA5DBEP
S_ALR_87003152	IMG Activity: SIMG_EURO_CS1095
S_ALR_87003153	IMG Activity: SIMG_CFMENUCX01_IT23
S_ALR_87003154	IMG Activity: SIMG_CFMENUORFBOB50
S_ALR_87003155	IMG Activity: SIMG_EURO_CS1030
S_ALR_87003156	IMG Activity: SIMG_CFMENUCX01_MD33
S_ALR_87003157	IMG Activity: SIMG_CFMENUORFBOBB3
S_ALR_87003158	IMG Activity: SIMG_EURO_CS1070
S_ALR_87003159	IMG Activity: SIMG_CFMENUCX01_CU02
S_ALR_87003160	IMG Activity: SIMG_CFMENUORFBOBAU
S_ALR_87003161	IMG Activity: SIMG_EURO_CS1060
S_ALR_87003162	IMG Activity: SIMG_CFMENUCX01_IT24
S_ALR_87003163	IMG Activity: SIMG_CFMENUORFBOBAT
S_ALR_87003164	IMG Activity: SIMG_CFMENUCX01_FL02
S_ALR_87003165	IMG Activity: SIMG_EURO_CS1080
S_ALR_87003166	IMG Activity: SIMG_CFMENUCX01_FL03
S_ALR_87003167	IMG Activity: SIMG_EURO_RCOPCA44
S_ALR_87003168	IMG Activity: SIMG_CFMENUCX01_FL04
S_ALR_87003169	IMG Activity: SIMG_EURO_EWUMEKAAX
S_ALR_87003170	IMG Activity: SIMG_CFMENUCX01_FL05
S_ALR_87003171	IMG Activity: SIMG_CFORFBOB55DBEP
S_ALR_87003172	IMG Activity: SIMG_CFMENUCX01_FL06
S_ALR_87003173	IMG Activity: SIMG_EURO_RM07MBST

S_ALR_87003174	IMG Activity: SIMG_CFMENUORFBOB19
S_ALR_87003175	IMG Activity: SIMG_CFMENUCX01_DITA
S_ALR_87003176	IMG Activity: SIMG_CFORFBCHKQLKR
S_ALR_87003177	IMG Activity: SIMG_CFMENUCX01_CU09
S_ALR_87003178	IMG Activity: SIMG_EURO_PAKET
S_ALR_87003179	IMG Activity: SIMG_CFORFBT055F_KRE
S_ALR_87003180	IMG Activity: SIMG_CFMENUCX01_CU07
S_ALR_87003181	IMG Activity: SIMG_EURO_UMSETZAKTI
S_ALR_87003182	IMG Activity: SIMG_CFMENUCX01_CU03
S_ALR_87003183	IMG Activity: SIMG_EURO_FISL-FIGL
S_ALR_87003184	IMG Activity: SIMG_CFMENUCX01_CU05
S_ALR_87003185	IMG Activity: EURO_FIAA_ARCH
S_ALR_87003186	IMG Activity: SIMG_CFMENUCX01_7500

2

Transaction Code	Text
S_ALR_87003187	IMG Activity: SIMG_CFMENUCX01_CU10
S_ALR_87003188	IMG Activity: EURO_FIAA_RASKABU
S_ALR_87003189	IMG Activity: SIMG_CFMENUCX01_CU06
S_ALR_87003190	IMG Activity: SIMG_CFMENUCX01_IT21
S_ALR_87003191	IMG Activity: SIMG_CFMENUORFBOBT5
S_ALR_87003192	IMG Activity: EURO_FIAA_ERIN
S_ALR_87003193	IMG Activity: SIMG_CFMENUCX01_3165
S_ALR_87003194	IMG Activity: SIMG_CFMENUCX01_2110
S_ALR_87003195	IMG Activity: SIMG_EURO_SALDOVOR
S_ALR_87003196	IMG Activity: SIMG_CFMENUCX01_2120
S_ALR_87003197	IMG Activity: SIMG_CFMENUORFBOBT4
S_ALR_87003198	IMG Activity: SIMG_CFMENUCX01_2130
S_ALR_87003199	IMG Activity: SIMG_EURO_BILTEST
S_ALR_87003200	IMG Activity: SIMG_CFMENUCX01_DI03
S_ALR_87003201	IMG Activity: SIMG_CFMENUORFBOBAS
S_ALR_87003202	IMG Activity: SIMG_CFMENUCX01_1201
S_ALR_87003203	IMG Activity: SIMG_EURO_KUNDEN06
S_ALR_87003204	IMG Activity: SIMG_CFMENUCX01_IT11
S_ALR_87003205	IMG Activity: SIMG_CFMENUCX01_2551
S_ALR_87003206	IMG Activity: SIMG_CFMENUORFBOBYY
S_ALR_87003207	IMG Activity: SIMG_EURO_KUNDON07
S_ALR_87003208	IMG Activity: SIMG_CFMENUORFBOBXM
S_ALR_87003209	IMG Activity: SIMG_CFMENUORFBOBCL
S_ALR_87003210	IMG Activity: SIMG_CFMENUCX01_MD37
S_ALR_87003211	IMG Activity: SIMG_CFMENUCX01_3310
S_ALR_87003212	IMG Activity: SIMG_CFORFBCMODNACH
S_ALR_87003213	IMG Activity: SIMG_CFORFBTBUVTX
S_ALR_87003214	IMG Activity: SIMG_EURO_VORALL
S_ALR_87003215	IMG Activity: SIMG_CFMENUORFBOB58
S_ALR_87003216	IMG Activity: SIMG_CFMENUORFBOB99
S_ALR_87003217	IMG Activity: SIMG_CFMENUORFBOBBQ
S_ALR_87003218	IMG Activity: SIMG_CFMENUORFBOB97
S_ALR_87003219	IMG Activity: SIMG_EURO_EWUAFALO
S_ALR_87003220	IMG Activity: SIMG_CFMENUORFBOBB2
S_ALR_87003221	IMG Activity: SIMG_CFORFBOBCYMTRW
S_ALR_87003222	IMG Activity: SIMG_CFMENUORFBOBDA

S_ALR_87003223	IMG Activity: J_1AASSIGN_FISC_TYPE
S_ALR_87003224	IMG Activity: SIMG_EURO_EWUORGLO
S_ALR_87003225	IMG Activity: SIMG_CFMENUORFBOBYP
S_ALR_87003226	IMG Activity: SIMG_CFMENUORFBOB40
S_ALR_87003227	IMG Activity: SIMG_CFORFBTAKOF
S_ALR_87003228	IMG Activity: SIMG_EURO_KUNDEN03
S_ALR_87003229	IMG Activity: SIMG_CFMENUORFBOBYG
S_ALR_87003230	IMG Activity: J_1BTAX_ICMS_COMPLEM
S_ALR_87003231	IMG Activity: SIMG_EURO_PAKUEBERS
S_ALR_87003232	IMG Activity: J_1BTAX_SUBST_TRIBUT
S_ALR_87003233	IMG Activity: SIMG_CFMENUORFBOB59
S_ALR_87003234	IMG Activity: SIMG_EURO_TEILWAEHR2
S_ALR_87003235	IMG Activity: SIMG_EURO_EWUARCHI
S_ALR_87003236	IMG Activity: J_1BTAX_SUBST_TRIBEX
S_ALR_87003237	IMG Activity: SIMG_CFMENUORFBOBA1
S_ALR_87003238	IMG Activity: SIMG_CFORFBCHKZAZA
S_ALR_87003239	IMG Activity: J_1BTXIS1
S_ALR_87003240	IMG Activity: SIMG_CFMENUORFBOBYE
S_ALR_87003241	IMG Activity: SIMG_EURO_KUNDEN04
S_ALR_87003242	IMG Activity: SIMG_CFORFBOBXP
S_ALR_87003243	IMG Activity: J_1AREASON_DEF4
S_ALR_87003244	IMG Activity: SIMG_CFORFBT0332
S_ALR_87003245	IMG Activity: SIMG_EURO_KUNDEN05
S_ALR_87003246	IMG Activity: J_1AREASON_PER_TAXC4
S_ALR_87003247	IMG Activity: SIMG_CFMENUORFBOBCM
S_ALR_87003248	IMG Activity: SIMG_EURO_SALDO01
S_ALR_87003249	IMG Activity: J_1AFISCAL_TYPE4
S_ALR_87003250	IMG Activity: CFORFBT059E
S_ALR_87003251	IMG Activity: SIMG_CFMENUORFBOB89
S_ALR_87003252	IMG Activity: SIMG_EURO_SALDO02
S_ALR_87003253	IMG Activity: SIMG_CFORFBOB27ZVORA
S_ALR_87003254	IMG Activity: SIMG_ORFB_V_SECCODE
S_ALR_87003255	IMG Activity: SIMG_CFMENUORFBOBCG
S_ALR_87003256	IMG Activity: SIMG_CFORFBCHKEPZA
S_ALR_87003257	IMG Activity: SIMG_EURO_BUCHUNG
S_ALR_87003258	IMG Activity: SIMG_ORFB_V_RGOFFICE
S_ALR_87003259	IMG Activity: SIMG_CFMENUORFBOBCH
S_ALR_87003260	IMG Activity: SIMG_ORFB_V_TAXOFF
S_ALR_87003261	IMG Activity: SIMG_CFORFBT007R
S_ALR_87003262	IMG Activity: SIMG_EURO_BELEG03
S_ALR_87003263	IMG Activity: SIMG_CFORFBOBXLZMAN
S_ALR_87003264	IMG Activity: SIMG_CFORFBT059PI
S_ALR_87003265	IMG Activity: SIMG_CFMENUORFBOBC6
S_ALR_87003266	IMG Activity: SIMG_CFORFBT059PP
S_ALR_87003267	IMG Activity: SIMG_EURO_BELEG02
S_ALR_87003268	IMG Activity: SIMG_CFMENUORFBOBYC
S_ALR_87003269	IMG Activity: SIMG_CFORFBT059C
S_ALR_87003270	IMG Activity: SIMG_EURO_WEREKTO99
S_ALR_87003271	IMG Activity: SIMG_CFORFBOBBEZMAN
S_ALR_87003272	IMG Activity: SIMG_CFORFBSE71UMME
S_ALR_87003273	IMG Activity: SIMG_CFMENUORFBOBC7
S_ALR_87003274	IMG Activity: SIMG_XXMENUORFBOBA3
S_ALR_87003275	IMG Activity: SIMG_CFORFBT000F3
S_ALR_87003276	IMG Activity: SIMG_EURO_TRANSRET

S_ALR_87003277	IMG Activity: SIMG_CFMENUORFBOB98
S_ALR_87003278	IMG Activity: SIMG_CFORFBOBCWZMAN
S_ALR_87003279	IMG Activity: SIMG_CFORFBTEURB
S_ALR_87003280	IMG Activity: SIMG_CFMENUORFBOBYS
S_ALR_87003281	IMG Activity: SIMG_EURO_BERECHT
S_ALR_87003282	IMG Activity: SIMG_CFMENUORFBOBCF
S_ALR_87003283	IMG Activity: SIMG_CFORFBT005Q
S_ALR_87003284	IMG Activity: SIMG_CFORFBT059O
S_ALR_87003285	IMG Activity: J_1ATYPE_OF_ID4
S_ALR_87003286	IMG Activity: SIMG_EURO_BATCH
S_ALR_87003287	IMG Activity: SIMG_CFORFBT059V
S_ALR_87003288	IMG Activity: SIMG_CFORFBOB27ZMAN
S_ALR_87003289	IMG Activity: SIMG_EURO_ADMICRIT45
S_ALR_87003290	IMG Activity: J_1BCUST_GROUPS_ST
S_ALR_87003291	IMG Activity: SIMG_CFORFBCHKBOPZA
S_ALR_87003292	IMG Activity: SIMG_EURO_SPOOL
S_ALR_87003293	IMG Activity: J_1ATAX_CAT
S_ALR_87003294	IMG Activity: SIMG_XXMENUORFBOB60
S_ALR_87003295	IMG Activity: J_1ATAXCAT_BKRS_INFD
S_ALR_87003296	IMG Activity: SIMG_CFMENUORFBOB44
S_ALR_87003297	IMG Activity: SIMG_EURO_KVORLED
S_ALR_87003298	IMG Activity: J_1ATAXCAT_BKRS_INFK
S_ALR_87003299	IMG Activity: EURO_FIAA_RAJWE
S_ALR_87003300	IMG Activity: J_1ATAX_MINIMUM4
S_ALR_87003301	IMG Activity: SIMG_CFMENUORFBOBD2
S_ALR_87003302	IMG Activity: EURO_FIAA_BWA
S_ALR_87003303	IMG Activity: J_1ATAX_CLASSIF4
S_ALR_87003304	IMG Activity: SIMG_CFMENUORFBOB21
S_ALR_87003305	IMG Activity: J_1BTAX_REG_EXPORT
S_ALR_87003306	IMG Activity: ORFA_FIAA_RAJABS
S_ALR_87003307	IMG Activity: SIMG_CFMENUORFBFCHV
S_ALR_87003308	IMG Activity: SIMG_CFORFBWERK
S_ALR_87003309	IMG Activity: SIMG_CFMENUORFBFCHI
S_ALR_87003310	IMG Activity: SIMG_EURO_MAHN
S_ALR_87003311	IMG Activity: SIMG_CFORFBT001N
S_ALR_87003312	IMG Activity: J_1BTAXSITUATIONIPI
S_ALR_87003313	IMG Activity: SIMG_CFORFBCHKZAZL
S_ALR_87003314	IMG Activity: SIMG_EURO_RUNDKONTO2
S_ALR_87003315	IMG Activity: J_1BATL2V
S_ALR_87003316	IMG Activity: SIMG_CFORFBOBAZEDIZA
S_ALR_87003317	IMG Activity: J_1BATL1V
S_ALR_87003318	IMG Activity: SIMG_EURO_RUNDKONT04
S_ALR_87003319	IMG Activity: J_1BTAX_REGIONS
S_ALR_87003320	IMG Activity: SIMG_CFORFBOBWREDIZA
S_ALR_87003321	IMG Activity: J_1BTXMMCV
S_ALR_87003322	IMG Activity: SIMG_EURO_RUNDKONTO3
S_ALR_87003323	IMG Activity: SIMG_CFORFBOBCZEDIZA
S_ALR_87003324	IMG Activity: J_1BTAX_DEFAULT_RATE
S_ALR_87003325	IMG Activity: SIMG_EURO_RUNDKONTO
S_ALR_87003326	IMG Activity: J_1BTAX_IPI
S_ALR_87003327	IMG Activity: SIMG_EURO_ZAHL
S_ALR_87003328	IMG Activity: SIMG_CFORFBSE71ZAHL
S_ALR_87003329	IMG Activity: J_1BTAX_IPI_EXCEPT
S_ALR_87003330	IMG Activity: SIMG_EURO_RFEWA012

S_ALR_87003331	IMG Activity: SIMG_CFORFBCMODDB
S_ALR_87003332	IMG Activity: J_1BTAX_ICMS_GENERAL
S_ALR_87003333	IMG Activity: SIMG_EURO_RFEWASHK
S_ALR_87003334	IMG Activity: J_1BTAX_ICMS_EXCEPTI
S_ALR_87003335	IMG Activity: SIMG_CFMENUORFBOB05D
S_ALR_87003336	IMG Activity: J_1BTXSDCV
S_ALR_87003337	IMG Activity: SIMG_ORFB_J_1BBRANCV
S_ALR_87003338	IMG Activity: SIMG_EURO_EWUMEKABX
S_ALR_87003339	IMG Activity: SIMG_CFORFBT042F
S_ALR_87003340	IMG Activity: SIMG_ORFB_J_1BT001WV
S_ALR_87003341	IMG Activity: SIMG_CFMENUORFBFTXP
S_ALR_87003342	IMG Activity: SIMG_EURO_EWUARCH2
S_ALR_87003343	IMG Activity: SIMG_CFMENUORFBOB20
S_ALR_87003344	IMG Activity: SIMG_CFMENUORFBOBCK
S_ALR_87003345	IMG Activity: SIMG_EURO_RFEWA011
S_ALR_87003346	IMG Activity: SIMG_CFORFBT042TZ
S_ALR_87003347	IMG Activity: SIMG_CFORFBOB69
S_ALR_87003348	IMG Activity: SIMG_CFORFBOBC8
S_ALR_87003349	IMG Activity: SIMG_EURO_EWUMMCHK
S_ALR_87003350	IMG Activity: SIMG_CFORFBOBA5DB
S_ALR_87003351	IMG Activity: SIMG_ORFB1_T001RWT
S_ALR_87003352	IMG Activity: SIMG_EURO_EWUMPOHD40
S_ALR_87003353	IMG Activity: SIMG_CFORFBT042ZZ
S_ALR_87003354	IMG Activity: SIMG_CFMENUORFBOB79
S_ALR_87003355	IMG Activity: SIMG_ORFB_BUSTYPEDEB
S_ALR_87003356	IMG Activity: SIMG_CFORFBCMODKORR
S_ALR_87003357	IMG Activity: SIMG_EURO_RFEWUC1O
S_ALR_87003358	IMG Activity: J_1ADISCOUNT_TYPE4
S_ALR_87003359	IMG Activity: SIMG_CFMENUORFBO7S4
S_ALR_87003360	IMG Activity: SIMG_EURO_RFEWUC1F
S_ALR_87003361	IMG Activity: SIMG_CFMENUORFBOBXV
S_ALR_87003362	IMG Activity: SIMG_CFMENUORFBO7S6
S_ALR_87003363	IMG Activity: SIMG_CFMENUORFBOBWC1
S_ALR_87003364	IMG Activity: SIMG_EURO_RKAABR01
S_ALR_87003365	IMG Activity: SIMG_CFMENUORFBOBWD1
S_ALR_87003366	IMG Activity: SIMG_CFMENUORFBOBXU
S_ALR_87003367	IMG Activity: SIMG_EURO_RFEWUS1C
S_ALR_87003368	IMG Activity: SIMG_EURO_RFEWUS1P
S_ALR_87003369	IMG Activity: SIMG_ORFB_OBXO
S_ALR_87003370	IMG Activity: SIMG_CFMENUORFBOBB1
S_ALR_87003371	IMG Activity: SIMG_EURO_RFEWACUS
S_ALR_87003372	IMG Activity: SIMG_CFORFBOB00ZA
S_ALR_87003373	IMG Activity: SIMG_EURO_EWULISLS
S_ALR_87003374	IMG Activity: J_1A_INFL_ACC_DET
S_ALR_87003375	IMG Activity: SIMG_CFORFBOB09ZA
S_ALR_87003376	IMG Activity: SIMG_EURO_RAEWUS1B
S_ALR_87003377	IMG Activity: SIMG_CFMENUORFBOB77
S_ALR_87003378	IMG Activity: SIMG_CFORFBT055F_DEB
S_ALR_87003379	IMG Activity: SIMG_EURO_EWUEISLS
S_ALR_87003380	IMG Activity: SIMG_CFORFB1T048A
S_ALR_87003381	IMG Activity: SIMG_CFMENUORFBOB78
S_ALR_87003382	IMG Activity: SIMG_EURO_EWUCOPLS
S_ALR_87003383	IMG Activity: SIMG_CFMENUORFBOB30
S_ALR_87003384	IMG Activity: SIMG_CFORFBSE71KORR

S_ALR_87003385	IMG Activity: SIMG_EURO_RAEWUAFA
S_ALR_87003386	IMG Activity: SIMG_CFMENUORFBOBWE1
S_ALR_87003387	IMG Activity: SIMG_CFMENUORFBOB96
S_ALR_87003388	IMG Activity: SIMG_EURO_RAEWUS1A
S_ALR_87003389	IMG Activity: SIMG_CFMENUORFBOB31
S_ALR_87003390	IMG Activity: SIMG_CFORFBSXDABLG
S_ALR_87003391	IMG Activity: SIMG_CFMENUORFBOBWQ
S_ALR_87003392	IMG Activity: SIMG_EURO_EWUMMPOA
S_ALR_87003393	IMG Activity: SIMG_CFMENUORFBOBDU
S_ALR_87003394	IMG Activity: SIMG_CFMENUORFBOBWP
S_ALR_87003395	IMG Activity: SIMG_EURO_EWUCOOLO
S_ALR_87003396	IMG Activity: SIMG_CFMENUORFBBMV0
S_ALR_87003397	IMG Activity: SIMG_CFORFBCHKBLZA
S_ALR_87003398	IMG Activity: SIMG_CFORFBOBR1DTBN
S_ALR_87003399	IMG Activity: SIMG_EURO_EWUMEBAN40
S_ALR_87003400	IMG Activity: SIMG_CFMENUORFBOBZ9
S_ALR_87003401	IMG Activity: SIMG_EURO_EWUFISLT
S_ALR_87003402	IMG Activity: SIMG_CFMENUORFBOBZ8
S_ALR_87003403	IMG Activity: SIMG_CFORFBOB27ZAFR
S_ALR_87003404	IMG Activity: SIMG_EURO_RAEWUC1B
S_ALR_87003405	IMG Activity: SIMG_CFORFBFIBF
S_ALR_87003406	IMG Activity: SIMG_CFORFBCMODWF
S_ALR_87003407	IMG Activity: SIMG_EURO_EWUFISLS
S_ALR_87003408	IMG Activity: SIMG_EURO_KOSTENSTE
S_ALR_87003409	IMG Activity: SIMG_CFMENUORFBOBWJ1
S_ALR_87003410	IMG Activity: SIMG_EURO_VORSTEUER
S_ALR_87003411	IMG Activity: SIMG_EURO_CS2391
S_ALR_87003412	IMG Activity: SIMG_EURO_CS3100
S_ALR_87003413	IMG Activity: SIMG_CFMENUORFBOBKU
S_ALR_87003414	IMG Activity: SIMG_EURO_BACKUPPLAN
S_ALR_87003415	IMG Activity: SIMG_CFMENUORFBOBKV
S_ALR_87003416	IMG Activity: SIMG_EURO_ARCHIVISRE
S_ALR_87003417	IMG Activity: SIMG_CFMENUORFBOBKW
S_ALR_87003418	IMG Activity: SIMG_EURO_ZAHLUNG
S_ALR_87003419	IMG Activity: SIMG_EURO_AUF
S_ALR_87003420	IMG Activity: SIMG_CFORFBT059M_C
S_ALR_87003421	IMG Activity: SIMG_EURO_INTRASTAT
S_ALR_87003422	IMG Activity: SIMG_EURO_CS2251
S_ALR_87003423	IMG Activity: SIMG_CFORFBT001WT
S_ALR_87003424	IMG Activity: SIMG_EURO_CS2243
S_ALR_87003425	IMG Activity: SIMG_CFORFBOBWW
S_ALR_87003426	IMG Activity: SIMG_EURO_CS2297
S_ALR_87003427	IMG Activity: SIMG_EURO_KONDITION
S_ALR_87003428	IMG Activity: SIMG_CFMENUORFBOBAR
S_ALR_87003429	IMG Activity: SIMG_EURO_BUCHPROT
S_ALR_87003430	IMG Activity: SIMG_EURO_BERICHISRE
S_ALR_87003431	IMG Activity: SIMG_CFORFBCHKQLZA
S_ALR_87003432	IMG Activity: SIMG_EURO_KORRES
S_ALR_87003433	IMG Activity: HAUSW_UMSTELLUNG_TR
S_ALR_87003434	IMG Activity: SIMG_CFMENUORFBXDN1
S_ALR_87003435	IMG Activity: SIMG_EURO_KUNDE
S_ALR_87003436	IMG Activity: EURO_TR_EMMIS_UMSTEL
S_ALR_87003437	IMG Activity: SIMG_CFMENUORFBOBT1
S_ALR_87003438	IMG Activity: EURO_TR_EMMIS_NACHBE

S_ALR_87003439	IMG Activity: SIMG_ORFB_OBXQ
S_ALR_87003440	IMG Activity: SIMG_EURO_TABUMSPRUF
S_ALR_87003441	IMG Activity: EURO_TR_VERTW_VORARB
S_ALR_87003442	IMG Activity: SIMG_XXMENUORFBOBXK
S_ALR_87003443	IMG Activity: SIMG_EURO_WERTANZEIG
S_ALR_87003444	IMG Activity: SIMG_CFMENUORFBOBWB1
S_ALR_87003445	IMG Activity: SIMG_EURO_OFFLINE
S_ALR_87003446	IMG Activity: EURO_TR_TRANS_VORARB
S_ALR_87003447	IMG Activity: SIMG_ORFB_INDUSTYPDE
S_ALR_87003448	IMG Activity: EURO_TR_TRANS_UMSTEL
S_ALR_87003449	IMG Activity: SIMG_CFMENUORFBOBWA1
S_ALR_87003450	IMG Activity: EURO_TR_TRANS_NACHBE
S_ALR_87003451	IMG Activity: SIMG_EURO_BACKUP02
S_ALR_87003452	IMG Activity: EURO_TR_EMMIS_VOARBE
S_ALR_87003453	IMG Activity: SIMG_CFMENUORFBOBT2
S_ALR_87003454	IMG Activity: EURO_TR_VERTW_UMSTEL
S_ALR_87003455	IMG Activity: OHEURDE102
S_ALR_87003456	IMG Activity: SIMG_EURO_REPWRITE
S_ALR_87003457	IMG Activity: SIMG_EURO_BACKUP3
S_ALR_87003458	IMG Activity: SIMG_EURO_BACKUP2
S_ALR_87003459	IMG Activity: SIMG_EURO_TEILWAEHR1
S_ALR_87003460	IMG Activity: SIMG_EURO_UMSATZREP
S_ALR_87003461	IMG Activity: SIMG_EURO_BILANZ
S_ALR_87003462	IMG Activity: EURO_TR_VERTW_NACHBE
S_ALR_87003463	IMG Activity: SIMG_EURO_DTAFORM
S_ALR_87003464	IMG Activity: SIMG_EURO_PLANPROZ
S_ALR_87003465	IMG Activity: SIMG_EURO_REVISION02
S_ALR_87003466	IMG Activity: SIMG_EURO_LC1010
S_ALR_87003467	IMG Activity: SIMG_EURO_LOGGING02
S_ALR_87003468	IMG Activity: SIMG_EURO_REVISION01
S_ALR_87003469	IMG Activity: SIMG_EURO_LC2251
S_ALR_87003470	IMG Activity: SIMG_EURO_LC2243
S_ALR_87003471	IMG Activity: SIMG_EURO_LC2297
S_ALR_87003472	IMG Activity: SIMG_EURO_LC1005
S_ALR_87003473	IMG Activity: SIMG_EURO_LC3100
S_ALR_87003474	IMG Activity: SIMG_EURO_LC2391
S_ALR_87003475	IMG Activity: SIMG_EURO_ARCHIV02
S_ALR_87003476	IMG Activity: SIMG_EURO_NACHBEREC2
S_ALR_87003477	IMG Activity: SIMG_EURO_SAPKKAE0
S_ALR_87003478	IMG Activity: SIMG_EURO_VORTR
S_ALR_87003479	IMG Activity: SIMG_EURO_LC2244
S_ALR_87003480	IMG Activity: SIMG_EURO_ROLLBACK01
S_ALR_87003481	IMG Activity: SIMG_EURO_LC2207
S_ALR_87003482	IMG Activity: SIMG_EURO_R3CHECK
S_ALR_87003483	IMG Activity: SIMG_EURO_LC2296
S_ALR_87003484	IMG Activity: SIMG_EURO_PEREXTRAKT
S_ALR_87003485	IMG Activity: SIMG_EURO_BACKUP01
S_ALR_87003486	IMG Activity: SIMG_EURO_LC2221
S_ALR_87003487	IMG Activity: SIMG_EURO_LC2242
S_ALR_87003488	IMG Activity: SIMG_EURO_REVAKT
S_ALR_87003489	IMG Activity: SIMG_EURO_BACKUP03
S_ALR_87003490	IMG Activity: SIMG_EURO_LOGGING01
S_ALR_87003491	IMG Activity: SIMG_EURO_LC2222
S_ALR_87003492	IMG Activity: SIMG_EURO_LC2208

S_ALR_87003493	IMG Activity: SIMG_EURO_CS2222
S_ALR_87003494	IMG Activity: SIMG_EURO_CS2208
S_ALR_87003495	IMG Activity: SIMG_EURO_CS2221
S_ALR_87003496	IMG Activity: SIMG_EURO_RECHNUNR40
S_ALR_87003497	IMG Activity: SIMG_EURO_CS2207
S_ALR_87003498	IMG Activity: SIMG_EURO_BESTELLR40
S_ALR_87003499	IMG Activity: SIMG_EURO_WAREINGR40
S_ALR_87003500	IMG Activity: SIMG_EURO_BONUS
S_ALR_87003501	IMG Activity: SIMG_EURO_NACHFI2
S_ALR_87003502	IMG Activity: SIMG_EURO_CS2244
S_ALR_87003503	IMG Activity: SIMG_EURO_CS2242
S_ALR_87003504	IMG Activity: SIMG_EURO_FIXKURSR40
S_ALR_87003505	IMG Activity: SIMG_EURO_MASSENLR40
S_ALR_87003506	IMG Activity: SIMG_EURO_ADMINUSER
S_ALR_87003507	IMG Activity: NACHBEARB_TR_TM
S_ALR_87003508	IMG Activity: SIMG_EURO_NACHCO
S_ALR_87003509	IMG Activity: SIMG_EURO_CS1010
S_ALR_87003510	IMG Activity: SIMG_EURO_CS1005
S_ALR_87003511	IMG Activity: SIMG_EURO_COPCACT
S_ALR_87003512	IMG Activity: SIMG_EURO_VOREIS2
S_ALR_87003513	IMG Activity: SIMG_EURO_MASSENKR40
S_ALR_87003514	IMG Activity: SIMG_EURO_SOLLSTELL
S_ALR_87003515	IMG Activity: SIMG_EURO_CS2296
S_ALR_87003516	IMG Activity: SIMG_EURO_ROLLBACK02
S_ALR_87003517	IMG Activity: SIMG_EURO_PCASALDO
S_ALR_87003518	IMG Activity: SIMG_EURO_VORPROFIT2
S_ALR_87003519	IMG Activity: ORIP_IMEQ
S_ALR_87003520	IMG Activity: ORIP_USER_INFO
S_ALR_87003521	IMG Activity: ORIP_IMET
S_ALR_87003522	IMG Activity: ORIP_IMEX
S_ALR_87003523	IMG Activity: ORIP_IMEZ
S_ALR_87003524	IMG Activity: ORIP_INF_UMSCHL
S_ALR_87003525	IMG Activity: ORIP_VERD_VERS
S_ALR_87003526	IMG Activity: ORIP_IMEY
S_ALR_87003527	IMG Activity: ORIP_STAT_SCHEMA
S_ALR_87003528	IMG Activity: ORIP_IMER
S_ALR_87003529	IMG Activity: ORIP_IMEP
S_ALR_87003530	IMG Activity: ORIP_OIT6
S_ALR_87003531	IMG Activity: ORIP_BUDG_ERW
S_ALR_87003532	IMG Activity: ORIP_BUDG_IST
S_ALR_87003533	IMG Activity: ORIP_BUDGETART
S_ALR_87003534	IMG Activity: ORIP_BUDG_AUF2
S_ALR_87003535	IMG Activity: ORIP_IMEO
S_ALR_87003536	IMG Activity: ORIP_IME1
S_ALR_87003537	IMG Activity: ORIP_IME4
S_ALR_87003538	IMG Activity: ORIP_IMEV
S_ALR_87003539	IMG Activity: ORIP_KONS1
S_ALR_87003540	IMG Activity: ORIP_SU02
S_ALR_87003541	IMG Activity: ORIP_SU01
S_ALR_87003542	IMG Activity: ORIP_VERD_LOESCH2
S_ALR_87003543	IMG Activity: ORIP_VERD_LOESCH
S_ALR_87003544	IMG Activity: ORIP_IMER_VERD
S_ALR_87003545	IMG Activity: SIMGORIP_EBENEN
S_ALR_87003546	IMG Activity: SIMGORIP_VORSELEKT

S_ALR_87003547	IMG Activity: SIMGORIP_AUSPRAEGUNG
S_ALR_87003548	IMG Activity: SIMGORIP_ORGDEF
S_ALR_87003549	IMG Activity: ORIP_UPLOAD
S_ALR_87003550	IMG Activity: ORIP_IMEQ_VERD
S_ALR_87003551	IMG Activity: ORIP_IME1_VERD
S_ALR_87003552	IMG Activity: ORIP_IME4_VERD
S_ALR_87003553	IMG Activity: ORIP_IMEV_VERD
S_ALR_87003554	IMG Activity: ORIP_VERD_CUST
S_ALR_87003555	IMG Activity: ORIP_VERD_EINZEL
S_ALR_87003556	IMG Activity: ORIP_IMET_VERD
S_ALR_87003557	IMG Activity: ORIP_IMEX_VERD
S_ALR_87003558	IMG Activity: ORIP_IMEZ_VERD
S_ALR_87003559	IMG Activity: ORIP_IMEP_VERD
S_ALR_87003560	IMG Activity: ORIP_IMEO_VERD
S_ALR_87003561	IMG Activity: ORIP_BUDG_AUF1
S_ALR_87003562	IMG Activity: ORIM_OIB1
S_ALR_87003563	IMG Activity: ORIP_PLAN_ART
S_ALR_87003564	IMG Activity: ORIP_USER
S_ALR_87003565	IMG Activity: ORIP_USER_KURZ
S_ALR_87003566	IMG Activity: ORIP_PLANVERSION
S_ALR_87003567	IMG Activity: ORIP_GENEHMPLAN1
S_ALR_87003568	IMG Activity: OANF_GENEHM_STUF
S_ALR_87003569	IMG Activity: OANF_GENEHM_STUF1
S_ALR_87003570	IMG Activity: SIMG_ORIPBS52
S_ALR_87003571	IMG Activity: ORIM_OIT1
S_ALR_87003572	IMG Activity: ORIM_OIT2
S_ALR_87003573	IMG Activity: ORIP_STATUS_ART
S_ALR_87003574	IMG Activity: ORIP_INST1
S_ALR_87003575	IMG Activity: ORIP_INST2
S_ALR_87003576	IMG Activity: ORIP_RUECKSETZEN
S_ALR_87003577	IMG Activity: ORIM_STATUS
S_ALR_87003578	IMG Activity: ORIP_OK11
S_ALR_87003579	IMG Activity: ORIP_FELD
S_ALR_87003580	IMG Activity: ORIM_OPS6
S_ALR_87003581	IMG Activity: ORIP_BUDG_PROJ2
S_ALR_87003582	IMG Activity: ORIP_BUDG_PROG1
S_ALR_87003583	IMG Activity: ORIP_BUDG_VERT_ART
S_ALR_87003584	IMG Activity: ORIM_OIT3
S_ALR_87003585	IMG Activity: ORIP_UMWELT
S_ALR_87003586	IMG Activity: ORIP_GROSS
S_ALR_87003587	IMG Activity: ORIM_BUDG_PROF
S_ALR_87003588	IMG Activity: ORIP_BUDG_ART
S_ALR_87003589	IMG Activity: ORIP_OK11X
S_ALR_87003590	IMG Activity: SIMG_XXLEIDW2008
S_ALR_87003591	IMG Activity: SIMG_XXLEIDW2009
S_ALR_87003592	IMG Activity: SIMG_XXLEIDW2014
S_ALR_87003593	IMG Activity: SIMG_XXLEIDW2032
S_ALR_87003594	IMG Activity: SIMG_XXLEIDW2013
S_ALR_87003595	IMG Activity: SIMG_XXLEIDW2031
S_ALR_87003596	IMG Activity: SIMG_XXLEIDW2011
S_ALR_87003597	IMG Activity: SIMG_XXLEIDW2010
S_ALR_87003598	IMG Activity: SIMG_XXLEIDW2012
S_ALR_87003599	IMG Activity: SIMG_XXLEIDW2006
S_ALR_87003600	IMG Activity: SIMG_XXLEIDW2007

S_ALR_87003601	IMG Activity: SIMG_XXLEIDW2016
S_ALR_87003602	IMG Activity: SIMG_XXLEIDW2017
S_ALR_87003603	IMG Activity: SIMG_XXLEIDW2018
S_ALR_87003604	IMG Activity: SIMG_XXLEIDW2020
S_ALR_87003605	IMG Activity: SIMG_XXLEIDW2022
S_ALR_87003606	IMG Activity: SIMG_XXLEIDW2023
S_ALR_87003607	IMG Activity: SIMG_XXLEIDW2024
S_ALR_87003608	IMG Activity: SIMG_XXLEIDW2025
S_ALR_87003609	IMG Activity: SIMG_XXLEIDW2026
S_ALR_87003610	IMG Activity: SIMG_XXLEIDW2028
S_ALR_87003611	IMG Activity: SIMG_XXLEIDW2029
S_ALR_87003612	IMG Activity: SIMG_CFORFBOBWU
S_ALR_87003613	IMG Activity: SIMG_CFORFBOBWS
S_ALR_87003614	IMG Activity: SIMG_CFORFBOBWO
S_ALR_87003615	IMG Activity: SIMG_CFORFBT059M_T
S_ALR_87003616	IMG Activity: SIMG_CFORFBT059PK
S_ALR_87003617	IMG Activity: SIMG_CFORFBT059Z
S_ALR_87003618	IMG Activity: SIMG_CFORFBT059FBH
S_ALR_87003619	IMG Activity: SIMG_CFORFBT059KN
S_ALR_87003620	IMG Activity: SIMG_CFORFBT059KT
S_ALR_87003621	IMG Activity: CFORFBT059PR
S_ALR_87003622	IMG Activity: SIMG_CFORFBWTCTNO3
S_ALR_87003623	IMG Activity: J_1A_INFLATION_METH
S_ALR_87003624	IMG Activity: J_1A_INFLATION_INDEX
S_ALR_87003625	IMG Activity: J_1A_TIME_BASE_VAR
S_ALR_87003626	IMG Activity: J_1A_POSTING_VARIANT
S_ALR_87003627	IMG Activity: J_1AGL_ACC_INFLATION
S_ALR_87003628	IMG Activity: SIMG_CFORFBWTCTNO2
S_ALR_87003629	IMG Activity: SIMG_CFORFBWTCTNCL
S_ALR_87003630	IMG Activity: SIMG_CFORFBWTCTNGR
S_ALR_87003631	IMG Activity: SIMG_CFMENUORK13KEI
S_ALR_87003632	IMG Activity: SIMG_CFORFBOBWZ
S_ALR_87003633	IMG Activity: SIMG_CFMENUORK13KEH
S_ALR_87003634	IMG Activity: SIMG_CFORFBWTCTNUM
S_ALR_87003635	IMG Activity: SIMG_CFMENUORK1GCO1
S_ALR_87003636	IMG Activity: SIMG_CFORFBWTCTNT005
S_ALR_87003637	IMG Activity: SIMG_CFMENUORK1OKB9
S_ALR_87003638	IMG Activity: SIMG_CFORFBWTCTNO1
S_ALR_87003639	IMG Activity: SIMG_CFMENUORK1CMOD
S_ALR_87003640	IMG Activity: SIMG_CFMENUORFBOBBP
S_ALR_87003641	IMG Activity: SIMG_CFMENUORK11KEF
S_ALR_87003642	IMG Activity: SIMG_CFMENUORFBOB52
S_ALR_87003643	IMG Activity: SIMG_CFMENUORK1GCO2
S_ALR_87003644	IMG Activity: SIMG_CFMENUORFBOBU1
S_ALR_87003645	IMG Activity: SIMG_CFMENUORK13KE7
S_ALR_87003646	IMG Activity: SIMG_CFMENUORFBOB63
S_ALR_87003647	IMG Activity: SIMG_CFMENUORK1OCCL
S_ALR_87003648	IMG Activity: SIMG_CFMENUORFBOB68
S_ALR_87003649	IMG Activity: SIMG_CFMENUORK1OKEU
S_ALR_87003650	IMG Activity: SIMG_CFMENUORFBO7E6
S_ALR_87003651	IMG Activity: SIMG_CFMENUORK18KER
S_ALR_87003652	IMG Activity: SIMG_CFMENUORFBO7Z2
S_ALR_87003653	IMG Activity: SIMG_CFMENUORK18KES
S_ALR_87003654	IMG Activity: SIMG_CFMENUORFBO7Z1

S_ALR_87003655	IMG Activity: SIMG_CFMENUORK10KET
S_ALR_87003656	IMG Activity: SIMG_CFMENUORFBO7V1
S_ALR_87003657	IMG Activity: SIMG_CFMENUORK1GCS6
S_ALR_87003658	IMG Activity: SIMG_CFMENUORFBFBN1
S_ALR_87003659	IMG Activity: SIMG_CFMENUORK12KET
S_ALR_87003660	IMG Activity: SIMG_CFMENUORFBOB32A
S_ALR_87003661	IMG Activity: SIMG_CFMENUORK1GCT0
S_ALR_87003662	IMG Activity: SIMG_CFMENUORFBOB29
S_ALR_87003663	IMG Activity: SIMG_CFMENUORK18KET
S_ALR_87003664	IMG Activity: SIMG_CFMENUORFBOBBM
S_ALR_87003665	IMG Activity: SIMG_CFMENUORK18KET3
S_ALR_87003666	IMG Activity: SIMG_CFMENUORFBOBBN
S_ALR_87003667	IMG Activity: SIMG_CFMENUORK10KE2
S_ALR_87003668	IMG Activity: SIMG_CFORFBT000F1
S_ALR_87003669	IMG Activity: SIMG_CFMENUORK1GP31
S_ALR_87003670	IMG Activity: SIMG_CFMENUORFBOB65
S_ALR_87003671	IMG Activity: SIMG_CFMENUORK1KP34
S_ALR_87003672	IMG Activity: SIMG_CFMENUORFBOBC2
S_ALR_87003673	IMG Activity: SIMG_CFMENUORK17KEK
S_ALR_87003674	IMG Activity: SIMG_CFORFBOBA5BELE
S_ALR_87003675	IMG Activity: SIMG_CFMENUORK17KEF
S_ALR_87003676	IMG Activity: SIMG_CFMENUORFBOBBO
S_ALR_87003677	IMG Activity: SIMG_CFMENUORK17KEA
S_ALR_87003678	IMG Activity: SIMG_CFMENUORFBO7E3
S_ALR_87003679	IMG Activity: SIMG_ORKS_KA06_UMPLA
S_ALR_87003680	IMG Activity: SIMG_CFMENUORFBOB37
S_ALR_87003681	IMG Activity: SIMG_CFMENUORK14KE7
S_ALR_87003682	IMG Activity: SIMG_CFMENUORFBOBC1
S_ALR_87003683	IMG Activity: SIMG_CFMENUORFBOB56
S_ALR_87003684	IMG Activity: SIMG_CFMENUORK1KEDP
S_ALR_87003685	IMG Activity: SIMG_CFMENUORK1KESF
S_ALR_87003686	IMG Activity: SIMG_CFMENUORFBOB64
S_ALR_87003687	IMG Activity: SIMG_CFMENUORK10KE1
S_ALR_87003688	IMG Activity: SIMG_CFMENUORFBOBBF
S_ALR_87003689	IMG Activity: SIMG_CFMENUORK18KET4
S_ALR_87003690	IMG Activity: SIMG_CFORFBT000F2
S_ALR_87003691	IMG Activity: SIMG_CFMENUORK18KET2
S_ALR_87003692	IMG Activity: SIMG_CFMENUORFBOB41
S_ALR_87003693	IMG Activity: SIMG_CFMENUORK18KET1
S_ALR_87003694	IMG Activity: J_1ACLASS_DOCFI4
S_ALR_87003695	IMG Activity: SIMG_CFMENUORK1GCBAA
S_ALR_87003696	IMG Activity: SIMG_CFMENUORFBOB28
S_ALR_87003697	IMG Activity: SIMG_CFMENUORK10KEH
S_ALR_87003698	IMG Activity: VORGANGORDNER
S_ALR_87003699	IMG Activity: NK-PRIMANOTA
S_ALR_87003700	IMG Activity: SIMG_CFMENUORK10KE4
S_ALR_87003701	IMG Activity: SIMG_CFMENUORFBOBBH
S_ALR_87003702	IMG Activity: FELDAUSW_SACHBEARB
S_ALR_87003703	IMG Activity: SIMG_CFMENUORK1KE8W
S_ALR_87003704	IMG Activity: FW-7
S_ALR_87003705	IMG Activity: W_DF_LT_0202
S_ALR_87003706	IMG Activity: SIMG_CFMENUORK1KE8L
S_ALR_87003707	IMG Activity: SIMG_CFMENUORFBOBT8
S_ALR_87003708	IMG Activity: SIMG_CFMENUORK1KE8U

S_ALR_87003709	IMG Activity: SIMG_LEARCHVFKK
S_ALR_87003710	IMG Activity: SACHBEARB_ZUORD
S_ALR_87003711	IMG Activity: W_DF_LT_0201
S_ALR_87003712	IMG Activity: SIMG_CFMENUFWMCFZ89
S_ALR_87003713	IMG Activity: SIMG_LEVERWPROF
S_ALR_87003714	IMG Activity: W_DF_LT_0203
S_ALR_87003715	IMG Activity: ORDNERVERWLOGFELDER
S_ALR_87003716	IMG Activity: SIMG_LEARCHVTTK
S_ALR_87003717	IMG Activity: LZB-KZ
S_ALR_87003718	IMG Activity: SIMG_CFMENUO000O1CL
S_ALR_87003719	IMG Activity: SIMG_CFMENUORK10KEQ
S_ALR_87003720	IMG Activity: SIMG_CFMENUORFBOB32
S_ALR_87003721	IMG Activity: SIMG_LEVERWBER
S_ALR_87003722	IMG Activity: ORD_VERW_REGIS_PFLEG
S_ALR_87003723	IMG Activity: SIMG_LEARCHLIKP
S_ALR_87003724	IMG Activity: SIMG_CFMENUFWMCFZ51
S_ALR_87003725	IMG Activity: SIMG_CFMENUO000O008
S_ALR_87003726	IMG Activity: SIMG_CFMENUORK1KE8P
S_ALR_87003727	IMG Activity: SIMG_LEARCHLVS
S_ALR_87003728	IMG Activity: REPORTFUNKTPFLEGEN
S_ALR_87003729	IMG Activity: SIMG_CFMENUOLPFOPKA
S_ALR_87003730	IMG Activity: SIMG_CFMENUORK1KE8O
S_ALR_87003731	IMG Activity: NK-BELEGE
S_ALR_87003732	IMG Activity: SIMG_CFMENUO000O016
S_ALR_87003733	IMG Activity: KORRESPONDENZ_KLASSE
S_ALR_87003734	IMG Activity: SIMG_CFMENU2OLPKCY39
S_ALR_87003735	IMG Activity: SIMG_CFMENUOLPFOPK9
S_ALR_87003736	IMG Activity: SIMG_OLPR_V_TBMOT
S_ALR_87003737	IMG Activity: SIMG_CFMENUORK10KEZ
S_ALR_87003738	IMG Activity: SIMG_CFMENUFWMCFWZA
S_ALR_87003739	IMG Activity: OLPR_IM_BUDGPROF
S_ALR_87003740	IMG Activity: SIMG_CFMENUFNMCFNCD
S_ALR_87003741	IMG Activity: SIMG_CFMENUO000O002
S_ALR_87003742	IMG Activity: SIMG_CFMENUOLPFOPKX
S_ALR_87003743	IMG Activity: SIMG_CFMENUOLPKOPG7
S_ALR_87003744	IMG Activity: SIMG_CFMENUORK1OBA5
S_ALR_87003745	IMG Activity: SIMG_OLPR_ODP4
S_ALR_87003746	IMG Activity: SIMG_CFMENUOLPSOP50
S_ALR_87003747	IMG Activity: OLPR_IM_PLANPROF
S_ALR_87003748	IMG Activity: SIMG_CFMENUFWMCFWR1
S_ALR_87003749	IMG Activity: SIMG_CFMENUOLPSBS02
S_ALR_87003750	IMG Activity: SIMG_CFMENUFNMCFNCZ
S_ALR_87003751	IMG Activity: SIMG_CFMENUOLPFOPLJ
S_ALR_87003752	IMG Activity: SIMG_CFMENUO000SMOD
S_ALR_87003753	IMG Activity: SIMG_CFMENUOLPKOPD3
S_ALR_87003754	IMG Activity: SIMG_OLPR_ODP3
S_ALR_87003755	IMG Activity: SIMG_CFMENUORK1PFCG
S_ALR_87003756	IMG Activity: SIMG_IMMENUOLPROKO7
S_ALR_87003757	IMG Activity: SIMG_CFMENUOLQSOQS1
S_ALR_87003758	IMG Activity: EXT_BEW_ART_DEFINIER
S_ALR_87003759	IMG Activity: SIMG_CFMENUFWMCFZ87
S_ALR_87003760	IMG Activity: SIMG_CFMENUOLPSOP5A
S_ALR_87003761	IMG Activity: CM_OLPSCC_V_TCC21T
S_ALR_87003762	IMG Activity: SIMG_CFMENUOLPFOPLI

S_ALR_87003763	IMG Activity: SIMG_CFMENUORK10KEP
S_ALR_87003764	IMG Activity: SIMG_OLPR_OITB
S_ALR_87003765	IMG Activity: SIMG_CFMENUO000MERK
S_ALR_87003766	IMG Activity: SIMG_CFMENUOLPKOPD2
S_ALR_87003767	IMG Activity: SIMG_OLPR_ODP2
S_ALR_87003768	IMG Activity: SIMG_CFMENUOLQSOQSS
S_ALR_87003769	IMG Activity: EXT_BEWART_REPORTTYP
S_ALR_87003770	IMG Activity: CM_OLPSCC_V_TCC21
S_ALR_87003771	IMG Activity: SIMG_CFMENUFWMCFZ52
S_ALR_87003772	IMG Activity: SIMG_CFMENUOLPSOP58
S_ALR_87003773	IMG Activity: SIMG_CFMENUOLPFOPMJ
S_ALR_87003774	IMG Activity: SIMG_CFMENUORK14KED
S_ALR_87003775	IMG Activity: SIMG_OLPR_OITA
S_ALR_87003776	IMG Activity: SIMG_OLPR_ODP1
S_ALR_87003777	IMG Activity: SIMG_CFMENUO000KLAS
S_ALR_87003778	IMG Activity: SIMG_CFMENUOLPKOPD1
S_ALR_87003779	IMG Activity: SIMG_OLQU-O
S_ALR_87003780	IMG Activity: EXT_BWART_INT_BWART
S_ALR_87003781	IMG Activity: CM_OLPSCC_V_TCC20T
S_ALR_87003782	IMG Activity: SIMG_CFMENUFWMCFW47
S_ALR_87003783	IMG Activity: SIMG_CFMENUOLPFOPJ4N
S_ALR_87003784	IMG Activity: OLQG-E
S_ALR_87003785	IMG Activity: SIMG_CFMENUOLPSOP04
S_ALR_87003786	IMG Activity: SIMG_CFMENUORK1KE87
S_ALR_87003787	IMG Activity: SIMG_OLPR_V_T100C
S_ALR_87003788	IMG Activity: OLPR_IM_GROSS
S_ALR_87003789	IMG Activity: SIMG_CFMENUO0002239
S_ALR_87003790	IMG Activity: OLQG-O
S_ALR_87003791	IMG Activity: SIMG_CFMENUFNMCFNFD
S_ALR_87003792	IMG Activity: SIMG_CFMENUOLPKOPDE
S_ALR_87003793	IMG Activity: CM_OLPSCC_V_TCC20
S_ALR_87003794	IMG Activity: SIMG_CFMENUFWMCFZ56
S_ALR_87003795	IMG Activity: OLQU-B0
S_ALR_87003796	IMG Activity: SIMG_CFMENUOLPFOPKW
S_ALR_87003797	IMG Activity: SIMG_CFMENUORK10KEB
S_ALR_87003798	IMG Activity: SIMG_CFMENUOLPSOP8A
S_ALR_87003799	IMG Activity: SIMG_OLPR_KANKFESTPR
S_ALR_87003800	IMG Activity: SIMG_IMMENUOLPROKO6
S_ALR_87003801	IMG Activity: SIMG_CFMENUFNMCFNFE
S_ALR_87003802	IMG Activity: SIMG_CFMENUO000O12A
S_ALR_87003803	IMG Activity: SIMG_CFMENUOLPKCY40
S_ALR_87003804	IMG Activity: CF_OLPSCC_VC_TC85
S_ALR_87003805	IMG Activity: SIMG_CFMENUFWMCFZ19
S_ALR_87003806	IMG Activity: SIMG_CFMENUOLPSOP8B
S_ALR_87003807	IMG Activity: OLPR_IM_STATI2
S_ALR_87003808	IMG Activity: SIMG_CFMENUORK10KEG
S_ALR_87003809	IMG Activity: SIMG_OLPR_FM_FS02
S_ALR_87003810	IMG Activity: SIMG_CFMENUOLPFOPKT
S_ALR_87003811	IMG Activity: SIMG_CFMENUFNMCFNFF
S_ALR_87003812	IMG Activity: SIMG_CFMENUO000O003
S_ALR_87003813	IMG Activity: SIMG_CFMENUOLPKCY39
S_ALR_87003814	IMG Activity: CF_OLPSCC_V_TC83
S_ALR_87003815	IMG Activity: OLPR_IM_STATI1
S_ALR_87003816	IMG Activity: SIMG_CFMENUOLPSCANM

S_ALR_87003817	IMG Activity: SIMG_CFMENUORK11KED
S_ALR_87003818	IMG Activity: SIMG_CFMENUFWMCFW49
S_ALR_87003819	IMG Activity: SIMG_CFMENUOLPFOPKS
S_ALR_87003820	IMG Activity: SIMG_CFMENUFNMCFZZ1
S_ALR_87003821	IMG Activity: SIMG_OLPR_FM_FM3U
S_ALR_87003822	IMG Activity: CF_OLPSCC_V_TC81
S_ALR_87003823	IMG Activity: SIMG_CFMENUOLPKCY38
S_ALR_87003824	IMG Activity: OLPR_IM_STATI0
S_ALR_87003825	IMG Activity: SIMG_CFMENUORK13KEG
S_ALR_87003826	IMG Activity: SIMG_CFMENUOLPSCANR
S_ALR_87003827	IMG Activity: SIMG_CFMENUOLPFKZA1
S_ALR_87003828	IMG Activity: SIMG_CFMENUFWMCFW-3
S_ALR_87003829	IMG Activity: SIMG_CFMENUFNMCFZZ2
S_ALR_87003830	IMG Activity: SIMG_OLPR_FM_OKJ3
S_ALR_87003831	IMG Activity: SIMG_CFMENUO000O005
S_ALR_87003832	IMG Activity: SIMG_IMOLPR_OKEU
S_ALR_87003833	IMG Activity: SIMG_CFMENUOLPKOPG2
S_ALR_87003834	IMG Activity: SIMG_CFMENUOLPSOS52
S_ALR_87003835	IMG Activity: WP-ZUSATZBEW.
S_ALR_87003836	IMG Activity: SIMG_CFMENUFNMCFZZB
S_ALR_87003837	IMG Activity: SIMG_CFMENUOLPFOKZ2
S_ALR_87003838	IMG Activity: SIMG_CFMENUORK17KEJ
S_ALR_87003839	IMG Activity: SIMG_CFMENUOLPSOP46
S_ALR_87003840	IMG Activity: SIMG_OLPR_FM_OKJ2
S_ALR_87003841	IMG Activity: OLPR_IM_TOLERANZ
S_ALR_87003842	IMG Activity: SIMG_CFMENUO000O004
S_ALR_87003843	IMG Activity: SIMG_CFMENUOLPKOPD4
S_ALR_87003844	IMG Activity: ORDVERWTRANSAKTIONEN
S_ALR_87003845	IMG Activity: SIMG_CF_OLPSCC_OP15
S_ALR_87003846	IMG Activity: WP-ZUORDNUNG
S_ALR_87003847	IMG Activity: SIMG_CFMENUOLPFOKK1
S_ALR_87003848	IMG Activity: SIMG_CFMENUORK13KE1
S_ALR_87003849	IMG Activity: SIMG_CFMENUOLPSOP71
S_ALR_87003850	IMG Activity: OLPR_IM_WORKFLOW
S_ALR_87003851	IMG Activity: SIMG_OLPR_FM_OKJ1
S_ALR_87003852	IMG Activity: SIMG_CFMENUO000O017
S_ALR_87003853	IMG Activity: ORDVERW_FUNK_REG_PFL
S_ALR_87003854	IMG Activity: SIMG_CFMENUOLPKOPDB
S_ALR_87003855	IMG Activity: SIMG_CFMENUFWMCFZ18
S_ALR_87003856	IMG Activity: SIMG_CFMENUOLPFOKK4
S_ALR_87003857	IMG Activity: SIMG_CF_OLPSCC_OSSZ
S_ALR_87003858	IMG Activity: SIMG_IMMENUORFAAM01
S_ALR_87003859	IMG Activity: SIMG_OLPR_UEFAKTURA
S_ALR_87003860	IMG Activity: SIMG_CFMENUOLPSOP18
S_ALR_87003861	IMG Activity: VORGANGSARTPRO
S_ALR_87003862	IMG Activity: SIMG_CFMENUOLPKOPC5
S_ALR_87003863	IMG Activity: SIMG_CFMENUO000O006
S_ALR_87003864	IMG Activity: SIMG_CFMENUFWMCFW45
S_ALR_87003865	IMG Activity: SIMG_CFMENUOLPFOKK3
S_ALR_87003866	IMG Activity: SIMG_CFMENUORK14KE1
S_ALR_87003867	IMG Activity: SIMG_CFMENUOLPSOS53
S_ALR_87003868	IMG Activity: OLPR_IM_BILD
S_ALR_87003869	IMG Activity: SIMG_OLPR_OKI0
S_ALR_87003870	IMG Activity: SIMG_CFMENUFNMCFNFA

S_ALR_87003871	IMG Activity: SIMG_CFMENUOLPSOPJS
S_ALR_87003872	IMG Activity: KAP_ART
S_ALR_87003873	IMG Activity: SIMG_CFMENUOLPKOPA9
S_ALR_87003874	IMG Activity: SIMG_CFMENUOLPFOPTT
S_ALR_87003875	IMG Activity: SIMG_CFMENUORK10KES
S_ALR_87003876	IMG Activity: SIMG_CFMENUOLPSOS59
S_ALR_87003877	IMG Activity: SIMG_OLPR_OKGL
S_ALR_87003878	IMG Activity: SIMG_CFMENUFNMCFNFB
S_ALR_87003879	IMG Activity: SIMG_CFMENUOLPSOP67
S_ALR_87003880	IMG Activity: SIMG_OLPR_V_TKFPA_VR
S_ALR_87003881	IMG Activity: NUM_KAP
S_ALR_87003882	IMG Activity: SIMG_CFMENUOLPFOPKB
S_ALR_87003883	IMG Activity: SIMG_CFMENUORK1GB02
S_ALR_87003884	IMG Activity: SIMG_CFMENUOLPKCNG8
S_ALR_87003885	IMG Activity: SIMG_CFMENUOLPSCCW1
S_ALR_87003886	IMG Activity: SIMG_OLPR_OKG1
S_ALR_87003887	IMG Activity: SIMG_CFMENUFNMCFNFC
S_ALR_87003888	IMG Activity: SIMG_OLPR_KA01_AUF
S_ALR_87003889	IMG Activity: SIMG_OLPS_UBERSICHT
S_ALR_87003890	IMG Activity: SIMG_CFMENUFWMCFWFO
S_ALR_87003891	IMG Activity: SIMG_CFMENUOLPFOPKC
S_ALR_87003892	IMG Activity: SIMG_CFMENUORK1KE8R
S_ALR_87003893	IMG Activity: SIMG_CFMENUOLPKOPA6
S_ALR_87003894	IMG Activity: SIMG_CFMENUOLPSOS58
S_ALR_87003895	IMG Activity: SIMG_IMMENUORFAOAE3
S_ALR_87003896	IMG Activity: ROLLE/DOK.GRUPPE
S_ALR_87003897	IMG Activity: SIMG_CFMENUOLPROKG6
S_ALR_87003898	IMG Activity: SIMG_CFMENUOLPFOPKI
S_ALR_87003899	IMG Activity: SIMG_CFMENUORK1KE8Q
S_ALR_87003900	IMG Activity: SIMG_CFMENUFWMCTBCC
S_ALR_87003901	IMG Activity: OLPR_IM_UMWELT
S_ALR_87003902	IMG Activity: SIMG_CFMENUOLPSOS56
S_ALR_87003903	IMG Activity: SIMG_CFMENUOLPKOPA5
S_ALR_87003904	IMG Activity: SIMG_CFMENUFNMCFNQE
S_ALR_87003905	IMG Activity: SIMG_CFMENUORK10KER
S_ALR_87003906	IMG Activity: OLPR_IM_GRUND
S_ALR_87003907	IMG Activity: SIMG_CFMENUORFBOBH1
S_ALR_87003908	IMG Activity: SIMG_CFMENUOLPFOPK4
S_ALR_87003909	IMG Activity: SIMG_OLPR_T399X_N1
S_ALR_87003910	IMG Activity: SIMG_CFMENUFWMCFW43
S_ALR_87003911	IMG Activity: CFMENUOLPS_TCC10T
S_ALR_87003912	IMG Activity: SIMG_CFMENUOLPKOPA4
S_ALR_87003913	IMG Activity: SIMG_CFMENUOLPSOP48
S_ALR_87003914	IMG Activity: SIMG_CFMENUFNMCFOC9
S_ALR_87003915	IMG Activity: OLPR_IM_SELEKT
S_ALR_87003916	IMG Activity: SIMG_CFORFBOB28BPOS
S_ALR_87003917	IMG Activity: SIMG_CFMENUORK1KE8C
S_ALR_87003918	IMG Activity: SIMG_CFMENUOLPFOPL7
S_ALR_87003919	IMG Activity: SIMG_OLPR_TCJ41_6
S_ALR_87003920	IMG Activity: SIMG_CFMENUFWMCFZ76
S_ALR_87003921	IMG Activity: SIMG_CFMENUOLPSTCC10
S_ALR_87003922	IMG Activity: SIMG_CFMENUOLPKOPA3
S_ALR_87003923	IMG Activity: SIMG_CFMENUOLPSOP44
S_ALR_87003924	IMG Activity: SIMG_CFMENUFNMCFNC1

S_ALR_87003925	IMG Activity: SIMG_IMMENUOLPROPSA
S_ALR_87003926	IMG Activity: SIMG_CFMENUORK1GCT6
S_ALR_87003927	IMG Activity: SIMG_CFMENUOLPFOPL9
S_ALR_87003928	IMG Activity: SIMG_CFORFBOBBHBPOS
S_ALR_87003929	IMG Activity: SIMG_CFMENUOLPSOS61
S_ALR_87003930	IMG Activity: SIMG_CFMENUOLPROKG8
S_ALR_87003931	IMG Activity: SIMG_CFMENUFWMCFZ63
S_ALR_87003932	IMG Activity: SIMG_CFMENUOLPKOPB1
S_ALR_87003933	IMG Activity: SIMG_CFMENUOLPSOP63
S_ALR_87003934	IMG Activity: OLPR_IM_BILDPS
S_ALR_87003935	IMG Activity: SIMG_CFMENUFNMCFND1
S_ALR_87003936	IMG Activity: SIMG_CFMENUORK10KEA
S_ALR_87003937	IMG Activity: SIMG_CFMENUOLPFOPK2
S_ALR_87003938	IMG Activity: SIMG_CFMENUORFBOXK1
S_ALR_87003940	IMG Activity: SIMG_CFMENUOLPROKG4
S_ALR_87003941	IMG Activity: SIMG_CFMENUOLPKOPA8
S_ALR_87003942	IMG Activity: SIMG_CFMENUOLPSOPB4
S_ALR_87003943	IMG Activity: SIMG_CFMENUFWMCFZ85
S_ALR_87003944	IMG Activity: BUERGSCHAFTSART_II
S_ALR_87003945	IMG Activity: SIMG_CFMENUORK17KEI
S_ALR_87003946	IMG Activity: SIMG_ORK2_SELVAR
S_ALR_87003947	IMG Activity: SIMG_CFMENUORFBOBA7
S_ALR_87003948	IMG Activity: SIMG_CFMENUOLPSOS62
S_ALR_87003949	IMG Activity: SIMG_CFMENUOLPFOP4A
S_ALR_87003950	IMG Activity: SIMG_CFMENUOLPROKG5
S_ALR_87003951	IMG Activity: SIMG_CFMENUOLPKCNG3
S_ALR_87003952	IMG Activity: VERSICHERUNGSSPARTE
S_ALR_87003953	IMG Activity: SIMG_CFMENUOLPSOPB3
S_ALR_87003954	IMG Activity: SIMG_CFMENUFNMCFNCY
S_ALR_87003955	IMG Activity: SIMG_CFMENUORK11KEE
S_ALR_87003956	IMG Activity: SIMG_CFMENUORK2KALI
S_ALR_87003957	IMG Activity: SIMG_CFMENUORFBOBC4
S_ALR_87003958	IMG Activity: SIMG_CFMENUOLPFOPKV
S_ALR_87003959	IMG Activity: SIMG_CFMENUOLPSOS60
S_ALR_87003960	IMG Activity: SIMG_OLPR_V_TKFPA_VB
S_ALR_87003961	IMG Activity: SIMG_CFMENUOLPKOPDT
S_ALR_87003962	IMG Activity: SIMG_CFMENUFWMCFZ67
S_ALR_87003963	IMG Activity: SIMG_CFMENUOLPSOP21
S_ALR_87003964	IMG Activity: SIMG_CFMENUORK17KEQ
S_ALR_87003965	IMG Activity: SIMG_CFMENUFNMCFNQA
S_ALR_87003966	IMG Activity: SIMG_CFMENUORK2GCRS
S_ALR_87003967	IMG Activity: SIMG_CFMENUOLPFOPLP
S_ALR_87003968	IMG Activity: SIMG_CFMENUORFBOBC5
S_ALR_87003969	IMG Activity: SIMG_CFMENUOLPSOS54
S_ALR_87003970	IMG Activity: SIMG_OLPR_OFP1
S_ALR_87003971	IMG Activity: SIMG_CFMENUOLPKBCG1
S_ALR_87003972	IMG Activity: SIMG_CFMENUORK11KEB
S_ALR_87003973	IMG Activity: SIMG_CFMENUOLPSOP17
S_ALR_87003974	IMG Activity: SIMG_CFMENUFWMCFZ70
S_ALR_87003975	IMG Activity: SIMG_CFMENUFNMCFNCN
S_ALR_87003976	IMG Activity: SIMG_CFMENUORK2KAL8
S_ALR_87003977	IMG Activity: SIMG_CFMENUOLPFOPK8
S_ALR_87003978	IMG Activity: SIMG_CFMENUOLPSOS57
S_ALR_87003979	IMG Activity: SIMG_CFMENUORFBOB71

S_ALR_87003980	IMG Activity: SIMG_OLPR_USER_AE
S_ALR_87003981	IMG Activity: SIMG_CFMENUOLPKOPA0
S_ALR_87003982	IMG Activity: SIMG_CFMENUOLPSOP28
S_ALR_87003983	IMG Activity: SIMG_CFMENUORK1GS01
S_ALR_87003984	IMG Activity: SERVICEREPORT_BW_PR
S_ALR_87003985	IMG Activity: SIMG_CFMENUFNMCFOCA
S_ALR_87003986	IMG Activity: SIMG_CFMENUORK2GCRS1
S_ALR_87003987	IMG Activity: SIMG_OLPR_OPI2_AUF
S_ALR_87003988	IMG Activity: SIMG_CFMENUOLPFHJOB
S_ALR_87003989	IMG Activity: SIMG_CFMENUOLPSOS55
S_ALR_87003990	IMG Activity: SIMG_CFMENUOLPKOPC0
S_ALR_87003991	IMG Activity: SIMG_CFMENUOLPSOP37
S_ALR_87003992	IMG Activity: SIMG_CFMENUORK11KE4
S_ALR_87003993	IMG Activity: SIMG_CFMENUORFBOBH2
S_ALR_87003994	IMG Activity: SIMG_CFMENUFWMCFWS2
S_ALR_87003995	IMG Activity: SIMG_CFMENUOLPFCI41
S_ALR_87003996	IMG Activity: SIMG_OLPR_KEI1
S_ALR_87003997	IMG Activity: SIMG_CFMENUORK2OKRS1
S_ALR_87003998	IMG Activity: SIMG_CFMENUOLPSOS51
S_ALR_87003999	IMG Activity: SIMG_CFMENUFNMCFNQB
S_ALR_87004000	IMG Activity: SIMG_CFMENUOLPKCO44
S_ALR_87004001	IMG Activity: SIMG_CFMENUORK1GS11
S_ALR_87004002	IMG Activity: SIMG_CFMENUOLPSOP11
S_ALR_87004003	IMG Activity: SIMG_CFMENUORFBOBYZ
S_ALR_87004004	IMG Activity: SIMG_CFMENUOLPFOPK6
S_ALR_87004005	IMG Activity: SIMG_CFMENUFWMCFWS1
S_ALR_87004006	IMG Activity: SIMG_OLPR_V_TORB2
S_ALR_87004007	IMG Activity: SIMG_CFMENUORK2KSAZ
S_ALR_87004008	IMG Activity: SIMG_CFMENUOLPKOPC3
S_ALR_87004009	IMG Activity: SIMG_CFMENUFNMCFNQC
S_ALR_87004010	IMG Activity: SIMG_CFMENUORK18KEO
S_ALR_87004011	IMG Activity: SIMG_CFMENUORFBOBBG
S_ALR_87004012	IMG Activity: SIMG_CFMENUOLPSOP4A
S_ALR_87004031	IMG Activity: SIMG_CFMENUOLPFCO86
S_ALR_87004032	IMG Activity: SIMG_OLPR_V_TORB1
S_ALR_87004033	IMG Activity: SIMG_CFMENUFWMCFZW2
S_ALR_87004034	IMG Activity: SIMG_CFMENUORK2KALA
S_ALR_87004035	IMG Activity: SIMG_CFMENUOLPKOPC2
S_ALR_87004036	IMG Activity: SIMG_CFMENUFNMCFNQD
S_ALR_87004037	IMG Activity: SIMG_CFMENUORK1Z051
S_ALR_87004038	IMG Activity: SIMG_CFMENUORFBOB87
S_ALR_87004039	IMG Activity: SIMG_CFMENUOLPSOPB5
S_ALR_87004040	IMG Activity: SIMG_CFMENUOLPFOPK5
S_ALR_87004041	IMG Activity: SIMG_CFMENUFWMCFZW0
S_ALR_87004042	IMG Activity: SIMG_OLPR_FM_FM3N
S_ALR_87004043	IMG Activity: SIMG_CFMENUOLPKOPD0
S_ALR_87004044	IMG Activity: SIMG_CFMENUORK2OBYB
S_ALR_87004045	IMG Activity: SIMG_CFMENUFNMCFNC4
S_ALR_87004046	IMG Activity: SIMG_CFMENUORK1Z053
S_ALR_87004047	IMG Activity: SIMG_CFMENUORFBOBCN
S_ALR_87004048	IMG Activity: SIMG_CFMENUOLPSOP62
S_ALR_87004049	IMG Activity: SIMG_OLPF_SMOD_WABE
S_ALR_87004050	IMG Activity: SIMG_CFMENUFWMCFZ65
S_ALR_87004051	IMG Activity: SIMG_CFMENUOLPKOPDH

S_ALR_87004052	IMG Activity: SIMG_CFMENUOLPROPCV
S_ALR_87004053	IMG Activity: SIMG_CFMENUORK11KE6
S_ALR_87004054	IMG Activity: SIMG_CFMENUFNMCFODP
S_ALR_87004055	IMG Activity: SIMG_CFMENUORK2OK13
S_ALR_87004056	IMG Activity: SIMG_OLPF_SMOD_OCM02
S_ALR_87004057	IMG Activity: SIMG_CFMENUORFBOBCO
S_ALR_87004058	IMG Activity: SIMG_CFMENUOLPSOP41
S_ALR_87004059	IMG Activity: SIMG_CFMENUFWMCFWT4
S_ALR_87004060	IMG Activity: SIMG_CFMENUORK1KKP2
S_ALR_87004061	IMG Activity: SIMG_CFMENUOLPKOPG5
S_ALR_87004062	IMG Activity: SIMG_CFMENUOLPROPJS
S_ALR_87004063	IMG Activity: SIMG_CFMENUFNMCFODQ
S_ALR_87004064	IMG Activity: SIMG_OLPF_SMOD_OCM01
S_ALR_87004065	IMG Activity: SIMG_ORK2_KALH_REGEL
S_ALR_87004066	IMG Activity: SIMG_CFMENUOLPSOP39
S_ALR_87004067	IMG Activity: SIMG_CFORFBT001EXT
S_ALR_87004068	IMG Activity: SIMG_CFMENUOLPKGRAF
S_ALR_87004069	IMG Activity: BERICHTSAUSWAHL_WP
S_ALR_87004070	IMG Activity: SIMG_CFMENUORK1KKF2
S_ALR_87004071	IMG Activity: SIMG_OLPF_SMOD_EXPMT
S_ALR_87004072	IMG Activity: SIMG_ORK2_SELEK_RPAN
S_ALR_87004073	IMG Activity: SIMG_CFMENUORFBOBWH
S_ALR_87004074	IMG Activity: SIMG_CFMENUFNMCFZTA
S_ALR_87004075	IMG Activity: SIMG_CFMENUOLPROPJO
S_ALR_87004076	IMG Activity: SIMG_CFMENUOLPSOP13
S_ALR_87004077	IMG Activity: SIMG_CFMENUOLPKOPC1
S_ALR_87004078	IMG Activity: SIMG_CFMENUORK1COR2
S_ALR_87004079	IMG Activity: SIMG_CFMENUFWMCFW53
S_ALR_87004080	IMG Activity: SIMG_OLPF_SMOD_EXPCG
S_ALR_87004081	IMG Activity: SIMG_ORK2_EXTRA_GRE9
S_ALR_87004082	IMG Activity: SIMG_CFMENUORFBOBWI
S_ALR_87004083	IMG Activity: KORRESPONDENZ
S_ALR_87004084	IMG Activity: SIMG_CFMENUOLPSOP54
S_ALR_87004085	IMG Activity: SIMG_CFMENUOLPROPJN
S_ALR_87004086	IMG Activity: SIMG_CFMENUORK1CO02
S_ALR_87004087	IMG Activity: SIMG_CFMENUORK2OK19
S_ALR_87004088	IMG Activity: SIMG_CFMENUORFBOBWK
S_ALR_87004089	IMG Activity: SIMG_OLPF_SMOD_ORDCR
S_ALR_87004090	IMG Activity: SIMG_CFMENUOLPKOPDF
S_ALR_87004091	IMG Activity: SIMG_CFMENUFWMCFW50
S_ALR_87004092	IMG Activity: SIMG_CFMENUORK1VA02
S_ALR_87004093	IMG Activity: SIMG_CFMENUORK2SU03
S_ALR_87004094	IMG Activity: SIMG_OLPR_OPH7
S_ALR_87004095	IMG Activity: SIMG_CFMENUOLPSOP51
S_ALR_87004096	IMG Activity: SIMG_CFORFBCMODBLVOR
S_ALR_87004097	IMG Activity: SIMG_OLPF_SMOD_COMK
S_ALR_87004098	IMG Activity: TRANSZUKORRESPONDENZ
S_ALR_87004099	IMG Activity: SIMG_OLPR_FM_OPH6
S_ALR_87004100	IMG Activity: SIMG_OLPF_SMOD_STATX
S_ALR_87004101	IMG Activity: SIMG_CFMENUORK10KEL
S_ALR_87004102	IMG Activity: SIMG_CFMENUOLPSOP35
S_ALR_87004103	IMG Activity: SIMG_CFMENUOLPKCES
S_ALR_87004104	IMG Activity: SIMG_CFMENUORK2SU02
S_ALR_87004105	IMG Activity: SIMG_CFMENUFNMCFND8

S_ALR_87004106	IMG Activity: SIMG_CFMENUORFBOBBZ
S_ALR_87004107	IMG Activity: ABGRENZUNG_WERTP
S_ALR_87004108	IMG Activity: SIMG_CFMENUORK10KEM
S_ALR_87004109	IMG Activity: SIMG_CFMENUOLPFOPJ1
S_ALR_87004110	IMG Activity: SIMG_ORK2_PARAM_RPXN
S_ALR_87004111	IMG Activity: SIMG_CFMENUOLPSOP36
S_ALR_87004112	IMG Activity: SONDERVEREINBARUNGEN
S_ALR_87004113	IMG Activity: SIMG_OLPR_FM_OPH5
S_ALR_87004114	IMG Activity: SIMG_CFMENUFWMCFWTR
S_ALR_87004115	IMG Activity: SIMG_CFMENUOLPKCEV
S_ALR_87004116	IMG Activity: SIMG_CFMENUORFBTXDE
S_ALR_87004117	IMG Activity: SIMG_CFMENUORK1MM02
S_ALR_87004118	IMG Activity: SIMG_CFMENUOLPFOPJ3
S_ALR_87004119	IMG Activity: SIMG_CFMENUOLPSOP7A
S_ALR_87004120	IMG Activity: SIMG_CFMENUORK2GR21
S_ALR_87004121	IMG Activity: SIMG_CFMENUOLPROP421
S_ALR_87004122	IMG Activity: AKTENART
S_ALR_87004123	IMG Activity: SIMG_CMMENUOLPKOPDM
S_ALR_87004124	IMG Activity: FINANZAMT
S_ALR_87004125	IMG Activity: SIMG_CFMENUORFBTRWC
S_ALR_87004126	IMG Activity: SIMG_CFMENUORK10KE8
S_ALR_87004127	IMG Activity: SIMG_OLPF_SMOD_CON05
S_ALR_87004128	IMG Activity: SIMG_CFMENUOLPSOP82
S_ALR_87004129	IMG Activity: SIMG_CFMENUOLPROP101
S_ALR_87004130	IMG Activity: SIMG_CFMENUORK2OCMI
S_ALR_87004131	IMG Activity: SIMG_CFMENUFNMCFNC6
S_ALR_87004132	IMG Activity: BAV_ANZEIGEN
S_ALR_87004133	IMG Activity: SIMG_CFORFBCMODEXST
S_ALR_87004134	IMG Activity: SIMG_OLPF_SMOD_CON04
S_ALR_87004135	IMG Activity: SIMG_CFMENUORK10KE6
S_ALR_87004136	IMG Activity: SIMG_CFMENUOLPKOPG1
S_ALR_87004137	IMG Activity: SIMG_CFMENUOLPSOP65
S_ALR_87004138	IMG Activity: SIMG_CFMENUOLPROP451
S_ALR_87004139	IMG Activity: SIMG_OLPF_SMOD_CON03
S_ALR_87004140	IMG Activity: SIMG_CFMENUORK2FGRP
S_ALR_87004141	IMG Activity: SIMG_CFMENUFNMCFNCE
S_ALR_87004142	IMG Activity: SIMG_CFMENUOLPSOP72
S_ALR_87004143	IMG Activity: SIMG_CFMENUFWMCFWID
S_ALR_87004144	IMG Activity: SIMG_CFMENUORK10KEO
S_ALR_87004145	IMG Activity: SIMG_CFMENUORFBOBAD
S_ALR_87004146	IMG Activity: SIMG_CFMENUOLPROP401
S_ALR_87004147	IMG Activity: SIMG_OLPF_SMOD_CON02
S_ALR_87004148	IMG Activity: SIMG_CFMENUOLPKOPG4
S_ALR_87004149	IMG Activity: SIMG_CFMENUORK2GR5G
S_ALR_87004150	IMG Activity: SIMG_CFMENUFNMCFNC2
S_ALR_87004151	IMG Activity: SIMG_CFMENUORK11KE1
S_ALR_87004152	IMG Activity: RENTENFONDS_ZUORD
S_ALR_87004153	IMG Activity: SIMG_CFMENUORFBOBAE
S_ALR_87004154	IMG Activity: SIMG_OLPS_UBERSI_FHM
S_ALR_87004155	IMG Activity: SIMG_OLPR_LSTVR_TRM
S_ALR_87004156	IMG Activity: SIMG_OLPF_SMOD_CON01
S_ALR_87004157	IMG Activity: SIMG_CFMENUOLPKOPDQ
S_ALR_87004158	IMG Activity: SIMG_CFMENUORK2KALN
S_ALR_87004159	IMG Activity: SIMG_CFMENUFNMCFNCU

S_ALR_87004160	IMG Activity: SIMG_CFMENUORK10KE5
S_ALR_87004161	IMG Activity: SIMG_CFMENUORFBTTXC
S_ALR_87004162	IMG Activity: SIMG_OLPR_TRMPLOPT8
S_ALR_87004163	IMG Activity: SIMG_CFMENUOLPSOP74
S_ALR_87004164	IMG Activity: SIMG_OLPF_SMOD_CONF
S_ALR_87004165	IMG Activity: SIMG_CFMENUORK10KKS
S_ALR_87004166	IMG Activity: SIMG_CFMENUORK2KAH2
S_ALR_87004167	IMG Activity: SIMG_OLPRPSPTERMOPTQ
S_ALR_87004168	IMG Activity: SIMG_CFMENUOLPKOPDJ
S_ALR_87004169	IMG Activity: SIMG_CFMENUOLPFOPL6
S_ALR_87004170	IMG Activity: SIMG_CFMENUOLPSOP47
S_ALR_87004171	IMG Activity: SIMG_CFMENUORFBOBCP
S_ALR_87004172	IMG Activity: SIMG_CFMENUFWMCFW40
S_ALR_87004173	IMG Activity: SIMG_CFMENUFNMCFNS4
S_ALR_87004174	IMG Activity: SIMG_OLPR_FM_OPH4
S_ALR_87004175	IMG Activity: SIMG_CMMENUOLPKOPDK
S_ALR_87004176	IMG Activity: KURSZUSATZ_WP
S_ALR_87004177	IMG-Aktivität: SIMG_CFMENUOLPFOPL4
S_ALR_87004178	IMG Activity: SIMG_CFMENUOLPSOP80
S_ALR_87004179	IMG Activity: SIMG_CFMENUFNMCFWRE
S_ALR_87004180	IMG Activity: SIMG_CFMENUOLPSOPE0
S_ALR_87004181	IMG Activity: SIMG_CFMENUOLPKOPDL
S_ALR_87004182	IMG Activity: SIMG_OLPR_OK60_FIN
S_ALR_87004183	IMG Activity: SIMG_CFMENUFWMCFW80
S_ALR_87004184	IMG Activity: SIMG_CFMENUOLPFCOMP
S_ALR_87004185	IMG Activity: SIMG_CFMENUFNMCFZID
S_ALR_87004186	IMG Activity: SIMG_CFMENUOLPSOP15
S_ALR_87004187	IMG Activity: SIMG_OLPR_FINPLANTAG
S_ALR_87004188	IMG Activity: SIMG_CFMENUOLPKOPG3
S_ALR_87004189	IMG Activity: WP-TYP
S_ALR_87004190	IMG Activity: SIMG_CFMENUOLPFKOMM
S_ALR_87004191	IMG Activity: SIMG_CFMENUFNMCFZ32
S_ALR_87004192	IMG Activity: SIMG_CFMENUOLPSOSSZ
S_ALR_87004193	IMG Activity: SIMG_OLPR_TCJ41_2
S_ALR_87004194	IMG Activity: SIMG_CFMENUOLPFCOIS
S_ALR_87004195	IMG Activity: SIMG_CFMENUOLPKOPG0
S_ALR_87004196	IMG Activity: VERWAHRART_PFLEGEN
S_ALR_87004197	IMG Activity: SIMG_CFMENUFNMCFZ34
S_ALR_87004198	IMG Activity: SIMG_CFMENUOLPSOPE8
S_ALR_87004199	IMG Activity: SIMG_CFMENUOLPFCOS1
S_ALR_87004200	IMG Activity: SIMG_OLPR_OPTM
S_ALR_87004201	IMG Activity: SIMG_CFMENUFWMCFW46
S_ALR_87004202	IMG Activity: SIMG_CFMENUFNMCFZ33
S_ALR_87004203	IMG Activity: SIMG_CFMENUOLPSOPE6
S_ALR_87004204	IMG Activity: SIMG_OLPR_CJVC_FIN
S_ALR_87004205	IMG Activity: SIMG_CFMENUOLPFCOF1
S_ALR_87004206	IMG Activity: MAHNW_ZEWG_MAHNBAR
S_ALR_87004207	IMG Activity: SIMG_CFMENUFWMCFW42
S_ALR_87004208	IMG Activity: SIMG_CFMENUOLPKOPA2
S_ALR_87004209	IMG Activity: SIMG_CFMENUOLPFOPKE
S_ALR_87004210	IMG Activity: SIMG_OLPR_OPI4
S_ALR_87004211	IMG Activity: SIMG_CFMENUOLPSOPE4
S_ALR_87004212	IMG Activity: SIMG_CFMENUORK10KEX
S_ALR_87004213	IMG Activity: MAHNW_FORMULARE_MSTF

S_ALR_87004214	IMG Activity: SIMG_CFMENUFWMCFW41
S_ALR_87004215	IMG Activity: SIMG_CFMENUOLPKOPCS
S_ALR_87004216	IMG Activity: SIMG_CFMENUOLPSOPE3
S_ALR_87004217	IMG Activity: SIMG_OLPR_OFD8
S_ALR_87004218	IMG Activity: SIMG_OLPF_SMOD_ASSMB
S_ALR_87004219	IMG Activity: SIMG_CFMENUORK2OKA6
S_ALR_87004220	IMG Activity: SIMG_CFORFBOBA5STEU
S_ALR_87004221	IMG Activity: FONDSTYP
S_ALR_87004222	IMG Activity: MAHNW_GERMAHNVERFAHR
S_ALR_87004223	IMG Activity: SIMG_CFMENUOLPKOPCR
S_ALR_87004224	IMG Activity: SIMG_CFMENUORK10KEY
S_ALR_87004225	IMG Activity: SIMG_OLPF_SMOD_DELTN
S_ALR_87004226	IMG Activity: SIMG_CFMENUOLPSOPE2
S_ALR_87004227	IMG Activity: SIMG_OLPR_FM_OPH3
S_ALR_87004228	IMG Activity: SIMG_CFMENUORK2OKA4
S_ALR_87004229	IMG Activity: SIMG_CFMENUORFBOB88
S_ALR_87004230	IMG Activity: SIMG_CMMENUOLPKSEQUE
S_ALR_87004231	IMG Activity: SIMG_CFMENUFWMCFW55
S_ALR_87004232	IMG Activity: SIMG_CFMENUORK1KCH1
S_ALR_87004233	IMG Activity: SIMG_CFMENUFNMCFZBK
S_ALR_87004234	IMG Activity: SIMG_OLPF_SMOD_SAVE2
S_ALR_87004235	IMG Activity: SIMG_CFMENUOLPSOPE1
S_ALR_87004236	IMG Activity: SIMG_OLPR_FM_OPH2
S_ALR_87004237	IMG Activity: SIMG_CFMENUORK2OKEC
S_ALR_87004238	IMG Activity: SIMG_CFMENUORFBOBY6
S_ALR_87004239	IMG Activity: SIMG_CFMENUORK1KSKO
S_ALR_87004240	IMG Activity: SIMG_CFMENUOLPKOPDU
S_ALR_87004241	IMG Activity: SIMG_OLPF_SMOD_SAVE
S_ALR_87004242	IMG Activity: SIMG_CFMENUOLPSOP73
S_ALR_87004243	IMG Activity: BERICHTSAUSWAHL_DL
S_ALR_87004244	IMG Activity: SIMG_CFMENUFWMCFZC6
S_ALR_87004245	IMG Activity: SIMG_OLPR_FM_OPH1
S_ALR_87004246	IMG Activity: SIMG_CFMENUORK1KE51
S_ALR_87004247	IMG Activity: SIMG_CFMENUORK2OKEK
S_ALR_87004248	IMG Activity: SIMG_CFMENUOLPKOP4A
S_ALR_87004249	IMG Activity: SIMG_OLPF_SMOD_CREAT
S_ALR_87004250	IMG Activity: SIMG_CFMENUOLPSOPEA
S_ALR_87004251	IMG Activity: SIMG_CFMENUORFBSM59
S_ALR_87004252	IMG Activity: SIMG_OLPR_FM_OPI6
S_ALR_87004253	IMG Activity: FELD_DEPOT
S_ALR_87004254	IMG Activity: SIMG_CFMENUFNMCFNS6
S_ALR_87004255	IMG Activity: SIMG_CFMENUORK1KE59
S_ALR_87004256	IMG Activity: SIMG_CMMENUOLPKVORG
S_ALR_87004257	IMG Activity: SIMG_CFMENUORK2OKB2
S_ALR_87004258	IMG Activity: SIMG_CFMENUOLPSOPL2
S_ALR_87004259	IMG Activity: SIMG_CFMENOLPFOPJB
S_ALR_87004260	IMG Activity: SIMG_OLPR_OPIC_FIN
S_ALR_87004261	IMG Activity: SIMG_CFMENUORFBOBWB
S_ALR_87004262	IMG Activity: WP-KURSART
S_ALR_87004263	IMG Activity: SIMG_CFMENUORK10KE7
S_ALR_87004264	IMG Activity: SIMG_CFMENUOLPKOPJF
S_ALR_87004265	IMG Activity: SIMG_CFMENUOLPSOPL3
S_ALR_87004266	IMG Activity: SIMG_CFMENUORK2OKB3
S_ALR_87004267	IMG Activity: SIMG_CFMENUFNMCFZ81

S_ALR_87004268	IMG Activity: SIMG_CFMENUOLPFOPLM
S_ALR_87004269	IMG Activity: SIMG_OLPR_KANK1
S_ALR_87004270	IMG Activity: SIMG_CFMENUORK11KEM
S_ALR_87004271	IMG Activity: SIMG_CFMENUOLPKOPJE
S_ALR_87004272	IMG Activity: SIMG_CFMENUOLPSOKK7
S_ALR_87004273	IMG Activity: SIMG_CFMENUORFBOBWJ
S_ALR_87004274	IMG Activity: SIMG_CFMENUFWMCFW58
S_ALR_87004275	IMG Activity: SIMG_CFMENUOLPFOPLK
S_ALR_87004276	IMG Activity: SIMG_CFMENUORK2SM35
S_ALR_87004277	IMG Activity: SIMG_CFMENUFNMCFZW0
S_ALR_87004278	IMG Activity: SIMG_OLPR_FMU1_ZAHL
S_ALR_87004279	IMG Activity: SIMG_CFMENUORK1KCH4
S_ALR_87004280	IMG Activity: SIMG_CFMENUOLPKOPCF
S_ALR_87004281	IMG Activity: SIMG_CFMENUOLQNOQNM3
S_ALR_87004282	IMG Activity: SIMG_CFMENUORFBOBR8
S_ALR_87004283	IMG Activity: SIMG_CFMENUOLPFOPJW
S_ALR_87004284	IMG Activity: SIMG_CFMENUFWMCFZWE
S_ALR_87004285	IMG Activity: SIMG_CFMENUORK2KA02
S_ALR_87004286	IMG Activity: SIMG_CFMENUOLPSOP4F
S_ALR_87004287	IMG Activity: SIMG_CFMENUORK10KEW
S_ALR_87004288	IMG Activity: SIMG_CFMENUFNMCFZW2
S_ALR_87004289	IMG Activity: SIMG_CFMENUOLPROKO7
S_ALR_87004290	IMG Activity: SIMG_CFMENUOLPKOPCH
S_ALR_87004291	IMG Activity: SIMG_CFMENUOLPFOPKZ
S_ALR_87004292	IMG Activity: OLQN-MDD
S_ALR_87004293	IMG Activity: SIMG_CFMENUORFBOBWA
S_ALR_87004294	IMG Activity: SIMG_CFMENUOLPSOPEC
S_ALR_87004295	IMG Activity: SIMG_CFMENUFWMCFW59
S_ALR_87004296	IMG Activity: SIMG_CFMENUORK1CJ07
S_ALR_87004297	IMG Activity: SIMG_ORK2_KM5V
S_ALR_87004298	IMG Activity: TEXTBAUSTEINE_KOP
S_ALR_87004299	IMG Activity: SIMG_CFMENUOLPRKEI1
S_ALR_87004300	IMG Activity: SIMG_CFMENUOLPFOPJ9
S_ALR_87004301	IMG Activity: SIMG_CFMENUOLPKOPJN
S_ALR_87004302	IMG Activity: SIMG_CFMENUOLQNOQND
S_ALR_87004303	IMG Activity: SIMG_CFMENUORK11KE0
S_ALR_87004304	IMG Activity: SIMG_CFMENUOLPSOP78
S_ALR_87004305	IMG Activity: WZ_KOP_TEXTE_MANDANT
S_ALR_87004306	IMG Activity: SIMG_OLPR_OKEU
S_ALR_87004307	IMG Activity: NK_GATTUNG
S_ALR_87004308	IMG Activity: SIMG_CFMENUORK2KA01
S_ALR_87004309	IMG Activity: SIMG_CFMENUORFBO7E4
S_ALR_87004310	IMG Activity: SIMG_CFMENUOLPFCO80
S_ALR_87004311	IMG Activity: SIMG_CMMENUOLPKTABLE
S_ALR_87004312	IMG Activity: SIMG_CFMENUOLQNOQNA
S_ALR_87004313	IMG Activity: SIMG_CFMENUORK10KEN
S_ALR_87004314	IMG Activity: SIMG_CFMENUOLPSOP76
S_ALR_87004315	IMG Activity: SIMG_CFMENUOLPROKO6
S_ALR_87004316	IMG Activity: SIMG_CFMENUFNMCOBY4
S_ALR_87004317	IMG Activity: SIMG_CFMENUORK2KA021
S_ALR_87004318	IMG Activity: SIMG_CFMENUFWMCFW-1
S_ALR_87004319	IMG Activity: SIMG_CFMENUOLPFCO83
S_ALR_87004320	IMG Activity: SIMG_CFMENUOLPKOPCM
S_ALR_87004321	IMG Activity: OLQN-OQN8

S_ALR_87004322	IMG Activity: SIMG_CFMENUORK1Z042
S_ALR_87004323	IMG Activity: SIMG_CFMENUOLPSOPEB
S_ALR_87004324	IMG Activity: SIMG_CFMENUORFBOBD1
S_ALR_87004325	IMG Activity: SIMG_OLPR_K01_ABR
S_ALR_87004326	IMG Activity: OLQN-MLB
S_ALR_87004327	IMG Activity: SIMG_CFMENUFNMCFZ53
S_ALR_87004328	IMG Activity: SIMG_ORK2_EWKRT_CMOD
S_ALR_87004329	IMG Activity: SIMG_CFMENUOLPFOPKP
S_ALR_87004330	IMG Activity: ALLGEMKLASSIF_WP
S_ALR_87004331	IMG Activity: SIMG_CFMENUOLPKOP7B
S_ALR_87004332	IMG Activity: SIMG_CFMENUORK18KEN
S_ALR_87004333	IMG Activity: SIMG_OLPS_NUM_GROBPL
S_ALR_87004334	IMG Activity: SIMG_CFMENUORK2AG_VF
S_ALR_87004335	IMG Activity: SIMG_CFORFBCMODARCH
S_ALR_87004336	IMG Activity: SIMG_OLPR_USEREXITS
S_ALR_87004337	IMG Activity: OLQN-MF
S_ALR_87004338	IMG Activity: SIMG_CFMENUFNMCFZ54
S_ALR_87004339	IMG Activity: SIMG_CFMENUORK10KEK
S_ALR_87004340	IMG Activity: SIMG_CMMENUOLPKFELDR
S_ALR_87004341	IMG Activity: SIMG_CFMENUOLPFOPL2
S_ALR_87004342	IMG Activity: SIMG_XXMENUORK2_P_V
S_ALR_87004343	IMG Activity: SIMG_CFMENUFWMCFW54
S_ALR_87004344	IMG Activity: SIMG_CFMENUOLPSOP77
S_ALR_87004345	IMG Activity: OLQN-AB
S_ALR_87004346	IMG Activity: SIMG_CFMENUORFBOBS2
S_ALR_87004347	IMG Activity: SIMG_OLPR_KANKVERZ
S_ALR_87004348	IMG Activity: SIMG_CFMENUORK11KE8
S_ALR_87004349	IMG Activity: SIMG_CMMENUOLPKSORTI
S_ALR_87004350	IMG Activity: SIMG_CFMENUFNMCFZ55
S_ALR_87004351	IMG Activity: SIMG_CFMENUOLPFOPJH
S_ALR_87004352	IMG Activity: SIMG_OLPS_CMOD_ARCH
S_ALR_87004353	IMG Activity: SIMG_CFMENUFWMCFZBW
S_ALR_87004354	IMG Activity: OLQL-MK
S_ALR_87004355	IMG Activity: SIMG_CFMENUOLPRKO8N
S_ALR_87004356	IMG Activity: SIMG_CFMENUOLPFOPJM
S_ALR_87004357	IMG Activity: SIMG_CFMENUOLPKOPCE
S_ALR_87004358	IMG Activity: SIMG_CFMENUORK18KEG
S_ALR_87004359	IMG Activity: SIMG_CFMENUORFBOBR3
S_ALR_87004360	IMG Activity: SIMG_CFMENUFNMCFZ84
S_ALR_87004361	IMG Activity: SIMG_CFMENUOLPSOP49
S_ALR_87004362	IMG Activity: OLQI-OQI4
S_ALR_87004363	IMG Activity: SIMG_CFMENUFWMCFZFD
S_ALR_87004364	IMG Activity: SIMG_CFMENUORK11KEA
S_ALR_87004365	IMG Activity: SIMG_ORKAOPI1
S_ALR_87004366	IMG Activity: SIMG_CFMENUOLPFOPJI
S_ALR_87004367	IMG Activity: SIMG_OLPR_V_TCJ41_11
S_ALR_87004368	IMG Activity: SIMG_CFMENUOLPKOPCN
S_ALR_87004369	IMG Activity: SIMG_CFMENUORFBOB22
S_ALR_87004370	IMG Activity: SIMG_CFMENUFNMCFZ62
S_ALR_87004371	IMG Activity: SIMG_CFMENUOLPSSXDA
S_ALR_87004372	IMG Activity: OLQN-OQNFB
S_ALR_87004373	IMG Activity: SIMG_OLPR_VC0SRG
S_ALR_87004374	IMG Activity: SIMG_CFMENUFWMCFZCT
S_ALR_87004375	IMG Activity: SIMG_CMMENUOLPKFIXI

S_ALR_87004376	IMG Activity: SIMG_CFMENUOLPFOPKN
S_ALR_87004377	IMG Activity: SIMG_CFMENUOLPSOP55
S_ALR_87004378	IMG Activity: OLQN-OQNFR
S_ALR_87004379	IMG Activity: SIMG_CFMENUFNMCFZ75
S_ALR_87004380	IMG Activity: SIMG_CFMENUORK1GCBA
S_ALR_87004381	IMG Activity: SIMG_CFMENUORFBOBWG
S_ALR_87004382	IMG Activity: SIMG_OLPR_T0030_N1
S_ALR_87004383	IMG Activity: SIMG_CFMENUOLPFOPJG
S_ALR_87004384	IMG Activity: SIMG_CFMENUOLPKOPCI
S_ALR_87004385	IMG Activity: SIMG_CFMENUOLPSOP52
S_ALR_87004386	IMG Activity: SIMG_CFMENUFWMCFZBB
S_ALR_87004387	IMG Activity: SIMG_CFMENUORK1KEE0
S_ALR_87004388	IMG Activity: MAHNW_ROLLENTYPEN
S_ALR_87004389	IMG Activity: OLQN-OQNFM
S_ALR_87004390	IMG Activity: SIMG_CFMENUORFBOBWF
S_ALR_87004391	IMG Activity: SIMG_OLPR_T399X_N0
S_ALR_87004392	IMG Activity: SIMG_CFMENUOLPFOPJF
S_ALR_87004393	IMG Activity: SIMG_CFMENUOLPKOPCG
S_ALR_87004394	IMG Activity: SIMG_CFMENUOLPSOP70
S_ALR_87004395	IMG Activity: SIMG_CFMENUORK1OKEQ
S_ALR_87004396	IMG Activity: BS_RESTP_AUSGL
S_ALR_87004397	IMG Activity: DEFAULT_ZUSATZBEW.
S_ALR_87004398	IMG Activity: OLQN-MLFM
S_ALR_87004399	IMG Activity: SIMG_OLPR_ABRECHOPTR
S_ALR_87004400	IMG Activity: SIMG_CFMENUORFBOBWE
S_ALR_87004401	IMG Activity: SIMG_CFMENUOLPFOPJE
S_ALR_87004402	IMG Activity: SIMG_CFMENUOLPSOS38
S_ALR_87004403	IMG Activity: SIMG_CFMENUOLPKOPDA
S_ALR_87004404	IMG Activity: SIMG_CFMENUORK1OKE0
S_ALR_87004405	IMG Activity: SIMG_CFMENUFNMCFNCG
S_ALR_87004406	IMG Activity: OLQN-MLF
S_ALR_87004407	IMG Activity: SIMG_CFMENUFWMCFZBE
S_ALR_87004408	IMG Activity: SIMG_OLPR_TCJ41_7
S_ALR_87004409	IMG Activity: SIMG_CFMENUORFBOBWD
S_ALR_87004410	IMG Activity: SIMG_CFMENUOLPFOPJA
S_ALR_87004411	IMG Activity: SIMG_CFMENUOLPSOS35
S_ALR_87004412	IMG Activity: SIMG_CMMENUOLPKINFO
S_ALR_87004413	IMG Activity: SIMG_CFMENUORK1OB08
S_ALR_87004414	IMG Activity: OLQN-MSS
S_ALR_87004415	IMG Activity: STEUERSAETZE
S_ALR_87004416	IMG Activity: SIMG_OLPR_ZINSZINS1
S_ALR_87004417	IMG Activity: SIMG_CFMENUOLPFOPJC
S_ALR_87004418	IMG Activity: SIMG_CFMENUOLPSOS33
S_ALR_87004419	IMG Activity: SIMG_CFMENUFWMCFZCE
S_ALR_87004420	IMG Activity: SIMG_CFMENUORFBOBWC
S_ALR_87004421	IMG Activity: SIMG_CFMENUORK1OB07
S_ALR_87004422	IMG Activity: SIMG_CFMENUOLPKOPCD
S_ALR_87004423	IMG Activity: OLQN-MW
S_ALR_87004424	IMG Activity: SIMG_CFMENUFNMCFZ58
S_ALR_87004425	IMG Activity: SIMG_CFMENUOLPSOS32
S_ALR_87004426	IMG Activity: SIMG_OLPR_OB83
S_ALR_87004427	IMG Activity: SIMG_CFMENUOLPFOS15
S_ALR_87004429	IMG Activity: SIMG_CFMENUOLPKOPB4
S_ALR_87004430	IMG Activity: SIMG_CFMENUORFBOBR7

S_ALR_87004431	IMG Activity: SIMG_CFMENUFWMCFZCG
S_ALR_87004432	IMG Activity: OLQN-MPL
S_ALR_87004433	IMG Activity: SIMG_CFMENUOLPFOP76
S_ALR_87004434	IMG Activity: SIMG_CFMENUOLPSOS30
S_ALR_87004435	IMG Activity: SIMG_OLPR_OBAC
S_ALR_87004436	IMG Activity: SIMG_CFMENUFNMCFWR1
S_ALR_87004437	IMG Activity: SIMG_CFMENUORK11KEC
S_ALR_87004438	IMG Activity: SIMG_CFMENUOLPKOPB3
S_ALR_87004439	IMG Activity: SIMG_CFMENUORK11KE9
S_ALR_87004440	IMG Activity: STATUS
S_ALR_87004441	IMG Activity: OLQN-OQNP
S_ALR_87004442	IMG Activity: SIMG_CFMENUOLPFOPJD
S_ALR_87004443	IMG Activity: SIMG_CFMENUFNMCFNZA
S_ALR_87004444	IMG Activity: SIMG_CFMENUOLPSOS31
S_ALR_87004445	IMG Activity: SIMG_OLPR_OPIH
S_ALR_87004446	IMG Activity: SIMG_CFMENUOLPKBCG9
S_ALR_87004447	IMG Activity: SIMG_CFMENUORK1FO62
S_ALR_87004448	IMG Activity: OLQN-OQNN
S_ALR_87004449	IMG Activity: SIMG_CFMENUFWMCFZC7
S_ALR_87004450	IMG Activity: SIMG_CFMENUOLPSOKK9
S_ALR_87004451	IMG Activity: SIMG_CFMENUOLPFOPEC
S_ALR_87004452	IMG Activity: SIMG_CFMENUFNMCFZZE
S_ALR_87004453	IMG Activity: SIMG_OLPR_OPIE
S_ALR_87004454	IMG Activity: SIMG_CFMENUORK1AS02
S_ALR_87004455	IMG Activity: SIMG_CFMENUOLPKOPCY
S_ALR_87004456	IMG Activity: OLQN-SCR
S_ALR_87004457	IMG Activity: SIMG_CFMENUOLPFOPKJ
S_ALR_87004458	IMG Activity: SIMG_CFMENUFNMCFZZD
S_ALR_87004459	IMG Activity: SIMG_CFMENUOLPSOVT6
S_ALR_87004460	IMG Activity: SIMG_CFMENUORK11W32
S_ALR_87004461	IMG Activity: SIMG_OLPR_ABC_ZUORDN
S_ALR_87004462	IMG Activity: SIMG_CFMENUOLPKOPCX
S_ALR_87004463	IMG Activity: SIMG_CFMENUOLQNOQNM1
S_ALR_87004464	IMG Activity: SIMG_CFMENUFNMCFNCM
S_ALR_87004465	IMG Activity: SIMG_CFMENUORK1CP02
S_ALR_87004466	IMG Activity: SIMG_CFMENUOLPSOS41
S_ALR_87004467	IMG Activity: SIMG_CFMENUOLPFCO81
S_ALR_87004468	IMG Activity: SIMG_OLPR_ABC_SCHEMA
S_ALR_87004469	IMG Activity: OLQN-OQN6
S_ALR_87004470	IMG Activity: SIMG_CFMENUOLPKOPB5
S_ALR_87004471	IMG Activity: SIMG_CFMENUFNMCFNCT
S_ALR_87004472	IMG Activity: SIMG_CFMENUOLPFOPL3
S_ALR_87004473	IMG Activity: SIMG_CFMENUORK1KO02
S_ALR_87004474	IMG Activity: SIMG_CFMENUOLPSSDT
S_ALR_87004475	IMG Activity: SIMG_OLPR_ABC_UMGEB
S_ALR_87004476	IMG Activity: SIMG_CMMENUOLQNOQNS1
S_ALR_87004477	IMG Activity: SIMG_CFMENUOLPKBCG5
S_ALR_87004478	IMG Activity: SIMG_CFMENUORK1KS02
S_ALR_87004479	IMG Activity: SIMG_CFMENUFNMCFZZ5
S_ALR_87004480	IMG Activity: SIMG_CFMENUOLPSCLVL
S_ALR_87004481	IMG Activity: SIMG_CFMENUOLPFCO84
S_ALR_87004482	IMG Activity: SIMG_OLPR_KA06_VERZ
S_ALR_87004483	IMG Activity: SIMG_CFMENUOLQNOQNM2
S_ALR_87004484	IMG Activity: SIMG_CFMENUOLPKAWSS

S_ALR_87004485	IMG Activity: SIMG_CFMENUOLPFOPKM
S_ALR_87004486	IMG Activity: SIMG_CFMENUORK18KEH
S_ALR_87004487	IMG Activity: SIMG_CFMENUFNMCFND3
S_ALR_87004488	IMG Activity: SIMG_CFMENUOLPSOS70
S_ALR_87004489	IMG Activity: SIMG_OLPR_OPID
S_ALR_87004490	IMG Activity: OLQN-MPN
S_ALR_87004492	IMG Activity: SIMG_CFMENUOLPFOPKL
S_ALR_87004493	IMG Activity: OLQN-WL
S_ALR_87004494	IMG Activity: SIMG_CFMENUOLPKAWSW
S_ALR_87004495	IMG Activity: SIMG_CFMENUFNMCFNDA
S_ALR_87004496	IMG Activity: SIMG_CFMENUOLPSOS29
S_ALR_87004497	IMG Activity: SIMG_OLPR_TCJ41_5
S_ALR_87004498	IMG Activity: OLQN-WK
S_ALR_87004500	IMG Activity: SIMG_CFMENUFNMCFZD4
S_ALR_87004501	IMG Activity: SIMG_CFMENUOLPFOPJ8
S_ALR_87004502	IMG Activity: SIMG_CFMENUOLPSOS37
S_ALR_87004503	IMG Activity: SIMG_CFMENUOLPKBCG3
S_ALR_87004504	IMG Activity: SIMG_OLPR_OPIC
S_ALR_87004505	IMG Activity: SIMG_CFMENUORK18KEB
S_ALR_87004506	IMG Activity: SIMG_CFMENUFNMCFZCX
S_ALR_87004507	IMG Activity: SIMG_CFMENUOLPSOS36
S_ALR_87004508	IMG Activity: SIMG_CFMENUOLPFCO44
S_ALR_87004509	IMG Activity: SIMG_CFMENUOLPKBCG4
S_ALR_87004510	IMG Activity: SIMG_CFMENUORK18KED
S_ALR_87004511	IMG Activity: MAHNW_GRUNDEINSTELLU
S_ALR_87004512	IMG Activity: SIMG_OLPR_OPIB
S_ALR_87004513	IMG Activity: SIMG_CFMENUOLPSOS34
S_ALR_87004514	IMG Activity: SIMG_CFMENUORK1VERT
S_ALR_87004515	IMG Activity: SIMG_CFMENUOLPFOPJO
S_ALR_87004516	IMG Activity: MANUELLE_MAHNSTUFE
S_ALR_87004517	IMG Activity: SIMG_CFMENUORK1FGRP
S_ALR_87004518	IMG Activity: SIMG_CFMENUOLPKBCG8
S_ALR_87004519	IMG Activity: SIMG_CFMENUOLPSOSVS
S_ALR_87004520	IMG Activity: SIMG_OLPR_OPIA
S_ALR_87004521	IMG Activity: SIMG_CFMENUORK1FGRW
S_ALR_87004522	IMG Activity: SIMG_CFMENUOLPFOPJN
S_ALR_87004523	IMG Activity: SIMG_CFMENUORK1Z009
S_ALR_87004524	IMG Activity: SIMG_CFMENUOLPKOPU7
S_ALR_87004525	IMG Activity: SIMG_CFMENUOLPSOS26
S_ALR_87004526	IMG Activity: SIMG_OLPR_OT03
S_ALR_87004527	IMG Activity: V_BEWART_EX_MAHN
S_ALR_87004528	IMG Activity: SIMG_CFMENUOLPKOPU4
S_ALR_87004529	IMG Activity: SIMG_CFMENUOLPSOS23
S_ALR_87004530	IMG Activity: SIMG_OLPR_CJ8V
S_ALR_87004531	IMG Activity: SIMG_CFMENUOLPFOPJS
S_ALR_87004532	IMG Activity: ABGRENZUNG_DARL
S_ALR_87004533	IMG Activity: SIMG_CFMENUOLPSOS24
S_ALR_87004534	IMG Activity: SIMG_CFMENUOLPKOPU5
S_ALR_87004535	IMG Activity: SIMG_CFMENUOLPKOPU3
S_ALR_87004536	IMG Activity: SIMG_OLPR_KANK5
S_ALR_87004537	IMG Activity: SIMG_CFMENUFNMCFZ52
S_ALR_87004538	IMG Activity: SIMG_CFMENUOLPSOS22
S_ALR_87004539	IMG Activity: SIMG_CFMENUOLPKOPU6
S_ALR_87004540	IMG Activity: SIMG_OLPR_OLPE1

S_ALR_87004541	IMG Activity: SIMG_CFMENUOLPFOPJ4
S_ALR_87004542	IMG Activity: VORGTYP_ZU_STRGRP
S_ALR_87004543	IMG Activity: SIMG_CFMENUOLPSOS21
S_ALR_87004544	IMG Activity: SIMG_OLPR_TBP1CFPART
S_ALR_87004546	IMG Activity: SIMG_CFMENUOLPSOS20
S_ALR_87004547	IMG Activity: SIMG_CFMENUOLPKOPUZ
S_ALR_87004549	IMG Activity: SIMG_OLPR_V_TFPLTWBS
S_ALR_87004550	IMG Activity: SIMG_CFMENUOLPSOS28
S_ALR_87004551	IMG Activity: SIMG_CFMENUOLPKBCG2
S_ALR_87004552	IMG Activity: SIMG_CFMENUFNMCFND9
S_ALR_87004553	IMG Activity: SIMG_CFMENUOLPSOS27
S_ALR_87004554	IMG Activity: SIMG_OLPR_TVTB
S_ALR_87004555	IMG Activity: SIMG_CFMENUORFB2OB83
S_ALR_87004556	IMG Activity: SIMG_CFMENUOLPKOPCB
S_ALR_87004557	IMG Activity: SIMG_CFMENUFNMCFOCP
S_ALR_87004558	IMG Activity: SIMG_CFMENUOLPSOS17
S_ALR_87004559	IMG Activity: SIMG_OLPR_V_TFPLAWBS
S_ALR_87004560	IMG Activity: SIMG_CFMENUOLPKOPUL
S_ALR_87004561	IMG Activity: SIMG_CFMENUORFB2OB85
S_ALR_87004562	IMG Activity: SIMG_CFMENUFNMCFN-6
S_ALR_87004563	IMG Activity: SIMG_CFMENUOLPSOS12
S_ALR_87004564	IMG Activity: SIMG_OLPR_ERLART_FPL
S_ALR_87004565	IMG Activity: SIMG_CFMENUOLPKOPJS
S_ALR_87004566	IMG Activity: FVVD_KSON
S_ALR_87004567	IMG Activity: SIMG_CFMENUOLPSOS11
S_ALR_87004568	IMG Activity: SIMG_OLPR_KUND_ZID
S_ALR_87004569	IMG Activity: DARLSICH
S_ALR_87004570	IMG Activity: SIMG_CFMENUOLPKOPCC
S_ALR_87004571	IMG Activity: SIMG_CFMENUOLPSOS15
S_ALR_87004572	IMG Activity: SIMG_CFMENUOLPROKG3
S_ALR_87004573	IMG Activity: SIMG_CFMENUOLPKAUFL
S_ALR_87004574	IMG Activity: SIMG_CFMENUFNMCFNCO
S_ALR_87004575	IMG Activity: SIMG_CFMENUOLPKGROB
S_ALR_87004576	IMG Activity: SIMG_CFMENUOLPROKG2
S_ALR_87004577	IMG Activity: DARLART_DEFINIEREN
S_ALR_87004578	IMG Activity: SIMG_CFMENUORFBOBL1
S_ALR_87004579	IMG Activity: SIMG_CFMENUOLPSOS14
S_ALR_87004580	IMG Activity: FVVD_BEKI
S_ALR_87004581	IMG Activity: SIMG_CFMENUOLPROKG1
S_ALR_87004582	IMG Activity: SIMG_CFMENUORFBOBV2
S_ALR_87004583	IMG Activity: SIMG_CFMENUOLPSOS16
S_ALR_87004584	IMG Activity: SIMG_CFMENUFNMCFZ19
S_ALR_87004585	IMG Activity: SIMG_OLPR_KA01_ABGR
S_ALR_87004586	IMG Activity: SIMG_CFMENUOLPSOS13
S_ALR_87004587	IMG Activity: SIMG_CFMENUORFBOBBT
S_ALR_87004588	IMG Activity: SIMG_OLPR_OPIC_ERL
S_ALR_87004589	IMG Activity: SIMG_CFMENUFNMCFZ17
S_ALR_87004590	IMG Activity: SIMG_CFMENUOLPSOS25
S_ALR_87004591	IMG Activity: SIMG_CFMENUORFB2OB81
S_ALR_87004592	IMG Activity: SIMG_CFMENUOLPRKBC4
S_ALR_87004593	IMG Activity: SIMG_CFMENUFNMCFZ18
S_ALR_87004594	IMG Activity: SIMG_CFMENUOLPSOP26
S_ALR_87004595	IMG Activity: SIMG_OLPR_OPO8_ERL
S_ALR_87004596	IMG Activity: SIMG_CFMENUFNMCFN-5

S_ALR_87004597	IMG Activity: SIMG_CFORFBSXDASAKO2
S_ALR_87004598	IMG Activity: SIMG_CFMENUOLPSOP32
S_ALR_87004599	IMG Activity: GRUNDBUCH
S_ALR_87004600	IMG Activity: SIMG_OLPR_KP65_ERL
S_ALR_87004601	IMG Activity: SIMG_CFMENUORFB2OB46
S_ALR_87004602	IMG Activity: SIMG_CFMENUOLPSOP42
S_ALR_87004603	IMG Activity: SIMG_OLPR_OKEQ1
S_ALR_87004604	IMG Activity: SIMG_CFMENUFNMCFNC8
S_ALR_87004605	IMG Activity: SIMG_CFMENUOLPSOP7B
S_ALR_87004606	IMG Activity: SIMG_CFMENUORFB2OBAA
S_ALR_87004607	IMG Activity: SIMG_CFMENUOLPFOP7B
S_ALR_87004608	IMG Activity: SIMG_OLPR_OB07_2
S_ALR_87004609	IMG Activity: SIMG_CFMENUFNMCFNC9
S_ALR_87004610	IMG Activity: SIMG_CFMENUOLPSOP34
S_ALR_87004611	IMG Activity: SIMG_CFMENUORFBOBL2
S_ALR_87004612	IMG Activity: SIMG_CFMENUOLPFOPJZ
S_ALR_87004613	IMG Activity: SIMG_OLPR_CJVC_ERL
S_ALR_87004614	IMG Activity: SIMG_CFMENUOLPSOP19
S_ALR_87004615	IMG Activity: SIMG_CFMENUFNMCFNC5
S_ALR_87004616	IMG Activity: SIMG_CFMENUORFB2OBAC
S_ALR_87004617	IMG Activity: SIMG_CFMENUOLPFOPJY
S_ALR_87004618	IMG Activity: SIMG_OLPR_OPI2_ERL
S_ALR_87004619	IMG Activity: SIMG_CFMENUOLPSOP30
S_ALR_87004620	IMG Activity: SIMG_CFORFBT894PL
S_ALR_87004621	IMG Activity: SIMG_CFMENUOLPSOM10
S_ALR_87004622	IMG Activity: SIMG_OLPR_OPI1_ERL
S_ALR_87004623	IMG Activity: SIMG_CFMENUFNMCFNC3
S_ALR_87004624	IMG Activity: SIMG_CFMENUOLPFOPJR
S_ALR_87004625	IMG Activity: SIMG_CFORFBGCD1
S_ALR_87004626	IMG Activity: SIMG_CFMENUOLPFOPJQ
S_ALR_87004627	IMG Activity: SIMG_OLPR_OB08
S_ALR_87004628	IMG Activity: SIMG_CFMENUOLPSOP10
S_ALR_87004629	IMG Activity: SIMG_CFMENUFNMCFNCB
S_ALR_87004630	IMG Activity: SIMG_CFORFBOBPL
S_ALR_87004631	IMG Activity: SIMG_CFMENUOLPFOPK3
S_ALR_87004632	IMG Activity: SIMG_CFMENUOLPSOP14
S_ALR_87004633	IMG Activity: SIMG_CFMENUOLPROK11
S_ALR_87004634	IMG Activity: SIMG_CFMENUFNMCFNCI
S_ALR_87004635	IMG Activity: SIMG_CFORFBOBP5
S_ALR_87004636	IMG Activity: SIMG_CFMENUOLPFOPJ2
S_ALR_87004637	IMG Activity: SIMG_CFMENUOLPSQSUB
S_ALR_87004638	IMG Activity: SIMG_OLPR_TCJ41_1
S_ALR_87004639	IMG Activity: SIMG_CFMENUFNMCFNCH
S_ALR_87004640	IMG Activity: SIMG_CFMENUORFBVKOA
S_ALR_87004641	IMG Activity: SIMG_CFMENUOLPFOPJL
S_ALR_87004642	IMG Activity: SIMG_CFMENUOLPSOP45
S_ALR_87004643	IMG Activity: SIMG_OLPR_OPSB
S_ALR_87004644	IMG Activity: SIMG_CFMENUFNMCFNCK
S_ALR_87004645	IMG Activity: SIMG_CFMENUOLPFOVZ2
S_ALR_87004646	IMG Activity: SIMG_CFMENUOLPSOP22
S_ALR_87004647	IMG Activity: SIMG_CFORFBOBCYVTRB
S_ALR_87004648	IMG Activity: SIMG_OLPR_KANK7
S_ALR_87004649	IMG Activity: KOND_NEUGESCHTAB
S_ALR_87004650	IMG Activity: SIMG_CFMENUOLPFOPJV

S_ALR_87004651	IMG Activity: SIMG_CFORFBV001NP
S_ALR_87004652	IMG Activity: SIMG_CFMENUOLPSOS43
S_ALR_87004653	IMG Activity: OLQU-BG
S_ALR_87004654	IMG Activity: OLQS-PAT
S_ALR_87004655	IMG Activity: SIMG_CFMENUFNMCFZCS
S_ALR_87004656	IMG Activity: SIMG_CFMENUOLPRKAH2
S_ALR_87004657	IMG Activity: SIMG_CFMENUOLPFBS02
S_ALR_87004658	IMG Activity: OLQU-D
S_ALR_87004659	IMG Activity: OLQS-PTYP
S_ALR_87004660	IMG Activity: SIMG_CFORFB2T041C
S_ALR_87004661	IMG Activity: SIMG_CFMENUOLPSOP20
S_ALR_87004662	IMG Activity: SIMG_CFMENUFNMCFZCJ
S_ALR_87004663	IMG Activity: SIMG_OLPR_KPH2_2
S_ALR_87004664	IMG Activity: SIMG_CFMENUOLPFOS35
S_ALR_87004665	IMG Activity: OLQU-K
S_ALR_87004666	IMG Activity: SIMG_CFMENUOLQSOQ62
S_ALR_87004667	IMG Activity: SIMG_CFMENUOLPSOP00
S_ALR_87004668	IMG Activity: SIMG_ORFB2T001B_PL2
S_ALR_87004669	IMG Activity: SIMG_OLPR_KP34_ERL
S_ALR_87004670	IMG Activity: SIMG_CFMENUFNMCFZBA
S_ALR_87004671	IMG Activity: SIMG_CFMENUOLPFOS32
S_ALR_87004672	IMG Activity: OLQU_SS02
S_ALR_87004673	IMG Activity: OLQS-PD
S_ALR_87004674	IMG Activity: SIMG_CFMENUOLPSOS45
S_ALR_87004675	IMG Activity: SIMG_CFMENUFNMCFZBD
S_ALR_87004676	IMG Activity: SIMG_ORFB2T894_PL2
S_ALR_87004677	IMG Activity: SIMG_CMMENUOLPROP131
S_ALR_87004678	IMG Activity: SIMG_CFMENUOLPFOPJJ
S_ALR_87004679	IMG Activity: OLQU_SS42
S_ALR_87004680	IMG Activity: SIMG_CFMENUOLQSOQ67
S_ALR_87004681	IMG Activity: SIMG_CFMENUOLPSOS44
S_ALR_87004682	IMG Activity: SIMG_CFMENUFNMCFNQ5
S_ALR_87004683	IMG Activity: SIMG_CFMENUOLPROKSR
S_ALR_87004684	IMG Activity: SIMG_CFMENUOLPFOPJK
S_ALR_87004685	IMG Activity: SIMG_CFMENUORFBOBP2
S_ALR_87004686	IMG Activity: OLQU-WF
S_ALR_87004687	IMG Activity: SIMG_CFMENUOLQSOQ58
S_ALR_87004688	IMG Activity: SIMG_CFMENUOLPSOPFA
S_ALR_87004689	IMG Activity: SIMG_CFMENUFNMCFN-1
S_ALR_87004690	IMG Activity: SIMG_OLPR_KBH1
S_ALR_87004691	IMG Activity: SIMG_CFMENUOLPF399X
S_ALR_87004692	IMG Activity: SIMG_CFMENUOLQIOQR0
S_ALR_87004693	IMG Activity: SIMG_ORFB_INVESTKONT
S_ALR_87004694	IMG Activity: SIMG_CFMENUOLQSOQ50
S_ALR_87004695	IMG Activity: SIMG_CFMENUOLPSOP40
S_ALR_87004696	IMG Activity: SIMG_CFMENUFNMCFZ21
S_ALR_87004697	IMG Activity: SIMG_OLQU-E
S_ALR_87004698	IMG Activity: SIMG_CFMENUOLPFOMIH
S_ALR_87004699	IMG Activity: SIMG_CFMENUOLPROKOH
S_ALR_87004700	IMG Activity: SIMG_CFMENUOLQSOQ44
S_ALR_87004701	IMG Activity: SIMG_CFORFBAO99
S_ALR_87004702	IMG Activity: SIMG_OLPFWORKFLOW
S_ALR_87004703	IMG Activity: KOMP/PART
S_ALR_87004704	IMG Activity: OLQU-T

S_ALR_87004705	IMG Activity: SIMG_OLPR_GRE9
S_ALR_87004706	IMG Activity: SIMG_CFMENUOLQSOQ46
S_ALR_87004707	IMG Activity: J_1AFOREIGN_PERSON4
S_ALR_87004708	IMG Activity: PROD_PRO_BUKRS
S_ALR_87004709	IMG Activity: SIMG_CFMENUOLQSOQ02
S_ALR_87004710	IMG Activity: SIMG_OLPR_RPPN
S_ALR_87004711	IMG Activity: SIMG_CFMENUOLQSOQ48
S_ALR_87004712	IMG Activity: FINANZDISPOEBENE
S_ALR_87004713	IMG Activity: J_1ATAX_ID4
S_ALR_87004714	IMG Activity: OLQU-H
S_ALR_87004715	IMG Activity: SIMG_OLPR_RPXN
S_ALR_87004716	IMG Activity: OLQS-PL
S_ALR_87004717	IMG Activity: SIMG_CFMENUFNMCFZCH
S_ALR_87004718	IMG Activity: SIMG_OLQU-SF
S_ALR_87004719	IMG Activity: SIMG_OLPR_USEREXITRE
S_ALR_87004720	IMG Activity: J_1ATIDSW
S_ALR_87004721	IMG Activity: SIMG_CFMENUOLQSOQEC
S_ALR_87004722	IMG Activity: SIMG_CFMENUFNMCFN-4
S_ALR_87004723	IMG Activity: OLQU-SM
S_ALR_87004724	IMG Activity: SIMG_OLPR_GR5G
S_ALR_87004725	IMG Activity: SIMG_CFMENUOLQBOQB3
S_ALR_87004726	IMG Activity: J_1BLB09
S_ALR_87004727	IMG Activity: SIMG_CFMENUFNMCFZKE
S_ALR_87004728	IMG Activity: OLQU-B
S_ALR_87004729	IMG Activity: SIMG_CFMENUOLQBOQB4
S_ALR_87004730	IMG Activity: SIMG_CFMENUOLPRFGRW
S_ALR_87004731	IMG Activity: SIMG_CFORFBTFE05
S_ALR_87004732	IMG Activity: OLQU-L
S_ALR_87004733	IMG Activity: SIMG_CFMENUFNMCFZCW
S_ALR_87004734	IMG Activity: SIMG_CFMENUOLQBOQBS
S_ALR_87004735	IMG Activity: SIMG_OLPR_OKMI
S_ALR_87004736	IMG Activity: SIMG_CFORFBTFE18
S_ALR_87004737	IMG Activity: SIMG_CFMENUFNMCFNCX
S_ALR_87004738	IMG Activity: OLQS_BS
S_ALR_87004739	IMG Activity: SIMG_CFORFBTFE19
S_ALR_87004740	IMG Activity: SIMG_OLPR_GR21
S_ALR_87004741	IMG Activity: SIMG_CFMENUFNMCFNQ7
S_ALR_87004742	IMG Activity: OLQB-L
S_ALR_87004743	IMG Activity: SIMG_OLPR_ORRS2
S_ALR_87004744	IMG Activity: SIMG_CFORFBOBCYANLG
S_ALR_87004745	IMG Activity: FVV_VORG
S_ALR_87004746	IMG Activity: SIMG_CFMENUOLQBOQB2
S_ALR_87004747	IMG Activity: SIMG_CFMENUOLPROKS7
S_ALR_87004748	IMG Activity: J_1BLB08
S_ALR_87004749	IMG Activity: SIMG_CFMENUFNMCFZCF
S_ALR_87004750	IMG Activity: OLQS-PVRS
S_ALR_87004751	IMG Activity: SIMG_CFMENUOLPRORRS
S_ALR_87004752	IMG Activity: SIMG_CFMENUORFBOBYD
S_ALR_87004753	IMG Activity: FVVD_KINT
S_ALR_87004754	IMG Activity: OLQS-OQ05
S_ALR_87004755	IMG Activity: SIMG_OLPR_STRK_CJET
S_ALR_87004756	IMG Activity: FVVD_RPNSP
S_ALR_87004757	IMG Activity: SIMG_CFMENUOLQSOQ76
S_ALR_87004758	IMG Activity: J_1AGI_PERCENTAGE4

S_ALR_87004759	IMG Activity: SIMG_OLPR_CJEO
S_ALR_87004760	IMG Activity: OLQS-OQCI
S_ALR_87004761	IMG Activity: J_1AMULT_AGREEMENT4
S_ALR_87004762	IMG Activity: SIMG_OLPR_CJEQ
S_ALR_87004763	IMG Activity: ANTEILSARTEN
S_ALR_87004764	IMG Activity: SIMG_CFMENUOLQBOQB1
S_ALR_87004765	IMG Activity: J_1AGI_LAYOUT4
S_ALR_87004766	IMG Activity: SIMG_OLPR_CJEB
S_ALR_87004767	IMG Activity: SIMG_CFMENUOLQSOQC4
S_ALR_87004768	IMG Activity: SIMG_CFMENUFNMCFW56
S_ALR_87004769	IMG Activity: SIMG_OLPR_CJEV
S_ALR_87004770	IMG Activity: SIMG_CFMENUOLQSQS39
S_ALR_87004771	IMG Activity: SIMG_CFMENUORFBOB53
S_ALR_87004772	IMG Activity: SIMG_CFMENUFNMCFNCC
S_ALR_87004773	IMG Activity: SIMG_OLPR_CJE1
S_ALR_87004774	IMG Activity: SIMG_CFMENUOLQSOQC7
S_ALR_87004775	IMG Activity: J_1AASSIGN_CODES4
S_ALR_87004776	IMG Activity: SIMG_CFMENUFNMCFNCA
S_ALR_87004777	IMG Activity: SIMG_CFMENUOLQSQS29
S_ALR_87004778	IMG Activity: SIMG_OLPR_CJE4
S_ALR_87004779	IMG Activity: MAHNWESEN_SUCHKENNZ
S_ALR_87004780	IMG Activity: SIMG_CFORFBVCT09304
S_ALR_87004781	IMG Activity: SIMG_CFMENUOLQSOQCS
S_ALR_87004782	IMG Activity: SIMG_OLPR_INF_OPU9
S_ALR_87004783	IMG Activity: J_1AOFF_TYPE_MAINT4
S_ALR_87004784	IMG Activity: SIMG_CFMENUFNMCFNCL
S_ALR_87004785	IMG Activity: SIMG_CFMENUOLQSOQCC
S_ALR_87004786	IMG Activity: SIMG_OLPR_CJBBS2
S_ALR_87004787	IMG Activity: SIMG_CFMENUFNMCFZ30
S_ALR_87004788	IMG Activity: SIMG_CFMENUOLQSOQCE
S_ALR_87004789	IMG Activity: J_1AOFF_DOC_ASSIGN4
S_ALR_87004790	IMG Activity: SIMG_OLPR_CJBBS1
S_ALR_87004791	IMG Activity: SIMG_CFMENUFNMCFNCF
S_ALR_87004792	IMG Activity: SIMG_CFMENUOLQSOQC2
S_ALR_87004793	IMG Activity: J_1ADRVERSION4
S_ALR_87004794	IMG Activity: SIMG_OLPR_CJEK
S_ALR_87004795	IMG Activity: SIMG_CFMENUFNMCFW57
S_ALR_87004796	IMG Activity: SIMG_CFMENUOLQSOQCA
S_ALR_87004797	IMG Activity: J_1ADEF_OFF_TAX_COD4
S_ALR_87004798	IMG Activity: SIMG_OLPR_CJ81
S_ALR_87004799	IMG Activity: SIMG_CFMENUFNMCFNCQ
S_ALR_87004800	IMG Activity: OLQWOQES3
S_ALR_87004801	IMG Activity: SIMG_OLPR_CJEX
S_ALR_87004802	IMG Activity: SIMG_CFORFBTFE02
S_ALR_87004803	IMG Activity: ERBBAURECHT_DEFINIER
S_ALR_87004804	IMG Activity: OLQWOQES2
S_ALR_87004805	IMG Activity: SIMG_OLPR_CJEZ
S_ALR_87004806	IMG Activity: GRUNDSTVERH_DEF
S_ALR_87004807	IMG Activity: SIMG_CFMENUORFBOBDB
S_ALR_87004808	IMG Activity: OLQWOQES1
S_ALR_87004809	IMG Activity: SIMG_OLPR_CJEY
S_ALR_87004810	IMG Activity: SIMG_CFMENUFNMCFZBM
S_ALR_87004811	IMG Activity: SIMG_CFORFBSE71QUST
S_ALR_87004812	IMG Activity: SIMG_CFMENUOLQSQDA1

S_ALR_87004813	IMG Activity: SIMG_OLPR_USER_EP
S_ALR_87004814	IMG Activity: INSTALL_PARAM
S_ALR_87004815	IMG Activity: SIMG_CFMENUOLQSOQEP
S_ALR_87004816	IMG Activity: SIMG_CFORFBOB91QUST
S_ALR_87004817	IMG Activity: SIMG_CFMENUOLPROPA6
S_ALR_87004818	IMG Activity: ROLLENTYP
S_ALR_87004819	IMG Activity: SIMG_CFMENUOLQSQDM1
S_ALR_87004820	IMG Activity: SIMG_CFORFBOB92QUST
S_ALR_87004821	IMG Activity: OLQS-PVP
S_ALR_87004822	IMG Activity: SIMG_CFMENUOLPROPA5
S_ALR_87004823	IMG Activity: SIMG_CFMENUFNMCFNCS
S_ALR_87004824	IMG Activity: OLQS-PROD
S_ALR_87004825	IMG Activity: SIMG_CFORFBSE91QUSTI
S_ALR_87004826	IMG Activity: SIMG_CFMENUOLPROPA4
S_ALR_87004827	IMG Activity: OLQS-V
S_ALR_87004828	IMG Activity: AUSTATTUNG_DEF
S_ALR_87004829	IMG Activity: SIMG_CFORFBOBCYCNTR
S_ALR_87004830	IMG Activity: SIMG_CFMENUOLPROPA3
S_ALR_87004831	IMG Activity: OBJEKTZUSTAND_DEF
S_ALR_87004832	IMG Activity: SIMG_CFMENUORFBOBCI
S_ALR_87004833	IMG Activity: SIMG_CFMENUOLPROPA2
S_ALR_87004834	IMG Activity: SIMG_CFMENUFNMCFZ91
S_ALR_87004835	IMG Activity: SIMG_CFMENUOLPROPA0
S_ALR_87004836	IMG Activity: SIMG_CFMENUORFBOBCJ
S_ALR_87004837	IMG Activity: SIMG_CFMENUFNMCFOCQ
S_ALR_87004838	IMG Activity: SIMG_CFMENUOLPRWSS
S_ALR_87004839	IMG Activity: SIMG_CFORFBSE71UMST
S_ALR_87004840	IMG Activity: SIMG_CFMENUFNMCFNCW
S_ALR_87004841	IMG Activity: SIMG_CFMENUOLPRSU02
S_ALR_87004842	IMG Activity: SIMG_CFORFBOB91UMST
S_ALR_87004843	IMG Activity: FVVD_KOBJ
S_ALR_87004844	IMG Activity: SIMG_OLPR_CMOD_BER
S_ALR_87004845	IMG Activity: SIMG_CFORFBOB92UMST
S_ALR_87004846	IMG Activity: SIMG_CFMENUFNMCFNCV
S_ALR_87004847	IMG Activity: SIMG_CFMENUOLPRSU03
S_ALR_87004848	IMG Activity: FVV_OBJNR
S_ALR_87004849	IMG Activity: SIMG_CFMENUOLPROPC5
S_ALR_87004850	IMG Activity: SIMG_CFMENUOLPROPB1
S_ALR_87004851	IMG Activity: FVVD_RBLNR
S_ALR_87004852	IMG Activity: SIMG_CFORFBT059PS
S_ALR_87004853	IMG Activity: SIMG_CFMENUOLPROPA8
S_ALR_87004854	IMG Activity: GEBIETSBESCH_DEF
S_ALR_87004855	IMG Activity: SIMG_CFORFBT059MTR
S_ALR_87004856	IMG Activity: SIMG_OLPR_OPDT
S_ALR_87004857	IMG Activity: SIMG_CFMENUFNMCFZ94
S_ALR_87004858	IMG Activity: SIMG_CFORFBT059MCR
S_ALR_87004859	IMG Activity: SIMG_CFMENUOLPRWSW
S_ALR_87004860	IMG Activity: SIMG_CFMENUFNMCFNCJ
S_ALR_87004861	IMG Activity: SIMG_CFMENUORFBOBA2
S_ALR_87004862	IMG Activity: SIMG_OLPR_RCJCLMIG
S_ALR_87004863	IMG Activity: SIMG_CFMENUFNMCFZ56
S_ALR_87004864	IMG Activity: SIMG_CFORFBTFE01
S_ALR_87004865	IMG Activity: SIMG_OLPR_USER_VERD
S_ALR_87004866	IMG Activity: SIMG_CFMENUFNMCFZ51

S_ALR_87004867	IMG Activity: SIMG_OLPR_V_TKKBH
S_ALR_87004868	IMG Activity: SIMG_CFMENUFNMCFZ89
S_ALR_87004869	IMG Activity: SIMG_CFORFBOB92QUSTI
S_ALR_87004870	IMG Activity: SIMG_OLPR_KKR0
S_ALR_87004871	IMG Activity: SIMG_OLPR_CJEN
S_ALR_87004872	IMG Activity: CFORFB2T059L
S_ALR_87004873	IMG Activity: SIMG_OLPR_CJVC_INFO
S_ALR_87004874	IMG Activity: SIMG_CFMENUORFBOBYB
S_ALR_87004875	IMG Activity: SIMG_OLPR_OPI3
S_ALR_87004876	IMG Activity: CFORFBT059REXT
S_ALR_87004877	IMG Activity: SIMG_OLPR_USER_EIS
S_ALR_87004878	IMG Activity: SIMG_OLPR_CJSB
S_ALR_87004879	IMG Activity: SIMG_CFMENUORFB2OB74
S_ALR_87004880	IMG Activity: SIMG_OLPR_TKKBH
S_ALR_87004881	IMG Activity: SIMG_CFORFBOB26A
S_ALR_87004882	IMG Activity: SIMG_CFMENUOLPROKRB
S_ALR_87004883	IMG Activity: SIMG_CFORFBCMODSAKOA
S_ALR_87004884	IMG Activity: SIMG_OLPR_T0030_N0
S_ALR_87004885	IMG Activity: SIMG_CFMENUORFBFSIR
S_ALR_87004886	IMG Activity: SIMG_CFMENUORFBOB15
S_ALR_87004887	IMG Activity: SIMG_CFMENUOLPROKRX
S_ALR_87004888	IMG Activity: SIMG_OLPR_OKQ4
S_ALR_87004889	IMG Activity: SIMG_OLPR_OPKB
S_ALR_87004890	IMG Activity: SIMG_CFMENUORFBFSK2
S_ALR_87004891	IMG Activity: SIMG_OLPR_OPKC
S_ALR_87004892	IMG Activity: SIMG_OLPR_CMOD_BANF2
S_ALR_87004893	IMG Activity: SIMG_CFORFBOBD4A
S_ALR_87004894	IMG Activity: SIMG_OLPR_CMOD_MAT
S_ALR_87004895	IMG Activity: SIMG_CFORFBSXDASAKO1
S_ALR_87004896	IMG Activity: SIMG_CFMENUORFBFS01
S_ALR_87004897	IMG Activity: SIMG_CFMENUOLPROPJK
S_ALR_87004898	IMG Activity: SIMG_CFMENUORFBFSIZ
S_ALR_87004899	IMG Activity: SIMG_CFMENUOLPROPJJ
S_ALR_87004900	IMG Activity: SIMG_CFORFBOB13A
S_ALR_87004901	IMG Activity: SIMG_OLPR_CMOD_CON03
S_ALR_87004902	IMG Activity: SIMG_CFORFBOB62A
S_ALR_87004903	IMG Activity: SIMG_OLPR_CMOD_CON02
S_ALR_87004904	IMG Activity: SIMG_OLPR_CMOD_CON01
S_ALR_87004905	IMG Activity: SIMG_OLPR_FELD_OPUD
S_ALR_87004906	IMG Activity: SIMG_CFMENUOLPROPK5
S_ALR_87004907	IMG Activity: SIMG_CFMENUORFBOB67
S_ALR_87004908	IMG Activity: SIMG_CFMENUOLPROPST
S_ALR_87004909	IMG Activity: SIMG_CFMENUORFB2OBR2
S_ALR_87004910	IMG Activity: SIMG_CFMENUORFBOBY8
S_ALR_87004911	IMG Activity: SIMG_OLPR_OPLI
S_ALR_87004912	IMG Activity: SIMG_CFMENUORFBOBY9
S_ALR_87004913	IMG Activity: SIMG_CFMENUOLPROPJL
S_ALR_87004914	IMG Activity: SIMG_CFMENUOLPROP17
S_ALR_87004915	IMG Activity: SIMG_CFMENUORFBFSI5
S_ALR_87004916	IMG Activity: SIMG_OLPR_MPP_CMPC
S_ALR_87004917	IMG Activity: SIMG_CFMENUORFBOBBI
S_ALR_87004918	IMG Activity: SIMG_OLPR_KAP_OPSP
S_ALR_87004919	IMG Activity: SIMG_CFMENUORFBFSIP
S_ALR_87004920	IMG Activity: SIMG_OLPR_OP4A

S_ALR_87004921	IMG Activity: SIMG_CFMENUORFBFSM1
S_ALR_87004922	IMG Activity: SIMG_CFMENUOLPROP28
S_ALR_87004923	IMG Activity: SIMG_CFORFBOBT6A
S_ALR_87004924	IMG Activity: SIMG_CFMENUORFBFSP1
S_ALR_87004925	IMG Activity: SIMG_CFMENUOLPROP34
S_ALR_87004926	IMG Activity: SIMG_CFORFBOBT7A
S_ALR_87004927	IMG Activity: SIMG_CFMENUOLPROP32
S_ALR_87004928	IMG Activity: SIMG_CFMENUORFBFSS1
S_ALR_87004929	IMG Activity: SIMG_OLPR_BEW_OPT1
S_ALR_87004930	IMG Activity: SIMG_OLPR_BANF_OPTT1
S_ALR_87004931	IMG Activity: SIMG_CFMENUORFBOBY7
S_ALR_87004932	IMG Activity: SIMG_CFMENUORFBOB62
S_ALR_87004933	IMG Activity: SIMG_OLPR_BKZ_OPS8
S_ALR_87004934	IMG Activity: SIMG_OLPR_OPB5
S_ALR_87004935	IMG Activity: SIMG_CFMENUORFBOBY2
S_ALR_87004936	IMG Activity: SIMG_OLPR_OPB4
S_ALR_87004937	IMG Activity: SIMG_OLPR_VERTOPB2
S_ALR_87004938	IMG Activity: SIMG_CFMENUORFBFSIO
S_ALR_87004939	IMG Activity: SIMG_CFMENUORFBOB13
S_ALR_87004940	IMG Activity: SIMG_CFMENUOLPROP21
S_ALR_87004941	IMG Activity: SIMG_OLPR_CMOD_CON04
S_ALR_87004942	IMG Activity: SIMG_CFMENUORFBFSIQ
S_ALR_87004943	IMG Activity: SIMG_CFMENUOLPROPSM
S_ALR_87004944	IMG Activity: SIMG_CFMENUORFBFSIY
S_ALR_87004945	IMG Activity: ORKA_IM_BUDG
S_ALR_87004946	IMG Activity: SIMG_OLPR_CMOD_SICHT
S_ALR_87004947	IMG Activity: SIMG_CFMENUORFBFSIT
S_ALR_87004948	IMG Activity: ORKA_IM_PLAN
S_ALR_87004949	IMG Activity: SIMG_ORKAKTPF_ZUORDN
S_ALR_87004950	IMG Activity: SIMG_CFMENUORK3OKE8
S_ALR_87004951	IMG Activity: SIMG_OLPR_SEL_CO44
S_ALR_87004952	IMG Activity: SIMG_CFMENUORFBFSIV
S_ALR_87004953	IMG Activity: SIMG_IMENUORKAOKO7
S_ALR_87004954	IMG Activity: SIMG_ORKACPT2_SCHEMA
S_ALR_87004955	IMG Activity: SIMG_CFMENUORK3OKE9
S_ALR_87004956	IMG Activity: SIMG_OLPR_SICHT_OPUR
S_ALR_87004957	IMG Activity: SIMG_CFMENUORKAOITBX
S_ALR_87004958	IMG Activity: SIMG_CFMENUORK30KWT
S_ALR_87004959	IMG Activity: SIMG_ORKACPT2_UMGEBG
S_ALR_87004960	IMG Activity: SIMG_OLPR_DB_OPTX
S_ALR_87004961	IMG Activity: SIMG_CFMENUORFBOBDC
S_ALR_87004962	IMG Activity: SIMG_CFMENUORKAOITA
S_ALR_87004963	IMG Activity: SIMG_CFMENUORK3OKC3
S_ALR_87004964	IMG Activity: SIMG_ORKAOKOV
S_ALR_87004965	IMG Activity: SIMG_OLPR_OPIS
S_ALR_87004966	IMG Activity: SIMG_CFMENUORFBFSIX
S_ALR_87004967	IMG Activity: ORKA_IM_GROSS
S_ALR_87004968	IMG Activity: SIMG_OLPR_OPIR
S_ALR_87004969	IMG Activity: SIMG_CFMENUORKAKO021
S_ALR_87004970	IMG Activity: SIMG_CFMENUORK3OKC5
S_ALR_87004971	IMG Activity: SIMG_IMMENUORKAOKO6
S_ALR_87004972	IMG Activity: SIMG_ORKAOKOG
S_ALR_87004973	IMG Activity: SIMG_CFMENUORK3OKC4
S_ALR_87004974	IMG Activity: SIMG_OLPR_INF_OPU8

S_ALR_87004975	IMG Activity: SIMG_CFMENUORFBOB26
S_ALR_87004976	IMG Activity: ORKA_IM_STATI2
S_ALR_87004977	IMG Activity: SIMG_CFMENUORKACMODZ
S_ALR_87004978	IMG Activity: SIMG_CFMENUORK3OKE5
S_ALR_87004979	IMG Activity: SIMG_OLPR_INF_OPTW
S_ALR_87004980	IMG Activity: ORKA_IM_STATI1
S_ALR_87004981	IMG Activity: SIMG_CFMENUORFBOBT6
S_ALR_87004982	IMG Activity: SIMG_ORKAKK06
S_ALR_87004983	IMG Activity: SIMG_OLPR_INF_OPTG
S_ALR_87004984	IMG Activity: SIMG_CFMENUORK3OKE6
S_ALR_87004985	IMG Activity: ORKA_IM_STATI0
S_ALR_87004986	IMG Activity: SIMG_ORKAOPIE
S_ALR_87004987	IMG Activity: SIMG_CFMENUORFBOBT7
S_ALR_87004988	IMG Activity: SIMG_IMMENUORKAOKEU
S_ALR_87004989	IMG Activity: SIMG_CFMENUORK3OKBF
S_ALR_87004990	IMG Activity: SIMG_OLPR_INF_OPTV
S_ALR_87004991	IMG Activity: SIMG_ORKAOPIG
S_ALR_87004992	IMG Activity: ORKA_IM_TOLERANZ
S_ALR_87004993	IMG Activity: SIMG_CFMENUORK3OKEX
S_ALR_87004994	IMG Activity: SIMG_OLPR_INF_OPTU
S_ALR_87004995	IMG Activity: SIMG_CFORFBCMODSAKO
S_ALR_87004996	IMG Activity: SIMG_ORKAKA06_VERZIN
S_ALR_87004997	IMG Activity: ORKA_IM_WORKFLOW
S_ALR_87004998	IMG Activity: SIMG_OLPR_FA_OPTI
S_ALR_87004999	IMG Activity: SIMG_CFMENUORK3OKE7
S_ALR_87005000	IMG Activity: SIMG_ORKAOPID
S_ALR_87005001	IMG Activity: SIMG_IMMENUORKAAM01
S_ALR_87005002	IMG Activity: SIMG_CFMENUORK3KPRN
S_ALR_87005003	IMG Activity: SIMG_CFMENUORFBOBD4
S_ALR_87005004	IMG Activity: SIMG_CFMENUOLPROPSL
S_ALR_87005005	IMG Activity: SIMG_ORKAKO02_ZINS
S_ALR_87005006	IMG Activity: ORKA_IM_BILD
S_ALR_87005007	IMG Activity: SIMG_CFMENUORK3OKBC
S_ALR_87005008	IMG Activity: SIMG_ORKAOPIC
S_ALR_87005009	IMG Activity: SIMG_CFMENUORFBOBG9
S_ALR_87005010	IMG Activity: SIMG_CFMENUORKAOKGL
S_ALR_87005011	IMG Activity: SIMG_OLPR_OWF1_PFCU
S_ALR_87005012	IMG Activity: SIMG_CFMENUORK3OKEP
S_ALR_87005031	IMG Activity: SIMG_ORKAOPIB
S_ALR_87005032	IMG Activity: SIMG_CFMENUORFBOBG8
S_ALR_87005033	IMG Activity: SIMG_CFMENUORKAOKG1
S_ALR_87005034	IMG Activity: SIMG_OLPR_FA_OPUF
S_ALR_87005035	IMG Activity: SIMG_CFMENUORK3OKBG
S_ALR_87005036	IMG Activity: SIMG_ORKAOPIA
S_ALR_87005037	IMG Activity: ORKA_IM_KONTEN
S_ALR_87005038	IMG Activity: SIMG_OLPR_EVSK
S_ALR_87005039	IMG Activity: SIMG_CFMENUORFBFSI2
S_ALR_87005040	IMG Activity: SIMG_CFMENUORK3KAL1
S_ALR_87005041	IMG Activity: SIMG_ORKAOT03
S_ALR_87005042	IMG Activity: ORKA_IM_UMWELT
S_ALR_87005043	IMG Activity: SIMG_OLPR_EVVS
S_ALR_87005044	IMG Activity: SIMG_ORKAOPIH
S_ALR_87005045	IMG Activity: ORKA_IM_INVGRUND
S_ALR_87005046	IMG Activity: SIMG_ORK3_GSCD

S_ALR_87005047	IMG Activity: SIMG_OLPR_VERSOPTS
S_ALR_87005048	IMG Activity: SIMG_CFMENUORKAKBC4
S_ALR_87005049	IMG Activity: ORKA_IM_SELEKT
S_ALR_87005050	IMG Activity: SIMG_ORK3_COEP_SM30
S_ALR_87005051	IMG Activity: SIMG_CFMENUORFBOBBJ
S_ALR_87005052	IMG Activity: SIMG_OLPR_SIM_OPS4
S_ALR_87005053	IMG Activity: SIMG_IMMENUORKAKOT2
S_ALR_87005054	IMG Activity: SIMG_CFMENUORKAKBC1
S_ALR_87005055	IMG Activity: SIMG_CFMENUORK3OKC6
S_ALR_87005056	IMG Activity: SIMG_CFORFBOB55SALD
S_ALR_87005057	IMG Activity: SIMG_OLPR_SIMNUMOPUS
S_ALR_87005058	IMG Activity: SIMG_ORKAKAK2_I
S_ALR_87005059	IMG Activity: SIMG_IMMENUORKAKO02
S_ALR_87005060	IMG Activity: SIMG_CFMENUORK3OKO5
S_ALR_87005061	IMG Activity: SIMG_CFMENUORKAOKEP
S_ALR_87005062	IMG Activity: SIMG_OLPR_CMOD_CON05
S_ALR_87005063	IMG Activity: SIMG_CFORFBOBY9DTUB
S_ALR_87005064	IMG Activity: SIMG_CFMENUORKKKKPV
S_ALR_87005065	IMG Activity: SIMG_CFMENUORKAOKB9
S_ALR_87005066	IMG Activity: SIMG_CFMENUOLPRKBC3
S_ALR_87005067	IMG Activity: SIMG_CFMENUORKKKKE5
S_ALR_87005068	IMG Activity: SIMG_CFORFBOBY7DTUB
S_ALR_87005069	IMG Activity: SIMG_CFMENUORKAKANKI
S_ALR_87005070	IMG Activity: SIMG_OLPR_KP85
S_ALR_87005071	IMG Activity: SIMG_CFMENUORK3OKBA
S_ALR_87005072	IMG Activity: SIMG_CFMENUORKAOK60
S_ALR_87005073	IMG Activity: SIMG_CFORFBCHKBLSK
S_ALR_87005074	IMG Activity: SIMG_CFMENUORK3OKBB
S_ALR_87005075	IMG Activity: SIMG_OLPR_TPIS3
S_ALR_87005076	IMG Activity: SIMG_ORKA_FMU1
S_ALR_87005077	IMG Activity: SIMG_CFORFBCHKBVSK
S_ALR_87005078	IMG Activity: SIMG_CFMENUORK3OKEV1
S_ALR_87005079	IMG Activity: SIMG_CFMENUOLPRKBH2
S_ALR_87005080	IMG Activity: SIMG_CFMENUORKAOVA
S_ALR_87005081	IMG Activity: SIMG_CFMENUORFB2O7V3
S_ALR_87005082	IMG Activity: SIMG_CFMENUORK3OBA5
S_ALR_87005083	IMG Activity: SIMG_OLPR_EVCE
S_ALR_87005084	IMG Activity: SIMG_CFMENUORKAKBC2
S_ALR_87005085	IMG Activity: SIMG_CFMENUORK3OKC7
S_ALR_87005086	IMG Activity: SIMG_OLPR_EVVDOR
S_ALR_87005087	IMG Activity: SIMG_ORKAKGF4
S_ALR_87005088	IMG Activity: SIMG_CFMENUORFB2O7F1
S_ALR_87005089	IMG Activity: SIMG_CFMENUORK3OKC9
S_ALR_87005090	IMG Activity: SIMG_OLPR_EVVD
S_ALR_87005091	IMG Activity: SIMG_CFMENUORKAKZE2
S_ALR_87005092	IMG Activity: SIMG_CFMENUORFB2O7F3
S_ALR_87005093	IMG Activity: SIMG_CFMENUOLPROP82
S_ALR_87005094	IMG Activity: SIMG_CFMENUORKAKZM2
S_ALR_87005095	IMG Activity: SIMG_ORK3_OKBI_VERD
S_ALR_87005096	IMG Activity: SIMG_CFMENUORFB2O7F2
S_ALR_87005097	IMG Activity: SIMG_CMMENUOLPROP13
S_ALR_87005098	IMG Activity: SIMG_CFMENUORKAKZZ2
S_ALR_87005099	IMG Activity: SIMG_ORK38KEM
S_ALR_87005100	IMG Activity: SIMG_CFMENUORKAKZB2

S_ALR_87005101	IMG Activity: SIMG_CFMENUOLPROP65
S_ALR_87005102	IMG Activity: SIMG_CFORFBOB55OFPO
S_ALR_87005103	IMG Activity: SIMG_CFMENUORK3OKKP
S_ALR_87005104	IMG Activity: SIMG_CFMENUORKAKZS2
S_ALR_87005105	IMG Activity: SIMG_CFMENUOLPROP72
S_ALR_87005106	IMG Activity: SIMG_CFMENUORK3KANK
S_ALR_87005107	IMG Activity: SIMG_CFORFBOBY8DTUB
S_ALR_87005108	IMG Activity: SIMG_CFMENUORKAKA06
S_ALR_87005109	IMG Activity: SIMG_CFMENUOLPROMD0
S_ALR_87005110	IMG Activity: SIMG_CFMENUORK3OKEQ
S_ALR_87005111	IMG Activity: SIMG_CFMENUORFB2OBXH
S_ALR_87005112	IMG Activity: SIMG_OLPR_NPL_OPTN
S_ALR_87005113	IMG Activity: SIMG_CFMENUORKAKOW1
S_ALR_87005114	IMG Activity: SIMG_CFMENUORK3SU03
S_ALR_87005115	IMG Activity: SIMG_CFMENUOLPROP45
S_ALR_87005116	IMG Activity: SIMG_CFMENUORKAKBC3
S_ALR_87005117	IMG Activity: SIMG_CFMENUORFB2OB09
S_ALR_87005118	IMG Activity: SIMG_ORKA_TKKBH
S_ALR_87005119	IMG Activity: SIMG_CFMENUORK3SU02
S_ALR_87005120	IMG Activity: SIMG_CFMENUOLPROP10
S_ALR_87005121	IMG Activity: SIMG_CFORFBOBIA
S_ALR_87005122	IMG Activity: SIMG_ORKA_KKR0
S_ALR_87005123	IMG Activity: SIMG_ORK3SM30_WAEHR
S_ALR_87005124	IMG Activity: SIMG_OLPR_OB08_1
S_ALR_87005125	IMG Activity: SIMG_CFORFBOBIB
S_ALR_87005126	IMG Activity: SIMG_ORKA_EXTRA_GRE9
S_ALR_87005127	IMG Activity: SIMG_ORK3OMX3
S_ALR_87005128	IMG Activity: SIMG_OLPR_OKEQ
S_ALR_87005129	IMG Activity: SIMG_ORKA_SELEK_RPON
S_ALR_87005130	IMG Activity: SIMG_CFORFBCHKOPGL
S_ALR_87005131	IMG Activity: SIMG_OLPR_KSTKR
S_ALR_87005132	IMG Activity: SIMG_ORK38KEP
S_ALR_87005133	IMG Activity: SIMG_ORKA_PARAM_RPXN
S_ALR_87005134	IMG Activity: SIMG_CFORFBCHKKOSK
S_ALR_87005135	IMG Activity: SIMG_ORK3OMX2
S_ALR_87005136	IMG Activity: SIMG_CFMENUOLPROP42
S_ALR_87005137	IMG Activity: SIMG_CFMENUORKAOKL1
S_ALR_87005138	IMG Activity: SIMG_ORK3OMX1
S_ALR_87005139	IMG Activity: SIMG_CFMENUORFBO7S5
S_ALR_87005140	IMG Activity: SIMG_CFMENUOLPRJOB
S_ALR_87005141	IMG Activity: SIMG_CFMENUORKAGR5G
S_ALR_87005142	IMG Activity: SIMG_ORK3OMX6
S_ALR_87005143	IMG Activity: SIMG_CFMENUORFB2OBKB
S_ALR_87005144	IMG Activity: SIMG_CFMENUOLPROPS3
S_ALR_87005145	IMG Activity: SIMG_CFMENUORKAFGRW
S_ALR_87005146	IMG Activity: SIMG_OLPR_CJBBS1_PLA
S_ALR_87005147	IMG Activity: SIMG_ORK3OKEQ_TRPR
S_ALR_87005148	IMG Activity: SIMG_CFMENUORKAORMI
S_ALR_87005149	IMG Activity: SIMG_CFMENUORFBOBYA
S_ALR_87005150	IMG Activity: SIMG_XXMENUORK3_AK
S_ALR_87005151	IMG Activity: SIMG_OLPR_BPOPT7
S_ALR_87005152	IMG Activity: SIMG_ORKA_ROLLUP_IS
S_ALR_87005153	IMG Activity: SIMG_OLPR_REG_NP
S_ALR_87005154	IMG Activity: SIMG_CFMENUORFB2O7Z4

S_ALR_87005155	IMG Activity: SIMG_CFMENUORKASU03
S_ALR_87005156	IMG Activity: SIMG_ORKAKOCM
S_ALR_87005157	IMG Activity: SIMG_OLPR_OPG3
S_ALR_87005158	IMG Activity: SIMG_CFMENUORFB2O7S7
S_ALR_87005159	IMG Activity: SIMG_XXMENUORKA_I_V
S_ALR_87005160	IMG Activity: SIMG_CFMENUOLPROP74
S_ALR_87005161	IMG Activity: SIMG_CFMENUORFB2O7R1
S_ALR_87005162	IMG Activity: SIMG_CFMENUORKATKKBH
S_ALR_87005163	IMG Activity: SIMG_CFMENUOLPROP47
S_ALR_87005164	IMG Activity: SIMG_CFMENUORFBOB48
S_ALR_87005165	IMG Activity: SIMG_CFMENUORKAOKRA
S_ALR_87005166	IMG Activity: SIMG_CFMENUOLPROP80
S_ALR_87005167	IMG Activity: SIMG_CFMENUORFB2O7V2
S_ALR_87005168	IMG Activity: SIMG_CFMENUORKAOKKD
S_ALR_87005169	IMG Activity: SIMG_CFMENUORKAKOT22
S_ALR_87005170	IMG Activity: SIMG_CFMENUOLPROP73
S_ALR_87005171	IMG Activity: SIMG_CFMENUORFB2O7F8
S_ALR_87005172	IMG Activity: SIMG_CFMENUORKACL00
S_ALR_87005173	IMG Activity: SIMG_CFORFBSQ02
S_ALR_87005174	IMG Activity: SIMG_CFMENUORKAOKRX
S_ALR_87005175	IMG Activity: SIMG_CFMENUOLPROPS0
S_ALR_87005176	IMG Activity: SIMG_CFMENUORFB2OB16
S_ALR_87005177	IMG Activity: SIMG_CFMENUORKAKO8N
S_ALR_87005178	IMG Activity: SIMG_CFMENUORKAOKOV1
S_ALR_87005179	IMG Activity: SIMG_OLPR_TLNTZOPTP
S_ALR_87005180	IMG Activity: SIMG_CFMENUORFB2O7Z3
S_ALR_87005181	IMG Activity: SIMG_CFMENUORKAOKO7
S_ALR_87005182	IMG Activity: SIMG_CFMENUOLPRKOT2
S_ALR_87005183	IMG Activity: SIMG_CFMENUORFB2O7R3
S_ALR_87005184	IMG Activity: SIMG_CFMENUORKAKEI1
S_ALR_87005185	IMG Activity: SIMG_OLPR_KPH1_1
S_ALR_87005186	IMG Activity: SIMG_CFMENUORFB2O7F4
S_ALR_87005187	IMG Activity: SIMG_CFMENUORKAOKEU
S_ALR_87005188	IMG Activity: SIMG_OLPR_KP34
S_ALR_87005189	IMG Activity: SIMG_CFMENUORFBOBRS
S_ALR_87005190	IMG Activity: SIMG_CFMENUORKAOKO6
S_ALR_87005191	IMG Activity: SIMG_CFMENUOLPROOPSP
S_ALR_87005192	IMG Activity: SIMG_CFORFBOB55SAKO
S_ALR_87005193	IMG Activity: SIMG_CFMENUORKAABR
S_ALR_87005194	IMG Activity: SIMG_CFMENUOLPROPS4
S_ALR_87005195	IMG Activity: SIMG_ORKACMOD_VERZIN
S_ALR_87005196	IMG Activity: SIMG_CFMENUORFB2O7R2
S_ALR_87005197	IMG Activity: SIMG_ORKAKANK_VERZIN
S_ALR_87005198	IMG Activity: SIMG_CFMENUOLPRCO82
S_ALR_87005199	IMG Activity: SIMG_CFMENUORFB2O7F7
S_ALR_87005200	IMG Activity: SIMG_CFMENUORKAKAH21
S_ALR_87005201	IMG Activity: SIMG_OLPR_KPRI
S_ALR_87005202	IMG Activity: SIMG_CFMENUORFB2O7F5
S_ALR_87005203	IMG Activity: SIMG_CFMENUORKAGR21
S_ALR_87005204	IMG Activity: SIMG_CFMENUOLPROK02
S_ALR_87005205	IMG Activity: SIMG_CFMENUORKAGCRS1
S_ALR_87005206	IMG Activity: SIMG_CFMENUORFBOBB4
S_ALR_87005207	IMG Activity: SIMG_OLPR_ANNPL_BS52
S_ALR_87005208	IMG Activity: SIMG_CFMENUORKAOKOV2

S_ALR_87005209	IMG Activity: SIMG_CFMENUORFB2O7F6
S_ALR_87005210	IMG Activity: SIMG_ORKA_EWEP_CMOD
S_ALR_87005211	IMG Activity: SIMG_CFMENUOLPRKLH2
S_ALR_87005212	IMG Activity: SIMG_CFMENUORKAOKSA
S_ALR_87005213	IMG Activity: SIMG_CFMENUOLPRKSH2
S_ALR_87005214	IMG Activity: SIMG_CFMENUORKAGCRS
S_ALR_87005215	IMG Activity: SIMG_OLPR_KAH2
S_ALR_87005216	IMG Activity: SIMG_CFMENUORKAOKD6
S_ALR_87005217	IMG Activity: SIMG_CFMENUORKAKBH21
S_ALR_87005218	IMG Activity: SIMG_OLPR_BANF_OPTT
S_ALR_87005219	IMG Activity: SIMG_CFMENUORKAKOH91
S_ALR_87005220	IMG Activity: SIMG_OLPR_OPI1
S_ALR_87005221	IMG Activity: SIMG_CFMENUORKAKOT21
S_ALR_87005222	IMG Activity: SIMG_CFMENUOLPROPSG
S_ALR_87005223	IMG Activity: SIMG_CFMENUORKAOK10
S_ALR_87005224	IMG Activity: SIMG_OLPR_T003O_N2
S_ALR_87005225	IMG Activity: SIMG_CFMENUORKAKANK
S_ALR_87005226	IMG Activity: SIMG_OLPR_TCJ41_10
S_ALR_87005227	IMG Activity: SIMG_CFMENUORKAOKC8
S_ALR_87005228	IMG Activity: SIMG_CFMENUOLPROP40
S_ALR_87005229	IMG Activity: SIMG_CFMENUORKAOKO9
S_ALR_87005230	IMG Activity: SIMG_ORKA_KO09_ALTDS
S_ALR_87005231	IMG Activity: SIMG_OLPR_KP65
S_ALR_87005232	IMG Activity: SIMG_CFMENUORKACMOD
S_ALR_87005233	IMG Activity: SIMG_CFMENUOLPROPSU
S_ALR_87005234	IMG Activity: SIMG_ORKASE71_DRUCK
S_ALR_87005235	IMG Activity: SIMG_OLPR_OB07_1
S_ALR_87005236	IMG Activity: SIMG_CFMENUORKACL001
S_ALR_87005237	IMG Activity: SIMG_CFMENUOLPROP26
S_ALR_87005238	IMG Activity: SIMG_CFMENUORKAOKK1
S_ALR_87005239	IMG Activity: SIMG_OLPR_CJVC
S_ALR_87005240	IMG Activity: SIMG_CFMENUORKAKPH2
S_ALR_87005241	IMG Activity: SIMG_CFMENUORKAKP34
S_ALR_87005242	IMG Activity: SIMG_OLPR_OPI2
S_ALR_87005243	IMG Activity: SIMG_CFMENUORKAKPH5
S_ALR_87005244	IMG Activity: SIMG_OLPR_STDNTOPS1
S_ALR_87005245	IMG Activity: SIMG_CFMENUORKAKPG5
S_ALR_87005246	IMG Activity: SIMG_CFMENUOLPROPSH
S_ALR_87005247	IMG Activity: SIMG_CFMENUORKAKBH22
S_ALR_87005248	IMG Activity: SIMG_OLPR_STDN_OPTN
S_ALR_87005249	IMG Activity: SIMG_CFMENUORKAKOH9
S_ALR_87005250	IMG Activity: SIMG_OLPR_CMOD_USER3
S_ALR_87005251	IMG Activity: SIMG_CFMENUORKAKAH2
S_ALR_87005252	IMG Activity: SIMG_CFMENUORKAKAK2
S_ALR_87005253	IMG Activity: SIMG_OLPR_CMOD_USER1
S_ALR_87005254	IMG Activity: SIMG_ORKASM34_LAYOUT
S_ALR_87005255	IMG Activity: SIMG_OLPR_CMOD_FLD4
S_ALR_87005256	IMG Activity: SIMG_ORKAKOT2_FELD
S_ALR_87005257	IMG Activity: SIMG_ORKAKOT2_STATUS
S_ALR_87005258	IMG Activity: SIMG_OLPR_CMOD_FLD9
S_ALR_87005259	IMG Activity: SIMG_CFMENUORKAKOV2
S_ALR_87005260	IMG Activity: SIMG_CFMENUOLPROPJ9
S_ALR_87005261	IMG Activity: SIMG_CFMENUORKABS52
S_ALR_87005262	IMG Activity: SIMG_CFMENUOLPROPS5

S_ALR_87005263	IMG Activity: SIMG_CFMENUORKAOK02
S_ALR_87005264	IMG Activity: SIMG_OLPR_TOP8B
S_ALR_87005265	IMG Activity: SIMG_CFMENUORKAKONK
S_ALR_87005266	IMG Activity: SIMG_CFMENUORKAKOT2
S_ALR_87005267	IMG Activity: SIMG_CFMENUORKAOKKP
S_ALR_87005268	IMG Activity: SIMG_OLPR_CMOD_FLD8
S_ALR_87005269	IMG Activity: SIMG_CFMENUOLPRCNN1
S_ALR_87005270	IMG Activity: SIMG_CFMENUOLPRCO44
S_ALR_87005271	IMG Activity: SIMG_OLPR_OPS6
S_ALR_87005272	IMG Activity: SIMG_OLPR_OPSO
S_ALR_87005273	IMG Activity: SIMG_OLPR_OPSA
S_ALR_87005274	IMG Activity: SIMG_OLPR_OPSJ
S_ALR_87005275	IMG Activity: SIMG_CFMENUORKAOKO1
S_ALR_87005276	IMG Activity: SIMG_OLPR_OPSK
S_ALR_87005277	IMG Activity: SIMG_OLPR_CMOD_FLD3
S_ALR_87005278	IMG Activity: SIMG_CFMENUORKAOKO8
S_ALR_87005279	IMG Activity: SIMG_OLPR_STPR_OPTZ
S_ALR_87005280	IMG Activity: SIMG_CFMENUORKAOKOU
S_ALR_87005281	IMG Activity: SIMG_CFMENUORKAOKOL
S_ALR_87005282	IMG Activity: SIMG_CFMENUOLPROPSR
S_ALR_87005283	IMG Activity: SIMG_CFMENUORKABS42
S_ALR_87005284	IMG Activity: SIMG_OLPR_STD_OPUI
S_ALR_87005285	IMG Activity: SIMG_CFMENUORKAOKOR
S_ALR_87005286	IMG Activity: SIMG_CFMENUORKAOKOV
S_ALR_87005287	IMG Activity: SIMG_OLPR_OPS1
S_ALR_87005288	IMG Activity: OLQW-PO
S_ALR_87005289	IMG Activity: OLQZ-FS2
S_ALR_87005290	IMG Activity: SIMG_CFMENUORKASE11
S_ALR_87005291	IMG Activity: SIMG_OLPR_STD_OPTN
S_ALR_87005292	IMG Activity: SIMG_CFMENUOLQWCQ85
S_ALR_87005293	IMG Activity: OLQZ-FS1
S_ALR_87005294	IMG Activity: SIMG_CFMENUORKAKO02
S_ALR_87005295	IMG Activity: SIMG_OLPR_CMOD_USER2
S_ALR_87005296	IMG Activity: OLQW-EK
S_ALR_87005297	IMG Activity: OLQZ-FB
S_ALR_87005298	IMG Activity: SIMG_ORKA_CPT2_UMG_P
S_ALR_87005299	IMG Activity: SIMG_OLPR_CMOD_FLD5
S_ALR_87005300	IMG Activity: OLQZ-FA
S_ALR_87005301	IMG Activity: OLQW-EH
S_ALR_87005302	IMG Activity: SIMG_CFMENUORKAOKOZ
S_ALR_87005303	IMG Activity: OLQZ-FF
S_ALR_87005304	IMG Activity: SIMG_CFMENUOLQSOQCH
S_ALR_87005305	IMG Activity: SIMG_CFMENUORKAKOW11
S_ALR_87005306	IMG Activity: SIMG_CFMENUOLPROPS1
S_ALR_87005307	IMG Activity: OLQW_OQLS2
S_ALR_87005308	IMG Activity: OLQZ-FK1
S_ALR_87005309	IMG Activity: SIMG_CFMENUOLPROPT4
S_ALR_87005310	IMG Activity: OLQZ-FKF
S_ALR_87005311	IMG Activity: OLQW-K
S_ALR_87005312	IMG Activity: SIMG_OLPR_LV_NPLN
S_ALR_87005313	IMG Activity: OLQZ-SA
S_ALR_87005314	IMG Activity: OLQW-PP
S_ALR_87005315	IMG Activity: OLQZ-ST
S_ALR_87005316	IMG Activity: OLQW-PN

S_ALR_87005317	IMG Activity: SIMG_OLPR_FA_STDNETZ
S_ALR_87005318	IMG Activity: OLQZ-SP
S_ALR_87005319	IMG Activity: OLQW-PG
S_ALR_87005320	IMG Activity: SIMG_OLPR_OPG4
S_ALR_87005321	IMG Activity: OLQZ-SAB
S_ALR_87005322	IMG Activity: SIMG_OLPR_ZTPR_OPTY
S_ALR_87005323	IMG Activity: OLQW-LV
S_ALR_87005324	IMG Activity: OLQZ-SAV
S_ALR_87005325	IMG Activity: SIMG_OLPR_TCSUB_VG
S_ALR_87005326	IMG Activity: OLQZ-SD
S_ALR_87005327	IMG Activity: SIMG_CFMENUOLQIOQI1
S_ALR_87005328	IMG Activity: SIMG_OLPR_OPT6
S_ALR_87005329	IMG Activity: OLQZ-FP
S_ALR_87005330	IMG Activity: SIMG_CFMENUOLQIOQI2
S_ALR_87005331	IMG Activity: OLQZ-VFK1
S_ALR_87005332	IMG Activity: SIMG_OLPR_STMLSTOPSR
S_ALR_87005333	IMG Activity: OLQW-IDI
S_ALR_87005334	IMG Activity: OLQZ-VS
S_ALR_87005335	IMG Activity: SIMG_OLPR_FA_NPL
S_ALR_87005336	IMG Activity: OLQL-STI
S_ALR_87005337	IMG Activity: OLQZ-VFKF
S_ALR_87005338	IMG Activity: OLQW_OQE6
S_ALR_87005339	IMG Activity: SIMG_CFMENUOLPROPT5
S_ALR_87005340	IMG Activity: OLQZ-VT
S_ALR_87005341	IMG Activity: SIMG_OLPR_CMOD_NUM
S_ALR_87005342	IMG Activity: SIMG_CFMENUOLQWOQE3
S_ALR_87005343	IMG Activity: OLQZ-VF
S_ALR_87005344	IMG Activity: SIMG_OLPR_CMOD_BANF1
S_ALR_87005345	IMG Activity: SIMG_CFMENUOLQWQE29
S_ALR_87005346	IMG Activity: OLQZ-VH
S_ALR_87005347	IMG Activity: SIMG_OLPR_STD_OP46
S_ALR_87005348	IMG Activity: OLQW-DR
S_ALR_87005349	IMG Activity: OLQZ-VFN
S_ALR_87005350	IMG Activity: SIMG_CFMENUOLPROPJ7
S_ALR_87005351	IMG Activity: OLQZ-VFS
S_ALR_87005352	IMG Activity: SIMG_OLPR_OP50
S_ALR_87005353	IMG Activity: OLQW-LF
S_ALR_87005354	IMG Activity: SIMG_ORKA_KPR6
S_ALR_87005355	IMG Activity: OLQZ-VFA
S_ALR_87005356	IMG Activity: OLQW_OQLS1
S_ALR_87005357	IMG Activity: SIMG_OLPR_LISTVR_FHM
S_ALR_87005358	IMG Activity: OLQZ-VZ
S_ALR_87005359	IMG Activity: OLQW-I
S_ALR_87005360	IMG Activity: SIMG_OLPR_NETZGRAFIK
S_ALR_87005361	IMG Activity: OLQW_OQLV
S_ALR_87005362	IMG Activity: SIMG_OLPR_LSTVR_ARPL
S_ALR_87005363	IMG Activity: OLQW-OQWP
S_ALR_87005364	IMG Activity: SIMG_OLPR_STD_OPUY
S_ALR_87005365	IMG Activity: OLQW-OQWT
S_ALR_87005366	IMG Activity: SIMG_OLPR_LV_STDNETZ
S_ALR_87005367	IMG Activity: OLQW-OQWB
S_ALR_87005368	IMG Activity: SIMG_CFMENUOLPROPS2
S_ALR_87005369	IMG Activity: SIMG_CFMENUOLQWOQL2
S_ALR_87005370	IMG Activity: SIMG_OLPR_KPRK

S_ALR_87005371	IMG Activity: SIMG_CFMENUOLQWQA09
S_ALR_87005372	IMG Activity: SIMG_OLPR_OKEP
S_ALR_87005373	IMG Activity: SIMG_CFMENUOLQWOQL4
S_ALR_87005374	IMG Activity: SIMG_CFMENUOLQWOQL1
S_ALR_87005375	IMG Activity: SIMG_CFMENUOLPROPS6
S_ALR_87005376	IMG Activity: OLQW-C
S_ALR_87005377	IMG Activity: SIMG_OLPR_PSP_OPTN
S_ALR_87005378	IMG Activity: OLQW-M
S_ALR_87005379	IMG Activity: SIMG_ORKA_BEW_VERS
S_ALR_87005380	IMG Activity: SIMG_OLPR_CJBN
S_ALR_87005381	IMG Activity: SIMG_CFMENUOLQWOQV1
S_ALR_87005382	IMG Activity: SIMG_CFMENUOLPROPTK
S_ALR_87005383	IMG Activity: OLQW-QA18
S_ALR_87005384	IMG Activity: SIMG_ORKA_KALK_BEW
S_ALR_87005385	IMG Activity: SIMG_CFMENUOLPROPS7
S_ALR_87005386	IMG Activity: SIMG_CFMENUOLQWOQV3
S_ALR_87005387	IMG Activity: SIMG_ORKA_BEW
S_ALR_87005388	IMG Activity: OLQW-SW
S_ALR_87005389	IMG Activity: SIMG_CFMENUOLPROPSA
S_ALR_87005390	IMG Activity: OLQW-ES
S_ALR_87005391	IMG Activity: SIMG_ORKA_KALK
S_ALR_87005392	IMG Activity: OLQW-F
S_ALR_87005393	IMG Activity: SIMG_CFMENUOLPROPSO
S_ALR_87005394	IMG Activity: SIMG_ORKA_CPT2_SCH_P
S_ALR_87005395	IMG Activity: SIMG_CFMENUORKSKSW1
S_ALR_87005396	IMG Activity: SIMG_CFMENUORKAOK14
S_ALR_87005397	IMG Activity: SIMG_OLPR_FMU1
S_ALR_87005398	IMG Activity: SIMG_CFMENUORKSKOT21
S_ALR_87005399	IMG Activity: SIMG_CFMENUORKACJBN
S_ALR_87005400	IMG Activity: SIMG_OLPR_OKBG
S_ALR_87005401	IMG Activity: SIMG_ORKSSM34_LAY_I
S_ALR_87005402	IMG Activity: SIMG_CFMENUORKAOPTK
S_ALR_87005403	IMG Activity: SIMG_OLPR_KANKANZ
S_ALR_87005404	IMG Activity: SIMG_CFMENUORKSKO011
S_ALR_87005405	IMG Activity: SIMG_CFMENUORKAOKOC
S_ALR_87005406	IMG Activity: SIMG_CFMENUORKSKS031
S_ALR_87005407	IMG Activity: SIMG_OLPR_TCN41RP
S_ALR_87005408	IMG Activity: SIMG_CFMENUORKAOK111
S_ALR_87005409	IMG Activity: SIMG_CFMENUORKSKCAP2
S_ALR_87005410	IMG Activity: SIMG_OLPR_V_TFPLTRP
S_ALR_87005411	IMG Activity: SIMG_CFMENUORKAOKOB
S_ALR_87005412	IMG Activity: SIMG_ORKSSM30_PERSKO
S_ALR_87005413	IMG Activity: SIMG_CFMENUORKAOKOA1
S_ALR_87005414	IMG Activity: SIMG_OLPR_TVTB_1
S_ALR_87005415	IMG Activity: SIMG_ORKSSM30_PERSAB
S_ALR_87005416	IMG Activity: SIMG_ORKA_KTPF
S_ALR_87005417	IMG Activity: SIMG_OLPR_V_TFPLARP
S_ALR_87005418	IMG Activity: SIMG_CFMENUORKSKK031
S_ALR_87005419	IMG Activity: SIMG_CFMENUORKAOK11
S_ALR_87005420	IMG Activity: SIMG_OLPR_TCSUB_PSP
S_ALR_87005421	IMG Activity: SIMG_CFMENUORKSKVA2
S_ALR_87005422	IMG Activity: SIMG_ORKA_KPRI
S_ALR_87005423	IMG Activity: SIMG_OLPR_REG_PSP
S_ALR_87005424	IMG Activity: SIMG_CFMENUORKSKVD2

S_ALR_87005425	IMG Activity: SIMG_CFMENUORKAPL
S_ALR_87005426	IMG Activity: SIMG_ORKS_KZS2
S_ALR_87005427	IMG Activity: SIMG_CFMENUOLPROPSC
S_ALR_87005428	IMG Activity: SIMG_CFMENUORKACKNR
S_ALR_87005429	IMG Activity: SIMG_ORKS_KZB2
S_ALR_87005430	IMG Activity: SIMG_CFMENUOLPRVKBN
S_ALR_87005431	IMG Activity: SIMG_ORKA_KPRK
S_ALR_87005432	IMG Activity: SIMG_ORKS_KZZ2
S_ALR_87005433	IMG Activity: SIMG_ORKA_KOND
S_ALR_87005434	IMG Activity: SIMG_OLPR_TCJ41_3
S_ALR_87005435	IMG Activity: SIMG_ORKS_KZM2
S_ALR_87005436	IMG Activity: SIMG_XXMENUORKA_P_V
S_ALR_87005437	IMG Activity: SIMG_XXMENUORKA_PL_A
S_ALR_87005438	IMG Activity: SIMG_CFMENUOLPROPS9
S_ALR_87005439	IMG Activity: SIMG_ORKS_KZE2
S_ALR_87005440	IMG Activity: SIMG_XXORKA_I_A
S_ALR_87005441	IMG Activity: W_MDS_0003
S_ALR_87005442	IMG Activity: SIMG_CFMENUOM00OM15
S_ALR_87005443	IMG Activity: SIMG_OLPR_OPSV1
S_ALR_87005444	IMG Activity: SIMG_ORKS_KA06
S_ALR_87005445	IMG Activity: W_MDS_0001
S_ALR_87005446	IMG Activity: SIMG_CFMENUOM00OM16
S_ALR_87005447	IMG Activity: SIMG_OLPR_KANK4
S_ALR_87005448	IMG Activity: SIMG_CFMENUORKSKA012
S_ALR_87005449	IMG Activity: W_MDS_0002
S_ALR_87005450	IMG Activity: SIMG_CFMENUOM00OM17
S_ALR_87005451	IMG Activity: SIMG_OLPR_KGF4
S_ALR_87005452	IMG Activity: W_MDS_0000
S_ALR_87005453	IMG Activity: SIMG_CFMENUOM00OJIN1
S_ALR_87005454	IMG Activity: SIMG_CFMENUOLPRKZE2
S_ALR_87005455	IMG Activity: SIMG_CFMENUORKSKSAJ
S_ALR_87005456	IMG Activity: SIMG_OLPR_KZM2
S_ALR_87005457	IMG Activity: SIMG_CFMENUOM00OM19
S_ALR_87005458	IMG Activity: SIMG_CFMENUORKSKA013
S_ALR_87005459	IMG Activity: SIMG_OLPR_KZZ2
S_ALR_87005460	IMG Activity: SIMG_CFMENUORKSKSAZI
S_ALR_87005461	IMG Activity: SIMG_CFMENUOM00OM20
S_ALR_87005462	IMG Activity: SIMG_ORKS_CMOD_ABGR
S_ALR_87005463	IMG Activity: SIMG_CFMENUOLPRKZB2
S_ALR_87005464	IMG Activity: SIMG_CFMENUOM00OJI1
S_ALR_87005465	IMG Activity: SIMG_ORKS_KBC5
S_ALR_87005466	IMG Activity: SIMG_OLPR_KK06
S_ALR_87005467	IMG Activity: SIMG_CFMENUOM00OJI2
S_ALR_87005468	IMG Activity: SIMG_ORKS_KL01_ILV_P
S_ALR_87005469	IMG Activity: SIMG_OLPR_KANK6
S_ALR_87005470	IMG Activity: SIMG_CFMENUOM00OJI3
S_ALR_87005471	IMG Activity: SIMG_CFMENUORKSKSC7
S_ALR_87005472	IMG Activity: SIMG_OLPR_TCK05_NP
S_ALR_87005473	IMG Activity: SIMG_CFMENUOM00OJIN5
S_ALR_87005474	IMG Activity: SIMG_OLPR_TCJ41_4
S_ALR_87005475	IMG Activity: SIMG_CFMENUORKSOKES
S_ALR_87005476	IMG Activity: SIMG_CFMENUOM00OM14
S_ALR_87005477	IMG Activity: SIMG_OLPR_OKOG
S_ALR_87005478	IMG Activity: SIMG_CFMENUOM00OM18

S_ALR_87005479	IMG Activity: SIMG_CFMENUOM00OJIN4
S_ALR_87005480	IMG Activity: SIMG_OLPR_CMODZUSCHL
S_ALR_87005481	IMG Activity: SIMG_CFMENUOM00OJIN3
S_ALR_87005482	IMG Activity: SIMG_CFMENUOLPRKBC2
S_ALR_87005483	IMG Activity: SIMG_CFMENUOM00OJIN2
S_ALR_87005484	IMG Activity: SIMG_CFMENUOLPRKBC1
S_ALR_87005485	IMG Activity: SIMG_CFMENUOM00OM13
S_ALR_87005486	IMG Activity: SIMG_CFMENUOM00OM12
S_ALR_87005487	IMG Activity: SIMG_OLPR_OK02
S_ALR_87005488	IMG Activity: SIMG_CFMENUOM00OM11
S_ALR_87005489	IMG Activity: SIMG_CFMENUORKSOKEW
S_ALR_87005490	IMG Activity: SIMG_OLPR_ANPSP_BS52
S_ALR_87005491	IMG Activity: SIMG_OLPR_OK60_2
S_ALR_87005492	IMG Activity: SIMG_CFMENUOLPROPSJ
S_ALR_87005493	IMG Activity: SIMG_CFMENUOLPRKZS2
S_ALR_87005494	IMG Activity: SIMG_OLPR_KA06
S_ALR_87005495	IMG Activity: SIMG_CFMENUOLPROPSK
S_ALR_87005496	IMG Activity: SIMG_OLPR_KSW1
S_ALR_87005497	IMG Activity: SIMG_OLPR_KSW7
S_ALR_87005498	IMG Activity: SIMG_OLPR_PSP_OPUK
S_ALR_87005499	IMG Activity: SIMG_OLPR_TCJ41_01
S_ALR_87005500	IMG Activity: SIMG_CFMENUOLPROPSB
S_ALR_87005501	IMG Activity: SIMG_CFMENUOLPRCKNR
S_ALR_87005502	IMG Activity: SIMG_CFMENUOLPROKK4
S_ALR_87005503	IMG Activity: SIMG_CFMENUOLPROKK1
S_ALR_87005504	IMG Activity: SIMG_OLPR_SUB_OPSN
S_ALR_87005505	IMG Activity: SIMG_CFMENUOMP0OMP9
S_ALR_87005506	IMG Activity: SIMG_CFMENUOLPROPL1
S_ALR_87005507	IMG Activity: SIMG_CFMENUORKSKCAL1
S_ALR_87005508	IMG Activity: SIMG_CFMENUOMP0OMPG
S_ALR_87005509	IMG Activity: SIMG_CFMENUORKSKCAU1
S_ALR_87005510	IMG Activity: SIMG_CFMENUOLPROPT3
S_ALR_87005511	IMG Activity: SIMG_CFMENUOMP0OMPA
S_ALR_87005512	IMG Activity: SIMG_CFMENUORKEKE4MI
S_ALR_87005513	IMG Activity: SIMG_OLPR_OPO8
S_ALR_87005514	IMG Activity: SIMG_CFMENUOMP0OMPS
S_ALR_87005515	IMG Activity: SIMG_CFMENUORKEKE4W
S_ALR_87005516	IMG Activity: SIMG_OLPR_OK11
S_ALR_87005517	IMG Activity: SIMG_CFMENUOMP0OMPH
S_ALR_87005518	IMG Activity: SIMG_CFMENUORKEKECM
S_ALR_87005519	IMG Activity: SIMG_CFMENUOMP0OSPA
S_ALR_87005520	IMG Activity: SIMG_CFMENUORKEKEI1
S_ALR_87005521	IMG Activity: SIMG_OLPR_ZUOR
S_ALR_87005522	IMG Activity: SIMG_CFMENUOMP0OPB2
S_ALR_87005523	IMG Activity: SIMG_CFMENUORKEOKO7
S_ALR_87005524	IMG Activity: SIMG_OLPR_BEW
S_ALR_87005525	IMG Activity: SIMG_CFMENUORKEKE4I2
S_ALR_87005526	IMG Activity: OMP0_DATTRANS_SXDA
S_ALR_87005527	IMG Activity: SIMG_OLPR_CMOD_USER
S_ALR_87005528	IMG Activity: SIMG_CFMENUOMP0OMI6
S_ALR_87005529	IMG Activity: SIMG_CFMENUORKEKEKF
S_ALR_87005530	IMG Activity: SIMG_OLPR_KALK
S_ALR_87005531	IMG Activity: OMP0_OMPP
S_ALR_87005532	IMG Activity: SIMG_CFMENUORKEKEAT

S_ALR_87005533	IMG Activity: SIMG_OLPR_KOND
S_ALR_87005534	IMG Activity: SIMG_CFMENUOMP0OMPD
S_ALR_87005535	IMG Activity: SIMG_CFMENUORKEKE4I
S_ALR_87005536	IMG Activity: SIMG_ORKS_KSES_PLAN
S_ALR_87005537	IMG Activity: SIMG_CFMENUOMP0OMP6
S_ALR_87005538	IMG Activity: SIMG_OLPR_CMOD_FLD6
S_ALR_87005539	IMG Activity: SIMG_CFMENUORKEKEI2
S_ALR_87005540	IMG Activity: SIMG_CFMENUORKSKSU7
S_ALR_87005541	IMG Activity: SIMG_CFMENUOMP0OMP4
S_ALR_87005542	IMG Activity: SIMG_OLPR_CMOD_FLD7
S_ALR_87005543	IMG Activity: SIMG_CFMENUORKEKEUH
S_ALR_87005544	IMG Activity: SIMG_CFMENUORKSKL02
S_ALR_87005545	IMG Activity: SIMG_CFMENUOMP0OMP8
S_ALR_87005546	IMG Activity: SIMG_CFMENUORKEKE3T
S_ALR_87005547	IMG Activity: SIMG_OLPR_KANK2
S_ALR_87005548	IMG Activity: SIMG_CFMENUORKSOKB9
S_ALR_87005549	IMG Activity: SIMG_CFMENUOMP0OMPJ
S_ALR_87005550	IMG Activity: SIMG_CFMENUORKEKEU1
S_ALR_87005551	IMG Activity: SIMG_OLPR_KPR6
S_ALR_87005552	IMG Activity: SIMG_CFMENUORKSKBC1
S_ALR_87005553	IMG Activity: SIMG_CFMENUOMP0OMPC
S_ALR_87005554	IMG Activity: SIMG_CFMENUORKSKBC4
S_ALR_87005555	IMG Activity: SIMG_OLPR_VERS
S_ALR_87005556	IMG Activity: OMP0_OMPO
S_ALR_87005557	IMG Activity: SIMG_CFMENUORKEKSES
S_ALR_87005558	IMG Activity: SIMG_OLPR_OKTZ
S_ALR_87005559	IMG Activity: SIMG_CFMENUORKEOKB9
S_ALR_87005560	IMG Activity: SIMG_CFMENUOMP0OMP1
S_ALR_87005561	IMG Activity: OMP0_OMIE
S_ALR_87005562	IMG Activity: SIMG_OLPR_T399X_N2
S_ALR_87005563	IMG Activity: SIMG_CFMENUORKEKEDV
S_ALR_87005564	IMG Activity: SIMG_CFMENUOMP0OMID
S_ALR_87005565	IMG Activity: SIMG_OLPR_OKYG
S_ALR_87005566	IMG Activity: SIMG_CFMENUORKE5310
S_ALR_87005567	IMG Activity: SIMG_CFMENUOMP0OMP2
S_ALR_87005568	IMG Activity: SIMG_CFMENUOMP0OPPU
S_ALR_87005569	IMG Activity: SIMG_CFMENUORKEKE3Z
S_ALR_87005570	IMG Activity: SIMG_CFMENUOMP0OPPT
S_ALR_87005571	IMG Activity: SIMG_OLPR_PSPOPS1
S_ALR_87005572	IMG Activity: SIMG_CFMENUORKEKE1T
S_ALR_87005573	IMG Activity: SIMG_CFMENUORKEKEPG
S_ALR_87005574	IMG Activity: SIMG_OLPR_VALID_OPSI
S_ALR_87005575	IMG Activity: SIMG_CFMENUOMP0OPPS
S_ALR_87005576	IMG Activity: SIMG_CFMENUORKEKE1R
S_ALR_87005577	IMG Activity: SIMG_CFMENUOMP0ORGRE
S_ALR_87005578	IMG Activity: SIMG_CFMENUORKEKE1I
S_ALR_87005579	IMG Activity: SIMG_OLPR_OKK4
S_ALR_87005580	IMG Activity: SIMG_CFMENUORKEKE1O
S_ALR_87005581	IMG Activity: SIMG_OLPR_OPR3
S_ALR_87005582	IMG Activity: SIMG_CFMENUORKEKEPE
S_ALR_87005583	IMG Activity: SIMG_CFMENUOLPROKK3
S_ALR_87005584	IMG Activity: SIMG_CFMENUORKEKE4S
S_ALR_87005585	IMG Activity: SIMG_OLPR_OKYF
S_ALR_87005586	IMG Activity: SIMG_CFMENUORKEKEF3

S_ALR_87005587	IMG Activity: SIMG_OLPR_ACCESS
S_ALR_87005588	IMG Activity: SIMG_CFMENUOLPRUMFK2
S_ALR_87005589	IMG Activity: SIMG_CFMENUOLPRUMFK1
S_ALR_87005590	IMG Activity: SIMG_OLPR_FM_SM35
S_ALR_87005591	IMG Activity: SIMG_CFMENUOLPRUMFK4
S_ALR_87005592	IMG Activity: SIMG_OLPR_KAPA
S_ALR_87005593	IMG Activity: SIMG_OLPR_HIERGRAFIK
S_ALR_87005594	IMG Activity: SIMG_OLPR_PSBERECHT
S_ALR_87005595	IMG Activity: SIMG_CMMENUOLPRKDPS
S_ALR_87005596	IMG Activity: SIMG_OLPR_PSSD_OPT9
S_ALR_87005597	IMG Activity: SIMG_CFMENUOLPRUMFK3
S_ALR_87005598	IMG Activity: SIMG_OLPR_BILDMITTEL
S_ALR_87005599	IMG Activity: SIMG_OLPR_ABRECH_ERL
S_ALR_87005600	IMG Activity: W_DF_VK_0120
S_ALR_87005601	IMG Activity: SIMG_OLPR_ROLLUP_IS
S_ALR_87005602	IMG Activity: W_DF_VK_0126
S_ALR_87005603	IMG Activity: SIMG_OLPR_OWF1_MLST
S_ALR_87005604	IMG Activity: W_DF_VK_0138
S_ALR_87005605	IMG Activity: SIMG_OLPR_NP_DRUCKE
S_ALR_87005606	IMG Activity: SIMG_OLPR_EISALLG
S_ALR_87005607	IMG Activity: W_DF_VK_0129
S_ALR_87005608	IMG Activity: SIMG_OLPR_ZUMBUCHUNG
S_ALR_87005609	IMG Activity: W_DF_VK_0110
S_ALR_87005610	IMG Activity: W_KO_0410
S_ALR_87005611	IMG Activity: SIMG_CFMENUORKEKEPH
S_ALR_87005612	IMG Activity: SIMG_CFMENUORKSOK60
S_ALR_87005613	IMG Activity: W_DF_VK_0141
S_ALR_87005614	IMG Activity: SIMG_CFMENUORKEKE4T
S_ALR_87005615	IMG Activity: W_DF_VK_0144
S_ALR_87005616	IMG Activity: SIMG_CFMENUORKEKEPS
S_ALR_87005617	IMG Activity: W_DF_VK_0111
S_ALR_87005618	IMG Activity: SIMG_CFMENUORKEKE3I
S_ALR_87005619	IMG Activity: W_DF_VK_0128
S_ALR_87005620	IMG Activity: SIMG_CFMENUORKEKEPA
S_ALR_87005621	IMG Activity: W_DF_VK_0112
S_ALR_87005622	IMG Activity: SIMG_CFMENUORKEKE4G
S_ALR_87005623	IMG Activity: W_DF_VK_0127
S_ALR_87005624	IMG Activity: SIMG_CFMENUORKEKE2S
S_ALR_87005625	IMG Activity: W_DF_VK_0124
S_ALR_87005626	IMG Activity: SIMG_CFMENUORKEKE4MS
S_ALR_87005627	IMG Activity: W_DF_VK_0123
S_ALR_87005628	IMG Activity: SIMG_CFMENUORKEKE4F
S_ALR_87005629	IMG Activity: W_DF_VK_0122
S_ALR_87005630	IMG Activity: SIMG_CFMENUORKEKE19
S_ALR_87005631	IMG Activity: W_DF_VK_0121
S_ALR_87005632	IMG Activity: SIMG_CFMENUORKEKE1Q
S_ALR_87005633	IMG Activity: W_DF_VK_0131
S_ALR_87005634	IMG Activity: SIMG_CFMENUORKEKE3J
S_ALR_87005635	IMG Activity: W_DF_VK_0134
S_ALR_87005636	IMG Activity: SIMG_CFMENUORKEKEN1
S_ALR_87005637	IMG Activity: W_DF_VK_0133
S_ALR_87005638	IMG Activity: SIMG_CFMENUORKEKE3D
S_ALR_87005639	IMG Activity: W_DF_VK_0132
S_ALR_87005640	IMG Activity: SIMG_CFMENUORKEKE3E

S_ALR_87005641	IMG Activity: W_DF_VK_0180
S_ALR_87005642	IMG Activity: SIMG_CFMENUORKEKE34
S_ALR_87005643	IMG Activity: W_KO_0110
S_ALR_87005644	IMG Activity: SIMG_CFMENUORKEKEPD
S_ALR_87005645	IMG Activity: W_DF_VK_0140
S_ALR_87005646	IMG Activity: SIMG_CFMENUORKEKES3
S_ALR_87005647	IMG Activity: W_DF_VK_0160
S_ALR_87005648	IMG Activity: SIMG_CFMENUORKEKE3K
S_ALR_87005649	IMG Activity: W_DF_EK_0154
S_ALR_87005650	IMG Activity: SIMG_CFMENUORKEKEKG
S_ALR_87005651	IMG Activity: W_DF_VK_0137
S_ALR_87005652	IMG Activity: SIMG_CFMENUORKEKE2K
S_ALR_87005653	IMG Activity: W_DF_VK_0191
S_ALR_87005654	IMG Activity: SIMG_CFMENUORKEKEKE
S_ALR_87005655	IMG Activity: W_DF_VK_0139
S_ALR_87005656	IMG Activity: SIMG_CFMENUORKEKEC3
S_ALR_87005657	IMG Activity: W_DF_VK_0136
S_ALR_87005658	IMG Activity: SIMG_CFMENUORKEKER1
S_ALR_87005659	IMG Activity: W_DF_VK_0135
S_ALR_87005660	IMG Activity: SIMG_CFMENUORKE6110
S_ALR_87005661	IMG Activity: SIMG_CFMENUORKEKE3F
S_ALR_87005662	IMG Activity: SIMG_CFMENUORKEKE3S
S_ALR_87005663	IMG Activity: SIMG_CFMENUORKEKE94
S_ALR_87005664	IMG Activity: SIMG_CFMENUORKEKE91
S_ALR_87005665	IMG Activity: SIMG_CFMENUORKEKE3Q
S_ALR_87005666	IMG Activity: SIMG_CFMENUORKEKE3X
S_ALR_87005667	IMG Activity: SIMG_CFMENUORKEKE31
S_ALR_87005668	IMG Activity: SIMG_CFMENUORKEOKU7
S_ALR_87005669	IMG Activity: SIMG_CFMENUORKSOKF1
S_ALR_87005670	IMG Activity: SIMG_CFMENUORKEKE3R
S_ALR_87005671	IMG Activity: SIMG_CFMENUORKSSOVA
S_ALR_87005672	IMG Activity: SIMG_CFMENUORKEKE3P
S_ALR_87005673	IMG Activity: SIMG_ORKS_FMU1
S_ALR_87005674	IMG Activity: SIMG_ORKS_KGF4
S_ALR_87005675	IMG Activity: SIMG_CFMENUORKSGCRS
S_ALR_87005676	IMG Activity: SIMG_CFMENUORKEKE3C
S_ALR_87005677	IMG Activity: SIMG_CFMENUORKSOKB6
S_ALR_87005678	IMG Activity: SIMG_CFMENUORKEKEVG
S_ALR_87005679	IMG Activity: SIMG_ORKS_EWEP_CMOD
S_ALR_87005680	IMG Activity: SIMG_CFMENUORKEKEAS
S_ALR_87005681	IMG Activity: SIMG_CFMENUORKSGCRS2
S_ALR_87005682	IMG Activity: W_ZF_VK_0463
S_ALR_87005683	IMG Activity: SIMG_CFMENUORKEKEI3
S_ALR_87005684	IMG Activity: SIMG_CFMENUORKSGR21
S_ALR_87005685	IMG Activity: W_ZF_VK_0810
S_ALR_87005686	IMG Activity: SIMG_CFMENUORKEKEG1
S_ALR_87005687	IMG Activity: SIMG_CFMENUORKSOKD3
S_ALR_87005688	IMG Activity: W_ZF_ST_0610
S_ALR_87005689	IMG Activity: SIMG_CFMENUORKE5065
S_ALR_87005690	IMG Activity: SIMG_CFMENUORKSKAH22
S_ALR_87005691	IMG Activity: W_ZF_ST_0620
S_ALR_87005692	IMG Activity: SIMG_CFMENUORKEKE9D
S_ALR_87005693	IMG Activity: SIMG_CFMENUORKSKSH21
S_ALR_87005694	IMG Activity: W_ZF_VK_0802

S_ALR_87005695	IMG Activity: SIMG_CFMENUORKSKLH22
S_ALR_87005696	IMG Activity: SIMG_CFMENUORKE5055
S_ALR_87005697	IMG Activity: SIMG_CFMENUORKSKBH22
S_ALR_87005698	IMG Activity: SIMG_CFMENUORKEKEAE
S_ALR_87005699	IMG Activity: SIMG_ORKS_SELVAR
S_ALR_87005700	IMG Activity: SIMG_CFMENUORKEOKOA
S_ALR_87005701	IMG Activity: SIMG_ORKS_EXTRA_GRE9
S_ALR_87005702	IMG Activity: SIMG_CFMENUORKEKES4
S_ALR_87005703	IMG Activity: SIMG_CFMENUORKEKE39
S_ALR_87005704	IMG Activity: SIMG_CFMENUORKE5610
S_ALR_87005705	IMG Activity: SIMG_CFMENUORKE5095
S_ALR_87005706	IMG Activity: SIMG_CFMENUORKSSU03
S_ALR_87005707	IMG Activity: SIMG_CFMENUORKECPT2
S_ALR_87005708	IMG Activity: SIMG_ORKS_EWZYK_CMOD
S_ALR_87005709	IMG Activity: SIMG_CFMENUORKEKEKW
S_ALR_87005710	IMG Activity: SIMG_CFMENUORKSSU02
S_ALR_87005711	IMG Activity: SIMG_ORKS_SELEK_RPCN
S_ALR_87005712	IMG Activity: SIMG_CFMENUORKEKE3A
S_ALR_87005713	IMG Activity: SIMG_CFMENUORKSOKMI
S_ALR_87005714	IMG Activity: SIMG_CFMENUORKEKE45
S_ALR_87005715	IMG Activity: SIMG_CFMENUORKSFGRP
S_ALR_87005716	IMG Activity: SIMG_CFMENUORKSGR5G
S_ALR_87005717	IMG Activity: SIMG_CFMENUORKEKE4L
S_ALR_87005718	IMG Activity: SIMG_CFMENUORKEKE17
S_ALR_87005719	IMG Activity: SIMG_CFMENUORKSOKLS
S_ALR_87005720	IMG Activity: SIMG_CFMENUORKEKEN2
S_ALR_87005721	IMG Activity: SIMG_ORKS_PARAM_RPXN
S_ALR_87005722	IMG Activity: SIMG_CFMENUORKEOKEQ
S_ALR_87005723	IMG Activity: SIMG_CFMENUORKEKE37
S_ALR_87005724	IMG Activity: SIMG_CFMENUORKEKE4A
S_ALR_87005725	IMG Activity: SIMG_CFMENUORKEKE48
S_ALR_87005726	IMG Activity: SIMG_CFMENUORKEKE47
S_ALR_87005727	IMG Activity: SIMG_CFMENUORKEKE46
S_ALR_87005728	IMG Activity: SIMG_CFMENUORKEKE4MP
S_ALR_87005729	IMG Activity: SIMG_CFMENUORKEKEVP
S_ALR_87005730	IMG Activity: SIMG_CFMENUORKEKE0F
S_ALR_87005731	IMG Activity: SIMG_CFMENUORKEKE0E
S_ALR_87005732	IMG Activity: SIMG_CFMENUORKEKE0C
S_ALR_87005733	IMG Activity: SIMG_CFMENUORKEKE14
S_ALR_87005734	IMG Activity: SIMG_CFMENUORKEKP34
S_ALR_87005735	IMG Activity: SIMG_CFMENUORKEKEQ3A
S_ALR_87005736	IMG Activity: SIMG_CFMENUORKEKEVF
S_ALR_87005737	IMG Activity: SIMG_CFMENUORKEKEA0
S_ALR_87005738	IMG Activity: SIMG_ORKS_KA06_UMIST
S_ALR_87005739	IMG Activity: SIMG_CFMENUORKEKECP
S_ALR_87005740	IMG Activity: SIMG_ORKS_KSES_IST
S_ALR_87005741	IMG Activity: SIMG_CFMENUORKEKEQ3
S_ALR_87005742	IMG Activity: SIMG_CFMENUORKSKSU1
S_ALR_87005743	IMG Activity: SIMG_CFMENUORKSKL03
S_ALR_87005744	IMG Activity: SIMG_CFMENUORKEKEBD
S_ALR_87005745	IMG Activity: SIMG_CFMENUORKSKCAL2
S_ALR_87005746	IMG Activity: SIMG_CFMENUORKEFILE
S_ALR_87005747	IMG Activity: SIMG_CFMENUORKEMODIF
S_ALR_87005748	IMG Activity: SIMG_CFMENUORKSKCAU2

S_ALR_87005749	IMG Activity: SIMG_ORKS_KK06
S_ALR_87005750	IMG Activity: SIMG_CFMENUORKESF07
S_ALR_87005751	IMG Activity: SIMG_ORKS_CMODZ
S_ALR_87005752	IMG Activity: SIMG_CFMENUORKESF01
S_ALR_87005753	IMG Activity: SIMG_ORKS_KM1V_GKZ
S_ALR_87005754	IMG Activity: SIMG_CFMENUORKEKEA5
S_ALR_87005755	IMG Activity: SIMG_CFMENUORKSKCAV2
S_ALR_87005756	IMG Activity: SIMG_CFMENUORKEKEA6
S_ALR_87005757	IMG Activity: SIMG_CFMENUORKSKSV1
S_ALR_87005758	IMG Activity: SIMG_CFMENUORKEKETR
S_ALR_87005759	IMG Activity: SIMG_CFMENUORKEKE40
S_ALR_87005760	IMG Activity: SIMG_CFMENUORKEKE4H
S_ALR_87005761	IMG Activity: SIMG_CFMENUORKEKE4J
S_ALR_87005762	IMG Activity: SIMG_CFMENUORKEKEPC
S_ALR_87005763	IMG Activity: SIMG_CFMENUORKEKE4R
S_ALR_87005764	IMG Activity: SIMG_CFMENUORKEKES1
S_ALR_87005765	IMG Activity: SIMG_CFMENUORKEKEDR
S_ALR_87005766	IMG Activity: SIMG_CFMENUORKEPFCG
S_ALR_87005767	IMG Activity: SIMG_CFMENUORKEKE4U
S_ALR_87005768	IMG Activity: SIMG_CFMENUORKEKE97
S_ALR_87005769	IMG Activity: SIMG_CFMENUORKEKE2U
S_ALR_87005770	IMG Activity: SIMG_CFMENUORKSOKA8
S_ALR_87005771	IMG Activity: SIMG_CFMENUORKEKE4D
S_ALR_87005772	IMG Activity: SIMG_CFMENUORKEKEDP
S_ALR_87005773	IMG Activity: SIMG_CFMENUORKEKEP1
S_ALR_87005774	IMG Activity: SIMG_CFMENUORKEKEV1
S_ALR_87005775	IMG Activity: SIMG_CFMENUORKEKEPF
S_ALR_87005776	IMG Activity: SIMG_CFMENUORKEKEF1
S_ALR_87005777	IMG Activity: SIMG_CFMENUORKE3075
S_ALR_87005778	IMG Activity: SIMG_CFMENUORKE3060
S_ALR_87005779	IMG Activity: SIMG_CFMENUORKE7410
S_ALR_87005780	IMG Activity: SIMG_CFMENUORKEKESF
S_ALR_87005781	IMG Activity: SIMG_CFMENUORKEKEG7
S_ALR_87005782	IMG Activity: SIMG_CFMENUORKEKEU7
S_ALR_87005783	IMG Activity: SIMG_CFMENUORKEWE60
S_ALR_87005784	IMG Activity: SIMG_CFMENUORKEKEPV
S_ALR_87005785	IMG Activity: SIMG_CFMENUORKE3065
S_ALR_87005786	IMG Activity: SIMG_CFMENUORKE3055
S_ALR_87005787	IMG Activity: SIMG_CFMENUORKEKEFA
S_ALR_87005788	IMG Activity: SIMG_CFMENUORKEKEFB
S_ALR_87005789	IMG Activity: SIMG_CMMENUORKE3065
S_ALR_87005790	IMG Activity: SIMG_CFMENUORKE7600
S_ALR_87005791	IMG Activity: SIMG_ORKS_KL01_ILV_I
S_ALR_87005792	IMG Activity: SIMG_CFMENUORKSKSC1
S_ALR_87005793	IMG Activity: SIMG_CFMENUORKSOKES1
S_ALR_87005794	IMG Activity: SIMG_CFMENUORKSOKEW1
S_ALR_87005795	IMG Activity: SIMG_CFMENUORKSKK01
S_ALR_87005796	IMG Activity: SIMG_CFMENUORKSKPT1
S_ALR_87005797	IMG Activity: SIMG_CFMENUORKSCTU1
S_ALR_87005798	IMG Activity: SIMG_CFMENUORKSKBH2
S_ALR_87005799	IMG Activity: SIMG_CFMENUORKSKPR6
S_ALR_87005800	IMG Activity: SIMG_CFMENUORKS_VERS
S_ALR_87005801	IMG Activity: SIMG_CFMENUORKSKPR2
S_ALR_87005802	IMG Activity: SIMG_CFMENUORKS_ZUOR

SAP Transaction Codes – Volume Two

S_ALR_87005803	IMG Activity: SIMG_CFMENUORKS_BEW
S_ALR_87005804	IMG Activity: SIMG_ORKSSM34_LAY_P
S_ALR_87005805	IMG Activity: SIMG_CFMENUORKSKOT2
S_ALR_87005806	IMG Activity: SIMG_CFMENUORKSKLH2
S_ALR_87005807	IMG Activity: SIMG_CFMENUORKSOKEE
S_ALR_87005808	IMG Activity: SIMG_CFMENUORKSKSW7
S_ALR_87005809	IMG Activity: SIMG_CFMENUORKSKCAP1
S_ALR_87005810	IMG Activity: SIMG_CFMENUOLSDARCH2
S_ALR_87005811	IMG Activity: SIMG_CFMENUORKSOKEI
S_ALR_87005812	IMG Activity: SIMG_CFMENUOLSDVOKO
S_ALR_87005813	IMG Activity: SIMG_ORKS_EWLRT_CMOD
S_ALR_87005814	IMG Activity: SIMG_CFMENUOLSDSXDA2
S_ALR_87005815	IMG Activity: SIMG_CFMENUORKSKPU1
S_ALR_87005816	IMG Activity: SIMG_CFMENUOLSDSXDA
S_ALR_87005817	IMG Activity: SIMG_CFMENUOLSDVOE3
S_ALR_87005818	IMG Activity: SIMG_CFMENUOLSDDAT07
S_ALR_87005819	IMG Activity: SIMG_XXMENUOLSDUSE15
S_ALR_87005820	IMG Activity: SIMG_CFMENUORKSOB08
S_ALR_87005821	IMG Activity: SIMG_CFMENUOLSDSMME
S_ALR_87005822	IMG Activity: SIMG_XXMENUOLSDUSE22
S_ALR_87005823	IMG Activity: SIMG_CFMENUOLSDVOE1
S_ALR_87005824	IMG Activity: SIMG_CFMENUORKSKP85
S_ALR_87005825	IMG Activity: SIMG_XXMENUOLSDUSE16
S_ALR_87005826	IMG Activity: SIMG_CFMENUOLSDPC02
S_ALR_87005827	IMG Activity: SIMG_CFMENUORKSKP75
S_ALR_87005828	IMG Activity: SIMG_XXMENUOLSDUSE31
S_ALR_87005829	IMG Activity: SIMG_CFMENUOLSDPC03
S_ALR_87005830	IMG Activity: SIMG_CFMENUORKSOKEV
S_ALR_87005831	IMG Activity: SIMG_XXMENUOLSDMODAA
S_ALR_87005832	IMG Activity: SIMG_CFMENUOLSDVOE2
S_ALR_87005833	IMG Activity: SIMG_CFMENUORKSKP65
S_ALR_87005834	IMG Activity: SIMG_CFMENUOLSDMODAD
S_ALR_87005835	IMG Activity: SIMG_CMMENUOLSDVOE4
S_ALR_87005836	IMG Activity: SIMG_CFMENUORKSKBH21
S_ALR_87005837	IMG Activity: SIMG_XXMENUOLSDUSE12
S_ALR_87005838	IMG Activity: SIMG_CFMENUORKSKAH2
S_ALR_87005839	IMG Activity: SIMG_XXMENUOLSDMODB3
S_ALR_87005840	IMG Activity: SIMG_CFMENUORKSKSH2
S_ALR_87005841	IMG Activity: SIMG_XXMENUOLSDMODB1
S_ALR_87005842	IMG Activity: SIMG_CFMENUORKSKLH21
S_ALR_87005843	IMG Activity: SIMG_XXMENUOLSDUSE14
S_ALR_87005844	IMG Activity: SIMG_CFMENUORKS_KALK
S_ALR_87005845	IMG Activity: SIMG_CFMENUORKS_KOND
S_ALR_87005846	IMG Activity: SIMG_CFMENUORKSKPRK
S_ALR_87005847	IMG Activity: SIMG_CFMENUORKSKPRI
S_ALR_87005848	IMG Activity: SIMG_CFMENUORKSOKY8
S_ALR_87005849	IMG Activity: SIMG_CFMENUORKSOB07
S_ALR_87005850	IMG Activity: SIMG_CFMENUORKSOKY4
S_ALR_87005851	IMG Activity: SIMG_CFMENUORKSKP81
S_ALR_87005852	IMG Activity: SIMG_CFMENUORKSKP34
S_ALR_87005853	IMG Activity: SIMG_CFMENUORKSKSH3
S_ALR_87005854	IMG Activity: SIMG_CFMENUORKSKPHR
S_ALR_87005855	IMG Activity: SIMG_CFMENUORKSOKEA
S_ALR_87005856	IMG Activity: SIMG_XXMENUOLSDUSE21

S_ALR_87005857	IMG Activity: SIMG_CFMENUORKSOKEG
S_ALR_87005858	IMG Activity: SIMG_XXMENUOLSDCASUE
S_ALR_87005859	IMG Activity: SIMG_CFMENUORKSKK03
S_ALR_87005860	IMG Activity: SIMG_XXMENUOLSDUSE13
S_ALR_87005861	IMG Activity: SIMG_ORKS_COPY_CMOD
S_ALR_87005862	IMG Activity: SIMG_CMMENUOLSDUS11
S_ALR_87005863	IMG Activity: SIMG_CFMENUORKSKSAZ
S_ALR_87005864	IMG Activity: SIMG_CFMENUOLSDUSE1
S_ALR_87005865	IMG Activity: SIMG_ORKS_KM1V
S_ALR_87005866	IMG Activity: SIMG_CFMENUORKSOKOZ
S_ALR_87005867	IMG Activity: SIMG_CMMENUOLSDUS10
S_ALR_87005868	IMG Activity: SIMG_ORKS_ERKOS_0KM1
S_ALR_87005869	IMG Activity: SIMG_XXMENUOLSDAUFW
S_ALR_87005870	IMG Activity: SIMG_XXMENUOLSDUSE17
S_ALR_87005871	IMG Activity: SIMG_CFMENUORKSKS02
S_ALR_87005872	IMG Activity: SIMG_CFMENUORKSOKEO
S_ALR_87005873	IMG Activity: SIMG_XXMENUOLSDMODA7
S_ALR_87005874	IMG Activity: SIMG_CFMENUORKSOMIK
S_ALR_87005875	IMG Activity: SIMG_XXMENUOLSDMODA6
S_ALR_87005876	IMG Activity: SIMG_CFMENUORKSAR13
S_ALR_87005877	IMG Activity: SIMG_CFMENUOLSDMODA6
S_ALR_87005878	IMG Activity: SIMG_CFMENUORKSKA04
S_ALR_87005879	IMG Activity: SIMG_XXMENUOLSDMODA5
S_ALR_87005880	IMG Activity: SIMG_CFMENUORKSKA01
S_ALR_87005881	IMG Activity: SIMG_XXMENUOLSDMODA4
S_ALR_87005882	IMG Activity: SIMG_ORKS_KM7V
S_ALR_87005883	IMG Activity: SIMG_XXMENUOLSDMODA3
S_ALR_87005884	IMG Activity: SIMG_CFMENUORKSKS03
S_ALR_87005885	IMG Activity: SIMG_XXMENUOLSDMODA2
S_ALR_87005886	IMG Activity: SIMG_CFMENUORKSKO01
S_ALR_87005887	IMG Activity: SIMG_CFMENUOLSDNATNF
S_ALR_87005888	IMG Activity: SIMG_CFMENUORKSKVD0
S_ALR_87005889	IMG Activity: SIMG_XXMENUOLSDMODAX
S_ALR_87005890	IMG Activity: SIMG_CFMENUORKSKL01
S_ALR_87005891	IMG Activity: SIMG_XXMENUOLSDMODB4
S_ALR_87005892	IMG Activity: SIMG_CFMENUORKSKVA0
S_ALR_87005893	IMG Activity: SIMG_XXMENUOLSDMODB2
S_ALR_87005894	IMG Activity: SIMG_ORKS_EWKOS_CMOD
S_ALR_87005895	IMG Activity: SIMG_XXMENUOLSDMODA0
S_ALR_87005896	IMG Activity: SIMG_CFMENUORKSOKA2
S_ALR_87005897	IMG Activity: SIMG_XXMENUOLSDMODA9
S_ALR_87005898	IMG Activity: SIMG_CFMENUORKSKA011
S_ALR_87005899	IMG Activity: SIMG_XXMENUOLSDMODAE
S_ALR_87005900	IMG Activity: SIMG_CFMENUORKSOKKP
S_ALR_87005901	IMG Activity: SIMG_XXMENUOLSDMODA8
S_ALR_87005902	IMG Activity: SIMG_CFMENUORKSKCAV1
S_ALR_87005903	IMG Activity: SIMG_CFMENUORKSKSV7
S_ALR_87005904	IMG Activity: SIMG_XXMENUORKS_PL_A
S_ALR_87005905	IMG Activity: SIMG_XXMENUORKS_P_V
S_ALR_87005906	IMG Activity: SIMG_XXORKS_I_A
S_ALR_87005907	IMG Activity: SIMG_CFMENUOLSDNV02
S_ALR_87005908	IMG Activity: SIMG_CFMENUOLSDSU02
S_ALR_87005909	IMG Activity: SIMG_CFMENUOLSDT_56
S_ALR_87005910	IMG Activity: SIMG_CFMENUOLSDVN08

S_ALR_87005911	IMG Activity: SIMG_CFMENUOLSDT_76
S_ALR_87005912	IMG Activity: SIMG_CFMENUOLSDT_60
S_ALR_87005913	IMG Activity: SIMG_CFMENUOLSDZUSAT
S_ALR_87005914	IMG Activity: SIMG_CFMENUOLSDT_57
S_ALR_87005915	IMG Activity: SIMG_CFMENUOLSDT_08
S_ALR_87005916	IMG Activity: SIMG_CFMENUOLSDT_07
S_ALR_87005917	IMG Activity: SIMG_CFMENUOLSDT_06
S_ALR_87005918	IMG Activity: SIMG_CFMENUOLSDTV24
S_ALR_87005919	IMG Activity: SIMG_CFMENUOLSD0VI1
S_ALR_87005920	IMG Activity: SIMG_CFMENUOLSD0VTL
S_ALR_87005921	IMG Activity: SIMG_CFMENUOLSDVEB9
S_ALR_87005922	IMG Activity: SIMG_CMMENUOLSDFLRF1
S_ALR_87005923	IMG Activity: SIMG_CFMENUOLSDNV04
S_ALR_87005924	IMG Activity: W_DF_LT_0510
S_ALR_87005925	IMG Activity: SIMG_CFMENUOLSDNV05
S_ALR_87005926	IMG Activity: SIMG_CFMENUOLSDOVLR
S_ALR_87005927	IMG Activity: SIMG_CFMENUOLSDNV06
S_ALR_87005928	IMG Activity: SIMG_CFMENUOLSDNV07
S_ALR_87005929	IMG Activity: SIMG_CFMENUOLSDOVLO
S_ALR_87005930	IMG Activity: SIMG_CFMENUOLSDNKO02
S_ALR_87005931	IMG Activity: SIMG_CFMENUOLSD0VRF
S_ALR_87005932	IMG Activity: SIMG_CMMENUOLSDFLRF2
S_ALR_87005933	IMG Activity: SIMG_CFMENUOLSDVT11
S_ALR_87005934	IMG Activity: SIMG_CFMENUOLSDOVTK
S_ALR_87005935	IMG Activity: SIMG_CFMENUOLSDOVTS
S_ALR_87005936	IMG Activity: SIMG_CFMENUOLSD0VTR
S_ALR_87005937	IMG Activity: SIMG_CFMENUOLSDVN07
S_ALR_87005938	IMG Activity: SIMG_CFMENUOLSDT_31
S_ALR_87005939	IMG Activity: SIMG_CFMENUOLSDNKO04
S_ALR_87005940	IMG Activity: SIMG_CFMENUOLSDWE20
S_ALR_87005941	IMG Activity: SIMG_CFMENUOLSDNKO05
S_ALR_87005942	IMG Activity: SIMG_CFMENUOLSDNKO06
S_ALR_87005943	IMG Activity: SIMG_CFMENUOLSDWE21
S_ALR_87005944	IMG Activity: SIMG_CFMENUOLSDNKO07
S_ALR_87005945	IMG Activity: SIMG_CFMENUOLSDBD64
S_ALR_87005946	IMG Activity: SIMG_CFMENUOLSDVOKR
S_ALR_87005947	IMG Activity: SIMG_CFMENUOLSDSM59
S_ALR_87005948	IMG Activity: SIMG_CFMENUOLSDBEKRE
S_ALR_87005949	IMG Activity: SIMG_CFMENUOLSDOMTB
S_ALR_87005950	IMG Activity: SIMG_CFMENUOLSDNVE02
S_ALR_87005951	IMG Activity: SIMG_CFMENUOLSD0VTP
S_ALR_87005952	IMG Activity: SIMG_CFMENUOPP1OMIO
S_ALR_87005953	IMG Activity: SIMG_CFMENUOPP2OPPN
S_ALR_87005954	IMG Activity: SIMG_CFMENUOPP1OMIW
S_ALR_87005955	IMG Activity: SIMG_CFMENUOLSDVII5
S_ALR_87005956	IMG Activity: SIMG_CFMENUOPP3OSPO
S_ALR_87005957	IMG Activity: SIMG_CFMENUOPP2OPPM
S_ALR_87005958	IMG Activity: W_GE_BE_0100
S_ALR_87005959	IMG Activity: SIMG_CFMENUGCU0GR22
S_ALR_87005960	IMG Activity: W_GE_0200
S_ALR_87005961	IMG Activity: SIMG_CFMENUOPP1OPPA
S_ALR_87005962	IMG Activity: PPPI_PC_100
S_ALR_87005963	IMG Activity: PPPI_MD_222
S_ALR_87005964	IMG Activity: SIMG_CFMENUOPP3OPKF

S_ALR_87005965	IMG Activity: SIMG_CFMENUOPP2OPPK
S_ALR_87005966	IMG Activity: SIMG_CFMENUORFAOA77
S_ALR_87005967	IMG Activity: SIMG_CFMENUGCU0GR12
S_ALR_87005968	IMG Activity: W_OE_EG_WL_0101
S_ALR_87005969	IMG Activity: PPPI_MD_2213
S_ALR_87005970	IMG Activity: SIMG_CFMENUOPP1OMDR
S_ALR_87005971	IMG Activity: SIMG_CFMENUOPP3OPKD
S_ALR_87005972	IMG Activity: SIMG_CFMENUORFAOA78
S_ALR_87005973	IMG Activity: SIMG_CFMENUOPP2OPPD
S_ALR_87005974	IMG Activity: W_GE_0100
S_ALR_87005975	IMG Activity: SIMG_CFMENUOPP2OMDM
S_ALR_87005976	IMG Activity: SIMG_CFMENUGCU0GCRB
S_ALR_87005977	IMG Activity: PPPI_MD_2212
S_ALR_87005978	IMG Activity: SIMG_CFMENUOPP1OMIL
S_ALR_87005979	IMG Activity: ORFA_LAYOUT
S_ALR_87005980	IMG Activity: SIMG_CFMENUOPP3RZ12
S_ALR_87005981	IMG Activity: PPPI_MD_2211
S_ALR_87005982	IMG Activity: SIMG_CFMENUGCU0GAR8
S_ALR_87005983	IMG Activity: SIMG_CFMENUOPP1OPPB
S_ALR_87005984	IMG Activity: ORFA_ALTD_REIHENF
S_ALR_87005985	IMG Activity: PPPI_MD_212
S_ALR_87005986	IMG Activity: SIMG_CFMENUOPP2OMI6
S_ALR_87005987	IMG Activity: SIMG_CFMENUOPP3OSP1
S_ALR_87005988	IMG Activity: SIMG_CFMENUGCU0GAR9
S_ALR_87005989	IMG Activity: SIMG_CFMENUOPP1CMD
S_ALR_87005990	IMG Activity: PPPI_MD_211
S_ALR_87005991	IMG Activity: SIMG_CFMENUOPP2OMD0
S_ALR_87005992	IMG Activity: SIMG_CFMENUORFAOAVA
S_ALR_87005993	IMG Activity: SIMG_CFMENUOPP3OPP5
S_ALR_87005994	IMG Activity: SIMG_CFMENUGCU0GCAG
S_ALR_87005995	IMG Activity: SIMG_CFMENUOPP1OPPC
S_ALR_87005996	IMG Activity: PPPI_MD_223
S_ALR_87005997	IMG Activity: SIMG_CFMENUOPP2OMDQ
S_ALR_87005998	IMG Activity: SIMG_CFMENUORFAOAV8
S_ALR_87005999	IMG Activity: SIMG_CFMENUOPP3OSPP
S_ALR_87006000	IMG Activity: SIMG_CFMENUGCU0GCS5
S_ALR_87006001	IMG Activity: SIMG_CFMENUOPP1MP1
S_ALR_87006002	IMG Activity: PPPI_MD_234
S_ALR_87006003	IMG Activity: ORFA_KLASS_LEAS
S_ALR_87006004	IMG Activity: SIMG_CFMENUOPP1OMDG
S_ALR_87006005	IMG Activity: PPPI_MD_233
S_ALR_87006006	IMG Activity: SIMG_CFMENUGCU0GCS7
S_ALR_87006007	IMG Activity: SIMG_CFMENUSPCUOSQ1
S_ALR_87006008	IMG Activity: ORFA_KONS_BEW2
S_ALR_87006009	IMG Activity: PPPI_MD_232
S_ALR_87006010	IMG Activity: SIMG_CFMENUOPP1OMI4
S_ALR_87006011	IMG Activity: SIMG_CFMENUSPCUOSQ2
S_ALR_87006012	IMG Activity: SIMG_CFMENUGCU0GCRS
S_ALR_87006031	IMG Activity: ORFA_KONS_TRANSFER
S_ALR_87006032	IMG Activity: PPPI_MD_231
S_ALR_87006033	IMG Activity: SIMG_CFMENUOPP3OSPN
S_ALR_87006034	IMG Activity: SIMG_OREHFXI1
S_ALR_87006035	IMG Activity: ORFA_ALTDATUM
S_ALR_87006036	IMG Activity: PPPI_MD_225

S_ALR_87006037	IMG Activity: SIMG_OREHFXIZ
S_ALR_87006038	IMG Activity: SIMG_CFMENUOPP3OMDM
S_ALR_87006039	IMG Activity: PPPI_MD_224
S_ALR_87006040	IMG Activity: SIMG_OREHFXIR
S_ALR_87006041	IMG Activity: PPPI_MD_422
S_ALR_87006042	IMG Activity: SIMG_CFMENUOPP3OMI6
S_ALR_87006043	IMG Activity: SIMG_OREHFXIP
S_ALR_87006044	IMG Activity: PPPI_MD_414
S_ALR_87006045	IMG Activity: SIMG_CFMENUOPP3OKRV
S_ALR_87006046	IMG Activity: SIMG_OREHFXI4
S_ALR_87006047	IMG Activity: PPPI_MD_421
S_ALR_87006048	IMG Activity: SIMG_CFMENUOPP3OKRC
S_ALR_87006049	IMG Activity: SIMG_CFMENUGCU0GCRE2
S_ALR_87006050	IMG Activity: SIMG_CFMENUOPP3OKS9
S_ALR_87006051	IMG Activity: PPPI_MD_413
S_ALR_87006052	IMG Activity: SIMG_CFMENUGCU0GCRE1
S_ALR_87006053	IMG Activity: SIMG_CFMENUOLSDNVE04
S_ALR_87006054	IMG Activity: PPPI_MD_412
S_ALR_87006055	IMG Activity: SIMG_CFMENUOPP3OKSP
S_ALR_87006056	IMG Activity: SIMG_CFMENUGCU0FGRP
S_ALR_87006057	IMG Activity: PPPI_MD_411
S_ALR_87006058	IMG Activity: SIMG_CFMENUOLSDNVE05
S_ALR_87006059	IMG Activity: SIMG_CFMENUOPP3OKZ3
S_ALR_87006060	IMG Activity: SIMG_CFMENUGCU0GCS6
S_ALR_87006061	IMG Activity: PPPI_MD_423
S_ALR_87006062	IMG Activity: SIMG_CFMENUOLSDNVE06
S_ALR_87006063	IMG Activity: SIMG_CFMENUOPP3OSP5
S_ALR_87006064	IMG Activity: PPPI_MD_434
S_ALR_87006065	IMG Activity: SIMG_CFMENUGCU0GCBR
S_ALR_87006066	IMG Activity: SIMG_CFMENUOLSDNL02
S_ALR_87006067	IMG Activity: SIMG_CFMENUOPP3OSPM
S_ALR_87006068	IMG Activity: PPPI_MD_435
S_ALR_87006069	IMG Activity: SIMG_CFMENUGCU0GCR5
S_ALR_87006070	IMG Activity: PPPI_MD_433
S_ALR_87006071	IMG Activity: SIMG_CFMENUOPP3OSPK
S_ALR_87006072	IMG Activity: SIMG_CFMENUGCU0GCR2
S_ALR_87006073	IMG Activity: PPPI_MD_436
S_ALR_87006074	IMG Activity: SIMG_CFMENUOPP3OSP4
S_ALR_87006075	IMG Activity: OADV1
S_ALR_87006076	IMG Activity: W_KO_NF_0212
S_ALR_87006077	IMG Activity: PPPI_MD_431
S_ALR_87006078	IMG Activity: SIMG_CFMENUGCU0GCA5
S_ALR_87006079	IMG Activity: SIMG_CFMENUOPP3OSPT
S_ALR_87006080	IMG Activity: SIMG_CFMENUOLSDNL04
S_ALR_87006081	IMG Activity: W_KO_NF_0211
S_ALR_87006082	IMG Activity: PPPI_MD_424
S_ALR_87006083	IMG Activity: SIMG_CFMENUGCU0GCA4
S_ALR_87006084	IMG Activity: PPPI_MD_235
S_ALR_87006085	IMG Activity: W_KO_NF_0219
S_ALR_87006086	IMG Activity: SIMG_CFMENUOLSDNL05
S_ALR_87006087	IMG Activity: SIMG_CFMENUGCU0GCA3
S_ALR_87006088	IMG Activity: PPPI_MD_471
S_ALR_87006089	IMG Activity: W_ZF_VK_0263
S_ALR_87006090	IMG Activity: SIMG_CFMENUOLSDNL06

S_ALR_87006091	IMG Activity: SIMG_CFMENUGCU0GCA7
S_ALR_87006092	IMG Activity: PPPI_MD_2612
S_ALR_87006093	IMG Activity: W_ZF_VK_0262
S_ALR_87006094	IMG Activity: SIMG_CFMENUOLSDNL07
S_ALR_87006095	IMG Activity: PPPI_MD_2613
S_ALR_87006096	IMG Activity: SIMG_CFMENUGCU0GCA2
S_ALR_87006097	IMG Activity: W_KO_NF_0213
S_ALR_87006098	IMG Activity: PPPI_MD_2611
S_ALR_87006099	IMG Activity: SIMG_CFMENUOLSDOVFD
S_ALR_87006100	IMG Activity: SIMG_CFMENUGCU0GL20
S_ALR_87006101	IMG Activity: W_KO_NF_0218
S_ALR_87006102	IMG Activity: PPPI_MD_250
S_ALR_87006103	IMG Activity: SIMG_CFMENUOLSDOMIH
S_ALR_87006104	IMG Activity: SIMG_CFMENUGCU0GCW6
S_ALR_87006105	IMG Activity: W_KO_NF_0217
S_ALR_87006106	IMG Activity: PPPI_MD_2446
S_ALR_87006107	IMG Activity: SIMG_CFMENUOLSDOVZJ
S_ALR_87006108	IMG Activity: SIMG_CFMENUGCU0GCRF
S_ALR_87006109	IMG Activity: PPPI_MD_472-1
S_ALR_87006110	IMG Activity: W_KO_NF_0216
S_ALR_87006111	IMG Activity: SIMG_CFMENUOLSDOVA8
S_ALR_87006112	IMG Activity: SIMG_CFMENUGCU0GCW8
S_ALR_87006113	IMG Activity: PPPI_MD_112
S_ALR_87006114	IMG Activity: W_KO_NF_0215
S_ALR_87006115	IMG Activity: SIMG_CFMENUOLSDOV1Z
S_ALR_87006116	IMG Activity: SIMG_CFMENUGCU0GCW5
S_ALR_87006117	IMG Activity: PPPI_MD_111
S_ALR_87006118	IMG Activity: W_KO_NF_0214
S_ALR_87006119	IMG Activity: PPPI_MD_460
S_ALR_87006120	IMG Activity: SIMG_CFMENUOLSDOV2Z
S_ALR_87006121	IMG Activity: W_KO_NF_0221
S_ALR_87006122	IMG Activity: SIMG_CFMENUGCU0GCW3
S_ALR_87006123	IMG Activity: W_ZF_VK_0230
S_ALR_87006124	IMG Activity: SIMG_CFMENUOLSDOV3Z
S_ALR_87006125	IMG Activity: PPPI_MD_450
S_ALR_87006126	IMG Activity: SIMG_CFMENUGCU0GCW2
S_ALR_87006127	IMG Activity: PPPI_MD_440
S_ALR_87006128	IMG Activity: W_ZF_VK_0220
S_ALR_87006129	IMG Activity: SIMG_CFMENUOLSDOVZ1
S_ALR_87006130	IMG Activity: SIMG_CFMENUGCU0GCW4
S_ALR_87006131	IMG Activity: OALE_CATSHR_19
S_ALR_87006132	IMG Activity: PPPI_MD_472-2
S_ALR_87006133	IMG Activity: W_ZF_VK_0210
S_ALR_87006134	IMG Activity: SIMG_CFMENUOLSDOVZ3
S_ALR_87006135	IMG Activity: SIMG_CFMENUGCU0GCW1
S_ALR_87006136	IMG Activity: PPPI_MD_241
S_ALR_87006137	IMG Activity: W_ZF_VK_0240
S_ALR_87006138	IMG Activity: SIMG_CFMENUOPP1OMD2
S_ALR_87006139	IMG Activity: PPPI_MD_2383
S_ALR_87006140	IMG Activity: SIMG_CFMENUOLSDOVZ9
S_ALR_87006141	IMG Activity: SIMG_CFMENUGCU0GCT0
S_ALR_87006142	IMG Activity: W_KO_NF_0222
S_ALR_87006143	IMG Activity: SIMG_CFMENUOPP1OMDC
S_ALR_87006144	IMG Activity: PPPI_MD_2382

S_ALR_87006145	IMG Activity: SIMG_CFMENUGCU0GCT9
S_ALR_87006146	IMG Activity: SIMG_CFMENUOLSDOVZ0
S_ALR_87006147	IMG Activity: OALE_CATSHR_11
S_ALR_87006148	IMG Activity: SIMG_CFMENUOPP1OMIT
S_ALR_87006149	IMG Activity: W_ZF_VK_0261
S_ALR_87006150	IMG Activity: PPPI_MD_2381
S_ALR_87006151	IMG Activity: OALE_CATSHR_02
S_ALR_87006152	IMG Activity: SIMG_CFMENUGCU0GCT8
S_ALR_87006153	IMG Activity: SIMG_CFMENUOLSDOVZ8X
S_ALR_87006154	IMG Activity: OALE_CATSHR_10
S_ALR_87006155	IMG Activity: PPPI_MD_237
S_ALR_87006156	IMG Activity: W_KO_NF_0301
S_ALR_87006157	IMG Activity: OALE_CATSHR_16
S_ALR_87006158	IMG Activity: SIMG_CFMENUGCU0GCT7
S_ALR_87006159	IMG Activity: SIMG_CFMENUOLSDOVZK
S_ALR_87006160	IMG Activity: OALE_CATSHR_15
S_ALR_87006161	IMG Activity: PPPI_MD_236
S_ALR_87006162	IMG Activity: W_ZF_VK_0253
S_ALR_87006163	IMG Activity: SIMG_CFMENUGCU0GCT6
S_ALR_87006164	IMG Activity: OALE_CATSHR_14
S_ALR_87006165	IMG Activity: SIMG_CFMENUOLSDOV5Z
S_ALR_87006166	IMG Activity: PPPI_MD_242
S_ALR_87006167	IMG Activity: OALE_CATSHR_13
S_ALR_87006168	IMG Activity: W_ZF_VK_0251
S_ALR_87006169	IMG Activity: SIMG_CFMENUGCU0GCT5
S_ALR_87006170	IMG Activity: PPPI_MD_2445
S_ALR_87006171	IMG Activity: OALE_CATSHR_12
S_ALR_87006172	IMG Activity: SIMG_CFMENUOLSDOVLY
S_ALR_87006173	IMG Activity: OALE_CATSHR_06
S_ALR_87006174	IMG Activity: W_ZF_VK_0252
S_ALR_87006175	IMG Activity: SIMG_CFMENUGCU0GCT4
S_ALR_87006176	IMG Activity: PPPI_MD_2444
S_ALR_87006177	IMG Activity: OALE_CATSHR_03
S_ALR_87006178	IMG Activity: SIMG_CFMENUOLSDOVLZ
S_ALR_87006179	IMG Activity: OALE_CATSHR_20
S_ALR_87006180	IMG Activity: PPPI_MD_2443
S_ALR_87006181	IMG Activity: SIMG_CFMENUGCU0GCT1
S_ALR_87006182	IMG Activity: OALE_CATSHR_17
S_ALR_87006183	IMG Activity: SIMG_CFMENUOLSDARBEI
S_ALR_87006184	IMG Activity: OALE_CATSHR_01
S_ALR_87006185	IMG Activity: PPPI_MD_2442
S_ALR_87006186	IMG Activity: SIMG_CFMENUGCU0GCTA
S_ALR_87006187	IMG Activity: OALE_CATSHR_09
S_ALR_87006188	IMG Activity: SIMG_CFMENUOLSDDAUER
S_ALR_87006189	IMG Activity: PPPI_MD_2441
S_ALR_87006190	IMG Activity: OALE_CATSHR_08
S_ALR_87006191	IMG Activity: SIMG_OREHGCGS
S_ALR_87006192	IMG Activity: PPPI_MD_243
S_ALR_87006193	IMG Activity: OALE_CATSHR_07
S_ALR_87006194	IMG Activity: SIMG_CFMENUOLSDOVA6
S_ALR_87006195	IMG Activity: SIMG_CFMENUOPP1OMDT
S_ALR_87006196	IMG Activity: OALE_CATSHR_04
S_ALR_87006197	IMG Activity: SIMG_CFMENUGCU0GCAC
S_ALR_87006198	IMG Activity: PPPI_MD_3333

S_ALR_87006199	IMG Activity: OALE_CATSHR_18
S_ALR_87006200	IMG Activity: SIMG_CFMENUOPP1OMI5
S_ALR_87006201	IMG Activity: SIMG_CFMENUGCU0GCDE
S_ALR_87006202	IMG Activity: PPPI_MD_3332
S_ALR_87006203	IMG Activity: SIMG_CFMENUOPP1OMIM
S_ALR_87006204	IMG Activity: PPPI_MD_332
S_ALR_87006205	IMG Activity: SIMG_CFMENUGCU0GAL2
S_ALR_87006206	IMG Activity: SIMG_CFMENUOLSDOV4Z
S_ALR_87006207	IMG Activity: SIMG_CFMENUOPP1OPVP
S_ALR_87006208	IMG Activity: PPPI_MD_331
S_ALR_87006209	IMG Activity: SIMG_CFMENUOLSDOV9Z
S_ALR_87006210	IMG Activity: SIMG_CFMENUGCU0GAL1
S_ALR_87006211	IMG Activity: SIMG_CFMENUOPP1OPP5
S_ALR_87006212	IMG Activity: PPPI_MD_325
S_ALR_87006213	IMG Activity: SIMG_CFMENUGCU0GCM1
S_ALR_87006214	IMG Activity: SIMG_CFMENUOLSDOV6Z
S_ALR_87006215	IMG Activity: PPPI_MD_3242
S_ALR_87006216	IMG Activity: SIMG_CFMENUOPP1OMD3
S_ALR_87006217	IMG Activity: SIMG_CFMENUOLSDBD50
S_ALR_87006218	IMG Activity: SIMG_CFMENUOLSDOV7Z
S_ALR_87006219	IMG Activity: PPPI_MD_3372
S_ALR_87006220	IMG Activity: SIMG_CFMENUGCU0GCTR
S_ALR_87006221	IMG Activity: SIMG_CFMENUOPP1OMIU
S_ALR_87006222	IMG Activity: PPPI_MD_3371
S_ALR_87006223	IMG Activity: SIMG_CFMENUOLSDOV8Z
S_ALR_87006224	IMG Activity: SIMG_CFMENUGCU0GCTS
S_ALR_87006225	IMG Activity: SIMG_CFMENUOLSDV/36
S_ALR_87006226	IMG Activity: SIMG_CFMENUOPP1OMIV
S_ALR_87006227	IMG Activity: PPPI_MD_3352
S_ALR_87006228	IMG Activity: SIMG_CFMENUOLSDOVAD
S_ALR_87006229	IMG Activity: SIMG_CFMENUGCU0GCT3
S_ALR_87006230	IMG Activity: SIMG_CFMENUOPP1OPPE
S_ALR_87006231	IMG Activity: SIMG_CFMENUOLSD0VTS
S_ALR_87006232	IMG Activity: PPPI_MD_3351
S_ALR_87006233	IMG Activity: SIMG_CFMENUOLSDNVE07
S_ALR_87006234	IMG Activity: SIMG_CFMENUOPP1OMDV
S_ALR_87006235	IMG Activity: SIMG_CFMENUGCU0GCD1
S_ALR_87006236	IMG Activity: PPPI_MD_334
S_ALR_87006237	IMG Activity: SIMG_CFMENUOLSD0VTG
S_ALR_87006238	IMG Activity: SIMG_CFMENUOLSDNF3
S_ALR_87006239	IMG Activity: PPPI_MD_3334
S_ALR_87006240	IMG Activity: SIMG_CFMENUGCU0GCE3
S_ALR_87006241	IMG Activity: SIMG_CFMENUOLSDT_80
S_ALR_87006242	IMG Activity: SIMG_OREHFXIY
S_ALR_87006243	IMG Activity: PPPI_MD_323
S_ALR_87006244	IMG Activity: SIMG_CFMENUOPP3OS81
S_ALR_87006245	IMG Activity: SIMG_CFMENUOLSDINDEX
S_ALR_87006246	IMG Activity: PPPI_MD_3142
S_ALR_87006247	IMG Activity: SIMG_OREHFXIT
S_ALR_87006248	IMG Activity: SIMG_CFMENUOPP1OPPH
S_ALR_87006249	IMG Activity: SIMG_CFMENUOPP3OS80
S_ALR_87006250	IMG Activity: SIMG_CFMENUOLSDT_VE
S_ALR_87006251	IMG Activity: PPPI_MD_3141
S_ALR_87006252	IMG Activity: SIMG_CFMENUOPP1OMIN

S_ALR_87006253	IMG Activity: SIMG_OREHFXIV
S_ALR_87006254	IMG Activity: SIMG_CFMENUOPP3OSP2
S_ALR_87006255	IMG Activity: PPPI_MD_313
S_ALR_87006256	IMG Activity: SIMG_CFMENUOLSDT_VD
S_ALR_87006257	IMG Activity: SIMG_CFMENUOPP1OMIB
S_ALR_87006258	IMG Activity: SIMG_OREHFXIX
S_ALR_87006259	IMG Activity: SIMG_CFMENUOLSDV/27
S_ALR_87006260	IMG Activity: SIMG_CFMENUOPP3OSPR
S_ALR_87006261	IMG Activity: PPPI_MD_318
S_ALR_87006262	IMG Activity: SIMG_OREHFXIQ
S_ALR_87006263	IMG Activity: SIMG_CFMENUOPP1OMIR
S_ALR_87006264	IMG Activity: SIMG_CFMENUOLSDVFBWG
S_ALR_87006265	IMG Activity: SIMG_CFMENUOPP3OPB4
S_ALR_87006266	IMG Activity: SIMG_CFMENUOLSDVP01
S_ALR_87006267	IMG Activity: OALE_DSTSCN_SALESINF
S_ALR_87006268	IMG Activity: PPPI_MD_2121
S_ALR_87006269	IMG Activity: SIMG_CFMENUOPP1OM0C
S_ALR_87006270	IMG Activity: SIMG_OREHFXIO
S_ALR_87006271	IMG Activity: OALE_DSTSCN_PURCHINF
S_ALR_87006272	IMG Activity: SIMG_CFMENUOLSDRUND
S_ALR_87006273	IMG Activity: SIMG_CFMENUOPP3OPB5
S_ALR_87006274	IMG Activity: SIMG_CFMENUOLSDOVNN
S_ALR_87006275	IMG Activity: PPPI_MD_312
S_ALR_87006276	IMG Activity: OALE_DSTSCN_INVCONTR
S_ALR_87006277	IMG Activity: SIMG_CFMENUOPP1OMIX
S_ALR_87006278	IMG Activity: OANF_WIRT_DAT
S_ALR_87006279	IMG Activity: SIMG_CFMENUGCU0GCD2
S_ALR_87006280	IMG Activity: OALE_DSTSCN_CDLIS
S_ALR_87006281	IMG Activity: SIMG_CFMENUOLSDOVNM
S_ALR_87006282	IMG Activity: PPPI_MD_321
S_ALR_87006283	IMG Activity: SIMG_CFMENUOPP1OMDA
S_ALR_87006284	IMG Activity: OANF_GEN_STUF
S_ALR_87006285	IMG Activity: SIMG_CFMENUOLSDKOPKO
S_ALR_87006286	IMG Activity: SIMG_CFMENUOPP3OSPA
S_ALR_87006287	IMG Activity: SIMG_CFMENUGCU0GCT2
S_ALR_87006288	IMG Activity: PPPI_MD_316
S_ALR_87006289	IMG Activity: SIMG_CFMENUOLSDV/G7
S_ALR_87006290	IMG Activity: SIMG_CFMENUOPP1OMD5
S_ALR_87006291	IMG Activity: SIMG_CFMENUOPP3OPB3
S_ALR_87006292	IMG Activity: OANF_GEN_WORK
S_ALR_87006293	IMG Activity: SIMG_CFMENUOLSDABSEN
S_ALR_87006294	IMG Activity: SIMG_CFMENUGCU0GCVZ
S_ALR_87006295	IMG Activity: PPPI_MD_317
S_ALR_87006296	IMG Activity: SIMG_OPP3KAPAPLANUNG
S_ALR_87006297	IMG Activity: SIMG_CFMENUOPP1OMDD
S_ALR_87006298	IMG Activity: SIMG_CFMENUOLSDV/G9
S_ALR_87006299	IMG Activity: OANF_BERICHT
S_ALR_87006300	IMG Activity: SIMG_CFMENUGCU0GGB1
S_ALR_87006301	IMG Activity: SIMG_CFMENUOLSDCOZU
S_ALR_87006302	IMG Activity: PPPI_MD_320
S_ALR_87006303	IMG Activity: SIMG_CFMENUOPP1OPPJ
S_ALR_87006304	IMG Activity: OANF_IMDV
S_ALR_87006305	IMG Activity: SIMG_CFMENUOLSDV/39
S_ALR_87006306	IMG Activity: SIMG_CFMENUOLSDSACHK

S_ALR_87006307	IMG Activity: SIMG_CFMENUGCU0GGB0
S_ALR_87006308	IMG Activity: PPPI_MD_319
S_ALR_87006309	IMG Activity: OANF_ZINS
S_ALR_87006310	IMG Activity: SIMG_CFMENUOLSDVONC
S_ALR_87006311	IMG Activity: OANF_EDITION1
S_ALR_87006312	IMG Activity: PPPI_MD_315
S_ALR_87006313	IMG Activity: SIMG_CFMENUGCU0GS12
S_ALR_87006314	IMG Activity: SIMG_CFMENUOLSDKONT
S_ALR_87006315	IMG Activity: SIMG_CFMENUOLSDV/81
S_ALR_87006316	IMG Activity: OANF_PLAN
S_ALR_87006317	IMG Activity: PPPI_MD_3373
S_ALR_87006318	IMG Activity: SIMG_CFMENUGCU0GS02
S_ALR_87006319	IMG Activity: SIMG_CFMENUOLSDT_53
S_ALR_87006320	IMG Activity: SIMG_KOPLAN1
S_ALR_87006321	IMG Activity: PPPI_MD_3422
S_ALR_87006322	IMG Activity: SIMG_CFMENUGCU0GCD3
S_ALR_87006323	IMG Activity: OANF_CASH_PLAN
S_ALR_87006324	IMG Activity: SIMG_CFMENUOLSDOVS8
S_ALR_87006325	IMG Activity: PPPI_MD_351
S_ALR_87006326	IMG Activity: OANF_KOPLA2
S_ALR_87006327	IMG Activity: SIMG_CFMENUOLSDOVA0
S_ALR_87006328	IMG Activity: SIMG_CFMENUGCU0GCD5
S_ALR_87006329	IMG Activity: PPPI_MD_361
S_ALR_87006330	IMG Activity: W_KO_NF_0114
S_ALR_87006331	IMG Activity: OANF_IMD4
S_ALR_87006332	IMG Activity: SIMG_CFMENUOLSDVOPA4
S_ALR_87006333	IMG Activity: SIMG_CFMENUGCU0GCA9
S_ALR_87006334	IMG Activity: PPPI_MD_370
S_ALR_87006335	IMG Activity: W_KO_NF_0113
S_ALR_87006336	IMG Activity: OANF_INF_CMOD
S_ALR_87006337	IMG Activity: SIMG_CFMENUOLSDVOPA3
S_ALR_87006338	IMG Activity: PPPI_MD_511
S_ALR_87006339	IMG Activity: SIMG_CFMENUGCU0GCVW
S_ALR_87006340	IMG Activity: W_KO_NF_0112
S_ALR_87006341	IMG Activity: ORIP_IMEQ_ANF
S_ALR_87006342	IMG Activity: PPPI_MD_512
S_ALR_87006343	IMG Activity: SIMG_CFMENUOLSDOVA2
S_ALR_87006344	IMG Activity: W_KO_NF_0111
S_ALR_87006345	IMG Activity: ORIP_IMER_ANF
S_ALR_87006346	IMG Activity: SIMG_CFMENUGCU0GCVV
S_ALR_87006347	IMG Activity: W_ZF_VK_0470
S_ALR_87006348	IMG Activity: PPPI_MD_513
S_ALR_87006349	IMG Activity: SIMG_XXMENUOLSDVOTX2
S_ALR_87006350	IMG Activity: ORIP_STAT_SCHEMA_ANF
S_ALR_87006351	IMG Activity: SIMG_CFMENUGCU0GD61
S_ALR_87006352	IMG Activity: W_ZF_VK_0650
S_ALR_87006353	IMG Activity: PPPI_MD_514
S_ALR_87006354	IMG Activity: SIMG_XXMENUOLSDVOTX5
S_ALR_87006355	IMG Activity: ORIP_IMEY_ANF
S_ALR_87006356	IMG Activity: SIMG_CFMENUGCU0GCUT
S_ALR_87006357	IMG Activity: W_ZF_VK_0640
S_ALR_87006358	IMG Activity: SIMG_XXMENUOLSDVOTX3
S_ALR_87006359	IMG Activity: OANF_IMDT
S_ALR_87006360	IMG Activity: SIMG_CFMENUOREH_T009

S_ALR_87006361	IMG Activity: PPPI_MD_515
S_ALR_87006362	IMG Activity: W_KO_NF_0115
S_ALR_87006363	IMG Activity: OANF_IMD1
S_ALR_87006364	IMG Activity: W_KO_NF_0122
S_ALR_87006365	IMG Activity: PPPI_MD_3421
S_ALR_87006366	IMG Activity: SIMG_CFMENUOLSDOV13
S_ALR_87006367	IMG Activity: SIMG_CFMENUGCU0CMOD
S_ALR_87006368	IMG Activity: OANF_IMDO
S_ALR_87006369	IMG Activity: W_KO_NF_0121
S_ALR_87006370	IMG Activity: PPPI_MD_338
S_ALR_87006371	IMG Activity: OANF_IMDP
S_ALR_87006372	IMG Activity: SIMG_CFMENUGCU0GCS1
S_ALR_87006373	IMG Activity: SIMG_CFMENUOLSDNT07
S_ALR_87006374	IMG Activity: PPPI_MD_341
S_ALR_87006375	IMG Activity: OANF_IMDZ
S_ALR_87006376	IMG Activity: W_KO_NF_0119
S_ALR_87006377	IMG Activity: SIMG_CFMENUGCU0GCB1
S_ALR_87006378	IMG Activity: SIMG_CFMENUOLSDNT06
S_ALR_87006379	IMG Activity: OANF_IMDX
S_ALR_87006380	IMG Activity: W_KO_NF_0118
S_ALR_87006381	IMG Activity: SIMG_CFMENUGCU0GCP3
S_ALR_87006382	IMG Activity: OANF_STATUS
S_ALR_87006383	IMG Activity: W_KO_NF_0117
S_ALR_87006384	IMG Activity: SIMG_CFMENUGCU0GCVP
S_ALR_87006385	IMG Activity: OANF_UMWELT
S_ALR_87006386	IMG Activity: W_KO_NF_0116
S_ALR_87006387	IMG Activity: SIMG_CFMENUGCU0GCP6
S_ALR_87006388	IMG Activity: W_ZF_VK_0490
S_ALR_87006389	IMG Activity: OANF_GROSS
S_ALR_87006390	IMG Activity: SIMG_CFMENUGCU0GCP5
S_ALR_87006391	IMG Activity: W_ZF_VK_0480
S_ALR_87006392	IMG Activity: OANF_PRIO
S_ALR_87006393	IMG Activity: SIMG_CFMENUGCU0GCX1
S_ALR_87006394	IMG Activity: OANF_PARTNER
S_ALR_87006395	IMG Activity: OANF_STAT_BER
S_ALR_87006396	IMG Activity: SIMG_CFMENUGCU0GCX2
S_ALR_87006397	IMG Activity: OANF_ANF_ART
S_ALR_87006398	IMG Activity: SIMG_CFMENUGCU0GCVY
S_ALR_87006399	IMG Activity: SIMG_CFMENUOLSDNT05
S_ALR_87006400	IMG Activity: OANF_NUMMERN
S_ALR_87006401	IMG Activity: SIMG_CFMENUGCU0GCVX
S_ALR_87006402	IMG Activity: SIMG_CFMENUOLSDVXTS
S_ALR_87006403	IMG Activity: OANF_STATUS4
S_ALR_87006404	IMG Activity: SIMG_CFMENUGCU0GCG2
S_ALR_87006405	IMG Activity: OANF_FELD
S_ALR_87006406	IMG Activity: SIMG_CFMENUOLSDVXTV
S_ALR_87006407	IMG Activity: SIMG_CFMENUGCU0GCCG
S_ALR_87006408	IMG Activity: OANF_EDITION
S_ALR_87006409	IMG Activity: SIMG_CFMENUOLSDVXTZ
S_ALR_87006410	IMG Activity: SIMG_CFMENUGCU0GCD6
S_ALR_87006411	IMG Activity: OANF_LANGTEXT
S_ALR_87006412	IMG Activity: SIMG_CFMENUOLSD0VTW
S_ALR_87006413	IMG Activity: OANF_BILD
S_ALR_87006414	IMG Activity: SIMG_CFMENUGCU0GCIQ

S_ALR_87006415	IMG Activity: SIMG_CFMENUOLSDOTF1
S_ALR_87006416	IMG Activity: OANF_USER
S_ALR_87006417	IMG Activity: SIMG_CFMENUGCU0GCI1
S_ALR_87006418	IMG Activity: SIMG_CFMENUOLSDOV14
S_ALR_87006419	IMG Activity: OANF_BEWERT
S_ALR_87006420	IMG Activity: SIMG_CFMENUOLSD0VTKT
S_ALR_87006421	IMG Activity: SIMG_CFMENUGCU0GCI2
S_ALR_87006422	IMG Activity: SIMG_CFMENUGCU0GCIN
S_ALR_87006423	IMG Activity: SIMG_CFMENUOLSDNT04
S_ALR_87006424	IMG Activity: SIMG_CFMENUOLSDOVRQ
S_ALR_87006425	IMG Activity: OANF_USER_KURZ
S_ALR_87006426	IMG Activity: SIMG_XXAK_OXK3
S_ALR_87006427	IMG Activity: SIMG_CMMENUOLSDFA
S_ALR_87006428	IMG Activity: SIMG_CFMENUGCU0GCVO
S_ALR_87006429	IMG Activity: SIMG_CFMENUOLSDVUA2
S_ALR_87006430	IMG Activity: SIMG_CFMENUGCU0GCL2
S_ALR_87006431	IMG Activity: SIMG_CFMENUGCU0GCF2
S_ALR_87006432	IMG Activity: SIMG_CFMENUGCU0GCV2
S_ALR_87006433	IMG Activity: SIMG_CFMENUOLSDNT02
S_ALR_87006434	IMG Activity: SIMG_CFMENUGCU0GCI4
S_ALR_87006435	IMG Activity: SIMG_CFMENUOLSDVOPA1
S_ALR_87006436	IMG Activity: SIMG_CFMENUOLSDVXVK
S_ALR_87006437	IMG Activity: SIMG_CFMENUGCUOGCI3
S_ALR_87006438	IMG Activity: SIMG_CFMENUOLSDV/X5
S_ALR_87006439	IMG Activity: SIMG_CFMENUGCU0GCVB
S_ALR_87006440	IMG Activity: SIMG_CFMENUOLSD0VTA
S_ALR_87006441	IMG Activity: SIMG_CFMENUGCU0GCU2
S_ALR_87006442	IMG Activity: SIMG_CFMENUOLSDOVR1
S_ALR_87006443	IMG Activity: SIMG_CFMENUGCU0GCGG
S_ALR_87006444	IMG Activity: SIMG_CFMENUOLSD0VTB
S_ALR_87006445	IMG Activity: SIMG_CFMENUGCU0GCLE
S_ALR_87006446	IMG Activity: SIMG_CFMENUOLSD0VTE
S_ALR_87006447	IMG Activity: SIMG_CFMENUGCU0GCA1
S_ALR_87006448	IMG Activity: SIMG_CFMENUGCU0GCBX
S_ALR_87006449	IMG Activity: SIMG_CFMENUOLSD0VTC
S_ALR_87006450	IMG Activity: SIMG_CFMENUGCU0GCA6
S_ALR_87006451	IMG Activity: SIMG_CFMENUGCU0GP32
S_ALR_87006452	IMG Activity: SIMG_CFMENUOLSD0VTD
S_ALR_87006453	IMG Activity: SIMG_CFMENUGCU0GB05
S_ALR_87006454	IMG Activity: SIMG_CFMENUOLSDOVSY
S_ALR_87006455	IMG Activity: SIMG_CFMENUGCU0GB04
S_ALR_87006456	IMG Activity: SIMG_CFMENUGCU0GB02
S_ALR_87006457	IMG Activity: SIMG_CFMENUGCU0GCGE
S_ALR_87006458	IMG Activity: SIMG_CFMENUOLSDOVL7
S_ALR_87006459	IMG Activity: SIMG_CFMENUGCU0GB03
S_ALR_87006460	IMG Activity: SIMG_CFMENUGCU0GCP4
S_ALR_87006461	IMG Activity: SIMG_CFMENUGCU0GCVI
S_ALR_87006462	IMG Activity: SIMG_CFMENUGCU0GCBA
S_ALR_87006463	IMG Activity: SIMG_CFMENUGCU0GCA8
S_ALR_87006464	IMG Activity: SIMG_CFMENUGCU0GP42
S_ALR_87006465	IMG Activity: SIMG_CFMENUGCU0GCP1
S_ALR_87006466	IMG Activity: SIMG_CFMENUGCU0GCP2
S_ALR_87006467	IMG Activity: SIMG_CFMENUORFALEA2
S_ALR_87006468	IMG Activity: ORFA_LEAS_FELD

S_ALR_87006469	IMG Activity: ORFA_ORD_SCHL
S_ALR_87006470	IMG Activity: SIMG_CFMENUORFAOA11
S_ALR_87006471	IMG Activity: ORFA_OARC
S_ALR_87006472	IMG Activity: ORFA_OAVC
S_ALR_87006473	IMG Activity: SIMG_ORFA_OACS
S_ALR_87006474	IMG Activity: SIMG_ORFA_OAKA
S_ALR_87006475	IMG Activity: ORFA_KLASS_SPEZ_ALLG
S_ALR_87006476	IMG Activity: ORFA_KOST_UEBER
S_ALR_87006477	IMG Activity: SIMG_CFMENUORFAOAW1
S_ALR_87006478	IMG Activity: ORFA_UMWELT
S_ALR_87006479	IMG Activity: ORFA_UEBERNR
S_ALR_87006480	IMG Activity: SIMG_CFMENUORFASTA8
S_ALR_87006481	IMG Activity: ORFA_KLASS_SPEZ3
S_ALR_87006482	IMG Activity: SIMG_CFMENUOPP1OMD0
S_ALR_87006483	IMG Activity: ORFA_GESUMB
S_ALR_87006484	IMG Activity: SIMG_CFMENUOPP1OMII
S_ALR_87006485	IMG Activity: SIMG_CFMENUOLSDIACIA
S_ALR_87006486	IMG Activity: SIMG_CFMENUORFAOAVC
S_ALR_87006487	IMG Activity: SIMG_CFMENUOLSDGRENZ
S_ALR_87006488	IMG Activity: SIMG_CFMENUOPP1OMDQ
S_ALR_87006489	IMG Activity: SIMG_CFMENUORFAVRM4
S_ALR_87006490	IMG Activity: SIMG_CFMENUOLSDVEB1
S_ALR_87006491	IMG Activity: ORFA_RESTW
S_ALR_87006492	IMG Activity: SIMG_CFMENUOPP1OMD9
S_ALR_87006493	IMG Activity: ORFA_VERM_ANHALT
S_ALR_87006494	IMG Activity: SIMG_CFMENUOPP1SP
S_ALR_87006495	IMG Activity: SIMG_CFMENUORFAVRM55
S_ALR_87006496	IMG Activity: SIMG_CFMENUOPP1OMDU
S_ALR_87006497	IMG Activity: ORFA_VERM_INDEX2
S_ALR_87006498	IMG Activity: SIMG_CFMENUOPP1OM01
S_ALR_87006499	IMG Activity: SIMG_CFMENUORFAOAVB
S_ALR_87006500	IMG Activity: SIMG_CFMENUOPP1OMIZ
S_ALR_87006501	IMG Activity: ORFA_ZINS_BEW
S_ALR_87006502	IMG Activity: SIMG_CFMENUOPP1OMIP
S_ALR_87006503	IMG Activity: ORFA_ZINS_KONTEN
S_ALR_87006504	IMG Activity: ORFA_ZINS_SCHL
S_ALR_87006505	IMG Activity: SIMG_CFMENUORFAOAE4
S_ALR_87006506	IMG Activity: SIMG_CFMENUORFAVRM1
S_ALR_87006507	IMG Activity: SIMG_CFMENUORFAOAVE
S_ALR_87006508	IMG Activity: ORFA_VERM_FELD
S_ALR_87006509	IMG Activity: ORFA_VERS_INDEX2
S_ALR_87006510	IMG Activity: ORFA_VERS_FELD
S_ALR_87006511	IMG Activity: SIMG_CFMENUORFAVRS7
S_ALR_87006512	IMG Activity: ORFA_KLASS_SPEZ1
S_ALR_87006513	IMG Activity: ORFA_DATUMAFA
S_ALR_87006514	IMG Activity: ORFA_KONS_BEW1
S_ALR_87006515	IMG Activity: SIMG_CFMENUORFAVRS5
S_ALR_87006516	IMG Activity: SIMG_CFMENUOPP1OPPQ
S_ALR_87006517	IMG Activity: SIMG_CFMENUORFAVRM7
S_ALR_87006518	IMG Activity: SIMG_CFMENUOPP1OMIQ
S_ALR_87006519	IMG Activity: ORFA_KLASS_SPEZ2
S_ALR_87006520	IMG Activity: SIMG_CFMENUOPP1OPPR
S_ALR_87006521	IMG Activity: SIMG_CFMENUORFAOAVD
S_ALR_87006522	IMG Activity: SIMG_CFMENUOPP1OMIG

S_ALR_87006523	IMG Activity: SIMG_CFMENUORFAOAVF
S_ALR_87006524	IMG Activity: SIMG_CFMENUOPP1OM0F
S_ALR_87006525	IMG Activity: SIMG_CFMENUORFAOAVT
S_ALR_87006526	IMG Activity: SIMG_CFMENUORFAVRS4
S_ALR_87006527	IMG Activity: SIMG_CFMENUOPP1OMI2
S_ALR_87006528	IMG Activity: SIMG_CFMENUOPP1OMI3
S_ALR_87006529	IMG Activity: SIMG_CFMENUORFAVOR48
S_ALR_87006530	IMG Activity: SIMG_CFMENUOPP1OMIY
S_ALR_87006531	IMG Activity: ORFA_AIB_NUMMERN
S_ALR_87006532	IMG Activity: SIMG_CFMENUORFAAIIO
S_ALR_87006533	IMG Activity: SIMG_CFMENUOPP1OMDX
S_ALR_87006534	IMG Activity: SIMG_CFMENUORFAVOR49
S_ALR_87006535	IMG Activity: SIMG_CFMENUOPP1OPPD
S_ALR_87006536	IMG Activity: SIMG_CFMENUOPP1OMDK
S_ALR_87006537	IMG Activity: ORFA_BEW_NACH
S_ALR_87006538	IMG Activity: SIMG_CFMENUOPP1OMI1
S_ALR_87006539	IMG Activity: SIMG_CFMENUORFAVOR71
S_ALR_87006540	IMG Activity: SIMG_CFMENUOPP1OPPI
S_ALR_87006541	IMG Activity: SIMG_CFMENUORFAOKO7
S_ALR_87006542	IMG Activity: SIMG_CFMENUOPP1OMDW
S_ALR_87006543	IMG Activity: ORFA_BEW_TRANFER
S_ALR_87006544	IMG Activity: SIMG_CFMENUORFAOAW3
S_ALR_87006545	IMG Activity: SIMG_CFMENUOPP1OMDY
S_ALR_87006546	IMG Activity: SIMG_CFMENUOPP1OMIA
S_ALR_87006547	IMG Activity: SIMG_CFMENUORFAOAVZ
S_ALR_87006548	IMG Activity: SIMG_CFMENUOPP1OMDZ
S_ALR_87006549	IMG Activity: SIMG_CFMENUORFAVOR41
S_ALR_87006550	IMG Activity: ORFA_BWA_AIB
S_ALR_87006551	IMG Activity: SIMG_CFMENUOPP1OMDM
S_ALR_87006552	IMG Activity: ORFA_AIB_KOSTART
S_ALR_87006553	IMG Activity: SIMG_CFMENUOPP1OPPS
S_ALR_87006554	IMG Activity: SIMG_CFMENUORFAOA90
S_ALR_87006555	IMG Activity: SIMG_CFMENUOPP1OPPT
S_ALR_87006556	IMG Activity: SIMG_CFMENUORFAOAV9
S_ALR_87006557	IMG Activity: SIMG_CFMENUOPP1OPPU
S_ALR_87006558	IMG Activity: ORFA_OATR
S_ALR_87006559	IMG Activity: SIMG_CFMENUOPP1OMPG
S_ALR_87006560	IMG Activity: SIMG_CFMENUORFAOAVI
S_ALR_87006561	IMG Activity: SIMG_CFMENUOPP1OMI6
S_ALR_87006562	IMG Activity: ORFA_SIMU
S_ALR_87006563	IMG Activity: SIMG_CFMENUORFAINF2
S_ALR_87006564	IMG Activity: SIMG_CFMENUORFAOA79
S_ALR_87006565	IMG Activity: ORFA_ERW_BUCH
S_ALR_87006566	IMG Activity: ORFA_STATI0
S_ALR_87006567	IMG Activity: ORFA_STAT_KONT
S_ALR_87006568	IMG Activity: ORFA_FELDST_VAR
S_ALR_87006569	IMG Activity: ORFA_BEW_VORSCHLAG
S_ALR_87006570	IMG Activity: ORFA_VORG_INT
S_ALR_87006571	IMG Activity: ORFA_BEZ_DAT
S_ALR_87006572	IMG Activity: SIMG_ORFA_OAZ1
S_ALR_87006573	IMG Activity: ORFA_IND_ANLNR
S_ALR_87006574	IMG Activity: SIMG_CFMENUORFAVOR21
S_ALR_87006575	IMG Activity: ORFA_IND_SCHL
S_ALR_87006576	IMG Activity: ORFA_ABG_SPEZ

S_ALR_87006577	IMG Activity: ORFA_BEW_MEHR
S_ALR_87006578	IMG Activity: ORFA_VORG_TABWI
S_ALR_87006579	IMG Activity: ORFA_ERW_INVENT
S_ALR_87006580	IMG Activity: SIMG_CFMENUOLSDOVSQ
S_ALR_87006581	IMG Activity: SIMG_CFMENUOLSDOVSG
S_ALR_87006582	IMG Activity: SIMG_CFMENUOLSDOVSE
S_ALR_87006583	IMG Activity: SIMG_CFMENUOLSDOVR4
S_ALR_87006584	IMG Activity: SIMG_CFMENUOLSDOVSC
S_ALR_87006585	IMG Activity: SIMG_CFMENUOLSDOVR3
S_ALR_87006586	IMG Activity: SIMG_CFMENUOLSDOVSD
S_ALR_87006587	IMG Activity: SIMG_CFMENUOLSDRESKX
S_ALR_87006588	IMG Activity: SIMG_CFMENUOLSDOVR0
S_ALR_87006589	IMG Activity: SIMG_CFMENUOLSDOVZA
S_ALR_87006590	IMG Activity: SIMG_CFMENUOLSDVOVK
S_ALR_87006591	IMG Activity: SIMG_CFMENUOLSDHR
S_ALR_87006592	IMG Activity: SIMG_XXCFMENUOLSDATT
S_ALR_87006593	IMG Activity: SIMG_CFMENUOLSDOVR7
S_ALR_87006594	IMG Activity: SIMG_CFMENUOLSDOVSM
S_ALR_87006595	IMG Activity: SIMG_CFMENUOLSDOVSW
S_ALR_87006596	IMG Activity: SIMG_CFMENUOLSDOVSR
S_ALR_87006597	IMG Activity: SIMG_CFMENUOLSDOVSN
S_ALR_87006598	IMG Activity: SIMG_CFMENUOLSDOVS9
S_ALR_87006599	IMG Activity: SIMG_CFMENUOLSDOVR2
S_ALR_87006600	IMG Activity: SIMG_CFMENUSAPCVOR2
S_ALR_87006601	IMG Activity: SIMG_CFMENUOLSDOVH4
S_ALR_87006602	IMG Activity: SIMG_CFMENUOLSDOVH3
S_ALR_87006603	IMG Activity: SIMG_CFMENUOLSDOVH2
S_ALR_87006604	IMG Activity: SIMG_CFMENUOLSDVOPA
S_ALR_87006605	IMG Activity: SIMG_CFMENUOLSDOVH1
S_ALR_87006606	IMG Activity: SIMG_CFMENUOLSDOV2
S_ALR_87006607	IMG Activity: SIMG_CFMENUSAPCVOR1
S_ALR_87006608	IMG Activity: SIMG_CFMENUOLSDOV1
S_ALR_87006609	IMG Activity: SIMG_CFMENUOLSDOVS6
S_ALR_87006610	IMG Activity: SIMG_CFMENUOLSDOVXZ
S_ALR_87006611	IMG Activity: ORFA_VORG_ZUG
S_ALR_87006612	IMG Activity: ORFA_KONT_TYP
S_ALR_87006613	IMG Activity: SIMG_CFMENUORFAOAE3
S_ALR_87006614	IMG Activity: ORFA_OAKB
S_ALR_87006615	IMG Activity: ORFA_UMB_VAR
S_ALR_87006616	IMG Activity: SIMG_CFMENUORFAVOR32
S_ALR_87006617	IMG Activity: ORFA_SE71
S_ALR_87006618	IMG Activity: ORFA_TRANS2
S_ALR_87006619	IMG Activity: ORFA_TRANS
S_ALR_87006620	IMG Activity: ORFA_ERW_TRANS
S_ALR_87006621	IMG Activity: SIMG_CFMENUORFAVOR31
S_ALR_87006622	IMG Activity: ORFA_OA01
S_ALR_87006623	IMG Activity: ORFA_VORG_ABG_FRZ
S_ALR_87006624	IMG Activity: SIMG_CFMENUORFAVOR26
S_ALR_87006625	IMG Activity: SIMG_CFMENUORFAVOR22
S_ALR_87006626	IMG Activity: ORFA_CMOD_ABG_KONT
S_ALR_87006627	IMG Activity: ORFA_IND_UMR
S_ALR_87006628	IMG Activity: ORFA_VERS_NEU
S_ALR_87006629	IMG Activity: SIMG_CFMENUORFAOA39
S_ALR_87006630	IMG Activity: OALE_FIVZROLLUP

S_ALR_87006631	IMG Activity: OALE_CLEARACT_OBV5
S_ALR_87006632	IMG Activity: OALE_POSTKEY_OBBT
S_ALR_87006633	IMG Activity: OALE_CHNGACCT_OBV6
S_ALR_87006634	IMG Activity: OALE_FICHECK
S_ALR_87006635	IMG Activity: OALE_DSTSCN_ACCCO
S_ALR_87006636	IMG Activity: SIMG_CFMENUORFABER43
S_ALR_87006637	IMG Activity: OALE_DSTSCN_CREDIT
S_ALR_87006638	IMG Activity: ORFA_BEW_GJAHR_VAR_B
S_ALR_87006639	IMG Activity: SIMG_OALE_ACOPA_063
S_ALR_87006640	IMG Activity: ORFA_BEW_GJAHR_VAR_A
S_ALR_87006641	IMG Activity: SIMG_CFMENUORFAOAV3
S_ALR_87006642	IMG Activity: SIMG_OALE_ACPSP_011
S_ALR_87006643	IMG Activity: ORFA_UMSTBETR
S_ALR_87006644	IMG Activity: OALE_LO_DEKR_0003
S_ALR_87006645	IMG Activity: SIMG_CFMENUORFAOAE1
S_ALR_87006646	IMG Activity: OALE_DSTSCN_ACCSL
S_ALR_87006647	IMG Activity: ORFA_BEREICH1
S_ALR_87006648	IMG Activity: ORFA_BEREICH_PARA
S_ALR_87006649	IMG Activity: ORFA_KLASS_BEW1
S_ALR_87006650	IMG Activity: SIMG_CFMENUORFAVOR13
S_ALR_87006651	IMG Activity: ORFA_RUND
S_ALR_87006652	IMG Activity: ORFA_RUMPF
S_ALR_87006653	IMG Activity: ORFA_KLASS_KOMPL
S_ALR_87006654	IMG Activity: ORFA_OAWF
S_ALR_87006655	IMG Activity: SIMG_CFMENUORFASU02
S_ALR_87006656	IMG Activity: ORFA_NORM_BEREICH
S_ALR_87006657	IMG Activity: ORFA_NORM_KONTEN
S_ALR_87006658	IMG Activity: SIMG_CFMENUORFAOA25
S_ALR_87006659	IMG Activity: SIMG_CFMENUOLSDNG07
S_ALR_87006660	IMG Activity: ORFA_KOMPLEX
S_ALR_87006661	IMG Activity: ORFA_RUMPF_RECH
S_ALR_87006662	IMG Activity: ORFA_BEW_GJAHR_VAR_H
S_ALR_87006663	IMG Activity: ORFA_445
S_ALR_87006664	IMG Activity: SIMG_CFMENUORFAOAV1
S_ALR_87006665	IMG Activity: ORFA_BEREICH_FREMD
S_ALR_87006666	IMG Activity: ORFA_BEW_FREMD_PAR
S_ALR_87006667	IMG Activity: SIMG_IND_NUMKR
S_ALR_87006668	IMG Activity: SIMG_CFMENUOLSDNG02
S_ALR_87006669	IMG Activity: SIMG_CFMENUOLSDNG04
S_ALR_87006670	IMG Activity: SIMG_CFMENUOLSDNG06
S_ALR_87006671	IMG Activity: OALE_DSTSCN_TRCM
S_ALR_87006672	IMG Activity: OALE_DSTSCN_COPA
S_ALR_87006673	IMG Activity: OALE_DSTSCN_KONSOL
S_ALR_87006674	IMG Activity: SIMG_XXAK_OXK3_ALE
S_ALR_87006675	IMG Activity: SIMG_CFMENUORFAORG2
S_ALR_87006676	IMG Activity: ORFA_BILDAUFBAU
S_ALR_87006677	IMG Activity: SIMG_CFMENUORFAAS08
S_ALR_87006678	IMG Activity: SIMG_CFMENUORFAAM01
S_ALR_87006679	IMG Activity: SIMG_CFMENUOLSDFP3
S_ALR_87006680	IMG Activity: ORFA_BKRS_NUMMERN
S_ALR_87006681	IMG Activity: SIMG_CFMENUOLSDVOK0
S_ALR_87006682	IMG Activity: ORFA_JAHR_RUECK
S_ALR_87006683	IMG Activity: SIMG_CFMENUOLSDVOKX
S_ALR_87006684	IMG Activity: SIMG_CFMENUOLSDLWM5

S_ALR_87006685	IMG Activity: SIMG_CFMENUOLSDLWM6
S_ALR_87006686	IMG Activity: SIMG_CFMENUOLSDLWM7
S_ALR_87006687	IMG Activity: SIMG_CFMENUOLSDLWM8
S_ALR_87006688	IMG Activity: SIMG_CFMENUOLSDLWM9
S_ALR_87006689	IMG Activity: SIMG_CFMENUOLSDOVLQ
S_ALR_87006690	IMG Activity: SIMG_CFMENUOLSDLWM4
S_ALR_87006691	IMG Activity: SIMG_CFMENUOLSDOVB6
S_ALR_87006692	IMG Activity: SIMG_CFMENUOLSDLWM1
S_ALR_87006693	IMG Activity: SIMG_CFMENUOLSDLWM2
S_ALR_87006694	IMG Activity: SIMG_CFMENUOLSDTOR
S_ALR_87006695	IMG Activity: SIMG_CFMENUOLSDBEREI
S_ALR_87006696	IMG Activity: SIMG_CFMENUOLSDLWM3
S_ALR_87006697	IMG Activity: SIMG_CMMENUOLSDKWLS
S_ALR_87006698	IMG Activity: ORFA_LAENDER
S_ALR_87006699	IMG Activity: SIMG_CMMENUOLSDKWLS3
S_ALR_87006700	IMG Activity: SIMG_CFMENUOLSDOMS6
S_ALR_87006701	IMG Activity: SIMG_CFMENUOLSDOVL3
S_ALR_87006702	IMG Activity: SIMG_CFMENUOLSDLOF2
S_ALR_87006703	IMG Activity: SIMG_CFMENUOLSDLOF1
S_ALR_87006704	IMG Activity: SIMG_CMMENUOLSDKWLS1
S_ALR_87006705	IMG Activity: SIMG_CMMENUOLSDKWLS2
S_ALR_87006706	IMG Activity: SIMG_CFMENUOLSDSDPI
S_ALR_87006707	IMG Activity: ORFA_KLASS_SPEZ
S_ALR_87006708	IMG Activity: SIMG_CFMENUOLSDVOLF
S_ALR_87006709	IMG Activity: SIMG_CFMENUOLSDVOLB
S_ALR_87006710	IMG Activity: SIMG_XXMENUOLSDVOLB
S_ALR_87006711	IMG Activity: SIMG_CFMENUOLSDOVV1
S_ALR_87006712	IMG Activity: SIMG_CFMENUOLSDOVLS
S_ALR_87006713	IMG Activity: SIMG_CFMENUOLSDKALK
S_ALR_87006714	IMG Activity: W_DF_LT_0003
S_ALR_87006715	IMG Activity: SIMG_CFMENUORFAOAB3
S_ALR_87006716	IMG Activity: SIMG_CFMENUOLSDBEST
S_ALR_87006717	IMG Activity: SIMG_CMMENUOLSDVBX1
S_ALR_87006718	IMG Activity: SIMG_CFMENUOLSDOVLP
S_ALR_87006719	IMG Activity: SIMG_CFMENUOLSDVSTK
S_ALR_87006720	IMG Activity: SIMG_CFMENUORFAOAMK
S_ALR_87006721	IMG Activity: J_1AASSIGN_DC_DT
S_ALR_87006722	IMG Activity: SIMG_CFMENUORFAOAPL
S_ALR_87006723	IMG Activity: SIMG_CFMENUOLSDOVM1
S_ALR_87006724	IMG Activity: SIMG_CFMENUOLSDVN01L
S_ALR_87006725	IMG Activity: SIMG_CFMENUOLSDMY12
S_ALR_87006726	IMG Activity: SIMG_CFMENUOLSDSPLLN
S_ALR_87006727	IMG Activity: J_1AASSIGN_BR_SHIP
S_ALR_87006728	IMG Activity: J_1ATVKO
S_ALR_87006729	IMG Activity: SIMG_CFMENUOLSDVOL1
S_ALR_87006730	IMG Activity: SIMG_CFMENUOLSDOVB9
S_ALR_87006731	IMG Activity: SIMG_CFMENUOLSDOMNG
S_ALR_87006732	IMG Activity: SIMG_CFMENUOLSDVL14
S_ALR_87006733	IMG Activity: SIMG_CFMENUOLSDV633
S_ALR_87006734	IMG Activity: SIMG_CFMENUOLSDVKDV
S_ALR_87006735	IMG Activity: SIMG_CFMENUOLSDSELKR
S_ALR_87006736	IMG Activity: SIMG_CFMENUOLSDOVVM
S_ALR_87006737	IMG Activity: SIMG_CFMENUOLSDVOGX
S_ALR_87006738	IMG Activity: SIMG_CFMENUOCA0OD65

S_ALR_87006739	IMG Activity: SIMG_CFMENUOLSDVSAY
S_ALR_87006741	IMG Activity: SIMG_CFMENUOCA0OD59
S_ALR_87006742	IMG Activity: SIMG_CFMENUOLSDTVINP
S_ALR_87006743	IMG Activity: SIMG_CFMENUOCA0OD58
S_ALR_87006744	IMG Activity: SIMG_CFMENUOLSDTVINM
S_ALR_87006745	IMG Activity: SIMG_CFMENUOCA0OD57
S_ALR_87006746	IMG Activity: SIMG_CFMENUOCA0OD56
S_ALR_87006747	IMG Activity: SIMG_CFMENUOCA0OD55
S_ALR_87006748	IMG Activity: SIMG_CFMENUOCA0OD51
S_ALR_87006749	IMG Activity: SIMG_XXMENUOLSDFLDV2
S_ALR_87006750	IMG Activity: ORFA_BUSCHL
S_ALR_87006751	IMG Activity: SIMG_XXMENUOLSDFLDV3
S_ALR_87006752	IMG Activity: ORFA_FELDST_ABG
S_ALR_87006753	IMG Activity: SIMG_CFMENUOLSDVCHP
S_ALR_87006754	IMG Activity: SIMG_CFMENUORFAOAI1
S_ALR_87006755	IMG Activity: SIMG_CFMENUORFAOAI2
S_ALR_87006756	IMG Activity: SIMG_CFMENUOLSDOVV5
S_ALR_87006757	IMG Activity: SIMG_CFMENUORFAOAI4
S_ALR_87006758	IMG Activity: SIMG_CFMENUORFAOAI3
S_ALR_87006759	IMG Activity: ORFA_BEW_FOERDER
S_ALR_87006760	IMG Activity: ORFA_BEWEG_RUECK
S_ALR_87006761	IMG Activity: ORFA_BER_SOPO_BN
S_ALR_87006762	IMG Activity: SIMG_XXMENUOLML1112
S_ALR_87006763	IMG Activity: SIMG_XXMENUOLML1113
S_ALR_87006764	IMG Activity: ORFA_IND_ALT
S_ALR_87006765	IMG Activity: ORFA_BER_RUECKL
S_ALR_87006766	IMG Activity: ORFA_RUECK_KONTEN
S_ALR_87006767	IMG Activity: SIMG_CMMENUOLSDSLV
S_ALR_87006768	IMG Activity: ORFA_BEW_ALT
S_ALR_87006769	IMG Activity: SIMG_CMMENUOLSDVZP
S_ALR_87006770	IMG Activity: SIMG_CMMENUOLSDWP
S_ALR_87006771	IMG Activity: SIMG_CMMENUOLSDZS
S_ALR_87006772	IMG Activity: SIMG_CMMENUOLSDWR
S_ALR_87006773	IMG Activity: SIMG_CFMENUORFAOAA2
S_ALR_87006774	IMG Activity: SIMG_CFMENUOLSDVLPP
S_ALR_87006775	IMG Activity: ORFA_AUFW_KONTEN
S_ALR_87006776	IMG Activity: SIMG_CFMENUOLSDVPBD
S_ALR_87006777	IMG Activity: ORFA_AUFW_KONTEN1
S_ALR_87006778	IMG Activity: SIMG_CFMENUOLSDVHAR
S_ALR_87006779	IMG Activity: ORFA_IND_AUFW
S_ALR_87006780	IMG Activity: SIMG_CFMENUOLSDVEGR
S_ALR_87006781	IMG Activity: SIMG_CFMENUOLSDVHZU
S_ALR_87006782	IMG Activity: ORFA_BEWEG_AUFW
S_ALR_87006783	IMG Activity: ORFA_AUFW_NEU
S_ALR_87006784	IMG Activity: SIMG_CFMENUOLSDVEG1
S_ALR_87006785	IMG Activity: ORFA_AUFW_BEREICH
S_ALR_87006786	IMG Activity: SIMG_CFMENUOLSDVNKP
S_ALR_87006787	IMG Activity: SIMG_XXMENUOLML1114
S_ALR_87006788	IMG Activity: SIMG_CFMENUORFAVOR64
S_ALR_87006789	IMG Activity: SIMG_CFMENUOLSDREGFD
S_ALR_87006790	IMG Activity: ORFA_IND_KONTEN
S_ALR_87006791	IMG Activity: SIMG_CFMENUOLSDWARFD
S_ALR_87006792	IMG Activity: ORFA_IND_KONTEN1
S_ALR_87006793	IMG Activity: SIMG_CFMENUOLSDROUTD

S_ALR_87006794	IMG Activity: SIMG_CFMENUORFAOAV5
S_ALR_87006795	IMG Activity: SIMG_CFMENUOLSDBZFWR
S_ALR_87006796	IMG Activity: ORFA_IND_KLASSEN
S_ALR_87006797	IMG Activity: SIMG_CFMENUOLSDBZFRR
S_ALR_87006798	IMG Activity: ORFA_ALT_FREMDW
S_ALR_87006799	IMG Activity: ORFA_BEWEG_AUSSER
S_ALR_87006800	IMG Activity: SIMG_CFMENUORFAOA27
S_ALR_87006801	IMG Activity: ORFA_AS81
S_ALR_87006802	IMG Activity: SIMG_CFMENUORFAOAVS
S_ALR_87006803	IMG Activity: SIMG_CFMENUOLSDUVSZ
S_ALR_87006804	IMG Activity: SIMG_CFMENUORFAOAVHX
S_ALR_87006805	IMG Activity: ORFA_PER_ZEIT
S_ALR_87006806	IMG Activity: SIMG_CFMENUOLSDOIS1
S_ALR_87006807	IMG Activity: SIMG_CFMENUOLSDOIS2
S_ALR_87006808	IMG Activity: SIMG_CFMENUORFASU03
S_ALR_87006809	IMG Activity: ORFA_SOND_BER
S_ALR_87006810	IMG Activity: ORFA_AFARFO
S_ALR_87006811	IMG Activity: ORFA_SOND_KONTEN
S_ALR_87006812	IMG Activity: SIMG_CFMENUORFABEWA1
S_ALR_87006813	IMG Activity: ORFA_AUSS_KONTEN
S_ALR_87006814	IMG Activity: ORFA_PER_GEN
S_ALR_87006815	IMG Activity: ORFA_IND_BEZ
S_ALR_87006816	IMG Activity: ORFA_IND_AFAMETH
S_ALR_87006817	IMG Activity: PPPI_PD_220
S_ALR_87006818	IMG Activity: ORFA_BEZUG_IND
S_ALR_87006819	IMG Activity: PPPI_PD_230
S_ALR_87006820	IMG Activity: SIMG_CFMENUORFAOAW2
S_ALR_87006821	IMG Activity: PPPI_PD_254
S_ALR_87006822	IMG Activity: PPPI_PD_253
S_ALR_87006823	IMG Activity: SIMG_CFMENUORFAOA29
S_ALR_87006824	IMG Activity: PPPI_PD_252
S_ALR_87006825	IMG Activity: ORFA_IND_UMST
S_ALR_87006826	IMG Activity: PPPI_PD_251
S_ALR_87006827	IMG Activity: SIMG_CFMENUORFAOA23
S_ALR_87006828	IMG Activity: PPPI_PD_300
S_ALR_87006829	IMG Activity: PPPI_PD_420
S_ALR_87006830	IMG Activity: PPPI_PD_410
S_ALR_87006831	IMG Activity: SIMG_CFMENUOLSDOVZG
S_ALR_87006832	IMG Activity: PPPI_PO_720
S_ALR_87006833	IMG Activity: PPPI_PO_740
S_ALR_87006834	IMG Activity: SIMG_CFMENUOLSDOVZH
S_ALR_87006835	IMG Activity: PPPI_PO_730
S_ALR_87006836	IMG Activity: SIMG_CFMENUOLSDOVZI
S_ALR_87006837	IMG Activity: PPPI_PD_255
S_ALR_87006838	IMG Activity: SIMG_CFMENUOLSDOVZ2
S_ALR_87006839	IMG Activity: SIMG_CFMENUOLSDVTTZ
S_ALR_87006840	IMG Activity: SIMG_CFMENUOLSDVTTV
S_ALR_87006841	IMG Activity: SIMG_CFMENUOLSD0VSH
S_ALR_87006842	IMG Activity: SIMG_CMMENUOLSDOVSF
S_ALR_87006843	IMG Activity: SIMG_CFMENUOLSDOVKH
S_ALR_87006844	IMG Activity: SIMG_CMMENUOLSDOVSX
S_ALR_87006845	IMG Activity: SIMG_CMMENUOLSDOVL2
S_ALR_87006846	IMG Activity: SIMG_CFMENUOLSDWAR
S_ALR_87006847	IMG Activity: SIMG_CFMENUOLSDVTTS

S_ALR_87006848	IMG Activity: SIMG_CFMENUOLSDV/T3
S_ALR_87006849	IMG Activity: SIMG_CFMENUOLSDV/T5
S_ALR_87006850	IMG Activity: SIMG_CFMENUOLSDVTVK
S_ALR_87006851	IMG Activity: SIMG_CFMENUOLMBOMCG
S_ALR_87006852	IMG Activity: SIMG_CFMENUOCU0CU24
S_ALR_87006853	IMG Activity: SIMG_CFMENUOFDIMERKM
S_ALR_87006854	IMG Activity: SIMG_XXOLMLCHA_04
S_ALR_87006855	IMG Activity: SIMG_CFMENUOFDIRUNDU
S_ALR_87006856	IMG Activity: SIMG_CFMENUOCU0CU30
S_ALR_87006857	IMG Activity: SIMG_CFMENUOLSDV/C3A
S_ALR_87006858	IMG Activity: SIMG_CFMENUOFDIFODE
S_ALR_87006859	IMG Activity: SIMG_CFMENUOFDIFOC3
S_ALR_87006860	IMG Activity: PPPI_PO_33015
S_ALR_87006861	IMG Activity: SIMG_CFMENUOCU0CU31
S_ALR_87006862	IMG Activity: SIMG_CFMENUOLPFOPLG
S_ALR_87006863	IMG Activity: SIMG_CMMENUOFDI0014
S_ALR_87006864	IMG Activity: SIMG_CFMENUOFDIBBVST
S_ALR_87006865	IMG Activity: SIMG_CFMENUOCU0CU22
S_ALR_87006866	IMG Activity: SIMG_CFMENUOCHAZCM
S_ALR_87006867	IMG Activity: SIMG_CFMENUOFDIFODJ
S_ALR_87006868	IMG Activity: SIMG_CFMENUOFDIFOZ0
S_ALR_87006869	IMG Activity: SIMG_CFMENUOCU0CU26
S_ALR_87006870	IMG Activity: SIMG_CFMENUOCHAZCK
S_ALR_87006871	IMG Activity: SIMG_CFMENUOCHAZCS
S_ALR_87006872	IMG Activity: SIMG_CFMENUOFDIFOC4
S_ALR_87006873	IMG Activity: SIMG_CFMENUOFDIFOO6
S_ALR_87006874	IMG Activity: SIMG_CFMENUOCU0CU27
S_ALR_87006875	IMG Activity: SIMG_CFMENUOCHACOCR
S_ALR_87006876	IMG Activity: SIMG_CFMENUOFDIFOM3
S_ALR_87006877	IMG Activity: SIMG_CFMENUOCU0CU23
S_ALR_87006878	IMG Activity: SIMG_CFMENUOFDIFOCN
S_ALR_87006879	IMG Activity: SIMG_CFMENUOCHAOLP8
S_ALR_87006880	IMG Activity: SIMG_CFMENUOCU0CU16
S_ALR_87006881	IMG Activity: SIMG_CFMENUOFDIFOBV
S_ALR_87006882	IMG Activity: SIMG_CFMENUOLMBOMCW
S_ALR_87006883	IMG Activity: SIMG_XXOLMLCHA_02
S_ALR_87006884	IMG Activity: SIMG_CFMENUOFDITIVN2
S_ALR_87006885	IMG Activity: SIMG_CFMENUOCU0CU18
S_ALR_87006886	IMG Activity: SIMG_CFMENUOLSDV/C2A
S_ALR_87006887	IMG Activity: SIMG_CFMENUOCU0CU29
S_ALR_87006888	IMG Activity: SIMG_CFMENUOFDITIVN1
S_ALR_87006889	IMG Activity: PPPI_PO_33014
S_ALR_87006890	IMG Activity: SIMG_CFMENUOCU0SMOD
S_ALR_87006891	IMG Activity: SIMG_CFMENUOLPFOPLF
S_ALR_87006892	IMG Activity: SIMG_CFMENUOFDIFOD8
S_ALR_87006893	IMG Activity: SIMG_CFMENUOLMBOMCY
S_ALR_87006894	IMG Activity: SIMG_LOVC_AUTH_01
S_ALR_87006895	IMG Activity: SIMG_CFMENUOFDIFP01
S_ALR_87006896	IMG Activity: SIMG_XXOLMLCHA_03
S_ALR_87006897	IMG Activity: SIMG_CFMENUOCU0CU14
S_ALR_87006898	IMG Activity: SIMG_CFMENUOLSDV/C1A
S_ALR_87006899	IMG Activity: SIMG_CFMENUOFDIFOPU
S_ALR_87006900	IMG Activity: PPPI_PO_33013
S_ALR_87006901	IMG Activity: SIMG_CFMENUOCU0CU15

S_ALR_87006902	IMG Activity: SIMG_CFMENUOFDI094C
S_ALR_87006903	IMG Activity: SIMG_CFMENUOLPFOPLE
S_ALR_87006904	IMG Activity: SIMG_CFMENUOCU0CU10
S_ALR_87006905	IMG Activity: SIMG_CFMENUOLSDV/C5A
S_ALR_87006906	IMG Activity: SIMG_CFMENUOFDIFOE0
S_ALR_87006907	IMG Activity: SIMG_CFMENUOCU0CU28
S_ALR_87006908	IMG Activity: SIMG_CFMENUOCHAWSMP
S_ALR_87006909	IMG Activity: SIMG_CFMENUOFDINUMM2
S_ALR_87006910	IMG Activity: OTMA
S_ALR_87006911	IMG Activity: SIMG_CFMENUOCU0CU25
S_ALR_87006912	IMG Activity: SIMG_CFMENUOCHAWSAKT
S_ALR_87006913	IMG Activity: OCHA_BMAPM
S_ALR_87006914	IMG Activity: OCHA_PMABM
S_ALR_87006915	IMG Activity: SIMG_CFMENUOFDIMSBTE
S_ALR_87006916	IMG Activity: OCHA_BMAAM
S_ALR_87006917	IMG Activity: SIMG_CFMENUOCU0CU11
S_ALR_87006918	IMG Activity: SIMG_CFMENUOCHAPMUMP
S_ALR_87006919	IMG Activity: SIMG_CFMENUOFDIFO49
S_ALR_87006920	IMG Activity: SIMG_CFMENUOCHAPMUMB
S_ALR_87006921	IMG Activity: SIMG_CFMENUOFDIFOPS
S_ALR_87006922	IMG Activity: SIMG_CFMENUOCHAPMMP
S_ALR_87006923	IMG Activity: SIMG_CFMENUOFDIFOPT
S_ALR_87006924	IMG Activity: SIMG_CFMENUOCHAPMAK
S_ALR_87006925	IMG Activity: SIMG_CFMENUOFDIOT25
S_ALR_87006926	IMG Activity: SIMG_CFMENUOCHAWSAMP
S_ALR_87006927	IMG Activity: SIMG_CFMENUOCHAKNNK
S_ALR_87006928	IMG Activity: SIMG_CFMENUOFDIOT26
S_ALR_87006929	IMG Activity: SIMG_CFMENUOLSDCU70
S_ALR_87006930	IMG Activity: SIMG_CFMENUOLSDCL01
S_ALR_87006931	IMG Activity: SIMG_CFMENUOFDIPLAIM
S_ALR_87006932	IMG Activity: SIMG_CFMENUOLSDV/CA
S_ALR_87006933	IMG Activity: SIMG_CFMENUOFDISTAKA
S_ALR_87006934	IMG Activity: SIMG_XXMENUOLML0023
S_ALR_87006935	IMG Activity: OCHA_AMABM
S_ALR_87006936	IMG Activity: SIMG_CFMENUOFDIKOPLA
S_ALR_87006937	IMG Activity: SIMG_CFMENUOCHAWSVMD
S_ALR_87006938	IMG Activity: OCHA_CSMEEDIT
S_ALR_87006939	IMG Activity: OCHA_CSMEAKT
S_ALR_87006940	IMG Activity: SIMG_CFMENUORKSKAH1
S_ALR_87006941	IMG Activity: SIMG_CFMENUOCHAOMBB
S_ALR_87006942	IMG Activity: SIMG_CFMENUOFDIFOD2
S_ALR_87006943	IMG Activity: SIMG_CFMENUOLMBOMCX
S_ALR_87006944	IMG Activity: CFMENU_OCHA_FAF
S_ALR_87006945	IMG Activity: SIMG_CFMENUOFDIPLATR
S_ALR_87006946	IMG Activity: SIMG_CFMENUOCHAXZ011
S_ALR_87006947	IMG Activity: SIMG_CFMENUOFDIKEI1
S_ALR_87006948	IMG Activity: SIMG_CFMENUOCHAXZ012
S_ALR_87006949	IMG Activity: SIMG_OFDI_OKEU
S_ALR_87006950	IMG Activity: SIMG_CFMENUOCHAXZ014
S_ALR_87006951	IMG Activity: SIMG_CFMENUOFDIOKO6
S_ALR_87006952	IMG Activity: SIMG_CFMENUOCHAXZ013
S_ALR_87006953	IMG Activity: SIMG_OFDI_K01_ABR
S_ALR_87006954	IMG Activity: SIMG_CFMENUOLMBCHNX
S_ALR_87006955	IMG Activity: SIMG_CFMENUOCHAMHDPK

S_ALR_87006956	IMG Activity: SIMG_CFMENUOFDIPLAPR
S_ALR_87006957	IMG Activity: SIMG_CFMENUOLMBCHNEU
S_ALR_87006958	IMG Activity: SIMG_CFMENUOFDIFODW
S_ALR_87006959	IMG Activity: CFMENU_OCHA_FAL
S_ALR_87006960	IMG Activity: SIMG_CFMENUOLSDNL12
S_ALR_87006961	IMG Activity: SIMG_CFMENUOFDITIV46
S_ALR_87006962	IMG Activity: SIMG_CFMENUOCHACUST
S_ALR_87006963	IMG Activity: RUND_VZ_PAUSCH
S_ALR_87006964	IMG Activity: SIMG_CFMENUOLMBCHNPP
S_ALR_87006965	IMG Activity: SIMG_CFMENUOLMBOMCV
S_ALR_87006966	IMG Activity: SIMG_CFMENUOCHAMMCF1
S_ALR_87006967	IMG Activity: SIMG_CFMENUOFDIETH
S_ALR_87006968	IMG Activity: SIMG_CFMENUOLSDNL11
S_ALR_87006969	IMG Activity: SIMG_CFMENUOLSDBA1
S_ALR_87006970	IMG Activity: SIMG_CFMENUOCHAMMCF2
S_ALR_87006971	IMG Activity: SIMG_XXMENUOLSDVL1
S_ALR_87006972	IMG Activity: SIMG_CFMENUOFDIKORUN
S_ALR_87006973	IMG Activity: SIMG_XXMENUOLSDFLDV1
S_ALR_87006974	IMG Activity: SIMG_CFMENUOCHABNCM
S_ALR_87006975	IMG Activity: SIMG_CFMENUOFDIFOCT
S_ALR_87006976	IMG Activity: SIMG_CFMENUOLMBOMA1
S_ALR_87006977	IMG Activity: SIMG_CFMENUOFDIFOCV
S_ALR_87006978	IMG Activity: SIMG_CFMENUOLPFCOND
S_ALR_87006979	IMG Activity: SIMG_CFMENUOFDIFOO7
S_ALR_87006980	IMG Activity: SIMG_CFMENUOLMSOMCT
S_ALR_87006981	IMG Activity: SIMG_CFMENUOLSDOVF2
S_ALR_87006982	IMG Activity: SIMG_CFMENUOFDIFOER
S_ALR_87006983	IMG Activity: PPPI_PO_33012
S_ALR_87006984	IMG Activity: SIMG_CFMENUOLSDOVF0
S_ALR_87006985	IMG Activity: SIMG_CFMENUOLSDV/C7A
S_ALR_87006986	IMG Activity: SIMG_CFMENUOFDIUSTAX
S_ALR_87006987	IMG Activity: SIMG_CFMENUOLSDOVF1
S_ALR_87006988	IMG Activity: SIMG_XXOLMLCHA_01
S_ALR_87006989	IMG Activity: SIMG_CFMENUOFDINUESR
S_ALR_87006990	IMG Activity: SIMG_CFMENUOCHABNNK
S_ALR_87006991	IMG Activity: SIMG_CFMENUOFDINUEIB
S_ALR_87006992	IMG Activity: SIMG_CFMENUOCHAOMCZ
S_ALR_87006993	IMG Activity: SIMG_CFMENUOFDIFOB0
S_ALR_87006994	IMG Activity: SIMG_XXMENUOLML0022
S_ALR_87006995	IMG Activity: SIMG_CFMENUOFDITIVFI
S_ALR_87006996	IMG Activity: SIMG_CFMENUOFDIZWBLA
S_ALR_87006997	IMG Activity: SIMG_CFMENUOFDIFZZ1
S_ALR_87006998	IMG Activity: SIMG_CMMENUOFDIFNZA
S_ALR_87006999	IMG Activity: SIMG_CMMENUOFDIFND3
S_ALR_87007000	IMG Activity: SIMG_CFMENUOFDIZEBWA
S_ALR_87007001	IMG Activity: SIMG_CFMENUOFDIKOAUS
S_ALR_87007002	IMG Activity: SIMG_CFMENUOFDITZV05
S_ALR_87007003	IMG Activity: SIMG_CFMENUOFDITTXBS
S_ALR_87007004	IMG Activity: SIMG_CFMENUOFDIFOLM
S_ALR_87007005	IMG Activity: SIMG_CFMENUOLSDBEDKA
S_ALR_87007006	IMG Activity: SIMG_CFMENUOFDIFOLR
S_ALR_87007007	IMG Activity: SIMG_CFMENUOFDITEXT
S_ALR_87007008	IMG Activity: SIMG_CFMENUOFDITIVWA
S_ALR_87007009	IMG Activity: SIMG_CFMENUOFDIVITXT

S_ALR_87007010	IMG Activity: SIMG_CFMENUOLSDOV64
S_ALR_87007011	IMG Activity: SIMG_CFMENUOFDIFZCL
S_ALR_87007012	IMG Activity: SIMG_CFMENUOLSDOVK5
S_ALR_87007013	IMG Activity: SIMG_CFMENUOFDITA7FC
S_ALR_87007014	IMG Activity: SIMG_CFMENUOLSDERLTY
S_ALR_87007015	IMG Activity: SIMG_CFMENUOFDICORDT
S_ALR_87007016	IMG Activity: SIMG_CFMENUOLSDERLKO
S_ALR_87007017	IMG Activity: SIMG_CFMENUOFDICORGP
S_ALR_87007018	IMG Activity: SIMG_CFMENUOFDIFOLX
S_ALR_87007019	IMG Activity: SIMG_CFMENUOFDIWB01
S_ALR_87007020	IMG Activity: SIMG_CFEMNUOFDITIVM6
S_ALR_87007021	IMG Activity: SIMG_CFMENUOFDITIVM5
S_ALR_87007022	IMG Activity: SIMG_CFMENUOFDITIVM4
S_ALR_87007023	IMG Activity: SIMG_CFMENUOFDITIVM7
S_ALR_87007024	IMG Activity: SIMG_CFMENUOFDIWB00
S_ALR_87007025	IMG Activity: ANPASSUNGSVERFAHREN
S_ALR_87007026	IMG Activity: SIMG_CFMENUOFDIWB03
S_ALR_87007027	IMG Activity: SIMG_CFMENUOFDIWB02
S_ALR_87007028	IMG Activity: SIMG_CFMENUOFDIWB51
S_ALR_87007029	IMG Activity: SIMG_CFMENUOFDIFOCO
S_ALR_87007030	IMG Activity: SIMG_CFMENUOFDIANPAS
S_ALR_87007031	IMG Activity: SIMG_CFMENUOFDIFOC2
S_ALR_87007032	IMG Activity: SIMG_CMMENUOFDIFOZW
S_ALR_87007033	IMG Activity: SIMG_CFMENUOFDIVERFA
S_ALR_87007034	IMG Activity: SIMG_CMMENUOLSDFKM
S_ALR_87007035	IMG Activity: SIMG_CFMENUOFDITIVM1
S_ALR_87007036	IMG Activity: SIMG_CFMENUOLSDVK09
S_ALR_87007037	IMG Activity: SIMG_CFMENUOFDIFODK
S_ALR_87007038	IMG Activity: SIMG_CFMENUOLSDVK11
S_ALR_87007039	IMG Activity: SIMG_CFMENUOLSDVOK11
S_ALR_87007040	IMG Activity: SIMG_CFMENUOFDIFOEJ
S_ALR_87007041	IMG Activity: SIMG_CFMENUOLSDVOK15
S_ALR_87007042	IMG Activity: SIMG_CFMENUOFDITIVM3
S_ALR_87007043	IMG Activity: SIMG_CFMENUOLSDOV66
S_ALR_87007044	IMG Activity: SIMG_CFMENUOLSDWIASZ
S_ALR_87007045	IMG Activity: SIMG_CFMENUOFDIOKO7
S_ALR_87007046	IMG Activity: SIMG_CFMENUOLSDOV65
S_ALR_87007047	IMG Activity: SIMG_CFMENUOFDIFO5V
S_ALR_87007048	IMG Activity: SIMG_CFMENUOLSDOV68
S_ALR_87007049	IMG Activity: SIMG_CFMENUOFDIFO79
S_ALR_87007050	IMG Activity: SIMG_CFMENUOLSDWIAFR
S_ALR_87007051	IMG Activity: SIMG_CMMENUOFDIALTMV
S_ALR_87007052	IMG Activity: SIMF_CFMENUOFDIALTME
S_ALR_87007053	IMG Activity: SIMG_CFMENUOFDIALTDT
S_ALR_87007054	IMG Activity: SIMG_CFMENUOLSDOV62
S_ALR_87007055	IMG Activity: SIMG_CFMENUOFDIFVOI
S_ALR_87007056	IMG Activity: SIMG_CFMENUOLSDOV60
S_ALR_87007057	IMG Activity: SIMG_CFMENUOLSDWIAME
S_ALR_87007058	IMG Activity: SIMG_CFMENUOFDIFVVD
S_ALR_87007059	IMG Activity: SIMG_CFMENUOLSDOV67
S_ALR_87007060	IMG Activity: SIMG_CFMENUOFDIFVVC
S_ALR_87007061	IMG Activity: SIMG_CFMENUOFDIFVVB
S_ALR_87007062	IMG Activity: SIMG_CFMENUOFDIFVIR
S_ALR_87007063	IMG Activity: SIMG_CFMENUOFDIFVIQ

S_ALR_87007064	IMG Activity: SIMG_CFMENUOFDIFZ55
S_ALR_87007065	IMG Activity: SIMG_CFMENUOFDIFZ35
S_ALR_87007066	IMG Activity: SIMG_CFMENUOFDIFZ33
S_ALR_87007067	IMG Activity: SIMG_CFMENUOFDIFZ34
S_ALR_87007068	IMG Activity: SIMG_CFMENUOFDIFZ32
S_ALR_87007069	IMG Activity: SIMG_CFMENUOLSDVOVR
S_ALR_87007070	IMG Activity: SIMG_CFMENUOLSDVOVO
S_ALR_87007071	IMG Activity: SIMG_CFMENUOFDIFZ66
S_ALR_87007072	IMG Activity: SIMG_CFMENUOLSDVOVP
S_ALR_87007073	IMG Activity: SIMG_CFMENUOFDIFZBN
S_ALR_87007074	IMG Activity: SIMG_CFMENUOLSDVOVQ
S_ALR_87007075	IMG Activity: SIMG_CFMENUOFDIFZ77
S_ALR_87007076	IMG Activity: SIMG_CFMENUOLSDVOVM
S_ALR_87007077	IMG Activity: SIMG_CFMENUOFDIFZ64
S_ALR_87007078	IMG Activity: SIMG_CFMENUOLSDVOVL
S_ALR_87007079	IMG Activity: SIMG_CFMENUOFDIFZ84
S_ALR_87007080	IMG Activity: SIMG_CFMENUOLSDVOVN
S_ALR_87007081	IMG Activity: SIMG_CFMENUOFDIFZ68
S_ALR_87007082	IMG Activity: SIMG_CFMENUOLSDOVAIX
S_ALR_87007083	IMG Activity: SIMG_CMMENUOLSDXWSN1
S_ALR_87007084	IMG Activity: SIMG_CFMENUOLSDPFTC
S_ALR_87007085	IMG Activity: SIMG_CFMENUOFDINUMM
S_ALR_87007086	IMG Activity: SIMG_CFMENUOLSDXVOV8
S_ALR_87007087	IMG Activity: SIMG_CFMENUOFDINART
S_ALR_87007088	IMG Activity: SIMG_CFMENUOLSDXVOV7
S_ALR_87007089	IMG Activity: SIMG_CFMENUOLSDXOVAW
S_ALR_87007090	IMG Activity: SIMG_CFMENUOFDIVERTR
S_ALR_87007091	IMG Activity: SIMG_CFMENUOLSDXVOV4
S_ALR_87007092	IMG Activity: SIMG_CFMENUOFDIGSART
S_ALR_87007093	IMG Activity: SIMG_CFMENUOLSDXV/06
S_ALR_87007094	IMG Activity: SIMG_CFMENUOFDIRECHT
S_ALR_87007095	IMG Activity: SIMG_CFMENUOFDIFELD
S_ALR_87007096	IMG Activity: SIMG_CFMENUOFIDTIVAR
S_ALR_87007097	IMG Activity: SIMG_CFMENUOLSDXVTAA
S_ALR_87007098	IMG Activity: SIMG_CFMENUOFDITTXIN
S_ALR_87007099	IMG Activity: SIMG_CFMENUOFDIFOLT
S_ALR_87007100	IMG Activity: SIMG_CFMENUOFDIFOLS
S_ALR_87007101	IMG Activity: SIMG_CFMENUOLSDOVA9X
S_ALR_87007102	IMG Activity: SIMG_CFMENUOFDIFLACH
S_ALR_87007103	IMG Activity: SIMG_CFMENUOFDIVAL
S_ALR_87007104	IMG Activity: SIMG_CMMENUOLSDVB
S_ALR_87007105	IMG Activity: SIMG_CFMENUOLSDVDF1
S_ALR_87007106	IMG Activity: SIMG_CFMENUOLSDVOKF
S_ALR_87007107	IMG Activity: W_DF_VK_0330
S_ALR_87007108	IMG Activity: W_DF_VK_0320
S_ALR_87007109	IMG Activity: SIMG_CFMENUOLSDLIEF
S_ALR_87007110	IMG Activity: SIMG_CFMENUOLSDOVAJX
S_ALR_87007111	IMG Activity: SIMG_CFMENUOLSDOVD0X
S_ALR_87007112	IMG Activity: SIMG_CFMENUOLSDOVD1X
S_ALR_87007113	IMG Activity: SIMG_CFMENUOLSDOVAB
S_ALR_87007114	IMG Activity: SIMG_CFMENUOLSDVOZP
S_ALR_87007115	IMG Activity: SIMG_CFMENUOLSDOVAS
S_ALR_87007116	IMG Activity: SIMG_CFMENUOLSDOVAH
S_ALR_87007117	IMG Activity: SIMG_CFMENUOLSDBS02

S_ALR_87007118	IMG Activity: SIMG_CFMENUOLSDOVSB
S_ALR_87007119	IMG Activity: OSD5_ODP1
S_ALR_87007120	IMG Activity: SIMG_CFMENUOLSDVOV4
S_ALR_87007121	IMG Activity: SIMG_CFMENUOLSDOVAG
S_ALR_87007122	IMG Activity: SIMG_CFMENUOLSDOVAZ
S_ALR_87007123	IMG Activity: SIMG_CFMENUOLSDOVV6
S_ALR_87007124	IMG Activity: SIMG_CFMENUOLSDOVA4
S_ALR_87007125	IMG Activity: SIMG_CFMENUOLSDOVAU
S_ALR_87007126	IMG Activity: SIMG_CFMENUOFDIPRUEF
S_ALR_87007127	IMG Activity: SIMG_CFMENUOLSDVOV5
S_ALR_87007128	IMG Activity: SIMG_CFMENUOFDIHEIZ
S_ALR_87007129	IMG Activity: SIMG_CFMENUOLSDVOVA
S_ALR_87007130	IMG Activity: SIMG_CFMENUOLSDVORB
S_ALR_87007131	IMG Activity: SIMG_CFMENUOFDINUMMP
S_ALR_87007132	IMG Activity: SIMG_CFMENUOLSDVORS
S_ALR_87007133	IMG Activity: SIMG_CFMENUOFDISUB
S_ALR_87007134	IMG Activity: SIMG_CFMENUOLSDOVAW
S_ALR_87007135	IMG Activity: SIMG_CFMENUOLSDVOV7
S_ALR_87007136	IMG Activity: SIMG_CFMENUOLSDSWE2
S_ALR_87007137	IMG Activity: SIMG_CFMENUOFDIFOBK
S_ALR_87007138	IMG Activity: SIMG_CFMENUOLSDVN01
S_ALR_87007139	IMG Activity: SIMG_CFMENUOFDIMANDT
S_ALR_87007140	IMG Activity: SIMG_CFMENUOLSDOVA3
S_ALR_87007141	IMG Activity: SIMG_CFMENUOFDIBKCOP
S_ALR_87007142	IMG Activity: SIMG_CFMENUOLSDVORP
S_ALR_87007143	IMG Activity: SIMG_CFMENUOLSDVORV
S_ALR_87007144	IMG Activity: SIMG_CFMENUOLMBCHNUM
S_ALR_87007145	IMG Activity: SIMG_CFMENUOFDIBTE
S_ALR_87007146	IMG Activity: SIMG_CFMENUOLSDVOV8
S_ALR_87007147	IMG Activity: SIMG_CFMENUOFDIBELEI
S_ALR_87007148	IMG Activity: SIMG_CFMENUOFIDVERK2
S_ALR_87007149	IMG Activity: SIMG_CFMENUOCHAXD001
S_ALR_87007150	IMG Activity: SIMG_CFMENUOFDIFOEC
S_ALR_87007151	IMG Activity: SIMG_CFMENUOLSDOVVW
S_ALR_87007152	IMG Activity: SIMG_CFMENUOCHASYSM
S_ALR_87007153	IMG Activity: SIMG_CFMENUOFDIFOEN
S_ALR_87007154	IMG Activity: SIMG_CFMENUOFDIFOEO
S_ALR_87007155	IMG Activity: SIMG_CFMENUOFDIFOBR
S_ALR_87007156	IMG Activity: SIMG_CFMENUOFDIFOB3
S_ALR_87007157	IMG Activity: SIMG_CFMENUOFDIFOC8
S_ALR_87007158	IMG Activity: SIMG_CFMENUOFDI26A
S_ALR_87007159	IMG Activity: SIMG_CFMENUOFDIFOBP
S_ALR_87007160	IMG Activity: SIMG_CFMENUOFDIFOBQ
S_ALR_87007161	IMG Activity: SIMG_CFMENUOFDIFOCR
S_ALR_87007162	IMG Activity: SIMG_CFMENUOFDIVVFEL
S_ALR_87007163	IMG Activity: SIMG_CFMENUOFDINUMM3
S_ALR_87007164	IMG Activity: SIMG_CFMENUOFDIKO8N
S_ALR_87007165	IMG Activity: SIMG_OFDILPR_CJ8VABR
S_ALR_87007166	IMG Activity: SIMG_CFMENUOFDIFOEB
S_ALR_87007167	IMG Activity: SIMG_CFMENUOFDIIV95
S_ALR_87007168	IMG Activity: SIMG_CFMENUOFDIIV96
S_ALR_87007169	IMG Activity: SIMG_CFMENUOFDIIV94
S_ALR_87007170	IMG Activity: SIMG_CFMENUOFDITIVC7
S_ALR_87007171	IMG Activity: SIMG_CFMENUOFDIFOEE

S_ALR_87007172	IMG Activity: SIMG_CFMENUOFDIRECH3
S_ALR_87007173	IMG Activity: SIMG_CFMENUOFDI_JBWT
S_ALR_87007174	IMG Activity: SIMG_CFMENUOFDIRECH2
S_ALR_87007175	IMG Activity: SIMG_CFMENUOFDIRECH1
S_ALR_87007176	IMG Activity: SIMG_CFMENUOFDILISMV
S_ALR_87007177	IMG Activity: SIMG_CFMENUOFDIJBWW
S_ALR_87007178	IMG Activity: SIMG_CFMENUOFDIFZID
S_ALR_87007179	IMG Activity: SIMG_OFDIBERICHTSBAU
S_ALR_87007180	IMG Activity: SIMG_CFMENUOFDIFO4W
S_ALR_87007181	IMG Activity: SIMG_CFMENUOFDIRECH5
S_ALR_87007182	IMG Activity: SIMG_CFMENUOFDIRECH4
S_ALR_87007183	IMG Activity: SIMG_CFMENUOFDISTAID
S_ALR_87007184	IMG Activity: SIMG_CFMENUOFDIBBKON
S_ALR_87007185	IMG Activity: SIMG_CFMENUOFDIBERRI
S_ALR_87007186	IMG Activity: W_STW_WE_0005
S_ALR_87007187	IMG Activity: SIMG_CFMENUOFDIFO4O
S_ALR_87007188	IMG Activity: W_STW_WE_0006
S_ALR_87007189	IMG Activity: SIMG_CFMENUOFDILISME
S_ALR_87007190	IMG Activity: W_STW_WE_0007
S_ALR_87007191	IMG Activity: SIMG_CFMENUOFDILISGB
S_ALR_87007192	IMG Activity: W_ZF_VK_0130
S_ALR_87007193	IMG Activity: W_STW_WE_0016
S_ALR_87007194	IMG Activity: W_ZF_VK_0109
S_ALR_87007195	IMG Activity: SIMG_CFMENUOFDILISGR
S_ALR_87007196	IMG Activity: W_STW_SL_0001
S_ALR_87007197	IMG Activity: SIMG_CFMENUOLSDVVCB
S_ALR_87007198	IMG Activity: W_ZF_VK_0106
S_ALR_87007199	IMG Activity: SIMG_CFMENUOFDILISWE
S_ALR_87007200	IMG Activity: W_STW_WE_0002
S_ALR_87007201	IMG Activity: SIMG_CMMENUOLSDVBX3
S_ALR_87007202	IMG Activity: W_DF_EK_0155
S_ALR_87007203	IMG Activity: W_STW_WE_0003
S_ALR_87007204	IMG Activity: SIMG_CFMENUOFDIFO4A
S_ALR_87007205	IMG Activity: W_DF_EK_0160
S_ALR_87007206	IMG Activity: W_STW_KA_0001
S_ALR_87007207	IMG Activity: W_DF_EK_0151
S_ALR_87007208	IMG Activity: W_STW_PK_0000
S_ALR_87007209	IMG Activity: SIMG_CFMENUOFDIKUEN1
S_ALR_87007210	IMG Activity: W_STW_IN_0000
S_ALR_87007211	IMG Activity: W_DF_EK_0153
S_ALR_87007212	IMG Activity: W_STW_HA_0000
S_ALR_87007213	IMG Activity: SIMG_CFMENUOFDIFODT
S_ALR_87007214	IMG Activity: W_STW_AU_0000
S_ALR_87007215	IMG Activity: W_ZF_VK_0140
S_ALR_87007216	IMG Activity: SIMG_CFMENUOFDITIVG1
S_ALR_87007217	IMG Activity: W_ZF_VK_0105
S_ALR_87007218	IMG Activity: W_ZF_VK_0111
S_ALR_87007219	IMG Activity: SIMG_CFMENUOFDITIVG2
S_ALR_87007220	IMG Activity: W_ZF_VK_0110
S_ALR_87007221	IMG Activity: W_ZF_VK_0120
S_ALR_87007222	IMG Activity: W_ZF_VK_0150
S_ALR_87007223	IMG Activity: SIMG_CFMENUOLSDOVCD
S_ALR_87007224	IMG Activity: SIMG_CFMENUOFDITIV56
S_ALR_87007225	IMG Activity: SIMG_CFMENUOLSDOVCB

S_ALR_87007226	IMG Activity: SIMG_CFMENUOLSDOVCC
S_ALR_87007227	IMG Activity: SIMG_CFMENUOLSDOVCE
S_ALR_87007228	IMG Activity: SIMG_CFMENUOLSDOVCW
S_ALR_87007229	IMG Activity: SIMG_CFMENUOLSDOVCM
S_ALR_87007230	IMG Activity: SIMG_CFMENUOLSDVN05
S_ALR_87007231	IMG Activity: SIMG_CFMENUOLSDOVCK
S_ALR_87007232	IMG Activity: SIMG_CFMENUOLSDMY11
S_ALR_87007233	IMG Activity: SIMG_CFMENUOLSDOVC3
S_ALR_87007234	IMG Activity: SIMG_CFMENUOLSDOVC2
S_ALR_87007235	IMG Activity: SIMG_CFMENUOLSDVK01
S_ALR_87007236	IMG Activity: SIMG_CFMENUOFDITIV57
S_ALR_87007237	IMG Activity: SIMG_CFMENUOLSDOVC4
S_ALR_87007238	IMG Activity: SIMG_CFMENUOLSDOVC1
S_ALR_87007239	IMG Activity: SIMG_CMMENUOLSDPOTA
S_ALR_87007240	IMG Activity: SIMG_CFMENUOFDITIV58
S_ALR_87007241	IMG Activity: SIMG_CFMENUOFDITIV59
S_ALR_87007242	IMG Activity: SIMG_CFMENUOFDITIVB3
S_ALR_87007243	IMG Activity: PPPI_PO_3561
S_ALR_87007244	IMG Activity: SIMG_CFMENUOFDIOAA
S_ALR_87007245	IMG Activity: PPPI_PO_355
S_ALR_87007246	IMG Activity: SIMG_CFMENUOFDIOBJME
S_ALR_87007247	IMG Activity: PPPI_PO_354
S_ALR_87007248	IMG Activity: SIMG_CFMENUOFDIUNO
S_ALR_87007249	IMG Activity: PPPI_PO_352
S_ALR_87007250	IMG Activity: SIMG_OFDICFMENUFOO8
S_ALR_87007251	IMG Activity: PPPI_PO_351
S_ALR_87007252	IMG Activity: SIMG_CFMENUOFDIFIBF
S_ALR_87007253	IMG Activity: PPPI_PO_3562
S_ALR_87007254	IMG Activity: SIMG_CFMENUOFIDADRES
S_ALR_87007255	IMG Activity: PPPI_PO_372
S_ALR_87007256	IMG Activity: SIMG_CFMENUOFDIOG
S_ALR_87007257	IMG Activity: PPPI_PO_377
S_ALR_87007258	IMG Activity: SIMG_CFMENUOFTDOT47
S_ALR_87007259	IMG Activity: PPPI_PO_376
S_ALR_87007260	IMG Activity: SIMG_CFMENUOFDIFOWE
S_ALR_87007261	IMG Activity: SIMG_CFMENUOFTDOT23
S_ALR_87007262	IMG Activity: PPPI_PO_378
S_ALR_87007263	IMG Activity: SIMG_CFMENUOFDITIVC4
S_ALR_87007264	IMG Activity: SIMG_CFMENUOFTDOT48
S_ALR_87007265	IMG Activity: PPPI_PO_371
S_ALR_87007266	IMG Activity: SIMG_CFMENUOFDIFOCF
S_ALR_87007267	IMG Activity: SIMG_CFMENUOFTDOBXR
S_ALR_87007268	IMG Activity: PPPI_PO_348
S_ALR_87007269	IMG Activity: SIMG_CFMENUOFTDOBYN
S_ALR_87007270	IMG Activity: SIMG_CFMENUOFDIFOME2
S_ALR_87007271	IMG Activity: SIMG_CFMENUOFTDOT21
S_ALR_87007272	IMG Activity: PPPI_PO_341
S_ALR_87007273	IMG Activity: SIMG_CFMENUOFDIFOME3
S_ALR_87007274	IMG Activity: SIMG_CFMENUOFTDOT17
S_ALR_87007275	IMG Activity: PPPI_PO_334
S_ALR_87007276	IMG Activity: SIMG_CFMENUOFDITILG1
S_ALR_87007277	IMG Activity: PPPI_PO_333
S_ALR_87007278	IMG Activity: SIMG_CFMENUOFTDOT18
S_ALR_87007279	IMG Activity: SIMG_CFMENUOFDITIVC6

S_ALR_87007280	IMG Activity: SIMG_CFMENUOFTDOT19
S_ALR_87007281	IMG Activity: PPPI_PO_332
S_ALR_87007282	IMG Activity: SIMG_CFMENUOFDIFODP
S_ALR_87007283	IMG Activity: SIMG_CFMENUOFTDOT22
S_ALR_87007284	IMG Activity: PPPI_PO_342
S_ALR_87007285	IMG Activity: SIMG_CFMENUOFDIOK02
S_ALR_87007286	IMG Activity: SIMG_CFMENUOFTDOT20
S_ALR_87007287	IMG Activity: PPPI_PO_349
S_ALR_87007288	IMG Activity: SIMG_CFMENUOFDIBEREG
S_ALR_87007289	IMG Activity: SIMG_CFMENUOLSDVB(5
S_ALR_87007290	IMG Activity: SIMG_CFMENUOFTDOBXY
S_ALR_87007291	IMG Activity: PPPI_PO_347
S_ALR_87007292	IMG Activity: SIMG_CFMENUOLSDVB(4
S_ALR_87007293	IMG Activity: SIMG_CFMENUOFTDOT38
S_ALR_87007294	IMG Activity: PPPI_PO_3442
S_ALR_87007295	IMG Activity: SIMG_CFMENUOFDITIV83
S_ALR_87007296	IMG Activity: SIMG_CFMENUOFTDOT24
S_ALR_87007297	IMG Activity: SIMG_CFMENUOLSDVB(3
S_ALR_87007298	IMG Activity: PPPI_PO_3441
S_ALR_87007299	IMG Activity: SIMG_CFMENUOFDITIV5A
S_ALR_87007300	IMG Activity: SIMG_CFMENUOFTDOT27
S_ALR_87007301	IMG Activity: PPPI_PO_343
S_ALR_87007302	IMG Activity: SIMG_CFMENUOLSDVB(2
S_ALR_87007303	IMG Activity: SIMG_CFMENUOFTDOTZ2
S_ALR_87007304	IMG Activity: SIMG_CFMENUOFDITIV00
S_ALR_87007305	IMG Activity: PPPI_PO_373
S_ALR_87007306	IMG Activity: SIMG_CFMENUOLSDBD
S_ALR_87007307	IMG Activity: PPPI_PF_300
S_ALR_87007308	IMG Activity: COCB420
S_ALR_87007309	IMG Activity: SIMG_CFMENUOFTDOTZ3
S_ALR_87007310	IMG Activity: SIMG_CFMENUOFDIFOCA
S_ALR_87007311	IMG Activity: SIMG_CFMENUSAPCOX18
S_ALR_87007312	IMG Activity: PPPI_PO_630
S_ALR_87007313	IMG Activity: PPPI_PF_100
S_ALR_87007314	IMG Activity: COCB440
S_ALR_87007315	IMG Activity: SIMG_CFMENUOFTDOT39
S_ALR_87007316	IMG Activity: SIMG_CFMENUOLSDBONU7
S_ALR_87007317	IMG Activity: SIMG_CFMENUSAPCOMJ7
S_ALR_87007318	IMG Activity: TRMV
S_ALR_87007319	IMG Activity: PPPI_PF_220
S_ALR_87007320	IMG Activity: PPPI_PO_620
S_ALR_87007321	IMG Activity: COCB433-54
S_ALR_87007322	IMG Activity: SIMG_CFMENUOFTDOT29
S_ALR_87007323	IMG Activity: SIMG_CFMENUOFDIFZV5
S_ALR_87007324	IMG Activity: PPPI_PF_210
S_ALR_87007325	IMG Activity: VARIANTENGRP_REORG
S_ALR_87007326	IMG Activity: SIMG_CFMENUSAPCOMJM
S_ALR_87007327	IMG Activity: SIMG_CFMENUOLSDBONU3
S_ALR_87007328	IMG Activity: COCB436-4
S_ALR_87007329	IMG Activity: PPPI_PO_521
S_ALR_87007330	IMG Activity: SIMG_CFMENUOFTDOBYR
S_ALR_87007331	IMG Activity: SIMG_SAPZOZCG
S_ALR_87007332	IMG Activity: SIMG_CFMENUSAPCOVX3
S_ALR_87007333	IMG Activity: AUTOERMITTLUNG_DE

S_ALR_87007334	IMG Activity: VARIANTGRUPPEN_EINPL
S_ALR_87007335	IMG Activity: SIMG_CFMENUOFDIFOME
S_ALR_87007336	IMG Activity: COCB431
S_ALR_87007337	IMG Activity: PPPI_PO_440
S_ALR_87007338	IMG Activity: SIMG_CFMENUSAPCOVXK
S_ALR_87007339	IMG Activity: SIMG_CFMENUOLSDOVBB
S_ALR_87007341	IMG Activity: KONTREF_DEF_DE
S_ALR_87007342	IMG Activity: SIMG_CFMENUOFTDOBYM
S_ALR_87007343	IMG Activity: VARIANTGRUPPEN_PFLEG
S_ALR_87007344	IMG Activity: COCB432
S_ALR_87007345	IMG Activity: SIMG_CFMENUOFDIFOCM
S_ALR_87007346	IMG Activity: SIMG_CFMENUSAPCOVXA
S_ALR_87007347	IMG Activity: PPPI_PO_436
S_ALR_87007348	IMG Activity: SIMG_SAPZOZBP
S_ALR_87007349	IMG Activity: SIMG_CFMENUOLSDUEB02
S_ALR_87007350	IMG Activity: NUMMERNKR_BUCH_BELEG
S_ALR_87007351	IMG Activity: SIMG_CFMENUOFTDOBXT
S_ALR_87007352	IMG Activity: VARIGRUPPEN_DEFINIER
S_ALR_87007353	IMG Activity: BRIEFANREDE_GP_I
S_ALR_87007354	IMG Activity: SIMG_CFMENUSAPCOVXG
S_ALR_87007355	IMG Activity: PPPI_PO_810
S_ALR_87007356	IMG Activity: SIMG_SAPZOZAP
S_ALR_87007357	IMG Activity: BEWEGUNGSARTEN_ZUORD
S_ALR_87007358	IMG Activity: SIMG_CFMENUOLSDVB(1
S_ALR_87007359	IMG Activity: CM_ZA
S_ALR_87007360	IMG Activity: VARIANTEN_DEFINIEREN
S_ALR_87007361	IMG Activity: ANSCHRIFTSKENN_GP_I
S_ALR_87007362	IMG Activity: SIMG_CFMENUSAPCKEKK
S_ALR_87007363	IMG Activity: PPPI_PO_122
S_ALR_87007364	IMG Activity: BEWEGUNGSARTEN_DEF
S_ALR_87007365	IMG Activity: TRMY
S_ALR_87007366	IMG Activity: RFTREY60
S_ALR_87007367	IMG Activity: SIMG_CFMENUSAPCOIX0
S_ALR_87007368	IMG Activity: SIMG_CFMENUOLSDLIST
S_ALR_87007369	IMG Activity: RECHTSFORM_GP_I
S_ALR_87007370	IMG Activity: TRMT
S_ALR_87007371	IMG Activity: TELEFAXOPTIONEN_DE
S_ALR_87007372	IMG Activity: V_T243D
S_ALR_87007373	IMG Activity: PPPI_PO_121
S_ALR_87007374	IMG Activity: SIMG_CFMENUSAPCOX16
S_ALR_87007375	IMG Activity: SIMG_CFMENUOLSDOV85
S_ALR_87007376	IMG Activity: SF07
S_ALR_87007377	IMG Activity: DRUCKEROPTIONEN_DE
S_ALR_87007378	IMG Activity: SIMG_CFMENUOFTDOT10
S_ALR_87007379	IMG Activity: SIMG_CFMENUSAPCOB38
S_ALR_87007380	IMG Activity: PPPI_PO_910
S_ALR_87007381	IMG Activity: FAMILIENSTAND_GP_I
S_ALR_87007382	IMG Activity: SF01
S_ALR_87007383	IMG Activity: SIMG_CFMENUOLSDOV84
S_ALR_87007384	IMG Activity: FORMULARE_DE
S_ALR_87007385	IMG Activity: SIMG_CFMENUSAPCOBB6
S_ALR_87007386	IMG Activity: SIMG_CFMENUOFTDOT06
S_ALR_87007387	IMG Activity: TRMG
S_ALR_87007388	IMG Activity: PPPI_PO_820

S_ALR_87007389	IMG Activity: GART_KONDART_DE
S_ALR_87007390	IMG Activity: SIMG_CFMENUSAPCOF18
S_ALR_87007391	IMG Activity: SIMG_CFMENUOLSDOV81
S_ALR_87007392	IMG Activity: SIMG_CFMENUOFTDOT07
S_ALR_87007393	IMG Activity: BERICHTSAUSWAHL_DE
S_ALR_87007394	IMG Activity: OKUL
S_ALR_87007395	IMG Activity: PPPI_PO_815
S_ALR_87007396	IMG Activity: SIMG_CFMENUSAPCOFC11
S_ALR_87007397	IMG Activity: SIMG_CFMENUOFTDOT12
S_ALR_87007398	IMG Activity: MITARBEITERGRUP_GP_I
S_ALR_87007399	IMG Activity: TRDE_ZAHLUNGSAVISE
S_ALR_87007400	IMG Activity: TRMK
S_ALR_87007401	IMG Activity: SIMG_CFMENUSAPCOX19
S_ALR_87007402	IMG Activity: PPPI_PO_420
S_ALR_87007403	IMG Activity: TRCM_BERAUSWAHL
S_ALR_87007404	IMG Activity: UMBUCHUNG_DE
S_ALR_87007405	IMG Activity: TRMW
S_ALR_87007406	IMG Activity: SIMG_CFMENUSAPCOX17
S_ALR_87007407	IMG Activity: PPPI_PO_410
S_ALR_87007408	IMG Activity: ABGRENZUNG_DE
S_ALR_87007409	IMG Activity: SIMG_CFMENUOFTDOT01
S_ALR_87007410	IMG Activity: SIMG_CFMENUSAPCOMKI
S_ALR_87007411	IMG Activity: TR_IMG_KURST_WAEHRG
S_ALR_87007412	IMG Activity: SIMG_CFMENUOFDIFOO9
S_ALR_87007413	IMG Activity: SIMG_CFMENUOLSDOV83
S_ALR_87007414	IMG Activity: BEWERTG_DE
S_ALR_87007415	IMG Activity: SIMG_CFMENUSAPCOMKJ
S_ALR_87007416	IMG Activity: PPPI_PO_390
S_ALR_87007417	IMG Activity: SIMG_CFMENUOFTDOT05
S_ALR_87007418	IMG Activity: TRM1
S_ALR_87007419	IMG Activity: SIMG_SAPCOML2
S_ALR_87007420	IMG Activity: SIMG_CMMENUOFDIFB01
S_ALR_87007421	IMG Activity: TRDE_BEWBEW
S_ALR_87007422	IMG Activity: SIMG_CFMENUOLSDOVGD
S_ALR_87007423	IMG Activity: TRMR
S_ALR_87007424	IMG Activity: SIMG_CFMENUOFTDOT37
S_ALR_87007425	IMG Activity: PPPI_PO_383
S_ALR_87007426	IMG Activity: SIMG_CFMENUSAPCOVXC
S_ALR_87007427	IMG Activity: MARGINVERWALTUNG_DEF
S_ALR_87007428	IMG Activity: TRMZ
S_ALR_87007429	IMG Activity: SIMG_CFMENUOFDIPM
S_ALR_87007430	IMG Activity: SIMG_CFMENUOFTDOT32
S_ALR_87007431	IMG Activity: SIMG_CFMENUOLSDOCR4
S_ALR_87007432	IMG Activity: PPPI_PO_374
S_ALR_87007433	IMG Activity: SIMG_CFMENUSAPCOIX1
S_ALR_87007434	IMG Activity: TRMP
S_ALR_87007435	IMG Activity: SIMG_CFMENUOFDITIV03
S_ALR_87007436	IMG Activity: SIMG_CFMENUOFTDOT14
S_ALR_87007437	IMG Activity: SIMG_CFMENUSAPCOVX8
S_ALR_87007438	IMG Activity: PPPI_PO_425
S_ALR_87007439	IMG Activity: DEFINITION_DE
S_ALR_87007440	IMG Activity: SIMG_CFMENUOLSDMERCH
S_ALR_87007441	IMG Activity: TRM5
S_ALR_87007442	IMG Activity: SIMG_CFMENUOFDIAM02

S_ALR_87007443	IMG Activity: SIMG_CFMENUSAPCOX01
S_ALR_87007444	IMG Activity: BEWEGUNGSARTEN_DE
S_ALR_87007445	IMG Activity: TRM4
S_ALR_87007446	IMG Activity: SIMG_CFMENUOFTDOT13
S_ALR_87007447	IMG Activity: PPPI_PO_435
S_ALR_87007448	IMG Activity: SIMG_CFMENUOLSDOVFF1
S_ALR_87007449	IMG Activity: ANREDE_GP_I
S_ALR_87007450	IMG Activity: SIMG_CFMENUSAPCOVXM
S_ALR_87007451	IMG Activity: COCB340
S_ALR_87007452	IMG Activity: V_T243B
S_ALR_87007453	IMG Activity: TRM2
S_ALR_87007454	IMG Activity: PPPI_PO_434
S_ALR_87007455	IMG Activity: SIMG_CFMENUOLSDOV87
S_ALR_87007456	IMG Activity: SIMG_CFMENUSAPCOVXJ
S_ALR_87007457	IMG Activity: SIMG_CFMENUOFDIPAPA
S_ALR_87007458	IMG Activity: GART_DEFINITION_DE
S_ALR_87007459	IMG Activity: COCB350
S_ALR_87007460	IMG Activity: TRTM-OBJEKT
S_ALR_87007461	IMG Activity: SIMG_CFMENUOFTDOT16
S_ALR_87007462	IMG Activity: PPPI_PO_433
S_ALR_87007463	IMG Activity: SIMG_CFMENUSAPCOVX6
S_ALR_87007464	IMG Activity: PR_NUMMERNKREIS_DE
S_ALR_87007465	IMG Activity: TRMQ
S_ALR_87007466	IMG Activity: SIMG_CFMENUOLSDOV86
S_ALR_87007467	IMG Activity: COCB411
S_ALR_87007468	IMG Activity: V_T243A
S_ALR_87007469	IMG Activity: SIMG_CFMENUSAPOVFL
S_ALR_87007470	IMG Activity: ROLLENART_GP_I
S_ALR_87007471	IMG Activity: PPPI_PO_432
S_ALR_87007472	IMG Activity: NUMKR_GATT_OPTFUT
S_ALR_87007473	IMG Activity: TRMX
S_ALR_87007474	IMG Activity: COCB412
S_ALR_87007475	IMG Activity: SIMG_CMMENUOLSDBONU4
S_ALR_87007476	IMG Activity: SIMG_CFMENUOFTDOT11
S_ALR_87007477	IMG Activity: KONDITIONSARTEN_DE
S_ALR_87007478	IMG Activity: SIMG_CFMENUOFDI002_I
S_ALR_87007479	IMG Activity: TRMO
S_ALR_87007480	IMG Activity: PPPI_PO_431
S_ALR_87007481	IMG Activity: V_T243C
S_ALR_87007482	IMG Activity: COCB412-1
S_ALR_87007483	IMG Activity: SIMG_CFMENUOLSDOVBK
S_ALR_87007484	IMG Activity: PPPI_PO_225
S_ALR_87007485	IMG Activity: SIMG_CFMENUFNMAFZ96I
S_ALR_87007486	IMG Activity: COCB437
S_ALR_87007487	IMG Activity: PRODUKTARTEN_DE
S_ALR_87007488	IMG Activity: SIMG_CFMENUOFTDOT08
S_ALR_87007489	IMG Activity: ROLLE-SICHT-ZUORD_GI
S_ALR_87007490	IMG Activity: PPPI_PO_2242
S_ALR_87007491	IMG Activity: SIMG_CFMENUOLSDOVBP
S_ALR_87007492	IMG Activity: COCB610
S_ALR_87007493	IMG Activity: SIMG_CFMENUOLSDOVXT
S_ALR_87007494	IMG Activity: SIMG_CFMENUOFTDOT09
S_ALR_87007495	IMG Activity: SIMG_CFMENUOFDI103_I
S_ALR_87007496	IMG Activity: BEWEGUNGSART_DE

S_ALR_87007497	IMG Activity: TRCM_BA
S_ALR_87007498	IMG Activity: PPPI_PO_227
S_ALR_87007499	IMG Activity: SIMG_CFMENUOLSDOVBM
S_ALR_87007500	IMG Activity: SIMG_CFMENUSAPCKEP8
S_ALR_87007501	IMG Activity: COCB620
S_ALR_87007502	IMG Activity: SIMG_CFMENUOFDIMAHGP
S_ALR_87007503	IMG Activity: SIMG_CFMENUSAPCOX14
S_ALR_87007504	IMG Activity: COCB630
S_ALR_87007505	IMG Activity: SIMG_CFMENUOLSDOVBJ
S_ALR_87007506	IMG Activity: PPPI_PO_221
S_ALR_87007507	IMG Activity: SIMG_CFMENUSAPCOX10
S_ALR_87007508	IMG Activity: SIMG_CFMENUOFDIFOCL
S_ALR_87007509	IMG Activity: COCB111
S_ALR_87007510	IMG Activity: SIMG_CFMENUOLSDOVBN
S_ALR_87007511	IMG Activity: PPPI_PO_216
S_ALR_87007512	IMG Activity: BP_ZIELGRUPPE2_GP
S_ALR_87007513	IMG Activity: SAPC_STANDORT
S_ALR_87007514	IMG Activity: COCB112
S_ALR_87007515	IMG Activity: SIMG_CFMENUOLSDVOF2
S_ALR_87007516	IMG Activity: PPPI_PO_260
S_ALR_87007517	IMG Activity: SIMG_CFMENUOFDIBONIB
S_ALR_87007518	IMG Activity: SIMG_CFMENUSAPCOVXB
S_ALR_87007519	IMG Activity: COCB433
S_ALR_87007520	IMG Activity: PPPI_PO_360
S_ALR_87007521	IMG Activity: INSTITUT_GP_I
S_ALR_87007522	IMG Activity: PPPI_PO_232
S_ALR_87007523	IMG Activity: SIMG_CFMENUSAPCOVX5
S_ALR_87007524	IMG Activity: COCB434
S_ALR_87007525	IMG Activity: SIMG_CFMENUSAPCOVXI
S_ALR_87007526	IMG Activity: SIMG_CFMENUOFDIZUSGP
S_ALR_87007527	IMG Activity: SIMG_CFMENUSAPCOX06
S_ALR_87007528	IMG Activity: COCB435
S_ALR_87007529	IMG Activity: PPPI_PO_231
S_ALR_87007530	IMG Activity: SIMG_CFMENUSAPCOX15
S_ALR_87007531	IMG Activity: SIMG_CFMENUOFDINOTEI
S_ALR_87007532	IMG Activity: COCB436
S_ALR_87007533	IMG Activity: PPPI_PO_226
S_ALR_87007534	IMG Activity: SIMG_CFMENUSAPCOB45
S_ALR_87007535	IMG Activity: PHONETISCHE_SUCHE_RE
S_ALR_87007536	IMG Activity: PPPI_PO_217
S_ALR_87007537	IMG Activity: SIMG_CFMENUSAPCOX02
S_ALR_87007538	IMG Activity: COCB540
S_ALR_87007539	IMG Activity: SIMG_CFMENUOFDITPZ2I
S_ALR_87007540	IMG Activity: SIMG_CFMENUSAPCOX03
S_ALR_87007541	IMG Activity: PPPI_PO_2141
S_ALR_87007542	IMG Activity: COCB530
S_ALR_87007543	IMG Activity: SIMG_CFMENUOFIDBC15I
S_ALR_87007544	IMG Activity: SAPC-OKBD
S_ALR_87007545	IMG Activity: COCB520
S_ALR_87007546	IMG Activity: SIMG_CFMENUSAPCOCC1
S_ALR_87007547	IMG Activity: SIMG_CFMENUSAPCOF01
S_ALR_87007548	IMG Activity: SIMG_CFMENUOFDIFOO4
S_ALR_87007549	IMG Activity: SIMG_CFMENUSAPCOX09
S_ALR_87007550	IMG Activity: COCB510

S_ALR_87007551	IMG Activity: SIMG_CFMENUOFDINUMV
S_ALR_87007552	IMG Activity: SIMG_CFMENUSAPCOX08
S_ALR_87007553	IMG Activity: COCB553
S_ALR_87007554	IMG Activity: SIMG_CFMENUOLSDVOVPX
S_ALR_87007555	IMG Activity: SAPC_LGNUM
S_ALR_87007556	IMG Activity: SIMG_CFMENUOFDIFZC1
S_ALR_87007557	IMG Activity: COCB552
S_ALR_87007558	IMG Activity: SIMG_CFMENUOLSDOVBI
S_ALR_87007559	IMG Activity: SIMG_CFMENUSAPCOVXD
S_ALR_87007560	IMG Activity: COCB551
S_ALR_87007561	IMG Activity: PPPI_PO_211
S_ALR_87007562	IMG Activity: SIMG_CFMENUSAPCOVX7
S_ALR_87007563	IMG Activity: SIMG_CFMENUOLSDVOB3
S_ALR_87007564	IMG Activity: COCB642
S_ALR_87007565	IMG Activity: SIMG_CFMENUOFDIMIND
S_ALR_87007566	IMG Activity: SIMG_CFMENUSAPCOVX1
S_ALR_87007567	IMG Activity: PPPI_PO_113
S_ALR_87007568	IMG Activity: SIMG_CFMENUOLSDXXXB
S_ALR_87007569	IMG Activity: COCB641
S_ALR_87007570	IMG Activity: SIMG_CFMENUOFDITZK07
S_ALR_87007571	IMG Activity: SIMG_CFMENUSAPCOVX4
S_ALR_87007572	IMG Activity: PPPI_PO_112
S_ALR_87007573	IMG Activity: COCB332-1
S_ALR_87007574	IMG Activity: SIMG_CFMENUOLSDOVB3
S_ALR_87007575	IMG Activity: SIMG_CFMENUOFDIFZBC
S_ALR_87007576	IMG Activity: COCB310
S_ALR_87007577	IMG Activity: PPPI_PO_215
S_ALR_87007578	IMG Activity: SIMG_CFMENUOLSDBONU9
S_ALR_87007579	IMG Activity: SIMG_CFMENUOFDIBK01
S_ALR_87007580	IMG Activity: COCB310-11
S_ALR_87007581	IMG Activity: PPPI_PO_2145
S_ALR_87007582	IMG Activity: SIMG_CFMENUOLSDBONU6
S_ALR_87007583	IMG Activity: SIMG_CFMENUOFDITIVC8
S_ALR_87007584	IMG Activity: COCB310-12
S_ALR_87007585	IMG Activity: PPPI_PO_2144
S_ALR_87007586	IMG Activity: SIMG_CFMENUOLSDAUKRE
S_ALR_87007587	IMG Activity: SIMG_CFMENUOFDITIVC9
S_ALR_87007588	IMG Activity: COCB310-13
S_ALR_87007589	IMG Activity: PPPI_PO_2143
S_ALR_87007590	IMG Activity: SIMG_CFMENUOLSDOVVA
S_ALR_87007591	IMG Activity: SIMG_CFMENUOFDIFOCH
S_ALR_87007592	IMG Activity: COCB332
S_ALR_87007593	IMG Activity: PPPI_PO_2142
S_ALR_87007594	IMG Activity: SIMG_CFMENUOLSDOVV9
S_ALR_87007595	IMG Activity: SIMG_CFMENUOFDIFZCV
S_ALR_87007596	IMG Activity: COCB331
S_ALR_87007597	IMG Activity: PPPI_PO_312
S_ALR_87007598	IMG Activity: SIMG_CFMENUOLSDOVV8
S_ALR_87007599	IMG Activity: COCB554
S_ALR_87007600	IMG Activity: SIMG_CFMENUOFDIZPAIF
S_ALR_87007601	IMG Activity: PPPI_PO_313
S_ALR_87007602	IMG Activity: SIMG_CFMENUOLSDXXXA
S_ALR_87007603	IMG Activity: SIMG_CFMENUOFDIFZBF
S_ALR_87007604	IMG Activity: PPPI_PO_335

S_ALR_87007605	IMG Activity: SIMG_CFMENUOLSDOVPG
S_ALR_87007606	IMG Activity: SIMG_CFMENUOFDIT033E
S_ALR_87007607	IMG Activity: PPPI_PO_324
S_ALR_87007608	IMG Activity: J_1BTVAKU
S_ALR_87007609	IMG Activity: PPPI_PO_323
S_ALR_87007610	IMG Activity: J_1ABRANCH_DELIVERY
S_ALR_87007611	IMG Activity: PPPI_PO_321
S_ALR_87007612	IMG Activity: SIMG_CFMENUOFDINUMM1
S_ALR_87007613	IMG Activity: J_1ASALES_ORG_EXT
S_ALR_87007614	IMG Activity: PPPI_PO_322
S_ALR_87007615	IMG Activity: J_1AASSIGN_BR_SA
S_ALR_87007616	IMG Activity: SIMG_CFMENUOFDIWBS
S_ALR_87007617	IMG Activity: PPPI_PO_270
S_ALR_87007618	IMG Activity: SIMG_CFMENUOFDITIVC1
S_ALR_87007619	IMG Activity: SIMG_CFMENUOLSDMXLIN
S_ALR_87007620	IMG Activity: PPPI_PO_328
S_ALR_87007621	IMG Activity: J_1BSDKON0
S_ALR_87007622	IMG Activity: SIMG_CFMENUOFDITIVC2
S_ALR_87007623	IMG Activity: PPPI_PO_327
S_ALR_87007624	IMG Activity: J_1BSDFK
S_ALR_87007625	IMG Activity: SIMG_CFMENUOFDITIVC3
S_ALR_87007626	IMG Activity: PPPI_PO_331
S_ALR_87007627	IMG Activity: J_1BSDIC
S_ALR_87007628	IMG Activity: SIMG_CFMENUOFDIANMI2
S_ALR_87007630	IMG Activity: PPPI_PO_311
S_ALR_87007631	IMG Activity: SIMG_OE_EG_WL_0226
S_ALR_87007632	IMG Activity: W_ZF_ST_0730
S_ALR_87007633	IMG Activity: SIMG_CFMENUOFDIFOZA
S_ALR_87007634	IMG Activity: J_1BSDICA
S_ALR_87007635	IMG Activity: CF_OVPS_V_TDIEX
S_ALR_87007636	IMG Activity: W_ZF_ST_0720
S_ALR_87007637	IMG Activity: SIMG_CFMENUOFDIVERK1
S_ALR_87007638	IMG Activity: SIMG_OE_EG_WL_0225
S_ALR_87007639	IMG Activity: J_1BAUTO_NFTEXTS
S_ALR_87007640	IMG Activity: CF_OVPS_V_TDIM
S_ALR_87007641	IMG Activity: W_ZF_ST_0710
S_ALR_87007642	IMG Activity: SIMG_OE_EG_WL_0224
S_ALR_87007643	IMG Activity: CF_OVPS_V_TDIMT
S_ALR_87007644	IMG Activity: SIMG_CFMENUOLSDNARL
S_ALR_87007645	IMG Activity: W_ZF_ST_0740
S_ALR_87007646	IMG Activity: SIMG_CFMENUOFDITZR1
S_ALR_87007647	IMG Activity: W_OE_EG_WL_0227
S_ALR_87007648	IMG Activity: CF_OVPS_V_TDIMCT
S_ALR_87007649	IMG Activity: CFMENUOFDIANGEBOT
S_ALR_87007650	IMG Activity: W_OE_EG_WL_0228
S_ALR_87007651	IMG Activity: SIMG_CFMENUOLSDREKO
S_ALR_87007652	IMG Activity: CF_OVPS_V_TDICO
S_ALR_87007653	IMG Activity: W_OE_EG_WL_0112
S_ALR_87007654	IMG Activity: SIMG_CFMENUOLSDOVV7
S_ALR_87007655	IMG Activity: CF_OVPS_V_TDICOT
S_ALR_87007656	IMG Activity: SIMG_CFMENUOFDIANMI1
S_ALR_87007657	IMG Activity: W_OE_EG_WL_0111
S_ALR_87007658	IMG Activity: SIMGCFMENUOFDITIVC61
S_ALR_87007659	IMG Activity: CF_OVPS_V_TDIPR

S_ALR_87007660	IMG Activity: W_OE_EG_WL_0225
S_ALR_87007661	IMG Activity: SIMG_CFMENUOLSDVN01F
S_ALR_87007662	IMG Activity: SIMG_CFMENUOFDIFOCJ
S_ALR_87007663	IMG Activity: CF_OVPS_V_TDICT
S_ALR_87007664	IMG Activity: W_OE_EG_WL_0224
S_ALR_87007665	IMG Activity: SIMG_CFMENUOLSDVOFA
S_ALR_87007666	IMG Activity: SIMG_CFMENUOFDIKUEN2
S_ALR_87007667	IMG Activity: W_OE_EG_WL_0221
S_ALR_87007668	IMG Activity: CF_OVPS_ODI4
S_ALR_87007669	IMG Activity: SIMG_CFMENUOFDIKUEN3
S_ALR_87007670	IMG Activity: SIMG_CFMENUOLSDOVV3
S_ALR_87007671	IMG Activity: W_OE_EG_WL_0172
S_ALR_87007672	IMG Activity: CF_OVPS_ODI5
S_ALR_87007673	IMG Activity: W_OE_EG_WL_0120
S_ALR_87007674	IMG Activity: SIMG_CMMENUOLSDVBX2
S_ALR_87007675	IMG Activity: CF_OVPS_ODI6
S_ALR_87007676	IMG Activity: SIMG_CFMENUOFDIFO1R
S_ALR_87007677	IMG Activity: W_OE_EG_WL_0170
S_ALR_87007678	IMG Activity: SIMG_CFMENUOFDICO2
S_ALR_87007679	IMG Activity: SIMG_CFMENUOLSDOVVR
S_ALR_87007680	IMG Activity: CF_OVPS_V_TDIBP
S_ALR_87007681	IMG Activity: SIMG_CMMENUOFDIBWA5
S_ALR_87007682	IMG Activity: W_OE_EG_WL_0110
S_ALR_87007683	IMG Activity: SIMG_CFMEUNUOFDICASH
S_ALR_87007684	IMG Activity: CF_OVPS_V_TDIBPT
S_ALR_87007685	IMG Activity: SIMG_XXMENUOLSDOVV5
S_ALR_87007686	IMG Activity: SIMG_CFMENUOFDIFIAA
S_ALR_87007687	IMG Activity: W_OE_EG_WL_0160
S_ALR_87007688	IMG Activity: SIMG_CMMENUOFDIBWA2
S_ALR_87007689	IMG Activity: CF_OVPS_V_TDIEV
S_ALR_87007690	IMG Activity: SIMG_CMMENUOFDIBWA7
S_ALR_87007691	IMG Activity: SIMG_CFMENUOLSDVSAX
S_ALR_87007692	IMG Activity: W_OE_EG_WL_0175
S_ALR_87007693	IMG Activity: SIMG_CFMENUOFDICO1
S_ALR_87007694	IMG Activity: CF_OVPS_V_TDIC
S_ALR_87007695	IMG Activity: SIMG_CFMENUOFDIFI3
S_ALR_87007696	IMG Activity: W_OE_EG_WL_0173
S_ALR_87007697	IMG Activity: SIMG_CFMENUOLSDVLIC
S_ALR_87007698	IMG Activity: SIMG_CMMENUOFDIBWA8
S_ALR_87007699	IMG Activity: SIMG_CFMENUOVPSOD79
S_ALR_87007700	IMG Activity: SIMG_CMEMENUOFDIGRUN
S_ALR_87007701	IMG Activity: W_OE_EG_WL_0226
S_ALR_87007702	IMG Activity: SIMG_CMMENUOFDIUNTER
S_ALR_87007703	IMG Activity: SIMG_CFMENUOVPSOD77
S_ALR_87007704	IMG Activity: SIMG_CMMENUOFDIBWA3
S_ALR_87007705	IMG Activity: SIMG_CFMENUOLSDOVXZ1
S_ALR_87007707	IMG Activity: SIMG_CFMENUOFDITABAE
S_ALR_87007708	IMG Activity: SIMG_CFMENUOVPSOD80
S_ALR_87007709	IMG Activity: SIMG_CMMENUOFDIBWA4
S_ALR_87007710	IMG Activity: SIMG_CFMENUOLSDOVFD1
S_ALR_87007711	IMG Activity: SIMG_CFMENUOFDIFI2
S_ALR_87007712	IMG Activity: SIMG_CFMENUOVPSOD81
S_ALR_87007713	IMG Activity: SIMG_CFMENUOFDIFI1
S_ALR_87007715	IMG Activity: SIMG_CFMENUOVPSDT

S_ALR_87007716	IMG Activity: SIMG_CFMENUOFDIANPBE
S_ALR_87007717	IMG Activity: SIMG_CMMENUOFDIANUEB
S_ALR_87007718	IMG Activity: SIMG_CFMENUOLSDOVK2
S_ALR_87007719	IMG Activity: SIMG_CFMENUOVPSOD922
S_ALR_87007720	IMG Activity: SIMG_CFMENUOFDIOPTAR
S_ALR_87007721	IMG Activity: SIMG_CFMENUOFDIBEREC
S_ALR_87007722	IMG Activity: SIMG_CFMENUOLSDOVK1
S_ALR_87007723	IMG Activity: SIMG_CFMENUOVPSOD02
S_ALR_87007724	IMG Activity: SIMG_CFMENUOFIDCO3
S_ALR_87007725	IMG Activity: SIMG_CFMENUOFDIBK01P
S_ALR_87007726	IMG Activity: SIMG_CFMENUOVPSOD75
S_ALR_87007727	IMG Activity: SIMG_CFMENUOLSDOVZP
S_ALR_87007728	IMG Activity: SIMG_CFMENUOFDISOLL
S_ALR_87007729	IMG Activity: CF_OVPS_V_TDWI
S_ALR_87007730	IMG Activity: SIMG_CFMENUOFDIEIGNU
S_ALR_87007731	IMG Activity: SIMG_CFMENUOLSDOVAC
S_ALR_87007732	IMG Activity: CF_OVPS_V_TDWIU
S_ALR_87007733	IMG Activity: SIMG_CFMENUOFDILEERS
S_ALR_87007734	IMG Activity: SIMG_CFMENUOFDINACHB
S_ALR_87007735	IMG Activity: SIMG_CFMENUOLSDESR
S_ALR_87007736	IMG Activity: CF_OVPS_V_TC81
S_ALR_87007737	IMG Activity: SIMG_CMMENUOFDIBWA9
S_ALR_87007738	IMG Activity: CF_OVPS_V_TC83
S_ALR_87007739	IMG Activity: SIMG_CFMENUOLSDVOFMZ
S_ALR_87007740	IMG Activity: SIMG_CFMENUOFDIBANKV
S_ALR_87007741	IMG Activity: SIMG_CMMENUOFDIBWA13
S_ALR_87007742	IMG Activity: CF_OVPS_VC_TC85
S_ALR_87007743	IMG Activity: SIMG_CMMENUOFDIBWA12
S_ALR_87007744	IMG Activity: SIMG_CFMENUOVPSCCV2
S_ALR_87007745	IMG Activity: SIMG_CMMENUOFDIBWA11
S_ALR_87007746	IMG Activity: SIMG_CMMENUOFDIBWA10
S_ALR_87007747	IMG Activity: SIMG_CFMENUOVPSOD71
S_ALR_87007748	IMG Activity: SIMG_CFMENUOFDIANMI3
S_ALR_87007749	IMG Activity: SIMG_CFMENUOFDIBATCH
S_ALR_87007750	IMG Activity: SIMG_CFMENUOVPSOS57
S_ALR_87007751	IMG Activity: SIMG_CFMENUOFDISTEUR
S_ALR_87007752	IMG Activity: SIMG_CFMENUSAPCFILE
S_ALR_87007753	IMG Activity: SIMG_CMMENUOFDIPS
S_ALR_87007754	IMG Activity: SIMG_CMMENUOIFDIPM
S_ALR_87007755	IMG Activity: SIMG_CFMENUOVPSOD11
S_ALR_87007756	IMG Activity: SIMG_CFEMNUOFDIRSP
S_ALR_87007757	IMG Activity: SIMG_CFMENUOFDIVORST
S_ALR_87007758	IMG Activity: SIMG_CFMENUOFDINKA
S_ALR_87007759	IMG Activity: SIMG_CFMENUOFDIABGRE
S_ALR_87007760	IMG Activity: SIMG_CFMENUOFDISOLLV
S_ALR_87007761	IMG Activity: SIMG_CFMENUOFDIEIGEN
S_ALR_87007762	IMG Activity: SIMG_CFMENUCVIX
S_ALR_87007763	IMG Activity: SIMG_CFMENUCVIY
S_ALR_87007764	IMG Activity: SIMG_CFMENUOVPSOD12
S_ALR_87007765	IMG Activity: SIMG_CFMENUOVPSOD30
S_ALR_87007766	IMG Activity: SIMG_CFMENUOVPSOD40
S_ALR_87007767	IMG Activity: SIMG_CFMENUOVPSOD41
S_ALR_87007768	IMG Activity: SIMG_CFMENU_SWU3
S_ALR_87007769	IMG Activity: CFMENU_T_SPAD

S_ALR_87007770	IMG Activity: CF_OVPS_ODI1
S_ALR_87007771	IMG Activity: CFMENU_V_SXCONV
S_ALR_87007772	IMG Activity: CF_OVPS_ODI2
S_ALR_87007773	IMG Activity: CF_OVPS_ODI3
S_ALR_87007774	IMG Activity: SIMG_CFMENU_SO16
S_ALR_87007775	IMG Activity: SIMG_CFMENUOVPSOD00
S_ALR_87007776	IMG Activity: CFMENU_T_SCOT
S_ALR_87007777	IMG Activity: OIW_SU02
S_ALR_87007778	IMG Activity: W_ZF_VK_0321
S_ALR_87007779	IMG Activity: OIW_SU03
S_ALR_87007780	IMG Activity: W_ZF_VK_0360
S_ALR_87007781	IMG Activity: OIW3
S_ALR_87007782	IMG Activity: W_ZF_VK_0330
S_ALR_87007783	IMG Activity: OIW2
S_ALR_87007784	IMG Activity: W_ZF_VK_0380
S_ALR_87007785	IMG Activity: OIW1
S_ALR_87007786	IMG Activity: W_ZF_VK_0322
S_ALR_87007787	IMG Activity: W_ZF_VK_0323
S_ALR_87007788	IMG Activity: W_ZF_VK_0381
S_ALR_87007789	IMG Activity: W_ZF_VK_0320
S_ALR_87007790	IMG Activity: W_ZF_VK_0303
S_ALR_87007791	IMG Activity: W_ZF_VK_0304
S_ALR_87007792	IMG Activity: W_ZF_VK_0302
S_ALR_87007793	IMG Activity: W_ZF_VK_0301
S_ALR_87007794	IMG Activity: W_ZF_VK_0350
S_ALR_87007795	IMG Activity: W_ZF_VK_0314
S_ALR_87007796	IMG Activity: W_ZF_VK_0312
S_ALR_87007797	IMG Activity: KONTREF_DEF_FX
S_ALR_87007798	IMG Activity: LIM_PROD_GRP_TR
S_ALR_87007799	IMG Activity: KONTREF_DEF_GH
S_ALR_87007800	IMG Activity: TELEFAXOPTIONEN_FX
S_ALR_87007801	IMG Activity: TEILNEHMENDE_WAEHRNG
S_ALR_87007802	IMG Activity: TELEFAXOPTIONEN_GH
S_ALR_87007803	IMG Activity: DRUCKEROPTIONEN_FX
S_ALR_87007804	IMG Activity: INDEXART_UMSCHLUESS
S_ALR_87007805	IMG Activity: KORRELATIOSART
S_ALR_87007806	IMG Activity: ARCHIV_MINDVWD_BUKRS
S_ALR_87007807	IMG Activity: DRUCKEROPTIONEN_GH
S_ALR_87007808	IMG Activity: FORMULARE_FX
S_ALR_87007809	IMG Activity: BARWERTARTEN
S_ALR_87007810	IMG Activity: W_WIC_0005
S_ALR_87007811	IMG Activity: FORMULARE_GH
S_ALR_87007812	IMG Activity: REFERENZ_DATAFEED
S_ALR_87007813	IMG Activity: ARCHIV_MINDVWD_PART
S_ALR_87007814	MRM-Relevant Flow Types
S_ALR_87007815	IMG Activity: W_WIC_0004
S_ALR_87007816	IMG Activity: RAHMENVERTR_ART_MM
S_ALR_87007817	Maintain Evaluaton Type
S_ALR_87007818	IMG Activity: TR_BASIS_KOPIER
S_ALR_87007819	IMG Activity: WERTPAPIERE_DATAFEED
S_ALR_87007820	IMG Activity: ABL_REGELN_FX
S_ALR_87007821	IMG Activity: W_WIC_0003
S_ALR_87007822	IMG Activity: RAHMENVERTRAG_NK_MM
S_ALR_87007823	IMG Activity: PRODUKTEINSTELLUNGEN

S_ALR_87007824	IMG Activity: ABL_VERF_FX
S_ALR_87007825	IMG Activity: LIM_ART_TR
S_ALR_87007826	IMG Activity: W_WIC_0002
S_ALR_87007827	IMG Activity: KONDARTZUORDNUNG_GH
S_ALR_87007828	IMG Activity: WPINF_DF_PROVIDER
S_ALR_87007829	IMG Activity: SZENARIOARTEN
S_ALR_87007830	IMG Activity: BERICHTSAUSWAHL_FX
S_ALR_87007831	IMG Activity: BER.GRUPPE
S_ALR_87007832	IMG Activity: ERMITTLUNG_GH
S_ALR_87007833	IMG Activity: W_WIC_0001
S_ALR_87007834	IMG Activity: DATAFEEDNAME
S_ALR_87007835	IMG Activity: BERICHTSAUSWAHL_MRM
S_ALR_87007836	IMG Activity: TRFX_ZAHLUNGSAVISE
S_ALR_87007837	IMG Activity: BERICHTSAUSWAHL_MM
S_ALR_87007838	IMG Activity: BEWPRINZ_DE
S_ALR_87007839	IMG Activity: W_WIC_0000
S_ALR_87007840	IMG Activity: REFERENZZINSEN
S_ALR_87007841	IMG Activity: BEWERT_FX
S_ALR_87007842	IMG Activity: TRMM_ZAHLUNGSAVISE
S_ALR_87007843	IMG Activity: DATAFEED_RFC
S_ALR_87007844	IMG Activity: 2STF_BEWPRINZ_WP
S_ALR_87007845	IMG Activity: KURVENARTEN
S_ALR_87007846	IMG Activity: ABGRENZUNG_GH
S_ALR_87007847	IMG Activity: TRFX_BEWBEW
S_ALR_87007848	IMG Activity: _V_JBD16CURR
S_ALR_87007849	IMG Activity: DATAFEED_RFC_ZUORDNG
S_ALR_87007850	IMG Activity: BEWERTG_GH
S_ALR_87007851	IMG Activity: VOLATILITAETSARTEN
S_ALR_87007852	IMG Activity: SIMG_CFMENUFWMCFW52
S_ALR_87007853	IMG Activity: TRMM_BEWBEW
S_ALR_87007854	IMG Activity: BED_WPBEZ_UMSCHLUESS
S_ALR_87007855	IMG Activity: DEFINITION_FX
S_ALR_87007856	IMG Activity: STATISTIKART
S_ALR_87007857	IMG Activity: STORNOARTEN_DE
S_ALR_87007858	IMG Activity: HANDPLATZ_UMSCHLUESS
S_ALR_87007859	IMG Activity: AUTOERMITTLUNG_FX
S_ALR_87007860	IMG Activity: KONTFINDUNG_DEF_GH
S_ALR_87007861	IMG Activity: TR_IS_KOPIER
S_ALR_87007862	IMG Activity: BEWEGUNGSART_FX
S_ALR_87007863	IMG Activity: WPKURSART_UMSCHLUESS
S_ALR_87007864	IMG Activity: KONDITIONSARTEN_GH
S_ALR_87007865	IMG Activity: TRFDUE_JBMU
S_ALR_87007866	IMG Activity: DEVISENATTRIBUTE_FX
S_ALR_87007867	IMG Activity: PRODUKTARTEN_GH
S_ALR_87007868	IMG Activity: COMMODITY_DF
S_ALR_87007869	IMG Activity: GART_DEFINITION_FX
S_ALR_87007870	IMG Activity: TRFDUE_KCLL
S_ALR_87007871	IMG Activity: BEWEGUNGSARTZUORDNG
S_ALR_87007872	IMG Activity: AZSBEZ_UMSCHLUESSELN
S_ALR_87007873	IMG Activity: TRFDUE_OKCG
S_ALR_87007874	IMG Activity: BEWEGUNGSARTEN_GH
S_ALR_87007875	IMG Activity: PRODUKTARTEN_FX
S_ALR_87007876	IMG Activity: TRFDUE_FU88
S_ALR_87007877	IMG Activity: INDICES_DATAFEED

S_ALR_87007878	IMG Activity: GART_DEFINITION_GH
S_ALR_87007879	IMG Activity: TR_LO_KOPIER
S_ALR_87007880	IMG Activity: INDEXBEZ_UMSCHLUESS
S_ALR_87007881	IMG Activity: TR_GP_KOPIER
S_ALR_87007882	IMG Activity: ABL_REGELN_MM
S_ALR_87007883	IMG Activity: PFLEGE_BENUTZER_TRGF
S_ALR_87007884	IMG Activity: TR_MM_KOPIER
S_ALR_87007885	IMG Activity: ABL_VERF_MM
S_ALR_87007886	IMG Activity: VOLAART_UMSCHL_DF
S_ALR_87007887	IMG Activity: TR_FX_KOPIER
S_ALR_87007888	IMG Activity: DATENQUELLEN_DF
S_ALR_87007889	IMG Activity: TR_DE_KOPIER
S_ALR_87007890	IMG Activity: SIMG_PPPI_SOP
S_ALR_87007891	IMG Activity: COMM_KURSARTEN_DF
S_ALR_87007892	IMG Activity: TR_SE_KOPIER
S_ALR_87007893	IMG Activity: SIMG_PPPI_PP
S_ALR_87007894	IMG Activity: SIMG_PDC_CI36
S_ALR_87007895	IMG Activity: FIXINGMARGEN_FX
S_ALR_87007896	IMG Activity: SIMG_PPPI_POI
S_ALR_87007897	IMG Activity: KORRESPONDENZART_GF
S_ALR_87007898	IMG Activity: UMSCHL_TAB_DF
S_ALR_87007899	IMG Activity: TR_IMG_PRQ_VEK
S_ALR_87007900	IMG Activity: SIMG_PPPI_MRP
S_ALR_87007901	IMG Activity: SIMG_PDC_HJOB_PM
S_ALR_87007902	IMG Activity: NOTIZBUCH_FX
S_ALR_87007903	IMG Activity: SIMG_PPPI_CRP
S_ALR_87007904	IMG Activity: BEWEGUNGSARTEN_FX
S_ALR_87007905	IMG Activity: WAEHRUNGSARTEN_DF
S_ALR_87007906	IMG Activity: TR_IMG_PRQ_GED
S_ALR_87007907	IMG Activity: SIMG_PDC_CI31
S_ALR_87007908	IMG Activity: WP_KURSARTEN_UM_DF
S_ALR_87007909	IMG Activity: TR_IMG_PRQ_FKP
S_ALR_87007910	IMG Activity: NACHRICHT_TRGF
S_ALR_87007911	IMG Activity: SIMG_PDC_HJOB_PP
S_ALR_87007912	IMG Activity: INDEXART_UMSCHL_DF
S_ALR_87007913	IMG Activity: TR_IMG_PRQ_KFD
S_ALR_87007914	IMG Activity: KALENDER
S_ALR_87007915	IMG Activity: SIMG_PDC_CI41
S_ALR_87007916	IMG Activity: DF_PRT_OPT
S_ALR_87007917	IMG Activity: NK_TR-KLAMMER
S_ALR_87007918	IMG Activity: TR_IMG_PRQ_ALE
S_ALR_87007919	IMG Activity: SIMG_PDCSU02
S_ALR_87007920	IMG Activity: DATAFEED_WHRG
S_ALR_87007921	IMG Activity: SIMG_CFMENUFWMCFZBH
S_ALR_87007922	IMG Activity: SIMG_PDCSU03
S_ALR_87007923	IMG Activity: TR_IMG_PRQ_FKW
S_ALR_87007924	IMG Activity: STAMMDATEN_DF
S_ALR_87007925	IMG Activity: SIMG_CFMENUFWMCFW32
S_ALR_87007926	IMG Activity: SIMG_PDC_HJOB_PPPK
S_ALR_87007927	IMG Activity: TR_IMG_PRQ_TDWD
S_ALR_87007928	IMG Activity: PORTFOLIO
S_ALR_87007929	IMG Activity: TR_INTERNET_DF
S_ALR_87007930	IMG Activity: SIMG_PDC_CI21
S_ALR_87007931	IMG Activity: TR_IMG_PRQ_NKZA

S_ALR_87007932	IMG Activity: WHGSBEZ_UMSCHL_DF
S_ALR_87007933	IMG Activity: BENUTZERDATEN
S_ALR_87007934	IMG Activity: SIMG_PDC_HJOB_PS
S_ALR_87007935	IMG Activity: TR_IMG_PRQ_KBB
S_ALR_87007936	IMG Activity: TRGFMD_WF
S_ALR_87007937	IMG Activity: BERECHTIGUNGEN
S_ALR_87007938	IMG Activity: TR_IMG_PRQ_VZA
S_ALR_87007939	IMG Activity: SIMG_PDC_BA11
S_ALR_87007940	IMG Activity: WORKFLOW_DEF_DF
S_ALR_87007941	IMG Activity: TR_PRQ_ZAHLBANK
S_ALR_87007942	IMG Activity: TRTM_RELEASE_WF_DEF
S_ALR_87007943	IMG Activity: SIMG_PDC_BA10
S_ALR_87007944	IMG Activity: SIMG_UMRECHNUNG
S_ALR_87007945	IMG Activity: SIMG_PDC_BDEGRUPPE
S_ALR_87007946	IMG Activity: TRTMGF_RELEASE
S_ALR_87007947	IMG Activity: UEBERSTZUNGSTABCHECK
S_ALR_87007948	IMG Activity: SIMG_PDC_HJOB_KK-ALL
S_ALR_87007949	IMG Activity: TRFDUE_SICHERHEITEN
S_ALR_87007950	IMG Activity: SIMG_PDC_PA06
S_ALR_87007951	IMG Activity: TRFDUE_OBJEKTE
S_ALR_87007952	IMG Activity: TRFDUE_VORGEHEN
S_ALR_87007955	IMG Activity: TRFDUE_CONDITIONS
S_ALR_87007956	IMG Activity: SIMG_REFERENZZI
S_ALR_87007957	IMG Activity: TRFDUE_JBIUDA1
S_ALR_87007958	IMG Activity: TRFDUE_JBIUDAB
S_ALR_87007959	IMG Activity: INDEX_VOLA_DF
S_ALR_87007960	IMG Activity: INDIZES_GF
S_ALR_87007961	IMG Activity: TRTMJOBS_DATAFEED
S_ALR_87007962	IMG Activity: VARIANTEN_DATAFEED
S_ALR_87007963	IMG Activity: SIMG_WAEHRUNGEN
S_ALR_87007964	IMG Activity: SIMG_DEZWAEHRUNGEN
S_ALR_87007965	IMG Activity: SIMG_KURST_WAEHRG
S_ALR_87007966	IMG Activity: SIMG_KURSSPANNE
S_ALR_87007967	IMG Activity: SIMG_RUNDUNGSREGELN
S_ALR_87007968	IMG Activity: INDEXARTEN_GF
S_ALR_87007969	IMG Activity: HERKUNFT_DEF_UMSCHL
S_ALR_87007970	IMG Activity: UMSCHLUESSELDATAFD
S_ALR_87007971	IMG Activity: WBZ_UMSCHLUESSELN
S_ALR_87007972	IMG Activity: WHRGSART_UMSCHLUESS
S_ALR_87007973	IMG Activity: SWAPSAETZE_DF
S_ALR_87007974	IMG Activity: KURS_UEBERWACHUNG
S_ALR_87007975	IMG Activity: INTR_VOLA_DF
S_ALR_87007976	IMG Activity: WP_VOLA_DF
S_ALR_87007977	IMG Activity: TR_VGWEIS_INBETR_DF
S_ALR_87007978	IMG Activity: SIMG_CFMENUORKKOPPT
S_ALR_87007979	IMG Activity: SIMG_CFMENUORKKOPPS
S_ALR_87007980	IMG Activity: SIMG_CFMENUORKKOVZ1
S_ALR_87007981	IMG Activity: SIMG_CFMENUORKKOVZH
S_ALR_87007982	IMG Activity: SIMG_CFMENUORKKOVZG
S_ALR_87007983	IMG Activity: SIMG_ORKK_OKTZ
S_ALR_87007984	IMG Activity: SIMG_CFMENUORKKVOV4
S_ALR_87007985	IMG Activity: SIMG_ORKKOVAW
S_ALR_87007986	IMG Activity: SIMG_CFMENUORKKVOV7
S_ALR_87007987	IMG Activity: SIMG_CFMENUORKKOPPU

S_ALR_87007988	IMG Activity: SIMG_CFMENUORKKOME9
S_ALR_87007989	IMG Activity: SIMG_ORKK_KUND_OKOG
S_ALR_87007990	IMG Activity: SIMG_ORKK_KUND_CMODZ
S_ALR_87007991	IMG Activity: SIMG_ORKK_KUND_KZE2
S_ALR_87007992	IMG Activity: SIMG_ORKK_KUND_KZM2
S_ALR_87007993	IMG Activity: SIMG_ORKK_KUND_KZZ2
S_ALR_87007994	IMG Activity: SIMG_CFMENUORKKVOFA
S_ALR_87007995	IMG Activity: SIMG_ORKK_ZUORDKAUF
S_ALR_87007996	IMG Activity: SIMG_ORKK_SCHEMAKAUF
S_ALR_87007997	IMG Activity: SIMG_ORKK_UMGEBKAUF
S_ALR_87007998	IMG Activity: SIMG_ORKK_KUND_OKZ2
S_ALR_87007999	IMG Activity: SIMG_ORKK_KUND_OKYW
S_ALR_87008000	IMG Activity: SIMG_CFMENUORKKOKG5
S_ALR_87008001	IMG Activity: SIMG_ORKK_KUND_ZID
S_ALR_87008002	IMG Activity: SIMG_CFMENUORKKOKG3
S_ALR_87008003	IMG Activity: SIMG_CFMENUORKKOKG2
S_ALR_87008004	IMG Activity: SIMG_CFMENUORKKOKG1
S_ALR_87008005	IMG Activity: SIMG_ORKK_ERG_CMOD
S_ALR_87008006	IMG Activity: SIMG_CFMENUORKKOKG6
S_ALR_87008007	IMG Activity: SIMG_CFMENUORKKOKG8
S_ALR_87008008	IMG Activity: SIMG_CFMENUORKKOKG4
S_ALR_87008009	IMG Activity: SIMG_ORKK_KUND_KA02
S_ALR_87008010	IMG Activity: SIMG_CFMENUORKKOKY7
S_ALR_87008011	IMG Activity: SIMG_ORKK_KUND_OKK6
S_ALR_87008012	IMG Activity: SIMG_ORKK_KUND_OKKM
S_ALR_87008013	IMG Activity: SIMG_CFMENUORKKOKY0
S_ALR_87008014	IMG Activity: SIMG_CFMENUORKKOKYA
S_ALR_87008015	IMG Activity: SIMG_CFMENUORKKOKY9
S_ALR_87008016	IMG Activity: SIMG_ORKK_KART_EINZ
S_ALR_87008017	IMG Activity: SIMG_CFMENUORKKOKY1
S_ALR_87008018	IMG Activity: SIMG_ORKK_KUND_OKYV
S_ALR_87008019	IMG Activity: SIMG_ORKK_KUND_OKK5
S_ALR_87008021	IMG Activity: SIMG_CFMENUORKKOKOS
S_ALR_87008022	IMG Activity: SIMG_CFMENUORKKOKZ3
S_ALR_87008023	IMG Activity: SIMG_CFMENUORKKKOT2
S_ALR_87008024	IMG Activity: SIMG_CFMENUORKKOKY5
S_ALR_87008025	IMG Activity: SIMG_CFMENUORKKOKY2
S_ALR_87008026	IMG Activity: SIMG_ORKK_WERK_ZID
S_ALR_87008027	IMG Activity: SIMG_KKSORKKOKG3
S_ALR_87008028	IMG Activity: SIMG_CFMENUORKKOKG9
S_ALR_87008029	IMG Activity: SIMG_KKSORKKOKG1
S_ALR_87008030	IMG Activity: SIMG_CFMENUORKKOPK9
S_ALR_87008031	IMG Activity: SIMG_CFMENUORKKOPN2
S_ALR_87008032	IMG Activity: SIMG_ORKK_UMGEBAUF
S_ALR_87008033	IMG Activity: SIMG_ORKK_WERK_OKZ2
S_ALR_87008034	IMG Activity: SIMG_ORKK_AUF_OKOG
S_ALR_87008035	IMG Activity: SIMG_ORKK_WERK_CMODZ
S_ALR_87008036	IMG Activity: SIMG_ORKK_WERK_KZE2
S_ALR_87008037	IMG Activity: SIMG_CFMENUORKKOPL1
S_ALR_87008038	IMG Activity: SIMG_ORKK_WERK_OPR4
S_ALR_87008039	IMG Activity: SIMG_ORKK_WERK_OPR1
S_ALR_87008040	IMG Activity: SIMG_ORKK_ZUORDAUF
S_ALR_87008041	IMG Activity: SIMG_ORKK_SCHEMAAUF
S_ALR_87008042	IMG Activity: SIMG_KKSORKKOKG5

S_ALR_87008043	IMG Activity: SIMG_CFMENUORKKKKEI1
S_ALR_87008044	IMG Activity: SIMG_CFMENUORKKOKEU
S_ALR_87008045	IMG Activity: SIMG_CFMENUORKKOKO6
S_ALR_87008046	IMG Activity: SIMG_ORKK_WERK_ABR
S_ALR_87008047	IMG Activity: SIMG_CFMENUORKKOKO7
S_ALR_87008048	IMG Activity: SIMG_ORKK_KUND_KZB2
S_ALR_87008049	IMG Activity: SIMG_ORKK_KUND_KZS2
S_ALR_87008050	IMG Activity: SIMG_ORKK_KUND_KA06
S_ALR_87008051	IMG Activity: SIMG_ORKK_KUND_OKZ1
S_ALR_87008052	IMG Activity: SIMG_CFMENUORKKKO8N
S_ALR_87008053	IMG Activity: SIMG_CFMENUORKKKANK
S_ALR_87008054	IMG Activity: SIMG_CFMENUORKKOKV1
S_ALR_87008055	IMG Activity: SIMG_KKSORKKOKG6
S_ALR_87008056	IMG Activity: SIMG_KKSORKKOKG8
S_ALR_87008057	IMG Activity: SIMG_KKSORKKOKG4
S_ALR_87008058	IMG Activity: SIMG_ORKK_WERK_KA02
S_ALR_87008059	IMG Activity: SIMG_CFMENUORKKOKA8
S_ALR_87008060	IMG Activity: SIMG_CFMENUORKKOKV6
S_ALR_87008061	IMG Activity: SIMG_ORKKBEWAUSAUF
S_ALR_87008062	IMG Activity: SIMG_CFMENUORKKOKVG
S_ALR_87008063	IMG Activity: SIMG_CFMENUORKKOKVW
S_ALR_87008064	IMG Activity: SIMG_SDORKKOKO7
S_ALR_87008065	IMG Activity: SIMG_CFMENUORKKKKON
S_ALR_87008066	IMG Activity: SIMG_CFMENUORKKKKOH
S_ALR_87008067	IMG Activity: SIMG_CFMENUORKKKKOI
S_ALR_87008068	IMG Activity: SIMG_CFMENUORKKKKOJ
S_ALR_87008069	IMG Activity: SIMG_CFMENUORKKKKOK
S_ALR_87008070	IMG Activity: SIMG_CFMENUORKKCO44
S_ALR_87008071	IMG Activity: SIMG_ORKK_WERK_EX
S_ALR_87008072	IMG Activity: SIMG_CFMENUORKKKKO8
S_ALR_87008073	IMG Activity: SIMG_CFMENUORKKKKOP
S_ALR_87008074	IMG Activity: SIMG_CFMENUORKKKKOO
S_ALR_87008075	IMG Activity: SIMG_ORKK_COPCIS_005
S_ALR_87008076	IMG Activity: COPCACT_INNAME
S_ALR_87008077	IMG Activity: COPCACT_ACTIVATE
S_ALR_87008078	IMG Activity: SIMG_CFMENUOLMWOMX8
S_ALR_87008079	IMG Activity: SIMG_CFMENUOLMWOMX9
S_ALR_87008080	IMG Activity: SIMG_CFMENUOLMWOMX0
S_ALR_87008081	IMG Activity: SIMG_CFMENUORKKOKSV
S_ALR_87008082	IMG Activity: SIMG_CFMENUORKKOKS8
S_ALR_87008083	IMG Activity: SIMG_CFMENUORKKOKSL
S_ALR_87008084	IMG Activity: SIMG_ORKK_COPCIS_004
S_ALR_87008085	IMG Activity: COPCACT_ASSIGN_NAME
S_ALR_87008086	IMG Activity: SIMG_CFMENUORKKKKR0
S_ALR_87008087	IMG Activity: SIMG_ORKK_COPCIS_010
S_ALR_87008088	IMG Activity: SIMG_CFMENUORKKOKT9
S_ALR_87008089	IMG Activity: SIMG_CFMENUORKKOKTA
S_ALR_87008090	IMG Activity: SIMG_ORKK_COPCIS_009
S_ALR_87008091	IMG Activity: SIMG_CFMENUORKKOKS3
S_ALR_87008092	IMG Activity: SIMG_CFMENUORKKKKO1
S_ALR_87008093	IMG Activity: SIMG_CFMENUORKKKKO4
S_ALR_87008094	IMG Activity: SIMG_CFMENUORKKKKO7
S_ALR_87008095	IMG Activity: SIMG_CFMENUORKKFGRP
S_ALR_87008096	IMG Activity: SIMG_ORKK_COPCIS_011

S_ALR_87008097	IMG Activity: SIMG_CFMENUORKKOKSD
S_ALR_87008098	IMG Activity: SIMG_CFMENUORKKOKSP
S_ALR_87008099	IMG Activity: SIMG_CFMENUORKKOKRA
S_ALR_87008100	IMG Activity: SIMG_CFMENUORKKOKKC
S_ALR_87008101	IMG Activity: SIMG_CFMENUORKKCL00
S_ALR_87008102	IMG Activity: SIMG_CFMENUORKKOKRX
S_ALR_87008103	IMG Activity: SIMG_ORKK_COPCIS_008
S_ALR_87008104	IMG Activity: SIMG_CFMENUORKKOKS2
S_ALR_87008105	IMG Activity: SIMG_CFMENUORKKOKSB
S_ALR_87008106	IMG Activity: SIMG_ORKK_COPCIS_007
S_ALR_87008107	IMG Activity: SIMG_CFMENUORKKOKS9
S_ALR_87008108	IMG Activity: SIMG_ORKK_IMMA_OKOG
S_ALR_87008109	IMG Activity: SIMG_ORKK_KTR_CMODZ
S_ALR_87008110	IMG Activity: SIMG_ORKK_KTR_KZE2
S_ALR_87008111	IMG Activity: SIMG_ORKK_KTR_KZM2
S_ALR_87008112	IMG Activity: SIMG_ORKK_KTR_KZZ2
S_ALR_87008114	IMG Activity: SIMG_ORKK_KTR_OPR1
S_ALR_87008115	IMG Activity: SIMG_ORKK_ZUORDIMMA
S_ALR_87008116	IMG Activity: SIMG_ORKK_SCHMEMAIMM
S_ALR_87008117	IMG Activity: SIMG_ORKK_UMGEBIMMA
S_ALR_87008118	IMG Activity: SIMG_ORKK_KTR_KZB2
S_ALR_87008119	IMG Activity: SIMG_SDORKKKO8N
S_ALR_87008120	IMG Activity: SIMG_SDORKKKEI1
S_ALR_87008121	IMG Activity: SIMG_SDORKKOKEU
S_ALR_87008122	IMG Activity: SIMG_SDORKKOKO6
S_ALR_87008123	IMG Activity: SIMG_ORKK_KUND_ABR
S_ALR_87008124	IMG Activity: SIMG_ORKK_KTR_KZS2
S_ALR_87008125	IMG Activity: SIMG_ORKK_KTR_KA06
S_ALR_87008126	IMG Activity: SIMG_ORKK_KTR_OKZ1
S_ALR_87008127	IMG Activity: SIMG_CFMENUORKKOKZ7
S_ALR_87008128	IMG Activity: SIMG_CFMENUORKKOKZ8
S_ALR_87008129	IMG Activity: SIMG_CFMENUORKKOKY3
S_ALR_87008130	IMG Activity: CFMENUOLMWOMX2
S_ALR_87008131	IMG Activity: CFMENUOLMWOMX1
S_ALR_87008132	IMG Activity: SIMG_ORKK_KTR_KO8N
S_ALR_87008133	IMG Activity: SIMG_ORKK_KTR_KEI1
S_ALR_87008134	IMG Activity: SIMG_ORKK_KTR_OKEU
S_ALR_87008135	IMG Activity: SIMG_CFMENUOLMWOMX7
S_ALR_87008136	IMG Activity: SIMG_CFMENUORKKOPR4
S_ALR_87008137	IMG Activity: SIMG_CFMENUOLMWOMX4
S_ALR_87008138	IMG Activity: CFMENUOLMWOMX3
S_ALR_87008139	IMG Activity: SIMG_ORKK_KTR_OKO6
S_ALR_87008140	IMG Activity: SIMG_CFMENUORKKKK03
S_ALR_87008141	IMG Activity: SIMG_CFMENUORKKKP34
S_ALR_87008142	IMG Activity: SIMG_CFMENUORKKKK95
S_ALR_87008143	IMG Activity: SIMG_CFMENUORKKKK65
S_ALR_87008144	IMG Activity: SIMG_CFMENUORKKOKY6
S_ALR_87008145	IMG Activity: SIMG_ORKK_KTR_ABR
S_ALR_87008146	IMG Activity: SIMG_ORKK_KTR_OKO7
S_ALR_87008147	IMG Activity: SIMG_CFMENUORKKKKVC2
S_ALR_87008148	IMG Activity: SIMG_CFMENUORKKKK02
S_ALR_87008149	IMG Activity: SIMG_CFMENUORKKKKVC0
S_ALR_87008150	IMG Activity: SIMG_ORKK_BAU_KA06
S_ALR_87008151	IMG Activity: SIMG_ORKK_SEIB_BV

S_ALR_87008152	IMG Activity: SIMG_ORKK_SEIB_KA
S_ALR_87008153	IMG Activity: SIMG_ORKK_SEIBAN
S_ALR_87008154	IMG Activity: SIMG_ORKK_ROHSTOFF
S_ALR_87008155	IMG Activity: SIMG_ORKK_BAU_KZE2
S_ALR_87008156	IMG Activity: SIMG_ORKK_BAU_KZM2
S_ALR_87008157	IMG Activity: SIMG_ORKK_BAU_KZZ2
S_ALR_87008158	IMG Activity: SIMG_ORKK_BAU_KZB2
S_ALR_87008159	IMG Activity: SIMG_ORKK_BAU_KZS2
S_ALR_87008160	IMG Activity: SIMG_ORKKOKK6
S_ALR_87008161	IMG Activity: SIMG_ORKKOKKM
S_ALR_87008162	IMG Activity: SIMG_ORKK_OKK4
S_ALR_87008163	IMG Activity: SIMG_ORKKOKKI
S_ALR_87008164	IMG Activity: SIMG_ORKKOKKN
S_ALR_87008165	IMG Activity: SIMG_ORKK_REFERENZ
S_ALR_87008166	IMG Activity: SIMG_ORKK_PARTNER
S_ALR_87008167	IMG Activity: SIMG_CFMENUORKKOKYW
S_ALR_87008168	IMG Activity: SIMG_CFMENUORKKOKYV
S_ALR_87008169	IMG Activity: SIMG_ORKK_KALKVERS
S_ALR_87008170	IMG Activity: SIMG_ORKK_BAU_CMODZ
S_ALR_87008171	IMG Activity: SIMG_ORKK_SERIE_KZZ2
S_ALR_87008172	IMG Activity: SIMG_ORKK_SERIE_KZB2
S_ALR_87008173	IMG Activity: SIMG_ORKK_SERIE_KZS2
S_ALR_87008174	IMG Activity: SIMG_ORKK_SERIE_KA06
S_ALR_87008175	IMG Activity: SIMG_ORKK_SERIE_OKZ1
S_ALR_87008176	IMG Activity: SIMG_ORKK_SERIE_OKZ2
S_ALR_87008177	IMG Activity: SIMG_ORKK_PER_OKOG
S_ALR_87008178	IMG Activity: SIMG_ORKK_SERIE_CMOD
S_ALR_87008179	IMG Activity: SIMG_ORKK_SERIE_KZE2
S_ALR_87008180	IMG Activity: SIMG_ORKK_SERIE_KZM2
S_ALR_87008181	IMG Activity: SIMG_KKEKORKKOKK4
S_ALR_87008182	IMG Activity: SIMG_ORKK_KA_BAUTEIL
S_ALR_87008183	IMG Activity: SIMG_CFMENUORKKOKKO
S_ALR_87008184	IMG Activity: SIMG_ORKK_BAU_OKOG
S_ALR_87008185	IMG Activity: SIMG_ORKK_HERK_MUNDS
S_ALR_87008186	IMG Activity: SIMG_CFMENUORKKOKK7
S_ALR_87008187	IMG Activity: SIMG_CFMENUORKKOKK9
S_ALR_87008188	IMG Activity: SIMG_CFMENUORKKOKZZ
S_ALR_87008189	IMG Activity: SIMG_CFMENUORKKCKNR
S_ALR_87008190	IMG Activity: SIMG_ORKK_EK_CMOD
S_ALR_87008191	IMG Activity: SIMG_CFMENUORKKCKC1
S_ALR_87008192	IMG Activity: SIMG_CFMENUORKKOKTZ
S_ALR_87008193	IMG Activity: SIMG_ORKK_KTPF
S_ALR_87008194	IMG Activity: SIMG_ORKK_SCHEMA
S_ALR_87008195	IMG Activity: SIMG_ORKK_UMGEB
S_ALR_87008196	IMG Activity: SIMG_CFMENUORKKOKK6
S_ALR_87008197	IMG Activity: SIMG_CFMENUORKKOKKM
S_ALR_87008198	IMG Activity: SIMG_CFMENUORKKOKK4
S_ALR_87008199	IMG Activity: SIMG_CFMENUORKKOKKI
S_ALR_87008200	IMG Activity: SIMG_CFMENUORKKOKKN
S_ALR_87008201	IMG Activity: SIMG_CFMENUORKKKZZ2
S_ALR_87008202	IMG Activity: SIMG_CFMENUORKKKZB2
S_ALR_87008203	IMG Activity: SIMG_CFMENUORKKKZS2
S_ALR_87008204	IMG Activity: SIMG_CFMENUORKKKA06
S_ALR_87008205	IMG Activity: SIMG_CFMENUORKKOKZ1

S_ALR_87008206	IMG Activity: SIMG_CFMENUORKKOKZ2
S_ALR_87008207	IMG Activity: SIMG_ORKK_PC_OKOG
S_ALR_87008208	IMG Activity: SIMG_CFMENUORKKCMODZ
S_ALR_87008209	IMG Activity: SIMG_CFMENUORKKKZE2
S_ALR_87008210	IMG Activity: SIMG_CFMENUORKKKZM2
S_ALR_87008212	IMG Activity: SIMG_ORKK_MISCH_OMXA
S_ALR_87008213	IMG Activity: SIMG_ORKK_KUPPEL_UR
S_ALR_87008214	IMG Activity: SIMG_CFMENUORKKOMD9
S_ALR_87008215	IMG Activity: SIMG_CFMENUORKKOS32
S_ALR_87008216	IMG Activity: SIMG_ORKK_ERZ_CMOD
S_ALR_87008217	IMG Activity: SIMG_CFMENUORKKOPR3
S_ALR_87008218	IMG Activity: SIMG_CFMENUORKKCCF1
S_ALR_87008219	IMG Activity: SIMG_CFMENUORKKOPR1
S_ALR_87008220	IMG Activity: SIMG_CFMENUORKKOPJG
S_ALR_87008221	IMG Activity: SIMG_CFMENUORKKOPJF
S_ALR_87008222	IMG Activity: SIMG_CFMENUORKKOSM2
S_ALR_87008223	IMG Activity: SIMG_CFMENUORKKOMS4
S_ALR_87008224	IMG Activity: SIMG_CFMENUORKKOKK5
S_ALR_87008225	IMG Activity: SIMG_CFMENUORKKOPJM
S_ALR_87008226	IMG Activity: SIMG_CFMENUORKKOPJI
S_ALR_87008227	IMG Activity: SIMG_CFMENUORKKOP54
S_ALR_87008228	IMG Activity: SIMG_CFMENUORKKOP51
S_ALR_87008229	IMG Activity: SIMG_CFMENUORKKOKZ4
S_ALR_87008230	IMG Activity: SIMG_ORKK_SERIE_ABR
S_ALR_87008231	IMG Activity: SIMG_PP3ORKKOKG1
S_ALR_87008232	IMG Activity: SIMG_PP3ORKKOKO7
S_ALR_87008233	IMG Activity: SIMG_PP3ORKKOKG9
S_ALR_87008234	IMG Activity: SIMG_PP3ORKKOKGD
S_ALR_87008235	IMG Activity: SIMG_PP3ORKKKANK
S_ALR_87008236	IMG Activity: SIMG_ORKK_EINSKTHIER
S_ALR_87008237	IMG Activity: SIMG_ORKKBEWWIPPER
S_ALR_87008238	IMG Activity: SIMG_PP3ORKKOKO6
S_ALR_87008239	IMG Activity: SIMG_CFMENUORKKOKZ5
S_ALR_87008240	IMG Activity: SIMG_CFMENUORKKOKYC
S_ALR_87008241	IMG Activity: SIMG_CFMENUORKKOSP3
S_ALR_87008242	IMG Activity: SIMG_PP3ORKKKO8N
S_ALR_87008243	IMG Activity: SIMG_CFMENUORKKOSP5
S_ALR_87008244	IMG Activity: SIMG_PP3ORKKKEI1
S_ALR_87008245	IMG Activity: SIMG_PP3ORKKOPK9
S_ALR_87008246	IMG Activity: SIMG_PP3ORKKOKEU
S_ALR_87008247	IMG Activity: SIMG_PP3ORKKOKG8
S_ALR_87008248	IMG Activity: SIMG_PP3ORKKOKG6
S_ALR_87008249	IMG Activity: SIMG_PP3ORKKOKA8
S_ALR_87008250	IMG Activity: SIMG_PP3ORKKOKV6
S_ALR_87008251	IMG Activity: SIMG_PP3ORKKOKV1
S_ALR_87008252	IMG Activity: SIMG_PP3ORKKOKVW
S_ALR_87008253	IMG Activity: SIMG_PP3ORKKOKVG
S_ALR_87008254	IMG Activity: SIMG_ORKK_BEWAUSPER
S_ALR_87008255	IMG Activity: SIMG_CFMENUORKKOKV2
S_ALR_87008256	IMG Activity: SIMG_CFMENUORKKOKV7
S_ALR_87008257	IMG Activity: SIMG_ORKK_BEWAUSKTHI
S_ALR_87008258	IMG Activity: SIMGORKKBEWWIPZUORD
S_ALR_87008259	IMG Activity: SIMG_ORKK_SERIE_ZID
S_ALR_87008260	IMG Activity: SIMG_CFMENUORKKOKVH

S_ALR_87008261	IMG Activity: SIMG_PP3ORKKOKG5
S_ALR_87008262	IMG Activity: SIMG_ORKK_SERIE_KA02
S_ALR_87008263	IMG Activity: SIMG_PP3ORKKOKG4
S_ALR_87008264	IMG Activity: SIMG_PP3ORKKKOT2
S_ALR_87008265	IMG Activity: SIMG_ORKK_SERIE_OPR1
S_ALR_87008266	IMG Activity: SIMG_ORKK_SCHEMAPER1
S_ALR_87008267	IMG Activity: SIMG_PP3ORKKOPN2
S_ALR_87008268	IMG Activity: SIMG_ORKK_WERK_KZS2
S_ALR_87008269	IMG Activity: SIMG_ORKK_FINDPER
S_ALR_87008270	IMG Activity: SIMG_ORKK_WERK_KA06
S_ALR_87008271	IMG Activity: SIMG_PP3ORKKOPL1
S_ALR_87008272	IMG Activity: SIMG_ORKK_WERK_KZM2
S_ALR_87008273	IMG Activity: SIMG_ORKK_SERIE_OPR4
S_ALR_87008274	IMG Activity: SIMG_ORKK_WERK_KZB2
S_ALR_87008275	IMG Activity: SIMG_ORKK_WERK_KZZ2
S_ALR_87008276	IMG Activity: SIMG_ORKK_UMGEBPER
S_ALR_87008277	IMG Activity: SIMG_PP3ORKKOKZ3
S_ALR_87008278	IMG Activity: SIMG_ORKK_WERK_OKZ1
S_ALR_87008279	IMG Activity: SIMG_CFMENUORKKOKZ6
S_ALR_87008280	IMG Activity: SIMG_CFMENUOLMEOMGA
S_ALR_87008281	IMG Activity: W_DF_LT_0800
S_ALR_87008282	IMG Activity: SIMG_OLME1FS02
S_ALR_87008283	IMG Activity: W_FD_0000
S_ALR_87008284	IMG Activity: SIMG_OLME1OMGG
S_ALR_87008285	IMG Activity: SIMG_OLME1OMER
S_ALR_87008286	IMG Activity: SIMG_OLMEFELDFORMAT
S_ALR_87008287	IMG Activity: SIMG_OLME2FS02
S_ALR_87008288	IMG Activity: SIMG_OLMEOLIS004
S_ALR_87008289	IMG Activity: SIMG_OLME2AORKSOVA
S_ALR_87008290	IMG Activity: SIMG_OLME2OMER
S_ALR_87008291	IMG Activity: SIMG_OLME2OMGG
S_ALR_87008292	IMG Activity: SIMG_OLMEVORAUSSETZ
S_ALR_87008311	IMG-Aktivität: J_1ADOC_CLASS4
S_ALR_87008312	IMG-Aktivität: J_1ASUB_NUMBER4
S_ALR_87008313	IMG-Aktivität: J_1ACPA_LETTER4
S_ALR_87008314	IMG-Aktivität: J_1ADOC_NUMBER_RANGE
S_ALR_87008315	IMG-Aktivität: J_1AARG_DOC_NUM_GRP4
S_ALR_87008316	IMG-Aktivität: J_1AARG_DOC_NO4
S_ALR_87008317	IMG Activity: J_1A_AA_REV_ADD_SET
S_ALR_87008318	IMG Activity: J_1A_AA_INFL_KLASSE
S_ALR_87008319	IMG Activity: J_1A_AA_REV_SCHL
S_ALR_87008320	IMG Activity: J_1A_AA_REV_BEREICH
S_ALR_87008321	IMG Activity: J_1A_AA_PER_KONTR
S_ALR_87008322	IMG Activity: J_1AAA_FORM
S_ALR_87008323	IMG Activity: J_1AAA_DOC_KLASSE
S_ALR_87008324	IMG-Aktivität: J_1BPROCESSING_PROGS
S_ALR_87008325	IMG-Aktivität: J_1BOUT_COND_DISPLAY
S_ALR_87008326	IMG-Aktivität: J_1BOUT_COND_CHANGE
S_ALR_87008327	IMG-Aktivität: J_1BOUT_COND_CREATE
S_ALR_87008328	IMG-Aktivität: J_1BSERIES_NFNUMBER
S_ALR_87008329	IMG-Aktivität: J_1BFORM_NUMBER_RANG
S_ALR_87008330	IMG-Aktivität: J_1BGROUP_NUMBER
S_ALR_87008331	IMG-Aktivität: J_1BCONTAB_CREATE
S_ALR_87008332	IMG-Aktivität: J_1BREF_ASSIGNMENT

S_ALR_87008333	IMG-Aktivität: J_1BOUTPUT_DET_PROC
S_ALR_87008334	IMG-Aktivität: J_1BCONDITION_TYPES
S_ALR_87008335	IMG-Aktivität: J_1BACCESS_SEQUENCES
S_ALR_87008336	IMG-Aktivität: J_1BCONTAB_FIELD_CAT
S_ALR_87008337	IMG-Aktivität: J_1BCONTAB_DISPLAY
S_ALR_87008338	IMG-Aktivität: J_1BCONTAB_CHANGE
S_ALR_87008339	IMG-Aktivität: J_1BNUMBER_RANGES
S_ALR_87008340	IMG-Aktivität: J_1BMGROUP
S_ALR_87008341	IMG-Aktivität: J_1BNF_TYPE_MASTER
S_ALR_87008342	IMG-Aktivität: J_1BNBMCODE
S_ALR_87008343	IMG-Aktivität: J_1BBRCREATE
S_ALR_87008344	IMG-Aktivität: J_1BASSBRANCH
S_ALR_87008345	IMG-Aktivität: J_1BCFOP_SD
S_ALR_87008346	IMG-Aktivität: J_1BFORM_MASTER
S_ALR_87008347	IMG-Aktivität: J_1BCFOP_MM
S_ALR_87008348	IMG-Aktivität: J_1BCFOP_DESCRIPT
S_ALR_87008526	IMG activity: CURRENCY_VOLA_INPUT
S_ALR_87008527	IMG activity: STOCK_PRC_VOLA_INPUT
S_ALR_87008528	IMG activity: INTEREST_VOLA_INPUT
S_ALR_87008529	IMG activity: INTR_VOLA_CURV_MRM
S_ALR_87008530	IMG activity: INTEREST_CURVE_INPUT
S_ALR_87008531	IMG activity: BARWERT_OTC
S_ALR_87008532	IMG activity: KORR_MAINTAIN
S_ALR_87008533	IMG Activity: BETAFAK_PFLEGEN
S_ALR_87008534	IMG activity: INDEX_VOLA_PFLEGEN
S_ALR_87008535	IMG Activity: SIMG_WAEHRUNGSPFLEGE
S_ALR_87008536	IMG Activity: STOCK_PRICES_INPUT
S_ALR_87008537	IMG Activity: SIMG_ZINSWERTE
S_ALR_87008538	IMG Activity: INDEX_INPUT
S_ALR_87008539	IMG Activity: SWAP_RATE_INPUT
S_ALR_87008554	IMG Activity: SIMG_CFMENUOLSDV/36
S_ALR_87008555	IMG Activity: OALE_DSTSCN_DSTCNTRK
S_ALR_87008556	IMG Activity: OALE_DSTSCN_DSALCSHP
S_ALR_87008557	IMG Activity: OALE_DSTSCN_SDMM
S_ALR_87008558	IMG Activity: SIMG_CFMENUOLSDBD50
S_ALR_87008559	IMG Activity: SIMG_XXMENUOLML0005
S_ALR_87008560	IMG Activity: OALE_LO_DEKR_0003
S_ALR_87008561	IMG Activity: SIMG_OALE_PDMFGOS48
S_ALR_87008562	IMG Activity: SIMG_CFMENUOLSD0VTS
S_ALR_87008563	IMG Activity: OALE_DSTSCN_CREDIT
S_ALR_87008564	IMG Activity: SIMG_CFMENUOLSDOMTB
S_ALR_87008565	IMG Activity: SIMG_CFMENUOLSDSM59
S_ALR_87008566	IMG Activity: SIMG_CFMENUOLSDBD64
S_ALR_87008567	IMG Activity: SIMG_CFMENUOLSDWE21
S_ALR_87008568	IMG Activity: SIMG_CFMENUOLSDWE20
S_ALR_87008569	IMG Activity: SIMG_CFMENUOLSD0VTP
S_ALR_87008570	IMG Activity: SIMG_CFMENUOLSD0VTG
S_ALR_87008571	IMG Activity: SIMG_OALE_PDMFGOS47
S_ALR_87008572	IMG Activity: SIMG_OALE_PDMSTAMAT
S_ALR_87008573	IMG Activity: SIMG_OALE_PDMSTABOM
S_ALR_87008574	IMG Activity: SIMG_OALE_PDMOCP4
S_ALR_87008575	IMG Activity: SIMG_OALE_PDMOCP3
S_ALR_87008576	IMG Activity: SIMG_OALE_PDMOCP2
S_ALR_87008577	IMG Activity: SIMG_OALE_PDMOCP1

S_ALR_87008578	IMG Activity: SIMG_OALE_LOPSP_011
S_ALR_87008579	IMG Activity: SIMG_OALE_PDMSTADOC
S_ALR_87008580	IMG Activity: SIMG_OALE_PDMSTACLA
S_ALR_87008581	IMG Activity: SIMG_OALE_PDMSTACHAR
S_ALR_87008582	IMG Activity: OALE_HRDST_07
S_ALR_87008583	IMG Activity: OALE_HRDST_08
S_ALR_87008584	IMG Activity: OALE_DSTSCN_PPPOI
S_ALR_87008585	IMG Activity: OALE_HRDST_13
S_ALR_87008586	IMG Activity: OALE_HRDST_12
S_ALR_87008587	IMG Activity: OALE_DSTSCN_SALESINF
S_ALR_87008588	IMG Activity: OALE_DSTSCN_PURCHINF
S_ALR_87008589	IMG Activity: OALE_DSTSCN_INVCONTR
S_ALR_87008590	IMG Activity: OALE_DSTSCN_CDLIS
S_ALR_87008591	IMG Activity: OALE_DSTSCN_PPCOPA
S_ALR_87008592	IMG Activity: OALE_DSTSCN_PPREP
S_ALR_87008593	IMG Activity: OALE_DSTSCN_SOP
S_ALR_87008594	IMG Activity: OALE_HRDST_04
S_ALR_87008595	IMG Activity: OALE_HRDST_PP08004
S_ALR_87008596	IMG Activity: OALE_HRDST_PP08002
S_ALR_87008597	IMG Activity: OALE_HRDST_PP08003
S_ALR_87008598	IMG Activity: OALE_HRDST_PP08005
S_ALR_87008599	IMG Activity: OALE_HRDST_PP08001
S_ALR_87008600	IMG Activity: OALE_HRDST_PAINW
S_ALR_87008601	IMG Activity: OALE_HRDST_15
S_ALR_87008602	IMG Activity: OALE_HRDST_14
S_ALR_87008612	IMG Activity: OALE_CATSHR_19
S_ALR_87008613	IMG Activity: OALE_CATSHR_11
S_ALR_87008614	IMG Activity: OALE_CATSHR_02
S_ALR_87008615	IMG Activity: OALE_CATSHR_10
S_ALR_87008616	IMG Activity: OALE_CATSHR_16
S_ALR_87008617	IMG Activity: OALE_CATSHR_15
S_ALR_87008618	IMG Activity: OALE_CATSHR_14
S_ALR_87008619	IMG Activity: OALE_CATSHR_13
S_ALR_87008620	IMG Activity: OALE_CATSHR_12
S_ALR_87008621	IMG Activity: OALE_CATSHR_06
S_ALR_87008622	IMG Activity: OALE_CATSHR_03
S_ALR_87008623	IMG Activity: OALE_CATSHR_20
S_ALR_87008624	IMG Activity: OALE_CATSHR_17
S_ALR_87008625	IMG Activity: OALE_CATSHR_01
S_ALR_87008626	IMG Activity: OALE_CATSHR_09
S_ALR_87008627	IMG Activity: OALE_CATSHR_08
S_ALR_87008628	IMG Activity: OALE_CATSHR_07
S_ALR_87008629	IMG Activity: OALE_CATSHR_04
S_ALR_87008630	IMG Activity: OALE_CATSHR_18
S_ALR_87008648	IMG Activity: W_KO_NF_0114
S_ALR_87008649	IMG Activity: W_KO_NF_0113
S_ALR_87008650	IMG Activity: W_KO_NF_0112
S_ALR_87008651	IMG Activity: W_KO_NF_0111
S_ALR_87008652	IMG Activity: W_ZF_VK_0470
S_ALR_87008653	IMG Activity: W_ZF_VK_0650
S_ALR_87008654	IMG Activity: W_ZF_VK_0640
S_ALR_87008655	IMG Activity: W_KO_NF_0115
S_ALR_87008656	IMG Activity: W_KO_NF_0122
S_ALR_87008657	IMG Activity: W_KO_NF_0121

S_ALR_87008658	IMG Activity: W_KO_NF_0301
S_ALR_87008659	IMG Activity: W_KO_NF_0119
S_ALR_87008660	IMG Activity: W_KO_NF_0118
S_ALR_87008661	IMG Activity: W_KO_NF_0117
S_ALR_87008662	IMG Activity: W_KO_NF_0116
S_ALR_87008663	IMG Activity: W_ZF_VK_0490
S_ALR_87008664	IMG Activity: W_ZF_VK_0480
S_ALR_87008665	IMG Activity: W_ZF_VK_0463
S_ALR_87008666	IMG activity: W_ZF_VK_0462
S_ALR_87008667	IMG activity: W_ZF_VK_0450
S_ALR_87008668	IMG activity: W_ZF_VK_0440
S_ALR_87008669	IMG activity: W_ZF_VK_0430
S_ALR_87008670	IMG activity: W_ZF_VK_0620
S_ALR_87008671	IMG activity: W_ZF_VK_0410
S_ALR_87008672	IMG activity: W_ZF_VK_0630
S_ALR_87008673	IMG activity: W_ZF_VK_0610
S_ALR_87008674	IMG activity: W_ZF_VK_0420
S_ALR_87008684	IMG Activity: EHS_SD_100_20_013_40
S_ALR_87008685	IMG Activity: EHS_SD_100_20_023
S_ALR_87008686	IMG Activity: EHS_SD_100_10_15
S_ALR_87008687	IMG Activity: EHS_MD_130_20_2B
S_ALR_87008688	IMG Activity: EHS_SD_100_20_10
S_ALR_87008689	IMG Activity: EHS_SR_225_40
S_ALR_87008690	IMG Activity: EHS_SD_100_20_013_20
S_ALR_87008691	IMG Activity: EHS_SR_230_10_1
،S_ALR_87008692	IMG Activity: EHS_SD_100_20_013_10
S_ALR_87008693	IMG Activity: EHS_SD_100_20_013_30
S_ALR_87008694	IMG Activity: EHS_SR_225_50
S_ALR_87008695	IMG Activity: EHS_SD_100_20_20
S_ALR_87008696	IMG Activity: EHS_SR_210_30_01
S_ALR_87008697	IMG Activity: EHS_SR_210_10_15
S_ALR_87008698	IMG Activity: EHS_SR_210_10_12
S_ALR_87008699	IMG Activity: EHS_SR_210_10_10
S_ALR_87008700	IMG Activity: EHS_SR_210_10_05
S_ALR_87008701	IMG Activity: EHS_SD_200_10_20
S_ALR_87008702	IMG Activity: EHS_SD_100_20_30
S_ALR_87008703	IMG Activity: EHS_SR_210_20_30
S_ALR_87008704	IMG Activity: EHS_SR_210_20_10
S_ALR_87008705	IMG Activity: EHS_SD_100_20_40
S_ALR_87008706	IMG Activity: EHS_SD_200_10_10
S_ALR_87008707	IMG Activity: EHS_SD_100_10_10
S_ALR_87008708	IMG Activity: EHS_DDS_100_10_22
S_ALR_87008709	IMG Activity: EHS_DDS_100_10_30
S_ALR_87008710	IMG Activity: EHS_DDS_100_10_26
S_ALR_87008711	IMG Activity: EHS_DDS_100_10_60
S_ALR_87008712	IMG Activity: EHS_DDS_100_10_10
S_ALR_87008713	IMG Activity: EHS_SD_100_10_013_20
S_ALR_87008714	IMG Activity: EHS_DDS_100_10_50
S_ALR_87008715	IMG Activity: EHS_SD_100_10_013_10
S_ALR_87008716	IMG Activity: EHS_DDS_100_10_07
S_ALR_87008717	IMG Activity: EHS_DDS_100_10_20
S_ALR_87008718	IMG Activity: EHS_DDS_100_10_29
S_ALR_87008719	IMG Activity: EHS_SR_250_01
S_ALR_87008720	IMG Activity: EHS_SD_100_10_023

S_ALR_87008721	IMG Activity: EHS_MD_120_30_3B
S_ALR_87008722	IMG Activity: EHS_SR_230_10_5
S_ALR_87008723	IMG Activity: EHS_SR_230_10_4
S_ALR_87008724	IMG Activity: EHS_SD_100_10_013_40
S_ALR_87008725	IMG Activity: EHS_DDS_100_10_28
S_ALR_87008726	IMG Activity: EHS_DDS_100_10_27
S_ALR_87008727	IMG Activity: EHS_DDS_100_10_05
S_ALR_87008728	IMG Activity: EHS_DDS_100_10_03
S_ALR_87008729	IMG Activity: EHS_SD_100_10_013_30
S_ALR_87008730	IMG Activity: EHS_MD_110_02_1
S_ALR_87008731	IMG Activity: EHS_SRE_IMP_70
S_ALR_87008732	IMG Activity: EHS_MD_100_6
S_ALR_87008733	IMG Activity: EHS_MD_120_10_10_5
S_ALR_87008734	IMG Activity: EHS_MD_120_10_10_1
S_ALR_87008735	IMG Activity: EHS_MD_120_30_3
S_ALR_87008736	IMG Activity: EHS_MD_160_10
S_ALR_87008737	IMG Activity: EHS_MD_120_30_01
S_ALR_87008738	IMG Activity: EHS_MD_120_30_00
S_ALR_87008739	IMG Activity: EHS_MD_120_30_20
S_ALR_87008740	IMG Activity: EHS_MD_120_10_10_0
S_ALR_87008741	IMG Activity: EHS_MD_110_05_2
S_ALR_87008742	IMG Activity: EHS_MD_110_05_1
S_ALR_87008743	IMG Activity: EHS_MD_110_01_1
S_ALR_87008744	IMG Activity: EHS_MD_150_01_1
S_ALR_87008745	IMG Activity: EHS_MD_150_01_2
S_ALR_87008746	IMG Activity: EHS_MD_100_3
S_ALR_87008747	IMG Activity: EHS_MD_100_4
S_ALR_87008748	IMG Activity: EHS_MD_110_05_4
S_ALR_87008749	IMG Activity: EHS_MD_110_05_32
S_ALR_87008750	IMG Activity: EHS_MD_110_05_3
S_ALR_87008751	IMG Activity: EHS_MD_130_30
S_ALR_87008752	IMG Activity: EHS_MD_130_20_3
S_ALR_87008753	IMG Activity: EHS_MD_130_20_2
S_ALR_87008754	IMG Activity: EHS_MD_130_20_1
S_ALR_87008755	IMG Activity: EHS_SD_200_10_03
S_ALR_87008756	IMG Activity: EHS_MD_130_10_1
S_ALR_87008757	IMG Activity: EHS_SD_200_10_01
S_ALR_87008758	IMG Activity: EHS_MD_140_05_1
S_ALR_87008759	IMG Activity: EHS_MD_140_01_4
S_ALR_87008760	IMG Activity: EHS_MD_140_01_3
S_ALR_87008761	IMG Activity: EHS_MD_140_01_1
S_ALR_87008762	IMG Activity: EHS_SD_200_10_02
S_ALR_87008763	IMG Activity: EHS_MD_130_30_0
S_ALR_87008764	IMG Activity: EHS_MD_130_30_1
S_ALR_87008765	IMG Activity: EHS_MD_120_30_5
S_ALR_87008766	IMG Activity: EHS_SD_200_10_04
S_ALR_87008767	IMG Activity: EHS_MD_130_01_2
S_ALR_87008768	IMG Activity: EHS_MD_130_05_1
S_ALR_87008769	IMG Activity: EHS_MD_120_30_4
S_ALR_87008770	IMG Activity: EHS_MD_120_10_20_5
S_ALR_87008771	IMG Activity: EHS_SRE_IMP_100_01
S_ALR_87008772	IMG Activity: EHS_SRE_IMP_120
S_ALR_87008773	IMG Activity: EHS_MD_120_20_40_2
S_ALR_87008774	IMG Activity: EHS_SRE_IMP_80

S_ALR_87008775	IMG Activity: EHS_MD_160_20
S_ALR_87008776	IMG Activity: EHS_MD_120_30_2
S_ALR_87008777	IMG Activity: EHS_MD_120_30_1
S_ALR_87008778	IMG Activity: EHS_MD_120_10_20_1
S_ALR_87008779	IMG Activity: EHS_SR_225_20
S_ALR_87008780	IMG Activity: EHS_SR_225_60
S_ALR_87008781	IMG Activity: EHS_SR_230_10_2
S_ALR_87008782	IMG Activity: EHS_SRE_IMP_90
S_ALR_87008783	IMG Activity: EHS_SD_100_10_033
S_ALR_87008784	IMG Activity: EHS_SD_100_10_005
S_ALR_87008785	IMG Activity: EHS_SD_100_10_013_50
S_ALR_87008786	IMG Activity: EHS_DDS_100_10_40
S_ALR_87008787	IMG Activity: EHS_SD_100_20_013_50
S_ALR_87008788	IMG Activity: EHS_SR_220_01
S_ALR_87008789	IMG Activity: EHS_SR_210_20_40
S_ALR_87008790	IMG Activity: EHS_SR_220_08_01
S_ALR_87008791	IMG Activity: EHS_SR_220_08
S_ALR_87008792	IMG Activity: EHS_SR_220_09
S_ALR_87008793	IMG Activity: EHS_SD_100_10_20
S_ALR_87008794	IMG Activity: EHS_SR_220_10
S_ALR_87008795	IMG Activity: EHS_SR_225_10
S_ALR_87008811	IMG Activity: PPPI_PO_212
S_ALR_87008812	IMG Activity: COCB320
S_ALR_87008813	IMG Activity: SIMG_CFMENUOLIAOIDF
S_ALR_87008814	IMG Activity: SIMG_CFMENUOLIAOIDA
S_ALR_87008815	IMG Activity: SIMGOLMEVNE3
S_ALR_87008816	IMG Activity: SIMG_CFMENUORFBOBD5
S_ALR_87008817	IMG Activity: SIMG_CFORFBOAC5
S_ALR_87008818	IMG Activity: SIMG_CFMENUOLSDVNOX
S_ALR_87008819	IMG Activity: SIMG_CFMENUOLSDNK03
S_ALR_87008820	IMG Activity: SIMG_CFMENUOLSDNL03
S_ALR_87008821	IMG Activity: SIMG_CFMENUOLSDNVE03
S_ALR_87008822	IMG Activity: SIMG_CFMENUOLSDNG03
S_ALR_87008823	IMG Activity: SIMG_CFMENUOLSDNT03
S_ALR_87008824	IMG Activity: SIMG_CFMENUOLSDNF03
S_ALR_87008825	IMG Activity: SIMG_CFMENUOLSDNV03
S_ALR_87008826	IMG Activity: SIMG_CFMENUOLSDNKO03
S_ALR_87008827	IMG Activity: SIMG_CFORFBOAC5
S_ALR_87008828	IMG Activity: SIMG_CFMENUORFBOBD5
S_ALR_87008829	IMG Activity: SIMG_VC_DVS30
S_ALR_87008830	IMG Activity: SIMG_VC_DVS10
S_ALR_87008831	IMG Activity: SIMG_VC_DVS10
S_ALR_87008832	IMG Activity: SIMG_VC_DVS21
S_ALR_87008839	IMG Activity: GGA_300_140
S_ALR_87008840	IMG Activity: GGA_300_160
S_ALR_87008841	IMG Activity: GGA_300_170_100
S_ALR_87008842	IMG Activity: GGA_300_170_200
S_ALR_87008843	IMG Activity: GGA_300_170_300
S_ALR_87008844	IMG Activity: GGA_300_180
S_ALR_87008845	IMG Activity: GGA_200_200_100
S_ALR_87008846	IMG Activity: GGA_200_200_110
S_ALR_87008847	IMG Activity: GGA_200_200_120
S_ALR_87008848	IMG Activity: GGA_200_200_150
S_ALR_87008849	IMG Activity: GGA_200_200_160

SAP Transaction Codes – Volume Two

S_ALR_87008850	IMG Activity: GGA_820_100
S_ALR_87008851	IMG Activity: GGA_300_200
S_ALR_87008852	IMG Activity: GGA_400_100
S_ALR_87008853	IMG Activity: GGA_400_120
S_ALR_87008855	IMG Activity: GGA_400_180
S_ALR_87008856	IMG Activity: GGA_400_200
S_ALR_87008857	IMG Activity: GGA_700_100
S_ALR_87008858	IMG Activity: GGA_300_202
S_ALR_87008859	IMG Activity: GGA_300_120
S_ALR_87008860	IMG Activity: GGA_300_112
S_ALR_87008861	IMG Activity: GGA_300_100
S_ALR_87008862	IMG Activity: GGA_700_150
S_ALR_87008864	IMG Activity: GGA_200_100_200
S_ALR_87008865	IMG Activity: GGA_100_150
S_ALR_87008866	IMG Activity: GGA_800_140
S_ALR_87008867	IMG Activity: GGA_800_120
S_ALR_87008868	IMG Activity: GGA_100_100
S_ALR_87008869	IMG Activity: GGA_200_100_100
S_ALR_87008870	IMG Activity: GGA_100_200
S_ALR_87008871	IMG Activity: GGA_100_250
S_ALR_87008872	IMG Activity: GGA_100_270
S_ALR_87008873	IMG Activity: GGA_100_260
S_ALR_87008874	IMG Activity: GGA_100_300
S_ALR_87008875	IMG Activity: GGA_100_350
S_ALR_87008876	IMG Activity: GGA_200_300_100
S_ALR_87008877	IMG Activity: GGA_200_300_110
S_ALR_87008878	IMG Activity: GGA_200_300_120
S_ALR_87008879	IMG Activity: GGA_200_300_140
S_ALR_87008880	IMG Activity: GGA_200_300_160
S_ALR_87008881	IMG Activity: GGA_800_180
S_ALR_87008882	IMG Activity: GGA_200_100_110
S_ALR_87008883	IMG Activity: GGA_200_100_140
S_ALR_87008884	IMG Activity: GGA_200_100_130
S_ALR_87008885	IMG Activity: GGA_800_160
S_ALR_87008886	IMG Activity: GGA_200_100_145
S_ALR_87008887	IMG Activity: GGA_200_100_150
S_ALR_87008888	IMG Activity: GGA_770_100
S_ALR_87008889	IMG Activity: GGA_800_110
S_ALR_87008890	IMG Activity: GGA_800_100
S_ALR_87008898	IMG Activity: SIMG_XXCMMENUORFBKPU
S_ALR_87008900	IMG Activity: SIMG_GLT0GCT6
S_ALR_87008901	IMG Activity: SIMG_GLT0GA27
S_ALR_87008902	IMG Activity: SIMG_GLT0GA47
S_ALR_87008903	IMG Activity: SIMG_GLT0OB53
S_ALR_87008904	IMG Activity: SIMG_GLT0GLCF
S_ALR_87008905	IMG Activity: SIMG_GLT0GLGCU1
S_ALR_87008906	IMG Activity: SIMG_GLT0GLGCU2
S_ALR_87008907	IMG Activity: SIMG_GLT0FGI4
S_ALR_87008908	IMG Activity: SIMG_ORFB2GCR2
S_ALR_87008909	IMG Activity: SIMG_ORFB2T892U
S_ALR_87008910	IMG Activity: SIMG_GLT0GCT4
S_ALR_87008911	IMG Activity: SIMG_ORFB2T001B_PL
S_ALR_87008912	IMG Activity: SIMG_ORFB2T894_PL
S_ALR_87008913	IMG Activity: SIMG_ORFB2T895

S_ALR_87008914	IMG Activity: SIMG_ORFB2GP32
S_ALR_87008915	IMG Activity: SIMG_ORFB2GCLE
S_ALR_87008916	IMG Activity: SIMG_GLT0FGIP
S_ALR_87008917	IMG Activity: SIMG_GLT0FGIT
S_ALR_87008918	IMG Activity: SIMG_GLT0OBRX
S_ALR_87008919	IMG Activity: SIMG_CFORFBGCUT
S_ALR_87008920	IMG Activity: SIMG_GLT0GS02
S_ALR_87008921	IMG Activity: SIMG_GLT0GS12
S_ALR_87008922	IMG Activity: SIMG_GLT0GCTS
S_ALR_87008923	IMG Activity: SIMG_GLT0GCAC
S_ALR_87008924	IMG Activity: SIMG_GLT0GLDE
S_ALR_87008925	IMG Activity: SIMG_GLT0FGIR
S_ALR_87008926	IMG Activity: SIMG_GLT0FGIZ
S_ALR_87008927	IMG Activity: SIMG_GLT0FGI1
S_ALR_87008928	IMG Activity: SIMG_GLT0FGIO
S_ALR_87008929	IMG Activity: SIMG_GLT0FGIQ
S_ALR_87008930	IMG Activity: SIMG_GLT0FGIX
S_ALR_87008931	IMG Activity: SIMG_GLT0FGIY
S_ALR_87008932	IMG Activity: SIMG_GLT0FGIV
S_ALR_87008933	IMG Activity: SIMG_GLT0GBEB_ACCDET
S_ALR_87008934	IMG Activity: SIMG_GLT0GINS
S_ALR_87008935	IMG Activity: SIMG_GLT0GLL2_SPLIT
S_ALR_87008936	IMG Activity: SIMG_GLT0GLL2
S_ALR_87008937	IMG Activity: SIMG_GLT0V_001_GKF
S_ALR_87008938	IMG Activity: SIMG_GLT0OBG1
S_ALR_87008939	IMG Activity: SIMG_GLT0GCHE
S_ALR_87008940	IMG Activity: SIMG_GLT0T000GL
S_ALR_87008941	IMG Activity: SIMG_GLT0GLR2
S_ALR_87008942	IMG Activity: SIMG_GLT0_T800D
S_ALR_87008943	IMG Activity: SIMG_GLT0_T8G17
S_ALR_87008944	IMG Activity: SIMG_GLT0_T8G12
S_ALR_87008945	IMG Activity: SIMG_GLT0T882G_GL
S_ALR_87008946	IMG Activity: SIMG_ORFB2T811I
S_ALR_87008947	IMG Activity: SIMG_ORFB2T811I2
S_ALR_87008948	IMG Activity: SIMG_ORFBT811U
S_ALR_87008949	IMG Activity: SIMG_ORFB2GCA9
S_ALR_87008950	IMG Activity: SIMG_GLT0GCT7
S_ALR_87008951	IMG Activity: SIMG_GLT0GL21
S_ALR_87008952	IMG Activity: SIMG_GLT0T001A
S_ALR_87008953	IMG Activity: SIMG_GLT0GA11
S_ALR_87008954	IMG Activity: SIMG_GLT0GA31
S_ALR_87008998	IMG Activity: SIMG_ORFA_OACS
S_ALR_87008999	IMG Activity: SIMG_ORFA_OAKA
S_ALR_87009000	IMG Activity: ORFA_ERW_INVENT
S_ALR_87009001	IMG Activity: ORFA_VORG_ZUG
S_ALR_87009002	IMG Activity: ORFA_KONT_TYP
S_ALR_87009003	IMG Activity: ORFA_BESTANLKL
S_ALR_87009004	IMG Activity: SIMG_CFMENUORFAOAE3
S_ALR_87009005	IMG Activity: ORFA_OAVC
S_ALR_87009006	IMG Activity: ORFA_UEBERNR
S_ALR_87009007	IMG Activity: SIMG_CFMENUORFASTA8
S_ALR_87009008	IMG Activity: ORFA_KLASS_SPEZ3
S_ALR_87009009	IMG Activity: ORFA_GESUMB
S_ALR_87009010	IMG Activity: ORFA_KOST_UEBER

S_ALR_87009011	IMG Activity: SIMG_CFMENUORFAOA11
S_ALR_87009012	IMG Activity: ORFA_OARC
S_ALR_87009013	IMG Activity: SIMG_CFMENUORFAVOR26
S_ALR_87009014	IMG Activity: SIMG_CFMENUORFAVOR22
S_ALR_87009015	IMG Activity: ORFA_CMOD_ABG_KONT
S_ALR_87009016	IMG Activity: SIMG_CFMENUORFAVOR31
S_ALR_87009017	IMG Activity: ORFA_UMB_VAR
S_ALR_87009018	IMG Activity: SIMG_CFMENUORFAVOR32
S_ALR_87009019	IMG Activity: ORFA_TRANS2
S_ALR_87009020	IMG Activity: ORFA_VORG_ABG_FRZ
S_ALR_87009021	IMG Activity: ORFA_VORG_TABWI
S_ALR_87009022	IMG Activity: SIMG_ORFA_OAZ1
S_ALR_87009023	IMG Activity: SIMG_CFMENUORFAVOR21
S_ALR_87009024	IMG Activity: ORFA_ABG_SPEZ
S_ALR_87009025	IMG Activity: ORFA_BEW_MEHR
S_ALR_87009026	IMG Activity: ORFA_OAKB
S_ALR_87009027	IMG Activity: ORFA_OA01
S_ALR_87009028	IMG Activity: ORFA_UMWELT
S_ALR_87009029	IMG Activity: SIMG_CFMENUORFAOAVF
S_ALR_87009030	IMG Activity: SIMG_CFMENUORFAOAVT
S_ALR_87009031	IMG Activity: SIMG_CFMENUORFAVRS4
S_ALR_87009032	IMG Activity: SIMG_CFMENUORFAVRS5
S_ALR_87009033	IMG Activity: ORFA_VERS_INDEX2
S_ALR_87009034	IMG Activity: ORFA_VERS_FELD
S_ALR_87009035	IMG Activity: SIMG_CFMENUORFAVRS7
S_ALR_87009036	IMG Activity: SIMG_CFMENUORFAOAVD
S_ALR_87009037	IMG Activity: SIMG_CFMENUORFAVRM4
S_ALR_87009038	IMG Activity: ORFA_VERM_ANHALT
S_ALR_87009039	IMG Activity: SIMG_CFMENUORFAVRM55
S_ALR_87009040	IMG Activity: ORFA_VERM_INDEX2
S_ALR_87009041	IMG Activity: ORFA_VERM_FELD
S_ALR_87009042	IMG Activity: SIMG_CFMENUORFAVRM7
S_ALR_87009043	IMG Activity: ORFA_KLASS_SPEZ2
S_ALR_87009044	IMG Activity: SIMG_CFMENUORFAOA77
S_ALR_87009045	IMG Activity: SIMG_CFMENUORFAOA78
S_ALR_87009046	IMG Activity: ORFA_LAYOUT
S_ALR_87009047	IMG Activity: SIMG_CFMENUORFAOAVA
S_ALR_87009048	IMG Activity: SIMG_CFMENUORFAOAV8
S_ALR_87009049	IMG Activity: ORFA_ORD_SCHL
S_ALR_87009050	IMG Activity: SIMG_CFMENUORFAOAW1
S_ALR_87009051	IMG Activity: ORFA_KLASS_LEAS
S_ALR_87009052	IMG Activity: ORFA_KLASS_SPEZ1
S_ALR_87009053	IMG Activity: ORFA_KONS_BEW1
S_ALR_87009054	IMG Activity: ORFA_KONS_BEW2
S_ALR_87009055	IMG Activity: ORFA_KONS_TRANSFER
S_ALR_87009056	IMG Activity: SIMG_CFMENUORFAOAC1
S_ALR_87009057	IMG Activity: SIMG_CFMENUORFALEA2
S_ALR_87009058	IMG Activity: ORFA_LEAS_FELD
S_ALR_87009059	IMG Activity: ORFA_TRANS
S_ALR_87009060	IMG Activity: ORFA_VERS_NEU
S_ALR_87009061	IMG Activity: ORFA_AUFW_NEU
S_ALR_87009062	IMG Activity: ORFA_ALT_FREMDW
S_ALR_87009063	IMG Activity: ORFA_BEW_ALT
S_ALR_87009064	IMG Activity: SIMG_CFMENUORFAOA13

S_ALR_87009065	IMG Activity: ORFA_IND_ALT
S_ALR_87009066	IMG Activity: ORFA_AS91
S_ALR_87009067	IMG Activity: SIMG_CFMENUORFAOAE4
S_ALR_87009068	IMG Activity: ORFA_IND_SCHL
S_ALR_87009069	IMG Activity: ORFA_IND_ANLNR
S_ALR_87009070	IMG Activity: SIMG_CFMENUORFAALT9
S_ALR_87009071	IMG Activity: ORFA_ALTD_REIHENF
S_ALR_87009072	IMG Activity: ORFA_ALTDATUM
S_ALR_87009073	IMG Activity: ORFA_DATUMAFA
S_ALR_87009074	IMG Activity: ORFA_RESTW
S_ALR_87009075	IMG Activity: SIMG_CFMENUORFAOAK5
S_ALR_87009076	IMG Activity: SIMG_CFMENUORFAOAMK
S_ALR_87009077	IMG Activity: SIMG_CFMENUORFAOASV
S_ALR_87009078	IMG Activity: SIMG_CFMENUORFAOABP
S_ALR_87009079	IMG Activity: SIMG_CFMENUORFAOABL
S_ALR_87009080	IMG Activity: SIMG_CFMENUORFAOAGL
S_ALR_87009081	IMG Activity: ORFA_JAHR_RUECK
S_ALR_87009082	IMG Activity: SIMG_CFMENUORFAOAK1
S_ALR_87009083	IMG Activity: ORFA_AS81
S_ALR_87009084	IMG Activity: SIMG_CFMENUORFASU03
S_ALR_87009085	IMG Activity: SIMG_CFMENUORFASU02
S_ALR_87009086	IMG Activity: ORFA_OAWF
S_ALR_87009087	IMG Activity: SIMG_CFMENUORFAOAV1
S_ALR_87009088	IMG Activity: SIMG_CFMENUORFAOAV3
S_ALR_87009089	IMG Activity: SIMG_CFMENUORFABER43
S_ALR_87009090	IMG Activity: ORFA_IND_UMR
S_ALR_87009091	IMG Activity: SIMG_CFMENUORFAAIIO
S_ALR_87009092	IMG Activity: SIMG_CFMENUORFAVOR49
S_ALR_87009093	IMG Activity: ORFA_BEW_NACH
S_ALR_87009094	IMG Activity: SIMG_CFMENUORFAVOR71
S_ALR_87009095	IMG Activity: ORFA_STATI0
S_ALR_87009096	IMG Activity: ORFA_STAT_KONT
S_ALR_87009097	IMG Activity: ORFA_FELDST_VAR
S_ALR_87009098	IMG Activity: ORFA_AIB_NUMMERN
S_ALR_87009099	IMG Activity: ORFA_ERW_TRANS
S_ALR_87009100	IMG Activity: ORFA_BEW_TRANFER
S_ALR_87009101	IMG Activity: SIMG_CFMENUORFAVOR41
S_ALR_87009102	IMG Activity: ORFA_BWA_AIB
S_ALR_87009103	IMG Activity: ORFA_AIB_KOSTART
S_ALR_87009104	IMG Activity: SIMG_CFMENUORFAOKO7
S_ALR_87009105	IMG Activity: SIMG_CFMENUORFAVOR48
S_ALR_87009106	IMG Activity: SIMG_CFMENUORFAINF2
S_ALR_87009107	IMG Activity: SIMG_CFMENUORFAOA79
S_ALR_87009108	IMG Activity: SIMG_CFMENUORFAOAV9
S_ALR_87009109	IMG Activity: SIMG_CFMENUORFAOA90
S_ALR_87009110	IMG Activity: SIMG_CFMENUORFAOAVZ
S_ALR_87009111	IMG Activity: SIMG_CFMENUORFAOAW3
S_ALR_87009112	IMG Activity: ORFA_SE71
S_ALR_87009113	IMG Activity: ORFA_SIMU
S_ALR_87009114	IMG Activity: ORFA_BEW_VORSCHLAG
S_ALR_87009115	IMG Activity: ORFA_VORG_INT
S_ALR_87009116	IMG Activity: ORFA_BEZ_DAT
S_ALR_87009117	IMG Activity: ORFA_BUCH_ZEIL
S_ALR_87009118	IMG Activity: ORFA_ERW_BUCH

S_ALR_87009119	IMG Activity: ORFA_OATR
S_ALR_87009120	IMG Activity: SIMG_CFMENUORFAOAVI
S_ALR_87009121	IMG Activity: ORFA_FELDST_ABG
S_ALR_87009122	IMG Activity: ORFA_BEWEG_AUSSER
S_ALR_87009123	IMG Activity: SIMG_CFMENUORFAOA27
S_ALR_87009124	IMG Activity: ORFA_BUSCHL
S_ALR_87009125	IMG Activity: ORFA_HAUPT_KONT
S_ALR_87009126	IMG Activity: SIMG_CFMENUORFAOAVS
S_ALR_87009127	IMG Activity: SIMG_CFMENUORFAOAB3
S_ALR_87009128	IMG Activity: ORFA_SOND_KONTEN
S_ALR_87009129	IMG Activity: SIMG_CFMENUORFAINF9
S_ALR_87009130	IMG Activity: SIMG_CFMENUORFABEWA1
S_ALR_87009131	IMG Activity: ORFA_AUSS_KONTEN
S_ALR_87009132	IMG Activity: ORFA_VORSTEUER
S_ALR_87009133	IMG Activity: SIMG_CFMENUORFAOAVHX
S_ALR_87009134	IMG Activity: ORFA_MIT_BEREICH
S_ALR_87009135	IMG Activity: ORFA_IND_BEZ
S_ALR_87009136	IMG Activity: ORFA_IND_AFAMETH
S_ALR_87009137	IMG Activity: ORFA_IND_UMST
S_ALR_87009138	IMG Activity: RSL_DEGRESSIV
S_ALR_87009139	IMG Activity: RSL_RECHENSCHLUSSEL
S_ALR_87009140	IMG Activity: ORFA_PER_ZEIT
S_ALR_87009141	IMG Activity: ORFA_PER_GEN
S_ALR_87009142	IMG Activity: SIMG_CFMENUORFAOA23
S_ALR_87009143	IMG Activity: SIMG_CFMENUORFAOA29
S_ALR_87009144	IMG Activity: SIMG_CFMENUORFAOAW2
S_ALR_87009145	IMG Activity: ORFA_BEZUG_IND
S_ALR_87009146	IMG Activity: ORFA_BEREICH1
S_ALR_87009147	IMG Activity: ORFA_BEW_GJAHR_VAR_B
S_ALR_87009148	IMG Activity: ORFA_BEW_GJAHR_VAR_A
S_ALR_87009149	IMG Activity: SIMG_CFMENUORFAOAE1
S_ALR_87009150	IMG Activity: ORFA_RUMPF
S_ALR_87009151	IMG Activity: ORFA_RUMPF_RECH
S_ALR_87009152	IMG Activity: ORFA_KLASS_BEW1
S_ALR_87009153	IMG Activity: SIMG_CFMENUORFAVOR13
S_ALR_87009154	IMG Activity: ORFA_RUND
S_ALR_87009155	IMG Activity: ORFA_UMSTBETR
S_ALR_87009156	IMG Activity: SIMG_CFMENUORFAOA39
S_ALR_87009157	IMG Activity: ORFA_BEREICH_PARA
S_ALR_87009158	IMG Activity: ORFA_BEW_GJAHR_VAR_H
S_ALR_87009159	IMG Activity: ORFA_NORM_BEREICH
S_ALR_87009160	IMG Activity: ORFA_NORM_KONTEN
S_ALR_87009161	IMG Activity: SIMG_CFMENUORFAOA25
S_ALR_87009162	IMG Activity: SIMG_CFMENUORFAOAEA
S_ALR_87009163	IMG Activity: ORFA_SOND_BER
S_ALR_87009164	IMG Activity: ORFA_AFARFO
S_ALR_87009165	IMG Activity: ORFA_445
S_ALR_87009166	IMG Activity: ORFA_BEREICH_FREMD
S_ALR_87009167	IMG Activity: ORFA_BEW_FREMD_PAR
S_ALR_87009168	IMG Activity: SIMG_CFMENUORFAOAPL
S_ALR_87009169	IMG Activity: ORFA_KOMPLEX
S_ALR_87009170	IMG Activity: ORFA_KLASS_KOMPL
S_ALR_87009171	IMG Activity: ORFA_IND_KLASSEN
S_ALR_87009172	IMG Activity: ORFA_BKRS_NUMMERN

S_ALR_87009173	IMG Activity: ORFA_LAENDER
S_ALR_87009174	IMG Activity: ORFA_AUFW_BEREICH
S_ALR_87009175	IMG Activity: SIMG_CFMENUORFAOAA2
S_ALR_87009176	IMG Activity: ORFA_AUFW_KONTEN
S_ALR_87009177	IMG Activity: ORFA_S_KLASSEN
S_ALR_87009178	IMG Activity: SIMG_CFMENUORFAVOR64
S_ALR_87009179	IMG Activity: ORFA_IND_KONTEN
S_ALR_87009180	IMG Activity: ORFA_IND_KONTEN1
S_ALR_87009181	IMG Activity: SIMG_IND_NUMKR
S_ALR_87009182	IMG Activity: SIMG_CFMENUORFAOAV5
S_ALR_87009183	IMG Activity: ORFA_ZINS_KONTEN
S_ALR_87009184	IMG Activity: ORFA_ZINS_SCHL
S_ALR_87009185	IMG Activity: SIMG_CFMENUORFAVRM1
S_ALR_87009186	IMG Activity: SIMG_CFMENUORFAOAVE
S_ALR_87009187	IMG Activity: SIMG_CFMENUORFAOAVB
S_ALR_87009188	IMG Activity: SIMG_CFMENUORFAOAVC
S_ALR_87009189	IMG Activity: ORFA_AUFW_KONTEN1
S_ALR_87009190	IMG Activity: ORFA_IND_AUFW
S_ALR_87009191	IMG Activity: ORFA_BEWEG_AUFW
S_ALR_87009192	IMG Activity: SIMG_CFMENUORFAOAB1
S_ALR_87009193	IMG Activity: ORFA_ZINS_BEW
S_ALR_87009194	IMG Activity: SIMG_CFMENUORFAOAP1
S_ALR_87009195	IMG Activity: SIMG_CFMENUORFAORG2
S_ALR_87009196	IMG Activity: ORFA_BER_SOPO_BN
S_ALR_87009197	IMG Activity: ORFA_SONDER_KONTEN
S_ALR_87009198	IMG Activity: SIMG_CFMENUORFAAS08
S_ALR_87009199	IMG Activity: ORFA_BER_RUECKL
S_ALR_87009200	IMG Activity: ORFA_RUECK_KONTEN
S_ALR_87009201	IMG Activity: ORFA_BEWEG_RUECK
S_ALR_87009202	IMG Activity: SIMGRSL_MAX_BETRAG
S_ALR_87009203	IMG Activity: RSL_STUFEN
S_ALR_87009204	IMG Activity: RSL_PER
S_ALR_87009205	IMG Activity: RSL_ZUORDNUNG
S_ALR_87009206	IMG Activity: ORFA_KLASS_SPEZ
S_ALR_87009207	IMG Activity: SIMG_CFMENUORFAAM01
S_ALR_87009208	IMG Activity: SIMG_CFMENUORFAOAI3
S_ALR_87009209	IMG Activity: ORFA_BILDAUFBAU
S_ALR_87009210	IMG Activity: SIMG_CFMENUORFAOAI4
S_ALR_87009211	IMG Activity: SIMG_CFMENUORFAOAI2
S_ALR_87009212	IMG Activity: ORFA_BEW_FOERDER
S_ALR_87009213	IMG Activity: SIMG_CFMENUORFAOAI1
S_ALR_87009214	IMG Activity: OLPA_VERFUG1
S_ALR_87009215	IMG Activity: OLPA_VERFUG2
S_ALR_87009238	IMG Activity: SIMG_OLPR_CMOD_STULI
S_ALR_87009239	IMG Activity: SIMG_CFMENUOFTFOFG1
S_ALR_87009240	IMG Activity: SIMG_CFMENUOFTFOFD8
S_ALR_87009241	IMG Activity: SIMG_CFMENUOFTFOFRB
S_ALR_87009242	IMG Activity: SIMG_CFMENUOFTFFMEN
S_ALR_87009243	IMG Activity: SIMG_CFMENUOFTFFMEO
S_ALR_87009244	IMG Activity: SIMG_CFMENUOFTFFMEP
S_ALR_87009245	IMG Activity: SIMG_CFMENUOFTFOF03
S_ALR_87009246	IMG Activity: SIMG_CFMENUOFTFOFG3
S_ALR_87009247	IMG Activity: SIMG_CFMENUOFTFOFG4
S_ALR_87009248	IMG Activity: SIMG_CFMENUOFTFOFG9

S_ALR_87009249	IMG Activity: SIMG_CFMENUOFTFOFGA
S_ALR_87009250	IMG Activity: SIMG_CFMENUOFTFOFG2
S_ALR_87009251	IMG Activity: SIMG_CFMENUOFTFFME4
S_ALR_87009252	IMG Activity: SIMG_CFMENUOFTFFME6
S_ALR_87009253	IMG Activity: SIMG_CFMENUOFTFFME2
S_ALR_87009254	IMG Activity: SIMG_CFMENUOFTFFME7
S_ALR_87009255	IMG Activity: SIMG_CFMENUOFTFFMEV
S_ALR_87009256	IMG Activity: SIMG_CFMENUOFTFFME9
S_ALR_87009257	IMG Activity: SIMG_CFMENUOFTFFME3
S_ALR_87009258	IMG Activity: SIMG_CFMENUOFTFFME5
S_ALR_87009259	IMG Activity: SIMG_CFMENUOFTFFME1
S_ALR_87009260	IMG Activity: SIMG_CFMENUOFTFFMEK
S_ALR_87009261	IMG Activity: SIMG_CFMENUOFTFFMEL
S_ALR_87009262	IMG Activity: SIMG_CFMENUOFTFFMEM
S_ALR_87009263	IMG Activity: SIMG_CFMENUOFTFOFD3
S_ALR_87009264	IMG Activity: SIMG_CFMENUOFTFOF22
S_ALR_87009265	IMG Activity: SIMG_CFMENUOFTFOF31
S_ALR_87009266	IMG Activity: SIMG_CFMENUOFTFOF10
S_ALR_87009267	IMG Activity: SIMG_CFMENUOFTFOFD1
S_ALR_87009268	IMG Activity: SIMG_CFMENUOFTFOF07
S_ALR_87009269	IMG Activity: SIMG_CFMENUOFTFOF30
S_ALR_87009270	IMG Activity: SIMG_CFMENUOFTFOB29
S_ALR_87009271	IMG Activity: SIMG_CFMENUOFTFOF01
S_ALR_87009272	IMG Activity: SIMG_CFMENUOFTFOK60
S_ALR_87009273	IMG Activity: SIMG_CFMENUOFTFOFGE
S_ALR_87009274	IMG Activity: SIMG_CFMENUOFTFOFGG
S_ALR_87009275	IMG Activity: SIMG_CFMENUOFTFOF06
S_ALR_87009276	IMG Activity: SIMG_CFMENUOFTFOFD2
S_ALR_87009277	IMG Activity: SIMG_CFMENUOFTFOF05
S_ALR_87009287	Securities: Fin. Transaction Types
S_ALR_87009293	Securities: Flow Types
S_ALR_87009294	Assign Flow Types
S_ALR_87009295	Assign Flow Types to Transact. Types
S_ALR_87009296	Define Derivation Procedures
S_ALR_87009301	IMG Activity: RECHTSTRAGER_GP_I
S_ALR_87009302	IMG Activity: HANDLER
S_ALR_87009303	IMG Activity: STORNOGRUNDE_DE
S_ALR_87009304	IMG Activity: LEITWAHRUNGEN
S_ALR_87009305	IMG Activity: ERTRAGE_TREASURY_WP
S_ALR_87009306	IMG Activity: GESCHAFT_GH
S_ALR_87009307	IMG Activity: KONTFIND_PRUFUNG_GH
S_ALR_87009308	IMG Activity: GESCHAFT_FX
S_ALR_87009309	IMG Activity: UNDERLYINGGESCHAFTFX
S_ALR_87009310	IMG Activity: ORDERLIMITPRUF_FX
S_ALR_87009311	IMG activity: PRUFUNG_FX
S_ALR_87009312	IMG Activity: GESCHAFT_DE
S_ALR_87009313	IMG Activity: UNDERLYINGGESCHAFTDE
S_ALR_87009314	IMG Activity: PRUFUNG_DE
S_ALR_87009315	IMG Activity: KUNDIGUNGSGRUNDE
S_ALR_87009316	IMG Activity: KUNDIGUNGSVEREINB_DG
S_ALR_87009317	IMG Activity: KUNDIGUNGSVEREINB_DN
S_ALR_87009318	IMG activity: WAHRUNGSVOLAS_DF
S_ALR_87009324	IMG Activity: SIMG_CFMENUOFTDOT33
S_ALR_87009325	IMG Activity: SIMG_CFORFBOB27ZAFR

S_ALR_87009326	IMG Activity: SIMG_CFMENUORFBOBAP
S_ALR_87009327	IMG Activity: SIMG_CFMENUORFBOB10
S_ALR_87009328	IMG Activity: SIMG_CFMENUORFBOBA3
S_ALR_87009329	IMG Activity: SIMG_CFMENUORFBOBAL
S_ALR_87009330	IMG Activity: SIMG_CFMENUORFBOB61
S_ALR_87009331	IMG Activity: SIMG_CFMENUORFBOB18
S_ALR_87009332	IMG Activity: SIMG_CFMENUORFB2OB16
S_ALR_87009333	IMG Activity: BRANCHE_GF
S_ALR_87009334	IMG Activity: RATING_GP
S_ALR_87009335	IMG Activity: INSTITUT_GP
S_ALR_87009336	IMG Activity: SIMG_CFMENUORFBOBCP
S_ALR_87009337	IMG Activity: ORGANKREDIT_GP
S_ALR_87009338	IMG Activity: KWG_AUSKUNFT_GP
S_ALR_87009339	IMG Activity: SIMG_CFMENUORFBOB47
S_ALR_87009340	IMG Activity: SIMG_CFMENUOFTDOT13
S_ALR_87009341	IMG Activity: GPZUSATZ7_GP
S_ALR_87009342	IMG Activity: GPZUSATZ8_GP
S_ALR_87009343	IMG Activity: GPZUSATZ9_GP
S_ALR_87009344	IMG Activity: GPZUSATZ10_GP
S_ALR_87009345	IMG Activity: GPZUSATZ11_GP
S_ALR_87009346	IMG Activity: TEXT-ID-ALLG_GP
S_ALR_87009347	IMG Activity: TEXT-ID-ROLLEN_GP
S_ALR_87009348	IMG Activity: TEXT-ID-ROLLE-Z_GP
S_ALR_87009349	IMG Activity: GPZUSATZ6_GP
S_ALR_87009350	IMG Activity: SIMG_CFMENUORFBOBAQ
S_ALR_87009351	IMG Activity: SIMG_CFMENUORFBFBMP
S_ALR_87009352	IMG Activity: SIMG_CFMENUORFBOB05K
S_ALR_87009353	IMG Activity: GPZUSATZ1_GP
S_ALR_87009354	IMG Activity: GPZUSATZ2_GP
S_ALR_87009355	IMG Activity: GPZUSATZ3_GP
S_ALR_87009356	IMG Activity: GPZUSATZ4_GP
S_ALR_87009357	IMG Activity: GPZUSATZ5_GP
S_ALR_87009358	IMG Activity: ANREDE_GP
S_ALR_87009359	IMG Activity: BRIEFANREDE_GP
S_ALR_87009360	IMG Activity: ANSCHRIFTSKENNUNG_GP
S_ALR_87009361	IMG Activity: BP_FM_ROLLENTYP
S_ALR_87009362	IMG Activity: BP_FM_AKT
S_ALR_87009363	IMG Activity: RECHTSFORM_GP
S_ALR_87009364	IMG Activity: BEZIEHUNGSART_GP
S_ALR_87009365	IMG Activity: FUNKTION_GP
S_ALR_87009366	IMG Activity: ABTEILUNG_GP
S_ALR_87009367	IMG Activity: ROLLENART_GP
S_ALR_87009368	IMG Activity: FREIGABEPARAMETER_GP
S_ALR_87009369	IMG Activity: AKTIVIERUNG_GP
S_ALR_87009370	IMG Activity: ROLLE-SICHT-ZUORD_GP
S_ALR_87009371	IMG Activity: GUTERSTAND_GP
S_ALR_87009372	IMG Activity: NUMMERNKREISE_GP
S_ALR_87009373	IMG Activity: BESCHAFTSTATUS_GP
S_ALR_87009374	IMG Activity: MITARBEITERGRUPPE_GP
S_ALR_87009375	IMG Activity: BP_ZIELGRUPPE2_GP
S_ALR_87009376	IMG Activity: RECHTSTRAGER_GP
S_ALR_87009377	IMG Activity: PHONETISCHE_SUCHE_GP
S_ALR_87009378	IMG Activity: GP-GRUPPIERUNG
S_ALR_87009379	IMG Activity: FAMILIENSTAND_GP

S_ALR_87009380	IMG Activity: SIMG_CFMENUOFTDOT33
S_ALR_87009381	IMG Activity: SIMG_CFORFBOB27ZAFR
S_ALR_87009382	IMG Activity: SIMG_CFMENUORFBOBAP
S_ALR_87009383	IMG Activity: SIMG_CFMENUORFBOB10
S_ALR_87009384	IMG Activity: SIMG_CFMENUORFBOBA3
S_ALR_87009385	IMG Activity: SIMG_CFMENUORFBOBAL
S_ALR_87009386	IMG Activity: SIMG_CFMENUORFBOB61
S_ALR_87009387	IMG Activity: SIMG_CFMENUORFBOB18
S_ALR_87009388	IMG Activity: SIMG_CFMENUORFB2OB16
S_ALR_87009389	IMG Activity: BRANCHE_GF
S_ALR_87009390	IMG Activity: RATING_GP
S_ALR_87009391	IMG Activity: INSTITUT_GP
S_ALR_87009392	IMG Activity: SIMG_CFMENUORFBOBCP
S_ALR_87009393	IMG Activity: ORGANKREDIT_GP
S_ALR_87009394	IMG Activity: KWG_AUSKUNFT_GP
S_ALR_87009395	IMG Activity: SIMG_CFMENUORFBOB47
S_ALR_87009396	IMG Activity: SIMG_CFMENUOFTDOT13
S_ALR_87009397	IMG Activity: GPZUSATZ7_GP
S_ALR_87009398	IMG Activity: GPZUSATZ8_GP
S_ALR_87009399	IMG Activity: GPZUSATZ9_GP
S_ALR_87009400	IMG Activity: GPZUSATZ10_GP
S_ALR_87009401	IMG Activity: GPZUSATZ11_GP
S_ALR_87009402	IMG Activity: TEXT-ID-ALLG_GP
S_ALR_87009403	IMG Activity: TEXT-ID-ROLLEN_GP
S_ALR_87009404	IMG Activity: TEXT-ID-ROLLE-Z_GP
S_ALR_87009405	IMG Activity: GPZUSATZ6_GP
S_ALR_87009406	IMG Activity: SIMG_CFMENUORFBOBAQ
S_ALR_87009407	IMG Activity: SIMG_CFMENUORFBFBMP
S_ALR_87009408	IMG Activity: SIMG_CFMENUORFBOB05K
S_ALR_87009409	IMG Activity: GPZUSATZ1_GP
S_ALR_87009410	IMG Activity: GPZUSATZ2_GP
S_ALR_87009411	IMG Activity: GPZUSATZ3_GP
S_ALR_87009412	IMG Activity: GPZUSATZ4_GP
S_ALR_87009413	IMG Activity: GPZUSATZ5_GP
S_ALR_87009414	IMG Activity: ANREDE_GP
S_ALR_87009415	IMG Activity: BRIEFANREDE_GP
S_ALR_87009416	IMG Activity: ANSCHRIFTSKENNUNG_GP
S_ALR_87009417	IMG Activity: BP_FM_ROLLENTYP
S_ALR_87009418	IMG Activity: BP_FM_AKT
S_ALR_87009419	IMG Activity: RECHTSFORM_GP
S_ALR_87009420	IMG Activity: BEZIEHUNGSART_GP
S_ALR_87009421	IMG Activity: FUNKTION_GP
S_ALR_87009422	IMG Activity: ABTEILUNG_GP
S_ALR_87009423	IMG Activity: ROLLENART_GP
S_ALR_87009424	IMG Activity: FREIGABEPARAMETER_GP
S_ALR_87009425	IMG Activity: AKTIVIERUNG_GP
S_ALR_87009426	IMG Activity: ROLLE-SICHT-ZUORD_GP
S_ALR_87009427	IMG Activity: GUTERSTAND_GP
S_ALR_87009428	IMG Activity: NUMMERNKREISE_GP
S_ALR_87009429	IMG Activity: BESCHAFTSTATUS_GP
S_ALR_87009430	IMG Activity: MITARBEITERGRUPPE_GP
S_ALR_87009431	IMG Activity: BP_ZIELGRUPPE2_GP
S_ALR_87009432	IMG Activity: RECHTSTRAGER_GP
S_ALR_87009433	IMG Activity: PHONETISCHE_SUCHE_GP

S_ALR_87009434	IMG Activity: GP-GRUPPIERUNG
S_ALR_87009435	IMG Activity: FAMILIENSTAND_GP
S_ALR_87009436	IMG Activity: SIMG_CFMENUOFTDOT33
S_ALR_87009437	IMG Activity: SIMG_CFORFBOB27ZAFR
S_ALR_87009438	IMG Activity: SIMG_CFMENUORFBOBAP
S_ALR_87009439	IMG Activity: SIMG_CFMENUORFBOB10
S_ALR_87009440	IMG Activity: SIMG_CFMENUORFBOBA3
S_ALR_87009441	IMG Activity: SIMG_CFMENUORFBOBAL
S_ALR_87009442	IMG Activity: SIMG_CFMENUORFBOB61
S_ALR_87009443	IMG Activity: SIMG_CFMENUORFBOB18
S_ALR_87009444	IMG Activity: SIMG_CFMENUORFB2OB16
S_ALR_87009445	IMG Activity: BRANCHE_GF
S_ALR_87009446	IMG Activity: RATING_GP
S_ALR_87009447	IMG Activity: INSTITUT_GP
S_ALR_87009448	IMG Activity: SIMG_CFMENUORFBOBCP
S_ALR_87009449	IMG Activity: ORGANKREDIT_GP
S_ALR_87009450	IMG Activity: KWG_AUSKUNFT_GP
S_ALR_87009451	IMG Activity: SIMG_CFMENUORFBOB47
S_ALR_87009452	IMG Activity: SIMG_CFMENUOFTDOT13
S_ALR_87009453	IMG Activity: GPZUSATZ7_GP
S_ALR_87009454	IMG Activity: GPZUSATZ8_GP
S_ALR_87009455	IMG Activity: GPZUSATZ9_GP
S_ALR_87009456	IMG Activity: GPZUSATZ10_GP
S_ALR_87009457	IMG Activity: GPZUSATZ11_GP
S_ALR_87009458	IMG Activity: TEXT-ID-ALLG_GP
S_ALR_87009459	IMG Activity: TEXT-ID-ROLLEN_GP
S_ALR_87009460	IMG Activity: TEXT-ID-ROLLE-Z_GP
S_ALR_87009461	IMG Activity: GPZUSATZ6_GP
S_ALR_87009462	IMG Activity: SIMG_CFMENUORFBOBAQ
S_ALR_87009463	IMG Activity: SIMG_CFMENUORFBFBMP
S_ALR_87009464	IMG Activity: SIMG_CFMENUORFBOB05K
S_ALR_87009465	IMG Activity: GPZUSATZ1_GP
S_ALR_87009466	IMG Activity: GPZUSATZ2_GP
S_ALR_87009467	IMG Activity: GPZUSATZ3_GP
S_ALR_87009468	IMG Activity: GPZUSATZ4_GP
S_ALR_87009469	IMG Activity: GPZUSATZ5_GP
S_ALR_87009470	IMG Activity: ANREDE_GP
S_ALR_87009471	IMG Activity: BRIEFANREDE_GP
S_ALR_87009472	IMG Activity: ANSCHRIFTSKENNUNG_GP
S_ALR_87009473	IMG Activity: BP_FM_ROLLENTYP
S_ALR_87009474	IMG Activity: BP_FM_AKT
S_ALR_87009475	IMG Activity: RECHTSFORM_GP
S_ALR_87009476	IMG Activity: BEZIEHUNGSART_GP
S_ALR_87009477	IMG Activity: FUNKTION_GP
S_ALR_87009478	IMG Activity: ABTEILUNG_GP
S_ALR_87009479	IMG Activity: ROLLENART_GP
S_ALR_87009480	IMG Activity: FREIGABEPARAMETER_GP
S_ALR_87009481	IMG Activity: AKTIVIERUNG_GP
S_ALR_87009482	IMG Activity: ROLLE-SICHT-ZUORD_GP
S_ALR_87009483	IMG Activity: GUTERSTAND_GP
S_ALR_87009484	IMG Activity: NUMMERNKREISE_GP
S_ALR_87009485	IMG Activity: BESCHAFTSTATUS_GP
S_ALR_87009486	IMG Activity: MITARBEITERGRUPPE_GP
S_ALR_87009487	IMG Activity: BP_ZIELGRUPPE2_GP

S_ALR_87009488	IMG Activity: RECHTSTRAGER_GP
S_ALR_87009489	IMG Activity: PHONETISCHE_SUCHE_GP
S_ALR_87009490	IMG Activity: GP-GRUPPIERUNG
S_ALR_87009491	IMG Activity: FAMILIENSTAND_GP
S_ALR_87009492	IMG Activity: SIMG_CFMENUOFTDOT33
S_ALR_87009493	IMG Activity: SIMG_CFORFBOB27ZAFR
S_ALR_87009494	IMG Activity: SIMG_CFMENUORFBOBAP
S_ALR_87009495	IMG Activity: SIMG_CFMENUORFBOB10
S_ALR_87009496	IMG Activity: SIMG_CFMENUORFBOBA3
S_ALR_87009497	IMG Activity: SIMG_CFMENUORFBOBAL
S_ALR_87009498	IMG Activity: SIMG_CFMENUORFBOB61
S_ALR_87009499	IMG Activity: SIMG_CFMENUORFBOB18
S_ALR_87009500	IMG Activity: SIMG_CFMENUORFB2OB16
S_ALR_87009501	IMG Activity: BRANCHE_GF
S_ALR_87009502	IMG Activity: RATING_GP
S_ALR_87009503	IMG Activity: INSTITUT_GP
S_ALR_87009504	IMG Activity: SIMG_CFMENUORFBOBCP
S_ALR_87009505	IMG Activity: ORGANKREDIT_GP
S_ALR_87009506	IMG Activity: KWG_AUSKUNFT_GP
S_ALR_87009507	IMG Activity: SIMG_CFMENUORFBOB47
S_ALR_87009508	IMG Activity: SIMG_CFMENUOFTDOT13
S_ALR_87009509	IMG Activity: GPZUSATZ7_GP
S_ALR_87009510	IMG Activity: GPZUSATZ8_GP
S_ALR_87009511	IMG Activity: GPZUSATZ9_GP
S_ALR_87009512	IMG Activity: GPZUSATZ10_GP
S_ALR_87009513	IMG Activity: GPZUSATZ11_GP
S_ALR_87009514	IMG Activity: TEXT-ID-ALLG_GP
S_ALR_87009515	IMG Activity: TEXT-ID-ROLLEN_GP
S_ALR_87009516	IMG Activity: TEXT-ID-ROLLE-Z_GP
S_ALR_87009517	IMG Activity: GPZUSATZ6_GP
S_ALR_87009518	IMG Activity: SIMG_CFMENUORFBOBAQ
S_ALR_87009519	IMG Activity: SIMG_CFMENUORFBFBMP
S_ALR_87009520	IMG Activity: SIMG_CFMENUORFBOB05K
S_ALR_87009521	IMG Activity: GPZUSATZ1_GP
S_ALR_87009522	IMG Activity: GPZUSATZ2_GP
S_ALR_87009523	IMG Activity: GPZUSATZ3_GP
S_ALR_87009524	IMG Activity: GPZUSATZ4_GP
S_ALR_87009525	IMG Activity: GPZUSATZ5_GP
S_ALR_87009526	IMG Activity: ANREDE_GP
S_ALR_87009527	IMG Activity: BRIEFANREDE_GP
S_ALR_87009528	IMG Activity: ANSCHRIFTSKENNUNG_GP
S_ALR_87009529	IMG Activity: BP_FM_ROLLENTYP
S_ALR_87009530	IMG Activity: BP_FM_AKT
S_ALR_87009531	IMG Activity: RECHTSFORM_GP
S_ALR_87009532	IMG Activity: BEZIEHUNGSART_GP
S_ALR_87009533	IMG Activity: FUNKTION_GP
S_ALR_87009534	IMG Activity: ABTEILUNG_GP
S_ALR_87009535	IMG Activity: ROLLENART_GP
S_ALR_87009536	IMG Activity: FREIGABEPARAMETER_GP
S_ALR_87009537	IMG Activity: AKTIVIERUNG_GP
S_ALR_87009538	IMG Activity: ROLLE-SICHT-ZUORD_GP
S_ALR_87009539	IMG Activity: GUTERSTAND_GP
S_ALR_87009540	IMG Activity: NUMMERNKREISE_GP
S_ALR_87009541	IMG Activity: BESCHAFTSTATUS_GP

S_ALR_87009542	IMG Activity: MITARBEITERGRUPPE_GP
S_ALR_87009543	IMG Activity: BP_ZIELGRUPPE2_GP
S_ALR_87009544	IMG Activity: RECHTSTRAGER_GP
S_ALR_87009545	IMG Activity: PHONETISCHE_SUCHE_GP
S_ALR_87009546	IMG Activity: GP-GRUPPIERUNG
S_ALR_87009547	IMG Activity: FAMILIENSTAND_GP
S_ALR_87009572	IMG Activity: GUTERSTAND_GP_I
S_ALR_87009573	IMG Activity: BESCHAFTSTATUS_GP_I
S_ALR_87009588	.
S_ALR_87009625	SAPLS_CUS_IMG_ACTIVITY
S_ALR_87009626	SAPLS_CUS_IMG_ACTIVITY
S_ALR_87009630	Plan/Actual Comparison
S_ALR_87009631	Division Comparison
S_ALR_87009632	Ranking List by Customer Group
S_ALR_87009633	CM: Region/Business Area/Product Grp
S_ALR_87009634	Percentage
S_ALR_87009635	Comparison: Current Year/Prev. Year
S_ALR_87009636	Quarters: Customer Group/Division
S_ALR_87009637	Quarterly Comparision: State List
S_ALR_87009638	Quarters: Product Group List
S_ALR_87009639	Group: Prev. Year in Group Currency
S_ALR_87009640	Company: Prev. Year Comp. in Loc.Cur
S_ALR_87009641	Company Code Overview: Key Figures
S_ALR_87009642	Company Code: Prev.Year Comp. in GC
S_ALR_87009643	Company Code: Bal. Sheet Str., Prev.
S_ALR_87009644	Company Code: Profit Breakdown Comp.
S_ALR_87009645	Value Development in Group Currency
S_ALR_87009646	Value Development in Local Currency
S_ALR_87009665	Line Item Report
S_ALR_87009666	EC-CS Master Data List: Consolid.
S_ALR_87009667	Where Used in Consolidation
S_ALR_87009668	EC-CS Master Data List: Consolid.
S_ALR_87009669	Where Used in Consolidation
S_ALR_87009670	EC-CS Master Data List: Items
S_ALR_87009671	EC-CS Master Data List: Subitems
S_ALR_87009672	Consolidation Versions
S_ALR_87009673	Methods for Interunit Elimination
S_ALR_87009674	Customizing of Cons. of Investments
S_ALR_87009675	Methods for Group Reclassifications
S_ALR_87009676	FICIPI85
S_ALR_87009677	FICIPI86
S_ALR_87009678	Changes in Investments
S_ALR_87009679	Changes in Investee Equity
S_ALR_87009680	Amortization of Goodwill
S_ALR_87009681	Equity Holdings Adjustments
S_ALR_87009682	Group Shares
S_ALR_87009683	Database List of Totals Records
S_ALR_87009684	Database List of Journal Entries
S_ALR_87009685	Analysis of PCA Transaction Data
S_ALR_87009686	Analysis of PCA Transaction Data
S_ALR_87009687	EC-CS Integration: Cons. Units Used
S_ALR_87009688	Plan/Actual/Variance: Profit Ctr Grp
S_ALR_87009689	Plan/Actual/Variance: Profit Center
S_ALR_87009690	Plan/Actual/Variance: Profit Centers

S_ALR_87009691	Plan/Plan/Actual:Versions,PrCtrGrp
S_ALR_87009692	Plan/Plan/Actual:Versions,Profit Ctr
S_ALR_87009693	Plan/Actual Bal.Sheet Accts: PrCtr
S_ALR_87009694	Plan/Actual Bal.Sheet Accts: PrCtr
S_ALR_87009695	Plan/Actual/Variance: PrCtrs,Periods
S_ALR_87009696	Plan/Actual/Variance: PrCtrs,Periods
S_ALR_87009697	Curr.Period,Aggreg.,Year Pl/Act.PrCt
S_ALR_87009698	Curr.Period,Aggreg.,Year Pl/Act.PrCt
S_ALR_87009699	Curr.Period,Aggreg.,Year PrCtr Comp.
S_ALR_87009700	Actual Quarters Over Two Years:PCG
S_ALR_87009701	Actual Quarters Over Two Years:PrCtr
S_ALR_87009702	Plan Quarters Over Two Years: PrCtr
S_ALR_87009703	Plan Quarters Over Two Years: PrCtr
S_ALR_87009704	Return on Investment Profit Center G
S_ALR_87009705	Return on Investment: Profit Center
S_ALR_87009706	Return on Investment: PrCtr Comp.
S_ALR_87009707	EC-PCA: Actual Line Items
S_ALR_87009708	EC-PCA: Plan Line Items
S_ALR_87009709	Statistical Key Figures
S_ALR_87009710	ALE: Plan/Actl/Variance Profit Ctr
S_ALR_87009711	ALE: Plan/Actual/Variance by PrCtr
S_ALR_87009712	Profit Center: Area list plan/act.
S_ALR_87009713	Profit Center: Periods, Plan/Actual
S_ALR_87009714	PrCtr: Return on Investment
S_ALR_87009715	PCtr Grp: Actual Comparison
S_ALR_87009716	Profit Center Group: Actual Comp.
S_ALR_87009717	PrCtr Group: Quarterly Comp, Actual
S_ALR_87009718	PrCtr Group: Balance Sheet Items
S_ALR_87009719	PrCtr Group: Plan Comparison
S_ALR_87009720	PrCtr Grp: Plan in 2 Time Periods
S_ALR_87009721	PrCtr Grp:Quarterly Plan Comparison
S_ALR_87009722	P/A Comp. of Profit Center Group
S_ALR_87009723	PrCtr Group: Curr.Per.+ Cum. + FYear
S_ALR_87009724	PrCtr Group: Actual/2 Plan Versions
S_ALR_87009725	PrCtr Group: P/A Comp. (Local Crcy)
S_ALR_87009726	PrCtr Group: P/A Comp. (by Origin)
S_ALR_87009727	P/A Comp. of PrCtrGrp (Partner PrC)
S_ALR_87009728	Plan/Act.Comp. PrCtr Grp(Fxd Prices)
S_ALR_87009729	Profit Center Group: Forecast
S_ALR_87009730	PCtr Rep.: Plan/Actual Comparison
S_ALR_87009731	PCtr: Current/Cumulated/Fiscal Year
S_ALR_87009732	PCtr: Actual in 2 Time Periods
S_ALR_87009733	PCtr: Plan in 2 Time Periods
S_ALR_87009734	Profit Center Report: 2 Versions
S_ALR_87009735	Actual/Plan Comparison by Accts
S_ALR_87009736	PCtr: Area List Plan/Act.(Var.Cur.)
S_ALR_87009737	PCtr Grp: Plan/Actual Comparison
S_ALR_87009738	PrCtr Grp: Plan/Act.(Var.Cur./Orig)
S_ALR_87009739	PCtr Grp: Qr Actual Comp.(Var.Cur.)
S_ALR_87009740	PrCtr Grp: Qtr Plan Comp.(Var.Cur.)
S_ALR_87009741	PrCtr: Plan/Actual Comp. (Var.Cur.)
S_ALR_87009742	Average Balance YTD / Accounts
S_ALR_87009743	Average Balance YTD/Profit Centers
S_ALR_87009744	Average Balance Period / Accounts

S_ALR_87009745	Average Balance Period/Profit Ctrs
S_ALR_87009746	EC-PCA: Drilldown Receivables
S_ALR_87009747	EC-PCA: Drilldown Payables
S_ALR_87009748	Line Items: Periodic Transfer, AR
S_ALR_87009749	Line Items: Periodic Transfer, AP
S_ALR_87009750	Line Items:Periodic Transfer, Assets
S_ALR_87009751	Line Items: Periodic Transfer, Mat.
S_ALR_87009752	Transfer Prices: Reconciliation for
S_ALR_87009753	Print Companies
S_ALR_87009754	Print Subgroups
S_ALR_87009755	Consolidation Items
S_ALR_87009756	Transaction Types for Consolidation
S_ALR_87009757	List of Ownership
S_ALR_87009758	Equity Structure of Investee Cos
S_ALR_87009759	Changes in Investments
S_ALR_87009760	Changes in Investee Equity
S_ALR_87009761	Fair Value Adjustments
S_ALR_87009762	Changes in Hidden Reserves
S_ALR_87009763	Profit Trends: Affiliated Companies
S_ALR_87009764	Elimin. Internal Business: Balance
S_ALR_87009765	Elimin. Internal Business: Delivery
S_ALR_87009766	Print Asset Transfers
S_ALR_87009767	Changes in Asset Transfer Depr.
S_ALR_87009768	Print Currency Translation Method
S_ALR_87009769	Print Cons. of Investments Method
S_ALR_87009770	Print Intercompany Eliminations
S_ALR_87009771	Versions of Consolidation
S_ALR_87009772	Selected Items in Consolidation
S_ALR_87009773	Journal Entries by Company
S_ALR_87009774	Totals Report - Hierarchy
S_ALR_87009775	Standard Reports
S_ALR_87009776	Comparisons
S_ALR_87009777	Value Developments
S_ALR_87009778	Exp. Balance Sheet Eval: Grid
S_ALR_87009779	Exp. Balance Sheet Eval: Runtimes
S_ALR_87009780	Expanded P+L Evaluations
S_ALR_87009781	Interactive Reporting for Consolid.
S_ALR_87009782	Create Data Extract from Subgroup
S_ALR_87009783	Data Selection FI-LC for EIS Report
S_ALR_87009784	Database List of Totals Records
S_ALR_87009785	Database List of Journal Entries
S_ALR_87009786	Database Listing, Prep. for Cons.
S_ALR_87009787	Actual/Actual Comparison for Year
S_ALR_87009788	Half-Year Actual/Actual Comparison
S_ALR_87009789	Quarterly Actual/Actual Comparison
S_ALR_87009790	Periodic Actual/Actual Comparison
S_ALR_87009791	Annual Plan/Actual Comparison
S_ALR_87009792	Half-Year Plan/Actual Comparison
S_ALR_87009793	Quarterly Plan/Actual Comparison
S_ALR_87009794	Periodic Plan/Actual Comparison
S_ALR_87009795	10-Year Actual/Actual Comparison
S_ALR_87009796	Balance Sheet for Portugal: Assets
S_ALR_87009797	Balance Sheet Portugal: Liabilities
S_ALR_87009798	Balance Sheet for Portugal: P+L Part

SAP Transaction Codes – Volume Two

S_ALR_87009799	Balance Sheet - Assets (Slovakia)
S_ALR_87009800	Balance Sheet:Liabilities (Slovakia)
S_ALR_87009801	Profit and Loss Statement (Slovakia)
S_ALR_87009802	Cash Flow (Slovakia)
S_ALR_87009803	Balance Sheet: Assets (Czech Rep.)
S_ALR_87009804	Bal. Sheet: Liabilities (Czech Rep.)
S_ALR_87009805	Profit/Loss: Czech Republic
S_ALR_87009806	Cash flow: Czech Republic
S_ALR_87009807	Balance using C/S (German Trade Law)
S_ALR_87009808	Profit and Loss Statement(Per.Acctg)
S_ALR_87009809	Cash Flow (Direct Method)
S_ALR_87009810	Cash Flow (Indirect Method) Variant
S_ALR_87009811	Cash Flow (Indirect Method) Variant
S_ALR_87009812	Cash Flow (AJI-03 Form)
S_ALR_87009813	Totals and Balances
S_ALR_87009814	G/L Account Balances
S_ALR_87009815	G/L Account Balances
S_ALR_87009816	Structured Account Balances
S_ALR_87009817	Structured Account Balances
S_ALR_87009818	General Ledger Line Items
S_ALR_87009819	General Ledger Line Items
S_ALR_87009820	General Ledger Line Items
S_ALR_87009821	Balance Sheet/P+L
S_ALR_87009822	Balance Sheet/P+L
S_ALR_87009823	Adjusted Balance Sheet Comparison
S_ALR_87009824	Document Journal
S_ALR_87009825	Document Journal
S_ALR_87009826	Compact Document Journal
S_ALR_87009827	Compact Document Journal
S_ALR_87009828	Line Item Journal
S_ALR_87009829	Line Item Journal
S_ALR_87009830	Display of Changed Documents
S_ALR_87009831	Display of Changed Documents
S_ALR_87009832	Compact Document Journal
S_ALR_87009833	Daily Report for Bank and Payment
S_ALR_87009834	Journal
S_ALR_87009835	Compact Journal (Poland)
S_ALR_87009836	Balance Sheet/P+L
S_ALR_87009837	Balance Sheet/P+L
S_ALR_87009838	G/L Account Balances
S_ALR_87009839	G/L Account Balances
S_ALR_87009840	G/L Account Balances
S_ALR_87009841	G/L Account Balances
S_ALR_87009842	General Ledger Line Items
S_ALR_87009843	General Ledger Line Items
S_ALR_87009844	General Ledger Line Items
S_ALR_87009845	Display Changes to G/L Accounts
S_ALR_87009846	Display Changes to G/L Accounts
S_ALR_87009847	Cash Journal
S_ALR_87009848	Preliminary Bal. Sheet -Requirement:
S_ALR_87009849	G/L Account Balances (Poland)
S_ALR_87009850	General Ledger from Document File
S_ALR_87009851	G/L Corresponding Accounts (Russia)
S_ALR_87009852	Extract for Aggregated Classic

S_ALR_87009853	Account Balance from Aggregated
S_ALR_87009854	Historical Balance Audit Trail Acc.
S_ALR_87009855	Open Item Balance Audit Trail from
S_ALR_87009856	Extract for Aggregated Open Item Bal
S_ALR_87009857	Account Balance from Aggregated
S_ALR_87009858	Open Item Balance Audit Trail Acc.
S_ALR_87009859	Bill of Exchange List
S_ALR_87009860	Bill of Exchange List
S_ALR_87009861	Extended Bill of Exchange Info
S_ALR_87009862	Extended Bill of Exchange Info
S_ALR_87009863	Chart of Accounts
S_ALR_87009864	Chart of Accounts
S_ALR_87009865	G/L Account List
S_ALR_87009866	G/L Account List
S_ALR_87009867	Account Assignment Manual
S_ALR_87009868	Account Assignment Manual
S_ALR_87009869	Customer / Vendor / G/L Account
S_ALR_87009870	Customer / Vendor / G/L Account
S_ALR_87009871	G/L Accounts List
S_ALR_87009872	Avg. Bal.: Period Version LC
S_ALR_87009873	Avg. Bal.: Period Version TC
S_ALR_87009874	Avg.balances daily vers.post.date
S_ALR_87009875	Avg.balances day vers.fix.val.date
S_ALR_87009876	Avg. Bal.: Period Version LC YTD
S_ALR_87009877	Avg.Balances Period Version TC YTD
S_ALR_87009878	Invoice Numbers Allocated Twice
S_ALR_87009879	Invoice Numbers Allocated Twice
S_ALR_87009880	Gaps in Document Number Assignment
S_ALR_87009881	Posting Totals
S_ALR_87009882	Posting Totals
S_ALR_87009883	Recurring Entry Documents
S_ALR_87009884	Recurring Entry Documents
S_ALR_87009885	Document Items Extract
S_ALR_87009886	Cashed checks per bank account
S_ALR_87009887	Outstanding Checks per G/L Account
S_ALR_87009888	Payment Advice Overview
S_ALR_87009889	Payment Advice Overview
S_ALR_87009890	Payment Advice Overview(Header/Item)
S_ALR_87009891	Payment Advice Overview(Header/Item)
S_ALR_87009892	Payment Advice Notes: Reorganization
S_ALR_87009893	Payment Advice Notes: Reorganization
S_ALR_87009894	Advance Return for Tax on Sales/Pur.
S_ALR_87009895	Advance Return for Tax on Sales/Pur.
S_ALR_87009896	Additional List for Advance Return f
S_ALR_87009897	Additional List for Advance Return f
S_ALR_87009898	Deferred Tax Transfer
S_ALR_87009899	Tax Adjustment
S_ALR_87009900	Input Tax from Parked Documents
S_ALR_87009901	Cross-Company Code Tax
S_ALR_87009902	Cross-Company Tax(Japan and Denmark)
S_ALR_87009903	Tax Information (Country)
S_ALR_87009904	Daily Report for VAT
S_ALR_87009905	Extended Tax Journal
S_ALR_87009906	VAT Report with Magnetic Output for

SAP Transaction Codes – Volume Two

S_ALR_87009907	Data Medium Exchange with Hard Disk
S_ALR_87009908	Print Program:Adv.Return for SalesTx
S_ALR_87009909	Annual Tax Return (Belgium) ---->
S_ALR_87009910	Data Medium Exchange with Disk
S_ALR_87009911	Advance Return for Tax on Sales/Pur.
S_ALR_87009912	Advance Return for Tax on Sales/Pur.
S_ALR_87009913	Print Program:Adv.Return for SalesTx
S_ALR_87009914	Annual Tax Return
S_ALR_87009915	Adv.Return for Sales Tax (Italy/Sp.)
S_ALR_87009916	Annual Tax Return
S_ALR_87009917	Annual Tax Return: Customers/Vendors
S_ALR_87009918	Annual Tax Return: Customers/Vendors
S_ALR_87009919	Taxes/Dues, Prepaid Exp., Donations
S_ALR_87009920	VAT Report for Korea (Cust./Vendors)
S_ALR_87009921	Entertainment Expense List
S_ALR_87009922	Sales/Purchase Tax Rep.(South Korea)
S_ALR_87009923	VAT Register (Poland)
S_ALR_87009924	VAT Report for Portugal
S_ALR_87009925	Annual Sales Ret. to Tax Office (PT)
S_ALR_87009926	VAT Report (Russia)
S_ALR_87009927	Tax on Operating Profit: Russia
S_ALR_87009928	Tax List Domestic/Foreign Banks(RU)
S_ALR_87009929	Adv.Return for Sales Tax (Italy/Sp.)
S_ALR_87009930	Annual Sales Report (Spain)
S_ALR_87009931	Data Medium Exchange with Disk
S_ALR_87009932	Record of Use and Sales Taxes (USA)
S_ALR_87009933	Forced Update of the external audit
S_ALR_87009934	Display utility for Audit File index
S_ALR_87009935	Update Audit Files/Sales Ta
S_ALR_87009936	Purchase Ledger
S_ALR_87009937	Sales Ledger
S_ALR_87009938	EC Sales List
S_ALR_87009939	Payment Medium International - Load
S_ALR_87009940	EC Sales List (Belgium)
S_ALR_87009941	EC Sales List (Spain)
S_ALR_87009942	EC Sales List (Austria)
S_ALR_87009943	German Foreign Trade Regulations
S_ALR_87009944	Direct Reporting of Bank Transfers
S_ALR_87009945	Accounts Rec. Information System
S_ALR_87009946	Due Date Analysis for Open Items
S_ALR_87009947	Transaction Figures: Account Balance
S_ALR_87009948	Transaction Figures: Special Sales
S_ALR_87009949	Transaction Figures: Sales
S_ALR_87009950	Customer Balances in Local Currency
S_ALR_87009951	List of Customer Open Items
S_ALR_87009952	List of Customer Open Items
S_ALR_87009953	Open Items: Customer Due Date Forec.
S_ALR_87009954	Customer Eval. with OI Sorted List
S_ALR_87009955	Customer Payment History
S_ALR_87009956	Customer Open Item Analysis(Overdue)
S_ALR_87009957	Customer List
S_ALR_87009958	List of Customer Addresses
S_ALR_87009959	F2
S_ALR_87009960	Display Changes to Customers

S_ALR_87009961	Display Critical Customer Changes
S_ALR_87009962	Customer Balances in Local Currency
S_ALR_87009963	List of Customer Open Items
S_ALR_87009964	Customer Sales
S_ALR_87009965	Extract for Aggregated Classic
S_ALR_87009966	Account Balance from Aggregated
S_ALR_87009967	Historical Balance Audit Trail Acc.
S_ALR_87009968	Open Item Balance Audit Trail from
S_ALR_87009969	Extract for Aggregated Open Item Bal
S_ALR_87009970	Account Balance from Aggregated
S_ALR_87009971	Open Item Balance Audit Trail Acc.
S_ALR_87009972	Open Down Payments
S_ALR_87009973	Customer Master Data Comparison
S_ALR_87009974	Customer Payment History
S_ALR_87009975	List of Customer Line Items
S_ALR_87009976	List of Cleared Customer Items
S_ALR_87009977	Open Down Payments
S_ALR_87009978	Payment Advice Overview
S_ALR_87009979	Payment Advice Overview
S_ALR_87009980	Payment Advice Overview(Header/Item)
S_ALR_87009981	Payment Advice Overview(Header/Item)
S_ALR_87009982	Payment Advice Notes: Reorganization
S_ALR_87009983	Payment Advice Notes: Reorganization
S_ALR_87009984	Calculation of Interest on Arrears
S_ALR_87009985	Customer Interest Scale
S_ALR_87009986	Bill of Exchange List
S_ALR_87009987	Extended Bill of Exchange List (ALV)
S_ALR_87009988	Data Medium Exchange with Disk
S_ALR_87009989	Maintain Bill of Exchange Liability
S_ALR_87009990	Multi-Level Dunning Bill of Exch.Req
S_ALR_87009991	Bill of Exchange Management
S_ALR_87009992	Customers With Missing Credit Data
S_ALR_87009993	Display Changes to Credit Management
S_ALR_87009994	Credit Limit Overview
S_ALR_87009995	Credit Overview
S_ALR_87009996	Credit Master Sheet
S_ALR_87009997	Credit Mgmt: Early Warning List
S_ALR_87009998	Reset Credit Limit for Customers
S_ALR_87009999	Credit Limit Data Mass Change
S_ALR_87010000	Printing of Documents (No Payments)
S_ALR_87010001	Payment Notice (Accounts Receivable)
S_ALR_87010002	Gross Income Additional Tax Listing
S_ALR_87010003	Multilateral agreement coefficient
S_ALR_87010004	Gross income declaration
S_ALR_87010005	Significant Trans. Cross Check CTTI
S_ALR_87010006	Data Medium Exchange with Hard Disk
S_ALR_87010007	Belgium:BLIW-IBLC:Open Items Foreign
S_ALR_87010008	Registro de Entradas (Mod.1) + Lista
S_ALR_87010009	List of Outgoing Documents
S_ALR_87010010	Production Control Record
S_ALR_87010011	Physical Inventory Overview
S_ALR_87010012	Registro de Apuração do IPI (Modelo
S_ALR_87010013	Registro de Apuração do ICMS (Modelo
S_ALR_87010014	List of Interstate Operations

S_ALR_87010015	Directory for Calculating ISS Tax
S_ALR_87010016	Arquivo Magnético / Convênio ICMS 13
S_ALR_87010017	IN68: Master Data, Doc.Files, Tables
S_ALR_87010018	Customer / Vendor / G/L Account
S_ALR_87010019	List of Open Items
S_ALR_87010020	Issued Notas Fiscais
S_ALR_87010021	German Foreign Trade Regulations
S_ALR_87010022	German Foreign Trade Reg. Report
S_ALR_87010023	Top Customers Report
S_ALR_87010024	Top Customers Report
S_ALR_87010025	Customer Balances in Local Currency
S_ALR_87010026	Tax Customer List (Russia)
S_ALR_87010027	Vendor Information System
S_ALR_87010028	Due Date Analysis for Open Items
S_ALR_87010029	Transaction Figures: Account Balance
S_ALR_87010030	Transaction Figures: Special Sales
S_ALR_87010031	Transaction Figures: Sales
S_ALR_87010032	Vendor Balances in Local Currency
S_ALR_87010033	List of Vendor Open Items
S_ALR_87010034	Open Items: Vendor Due Date Forecast
S_ALR_87010035	Vendor Payment History
S_ALR_87010036	Vendor List
S_ALR_87010037	F1
S_ALR_87010038	F2
S_ALR_87010039	Display Changes to Vendors
S_ALR_87010040	Display Critical Vendor Changes
S_ALR_87010041	Vendor Balances in Local Currency
S_ALR_87010042	List of Vendor Open Items
S_ALR_87010043	Vendor Business
S_ALR_87010044	Open Bus. Transactions by Delivery
S_ALR_87010045	Extract for Aggregated Classic
S_ALR_87010046	Account Balance from Aggregated
S_ALR_87010047	Historical Balance Audit Trail Acc.
S_ALR_87010048	Open Item Balance Audit Trail from
S_ALR_87010049	Extract for Aggregated Open Item Bal
S_ALR_87010050	Account Balance from Aggregated
S_ALR_87010051	Open Item Balance Audit Trail Acc.
S_ALR_87010052	Vendor Master Data Comparison
S_ALR_87010053	List of Vendor Line Items
S_ALR_87010054	List Of Cleared Vendor Items
S_ALR_87010055	List Of Down Payments Open
S_ALR_87010056	Payment Advice Overview
S_ALR_87010057	Payment Advice Overview
S_ALR_87010058	Payment Advice Overview(Header/Item)
S_ALR_87010059	Payment Advice Overview(Header/Item)
S_ALR_87010060	Payment Advice Notes: Reorganization
S_ALR_87010061	Payment Advice Notes: Reorganization
S_ALR_87010062	Calculation of Interest on Arrears
S_ALR_87010063	Interest scale for vendors
S_ALR_87010064	Bill of Exchange List
S_ALR_87010065	Extended Bill of Exchange List (ALV)
S_ALR_87010066	Copy Payment Advice for Due B./Exch.
S_ALR_87010067	Copy Payment Advice to Due B./Exch.
S_ALR_87010068	Bill of Exchange & Check Usage List

S_ALR_87010069	Cashed Checks
S_ALR_87010070	Payment Settlement List
S_ALR_87010071	Payment Regulation: List of
S_ALR_87010072	Withholding Tax Report for Vendor
S_ALR_87010073	Withholding Tax Amounts and Income
S_ALR_87010074	Self Withholding
S_ALR_87010075	Social security withholding tax
S_ALR_87010076	Data Medium Exchange with Hard Disk
S_ALR_87010077	Payts with Withholding Tax:Argentina
S_ALR_87010078	Withholding Tax Certificates
S_ALR_87010079	DIRF
S_ALR_87010080	Withholding Tax Rep. (Belgium,281.50
S_ALR_87010081	Withholding Tax Report to Tax Auth.
S_ALR_87010082	Withholding Tax Report - France
S_ALR_87010083	Form 770 Withholding Tax Report
S_ALR_87010084	Withholding Tax Report for Vendor
S_ALR_87010085	Withholding Tax Report to Tax Auth.
S_ALR_87010086	Detailed Information/Total of Earnin
S_ALR_87010087	Refundable Withholding Tax
S_ALR_87010088	WH Tax Certificates (South Korea)
S_ALR_87010089	Withholding Tax frm Business Earning
S_ALR_87010090	Withh.Tax Return (DTA) to Tax Office
S_ALR_87010091	Withh.Tax Return Model 210 Spain
S_ALR_87010092	Postcard Printout 1099 Vendor Addr.
S_ALR_87010093	1099 Listings
S_ALR_87010094	1099 MISC Form, Tape Reporting
S_ALR_87010095	1042 Reporting (USA)
S_ALR_87010096	Payment notice (+/-)
S_ALR_87010097	Significant Trans. Cross Check CTTI
S_ALR_87010098	Data Medium Exchange with Hard Disk
S_ALR_87010099	Belgium : BLIW-IBLC : Open Items
S_ALR_87010100	Registro de Entradas (Mod.1) + Lista
S_ALR_87010101	List of Outgoing Documents
S_ALR_87010102	Production Control Record
S_ALR_87010103	Physical Inventory Overview
S_ALR_87010104	Registro de Apuração do IPI (Modelo
S_ALR_87010105	Registro de Apuração do ICMS (Modelo
S_ALR_87010106	List of Interstate Operations
S_ALR_87010107	Directory for Calculating ISS Tax
S_ALR_87010108	Arquivo Magnético / Convênio ICMS 13
S_ALR_87010109	IN68: Master Data, Doc.Files, Tables
S_ALR_87010110	Customer / Vendor / G/L Account
S_ALR_87010111	German Foreign Trade Regulations
S_ALR_87010112	German Foreign Trade Reg. Report
S_ALR_87010113	Top Vendors Report
S_ALR_87010114	Vendor Balances in Local Currency
S_ALR_87010115	Tax Vendor List (Russian Federation)
S_ALR_87010116	Asset Balances
S_ALR_87010117	Asset Balances
S_ALR_87010118	Asset Balances
S_ALR_87010119	Asset Balances
S_ALR_87010120	Asset Balances
S_ALR_87010121	Asset Balances
S_ALR_87010122	Asset Balances

S_ALR_87010123	Asset Balances
S_ALR_87010124	Asset Balances
S_ALR_87010125	Sample for Address Data for Asset
S_ALR_87010126	Sample for Address Data for Asset
S_ALR_87010127	Real Estate and Similar Rights
S_ALR_87010128	Real Estate and Similar Rights
S_ALR_87010129	Vehicles
S_ALR_87010130	Vehicles
S_ALR_87010131	Asset Balances for Group Assets
S_ALR_87010132	Physical Inventory List
S_ALR_87010133	Physical Inventory List
S_ALR_87010134	Physical Inventory List
S_ALR_87010135	Physical Inventory List
S_ALR_87010136	Physical Inventory List
S_ALR_87010137	Bar Codes
S_ALR_87010138	Bar Codes
S_ALR_87010139	Leasing
S_ALR_87010140	Leasing
S_ALR_87010141	Liabilities from Leasing Agreements
S_ALR_87010142	Liabilities from Leasing Agreements
S_ALR_87010143	Asset History Sheet
S_ALR_87010144	Asset History Sheet
S_ALR_87010145	Liabilities from Leasing Agreements
S_ALR_87010146	Liabilities from Leasing Agreements
S_ALR_87010147	Asset Balances
S_ALR_87010148	Asset Balances
S_ALR_87010149	Asset History Sheet
S_ALR_87010150	Asset History Sheet
S_ALR_87010151	Asset History Sheet
S_ALR_87010152	Asset History Sheet
S_ALR_87010153	Asset Register (Italy)
S_ALR_87010154	Asset Register (Italy)
S_ALR_87010155	Asset Register by Third Party Loc.
S_ALR_87010156	Asset Register by Third Party Loc.
S_ALR_87010157	Depreciation
S_ALR_87010158	Depreciation
S_ALR_87010159	Depreciation
S_ALR_87010160	Depreciation
S_ALR_87010161	Depreciation
S_ALR_87010162	Depreciation
S_ALR_87010163	Depreciation
S_ALR_87010164	Write-Ups
S_ALR_87010165	Write-Ups
S_ALR_87010166	Depreciation Comparison
S_ALR_87010167	Depreciation Comparison
S_ALR_87010168	Manual Depreciation
S_ALR_87010169	Manual Depreciation
S_ALR_87010170	Asset Balances for Group Assets
S_ALR_87010171	Depreciation and Interest
S_ALR_87010172	Depreciation and Interest
S_ALR_87010173	Revaluation
S_ALR_87010174	Revaluation
S_ALR_87010175	Depreciation Posted to Cost Center
S_ALR_87010176	Depreciation Posted to Cost Center

S_ALR_87010177	Depreciation Simulation
S_ALR_87010178	Depreciation Simulation
S_ALR_87010179	Depreciation
S_ALR_87010180	Depreciation
S_ALR_87010181	Net Worth Valuation
S_ALR_87010182	Net Worth Valuation
S_ALR_87010183	Insurance Values
S_ALR_87010184	Insurance Values
S_ALR_87010185	Statement of Net Assets (Japan)
S_ALR_87010186	Gain for Transfer of Reserves
S_ALR_87010187	Gain for Transfer of Reserves
S_ALR_87010188	Depreciation
S_ALR_87010189	Depreciation
S_ALR_87010190	Changes to Asset Master Records
S_ALR_87010191	Changes to Asset Master Records
S_ALR_87010192	Asset Transactions
S_ALR_87010193	Asset Transactions
S_ALR_87010194	Asset Balances
S_ALR_87010195	Asset Balances
S_ALR_87010196	G/L Account Balances
S_ALR_87010197	G/L Account Balances
S_ALR_87010198	Fixed Asset Ledger
S_ALR_87010199	Asset Acquisitions(Mid-Quarter-Conv)
S_ALR_87010200	Asset Acquisitions(Mid-Quarter-Conv)
S_ALR_87010201	Asset Transactions
S_ALR_87010202	Asset Transactions
S_ALR_87010203	Asset Acquisitions
S_ALR_87010204	Asset Acquisitions
S_ALR_87010205	Asset Retirements
S_ALR_87010206	Asset Retirements
S_ALR_87010207	Intracompany Asset Transfers
S_ALR_87010208	Intracompany Asset Transfers
S_ALR_87010777	Plan/Actual Comparison
S_ALR_87010778	CM I: Districts/Plants/Mat. Groups
S_ALR_87010779	Comparison: Current Year/Prev. Year
S_ALR_87010780	Quarterly Comp.: Cust. Grp/Mat. Grp
S_ALR_87010781	Quarterly Comparison: Customer List
S_ALR_87010782	Quarterly Comparison: Product List
S_ALR_87010783	Division Comparison
S_ALR_87010784	Ranking List by Customer Group
S_ALR_87010785	Cost Element Report
S_ALR_87010786	Profit Center Report
S_ALR_87010787	Plan/Actual Comp. (COArea Currency)
S_ALR_87010788	Plan/Actual Comp. (CoCd Currency)
S_ALR_87010789	Automatic Currency Translation
S_ALR_87011758	.
S_ALR_87011760	Processes: Actual/plan/variance
S_ALR_87011761	List: Processes
S_ALR_87011762	Processes: Breakdown by Partner
S_ALR_87011763	List with partner
S_ALR_87011764	Processes: Actual/Target/Variance
S_ALR_87011765	List: Processes
S_ALR_87011766	List: Variances
S_ALR_87011767	List: Plan reconciliation

S_ALR_87011768	Processes: Value Added/Partner
S_ALR_87011769	Processes: Value Added Development
S_ALR_87011770	List: Prices/value added
S_ALR_87011771	List: Breakdown by process category
S_ALR_87011772	List: Breakdown by cost behavior
S_ALR_87011773	List: Cost component split
S_ALR_87011774	Stat. Key Figure: Monthly breakdown
S_ALR_87011775	Cost Centers: Actual/Plan/Variance
S_ALR_87011776	Cost Centers: Actl/target/variance
S_ALR_87011777	Activity Type: Load
S_ALR_87011778	Plan/Actual Comparison
S_ALR_87011779	CM I: Districts/Plants/Mat. Groups
S_ALR_87011780	Comparison: Current Year/Prev. Year
S_ALR_87011781	Quarterly Comp.: Cust. Grp/Mat. Grp
S_ALR_87011782	Quarterly Comparison: Customer List
S_ALR_87011783	Quarterly Comparison: Product List
S_ALR_87011784	Division Comparison
S_ALR_87011785	Ranking List by Customer Group
S_ALR_87011786	Cost Element Report
S_ALR_87011787	Profit Center Report
S_ALR_87011788	Plan/Actual Comp. (COArea Currency)
S_ALR_87011789	Plan/Actual Comp. (CoCd Currency)
S_ALR_87011790	Automatic Currency Translation
S_ALR_87011791	Current Year with Percentage Bal. Sh
S_ALR_87011792	Comparison Previous Year with Varian
S_ALR_87011793	Comparison of Years
S_ALR_87011794	Quarterly Comparison
S_ALR_87011795	Period Comparison
S_ALR_87011796	Local and Group Currency Comparison
S_ALR_87011797	Version Comparison
S_ALR_87011798	Comparison of Consolidation Units
S_ALR_87011799	Comparison of Consolidation Groups
S_ALR_87011800	Comparision Consolidation Units/Grou
S_ALR_87011801	Changes from Local Values to Cons.Va
S_ALR_87011802	Quarterly Changes Income Statement
S_ALR_87011803	Quarterly Changes Balance Sheet
S_ALR_87011804	Monthly Changes
S_ALR_87011805	Sales by Region
S_ALR_87011806	Profit and Loss by Functional Area
S_ALR_87011807	Changes in Investee Equity
S_ALR_87011808	Asset History Sheet
S_ALR_87011809	Line Item Report
S_ALR_87011810	EC-CS Master Data List: Consolid.
S_ALR_87011811	Where Used in Consolidation
S_ALR_87011812	EC-CS Master Data List: Consolid.
S_ALR_87011813	Where Used in Consolidation
S_ALR_87011814	EC-CS Master Data List: Items
S_ALR_87011815	FS Items Where-Used List
S_ALR_87011816	EC-CS Master Data List: Subitems
S_ALR_87011817	Consolidation Versions
S_ALR_87011818	Methods for Interunit Elimination
S_ALR_87011819	Customizing of Cons. of Investments
S_ALR_87011820	Methods for Group Reclassifications
S_ALR_87011821	FICIPI85

S_ALR_87011822	FICIPI86
S_ALR_87011823	Changes in investments
S_ALR_87011824	Changes in Investee Equity
S_ALR_87011825	Amortization of Goodwill
S_ALR_87011826	Equity Holdings Adjustments
S_ALR_87011827	Group Shares
S_ALR_87011828	Database List of Totals Records
S_ALR_87011829	Database List of Journal Entries
S_ALR_87011830	Analysis of PCA Transaction Data
S_ALR_87011831	Analysis of PCA Transaction Data
S_ALR_87011832	EC-CS Integration: Cons. Units Used
S_ALR_87011833	Plan/Actual Comparison
S_ALR_87011834	CM: Region/Business Area/Product Grp
S_ALR_87011835	Comparison: Current Year/Prev. Year
S_ALR_87011836	Quarters: Customer Group/Division
S_ALR_87011837	Quarterly Comparision: State List
S_ALR_87011838	Quarters: Product Group List
S_ALR_87011839	Division Comparison
S_ALR_87011840	Ranking List by Customer Group
S_ALR_87011841	Group: Prev. Year in Group Currency
S_ALR_87011842	Company: Prev. Year Comp. in Loc.Cur
S_ALR_87011843	Company Code: Prev.Year Comp. in GC
S_ALR_87011844	Company Code: Bal. Sheet Str., Prev.
S_ALR_87011845	Company Code: Profit Breakdown Comp.
S_ALR_87011846	Value Development in Group Currency
S_ALR_87011847	Value Development in Local Currency
S_ALR_87011848	Company Code Overview: Key Figures
S_ALR_87011849	Asset Balances
S_ALR_87011850	Asset Balances
S_ALR_87011851	Asset Balances
S_ALR_87011852	Asset Balances
S_ALR_87011853	Asset Balances
S_ALR_87011854	Asset Balances
S_ALR_87011855	Asset Balances
S_ALR_87011856	Asset Balances
S_ALR_87011857	Asset Balances
S_ALR_87011858	Sample for Address Data for Asset
S_ALR_87011859	Sample for Address Data for Asset
S_ALR_87011860	Real Estate and Similar Rights
S_ALR_87011861	Real estate and similar rights
S_ALR_87011862	Vehicles
S_ALR_87011863	Vehicles
S_ALR_87011864	Asset Balances for Group Assets
S_ALR_87011865	Physical Inventory List
S_ALR_87011866	Physical Inventory List
S_ALR_87011867	Physical Inventory List
S_ALR_87011868	Physical Inventory List
S_ALR_87011869	Inventory list
S_ALR_87011870	Bar Codes
S_ALR_87011871	Bar Codes
S_ALR_87011872	Leasing
S_ALR_87011873	Leasing
S_ALR_87011874	Liabilities from Leasing Agreements
S_ALR_87011875	Liabilities from Leasing Agreements

S_ALR_87011876	Asset History Sheet
S_ALR_87011877	Asset History Sheet
S_ALR_87011878	Liabilities from Leasing Agreements
S_ALR_87011879	Liabilities from Leasing Agreements
S_ALR_87011880	Asset Balances
S_ALR_87011881	Asset Balances
S_ALR_87011882	Asset History Sheet
S_ALR_87011883	Asset History Sheet
S_ALR_87011884	Asset History Sheet
S_ALR_87011885	Asset History Sheet
S_ALR_87011886	Asset Register (Italy)
S_ALR_87011887	Asset Register (Italy)
S_ALR_87011888	Asset Register by Third Party Loc.
S_ALR_87011889	Asset Register by Third Party Loc.
S_ALR_87011890	Depreciation
S_ALR_87011891	Depreciation
S_ALR_87011892	Depreciation
S_ALR_87011893	Depreciation
S_ALR_87011894	Depreciation
S_ALR_87011895	Depreciation
S_ALR_87011896	Depreciation
S_ALR_87011897	Write-Ups
S_ALR_87011898	Write-ups
S_ALR_87011899	Depreciation Comparison
S_ALR_87011900	Depreciation Comparison
S_ALR_87011901	Manual Depreciation
S_ALR_87011902	Manual Depreciation
S_ALR_87011903	Asset Balances for Group Assets
S_ALR_87011904	Depreciation and Interest
S_ALR_87011905	Depreciation and Interest
S_ALR_87011906	Revaluation
S_ALR_87011907	Revaluation
S_ALR_87011908	Depreciation Posted to Cost Center
S_ALR_87011909	Depreciation Posted to Cost Center
S_ALR_87011910	Depreciation Simulation
S_ALR_87011911	Depreciation Simulation
S_ALR_87011912	Depreciation
S_ALR_87011913	Depreciation
S_ALR_87011914	Net Worth Valuation
S_ALR_87011915	Net Worth Valuation
S_ALR_87011916	Insurance Values
S_ALR_87011917	Insurance Values
S_ALR_87011918	Statement of Net Assets (Japan)
S_ALR_87011919	Gain for Transfer of Reserves
S_ALR_87011920	Gain for transfer of reserves
S_ALR_87011921	Depreciation
S_ALR_87011922	Depreciation
S_ALR_87011923	Changes to Asset Master Records
S_ALR_87011924	Changes to Asset Master Records
S_ALR_87011925	Asset Transactions
S_ALR_87011926	Asset Transactions
S_ALR_87011927	Asset Balances
S_ALR_87011928	Asset Balances
S_ALR_87011929	G/L Account Balances

S_ALR_87011930	G/L Account Balances
S_ALR_87011931	Fixed Asset Ledger
S_ALR_87011932	Asset Acquisitions(Mid-Quarter-Conv)
S_ALR_87011933	Asset Acquisitions(Mid-Quarter-Conv)
S_ALR_87011934	Asset Transactions
S_ALR_87011935	Asset Transactions
S_ALR_87011936	Asset Acquisitions
S_ALR_87011937	Asset Acquisitions
S_ALR_87011938	Asset Retirements
S_ALR_87011939	Asset Retirements
S_ALR_87011940	Intracompany Asset Transfers
S_ALR_87011941	Intracompany Asset Transfers
S_ALR_87011942	Directory of Unposted Assets
S_ALR_87011943	Directory of Unposted Assets
S_ALR_87011944	List of Origins of Asset Charges
S_ALR_87011945	List of Origins of Asset Charges
S_ALR_87011946	List of Origins by Cost Elements
S_ALR_87011947	List of Origins by Cost Elements
S_ALR_87011948	Asset Retirements (French Law)
S_ALR_87011949	Asset Retirements (French Law)
S_ALR_87011950	Depreciation
S_ALR_87011951	Depreciation
S_ALR_87011952	Analysis of Retirement Revenue
S_ALR_87011953	Depreciation of Tang./Intang. Assets
S_ALR_87011954	Depreciation of Tangible Assets
S_ALR_87011955	Depreciation of Tang./Intang. Assets
S_ALR_87011956	Depreciation of Tangible Assets
S_ALR_87011957	Asset Depreciation and Tax Limits
S_ALR_87011958	Scrap Value Depr. (Uniform Depr.)
S_ALR_87011959	Depreciation of Tangible Assets
S_ALR_87011960	Intangible Assets: Depreciation
S_ALR_87011961	Asset History
S_ALR_87011962	Asset History
S_ALR_87011963	Asset Balances
S_ALR_87011964	Asset Balances
S_ALR_87011965	Asset Balances
S_ALR_87011966	Asset Balances
S_ALR_87011967	Asset Balances
S_ALR_87011968	Asset Balances
S_ALR_87011969	Asset Balances
S_ALR_87011970	Asset Balances
S_ALR_87011971	Asset Balances
S_ALR_87011972	Sample for Address Data for Asset
S_ALR_87011973	Sample for Address Data for Asset
S_ALR_87011974	Real Estate and Similar Rights
S_ALR_87011975	Real Estate and Similar Rights
S_ALR_87011976	Vehicles
S_ALR_87011977	Vehicles
S_ALR_87011978	Asset Balances for Group Assets
S_ALR_87011979	Physical Inventory List
S_ALR_87011980	Physical Inventory List
S_ALR_87011981	Physical Inventory List
S_ALR_87011982	Physical Inventory List
S_ALR_87011983	Physical Inventory List

S_ALR_87011984	Bar Codes
S_ALR_87011985	Bar Codes
S_ALR_87011986	Leasing
S_ALR_87011987	Leasing
S_ALR_87011988	Liabilities from Leasing Agreements
S_ALR_87011989	Liabilities from Leasing Agreements
S_ALR_87011990	Asset History Sheet
S_ALR_87011991	Asset History Sheet
S_ALR_87011992	Liabilities from Leasing Agreements
S_ALR_87011993	Liabilities from Leasing Agreements
S_ALR_87011994	Asset Balances
S_ALR_87011995	Asset Balances
S_ALR_87011996	Asset History Sheet
S_ALR_87011997	Asset History Sheet
S_ALR_87011998	Asset History Sheet
S_ALR_87011999	Asset History Sheet
S_ALR_87012000	Asset Register (Italy)
S_ALR_87012001	Asset Register (Italy)
S_ALR_87012002	Asset Register by Third Party Loc.
S_ALR_87012003	Asset Register by Third Party Loc.
S_ALR_87012004	Depreciation
S_ALR_87012005	Depreciation
S_ALR_87012006	Depreciation
S_ALR_87012007	Depreciation
S_ALR_87012008	Depreciation
S_ALR_87012009	Depreciation
S_ALR_87012010	Depreciation
S_ALR_87012011	Write-Ups
S_ALR_87012012	Write-Ups
S_ALR_87012013	Depreciation Comparison
S_ALR_87012014	Depreciation Comparison
S_ALR_87012015	Manual Depreciation
S_ALR_87012016	Manual Depreciation
S_ALR_87012017	Asset Balances for Group Assets
S_ALR_87012018	Depreciation and Interest
S_ALR_87012019	Depreciation and Interest
S_ALR_87012020	Revaluation
S_ALR_87012021	Revaluation
S_ALR_87012022	Depreciation Posted to Cost Center
S_ALR_87012023	Depreciation Posted to Cost Center
S_ALR_87012024	Depreciation Simulation
S_ALR_87012025	Depreciation Simulation
S_ALR_87012026	Depreciation
S_ALR_87012027	Depreciation
S_ALR_87012028	Net Worth Valuation
S_ALR_87012029	Net Worth Valuation
S_ALR_87012030	Insurance Values
S_ALR_87012031	Insurance Values
S_ALR_87012032	Statement of Net Assets (Japan)
S_ALR_87012033	Gain for Transfer of Reserves
S_ALR_87012034	Gain for Transfer of Reserves
S_ALR_87012035	Depreciation
S_ALR_87012036	Depreciation
S_ALR_87012037	Changes to Asset Master Records

S_ALR_87012038	Changes to Asset Master Records
S_ALR_87012039	Asset Transactions
S_ALR_87012040	Asset Transactions
S_ALR_87012041	Asset Balances
S_ALR_87012042	Asset Balances
S_ALR_87012043	G/L Account Balances
S_ALR_87012044	G/L Account Balances
S_ALR_87012045	Fixed Asset Ledger
S_ALR_87012046	Asset Acquisitions(Mid-Quarter-Conv)
S_ALR_87012047	Asset Acquisitions(Mid-Quarter-Conv)
S_ALR_87012048	Asset Transactions
S_ALR_87012049	Asset Transactions
S_ALR_87012050	Asset Acquisitions
S_ALR_87012051	Asset Acquisitions
S_ALR_87012052	Asset Retirements
S_ALR_87012053	Asset Retirements
S_ALR_87012054	Intracompany Asset Transfers
S_ALR_87012055	Intracompany Asset Transfers
S_ALR_87012056	Directory of Unposted Assets
S_ALR_87012057	Directory of Unposted Assets
S_ALR_87012058	List of Origins of Asset Charges
S_ALR_87012059	List of Origins of Asset Charges
S_ALR_87012060	List of Origins by Cost Elements
S_ALR_87012061	List of Origins by Cost Elements
S_ALR_87012062	Asset Retirements (French Law)
S_ALR_87012063	Asset Retirements (French Law)
S_ALR_87012064	Depreciation
S_ALR_87012065	Depreciation
S_ALR_87012066	Analysis of Retirement Revenue
S_ALR_87012067	Depreciation of Tang./Intang. Assets
S_ALR_87012068	Depreciation of Tangible Assets
S_ALR_87012069	Depreciation of Tang./Intang. Assets
S_ALR_87012070	Depreciation of Tangible Assets
S_ALR_87012071	Asset Depreciation and Tax Limits
S_ALR_87012072	Scrap Value Depr. (Uniform Depr.)
S_ALR_87012073	Depreciation of Tangible Assets
S_ALR_87012074	Intangible Assets: Depreciation
S_ALR_87012075	Asset History
S_ALR_87012076	Asset History
S_ALR_87012077	Vendor Information System
S_ALR_87012078	Due Date Analysis for Open Items
S_ALR_87012079	Transaction Figures: Account Balance
S_ALR_87012080	Transaction Figures: Special Sales
S_ALR_87012081	Transaction Figures: Sales
S_ALR_87012082	Vendor Balances in Local Currency
S_ALR_87012083	List of Vendor Open Items
S_ALR_87012084	Open Items: Vendor Due Date Forecast
S_ALR_87012085	Vendor Payment History
S_ALR_87012086	Vendor List
S_ALR_87012087	F1
S_ALR_87012088	F2
S_ALR_87012089	Display Changes to Vendors
S_ALR_87012090	Display Critical Vendor Changes
S_ALR_87012091	Vendor Balances in Local Currency

S_ALR_87012092	List of Vendor Open Items
S_ALR_87012093	Vendor Business
S_ALR_87012094	Open Bus. Transactions by Delivery
S_ALR_87012095	Extract for Aggregated Classic
S_ALR_87012096	Account Balance from Aggregated
S_ALR_87012097	Historical Balance Audit Trail Acc.
S_ALR_87012098	Open Item Balance Audit Trail from
S_ALR_87012099	Extract for Aggregated Open Item Bal
S_ALR_87012100	Account Balance from Aggregated
S_ALR_87012101	Open Item Balance Audit Trail Acc.
S_ALR_87012102	Vendor Master Data Comparison
S_ALR_87012103	List of Vendor Line Items
S_ALR_87012104	List Of Cleared Vendor Items
S_ALR_87012105	List Of Down Payments Open
S_ALR_87012106	Payment Advice Overview
S_ALR_87012107	Payment Advice Overview
S_ALR_87012108	Payment Advice Overview(Header/Item)
S_ALR_87012109	Payment Advice Overview(Header/Item)
S_ALR_87012110	Payment Advice Notes: Reorganization
S_ALR_87012111	Payment Advice Notes: Reorganization
S_ALR_87012112	Calculation of Interest on Arrears
S_ALR_87012113	Interest scale for vendors
S_ALR_87012114	Bill of Exchange List
S_ALR_87012115	Extended Bill of Exchange List (ALV)
S_ALR_87012116	Copy Payment Advice for Due B./Exch.
S_ALR_87012117	Copy Payment Advice to Due B./Exch.
S_ALR_87012118	Bill of Exchange & Check Usage List
S_ALR_87012119	Cashed Checks
S_ALR_87012120	Payment Settlement List
S_ALR_87012121	Payment Regulation: List of
S_ALR_87012122	Withholding Tax Report for Vendor
S_ALR_87012123	Withholding Tax Amounts and Income
S_ALR_87012124	Self Withholding
S_ALR_87012125	Social Security Withholding Tax
S_ALR_87012126	Data Medium Exchange with Hard Disk
S_ALR_87012127	Payts with Withholding Tax:Argentina
S_ALR_87012128	Withholding Tax Certificates
S_ALR_87012129	DIRF
S_ALR_87012130	Withholding Tax Rep. (Belgium,281.50
S_ALR_87012131	Withholding Tax Report to Tax Auth.
S_ALR_87012132	Withholding Tax Report - France
S_ALR_87012133	Form 770 Withholding Tax Report
S_ALR_87012134	Withholding Tax Report for Vendor
S_ALR_87012135	Withholding Tax Report to Tax Auth.
S_ALR_87012136	Detailed Information/Total of Earnin
S_ALR_87012137	Refundable Withholding Tax
S_ALR_87012138	WH Tax Certificates (South Korea)
S_ALR_87012139	Withholding Tax frm Business Earning
S_ALR_87012140	Withh.Tax Return (DTA) to Tax Office
S_ALR_87012141	Withh.Tax Return Model 210 Spain
S_ALR_87012142	Postcard Printout 1099 Vendor Addr.
S_ALR_87012143	1099 Listings
S_ALR_87012144	1099 MISC form, tape reporting
S_ALR_87012145	1042 Reporting (USA)

S_ALR_87012146	Payment notice (+/-)
S_ALR_87012147	Significant Trans. Cross Check CTTI
S_ALR_87012148	Data Medium Exchange with Hard Disk
S_ALR_87012149	Belgium : BLIW-IBLC : Open Items
S_ALR_87012150	Registro de Entradas (Mod.1) + Lista
S_ALR_87012151	List of Outgoing Documents
S_ALR_87012152	Production Control Record
S_ALR_87012153	Physical Inventory Overview
S_ALR_87012154	Registro de Apuração do IPI (Modelo
S_ALR_87012155	Registro de Apuração do ICMS (Modelo
S_ALR_87012156	List of Interstate Operations
S_ALR_87012157	Directory for Calculating ISS Tax
S_ALR_87012158	Arquivo Magnético / Convênio ICMS 13
S_ALR_87012159	IN68: Master Data, Doc.Files, Tables
S_ALR_87012160	Customer / Vendor / G/L Account
S_ALR_87012161	Requirement to Report Payments
S_ALR_87012162	German Foreign Trade Regulations
S_ALR_87012163	German Foreign Trade Reg. Report
S_ALR_87012164	Top Vendors Report
S_ALR_87012165	Vendor Balances (Poland)
S_ALR_87012166	Tax Vendor List (Russian Federation)
S_ALR_87012167	Accounts Rec. Information System
S_ALR_87012168	Due Date Analysis for Open Items
S_ALR_87012169	Transaction Figures: Account Balance
S_ALR_87012170	Transaction Figures: Special Sales
S_ALR_87012171	Transaction Figures: Sales
S_ALR_87012172	Customer Balances in Local Currency
S_ALR_87012173	List of Customer Open Items
S_ALR_87012174	List of Customer Open Items
S_ALR_87012175	Open Items: Customer Due Date Forec.
S_ALR_87012176	Customer Eval. with OI Sorted List
S_ALR_87012177	Customer Payment History
S_ALR_87012178	Customer Open Item Analysis(Overdue)
S_ALR_87012179	Customer List
S_ALR_87012180	List of customer addresses
S_ALR_87012181	F2
S_ALR_87012182	Display Changes to Customers
S_ALR_87012183	Display Critical Customer Changes
S_ALR_87012184	Customer Balances in Local Currency
S_ALR_87012185	List of Customer Open Items
S_ALR_87012186	Customer Sales
S_ALR_87012187	Extract for Aggregated Classic
S_ALR_87012188	Account Balance from Aggregated
S_ALR_87012189	Historical Balance Audit Trail Acc.
S_ALR_87012190	Open Item Balance Audit Trail from
S_ALR_87012191	Extract for Aggregated Open Item Bal
S_ALR_87012192	Account Balance from Aggregated
S_ALR_87012193	Open Item Balance Audit Trail Acc.
S_ALR_87012194	Open Down Payments
S_ALR_87012195	Customer Master Data Comparison
S_ALR_87012196	Customer Payment History
S_ALR_87012197	List of Customer Line Items
S_ALR_87012198	List of Cleared Customer Items
S_ALR_87012199	Open Down Payments

S_ALR_87012200	Payment Advice Overview
S_ALR_87012201	Payment Advice Overview
S_ALR_87012202	Payment Advice Overview(Header/Item)
S_ALR_87012203	Payment Advice Overview(Header/Item)
S_ALR_87012204	Payment Advice Notes: Reorganization
S_ALR_87012205	Payment Advice Notes: Reorganization
S_ALR_87012206	Calculation of Interest on Arrears
S_ALR_87012207	Customer Interest Scale
S_ALR_87012208	Bill of Exchange List
S_ALR_87012209	Extended Bill of Exchange List (ALV)
S_ALR_87012210	Data Medium Exchange with Disk
S_ALR_87012211	Maintain Bill of Exchange Liability
S_ALR_87012212	Multi-Level Dunning Bill of Exch.Req
S_ALR_87012213	Bill of Exchange Management
S_ALR_87012214	Customers With Missing Credit Data
S_ALR_87012215	Display Changes to Credit Management
S_ALR_87012216	Credit Limit Overview
S_ALR_87012217	Credit Overview
S_ALR_87012218	Credit Master Sheet
S_ALR_87012219	Credit Mgmt: Early Warning List
S_ALR_87012220	Reset Credit Limit for Customers
S_ALR_87012221	Credit Limit Data Mass Change
S_ALR_87012222	Printing of Documents (No Payments)
S_ALR_87012223	Payment Notice (Accounts Receivable)
S_ALR_87012224	Gross Income Additional Tax Listing
S_ALR_87012225	Multilateral Agreement Coefficient
S_ALR_87012226	Gross Income Declaration
S_ALR_87012227	Significant Trans. Cross Check CTTI
S_ALR_87012228	Data Medium Exchange with Hard Disk
S_ALR_87012229	Belgium:BLIW-IBLC:Open Items Foreign
S_ALR_87012230	Registro de Entradas (Mod.1) + Lista
S_ALR_87012231	List of Outgoing Documents
S_ALR_87012232	Production Control Record
S_ALR_87012233	Physical Inventory Overview
S_ALR_87012234	Registro de Apuração do IPI (Modelo
S_ALR_87012235	Registro de Apuração do ICMS (Modelo
S_ALR_87012236	List of Interstate Operations
S_ALR_87012237	Directory for Calculating ISS Tax
S_ALR_87012238	Arquivo Magnético / Convênio ICMS 13
S_ALR_87012239	IN68: Master Data, Doc.Files, Tables
S_ALR_87012240	Customer / Vendor / G/L Account
S_ALR_87012241	List of Open Items
S_ALR_87012242	Issued Notas Fiscais
S_ALR_87012243	German Foreign Trade Regulations
S_ALR_87012244	German Foreign Trade Reg. Report
S_ALR_87012245	Top Customers Report
S_ALR_87012246	Top Customers Report
S_ALR_87012247	Customer Balances (Poland)
S_ALR_87012248	Tax Customer List (Russia)
S_ALR_87012249	Actual/Actual Comparison for Year
S_ALR_87012250	Half-Year Actual/Actual Comparison
S_ALR_87012251	Quarterly Actual/Actual Comparison
S_ALR_87012252	Periodic Actual/Actual Comparison
S_ALR_87012253	Annual plan/actual comparison

S_ALR_87012254	Half-Year Plan/Actual Comparison
S_ALR_87012255	Quarterly Plan/Actual Comparison
S_ALR_87012256	Periodic Plan/Actual Comparison
S_ALR_87012257	10-Year Actual/Actual Comparison
S_ALR_87012258	Balance sheet for Portugal: Assets
S_ALR_87012259	Balance Sheet Portugal: Liabilities
S_ALR_87012260	Balance Sheet for Portugal: P+L Part
S_ALR_87012261	Balance Sheet - Assets (Slovakia)
S_ALR_87012262	Balance Sheet:Liabilities (Slovakia)
S_ALR_87012263	Profit and Loss Statement (Slovakia)
S_ALR_87012264	Cash flow (Slovakia)
S_ALR_87012265	Balance Sheet: Assets (Czech Rep.)
S_ALR_87012266	Bal. Sheet: Liabilities (Czech Rep.)
S_ALR_87012267	Profit/Loss: Czech Republic
S_ALR_87012268	Cash flow: Czech Republic
S_ALR_87012269	Balance using C/S (German Trade Law)
S_ALR_87012270	Profit and Loss Statement(Per.Acctg)
S_ALR_87012271	Cash Flow (Direct Method)
S_ALR_87012272	Cash Flow (Indirect Method) Variant
S_ALR_87012273	Cash Flow (Indirect Method) Variant
S_ALR_87012274	Cash Flow (AJI-03 Form)
S_ALR_87012275	Totals and Balances
S_ALR_87012276	G/L Account Balances
S_ALR_87012277	G/L Account Balances
S_ALR_87012278	Structured Account Balances
S_ALR_87012279	Structured Account Balances
S_ALR_87012280	General Ledger Line Items
S_ALR_87012281	General Ledger Line Items
S_ALR_87012282	General Ledger Line Items
S_ALR_87012283	Balance Sheet/P+L Statement
S_ALR_87012284	Balance Sheet/P+L Statement
S_ALR_87012285	Adjusted Balance Sheet Comparison
S_ALR_87012286	Document Journal
S_ALR_87012287	Document Journal
S_ALR_87012288	Compact Document Journal
S_ALR_87012289	Compact Document Journal
S_ALR_87012290	Line Item Journal
S_ALR_87012291	Line Item Journal
S_ALR_87012292	Display of Changed Documents
S_ALR_87012293	Display of Changed Documents
S_ALR_87012294	Compact Document Journal
S_ALR_87012295	Daily Report for Bank and Payment
S_ALR_87012296	Journal
S_ALR_87012297	Compact Journal (Poland)
S_ALR_87012298	Balance Sheet/P+L Statement
S_ALR_87012299	Balance Sheet/P+L Statement
S_ALR_87012300	G/L Account Balances
S_ALR_87012301	G/L Account Balances
S_ALR_87012302	G/L Account Balances
S_ALR_87012303	G/L Account Balances
S_ALR_87012304	General Ledger Line Items
S_ALR_87012305	General Ledger Line Items
S_ALR_87012306	General Ledger Line Items
S_ALR_87012307	Display Changes to G/L Accounts

S_ALR_87012308	Display Changes to G/L Accounts
S_ALR_87012309	Cash Journal
S_ALR_87012310	Preliminary Bal. Sheet -Requirement:
S_ALR_87012311	G/L Account Balances (Poland)
S_ALR_87012312	General Ledger from Document File
S_ALR_87012313	G/L Corresponding Accounts (Russia)
S_ALR_87012314	Extract for Aggregated Classic
S_ALR_87012315	Account Balance from Aggregated
S_ALR_87012316	Historical Balance Audit Trail Acc.
S_ALR_87012317	Open Item Balance Audit Trail from
S_ALR_87012318	Extract for Aggregated Open Item Bal
S_ALR_87012319	Account Balance from Aggregated
S_ALR_87012320	Open Item Balance Audit Trail Acc.
S_ALR_87012321	Bill of Exchange List
S_ALR_87012322	Bill of Exchange List
S_ALR_87012323	Extended Bill of Exchange Info
S_ALR_87012324	Extended Bill of Exchange Info
S_ALR_87012325	Chart of Accounts
S_ALR_87012326	Chart of Accounts
S_ALR_87012327	G/L Account List
S_ALR_87012328	G/L Account List
S_ALR_87012329	Account Assignment Manual
S_ALR_87012330	Account Assignment Manual
S_ALR_87012331	Customer / Vendor / G/L Account
S_ALR_87012332	Customer / Vendor / G/L Account
S_ALR_87012333	G/L accounts list
S_ALR_87012334	Average Balances Period Version LC
S_ALR_87012335	Average Balances Period Version TC
S_ALR_87012336	Avg.Balances Daily Vers.Posting Date
S_ALR_87012337	Avg.Balances Daily Vers.Fxd Val.Date
S_ALR_87012338	Avg.Balances Period Version LC YTD
S_ALR_87012339	Avg.Balances Period Version TC YTD
S_ALR_87012340	Invoice Numbers Allocated Twice
S_ALR_87012341	Invoice Numbers Allocated Twice
S_ALR_87012342	Gaps in Document Number Assignment
S_ALR_87012343	Posting Totals
S_ALR_87012344	Posting Totals
S_ALR_87012345	Recurring Entry Documents
S_ALR_87012346	Recurring Entry Documents
S_ALR_87012347	Document Items Extract
S_ALR_87012348	Cashed Checks per Bank Account
S_ALR_87012349	Outstanding Checks per G/L Account
S_ALR_87012350	Payment Advice Overview
S_ALR_87012351	Payment Advice Overview
S_ALR_87012352	Payment Advice Overview(Header/Item)
S_ALR_87012353	Payment Advice Overview(Header/Item)
S_ALR_87012354	Payment Advice Notes: Reorganization
S_ALR_87012355	Payment Advice Notes: Reorganization
S_ALR_87012356	Advance Return for Tax on Sales/Pur.
S_ALR_87012357	Advance Return for Tax on Sales/Pur.
S_ALR_87012358	Additional List for Advance Return f
S_ALR_87012359	Additional List for Advance Return f
S_ALR_87012360	Deferred Tax Transfer
S_ALR_87012361	Tax Adjustment

S_ALR_87012362	Input Tax from Parked Documents
S_ALR_87012363	Cross-Company Code Tax
S_ALR_87012364	Cross-Company Tax(Japan and Denmark)
S_ALR_87012365	Tax Information (Country)
S_ALR_87012366	Daily Report for VAT
S_ALR_87012367	Extended Tax Journal
S_ALR_87012368	VAT Report with Magnetic Output for
S_ALR_87012369	Data Medium Exchange with Hard Disk
S_ALR_87012370	Print Program:Adv.Return for SalesTx
S_ALR_87012371	Annual Tax Return (Belgium) ---->
S_ALR_87012372	Data Medium Exchange with Disk
S_ALR_87012373	Advance Return for Tax on Sales/Pur.
S_ALR_87012374	Advance Return for Tax on Sales/Pur.
S_ALR_87012375	Print Program:Adv.Return for SalesTx
S_ALR_87012376	Annual Tax Return
S_ALR_87012377	Adv.Return for Sales Tax (Italy/Sp.)
S_ALR_87012378	Annual Tax Return
S_ALR_87012379	Annual Tax Return: Customers/Vendors
S_ALR_87012380	Annual Tax Return: Customers/Vendors
S_ALR_87012381	Taxes/Dues, Prepaid Exp., Donations
S_ALR_87012382	VAT Report for Korea (Cust./Vendors)
S_ALR_87012383	Entertainment Expense List
S_ALR_87012384	Sales/Purchase Tax Rep.(South Korea)
S_ALR_87012385	VAT Register (Poland)
S_ALR_87012386	VAT Report for Portugal
S_ALR_87012387	Annual Sales Ret. to Tax Office (PT)
S_ALR_87012388	VAT Report (Russia)
S_ALR_87012389	Tax on Operating Profit: Russia
S_ALR_87012390	Tax List Domestic/Foreign Banks(RU)
S_ALR_87012391	Adv.Return for Sales Tax (Italy/Sp.)
S_ALR_87012392	Annual Sales Report (Spain)
S_ALR_87012393	Data Medium Exchange with Disk
S_ALR_87012394	Record of Use and Sales Taxes (USA)
S_ALR_87012395	Forced Update of the external audit
S_ALR_87012396	Display utility for Audit File index
S_ALR_87012397	Update Audit Files/Sales Ta
S_ALR_87012398	Purchase Ledger
S_ALR_87012399	Sales Ledger
S_ALR_87012400	EC Sales List
S_ALR_87012401	Payment Medium International - Load
S_ALR_87012402	EC Sales List (Belgium)
S_ALR_87012403	EC Sales List (Spain)
S_ALR_87012404	EC Sales List (Austria)
S_ALR_87012405	German Foreign Trade Regulations
S_ALR_87012406	Direct Reporting of Bank Transfers
S_ALR_87012407	Financial Statement, Act. Year Comp.
S_ALR_87012408	Transaction Figures: Account Balance
S_ALR_87012409	G/L Account Balances
S_ALR_87012410	Print Companies
S_ALR_87012411	Print Subgroups
S_ALR_87012412	Print Subgroup Hierarchy
S_ALR_87012413	Consolidation Items
S_ALR_87012414	Transaction Types for Consolidation
S_ALR_87012415	List of Ownership

S_ALR_87012416	Equity Structure of Investee Cos
S_ALR_87012417	Changes in Investments
S_ALR_87012418	Changes in Investee Equity
S_ALR_87012419	Fair Value Adjustments
S_ALR_87012420	Changes in Hidden Reserves
S_ALR_87012421	Profit Trends: Affiliated Companies
S_ALR_87012422	Elimin. Internal Business: Balance
S_ALR_87012423	Elimin. Internal Business: Delivery
S_ALR_87012424	Print Asset Transfers
S_ALR_87012425	Changes in Asset Transfer Depr.
S_ALR_87012426	Print Currency Translation Method
S_ALR_87012427	Print Cons. of Investments Method
S_ALR_87012428	Print Intercompany Eliminations
S_ALR_87012429	Versions of Consolidation
S_ALR_87012430	Selected Items in Consolidation
S_ALR_87012431	Journal Entries by Company
S_ALR_87012432	Totals Report - Hierarchy
S_ALR_87012433	Standard Reports
S_ALR_87012434	Comparisons
S_ALR_87012435	Value Developments
S_ALR_87012436	Exp. Balance Sheet Eval: Grid
S_ALR_87012437	Exp. Balance Sheet Eval: Runtimes
S_ALR_87012438	Expanded P+L Evaluations
S_ALR_87012439	Interactive Reporting for Consolid.
S_ALR_87012440	Create Data Extract from Subgroup
S_ALR_87012441	Data Selection FI-LC for EIS Report
S_ALR_87012442	Database List of Totals Records
S_ALR_87012443	Database List of Journal Entries
S_ALR_87012444	Database Listing, Prep. for Cons.
S_ALR_87012605	Assign Commitment Items to Cost Elem
S_ALR_87012609	FM Acct Assignts for Revs Incr. Bdgt
S_ALR_87012610	Assign Cost Centers to Funds Centers
S_ALR_87012611	Assigning CO Orders to Funds Centers
S_ALR_87012612	Assign WBS Elements to Funds Centers
S_ALR_87012613	Assign Profit Centers to Funds Ctrs
S_ALR_87012636	Level Line Items and Totals Records
S_ALR_87012637	Compare FM Totals with FI Totals
S_ALR_87012638	Compare Line Items in FI and FM
S_ALR_87012640	Reconciliation: C.F. Line Items
S_ALR_87012641	Index of Commitment Items
S_ALR_87012642	Asmt of Commitment Item to G/L Accts
S_ALR_87012643	Commitment/Plan/Actual
S_ALR_87012644	Commitment/Actual/Inventory
S_ALR_87012645	Commitment Actual Line Item by Doc.#
S_ALR_87012646	Commitment/Actual Items by Comm.Item
S_ALR_87012794	Plan from Measures/Approp. Request
S_ALR_87012795	Plan in Program, Approp. Req., Meas.
S_ALR_87012796	Request Plan: Investments/Expenses
S_ALR_87012797	Budget Distribution to Measures
S_ALR_87012798	Request Plan/Budget for Measures
S_ALR_87012799	Cons. Request Plan/Budget for Meas.
S_ALR_87012800	Program Budget/Committed Funds
S_ALR_87012801	Budget for Measures/Committed Funds
S_ALR_87012802	Request Plan/Assigned

S_ALR_87012803	Budget for Measures by Org. Unit
S_ALR_87012804	Assigned Funds per Summ. Version
S_ALR_87012805	Structure and Value List
S_ALR_87012806	Structure and Value List
S_ALR_87012808	Overall Plan/Annual Plan in Program
S_ALR_87012809	Plan from Approp. Requests and Meas.
S_ALR_87012810	Plan Program, Requests, Measures
S_ALR_87012811	Investment/Expense Plan, Approp.Req.
S_ALR_87012812	Plan Version Comp.: Prog./Meas./App.
S_ALR_87012813	Plan/Budget Comparison in Program
S_ALR_87012814	Distribution of Overall Bdgt in Prog
S_ALR_87012815	Distribution of Annual Bdgt in Prog.
S_ALR_87012816	Overall/Annual Budget in Program
S_ALR_87012817	Budget Update in Program
S_ALR_87012818	Prog. Budget/Standard Invstmt Reason
S_ALR_87012819	Budget Distribution to Measures
S_ALR_87012820	Overall/Annual Budget in Measures
S_ALR_87012821	Distrib. of Bdgt to Meas. by Budget
S_ALR_87012822	Request Plan/Budget for Measures
S_ALR_87012823	Cons. Request Plan/Budget for Meas.
S_ALR_87012824	Budget Availability in Program
S_ALR_87012825	Budget Available for Measures
S_ALR_87012826	Available Meas. Budget by Org. Units
S_ALR_87012827	Available Meas.Budget by Person Resp
S_ALR_87012828	Measure Budget/DownPayments/Assignd
S_ALR_87012829	Available Budget in Prog. by Budget
S_ALR_87012830	Annual Expected Value from Measures
S_ALR_87012831	Request Plan/Assigned
S_ALR_87012832	Depreciation Simulation
S_ALR_87012833	Depreciation Simulation
S_ALR_87012834	Depreciation Simulation
S_ALR_87012835	Depreciation Simulation
S_ALR_87012836	Depreciation Simulation
S_ALR_87012837	Overall Plan/Annual Plan from Req.
S_ALR_87012838	Investment/Expense Plan
S_ALR_87012839	Plan Version Comparison: Requests
S_ALR_87012840	Request Plan By Status
S_ALR_87012841	Request/Measure Plan
S_ALR_87012842	Request Plan/Budget for Measures
S_ALR_87012843	Request Plan/Assigned
S_ALR_87012853	Costing Items
S_ALR_87012888	Overview: Project Hierarchies
S_ALR_87012890	Order profit
S_ALR_87012891	Plan/Actual/Variance
S_ALR_87012892	Plan/Actual/Commitment
S_ALR_87012893	Summarization Object: Plan/Actual
S_ALR_87012894	Summ. Object: Actual/Plan/Commitment
S_ALR_87012895	Budget/Actual/Variance
S_ALR_87012896	Budget/Actual/Commitment
S_ALR_87012897	Plan/Actual/Variance
S_ALR_87012898	Planned Contribution Margin
S_ALR_87012899	Actual Contribution Margin
S_ALR_87012900	Summarization Object: Plan/Actual
S_ALR_87012901	Order Profit

S_ALR_87012902	Overview
S_ALR_87012903	Orders: Actual/Plan/Variance
S_ALR_87012904	Orders: Current Period/Cumulative
S_ALR_87012905	List: Orders
S_ALR_87012906	List: Orders by Cost Element
S_ALR_87012907	List: Cost Elements by Order
S_ALR_87012908	Orders: Breakdown by Partner
S_ALR_87012909	Orders: Actual/Plan/Commitments
S_ALR_87012910	List: Actual/Plan/Commitments
S_ALR_87012911	Orders: Yearly Comparison - Actual
S_ALR_87012912	Orders: Quarterly Comparison - Act.
S_ALR_87012913	Orders: Period Comparison - Actual
S_ALR_87012914	Orders: Yearly Comparison - Plan
S_ALR_87012915	Orders: Quarterly Comparison - Plan
S_ALR_87012916	Orders: Period Comparison - Plan
S_ALR_87012917	SObj: Actual/Plan/Variance
S_ALR_87012918	SObj: Actual/Plan/Commitment
S_ALR_87012919	SObj: Current/Cumulated/Total
S_ALR_87012920	Orders: Breakdown by Period
S_ALR_87012921	Orders: Actual/Plan/Price Variance
S_ALR_87012922	Orders: Actual/Plan/Consumption
S_ALR_87012923	Orders: Actual TCrcy/OCrcy/CAcrcy
S_ALR_87012924	List: Cost Elements (True Postings)
S_ALR_87012925	List: Actual Debit/Credit
S_ALR_87012926	List: Plan Debit/Credit
S_ALR_87012927	List: Actual/Plan/Var. Cumulative
S_ALR_87012928	List: Total Plan/Actual/Commitments
S_ALR_87012929	List: Budget/Actual/Commitments
S_ALR_87012930	List of Origins of Asset Charges
S_ALR_87012931	List of Origins of Asset Charges
S_ALR_87012932	List of Origins by Cost Elements
S_ALR_87012933	List of Origins by Cost Elements
S_ALR_87012934	Asset Acquisitions
S_ALR_87012935	Asset Acquisitions
S_ALR_87012936	Depreciation Simulation
S_ALR_87012937	Depreciation Simulation
S_ALR_87012938	Overall/Annual Plan from Approp.Req.
S_ALR_87012939	Plan Version Comp.:Appropiation Req.
S_ALR_87012940	Investment/Expense Plan, Approp.Req.
S_ALR_87012941	Plan from Approp. Requests and Meas.
S_ALR_87012942	Plan Versions in Approp.Req./Measure
S_ALR_87012943	Request Plan/Budget for Measures
S_ALR_87012944	Request Plan/Assigned
S_ALR_87012945	Overall Plan/Annual Plan from Req.
S_ALR_87012946	Investment/Expense Plan
S_ALR_87012947	Plan Version Comparison: Requests
S_ALR_87012948	Request Plan By Status
S_ALR_87012949	Request/Measure Plan
S_ALR_87012950	Request Plan/Budget for Measures
S_ALR_87012951	Request Plan/Assigned
S_ALR_87012952	Document Structure Distribution
S_ALR_87012953	Material BOM Distribution
S_ALR_87012954	Plant Allocations to Mat. BOMs
S_ALR_87012955	Display Batch Input Data from Seq.

SAP Transaction Codes – Volume Two

S_ALR_87012956	Display Batch Input Data from Seq.
S_ALR_87012957	BOM Changes for a Change Number
S_ALR_87012958	Display BOM Level by Level
S_ALR_87012959	Display Doc.Structure Level by Level
S_ALR_87012960	Display Multilevel BOM
S_ALR_87012961	Summarized BOM - Multilevel
S_ALR_87012962	BOM Comparison
S_ALR_87012963	Material Where-Used List
S_ALR_87012964	Single-Level Document Where-Used
S_ALR_87012965	Single-Level Class Where-Used List
S_ALR_87012966	Create BOMs using Batch Input
S_ALR_87012967	Change BOMs using Batch Input
S_ALR_87012968	Create Variant BOMs via Batch Input
S_ALR_87012969	Create BOMs using Batch Input
S_ALR_87012970	Validate Stock Data (Release 4.0)
S_ALR_87012971	Validate Stock Data (Release 4.5)
S_ALR_87012972	Pick-Up List for Batch Where-Used
S_ALR_87012973	Where-Used for Func. in Object Dep.
S_ALR_87012974	Where-Used for Var.Table in Obj.Dep.
S_ALR_87012975	Materials for Change Number
S_ALR_87012976	All Changes for Change Number
S_ALR_87012977	BOM Changes for a Change Number
S_ALR_87012978	Engineering Change Mgmt Status Rep.
S_ALR_87012979	ECH: Change Number Overview
S_ALR_87012980	ECM Browser:Engineering Change Hier.
S_ALR_87012981	ECH: ALE Distribution of Chge Master
S_ALR_87012982	Characteristics Mgmt: Display Char.
S_ALR_87012983	Display All Characteristics of Class
S_ALR_87012984	Classification: Use of Change Number
S_ALR_87012985	Display Obj. Dep. for Change Numbers
S_ALR_87012986	Overview of Configuration Profiles
S_ALR_87012987	Documents for Change Number
S_ALR_87012988	All Task List Changes for Change No.
S_ALR_87012989	Overview of Variant Table Lines for
S_ALR_87012990	Evaluation Comparison
S_ALR_87012991	Accounting Documents for Material
S_ALR_87012992	List of Parked Documents
S_ALR_87012993	Orders: Actual/plan/variance
S_ALR_87012994	Orders: Current Period/Cumulative
S_ALR_87012995	List: Orders
S_ALR_87012996	List: Orders by Cost Element
S_ALR_87012997	List: Cost Elements by Order
S_ALR_87012998	Orders: Breakdown by Partner
S_ALR_87012999	Orders: Actual/Plan/Commitments
S_ALR_87013000	List: Actual/Plan/Commitments
S_ALR_87013001	Orders: Yearly Comparison - Actual
S_ALR_87013002	Orders: Quarterly Comparison - Act.
S_ALR_87013003	Orders: Period Comparison - Actual
S_ALR_87013004	Orders: Yearly Comparison - Plan
S_ALR_87013005	Orders: Quarterly Comparison - Plan
S_ALR_87013006	Orders: Period Comparison - Plan
S_ALR_87013007	SObj: Actual/Plan/Variance
S_ALR_87013008	SObj: Actual/Plan/Commitment
S_ALR_87013009	SObj: Current/Cumulated/Total

SAP Transaction Codes – Volume Two

S_ALR_87013010	Orders: Breakdown by Period
S_ALR_87013011	Orders: Actual/Plan/Price Variance
S_ALR_87013012	Orders: Actual/Plan/Consumption
S_ALR_87013013	Orders: Actual TCrcy/OCrcy/CAcrcy
S_ALR_87013014	List: Cost Elements (True Postings)
S_ALR_87013015	List: Actual Debit/Credit
S_ALR_87013016	List: Plan Debit/Credit
S_ALR_87013017	List: Actual/Plan/Var. Cumulative
S_ALR_87013018	List: Total Plan/Actual/Commitments
S_ALR_87013019	List: Budget/Actual/Commitments
S_ALR_87013023	Analyze Costing Run
S_ALR_87013024	Analyze Costing Run
S_ALR_87013025	Analyze Costing Run
S_ALR_87013026	Analyze Costing Run
S_ALR_87013027	List of Existing Mat. Cost Estimates
S_ALR_87013028	Base Planning Object Overview
S_ALR_87013029	Where-used List Base Planning Obj.
S_ALR_87013030	Cost Components
S_ALR_87013031	Cost Elements
S_ALR_87013032	Costing Items
S_ALR_87013033	Cost Elements and Items
S_ALR_87013034	Cost Elements and Origins
S_ALR_87013035	Transactions and Items
S_ALR_87013036	Multilevel Expl.of Base Planning Obj
S_ALR_87013037	Costing Items
S_ALR_87013038	Cost Elements and Items
S_ALR_87013039	Cost Elements and Origins
S_ALR_87013040	Cost Components
S_ALR_87013041	Cost Elements
S_ALR_87013042	Costing Items
S_ALR_87013043	Cost Elements and Items
S_ALR_87013044	Cost Elements and Origins
S_ALR_87013046	Planned Costs
S_ALR_87013047	Cost Components
S_ALR_87013048	Cost Elements
S_ALR_87013049	Comparison of Unit Cost Estimates
S_ALR_87013050	Target/Actual/Production Variance
S_ALR_87013051	Target/Actual/Prod.Variances: Cum.
S_ALR_87013052	Target/Actual/Prod.Variances: Period
S_ALR_87013053	Target/Actual Comparison
S_ALR_87013054	Target/Actual Comparison: Cumulative
S_ALR_87013055	Target/Actual Comparison: Periods
S_ALR_87013056	Plan/Actual Comparison
S_ALR_87013057	Plan/Actual Comparison: Cumulative
S_ALR_87013058	Plan/Actual Comparison: Periods
S_ALR_87013059	Variance Categories
S_ALR_87013060	Variance Categories: Cumulative
S_ALR_87013061	Variance Categories: Periods
S_ALR_87013062	Work in Process
S_ALR_87013063	Actual/WIP: Cumulative
S_ALR_87013064	Actual/WIP: Periods
S_ALR_87013065	Planned Costs
S_ALR_87013066	Planned Costs: Cumulative
S_ALR_87013067	Planned Costs: Periodic

S_ALR_87013068	Actual Costs
S_ALR_87013069	Cumulated Actual Costs
S_ALR_87013070	Actual Costs: Periods
S_ALR_87013071	Order Selection
S_ALR_87013072	Order Selection
S_ALR_87013073	Overview of Order Hierarchies
S_ALR_87013074	GUI for Library 7KV
S_ALR_87013075	Work in Process
S_ALR_87013076	Actual Costs
S_ALR_87013077	Target/Actual/Production Variance
S_ALR_87013078	Target/Actual Comparison
S_ALR_87013079	Variance Categories
S_ALR_87013080	GUI for Library 7KV
S_ALR_87013081	Actual Costs
S_ALR_87013082	Target/Actual/Production Variance
S_ALR_87013083	Plan/Actual Comparison
S_ALR_87013084	Variance Categories
S_ALR_87013085	Work in Process
S_ALR_87013086	Planned Costs
S_ALR_87013087	Actual Costs
S_ALR_87013088	Target/Actual/Production Variance
S_ALR_87013089	Target/Actual Comparison
S_ALR_87013090	Plan/Actual Comparison
S_ALR_87013091	Variance Categories
S_ALR_87013092	Work in Process
S_ALR_87013093	Planned Costs
S_ALR_87013094	Actual Costs
S_ALR_87013095	Target/Actual/Production Variance
S_ALR_87013096	Target/Actual Comparison
S_ALR_87013097	Plan/Actual Comparison
S_ALR_87013098	Variance Categories
S_ALR_87013099	Plan/Actual Comparison
S_ALR_87013100	Plan/Actual Comparison
S_ALR_87013101	Sales Order Selection
S_ALR_87013102	Sales Order Selection
S_ALR_87013103	Sales Order Selection
S_ALR_87013104	Sales Order Selection
S_ALR_87013105	Plan/Actual Comparison
S_ALR_87013106	Work in Process
S_ALR_87013107	Order Profit
S_ALR_87013108	Reserves for Imminent Loss
S_ALR_87013109	Reserves for Unrealized Costs
S_ALR_87013110	Planned Costs
S_ALR_87013111	Actual Costs
S_ALR_87013112	Funds Commitment
S_ALR_87013113	Cost components
S_ALR_87013114	Cost Elements
S_ALR_87013115	Costing Items
S_ALR_87013116	Cost Elements and Items
S_ALR_87013117	Cost Elements and Origins
S_ALR_87013119	Plan/Actual Comparison
S_ALR_87013120	Work in Process
S_ALR_87013121	Order Profit
S_ALR_87013122	Reserves for Unrealized Costs

S_ALR_87013123	Reserves for Imminent Loss
S_ALR_87013124	Planned Costs
S_ALR_87013125	Actual Costs
S_ALR_87013126	Overview of Order Hierarchies
S_ALR_87013127	Order Selection
S_ALR_87013128	Order Selection
S_ALR_87013129	Plan/Actual Comparison
S_ALR_87013130	Plan/Actual Comparison
S_ALR_87013131	Work in Process
S_ALR_87013132	Order Profit
S_ALR_87013133	Reserves for Unrealized Costs
S_ALR_87013134	Reserves for Imminent Loss
S_ALR_87013135	Planned Costs
S_ALR_87013136	Actual Costs
S_ALR_87013137	Plan/Actual Comparison
S_ALR_87013138	Target/Actual/Production Variance
S_ALR_87013139	Target/Actual/Prod.Variances: Cum.
S_ALR_87013140	Target/Actual/Prod.Variances: Period
S_ALR_87013141	Target/Actual Comparison
S_ALR_87013142	Target/Actual Comparison: Cumulative
S_ALR_87013143	Target/Actual Comparison: Periods
S_ALR_87013144	Plan/Actual Comparison
S_ALR_87013145	Plan/Actual Comparison: Cumulative
S_ALR_87013146	Plan/Actual Comparison: Periods
S_ALR_87013147	Variance Categories
S_ALR_87013148	Variance Categories: Cumulative
S_ALR_87013149	Variance Categories: Periods
S_ALR_87013150	Work in Process
S_ALR_87013151	Actual/WIP: Cumulative
S_ALR_87013152	Actual/WIP: Periods
S_ALR_87013153	Planned Costs
S_ALR_87013154	Planned Costs: Cumulative
S_ALR_87013155	Planned Costs: Periodic
S_ALR_87013156	Actual Costs
S_ALR_87013157	Cumulated Actual Costs
S_ALR_87013158	Actual Costs: Periods
S_ALR_87013159	Order Selection
S_ALR_87013160	Order Selection
S_ALR_87013161	Order Selection
S_ALR_87013162	Overview of Order Hierarchies
S_ALR_87013163	Work in Process
S_ALR_87013164	Planned Costs
S_ALR_87013165	Actual Costs
S_ALR_87013166	Target/Actual/Production Variance
S_ALR_87013167	Target/Actual Comparison
S_ALR_87013168	Plan/Actual Comparison
S_ALR_87013169	Variance Categories
S_ALR_87013170	Planned Costs
S_ALR_87013171	Plan/Actual Comparison
S_ALR_87013172	Plan/Actual Comparison
S_ALR_87013173	Work in Process
S_ALR_87013174	Planned Costs
S_ALR_87013175	Actual Costs
S_ALR_87013176	Target/Actual/Production Variance

SAP Transaction Codes – Volume Two

S_ALR_87013177	Target/Actual Comparison
S_ALR_87013178	Plan/Actual Comparison
S_ALR_87013179	Variance Categories
S_ALR_87013180	Listing of Materials by Period
S_ALR_87013181	Material Ledger Data Over Sev.Period
S_ALR_87013182	Transaction History for a Material
S_ALR_87013198	Overview of Order Hierarchies
S_ALR_87013199	Planned Costs
S_ALR_87013200	Plan/Actual Comparison
S_ALR_87013201	Target/Actual Comparison
S_ALR_87013202	Target/Actual/Production Variance
S_ALR_87013203	Variance Categories
S_ALR_87013204	Work in Process
S_ALR_87013205	Actual Costs
S_ALR_87013206	Planned Costs
S_ALR_87013207	Plan/Actual Comparison
S_ALR_87013208	Target/Actual Comparison
S_ALR_87013209	Target/Actual/Production Variance
S_ALR_87013210	Variance Categories
S_ALR_87013211	Work in Process
S_ALR_87013212	Actual Costs
S_ALR_87013213	Plan/Actual Comparison
S_ALR_87013214	Plan/Actual Comparison
S_ALR_87013215	Planned Costs
S_ALR_87013231	Overview of Order Hierarchies
S_ALR_87013232	Planned Costs
S_ALR_87013233	Plan/Actual Comparison
S_ALR_87013234	Target/Actual Comparison
S_ALR_87013235	Target/Actual/Production Variance
S_ALR_87013236	Variance Categories
S_ALR_87013237	Work in Process
S_ALR_87013238	Actual Costs
S_ALR_87013239	Planned Costs
S_ALR_87013240	Plan/Actual Comparison
S_ALR_87013241	Target/Actual Comparison
S_ALR_87013242	Target/Actual/Production Variance
S_ALR_87013243	Variance Categories
S_ALR_87013244	Work in Process
S_ALR_87013245	Actual Costs
S_ALR_87013246	Plan/Actual Comparison
S_ALR_87013247	Plan/Actual Comparison
S_ALR_87013248	Planned Costs
S_ALR_87013249	Sales Order Selection
S_ALR_87013250	Planned Costs
S_ALR_87013251	Plan/Actual Comparison
S_ALR_87013252	Work in Process
S_ALR_87013253	Reserves for Unrealized Costs
S_ALR_87013254	Reserves for Imminent Loss
S_ALR_87013255	Order Profit
S_ALR_87013256	Actual Costs
S_ALR_87013257	Overview of Order Hierarchies
S_ALR_87013258	Planned Costs
S_ALR_87013259	Plan/Actual Comparison
S_ALR_87013260	Reserves for Unrealized Costs

S_ALR_87013261	Reserves for Imminent Loss
S_ALR_87013262	Order profit
S_ALR_87013263	Actual Costs
S_ALR_87013264	Planned Costs
S_ALR_87013265	Plan/Actual Comparison
S_ALR_87013266	Work in Process
S_ALR_87013267	Reserves for Unrealized Costs
S_ALR_87013268	Reserves for Imminent Loss
S_ALR_87013269	Order Profit
S_ALR_87013270	Actual Costs
S_ALR_87013271	Sales Order Selection
S_ALR_87013272	Overview of Order Hierarchies
S_ALR_87013273	Planned Costs
S_ALR_87013274	Plan/Actual Comparison
S_ALR_87013275	Work in Process
S_ALR_87013276	Reserves for Unrealized Costs
S_ALR_87013277	Reserves for Imminent Loss
S_ALR_87013278	Order Profit
S_ALR_87013279	Actual Costs
S_ALR_87013280	Planned Costs
S_ALR_87013281	Plan/Actual Comparison
S_ALR_87013282	Work in Process
S_ALR_87013283	Reserves for Unrealized Costs
S_ALR_87013284	Reserves for Imminent Loss
S_ALR_87013285	Order Profit
S_ALR_87013286	Actual Costs
S_ALR_87013287	Planned Costs
S_ALR_87013288	Plan/Actual Comparison
S_ALR_87013289	Work in Process
S_ALR_87013290	Reserves for Unrealized Costs
S_ALR_87013291	Reserves for Imminent Loss
S_ALR_87013292	Order Profit
S_ALR_87013293	Actual Costs
S_ALR_87013294	Line Items for Sales Document
S_ALR_87013295	Cost Elements
S_ALR_87013296	Cost Components
S_ALR_87013297	Costing Items
S_ALR_87013298	Cost Elements and Origins
S_ALR_87013299	Cost Elements and Items
S_ALR_87013300	Transactions and items
S_ALR_87013301	Overview of Order Hierarchies
S_ALR_87013302	Base Planning Object Overview
S_ALR_87013303	Where-Used List Base Planning Obj.
S_ALR_87013305	Cost Elements and Origins
S_ALR_87013306	Multilevel Expl.of Base Planning Obj
S_ALR_87013307	Comparison of Unit Cost Estimates
S_ALR_87013308	Overview Unit Cost Est. for Project
S_ALR_87013309	List of Existing Mat.Cost Estimates
S_ALR_87013310	Cost Elements
S_ALR_87013311	Cost Elements
S_ALR_87013312	Cost Components
S_ALR_87013313	Cost Components
S_ALR_87013314	Costing Items
S_ALR_87013315	Cost Elements and Origins

S_ALR_87013316	Cost Elements and Items
S_ALR_87013317	Transactions and Items
S_ALR_87013318	Costing Items
S_ALR_87013319	Cost Elements and Origins
S_ALR_87013320	Cost Elements and Items
S_ALR_87013321	Transactions and items
S_ALR_87013322	Cost Components
S_ALR_87013323	Cost Elements
S_ALR_87013325	Profit Center: Plan/Actual/Variance
S_ALR_87013326	Plan/Actual/Variance: Profit Ctr Grp
S_ALR_87013327	Plan/Actual/Variance: Profit Centers
S_ALR_87013328	Profit Ctr Grps: Plan/Actual Comp.
S_ALR_87013329	Plan/Plan/Actual:Versions,Profit Ctr
S_ALR_87013330	Plan/Plan/Actual:Versions,PrCtrGrp
S_ALR_87013331	Curr.Period,Aggreg.,Year Pl/Act.PrCt
S_ALR_87013332	Curr.Period,Aggreg.,Year Pl/Act.PrCt
S_ALR_87013333	Actual Quarters Over Two Years:PrCtr
S_ALR_87013334	Actual Quarters Over Two Years:PCG
S_ALR_87013335	Plan/Actual Bal.Sheet Accts: PrCtr
S_ALR_87013336	Plan/Actual Bal.Sheet Accts: PrCtr
S_ALR_87013337	Profit Center Group: Key Figures
S_ALR_87013338	Profit Center: Key Figures
S_ALR_87013339	PrCtr Comp.: Return on Investment
S_ALR_87013340	PrCtr Group: Plan/Actual Comparison
S_ALR_87013341	PrCtr Group: Actual/2 plan versions
S_ALR_87013342	Statistical Key Figures
S_ALR_87013343	Profit Center: Receivables
S_ALR_87013344	Profit Center: Payables
S_ALR_87013345	Line Items: Periodic transfer, AR
S_ALR_87013346	Line Items: Periodic transfer, AP
S_ALR_87013347	Line Items:Periodic Transfer, Assets
S_ALR_87013348	Line Items: Periodic Transfer, Mat.
S_ALR_87013349	Average Balance YTD / Accounts
S_ALR_87013350	Average Balance YTD/Profit Centers
S_ALR_87013351	Average Balance Period / Accounts
S_ALR_87013352	Average Balance Period/Profit Ctrs
S_ALR_87013353	ALE: Plan/Actual/Variance by PrCtr
S_ALR_87013354	ALE: Plan/Actl/Variance Profit Ctr
S_ALR_87013355	Transfer Prices: Reconciliation for
S_ALR_87013357	Overview of CO Prod. Orders/Product
S_ALR_87013364	Planned Costs
S_ALR_87013371	Cost Elements
S_ALR_87013372	Cost Components
S_ALR_87013377	Costing Items
S_ALR_87013378	Cost Elements and Origins
S_ALR_87013383	Cost Elements
S_ALR_87013385	Cost Components
S_ALR_87013394	Summarization Object: Plan/Actual
S_ALR_87013396	Plan/Actual Comparison
S_ALR_87013402	Overview of Order Hierarchies
S_ALR_87013403	GUI for Library 7KV
S_ALR_87013404	Planned Costs
S_ALR_87013405	Plan/Actual Comparison
S_ALR_87013406	Target/Actual Comparison

S_ALR_87013407	Target/Actual/Production Variance
S_ALR_87013408	Variance Categories
S_ALR_87013409	Work in Process
S_ALR_87013410	Actual Costs
S_ALR_87013411	Planned Costs
S_ALR_87013412	Plan/Actual Comparison
S_ALR_87013413	Target/Actual Comparison
S_ALR_87013414	Target/Actual/Production Variance
S_ALR_87013415	Variance Categories
S_ALR_87013416	Work in Process
S_ALR_87013417	Actual Costs
S_ALR_87013418	Plan/Actual Comparison
S_ALR_87013419	Plan/Actual Comparison
S_ALR_87013420	Planned Costs
S_ALR_87013421	Display Meas. Reading Entry List
S_ALR_87013422	Display Measuremt Docs from Archive
S_ALR_87013423	Validate Stock Data (Release 4.5)
S_ALR_87013424	Validate Stock Data (Release 4.0)
S_ALR_87013425	Maintenance Scheduling Overview
S_ALR_87013426	Maintenance Plan Costing
S_ALR_87013427	Object Costing
S_ALR_87013428	Package Sequence
S_ALR_87013429	Display Document Flow
S_ALR_87013430	Postprocessing of PDC Error Records
S_ALR_87013431	Confirmation Using Operation List
S_ALR_87013432	Display Confirmations
S_ALR_87013433	Display Document Flow
S_ALR_87013434	Material Where-used List
S_ALR_87013435	Output Usage Probability
S_ALR_87013437	Project Info System: Outl. Rep. Proj
S_ALR_87013438	Project Info System: Outl. Rep WBS-
S_ALR_87013439	Project Info System: Main Program Pl
S_ALR_87013440	Project Info System: Main prog. ord.
S_ALR_87013441	Project Info System: Main prog. netw
S_ALR_87013442	Project Info System: Main prog. act.
S_ALR_87013443	Project Info System: Main prog. conf
S_ALR_87013444	Project Info System: Main prog. rel.
S_ALR_87013445	Project Info System: Main prog. mile
S_ALR_87013446	Project Info System: Main prog. cap.
S_ALR_87013447	Project Info System: Main prog. prod
S_ALR_87013448	Project Info System: Main prog. comp
S_ALR_87013449	Project Info System: Main prog. dist
S_ALR_87013450	Project Info System: Main prog. dist
S_ALR_87013499	Overview: Project Hierarchies
S_ALR_87013503	SObj: Actual/Plan/Variance
S_ALR_87013504	SObj: Actual/Plan/Commitment
S_ALR_87013505	SObj: Current/Cumulated/Total
S_ALR_87013511	Order Profit
S_ALR_87013512	SObj: Actual/Plan/Variance
S_ALR_87013513	SObj: Current/Cumulated/Total
S_ALR_87013517	Project Info System: Outl. Rep. Proj
S_ALR_87013518	Project Info System: Outl. Rep WBS-
S_ALR_87013519	Project Info System: Main Prog.Dist.
S_ALR_87013520	Project Info System: Main Prog.Dist.

S_ALR_87013521	Project Info System: Main Program Pl
S_ALR_87013522	Project Info System: Main Prog.Order
S_ALR_87013523	Project Info System:Network Overview
S_ALR_87013524	Project Info System: Acty Overview
S_ALR_87013525	Project Info System:Confirmation Ov.
S_ALR_87013526	Project Info System: Main prog. rel.
S_ALR_87013527	Project Info System: Overview Milest
S_ALR_87013528	Project Info System: Overview Cap.
S_ALR_87013529	Project Info System: PRT Overview
S_ALR_87013530	Project Info System: Main Prog. Comp
S_ALR_87013531	Costs/Revenues/Expenditures/Receipts
S_ALR_87013532	Plan/Actual/Variance
S_ALR_87013533	Plan/Actual/Cmmt/Rem.Plan/Assigned
S_ALR_87013534	Plan 1/Plan 2/Actual/Commitments
S_ALR_87013535	Actual in COArea/Object/Trans. Curr.
S_ALR_87013536	Plan/Actual/Down Payment as Expense
S_ALR_87013537	Commitment Detail
S_ALR_87013538	Project Version Comparison:Act./Plan
S_ALR_87013539	Project Version Comparison: Plan
S_ALR_87013540	Forecast
S_ALR_87013541	Project Interest: Plan/Actual
S_ALR_87013542	Actual/Comm/Total/Plan in COAr crcy
S_ALR_87013543	Act/plan/variance abs./ % var.
S_ALR_87013544	Actual/Plan Comparison: Periods
S_ALR_87013545	Period Comparison - Actual
S_ALR_87013546	Commitments: Period comparison
S_ALR_87013547	Period Comparison - Plan
S_ALR_87013548	Stat. key figures/periods
S_ALR_87013549	Act/plan compare with partner
S_ALR_87013550	Debit in object/CO area currency
S_ALR_87013551	Plan: Debits in obj./CO area crcy
S_ALR_87013552	Debit/credit actual
S_ALR_87013553	Debit/credit plan
S_ALR_87013554	Comparison of 2 plan versions
S_ALR_87013555	Project results
S_ALR_87013556	Funds Overview
S_ALR_87013557	Budget/Actual/Variance
S_ALR_87013558	Budget/Actual/Commitmt/Rem.Plan/Assg
S_ALR_87013559	Budget/Distributed/Plan/Distributed
S_ALR_87013560	Budget updates
S_ALR_87013561	Availability Control
S_ALR_87013562	Annual Overview
S_ALR_87013563	Structure
S_ALR_87013564	Plan/Actual/Variance
S_ALR_87013565	Planned Contribution Margin
S_ALR_87013566	Actual Contribution Margin
S_ALR_87013567	Quotation/Order/Plan/Actual
S_ALR_87013568	Project Results
S_ALR_87013569	Incoming Orders/Balance
S_ALR_87013570	Act/plan/variance abs./ % var.
S_ALR_87013571	Actual/Plan Comparison: Periods
S_ALR_87013572	Project results
S_ALR_87013573	Overview
S_ALR_87013574	Expenditures

S_ALR_87013575	Revenues
S_ALR_87013576	Overview: Project Hierarchies
S_ALR_87013577	Costs/Revenues/Expenditures/Receipts
S_ALR_87013578	Plan/Actual/Variance
S_ALR_87013579	Plan/Actual/Commitment
S_ALR_87013580	SObj: Actual/Plan/Variance
S_ALR_87013581	SObj: Actual/Plan/Commitment
S_ALR_87013582	SObj: Current/Cumulated/Total
S_ALR_87013583	Budget/Actual/Variance
S_ALR_87013584	Budget/Actual/Commitment
S_ALR_87013585	Plan/Actual/Variance
S_ALR_87013586	Planned Contribution Margin
S_ALR_87013587	Actual Contribution Margin
S_ALR_87013588	Order Profit
S_ALR_87013589	SObj: Actual/Plan/Variance
S_ALR_87013590	SObj: Current/Cumulated/Total
S_ALR_87013591	Overview
S_ALR_87013592	Master Data Recon.Report:Consistency
S_ALR_87013593	Master Data Recon.Report:Consistency
S_ALR_87013594	Master Data Recon.Report:Consistency
S_ALR_87013595	Master Data Recon.Report:Consistency
S_ALR_87013596	Master Data Recon.Report:Consistency
S_ALR_87013597	Master Data Recon.Report:Consistency
S_ALR_87013598	Cost Elements: Breakdown by Bus.Area
S_ALR_87013599	Cost Elements: Breakdown by FuncArea
S_ALR_87013600	Cost Elem.: Obj. Class in Columns
S_ALR_87013601	Cost Elements: Breakdown by Obj.Type
S_ALR_87013602	Cost Elements: Obj. Type in Columns
S_ALR_87013603	CO/FI Reconciliation in Co.Code Crcy
S_ALR_87013604	CO/FI Reconciliation in Group Crcy
S_ALR_87013605	CO/FI Reconcil. CCode Crcy (BArea)
S_ALR_87013606	CO/FI Reconcil. Group Crcy (BArea)
S_ALR_87013607	CElem.: Company Code Allocations
S_ALR_87013608	CElem.: Business Area Allocations
S_ALR_87013609	CElem.: Functional Area Allocations
S_ALR_87013610	Cost Elements: Accrued Costs
S_ALR_87013611	Cost Centers: Actual/Plan/Variance
S_ALR_87013612	Area: Cost Centers
S_ALR_87013613	Range: Cost Elements
S_ALR_87013614	CCtrs: Current Period / Cumulative
S_ALR_87013615	Cost Centers: Breakdown by partner
S_ALR_87013616	Cost Centers: Breakdown by BusTrans
S_ALR_87013617	Range: Activity Types
S_ALR_87013618	Range: Statistical Key Figures
S_ALR_87013619	Areas: Assigned Orders/WBS Elements
S_ALR_87013620	Cost Centers: Act./Plan/Commitments
S_ALR_87013621	Range: Actual/Plan/Commitments
S_ALR_87013622	Cost Centers: Projection
S_ALR_87013623	Cost Centers: Quarterly Comparison
S_ALR_87013624	Cost Ctrs: Fiscal Year Comparison
S_ALR_87013625	Cost Centers: Actual/Target/Variance
S_ALR_87013626	Range: Cost Elements
S_ALR_87013627	Cost Centers: Variances
S_ALR_87013628	Cost Centers: Splitting

SAP Transaction Codes – Volume Two

S_ALR_87013629	Activity Types: Reconciliation
S_ALR_87013630	Activity Types: Plan receivers
S_ALR_87013631	Cost Centers: Rolling Year
S_ALR_87013632	Cost Centers: Average Costs
S_ALR_87013633	Cost Centers: Act./Plan/Var./Prev.Yr
S_ALR_87013634	Cost Centers: Currency Translation
S_ALR_87013635	Area: Actual/Plan 2 Currencies
S_ALR_87013636	Cost Centers: Object Comparison
S_ALR_87013637	Area: Internal Business Volume
S_ALR_87013638	Cost Centers: Curr./Cum./Total Year
S_ALR_87013639	Cost Centers: Act/Target from Summ.
S_ALR_87013640	CCtrs: Period Breakdown Actual/Plan
S_ALR_87013641	CCtrs: Period Breakdown Act./Target
S_ALR_87013642	Cost Centers: Breakdown Resources
S_ALR_87013643	Range: Orders
S_ALR_87013644	Cost Centers: Cost Component Split
S_ALR_87013645	Stat. Key Figs: Period Breakdown
S_ALR_87013646	Activity Types: Period Breakdown
S_ALR_87013647	Activity Types: Scheduled/Plan
S_ALR_87013648	Range: Actual/Budget/Commitments
S_ALR_87013649	Plan/Actual Comparison
S_ALR_87013650	Division Comparison
S_ALR_87013651	Ranking List by Customer Group
S_ALR_87013652	CM: Region/Business Area/Product Grp
S_ALR_87013653	Percentage
S_ALR_87013654	Comparison: Current Year/Prev. Year
S_ALR_87013655	Quarters: Customer Group/Division
S_ALR_87013656	Quarterly Comparision: State List
S_ALR_87013657	Quarters: Product Group List
S_ALR_87013658	Print Companies
S_ALR_87013659	Print Subgroups
S_ALR_87013660	Consolidation Items
S_ALR_87013661	Transaction Types for Consolidation
S_ALR_87013662	List of Ownership
S_ALR_87013663	Equity Structure of Investee Cos
S_ALR_87013664	Changes in Investments
S_ALR_87013665	Changes in Investee Equity
S_ALR_87013666	Fair Value Adjustments
S_ALR_87013667	Changes in Hidden Reserves
S_ALR_87013668	Profit Trends: Affiliated Companies
S_ALR_87013669	Elimin. Internal Business: Balance
S_ALR_87013670	Elimin. Internal Business: Delivery
S_ALR_87013671	Print Asset Transfers
S_ALR_87013672	Changes in Asset Transfer Depr.
S_ALR_87013673	Print Currency Translation Method
S_ALR_87013674	Print Cons. of Investments Method
S_ALR_87013675	Print Intercompany Eliminations
S_ALR_87013676	Versions of Consolidation
S_ALR_87013677	Selected Items in Consolidation
S_ALR_87013678	Journal Entries by Company
S_ALR_87013679	Totals Report - Hierarchy
S_ALR_87013680	Standard Reports
S_ALR_87013681	Comparisons
S_ALR_87013682	Value Developments

SAP Transaction Codes – Volume Two

S_ALR_87013683	Exp. Balance Sheet Eval: Grid
S_ALR_87013684	Exp. Balance Sheet Eval: Runtimes
S_ALR_87013685	Expanded P+L Evaluations
S_ALR_87013686	Interactive Reporting for Consolid.
S_ALR_87013687	Create Data Extract from Subgroup
S_ALR_87013688	Data Selection FI-LC for EIS Report
S_ALR_87013689	Database List of Totals Records
S_ALR_87013690	Database List: Journal Entries
S_ALR_87013691	Database Listing, Prep. for Cons.
S_ALR_87013692	Actual/Actual Comparison for Year
S_ALR_87013693	Half-Year Actual/Actual Comparison
S_ALR_87013694	Quarterly Actual/Actual Comparison
S_ALR_87013695	Periodic Actual/Actual Comparison
S_ALR_87013696	10-Year Actual/Actual Comparison
S_ALR_87013697	Annual Plan/Actual Comparison
S_ALR_87013698	Half-Year Plan/Actual Comparison
S_ALR_87013699	Quarterly Plan/Actual Comparison
S_ALR_87013700	Periodic Plan/Actual Comparison
S_ALR_87013701	Cash Flow (Direct Method)
S_ALR_87013702	Cash Flow (Indirect Method) Variant
S_ALR_87013703	Accounts Rec. Information System
S_ALR_87013704	Vendor Information System
S_ALR_87013705	Asset Balances
S_ALR_87013706	Asset Balances
S_ALR_87013707	Asset Balances
S_ALR_87013708	Asset Balances
S_ALR_87013709	Asset Balances
S_ALR_87013710	Asset Balances
S_ALR_87013711	Asset Balances
S_ALR_87013712	Asset Balances
S_ALR_87013713	Asset Balances
S_ALR_87013714	Asset Balances
S_ALR_87013715	Asset Balances
S_ALR_87013716	Asset Balances
S_ALR_87013717	Asset Balances
S_ALR_87013718	Asset Balances
S_ALR_87013719	Asset Balances
S_ALR_87013720	Asset Balances
S_ALR_87013721	Asset Balances
S_ALR_87013722	RAQ01INV
S_ALR_87013723	RAQ01INV
S_ALR_87013724	RAQ01INV
S_ALR_87013725	RAQ01INV
S_ALR_87013726	RAQ01INV
S_ALR_87013727	RAQ01INV
S_ALR_87013728	RAQ01INV
S_ALR_87013729	RAQ01INV
S_ALR_87013730	Bar Codes
S_ALR_87013731	Bar codes
S_ALR_87013732	RAQ02GRD
S_ALR_87013733	RAQ02GRD
S_ALR_87013734	RAQ03CAR
S_ALR_87013735	RAQ03CAR
S_ALR_87013736	RAQ04LEA

S_ALR_87013737	RAQ04LEA
S_ALR_87013738	Asset History Sheet
S_ALR_87013739	Asset History Sheet
S_ALR_87013740	Changes to Special Reserves
S_ALR_87013741	Changes to Special Reserves
S_ALR_87013742	Liabilities from Leasing Agreements
S_ALR_87013743	Liabilities from Leasing Agreements
S_ALR_87013744	Asset Balances
S_ALR_87013745	Asset Balances
S_ALR_87013746	Asset Register (Italy)
S_ALR_87013747	Asset Register (Italy)
S_ALR_87013748	Asset Register (Italy)
S_ALR_87013749	Asset Register (Italy)
S_ALR_87013750	Depreciation
S_ALR_87013751	Depreciation
S_ALR_87013752	RAQ07AFN
S_ALR_87013753	RAQ07AFN
S_ALR_87013754	RAQ09AFA
S_ALR_87013755	RAQ09AFA
S_ALR_87013756	RAQ08AFS
S_ALR_87013757	RAQ08AFS
S_ALR_87013758	RAQ11ZUS
S_ALR_87013759	RAQ11ZUS
S_ALR_87013760	RAQ10BAC
S_ALR_87013761	RAQ10BAC
S_ALR_87013762	Depreciation and Interest
S_ALR_87013763	Depreciation and Interest
S_ALR_87013764	RAQ12AUF
S_ALR_87013765	RAQ12AUF
S_ALR_87013766	RAQ27KOS
S_ALR_87013767	RAQ27KOS
S_ALR_87013768	Depreciation and Interest
S_ALR_87013769	Depreciation and Interest
S_ALR_87013770	Depreciation Simulation
S_ALR_87013771	Depreciation Simulation
S_ALR_87013772	Depreciation
S_ALR_87013773	Depreciation
S_ALR_87013774	Net Worth Valuation
S_ALR_87013775	Net Worth Valuation
S_ALR_87013776	Net Worth Valuation
S_ALR_87013777	Insurance Values
S_ALR_87013778	Insurance Values
S_ALR_87013779	Insurance Values
S_ALR_87013780	RAAKTB01
S_ALR_87013781	RAAKTB01
S_ALR_87013782	RAQ13MEH
S_ALR_87013783	RAQ13MEH
S_ALR_87013784	Asset Acquisitions(Mid-Quarter-Conv)
S_ALR_87013785	Asset Acquisitions(Mid-Quarter-Conv)
S_ALR_87013786	Depreciation
S_ALR_87013787	Changes to Asset Master Records
S_ALR_87013788	Changes to Asset Master Records
S_ALR_87013789	Asset Transactions
S_ALR_87013790	Asset Transactions

S_ALR_87013791	Asset Acquisitions
S_ALR_87013792	Asset Acquisitions
S_ALR_87013793	Asset Retirements
S_ALR_87013794	Asset Retirements
S_ALR_87013795	Intracompany Asset Transfers
S_ALR_87013796	Intracompany Asset Transfers
S_ALR_87013797	Directory of Unposted Assets
S_ALR_87013798	Directory of Unposted Assets
S_ALR_87013799	List of Origins of Asset Charges
S_ALR_87013800	List of Origins of Asset Charges
S_ALR_87013801	Application Log
S_ALR_87013802	Depreciation
S_ALR_87013803	Depreciation
S_ALR_87013804	Retirement Comparison
S_ALR_87013805	Retirement Comparison
S_ALR_87013806	Asset History
S_ALR_87013807	Asset History
S_ALR_87013809	Assign Cost Centers to Funds Centers
S_ALR_87013810	Assigning CO Orders to Funds Centers
S_ALR_87013811	Assign WBS Elements to Funds Centers
S_ALR_87013812	Assign Profit Centers to Funds Ctrs
S_ALR_87013815	Assign Commitment Items to Cost Elem
S_ALR_87013829	RFFMIEP1
S_ALR_87013840	Cost Elements: Breakdown by FuncArea
S_ALR_87013841	Cost Elements: Breakdown by Obj.Type
S_ALR_87013842	Cost Elements: Obj. Type in Columns
S_ALR_87013843	Cost Elem.: Obj. Class in Columns
S_ALR_87013844	CO/FI Reconciliation in Co.Code Crcy
S_ALR_87013845	CO/FI Reconciliation in Group Crcy
S_ALR_87013846	CElem.: Company Code Allocations
S_ALR_87013849	Cost Elements: Accrued Costs
S_ALR_87013851	Cost Centers: Actual/Plan/Variance
S_ALR_87013852	Area: Cost Centers
S_ALR_87013853	Range: Cost Elements
S_ALR_87013854	CCtrs: Current Period / Cumulative
S_ALR_87013855	Cost Centers: Breakdown by Partner
S_ALR_87013856	Cost Centers: Breakdown by BusTrans
S_ALR_87013857	Range: Activity Types
S_ALR_87013858	Range: Statistical Key Figures
S_ALR_87013859	Cost Centers: Act./Plan/Commitments
S_ALR_87013860	Range: Actual/Plan/Commitments
S_ALR_87013861	Cost Centers: Projection
S_ALR_87013862	Cost Centers: Quarterly Comparison
S_ALR_87013863	Cost Ctrs: Fiscal Year Comparison
S_ALR_87013864	Cost Centers: Actual/Target/Variance
S_ALR_87013865	Range: Cost Elements
S_ALR_87013867	Cost Centers: Breakdown by BusTrans
S_ALR_87013868	Cost Centers: Variances
S_ALR_87013869	Cost Centers: Splitting
S_ALR_87013870	Activity Types: Reconciliation
S_ALR_87013871	Activity Types: Plan Receivers
S_ALR_87013872	Range: Statistical Key Figures
S_ALR_87013873	Cost Centers: Rolling Year
S_ALR_87013874	Cost Centers: Currency Translation

S_ALR_87013875	Cost Centers: Object Comparison
S_ALR_87013876	Area: Internal Business Volume
S_ALR_87013877	Cost Centers: Curr./Cum./Total Year
S_ALR_87013878	Stat. Key Figs: Period Breakdown
S_ALR_87013879	Activity Types: Period Breakdown
S_ALR_87013880	Activity Types: Scheduled/Plan
S_ALR_87013881	CCtrs: Period Breakdown Actual/Plan
S_ALR_87013882	CCtrs: Period Breakdown Act./Target
S_ALR_87013883	Orders: Actual/Plan/Variance
S_ALR_87013884	Orders: Current Period/Cumulative
S_ALR_87013885	List: Actual Debit/Credit
S_ALR_87013886	List: Orders
S_ALR_87013887	List: Cost Elements by Order
S_ALR_87013888	Orders: Breakdown by Partner
S_ALR_87013889	Orders: Actual/Plan/Commitments
S_ALR_87013890	List: Actual/Plan/Commitments
S_ALR_87013891	Orders: Yearly Comparison - Actual
S_ALR_87013892	Orders: Quarterly Comparison - Act.
S_ALR_87013893	Orders: Period Comparison - Actual
S_ALR_87013894	Orders: Yearly Comparison - Plan
S_ALR_87013895	Orders: Quarterly Comparison - Plan
S_ALR_87013896	Orders: Period Comparison - Plan
S_ALR_87013897	SObj: Actual/Plan/Variance
S_ALR_87013898	SObj: Actual/Plan/Commitment
S_ALR_87013899	SObj: Current/Cumulated/Total
S_ALR_87013900	Orders: Breakdown by Period
S_ALR_87013901	Orders: Actual/Plan/Price Variance
S_ALR_87013902	Orders: Actual/Plan/Consumption
S_ALR_87013904	Orders: Actual TCrcy/OCrcy/CAcrcy
S_ALR_87013905	List: Actual/Plan/Var. Cumulative
S_ALR_87013907	RCNCO010
S_ALR_87013916	Processes: Breakdown by Partner
S_ALR_87013928	Plan/Actual Comparison
S_ALR_87013929	CM I: Districts/Plants/Mat. Groups
S_ALR_87013930	Comparison: Current Year/Prev. Year
S_ALR_87013931	Quarterly Comp.: Cust. Grp/Mat. Grp
S_ALR_87013932	Quarterly Comparison: Customer List
S_ALR_87013933	Quarterly Comparison: Product List
S_ALR_87013934	Division Comparison
S_ALR_87013935	Ranking List by Customer Group
S_ALR_87013936	Cost Element Report
S_ALR_87013937	Profit Center: Area List Plan/Act.
S_ALR_87013938	Profit Center: Periods, Plan/Actual
S_ALR_87013939	PrCtr: Return on Investment
S_ALR_87013940	PCtr Grp: Actual Comparison
S_ALR_87013941	PrCtr Group: Act./Act. Comparison
S_ALR_87013942	PrCtr Group: Actual/2 Plan Versions
S_ALR_87013943	PrCtr Group: Plan/Plan Comparison
S_ALR_87013944	PrCtr Grp: Plan in 2 Time Periods
S_ALR_87013945	PrCtr Group: Plan/Actual Comparison
S_ALR_87013946	PrCtr Group: Curr.Per.+ Cum. + FYear
S_ALR_87013947	PrCtr Group: Actual/2 Plan Versions
S_ALR_87013948	PrCtr Group: P/A Comp. (Local Crcy)
S_ALR_87013949	PrCtr Group: P/A Comp. (by Origin)

S_ALR_87013950	P/A Comp. of PrCtrGrp (Partner PrC)
S_ALR_87013951	Plan/Act.Comp. PrCtr Grp(Fxd Prices)
S_ALR_87013952	Profit Center Group: Forecast
S_ALR_87013953	PCtr Rep.: Plan/Actual Comparison
S_ALR_87013954	PCtr: Current/Cumulated/Fiscal Year
S_ALR_87013955	PCtr: Actual in 2 Time Periods
S_ALR_87013956	PCtr: Plan in 2 Time Periods
S_ALR_87013957	Profit Center Report: 2 Versions
S_ALR_87013958	Actual/Plan Comparison by Accts
S_ALR_87013959	EC-PCA: Actual Line Items
S_ALR_87013960	EC-PCA: Plan Line Items
S_ALR_87013961	Overall Plan/Annual Plan in Program
S_ALR_87013962	Overall/Annual Plan from Measures
S_ALR_87013963	Plan Program, Requests, Measures
S_ALR_87013964	Plan/Budget Comparison in Program
S_ALR_87013965	Overall/Annual Budget in Program
S_ALR_87013966	Overall/Annual Budget in Measures
S_ALR_87013967	Budget Distribution to Measures
S_ALR_87013969	Budget Available for Measures
S_ALR_87013971	Budget Availability in Program
S_ALR_87013972	Depreciation Simulation
S_ALR_87013973	Depreciation Simulation
S_ALR_87013974	Orders: Actual/Plan/Variance
S_ALR_87013975	Orders: Current Period/Cumulative
S_ALR_87013976	List: Actual Debit/Credit
S_ALR_87013977	List: Orders
S_ALR_87013978	List: Cost Elements by Order
S_ALR_87013979	Orders: Breakdown by Partner
S_ALR_87013980	Orders: Actual/Plan/Commitments
S_ALR_87013981	List: Actual/Plan/Commitments
S_ALR_87013982	Orders: Yearly Comparison - Actual
S_ALR_87013983	Orders: Quarterly Comparison - Act.
S_ALR_87013984	Orders: Period Comparison - Actual
S_ALR_87013985	Orders: Yearly Comparison - Plan
S_ALR_87013986	Orders: Quarterly Comparison - Plan
S_ALR_87013987	Orders: Period Comparison - Plan
S_ALR_87013988	SObj: Actual/Plan/Variance
S_ALR_87013989	SObj: Actual/Plan/Commitment
S_ALR_87013990	SObj: Current/Cumulated/Total
S_ALR_87013991	Orders: Breakdown by Period
S_ALR_87013992	Orders: Actual/Plan/Price Variance
S_ALR_87013993	Orders: Actual/Plan/Consumption
S_ALR_87013995	Orders: Actual TCrcy/OCrcy/CAcrcy
S_ALR_87013996	List: Actual/Plan/Var. Cumulative
S_ALR_87013998	List: Actual/Plan/Var. Cumulative
S_ALR_87014000	List: Actual Debit/Credit
S_ALR_87014001	List: Orders
S_ALR_87014002	List: Cost Elements by Order
S_ALR_87014003	List: Actual/Plan/Commitments
S_ALR_87014004	Order Report:Overall Plan/Actual Cst
S_ALR_87014005	Order Report: Budget
S_ALR_87014006	Orders: Yearly Comparison - Plan
S_ALR_87014007	Orders: Quarterly Comparison - Plan
S_ALR_87014008	Orders: Period Comparison - Plan

S_ALR_87014009	Orders: Yearly Comparison - Actual
S_ALR_87014010	Orders: Quarterly Comparison - Act.
S_ALR_87014011	Orders: Period Comparison - Actual
S_ALR_87014012	Orders: Actual/Plan/Variance
S_ALR_87014013	Orders: Actual/Plan/Price Variance
S_ALR_87014014	Orders: Actual/Plan/Consumption
S_ALR_87014015	Orders: Current Period/Cumulative
S_ALR_87014017	Orders: Breakdown by Partner
S_ALR_87014020	Orders: Actual/Plan/Commitments
S_ALR_87014022	Orders: Actual TCrcy/OCrcy/CAcrcy
S_ALR_87014023	Orders: Actual Periods
S_ALR_87014024	Orders: Plan Periods
S_ALR_87014025	Orders: Breakdown by Period
S_ALR_87014027	Summarization Object: Plan/Actual
S_ALR_87014028	Summ. Object: Actual/Plan/Commitment
S_ALR_87014030	Planned Costs
S_ALR_87014031	Plan/Actual Comparison
S_ALR_87014032	Depreciation Simulation
S_ALR_87014033	Depreciation Simulation
S_ALR_87014034	Depreciation Simulation
S_ALR_87014035	Depreciation Simulation
S_ALR_87014036	Depreciation Simulation
S_ALR_87014037	Depreciation Simulation
S_ALR_87014038	Depreciation Simulation
S_ALR_87014039	Depreciation Simulation
S_ALR_87014040	Depreciation Simulation
S_ALR_87014041	Depreciation Simulation
S_ALR_87014042	Primary Cost Planning Dep./Interest
S_ALR_87014043	Primary Cost Planning Dep./Interest
S_ALR_87014044	Organizational Structure
S_ALR_87014045	Org. Structure with Persons
S_ALR_87014046	Staff Assignments
S_ALR_87014047	Applicants by Name
S_ALR_87014048	Applicants by Action
S_ALR_87014049	Applications
S_ALR_87014050	Applicant Statistics
S_ALR_87014051	Planned Activities for Personnel Off
S_ALR_87014052	Vacancy Assignments
S_ALR_87014053	Vacancies
S_ALR_87014054	Job Advertisements
S_ALR_87014055	Evaluate Recruitment Instruments
S_ALR_87014056	HR Master Data Sheet
S_ALR_87014058	Family Members
S_ALR_87014059	Birthday List
S_ALR_87014060	Birthdays
S_ALR_87014061	Flexible Employee Data
S_ALR_87014063	Vehicle - Search List
S_ALR_87014064	Who's Who
S_ALR_87014065	Overview of Maternity Data
S_ALR_87014066	Education and Training
S_ALR_87014067	Telephone Directory
S_ALR_87014068	Employees with Powers of Attorney
S_ALR_87014069	Time Spent in Pay Scale Group/Level
S_ALR_87014070	Defaults for Pay Scale Reclass.

SAP Transaction Codes – Volume Two

S_ALR_87014071	Reference Personnel Numbers
S_ALR_87014072	Severely Challenged
S_ALR_87014073	Seniority and Age
S_ALR_87014074	Headcount Development
S_ALR_87014075	Nationalities
S_ALR_87014076	Employee Structure
S_ALR_87014077	Salary According to Seniority
S_ALR_87014078	Time-Related Statistical Evaluations
S_ALR_87014079	Assignment to Wage Level
S_ALR_87014081	Logged Changes in Infotype Data
S_ALR_87014082	Log of Report Starts
S_ALR_87014083	Date Monitoring
S_ALR_87014084	RHXQCAT0
S_ALR_87014085	Attendance Statistics
S_ALR_87014086	Business Event Hierarchy
S_ALR_87014087	Resource Reservation
S_ALR_87014088	Participation
S_ALR_87014089	Eligible Employees
S_ALR_87014090	Changes in Eligibility
S_ALR_87014091	Employee Demographics
S_ALR_87014092	Flexible Spending Acct Contributions
S_ALR_87014093	Health Premiums
S_ALR_87014094	Insurance Premiums
S_ALR_87014095	Savings Plan Premium
S_ALR_87014096	Vesting Percentage
S_ALR_87014097	Changes in Benefits Elections
S_ALR_87014098	Personal Work Schedule
S_ALR_87014099	Daily Work Schedule
S_ALR_87014100	Attendance/Absence for Each Employee
S_ALR_87014101	Attendance/Absence for Each Employee
S_ALR_87014102	Attendance Check
S_ALR_87014103	Att./Absences: Graphical Overview
S_ALR_87014104	Att./Absences: Graphical Overview
S_ALR_87014105	Attendance/Absence Data: Overview
S_ALR_87014106	Leave Overview
S_ALR_87014107	Att./Absences: Graphical Overview
S_ALR_87014108	Att./Absences: Graphical Overview
S_ALR_87014109	Time Leveling
S_ALR_87014110	Time Leveling
S_ALR_87014111	Time Statement Form
S_ALR_87014112	Time Statement Form
S_ALR_87014113	Time Statement Form
S_ALR_87014114	Time Statement Form
S_ALR_87014115	Time Accounts
S_ALR_87014116	Time Leveling
S_ALR_87014117	Time Leveling
S_ALR_87014118	Working Times of Time and Incentive
S_ALR_87014119	Reassignment Proposals for Wage Grps
S_ALR_87014120	Remuneration Statements
S_ALR_87014121	Remuneration Statements
S_ALR_87014122	Disp. Weekly Overview of Target Req.
S_ALR_87014123	Display Target Req.in Daily Overview
S_ALR_87014124	Display Personal Shift Plan
S_ALR_87014125	Display Attendance List

417

S_ALR_87014126	Remuneration Statements
S_ALR_87014127	Payroll Accounts
S_ALR_87014128	Payments and Deductions
S_ALR_87014129	Bank Details
S_ALR_87014130	Overview of Company Loans
S_ALR_87014131	Calc. Present Value for Company Loan
S_ALR_87014132	Account Statement for Company Loans
S_ALR_87014133	Payroll Journal --- International
S_ALR_87014134	Wage Type Statement
S_ALR_87014135	Wage Type Distribution
S_ALR_87014136	Paydays on Holidays or Weekends
S_ALR_87014137	Payday Calendar
S_ALR_87014138	Remuneration Statements
S_ALR_87014139	Payroll Accounts
S_ALR_87014140	Payments and Deductions
S_ALR_87014141	Bank Details
S_ALR_87014142	Overview of Company Loans
S_ALR_87014143	Calc. Present Value for Company Loan
S_ALR_87014144	Account Statement for Company Loans
S_ALR_87014145	Payroll Journal
S_ALR_87014146	Wage Type Statement
S_ALR_87014147	Wage Type Distribution
S_ALR_87014148	Posting to Accounting: Wage Type
S_ALR_87014149	Paydays on Holidays or Weekends
S_ALR_87014150	Payday Calendar
S_ALR_87014151	Remuneration Statements
S_ALR_87014152	Payroll Accounts
S_ALR_87014153	Payments and Deductions
S_ALR_87014154	Bank Details
S_ALR_87014155	Overview of Company Loans
S_ALR_87014156	Calc. Present Value for Company Loan
S_ALR_87014157	Account Statement for Company Loans
S_ALR_87014158	Payroll Journal --- International
S_ALR_87014159	Wage Type Statement
S_ALR_87014160	Wage Type Distribution
S_ALR_87014161	Posting to Accounting: Wage Type
S_ALR_87014162	Paydays on Holidays or Weekends
S_ALR_87014163	Payday Calendar
S_ALR_87014164	Remuneration statements
S_ALR_87014165	Payroll Accounts
S_ALR_87014166	Payments and Deductions
S_ALR_87014167	Bank Details
S_ALR_87014168	Overview of Company Loans
S_ALR_87014169	Calc. Present Value for Company Loan
S_ALR_87014170	Account Statement for Company Loans
S_ALR_87014171	Statutory Maternity Pay Record Sheet
S_ALR_87014172	Wage Type Statement
S_ALR_87014173	Wage Type Distribution
S_ALR_87014174	Posting to Accounting: Wage Type
S_ALR_87014175	Paydays on Holidays or Weekends
S_ALR_87014176	Payday Calendar
S_ALR_87014177	Remuneration statements
S_ALR_87014178	Payroll accounts
S_ALR_87014179	Payments and Deductions

S_ALR_87014180	Bank Details
S_ALR_87014181	Overview of Company Loans
S_ALR_87014182	Calc. Present Value for Company Loan
S_ALR_87014183	Account Statement for Company Loans
S_ALR_87014184	Payroll Journal
S_ALR_87014185	Wage Type Statement
S_ALR_87014186	Wage Type Distribution
S_ALR_87014187	Posting to Accounting: Wage Type
S_ALR_87014188	Paydays on Holidays or Weekends
S_ALR_87014189	Payday Calendar
S_ALR_87014190	Indiv.Statement Current Profit Shar.
S_ALR_87014191	List of Current Profit Sharing
S_ALR_87014192	List of Paid Profit Sharing
S_ALR_87014193	Details of Payment (Japan)
S_ALR_87014194	Wage Account (Japan)
S_ALR_87014195	Payments and Deductions
S_ALR_87014196	Overview of Company Loans
S_ALR_87014197	Calc. Present Value for Company Loan
S_ALR_87014198	Account Statement for Company Loans
S_ALR_87014199	Posting to Accounting: Wage Type
S_ALR_87014200	Paydays on Holidays or Weekends
S_ALR_87014201	Payday Calendar
S_ALR_87014202	Remuneration Statements
S_ALR_87014203	Payroll Account (NL)
S_ALR_87014204	Payments and Deductions
S_ALR_87014205	Bank Details
S_ALR_87014206	Overview of Company Loans
S_ALR_87014207	Calc. Present Value for Company Loan
S_ALR_87014208	Account Statement for Company Loans
S_ALR_87014209	Wage Type Statement
S_ALR_87014210	Wage Type Distribution
S_ALR_87014211	Posting to Accounting: Wage Type
S_ALR_87014212	Paydays on Holidays or Weekends
S_ALR_87014213	Payday Calendar
S_ALR_87014214	Remuneration Statements
S_ALR_87014215	Payroll accounts
S_ALR_87014216	Payments and Deductions
S_ALR_87014217	Bank Details
S_ALR_87014218	Overview of Company Loans
S_ALR_87014219	Calc. Present Value for Company Loan
S_ALR_87014220	Account Statement for Company Loans
S_ALR_87014221	Payroll journal (Austria)
S_ALR_87014222	Wage Type Statement
S_ALR_87014223	Wage Type Distribution
S_ALR_87014224	Posting to Accounting: Wage Type
S_ALR_87014225	Paydays on Holidays or Weekends
S_ALR_87014226	Payday Calendar
S_ALR_87014227	Remuneration Statements
S_ALR_87014228	Payroll Account
S_ALR_87014229	Payments and Deductions
S_ALR_87014230	Bank Details
S_ALR_87014231	Overview of Company Loans
S_ALR_87014232	Calc. Present Value for Company Loan
S_ALR_87014233	Account Statement for Company Loans

S_ALR_87014234	Payroll Journal (Switzerland)
S_ALR_87014235	Wage Type Statement
S_ALR_87014236	Wage Type Distribution
S_ALR_87014237	Posting to Accounting: Wage Type
S_ALR_87014238	Paydays on Holidays or Weekends
S_ALR_87014239	Payday Calendar
S_ALR_87014240	Remuneration Statement
S_ALR_87014241	Payroll Accounts
S_ALR_87014242	Payments and Deductions
S_ALR_87014243	Bank Details
S_ALR_87014244	Overview of Company Loans
S_ALR_87014245	Calc. Present Value for Company Loan
S_ALR_87014246	Account Statement for Company Loans
S_ALR_87014247	Monthly Overview of Payroll Results
S_ALR_87014248	Wage Type Statement
S_ALR_87014249	Wage Type Distribution
S_ALR_87014250	Posting to Accounting: Wage Type
S_ALR_87014251	Paydays on Holidays or Weekends
S_ALR_87014252	Payday Calendar
S_ALR_87014253	Remuneration Statements
S_ALR_87014254	Payments and Deductions
S_ALR_87014255	Bank Details
S_ALR_87014256	Overview of Company Loans
S_ALR_87014257	Calc. Present Value for Company Loan
S_ALR_87014258	Account Statement for Company Loans
S_ALR_87014259	Payroll Journal
S_ALR_87014260	Wage Type Statement
S_ALR_87014261	Wage Type Distribution
S_ALR_87014262	Posting to Accounting: Wage Type
S_ALR_87014263	Paydays on Holidays or Weekends
S_ALR_87014264	Payday Calendar
S_ALR_87014265	Remuneration Statements
S_ALR_87014266	Payroll Accounts
S_ALR_87014267	Payments and Deductions
S_ALR_87014268	Bank Details
S_ALR_87014269	Overview of Company Loans
S_ALR_87014270	Calc. Present Value for Company Loan
S_ALR_87014271	Account Statement for Company Loans
S_ALR_87014272	Payroll Journal
S_ALR_87014273	Wage Type Statement
S_ALR_87014274	Wage Type Distribution
S_ALR_87014275	Posting to Accounting: Wage Type
S_ALR_87014276	Paydays on Holidays or Weekends
S_ALR_87014277	Payday Calendar
S_ALR_87014278	Plan Scenarios of Personnel Costs
S_ALR_87014279	Travel Expense Reporting by Period
S_ALR_87014327	Aggregated Values
S_ALR_87014328	Transfer:Treasury/Money Market->EIS
S_ALR_87014329	Transfer:Treasury/Money Market->EIS
S_ALR_87014330	Amounts in DEM-USD-FRF-ITL
S_ALR_87014331	Transfer:Treasury/Foreign Exch.->EIS
S_ALR_87014332	Transfer:Treasury/Foreign Exch.->EIS
S_ALR_87014333	Transfer:Treasury/Securities -> EIS
S_ALR_87014334	Transfer:Treasury/Securities -> EIS

S_ALR_87014335	Transfer:Treasury/Derivatives -> EIS
S_ALR_87014336	Transfer:Treasury/Derivatives -> EIS
S_ALR_87014337	Payables and Receivables
S_ALR_87014338	Payables and Receivables
S_ALR_87014339	Money Market Position
S_ALR_87014340	Comparison: 1995, 1996, 1997
S_ALR_87014341	Transfer:Treasury/Money Market->EIS
S_ALR_87014342	Transfer:Treasury/Money Market->EIS
S_ALR_87014343	DEM/US$ Transactions
S_ALR_87014344	Transfer:Treasury/Foreign Exch.->EIS
S_ALR_87014345	Transfer:Treasury/Foreign Exch.->EIS
S_ALR_87014346	Transfer:Treasury/Securities -> EIS
S_ALR_87014347	Transfer:Treasury/Securities -> EIS
S_ALR_87014353	Position List:Traded Options/Futures
S_ALR_87014354	Transfer:Treasury/Derivatives -> EIS
S_ALR_87014355	Transfer:Treasury/Derivatives -> EIS
S_ALR_87014357	List of Sales Deals
S_ALR_87014358	List of Promotions
S_ALR_87014359	Expiring Quotations
S_ALR_87014360	Expired Quotations
S_ALR_87014361	Completed Quotations
S_ALR_87014362	Open Purch.Req. Ref. Archived/Compl.
S_ALR_87014363	RVAUFEIN
S_ALR_87014364	Expiring Contracts
S_ALR_87014365	Expired Contracts
S_ALR_87014366	Completed Contracts
S_ALR_87014367	Quantity Flow Monitoring
S_ALR_87014368	Payment Cards: Worklist
S_ALR_87014369	Payment Cards: SD Documents
S_ALR_87014370	Payment Cards: Maintenance
S_ALR_87014371	Customer for Payment Cards
S_ALR_87014372	Payment Cards Invalid in a Period
S_ALR_87014373	Standard Sel. Report for Addresses
S_ALR_87014374	Address Selection - Birthday List
S_ALR_87014375	Address Selection -Business Partners
S_ALR_87014376	Create Address List w.Ref.to Mailing
S_ALR_87014377	Standard Address Selection Report
S_ALR_87014378	Address Selection - Birthday List
S_ALR_87014379	Validate Stock Data (Release 4.5)
S_ALR_87014380	Validate Stock Data (Release 4.0)
S_ALR_87014381	Display Meas. Reading Entry List
S_ALR_87014382	Organization/Agent Call Vol. Report
S_ALR_87014383	CCM Agent Activity Report
S_ALR_87014384	CCM Profile Report
S_ALR_87014385	CCM Agent Profile Summary
S_ALR_87014386	CTI Profile/Framework:Detail Display
S_ALR_87014387	Display Document Flow
S_ALR_87014388	Display Confirmations
S_ALR_87014389	Maintenance Scheduling Overview
S_ALR_87014390	Maintenance Plan Costing
S_ALR_87014391	Object Costing
S_ALR_87014392	Display Document Flow
S_ALR_87014393	Transfer: Treasury/Cash Mgmt -> EIS
S_ALR_87014394	Transfer: Treasury/Cash Mgmt -> EIS

S_ALR_87014395	Currencies and Time Frame
S_ALR_87014396	Dynamic Currency and Time Frame
S_ALR_87014397	Data Transfer: Treasury/Loans -> EIS
S_ALR_87014398	Data Transfer: Treasury/Loans -> EIS
S_ALR_87014399	Guarantee Fee in Display Currency
S_ALR_87014400	Guarantee Charge in Payment Currency
S_ALR_87014401	Data Transfer: Treasury/Loans -> EIS
S_ALR_87014402	Data Transfer: Treasury/Loans -> EIS
S_ALR_87014403	Loan Commitment in Display Currency
S_ALR_87014404	Loan Commitment in Position Currency
S_ALR_87014405	Balance List in Display Currency
S_ALR_87014406	Balance List in Position Currency
S_ALR_87014407	Journal of Financial Transactions
S_ALR_87014408	Journal of Financial Transactions
S_ALR_87014409	Correspondence Overview
S_ALR_87014410	Correspondence Overview
S_ALR_87014413	Evaluate Offers
S_ALR_87014414	Evaluate Offers
S_ALR_87014415	Journal: Transactions w. Cash Flows
S_ALR_87014416	Journal: Transactions w. Cash Flows
S_ALR_87014417	Aggregated Values
S_ALR_87014418	Transfer:Treasury/Money Market->EIS
S_ALR_87014419	Transfer:Treasury/Money Market->EIS
S_ALR_87014420	Money Market Position
S_ALR_87014421	Comparison: 1995, 1996, 1997
S_ALR_87014422	Transfer:Treasury/Money Market->EIS
S_ALR_87014423	Transfer:Treasury/Money Market->EIS
S_ALR_87014424	Posting Journal
S_ALR_87014425	Posting Journal
S_ALR_87014426	Posting Overview
S_ALR_87014427	Posting Overview
S_ALR_87014428	Treasury: Payment Schedule
S_ALR_87014429	Treasury: Payment Schedule
S_ALR_87014430	IPD Property File
S_ALR_87014431	ROZ Annual File 1: Areas
S_ALR_87014432	ROZ Annual File 3: Rents
S_ALR_87014433	ROZ Annual File 3: Rents (2)
S_ALR_87014434	ROZ Annual File 5: Operating costs
S_ALR_87014435	Journal of Financial Transactions
S_ALR_87014436	Journal of Financial Transactions
S_ALR_87014437	Correspondence Overview
S_ALR_87014438	Correspondence Overview
S_ALR_87014441	Journal: Transactions w. Cash Flows
S_ALR_87014442	Journal: Transactions w. Cash Flows
S_ALR_87014443	Transfer:Treasury/Derivatives -> EIS
S_ALR_87014444	Transfer:Treasury/Derivatives -> EIS
S_ALR_87014445	Position List:Traded Options/Futures
S_ALR_87014446	Transfer:Treasury/Derivatives -> EIS
S_ALR_87014447	Transfer:Treasury/Derivatives -> EIS
S_ALR_87014448	Posting Journal
S_ALR_87014449	Posting Journal
S_ALR_87014450	Posting Overview
S_ALR_87014451	Posting Overview
S_ALR_87014452	Treasury: Payment Schedule

SAP Transaction Codes – Volume Two

S_ALR_87014453	Treasury: Payment Schedule
S_ALR_87014454	Journal of Financial Transactions
S_ALR_87014455	Journal of Financial Transactions
S_ALR_87014456	Correspondence Overview
S_ALR_87014457	Correspondence Overview
S_ALR_87014460	Evaluate Offers
S_ALR_87014461	Evaluate Offers
S_ALR_87014462	Journal: Transactions w. Cash Flows
S_ALR_87014463	Journal: Transactions w. Cash Flows
S_ALR_87014464	Amounts in DEM-USD-FRF-ITL
S_ALR_87014465	Transfer:Treasury/Foreign Exch.->EIS
S_ALR_87014466	Transfer:Treasury/Foreign Exch.->EIS
S_ALR_87014467	DEM/US$ Transactions
S_ALR_87014468	Transfer:Treasury/Foreign Exch.->EIS
S_ALR_87014469	Transfer:Treasury/Foreign Exch.->EIS
S_ALR_87014470	Posting Journal
S_ALR_87014471	Posting Journal
S_ALR_87014472	Posting Overview
S_ALR_87014473	Posting Overview
S_ALR_87014474	Treasury: Payment Schedule
S_ALR_87014475	Treasury: Payment Schedule
S_ALR_87014476	Transfer:Treasury/Securities -> EIS
S_ALR_87014477	Transfer:Treasury/Securities -> EIS
S_ALR_87014480	Transfer:Treasury/Securities -> EIS
S_ALR_87014481	Transfer:Treasury/Securities -> EIS
S_ALR_87014487	Treasury: Payment Schedule
S_ALR_87014488	Treasury: Payment Schedule
S_ALR_87014490	Land Register Standard Analysis
S_ALR_87014491	Business Entities Standard Analysis
S_ALR_87014492	Property Standard Analysis
S_ALR_87014493	Buildings Standard Analysis
S_ALR_87014494	Rental Units Standard Analysis
S_ALR_87014495	Partner Standard Analysis
S_ALR_87014496	Partner for Real Estate objects
S_ALR_87014497	Partner: Real Estate Objects,Address
S_ALR_87014498	Partner: Real Estate Objects,Address
S_ALR_87014499	Lease-Outs: Standard Analysis
S_ALR_87014500	Lease-Out Conditions
S_ALR_87014501	Maximum/minimum condition
S_ALR_87014502	Conditions: Tenants/Contracts
S_ALR_87014503	Rental unit conditions
S_ALR_87014504	Conditions: Tenants/Objects
S_ALR_87014505	Conditions Lease-Out/Rental Unit
S_ALR_87014506	Conditions by Owner
S_ALR_87014507	Key Figures Basic Rent
S_ALR_87014508	Rental Unit Areas
S_ALR_87014509	Rental Unit Areas by Tenants
S_ALR_87014510	Rental Unit Areas by Owners
S_ALR_87014511	Areas/Usage Types
S_ALR_87014512	Areas/Usage Types (%)
S_ALR_87014513	Rental Unit Area History
S_ALR_87014514	Property Areas
S_ALR_87014515	Property Areas by Owners
S_ALR_87014516	Property Area History

S_ALR_87014517	Building Areas
S_ALR_87014518	Building Areas by Owners
S_ALR_87014519	Building Area History
S_ALR_87014520	Property Areas/Buildings/Rental Unit
S_ALR_87014521	PR/BU/RU Areas by Owners
S_ALR_87014522	Areas, Rental Units (Display Unit)
S_ALR_87014523	Rental Unit Areas by Tenants (Disp.)
S_ALR_87014524	Rental Unit Areas by Owners (DU)
S_ALR_87014525	Areas/Usage Types (Display Unit)
S_ALR_87014526	Areas/Usage Types (%) (Display Unit)
S_ALR_87014527	Rental Unit Area History (Disp.Unit)
S_ALR_87014528	Areas, Properties (Display Unit)
S_ALR_87014529	Property Areas by Owners (Display)
S_ALR_87014530	Property Area History (Display)
S_ALR_87014531	Building Areas (Display Unit)
S_ALR_87014532	Building Areas by Owners
S_ALR_87014533	Building Area History (Display)
S_ALR_87014534	Property Areas/Buildings/RU(Displ.U)
S_ALR_87014535	PR/BU/RU Areas by Owners
S_ALR_87014536	Apportionment Units by Object
S_ALR_87014537	Apport. Units by Tenant/Agreement
S_ALR_87014538	Apport. Units by Tenant/Rental Unit
S_ALR_87014539	Deposits by Object
S_ALR_87014540	Deposits by Tenant/Contract
S_ALR_87014541	Deposits by Owner
S_ALR_87014542	Vacancies by Object
S_ALR_87014543	Areas/Usage Types (Display Unit)
S_ALR_87014544	Areas/Usage Types (%) (Display Unit)
S_ALR_87014545	Reasons for Vacancy
S_ALR_87014546	Rental Unit Occupancy History
S_ALR_87014547	Depreciation (Absolute/Relative)
S_ALR_87014548	Depreciation %
S_ALR_87014549	Acquisitions/Retirements
S_ALR_87014550	Period Overview - Actual
S_ALR_87014551	Commitments: Period Overview
S_ALR_87014552	Period Overview - Plan
S_ALR_87014553	Period Comparison - Actual
S_ALR_87014554	Commitments: Period comparison
S_ALR_87014555	Period Comparison - Plan
S_ALR_87014556	Year Overview - Actual
S_ALR_87014557	Commitments: Year Overview
S_ALR_87014558	Year Overview - Plan
S_ALR_87014559	Annual Comparison - Actual
S_ALR_87014560	Commitments: Annual Comparison
S_ALR_87014561	Annual Comparison - Plan
S_ALR_87014562	Actual/Commitments/Plan/Variances
S_ALR_87014563	Actual/Area Unit
S_ALR_87014564	Actual/Apportionment Unit
S_ALR_87014565	Actual: Cost Elements
S_ALR_87014566	Commitments: Cost Elements
S_ALR_87014567	Plan: Cost Elements
S_ALR_87014568	Period Comparison - Actual
S_ALR_87014569	Commitments: Period comparison
S_ALR_87014570	Period Comparison - Plan

SAP Transaction Codes – Volume Two

S_ALR_87014571	Year Overview - Actual
S_ALR_87014572	Commitments: Year Overview
S_ALR_87014573	Year Overview - Plan
S_ALR_87014574	Annual Comparison - Actual
S_ALR_87014575	Commitments: Annual Comparison
S_ALR_87014576	Annual Comparison - Plan
S_ALR_87014577	Cost Elements: Act./Cmmt/Plan/Var.
S_ALR_87014578	Line Items - Actual
S_ALR_87014579	Commitment Line Items
S_ALR_87014580	Management Contracts
S_ALR_87014581	Management Contracts, Current Period
S_ALR_87014582	Annual Overview
S_ALR_87014583	Year-To-Year Comparison
S_ALR_87014584	Period Overview - Actual
S_ALR_87014585	Period Comparison - Actual
S_ALR_87014586	Year Overview - Actual
S_ALR_87014587	Annual Comparison - Actual
S_ALR_87014588	Management Agreement Actual Line It.
S_ALR_87014589	Management Agrmnt:Commitment Line It
S_ALR_87014590	Overview of Extern. Heating Expenses
S_ALR_87014591	Itemization for Settlement Units
S_ALR_87014592	Eval.of SC Settlement: Apport.Result
S_ALR_87014593	SC Settlement
S_ALR_87014594	Credit/Receivables
S_ALR_87014595	Allocation per Tenant
S_ALR_87014596	Display Posting Log for Settlement
S_ALR_87014597	Settlement Unit Postings
S_ALR_87014598	Settlement Unit Postings
S_ALR_87014599	Settlement Unit Postings
S_ALR_87014600	Settlement Units: Actual Line Items
S_ALR_87014601	Settlement Units: Commitment Line It
S_ALR_87014602	Land Register Standard Analysis
S_ALR_87014603	Business Entities Standard Analysis
S_ALR_87014604	Property Standard Analysis
S_ALR_87014605	Buildings Standard Analysis
S_ALR_87014606	Rental Units Standard Analysis
S_ALR_87014607	Partner Standard Analysis
S_ALR_87014608	Partner for Real Estate Objects
S_ALR_87014609	Partner: Real Estate Objects,Address
S_ALR_87014610	Partner: Real Estate Objects,Address
S_ALR_87014611	Master SUs with Participating SUs
S_ALR_87014612	Lease-Outs: Standard Analysis
S_ALR_87014613	Index Data for Lease-Outs
S_ALR_87014614	Lease-Out Conditions
S_ALR_87014615	Maximum/Minimum Condition
S_ALR_87014616	Conditions: Tenants/Contracts
S_ALR_87014617	Rental Unit Conditions
S_ALR_87014618	Conditions: Tenants/Objects
S_ALR_87014619	Conditions Lease-Out/Rental Unit
S_ALR_87014620	Conditions by Owner
S_ALR_87014621	Key Figures Basic Rent
S_ALR_87014622	Rental Unit Areas
S_ALR_87014623	Rental Unit Areas by Tenants
S_ALR_87014624	Rental Unit Areas by Owners

S_ALR_87014625	Areas/Usage Types
S_ALR_87014626	Areas/Usage Types (%)
S_ALR_87014627	Rental Unit Area History
S_ALR_87014628	Property Areas
S_ALR_87014629	Property Areas by Owners
S_ALR_87014630	Property Area History
S_ALR_87014631	Building Areas
S_ALR_87014632	Building Areas by Owners
S_ALR_87014633	Building Area History
S_ALR_87014634	Property Areas/Buildings/Rental Unit
S_ALR_87014635	PR/BU/RU Areas by Owners
S_ALR_87014636	Areas, Rental Units (Display Unit)
S_ALR_87014637	Rental Unit Areas by Tenants (Disp.)
S_ALR_87014638	Rental Unit Areas by Owners (DU)
S_ALR_87014639	Areas/Usage Types (Display Unit)
S_ALR_87014640	Areas/Usage Types (%) (Display Unit)
S_ALR_87014641	Rental Unit Area History (Disp.Unit)
S_ALR_87014642	Areas, Properties (Display Unit)
S_ALR_87014643	Property Areas by Owners (Display)
S_ALR_87014644	Property Area History (Display)
S_ALR_87014645	Building Areas (Display Unit)
S_ALR_87014646	Building Areas by Owners
S_ALR_87014647	Building Area History (Display)
S_ALR_87014648	Property Areas/Buildings/RU(Displ.U)
S_ALR_87014649	PR/BU/RU Areas by Owners
S_ALR_87014650	Apportionment Units by Object
S_ALR_87014651	Apport. Units by Tenant/Agreement
S_ALR_87014652	Apport. Units by Tenant/Rental Unit
S_ALR_87014653	Deposits by Object
S_ALR_87014654	Deposits by Tenant/Contract
S_ALR_87014655	Deposits by Owner
S_ALR_87014656	Vacancies by Object
S_ALR_87014657	Areas/Usage Types (Display Unit)
S_ALR_87014658	Areas/Usage Types (%) (Display Unit)
S_ALR_87014659	Reasons for Vacancy
S_ALR_87014660	Rental Unit Occupancy History
S_ALR_87014661	Depreciation (Absolute/Relative)
S_ALR_87014662	Depreciation %
S_ALR_87014663	Acquisitions/Retirements
S_ALR_87014664	Period Overview - Actual
S_ALR_87014665	Commitments: Period Overview
S_ALR_87014666	Period Overview - Plan
S_ALR_87014667	Period Comparison - Actual
S_ALR_87014668	Commitments: Period comparison
S_ALR_87014669	Period Comparison - Plan
S_ALR_87014670	Year Overview - Actual
S_ALR_87014671	Commitments: Year Overview
S_ALR_87014672	Year Overview - Plan
S_ALR_87014673	Annual Comparison - Actual
S_ALR_87014674	Commitments: Annual Comparison
S_ALR_87014675	Annual Comparison - Plan
S_ALR_87014676	Actual/Commitments/Plan/Variances
S_ALR_87014677	Actual/Area Unit
S_ALR_87014678	Actual/Apportionment Unit

S_ALR_87014679	Maximum/Minimum Revenue
S_ALR_87014680	Period Overview - Actual
S_ALR_87014681	Commitments: Period Overview
S_ALR_87014682	Period Overview - Plan
S_ALR_87014683	Period Comparison - Actual
S_ALR_87014684	Commitments: Period Comparison
S_ALR_87014685	Period Comparison - Plan
S_ALR_87014686	Year Overview - Actual
S_ALR_87014687	Commitments: Year Overview
S_ALR_87014688	Year Overview - Plan
S_ALR_87014689	Annual Comparison - Actual
S_ALR_87014690	Commitments: Annual Comparison
S_ALR_87014691	Annual Comparison - Plan
S_ALR_87014692	Period Overview - Actual
S_ALR_87014693	Commitments: Period Overview
S_ALR_87014694	Period Overview - Plan
S_ALR_87014695	Period Comparison - Actual
S_ALR_87014696	Commitments: Period Comparison
S_ALR_87014697	Period Comparison - Plan
S_ALR_87014698	Year Overview - Actual
S_ALR_87014699	Commitments: Year Overview
S_ALR_87014700	Year Overview - Plan
S_ALR_87014701	Annual Comparison - Actual
S_ALR_87014702	Commitments: Annual Comparison
S_ALR_87014703	Annual Comparison - Plan
S_ALR_87014704	Period Overview - Actual
S_ALR_87014705	Commitments: Period Overview
S_ALR_87014706	Period Overview - Plan
S_ALR_87014707	Period Comparison - Actual
S_ALR_87014708	Commitments: Period Comparison
S_ALR_87014709	Period Comparison - Plan
S_ALR_87014710	Year Overview - Actual
S_ALR_87014711	Commitments: Year Overview
S_ALR_87014712	Year Overview - Plan
S_ALR_87014713	Annual Comparison - Actual
S_ALR_87014714	Commitments: Annual Comparison
S_ALR_87014715	Annual Comparison - Plan
S_ALR_87014716	Actual/Commitments/Plan/Variance
S_ALR_87014717	Actual/Area Unit
S_ALR_87014718	Actual/Apportionment Unit
S_ALR_87014719	Period Overview - Actual
S_ALR_87014720	Commitments: Period Overview
S_ALR_87014721	Period Overview - Plan
S_ALR_87014722	Period Comparison - Actual
S_ALR_87014723	Commitments: Period Comparison
S_ALR_87014724	Period Comparison - Plan
S_ALR_87014725	Year Overview - Actual
S_ALR_87014726	Commitments: Year Overview
S_ALR_87014727	Year Overview - Plan
S_ALR_87014728	Annual Comparison - Actual
S_ALR_87014729	Commitments: Annual Comparison
S_ALR_87014730	Annual Comparison - Plan
S_ALR_87014731	Actual/Commitments/Plan/Variance
S_ALR_87014732	Actual/Area Unit

S_ALR_87014733	Actual/Apportionment Unit
S_ALR_87014734	Period Overview - Actual
S_ALR_87014735	Commitments: Period Overview
S_ALR_87014736	Period Overview - Plan
S_ALR_87014737	Period Comparison - Actual
S_ALR_87014738	Commitments: Period Comparison
S_ALR_87014739	Period Comparison - Plan
S_ALR_87014740	Year Overview - Actual
S_ALR_87014741	Commitments: Year Overview
S_ALR_87014742	Year Overview - Plan
S_ALR_87014743	Annual Comparison - Actual
S_ALR_87014744	Commitments: Annual Comparison
S_ALR_87014745	Annual Comparison - Plan
S_ALR_87014746	Period Overview - Actual
S_ALR_87014747	Commitments: Period Overview
S_ALR_87014748	Period Overview - Plan
S_ALR_87014749	Period Comparison - Actual
S_ALR_87014750	Commitments: Period Comparison
S_ALR_87014751	Period Comparison - Plan
S_ALR_87014752	Year Overview - Actual
S_ALR_87014753	Commitments: Year Overview
S_ALR_87014754	Year Overview - Plan
S_ALR_87014755	Annual Comparison - Actual
S_ALR_87014756	Commitments: Annual Comparison
S_ALR_87014757	Annual Comparison - Plan
S_ALR_87014758	Period Overview - Actual
S_ALR_87014759	Commitments: Period Overview
S_ALR_87014760	Period Overview - Plan
S_ALR_87014761	Period Comparison - Actual
S_ALR_87014762	Commitments: Period Comparison
S_ALR_87014763	Period Comparison - Plan
S_ALR_87014764	Year Overview - Actual
S_ALR_87014765	Commitments: Year Overview
S_ALR_87014766	Year Overview - Plan
S_ALR_87014767	Annual Comparison - Actual
S_ALR_87014768	Commitments: Annual Comparison
S_ALR_87014769	Annual Comparison - Plan
S_ALR_87014770	Actual/Commitments/Plan/Variance
S_ALR_87014771	Actual/Area Unit
S_ALR_87014772	Actual/Apportionment Unit
S_ALR_87014773	Line Items - Actual
S_ALR_87014774	Commitment Line Items
S_ALR_87014775	Management Contracts
S_ALR_87014776	Management Contracts, Current Period
S_ALR_87014777	Annual Overview
S_ALR_87014778	Year-To-Year Comparison
S_ALR_87014779	Period Overview - Actual
S_ALR_87014780	Period Comparison - Actual
S_ALR_87014781	Year Overview - Actual
S_ALR_87014782	Annual Comparison - Actual
S_ALR_87014783	Management Agreement Actual Line It.
S_ALR_87014784	Management Agrmnt:Commitment Line It
S_ALR_87014785	Overview of Extern. Heating Expenses
S_ALR_87014786	Itemization for Settlement Units

S_ALR_87014787	Eval.of SC Settlement: Apport.Result
S_ALR_87014788	SC Settlement
S_ALR_87014789	Credit/Receivables
S_ALR_87014790	Advance Payment Balances
S_ALR_87014791	Allocation per Tenant
S_ALR_87014792	Posting Log for SCS
S_ALR_87014793	Settlement Unit Postings
S_ALR_87014794	Settlement Unit Postings
S_ALR_87014795	Settlement Unit Postings
S_ALR_87014796	Settlement Units: Actual Line Items
S_ALR_87014797	Settlement Units: Commitment Line It
S_ALR_87014798	Real Estate Option Rate Data
S_ALR_87014799	Land Register Standard Analysis
S_ALR_87014800	Business Entities Standard Analysis
S_ALR_87014801	Property Standard Analysis
S_ALR_87014802	Buildings Standard Analysis
S_ALR_87014803	Rental Units Standard Analysis
S_ALR_87014804	Partner standard analysis
S_ALR_87014805	Partner for Real Estate Objects
S_ALR_87014806	Partner: Real Estate Objects,Address
S_ALR_87014807	Partner: Real Estate Objects,Address
S_ALR_87014808	Master SUs with Participating SUs
S_ALR_87014809	Lease-Out Form: Correspondence
S_ALR_87014810	Res. Rental Agreement Form: Corresp.
S_ALR_87014811	Comm.Rental Agreement Form: Corresp.
S_ALR_87014812	Garage Rental Agreement Form:Corresp
S_ALR_87014813	Accomp.Letter for Res.Rental Agreem.
S_ALR_87014814	Comm.Rental Agreement: Accomp.Letter
S_ALR_87014815	Accomp.Letter forGarage Rntl Agreem.
S_ALR_87014816	Lease-Out Conversion to EURO
S_ALR_87014817	General Info. on Tenancy: Corresp.
S_ALR_87014818	Cross-Method Rent Adj.: Corresp.
S_ALR_87014819	Sales-Based Rent Settlement:Corresp.
S_ALR_87014820	Confirmation of Tenant Notice
S_ALR_87014821	Confirmation of Tenant Notice
S_ALR_87014822	Invoice for Rent on Basis of FI Docs
S_ALR_87014823	Tenant Account Sheet: Screen List or
S_ALR_87014824	Service Charge Stt.for Settlement ID
S_ALR_87014825	Service Charge Stt. for Rntl Agrmnt
S_ALR_87014826	Owner Settlement: Correspondence
S_ALR_87014827	Bank Payt Guar.for Lease-Out:Corr.
S_ALR_87014828	Personal Guarantee for Rental Agreem
S_ALR_87014829	SCB Application for Index-Linked Ren
S_ALR_87014830	Lease-Out Conditions
S_ALR_87014831	Maximum/minimum condition
S_ALR_87014832	Conditions: Tenants/Contracts
S_ALR_87014833	Rental Unit Conditions
S_ALR_87014834	Conditions: Tenants/Objects
S_ALR_87014835	Conditions Lease-Out/Rental Unit
S_ALR_87014836	Conditions by Owner
S_ALR_87014837	Key Figures Basic Rent
S_ALR_87014838	Rental Unit Areas
S_ALR_87014839	Rental Unit Areas by Tenants
S_ALR_87014840	Rental Unit Areas by Owners

S_ALR_87014841	Areas/Usage Types
S_ALR_87014842	Areas/Usage Types (%)
S_ALR_87014843	Rental Unit Area History
S_ALR_87014844	Property Areas
S_ALR_87014845	Property Areas by Owners
S_ALR_87014846	Property Area History
S_ALR_87014847	Building Areas
S_ALR_87014848	Building Areas by Owners
S_ALR_87014849	Building Area History
S_ALR_87014850	Property Areas/Buildings/Rental Unit
S_ALR_87014851	PR/BU/RU Areas by Owners
S_ALR_87014852	Areas, Rental Units (Display Unit)
S_ALR_87014853	Rental Unit Areas by Tenants (Disp.)
S_ALR_87014854	Rental Unit Areas by Owners (DU)
S_ALR_87014855	Areas/Usage Types (Display Unit)
S_ALR_87014856	Areas/Usage Types (%) (Display Unit)
S_ALR_87014857	Rental Unit Area History (Disp.Unit)
S_ALR_87014858	Areas, Properties (Display Unit)
S_ALR_87014859	Property Areas by Owners (Display)
S_ALR_87014860	Property Area History (Display)
S_ALR_87014861	Building Areas (Display Unit)
S_ALR_87014862	Building Areas by Owners
S_ALR_87014863	Building Area History (Display)
S_ALR_87014864	Property Areas/Buildings/RU(Displ.U)
S_ALR_87014865	PR/BU/RU Areas by Owners
S_ALR_87014866	Apportionment Units by Object
S_ALR_87014867	Apport. Units by Tenant/Agreement
S_ALR_87014868	Apport. Units by Tenant/Rental Unit
S_ALR_87014869	Apportionment Units by Owner
S_ALR_87014870	Deposits by Object
S_ALR_87014871	Deposits by Tenant/Contract
S_ALR_87014872	Deposits by Owner
S_ALR_87014873	Vacancies by Object
S_ALR_87014874	Areas/Usage Types (Display Unit)
S_ALR_87014875	Areas/Usage Types (%) (Display Unit)
S_ALR_87014876	Reasons for Vacancy
S_ALR_87014877	Depreciation (Absolute/Relative)
S_ALR_87014878	Depreciation %
S_ALR_87014879	Acquisitions/Retirements
S_ALR_87014880	Period Overview - Actual
S_ALR_87014881	Commitments: Period Overview
S_ALR_87014882	Period Overview - Plan
S_ALR_87014883	Period Comparison - Actual
S_ALR_87014884	Commitments: Period Comparison
S_ALR_87014885	Period Comparison - Plan
S_ALR_87014886	Year Overview - Actual
S_ALR_87014887	Commitments: Year Overview
S_ALR_87014888	Year Overview - Plan
S_ALR_87014889	Annual Comparison - Actual
S_ALR_87014890	Commitments: Annual Comparison
S_ALR_87014891	Annual Comparison - Plan
S_ALR_87014892	Actual/Commitments/Plan/Variances
S_ALR_87014893	Actual/Area Unit
S_ALR_87014894	Actual/Apportionment Unit

S_ALR_87014895	Maximum/Minimum Revenue
S_ALR_87014896	Actual: periods by tenant
S_ALR_87014897	Commitments: Periods by Tenant
S_ALR_87014898	Plan: periods by tenant
S_ALR_87014899	Actual: period comparison by tenant
S_ALR_87014900	Commitments: Period Comp. by Tenant
S_ALR_87014901	Plan: period comparison by tenant
S_ALR_87014902	Actual: year overview by tenant
S_ALR_87014903	Commitments: year overview by tenant
S_ALR_87014904	Plan: year overview by tenant
S_ALR_87014905	Actual: yearly comparison by tenant
S_ALR_87014906	Commitments: Yearly Comp. by Tenant
S_ALR_87014907	Plan: yearly comparison by tenant
S_ALR_87014908	Actual Data: Periods by Owner
S_ALR_87014909	Commitments: Periods by Owner
S_ALR_87014910	Plan Data: Periods by Owner
S_ALR_87014911	Actual: Period Comparison by Owner
S_ALR_87014912	Commitments: Period Comp. by Owner
S_ALR_87014913	Plan: Period Comparison by Owner
S_ALR_87014914	Actual: year overview by owner
S_ALR_87014915	Commitments: Year Overview by Owner
S_ALR_87014916	Plan: Year Overview by Owner
S_ALR_87014917	Actual: yearly comparison by owner
S_ALR_87014918	Commitments: Year Comp. by Owner
S_ALR_87014919	Plan: Year Comparison by Owner
S_ALR_87014920	Actual: Cost Elements
S_ALR_87014921	Commitments: Cost Elements
S_ALR_87014922	Plan: Cost Elements
S_ALR_87014923	Period Comparison - Actual
S_ALR_87014924	Commitments: Period Comparison
S_ALR_87014925	Period Comparison - Plan
S_ALR_87014926	Year Overview - Actual
S_ALR_87014927	Commitments: Year Overview
S_ALR_87014928	Year Overview - Plan
S_ALR_87014929	Annual Comparison - Actual
S_ALR_87014930	Commitments: Annual Comparison
S_ALR_87014931	Annual Comparison - Plan
S_ALR_87014932	Cost Elements: Act./Cmmt/Plan/Var.
S_ALR_87014933	Period Overview - Actual
S_ALR_87014934	Commitments: Period Overview
S_ALR_87014935	Period Overview - Plan
S_ALR_87014936	Period Comparison - Actual
S_ALR_87014937	Commitments: Period Comparison
S_ALR_87014938	Period Comparison - Plan
S_ALR_87014939	Year Overview - Actual
S_ALR_87014940	Commitments: year overview by tenant
S_ALR_87014941	Year Overview - Plan
S_ALR_87014942	Annual Comparison - Actual
S_ALR_87014943	Commitments: Annual Comparison
S_ALR_87014944	Annual Comparison - Plan
S_ALR_87014945	Actual/Commitment/Plan/Variance
S_ALR_87014946	Periods by tenant
S_ALR_87014947	Commitments: Periods by Tenant
S_ALR_87014948	Plan: periods by tenant

S_ALR_87014949	Actual: period comparison by tenant
S_ALR_87014950	Commitments: Period Comp. by Tenant
S_ALR_87014951	Plan: period comparison by tenant
S_ALR_87014952	Actual: year overview by tenant
S_ALR_87014953	Periods by owner
S_ALR_87014954	Commitments: Periods by Owner
S_ALR_87014955	Plan Data: Periods by Owner
S_ALR_87014956	Actual: Period Comparison by Owner
S_ALR_87014957	Commitments: Period Comp. by Owner
S_ALR_87014958	Plan: Period Comparison by Owner
S_ALR_87014959	Actual: year overview by owner
S_ALR_87014960	Commitments: Year Overview by Owner
S_ALR_87014961	Plan: Year Overview by Owner
S_ALR_87014962	Actual: yearly comparison by owner
S_ALR_87014963	Commitments: Year Comp. by Owner
S_ALR_87014964	Plan: Year Comparison by Owner
S_ALR_87014965	Period Overview - Actual
S_ALR_87014966	Commitments: Period Overview
S_ALR_87014967	Period Overview - Plan
S_ALR_87014968	Line Items - Actual
S_ALR_87014969	Commitment Line Items
S_ALR_87014970	Overview of Extern. Heating Expenses
S_ALR_87014971	Itemization for Settlement Units
S_ALR_87014972	Eval.of SC Settlement: Apport.Result
S_ALR_87014973	SC Settlement
S_ALR_87014974	Credit/Receivables
S_ALR_87014975	Allocation per Tenant
S_ALR_87014976	Display Posting Log for Settlement
S_ALR_87014977	Settlement Unit Postings
S_ALR_87014978	Settlement Unit Postings
S_ALR_87014979	Settlement Unit Postings
S_ALR_87014980	Settlement Units: Actual Line Items
S_ALR_87014981	Settlement Units: Commitment Line It
S_ALR_87014982	Real estate option rate data
S_ALR_87014983	Management contracts
S_ALR_87014984	Management contracts, current period
S_ALR_87014985	Annual Overview
S_ALR_87014986	Year-To-Year Comparison
S_ALR_87014987	Period Overview - Actual
S_ALR_87014988	Period Comparison - Actual
S_ALR_87014989	Year Overview - Actual
S_ALR_87014990	Annual Comparison - Actual
S_ALR_87014991	Management Agreement Actual Line It.
S_ALR_87014992	Management Agrmnt:Commitment Line It
S_ALR_87014993	Lease-Out Offer: Correspondence
S_ALR_87014994	Cancellation LO Offer:Correspondence
S_ALR_87014995	Lease-Out Form: Correspondence
S_ALR_87014996	Comm.Rental Agreement Form: Corresp.
S_ALR_87014997	Res. Rental Agreement Form: Corresp.
S_ALR_87014998	Garage Rental Agreement Form:Corresp
S_ALR_87014999	Comm.Rental Agreement: Accomp.Letter
S_ALR_87015000	Accomp.Letter for Res.Rental Agreem.
S_ALR_87015001	Accomp.Letter forGarage Rntl Agreem.
S_ALR_87015002	General Info. on Tenancy: Corresp.

SAP Transaction Codes – Volume Two

S_ALR_87015003	Rental Unit Insp. for Lease-Out
S_ALR_87015004	Rental Collateral Release: Corresp.
S_ALR_87015005	Invoice for Rent on Basis of FI Docs
S_ALR_87015006	Print Sales-Based Rent Settlement
S_ALR_87015007	Tenant Account Sheet: Screen List or
S_ALR_87015008	Service Charge Stt. for Rntl Agrmnt
S_ALR_87015009	Service Charge Stt.for Settlement ID
S_ALR_87015010	Service Charge Settlm.: Print Letter
S_ALR_87015011	Cross-Method Rent Adj.: Corresp.
S_ALR_87015012	Rent Adjustment Switzerland:Corresp.
S_ALR_87015013	General Info. on Tenancy: Corresp.
S_ALR_87015014	Bank Payt Guar.for Lease-Out:Corr.
S_ALR_87015015	Personal Guarantee for Rental Agreem
S_ALR_87015016	SCB Application for Index-Linked Ren
S_ALR_87015017	Owner Settlement: Correspondence
S_ALR_87015018	Lease-Out Conversion to EURO
S_ALR_87015019	New LO No.After Legacy Data Transfer
S_ALR_87015020	Tenant Account Sheet: Screen List or
S_ALR_87015021	List of Customer Open Items with Ren
S_ALR_87015022	Open Item List Grouped According to
S_ALR_87015023	Real Estate Balance List
S_ALR_87015024	Incoming Payments Sorted by Posting
S_ALR_87015025	Deposits by Object
S_ALR_87015026	Cost centers: Actual/plan/variance
S_ALR_87015027	Area: Cost Centers
S_ALR_87015028	Range: Cost Elements
S_ALR_87015029	CCtrs: Current period / cumulative
S_ALR_87015030	Cost Centers: Breakdown by partner
S_ALR_87015031	Cost Centers: Breakdown by BusTrans
S_ALR_87015032	Range: Activity Types
S_ALR_87015033	Range: Statistical Key Figures
S_ALR_87015034	Cost Centers: Act./Plan/Commitments
S_ALR_87015035	Range: Actual/Plan/Commitments
S_ALR_87015036	Cost Centers: Projection
S_ALR_87015037	Cost Centers: Quarterly Comparison
S_ALR_87015038	Cost Ctrs: Fiscal Year Comparison
S_ALR_87015039	Cost Centers: Actual/Target/Variance
S_ALR_87015040	Range: Cost Elements
S_ALR_87015042	Cost Centers: Breakdown by BusTrans
S_ALR_87015043	Cost Centers: Variances
S_ALR_87015044	Cost Centers: Splitting
S_ALR_87015045	Activity Types: Reconciliation
S_ALR_87015046	Activity Types: Plan receivers
S_ALR_87015047	Cost Centers: Rolling year
S_ALR_87015048	Cost Centers: Average costs
S_ALR_87015049	Cost Centers: Act./plan/var./prv.yr
S_ALR_87015050	Cost Centers: Currency translation
S_ALR_87015051	Area: Actual/plan 2 currencies
S_ALR_87015052	Cost Centers: Object Comparison
S_ALR_87015053	Area: Internal business volume
S_ALR_87015054	Cost Centers: Curr./cum./total year
S_ALR_87015055	Cost Centers: Act/Target from Summ.
S_ALR_87015056	CCtrs: Period breakdown actual/plan
S_ALR_87015057	CCtrs: Period breakdown act./target

S_ALR_87015058	Range: Orders
S_ALR_87015059	Cost Centers: Cost component split
S_ALR_87015060	Stat. Key Figs: Period breakdown
S_ALR_87015061	Activity Types: Period breakdown
S_ALR_87015062	Activity types: Scheduled/plan
S_ALR_87015065	Project Info System: Outl. Rep. Proj
S_ALR_87015066	Project Info System: Outl. Rep WBS-
S_ALR_87015067	Project Info System: Main Program Pl
S_ALR_87015068	Project Info System: Main Prog.Order
S_ALR_87015069	Project Info System:Network Overview
S_ALR_87015070	Project Info System: Main prog. act.
S_ALR_87015071	Project Info System:Confirmation Ov.
S_ALR_87015072	Project Info System: Main prog. rel.
S_ALR_87015073	Project Info System: Main prog. mile
S_ALR_87015074	Project Info System: Main prog. cap.
S_ALR_87015075	Project Info System: Main prog. prod
S_ALR_87015076	Project Info System: Main Prog. Comp
S_ALR_87015077	Project Info System: Main Prog.Dist.
S_ALR_87015078	Project Info System: Main Prog.Dist.
S_ALR_87015124	Progress Analysis
S_ALR_87015125	Progress Analysis: Detail
S_ALR_87015172	SAPLS_CUS_IMG_ACTIVITY
S_ALR_87015177	Guarantee Fee in Display Currency
S_ALR_87015178	Guarantee Charge in Payment Currency
S_ALR_87015179	LO Guarantee Fee
S_ALR_87015180	Loans: Deadline Monitoring
S_ALR_87015181	LO Accounting Assets
S_ALR_87015182	LO Accounting Liabilities
S_ALR_87015183	LO Borrower's Note Loans Assets
S_ALR_87015184	LO Stock List BNL Liabilities
S_ALR_87015185	LO Stock Development
S_ALR_87015186	LO Interest Flow List
S_ALR_87015187	Loan Commitment in Display Currency
S_ALR_87015188	Loan Commitment in Position Currency
S_ALR_87015189	Balance List in Display Currency
S_ALR_87015190	Balance List in Position Currency
S_ALR_87015191	LO Revenue List
S_ALR_87015192	Simulate Debit Position List
S_ALR_87015193	Compare Report: Compare Loans to FI
S_ALR_87015194	Evaluate Offers
S_ALR_87015195	Evaluate Offers
S_ALR_87015196	Journal of Financial Transactions
S_ALR_87015197	Journal of Financial Transactions
S_ALR_87015198	Correspondence Overview
S_ALR_87015199	Correspondence Overview
S_ALR_87015200	Transact.Release: Work Item Overview
S_ALR_87015202	Journal: Transactions w. Cash Flows
S_ALR_87015203	Journal: Transactions w. Cash Flows
S_ALR_87015204	Aggregated Values
S_ALR_87015205	Treasury: Payment Schedule
S_ALR_87015206	Treasury: Payment Schedule
S_ALR_87015207	Money Market Position
S_ALR_87015208	MM Stock Overview: Assets
S_ALR_87015209	MM Stock List: Liabilities

S_ALR_87015210	Comparison: 1995, 1996, 1997
S_ALR_87015212	MM Remaining Shelf Life Stats:Assets
S_ALR_87015213	MM Remaining Shelf Life Stats: Liab.
S_ALR_87015216	Posting Overview
S_ALR_87015217	Posting Overview
S_ALR_87015218	Posting Journal
S_ALR_87015219	Posting Journal
S_ALR_87015220	Treasury:Journal of Financial Trans.
S_ALR_87015221	Journal of Financial Transactions
S_ALR_87015222	Correspondence Overview
S_ALR_87015223	Correspondence Overview
S_ALR_87015226	Journal: Transactions w. Cash Flows
S_ALR_87015227	Journal: Transactions w. Cash Flows
S_ALR_87015228	Treasury: Payment Schedule
S_ALR_87015229	Treasury: Payment Schedule
S_ALR_87015230	Position List:Traded Options/Futures
S_ALR_87015232	Posting Overview
S_ALR_87015233	Posting Overview
S_ALR_87015234	Posting Journal
S_ALR_87015235	Posting Journal
S_ALR_87015236	Evaluate Offers
S_ALR_87015237	Evaluate Offers
S_ALR_87015239	Treasury:Journal of Financial Trans.
S_ALR_87015240	Journal of Financial Transactions
S_ALR_87015241	Correspondence Overview
S_ALR_87015242	Correspondence Overview
S_ALR_87015243	Transact.Release: Work Item Overview
S_ALR_87015244	Transact.Release: Work Item Overview
S_ALR_87015245	Journal: Transactions w. Cash Flows
S_ALR_87015246	Journal: Transactions w. Cash Flows
S_ALR_87015247	Amounts in DEM-USD-FRF-ITL
S_ALR_87015248	Treasury: Payment Schedule
S_ALR_87015249	Treasury: Payment Schedule
S_ALR_87015252	DEM/US$ Transactions
S_ALR_87015254	Posting Overview
S_ALR_87015255	Posting Overview
S_ALR_87015256	Posting Journal
S_ALR_87015257	Posting Journal
S_ALR_87015258	Treasury:Journal of Financial Trans.
S_ALR_87015259	Journal of Financial Transactions
S_ALR_87015262	Treasury: Payment Schedule
S_ALR_87015263	Treasury: Payment Schedule
S_ALR_87015270	SE Position: Comparison of Key Dates
S_ALR_87015277	Posting Overview
S_ALR_87015278	Posting Overview
S_ALR_87015279	Posting Journal
S_ALR_87015280	Posting Journal
S_ALR_87099606	FX Sensitivities (Example)
S_ALR_87099607	Interest Rate Sensitivities
S_ALR_87099608	MRM Crash Scenario Analysis
S_ALR_87099612	MM Remaining Term Statistics
S_ALR_87099613	MM Position Overview
S_ALR_87099617	Currencies and Time Frame
S_ALR_87099618	Dynamic Currency and Time Frame

SAP Transaction Codes – Volume Two

S_ALR_87099621	Interest Rate Sensitivities
S_ALR_87099622	FX Sensitivities (Example)
S_ALR_87099623	MRM Crash Scenario Analysis
S_ALR_87099625	Aggregated Values
S_ALR_87099626	Amounts in DEM-USD-FRF-ITL
S_ALR_87099627	Guarantee Fee in Display Currency
S_ALR_87099628	Guarantee Charge in Payment Currency
S_ALR_87099629	LO Guarantee Fee
S_ALR_87099630	Loans: Deadline Monitoring
S_ALR_87099631	Money Market Position
S_ALR_87099632	MM Stock Overview: Assets
S_ALR_87099633	MM Stock List: Liabilities
S_ALR_87099634	Comparison: 1995, 1996, 1997
S_ALR_87099636	MM Remaining Shelf Life Stats:Assets
S_ALR_87099637	MM Remaining Shelf Life Stats: Liab.
S_ALR_87099640	DEM/US$ Transactions
S_ALR_87099641	Position List:Traded Options/Futures
S_ALR_87099648	LO Accounting Assets
S_ALR_87099649	LO Accounting Liabilities
S_ALR_87099650	LO Borrower's Note Loans Assets
S_ALR_87099651	LO Stock List BNL Liabilities
S_ALR_87099652	LO Stock Development
S_ALR_87099653	LO Interest Flow List
S_ALR_87099654	Loan Commitment in Display Currency
S_ALR_87099655	Loan Commitment in Position Currency
S_ALR_87099656	Balance List in Display Currency
S_ALR_87099657	Balance List in Position Currency
S_ALR_87099661	LO Revenue List
S_ALR_87099662	Simulate Debit Position List
S_ALR_87099663	Compare Report: Compare Loans to FI
S_ALR_87099664	Define Authorization Group
S_ALR_87099665	Assign Position Management Procedure
S_ALR_87099668	TR Partial Positions
S_ALR_87099669	TR Position Accounting
S_ALR_87099670	TR Position Overview
S_ALR_87099671	TR Remaining Terms
S_ALR_87099679	IMG Activity: SIMG_CFMENUOPP1OM0K
S_ALR_87099680	Number Range Maintenance
S_ALR_87099703	SAPLS_CUS_IMG_ACTIVITY
S_ALR_87099704	SAPLS_CUS_IMG_ACTIVITY
S_ALR_87099706	SAPLS_CUS_IMG_ACTIVITY
S_ALR_87099707	SAPLS_CUS_IMG_ACTIVITY
S_ALR_87099708	SAPLS_CUS_IMG_ACTIVITY
S_ALR_87099709	SAPLS_CUS_IMG_ACTIVITY
S_ALR_87099710	SAPLS_CUS_IMG_ACTIVITY
S_ALR_87099711	SAPLS_CUS_IMG_ACTIVITY
S_ALR_87099728	Field Selection Control Cycle Data
S_ALR_87099731	Alternative Error Handling KANBAN
S_ALR_87099732	Field Selection Control Cycle Data
S_ALR_87099733	Display of Kanbans
S_ALR_87099735	Quick Info for Kanbans
S_ALR_87099789	SAPLS_CUS_IMG_ACTIVITY
S_ALR_87099809	Program FW_STATISTIK2
S_ALR_87099821	Definition of verification profile

S_ALR_87099822	Verification profile search
S_ALR_87099833	Program FW_STATISTIK2
S_ALR_87099856	IMG Activity: SIMG_CFMENUOLISAKTI
S_ALR_87099913	Clearing Line Layout
S_ALR_87099914	Clearing Line Layout
S_ALR_87099918	Primary Cost Planning Dep./Interest
S_ALR_87099919	Maintain Real Estate Object Set:
S_ALR_87099930	Analyze Costing Run
S_ALR_87099931	Analyze Costing Run
S_ALR_87099932	Variances Between Costing Runs
S_ALR_87099938	Archiving Deliveries: Reload Program
S_ALR_87099943	Dispatching of function requests
S_ALR_87099946	Sales Ledger (Chile, Peru)
S_ALR_87099947	Purchase Ledger (Chile, Peru)
S_ALR_87099948	Cash Journal (Chile, Peru)
S_ALR_87099949	General Ledger (Chile, Peru)
S_ALR_87099950	Journal (Chile, Peru)
S_ALR_87099970	Account Assignment Allocation
S_ALR_87099971	Acct Assign. Allocation for Sett.
S_ALR_87099972	Acct Assign. Allocation for Mgmt
S_ALR_87100025	Rent Adj. Acc. to Apt. Valuation
S_ALR_87100026	Rent Adjustment-Dunning Not Approved
S_ALR_87100028	Rent Collateral for LO: Adjustment
S_ALR_87100067	TR Position Trend List
S_ALR_87100068	TR Comparison of Key Dates
S_ALR_87100069	SE Remaining Term Statistics
S_ALR_87100087	5-Yr Int. Repayment Sheet for Bonds
S_ALR_87100088	DE Listed Futures: Position Overview
S_ALR_87100089	DE Listed Futures: Date Comparison
S_ALR_87100090	DE OTC Interest Revenue List
S_ALR_87100101	SAPLS_CUS_IMG_ACTIVITY
S_ALR_87100105	LO Borrower's Note Loans
S_ALR_87100107	IMG Activity: DRUCKEROPTIONEN_WP
S_ALR_87100109	Securities: Correspond. Fax Option
S_ALR_87100137	Order Selection
S_ALR_87100140	Posting journal
S_ALR_87100141	Export Taxes
S_ALR_87100142	Price List
S_ALR_87100143	Individual Prices
S_ALR_87100144	Discounts and Surcharges by Material
S_ALR_87100145	Discounts and Surcharges by Customer
S_ALR_87100146	Discounts and Surch. by Price Group
S_ALR_87100147	Discounts and Surch. by Mat. Group
S_ALR_87100148	Discounts/Surch. by Cust/Material
S_ALR_87100149	Disc. and Surch. for Cust./Mat. Grp
S_ALR_87100150	Disc. and Surch. for Price Grp/Mat
S_ALR_87100151	Disc. and Surch. for Price Grp/Mat.
S_ALR_87100152	Disc. and Surch. for Price Grp/Mat
S_ALR_87100153	Disc. and Surch. for Cust./Mat. Grp
S_ALR_87100154	Discounts/Surch. by Cust/Material
S_ALR_87100155	Discounts and Surch. by Mat. Group
S_ALR_87100156	Discounts and Surch. by Price Group
S_ALR_87100157	Discounts and Surcharges by Customer
S_ALR_87100158	Discounts and Surcharges by Material

S_ALR_87100159	Individual Prices
S_ALR_87100160	Price List
S_ALR_87100161	Export Taxes
S_ALR_87100162	Freight Incoterms 1
S_ALR_87100163	VAT
S_ALR_87100164	Canada/USA
S_ALR_87100165	I.E.P.S Mexico
S_ALR_87100166	Conditions by Customer
S_ALR_87100167	Conditions by Material
S_ALR_87100168	Conditions by Customer Hierarchy
S_ALR_87100171	Correspondence Overview
S_ALR_87100173	Correspondence Overview
S_ALR_87100174	Correspondence Overview
S_ALR_87100175	Correspondence Overview
S_ALR_87100176	Treasury: Call Up Correspondence
S_ALR_87100177	Correspondence Overview
S_ALR_87100178	Overdue List: Counterconfirmations
S_ALR_87100179	Overdue List: Counterconfirmations
S_ALR_87100180	Overdue List: Counterconfirmations
S_ALR_87100181	Overdue List: Counterconfirmations
S_ALR_87100182	Overdue List: Counterconfirmations
S_ALR_87100184	IMG Activity: PPPI_PO_338
S_ALR_87100185	Actual Costs Per Month, Current FY
S_ALR_87100186	Plan Costs per Month, Current FY
S_ALR_87100187	Commitment per Month, Current FY
S_ALR_87100188	Cumulated Actual Costs
S_ALR_87100189	Actual/Planned Time Series
S_ALR_87100190	Actual/Plan/Var Project + Respons
S_ALR_87100191	Receipts/Expenditures in Fiscal Year
S_ALR_87100195	IMG activity: W_WLFA_0014
S_ALR_87100198	Offsetting Account Program
S_ALR_87100205	General Ledger from Document File
S_ALR_87100571	Eval.of SC Settlement: Apport.Result
S_ALR_87100623	Asset Retirements (French Law)
S_ALR_87100634	e
S_ALR_87100639	Commitment Line Items
S_ALR_87100645	SAPLS_CUS_IMG_ACTIVITY
S_ALR_87100646	Flow Types for Valuation
S_ALR_87100684	Simulate APs to be Taken into Acct
S_ALR_87100802	Assign Open Items from OI Management
S_ALR_87100803	Input Tax Refund
S_ALR_87100819	Capital Allowance Report (Singapore)
S_ALR_87100820	Balancing Adjustment Report
S_ALR_87100833	Standard for Italy, Spain
S_ALR_87100875	Buffer Information for Number Ranges
S_ALR_87100876	Audit
S_ALR_87100886	Balance Sheet Key Figures
S_ALR_87100887	Balance Sheet Key Figures
S_ALR_87100974	Comparison
S_ALR_87100975	Audit
S_ALR_87100976	History Display
S_ALR_87100977	History Display
S_ALR_87100978	Transaction Figures (Batch)
S_ALR_87100979	Total of Documents (Batch)

SAP Transaction Codes – Volume Two

S_ALR_87100980	Balances (Batch)
S_ALR_87100981	Open Items (Batch)
S_ALR_87100982	Last Year's Balance Sheet
S_ALR_87100983	Profit and Loss Projection
S_ALR_87100984	P&L Plan Data
S_ALR_87100985	Balance Sheet and P&L (ABAP)
S_ALR_87100986	Balance Sheet Key Figures
S_ALR_87100987	Account Balances to be Compared
S_ALR_87100988	Structured Account Balances
S_ALR_87100989	Audit
S_ALR_87100990	Comparison
S_ALR_87100991	Chart of Accounts
S_ALR_87100992	Account Assignment Manual
S_ALR_87100993	Account List for Company Code
S_ALR_87100994	Account Detail Information
S_ALR_87100995	G/L Accounts
S_ALR_87100996	G/L Accounts Marked for Deletion...
S_ALR_87100997	List (Batch)
S_ALR_87100998	Audit
S_ALR_87100999	Audit Interactive List
S_ALR_87101000	Posting Totals (Batch !)
S_ALR_87101001	Line Item Journal (Batch)
S_ALR_87101002	Compact Document Journal (Batch)
S_ALR_87101003	General Audit
S_ALR_87101004	Update Interrupted?
S_ALR_87101005	Document Journal
S_ALR_87101006	Document Analysis Doc. Database BRF
S_ALR_87101007	Request
S_ALR_87101008	List (Batch)
S_ALR_87101009	G/L Account Balances
S_ALR_87101010	Financial Statement Data (Baetge)
S_ALR_87101011	General, Single Phase, Dialog
S_ALR_87101012	Data Procurement
S_ALR_87101013	Download / Export (2nd Phase,Online)
S_ALR_87101014	Program Description
S_ALR_87101015	Export from SDF
S_ALR_87101016	sdfg
S_ALR_87101017	Audit Private Folder
S_ALR_87101018	Export from BRF
S_ALR_87101019	Export from BRF
S_ALR_87101021	Fixed Values
S_ALR_87101023	BRF Document Database
S_ALR_87101024	DDF Customer Database
S_ALR_87101025	KDF Vendor Database
S_ALR_87101026	SDF G/L Account Database
S_ALR_87101027	BRF Document Database
S_ALR_87101028	DDF Customer Database
S_ALR_87101029	KDF Vendor Database
S_ALR_87101030	SDF General Ledger Account Database
S_ALR_87101031	Audit
S_ALR_87101046	Reconciliation Accounts
S_ALR_87101047	Transaction -> G/L Accounts
S_ALR_87101048	G/L Account -> Transactions
S_ALR_87101049	Number of G/L Accounts

S_ALR_87101050	Number of Assets (Main No.)
S_ALR_87101051	Number of Customers
S_ALR_87101052	Number of Vendors
S_ALR_87101053	Number of Materials
S_ALR_87101054	Normal Documents
S_ALR_87101055	Items, Normal Documents (Batch)
S_ALR_87101057	Comparison
S_ALR_87101058	Transaction Figures (Batch !)
S_ALR_87101059	Open Items (Batch !)
S_ALR_87101061	Account List
S_ALR_87101062	Account List for Company Code
S_ALR_87101063	Account Detail Information
S_ALR_87101064	New Customers for CoCode in Check
S_ALR_87101065	Marked for Deletion
S_ALR_87101066	List (Batch)
S_ALR_87101067	Audit
S_ALR_87101068	Document Analysis Customer Doc. Data
S_ALR_87101069	FI Outgoing Invoice List
S_ALR_87101070	FI Invoice Nos Used Multiple Times
S_ALR_87101071	Audit
S_ALR_87101072	Reconciliation
S_ALR_87101073	Program Description
S_ALR_87101074	Program Description
S_ALR_87101075	General, Single Phase, Dialog
S_ALR_87101076	Data Procurement
S_ALR_87101077	Domestic
S_ALR_87101078	International
S_ALR_87101079	Affiliated Companies
S_ALR_87101080	Domestic
S_ALR_87101081	International
S_ALR_87101082	Domestic
S_ALR_87101083	International
S_ALR_87101084	Domestic
S_ALR_87101085	International
S_ALR_87101086	Affiliated Companies
S_ALR_87101087	Vendor Accnt Balances: Credit Memos
S_ALR_87101088	Trial Balance: Down Payments Made
S_ALR_87101089	Line Item List
S_ALR_87101090	Trial Balance: Security Deposits
S_ALR_87101091	Line Item List
S_ALR_87101092	Domestic
S_ALR_87101093	International
S_ALR_87101094	Domestic
S_ALR_87101095	International
S_ALR_87101096	Accnt Bals: Individual Value Adjmnts
S_ALR_87101097	Individual Value Adjustments
S_ALR_87101098	Trial Balance: Bills Receivable
S_ALR_87101099	Bill of Exchange List
S_ALR_87101100	Bills of Exchange Receivable
S_ALR_87101101	Line Item List
S_ALR_87101102	Account Balance: Bills of Exchange
S_ALR_87101103	Line Item List
S_ALR_87101104	Trial Balance: Guarantees
S_ALR_87101105	Line Item List

S_ALR_87101106	Brief Overview
S_ALR_87101107	Audit
S_ALR_87101108	Missing Credit Data
S_ALR_87101109	Master Data Changes
S_ALR_87101110	Cut-off AR-List Customers
S_ALR_87101111	Audit Cut-off
S_ALR_87101112	Audit Cut-off
S_ALR_87101113	Due Date List
S_ALR_87101114	Open Items List
S_ALR_87101115	Due Date List
S_ALR_87101116	Transaction Figures (Batch !)
S_ALR_87101117	Open Items (Batch !)
S_ALR_87101118	Account List
S_ALR_87101119	Account List for Company Code
S_ALR_87101120	Account Detail Information
S_ALR_87101121	Directory, New Acquisitions
S_ALR_87101122	Deletion Flag
S_ALR_87101123	Audit
S_ALR_87101124	Audit
S_ALR_87101125	Audit Interactive List
S_ALR_87101126	FI Incoming Invoice List
S_ALR_87101127	Invoice Nos Assigned Multiple Times
S_ALR_87101128	Audit
S_ALR_87101129	Audit
S_ALR_87101130	Audit File Storage
S_ALR_87101131	Audit Private Folder
S_ALR_87101132	Export from KDF
S_ALR_87101137	Local Currency, Domestic
S_ALR_87101138	Foreign Account Balances
S_ALR_87101139	Affiliated Companies
S_ALR_87101140	Domestic One-Time Accounts
S_ALR_87101141	Foreign One-Time Accounts
S_ALR_87101142	Balances > n, Domestic
S_ALR_87101143	Balances > n, Foreign
S_ALR_87101144	Domestic Sales
S_ALR_87101145	Foreign Sales
S_ALR_87101146	Sales to Affiliated Companies
S_ALR_87101147	Customers with Credit Balances
S_ALR_87101148	Cust.with Credit Bal. Down Payment
S_ALR_87101149	Credit Customers Down Payments
S_ALR_87101150	Security Deposit
S_ALR_87101151	Security Deposit
S_ALR_87101152	Domestic
S_ALR_87101153	International
S_ALR_87101154	Domestic
S_ALR_87101155	International
S_ALR_87101156	Bills of Exchange Payable
S_ALR_87101157	Bills of Exchange Payable
S_ALR_87101158	Bills of Exchange Payable
S_ALR_87101159	Bills of Exchange Payable
S_ALR_87101160	Bill of Exchange Own Liability
S_ALR_87101161	Guarantees Given
S_ALR_87101162	Guarantees Given
S_ALR_87101163	Cut-off AR List Debitor

S_ALR_87101164	Cut-off Incomng Invoice List Vendors
S_ALR_87101165	Cut-off Incomng Invoice List Vendors
S_ALR_87101166	Cut-off AR List Debitor
S_ALR_87101167	Due Date Analysis for Open Items
S_ALR_87101168	Totals and Balances
S_ALR_87101169	Audit
S_ALR_87101170	Audit
S_ALR_87101171	Audit
S_ALR_87101172	Audit
S_ALR_87101173	Depreciation Simulation
S_ALR_87101174	Audit
S_ALR_87101175	Audit
S_ALR_87101176	Audit
S_ALR_87101177	Audit
S_ALR_87101178	Depreciation
S_ALR_87101179	Depreciation
S_ALR_87101180	Audit
S_ALR_87101181	Investment Support
S_ALR_87101182	Insurance List
S_ALR_87101183	Other Capitlzd In-House Prod.
S_ALR_87101184	Audit
S_ALR_87101185	Audit Asset Balances
S_ALR_87101186	Audit Current Book Value
S_ALR_87101187	Audit
S_ALR_87101188	Asset Acquisitions in Foreign Currcy
S_ALR_87101189	Audit
S_ALR_87101190	Audit
S_ALR_87101191	Audit
S_ALR_87101193	Hardcoded SAP*
S_ALR_87101194	Check standard user passwords
S_ALR_87101195	Rules for Logging on
S_ALR_87101196	Where-Used List: Authorization Objct
S_ALR_87101197	All Authorizations
S_ALR_87101198	All Authorizations
S_ALR_87101199	Number of User Master Records
S_ALR_87101200	List Users
S_ALR_87101201	Currently Active Users
S_ALR_87101202	Users with Initial Password
S_ALR_87101203	Not logged on for 30 Days
S_ALR_87101204	Unchanged for 180 Days
S_ALR_87101205	Users who can call OS Commands
S_ALR_87101206	Users with ABAP Authorization
S_ALR_87101207	Users who can use CTS
S_ALR_87101208	Update Accounting Periods
S_ALR_87101209	Update Company Codes
S_ALR_87101210	Update Chart of Accounts
S_ALR_87101211	Users who can Execute RFC Function
S_ALR_87101212	List of Internet users
S_ALR_87101213	Profile Generator
S_ALR_87101219	Check Table Logging
S_ALR_87101220	Display
S_ALR_87101223	Table Recording
S_ALR_87101225	Cust. Tables without Log
S_ALR_87101226	Standard Variant

SAP Transaction Codes – Volume Two

S_ALR_87101228	AIS Financial Accounting
S_ALR_87101235	AIS Accounting
S_ALR_87101236	AIS Finances
S_ALR_87101237	Table Access Statistics
S_ALR_87101238	Display Change Documents
S_ALR_87101239	Display Change Documents
S_ALR_87101247	Call System
S_ALR_87101248	Parameters for External Tools
S_ALR_87101249	System Overview
S_ALR_87101250	SAP Gateway
S_ALR_87101252	Installation Check for R/3 Spool
S_ALR_87101253	Spool Parameters
S_ALR_87101254	SNC Status
S_ALR_87101255	TMS: Display Configuration
S_ALR_87101256	TMS: Display Configuration
S_ALR_87101257	Import Overview
S_ALR_87101258	System Overview
S_ALR_87101259	TMS: Alert Viewer
S_ALR_87101260	Verbose
S_ALR_87101261	Transport Monitor ALOG
S_ALR_87101262	Transport Monitor SLOG
S_ALR_87101263	Search for Objects in Requests/Tasks
S_ALR_87101265	Requests with USR Tables
S_ALR_87101266	Requests with PA Tables
S_ALR_87101267	Analyze Objects in Requests/Tasks
S_ALR_87101268	RSWBOSSR
S_ALR_87101269	Set System Change Option
S_ALR_87101270	Syslog parameters
S_ALR_87101271	Performance Analysis
S_ALR_87101272	Performance analysis
S_ALR_87101273	Workload Statistics
S_ALR_87101274	Statistical Evaluations
S_ALR_87101275	Consistency Check
S_ALR_87101276	IDoc List
S_ALR_87101277	RFC Statistics
S_ALR_87101278	Remote Function Call
S_ALR_87101279	RFC Trace
S_ALR_87101280	Customer Exits
S_ALR_87101281	Customer Exits
S_ALR_87101282	Objects in Customer Namespace
S_ALR_87101283	Audit Info System: Locked/Unlocked
S_ALR_87101284	Authorization Group Transfer
S_ALR_87101285	Authorization Groups
S_ALR_87101286	Maintain/Restore Authorization Grps
S_ALR_87101287	Program Analysis
S_ALR_87101305	G/L Account Balances
S_ALR_87101308	Where-Used List
S_ALR_87101309	Personnel Number
S_ALR_87101310	Applicants
S_ALR_87101311	Vendors
S_ALR_87101312	Customers
S_ALR_87101313	Partner
S_ALR_87101314	Accounting Clerks
S_ALR_87101315	Sales Group

SAP Transaction Codes – Volume Two

S_ALR_87101316		Patients
S_ALR_87101317		User
S_ALR_87101318		Field Documentation
S_ALR_87101319		Balance Sheet Values by Account
S_ALR_87101320		Display Infotype Definitions
S_ALR_87101321		Authorized Objects per User/Profile
S_ALR_87101322		Display Infotypes of an Object
S_ALR_87101323		Display Infotypes According to DDic
S_ALR_87101324		Infotypes and Subtypes
S_ALR_87101325		Schema Directory
S_ALR_87101326		Directory of Personnel Calctn Rules
S_ANI_44000033		Backgroud job for convert the data i
S_ANI_44000034		Background job for history cleanup
S_AUT01	Maintain Logging Setting	
S_AUT02	Maintain Navigation Help	
S_AUT03	Display Logging Setting	
S_AUT04	Maintain Long Text Logging	
S_AUT05	Delete Long Text Logs	
S_AUT10	Evaluate New Audit Trail	
S_AX6_42000002		IMG Activity: BWCLBW_CTBW
S_AX6_42000003		IMG Activity: BWCOPA_KEB3
S_AX6_42000004		IMG Activity: BWCOPA_KEB5
S_AX6_42000005		IMG Activity: BWCOPA_KEB2
S_AX6_42000006		IMG Activity: BWCOPA_KEB0
S_AX6_42000007		IMG Activity: BWCOPA_KEB1
S_AX6_42000008		IMG Activity: BWCOPA_REPL
S_AX6_42000009		IMG Activity: BWANWENDERSTATUS
S_AX6_42000010		IMG Activity: R3BWSTATUS
S_AX6_42000011		IMG Activity: IOANLEGEN
S_AX6_42000012		IMG Activity: BWP4
S_AX6_42000013		IMG Activity: BWP3
S_AX6_42000014		IMG Activity: BWP5
S_AX6_42000015		IMG Activity: BWP6
S_AX6_42000016		IMG Activity: BWP7
S_AX6_42000017		IMG Activity: BWP1
S_AX6_42000018		IMG Activity: BWP2
S_AX6_42000019		IMG Activity: BWP0
S_AX6_42000020		IMG Activity: BW_RT_VGSCHLUSSEL
S_AX6_42000021		IMG Activity: BW_RT_BRANCHE
S_AX6_42000022		IMG Activity: BW_RT_BESTINITIAL
S_AX6_42000024		IMG Activity: BW_GENERICDS_DEFINE
S_AX6_42000025		IMG Activity: BW_CONTENTDS_EDIT
S_AX6_42000026		IMG Activity: BW_CONTENTDS_TAKEOV
S_AX6_42000027		IMG Activity: BW_DATAEX_RESTRICT
S_AX6_42000028		IMG Activity: BWLIS_DSGENHIER
S_AX6_42000029		IMG Activity: BWLIS_COCKPIT_LBWE
S_AX6_42000030		IMG Activity: BWLIS_PROTOKOLL_LBWF
S_AX6_42000031		IMG Activity: BWLIS_SETUPQM
S_AX6_42000032		IMG Activity: BWLIS_SETUPPRODUCT
S_AX6_42000033		IMG Activity: BWLIS_INITIALEXTR
S_AX6_42000034		IMG Activity: BWLIS_CASELECTION
S_AX7_53000006		IMG Activity: RETRAKTOR_TRANSFER
S_AX7_53000007		IMG Activity: RETRAKTOR_CUST
S_AX7_53000011		IMG Activity: BW_APPLHIER_TAKEOV

S_AX7_53000012	IMG Activity: BW_APPLHIER_CHANGE
S_AX7_53000016	IMG Activity: ECEIS_EXTRACTOR
S_AX7_53000019	IMG Activity: BW_DELTAQUEUE
S_AX7_68000098	IMG Activity: BWRE_V_TIVBW01
S_AX7_68000106	IMG Activity: BW_RT_AA_QUERY
S_AX7_68000107	IMG Activity: BW_RT_AA_APP
S_AX7_68000108	IMG Activity: BW_RT_AA_METH
S_AX7_68000115	IMG Activity: PORT_MAN_BIRTH_001
S_AX7_68000116	IMG Activity: PORT_MAN_EMPRO_001
S_AX7_68000117	IMG Activity: PORT_MAN_ATTA_001
S_AX7_68000118	IMG Activity: PORT_MAN_COLUMN_010
S_AX7_68000119	IMG Activity: PORT_MAN_COLUMN_009
S_AX7_68000120	IMG Activity: PORT_MAN_COLUMN_008
S_AX7_68000121	IMG Activity: PORT_MAN_ANNIV_001
S_AX7_68000122	IMG Activity: PORT_MAN_CCMO_004
S_AX7_68000123	IMG Activity: PORT_MAN_CCMO_003
S_AX7_68000124	IMG Activity: PORT_MAN_CCMO_002
S_AX7_68000125	IMG Activity: PORT_MAN_CCMO_001
S_AX7_68000126	IMG Activity: PORT_MAN_ETP_002
S_AX7_68000127	IMG Activity: PORT_MAN_ETP_001
S_AX7_68000128	IMG Activity: PORT_MAN_COLUMN_007
S_AX7_68000129	IMG Activity: PORT_MAN_COLUMN_001
S_AX7_68000130	IMG Activity: PORT_MAN_PERS_002
S_AX7_68000131	IMG Activity: PORT_MAN_COLUMN_002
S_AX7_68000132	IMG Activity: PORT_MAN_PERS_003
S_AX7_68000133	IMG Activity: PORT_MAN_COLUMN_003
S_AX7_68000134	IMG Activity: PORT_MAN_PERS_004
S_AX7_68000135	IMG Activity: PORT_MAN_COLUMN_004
S_AX7_68000136	IMG Activity: PORT_MAN_COLUMN_005
S_AX7_68000137	IMG Activity: PORT_MAN_COLUMN_006
S_AX7_68000138	IMG Activity: PORT_MAN_PERS_001
S_AX7_68000143	Personalization: Trip Approval
S_AX7_68000149	Services for Request Types
S_AX7_68000164	Rule: Critical Postings Requests
S_AX7_68000165	Rule Maintenance for Order Monitor
S_AX7_68000166	Extracts of Critical Line Items ORD
S_AX7_68000167	Write Extracts for ORDMonitor
S_AX7_68000168	Rule Maintenance for IAA Monitor
S_AX7_68000169	Write Extracts for IAA Monitor
S_AX7_68000170	Personalization: Collective Maint
S_AX7_68000171	BCT-CO: Change Report Row Hierarchy
S_AX7_68000172	BCT-CO: Displ/Check Report Row Hier.
S_AX7_68000190	Filter and Selection Block Size
S_AX7_68000200	Target Sys, Op. Mode, and Queue Type
S_AX7_68000267	IMG
S_AX7_68000268	IMG
S_AX7_68000269	IMG
S_AX7_68000270	IMG
S_AX7_68000271	IMG
S_AX7_68000272	IMG
S_AX7_68000273	Profile Maintenance Ext.Requirements
S_AX7_68000274	Procurement. Maint. Ext.Requirements
S_AX7_68000275	Project Maint. for Cust. Enhancement
S_AX7_68000276	BADI External Procurement

S_AX7_68000277	BADI Transfer Extended PO
S_AX7_68000283	BADI Contract Replication
S_AX7_68000287	S_AX7_68000287
S_AX7_68000288	S_AX7_68000288
S_AX8_68000130	Category Management IMG
S_AX8_68000131	Category Management IMG
S_AX8_68000135	Generated
S_AX8_68000136	BW Reconstruction
S_AX8_68000142	IMG Activity: HR_LSO_M1C3A1
S_AX8_68000168	ISR Enhancements
S_AX8_68000170	IMG Activity: HR_LSO_M1C3A2
S_AX8_68000171	IMG Activity: HR_LSO_M1C3A3
S_AX8_68000172	IMG Activity: HR_LSO_M1C3A4
S_AX8_68000173	IMG Activity: HR_LSO_M1C3A5
S_AX8_68000174	IMG Activity: HR_LSO_M1C3A6
S_AX8_68000175	IMG Activity: HR_LSO_M1C4A1
S_AX8_68000176	IMG Activity: HR_LSO_M1C5A1
S_AX8_68000177	IMG Activity: HR_LSO_M1C5A2
S_AX8_68000178	IMG Activity: HR_LSO_M1C6A1
S_AX8_68000179	IMG Activity: HR_LSO_M1C7A1
S_AX8_68000180	IMG Activity: HR_LSO_M1C7A2
S_AX8_68000181	IMG Activity: HR_LSO_M2A1
S_AX8_68000182	IMG Activity: HR_LSO_M2A2
S_AX8_68000183	IMG Activity: HR_LSO_M2A3
S_AX8_68000184	IMG Activity: HR_LSO_M2A4
S_AX8_68000185	IMG Activity: HR_LSO_M1C1D1A1
S_AX8_68000186	IMG Activity: HR_LSO_M1C1D1A2
S_AX8_68000187	IMG Activity: HR_LSO_M1C1D2A1
S_AX8_68000188	IMG Activity: SIMG_OHP3NR
S_AX8_68000189	IMG Activity: HR_LSO_M1C1D2A3
S_AX8_68000190	IMG Activity: HR_LSO_M1C1D3E1A1
S_AX8_68000191	IMG Activity: HR_LSO_M1C1D2A4
S_AX8_68000192	IMG Activity: HR_LSO_M1C1D3E2A1
S_AX8_68000193	IMG Activity: HR_LSO_M1C1D3E2A2
S_AX8_68000194	IMG Activity: HR_LSO_M1C1D3E2A3
S_AX8_68000195	IMG Activity: HR_LSO_M1C1D3E2F1A1
S_AX8_68000196	IMG Activity: HR_LSO_M1C1D3E2F1A2
S_AX8_68000197	IMG Activity: HR_LSO_M1C1D3E3A1
S_AX8_68000198	IMG Activity: HR_LSO_M1C1D3E3A2
S_AX8_68000199	IMG Activity: HR_LSO_M1C1D4A1
S_AX8_68000200	IMG Activity: HR_LSO_M1C1D4A2
S_AX8_68000201	IMG Activity: HR_LSO_M1C1D5E1A1
S_AX8_68000202	IMG Activity: HR_LSO_M1C1D5E1A2
S_AX8_68000203	IMG Activity: HR_LSO_M1C1D5E1A3
S_AX8_68000204	IMG Activity: HR_LSO_M1C1D5E2A1
S_AX8_68000205	IMG Activity: HR_LSO_M1C1D5E2A2
S_AX8_68000206	IMG Activity: HR_LSO_M1C1D5E2A3
S_AX8_68000207	IMG Activity: HR_LSO_M1C1D5E2A4
S_AX8_68000208	IMG Activity: HR_LSO_M1C1D5E2A5
S_AX8_68000209	IMG Activity: HR_LSO_M1C1D5E2F1A1
S_AX8_68000210	IMG Activity: HR_LSO_M1C1D5E2F1A2
S_AX8_68000211	IMG Activity: HR_LSO_M1C1D6E1A1
S_AX8_68000212	IMG Activity: HR_LSO_M1C1D6E2A1
S_AX8_68000213	IMG Activity: HR_LSO_M1C1D6E2A2

S_AX8_68000214	IMG Activity: HR_LSO_M1C1D6E2A3
S_AX8_68000215	IMG Activity: HR_LSO_M1C1D7A1
S_AX8_68000216	IMG Activity: HR_LSO_M1C1D7A2
S_AX8_68000217	IMG Activity: HR_LSO_M1C1D7A3
S_AX8_68000218	IMG Activity: HR_LSO_M1C1D7A4
S_AX8_68000219	IMG Activity: HR_LSO_M1C1D7A5
S_AX8_68000220	IMG Activity: HR_LSO_M1C1D8E1A1
S_AX8_68000221	IMG Activity: HR_LSO_M1C1D8E1A2
S_AX8_68000222	IMG Activity: HR_LSO_M1C1D8E1A3
S_AX8_68000223	IMG Activity: HR_LSO_M1C1D8E1A4
S_AX8_68000224	IMG Activity: HR_LSO_M1C1D8E1A5
S_AX8_68000225	IMG Activity: HR_LSO_M1C1D8E2A1
S_AX8_68000226	IMG Activity: HR_LSO_M1C1D8E2F1A1
S_AX8_68000227	IMG Activity: HR_LSO_M1C1D8E2F1A2
S_AX8_68000228	IMG Activity: HR_LSO_M1C1D9A1
S_AX8_68000229	IMG Activity: HR_LSO_M1C1D9A2
S_AX8_68000230	IMG Activity: HR_LSO_M1C1D9A3
S_AX8_68000231	IMG Activity: HR_LSO_M1C1D9E2A3
S_AX8_68000232	IMG Activity: HR_LSO_M1C1D9E2A2
S_AX8_68000233	IMG Activity: HR_LSO_M1C1D9E2A1
S_AX8_68000234	IMG Activity: HR_LSO_M1C1D9E1A3
S_AX8_68000235	IMG Activity: HR_LSO_M1C1D9E1A2
S_AX8_68000236	IMG Activity: HR_LSO_M1C1D9E1A1
S_AX8_68000237	IMG Activity: HR_LSO_M1C2D1A1
S_AX8_68000238	IMG Activity: HR_LSO_M1C2D1A2
S_AX8_68000239	IMG Activity: HR_LSO_M1C2D1A3
S_AX8_68000240	IMG Activity: HR_LSO_M1C2D2A5
S_AX8_68000241	IMG Activity: HR_LSO_M1C2D2A4
S_AX8_68000242	IMG Activity: HR_LSO_M1C2D2A3
S_AX8_68000243	IMG Activity: HR_LSO_M1C2D2A2
S_AX8_68000244	IMG Activity: HR_LSO_M1C2D2A1
S_AX8_68000245	IMG Activity: HR_LSO_M1C2D3A3
S_AX8_68000246	IMG Activity: HR_LSO_M1C2D3A2
S_AX8_68000247	IMG Activity: HR_LSO_M1C2D3A1
S_AX8_68000248	IMG Activity: HR_LSO_M1C2D4E1A6
S_AX8_68000249	IMG Activity: HR_LSO_M1C2D4E1A5
S_AX8_68000250	IMG Activity: HR_LSO_M1C2D4E1A4
S_AX8_68000251	IMG Activity: HR_LSO_M1C2D4E1A3
S_AX8_68000252	IMG Activity: HR_LSO_M1C2D4E1A2
S_AX8_68000253	IMG Activity: HR_LSO_M1C2D4E1A1
S_AX8_68000254	IMG Activity: HR_LSO_M1C2D4E2A5
S_AX8_68000255	IMG Activity: HR_LSO_M1C2D4E2A4
S_AX8_68000256	IMG Activity: HR_LSO_M1C2D4E2A3
S_AX8_68000257	IMG Activity: HR_LSO_M1C2D4E2A2
S_AX8_68000258	IMG Activity: HR_LSO_M1C2D4E2A1
S_AX8_68000259	IMG Activity: HR_LSO_M1C2D4E3A5
S_AX8_68000260	IMG Activity: HR_LSO_M1C2D4E3A4
S_AX8_68000261	IMG Activity: HR_LSO_M1C2D4E3A3
S_AX8_68000262	IMG Activity: HR_LSO_M1C2D4E3A2
S_AX8_68000263	IMG Activity: HR_LSO_M1C2D4E3A1
S_AX8_68000264	IMG Activity: HR_LSO_M1C2D5A2
S_AX8_68000265	IMG Activity: HR_LSO_M1C2D5A1
S_AX8_68000266	IMG Activity: HR_LSO_M1C2D6A2
S_AX8_68000267	IMG Activity: HR_LSO_M1C2D6A1

S_AX8_68000268	IMG Activity: HR_LSO_M1C2D7E1A2
S_AX8_68000269	IMG Activity: HR_LSO_M1C2D7E1A1
S_AX8_68000270	IMG Activity: HR_LSO_M1C2D7E2A4
S_AX8_68000271	IMG Activity: HR_LSO_M1C2D7E2A3
S_AX8_68000272	IMG Activity: HR_LSO_M1C2D7E2A2
S_AX8_68000273	IMG Activity: HR_LSO_M1C2D7E2A1
S_AX8_68000274	IMG Activity: HR_LSO_M1C2D7E3A3
S_AX8_68000275	IMG Activity: HR_LSO_M1C2D7E3A2
S_AX8_68000276	IMG Activity: HR_LSO_M1C2D7E3A1
S_AX8_68000277	IMG Activity: HR_LSO_M1C2D7E3F1A5
S_AX8_68000278	IMG Activity: HR_LSO_M1C2D7E3F1A4
S_AX8_68000279	IMG Activity: HR_LSO_M1C2D7E3F1A3
S_AX8_68000280	IMG Activity: HR_LSO_M1C2D7E3F1A2
S_AX8_68000281	IMG Activity: HR_LSO_M1C2D7E3F1A1
S_AX8_68000282	IMG Activity: HR_LSO_M1C3D1A2
S_AX8_68000283	IMG Activity: HR_LSO_M1C3D1A1
S_AX8_68000284	IMG Activity: HR_LSO_M1C3D2A3
S_AX8_68000285	IMG Activity: HR_LSO_M1C3D2A2
S_AX8_68000286	IMG Activity: HR_LSO_M1C3D2A1
S_AX8_68000287	IMG Activity: HR_LSO_M1C3D3A1
S_AX8_68000288	IMG Activity: HR_LSO_M1C3D3A2
S_AX8_68000289	IMG Activity: HR_LSO_M1C3D4A2
S_AX8_68000290	IMG Activity: HR_LSO_M1C3D4A1
S_AX8_68000291	IMG Activity: HR_LSO_M1C3D4E1A3
S_AX8_68000292	IMG Activity: HR_LSO_M1C3D4E1A2
S_AX8_68000293	IMG Activity: HR_LSO_M1C3D4E1A1
S_AX8_68000294	IMG Activity: HR_LSO_M1C3D4E1F1A2
S_AX8_68000295	IMG Activity: HR_LSO_M1C3D4E1F1A1
S_AX8_68000296	IMG Activity: HR_LSO_M1C5D1A5
S_AX8_68000297	IMG Activity: HR_LSO_M1C5D1A4
S_AX8_68000298	IMG Activity: HR_LSO_M1C5D1A3
S_AX8_68000299	IMG Activity: HR_LSO_M1C5D1A2
S_AX8_68000300	IMG Activity: HR_LSO_M1C5D1A1
S_AX8_68000301	IMG Activity: HR_LSO_M1C5D2A2
S_AX8_68000302	IMG Activity: HR_LSO_M1C5D2A1
S_AX8_68000303	IMG Activity: HR_LSO_M1C5D2A3
S_AX8_68000304	IMG Activity: HR_LSO_M1C5D3E1A4
S_AX8_68000305	IMG Activity: HR_LSO_M1C5D3E1A3
S_AX8_68000306	IMG Activity: HR_LSO_M1C5D3E1A2
S_AX8_68000307	IMG Activity: HR_LSO_M1C5D3E1A1
S_AX8_68000308	IMG Activity: HR_LSO_M1C5D3E2A3
S_AX8_68000309	IMG Activity: HR_LSO_M1C5D3E2A2
S_AX8_68000310	IMG Activity: HR_LSO_M1C5D3E2A1
S_AX8_68000311	IMG Activity: HR_LSO_M1C5D3E3A4
S_AX8_68000312	IMG Activity: HR_LSO_M1C5D3E3A3
S_AX8_68000313	IMG Activity: HR_LSO_M1C5D3E3A2
S_AX8_68000314	IMG Activity: HR_LSO_M1C5D3E3A1
S_AX8_68000315	IMG Activity: HR_LSO_M1C5D3E4A4
S_AX8_68000316	IMG Activity: HR_LSO_M1C5D3E4A3
S_AX8_68000317	IMG Activity: HR_LSO_M1C5D3E4A2
S_AX8_68000318	IMG Activity: HR_LSO_M1C5D3E4A1
S_AX8_68000319	IMG Activity: HR_LSO_M1C6D1A2
S_AX8_68000320	IMG Activity: HR_LSO_M1C6D1A1
S_AX8_68000321	IMG Activity: HR_LSO_M1C6D2A5

SAP Transaction Codes – Volume Two

S_AX8_68000322	IMG Activity: HR_LSO_M1C6D2A4
S_AX8_68000323	IMG Activity: HR_LSO_M1C6D2A3
S_AX8_68000324	IMG Activity: HR_LSO_M1C6D2A2
S_AX8_68000325	IMG Activity: HR_LSO_M1C6D2A1
S_AX8_68000326	IMG Activity: FIAP_V_T042ZEBPP
S_AX8_68000327	IMG Activity: FIAP_V_T042FCL
S_AX8_68000328	IMG Activity: FIAP_V_T042ICC
S_AX8_68000329	IMG activity: ECP_FIELDS
S_AX8_68000330	IMG Activity: PSREP_CPRO_PROJSCEN
S_AX8_68000337	IMG activity: ECP_BATCHPROCESS
S_AX8_68000338	IMG activity: ECP_PORTAL1
S_AX8_68000339	IMG Activity: FIAP_EBPP_TTXID
S_AX8_68000340	IMG Activity: FIAP_EBPP_LOG_CUST
S_AX8_68000341	IMG Activity: PORT_MAN_PCR_WFL_001
S_AX8_68000342	IMG Activity: PORT_MAN_RC_WFL_001
S_AX8_68000343	IMG Activity: PORT_MAN_CM_WFL_001
S_AX8_68000344	IMG Activity: HRWPC_PCR_APPR_FORM
S_AX8_68000345	IMG Activity: HRWPC_PCR_APPR_NEXT
S_AX8_68000346	IMG Activity: HRWPC_PCR_CHECK_DATE
S_AX8_68000349	IMG Activity: CRM_SRV_SCENARIO
S_AX8_68000351	IMG Activity: SIMG_CRM_COABR_BEMOT
S_AX8_68000352	IMG Activity: SIMG_CRM_BEMOT
S_AX8_68000355	IMG Activity: CATSNB_010
S_AX8_68000356	IMG activity: ECP_FUNCTION
S_AX8_68000357	IMG activity: ECP_FUNCTION_TYPE
S_AX8_68000358	IMG Activity: CATSNB_020
S_AX8_68000359	IMG Activity: CATSNB_030
S_AX8_68000360	IMG Activity: CATSNB_040
S_AX8_68000361	IMG Activity: CATSNB_050
S_AX8_68000362	IMG Activity: CATSNB_060
S_AX8_68000363	IMG Activity: CATSNB_070
S_AX8_68000364	IMG Activity: CPR_FINR3_COSCEN
S_AX8_68000365	IMG Activity: CPR_FINR3_FINDCOSCEN
S_AX8_68000366	IMG Activity: CPR_FINR3_KOSERSZUOG
S_AX8_68000367	IMG Activity: CATSNB_005
S_AX8_68000368	IMG Activity: WRB_BADI_001
S_AX8_68000369	IMG Activity: WRB_BADI_002
S_AX8_68000381	IMG Activity: CRM_SRV_ORKAOKEU
S_AX8_68000382	IMG Activity: CRM_COOMOPA_CL_KSR
S_AX8_68000383	IMG Activity: WOST_PI_BADI_001
S_AX8_68000384	IMG Activity: WOST_PI_BADI_002
S_AX8_68000386	IMG Activity: PT_WFMCORE
S_AX8_68000388	IMG Activity: FIAP_V_EBPP_T043G
S_AX8_68000391	IMG Activity: FBD_BADI_GETDATA
S_AX8_68000392	IMG Activity: FBD_BADI_INVDET
S_AX8_68000393	IMG Activity: FBD_BADI_USAPPLREF
S_AX8_68000394	IMG Activity: FBD_BADI_DEBITSL
S_AX8_68000395	IMG Activity: FBD_BADI_NOTIFY
S_AX8_68000396	IMG Activity: FBD_BADI_NOTIFY2
S_AX8_68000415	IMG activity: W_FRE_INT_0001
S_AX8_68000416	IMG activity: W_FRE_INT_0002
S_AX8_68000417	IMG activity: W_FRE_INT_0003
S_AX8_68000418	IMG activity: W_FRE_INT_0004
S_AX8_68000419	IMG activity: W_FRE_INT_0005

S_AX8_68000420	IMG Activity: IHC_PI_001
S_AX8_68000421	IMG activity: APO_CIF_PS_NETW_IN
S_AX8_68000427	IMG Activity: FIAP_VEBPP_REC_INV_C
S_AX8_68000428	IMG Activity: APAR_EBPP_CHECK_INV
S_AX8_68000429	IMG Activity: FIAP_EBPP_T000
S_AXA_22000023	IMG Aktivity: APOCIF_V_CIFVMISD
S_AXB_19000002	SAP Biller Direct: Program
S_B20_88000001	IMG Activity: SIMG_OCNG_CMOD_UEX17
S_B20_88000002	IMG Activity: SIMG_CFMENUOCNGCNG9
S_B20_88000003	IMG Activity: SIMG_CFMENUOCNGCNG8
S_B20_88000004	IMG Activity: SIMG_CFMENUOCNGCNG2
S_B20_88000005	IMG Activity: SIMG_CFMENUOCNGCNG3
S_B20_88000006	IMG Activity: SIMG_CFMENUOCNGCNG5
S_B20_88000007	IMG Activity: SIMG_CFMENUOCNGCNG1
S_B20_88000008	IMG Activity: SIMG_CFMENUOCNGCNG7
S_B20_88000009	IMG Activity: SESSION_MANAGER
S_B20_88000011	IMG Activity: SIMG_OCNG_CMOD_UEX23
S_B20_88000012	IMG Activity: SIMG_OCNG_CMOD_UEX22
S_B20_88000013	IMG Activity: SIMG_OCNG_CMOD_UEX21
S_B20_88000014	IMG Activity: SIMG_OCNG_CMOD_UEX20
S_B20_88000015	IMG Activity: SIMG_OCNG_CMOD_UEX19
S_B20_88000016	IMG Activity: SIMG_OCNG_CMOD_UEX18
S_B20_88000017	IMG Activity: SIMG_CFMENUOCNGBCG6
S_B20_88000018	IMG Activity: SIMG_CFMENUOCNGBCG4
S_B20_88000019	IMG Activity: SIMG_CFMENUOCNGBCG3
S_B20_88000020	IMG Activity: SIMG_CFMENUOCNGBCG5
S_B20_88000021	IMG Activity: SIMG_CFMENUOCNGBCG8
S_B20_88000022	IMG Activity: SIMG_CFMENUOCNGBCG9
S_B20_88000023	IMG Activity: SIMG_CFMENUOCNGBCG2
S_B20_88000024	IMG Activity: SIMG_CFMENUOCNGCNG6
S_B20_88000025	IMG Activity: SIMG_CFMENUOCNGCNG4
S_B20_88000026	IMG Activity: SIMG_OCNG_CMOD_UEX24
S_B20_88000027	IMG Activity: SIMG_CFMENUOCNGBCG7
S_B20_88000028	IMG Activity: SIMG_CFMENUOCNGBCG1
S_B20_88000029	IMG Activity: SIMG_CFMENUOCNGBCG0
S_B20_88000033	Navigation IMG -> TMS
S_B20_88000034	Navigation IMG -> Trans.Route Editor
S_B20_88000035	Navigation IMG->Syst. Change Option
S_B20_88000036	Navigation IMG -> Client Admin.
S_B20_88000153	S_B20_88000153
S_B5A_57000001	IMG-Activity: CFMENUORFBWKST
S_B5A_57000002	IMG Activity: CFMENUORFBWKRT
S_B5T_17000001	IMG Activity: SRM_CUST_02
S_B5T_17000004	IMG Activity: SRMCMCREATE
S_B6A_52000011	RSXMB_RZ20_CALL
S_B6A_52000012	Remote System for Monitoring Using
S_B6A_52000013	New System to Be Monitored in System
S_B6A_52000014	Administrator Registration for
S_B90_38000009	Tasks for Document Integration
S_B90_38000076	IMG
S_B90_38000089	zrez
S_B9R_99000001	System Administration Assistant
S_B9R_99000002	System Administration Assistant
S_BCE_68000046	IMG: SAPG_0004

S_BCE_68000047	IMG Activity: CATT_ETT
S_BCE_68000155	IMG activity: SIMG_CFMENUORFBOB08
S_BCE_68000156	IMG Activity: SIMG_CFMENUORFBOBBS
S_BCE_68000157	IMG Activity: SIMG_CFMENUORFBOB90
S_BCE_68000158	IMG Activity: SIMG_CFORFBSAPGOBD6
S_BCE_68000159	IMG Activity: SIMG_CFMENUORFBOB07
S_BCE_68000160	IMG Activity: OCNG_GW3
S_BCE_68000161	IMG Activity: OCNG_GW2
S_BCE_68000162	IMG Activity: SAPG_0004
S_BCE_68000163	IMG Activity: SIMG_CFMENUSAPCOY05
S_BCE_68000164	IMG Activity: SIMG_CFMENUOLMSOMSC
S_BCE_68000165	IMG Activity: SIMG_CFMENUSAPCOY04
S_BCE_68000166	IMG Activity: SIMG_CFMENUSAPCOY01
S_BCE_68000167	IMG Activity: SIMG_CFMENUSAPCOY17
S_BCE_68000168	IMG Activity: SIMG_CFMENUSAPCOVK2
S_BCE_68000169	IMG Activity: SAPG_0001
S_BCE_68000170	IMG Activity: SAPG_0002
S_BCE_68000171	IMG Activity: SAPG_0003
S_BCE_68000172	IMG Activity: SIMG_CFMENUSAPCOY03
S_BCE_68000173	IMG Activity: OCNG_GW1
S_BCE_68000174	IMG activity: SIMG_CFMENUORFBOB08
S_BCE_68000175	IMG Activity: SIMG_CFMENUORFBOBBS
S_BCE_68000177	IMG Activity: SIMG_CFORFBSAPGOBD6
S_BCE_68000178	IMG Activity: SIMG_CFMENUORFBOB07
S_BCE_68000179	IMG Activity: OCNG_GW3
S_BCE_68000180	IMG Activity: OCNG_GW2
S_BCE_68000181	IMG Activity: SAPG_0004
S_BCE_68000182	IMG Activity: SIMG_CFMENUSAPCOY05
S_BCE_68000183	IMG Activity: SIMG_CFMENUOLMSOMSC
S_BCE_68000184	IMG Activity: SIMG_CFMENUSAPCOY04
S_BCE_68000187	IMG Activity: SIMG_CFMENUSAPCOVK2
S_BCE_68000188	IMG Activity: SAPG_0001
S_BCE_68000189	IMG Activity: SAPG_0002
S_BCE_68000190	IMG Activity: SAPG_0003
S_BCE_68000191	IMG Activity: SIMG_CFMENUSAPCOY03
S_BCE_68000192	IMG Activity: OCNG_GW1
S_BCE_68000195	IMG Activity: SIMG_CFMENUORFBOBD5
S_BCE_68000196	IMG Activity: SIMG_CFORFBOAC5
S_BCE_68000201	IMG Activity: SIMG_SALWFPARAMOACA
S_BCE_68000202	IMG Activity: SIMG_SALWFDOKARTSOA0
S_BCE_68000203	IMG Activity: SIMGSIMG_WORKFLOW
S_BCE_68000204	IMG Activity: SIMG_SALCUCHECKOACK
S_BCE_68000205	IMG Activity: SIMG_SALABLAGEOAC0
S_BCE_68000206	IMG Activity: SIMG_SALPROTOOAA3
S_BCE_68000207	IMG Activity: SIMG_SALAPPLIKOAA4
S_BCE_68000214	IMG Activity: SIMG_CFMENUSAPCOBC3
S_BCE_68000215	IMG Activity: SIMG_PHON220
S_BCE_68000216	IMG Activity: SIMG_PHON310
S_BCE_68000217	IMG Activity: SIMG_PHON320
S_BCE_68000226	IMG Activity: SIMG_SALWWIZOAWW
S_BCE_68000227	IMG Activity: SIMG_SALARCHGEROAD6
S_BCE_68000228	IMG Activity: SIMG_SALCUCHECKOACK
S_BCE_68000229	IMG Activity: SIMG_SALPROTOOAA3
S_BCE_68000230	IMG Activity: SIMG_SALAPPLIKOAA4

S_BCE_68000231	IMG Activity: SIMG_SALBENAROAA1
S_BCE_68000232	IMG Activity: SIMG_SALBARARCHOAC5
S_BCE_68000233	IMG Activity: SIMG_CMMENUOEDISU01
S_BCE_68000234	IMG Activity: SIMG_SALERGVERKNOABA
S_BCE_68000235	IMG Activity: SIMG_SALGRUNDOAG1
S_BCE_68000236	IMG Activity: SIMG_SALABLAGEOAC0
S_BCE_68000237	IMG Activity: SIMG_CFMENUOEDIOAC3
S_BCE_68000238	IMG Activity: SIMG_SALQUEUEOAQ1
S_BCE_68000239	IMG Activity: SIMG_SALJOBSOAAT
S_BCE_68000240	IMG Activity: SIMG_SALNUMMOANR
S_BCE_68000241	IMG Activity: SIMG_SALVERPRÜFOACH
S_BCE_68000242	IMG Activity: SIMG_CMMENUOEDISU03
S_BCE_68000243	IMG Activity: SIMG_SALCUCHECKOACK
S_BCE_68000244	IMG Activity: SIMG_SALVOREINOAWS
S_BCE_68000245	IMG Activity: SIMG_SALVERKNTABOAD3
S_BCE_68000246	IMG Activity: SIMG_SALDOKARTENOAC2
S_BCE_68000247	IMG Activity: SIMG_SALDOKTYPENOAD2
S_BCE_68000248	IMG Activity: SIMG_SALBARCODEOAD4
S_BCE_68000249	IMG Activity: SIMG_SALCUCHECKOACK
S_BCE_68000250	IMG Activity: SIMG_SALDOKWIZOAD5
S_BCE_68000251	IMG Activity: SIMG_CMMENUOEDISU02
S_BCE_68000252	IMG Activity: SIMG_OSC1
S_BCE_68000254	IMG Activity: CFMENUSAPCFILE
S_BCE_68000255	IMG Activity: SIMG_CFMENUSAPCSF01
S_BCE_68000256	IMG Activity: SIMG_CFMENUSAPCSF07
S_BCE_68000257	IMG Activity: PROF_GEN_PFCG
S_BCE_68000258	IMG Activity: PROF_GEN_SSM1
S_BCE_68000259	IMG Activity: PROF_GEN_SU25
S_BCE_68000260	IMG Activity: PROF_GEN_PAR
S_BCE_68000261	IMG Activity: PROF_GEN_AUTH_OFF
S_BCE_68000262	IMG Activity: SIMG_APPL_LOG_NUMRA
S_BCE_68000263	IMG Activity: SIMG_CFMENUSAPCOY22
S_BCE_68000264	IMG Activity: SIMG_CFMENUSAPCOY20
S_BCE_68000265	IMG Activity: SIMG_CFMENUSAPCSUCU
S_BCE_68000266	IMG Activity: PROF_GEN_AUTH
S_BCE_68000267	IMG Activity: SIMG_SAPB_REC_CLIENT
S_BCE_68000268	IMG Activity: SIMG_SAPB_MAPPENREOR
S_BCE_68000269	IMG Activity: SIMG_SAPB_DUMPREORG
S_BCE_68000270	IMG Activity: SIMG_SAPB_SPOOLREORG
S_BCE_68000271	IMG Activity: USR40
S_BCE_68000272	IMG Activity: PROF_GEN_RHAUTUP1
S_BCE_68000273	IMG-Aktivität: BCDIGSI_ADMIN
S_BCE_68000274	IMG Activity: SIMG_WF18SWWD
S_BCE_68000275	IMG Activity: SIMG_WF15OOW4
S_BCE_68000276	IMG Activity: SIMG_WF_SWL_SYSTEM
S_BCE_68000277	IMG Activity: SIMG_WF46SWUT
S_BCE_68000278	IMG Activity: SIMG_SAPA_ADR_VERS
S_BCE_68000279	IMG Activity: SIMG_ADDRESSES_SA14
S_BCE_68000280	IMG Activity: SIMG_REGSTRUC_SRN1
S_BCE_68000281	IMG Activity: SIMG_REGSTRUC_SRN2
S_BCE_68000282	IMG Activity: SIMG_REGSTRUC_SRN3
S_BCE_68000283	IMG Activity: SIMG_REGSTRUC_STTYPE
S_BCE_68000284	IMG Activity: SIMG_REGSTRUC_GROUP
S_BCE_68000285	IMG Activity: SIMG_ADDRESSES_SA01

S_BCE_68000286	IMG Activity: SIMG_ADDRESSES_SA03
S_BCE_68000287	IMG Activity: SIMG_ADDRESSES_SA02
S_BCE_68000288	IMG Activity: SIMG_ADDRESSES_SA04
S_BCE_68000289	IMG Activity: SIMG_ADDRESSES_SA13
S_BCE_68000290	IMG Activity: SIMG_ADDRESSES_SA05
S_BCE_68000291	IMG Activity: CATT_ETT
S_BCE_68000292	IMG Activity: SIMG_GTFMCCOMMHIER
S_BCE_68000294	IMG Activity: OALE_RBDSERCHECK
S_BCE_68000295	IMG Activity: OALE_MAINTAIN_TBD55
S_BCE_68000296	IMG Activity: OALE_MAINTAIN_TBD56
S_BCE_68000297	IMG Activity: OALE_SERDIST_SM36
S_BCE_68000299	IMG Activity: OALE_INPUTVAR_SE38
S_BCE_68000300	IMG Activity: OALE_STATUSJOB_SM36
S_BCE_68000301	IMG Activity: OALE_SENDVARMSG_SE38
S_BCE_68000302	IMG Activity: OALE_LISTMODELL_BD64
S_BCE_68000303	IMG Activity: OALE_LISTINGS_BD68
S_BCE_68000304	IMG Activity: OALE_SERDIST_SE38
S_BCE_68000305	IMG Activity: OALE_IDOCRED_BD53
S_BCE_68000306	IMG Activity: OALE_VARIANTMSG_SM36
S_BCE_68000307	IMG Activity: OALE_VARIANTMSG_SE38
S_BCE_68000308	IMG Activity: OALE_CHGPNTMSGT_BD50
S_BCE_68000309	IMG Activity: OALE_CHGPNTRALL_BD61
S_BCE_68000311	IMG Activity: OALE_SERGRP_INBOUND
S_BCE_68000312	IMG Activity: OALE_SERGRP_MODEL
S_BCE_68000313	IMG Activity: OALE_SERGRP_ASSIGN
S_BCE_68000314	IMG Activity: OALE_FILTEROUT_BD56
S_BCE_68000315	IMG Activity: OALE_MSGTRANS_BD63
S_BCE_68000316	IMG Activity: SIMG_CFMENUOEDIWE46
S_BCE_68000318	IMG Activity: OALE_WFBASICS
S_BCE_68000319	IMG Activity: OALE_ACTIVMONI_SM36
S_BCE_68000320	IMG Activity: OALE_ACTIVMONI_SE38
S_BCE_68000321	IMG Activity: OALE_ERRPROCODE_WE40
S_BCE_68000324	IMG Activity: OALE_AUTOPARTN_BD82
S_BCE_68000325	IMG Activity: OALE_PRTNRDEFOU_WE20
S_BCE_68000326	IMG Activity: OALE_MODMAINT_BD64
S_BCE_68000327	IMG Activity: OALE_AUDITJOB_SM36
S_BCE_68000328	IMG Activity: OALE_IDOCONVOUT_BD55
S_BCE_68000332	IMG Activity: OALE_INPUTJOB_SM36
S_BCE_68000333	IMG Activity: OALE_CUSPARTCHK_BDM3
S_BCE_68000334	IMG Activity: OALE_AUDITVAR_SE38
S_BCE_68000335	IMG Activity: SVARA
S_BCE_68000336	IMG Activity: OALE_CONSCHECK_SM36
S_BCE_68000337	IMG Activity: OALE_CONSCHECK_SE38
S_BCE_68000338	IMG Activity: OALE_COMPNRANGE_BD70
S_BCE_68000339	IMG Activity: OALE_PORTDESCRP_WE21
S_BCE_68000340	IMG Activity: OALE_USER_DIST_CENTR
S_BCE_68000341	IMG Activity: OALE_USER_DIST_FIELD
S_BCE_68000342	IMG Activity: OALE_LOGSYSDEST_BD97
S_BCE_68000343	IMG Activity: OALE_USER_DIST_NEW
S_BCE_68000344	IMG Activity: OALE_RFCDEST_SM59
S_BCE_68000345	IMG Activity: OALE_USER_DIST_MODEL
S_BCE_68000348	IMG Activity: OALE_STATUSJOB_SM36
S_BCE_68000349	IMG Activity: OALE_ISOCODES
S_BCE_68000350	IMG Activity: OALE_STATUSVAR_SE38

S_BCE_68000353	IMG Activity: OBIL-ALE-11
S_BCE_68000354	IMG Activity: OALE_CHECKCONTRMODEL
S_BCE_68000356	IMG Activity: OALE_AUTHOR_SU03
S_BCE_68000358	IMG Activity: OALE_NUMCHGPNTR_BDCP
S_BCE_68000359	IMG Activity: OALE_PORTNUMR_OYSM
S_BCE_68000360	IMG Activity: OALE_LSYS_RENAME
S_BCE_68000361	IMG Activity: OBIL-ALE-12
S_BCE_68000362	IMG Activity: OALE_CONTROLMOD_BD64
S_BCE_68000363	IMG Activity: SIMG_OBPTAUTOCUSTOM
S_BCE_68000364	IMG Activity: SIMG_OBPTEVENTCOUP
S_BCE_68000365	IMG Activity: SIMG_CFMENUOEDIWE46
S_BCE_68000366	IMG Activity: SIMG_OBPTDEFAULT
S_BCE_68000367	IMG Activity: SIMG_OBPTIMAGING
S_BCE_68000368	IMG Activity: EDI-03
S_BCE_68000369	IMG Activity: SIMG_OBPTNUMBERRANGE
S_BCE_68000370	IMG Activity: SIMG_OBPTFEHLER
S_BCE_68000371	IMG Activity: SIMG_OBPTEDISEDIR
S_BCE_68000372	IMG Activity: SIMG_OBPTDELOLDAPPL
S_BCE_68000373	IMG Activity: PROF_GEN_PFCG
S_BCE_68000374	IMG Activity: PROF_GEN_PAR
S_BCE_68000375	IMG Activity: PROF_GEN_SSM1
S_BCE_68000376	IMG Activity: SESSION_MANAGER
S_BCE_68000377	IMG Activity: OCNG_GW3
S_BCE_68000378	IMG Activity: OCNG_GW2
S_BCE_68000379	IMG Activity: OCNG_GW1
S_BCE_68000380	IMG Activity: SIMG_SAPB_DEINDEX
S_BCE_68000382	IMG Activity: SIMG_CFMENUSAPCOY30
S_BCE_68000383	IMG Activity: SIMG_DOCU_AUTH
S_BCE_68000384	IMG Activity: SAPA_SXDA
S_BCE_68000392	Link Check
S_BCE_68000394	S_BCE_68000394
S_BCE_68000542	S_BCE_68000542
S_BCE_68000561	S_BCE_68000561
S_BCE_68000562	S_BCE_68000562
S_BCE_68000565	S_BCE_68000565
S_BCE_68000569	IMG Activity: SIMG_WF16SWWE
S_BCE_68000570	IMG Activity: SIMG_WF31OOCU
S_BCE_68000571	IMG Activity: SIMG_WF18SM59
S_BCE_68000572	IMG Activity: SIMG_WF19OO91
S_BCE_68000573	IMG Activity: SIMG_WF18SWLV
S_BCE_68000574	IMG Activity: SIMG_WF17OOW3
S_BCE_68000575	IMG Activity: SIMG_WF21OOOE
S_BCE_68000576	IMG Activity: SIMG_WF46SWUT
S_BCE_68000577	IMG Activity: SIMG_WF_SWL_SYSTEM
S_BCE_68000578	IMG Activity: SIMG_WF42SWL1
S_BCE_68000579	IMG Activity: SIMG_WF43SWP
S_BCE_68000580	IMG Activity: SIMG_WF19SWDC
S_BCE_68000581	IMG Activity: SIMG_WF44OOCU
S_BCE_68000582	IMG Activity: SIMG_WF50SWT0
S_BCE_68000583	IMG Activity: SIMG_CFMENUOHPWFUE01
S_BCE_68000584	IMG Activity: SIMG_CFMENUOHPWFOONR
S_BCE_68000585	IMG Activity: SIMG_CFMENUOHPWFOONC
S_BCE_68000587	IMG Activity: SIMG_WF14OOAP
S_BCE_68000588	IMG Activity: SIMG_WF11OOPR

S_BCE_68000589	IMG Activity: SIMG_WF0900
S_BCE_68000590	IMG Activity: SIMG_WF1140
S_BCE_68000591	IMG Activity: SIMG_CFMENUOHPWFOOAW
S_BCE_68000592	IMG Activity: SIMG_WF173OOW2
S_BCE_68000593	IMG Activity: SIMG_WF45SWUR
S_BCE_68000594	IMG Activity: SIMG_WF15OOW1
S_BCE_68000595	IMG Activity: SIMG_WF15OOW4
S_BCE_68000596	IMG Activity: SIMG_CFMENUOHPWFOOCH
S_BCE_68000597	IMG Activity: SIMG_CFMENUOHPWFOOLG
S_BCE_68000614	S_BCE_68000614
S_BCE_68000615	S_BCE_68000615
S_BCE_68000646	S_BCE_68000646
S_BCE_68000647	S_BCE_68000647
S_BCE_68000650	S_BCE_68000650
S_BCE_68000651	S_BCE_68000651
S_BCE_68000657	S_BCE_68000657
S_BCE_68000659	S_BCE_68000659
S_BCE_68000661	S_BCE_68000661
S_BCE_68000662	S_BCE_68000662
S_BCE_68000663	S_BCE_68000663
S_BCE_68001272	S_BCE_68001272
S_BCE_68001273	S_BCE_68001273
S_BCE_68001290	Search Server Relation
S_BCE_68001293	IMG activity: SIMG_ADDRESSES_SA15
S_BCE_68001393	Users by address data
S_BCE_68001394	Users According to Complex Criteria
S_BCE_68001395	Users According to Complex Criteria
S_BCE_68001396	Users According to Complex Criteria
S_BCE_68001397	Users According to Complex Criteria
S_BCE_68001398	Users According to Complex Criteria
S_BCE_68001399	Users According to Complex Criteria
S_BCE_68001400	Users According to Complex Criteria
S_BCE_68001401	Critical Combinations of Auth.
S_BCE_68001402	With Unsuccessful Logons
S_BCE_68001403	With Critical Authorizations
S_BCE_68001404	Profiles by Contained Profiles
S_BCE_68001405	Profiles by Authorization Name
S_BCE_68001406	Profiles by Values
S_BCE_68001407	Profiles by Changes
S_BCE_68001408	Profiles by Roles
S_BCE_68001409	Profiles According to Complex Crit.
S_BCE_68001410	Auth. Objects According to Complex
S_BCE_68001411	Auth. Objects According to Complex
S_BCE_68001412	Auth. Objects According to Complex
S_BCE_68001413	Auth. Objects According to Complex
S_BCE_68001414	Auth. According to Complex Criteria
S_BCE_68001415	Authorizations by Values
S_BCE_68001416	Authorizations by Changes
S_BCE_68001417	Auth. According to Complex Criteria
S_BCE_68001418	Roles by Role Name
S_BCE_68001419	Roles by User Assignment
S_BCE_68001420	Roles by Transaction Assignment
S_BCE_68001421	Roles by Profile Assignment
S_BCE_68001422	Roles by Authorization Object

S_BCE_68001423	Roles by Authorization Values
S_BCE_68001424	Roles by Change Data
S_BCE_68001425	Roles by Complex Criteria
S_BCE_68001426	Transactions for User
S_BCE_68001427	Transactions for User
S_BCE_68001428	Transactions for User
S_BCE_68001429	Transactions for User
S_BCE_68001430	Compare Users
S_BCE_68001431	Compare Profiles
S_BCE_68001432	Compare Authorizations
S_BCE_68001433	Comparisons
S_BCE_68001434	Where-used lists
S_BCE_68001435	Where-used lists
S_BCE_68001436	Where-used lists
S_BCE_68001437	Where-used lists
S_BCE_68001438	Where-used lists
S_BCE_68001439	For user
S_BCE_68001440	For profiles
S_BCE_68001441	For authorizations
S_BCE_68001452	IMG Activity: SIMG_OBIL_08
S_BCE_68001453	IMG Activity: MAND_0002
S_BCE_68001455	IMG Activity: OBIL_PAT06
S_BCE_68001456	IMG Activity: AUFT01
S_BCE_68001457	IMG Activity: ERWEIT-0001
S_BCE_68001458	IMG Activity: ERWEIT-0004
S_BCE_68001459	IMG Activity: ERWEIT-0003
S_BCE_68001461	IMG Activity: SIMG_SAPB_SLAKNUM
S_BCE_68001462	IMG Activity: SIMG_SAPB_SLDATWECHS
S_BCE_68001463	IMG Activity: SIMG_OBIL_11
S_BCE_68001464	hfdhgdf
S_BCE_68001467	IMG Activity: CUS_INFO_1_500
S_BCE_68001468	IMG Activity: CUS_INFO_1_100
S_BCE_68001469	IMG Activity: CUS_INFO_1_400
S_BCE_68001470	IMG Activity: CUS_INFO_1_300
S_BCE_68001471	IMG Activity: CUS_INFO_2_600
S_BCE_68001472	IMG Activity: CUS_INFO_2_400
S_BCE_68001473	IMG Activity: CUS_INFO_2_500
S_BCE_68001474	IMG Activity: CUS_INFO_2_300
S_BCE_68001475	IMG Activity: CUS_INFO_2_200
S_BCE_68001476	IMG Activity: CUS_INFO_2_600
S_BCE_68001477	IMG Activity: CUS_INF3_300
S_BCE_68001478	IMG Activity: CUS_INF3_200
S_BCE_68001479	IMG Activity: CUS_INF3_100
S_BCE_68001484	xxx
S_BCE_68001485	x
S_BCE_68001767	By Profile Name or Text
S_BCE_68001777	Compare Roles
S_BCE_68001821	.
S_BCE_68001822	.
S_BCE_68002030	Where-Used List for Authorization
S_BCE_68002040	Central Test Workbench Settings
S_BCE_68002041	Executable for Role
S_BCE_68002111	RSUSR008_009_NEW
S_BCE_68002311	Change Documents for Users

S_BIE_59000002	IMG Activity: SIMG_KEN_R3LINK31
S_BIE_59000003	IMG Activity: SIMG_KEN_LINK40ADEST
S_BIE_59000004	IMG Activity: SIMG_KEN_FORMATS
S_BIE_59000005	IMG Activity: SIMG_KEN_EXTCHAIN
S_BIE_59000006	IMG Activity: SIMG_KEN_EXTENSION
S_BIE_59000007	IMG Activity: IMS_TRAIN
S_BIE_59000008	IMG Activity: IMS_SSR
S_BIE_59000009	IMG Activity: SIMG_KEN_FLDRGRP
S_BIE_59000010	IMG Activity: SIMG_KEN_EXP_RANGE
S_BIE_59000011	IMG Activity: SIMG_KEN_EXRTAB
S_BIE_59000012	IMG Activity: SIMG_KEN_EXP_VARIANT
S_BIE_59000013	IMG Activity: SIMG_KEN_AUT_AUSH
S_BIE_59000014	IMG Activity: SIMG_KEN_EXP_ASSIGN
S_BIE_59000015	IMG Activity: SIMG_KEN_EXP_SERVER
S_BIE_59000016	IMG Activity: SIMG_KEN_EXP_SYSTEM
S_BIE_59000017	IMG Activity: SIMG_KEN_PROFILES
S_BIE_59000018	IMG Activity: DMS_SKPROG
S_BIE_59000019	IMG Activity: CMS_OALO
S_BIE_59000020	IMG Activity: CMS_OACT
S_BIE_59000021	IMG Activity: CMS_OACR
S_BIE_59000022	IMG Activity: SIMGZERTOAHT
S_BIE_59000023	IMG Activity: CMS_OAC0
S_BIE_59000024	IMG Activity: SIMG_KEN_EXT_APPL
S_BIE_59000025	IMG Activity: SIMG_KEN_VIEWDEST
S_BIE_59000026	IMG Activity: SIMG_KEN_HELPTYPE
S_BIE_59000027	IMG Activity: CMS_OADI
S_BIE_59000028	IMG Activity: DMS_SKPR04
S_BIE_59000029	IMG Activity: DMS_SKPR02
S_BIE_59000142	S_BIE_59000142
S_BIE_59000143	S_BIE_59000143
S_BIE_59000144	Priorities for appt. management
S_BIE_59000182	IMG activity: SIMG_REGSTRUC_SR30
S_BIE_59000183	IMG activity: SIMG_REGSTRUC_SR31
S_BIE_59000184	IMG activity: SIMG_REGSTRUC_SR32
S_BIE_59000185	IMG activity: SIMG_REGSTRUC_SR10
S_BIE_59000186	IMG activity: SIMG_REGSTRUC_SR11
S_BIE_59000187	IMG activity: SIMG_REGSTRUC_SR12
S_BIE_59000188	IMG activity: SIMG_REGSTRUC_SR20
S_BIE_59000189	IMG activity: SIMG_REGSTRUC_SR21
S_BIE_59000190	IMG activity: SIMG_REGSTRUC_SR22
S_BIE_59000191	IMG activity: SIMG_REGSTRUC_FILL
S_BIE_59000194	IMG activity: SIMG_ADDRESSES_SA16
S_BIE_59000197	Report cross-system information
S_BIE_59000198	Report cross-system information
S_BIE_59000199	Report cross-system information
S_BIE_59000219	IMG activity: SIMG_ADDRESSES_SA17
S_BIE_59000222	SAPLS_CUS_IMG_ACTIVITY
S_BIE_59000227	x
S_BIE_59000228	x
S_BIE_59000229	Display/Assign status of all roles
S_BIE_59000232	SAPLS_CUS_IMG_ACTIVITY
S_BIE_59000235	x
S_BIE_59000236	x
S_BIE_59000238	SAPLS_CUS_IMG_ACTIVITY

S_BIE_59000239	SAPLS_CUS_IMG_ACTIVITY
S_BIE_59000240	SAPLS_CUS_IMG_ACTIVITY
S_BIE_59000247	x
S_BIE_59000249	Roles By MiniApp
S_BIE_59000250	SAPLS_CUS_IMG_ACTIVITY
S_BIE_59000253	SAPLS_CUS_IMG_ACTIVITY
S_BIE_59000254	SAPLS_CUS_IMG_ACTIVITY
S_BIE_59000255	x
S_BIN_67000001	IMG-Aktivität: SIMG_BCSNC_SM54
S_BIN_67000002	IMG-Aktivität: SIMG_BCSNC_RFCDESSEC
S_BIN_67000003	IMG-Aktivität: SIMG_BCSNC_SM59
S_BIN_67000004	IMG-Aktivität: SIMG_BCSNC_SPAD
S_BIN_67000005	IMG-Aktivität: SIMG_BCSNC_SNCSYSACL
S_BIN_67000006	IMG-Aktivität: SIMG_BCSNC_USRACLEXT
S_BIN_67000007	IMG-Aktivität: SIMG_BCSNC_EXTID_DN
S_BIN_67000008	IMG-Aktivität: SIMG_BCSNC_EXTID_ID
S_BIN_67000009	IMG-Aktivität: SIMG_BCSNC_EXTID
S_BIN_67000010	IMG-Aktivität: SIMG_BCSNC_RSSNCCHK
S_BIN_67000011	IMG-Aktivität: SIMG_BCSNC_RSUSR402
S_BIN_67000012	IMG-Aktivität: SIMG_BCSNC_TXCOMSECU
S_BIN_67000013	IMG-Aktivität: SIMG_BCSNC_USRACL
S_BIN_67000014	IMG-Aktivität: SIMG_BCSNC_SSF_USER
S_BIN_67000015	IMG-Aktivität: SIMG_BCSNC_SSF_APPL
S_BIN_67000016	IMG-Aktivität: SIMG_BCSNC_SU01
S_BIN_67000017	IMG-Aktivität: SIMG_BCSNC_RSSNC40A
S_BIN_67000018	IMG-Aktivität: SIMG_BCSNC_RSUSR300
S_BIN_67000019	IMG-Aktivität: SIMG_BCSNC_RFCUSRACL
S_BIN_67000020	IMG-Aktivität: SIMG_BCSNC_PARAM
S_BIN_67000021	IMG-Aktivität: SIMG_BCSNC_RSSNCIMP
S_BIN_67000022	IMG Activity: HTTPPROXY
S_BIN_67000023	IMG Activity: TVARV-0001
S_BIN_67000029	IMG Activity: SICF_INST
S_BIO_23000001	IMG -> BAdI CTS_IMPORT_FEEDBACK
S_BIO_23000002	IMG -> BAdI CTS_EXPORT_FEEDBACK
S_BIO_23000003	IMG -> BAdI CTS_REQUEST_CHECK
S_BIO_23000006	IMG -> BAdI CTS_TASKDOC_TEMPLATE
S_BIO_23000007	IMG -> BAdI CTS_CURRENT_PROJECT
S_BR3_49000001	IMG Activity: BW_RSKC
S_BR3_49000002	IMG Activity: BWSIMG_ALEUSU01
S_BR3_49000003	IMG Activity: BW_LOGSYSSM30
S_BR3_49000004	IMG Activity: BW_WFSWU3
S_BR3_49000005	IMG Activity: BW_VARCMOD
S_BR3_49000006	IMG Activity: BW_VIRTCMOD
S_BR3_49000007	IMG Activity: BW_SPADPRINT
S_BR3_49000008	IMG Activity: BW_FISCALYEAR
S_BR3_49000009	IMG Activity: BW_RSADMIN
S_BR3_49000010	IMG Activity: BW_NUKSNUM
S_BR3_49000011	IMG Activity: BW_RSLGMP
S_BR3_49000012	IMG Activity: BW_BATCHRZ11
S_BYA_47000043	RCPE_CHKPRICEQUOT
S_BYA_47000046	RCPE_CHKPRICEQUOT
S_BYA_47000049	MDMGX
S_BYA_47000051	MDMGX
S_CUS_ACTIVITY	Customizing maint. obj. maintenance

SAP Transaction Codes – Volume Two

S_CUS_ATTRIBUTES	IMG attribute maintenance
S_CUS_IMG_ACTIVITY	IMG activity maintenance
S_CWE_15000044	IMG Activity: CON_FAIC02
S_DTR_07000013	IMG Activity: SIMG_LTRM001
S_DTR_07000017	IMG Activity: SIMG_LTBN003
S_DTR_07000018	IMG Activity: SIMG_LTBN004
S_DTR_07000019	IMG Activity: SIMG_LTBN005
S_DTR_07000021	IMG Activity: SIMG_LTRM_USEXIT002
S_DTR_07000022	IMG Activity: SIMG_LTRM_USEXIT003
S_DTR_07000023	IMG Activity: SIMG_LMBP001
S_DTR_07000024	IMG Activity: SIMG_LMBP002
S_DTR_07000025	S_DTR_07000025
S_DTR_07000026	IMG Activity: SIMG_LMBP004
S_DTR_07000028	IMG Activity: SIMG_LMBP006
S_DTR_07000029	IMG Activity: SIMG_LESI001
S_DTR_07000032	IMG Activity: SIMG_LTRT003
S_DTR_07000033	IMG Activity: SIMG_LTRT001
S_DTR_07000034	IMG Activity: SIMG_LTRT002
S_DTR_07000038	IMG Activity: SIMG_LTBN007
S_DTR_07000039	IMG Activity: SIMG_LTRM_USEXIT004
S_DTR_07000041	IMG Activity: SIMG_LMON001
S_DTR_07000042	IMG Activity: SIMGH_LMON002
S_DTR_07000043	IMG Activity: SIMGH_LMON003
S_DTR_07000044	IMG Activity: SIMGH_LMON004
S_E36_82000096	IMG Activity
S_E38_98000034	IMG Activity
S_E38_98000046	IMG Activity
S_E38_98000088	PrCtr Group: Plan/Actual Variance
S_E38_98000089	PrCtr Group: Plan/Plan/Actual
S_E38_98000090	PrCtr Group: Key Figures
S_E38_98000091	Profit Center Comparison: ROI
S_E38_98000092	Segment: Plan/Actual Variance
S_E38_98000093	Segment: Plan/Plan/Actual
S_E38_98000094	Segment: Key Figures
S_E38_98000095	Segment Comparison: ROI
S_E4A_94000025	Segment Catalog
S_E4A_94000026	DARTX: Field Catalog
S_E4A_94000027	DARTX: Data Extract Browser
S_E4A_94000036	Down-Payment Monitoring for PO
S_E4A_94000042	IMG Activity
S_E4A_94000109	Cost Elements (PS): Objects
S_E4A_94000110	Order (PS): Actual/Plan/Variance
S_E4A_94000111	Cost Centers (PSM):Actual/Plan/Var.
S_E4A_94000116	IMG
S_E4A_94000117	IMG
S_E4A_94000136	IMG
S_E4A_94000137	IMG
S_E4A_94000138	IMG
S_E4A_94000175	DART: XML File Creation
S_E4A_94000176	DART: XML File Merger
S_E4A_94000185	IMG Activity
S_E4A_94000186	IMG Activity
S_E4A_94000284	IMG Activity
S_E4A_94000320	Important Transactions Cross Check C

S_E4A_94000353	Update Liability of Monotributo Vend
S_E4A_94000354	Update cumulative amounts for vendor
S_E4A_94000356	Report RFIDESM340
S_E4A_94000367	Cash Ledger, Peru
S_E4A_94000368	Journal Ledger, Peru
S_E4A_94000369	General Ledger, Peru
S_E4A_94000372	Report RFCLLIB04_PE
S_E4A_94000381	Update Tax Payer List
S_E4A_94000385	Sales Ledger, Peru
S_E4E_66000026	SMI_PROFILE
S_E4E_66000086	IMG Activity
S_E4E_66000205	IMG Activity
S_E4I_14000028	IMG Activity
S_E4J_98000014	Assign Budget Type Group to Process
S_E4J_98000015	Define Statistical Budget Type Group
S_E4J_98000016	Assign Stat. Bdt Type Grp to Process
S_E4M_69000019	IMG Activity
S_E4M_69000194	IMG Activity
S_E4M_69000197	IMG Activity
S_E4M_69000198	IMG Activity
S_E4M_69000205	IMG Activity
S_E4M_69000211	IMG Activity
S_E4M_85000015	IMG Activity
S_E7Z_56000001	Display classifications
S_E7Z_56000002	Default variant
S_E7Z_56000003	Default variant
S_EAC_24000046	IMG Activity
S_EAI_14000027	IMG Activity
S_EAJ_88000021	Design Time for Processes/Forms
S_EAV_19000015	IMG Activity
S_EB5_05000041	Audit Private Folder
S_EB5_05000042	Audit Private Folder
S_EB5_05000043	Audit Private Folder
S_EB5_05000044	SAP Tax Audit Private Folder
S_EB5_05000045	Audit Private Folder
S_EB5_05000046	Audit Private Folder
S_EB5_05000047	Audit List Viewer
S_EB5_05000048	Audit List Viewer
S_EB5_05000049	Reconciliation Analysis FI-AA
S_EB5_05000050	Reconciliation Analysis FI-AA
S_EB5_05000051	Audit
S_EB5_05000052	Audit Information System
S_EB5_05000053	Audit
S_EB5_05000054	Audit Environment of Asset
S_EB5_05000055	Audit Asset Balances
S_EB5_05000056	Audit Current Book Value
S_EB5_05000057	Audit
S_EB5_05000058	Audit
S_EB5_05000059	Audit
S_EB5_05000060	Audit
S_EB5_05000061	Depreciation Log
S_EB5_05000062	Depreciation
S_EB5_05000063	Audit
S_EB5_05000064	Audit

S_EB5_05000065	Audit
S_EB5_05000067	Audit Information System
S_EB5_05000068	Audit
S_EB5_05000069	Audit
S_EB5_05000070	Audit Information System
S_EB5_05000071	Audit Information System
S_EB5_05000072	Audit Information System
S_EB5_05000073	Other Capitalized Internal Activity
S_EB5_05000074	AIS Tangible Fixed Assets
S_EB5_05000086	Audit Interactive List
S_EB5_05000087	Audit Interactive List
S_EB5_05000088	Audit Interactive List
S_EG4_04000077	IMG Activity
S_EG4_04000090	Account Statement for Company Loans
S_EG4_04000251	DMA Report
S_EG4_04000252	Programma per la compilazione del m
S_EG4_04000289	IMG Activity
S_EH1_67000058	IMG activity: OHBPSWTTRT
S_EH1_67000059	IMG activity: OHBPSASSWTRT
S_EH1_67000060	IMG activity: OHBPSUSEREXIT1
S_EH1_67000061	IMG activity: OHBPSUSEREXIT2
S_EH1_67000062	IMG activity: OHBPSUSEREXIT3
S_EH1_67000063	IMG activity: OHBPSESS
S_EH1_67000064	IMG activity: SIMGOHA_EFI_004
S_EH1_67000065	IMG activity: SIMGOHA_EFIGB_001
S_EH1_67000066	IMG activity: SIMGOHA_EFIGB_002
S_EH1_67000067	IMG activity: SIMGOHA_EFIGB_003
S_EH1_67000068	IMG activity: SIMGOHA_EFIGB_004
S_EH1_67000069	IMG activity: SIMGOHA_EFIGB_005
S_EH1_67000070	IMG activity: SIMGOHA_EFIGB_006
S_EH1_67000071	IMG activity: PBS_NO_BAS_100
S_EH1_67000072	IMG activity: PBS_NO_BAS_200
S_EH1_67000073	IMG activity: PBS_NO_BAS_300
S_EH1_67000074	IMG activity: PBS_NO_BAS_400
S_EH1_67000075	IMG activity: PBS_NO_BAS_500
S_EH1_67000076	IMG activity: PBS_NO_BAS_600
S_EH1_67000077	IMG activity: PBS_NO_BAS_700
S_EH1_67000079	IMG activity: PBS_NO_ADD_100
S_EH1_67000080	IMG activity: PBS_NO_ADD_200
S_EH1_67000082	IMG activity: PBS_NO_ADD_400
S_EH1_67000083	IMG activity: PBS_NO_ADD_500
S_EH1_67000084	IMG activity: PBS_NO_ADD_600
S_EH1_67000085	IMG activity: PBS_NO_PAY_100
S_EH1_67000086	IMG activity: PBS_NO_PAY_200
S_EH1_67000087	IMG activity: PBS_NO_PAY_300
S_EH1_67000088	IMG activity: PBS_NO_PAY_400
S_EH1_67000089	IMG activity: PBS_NO_PEN_100
S_EH1_67000090	IMG activity: PBS_NO_PEN_200
S_EH1_67000091	IMG activity: PBS_NO_ABS_100
S_EH1_67000092	IMG activity: PBS_NO_ABS_200
S_EH1_67000093	IMG activity: PBS_NO_ABS_300
S_EH1_67000096	IMG activity: PBS_NO_BAS_350
S_EH1_67000097	IMG activity: PBS_NO_REP_SPK_100
S_EH1_67000098	IMG activity: PBS_NO_REP_SPK_200

S_EH1_67000099	IMG activity: PBS_NO_REP_SPK_300
S_EH1_67000100	IMG activity: PBS_NO_REP_SPK_400
S_EH1_67000101	IMG activity: PBS_NO_BAS_800
S_EH1_67000102	IMG activity: PBS_NO_BAS_750
S_EH4_55000023	Report RP_US_EFFR_BUND_DUNNING
S_EH4_55000024	Actual Effort Certification by Emplo
S_EH4_55000031	IMG Activity
S_EH5_01000312	Relevant Receipts for EU VAT Refund
S_EI4_11000013	Cost Elements (PS): Objects
S_EI4_11000014	Cost Centers (PSM):Actual/Plan/Var.
S_EI4_11000015	Order (PS): Actual/Plan/Variance
S_EI4_11000036	IMG Activity
S_ELN_06000002	IMG Activity: V_FAGLCOFIVARC
S_FAD_62000042	IMG Activity: PCUI_HPF_020
S_FID_08000185	Payment Medium: Creation
S_FID_08000218	Remuneration Statement Finland as El
S_FID_08000225	SAP standard variant
S_FNO_22000130	Test
S_HC2_76000010	Creation of Instance Documents
S_HRJ_73000013	Shukko-in/-out overview
S_HRJ_73000014	Wage Amount for Fixed Labor Insuranc
S_HRJ_73000019	Shukko Cost Settlement Report
S_HRM_42000003	Pillai's variant -India
S_HRM_42000004	Wage Type Statement
S_HRM_42000005	Wage Type Distribution
S_HRM_42000006	Remuneration Statements
S_HRM_42000007	pillai's variant - India
S_HRM_42000008	Payroll Accounts
S_HRM_42000009	Payroll Journal --- International
S_HRM_42000010	Ptax Tesing
S_HRM_42000011	Rent receipt updation report
S_HRM_42000012	Batch program for DA
S_IMG_EXTENSION	IMG maintenance
S_IWB	Initial Screen Knowledge Warehouse
S_J10_96000008	SAPLS_CUS_IMG_ACTIVITY
S_J10_96000009	SAPLS_CUS_IMG_ACTIVITY
S_J10_96000010	SAPLS_CUS_IMG_ACTIVITY
S_J10_96000011	SAPLS_CUS_IMG_ACTIVITY
S_J16_56000017	IMG Activity: BW_CACHE
S_J16_56000033	IMG Activity: BW_BADI_OPENHUB
S_J16_56000034	IMG Activity: BW_ODS
S_J16_56000035	IMG Activity: BW_WEBPROTOCOL
S_J16_56000036	IMG Activity: BW_CONTENT_DOCU
S_J16_56000037	IMG Activity: BW_AUTH
S_KA5_12000001	IMG Activity: SIMG_SD_BOS_ML91
S_KA5_12000002	IMG Activity: SIMG_SD_BOS_ML90
S_KA5_12000003	IMG Activity: SIMG_SD_BOS_CMOD
S_KA5_12000004	IMG Activity: SIMG_SD_BOS_ADTBOS01
S_KA5_12000005	IMG Activity: SIMG_SD_BOS2
S_KA5_12000006	IMG Activity: SIMG_BOS_UC_OKYR
S_KA5_12000007	IMG Activity: SIMG_BOS_UC_OKYC
S_KA5_12000008	IMG Activity: SIMG_SD_BOS_OMV2
S_KA5_12000009	IMG Activity: SIMG_SD_BOS_OXA1
S_KA5_12000013	IMG-Activity: SPEC2000_CSPCICC

S_KA5_12000014	IMG-Activity: SPEC2000_CSPCTAX
S_KA5_12000015	IMG-Activity: SPEC2000_CSPCS1S
S_KA5_12000016	IMG-Activity: SPEC2000_CSPCPRI
S_KA5_12000017	IMG-Activity: SPEC2000_V_MOI
S_KA5_12000018	IMG-Aktivität: SIMG_CFMENUOLSDVOK2X
S_KA5_12000019	IMG-Aktivität: SIMG_CFMENUOLSDVOK25
S_KA5_12000020	IMG-Aktivität: AD10PROFILE
S_KA5_12000021	IMG-Aktivität: AD01PRNFLD
S_KA5_12000022	IMG-Aktivität: AD01CONDUSE
S_KA5_12000023	IMG-Aktivität: AD03PHP
S_KA5_12000024	IMG-Aktivität: PS_PARTNERSCHEMA
S_KA5_12000025	IMG-Aktivität: V_TPGPRF
S_KA5_12000026	IMG-Activity : SIMG_CFMENUOLSDV/G5
S_KA5_12000027	IMG-Aktivität: AD04CUMOH
S_KA5_12000028	IMG-Aktivität: AD01CT
S_KA5_12000029	IMG-Aktivität: SIMG_BOS_BILL_VBX2
S_KA5_12000030	IMG-Aktivität: SIMG_BOS_SALES_SDVB
S_KA5_12000031	IMG-Aktivität: SIMG_BOS_SALES_SPRO
S_KA5_12000032	IMG-Aktivität: SIMG_BOS_SALES_VOV7
S_KA5_12000033	IMG-Aktivität: SIMG_BOS_SALES_VOV8
S_KA5_12000034	IMG Activity: SIMG_OLMEML99
S_KA5_12000035	IMG Activity: SIMG_OLMEML89
S_KA5_12000038	IMG Activity: SIMG_CFMENUOLMEOMYB
S_KA5_12000040	IMG Activity: SIMG_SD_BOS_ADTBOS01
S_KA5_12000042	IMG Activity: SIMG_BOS_UC_OKYR
S_KA5_12000043	IMG Activity: SIMG_BOS_UC_OKYC
S_KA5_12000045	IMG Activity: SIMG_CFMENUOLMEOMV1
S_KA5_12000046	IMG Activity: SIMG_CFMENUOLMEACNR
S_KA5_12000048	IMG Activity: SIMG_CFMENUOLMEOMY8
S_KA5_12000049	IMG Activity: SIMG_CFMENUOLMEOXA3
S_KA5_12000050	IMG Activity: SIMG_CFMENUOLMEOXA2
S_KA5_12000051	IMG-Activity: MPN_COMMON_FIELDS
S_KA5_12000052	IMG-Activity: MPN_CONV_EXIT
S_KA5_12000053	IMG-Activity: MPN_V_TMEX_MPN06
S_KA5_12000054	IMG-Activity: SPEC2000_CSPCICC
S_KA5_12000055	IMG-Activity: SPEC2000_CSPCTAX
S_KA5_12000056	IMG-Activity: SPEC2000_CSPCS1S
S_KA5_12000057	IMG-Activity: SPEC2000_CSPCPRI
S_KA5_12000058	IMG-Activity: SPEC2000_V_MOI
S_KA5_12000059	IMG-Activity : SIMG_CFMENUOLSDNF04
S_KA5_12000060	IMG-Activity : SIMG_CFMENUOLSDNF05
S_KA5_12000061	IMG-Activity: SIMG_CFMENUOLSDNF06
S_KA5_12000062	IMG-Activity : SIMG_CFMENUOLSDNF07
S_KA5_12000063	IMG-Aktivität: SIMG_CFMENUOLSDVOK2X
S_KA5_12000064	IMG-Aktivität: SIMG_CFMENUOLSDVOK25
S_KA5_12000065	IMG-Aktivität: SIMG_CFMENUOLSDNV04
S_KA5_12000066	IMG-Aktivität: SIMG_CFMENUOLSDNV05
S_KA5_12000067	IMG-Aktivität: SIMG_CFMENUOLSDNV06
S_KA5_12000068	IMG-Aktivität: SIMG_CFMENUOLSDNV07
S_KA5_12000069	IMG-Activity : SIMG_CFMENUOLSDNF02
S_KA5_12000070	IMG-Aktivität: SIMG_CFMENUOLSDNF03
S_KA5_12000071	IMG-Aktivität: SIMG_CMMENUOLSDNFF
S_KA5_12000072	IMG-Aktivität: AD10PROFILE
S_KA5_12000073	IMG-Aktivität: AD01PRNFLD

S_KA5_12000074	IMG-Aktivität: AD01CONDUSE
S_KA5_12000075	IMG-Aktivität: AD03PHP
S_KA5_12000076	IMG-Aktivität: PS_PARTNERSCHEMA
S_KA5_12000077	IMG-Aktivität: V_TPGPRF
S_KA5_12000078	IMG-Activity : SIMG_CFMENUOLSDV/G5
S_KA5_12000079	IMG-Activity : SIMG_CFMENUOLSDV/G7
S_KA5_12000080	IMG-Activity : SIMG_CFMENUOLSDV/83
S_KA5_12000081	IMG-Aktivität: SIMG_CFMENUOLSDNF3
S_KA5_12000083	IMG-Aktivität: AD01CT
S_KA5_12000086	IMG-Aktivität: SIMG_CFMENUOLSDVOV5
S_KA5_12000087	IMG-Aktivität: SIMG_CFMENUOLSDVOV4
S_KA5_12000090	IMG-Aktivität: SIMG_CFMENUOLSDOVAZ
S_KA5_12000091	IMG-Aktivität: SIMG_CFMENUOLSDOVA3
S_KA5_12000093	IMG-Aktivität: SIMG_CFMENUOLSDNKO02
S_KA5_12000094	IMG-Aktivität: SIMG_CFMENUOLSDNKO06
S_KA5_12000095	IMG-Aktivität: SIMG_CFMENUOLSDNKO03
S_KA5_12000096	IMG-Aktivität: SIMG_CFMENUOLSDNKO05
S_KA5_12000097	IMG-Aktivität: SIMG_CFMENUOLSDNV03
S_KA5_12000098	IMG-Aktivität: SIMG_CFMENUOLSDNV02
S_KA5_12000099	IMG-Aktivität: SIMG_CFMENUOLSDNKO04
S_KA5_12000100	IMG-Aktivität: SIMG_CFMENUOLSDNKO07
S_KA5_12000261	IMG / HBS Sales units Types
S_KA5_12000262	IMG / HBS Relation Types
S_KA5_12000263	IMG / HBS Income Types
S_KA5_12000264	IMG / HBS Fit relevant bldg type
S_KA5_12000265	IMG / HBS Fit relevant charctr grps
S_KA5_12000266	IMG / HBS Fit relevant mtral class
S_KA5_12000267	IMG / HBS Pre-sale report
S_KA5_12000268	IMG / HBS maintenace view for TVAK
S_KA5_12000276	Customizing STEP
S_KA5_12000287	Number Ranges for RP Accounts
S_KA5_12000288	Number Ranges for Account Statements
S_KA5_12000289	Number Ranges for Account Postings
S_KA5_12000290	No. Ranges for Partner Relationships
S_KA5_12000291	No. Ranges f. Rel. f. RP Accounts
S_KA5_12000292	No. R. for Internal EDI Transm. No.
S_KA5_12000404	Maintain Account Posting Types
S_KA5_12000405	Posting Types -> Movement Types
S_KA5_12000417	SAPLS_CUS_IMG_ACTIVITY
S_KA5_12000467	IMG-Activity: SIMG_CFMENULEOJIT14
S_KA5_12000473	IMG activity: AD_CUS_SPCPRTNRINF
S_KA5_12000484	IMG-Activity: SIMG_CFMENULEOJIT24
S_KA5_12000485	SAPLS_CUS_IMG_ACTIVITY
S_KA5_12000510	S_KA5_12000510
S_KA5_12000511	S_KA5_12000511
S_KA5_12000512	S_KA5_12000512
S_KA5_12000513	S_KA5_12000513
S_KA5_12000568	S_KA5_12000568
S_KA5_12000569	S_KA5_12000569
S_KA5_12000588	SAPLS_CUS_IMG_ACTIVITY
S_KA5_12000589	SAPLS_CUS_IMG_ACTIVITY
S_KA5_12000590	SAPLS_CUS_IMG_ACTIVITY
S_KA5_12000637	Customizing
S_KA5_12000639	Customizing

SAP Transaction Codes – Volume Two

S_KA5_12000640	Customizing
S_KA5_12000641	SAPLS_CUS_IMG_ACTIVITY
S_KA5_12000643	Customizing
S_KA5_12000646	S_KA5_12000646
S_KA5_12000684	SAPLS_CUS_IMG_ACTIVITY
S_KA5_12000687	IMG-Aktivität: IP_PROFILES
S_KA5_12000773	IMG Activity: IWB_MPLT
S_KA5_12000774	IMG-Activity: SIMG_BOS_ECP_03
S_KA5_12000775	IMG-Activity: SIMG_BOS_ECP_04
S_KA5_12000792	S_KA5_12000792
S_KA5_12000824	S_KA5_12000824
S_KA5_12000825	Global profile parameter
S_KA5_12000826	Size of Memory Block
S_KA5_12000829	Customizing
S_KA5_12000835	Customizing
S_KA5_12000848	Customizing
S_KA5_12000849	Customizing
S_KA5_12000851	Customizing
S_KA5_12000860	Customizing
S_KA5_12000872	IMG activity: IS-AD_STOCK_CALC_MTB
S_KA5_12000902	S_KA5_12000902
S_KA5_12000903	SAPLS_CUS_IMG_ACTIVITY
S_KA5_12000904	SAPLS_CUS_IMG_ACTIVITY
S_KA5_12000905	SAPLS_CUS_IMG_ACTIVITY
S_KA5_12000906	SAPLS_CUS_IMG_ACTIVITY
S_KA5_12000910	S_KA5_12000910
S_KA5_12000912	BAdI for Classification Data
S_KA5_12000916	Customizing
S_KA5_12000919	IMG Activity: CFMENULEBORFUNK
S_KA5_12000920	IMG Activity: CFMENULEBOROBJE
S_KA5_12000921	IMG Activity: CFMENULEBORSELE
S_KA5_12000922	IMG Activity: CFMENULEBORSPAL
S_KA5_12000923	IMG Activity: CFMENULEBORFILT
S_KA5_12000924	IMG Activity: CFMENULEBORKONF
S_KA5_12000933	IMG activity: DI_0MVTPM
S_KA5_12000934	IMG activity: IS-AD_CMC_ORCO
S_KA5_12000935	IMG activity: IS-AD_CMC_PROF
S_KA5_12000936	IMG activity: IS-AD_CMC_INVG
S_KA5_12000937	IMG activity: IS-AD_CMC_US
S_KA5_12000966	IMG activity: DI_0PCS1
S_KA5_12000967	IMG activity: DI_0PCS2
S_KA5_12000968	IMG activity: DI_0PCS3
S_KA5_12000969	IMG Activity: 0PEG01
S_KA5_12000970	IMG Activity: 0PEG02
S_KA5_12000971	IMG Activity: 0DIS01
S_KA5_12000990	IMG Activity: SIMG_CFMENUOPP3OCPR
S_KA5_12001001	Time horizon to calculate periods ba
S_KA5_12001028	Customizing
S_KA5_12001029	Customizing
S_KA5_12001031	Customizing
S_KA5_12001032	Customizing
S_KA5_12001033	Customizing
S_KA5_12001046	SAPLS_CUS_IMG_ACTIVITY
S_KA5_12001047	SAPLS_CUS_IMG_ACTIVITY

S_KA5_12001067	SAPLS_CUS_IMG_ACTIVITY
S_KA5_12001068	SAPLS_CUS_IMG_ACTIVITY
S_KA5_12001069	SAPLS_CUS_IMG_ACTIVITY
S_KA5_12001084	SAPLS_CUS_IMG_ACTIVITY
S_KA5_12001086	Customizing
S_KA5_12001105	Customizing
S_KA5_12001106	S_KA5_12001106
S_KA5_12001107	S_KA5_12001107
S_KA5_12001127	IMG activity: VADS2KIPUPL_DTEL
S_KA5_12001128	IMG activity: VADS2KIPUPL_GSET
S_KA5_12001129	IMG activity: FILENAME
S_KA5_12001135	Update IP status after creating mast
S_KA5_12001137	IMG Activity: WTY_RECALL_IDTYPE
S_KA5_12001138	IMG Activity: WTY_REFOBJECTS
S_KA5_12001139	IMG Activity: WTY_DOCTYPE
S_KA5_12001140	IMG Activity: CWTY_ADDACCASS
S_KA5_12001141	IMG Activity: CWTY_PATRANS
S_KA5_12001148	IMG Activity: CWTY_VSEXITS
S_KA5_12001149	IMG Activity: CWTY_VALIDATION
S_KA5_12001150	IMG Activity: CWTY_SUBSTITUTION
S_KA5_12001153	IMG activity: ADS2KIPUPL_HDR_API
S_KA5_12001154	IMG activity: ADS2KIPUPL_PART_API
S_KA5_12001155	IMG activity: ADS2KIPUPL_S_PARSER
S_KA5_12001156	IMG activity: ADS2KIPUPL_S_READER
S_KA5_12001157	IMG activity: ADS2KIPUPL_T_PARSER
S_KA5_12001158	IMG activity: ADS2KIPUPL_T_READER
S_KA5_12001159	IMG activity: ADS2KIPUPL_V_PARSER
S_KA5_12001160	IMG activity: ADS2KIPUPL_V_READER
S_KA5_12001161	IMG activity: AD_SPC_IP_MD_TAB
S_KA5_12001164	IMG Activity: S2P_PLNG_SEG_EXTEN
S_KA5_12001165	IMG Activity: S2P_PLNG_ITEM_EXTEN
S_KA5_12001166	IMG Activity: S2P_GROUP_PLNG_ITEMS
S_KA5_12001167	IMG Activity: S2P_PLN_CALC_FACTORY
S_KA5_12001168	IMG Activity: S2P_PROPOSAL_CREATOR
S_KA5_12001169	IMG Activity: S2P_PSEG_CTR_FACTORY
S_KA5_12001170	IMG Activity: MILL_CUT_ADDIN2
S_KA5_12001272	IMG Activity: IE4NCGP
S_KA5_12001399	SAPLS_CUS_IMG_ACTIVITY
S_KA5_12001400	SAPLS_CUS_IMG_ACTIVITY
S_KA5_12001401	SAPLS_CUS_IMG_ACTIVITY
S_KA5_12001402	SAPLS_CUS_IMG_ACTIVITY
S_KA5_12001403	SAPLS_CUS_IMG_ACTIVITY
S_KA5_12001404	SAPLS_CUS_IMG_ACTIVITY
S_KA5_12001405	SAPLS_CUS_IMG_ACTIVITY
S_KA5_12001406	SAPLS_CUS_IMG_ACTIVITY
S_KA5_12001407	SAPLS_CUS_IMG_ACTIVITY
S_KA5_12001408	SAPLS_CUS_IMG_ACTIVITY
S_KA5_12001409	SAPLS_CUS_IMG_ACTIVITY
S_KA5_12001410	SAPLS_CUS_IMG_ACTIVITY
S_KA5_12001417	SAPLS_CUS_IMG_ACTIVITY
S_KBI_67000019	Maintain Change Document Objects
S_KBI_67000020	Maintain Change Objects (Technical)
S_KBI_67000132	...
S_KBI_67000144	...

S_KBI_67000145	...
S_KBI_67000146	...
S_KBI_67000169	Maintenance of Texts for Status
S_KBI_67000208	Test
S_KBI_67000378	IMG Activity: _AM_FS_PR_CD
S_KBI_67000410	IMG Activity: _AM_PR_CORR
S_KER_43000132	InfoSet Query
S_KFM_59000003	Test
S_KFM_59000006	LO NPVs of Current BNLs
S_KFM_86000002	SAPLS_CUS_IMG_ACTIVITY
S_KFM_86000003	SAPLS_CUS_IMG_ACTIVITY
S_KFM_86000021	IMG: Events System/Applic. Status
S_KFM_86000022	IMG: Change Status Profile
S_KFM_86000050	IMG: Change Derivation Procedure
S_KFM_86000054	Pos.Class. for Ext.Sec.Act Statement
S_KFM_86000055	Name for Ext. Sec. Acct Statements
S_KFM_86000056	Define Status for Ext. SA Statement
S_KFM_86000057	IMG Activity: MUSTER_VOREINST
S_KFM_86000058	IMG Activity: RUECKZ_ALLG_STEUER
S_KFM_86000059	IMG Activity: RUECKZ_BEWEG_FELD
S_KFM_86000060	IMG-Activity: RUECKZ_KONDIS_FEST
S_KFM_86000061	IMG Activity: RUECKZ_GRUENDE_DEF
S_KFM_86000062	IMG Activity: RUECKZ_ABLEHN_DEF
S_KFM_86000063	IMG: Change Price Index
S_KFM_86000076	IMG Activity: VORSCHL_BELPOSTEXT
S_KFM_86000099	SAPLS_CUS_IMG_ACTIVITY
S_KFM_86000100	Define Date Rule
S_KFM_86000101	Define Rounding Rule
S_KFM_86000102	Update Types for Rights
S_KFM_86000103	Define Consumption Sequence
S_KFM_86000111	Define Update Type for Sec.Act.Mgmt
S_KFM_86000112	Assign Update Type for Accrued Int.
S_KFM_86000113	Update Type for Nominal Adjustment
S_KFM_86000114	Update Type for Sec. Acct Transfer
S_KFM_86000115	IMG View: TRF Update Types
S_KFM_86000116	IMG: Assign Update Type to Flow Cat.
S_KFM_86000117	Assign Update Types for Hedge Acc.
S_KFM_86000119	View: Activate Free Characteristics
S_KFM_86000120	View: Global+Sngl.Pos.Rel.Collataral
S_KFM_86000125	View: The Display Filter and Texts
S_KFM_86000126	View: Define Limit Types
S_KFM_86000130	View: Maintain Notes for Reservation
S_KFM_86000133	IMG: Price Index Main Entity
S_KFM_86000134	IMG: Change Price Index Values
S_KFM_86000135	IMG: Business Address Services
S_KFM_86000136	IMG: Address Screen Variants
S_KFM_86000137	IMG: View for Titles
S_KFM_86000138	IMG: Academic Titles
S_KFM_86000139	IMG: Name Prefixes
S_KFM_86000140	IMG: Name Supplements
S_KFM_86000141	IMG: Name Formats
S_KFM_86000142	IMG: International Address Versions
S_KFM_86000143	IMG: Subtype for Pager Services
S_KFM_86000144	IMG: Address Mgmt Transport Zones

S_KFM_86000145	IMG: Logical Search Pools
S_KFM_86000146	IMG: Postal Codes
S_KFM_86000147	IMG: Create Postal Code
S_KFM_86000148	IMG: Change Postal Code
S_KFM_86000149	IMG: Display Postal Code
S_KFM_86000150	IMG: Postal Cities (Reg. Structure)
S_KFM_86000151	IMG: Create City: Initial Screen
S_KFM_86000152	IMG: Change City: Initial Screen
S_KFM_86000153	IMG: Display City: Initial Screen
S_KFM_86000154	IMG: Postal Streets (Reg. Structure)
S_KFM_86000155	IMG: Change Street Type
S_KFM_86000156	IMG: Create Street: Initial Screen
S_KFM_86000157	IMG: Change Street: Initial Screen
S_KFM_86000158	IMG: Display Street: Initial Screen
S_KFM_86000159	IMG: Grouping for Regional Structure
S_KFM_86000160	IMG: Initial Table for Mirror Deals
S_KFM_86000161	Update Types for Corporate Action
S_KFM_86000162	IMG: Mapping Product/Mirror Trans.
S_KFM_86000163	IMG: Inbound Function Mirror Trans.
S_KFM_86000165	Display Limits for Limit Type:
S_KFM_86000166	Overview of Limit Utilizations
S_KFM_86000167	Maintain ALM Valuation Type
S_KFM_86000176	IMG: Flow Types for Hedge Acc.FX Fwd
S_KFM_86000177	IMG: Flow Types for Hedge Acc.Deriv.
S_KFM_86000178	IMG: Flow Types for Effectiven.Meas.
S_KFM_86000179	IMG: Change Retr.Effectiv.Meas.Types
S_KFM_86000180	IMG: Adjust Hedge Strategy
S_KFM_86000182	SAPLS_CUS_IMG_ACTIVITY
S_KFM_86000184	BAdI Builder
S_KFM_86000185	BAdI Builder: Create Implementation
S_KFM_86000197	IMG: Update Type Acc.Ass.Ref.Transf.
S_KFM_86000199	IMG: Swift Code/BP Assignment
S_KFM_86000200	Maintain Standard Task
S_KFM_86000203	SAPLS_CUS_IMG_ACTIVITY
S_KFM_86000211	Determine Rate Cat. - Currency Swap
S_KFM_86000212	Bal. Sheet Accts for Currency Swap
S_KFM_86000214	SAPLS_CUS_IMG_ACTIVITY
S_KFM_86000215	View Cluster: Update Types f. SA Mgt
S_KFM_86000217	Dispatcher per Account Number
S_KFM_86000218	IMG: Settings for Hedge Management
S_KFM_86000226	IMG: View Update Type / Flow Type
S_KFM_86000251	*
S_KFM_86000254	*
S_KFM_86000255	*
S_KFM_86000256	*
S_KFM_86000259	Maint.View: Limit-Rel. Analysis Char
S_KFM_86000260	View Maint.: Limit Transfer Notes
S_KFM_86000261	IMG Activity
S_KFM_86000262	IMG Activity
S_KFM_86000263	IMG Activity
S_KFM_86000267	Activate Bank Area as IHC Center
S_KFM_86000268	Initial Screen for Processing Char.
S_KFM_86000269	Maintain Analysis Structure
S_KFM_86000270	Choose Characteristics

S_KFM_86000271	Valuation Rules for Risk Management
S_KFM_86000272	Edit Characteristic Values
S_KFM_86000273	Derivation Strategy of Analys.Struct
S_KFM_86000274	Derivation Strategy of Analys.Struct
S_KFM_86000275	IMG
S_KFM_86000276	IMG
S_KFM_86000277	Reorganize Analysis Characteristics
S_KFM_86000278	Delete Limit Utilizations
S_KFM_86000279	Delete Data for Limit Types
S_KFM_86000280	Reorg. Logs of Single Trans. Form
S_KFM_86000281	Reorganize Reservations
S_KFM_86000286	List and Check Routing Instructions
S_KFM_86000287	.
S_KFM_86000288	.
S_KFM_86000295	Auth. Group - Obj. Assignment in IMG
S_KFM_86000297	IMG Activity: BP_ENTWICKLKL
S_KFM_86000298	IMG Activity: BP_DOMAENEN
S_KFM_86000299	IMG Activity: BP_DATENELEMENTE
S_KFM_86000300	IMG Activity: BP_TABELLEN
S_KFM_86000301	IMG Activity: BP_TABELLENUM
S_KFM_86000306	Delete memo items (payment orders an
S_KFM_86000307	Delete memo items (payment orders an
S_KFM_86000308	Report: Output of application log me
S_KFM_86000309	Memo item
S_KI4_29000004	IMG Activity: SIMG_OHPIQ_3400
S_KI4_29000008	IMG Activity: SIMG_OHPIQ_3330
S_KI4_29000009	IMG Activity: SIMG_OHPIQ_3110
S_KI4_29000010	IMG Activity: SIMG_OHPIQ_3111
S_KI4_29000011	IMG Activity: SIMG_OHPIQ_3112
S_KI4_29000012	IMG Activity: SIMG_OHPIQ_3115
S_KI4_29000013	IMG Activity: SIMG_OHPIQ_0510
S_KI4_29000025	IMG Activity: SIMG_OHPIQ_6024
S_KI4_29000026	IMG Activity: SIMG_OHPIQ_6023
S_KI4_29000027	IMG Activity: SIMG_OHPIQ_6025
S_KI4_29000028	IMG Activity: SIMG_OHPIQ_6028
S_KI4_29000029	IMG Activity: SIMG_OHPIQ_6110
S_KI4_29000030	IMG Activity: SIMG_OHPIQ_6120
S_KI4_29000031	IMG Activity: SIMG_OHPIQ_6022
S_KI4_29000032	IMG Activity: SIMG_OHPIQ_6300
S_KI4_29000033	IMG Activity: SIMG_OHPIQ_3370
S_KI4_29000034	IMG Activity: SIMG_OHPIQ_3340
S_KI4_29000035	IMG Activity: SIMG_OHPIQ_3350
S_KI4_29000036	IMG Activity: SIMG_OHPIQ_3310
S_KI4_29000037	IMG Activity: SIMG_OHPIQ_3320
S_KI4_29000038	IMG Activity: SIMG_OHPIQ_32512
S_KI4_29000039	IMG Activity: SIMG_OHPIQ_32511
S_KI4_29000040	IMG Activity: SIMG_OHPIQ_0640
S_KI4_29000042	IMG Activity: SIMG_OHPIQ_0638
S_KI4_29000043	IMG Activity: SIMG_OHPIQ_2120
S_KI4_29000045	IMG Activity: SIMG_OHPIQ_0635
S_KI4_29000046	IMG-Aktivität: OHPSUS1042S008
S_KI4_29000047	IMG-Aktivität: OHPSUS1042S007
S_KI4_29000048	IMG-Aktivität: OHPSUS1042S005
S_KI4_29000049	IMG-Aktivität: OHPSUS1042S004

S_KI4_29000050	IMG-Aktivität: OHPSUS1042S003
S_KI4_29000051	IMG-Aktivität: OHPSUS1042S014
S_KI4_29000052	IMG-Aktivität: OHPSUS1042S013
S_KI4_29000053	IMG-Aktivität: OHPSUS1042S010
S_KI4_29000054	IMG-Aktivität: OHPSUS1042S011
S_KI4_29000055	IMG-Aktivität: OHPSUS1042S012
S_KI4_29000056	IMG-Aktivität: OHPSUS1042S002
S_KI4_29000057	IMG-Aktivität: OHPSUSEEO002
S_KI4_29000058	IMG-Aktivität: OHPSUSEEO003
S_KI4_29000059	IMG-Aktivität: OHPSUSEEO004
S_KI4_29000060	IMG-Aktivität: OHPSUSEEO005
S_KI4_29000061	IMG-Aktivität: OHPSUSEEO006
S_KI4_29000063	IMG-Aktivität: OHIGBPBS0302060401
S_KI4_29000064	IMG-Aktivität: OHIGBPBS0302060402
S_KI4_29000065	IMG-Aktivität: OHIGBPBS0302060501
S_KI4_29000066	IMG-Aktivität: OHIGBPBS0302060601
S_KI4_29000067	IMG-Aktivität: OHIGBPBS0302060701
S_KI4_29000068	IMG-Aktivität: OHIGBPBS0302060702
S_KI4_29000069	IMG-Aktivität: OHIGBPBS0302060304
S_KI4_29000070	IMG-Aktivität: OHIGBPBS0302060201
S_KI4_29000071	IMG-Aktivität: OHIGBPBS0302060202
S_KI4_29000072	IMG-Aktivität: OHIGBPBS0302060203
S_KI4_29000073	IMG-Aktivität: OHIGBPBS0302060301
S_KI4_29000074	IMG-Aktivität: OHIGBPBS0302060302
S_KI4_29000075	IMG-Aktivität: OHIGBPBS0302060303
S_KI4_29000076	IMG-Aktivität: OHIGBPBS0302060703
S_KI4_29000077	IMG-Aktivität: OHIGBPBS020201
S_KI4_29000078	IMG-Aktivität: OHIGBPBS020202
S_KI4_29000079	IMG-Aktivität: OHIGBPBS020203
S_KI4_29000080	IMG-Aktivität: OHIGBPBS0103
S_KI4_29000081	IMG-Aktivität: IHOGBPBS0101
S_KI4_29000082	IMG-Aktivität: IHOGBPBS0102
S_KI4_29000083	IMG-Aktivität: OHIGBPBS020101
S_KI4_29000084	IMG-Aktivität: OHIGBPBS0302060704
S_KI4_29000085	IMG-Aktivität: OHIGBPBS0302060801
S_KI4_29000086	IMG-Aktivität: OHIGBPBS0302060802
S_KI4_29000087	IMG-Aktivität: OHIGBPBS03020609
S_KI4_29000088	IMG-Aktivität: OHIGBPBS030301
S_KI4_29000089	IMG-Aktivität: OHIGBPBS030302
S_KI4_29000090	IMG-Aktivität: OHIGBPBS03020201
S_KI4_29000091	IMG-Aktivität: OHIGBPBS03020202
S_KI4_29000092	IMG-Aktivität: OHIGBPBS03020203
S_KI4_29000093	IMG-Aktivität: OHIGBPBS03020301
S_KI4_29000094	IMG-Aktivität: OHIGBPBS03020302
S_KI4_29000095	IMG-Aktivität: OHIGBPBS03020102
S_KI4_29000096	IMG-Aktivität: OHIGBPBS030101
S_KI4_29000097	IMG-Aktivität: OHIGBPBS030102
S_KI4_29000098	IMG-Aktivität: OHIGBPBS030103
S_KI4_29000099	IMG-Aktivität: OHIGBPBS030104
S_KI4_29000100	IMG-Aktivität: OHIGBPBS03020101
S_KI4_29000101	IMG-Aktivität: OHIGBPBS03020501
S_KI4_29000102	IMG-Aktivität: OHIGBPBS03020401
S_KI4_29000103	IMG-Aktivität: OHIGBPBS0302060101
S_KI4_29000104	IMG-Aktivität: OHIGBPBS03020303

S_KI4_29000105	IMG Activity : OHIFRPBS049
S_KI4_29000106	IMG Activity : OHIFRPBS045
S_KI4_29000107	IMG Activity : OHIFRPBS046
S_KI4_29000108	IMG Activity : OHIFRPBS051
S_KI4_29000109	IMG Activity : OHIFRPBS052
S_KI4_29000110	IMG Activity : OHIFRPBS053
S_KI4_29000111	IMG Activity : OHIFRPBS054
S_KI4_29000112	IMG Activity: OHIFRPBS043
S_KI4_29000113	IMG Activity: OHIFRPBS04D
S_KI4_29000114	IMG Activity: OHIFRPBS04E
S_KI4_29000115	IMG Activity: OHIFRPBS048
S_KI4_29000116	IMG Activity: OHIFRPBS04B
S_KI4_29000117	IMG Activity: OHIFRPBS04F
S_KI4_29000118	IMG Activity: OHIFRPBS044
S_KI4_29000119	IMG Activity: OHAFRPBS512
S_KI4_29000120	IMG Activity: OHAFRPBS520
S_KI4_29000121	IMG Activity: OHAFRPBS531
S_KI4_29000122	IMG Activity: OHAFRPBS532
S_KI4_29000123	IMG Activity: OHAFRPBS540
S_KI4_29000124	IMG Activity: OHAFRPBS551
S_KI4_29000125	IMG Activity: OHAFRPBS552
S_KI4_29000126	IMG Activity: OHIFRPBS055
S_KI4_29000127	IMG Activity: OHIFRPBS061
S_KI4_29000128	IMG Activity: OHIFRPBS072
S_KI4_29000129	IMG Activity: OHIFRPBS073
S_KI4_29000130	IMG Activity: OHIFRPBS071
S_KI4_29000131	IMG Activity: OHAFRPBS501
S_KI4_29000132	IMG Activity: OHAFRPBS511
S_KI4_29000133	IMG Activity: OHIFRPBS047
S_KI4_29000134	IMG Activity: OHIFRPBS021
S_KI4_29000135	IMG Activity: OHIFRPBS022
S_KI4_29000136	IMG Activity: OHIFRPBS023
S_KI4_29000137	IMG Activity: OHIFRPBS002
S_KI4_29000138	IMG Activity: OHIFRPBS004
S_KI4_29000139	IMG Activity: OHIFRPBS003
S_KI4_29000140	IMG Activity: OHIFRPBS013
S_KI4_29000141	IMG Activity: OHIFRPBS014
S_KI4_29000142	IMG Activity: OHIFRPBS018
S_KI4_29000143	IMG Activity: OHIFRPBS019
S_KI4_29000144	IMG Activity: OHIFRPBS012
S_KI4_29000145	IMG Activity: OHIFRPBS011
S_KI4_29000146	IMG Activity: OHIFRPBS031
S_KI4_29000147	IMG Activity: OHIFRPBS04A
S_KI4_29000148	IMG Activity: OHIFRPBS036
S_KI4_29000149	IMG Activity: OHIFRPBS041
S_KI4_29000150	IMG Activity: OHIFRPBS042
S_KI4_29000151	IMG Activity: OHIFRPBS035
S_KI4_29000152	IMG Activity: OHIFRPBS034
S_KI4_29000153	IMG Activity: OHIFRPBS032
S_KI4_29000154	IMG Activity: OHIFRPBS033
S_KI4_29000155	IMG Activity: OHIFRPBS001
S_KI4_29000156	IMG Activity: OHAFRPBS560
S_KI4_29000157	IMG Activity: OHIFRPBS04C
S_KI4_29000158	IMG Activity: OHIFRPBS062

S_KI4_29000159	IMG activity: PBS_AU_LAP_SI_040
S_KI4_29000160	IMG activity: PBS_AU_LAP_SI_030
S_KI4_29000161	IMG activity: PBS_AU_LAP_SI_020
S_KI4_29000162	IMG activity: PBS_AU_LAP_SI_010
S_KI4_29000163	IMG activity: PBS_AU_LAP_SI_001
S_KI4_29000164	IMG activity: PBS_AU_PAY_HD_001
S_KI4_29000165	IMG activity: PBS_AU_LAP_PO_030
S_KI4_29000166	IMG activity: PBS_AU_LAP_PO_020
S_KI4_29000167	IMG activity: PBS_AU_LAP_PO_010
S_KI4_29000168	IMG activity: PBS_AU_LAP_PO_001
S_KI4_29000169	IMG activity: PBS_AU_LAP_WT_001
S_KI4_29000170	IMG activity: PBS_AU_LAP_001
S_KI4_29000171	IMG activity: PBS_AU_ADV_040
S_KI4_29000172	IMG activity: PBS_AU_ADV_030
S_KI4_29000173	IMG activity: PBS_AU_ADV_020
S_KI4_29000174	IMG activity: PBS_AU_LAP_WT_050
S_KI4_29000175	IMG activity: PBS_AU_LAP_WT_040
S_KI4_29000176	IMG activity: PBS_AU_LAP_WT_030
S_KI4_29000177	IMG activity: PBS_AU_LAP_WT_020
S_KI4_29000178	IMG activity: PBS_AU_LAP_WT_010
S_KI4_29000179	IMG activity: PBS_AU_TIM_AC_010
S_KI4_29000180	IMG activity: PBS_AU_TIM_AC_001
S_KI4_29000181	IMG activity: PBS_AU_TIM_LA_040
S_KI4_29000182	IMG activity: PBS_AU_TIM_LA_030
S_KI4_29000183	IMG activity: PBS_AU_TIM_LA_020
S_KI4_29000184	IMG activity: PBS_AU_TIM_AC_060
S_KI4_29000185	IMG activity: PBS_AU_TIM_AC_050
S_KI4_29000186	IMG activity: PBS_AU_TIM_AC_040
S_KI4_29000187	IMG activity: PBS_AU_TIM_AC_030
S_KI4_29000188	IMG activity: PBS_AU_TIM_AC_020
S_KI4_29000189	IMG activity: PBS_AU_PAY_SA_020
S_KI4_29000190	IMG activity: PBS_AU_PAY_SA_010
S_KI4_29000191	IMG activity: PBS_AU_PAY_SA_001
S_KI4_29000192	IMG activity: PBS_AU_PAY_HD_020
S_KI4_29000193	IMG activity: PBS_AU_PAY_HD_010
S_KI4_29000194	IMG activity: PBS_AU_TIM_LA_010
S_KI4_29000195	IMG activity: PBS_AU_TIM_LA_001
S_KI4_29000196	IMG activity: PBS_AU_TIM_PS_001
S_KI4_29000197	IMG activity: PBS_AU_PAY_SA_040
S_KI4_29000198	IMG activity: PBS_AU_PAY_SA_030
S_KI4_29000199	IMG activity: PBS_AU_TER_BS_030
S_KI4_29000200	IMG activity: PBS_AU_TER_BS_040
S_KI4_29000201	IMG activity: PBS_AU_PAD_SA_010
S_KI4_29000202	IMG activity: PBS_AU_INC_010
S_KI4_29000203	IMG activity: PBS_AU_TER_001
S_KI4_29000204	IMG activity: PBS_AU_TER_010
S_KI4_29000205	IMG activity: PBS_AU_BS_001
S_KI4_29000206	IMG activity: PBS_AU_PAD_HD_020
S_KI4_29000207	IMG activity: PBS_AU_TER_BS_001
S_KI4_29000208	IMG activity: PBS_AU_PAD_HD_010
S_KI4_29000209	IMG activity: PBS_AU_PAD_HD_001
S_KI4_29000210	IMG activity: PBS_AU_TER_BS_010
S_KI4_29000211	IMG activity: PBS_AU_TER_BS_020
S_KI4_29000212	IMG activity: PBS_AU_PAD_SA_001

S_KI4_29000213	IMG activity: PBS_AU_TER_TP_001
S_KI4_29000214	IMG activity: PBS_AU_TER_LP_020
S_KI4_29000215	IMG activity: PBS_AU_PAD_SA_040
S_KI4_29000216	IMG activity: PBS_AU_TER_LP_030
S_KI4_29000217	IMG activity: PBS_AU_PAD_SA_030
S_KI4_29000218	IMG activity: PBS_AU_ADV_001
S_KI4_29000219	IMG activity: PBS_AU_ADV_010
S_KI4_29000220	IMG activity: PBS_AU_TER_LP_010
S_KI4_29000221	IMG activity: PBS_AU_INC_001
S_KI4_29000222	IMG activity: PBS_AU_TER_TP_020
S_KI4_29000223	IMG activity: PBS_AU_TER_TP_010
S_KI4_29000224	IMG activity: PBS_AU_TER_TP_030
S_KI4_29000225	IMG activity: PBS_AU_PAD_SA_020
S_KI4_29000226	IMG activity: PBS_AU_TER_LP_001
S_KI4_38000034	Index of Commitment Items
S_KI4_38000035	Account Determination for Requests
S_KI4_38000036	Assign Commitment Items to G/L Acct
S_KI4_38000038	Index of Funds Centers
S_KI4_38000039	Index of Funds
S_KI4_38000040	Index of Applications of Funds
S_KI4_38000041	FM Acct Assignments with Budget Memo
S_KI4_38000046	Assgd Funds (Overall Bdgt, Cmmt Bgt)
S_KI4_38000047	Assgd Funds (Annual Bdgt, Cmmt Bdgt)
S_KI4_38000048	Assgd Funds (Annual Bdgt, Cmmt Bdgt)
S_KI4_38000049	Assgd Funds (Overall Bgt, Rels, CB)
S_KI4_38000050	Assgd Funds (Annual Bdgt, Rels, CB)
S_KI4_38000054	Revenues Increasing the Budget
S_KI4_38000055	Collective Expenditures
S_KI4_38000056	Budget: Entry Documents
S_KI4_38000058	Document Lists of Requests
S_KI4_38000059	Budget Consistency Check
S_KI4_38000061	Worklist FMRC07 for Payment Matching
S_KI4_38000104	IMG Activity: _EURO_FMAREA_ACTIVE
S_KI4_38000105	IMG Activity: _EURO_KO_BUDVER_IMPO
S_KI4_38000106	IMG Activity: _EURO_KO_BUDVER_EXP0
S_KI4_38000107	IMG Activity: _EURO_ADMINREC_SHOW
S_KI4_38000108	IMG Activity: _EURO_MASTERDAT_COPY
S_KI4_38000109	IMG Activity: _EURO_FMAREA_CREATE
S_KI4_38000110	IMG Activity: SIMG_CFMENUOFTCOFD7
S_KI4_38000117	IMG Activity: _EURO_BUDVERS_IMPORT
S_KI4_38000118	IMG Activity: _EURO_BUDVERS_EXPORT
S_KI4_38000120	Reconciliation of Parked Docs FM
S_KI4_38000121	Maintain Tolerance for Bdgt Cnsstcy
S_KI4_38000122	Maintain Tolerance for Bdgt Cnsstcy
S_KI4_38000316	IMG activity: _ISPSFM_OFMFG_PO
S_KI4_38000317	IMG activity: _ISPSFM_V_T042F_FMFG
S_KI4_38000318	IMG Activity: _ISPSFM_N_V_FMBUDCAT
S_KI4_38000319	IMG Activity: SIMG_ISPSFM_F8P6
S_KI4_38000320	IMG Activity: _ISPSFM_N_FMLINR
S_KI4_38000328	IMG Activity: _ISPSFM_N_VERSION_A
S_KI4_38000333	IMG-Aktivität: _ISPSFM_V_FMFGT_ALC
S_KI4_38000335	IMG Activity: _ISPSFM_N_FMEDNR
S_KI4_38000336	IMG-Aktivität: _ISPSFM_FMUSFG1
S_KI4_38000339	IMG Activity: _ISPSFM_N_V_FMPTCOMB

S_KI4_38000341	IMG Activity: CMMENUORFA_MITKO2
S_KI4_38000346	IMG activity: _ISPSFM_V_FMBPCL_FUN
S_KI4_38000347	IMG activity: _ISPSFM_V_FMBPCL_FTY
S_KI4_38000350	IMG Activity: SIMG_ISPSFM_F8P5
S_KI4_38000352	IMG Activity: CMMENUORFA_MITKO3
S_KI4_38000353	IMG Activity: _ISPSFM_V_FMFGT_DIT
S_KI4_38000356	Program GMCOACTIVATE
S_KI4_55000001	IMG Activity: _ISPSDE_FMZT
S_KI4_55000002	IMG Activity: _ISPSDE_VERDSCHL
S_KI4_55000003	IMG Activity: _ISPSDE_FMTA
S_KI4_55000004	IMG Activity: _ISPSDE_F8R1
S_KI4_55000005	IMG Activity: _ISPSDE_F8R2
S_KI4_55000006	IMG Activity: _ISPSDE_MNTF
S_KI4_55000007	IMG Activity: _ISPSDE_MNTB
S_KI4_55000008	IMG Activity: _ISPSDE_V_FMBGACT
S_KI4_55000009	IMG Activity: _ISPSFM_FM+3
S_KI4_55000010	IMG Activity: _ISPSDE_FMBGAGLOB
S_KI4_55000011	IMG Activity: _ISPSDE_V_FMBGADEF
S_KI4_55000012	IMG Activity: _ISPSDE_V_FMBGAHHST
S_KI4_55000013	IMG Activity: _ISPSDE_V_FMBGAKONT
S_KI4_55000015	IMG Activity: _ISPSDE_FMNO
S_KI4_55000016	IMG Activity: _ISPSDE_V_FMPY
S_KI4_55000017	IMG Activity: _ISPSDE_V_FMAC
S_KI4_55000018	IMG Activity: _ISPSDE_REWR
S_KI4_55000019	IMG Activity: _ISPSFM_OF37
S_KI4_55000020	IMG Activity: _ISPSFM_OF36
S_KI4_55000021	IMG Activity: _ISPSFM_OFUP
S_KI4_55000022	IMG Activity: _ISPSDE_F839
S_KI4_55000023	IMG Activity: _ISPSDE_F843
S_KI4_55000024	IMG Activity: _ISPSDE_F855
S_KI4_55000025	IMG Activity: _ISPSDE_F850
S_KI4_55000026	IMG Activity: _ISPSDE_V_PSO51
S_KI4_55000027	IMG Activity: _ISPSDE_F858
S_KI4_55000028	IMG Activity: _ISPSDE_F859
S_KI4_55000030	IMG Activity: _ISPSDE_F860
S_KI4_55000031	IMG Activity: _ISPSDE_F865
S_KI4_55000032	IMG Activity: _ISPSDE_F838
S_KI4_55000033	IMG Activity: _ISPSDE_F823
S_KI4_55000034	IMG Activity: _ISPSDE_OB61
S_KI4_55000035	IMG Activity: _ISPSDE_F861
S_KI4_55000036	IMG Activity: _ISPSDE_F862
S_KI4_55000037	IMG Activity: _ISPSDE_F869
S_KI4_55000038	IMG Activity: _ISPSDE_F822
S_KI4_55000039	IMG Activity: _ISPSDE_F8O3
S_KI4_55000040	IMG Activity: _ISPSFM_F8O8
S_KI4_55000041	IMG Activity: _ISPSFM_F8O9
S_KI4_55000042	IMG Activity: _ISPSDE_F868
S_KI4_55000043	IMG Activity: _ISPSDE_F8O4
S_KI4_55000044	IMG Activity: _ISPSDE_F821
S_KI4_55000045	IMG Activity: _ISPSDE_F8O5
S_KI4_55000046	IMG Activity: _ISPSDE_V_FMFORMAN
S_KI4_55000047	IMG Activity: _ISPSFM_V_C_PSOFST
S_KI4_55000048	IMG Activity: _ISPSFM_PSOBLAFST
S_KI4_55000049	IMG Activity: _ISPSDE_F867

S_KI4_55000050	IMG Activity: _ISPSDE_FMHQ
S_KI4_55000051	IMG Activity: _ISPSDE_FMFU
S_KI4_55000052	IMG Activity: _ISPSDE_FMKS
S_KI4_55000053	IMG Activity: _ISPSDE_FMKF
S_KI4_55000054	IMG Activity: _ISPSDE_HHSU
S_KI4_55000055	IMG Activity: SIMG_ISPSDEOFRA
S_KI4_55000056	IMG Activity: _ISPSDE_FMGS
S_KI4_55000057	IMG Activity: _ISPSDE_OFR2
S_KI4_55000058	IMG Activity: _ISPSFM_OFCV
S_KI4_55000059	IMG Activity: _ISPSDE_OFEW
S_KI4_55000060	IMG Activity: _ISPSDE_FMK3
S_KI4_55000061	IMG Activity: _ISPSDE_FMFV
S_KI4_55000062	IMG Activity: _ISPSDE_FMEG
S_KI4_55000063	IMG Activity: _ISPSDE_FMIV
S_KI4_55000064	IMG Activity: _ISPSDE_OFR1
S_KI4_55000065	IMG Activity: _ISPSFM_OF09
S_KI4_55000066	IMG Activity: _ISPSFM_OFY3
S_KI4_55000067	IMG Activity: _ISPSFM_OFKA
S_KI4_55000068	IMG Activity: _ISPSDE_OFCC
S_KI4_55000069	IMG Activity: _ISPSDE_OFUD
S_KI4_55000072	IMG Activity: _ISPSFM_OF16
S_KI4_55000073	IMG Activity: _ISPSDE_FMHV
S_KI4_55000074	IMG Activity: _ISPSFM_OFYA
S_KI4_55000076	IMG Activity: _ISPSFM_OFY1
S_KI4_55000077	IMG Activity: _ISPSFM_FMSX
S_KI4_55000078	IMG Activity: _ISPSFM_OF12
S_KI4_55000079	IMG Activity: _ISPSDE_OFSN
S_KI4_55000080	IMG Activity: _ISPSDE_FM01
S_KI4_55000082	IMG Activity: _ISPSFM_BAFISTLLT
S_KI4_55000083	IMG Activity: _ISPSDE_F8O1
S_KI4_55000084	IMG Activity: _ISPSDE_F8O0
S_KI4_55000085	IMG Activity: _ISPSFM_FMSY
S_KI4_55000086	IMG Activity: _ISPSFM_AKTVERF
S_KI4_55000087	IMG Activity: _ISPSDE_BVERSAKT
S_KI4_55000089	IMG Activity: _ISPSFM_FM9X
S_KI4_55000090	IMG Activity: _ISPSFM_V_FM01_M
S_KI4_55000091	IMG Activity: _ISPSDE_V_FMFRG
S_KI4_55000092	IMG Activity: _ISPSFM_FMSG
S_KI4_55000093	IMG Activity: _ISPSFM_OK10
S_KI4_55000094	IMG Activity: _ISPSFM_FMSF
S_KI4_55000095	IMG Activity: _ISPSFM_OFES
S_KI4_55000096	IMG Activity: _ISPSDE_FMK2
S_KI4_55000097	IMG Activity: _ISPSDE_FMK4
S_KI4_55000098	IMG Activity: _ISPSDE_FMGL
S_KI4_55000099	IMG Activity: _ISPSDE_FMGR
S_KI4_55000100	IMG Activity: _ISPSDE_FM30
S_KI4_55000101	IMG Activity: _ISPSFM_FMGX
S_KI4_55000102	IMG Activity: _ISPSFM_FMGY
S_KI4_55000103	IMG Activity: _ISPSFM_BAFIPOSLT
S_KI4_55000104	IMG Activity: _ISPSDE_OFM_HSART
S_KI4_55000105	IMG Activity: _ISPSFM_OFED
S_KI4_55000106	IMG Activity: _ISPSFM_BAFONDSLT
S_KI4_55000107	IMG Activity: _ISPSFM_STATUS_DELET
S_KI4_55000109	IMG Activity: _ISPSFM_OFDE

S_KI4_55000110	IMG Activity: _ISPSFM_OFDF
S_KI4_55000111	IMG Activity: _ISPSFM_OFDG
S_KI4_55000112	IMG Activity: _ISPSFM_OFD5
S_KI4_55000116	IMG Activity: _ISPSFM_FMREW
S_KI4_55000117	IMG Activity: _ISPSFM_OFDM2
S_KI4_55000118	IMG Activity: _ISPSFM_MV_SM30
S_KI4_55000119	IMG Activity: _ISPSFM_FMUV
S_KI4_55000120	IMG Activity: _ISPSDE_FMDV
S_KI4_55000121	IMG Activity: _ISPSDE_FMDW
S_KI4_55000122	IMG Activity: _ISPSFM_OFMR3
S_KI4_55000123	IMG Activity: _ISPSDE_FMDX
S_KI4_55000124	IMG Activity: _ISPSDE_FMDY
S_KI4_55000125	IMG Activity: _ISPSFM_OFMR5
S_KI4_55000126	IMG Activity: _ISPSFM_OFMR6
S_KI4_55000127	IMG Activity: _ISPSFM_OK60
S_KI4_55000128	IMG Activity: _ISPSFM_FMU1
S_KI4_55000129	IMG Activity: _ISPSDE_FMDZ
S_KI4_55000130	IMG Activity: _ISPSFM_OFDM1
S_KI4_55000131	IMG Activity: _ISPSFM_OF27
S_KI4_55000132	IMG Activity: _ISPSDE_F853
S_KI4_55000133	IMG Activity: _ISPSDE_F854
S_KI4_55000134	IMG Activity: _ISPSFM_OF20
S_KI4_55000135	IMG Activity: _ISPSDE_F851
S_KI4_55000136	IMG Activity: _ISPSDE_F852
S_KI4_55000137	IMG Activity: _ISPSFM_OFM_ACT_MD_Y
S_KI4_55000138	IMG Activity: _ISPSDE_OFM_FM01_KOM
S_KI4_55000139	IMG Activity: _ISPSDE_OFM_ACT_KOMU
S_KI4_55000140	IMG Activity: _ISPSFM_OF38
S_KI4_55000141	IMG Activity: _ISPSDE_F8O2
S_KI4_55000142	IMG Activity: _ISPSFM_OF28
S_KI4_55000143	IMG Activity: _XXISPSFMEIN
S_KI4_55000144	IMG Activity: _ISPSFM_WOROLAN
S_KI4_55000145	IMG Activity: _ISPSFM_WOROLMI
S_KI4_55000146	IMG Activity: _ISPSFM_V_FM01I_CE
S_KI4_55000147	IMG Activity: _ISPSFM_F866
S_KI4_55000148	IMG Activity: _ISPSFM_OFUC
S_KI4_55000149	IMG Activity: _ISPSFM_CEPROFMAINT
S_KI4_55000150	IMG Activity: _ISPSFM_F8O2
S_KI4_55000153	IMG Activity: _ISPSFM_OFUG
S_KI4_55000155	IMG Activity: _ISPSFM_OFUT
S_KI4_55000156	IMG Activity: _ISPSFM_OFUD
S_KI4_55000157	IMG Activity: _ISPSFM_OF39
S_KI4_55000158	IMG Activity: _ISPSFM_OFK1
S_KI4_55000159	IMG Activity: _ISPSFM_OFK4
S_KI4_55000160	IMG Activity: _ISPSFM_BSP_FM9Y
S_KI4_55000161	IMG Activity: _ISPSFM_OFM_ACT_ISPS
S_KI4_55000162	IMG Activity: _ISPSFM_OFMR0
S_KI4_55000163	IMG Activity: _ISPSFM_F8P3
S_KI4_55000164	IMG Activity: _ISPSFM_WOROLBU
S_KI4_55000300	Form 1042S Printing
S_KI4_55000301	Substantial Presence Test
S_KI4_55000302	EEO (Equal Employment Opportunity) R
S_KI4_55000303	Substantial Presence Test
S_KI4_55000304	EEO (Equal Employment Opportunity) R

S_KI4_55000305	Selection of Promotable Agents
S_KI4_55000307	Grade Promotion: Nomination to
S_KI4_55000312	Download Data Medium to Disk
S_KI4_55000313	HESA Reporting (Interface to ALV)
S_KI4_55000314	USS Contributions (Interface to ALV)
S_KI4_55000315	USS Salary Changes (Interface to ALV
S_KI4_55000550	CUS_IMG_ACTIVITY
S_KI4_55000551	CUS_IMG_ACTIVITY
S_KI4_55000552	Wage Type Assignment - Enhancd Leave
S_KI4_55000610	IMG activity: OHPSUSSICK22
S_KI4_55000614	IMG activity: PBS_AU_TIM_LA_060
S_KI4_55000615	IMG activity: OHPSUSNOA004
S_KJ4_38000001	IMG activity: PBS_00_1_1_101
S_KJ4_38000002	IMG activity: PBS_00_1_1_102
S_KJ4_38000003	IMG activity: HR_PBS_00_PW_1_1
S_KJ4_38000004	IMG activity: HR_PBS_00_01_1_1
S_KJ4_38000005	IMG activity: HR_PBS_00_02_1_1
S_KJ4_38000006	IMG activity: HR_PBS_00_PW_2_2
S_KJ4_38000007	IMG activity: HR_PBS_00_03_1_1
S_KJ4_38000008	IMG activity: HR_PBS_00_04_1_1
S_KJ4_38000009	IMG activity: HR_PBS_00_05_1_1
S_KJ4_38000010	IMG activity: HR_PBS_00_06_2_2
S_KJ4_38000011	IMG activity: HR_PBS_00_07_1_1
S_KJ4_38000012	IMG activity: HR_PBS_00_08_2_2
S_KJ4_38000013	IMG activity: HR_PBS_00_09_1_1
S_KJ4_38000014	IMG activity: HR_PBS_00_10_1_1
S_KJ4_38000015	IMG activity: HR_PBS_00_11_1_1
S_KJ4_38000016	IMG activity: HR_PBS_00_12_2_2
S_KJ4_38000017	IMG activity: HR_PBS_00_13_2_2
S_KJ4_38000018	IMG activity: HR_PBS_00_14_1_1
S_KJ4_38000019	IMG activity: HR_PBS_00_15_1_1
S_KJ4_38000020	IMG activity: HR_PBS_00_17_1_1
S_KJ4_38000021	IMG activity: HR_PBS_00_18_1_1
S_KJ4_38000022	IMG activity: HR_PBS_00_20_1_1
S_KJ4_38000023	IMG activity: HR_PBS_00_21_1_1
S_KJ4_38000024	IMG activity: HR_PBS_00_22_1_1
S_KJ4_38000025	IMG activity: HR_PBS_00_24_1_1
S_KJ4_38000026	IMG activity: HR_PBS_00_25_1_1
S_KJ4_38000027	IMG activity: HR_PBS_00_16_1_1
S_KJ4_38000028	IMG activity: HR_PBS_00_30_1_1
S_KJ4_38000029	IMG activity: HR_PBS_00_31_1_1
S_KJ4_38000030	IMG activity: HR_PBS_00_99_1_1
S_KJ4_38000031	IMG activity: HR_PBS_00_40_1_1
S_KJ4_38000032	IMG activity: HR_VADM_NO_001_001
S_KJ4_38000033	IMG activity: HR_VADM_NO_001_002
S_KJ4_38000034	IMG activity: HR_VADM_NO_001_003
S_KJ4_38000035	IMG activity: HR_VADM_NO_001_004
S_KJ4_38000036	IMG activity: HR_VADM_NO_002_001
S_KJ4_38000037	IMG activity: HR_VADM_NO_002_002
S_KJ4_38000038	IMG activity: HR_VADM_NO_003_001
S_KJ4_38000039	IMG activity: HR_VADM_NO_003_002
S_KJ4_38000040	IMG activity: HR_VADM_NO_003_003
S_KJ4_38000041	IMG activity: HR_VADM_NO_003_004
S_KJ4_38000042	IMG activity: HR_VADM_NO_001_005

S_KJ4_38000043	IMG activity: HR_VADM_NO_001_006
S_KJ4_38000045	IMG Activity: HR_PBS_00_WB_RP1
S_KJ4_38000046	IMG Activity: HR_PBS_00_WB_RP2
S_KJ4_38000048	IMG Activity: HR_PBS_00_WB_RP4
S_KJ4_38000049	IMG Activity: HR_PBS_00_WB_RP5
S_KJ4_38000050	IMG Activity: HR_PBS_00_WB_RP6
S_KJ4_38000051	IMG Activity: HR_PBS_00_WB_RP8
S_KJ4_38000052	IMG activity: MDTOOLI_1
S_KJ4_38000053	IMG activity: MDTOOLI_2
S_KJ4_38000054	IMG activity: MDTOOLI_3
S_KJ4_38000055	IMG Activity: HR_PBS_DE_VA
S_KJ4_38000056	IMG Activity: HR_PBS_00_WB_VA1
S_KJ4_38000057	IMG Activity: HR_PBS_00_CA_01
S_KJ4_38000058	IMG Activity: HR_PBS_00_CA_02
S_KJ4_38000059	IMG Activity: HR_PBS_00_CA_03
S_KJ4_38000060	IMG Activity: HR_PBS_00_CA_04
S_KJ4_38000061	IMG Activity: HR_PBS_00_CA_05
S_KJ4_38000063	IMG Activity: HR_PBS_01_VG_EP_01
S_KJ4_38000065	IMG Activity: HR_PBS_01_VG_EP_02
S_KJ4_38000066	IMG Activity: HR_PBS_01_VG_EP_03
S_KJ4_38000067	IMG Activity: HR_PBS_01_VG_EP_04
S_KJ4_38000068	IMG Activity: HR_PBS_00_SCALE_01
S_KJ4_38000069	IMG Activity: HR_PBS_00_SCALE_02
S_KJ4_38000070	IMG Activity: HR_PBS_00_SCALE_03
S_KJ4_38000071	IMG Activity: HR_PBS_00_SEN_525TR
S_KJ4_38000072	IMG Activity: HR_PBS_00_SEN_525TRP
S_KJ4_38000073	IMG Activity: HR_PBS_00_SEN_525NI
S_KJ4_38000074	IMG Activity: HR_PBS_00_SEN_525OL
S_KJ4_38000075	IMG Activity: HR_PBS_01_VG_SEN_01
S_KJ4_38000076	IMG Activity: HR_PBS_01_VG_AG_01
S_KJ4_38000077	IMG Activity: HR_PBS_01_VG_AG_02
S_KJ4_38000078	IMG Activity: HR_PBS_01_VG_AG_03
S_KK4_08000006	IMG Activity:
S_KK4_08000015	IMG Activity:
S_KK4_08000017	IMG Activity:
S_KK4_08000020	IMG Activity:
S_KK4_08000022	IMG Activity:
S_KK4_08000023	IMG Activity:
S_KK4_08000028	IMG Activity:
S_KK4_08000029	IMG Activity:
S_KK4_08000030	IMG Activity:
S_KK4_08000031	IMG Activity:
S_KK4_08000033	IMG Activity:
S_KK4_08000034	IMG Activity:
S_KK4_08000035	IMG Activity:
S_KK4_08000036	IMG Activity:
S_KK4_08000037	IMG Activity:
S_KK4_08000039	IMG Activity:
S_KK4_08000040	IMG Activity:
S_KK4_08000041	IMG Activity:
S_KK4_08000044	IMG Activity:
S_KK4_08000046	IMG Activity:
S_KK4_08000047	IMG Activity:
S_KK4_08000063	IMG Activity:

S_KK4_08000065	IMG Activity:
S_KK4_08000067	IMG Activity:
S_KK4_08000068	IMG Activity:
S_KK4_08000069	IMG Activity:
S_KK4_08000070	IMG Activity:
S_KK4_08000071	IMG Activity:
S_KK4_08000072	IMG Activity:
S_KK4_08000073	IMG Activity:
S_KK4_08000074	IMG Activity:
S_KK4_08000075	IMG Activity:
S_KK4_08000076	IMG Activity:
S_KK4_08000077	IMG Activity:
S_KK4_08000081	IMG Activity:
S_KK4_08000082	IMG Activity:
S_KK4_08000083	IMG Activity:
S_KK4_08000084	IMG Activity:
S_KK4_08000085	IMG Activity:
S_KK4_08000086	IMG Activity:
S_KK4_08000087	IMG Activity:
S_KK4_08000089	IMG Activity:
S_KK4_08000094	S_KK4_08000094
S_KK4_08000096	S_KK4_08000096
S_KK4_08000097	IMG Activity:
S_KK4_08000100	IMG Activity:
S_KK4_08000102	IMG Activity:
S_KK4_08000103	IMG Activity:
S_KK4_08000104	IMG Activity:
S_KK4_08000114	IMG Activity:
S_KK4_08000115	IMG Activity:
S_KK4_08000117	S_KK4_08000117
S_KK4_08000118	S_KK4_08000118
S_KK4_08000119	S_KK4_08000119
S_KK4_08000120	S_KK4_08000120
S_KK4_08000129	IMG Activity:
S_KK4_08000130	IMG Activity:
S_KK4_08000146	IMG Activity:
S_KK4_08000160	IMG Activity:
S_KK4_08000162	IMG Activity:
S_KK4_08000172	IMG Activity:
S_KK4_08000175	IMG Activity:
S_KK4_08000176	IMG Activity:
S_KK4_08000177	IMG Activity:
S_KK4_08000182	IMG Activity:
S_KK4_08000183	IMG Activity:
S_KK4_08000184	IMG Activity:
S_KK4_08000185	IMG Activity:
S_KK4_08000186	IMG Activity:
S_KK4_08000189	IMG Activity:
S_KK4_08000190	IMG Activity:
S_KK4_08000191	IMG Activity:
S_KK4_08000192	IMG Activity:
S_KK4_08000193	IMG Activity:
S_KK4_08000194	Facts Capture Category
S_KK4_08000195	IMG Activity:

S_KK4_08000203	IMG Activity:
S_KK4_08000204	IMG Activity:
S_KK4_08000205	IMG Activity:
S_KK4_08000206	IMG Activity:
S_KK4_08000207	IMG Activity:
S_KK4_08000208	IMG Activity:
S_KK4_08000212	IMG Activity:
S_KK4_08000214	IMG Activity:
S_KK4_08000218	IMG Activity:
S_KK4_08000233	IMG Activity:
S_KK4_08000234	IMG Activity:
S_KK4_08000238	IMG Activity:
S_KK4_08000239	IMG Activity:
S_KK4_08000240	IMG Activity:
S_KK4_08000241	IMG Activity:
S_KK4_08000242	IMG Activity:
S_KK4_08000243	IMG Activity:
S_KK4_08000244	IMG Activity:
S_KK4_08000245	IMG Activity:
S_KK4_08000246	IMG Activity:
S_KK4_08000247	IMG Activity:
S_KK4_08000248	IMG Activity:
S_KK4_08000249	IMG Activity:
S_KK4_08000250	IMG Activity:
S_KK4_08000251	IMG Activity:
S_KK4_08000252	IMG Activity:
S_KK4_08000253	IMG Activity:
S_KK4_08000254	IMG Activity:
S_KK4_08000255	IMG Activity:
S_KK4_08000256	IMG Activity:
S_KK4_08000257	IMG Activity:
S_KK4_08000258	IMG Activity:
S_KK4_08000259	IMG Activity:
S_KK4_08000260	IMG Activity:
S_KK4_08000261	IMG Activity:
S_KK4_08000263	IMG Activity:
S_KK4_08000264	IMG Activity:
S_KK4_08000265	IMG Activity:
S_KK4_08000266	Create Seq. File Condition Transfer
S_KK4_08000267	Batch-Input StandRecs For Conditions
S_KK4_08000268	Batch Input: Session Overview
S_KK4_08000269	IMG Activity:
S_KK4_08000270	IMG Activity:
S_KK4_08000271	IMG Activity:
S_KK4_08000272	IMG Activity:
S_KK4_08000273	IMG Activity:
S_KK4_08000274	IMG Activity:
S_KK4_08000275	IMG Activity:
S_KK4_08000276	IMG Activity:
S_KK4_08000278	IMG Activity:
S_KK4_08000279	IMG Activity:
S_KK4_08000285	IMG Activity:
S_KK4_08000286	IMG Activity:
S_KK4_08000288	IMG Activity:

S_KK4_08000289	IMG Activity:
S_KK4_08000292	IMG Activity:
S_KK4_08000293	IMG Activity:
S_KK4_08000294	IMG Activity:
S_KK4_08000295	IMG Activity:
S_KK4_08000303	IMG Activity:
S_KK4_08000304	IMG Activity:
S_KK4_08000305	IMG Activity:
S_KK4_08000307	IMG Activity:
S_KK4_08000308	IMG Activity:
S_KK4_08000309	IMG Activity:
S_KK4_08000310	IMG Activity:
S_KK4_08000311	IMG Activity:
S_KK4_08000312	IMG Activity:
S_KK4_08000322	IMG Activity:
S_KK4_08000323	IMG Activity:
S_KK4_08000324	IMG Activity:
S_KK4_08000327	IMG Activity: Upload Screens
S_KK4_08000340	IMG Activity:
S_KK4_08000344	IMG Activity:
S_KK4_08000345	IMG Activity:
S_KK4_08000348	Reassignment Report
S_KK4_08000349	Status Report
S_KK4_08000352	List of Payments Over Limit
S_KK4_08000353	Claim List
S_KK4_08000359	Reassignment Report
S_KK4_08000360	IMG Activity:
S_KK4_08000363	IMG Activity:
S_KK4_08000364	IMG Activity:
S_KK4_08000365	IMG Activity:
S_KK4_08000366	IMG Activity:
S_KK4_08000367	IMG Activity:
S_KK4_08000368	IMG Activity:
S_KK4_08000369	IMG Activity:
S_KK4_08000370	IMG Activity:
S_KK4_08000384	IMG Activity:
S_KK4_08000385	IMG Activity:
S_KK4_08000394	IMG Activity:
S_KK4_08000395	IMG Activity:
S_KK4_08000396	IMG Activity:
S_KK4_08000399	IMG Activity:
S_KK4_08000403	IMG Activity:
S_KK4_08000404	IMG Activity:
S_KK4_08000405	IMG Activity:
S_KK4_08000406	IMG Activity:
S_KK4_08000407	IMG Activity:
S_KK4_08000408	IMG Activity:
S_KK4_08000409	IMG Activity:
S_KK4_08000411	IMG Activity:
S_KK4_08000412	IMG Activity:
S_KK4_08000415	IMG Activity:
S_KK4_08000416	IMG Activity:
S_KK4_08000417	IMG Activity:
S_KK4_08000418	IMG Activity:

S_KK4_08000419	IMG Activity:
S_KK4_08000420	IMG Activity:
S_KK4_08000421	IMG Activity:
S_KK4_08000422	IMG Activity:
S_KK4_08000423	IMG Activity:
S_KK4_08000424	IMG Activity:
S_KK4_08000425	IMG Activity:
S_KK4_08000426	IMG Activity:
S_KK4_08000444	IMG Activity:
S_KK4_08000445	IMG Activity:
S_KK4_08000446	IMG Activity:
S_KK4_08000447	IMG Activity:
S_KK4_08000448	IMG Activity:
S_KK4_08000449	IMG Activity:
S_KK4_08000450	IMG Activity:
S_KK4_08000451	IMG Activity:
S_KK4_08000458	IMG Activity:
S_KK4_08000460	IMG Activity:
S_KK4_08000461	IMG Activity:
S_KK4_08000462	IMG Activity:
S_KK4_08000463	IMG Activity:
S_KK4_08000464	IMG Activity:
S_KK4_08000465	IMG Activity:
S_KK4_08000466	IMG Activity:
S_KK4_08000467	IMG Activity:
S_KK4_08000468	IMG Activity: _ISISFICA_COINHVTV
S_KK4_08000469	IMG Activity: SIMG_ICL_TICL331
S_KK4_08000472	IMG Activity: SIMG_ICL_BDT_SH_CL
S_KK4_08000473	IMG Activity: SIMG_ICL_BDT_SH_BP
S_KK4_08000474	IMG Activity: _CACS_VC_TCACS_LSSEG
S_KK4_08000475	IMG Activity: SIMGH_ICL_CD
S_KK4_08000476	IMG Activity: SIMG_ICL_CMC_BRT_BRF
S_KK4_08000477	IMG Activity: _ISISFICA_V_TKKV007D
S_KK4_08000478	IMG Activity: _ISISFICA_V_TKKV007E
S_KK4_08000479	IMG Activity: _ISISFICA_V_TKKV007C
S_KK4_08000480	IMG Activity: _ISISFICA_VYTAX1
S_KK4_08000481	IMG Activity: _ISISFICA_VYAC23
S_KK4_08000482	IMG Activity: _ISISFICA_VYAS43
S_KK4_08000483	IMG Activity: _ISISFICA_ARCHBALINT
S_KK4_08000484	IMG Activity: _ISISFICA_ARCHCOIN
S_KK4_08000485	IMG Activity: SIMG_ICL_TICL271
S_KK4_08000486	IMG Activity: SIMG_ICL_TICL363
S_KK4_08000487	IMG Activity: SIMG_ICL_TICL364
S_KK4_08000488	IMG Activity: SIMG_ICL_BRF_EV
S_KK4_08000489	IMG Activity: SIMG_ICL_BRF_TBRF141
S_KK4_08000490	IMG Activity: SIMG_ICL_BRF_ACTIONS
S_KK4_08000491	IMG Activity: SIMG_ICLN_FNOL_VALI
S_KK4_08000492	IMG Activity: SIMG_ICLN_TICL254
S_KK4_08000493	IMG Activity: SIMG_ICLN_TICL252
S_KK4_08000494	IMG Activity: SIMG_ICLN_CHECK_BP
S_KK4_08000495	IMG Activity: SIMG_ICLN_SUBCL_DET
S_KK4_08000496	IMG Activity: SIMG_ICLN_TICL251
S_KK4_08000497	IMG Activity: SIMG_ICLN_TICL272
S_KK4_08000498	IMG Activity: SIMG_ICLN_DUP_CHK_BP

S_KK4_08000499	IMG Activity: SIMG_ICLN_DUP_CHECK
S_KK4_08000500	IMG Activity: SIMG_ICLN_CHECK_RE
S_KK4_08000501	IMG Activity: _ISISFICA_BROK_FQKPT
S_KK4_08000502	IMG Activity: SIMG_ICL_TICL366
S_KK4_08000503	IMG Activity: SIMG_ICL_TICL367
S_KK4_08000505	IMG Activity: SIMG_ICL_TICL369
S_KK4_08000506	IMG Activity: SIMG_ICL_LOSSALLOCAT
S_KK4_08000507	IMG Activity: SIMG_ICL_TICL138
S_KK4_08000508	IMG Activity: ICL_IND_IBNR_SUP
S_KK4_08000509	IMG Activity: SIMG_ICL_SE75
S_KK4_08000510	IMG Activity: SIMG_ICL_STXH
S_KK4_08000511	IMG Activity: _ISISFICA_VY_V131
S_KK4_08000512	IMG Activity: _ISISFICA_VY_V132
S_KK4_08000513	IMG Activity: SIMG_ICL_TICL349
S_KK4_08000514	IMG Activity: SIMGH_ICL_TICL321_CD
S_KK4_08000515	IMG Activity: SIMG_ICL_TICL321_CD
S_KK4_08000516	IMG Activity: SIMG_ICL_TICL160
S_KK4_08000520	IMG Activity:
S_KK4_08000527	IMG Activity:
S_KK4_08000528	IMG Activity:
S_KK4_08000535	IMG Activity:
S_KK4_08000580	IMG Activity: SIMG_M_TICL952
S_KK4_08000654	IMG Activity: SIMG_M_TICL096
S_KK4_08000694	IMG Activity: SIMG_TICL936
S_KK4_13000001	IMG Activity: SIMG_CFJB01KEN1
S_KK4_13000002	IMG Activity: SIMG_CFJB01JBN5
S_KK4_13000003	IMG Activity: SIMG_CFJB0BJB_VTNUMI
S_KK4_13000004	IMG Activity: SIMG_CFJB0BJB_VTNUM
S_KK4_13000005	IMG Activity: SIMG_CFJB0BJB_TONUMI
S_KK4_13000006	IMG Activity: SIMG_CFJB0BJB_TONUM
S_KK4_13000007	IMG Activity: SIMG_CFJB01JB0O
S_KK4_13000008	IMG Activity: SIMG_CFJB01JBM0
S_KK4_13000009	IMG Activity: SIMG_CFJB0BJB1C
S_KK4_13000010	IMG Activity: SIMG_CFJB01JBN4
S_KK4_13000011	IMG Activity: SIMG_CFJB01JBN1
S_KK4_13000012	IMG Activity: SIMG_JB01_VORKALK001
S_KK4_13000013	IMG Activity: SIMG_JB01_JBM2
S_KK4_13000014	IMG Activity: SIMG_CFJB0BJB1E
S_KK4_13000015	IMG Activity: SIMG_CFJB0BVCCDPERTY
S_KK4_13000016	IMG Activity: SIMG_CFJB0BJBCDLI
S_KK4_13000017	IMG Activity: SIMG_CFJB01OV/5
S_KK4_13000020	IMG Activity: SIMG_CFJB01SU03
S_KK4_13000021	IMG Activity: SIMG_CFJB01SU02
S_KK4_13000022	IMG Activity: _OBJTRANS
S_KK4_13000023	IMG Activity: _USEREXIT
S_KK4_13000024	IMG Activity: SIMG_CFJB08JB0L
S_KK4_13000025	IMG Activity: SIMG_CFJB08JB0M
S_KK4_13000026	IMG Activity: SIMG_JBDBALCOST
S_KK4_13000027	IMG Activity: _JBPD
S_KK4_13000028	IMG Activity: _KEI1
S_KK4_13000029	IMG Activity: _CPT1
S_KK4_13000030	IMG Activity: SIMG_CFJB01JB91
S_KK4_13000031	IMG Activity: SIMG_CFJB08JBTA
S_KK4_13000032	IMG Activity: SIMG_CFJB01JBDDRBCA1

S_KK4_13000033	IMG Activity: SIMG_CFJB01JBCAPAACT
S_KK4_13000034	IMG Activity: SIMG_CFJB08KE4U
S_KK4_13000035	IMG Activity: SIMG_CFJB01JB1F
S_KK4_13000036	IMG Activity: V_TKEVA01
S_KK4_13000037	IMG Activity: SIMG_CFJB08JB21
S_KK4_13000038	IMG Activity: SIMG_CFJB08JB20
S_KK4_13000039	IMG Activity: _CTU1
S_KK4_13000040	IMG Activity: SIMG_CFJB01JB0U
S_KK4_13000041	IMG Activity: SIMG_CFJB08JB41
S_KK4_13000042	IMG Activity: SIMG_CFJB01JB0W
S_KK4_13000043	IMG Activity: SIMG_CFJB08JB47
S_KK4_13000044	IMG Activity: SIMG_CFJB08JB48
S_KK4_13000045	IMG Activity: SIMG_CFJB08JB49
S_KK4_13000046	IMG Activity: SIMG_CFJB08JBT1
S_KK4_13000047	IMG Activity: SIMG_CFJB08JB4C
S_KK4_13000048	IMG Activity: SIMG_CFJB01KEP1
S_KK4_13000049	IMG Activity: SIMG_CFJB08JBKA
S_KK4_13000050	IMG Activity: SIMG_CFJB08JB4Q
S_KK4_13000051	IMG Activity: SIMG_CFJB08JB4L
S_KK4_13000052	IMG Activity: SIMG_CFJB01JB09
S_KK4_13000053	IMG Activity: SIMG_CFJB08JB45
S_KK4_13000054	IMG Activity: SIMG_CFJB08JB46
S_KK4_13000055	IMG Activity: SIMG_CFJB01JBG0
S_KK4_13000056	IMG Activity: SIMG_CFJB01JBDDRORD1
S_KK4_13000057	IMG Activity: SIMG_CFJB01KEQ3
S_KK4_13000058	IMG Activity: SIMG_CFJB01KEBD
S_KK4_13000059	IMG Activity: SIMG_CFJB01JBDDRFX1
S_KK4_13000060	IMG Activity: SIMG_CFJB01OKEQ
S_KK4_13000061	IMG Activity: SIMG_CFJB01JBDDRMM1
S_KK4_13000062	IMG Activity: _USEREXITEGK
S_KK4_13000063	IMG Activity: SIMGCFJB01JBDDRFGDT1
S_KK4_13000064	IMG Activity: SIMG_CFJB01JBRCPAACT
S_KK4_13000065	IMG Activity: SIMG_CFJB01JBDDRDERI
S_KK4_13000066	IMG Activity: SIMG_CMJB01JBB5
S_KK4_13000067	IMG Activity: SIMG_CFJB01JBB6
S_KK4_13000068	IMG Activity: SIMG_CFJB01JBDDRSTX1
S_KK4_13000069	IMG Activity: _JBDRDARL
S_KK4_13000070	IMG Activity: SIMG_CFJB01JBDDRVT1
S_KK4_13000071	IMG-Activity: SIMG_CFJB01JBVTPAACT
S_KK4_13000072	IMG Activity: SIMG_CFJB01JBDDRLOAN
S_KK4_13000073	IMG Activity: SIMG_CMJB010003
S_KK4_13000074	IMG Activity: SIMG_CMJB010004
S_KK4_13000075	IMG Activity: SIMG_BA-V_TBKKG33
S_KK4_13000076	IMG Activity: SIMG_BA-CA-V_TBKKG31
S_KK4_13000077	IMG Activity: SIMG_BA-CA-V_TBKKM3
S_KK4_13000078	IMG Activity: SIMG_BA-V_TBKKM2
S_KK4_13000079	IMG Activity: SIMG_BA-CA-V_TBKKI1
S_KK4_13000080	IMG Activity: SIMG_BA-CA-V_TBKK01D
S_KK4_13000081	IMG Activity: SIMG_BA-CA-V_TBKKG1
S_KK4_13000082	IMG Activity: SIMG_BA-VC_TBKK34
S_KK4_13000083	IMG Activity: SIMG-BA-V_TBKKCVAR
S_KK4_13000084	IMG Activity: IS-B-BCA-IC-V_TBKK92
S_KK4_13000085	IMG Activity: BA-CA-V_TBKKG2_DATE
S_KK4_13000086	IMG Activity: _BA-CA-PT-F9POWFCU

S_KK4_13000087	IMG Activity: _BA-CA-PT-WF-OOOE
S_KK4_13000088	IMG Activity: SIMG_BA-CA-PT-SM59
S_KK4_13000089	IMG Activity: SIMG_BA-CA-V_TBKKIDF
S_KK4_13000090	IMG Activity: SIMG_BA-CA-V_TBKKG2
S_KK4_13000091	IMG Activity: SIMG_BA-CA-V_TBKK65
S_KK4_13000092	IMG Activity: SIMG_BA-CA-V_TBKK60
S_KK4_13000093	IMG Activity: SIMG_BA-CA-VC_TBKKG6
S_KK4_13000094	IMG Activity: SIMG_BA-CA-PR-ASR
S_KK4_13000095	IMG Activity: _BA-CA-MD-F9MBP
S_KK4_13000096	IMG Activity: _BA-CA-MD-FIPRD4
S_KK4_13000097	IMG Activity: _BA-CA-MD-FIPRD3
S_KK4_13000098	IMG Activity: _B-BCA-MDAC-V_TBKKM9
S_KK4_13000099	IMG Activity: SIMG_BA-V_TBKKG32
S_KK4_13000100	IMG Activity: SIMG_BA-CA-V_TBKKG3
S_KK4_13000101	IMG Activity: SIMG_BA-CA-V_TBKKM8
S_KK4_13000102	IMG Activity: SIMG_BA-CA-V_TBKKA3
S_KK4_13000103	IMG Activity: SIMG_BA-CA-V_TBKKA2
S_KK4_13000104	IMG Activity: SIMG_B-BCA-V_TBKKA1
S_KK4_13000105	IMG Activity: SIMG_BA-CA-V_TBKKM5
S_KK4_13000106	IMG Activity: SIMG_BA-CA-SU02
S_KK4_13000107	IMG Activity: SIMG_BA-CA-SU03
S_KK4_13000108	IMG Activity: SIMG_BA-V_TB030/F9C]
S_KK4_13000109	IMG-Activity: SIMG_BA-F9CSO02
S_KK4_13000110	IMG Activity: SIMG_BA-V_TB030/F9C{
S_KK4_13000111	IMG Activity: SIMG_BA-V_TB030/F9C}
S_KK4_13000112	IMG Activity: SIMG_BA-V_TB030/F9C[
S_KK4_13000113	IMG Activity: _BA-CA-V_TBKKOAUTH
S_KK4_13000114	IMG Activity: SIMG_BA-CA-V_TBKK12
S_KK4_13000115	IMG Activity: SIMG_BA-CA-KCLP
S_KK4_13000116	IMG Activity: SIMG_BA-CA-KCLJ
S_KK4_13000117	IMG Activity: SIMG_BA-CA-OKCG
S_KK4_13000118	IMG Activity: SIMG_BA-CA-KCLL
S_KK4_13000119	IMG Activity: _BA-CA-V_TBKKSOAUTH
S_KK4_13000120	IMG Activity: _BA-CA-V_TBKKIAUTH
S_KK4_13000121	IMG Activity: SIMG_BA-V_TB030/F9C4
S_KK4_13000122	IMG Activity: _BA-CA-GL-F9HC4
S_KK4_13000123	IMG Activity: _BA-CA-GL-F9HC5
S_KK4_13000124	IMG Activity: SIMG_BA-V_TBKKCAS2
S_KK4_13000125	IMG Activity: SIMG-BA-V_TBKKCASS
S_KK4_13000126	IMG Activity: SIMG-BA-V_TBKKCGRP
S_KK4_13000127	IMG Activity: SIMG-BA-V_TBKKCTTP
S_KK4_13000128	IMG Activity: SIMG-BA-V_TBKKCACT
S_KK4_13000129	IMG Activity: SIMG_BA-V_TBKKCAS3
S_KK4_13000130	IMG Activity: _IS-B-BCA-IS-F9CRT1
S_KK4_13000131	IMG Activity: SIMG_BA-V_TBKKMHOS
S_KK4_13000132	IMG Activity: SIMG_BA-V_TBKKMDIS
S_KK4_13000133	IMG Activity BA-CA_F9CAPPLREL
S_KK4_13000134	IMG Activity: IS-BCA-V_TBKKREPORTS
S_KK4_13000135	IMG Activity: SIMGV_TBKKMCHAINCLST
S_KK4_13000136	IMG Activity: SIMG_BA-V_TBKKCCLR
S_KK4_13000137	IMG Activity: _BA-CA-MD-FIPRD2
S_KK4_13000138	IMG Activity: SIMG_BA-CA-V_TBKK82
S_KK4_13000139	IMG Activity: SIMG_BA-CA-V_TBKK02
S_KK4_13000140	IMG Activity: SIMG-BA-CA-F9CX

S_KK4_13000141	IMG Activity: SIMG_BA-CA-VC_TBKK03
S_KK4_13000142	IMG Activity: SIMG_BA-CA-V_TBKK81
S_KK4_13000143	IMG Activity: SIMG_BA-CA-BF11
S_KK4_13000144	IMG Activity: SIMG_BA-CA-V_TBKK8A
S_KK4_13000145	IMG Activity: SIMG_BA-V_TBKKG9
S_KK4_13000146	IMG Activity: SIMG_V_TBKK8K/TBKK8L
S_KK4_13000147	IMG Activity: SIMG_BA-CA-V_T056P
S_KK4_13000148	IMG Activity: SIMG_BA-CA-V_T056R
S_KK4_13000149	IMG Activity: SIMG_BA-CA-V_TBKK85
S_KK4_13000150	IMG Activity: SIMG_BA-CA-V_BNKA
S_KK4_13000151	IMG Activity: SIMG_BA-CA-F9BTEINFO
S_KK4_13000152	IMG Activity: SIMG_BA-CA-BF34
S_KK4_13000153	IMG Activity: SIMG_BA-CA-BF24
S_KK4_13000154	IMG Activity: SIMG-BA-CA-BF32
S_KK4_13000155	IMG Activity: SIMG_BA-CA-BF22
S_KK4_13000156	IMG Activity: SIMG_BA-CA-BF23
S_KK4_13000157	IMG Activity: SIMG_BA-CA-BF-F9MBC
S_KK4_13000158	IMG Activity: SIMG_BA-CA-V_TBKK80
S_KK4_13000159	IMG Activity: SIMG_BA-CA-BF31
S_KK4_13000160	IMG Activity: SIMG_BA-CA-TBKK80BAS
S_KK4_13000161	IMG Activity: SIMG_BA-CA-BF12
S_KK4_13000162	IMG Activity: SIMG_BA-CA_F9D1
S_KK4_13000163	IMG Activity: SIMG_BA-CA-BF-F9MDB
S_KK4_13000164	IMG Activity: _BA-CA-MD-FIPRC11
S_KK4_13000165	IMG Activity: SIMG_BA-CA-V_TBKKE1
S_KK4_13000166	IMG Activity: _BA-CA-MD-FIPRC10
S_KK4_13000167	IMG Activity: SIMG_BA-CA-V_TBKKE2
S_KK4_13000168	IMG Activity: _BA-V_TBKKE_FOUR_EYS
S_KK4_13000169	IMG Activity: SIMG_BA-CA-SNUM/F9A5
S_KK4_13000170	IMG Activity: _BA-CA-MD-FIPRC3
S_KK4_13000171	IMG Activity: SIMG_BA-CA-BF-BA-01
S_KK4_13000172	IMG Activity: _BA-CA-MD-FIPRC4
S_KK4_13000173	IMG Activity: SIMG_BA-CA_TBKK00
S_KK4_13000174	IMG Activity: SIMG_BA-CA-V_TBKK8M
S_KK4_13000175	IMG Activity: SIMG_BA-CA-V_TBKK8J
S_KK4_13000176	IMG Activity: SIMG_BA-CA-PCTR/DIV
S_KK4_13000177	IMG Activity: SIMG_BA-CA-TBKK00T
S_KK4_13000178	IMG Activity: SIMG_BA-CA-V_TBKK8H
S_KK4_13000179	IMG Activity: SIMG_BA-CA-V_TBKK8I
S_KK4_13000180	IMG Activity: _CA-BA-MD-FIPRD1
S_KK4_13000181	IMG Activity: SIMG_BA-CA-V_TBKK8N
S_KK4_13000182	IMG Activity: SIMG_BA-CA-GL-GLT
S_KK4_13000183	IMG Activity: SIMG_JBVCLZB
S_KK4_13000184	IMG Activity: _JBVSIMZ
S_KK4_13000185	IMG Activity: _JBVCPBL
S_KK4_13000186	IMG Activity: _JBVCFSZ
S_KK4_13000187	IMG Activity: _JBVBRFS
S_KK4_13000188	IMG Activity: _JBWV
S_KK4_13000189	IMG Activity: _OKUL
S_KK4_13000190	IMG Activity: _JBWK
S_KK4_13000191	IMG Activity: _JBWR
S_KK4_13000192	IMG Activity: _JBVIDXG
S_KK4_13000193	IMG Activity: _JBRSVRCFK
S_KK4_13000194	IMG Activity: _JBVCFART

S_KK4_13000195	IMG Activity: _JBR3
S_KK4_13000196	IMG Activity: _VTVBWCFV
S_KK4_13000197	IMG Activity: _V_VTVTRBW
S_KK4_13000198	IMG Activity: _V_VTVBKKBW
S_KK4_13000199	IMG Activity: SIMG_JBSTNK
S_KK4_13000200	IMG Activity: _VC_AUSWT
S_KK4_13000201	IMG Activity: SIMG_JBVBV2
S_KK4_13000202	IMG Activity: _JBW4
S_KK4_13000203	IMG Activity: _JBWB
S_KK4_13000204	IMG Activity: _JBWZ
S_KK4_13000205	IMG Activity: _JBWX
S_KK4_13000206	IMG Activity: _JBWY
S_KK4_13000207	IMG Activity: _BERECHTIGUNG
S_KK4_13000208	IMG Activity: _PROFILE
S_KK4_13000209	IMG Activity: SIMG_V_VTVAUTGR
S_KK4_13000211	IMG Activity: _JBW5
S_KK4_13000212	IMG Activity: _JBWP
S_KK4_13000213	IMG Activity: _JBWG
S_KK4_13000214	IMG Activity: _JBWW
S_KK4_13000215	IMG Activity: _JBWQ
S_KK4_13000216	IMG Activity: _JBW1
S_KK4_13000217	IMG Activity: _JBW2
S_KK4_13000218	IMG Activity: _JBWO
S_KK4_13000219	IMG Activity: _JBWT
S_KK4_13000220	IMG Activity: _JBRSVRBR
S_KK4_13000221	IMG Activity: SIMG_RMIJBVT
S_KK4_13000222	IMG Activity: SIMG_RMVT1
S_KK4_13000223	IMG Activity: SIMG_JBRCT
S_KK4_13000224	IMG Activity: SIMG_JBRCU
S_KK4_13000226	IMG Activity: _JBRGV
S_KK4_13000227	IMG Activity: SIMG_RMIBKKA
S_KK4_13000228	IMG Activity: _JBRZ
S_KK4_13000229	IMG Activity: SIMG_RMBK1
S_KK4_13000230	IMG Activity: SIMG_RMIFGDT
S_KK4_13000231	IMG Activity: SIMG_RMDR1
S_KK4_13000232	IMG Activity: _JBRDG
S_KK4_13000233	IMG Activity: _JBVDERI
S_KK4_13000234	IMG Activity: SIMG_JBVABREG
S_KK4_13000235	IMG Activity: _TMA5
S_KK4_13000236	IMG Activity: SIMG_JBVCPH
S_KK4_13000237	IMG Activity: SIMG_JBVCSI
S_KK4_13000238	IMG Activity: _JBR6
S_KK4_13000239	IMG Activity: _JBVVREG
S_KK4_13000240	IMG Activity: _JBVBEWREG
S_KK4_13000241	IMG Activity: _JBR1
S_KK4_13000242	IMG Activity: _JBRNR
S_KK4_13000243	IMG Activity: SIMG_RMD01
S_KK4_13000244	IMG Activity: _JBAP
S_KK4_13000245	IMG Activity: SIMG_JB02_CMOD
S_KK4_13000253	IMG Activity: SIMG_JBVCBGR
S_KK4_13000255	IMG Activity: _ALM_01
S_KK4_13000256	IMG Activity: SIMG_V_JBROZAKT
S_KK4_13000257	IMG Activity: SIMG_V_JBRKNZTYPTAB
S_KK4_13000258	IMG Activity: SIMG_V_DFCU30

S_KK4_13000259	IMG Activity: _V_ATVSZ
S_KK4_13000260	IMG Activity: _ATVO61
S_KK4_13000261	IMG Activity: _ATVO62
S_KK4_13000262	IMG Activity: SIMG_CFJB01JBGK
S_KK4_13000263	IMG Activity: _ATVO63
S_KK4_13000264	IMG Activity: _JBDRATEBAR
S_KK4_13000265	IMG Activity: _ATVO64
S_KK4_13000266	IMG Activity: SIMG_CFJB01JB62
S_KK4_13000267	IMG Activity: _VC_VOLA
S_KK4_13000268	IMG Activity: _V_INDEXA
S_KK4_13000269	IMG Activity: _V_ATVO3
S_KK4_13000270	IMG Activity: _V_ATV01
S_KK4_13000271	IMG Activity: _V_ATK01
S_KK4_13000272	IMG Activity: _JBVBFART
S_KK4_13000273	IMG Activity: SIMG_V_ATRFART
S_KK4_13000274	IMG Activity: SIMG_V_ATRFVOLA
S_KK4_13000275	IMG Activity: SIMG_V_ATRFVO
S_KK4_13000276	IMG Activity: SIMG_V_ATRFKORR
S_KK4_13000277	IMG Activity: SIMG_V_ATRF
S_KK4_13000278	IMG Activity: SIMG_V_ATRFBETA
S_KK4_13000279	IMG Activity: _TLMK
S_KK4_13000280	IMG Activity: _TLMR
S_KK4_13000281	IMG Activity: _TLM4
S_KK4_13000282	IMG Activity: _TLM5
S_KK4_13000283	IMG Activity: _TLMP
S_KK4_13000284	IMG Activity: _TLMG
S_KK4_13000285	IMG Activity: _V_KLREGDEF
S_KK4_13000286	IMG Activity: _V_KLEVC
S_KK4_13000287	IMG Activity: _V_KLADDONFAK
S_KK4_13000288	IMG Activity: _V_KLAUSFWKT
S_KK4_13000289	IMG Activity: SIMG_KLRRDEF
S_KK4_13000290	IMG Activity: _TLMV
S_KK4_13000291	IMG Activity: _TLMB
S_KK4_13000292	IMG Activity: _TLMZ
S_KK4_13000293	IMG Activity: _TLMX
S_KK4_13000294	IMG Activity: _TLMY
S_KK4_13000295	IMG Activity: _TLMW
S_KK4_13000296	IMG Activity: _TLMQ
S_KK4_13000297	IMG Activity: _TLM1
S_KK4_13000298	IMG Activity: _TLM2
S_KK4_13000299	IMG Activity: _TLMO
S_KK4_13000300	IMG Activity: _TLMT
S_KK4_13000301	IMG Activity: SIMG_V_KLRATINGRRFZU
S_KK4_13000302	IMG Activity: SIMG_V_KLRRFINDDEF
S_KK4_13000303	IMG Activity: _V_KLARRC
S_KK4_13000304	IMG Activity: SIMG_V_KLNT01
S_KK4_13000305	IMG Activity: _V_KLARRCRS
S_KK4_13000306	IMG Activity: SIMG_KLABL
S_KK4_13000307	IMG Activity: _V_KLRISKSENSI
S_KK4_13000308	IMG Activity: _V_KLXAKT
S_KK4_13000309	IMG Activity: SIMG_LMIBKKA
S_KK4_13000310	IMG Activity: SIMG_LMIJBVT
S_KK4_13000311	IMG Activity: SIMG_KLBEWFAK
S_KK4_13000312	IMG Activity: _V_KLEVDEF

S_KK4_13000313	IMG Activity: SIMG_V_KLARRZU04
S_KK4_13000314	IMG Activity: _V_KLARRZU01
S_KK4_13000315	IMG Activity: _V_KLARRZU02
S_KK4_13000316	IMG Activity: _V_KLEGZU
S_KK4_13000317	IMG Activity: _V_KLBESTZU
S_KK4_13000318	IMG Activity: _V_KLORDERZUARR
S_KK4_13000319	IMG Activity: FTLM_NOTIZEN
S_KK4_13000320	IMG Activity: FTLM_KUNDENMERKMALE
S_KK4_13000321	IMG Activity: FTLM_LIMITPRODUKTGR
S_KK4_13000322	IMG Activity: FTLM_FELDAUSWAHL
S_KK4_13000323	IMG Activity: FTLM_LIMITART
S_KK4_13000324	IMG Activity: FTLM_RESERV
S_KK4_13000329	Automatic Payments
S_KK4_13000330	ALM: Customizing: Due Date Scenarios
S_KK4_13000331	*
S_KK4_13000333	IMG: Activity
S_KK4_13000337	IMG: Activity
S_KK4_13000338	Bank Statement Interpretation
S_KK4_13000342	IMG: Activity
S_KK4_16000001	IMG Activity: _WCMMD_000021
S_KK4_16000002	IMG Activity: _WCMMD_000022
S_KK4_16000003	IMG Activity: _WCMPE_000004
S_KK4_16000004	IMG Activity: _WCMPE_000006
S_KK4_16000005	IMG Activity: _WCMPE_000007
S_KK4_16000006	IMG Activity: _WCMPE_000008
S_KK4_16000007	IMG Activity: _WCMPE_000009
S_KK4_16000008	IMG Activity: _WCMMD_000041
S_KK4_16000009	IMG Activity: _WCMMD_000004
S_KK4_16000010	IMG Activity: _WCMMD_000019
S_KK4_16000011	IMG Activity: _WCMMD_000044
S_KK4_16000012	IMG Activity: _WCMMD_000015
S_KK4_16000013	IMG Activity: _WCMMD_000016
S_KK4_16000014	IMG Activity: _WCMMD_000017
S_KK4_16000015	IMG Activity: _WCMMD_000040
S_KK4_16000016	IMG Activity: _WCMTC_000006
S_KK4_16000017	IMG Activity: _WCMTC_000007
S_KK4_16000018	IMG Activity: _WCMTC_000008
S_KK4_16000019	IMG Activity: _WCMTC_000011
S_KK4_16000020	IMG Activity: _WCMTC_000013
S_KK4_16000021	IMG Activity: _WCMTC_000014
S_KK4_16000022	IMG Activity: _WCMTC_000015
S_KK4_16000023	IMG Activity: _WCMTC_000004
S_KK4_16000024	IMG Activity: _WCMPE_000015
S_KK4_16000025	IMG Activity: _WCMPE_000010
S_KK4_16000026	IMG Activity: _WCMPE_000012
S_KK4_16000027	IMG Activity: _WCMPE_000014
S_KK4_16000028	IMG Activity: _WCMMD_000013
S_KK4_16000029	IMG Activity: _WCMTC_000005
S_KK4_16000030	IMG Activity: _WCMTC_000003
S_KK4_16000031	IMG Activity: _WCMMD_000006
S_KK4_16000032	IMG Activity: _WCMMD_000007
S_KK4_16000033	IMG Activity: _WCMMD_000008
S_KK4_16000034	IMG Activity: _WCMTC_000009
S_KK4_16000035	IMG Activity: _WCMMD_000009

S_KK4_16000036	IMG Activity: _WCMMD_000011
S_KK4_16000037	IMG Activity: _WCMMD_000012
S_KK4_16000038	IMG Activity: _WCMMD_000002
S_KK4_16000039	IMG Activity: _WCMMD_000043
S_KK4_16000040	IMG Activity: _WCMMD_000042
S_KK4_16000041	IMG Activity: _WCMMD_000035
S_KK4_16000042	IMG Activity: _WCMMC_000003
S_KK4_16000043	IMG Activity: _WCMMD_000036
S_KK4_16000044	IMG Activity: _WCMMD_000037
S_KK4_16000045	IMG Activity: _WCMMD_000032
S_KK4_16000046	IMG Activity: _WCMMD_000025
S_KK4_16000047	IMG Activity: _WCMMD_000030
S_KK4_16000048	IMG Activity: _WCMMD_000029
S_KK4_16000049	IMG Activity: _WCMMD_000027
S_KK4_16000050	IMG Activity: _WCMMD_000034
S_KK4_16000051	IMG Activity: _WCMPE_000003
S_KK4_16000052	IMG Activity: _WCMMD_000039
S_KK4_38000037	IMG Activity: IST_IF_TOICOPA001
S_KK4_38000038	IMG Activity: IST_BS_DEFSERVICES
S_KK4_66000001	IMG activity: SIMG_PRO_0021
S_KK4_66000002	IMG activity: SIMG_PRO_0020
S_KK4_66000003	IMG activity: SIMG_PRO_0019
S_KK4_66000004	IMG activity: SIMG_PRO_0018
S_KK4_66000005	IMG activity: SIMG_PRO_0017
S_KK4_66000006	IMG activity: SIMG_PRO_0016
S_KK4_66000007	IMG activity: SIMG_PRO_0015
S_KK4_66000008	IMG activity: SIMG_PRO_0014
S_KK4_66000009	IMG activity: SIMG_PRO_0013
S_KK4_66000010	IMG activity: SIMG_PRO_0022
S_KK4_66000011	IMG activity: SIMG_BIL_0002
S_KK4_66000012	IMG activity: SIMG_BIL_0001
S_KK4_66000013	IMG activity: SIMG_PRO_0029
S_KK4_66000014	IMG activity: SIMG_PRO_0028
S_KK4_66000015	IMG activity: SIMG_PRO_0027
S_KK4_66000016	IMG activity: SIMG_PRO_0026
S_KK4_66000017	IMG activity: SIMG_PRO_0025
S_KK4_66000018	IMG activity: SIMG_PRO_0024
S_KK4_66000019	IMG activity: SIMG_PRO_0023
S_KK4_66000020	IMG activity: SIMG_PRO_0011E
S_KK4_66000021	IMG activity: SIMG_PRO_0011F
S_KK4_66000022	IMG activity: SIMG_PRO_0011G
S_KK4_66000023	IMG activity: SIMG_PRO_0010
S_KK4_66000024	IMG activity: SIMG_PRO_009A
S_KK4_66000025	IMG activity: SIMG_PRO_0009
S_KK4_66000026	IMG activity: SIMG_PRO_0008
S_KK4_66000027	IMG activity: SIMG_PRO_0030
S_KK4_66000028	IMG activity: SIMG_PRO_0007
S_KK4_66000029	IMG activity: SIMG_PRO_0011B
S_KK4_66000030	IMG activity: SIMG_PRO_0012
S_KK4_66000031	IMG activity: SIMG_PRO_0011L
S_KK4_66000032	IMG-Aktivität: SIMG_PRO_0011K
S_KK4_66000033	IMG-Aktivität: SIMG_PRO_0011J
S_KK4_66000034	IMG-Aktivität: SIMG_PRO_0011I
S_KK4_66000035	IMG-Aktivität: SIMG_PRO_0011H

S_KK4_66000036	IMG-Aktivität: SIMG_PRO_0011D
S_KK4_66000037	IMG-Aktivität: SIMG_PRO_0011C
S_KK4_66000038	IMG-Aktivität: SIMG_PRO_0011A
S_KK4_66000039	IMG-Aktivität: SIMG_NOP_0006
S_KK4_66000040	IMG-Aktivität: SIMG_NOP_0005
S_KK4_66000041	IMG-Aktivität: SIMG_NOP_0004
S_KK4_66000042	IMG-Aktivität: SIMG_NOP_0003
S_KK4_66000043	IMG-Aktivität: SIMG_NOP_0002
S_KK4_66000044	IMG-Aktivität: SIMG_NOP_0001
S_KK4_66000045	IMG-Aktivität: SIMG_BIL_0024
S_KK4_66000046	IMG-Aktivität: SIMG_BIL_0011
S_KK4_66000047	IMG-Aktivität: SIMG_BIL_0010
S_KK4_66000048	IMG-Aktivität: SIMG_NOP_0007
S_KK4_66000049	IMG-Aktivität: SIMG_TLS_0015
S_KK4_66000050	IMG-Aktivität: SIMG_TLS_0013
S_KK4_66000051	IMG-Aktivität: SIMG_TLS_0012
S_KK4_66000052	IMG-Aktivität: SIMG_TLS_0014
S_KK4_66000053	IMG-Aktivität: SIMG_TLS_0011
S_KK4_66000054	IMG-Aktivität: SIMG_TLS_0010
S_KK4_66000055	IMG-Aktivität: SIMG_TLS_0009
S_KK4_66000056	IMG-Aktivität: SIMG_TLS_0002
S_KK4_66000057	IMG-Aktivität: SIMG_TLS_0001
S_KK4_66000058	IMG-Aktivität: SIMG_BIL_0014
S_KK4_66000059	IMG-Aktivität: SIMG_BIL_0016
S_KK4_66000060	IMG-Aktivität: SIMG_BIL_0015
S_KK4_66000061	IMG-Aktivität: SIMG_BIL_0013
S_KK4_66000062	IMG-Aktivität: SIMG_BIL_0012
S_KK4_66000063	IMG-Aktivität: SIMG_BIL_0006
S_KK4_66000064	IMG-Aktivität: SIMG_BIL_0005
S_KK4_66000065	IMG-Aktivität: SIMG_BIL_0004
S_KK4_66000066	IMG-Aktivität: SIMG_BIL_0003
S_KK4_66000067	IMG-Aktivität: SIMG_BIL_0017
S_KK4_66000068	IMG-Aktivität: SIMG_BIL_0009
S_KK4_66000069	IMG-Aktivität: SIMG_BIL_0008
S_KK4_66000070	IMG-Aktivität: SIMG_BIL_0007
S_KK4_66000071	IMG-Aktivität: SIMG_BIL_0023
S_KK4_66000072	IMG-Aktivität: SIMG_BIL_0022
S_KK4_66000073	IMG-Aktivität: SIMG_BIL_0021
S_KK4_66000074	IMG-Aktivität: SIMG_BIL_0020
S_KK4_66000075	IMG-Aktivität: SIMG_BIL_0019
S_KK4_66000076	IMG-Aktivität: SIMG_BIL_0018
S_KK4_66000077	IMG-Aktivität: SIMG_MAS_0008
S_KK4_66000078	IMG-Aktivität: SIMG_MAS_0007
S_KK4_66000079	IMG-Aktivität: SIMG_MAS_0006
S_KK4_66000080	IMG-Aktivität: SIMG_MAS_0029
S_KK4_66000081	IMG-Aktivität: SIMG_MAS_0005
S_KK4_66000082	IMG-Aktivität: SIMG_MAS_0004
S_KK4_66000083	IMG-Aktivität: SIMG_MAS_0003
S_KK4_66000084	IMG-Aktivität: SIMG_MAS_0002
S_KK4_66000085	IMG-Aktivität: SIMG_MAS_0001
S_KK4_66000086	IMG-Aktivität: SIMG_MAS_0017
S_KK4_66000087	IMG-Aktivität: SIMG_MAS_0016
S_KK4_66000088	IMG-Aktivität: SIMG_MAS_0015
S_KK4_66000089	IMG-Aktivität: SIMG_MAS_0014

S_KK4_66000090	IMG-Aktivität: SIMG_MAS_0013
S_KK4_66000091	IMG-Aktivität: SIMG_MAS_0012
S_KK4_66000092	IMG-Aktivität: SIMG_MAS_0011
S_KK4_66000093	IMG-Aktivität: SIMG_MAS_0010
S_KK4_66000094	IMG-Aktivität: SIMG_MAS_0009
S_KK4_66000095	IMG-Aktivität: SIMG_ENV_0009
S_KK4_66000096	IMG-Aktivität: SIMG_ENV_0008
S_KK4_66000097	IMG-Aktivität: SIMG_ENV_0007
S_KK4_66000098	IMG-Aktivität: SIMG_ENV_0006
S_KK4_66000099	IMG-Aktivität: SIMG_ENV_0005
S_KK4_66000100	IMG-Aktivität: SIMG_ENV_0004
S_KK4_66000101	IMG-Aktivität: SIMG_ENV_0003
S_KK4_66000102	IMG-Aktivität: SIMG_ENV_0002
S_KK4_66000103	IMG-Aktivität: SIMG_ENV_0001
S_KK4_66000104	IMG-Aktivität: SIMG_ENV_0015B
S_KK4_66000105	IMG-Aktivität: SIMG_ENV_0015A
S_KK4_66000106	IMG-Aktivität: SIMG_ENV_0007C
S_KK4_66000107	IMG-Aktivität: SIMG_ENV_0007B
S_KK4_66000108	IMG-Aktivität: SIMG_ENV_0014
S_KK4_66000109	IMG-Aktivität: SIMG_ENV_0012
S_KK4_66000110	IMG-Aktivität: SIMG_ENV_0013
S_KK4_66000111	IMG-Aktivität: SIMG_ENV_0007A
S_KK4_66000112	IMG-Aktivität: SIMG_ENV_0010
S_KK4_66000113	IMG-Aktivität: SIMG_PRO_0003
S_KK4_66000114	IMG-Aktivität: SIMG_MAS_0025
S_KK4_66000115	IMG-Aktivität: SIMG_MAS_0021
S_KK4_66000116	IMG-Aktivität: SIMG_PRO_0004
S_KK4_66000117	IMG-Aktivität: SIMG_MAS_0024
S_KK4_66000118	IMG-Aktivität: SIMG_MAS_0022
S_KK4_66000119	IMG-Aktivität: SIMG_MAS_0027
S_KK4_66000120	IMG-Aktivität: SIMG_MAS_0023
S_KK4_66000121	IMG-Aktivität: SIMG_MAS_0026
S_KK4_66000122	IMG-Aktivität: SIMG_MAS_0018
S_KK4_66000123	IMG-Aktivität: SIMG_MAS_0019
S_KK4_66000124	IMG-Aktivität: SIMG_PRO_0002
S_KK4_66000125	IMG-Aktivität: SIMG_PRO_0001
S_KK4_66000126	IMG-Aktivität: SIMG_MAS_0028
S_KK4_66000127	IMG-Aktivität: SIMG_PRO_0005
S_KK4_66000128	IMG-Aktivität: SIMG_PRO_0006
S_KK4_66000129	IMG-Aktivität: SIMG_MAS_0020
S_KK4_74000001	IMG Activity: ISH_CH_PROZ_ZULEIST
S_KK4_74000002	IMG Activity: ISH_CH_ZEIT_ZULEIST
S_KK4_74000003	IMG Activity: ISH_AT_ZEIT_ZULEIST
S_KK4_74000004	IMG Activity: ISH_BG_ABRECHNUNG
S_KK4_74000005	IMG Activity: SIMG_CMMENUNMO3SPEZ7
S_KK4_74000006	IMG Activity: ISH_ABSCHLAG_APS
S_KK4_74000007	IMG Activity: SIMG_CFMENUNMOEOVV4
S_KK4_74000008	IMG Activity: ISH_CH_EXAUF_AFART
S_KK4_74000009	IMG Activity: SIMG_EXTAUFANW
S_KK4_74000010	IMG Activity: ISH_CH_EXAUF_PFLGGEB
S_KK4_74000011	IMG Activity: ISHCH_AUFTCD_EXTAUF
S_KK4_74000012	IMG Activity: ISH_CH_EXAUF_POINTS
S_KK4_74000013	IMG Activity: ISH_CH_EXAUF_ABRART
S_KK4_74000014	IMG Activity: ISH_CH_PROZ_REDUKT

S_KK4_74000015	IMG Activity: ISH_ABR_ABTYP
S_KK4_74000016	IMG Activity: ISH_ABR_PARAM
S_KK4_74000017	IMG Activity: SIMG_CFMENUNMAGONOA
S_KK4_74000018	IMG Activity: SIMG_CFMENUNMOGON/1
S_KK4_74000019	IMG Activity: SIMG_CFMENUNMOGON38
S_KK4_74000020	IMG Activity: SIMG_CFMENUNMOGON69
S_KK4_74000021	IMG Activity: SIMG_CFMENUNMOGNT50
S_KK4_74000022	IMG Activity: SIMG_CFMENUNMOEOVV3
S_KK4_74000023	IMG Activity: SIMG_CFMENUNMOEOVV2
S_KK4_74000024	IMG Activity: SIMG_CFMENUNMOEVOPA
S_KK4_74000025	IMG Activity: SIMG_CFMENUNMOEVOFB
S_KK4_74000026	IMG Activity: SIMG_CFMENUNMOEVOV1
S_KK4_74000027	IMG Activity: SIMG_CFMENUNMOESNRO
S_KK4_74000028	IMG Activity: ISH_CH_ABR_ABTYP
S_KK4_74000029	IMG Activity: ISH_CH_EXAUF_AUTYP
S_KK4_74000030	IMG Activity: SIMG_CFMENUNMA3ONO1
S_KK4_74000031	IMG Activity: ISH_CH_HON_POINTS
S_KK4_74000032	IMG Activity: ISH_CH_HON_ABRART
S_KK4_74000033	IMG Activity: SIMG_ISHCH_KONTENF
S_KK4_74000034	IMG Activity: SIMG_ISHCH_BUCHVAR
S_KK4_74000035	IMG Activity: SIMG_ISHCH_VERRKTO
S_KK4_74000036	IMG Activity: SIMG_ISHCH_HONERM
S_KK4_74000037	IMG Activity: ISH_PA_TARIF01
S_KK4_74000038	IMG Activity: ISH_NL_PA_ALLG_EINRI
S_KK4_74000039	IMG Activity: SIMG_CFMENUNMA3ONO6
S_KK4_74000040	IMG Activity: SIMG_CFMENUNMA3ONO5
S_KK4_74000041	IMG Activity: SIMG_CFMENUNMA3ONO4
S_KK4_74000042	IMG Activity: SIMG_CFMENUNMA3ONO3
S_KK4_74000043	IMG Activity: IMG_CFMENUNMA3ONO2
S_KK4_74000044	IMG Activity: ISH_RNAACP00
S_KK4_74000045	IMG Activity: SIMG_CFMENUNMOESM32
S_KK4_74000046	IMG Activity: SIMG_CFMENUNMOEVOK1
S_KK4_74000047	IMG Activity: SIMG_CFMENUNMOEV/11
S_KK4_74000048	IMG Activity: SIMG_CFMENUNMOEV/09
S_KK4_74000049	IMG Activity: SIMG_CFMENUNMOEV/10
S_KK4_74000050	IMG Activity: ISH_ERLKONTAB_ANL
S_KK4_74000051	IMG Activity: SIMG_ISHCH_POOLS
S_KK4_74000052	IMG Activity: SIMG_ISHCH_AUFTCODE
S_KK4_74000053	IMG Activity: SIMG_ISHCH_AUFTKZ
S_KK4_74000054	IMG Activity: SIMG_ISHCH_HONBER
S_KK4_74000055	IMG Activity: SIMG_ISHCH_HONARTEN
S_KK4_74000056	IMG Activity: SIMG_ISHCH_HONREL
S_KK4_74000057	IMG Activity: SIMG_ISHCH_SYSTPAR
S_KK4_74000058	IMG Activity: SIMG_CFMENUNMOGON41
S_KK4_74000059	IMG Activity: SIMG_CFMENUNMOHONA1
S_KK4_74000060	IMG Activity: SIMG_CFMENUNMOHONAG
S_KK4_74000061	IMG Activity: SIMG_CFMENUNMOHNK35
S_KK4_74000062	IMG Activity: SIMG_CFMENUNMOHNK30
S_KK4_74000063	IMG Activity: SIMG_CFMENUNMOHON02
S_KK4_74000064	IMG Activity: SIMG_CFMENUNMOHON49
S_KK4_74000066	IMG Activity: ISH_PA_KU_NL01
S_KK4_74000067	IMG Activity: ISH_PA_KU_NL02
S_KK4_74000068	IMG Activity: ISH_NL_KU_KND
S_KK4_74000069	IMG Activity: SIMG_CFMENUON24

S_KK4_74000070	IMG Activity: SIMG_CFMENUNMOHON91
S_KK4_74000071	IMG Activity: SIMG_CFMENUNMOHON90
S_KK4_74000072	IMG Activity: SIMG_CFMENUNMOHONB5
S_KK4_74000073	IMG Activity: SIMG_CFMENUNMO3ONV5
S_KK4_74000074	IMG Activity: SIMG_CFMENUNMO3ONV3
S_KK4_74000075	IMG Activity: SIMG_CFMENUNMO3ONV1
S_KK4_74000076	IMG Activity: SIMG_CFMENUNMOJON86
S_KK4_74000077	IMG Activity: SIMG_CFMENUNMOJON57
S_KK4_74000078	IMG Activity: SIMG_CFMENUNMOJON96
S_KK4_74000079	IMG Activity: SIMG_CFMENUNMOJON95
S_KK4_74000080	IMG Activity: SIMG_CFMENUNMO3ON56
S_KK4_74000081	IMG Activity: SIMG_CFMENUNMO3ON55
S_KK4_74000082	IMG Activity: ISH_ZUZ_BETRAG_PRO_T
S_KK4_74000083	IMG Activity: SIMG_CFMENUNMO3ON33
S_KK4_74000084	IMG Activity: SIMG_CFMENUNMO3ON32
S_KK4_74000085	IMG Activity: ISH_CH_PATCLASS
S_KK4_74000086	IMG Activity: SIMG_ISHPAYCL
S_KK4_74000087	IMG Activity: ISH_NL_PA_SCHEINE01
S_KK4_74000088	IMG Activity: SIMG_CMMENUNMOGPR13
S_KK4_74000089	IMG Activity: SIMG_CFMENUNMOGV/06
S_KK4_74000090	IMG Activity: SIMG_CFMENUNMOGV/07
S_KK4_74000091	IMG Activity: SIMG_CFMENUNMOGPR12
S_KK4_74000092	IMG Activity: SIMG_CFMENUNMO3NT10
S_KK4_74000093	IMG Activity: SIMG_CFMENUNMO3ON66
S_KK4_74000094	IMG Activity: SIMG_CFMENUNMO3ON87
S_KK4_74000095	IMG Activity: SIMG_CFMENUNMOGV/08
S_KK4_74000096	IMG Activity: SIMG_CFMENUNMOGONV9
S_KK4_74000097	IMG Activity: ISH_CH_POINTS
S_KK4_74000098	IMG Activity: ISH_PA_PUNKT01
S_KK4_74000099	IMG Activity: SIMG_CFMENUNMOGONA8
S_KK4_74000100	IMG Activity: SIMG_CFMENUNMOGON88
S_KK4_74000101	IMG Activity: SIMG_CFMENUNMOGONA6
S_KK4_74000102	IMG Activity: ISH_CH_KUE_KLASSEN
S_KK4_74000103	IMG Actvity: ISH_CH_RUECKWEISCODE
S_KK4_74000104	IMG Activity: ISH_CH_KUECODE
S_KK4_74000105	IMG Activity: ISH_NL_PA_SCHEINE05
S_KK4_74000106	IMG Activity: ISH_NL_PA_SCHEINE04
S_KK4_74000107	IMG Activity: ISH_NL_PA_SCHEINE03
S_KK4_74000108	IMG Activity: ISH_NL_PA_SCHEINE02
S_KK4_74000109	IMG Activity: ISH_CH_ERM_ABRV
S_KK4_74000110	IMG Activity: ISH_CH_ABRV
S_KK4_74000111	IMG Activity: ISH_CH_STD_LEISTGEN
S_KK4_74000112	IMG Activity: ISH_CH_ABRART
S_KK4_74000113	IMG Activity: SIMG_CFMENUNMO3ON80
S_KK4_74000114	IMG Activity: SIMG_CFMENUNMO3NT50
S_KK4_74000115	IMG Activity: ISH_CH_KUE_LEIVERS
S_KK4_74000116	IMG Activity: SIMG_CFMENUNMO4ONCZ
S_KK4_74000117	IMG Activity: ISH_HCM_301_APPLSTAT
S_KK4_74000118	IMG Activity: ISH_HCM_301_CMSTATUS
S_KK4_74000119	IMG Activity: ISH_HCM_301_INSTIT
S_KK4_74000120	IMG Activity: ISH_HCM_301_ACTIV
S_KK4_74000121	IMG Activity: SIMG_CFMENUNMO4NRCM
S_KK4_74000122	IMG Activity: ISH_HCM_MONITORING
S_KK4_74000123	IMG Activity: ISH_HCM_301_NCMAPP

S_KK4_74000124	IMG Activity: ISH_HCM_301KTRNTYPEN
S_KK4_74000125	IMG Activity: ISH_HCM_301_PARTNER
S_KK4_74000126	IMG Activity: ISH_EDI_DCP_FILECMP
S_KK4_74000127	IMG Activity: ISH_EDI_DCP_MASGNMT
S_KK4_74000128	IMG Activity: ISH_EDI_DCP_INSPROV
S_KK4_74000129	IMG Activity: SIMG_CFMENUNMO4ONCW
S_KK4_74000130	IMG Activity: SIMG_CFMENUNMO4ONCV
S_KK4_74000131	IMG Activity: ISH_HCM_SYNC_VERS_M
S_KK4_74000132	IMG Activity: ISH_HCM_SYNC_VER_AUF
S_KK4_74000133	IMG Activity: SIMG_CFMENUNMO4ONCI
S_KK4_74000134	IMG Activity: SIMG_CFMENUNMO4ONCR
S_KK4_74000135	IMG Activity: SIMG_CFMENUNMO4ONCP
S_KK4_74000136	IMG Activity: SIMG_CFMENUNMO4ONCE
S_KK4_74000137	IMG Activity: ISH_HCM_MONITOR_PRF
S_KK4_74000138	IMG Activity: SIMG_CFMENUNMO4SM35
S_KK4_74000139	IMG Activity: SIMG_CFMENUNMO4SM37
S_KK4_74000140	IMG Activity: SIMG_CFMENUNMO4SM36
S_KK4_74000141	IMG Activity: SIMG_CFMENUNMO4ON01
S_KK4_74000142	IMG Activity: SIMG_CFMENUNMO4ONCN
S_KK4_74000143	IMG Activity: SIMG_CFMENUNMO4ONCK
S_KK4_74000144	IMG Activity: ISH_HCM_301_HILFSPRG
S_KK4_74000145	IMG Activity: SIMG_CFMENUNMO4ONR0
S_KK4_74000146	IMG Activity: SIMG_CFMENUNMO4ON78
S_KK4_74000147	IMG Activity: SIMG_CFMENUNMO4ON7C
S_KK4_74000148	IMG Activity: SIMG_CFMENUNMO4ON7F
S_KK4_74000149	IMG Activity: SIMG_CFMENUNMO4ON7A
S_KK4_74000150	IMG Activity: SIMG_CFMENUNMO4ON76
S_KK4_74000151	IMG Activity: SIMG_CFMENUNMO4ON75
S_KK4_74000152	IMG Activity: ISH_ARCH_CUST
S_KK4_74000153	IMG Activity: ISH_ARCH_FAKTURA
S_KK4_74000154	IMG Activity: SIMG_CFMENUNMO4ONRB
S_KK4_74000155	IMG Activity: SIMG_CFMENUNMO4ONRA
S_KK4_74000156	IMG Activity : SIMG_CFMENUNMO4ONR1
S_KK4_74000157	IMG Activity: SIMG_CFMENUNMO4ONR3
S_KK4_74000158	IMG Activity: SIMG_CFMENUNMO4ONR2
S_KK4_74000159	IMG Activity: SIMG_ISHCM_REPORTS
S_KK4_74000160	IMG Activity: SIMG_ISHCM_GD_ERRS
S_KK4_74000161	IMG Activity: SIMG_ISHCM_GD_CUFO
S_KK4_74000162	IMG Activity: SIMG_ISHCM_GD_RECV
S_KK4_74000163	IMG Activity: SIMG_ISHCM_GD_SEND
S_KK4_74000164	IMG Activity: ISH_HCM_CCPS_INDIC
S_KK4_74000165	IMG Activity: ISH_HCM_301_SERVASGN
S_KK4_74000166	IMG Activity: SIMG_CFMENUNMO4ON7B
S_KK4_74000167	IMG Activity: SIMG_CFMENUNMO4ON79
S_KK4_74000168	IMG Activity: SIMG_CFMENUNMO4ON77
S_KK4_74000169	IMG Activity: SIMG_CFMENUNMO4ON73
S_KK4_74000170	IMG Activity: SIMG_CFMENUNMO4ON72
S_KK4_74000171	IMG Activity: SIMG_CFMENUNMO4ON71
S_KK4_74000172	IMG Activity: SIMG_CFMENUNMO4ON70
S_KK4_74000173	IMG Activity: SIMG_CFMENUNMO4ONC5
S_KK4_74000174	IMG Activity: ISH_MM_TNM01
S_KK4_74000175	IMG Activity: ISH_MM_TNM02
S_KK4_74000176	IMG Activity: SIMG_CMMENUNMO3HCO2
S_KK4_74000177	IMG Activity: SIMG_CMMENUNMO3HCO13

S_KK4_74000178	IMG Activity: ISH_CH_SAMMELAUFTRAG
S_KK4_74000179	IMG Activity: ISH_CH_KUNDE_SAMMEL
S_KK4_74000180	IMG Activity: ISH_CH_SAP_SAMMEL
S_KK4_74000181	IMG Activity: ISH_MM_KAT_HIER
S_KK4_74000182	IMG Activity: ISH_MM_HIT_DEF
S_KK4_74000183	IMG Activity: ISH_MM_SET_OE
S_KK4_74000184	IMG Activity: ISH_MM_SET_DEF
S_KK4_74000185	IMG Activity: ISH_MM_KAT_OE
S_KK4_74000186	IMG Activity: ISH_MM_KAT_DEF
S_KK4_74000187	IMG Activity: ISH_MM_GEART
S_KK4_74000188	IMG Activity: ISH_TNHCO
S_KK4_74000189	IMG Activity: ISH_SG_EST_TABLES
S_KK4_74000190	IMG Activity: ISH_SG_CHARGE_SCHEME
S_KK4_74000191	IMG Activity: ISH_PA_SAMMEL04
S_KK4_74000192	IMG Activity: ISH_PA_SAMMEL03
S_KK4_74000193	IMG Activity: ISH_PA_SAMMEL02
S_KK4_74000194	IMG Activity: ISH_PA_SAMMEL01
S_KK4_74000195	IMG Activity: SIMG_CMMENUNMO3HCO16
S_KK4_74000196	IMG Activity: SIMG_CMMENUNMO3HCO15
S_KK4_74000197	IMG Activity: ISH_VORKALKULATION
S_KK4_74000198	IMG Activity: SIMG_CMMENUNMO3HCO12
S_KK4_74000199	IMG Activity: ISHCO_RNUNO2K0
S_KK4_74000200	IMG Activity: SIMG_CMMENUNMO3HCO11
S_KK4_74000201	IMG Activity: ISH_CH_TNHCO
S_KK4_74000202	IMG Activity: ISH_EIS_CUSTOMIZING
S_KK4_74000203	IMG Activity: SIMG_CFMENUNMO4ONCA
S_KK4_74000204	IMG Activity: SIMG_CFMENUNMO4ONC8
S_KK4_74000205	IMG Activity: SIMG_CFMENUNMO4ONC3
S_KK4_74000206	IMG Activity: SIMG_CFMENUNMO4NC20
S_KK4_74000207	IMG Activity: SIMG_CFMENUNMO4ONC1
S_KK4_74000208	IMG Activity: SIMG_CFMENUNMO4NC10
S_KK4_74000209	IMG Activity: ISH_V2_V3_PUNKTWERTE
S_KK4_74000210	IMG Activity: SIMG_CFMENUNMO4SM59
S_KK4_74000211	IMG Activity: SIMG_CFMENUNMO4SM54
S_KK4_74000212	IMG Activity: SIMG_CFMENUNMO4ONC6
S_KK4_74000213	IMG Activity: SIMG_CFMENUNMO4ONCT
S_KK4_74000214	IMG Activity: SIMG_CFMENUNMO4ONCH
S_KK4_74000215	IMG Activity: SIMG_CFMENUNMO4ONCG
S_KK4_74000216	IMG Activity: SIMG_CFMENUNMO4ONCC
S_KK4_74000217	IMG Activity: SIMG_CFMENUNMA4ONS1
S_KK4_74000218	IMG Activity: SIMG_CFMENUNMO4ONRK
S_KK4_74000219	IMG Activity: SIMG_CFMENUNMO4ONRF
S_KK4_74000220	IMG Activity: SIMG_CFMENUNMO4ONRL
S_KK4_74000221	IMG Activity: ISH_TNEI0
S_KK4_74000222	IMG Activity: ISH_TNFCL
S_KK4_74000223	IMG Activity: ISH_TNEIS
S_KK4_74000224	IMG Activity: SIMG_CFMENUNMO4ONRD
S_KK4_74000225	IMG Activity: SIMG_CFMENUNMO4ONRC
S_KK4_74000226	IMG Activity: SIMG_CFMENUNMO4ON88
S_KK4_74000227	IMG Activity: SIMG_CFMENUNMO4ONRE
S_KK4_74000228	IMG Activity: SIMG_TNABETTEN
S_KK4_74000229	IMG Activity: SIMG_N1FAPF
S_KK4_74000230	IMG Activity: SIMG_N1GES
S_KK4_74000231	IMG Activity: SIMG_CFMENUNMOJONA0

S_KK4_74000232	IMG Activity: SIMG_CFMENUNMO2ON44
S_KK4_74000233	IMG Activity: SIMG_CFMENUNMO2ON43
S_KK4_74000234	IMG Activity: SIMG_CFMENUNMO1ON03
S_KK4_74000235	IMG Activity: ISH_TN15D
S_KK4_74000236	IMG Activity: SIMG_CFMENUNMO1ON04
S_KK4_74000237	IMG Activity: TN15G
S_KK4_74000238	IMG Activity: ISH_TN40C
S_KK4_74000239	IMG Activity: SIMG_CFMENUNMO2ONDT
S_KK4_74000240	IMG Activity: SIMG_CFMENUNMO2ON59
S_KK4_74000241	IMG Activity: ISH_BAS_BENUTZER_ZUO
S_KK4_74000242	IMG Activity: SIMG_CFMENUNMO2ONB8
S_KK4_74000243	IMG Activity: ISH_CH_BEWART
S_KK4_74000244	IMG Activity: SIMG_CFMENUNMO2ONVC
S_KK4_74000245	IMG Activity: SIMG_CFMENUNMO2ON4A
S_KK4_74000246	IMG Activity: SIMG_CFMENUNMO2ON41
S_KK4_74000247	IMG Activity: SIMG_CFMENUNMO1ON17
S_KK4_74000248	IMG Activity: SIMG_CFMENUNMO2ONN5
S_KK4_74000249	IMG Activity: SIMG_CFMENUNMO1ON18
S_KK4_74000250	IMG Activity: ISH_CH_AHVNR
S_KK4_74000251	IMG Activity: ISH_TNDCV_IMG
S_KK4_74000252	IMG Activity: SIMG_CFMENUNMO2ONVB
S_KK4_74000253	IMG Activity: SIMG_CFMENUNMO2ON42
S_KK4_74000254	IMG Activity: SIMG_CFMENUNMO1ONP1
S_KK4_74000255	IMG Activity: SIMG_CFMENUNMO2ON30
S_KK4_74000256	IMG Activity: SIMG_CFMENUNMO2ON29
S_KK4_74000257	IMG Activity: ISH_NR_TERMINRESERV
S_KK4_74000258	IMG Activity: SIMG_CFMENUNMO2ON48
S_KK4_74000259	IMG Activity: SIMG_CFMENUNMO2ON47
S_KK4_74000260	IMG Activity: ISH_CH_OPKZ
S_KK4_74000261	IMG Activity: ISH_BAS_BENUTZER_PFL
S_KK4_74000262	IMG Activity: ISH_NRSF_SG
S_KK4_74000263	IMG Activity: SIMG_CFMENUNMO2ON39
S_KK4_74000264	IMG Activity: SIMG_ISHMED_TN26A
S_KK4_74000265	IMG Activity: SIMG_ISHMED_TN26G
S_KK4_74000266	IMG Activity: SIMG_ISHMED_TN26F
S_KK4_74000267	IMG Activity: ISH_TNDIA
S_KK4_74000268	IMG Activity: ISH_TN14O
S_KK4_74000269	IMG Activity: SIMG_CFMENUNMO2ON49
S_KK4_74000270	IMG Activity: SIMG_CFMENUNMO2ONVD
S_KK4_74000271	IMG Activity: ISH_V_N1STGR
S_KK4_74000272	IMG Activity: SIMG_CFMENUNMO2ON45
S_KK4_74000273	IMG Activity: ISH_TN14H
S_KK4_74000274	IMG Activity: ISH_TN14K
S_KK4_74000275	IMG Activity: ISH_TN14I
S_KK4_74000276	IMG Activity: SIMG_CFMENUNMO2ON34
S_KK4_74000277	IMG Activity: SIMG_CFMENUNMO2ONVI
S_KK4_74000278	IMG Activity: ISH_BAS_BENUTZER_GRP
S_KK4_74000279	IMG Activity: ISH_WAITINGLIST_STAT
S_KK4_74000280	IMG Activity: ISH_WAITINGLIST_RSN
S_KK4_74000281	IMG Activity: ISH_WAITINGLIST_TYPE
S_KK4_74000282	IMG Activity: ISH_PRIO_WARTELISTE
S_KK4_74000283	IMG Activity: ISH_CH_PATTYP
S_KK4_74000284	IMG Activity: SIMG_CFMENUNMOAON81
S_KK4_74000285	IMG Activity: SIMG_CFMENUNMO1ON74

S_KK4_74000286	IMG Activity: SIMG_CFMENUNMOB0NT2
S_KK4_74000287	IMG Activity: ISH_TN12R
S_KK4_74000288	IMG Activity: ISH_NL_ARZT_KTRAGER
S_KK4_74000289	IMG Activity: ISH_PA_GPART_KTR01
S_KK4_74000290	IMG Activity: ISH_CH_TARTYP
S_KK4_74000291	IMG Activity: ISH_CH_LEISTTXT_KZL
S_KK4_74000292	IMG Activity: ISH_LEIST_KATEGORIE
S_KK4_74000293	IMG Activity: SIMG_CFMENUNMOANT70
S_KK4_74000294	IMG Activity: SIMG_CFMENUNMOAON82
S_KK4_74000295	IMG Activity: SIMG_CFMENUNMO1ONN1
S_KK4_74000296	IMG Activity: SIMG_CFMENUNMO1ONN3
S_KK4_74000297	IMG Activity: SIMG_CFMENUNMO1ON62
S_KK4_74000298	IMG Activity: SIMG_CFMENUNMO1ONN2
S_KK4_74000299	IMG Activity: SIMG_CFMENUNMO1ON52
S_KK4_74000300	IMG Activity: SIMG_CFMENUNMO1ON50
S_KK4_74000301	IMG Activity: SIMG_CFMENUNMO1ONOB
S_KK4_74000302	IMG Activity: SIMG_CFMENUNMO1ON51
S_KK4_74000303	IMG Activity: SIMG_CFMENUNMO1ON54
S_KK4_74000304	IMG Activity: ISH_TNACC
S_KK4_74000305	IMG Activity: SIMG_CFMENUNMO1ON68
S_KK4_74000306	IMG Activity: SIMG_CFMENUNMO1ON61
S_KK4_74000307	IMG Activity: SIMG_CFMENUNMO1ON60
S_KK4_74000308	IMG Activity: SIMG_CFMENUNMO1ON64
S_KK4_74000309	IMG Activity: SIMG_CFMENUNMOAON99
S_KK4_74000310	IMG Activity: SIMG_CFMENUNMO2ON26
S_KK4_74000311	IMG Activity: ISH_TN17D
S_KK4_74000312	IMG Activity: SIMG_CFMENUNMO2ONN4
S_KK4_74000313	IMG Activity: SIMG_CFMENUNMO1ON14
S_KK4_74000314	IMG Activity: SIMG_CFMENUNMO2ONWA
S_KK4_74000315	IMG Activity: SIMG_CFMENUNMO2ON16
S_KK4_74000316	IMG Activity: ISH_CH_PATART
S_KK4_74000317	IMG Activity: ISH_TN17R
S_KK4_74000318	IMG Activity: SIMG_CFMENUNMO2ON25
S_KK4_74000319	IMG Activity: SIMG_CFMENUNMO1ON21
S_KK4_74000320	IMG Activity: SIMG_CFMENUNMO2ON28
S_KK4_74000321	IMG Activity: SIMG_CFMENUNMO2ON27
S_KK4_74000322	IMG Activity: ISH_CH_EINZG_KANTTAR
S_KK4_74000323	IMG Activity: ISH_CH_ABKOMMEN
S_KK4_74000324	IMG Activity: SIMG_CFMENUNMO2ON36
S_KK4_74000325	IMG Activity: ISH_CH_KANTONSTARIF
S_KK4_74000326	IMG Activity: ISH_NTPZ2
S_KK4_74000327	IMG Activity: ISH_NTPZ1
S_KK4_74000328	IMG Activity: SIMG_CFMENUNMOAON83
S_KK4_74000329	IMG Activity: ISH_PM_EINZUGSGEB
S_KK4_74000330	IMG Activity: ISH_POSTALCODES_SG
S_KK4_74000331	IMG Activity: ISH_POSTALCODES_ES
S_KK4_74000332	IMG Activity: ISH_INPUT_DIAKAT
S_KK4_74000333	IMG Activity: SIMG_CFMENUNMO2ON37
S_KK4_74000334	IMG Activity: ISH_CH_PLZ_REGION
S_KK4_74000335	IMG Activity: ISH_CH_LEISTAUFTEIL
S_KK4_74000336	IMG Activity: ISH_CH_HOECHSTWERTE
S_KK4_74000337	IMG Activity: ISH_CH_PAUSCHAL_ABRK
S_KK4_74000338	IMG Activity: SIMG_CFMENUNM01ON05
S_KK4_74000339	IMG Activity: ISH_AT_MAX_VALUES

S_KK4_74000340	IMG Activity: SIMG_CFMENUNMO1ON01
S_KK4_74000341	IMG Activity: ISH_PA_FPSE_REGELN
S_KK4_74000342	IMG Activity: ISH_SURCHARGESERVICE
S_KK4_74000343	IMG Activity: ISH_TNKRS
S_KK4_74000344	IMG Activity: ISH_CH_RADIOLOGIE
S_KK4_74000345	IMG Activity: ISH_CH_OPSZUS
S_KK4_74000346	IMG Activity: ISH_CH_LEISTZUS
S_KK4_74000347	IMG Activity: ISH_AT_MAX_GROUPS
S_KK4_74000348	IMG Activity: SIMG_CFMENUNMO1ON19
S_KK4_74000349	IMG Activity: SIMG_CFMENUNMO1ON06
S_KK4_74000350	IMG Activity: SIMG_CFMENUNMO1ON20
S_KK4_74000351	IMG Activity: SIMG_CFMENUNMO1ON02
S_KK4_74000352	IMG Activity: ISH_LATE_CHARGES
S_KK4_74000353	IMG Activity: ISH_MAX_GROUPS
S_KK4_74000354	IMG Activity: ISH_AT_LEIST_UMSCH
S_KK4_74000355	IMG Activity: ISH_AT_PAUSCHAL_ABRK
S_KK4_74000356	IMG Activity: ISH_NL_PA_INCLEXLC
S_KK4_74000357	IMG Activity: ISH_NL_REGEL_AUFN
S_KK4_74000358	IMG Activity: ISH_NL_LEI_REGELN02
S_KK4_74000359	IMG Activity: ISH_NL_LEI_REGELN01
S_KK4_74000360	IMG Activity: ISH_SG_EXTCONTRACT
S_KK4_74000361	IMG Activity: SIMG_VTRGKTART
S_KK4_74000362	IMG Activity: SIMG_TNWCH74
S_KK4_74000363	IMG Activity: ISH_SG_CONTRACT_CAT
S_KK4_74000364	IMG Activity: SIMG_CFMENUNMO3ONAA
S_KK4_74000365	IMG Activity: SIMG_CFMENUNMO3ON35
S_KK4_74000366	IMG Activity: SIMG_CFMENUNMOJFBMP
S_KK4_74000367	IMG Activity: SIMG_CFMENUNMOJOBVU
S_KK4_74000368	IMG Activity: SIMG_CFMENUNMOJOBB9
S_KK4_74000369	IMG Activity: SIMG_CFMENUNMOJOBD2
S_KK4_74000370	IMG Activity: SIMG_CFMENUNMOJXDN1
S_KK4_74000371	IMG Activity: ISH_SG_MEDISAVE_EST
S_KK4_74000372	IMG Activity: SIMG_CFMENUNMO3ON46
S_KK4_74000374	IMG Activity: SIMG_CFMENUNMOBON97
S_KK4_74000375	IMG Activity: SIMG_CFMENUNMOBON49
S_KK4_74000376	IMG Activity: ISH_MANDANT_RESET
S_KK4_74000377	IMG Activity: ISH_PA_FPSE_PARAM
S_KK4_74000378	IMG Activity: ISH_BAS_EINR_ANLEGEN
S_KK4_74000379	IMG Activity: ISH_SYSPARM_VV
S_KK4_74000380	IMG Activity: ISH_NL_PA_VVNL01
S_KK4_74000381	IMG Activity: ISH_PA_GPART_VV
S_KK4_74000382	IMG Activity: SIMG_INSPROVTYPE
S_KK4_74000383	IMG Activity: ISH_CH_KTARTEN
S_KK4_74000384	IMG Activity: SIMG_CFMENUNMOBONV7
S_KK4_74000385	IMG Activity: ISH_MAX_VALUES
S_KK4_74000386	IMG Activity: SIMG_CFMENUNMO1ONK2
S_KK4_74000387	IMG Activity: SIMG_CFMENUNMO1ONK5
S_KK4_74000388	IMG Activity: SIMG_CFMENUNMO2ON83
S_KK4_74000389	IMG Activity: SIMG_CFMENUNMO1ONB2
S_KK4_74000391	IMG Activity: SIMG_CFMENUNMO1ONK1
S_KK4_74000392	IMG Activity: SIMG_CFMENUNMO3ONBT
S_KK4_74000393	IMG Activity: ISH_TARAS_RULES
S_KK4_74000394	IMG Activity: ISH_CH_ABWESENHEITEN
S_KK4_74000395	IMG Activity: ISH_ABWES_1

S_KK4_74000396	IMG Activity: SIMG_CFMENUNMO3ON07
S_KK4_74000397	IMG Activity: ISH_UE_KUNDE
S_KK4_74000398	IMG Activity: ISH_KONFIGURATION
S_KK4_74000399	IMG Activity: SIMG_ISHMED_SWORT
S_KK4_74000400	IMG Activity: SIMG_ISHMED_N2HL
S_KK4_74000401	IMG Activity: SIMG_ISHMED_N2DZ
S_KK4_74000402	IMG Activity: ISH_DOKUMENTENART
S_KK4_74000403	IMG Activity: SIMG_CFMENUNMO2ON81
S_KK4_74000405	IMG Activity: ISH_UE_SAP
S_KK4_74000406	IMG Activity: SIMG_CFMENUNMO2ON80
S_KK4_74000407	IMG Activity: ISH_NUM_KREIS_DOKART
S_KK4_74000408	IMG Activity: ISH_ABR_ROLTP
S_KK4_74000409	IMG Activity: ISH_PA_RECH02
S_KK4_74000410	IMG Activity: ISH_PA_GPART_LEI03
S_KK4_74000411	IMG Activity: ISH_PA_RECH03
S_KK4_74000412	IMG Activity: ISH_PA_PFLEGE02
S_KK4_74000413	IMG Activity: SIMG_CFMENUNMO1ONK6
S_KK4_74000414	IMG Activity: SIMG_CFMENUNMO3ONL5
S_KK4_74000415	IMG Activity: ISH_PA_PFLEGE01
S_KK4_74000416	IMG Activity: ISH_BAS_SYSPAR_UEPFL
S_KK4_74000417	IMG Activity: SIMG_CFMENUNMO1ONK3
S_KK4_74000418	IMG Activity: SIMG_CFMENUNMO3ONL2
S_KK4_74000419	IMG Activity: SIMG_CFMENUNMO3ONL1
S_KK4_74000420	IMG Activity: SIMG_CFMENUNMO3ONB9
S_KK4_74000421	IMG Activity: ISH_PA_GPART_LEI01
S_KK4_74000422	IMG Activity: ISH_PA_RECH01
S_KK4_74000423	IMG Activity: ISH_PA_GPART_LEI02
S_KK4_74000424	IMG Activity: SIMG_CFMENUNMO3UMF2
S_KK4_74000425	IMG Activity: SIMG_CFMENUNMO1ONK4
S_KK4_74000426	IMG Activity: ISH_SD_FUNKTIONEN
S_KK4_74000427	IMG Activity: ISH_PA_BEISPIEL
S_KK4_74000428	IMG Activity: ISH_BERECHT_CUST
S_KK4_74000429	IMG Activity: ISH_HCM_P302_DO_CUST
S_KK4_74000430	IMG Activity: ISH_HCM_ELACH_DO_CUS
S_KK4_74000431	IMG Activity: ISH_HCM_CCPS_DO_CUST
S_KK4_74000432	IMG Activity: ISH_HCM_NPMI_DO_CUST
S_KK4_74000433	IMG Activity: SIMG_ISHCM_FCTDOC
S_KK4_74000434	IMG Activity: SIMG_ISHCM_GD_INST
S_KK4_74000435	IMG Activity: SIMG_CMMENUNMO3SPEZ5
S_KK4_74000436	IMG Activity: ISH_EIS_RFC
S_KK4_74000437	IMG Activity: SIMG_CFMENUNMO2ONE5
S_KK4_74000438	IMG Activity: ISH_SET_GET
S_KK4_74000439	IMG Activity: ISH_HCM_301_PRGLIST
S_KK4_74000440	IMG Activity: ISH_HCM_301_DO_CUST
S_KK4_74000441	IMG Activity: SIMG_ISHCM_TYPSPEC
S_KK4_74000442	IMG Activity: SIMG_CMMENUNMO3SPEZ2
S_KK4_74000443	IMG Activity: SIMG_CMMENUNMO3SPEZ4
S_KK4_74000444	IMG Activity: ISH_OM_BASICS
S_KK4_74000446	IMG Activity: SIMG_SE_ORG_ISH_O41
S_KK4_74000447	IMG Activity: SIMG_CMMENUNMO3SPEZ0
S_KK4_74000448	IMG Activity: SIMG_ISHCM_TRANSPORT
S_KK4_74000449	IMG Activity: SIMG_ISHCM_GD_CRIT
S_KK4_74000450	IMG Activity: ISH_CH_PA_BEISPIEL
S_KK4_74000451	IMG Activity: SIMG_CMMENUNMO3SPEZ6

S_KK4_74000452	IMG Activity: SIMG_ISHCM_EXTPROG
S_KK4_74000467	IMG Activity: ISH_COPA_BEWERTZUORD
S_KK4_74000558	IMG Activity: SIMG_ISHMED_TN2K4
S_KK4_74000559	IMG Activity: SIMG_ISHMED_N1STPL
S_KK4_74000560	IMG Activity: SIMG_ISHMED_TN2K2
S_KK4_74000561	IMG Activity: SIMG_ISHMED_N2GT
S_KK4_74000562	IMG Activity: SIMG_ISHMED_TN2K3
S_KK4_74000563	IMG Activity: SIMG_ISHMED_PERI002
S_KK4_74000564	IMG Activity: SIMG_ISHMED_PERI003
S_KK4_74000565	IMG Activity: SIMG_PERINAT_ANMANRI
S_KK4_74000566	IMG Activity: SIMG_PERINAT_ASSARI
S_KK4_74000567	IMG Activity: SIMG_ISHMED_N2PS
S_KK4_74000568	IMG Activity: SIMG_ISHMED_V_N1SR
S_KK4_74000569	IMG Activity: SIMG_ISHMED_V_N1SU
S_KK4_74000570	IMG Activity: ISHMED_N1LAGRG
S_KK4_74000571	IMG Activity: ISHMED_N1POBKL
S_KK4_74000572	IMG Activity: SIMG_ISHMED_OPDOKEIN
S_KK4_74000573	IMG Activity: SIMG_ISHMED_OPZEITEN
S_KK4_74000574	IMG Activity: SIMG_ISHMED_TN2K0
S_KK4_74000575	IMG Activity: SIMG_ISHMED_N2BK
S_KK4_74000576	IMG Activity: SIMG_ISHMED_TN2K1
S_KK4_74000577	IMG Activity: SIMG_PERINAT_AZGGIND
S_KK4_74000578	IMG Activity: SIMG_PERINAT_MITARB
S_KK4_74000579	IMG Activity: SIMG_PERINAT_NATION
S_KK4_74000580	IMG Activity: SIMG_PERINAT_NBERUF
S_KK4_74000581	IMG Activity: SIMG_PERINAT_PNDDIIC
S_KK4_74000582	IMG Activity: SIMG_PERINAT_PNDDRIC
S_KK4_74000583	IMG Activity: SIMG_PERINAT_PNDFBC
S_KK4_74000584	IMG Activity: SIMG_PERINAT_PNDSEIN
S_KK4_74000585	IMG Activity: SIMG_PERINAT_VEKL
S_KK4_74000586	IMG Activity: SIMG_ISHMED_RAD002
S_KK4_74000587	IMG Activity: SIMG_PERINAT_KATD
S_KK4_74000588	IMG Activity: SIMG_PERINAT_EKIERKR
S_KK4_74000589	IMG Activity: SIMG_PERINAT_EKIFBID
S_KK4_74000590	IMG Activity: SIMG_PERINAT_EKIVERG
S_KK4_74000591	IMG Activity: SIMG_PERINAT_GKIGM
S_KK4_74000592	IMG Activity: SIMG_PERINAT_GKIGPO
S_KK4_74000593	IMG Activity: SIMG_PERINAT_GKIGRIS
S_KK4_74000594	IMG Activity: SIMG_PERINAT_GKIGVW
S_KK4_74000595	IMG Activity: SIMG_PERINAT_GKIKLAG
S_KK4_74000596	IMG Activity: SIMG_PERINAT_KATB
S_KK4_74000597	IMG Activity: SIMG_ISHMED_NRKR_ATP
S_KK4_74000598	IMG Activity: SIMG_ISHMED_INTV_ZUO
S_KK4_74000599	IMG Activity: SIMG_ISHMED_V_N1AST
S_KK4_74000600	IMG Activity: SIMG_ISHMED_N1APRI
S_KK4_74000601	IMG Activity: SIMG_ISHMED_V_N1TA
S_KK4_74000602	IMG Activity: SIMG_ISHMED_BESUSTAT
S_KK4_74000603	IMG Activity: SIMG_ISHMED_NRKR_UNF
S_KK4_74000604	IMG Activity: SIMG_ISHMED_NRKR_ANF
S_KK4_74000605	IMG Activity: SIMG_ISHMED_KENNZEI
S_KK4_74000606	IMG Activity: SIMG_ISHMED_EINZEITU
S_KK4_74000607	IMG Activity: SIMG_ISHMED_EINZEITA
S_KK4_74000608	IMG Activity: SIMG_ISHMED_PARPFLEG
S_KK4_74000609	IMG Activity: SIMG_ISHMED_USRMA

S_KK4_74000610	IMG Activity: SIMG_ISHMED_TN2PCDES
S_KK4_74000611	IMG Activity: SIMG_ISHMED_V_N1LSTA
S_KK4_74000612	IMG Activity: SIMG_ISHMED_LSTGRTYP
S_KK4_74000613	IMG Activity: SIMG_ISHMED_V_N1STGR
S_KK4_74000614	IMG Activity: SIMG_ISHMED_OPNKRS
S_KK4_74000615	IMG Activity: SIMG_ISHMED_ANNR
S_KK4_74000616	IMG Activity: SIMG_ISHMED_N2ANART
S_KK4_74000617	IMG Activity: SIMG_ISHMED_NRKR_VKG
S_KK4_74000618	IMG Activity: SIMG_ISHMED_RAD001
S_KK4_74000619	IMG Activity: SIMG_ISHMED_PERI001
S_KK4_74000620	IMG Activity: ISHMED_OP_PROGRAMM
S_KK4_74000621	IMG Activity: SIMG_ISHMED_USEREXIT
S_KK4_74000622	IMG Activity: SIMG_ISHMED_SET_GET
S_KK4_74000623	IMG Activity: SIMG_ISHMED_TN2KUM01
S_KK4_74000624	IMG Activity: SIMG_ISHMED_TN2KUM06
S_KK4_74000625	IMG Activity: SIMG_ISHMED_TN2KUM03
S_KK4_74000626	IMG Activity: SIMG_ISHMED_TN2KUM05
S_KK4_74000627	IMG Activity: SIMG_ISHMED_MDV_01
S_KK4_74000628	IMG Activity: SIMG_ISHMED_OD03
S_KK4_74000629	IMG Activity: SIMG_ISHMED_TN26E
S_KK4_74000630	IMG Activity: SIMG_ISHMED_TN26C
S_KK4_74000631	IMG Activity: SIMG_ISHMED_TN26D
S_KK4_74000632	IMG Activity: SIMG_ISHMED_TN2KUM04
S_KK4_74000633	IMG Activity: SIMG_ISHMED_TN2KUM07
S_KK4_74000634	IMG Activity: SIMG_ISHMED_TN2KUM02
S_KK4_74000635	IMG Activity: SIMG_ISHMED_OD02
S_KK4_74000636	IMG Activity: SIMG_ISHMED_LABSLIST
S_KK4_74000637	IMG Activity: SIMG_ISHMED_N2LABS
S_KK4_74000638	IMG Activity: SIMG_ISHMED_FDBS
S_KK4_74000639	IMG Activity: SIMG_ISHMED_FD
S_KK4_74000640	IMG Activity: SIMG_ISHMED_FDBSNUM
S_KK4_74000641	IMG Activity: SIMG_ISHMED_BILDMOD
S_KK4_74000642	IMG Activity: SIMG_ISHMED_DVS10
S_KK4_74000643	IMG Activity: SIMG_ISHMED_OD11
S_KK4_74000644	IMG Activity: SIMG_ISHMED_OD00
S_KK4_74000645	IMG Activity: _ISUBS_000002
S_KK4_74000646	IMG Activity: _ISUBS_000001
S_KK4_74000647	IMG Activity: _ISUBFPS_000002
S_KK4_74000648	IMG Activity: _ISUBFPS_000006
S_KK4_74000649	IMG Activity: _ISUBFPS_000001
S_KK4_74000650	IMG Activity: _ISUBFPS_000008
S_KK4_74000651	IMG Activity: _ISUBFPS_000011
S_KK4_74000652	IMG Activity: _ISUBFRS_000007
S_KK4_74000653	IMG Activity: _ISUBFRS_000006
S_KK4_74000654	IMG Activity: _ISUBF_000004
S_KK4_74000655	IMG Activity: _ISUBF_000002
S_KK4_74000656	IMG Activity: _ISUBF_000003
S_KK4_74000657	IMG Activity: _ISUBFPS_000009
S_KK4_74000658	IMG Activity: _ISUBFPS_000004
S_KK4_74000659	IMG Activity: _ISUBFPS_000003
S_KK4_74000660	IMG Activity: _ISUBFPS_000007
S_KK4_74000661	IMG Activity: _ISUBFRS_000005
S_KK4_74000662	IMG Activity: _ISUBFRS_000002
S_KK4_74000663	IMG Activity: _ISUBFRS_000001

S_KK4_74000664	IMG Activity: _ISUBFRS_000012
S_KK4_74000665	IMG Activity: _ISUBFRS_000011
S_KK4_74000666	IMG Activity: _ISUBFRS_000009
S_KK4_74000667	IMG Activity: _ISUBFRS_000003
S_KK4_74000668	IMG Activity: _ISUBFRS_000004
S_KK4_74000669	IMG Activity: _ISUBDCO_000002
S_KK4_74000670	IMG Activity: _ISUBDCO_000003
S_KK4_74000671	IMG Activity: _ISUBDCO_000001
S_KK4_74000672	IMG Activity: _ISUBDIN_000007
S_KK4_74000673	IMG Activity: _ISUBDCT_000004
S_KK4_74000674	IMG Activity: _ISUBDCT_000003
S_KK4_74000675	IMG Activity: _ISUBDCT_000002
S_KK4_74000676	IMG Activity: _ISUBDCT_000005
S_KK4_74000677	IMG Activity: _ISUBDCO_000004
S_KK4_74000678	IMG Activity: _ISUBDIN_000001
S_KK4_74000679	IMG Activity: _ISUBDIN_000006
S_KK4_74000680	IMG Activity: _ISUBDPR_000006
S_KK4_74000681	IMG Activity: _ISUBDPR_000004
S_KK4_74000682	IMG Activity: _ISUBDPR_000002
S_KK4_74000683	IMG Activity: _ISUBDPR_000005
S_KK4_74000684	IMG Activity: _ISUBDPR_000001
S_KK4_74000685	IMG Activity: _ISUBDIN_000002
S_KK4_74000686	IMG Activity: _ISUBDBP_000010
S_KK4_74000687	IMG Activity: _ISUBDBP_000002
S_KK4_74000688	IMG Activity: _ISUBDIN_000008
S_KK4_74000689	IMG Activity: _ISUBDBP_000008
S_KK4_74000690	IMG Activity: _ISUBDIN_000009
S_KK4_74000691	IMG Activity: _ISUBD_000002
S_KK4_74000692	IMG Activity: _ISUBDDL_000002
S_KK4_74000693	IMG Activity: _ISUBDDL_000001
S_KK4_74000694	IMG Activity: _ISUBDCT_000001
S_KK4_74000695	IMG Activity: _ISUBDIN_000004
S_KK4_74000696	IMG Activity: _ISUBDBP_000007
S_KK4_74000697	IMG Activity: _ISUBDBP_000006
S_KK4_74000698	IMG Activity: _ISUBDBP_000011
S_KK4_74000699	IMG Activity: _ISUBDIN_000005
S_KK4_74000700	IMG Activity: _ISUBDBP_000004
S_KK4_74000701	IMG Activity: _ISUBDBP_000005
S_KK4_74000702	IMG Activity: _ISUDMMROR_000003
S_KK4_74000703	IMG Activity: _ISUDMMROS_000002
S_KK4_74000704	IMG Activity: _ISUDMMR_000027
S_KK4_74000705	IMG Activity: _ISUDMMR_000025
S_KK4_74000706	IMG Activity: _ISUDMMR_000024
S_KK4_74000707	IMG Activity: _ISUDMMR_000031
S_KK4_74000708	IMG Activity: _ISUDMMR_000021
S_KK4_74000709	IMG Activity: _ISUDMMRDC_000008
S_KK4_74000710	IMG Activity: _ISUDMMRDC_000003
S_KK4_74000714	IMG Activity: _ISUDMMRDC_000002
S_KK4_74000715	IMG Activity: _ISUDMMRDC_000013
S_KK4_74000716	IMG Activity: _ISUDMMR_000020
S_KK4_74000717	IMG Activity: _ISUDMMR_000036
S_KK4_74000718	IMG Activity: _ISUDMMR_000038
S_KK4_74000719	IMG Activity: _ISUDMMR_000037
S_KK4_74000720	IMG Activity: _ISUDMMR_000034

S_KK4_74000721	IMIMG Activity: _ISUDMMR_000033
S_KK4_74000722	IMG Activity: _ISUDMDIIS_000003
S_KK4_74000723	IMG Activity: _ISUDMDIMD_000002
S_KK4_74000724	IMG Activity: _ISUDMMR_000017
S_KK4_74000725	IMG Activity: _ISUDMMR_000035
S_KK4_74000726	IMG Activity: _ISUDMMR_000012
S_KK4_74000727	IMG Activity: _ISUDMMR_000004
S_KK4_74000728	IMG Activity: _ISUDMMR_000010
S_KK4_74000729	IMG Activity: _ISUDMMR_000028
S_KK4_74000730	IMG Activity: _ISUDMMR_000009
S_KK4_74000731	IMG Activity: _ISUDMMRDC_000005
S_KK4_74000732	IMG Activity: _ISUDMISSL_000010
S_KK4_74000733	IMG Activity: _ISUDMISSL_000009
S_KK4_74000734	IMG Activity: _ISUDMISSL_000004
S_KK4_74000735	IMG Activity: _ISUDMISSL_000003
S_KK4_74000736	IMG Activity: _ISUDMISSL_000006
S_KK4_74000737	IMG Activity: _ISUDMISSL_000005
S_KK4_74000738	IMG Activity: _ISUDMISSL_000002
S_KK4_74000739	IMG Activity: _ISUDMISCT_000002
S_KK4_74000740	IMG Activity: _ISUDMISCT_000004
S_KK4_74000741	IMG Activity: _ISUDMISWO_000002
S_KK4_74000742	IMG Activity: _ISUDMISPR_000002
S_KK4_74000743	IMG Activity: _ISUDMISPR_000003
S_KK4_74000744	IMG Activity: _ISUDMISSL_000011
S_KK4_74000745	IMG Activity: _ISUDMISSL_000008
S_KK4_74000746	IMG Activity: _ISUDMIS_000003
S_KK4_74000747	IMG Activity: _ISUDMMRDO_000004
S_KK4_74000748	IMG Activity: _ISUDMMRDO_000003
S_KK4_74000749	IMG Activity: _ISUDMMRDO_000002
S_KK4_74000750	IMG Activity: _ISUDMMRDC_000012
S_KK4_74000751	IMG Activity: _ISUDMMRDC_000011
S_KK4_74000752	IMG Activity: _ISUDMMRDC_000006
S_KK4_74000753	IMG Activity: _ISUDMMRDC_000004
S_KK4_74000754	IMG Activity: _ISUDMMRRA_000002
S_KK4_74000755	IMG Activity: _ISUDMMRRE_000002
S_KK4_74000756	IMG Activity: _ISUDMMRRE_000003
S_KK4_74000757	IMG Activity: _ISUDMMR_000003
S_KK4_74000760	IMG Activity: _ISUDMMRDO_000005
S_KK4_74000761	IMG Activity: _ISUDMTDDT_000008
S_KK4_74000762	IMG Activity: _ISUDMTDDT_000004
S_KK4_74000763	IMG Activity: _ISUDMTDDT_000003
S_KK4_74000764	IMG Activity: _ISUDMTD_000005
S_KK4_74000765	IMG Activity: _ISUDMTDDT_000009
S_KK4_74000766	IMG Activity: _ISUDMTDDT_000005
S_KK4_74000767	IMG Activity: _ISUDMTDIO_000008
S_KK4_74000768	IMG Activity: _ISUDMTDDV_000003
S_KK4_74000769	IMG Activity: _ISUDMTDDV_000004
S_KK4_74000770	IMG Activity: _ISUDMTDRG_000006
S_KK4_74000771	IMG Activity: _ISUDMTDDT_000006
S_KK4_74000772	IMG Activity: _ISUDMTDIO_000002
S_KK4_74000773	IMG Activity: _ISUDMTDDT_000007
S_KK4_74000774	IMG Activity: _ISUDMTDIO_000003
S_KK4_74000775	IMG Activity: _ISUDMTDCO_000003
S_KK4_74000776	IMG Activity: _ISUDMTDCO_000004

S_KK4_74000777	IMG Activity: _ISUDMTDCO_000002
S_KK4_74000778	IMG Activity: _ISUDMTDIO_000005
S_KK4_74000779	IMG Activity: _ISUDMTDIO_000006
S_KK4_74000780	IMG Activity: _ISUDMTDIO_000007
S_KK4_74000781	IMG Activity: _ISUDMTDIO_000004
S_KK4_74000782	IMG Activity: _ISUDMTDWG_000005
S_KK4_74000783	IMG Activity: _ISUDMTDWG_000007
S_KK4_74000784	IMG Activity: _ISUDMTDWG_000004
S_KK4_74000785	IMG Activity: _ISUDMTDWG_000003
S_KK4_74000786	IMG Activity: _ISUDMTDWG_000006
S_KK4_74000787	IMG Activity: _ISUDMTDWG_000002
S_KK4_74000788	IMG Activity: _ISUDMDIDG_000002
S_KK4_74000789	IMG Activity: _ISUDMDI_000006
S_KK4_74000790	IMG Activity: _ISUDMDI_000003
S_KK4_74000791	IMG Activity: _ISUDMDI_000005
S_KK4_74000792	IMG Activity: _ISUDMTDRG_000002
S_KK4_74000793	IMG Activity: _ISUDMTD_000003
S_KK4_74000794	IMG Activity: _ISUDMDIDG_000005
S_KK4_74000795	IMG Activity: _ISUDMDIDG_000004
S_KK4_74000796	IMG Activity: _ISUDMDIDG_000003
S_KK4_74000797	IMG Activity: _ISUDMTD_000004
S_KK4_74000798	IMG Activity: _ISUDMTDRG_000003
S_KK4_74000799	IMG Activity: _ISUDMTDRG_000004
S_KK4_74000800	IMG Activity: _ISUDMTDDV_000006
S_KK4_74000801	IMG Activity: _ISUDMTDDV_000005
S_KK4_74000802	IMG Activity: _ISUDMTDRG_000005
S_KK4_74000803	IMG Activity: _ISUDMDI_000004
S_KK4_74000804	IMG Activity: _ISUDMTDRG_000007
S_KK4_74000805	IMG Activity: _ISUDMDIIN_000003
S_KK4_74000806	IMG Activity: _ISUBISFGA_000007
S_KK4_74000807	IMG Activity: _ISUBISFGA_000006
S_KK4_74000808	IMG Activity: _ISUBISFGA_000005
S_KK4_74000809	IMG Activity: _ISUBISFGA_000004
S_KK4_74000810	IMG Activity: _ISUBISFGA_000032
S_KK4_74000811	IMG Activity: _ISUBISFGA_000031
S_KK4_74000812	IMG Activity: _ISUBISFGA_000026
S_KK4_74000813	IMG Activity: _ISUBISFGA_000027
S_KK4_74000814	IMG Activity: _ISUBISFGA_000033
S_KK4_74000815	IMG Activity: _ISUBISFGA_000025
S_KK4_74000816	IMG Activity: _ISUBISFGA_000035
S_KK4_74000817	IMG Activity: _ISUBISFGA_000020
S_KK4_74000818	IMG Activity: _ISUBISFGA_000019
S_KK4_74000819	IMG Activity: _ISUBISFGA_000017
S_KK4_74000820	IMG Activity: _ISUBIBDDS_000004
S_KK4_74000821	IMG Activity: _ISUBIBDDS_000003
S_KK4_74000822	IMG Activity: _ISUBIBDDS_000002
S_KK4_74000823	IMG Activity: _ISUBIBDRS_000055
S_KK4_74000824	IMG Activity: _ISUBIBDRS_000040
S_KK4_74000825	IMG Activity: _ISUBIBDRS_000039
S_KK4_74000826	IMG Activity: _ISUBIBDDS_000005
S_KK4_74000827	IMG Activity: _ISUBISFGA_000016
S_KK4_74000828	IMG Activity: _ISUBISFGA_000015
S_KK4_74000829	IMG Activity: _ISUBISFGA_000013
S_KK4_74000830	IMG Activity: _ISUBISFGA_000012

S_KK4_74000831	IMG Activity: _ISUBISFGA_000034
S_KK4_74000832	IMG Activity: _ISUBISFGA_000010
S_KK4_74000833	IMG Activity: _ISUBIPCCB_000002
S_KK4_74000834	IMG Activity: _ISUBIPCSI_000002
S_KK4_74000835	IMG Activity: _ISUBIPCSI_000003
S_KK4_74000836	IMG Activity: _ISUBIPCSI_000004
S_KK4_74000837	IMG Activity: _ISUBIPCAU_000005
S_KK4_74000839	IMG Activity: _ISUBIPCCB_000003
S_KK4_74000840	IMG Activity: _ISUBIPCOS_000005
S_KK4_74000841	IMG Activity: _ISUBIPCOS_000004
S_KK4_74000842	IMG Activity: _ISUBIPCOS_000002
S_KK4_74000843	IMG Activity: _ISUBIPCCB_000006
S_KK4_74000845	IMG Activity: _ISUBIPCCB_000004
S_KK4_74000846	IMG Activity: _ISUBIPCAU_000007
S_KK4_74000847	IMG Activity: _ISUBISFFC_000009
S_KK4_74000848	IMG Activity: _ISUBISFFC_000003
S_KK4_74000849	IMG Activity: _ISUBISFFC_000002
S_KK4_74000850	IMG Activity: _ISUBISFGA_000030
S_KK4_74000851	IMG Activity: _ISUBISFGA_000029
S_KK4_74000852	IMG Activity: _ISUBISFGA_000028
S_KK4_74000853	IMG Activity: _ISUBISFFC_000004
S_KK4_74000854	IMG Activity: _ISUBIPCAU_000008
S_KK4_74000855	IMG Activity: _ISUBIPCAU_000004
S_KK4_74000856	IMG Activity: _ISUBIPCAU_000003
S_KK4_74000858	IMG Activity: _ISUBIPC_000004
S_KK4_74000859	IMG Activity: _ISUBISFFC_000005
S_KK4_74000860	IMG Activity: _ISUBIBDRS_000038
S_KK4_74000861	IMG Activity: _ISUBIBDRS_000056
S_KK4_74000862	IMG Activity: _ISUBIBDRS_000051
S_KK4_74000863	IMG Activity: _ISUBIBDRS_000049
S_KK4_74000864	IMG Activity: _ISUBIBDRS_000048
S_KK4_74000865	IMG Activity: _ISUBIBDRS_000013
S_KK4_74000866	IMG Activity: _ISUBIBDRS_000005
S_KK4_74000867	IMG Activity: _ISUBIBDRS_000022
S_KK4_74000868	IMG Activity: _ISUBIBDRS_000045
S_KK4_74000869	IMG Activity: _ISUBIBDRS_000019
S_KK4_74000870	IMG Activity: _ISUBIBDRS_000018
S_KK4_74000871	IMG Activity: _ISUBIBDRS_000015
S_KK4_74000872	IMG Activity: _ISUBIBDRS_000012
S_KK4_74000874	IMG Activity: _ISUBIBDRS_000007
S_KK4_74000875	IMG Activity: _ISUBIBDBD_000003
S_KK4_74000876	IMG Activity: _ISUBIBDRS_000003
S_KK4_74000877	IMG Activity: _ISUBIBDBD_000002
S_KK4_74000878	IMG Activity: _ISUBIBDRS_000050
S_KK4_74000879	IMG Activity: _ISUBIBDRS_000044
S_KK4_74000880	IMG Activity: _ISUBIBDRS_000043
S_KK4_74000881	IMG Activity: _ISUBIBDRS_000042
S_KK4_74000882	IMG Activity: _ISUBIBDRS_000041
S_KK4_74000883	IMG Activity: _ISUBIBDRS_000010
S_KK4_74000884	IMG Activity: _ISUBIBDRS_000026
S_KK4_74000885	IMG Activity: _ISUBIBDRS_000054
S_KK4_74000886	IMG Activity: _ISUBIBDRS_000029
S_KK4_74000887	IMG Activity: _ISUBIBDRS_000030
S_KK4_74000888	IMG Activity: _ISUBIBDRS_000053

S_KK4_74000889	IMG Activity: _ISUBIBDRS_000035
S_KK4_74000890	IMG Activity: _ISUBIBDRS_000052
S_KK4_74000891	IMG Activity: _ISUBIBDRS_000034
S_KK4_74000892	IMG Activity: _ISUBIBDRS_000033
S_KK4_74000893	IMG Activity: _ISUBIBDRS_000023
S_KK4_74000894	IMG Activity: _ISUBIBDRS_000037
S_KK4_74000895	IMG Activity: _ISUBIBDRS_000032
S_KK4_74000896	IMG Activity: _ISUBIBDRS_000025
S_KK4_74000897	IMG Activity: _ISUBIBD_000003
S_KK4_74000898	IMG Activity: _ISUBIBD_000004
S_KK4_74000899	IMG Activity: _ISUBIBD_000005
S_KK4_74000900	IMG Activity: _ISUBIBDRS_000002
S_KK4_74000901	IMG Activity: _ISUINPC_000013
S_KK4_74000903	IMG Activity: _ISUINPC_000012
S_KK4_74000904	IMG Activity: _ISUINPC_000029
S_KK4_74000905	IMG Activity: _ISUINPC_000028
S_KK4_74000906	IMG Activity: _ISUINPC_000024
S_KK4_74000907	IMG Activity: _ISUINPC_000023
S_KK4_74000908	IMG Activity: _ISUINPC_000014
S_KK4_74000909	IMG Activity: _ISUINBB_000015
S_KK4_74000910	IMG Activity: _ISUINBB_000011
S_KK4_74000911	IMG Activity: _ISUINBB_000010
S_KK4_74000912	IMG Activity: _ISUINBB_000009
S_KK4_74000913	IMG Activity: _ISUINBB_000007
S_KK4_74000914	IMG Activity: _ISUINBB_000006
S_KK4_74000915	IMG Activity: _ISUINBB_000005
S_KK4_74000916	IMG Activity: _ISUINPC_000022
S_KK4_74000917	IMG Activity: _ISUINPC_000020
S_KK4_74000918	IMG Activity: _ISUINPC_000032
S_KK4_74000919	IMG Activity: _ISUINPC_000025
S_KK4_74000920	IMG Activity: _ISUINPC_000019
S_KK4_74000921	IMG Activity: _ISUINPC_000035
S_KK4_74000922	IMG Activity: _ISUINPC_000016
S_KK4_74000923	IMG Activity: _ISUINPC_000033
S_KK4_74000924	IMG Activity: _ISUINPC_000026
S_KK4_74000925	IMG Activity: _ISUINPC_000031
S_KK4_74000926	IMG Activity: _ISUINPC_000034
S_KK4_74000927	IMG Activity: _ISUCSBTIO_000002
S_KK4_74000928	IMG Activity: _ISUCSBTIO_000007
S_KK4_74000929	IMG Activity: _ISUCSBTIO_000008
S_KK4_74000930	IMG Activity: _ISUCSBTIO_000009
S_KK4_74000931	IMG Activity: _ISUCSBTIO_000013
S_KK4_74000932	IMG Activity: _ISUCSBTIO_000005
S_KK4_74000933	IMG Activity: _ISUCSBTIO_000016
S_KK4_74000934	IMG Activity: _ISUCSBTIO_000004
S_KK4_74000935	IMG Activity: _ISUCSBTIO_000021
S_KK4_74000936	IMG Activity: _ISUCSBTIO_000024
S_KK4_74000937	IMG Activity: _ISUCSBTIO_000025
S_KK4_74000938	IMG Activity: _ISUCSBTIO_000026
S_KK4_74000939	IMG Activity: _ISUCSBTIO_000027
S_KK4_74000940	IMG Activity: _ISUCSBTIO_000001
S_KK4_74000941	IMG Activity: _ISUCSBTIO_000015
S_KK4_74000942	IMG Activity: _ISUCSBTIO_000003
S_KK4_74000943	IMG Activity: _ISUCSBTIO_000023

S_KK4_74000944	IMG Activity: _ISUCSBTDR_000002
S_KK4_74000945	IMG Activity: _ISUCSBTDR_000006
S_KK4_74000946	IMG Activity: _ISUCSBTDR_000003
S_KK4_74000947	IMG Activity: _ISUCSBTDR_000007
S_KK4_74000948	IMG Activity: _ISUCSBTDR_000004
S_KK4_74000949	IMG Activity: _ISUCSBTDR_000005
S_KK4_74000950	IMG Activity: _ISUCS_000001
S_KK4_74000951	IMG Activity: _ISUCSBTIO_000006
S_KK4_74000952	IMG Activity: _ISUCSBTIO_000010
S_KK4_74000953	IMG Activity: _ISUCSBTIO_000011
S_KK4_74000954	IMG Activity: _ISUCSBTIO_000012
S_KK4_74000955	IMG Activity: _ISUCSBTIO_000014
S_KK4_74000956	IMG Activity: _ISUCSBTIO_000022
S_KK4_74000957	IMG Activity: _ISUCSBTIO_000018
S_KK4_74000958	IMG Activity: _ISUCSBTIO_000019
S_KK4_74000959	IMG Activity: _ISUCSFOCC_000015
S_KK4_74000960	IMG Activity: _ISUCSFOCC_000020
S_KK4_74000961	IMG Activity: _ISUCSFOCC_000001
S_KK4_74000962	IMG Activity: _ISUCSFO_000002
S_KK4_74000963	IMG Activity: _ISUCSFO_000005
S_KK4_74000964	IMG Activity: _ISUCSFOCC_000003
S_KK4_74000965	IMG Activity: _ISUCSCI_000003
S_KK4_74000966	IMG Activity: _ISUCSFO_000007
S_KK4_74000967	IMG Activity: _ISUCSFO_000004
S_KK4_74000968	IMG Activity: _ISUCSFO_000008
S_KK4_74000969	IMG Activity: _ISUCSFO_000003
S_KK4_74000970	IMG Activity: _ISUCSFO_000009
S_KK4_74000971	IMG Activity: _ISUCSFOCC_000008
S_KK4_74000972	IMG Activity: _ISUCSFOCC_000006
S_KK4_74000973	IMG Activity: _ISUCSFOCC_000013
S_KK4_74000974	IMG Activity: _ISUCSFOCC_000014
S_KK4_74000975	IMG Activity: _ISUCSFOCC_000010
S_KK4_74000976	IMG Activity: _ISUCSFOCC_000009
S_KK4_74000977	IMG Activity: _ISUCSFOCC_000011
S_KK4_74000978	IMG Activity: _ISUCSFOCC_000012
S_KK4_74000979	IMG Activity: _ISUCSFOCC_000005
S_KK4_74000980	IMG Activity: _ISUCS_000003
S_KK4_74000981	IMG Activity: _ISUWMPC_000005
S_KK4_74000982	IMG Activity: _ISUWMPC_000007
S_KK4_74000983	IMG Activity: _ISUWMPC_000008
S_KK4_74000984	IMG Activity: _ISUWMPC_000016
S_KK4_74000985	IMG Activity: _ISUWMPC_000017
S_KK4_74000986	IMG Activity: _ISUWMPC_000018
S_KK4_74000987	IMG Activity: _ISUWMPC_000019
S_KK4_74000988	IMG Activity: _ISUWMPC_000012
S_KK4_74000989	IMG Activity: _ISUWMIF_000002
S_KK4_74000990	IMG Activity: _ISUWMPC_000002
S_KK4_74000991	IMG Activity: _ISUWMMD_000002
S_KK4_74000992	IMG Activity: _ISUWMMD_000001
S_KK4_74000993	IMG Activity: _ISUWMPC_000006
S_KK4_74000994	IMG Activity: _ISUWMPC_000004
S_KK4_74000995	IMG Activity: _ISUWMPC_000011
S_KK4_74000996	IMG Activity: _ISUWMPC_000013
S_KK4_74000997	IMG Activity: _ISUWMPC_000009

S_KK4_74000998	IMG Activity: _ISUWAPC_000002
S_KK4_74000999	IMG Activity: _ISUWAMD_000003
S_KK4_74001000	IMG Activity: _ISUWAMD_000002
S_KK4_74001001	IMG Activity: _ISUWAMD_000004
S_KK4_74001002	IMG Activity: _ISUISST_000032
S_KK4_74001003	IMG Activity: _ISUISST_000040
S_KK4_74001004	IMG Activity: _ISUISST_000023
S_KK4_74001005	IMG Activity: _ISUISST_000022
S_KK4_74001006	IMG Activity: _ISUISST_000021
S_KK4_74001007	IMG Activity: _ISUISST_000020
S_KK4_74001008	IMG Activity: _ISUISST_000018
S_KK4_74001009	IMG Activity: _ISUISST_000015
S_KK4_74001010	IMG Activity: _ISUISST_000038
S_KK4_74001011	IMG Activity: _ISUISST_000028
S_KK4_74001012	IMG Activity: _ISUISST_000027
S_KK4_74001013	IMG Activity: _ISUISST_000036
S_KK4_74001014	IMG Activity: _ISUISST_000035
S_KK4_74001015	IMG Activity: _ISUISST_000042
S_KK4_74001016	IMG Activity: _ISUISST_000041
S_KK4_74001017	IMG Activity: _ISUISST_000033
S_KK4_74001018	IMG Activity: _ISUISST_000010
S_KK4_74001019	IMG Activity: _ISUISST_000003
S_KK4_74001020	IMG Activity: _ISUISST_000008
S_KK4_74001021	IMG Activity: _ISUISST_000012
S_KK4_74001022	IMG Activity: _ISUISST_000039
S_KK4_74001023	IMG Activity: _ISUISST_000013
S_KK4_74001024	IMG Activity: _ISUISST_000005
S_KK4_74001025	IMG Activity: _ISUUTSMIV_000007
S_KK4_74001026	IMG Activity: _ISUUTSMIV_000008
S_KK4_74001027	IMG Activity: _ISUUTAR_000002
S_KK4_74001028	IMG Activity: _ISUUTAR_000003
S_KK4_74001029	IMG Activity: _ISUUTSMIV_000009
S_KK4_74001030	IMG Activity: _ISUUTTR_000002
S_KK4_74001031	IMG Activity: _ISUUTDT_000002
S_KK4_74001032	IMG Activity: _ISUUTSMCV_000002
S_KK4_74001033	IMG Activity: _ISUUTDE_000015
S_KK4_74001034	IMG Activity: _ISUUTSMUE_000002
S_KK4_74001035	IMG Activity: _ISUUTSMCF_000007
S_KK4_74001036	IMG Activity: _ISUUTSMCF_000008
S_KK4_74001037	IMG Activity: _ISUUTSMCF_000005
S_KK4_74001038	IMG Activity: _ISUUTSMCF_000004
S_KK4_74001039	IMG Activity: _ISUUTSMIV_000005
S_KK4_74001040	IMG Activity: _ISUUTSMCF_000002
S_KK4_74001041	IMG Activity: _ISUUTSMIV_000002
S_KK4_74001042	IMG Activity: _ISUUTSMFM_000002
S_KK4_74001043	IMG Activity: _ISUUTSMIV_000003
S_KK4_74001046	IMG Activity: _ISUUTSMCO_000002
S_KK4_74001051	IMG Activity: _ISUUTDE_000003
S_KK4_74001052	IMG Activity: _ISUUTSMCO_000003
S_KK4_74001053	IMG Activity: _ISUUTDE_000014
S_KK4_74001054	IMG Activity: _ISUUTSMCV_000003
S_KK4_74001056	IMG Activity: _ISUUTDE_000007
S_KK4_74001057	IMG Activity: _ISUUTDE_000009
S_KK4_74001058	IMG Activity: _ISUUTDE_000012

S_KK4_74001059	IMG Activity: _ISUUTSMCE_000002
S_KK4_74001060	IMG Activity: _ISUUTDE_000018
S_KK4_74001061	IMG Activity: _ISUAU_000001
S_KK4_74001062	IMG Activity: _ISIS_TLXXMVZ
S_KK4_74001063	IMG Activity: _ISIS_TLXXMVL
S_KK4_74001064	IMG Activity: _ISIS_TLXXBEB
S_KK4_74001065	IMG Activity: _ISIS_TLXXFUB
S_KK4_74001066	IMG Activity: _ISIS_TLXXRSA
S_KK4_74001067	IMG Activity: _ISIS_TLXXMHK
S_KK4_74001068	IMG Activity: _ISIS_TLXXMBG
S_KK4_74001069	IMG Activity: _ISIS_TLXXMRS
S_KK4_74001070	IMG Activity: _ISIS_TLXXMBA
S_KK4_74001071	IMG Activity: _ISIS_TLXXMGA
S_KK4_74001072	IMG Activity: _ISIS_TLXXSDA
S_KK4_74001073	IMG Activity: _ISIS_VC_TLXX004
S_KK4_74001074	IMG Activity: _ISIS_TLXXVAL
S_KK4_74001075	IMG Activity: _ISIS_TLXXBSG
S_KK4_74001076	IMG Activity: _ISIS_TLXXLSL
S_KK4_74001077	IMG Activity: _ISIS_TLXXGZA
S_KK4_74001078	IMG Activity: _ISIS_TLXXGSA
S_KK4_74001079	IMG Activity: _ISIS_TLXXBSA
S_KK4_74001080	IMG Activity: _CACS_V_TCACS_ROLCON
S_KK4_74001081	IMG Activity: _CACS_CACS_STD_07
S_KK4_74001082	IMG Activity: _CACS_V_TCACS_PAYSER
S_KK4_74001083	IMG Activity: _CACS_V_TCACS_TRISYS
S_KK4_74001084	IMG Activity: _CACS_V_TCACS_ACCAS
S_KK4_74001085	IMG Activity: _CACS_V_TCACS_REMCLA
S_KK4_74001086	IMG Activity: _CACS_V_TCACS_REM
S_KK4_74001087	IMG Activity: _CACS_CACS_STD_06
S_KK4_74001088	IMG Activity: _CACS_V_TCACS_ROLE
S_KK4_74001089	IMG Activity: _CACS_V_CTRT_PROL
S_KK4_74001090	IMG Activity: _CACS_V_TCACS_TERMD
S_KK4_74001091	IMG Activity: _CACS_V_TCACS_TOFN
S_KK4_74001092	IMG Activity: _CACS_V_TCACS_CTRCH
S_KK4_74001093	IMG Activity: _CACS_SE75
S_KK4_74001094	IMG Activity: _CACS_V_COND_PRIO
S_KK4_74001095	IMG Activity: _CACS_CACS_DET_ACCAS
S_KK4_74001096	IMG Activity: _CACS_V_TCACS_STMTY
S_KK4_74001097	IMG Activity: _CACS_CACS_STD_09
S_KK4_74001098	IMG Activity: _CACS_V_CTRTST_STI
S_KK4_74001099	IMG Activity: _CACS_V_TCACS_ITITLE
S_KK4_74001100	IMG Activity: _CACS_CACSCOND0004
S_KK4_74001101	IMG Activity: _CACS_CACSCOND0006
S_KK4_74001102	IMG Activity: _CACS_CACSCOND0005
S_KK4_74001103	IMG Activity: _CACS_VOFM
S_KK4_74001104	IMG Activity: _CACS_CACSCOND0007
S_KK4_74001105	IMG Activity: _CACS_CACS_DET
S_KK4_74001106	IMG Activity: _CACS_V_COMB_CASSGN
S_KK4_74001107	IMG Activity: _CACS_CACSCOND0001
S_KK4_74001108	IMG Activity: _CACS_CACSCOND0002
S_KK4_74001109	IMG Activity: _CACS_CACSCOND0003
S_KK4_74001110	IMG Activity: _CACS_CACS_STD_08
S_KK4_74001111	IMG Activity: _CACS_V_TCACS_CDINTF
S_KK4_74001112	IMG Activity: _CACS_CACSCONDMAINT

S_KK4_74001113	IMG Activity: _CACS_CACS_STD_01
S_KK4_74001114	IMG Activity: _CACS_CACS_STD_12
S_KK4_74001115	IMG Activity: _CACS_V_TCACS_BUSOBJ
S_KK4_74001116	IMG Activity: _CACS_C_B
S_KK4_74001117	IMG Activity: _CACS_C_K
S_KK4_74001118	IMG Activity: _CACS_C_R
S_KK4_74001119	IMG Activity: _CACS_C_Q
S_KK4_74001120	IMG Activity: _CACS_C_P
S_KK4_74001121	IMG Activity: _CACS_C_C
S_KK4_74001122	IMG Activity: _CACS_C_G
S_KK4_74001123	IMG Activity: _CACS_C_M
S_KK4_74001124	IMG Activity: _CACS_C_S
S_KK4_74001125	IMG Activity: _CACS_C_T
S_KK4_74001126	IMG Activity: _CACS_V_TCACS_CTRTP
S_KK4_74001127	IMG Activity: _CACS_BDT_EINSTELL.
S_KK4_74001128	IMG Activity: _CACS_V_TBE37
S_KK4_74001129	IMG Activity: _CACS_TESTDATEN_LOSC
S_KK4_74001130	IMG Activity: _CACS_ANW_PRO_SETZEN
S_KK4_74001131	IMG Activity: _CACS_C_O
S_KK4_74001132	IMG Activity: _CACS_C_Z
S_KK4_74001133	IMG Activity: _CACS_C_X
S_KK4_74001134	IMG Activity: _CACS_C_Y
S_KK4_74001135	IMG Activity: _CACS_V_TB105
S_KK4_74001136	IMG Activity: _CACS_C_W
S_KK4_74001137	IMG Activity: _CACS_CACS_GENTEXT
S_KK4_74001138	IMG Activity: _CACS_V_TCACSFA
S_KK4_74001139	IMG Activity: _CACS_V_TCACSF
S_KK4_74001140	IMG Activity: _CACS_V_TCACSFD
S_KK4_74001141	IMG Activity: _CACS_C_V
S_KK4_74001142	IMG Activity: _CACS_V_TCACS_BUSCAS
S_KK4_74001143	IMG Activity: _CACS_V_TCACS_BUSIN
S_KK4_74001144	IMG Activity: _CACS_KCLL
S_KK4_74001145	IMG Activity: _CACS_V_TCACS_EDT
S_KK4_74001146	IMG Activity: _CACS_CACS_REPTYPE
S_KK4_74001147	IMG Activity: _CACS_C_3
S_KK4_74001148	IMG Activity: _CACS_C_0
S_KK4_74001149	IMG Activity: _CACS_V_TCACS_STDREP
S_KK4_74001150	IMG Activity: BERI-0002
S_KK4_74001151	IMG Activity: BERI-0001
S_KK4_74001152	IMG Activity: _CACS_C_4
S_KK4_74001153	IMG Activity: _CACS_C_5
S_KK4_74001154	IMG Activity: _CACS_C_6
S_KK4_74001155	IMG Activity: _CACS_C_1
S_KK4_74001156	IMG Activity: _CACS_C_2
S_KK4_74001159	IMG Activity: _CACS_V_TCACS_AUT05
S_KK4_74001160	IMG Activity: _CACS_V_TCACS_AUT04
S_KK4_74001161	IMG Activity: _FICABFCR_V_ARCHIVE
S_KK4_74001162	IMG Activity: _FICABFCR_V_ARC_DOC
S_KK4_74001163	IMG Activity: _FICABFCR_V_TFK070F
S_KK4_74001164	IMG Activity: _FICABFCR_V_FRMCLS
S_KK4_74001165	IMG Activity: _FICABFCR_V_TFK070L
S_KK4_74001167	IMG Activity: _CACS_V_CACS_T77MWBS
S_KK4_74001168	IMG Activity: _CACS_OOAW
S_KK4_74001169	IMG Activity: _CACS_V_TISIS_CNTTYP

S_KK4_74001170	IMG Activity: _CACS_V_TISIS_APPL
S_KK4_74001171	IMG Activity: _CACS_DUMMY1
S_KK4_74001172	IMG Activity: _CACS_V_TCACS_AUT01
S_KK4_74001174	IMG Activity: _FICABFCR_V_TFK070_A
S_KK4_74001175	IMG Activity: _CACS_V_TCACS_DOCRAN
S_KK4_74001176	IMG Activity: _CACS_CACS_DN01
S_KK4_74001177	IMG Activity: _CACS_V_TCACS_CASRAN
S_KK4_74001178	IMG Activity: _CACS_CACS_CN01
S_KK4_74001179	IMG Activity: _CACS_CACS_CSCCNR
S_KK4_74001180	IMG Activity: _CACS_CACSGEN2
S_KK4_74001181	IMG Activity: _CACS_V_TCACS_APRP3
S_KK4_74001183	IMG Activity: _CACS_V_TCACS_APPL
S_KK4_74001184	IMG Activity: _CACS_CACS_STMT
S_KK4_74001185	IMG Activity: _FICABFCR_VC_TFK070B
S_KK4_74001186	IMG Activity: _FICABFCR_VC_TFK0471
S_KK4_74001187	IMG Activity: _FICABFCR_V_TFK047H1
S_KK4_74001188	IMG Activity: _FICABFCR_VC_TFK070D
S_KK4_74001189	IMG Activity: _FICABFPW_ESENDC
S_KK4_74001190	IMG Activity: _ISUUTPW_000003
S_KK4_74001191	IMG Activity: _ISUUTPW_000009
S_KK4_74001192	IMG Activity: _ISUUTPW_000002
S_KK4_74001193	IMG Activity: _CACS_CACS_PAY
S_KK4_74001194	IMG Activity: _CACS_V_TCACS_ORG
S_KK4_74001195	IMG Activity: _CACS_CACSCOND0014
S_KK4_74001196	IMG Activity: _CACS_CACSCOND0016
S_KK4_74001197	IMG Activity: _CACS_CACSCOND0015
S_KK4_74001198	IMG Activity: _CACS_CACSCOND0017
S_KK4_74001199	IMG Activity: _CACS_V_RULEKIT_SERV
S_KK4_74001200	IMG Activity: _CACS_V_APRP3_VAL
S_KK4_74001201	IMG Activity: _CACS_CACSCOND0011
S_KK4_74001202	IMG Activity: _CACS_CACSCOND0012
S_KK4_74001203	IMG Activity: _CACS_CACSCOND0013
S_KK4_74001204	IMG Activity: _CACS_V_TCACS_RESP
S_KK4_74001205	IMG Activity: _CACS_VC_TVSC_PP_CS
S_KK4_74001206	IMG Activity: _CACS_V_TCACS_INPLAN
S_KK4_74001207	IMG Activity: _CACS_CACSCONDMAINTB
S_KK4_74001208	IMG Activity: _CACS_CACS_STD_02
S_KK4_74001209	IMG Activity: _CACS_CACS_STD_10
S_KK4_74001211	IMG Activity: _CACS_V_TCACS_CTRTP1
S_KK4_74001212	IMG Activity: _CACS_V_TCACS_OFFS
S_KK4_74001213	IMG Activity: _CACS_V_ACTGRP_ACT
S_KK4_74001214	IMG Activity: ISPSD_ABRPROVABRART
S_KK4_74001215	IMG Activity: ISPSD_ABRPROVLOHNART
S_KK4_74001216	IMG Activity: ISPSD_ABRKONDARTKAUT
S_KK4_74001217	IMG Activity: ISMSD_ABRPROVSPERR
S_KK4_74001218	IMG Activity: ISMSD_ABREINLNRPOST
S_KK4_74001219	IMG Activity: ISPSD_ABRPOSTABRART
S_KK4_74001220	IMG Activity: ISPSD_ABRNRDPOST
S_KK4_74001221	IMG Activity: ISPSD_ABRZUSTGPERSTZ
S_KK4_74001222	IMG Activity: ISMSD_ABRECHNDELIV
S_KK4_74001223	IMG Activity: ISPSD_ABRZUSTABRART
S_KK4_74001224	IMG Activity: ISPSD_ABRZUSTLOHNART
S_KK4_74001225	IMG Activity: ISPSD_ABRZUSTVERKMA
S_KK4_74001226	IMG Activity: ISPSD_ABRKLASSTAET

S_KK4_74001227	IMG Activity: ISPSD_ABRZUSTZUSCHL
S_KK4_74001228	IMG Activity: ISPSD_ABRZUSVERTRMOD
S_KK4_74001229	IMG Activity: ISPSD_ABRZUOANRTRAEG
S_KK4_74001230	IMG Activity: ISPAM_TJHAEIN
S_KK4_74001231	IMG Activity: ISMAM_TJHCENTACCESS
S_KK4_74001232	IMG Activity: ISPAM_WTYP
S_KK4_74001233	IMG Activity: ISPAM_RHYTHM
S_KK4_74001234	IMG Activity: ISPAM_TJJAD
S_KK4_74001235	IMG Activity: ISPAM_TJHB5
S_KK4_74001236	IMG Activity: ISPAM_TJHSTOG
S_KK4_74001237	IMG Activity: ISPAM_NUMMERNKREISEA
S_KK4_74001238	IMG Activity: ISPSD_ABRZUOANRBEILA
S_KK4_74001239	IMG Activity: ISPAM_KONTAKTARTEN
S_KK4_74001240	IMG Activity: ISPAM_KONTAKTSTATUS
S_KK4_74001241	IMG Activity: ISPAM_KONTAKTGRUND
S_KK4_74001242	IMG Activity: ISPAM_KONTAKTERG
S_KK4_74001243	IMG Activity: ISPAM_KONTAKTBESCHR
S_KK4_74001244	IMG Activity: ISPAM_NUMMERNKREISEK
S_KK4_74001245	IMG Activity: ISMSD_CCARD_KONSCHEM
S_KK4_74001246	IMG Activity: ISMSD_CCARD_KONTOZUO
S_KK4_74001247	IMG Activity: ISMSD_CCARD_KONAUT
S_KK4_74001248	IMG Activity: ISMSD_CCARD_MERCHID
S_KK4_74001249	IMG Activity: ISMSD_CCARD_TEXTERG
S_KK4_74001250	IMG Activity: ISPSD_FAKTUEBERLEITA
S_KK4_74001251	IMG Activity: ISPSD_FAKTFIBUBELEG
S_KK4_74001252	IMG Activity: ISMSD_CCARD_KONDART
S_KK4_74001253	IMG Activity: ISMSD_KARTENART
S_KK4_74001254	IMG Activity: ISMSD_KARTENTYP
S_KK4_74001255	IMG Activity: ISMSD_PRUEFGRUPPE
S_KK4_74001256	IMG Activity: ISMSD_AUTGUELTDAUER
S_KK4_74001257	IMG Activity: ISMSD_CCARD_FELDKAT
S_KK4_74001258	IMG Activity: ISMSD_CCARD_KONDTAB
S_KK4_74001259	IMG Activity: ISMSD_CCARD_ZUGRIFF
S_KK4_74001260	IMG Activity: ISPSD_FAKTBELARTERM
S_KK4_74001261	IMG Activity: ISPSD_ABRECHSTORNO
S_KK4_74001262	IMG Activity: ISPSD_ABRECHNRKRS
S_KK4_74001263	IMG Activity: ISPSD_ABRBELEGARTFI
S_KK4_74001264	IMG Activity: ISPSD_ABRBELARTFIND
S_KK4_74001265	IMG Activity: ISPSD_ABRSTEUERKZFI
S_KK4_74001266	IMG Activity: ISPSD_ABRSTEUERKZISP
S_KK4_74001267	IMG Activity: ISPSD_ABRSTKZFIND
S_KK4_74001268	IMG Activity: ISPSD_FAKTSPERRGUTSC
S_KK4_74001269	IMG Activity: ISPSD_FAKTMWSTKENNZ
S_KK4_74001270	IMG Activity: ISPSD_FAKTZAHLWEGAUS
S_KK4_74001271	IMG Activity: ISPSD_FAKTKTOMWSTDIF
S_KK4_74001272	IMG Activity: ISPSD_FAKTGRENZBETRD
S_KK4_74001273	IMG Activity: ISPSD_FAKTRECHART
S_KK4_74001274	IMG Activity: ISPSD_FAKTRECHERCHE
S_KK4_74001275	IMG Activity: ISPSD_FAKTBANKRINTER
S_KK4_74001276	IMG Activity: ISPAM_DRVZV
S_KK4_74001277	IMG Activity: ISPAM_PLAZANW
S_KK4_74001278	IMG Activity: ISPAM_TJJ65VB
S_KK4_74001279	IMG Activity: ISPAM_TJHB1
S_KK4_74001280	IMG Activity: ISPAM_SEITPOS

S_KK4_74001281	IMG Activity: ISPAM_TMOTKNZ
S_KK4_74001282	IMG Activity: ISPAM_TMOTLAGE
S_KK4_74001283	IMG Activity: ISPAM_CHINUMVKBUR
S_KK4_74001284	IMG Activity: ISPAM_TJHPSF
S_KK4_74001285	IMG Activity: ISPAM_KORRART
S_KK4_74001286	IMG Activity: ISPAM_TJH57
S_KK4_74001287	IMG Activity: ISPAM_TJH51
S_KK4_74001288	IMG Activity: ISPAM_TEILBEL
S_KK4_74001289	IMG Activity: ISPAM_CHIFFREKNZ
S_KK4_74001290	IMG Activity: ISPAM_NUMKRCHI
S_KK4_74001291	IMG Activity: ISPAM_RASTERUNGEN
S_KK4_74001292	IMG Activity: ISPAM_AZART_VORL
S_KK4_74001293	IMG Activity: ISPAM_AZART_SONDER
S_KK4_74001294	IMG Activity: ISPAM_AZART_PLAZ
S_KK4_74001295	IMG Activity: ISPAM_TJJ15VB
S_KK4_74001296	IMG Activity: ISP_FARBIGKEIT
S_KK4_74001297	IMG Activity: ISPAM_AZARTGEST
S_KK4_74001298	IMG Activity: ISPAM_AZART_FORMAT
S_KK4_74001299	IMG Activity: ISPAM_AZART_RECH
S_KK4_74001300	IMG Activity: ISPAM_RAHMENTYPEN
S_KK4_74001301	IMG Activity: ISPAM_FARBTYP
S_KK4_74001302	IMG Activity: ISPAM_FARBEN
S_KK4_74001303	IMG Activity: ISPAM_TJJAB
S_KK4_74001304	IMG Activity: ISPAM_TJHAG
S_KK4_74001305	IMG Activity: ISPAM_TJHB3
S_KK4_74001306	IMG Activity: ISPAM_AZART_FORM
S_KK4_74001307	IMG Activity: ISPAM_KOPIEVAR_DI
S_KK4_74001308	IMG Activity: ISPAM_KOPIEVAR_WS
S_KK4_74001309	IMG Activity: ISPAM_KOPIEVAR_VT
S_KK4_74001310	IMG Activity: ISPAM_KOPIEVAR_OL
S_KK4_74001311	IMG Activity: ISPAM_JHVAKO_GRFA
S_KK4_74001312	IMG Activity: ISPAM_JHVAKO_EINT
S_KK4_74001313	IMG Activity: ISPAM_TJHAD
S_KK4_74001314	IMG Activity: ISPAM_KOPIEVAR_SI
S_KK4_74001315	IMG Activity: ISMAM_CORRCAUSE
S_KK4_74001316	IMG Activity: ISPAM_TJHAF
S_KK4_74001317	IMG Activity: ISPAM_TJHAVMUPD
S_KK4_74001318	IMG Activity: ISPAM_MSTZ
S_KK4_74001319	IMG Activity: ISPAM_AMPEL
S_KK4_74001320	IMG Activity: ISPAM_JHVAKO_AVM
S_KK4_74001321	IMG Activity: ISPAM_KOPIEVAR_AZ
S_KK4_74001322	IMG Activity: ISPAM_VBEREIN
S_KK4_74001323	IMG Activity: ISPAM_AVMNUMINT
S_KK4_74001324	IMG Activity: ISPAM_NUMVK
S_KK4_74001325	IMG Activity: ISPAM_BESTART
S_KK4_74001326	IMG Activity: ISPAM_POSTYP
S_KK4_74001327	IMG Activity: ISPAM_TJHSTGVB
S_KK4_74001328	IMG Activity: ISPAM_TJHAKPZ
S_KK4_74001329	IMG Activity: ISPAM_POSART
S_KK4_74001330	IMG Activity: ISPAM_AUFART
S_KK4_74001331	IMG Activity: ISPAM_VBER_BONREAK
S_KK4_74001332	IMG Activity: ISPAM_DUBIOSITAET
S_KK4_74001333	IMG Activity: ISPAM_PRICE_BEZKO_2
S_KK4_74001334	IMG Activity: ISPAM_PRICE_BEZKO_3

S_KK4_74001335	IMG Activity: ISPAM_PRICE_BEZKO_4
S_KK4_74001336	IMG Activity: ISPAM_BELEGART
S_KK4_74001337	IMG Activity: ISPAM_TJHKD
S_KK4_74001338	IMG Activity: ISPSD_FAKT_FEHLERTYP
S_KK4_74001339	IMG Activity: ISMAM_CRED_MGMT_ASSI
S_KK4_74001340	IMG Activity: ISMAM_CRED_MGMT_MAIN
S_KK4_74001341	IMG Activity: ISMSD_ERLOSABGRRWINT
S_KK4_74001342	IMG Activity: ISMSD_TTYPV_RWIN
S_KK4_74001343	IMG Activity: ISPSD_KONTAKTDEF
S_KK4_74001344	IMG Activity: ISPSD_KONTAKTERGEBN
S_KK4_74001345	IMG Activity: ISPSD_NRKRSWERBKONT
S_KK4_74001346	IMG Activity: ISMAM_CRED_MGMT_KG
S_KK4_74001347	IMG Activity: ISPAM_FIND_TAX_1
S_KK4_74001348	IMG Activity: ISMSD_STEUERBEFRARTE
S_KK4_74001349	IMG Activity: ISMAM_USTAX_TXJCD_PL
S_KK4_74001350	IMG Activity: ISMAM_USTAX_TAXIW
S_KK4_74001351	IMG Activity: ISMAM_USTAX_TAXIW_PL
S_KK4_74001352	IMG Activity: ISMAM_CM_LIS_ACTIVE
S_KK4_74001353	IMG Activity: ISMAM_CM_BASIC_SET
S_KK4_74001354	IMG Activity: ISPSD_NRKREISEVK
S_KK4_74001355	IMG Activity: ISPSD_SPERRGRDAUFTRA
S_KK4_74001356	IMG Activity: ISMSD_PREISSCHLABO
S_KK4_74001357	IMG Activity: ISPSD_VKBRIEFTYPEN
S_KK4_74001358	IMG Activity: ISMSD_VKRENEWSTEUER
S_KK4_74001359	IMG Activity: ISMSD_VKRENFI
S_KK4_74001360	IMG Activity: ISMSD_RENKALKSCHEM
S_KK4_74001361	IMG Activity: ISMSD_VKRENVERSPZLG
S_KK4_74001362	IMG Activity: ISPSD_FAKTZAHLWEGEIN
S_KK4_74001363	IMG Activity: ISPSD_VKNRKRSKONDBEL
S_KK4_74001364	IMG Activity: ISPSD_VKALLGPARAM
S_KK4_74001365	IMG Activity: ISPSD_AUFTRAGSARTEN
S_KK4_74001366	IMG Activity: ISPSD_POSITIONSARTEN
S_KK4_74001367	IMG Activity: ISPSD_AUFTRARTBEZANG
S_KK4_74001368	IMG Activity: ISMSD_VKEREIGNVERMIT
S_KK4_74001369	IMG Activity: ISPSD_EINSTVKBELEGE
S_KK4_74001370	IMG Activity: ISPSD_KONTFINDERLOES
S_KK4_74001371	IMG Activity: ISPAM_GRUFU_KONT_A1
S_KK4_74001372	IMG Activity: ISPAM_GRUFU_KONT_A2
S_KK4_74001373	IMG Activity: ISPAM_GRUFU_KONT_A3
S_KK4_74001374	IMG Activity: ISPAM_GRUFU_KONT_A4
S_KK4_74001375	IMG Activity: ISPAM_GRUFU_KONT_A5
S_KK4_74001376	IMG Activity: ISPAM_DYN_MENU_KONTN
S_KK4_74001377	IMG Activity: ISPSD_KONTSCHLUESS
S_KK4_74001378	IMG Activity: ISPSD_AKONTSCHEMATA
S_KK4_74001379	IMG Activity: ISPSD_AKONTSCHLUESS
S_KK4_74001380	IMG Activity: ISPSD_AKONTSACHKTZUO
S_KK4_74001381	IMG Activity: ISPSD_KONTSTAMM
S_KK4_74001382	IMG Activity: ISPSD_KONTTABELLE
S_KK4_74001383	IMG Activity: ISPSD_KONTZUGRF
S_KK4_74001384	IMG Activity: ISPSD_KONTSCHEM
S_KK4_74001385	IMG Activity: ISPAM_GRUFU_KONT_A6
S_KK4_74001386	IMG Activity: ISPAM_KONT_ERLVT_2
S_KK4_74001387	IMG Activity: ISPAM_KONT_ERLVT_3
S_KK4_74001388	IMG Activity: ISPAM_KONT_ERLVT_4

S_KK4_74001389	IMG Activity: ISPAM_KONT_ERLVT_5
S_KK4_74001390	IMG Activity: ISPAM_MENU_KONT_EVT
S_KK4_74001391	IMG Activity: ISPAM_KONT_ERLVT_6
S_KK4_74001392	IMG Activity: ISPAM_FIND_TAX_2
S_KK4_74001393	IMG Activity: ISPAM_KONT_ERLVT_1
S_KK4_74001394	IMG Activity: ISPAM_KONT_STAMM_1
S_KK4_74001395	IMG Activity: ISPAM_KONT_STAMM_2
S_KK4_74001396	IMG Activity: ISPAM_KONT_STAMM_3
S_KK4_74001397	IMG Activity: ISPAM_KONT_STAMM_4
S_KK4_74001398	IMG Activity: ISPAM_KONT_STAMM_5
S_KK4_74001399	IMG Activity: ISPAM_DYN_MENU_KONTE
S_KK4_74001400	IMG Activity: ISPAM_KONT_STAMM_6
S_KK4_74001401	IMG Activity: ISPSD_VFUNKTBVERSPAP
S_KK4_74001402	IMG Activity: ISPSD_VERSPAPZUAB
S_KK4_74001403	IMG Activity: ISPSD_VERSEINLIEFNR
S_KK4_74001404	IMG Activity: ISPSD_VERSFEHLERNRKR
S_KK4_74001405	IMG Activity: ISPSD_VFEHLVERBR
S_KK4_74001406	IMG Activity: ISPSD_VGRDFEHLVERBR
S_KK4_74001407	IMG Activity: ISPSD_VFEHLVERBRVERU
S_KK4_74001408	IMG Activity: ISMSD_VERSZUSTBUCHFO
S_KK4_74001409	IMG Activity: ISPSD_VNUMARTBUNDE
S_KK4_74001410	IMG Activity: ISPSD_VSPOOLVERSANDP
S_KK4_74001411	IMG Activity: ISPSD_VERSPAPARTGRP
S_KK4_74001412	IMG Activity: ISPSD_VERSPAPARTEN
S_KK4_74001413	IMG Activity: ISPSD_VERSPAPDESTSU
S_KK4_74001414	IMG Activity: ISPSD_VERSPAPSORT
S_KK4_74001415	IMG Activity: ISPSD_VERSPAPFORM
S_KK4_74001416	IMG Activity: ISMSD_FKRENERLOSABGR
S_KK4_74001417	IMG Activity: ISPSD_NRKRSFAKT
S_KK4_74001418	IMG Activity: ISPSD_GLOBPARAMFAKT
S_KK4_74001419	IMG Activity: ISPSD_FAKTPERIOD
S_KK4_74001420	IMG Activity: ISPSD_FAKTMODALABO
S_KK4_74001421	IMG Activity: ISPSD_FAKTART
S_KK4_74001422	IMG Activity: ISMSD_FAKTBELTRENNKR
S_KK4_74001423	IMG Activity: ISPSD_FAKTBELEGFL
S_KK4_74001424	IMG Activity: ISPSD_STORNOGRDFAKT
S_KK4_74001425	IMG Activity: ISPSD_FAKTSACHINTERI
S_KK4_74001426	IMG Activity: ISPSD_FAKTBELARTDAUB
S_KK4_74001427	IMG Activity: ISMSD_FKREVUR
S_KK4_74001428	IMG Activity: ISMSD_ERLBELEGMITBEZ
S_KK4_74001429	IMG Activity: ISMSD_ERLBELEGOHNBEZ
S_KK4_74001430	IMG Activity: ISMSD_ERLBELEGPERIOD
S_KK4_74001431	IMG Activity: ISPSD_SPERRGRDFAKTUR
S_KK4_74001432	IMG Activity: ISPSD_BEZPFLEGEN
S_KK4_74001433	IMG Activity: ISPSD_WBZRECHENZENT
S_KK4_74001434	IMG Activity: ISPSD_WBZANRED
S_KK4_74001435	IMG Activity: ISPSD_WKZFRISTEN
S_KK4_74001436	IMG Activity: ISPSD_WBZAUFTEING
S_KK4_74001437	IMG Activity: ISPSD_WBZLIEFENDVORG
S_KK4_74001438	IMG Activity: ISPSD_LOGIDAT
S_KK4_74001439	IMG Activity: ISMSD_VKWBZDATEN
S_KK4_74001440	IMG Activity: ISMSD_VKRENSTUFENART
S_KK4_74001441	IMG Activity: ISMSD_REMSCHEMATA
S_KK4_74001442	IMG Activity: ISMSD_REMSCHEMFIND

S_KK4_74001443	IMG Activity: ISMSD_VKRENTRANSFTYP
S_KK4_74001444	IMG Activity: ISPSD_PROSPAUFTRUND
S_KK4_74001445	IMG Activity: ISPSD_VKNRKRSPROSPA
S_KK4_74001446	IMG Activity: ISPSD_VTBERFIND
S_KK4_74001447	IMG Activity: ISPSD_REMISSIONSMELD
S_KK4_74001448	IMG Activity: ISPSD_VERSDISPONRKRS
S_KK4_74001449	IMG Activity: ISMSD_VERSPAKETABLRE
S_KK4_74001450	IMG Activity: ISPSD_VERSPAKETFNRKR
S_KK4_74001451	IMG Activity: ISPSD_VFUNKTBAUSTPAK
S_KK4_74001452	IMG Activity: ISPSD_VKUNDFUNKTPAK
S_KK4_74001453	IMG Activity: ISPSD_VMINDESTGRBUND
S_KK4_74001454	IMG Activity: ISPSD_VMINSTCKGEBIND
S_KK4_74001455	IMG Activity: ISPSD_VERSGRP
S_KK4_74001456	IMG Activity: ISMSD_VKREMPERZUS
S_KK4_74001457	IMG Activity: ISMSD_AUFTRREKLAMGR
S_KK4_74001458	IMG Activity: ISMSD_REKLVERURSACH
S_KK4_74001459	IMG Activity: ISMSD_VERKREKLAM
S_KK4_74001460	IMG Activity: ISPSD_VKNRKRSRECHER
S_KK4_74001461	IMG Activity: ISPSD_VKRECHARTEN
S_KK4_74001462	IMG Activity: ISPSD_EINSTRECHERCHE
S_KK4_74001463	IMG Activity: ISP_IS-M:L_STAMM_NKER
S_KK4_74001464	IMG Activity: ISP_IS-M:L_FUNCPRPROF
S_KK4_74001465	IMG Activity: ISP_IS-M:L_FUNCPRNKPP
S_KK4_74001466	IMG Activity: ISP_IS-M:L_FUNCPRNKPW
S_KK4_74001467	IMG Activity: ISP_IS-M:L_FUNCMVAKT
S_KK4_74001468	IMG Activity: ISP_IS-M:L_FUNCMVKPRO
S_KK4_74001469	IMG Activity: ISP_IS-M:L_FUNCMVKZUO
S_KK4_74001470	IMG Activity: ISP_OS_PL_STAMM_NKMK
S_KK4_74001471	IMG Activity: ISP_IS_BFLA_TRANSPNR
S_KK4_74001472	IMG Activity: ISP_IS_BFLA_MASSGEN
S_KK4_74001473	IMG Activity: ISP_IS_BFLA_LAYOUTRE
S_KK4_74001474	IMG Activity: ISP_IS_BFLA_STDLAYOU
S_KK4_74001475	IMG Activity: ISP_IS_BFLA_SETS
S_KK4_74001476	IMG Activity: ISP_IS_BFLA_VARIAB
S_KK4_74001477	IMG Activity: ISP_IS-M:L_STAMM_PARA
S_KK4_74001478	IMG Activity: ISP_IS-M:L_FUNCMVUEPR
S_KK4_74001479	IMG Activity: ISP_IS_FKTERW_LDW_02
S_KK4_74001480	IMG Activity: ISP_IS_FKTERW_LDW_01
S_KK4_74001481	IMG Activity: ISP_IS-M:L_TOOL_PLTYP
S_KK4_74001482	IMG Activity: ISP_IS-M:L_TOOL_BMETH
S_KK4_74001483	IMG Activity: ISP_IS-M:L_TOOL_TSTAM
S_KK4_74001484	IMG Activity: ISP_IS-M:L_TOOL_BPARA
S_KK4_74001485	IMG Activity: ISP_IS_BERE_PFLEGEN
S_KK4_74001486	IMG Activity: ISP_IS_BERE_PROFILEP
S_KK4_74001487	IMG Activity: ISP_IS_LDWFS_VSG_KND
S_KK4_74001488	IMG Activity: ISP_IS_LDWFS_VSG_PVA
S_KK4_74001489	IMG Activity: ISP_IS_LDWFS_VSG_VBE
S_KK4_74001490	IMG Activity: ISP_IS_LDWFS_VSGZVBE
S_KK4_74001491	IMG Activity: ISP_IS_LDWFS_VSGZFKA
S_KK4_74001492	IMG Activity: ISP_IS_LDWFS_VSGZVBP
S_KK4_74001493	IMG Activity: ISP_IS_LDWFS_AKTIV
S_KK4_74001494	IMG Activity: ISP_IS_LDWDB_WERKZ4
S_KK4_74001495	IMG Activity: ISP_IS_LDWDB_WERKZ5
S_KK4_74001496	IMG Activity: ISP_IS_LDWFD_GR00001

S_KK4_74001497	IMG Activity: ISP_IS_LDWFD_REGEL01
S_KK4_74001498	IMG Activity: ISP_IS_LDWFD_BEDINGG
S_KK4_74001499	IMG Activity: ISP_IS_LDWFD_FORMELN
S_KK4_74001500	IMG Activity: ISP_IS_LDWFD_GENPROT
S_KK4_74001501	IMG Activity: ISPAM_BEGRP_STAT
S_KK4_74001502	IMG Activity: ISP_IS_LDWFS_STWAE
S_KK4_74001503	IMG Activity: ISP_IS_LDWFS_KONTPRO
S_KK4_74001504	IMG Activity: ISP_IS_LDWFS_KONTSIM
S_KK4_74001505	IMG Activity: ISP_IS_BSTA_EINST
S_KK4_74001506	IMG Activity: ISP_IS_BSTA_SELVERS
S_KK4_74001507	IMG Activity: ISP_IS_BFLA_LANG_DEF
S_KK4_74001508	IMG Activity: ISP_IS_BFLA_LANG_TRL
S_KK4_74001509	IMG Activity: ISPAM_JHVTJH05_S
S_KK4_74001510	IMG Activity: ISP_IS_LDWFS_VFG_VBK
S_KK4_74001511	IMG Activity: ISP_IS_LDWFS_VFG_VBP
S_KK4_74001512	IMG Activity: ISP_IS_LDWFS_VFG_LFG
S_KK4_74001513	IMG Activity: ISP_IS_LDWFS_VFG_LFZ
S_KK4_74001514	IMG Activity: ISPAM_TJHMC1
S_KK4_74001515	IMG Activity: ISPAM_TJHMC3
S_KK4_74001516	IMG Activity: ISPSD_WERKZDUEBAUFTR
S_KK4_74001517	IMG Activity: ISPSD_WERKZDUEBABO
S_KK4_74001518	IMG Activity: ISMSD_WKZDUEPRODSTRT
S_KK4_74001519	IMG Activity: ISMAM_WERKZDUE_GEN_N
S_KK4_74001520	IMG Activity: ISMAM_WERKZDUE_GEN_O
S_KK4_74001521	IMG Activity: ISMAM_WERKZDUE_DATEI
S_KK4_74001522	IMG Activity: ISMAM_WERKZDUE_CHECK
S_KK4_74001523	IMG Activity: ISMSD_WERKZDUEGOLIVE
S_KK4_74001524	IMG Activity: ISM_WERKZDUEPOSTIT1
S_KK4_74001525	IMG Activity: ISM_WERKZDUEPOSTIT2
S_KK4_74001526	IMG Activity: ISM_WERKZDUEPOSTIT3
S_KK4_74001527	IMG Activity: ISP_GP_NRKRS_PROT
S_KK4_74001528	IMG Activity: ISPSD_WERKZDUEBGP1
S_KK4_74001529	IMG Activity: ISPSD_WERKZDUEBGP2
S_KK4_74001530	IMG Activity: ISMSD_WERKZVACHTYPE
S_KK4_74001531	IMG Activity: ISMAM_WERKZDUE_AZSI
S_KK4_74001532	IMG Activity: ISP_WERKZARCHIV
S_KK4_74001533	IMG Activity: ISPAM_ARCHV_COND
S_KK4_74001534	IMG Activity: ISP_FOMELNBED
S_KK4_74001535	IMG Activity: ISP_BEDINGUNGEN
S_KK4_74001536	IMG Activity: ISP_BERECHTIGUNGEN
S_KK4_74001537	IMG Activity: ISP_BERECHTPROFILE
S_KK4_74001538	IMG Activity: ISP_BERECHTBENUTZER
S_KK4_74001539	IMG Activity: ISPAM_TJHVSW01
S_KK4_74001540	IMG Activity: ISMAM_WERKZDUE_WSVT
S_KK4_74001541	IMG Activity: ISMAM_WERKZDUE_ALT
S_KK4_74001542	IMG Activity: ISMAM_WERKZDUE_NOT
S_KK4_74001543	IMG Activity: ISPSD_ZEBUMODIF
S_KK4_74001544	IMG Activity: ISPSD_ERSTDATENZEBU
S_KK4_74001545	IMG Activity: ISPSD_WERKZDUEBZAEHL
S_KK4_74001546	IMG Activity: ISPAM_TJHVSW02
S_KK4_74001547	IMG Activity: ISPSD_PLZAUSWGEB
S_KK4_74001548	IMG Activity: ISPSD_WERKZKOMFUBRFC
S_KK4_74001549	IMG Activity: ISPSD_WERKZKOMMRFC
S_KK4_74001550	IMG Activity: ISPSD_WERKZKOMRFCIND

S_KK4_74001551	IMG Activity: ISPSD_WERKZKOMRFCZUO
S_KK4_74001552	IMG Activity: ISPSD_WERKZKOMEREIGA
S_KK4_74001553	IMG Activity: ISPSD_WERKZKOMMERZUO
S_KK4_74001554	IMG Activity: ISMSD_CIRCBOOK_NKRS
S_KK4_74001555	IMG Activity: ISPSD_AUFLMELDART
S_KK4_74001556	IMG Activity: ISPSD_AUFLMELDKATEGV
S_KK4_74001557	IMG Activity: ISPSD_AUFLMELDHIERAR
S_KK4_74001558	IMG Activity: ISMSD_RFCFI
S_KK4_74001559	IMG Activity: ISPSD_WERKZDUEBEXTST
S_KK4_74001560	IMG Activity: ISM_WERKZPOSTAKTDE1
S_KK4_74001561	IMG Activity: ISM_WERKZPOSTUSA1
S_KK4_74001562	IMG Activity: ISM_WERKZPOSTUSA2
S_KK4_74001563	IMG Activity: ISM_WERKZPOSTUSA3
S_KK4_74001564	IMG Activity: ISM_WERKZPOSTAKTUSA1
S_KK4_74001565	IMG Activity: ISM_WERKZPOSTAKTUSA2
S_KK4_74001566	IMG Activity: ISPSD_WERKZDUEBPOST8
S_KK4_74001567	IMG Activity: ISPSD_WERKZDUEBPOST1
S_KK4_74001568	IMG Activity: ISPSD_WERKZDUEBPOST2
S_KK4_74001569	IMG Activity: ISPSD_WERKZDUEBPOST3
S_KK4_74001570	IMG Activity: ISPSD_WERKZDUEBPOST4
S_KK4_74001571	IMG Activity: ISPSD_WERKZDUEBPOST5
S_KK4_74001572	IMG Activity: ISPSD_WERKZDUEBPOST6
S_KK4_74001573	IMG Activity: ISPSD_WERKZDUEBPOST7
S_KK4_74001574	IMG Activity: ISP_IS_LDWDB_WERKZ3
S_KK4_74001575	IMG Activity: ISM_COA_ASS_KONFL
S_KK4_74001576	IMG Activity: ISPAM_ABS_COND16
S_KK4_74001577	IMG Activity: ISMAM_BEZKOND_BEMGR
S_KK4_74001578	IMG Activity: ISPAM_TJHFACTOR
S_KK4_74001579	IMG Activity: ISM_MMCOA_KAUSSCHL
S_KK4_74001580	IMG Activity: ISM_MMCOA_ERFREGEL
S_KK4_74001581	IMG Activity: ISM_MMCOA_MXART
S_KK4_74001582	IMG Activity: ISMAM_COA_ASS_PART
S_KK4_74001583	IMG Activity: ISPAM_ABS_COND17
S_KK4_74001584	IMG Activity: ISPAM_ABSLIVAR_DEF
S_KK4_74001585	IMG Activity: ISPAM_ABSLIST
S_KK4_74001586	IMG Activity: ISPAM_VAR_LT_DEF
S_KK4_74001587	IMG Activity: ISPAM_ABSVBART
S_KK4_74001588	IMG Activity: ISPAM_ABSVAR1
S_KK4_74001589	IMG Activity: ISM_COA_PART
S_KK4_74001590	IMG Activity: ISM_MMCOA_PRUEF
S_KK4_74001591	IMG Activity: ISP_FIBLART_RUECK
S_KK4_74001592	IMG Activity: ISMAM_FK_COPA_ZUO_WE
S_KK4_74001593	IMG Activity: ISMAM_FK_COPA_RES_WE
S_KK4_74001594	IMG Activity: ISMAM_FK_COPA_ZUO_ME
S_KK4_74001595	IMG Activity: ISMAM_CCARD_INSTITUT
S_KK4_74001596	IMG Activity: ISMAM_CCARD_TYPE
S_KK4_74001597	IMG Activity: ISMAM_CCARD_EXCLCOND
S_KK4_74001598	IMG Activity: ISPAM_TTYPV_JHTFK
S_KK4_74001599	IMG Activity: ISPAM_SYSTEME
S_KK4_74001600	IMG Activity: ISPAM_ANWZUOSYSTEM
S_KK4_74001601	IMG Activity: ISPAM_EREIGZUOANWEND
S_KK4_74001602	IMG Activity: ISP_TBDLS_DEST_F
S_KK4_74001603	IMG Activity: ISPAM_JZ26
S_KK4_74001604	IMG Activity: ISPAM_SMARTNUMKI

S_KK4_74001605	IMG Activity: ISPAM_BELARTFIND_FI
S_KK4_74001606	IMG Activity: ISPAM_TJJW5
S_KK4_74001607	IMG Activity: ISPAM_TJJBEVTPA
S_KK4_74001608	IMG Activity: ISMAM_TJHUNITOL
S_KK4_74001609	IMG Activity: ISMAM_TJHBOOKL
S_KK4_74001610	IMG Activity: ISMAM_TJJPLZONL
S_KK4_74001611	IMG Activity: ISMAM_TJHTARGET
S_KK4_74001612	IMG Activity: ISMAM_TJHOLFMT
S_KK4_74001613	IMG Activity: ISPAM_TJJ41
S_KK4_74001614	IMG Activity: ISPAM_TJJ13VB
S_KK4_74001615	IMG Activity: ISPAM_AREA
S_KK4_74001616	IMG Activity: ISPAM_TJJAREAHIE
S_KK4_74001617	IMG Activity: ISPAM_NUMSI
S_KK4_74001618	IMG Activity: ISPAM_TJHSIBTYP
S_KK4_74001619	IMG Activity: ISPAM_SIBEARB
S_KK4_74001620	IMG Activity: ISPAM_SITYP
S_KK4_74001621	IMG Activity: ISMAM_TJHOLBME
S_KK4_74001622	IMG Activity: ISM_COA_OVERLAP
S_KK4_74001623	IMG Activity: ISPAM_ABSNRIV
S_KK4_74001624	IMG Activity: ISM_MMCOA_NRIV
S_KK4_74001625	IMG Activity: ISPAM_ABSBNRIV
S_KK4_74001626	IMG Activity: ISMAM_COA_UNITS
S_KK4_74001627	IMG Activity: ISPAM_COAA_SUM_TYPES
S_KK4_74001628	IMG Activity: ISPAM_ABS_COND_AUFR
S_KK4_74001629	IMG Activity: ISM_COA_AKTUA
S_KK4_74001630	IMG Activity: ISMAM_TJHOLHME
S_KK4_74001631	IMG Activity: ISM_COA_GPROLLEN
S_KK4_74001632	IMG Activity: ISM_COA_DONT_READ
S_KK4_74001633	IMG Activity: ISPAM_PAYROLL_FILE
S_KK4_74001634	IMG Activity: ISPAM_GP_VV_AK_PFL
S_KK4_74001635	IMG Activity: ISPAM_BELEGARTENPRAB
S_KK4_74001636	IMG Activity: ISPAM_FKARTPRAB
S_KK4_74001637	IMG Activity: ISPAM_TJHSTOG_ERLV
S_KK4_74001638	IMG Activity: ISPAM_FKART_ERLOES
S_KK4_74001639	IMG Activity: ISPAM_EFKART_ZUO
S_KK4_74001640	IMG Activity: ISPAM_JHVTJH49
S_KK4_74001641	IMG Activity: ISPAM_TECINTERFACE
S_KK4_74001642	IMG Activity: ISP_IS_LDWDB_KOMM11
S_KK4_74001643	IMG Activity: ISP_IS_LDWDB_KOMM12
S_KK4_74001644	IMG Activity: ISP_IS_LDWDB_KOMM2
S_KK4_74001645	IMG Activity: ISP_IS_LDWDB_FELDKEI
S_KK4_74001646	IMG Activity: ISP_IS_LDWDB_INFOST1
S_KK4_74001647	IMG Activity: ISP_IS_LDWDB_INFOST2
S_KK4_74001648	IMG Activity: ISP_IS_LDWDB_WERKZ1
S_KK4_74001649	IMG Activity: ISP_IS_LDWDB_EIGAPP1
S_KK4_74001650	IMG Activity: ISPAM_TECHSYS
S_KK4_74001651	IMG Activity: ISPAM_EDITSYS
S_KK4_74001652	IMG Activity: ISPAM_TJHA5
S_KK4_74001653	IMG Activity: ISPAM_PLZAVM
S_KK4_74001654	IMG Activity: ISPAM_RFCDES
S_KK4_74001655	IMG Activity: ISPAM_TJHTMMZ
S_KK4_74001656	IMG Activity: ISP_REPTREES
S_KK4_74001657	IMG Activity: ISMAM_CCARD_ACCASSGN
S_KK4_74001658	IMG Activity: ISMAM_CCARD_AUTCONTR

S_KK4_74001659	IMG Activity: ISMAM_CCARD_MERCHANT
S_KK4_74001660	IMG Activity: ISMAM_CCARD_AUTHTEXT
S_KK4_74001661	IMG Activity: ISPAM_BELEGARTEN
S_KK4_74001662	IMG Activity: ISPAM_FKARTAUFTRAG
S_KK4_74001663	IMG Activity: ISM_COA_STL_NUMKR
S_KK4_74001664	IMG Activity: ISMAM_CCARD_CHECKGRP
S_KK4_74001665	IMG Activity: ISMAM_CCARD_AUTH_VAL
S_KK4_74001666	IMG Activity: ISMAM_CCARD_FIELDCAT
S_KK4_74001667	IMG Activity: ISMAM_CCARD_CONDTAB
S_KK4_74001668	IMG Activity: ISMAM_CCARD_ACCSEQ
S_KK4_74001669	IMG Activity: ISMAM_CCARD_CONDTYPE
S_KK4_74001670	IMG Activity: ISMAM_CCARD_ACCSCHEM
S_KK4_74001671	IMG Activity: ISPAM_COAS_VBWIDE
S_KK4_74001672	IMG Activity: ISMAM_OUTBK_FKART_DF
S_KK4_74001673	IMG Activity: ISMAM_OUTBK_FKART_AS
S_KK4_74001674	IMG Activity: ISPAM_FKARTAABR
S_KK4_74001675	IMG Activity: ISPAM_COAS_SCALE
S_KK4_74001676	IMG Activity: ISPAM_XNOVABR
S_KK4_74001677	IMG Activity: ISPAM_COND_BMGR
S_KK4_74001678	IMG Activity: ISMAM_COAS_KSTEU
S_KK4_74001679	IMG Activity: ISMAM_TWIN_BILLNGGRP
S_KK4_74001680	IMG Activity: ISPAM_BELEGARTEN_AAB
S_KK4_74001681	IMG Activity: ISPSD_AKONTZUGRFOLG
S_KK4_74001682	IMG Activity: ISM_GPMAHNSCHLUESSEL
S_KK4_74001683	IMG Activity: ISMSD_STVERSLIEFART
S_KK4_74001684	IMG Activity: ISPSD_VERSANDAUSSTA
S_KK4_74001685	IMG Activity: ISM_GPMAHNBEREICHE
S_KK4_74001686	IMG Activity: ISPSD_VSUCHFPAKETBIL
S_KK4_74001687	IMG Activity: ISPSD_VPAKETFERTART
S_KK4_74001688	IMG Activity: ISM_GPMAHNSPERRGRND
S_KK4_74001689	IMG Activity: ISPSD_GPVTNRKRSGPER2
S_KK4_74001690	IMG Activity: ISMSD_STVERBRABLADB
S_KK4_74001691	IMG Activity: ISPSD_VERSABLREGNRKR
S_KK4_74001692	IMG Activity: ISPSD_VERSSTNRKRSVPV
S_KK4_74001693	IMG Activity: ISPSD_VERSSTNRKRSVPL
S_KK4_74001694	IMG Activity: ISPSD_VLAENDGRUPP
S_KK4_74001695	IMG Activity: ISPSD_VBUNDFERTSTUF
S_KK4_74001696	IMG Activity: ISPSD_INCOTERMS
S_KK4_74001697	IMG Activity: ISPSD_VPRODWDHGRP
S_KK4_74001698	IMG Activity: ISPSD_VPRODSEQ
S_KK4_74001699	IMG Activity: ISPSD_VNRKSPRODUKTIO
S_KK4_74001700	IMG Activity: ISPSD_WERBEART
S_KK4_74001701	IMG Activity: ISPSD_VREGARTBUNDF
S_KK4_74001702	IMG Activity: ISPSD_VPOSTSENDART
S_KK4_74001703	IMG Activity: ISPSD_VNETZEPOST
S_KK4_74001704	IMG Activity: ISPSD_VNETZLIEFART
S_KK4_74001705	IMG Activity: ISPSD_AUSNAHMELPLZ
S_KK4_74001706	IMG Activity: ISPSD_VGEBINDEART
S_KK4_74001707	IMG Activity: ISP_ZAHLUNGSBED
S_KK4_74001708	IMG Activity: ISMSD_STVERBREITALLG
S_KK4_74001709	IMG Activity: ISP_GP_BERUFE
S_KK4_74001710	IMG Activity: ISPSD_FREIEBEZKATEG
S_KK4_74001711	IMG Activity: ISP_BEZIRKSNR
S_KK4_74001712	IMG Activity: ISPSD_STRUKNKRSLAUFL

S_KK4_74001713	IMG Activity: ISP_GP_FAMSTAND
S_KK4_74001714	IMG Activity: ISP_GP_TITEL
S_KK4_74001715	IMG Activity: ISPSD_BEZKATEGORIEN
S_KK4_74001716	IMG Activity: ISM_STAMMGEOSTR
S_KK4_74001717	IMG Activity: ISM_STAMMGEOSEKADR
S_KK4_74001718	IMG Activity: ISP_GP_HERKUNFT
S_KK4_74001719	IMG Activity: ISP_GEOGRAPHARTEN
S_KK4_74001720	IMG Activity: ISPSD_STRUKNRKRSGEO
S_KK4_74001721	IMG Activity: ISPSD_GEO_POSTNRKRS
S_KK4_74001722	IMG Activity: ISPSD_VERSABLNRKRS
S_KK4_74001723	IMG Activity: ISPSD_VERSROUPVANRKR
S_KK4_74001724	IMG Activity: ISP_GP_ANREDE
S_KK4_74001725	IMG Activity: ISPSD_VLIEFERARTEN
S_KK4_74001726	IMG Activity: ISPSD_VERSLIEFNRKRS
S_KK4_74001727	IMG Activity: ISPSD_STRUKBEZRUND
S_KK4_74001728	IMG Activity: ISPSD_VERSROUTENRKRS
S_KK4_74001729	IMG Activity: ISPSD_ROUTENART
S_KK4_74001730	IMG Activity: ISPSD_STRUKROUTPERIO
S_KK4_74001731	IMG Activity: ISPSD_ROUTENKATEG
S_KK4_74001732	IMG Activity: ISPSD_FREIROUTENKAT
S_KK4_74001733	IMG Activity: ISPSD_VERKEHRSMART
S_KK4_74001734	IMG Activity: ISPSD_VERSRAUMABL
S_KK4_74001735	IMG Activity: ISPSD_NRKRSWERBEMAT
S_KK4_74001736	IMG Activity: ISPSD_PABRPRKONDTAB
S_KK4_74001737	IMG Activity: ISPSD_PABRPRKONDART
S_KK4_74001738	IMG Activity: ISPSD_PABRPRZUGRFOLG
S_KK4_74001739	IMG Activity: ISPSD_PABRPRKALKSCHE
S_KK4_74001740	IMG Activity: ISM_GPTEXTEBK
S_KK4_74001741	IMG Activity: ISM_GPTEXTEZK
S_KK4_74001742	IMG Activity: ISM_GPTEXTARTENVERK
S_KK4_74001743	IMG Activity: ISM_GPTEXTEVERKSCHEM
S_KK4_74001744	IMG Activity: ISPSD_PABRZUKONDAUSG
S_KK4_74001745	IMG Activity: ISPSD-PABRZUAUSSCHKZ
S_KK4_74001746	IMG Activity: ISM_GPTEXTVERKZUGR
S_KK4_74001747	IMG Activity: ISPSD_PABRZUMENSTAMM
S_KK4_74001748	IMG Activity: ISPSD_PABRZLISTKOND
S_KK4_74001749	IMG Activity: ISPSD-PABRPOKONDART
S_KK4_74001750	IMG Activity: ISPSD_PABRPOZUGRFOLG
S_KK4_74001751	IMG Activity: ISPSD_PABRPOKALKSCHE
S_KK4_74001752	IMG Activity: ISPAM_GPHITYP
S_KK4_74001753	IMG Activity: ISPSD_PABRPOKONDAUSG
S_KK4_74001754	IMG Activity: ISPSD_PABRPOAUSSCHKZ
S_KK4_74001755	IMG Activity: ISPSD_PABRPOKONDTAB
S_KK4_74001756	IMG Activity: ISPSD_PABRPRKONDAUSG
S_KK4_74001757	IMG Activity: ISPSD_PABRPRAUSSCHKZ
S_KK4_74001758	IMG Activity: ISM_GPTEXTBD
S_KK4_74001759	IMG Activity: ISPSD_PABRPRMENSTAMM
S_KK4_74001760	IMG Activity: ISPSD_PABRPRLISTKOND
S_KK4_74001761	IMG Activity: ISM_GPTEXTZD
S_KK4_74001762	IMG Activity: ISPSD_PABRZUKALKSCHE
S_KK4_74001763	IMG Activity: ISPSD_FAKTKONDGUTSCH
S_KK4_74001764	IMG Activity: ISPSD_KONDARTZUGR
S_KK4_74001765	IMG Activity: ISPSD_KALKSCHEMATA
S_KK4_74001766	IMG Activity: ISP_TAXKNZ_DEB

S_KK4_74001767	IMG Activity: ISPSD_KONDAUSSCHLGRP
S_KK4_74001768	IMG Activity: ISPSD_AUSSCHLKZKOND
S_KK4_74001769	IMG Activity: ISPSD_KONDART
S_KK4_74001770	IMG Activity: ISPSD_KUNDSTATISTGRP
S_KK4_74001771	IMG Activity: ISP_KUNDGRP
S_KK4_74001772	IMG Activity: ISPSD_GPSTAMMINFOZUO
S_KK4_74001773	IMG Activity: ISPSD_GPINFOBLOCK
S_KK4_74001774	IMG Activity: ISPSD_GPSTAMMINFOSI
S_KK4_74001775	IMG Activity: ISPSD_KONDTAB
S_KK4_74001776	IMG Activity: ISPSD_BEDINGPREIS
S_KK4_74001777	IMG Activity: ISPSD_FORMELNPREIS
S_KK4_74001778	IMG Activity: ISM_GPTEXTEEKORG
S_KK4_74001779	IMG Activity: ISPSD_PABRZUKONDTAB
S_KK4_74001780	IMG Activity: ISPSD_PABRZUKONDART
S_KK4_74001781	IMG Activity: ISPSD_PABRZUZUGRFOLG
S_KK4_74001782	IMG Activity: ISPSD_KONDLISTLAYOUT
S_KK4_74001783	IMG Activity: ISPSD_PREISRELEVFLD
S_KK4_74001784	IMG Activity: ISPSD_LANDGRPVERSAND
S_KK4_74001785	IMG Activity: ISP_PVAKONDGRP
S_KK4_74001786	IMG Activity: ISPSD_PREISPERIODIZ
S_KK4_74001787	IMG Activity: ISPSD_MENUESTAMMD
S_KK4_74001788	IMG Activity: ISP_KTO_ABSTIMM
S_KK4_74001789	IMG Activity: ISPSD_STRUKNRKRSSTRA
S_KK4_74001790	IMG Activity: ISPAM_TJJPOS
S_KK4_74001791	IMG Activity: ISPAM_TJJSPVM
S_KK4_74001792	IMG Activity: ISPAM_TJJVERT
S_KK4_74001793	IMG Activity: ISPSD_BESCHABWESENH
S_KK4_74001794	IMG Activity: ISP_DRUCKERZART
S_KK4_74001795	IMG Activity: ISP_TITELART
S_KK4_74001796	IMG Activity: ISPAM_TJJAMTL
S_KK4_74001797	IMG Activity: ISP_ADR_MONTFIND
S_KK4_74001798	IMG Activity: ISP_GEOPHONETSUCHE
S_KK4_74001799	IMG Activity: ISPSD_WERKZDUEBPHOSU
S_KK4_74001800	IMG Activity: ISPAM_VERBR_BEZ
S_KK4_74001801	IMG Activity: ISP0_PARTNER_AP
S_KK4_74001802	IMG Activity: ISPSD_BESCHABGANGSGR
S_KK4_74001803	IMG Activity: ISP_PERIODIZITAT
S_KK4_74001804	IMG Activity: ISPSD_BASPVASTATGRP
S_KK4_74001805	IMG Activity: ISP_BERICHTSGRP
S_KK4_74001806	IMG Activity: ISPSD_BEZTYP
S_KK4_74001807	IMG Activity: ISPSD_BEZPERZUS
S_KK4_74001808	IMG Activity: ISPSD_VKWOCHTAGBEZPE
S_KK4_74001809	IMG Activity: ISP_GENERIERUNGSGRUP
S_KK4_74001810	IMG Activity: ISP_NRKRSDRZ
S_KK4_74001811	IMG Activity: ISPSD_BESCHART
S_KK4_74001812	IMG Activity: ISP_NRKRSVERWGDRZ
S_KK4_74001813	IMG Activity: ISMSD_PRODSCHEM
S_KK4_74001814	IMG Activity: ISP_NRKRSBESCHVERH
S_KK4_74001815	IMG Activity: ISP_PVAART
S_KK4_74001816	IMG Activity: ISP_MTYP_INTSORTKEY
S_KK4_74001817	IMG Activity: ISPAM_FATBB
S_KK4_74001818	IMG Activity: ISPAM_GP_VV_VA_PFL
S_KK4_74001819	IMG Activity: ISPAM_BEDGRUPPE
S_KK4_74001820	IMG Activity: ISP_FAKTURATRENN

S_KK4_74001821	IMG Activity: ISPAM_GP_VV_VS_PFL
S_KK4_74001822	IMG Activity: ISPAM_GP_VV_BA_PFL
S_KK4_74001823	IMG Activity: ISP_ZAHLBEDGRUPPE
S_KK4_74001824	IMG Activity: ISPAM_GRUNDEINST_1
S_KK4_74001825	IMG Activity: ISPAM_VERMV_NUMKI
S_KK4_74001826	IMG Activity: ISP_JLVEKDLART_0020
S_KK4_74001827	IMG Activity: ISPAM_DEFAULTSPRAB
S_KK4_74001828	IMG Activity: ISP_ADR_DRFORMATE
S_KK4_74001829	IMG Activity: ISP_DRUCKSTEUER
S_KK4_74001830	IMG Activity: ISP_ADR_DRFORMULARE
S_KK4_74001831	IMG Activity: ISP_ADR_MTYP_NAMEN
S_KK4_74001832	IMG Activity: ISP_ADR_MTYP_DEBNAM
S_KK4_74001833	IMG Activity: ISP_ADR_MTYP_KREDNAM
S_KK4_74001834	IMG Activity: ISP_JGVTJG90C
S_KK4_74001835	IMG Activity: ISP_PROVSCHL
S_KK4_74001836	IMG Activity: ISPAM_STEUERKLASSKRE
S_KK4_74001837	IMG Activity: ISMAM_AGNTCONTRGROUP
S_KK4_74001838	IMG Activity: ISPAM_KONKAUS
S_KK4_74001839	IMG Activity: ISP_KUKARRIERE
S_KK4_74001840	IMG Activity: ISP_NRKRS_ADR
S_KK4_74001841	IMG Activity: ISPSD_VERMITTLERTYP
S_KK4_74001842	IMG Activity: ISPAM_TJJW9
S_KK4_74001843	IMG Activity: ISPAM_TJJBEVTMD
S_KK4_74001844	IMG Activity: ISPSD_SPERRGRDFAKT
S_KK4_74001845	IMG Activity: ISPSD_SPERRGRDAUFTR
S_KK4_74001846	IMG Activity: ISPAM_DIEN_NUMK
S_KK4_74001847	IMG Activity: ISP-FAKTKAL
S_KK4_74001848	IMG Activity: ISPAM_TJJW7
S_KK4_74001849	IMG Activity: ISPAM_JJTBEVRGRP
S_KK4_74001850	IMG Activity: ISPAM_BEHIEVERS
S_KK4_74001851	IMG Activity: ISPAM_TERMINSPEZ
S_KK4_74001852	IMG Activity: ISPAM_TJJW1
S_KK4_74001853	IMG Activity: ISPAM_TJJW3
S_KK4_74001854	IMG Activity: ISMSD_GPKUNDSCHEM
S_KK4_74001855	IMG Activity: ISPSD_HIERARCHTYPGEO
S_KK4_74001856	IMG Activity: ISP_GP_BRANCHENCODES
S_KK4_74001857	IMG Activity: ISP_GP_BRANCHE
S_KK4_74001858	IMG Activity: ISPSD_LANDSPEZPOSTHI
S_KK4_74001859	IMG Activity: ISPSD_KRGEMREGZUO
S_KK4_74001860	IMG Activity: ISPSD_AUSNAHMELPLZSD
S_KK4_74001861	IMG Activity: ISP_STRUKLESETIEFE
S_KK4_74001862	IMG Activity: ISPAM_DIENTYP
S_KK4_74001863	IMG Activity: ISPAM_TJHSEKL
S_KK4_74001864	IMG Activity: ISPAM_TJHGEWKL
S_KK4_74001865	IMG Activity: ISP_GP_AGENTART
S_KK4_74001866	IMG Activity: ISP_GP_BONITAET
S_KK4_74001867	IMG Activity: ISP_ANDERUNGSNR
S_KK4_74001868	IMG Activity: ISPAM_VTWOTAG
S_KK4_74001869	IMG Activity: ISPAM_IKOHIEVAR
S_KK4_74001870	IMG Activity: ISPAM_IKOHIEVERS
S_KK4_74001871	IMG Activity: ISP-LEISTKAL
S_KK4_74001872	IMG Activity: ISPAM_NRBE
S_KK4_74001873	IMG Activity: ISPAM_PENR
S_KK4_74001874	IMG Activity: ISPAM_BEGRPINH

S_KK4_74001875	IMG Activity: ISPAM_NRIKO
S_KK4_74001876	IMG Activity: ISPSD_GPVTNRKRSGPERS
S_KK4_74001877	IMG Activity: ISP_VAVARIANTENTYP
S_KK4_74001878	IMG Activity: ISPSD_ZUSTELLERSETZ
S_KK4_74001879	IMG Activity: ISP_NUMMERVA
S_KK4_74001880	IMG Activity: ISPSD_ZUSTELLGRP
S_KK4_74001881	IMG Activity: ISPSD_ZUSTELLTYP
S_KK4_74001882	IMG Activity: ISPAM_SFSP
S_KK4_74001883	IMG Activity: ISPAM_TJJFACSFP
S_KK4_74001884	IMG Activity: ISPAM_VTSI
S_KK4_74001885	IMG Activity: ISPSD_MBRSYST
S_KK4_74001886	IMG Activity: ISPAM_VTPE
S_KK4_74001887	IMG Activity: ISPAM_VTANZ
S_KK4_74001888	IMG Activity: ISPAM_SF
S_KK4_74001889	IMG Activity: ISPAM_BEGRPNUM
S_KK4_74001890	IMG Activity: ISPAM_LOCWIN
S_KK4_74001891	IMG Activity: ISPAM_BEGRP_PR
S_KK4_74001892	IMG Activity: ISPAM_TJJ39
S_KK4_74001893	IMG Activity: ISPSD_VERKSTELL
S_KK4_74001894	IMG Activity: ISPSD_PABRPOMENSTAMM
S_KK4_74001895	IMG Activity: ISPAM_AUFNACHRART
S_KK4_74001896	IMG Activity: ISPAM_AUFZUGRFOLG
S_KK4_74001897	IMG Activity: ISPAM_AUFNACHRSCHE
S_KK4_74001898	IMG Activity: ISPAM_AUFNACHR_PAR
S_KK4_74001899	IMG Activity: ISPMSD_VUEKORGBUKRS
S_KK4_74001900	IMG Activity: ISPAM_AUFKOND
S_KK4_74001901	IMG Activity: ISPAM_AUFKONDTAB
S_KK4_74001902	IMG Activity: ISPSD_VUVTWEGVKORG
S_KK4_74001903	IMG Activity: ISPSD_NFNRKRSRECHDRU
S_KK4_74001904	IMG Activity: ISPSD_NFKRITRECHDRU
S_KK4_74001905	IMG Activity: ISPSD_VUBUKRSVKORG
S_KK4_74001906	IMG Activity: ISPAM_NACHRZUGRNACHS
S_KK4_74001907	IMG Activity: ISPAM_AUFFELDKTLG
S_KK4_74001908	IMG Activity: ISPAM_ABSNACHR_PAR
S_KK4_74001909	IMG Activity: ISPAM_ABSKOND
S_KK4_74001910	IMG Activity: ISPAM_FKTFELDKTLG
S_KK4_74001911	IMG Activity: ISPAM_FKTKONDTAB
S_KK4_74001912	IMG Activity: ISPAM_FKTNACHRART
S_KK4_74001913	IMG Activity: ISPAM_FKTZUGRFOLG
S_KK4_74001914	IMG Activity: ISPAM_ABSNACHRSCHE
S_KK4_74001915	IMG Activity: ISPSD_VUWERKBUKRS
S_KK4_74001916	IMG Activity: ISPAM_ABSFELDKTLG
S_KK4_74001917	IMG Activity: ISPAM_ABSKONDTAB
S_KK4_74001918	IMG Activity: ISM_BUKRS_KKBER_ASS
S_KK4_74001919	IMG Activity: ISPAM_ABSNACHRART
S_KK4_74001920	IMG Activity: ISPAM_ABSZUGRFOLG
S_KK4_74001921	IMG Activity: ISM_VBER_KKBER_ASS
S_KK4_74001922	IMG Activity: ISPAM_ERLV_KSCHL_KOP
S_KK4_74001923	IMG Activity: ISPSD_VUVKORGVTWEGWK
S_KK4_74001924	IMG Activity: ISPAM_CONDIDX_ERLVT
S_KK4_74001925	IMG Activity: ISPAM_COND_COPY_EVT
S_KK4_74001926	IMG Activity: ISPAM_CND_IDX_OVERF3
S_KK4_74001927	IMG Activity: ISPAM_REV_ACC_DET_4
S_KK4_74001928	IMG Activity: ISPSD_VUSPARTJEVKEIN

S_KK4_74001929	IMG Activity: ISPAM_REV_ACC_DET_1
S_KK4_74001930	IMG Activity: ISPAM_COPY_KA_KS
S_KK4_74001931	IMG Activity: ISPAM_REV_ACC_DET_2
S_KK4_74001932	IMG Activity: ISPAM_REV_ACC_DET_3
S_KK4_74001933	IMG Activity: ISPSD_VUVTWEGJEVKORG
S_KK4_74001934	IMG Activity: ISPSD_VUVKBUEROVTBER
S_KK4_74001935	IMG Activity: ISPSD_NACHRSCHEMAZUO
S_KK4_74001936	IMG Activity: ISPSD_NACHRDYNMENKST
S_KK4_74001937	IMG Activity: ISPSD_NACHRDRUPARAM
S_KK4_74001938	IMG Activity: ISPSD_VUVTBEREICHE
S_KK4_74001939	IMG Activity: ISPSD_VUSPARTVKORG
S_KK4_74001940	IMG Activity: ISPSD_NACHRZUGRNACHS
S_KK4_74001941	IMG Activity: ISPAM_REV_ACC_DET_5
S_KK4_74001942	IMG Activity: ISPAM_REV_ACC_DET_6
S_KK4_74001943	IMG Activity: ISPAM_JJVTVBUR
S_KK4_74001944	IMG Activity: ISPSD_VUVKGRPVKBUERO
S_KK4_74001945	IMG Activity: ISPSD_EKORGVTBERZUO
S_KK4_74001946	IMG Activity: ISPSD_NACHRFKATKONDT
S_KK4_74001947	IMG Activity: ISPAM_FRMTXT_VKORG
S_KK4_74001948	IMG Activity: ISPAM_FRMTXT_EKORG
S_KK4_74001949	IMG Activity: ISPAM_ADRESSFORMAT
S_KK4_74001950	IMG Activity: ISPAM_ADRFRMT_FORM
S_KK4_74001951	IMG Activity: ISPAM_PRINT_OPT_NACH
S_KK4_74001952	IMG Activity: ISPAM_NACHR_DYNKOND
S_KK4_74001953	IMG Activity: ISPSD_VUWERKE
S_KK4_74001954	IMG Activity: ISPSD_VUSPARTEN
S_KK4_74001955	IMG Activity: ISPAM_PRGFRM_AUF
S_KK4_74001956	IMG Activity: ISPAM_PRGFRM_ABSCH
S_KK4_74001957	IMG Activity: ISPAM_PRGFRM_FAKT
S_KK4_74001958	IMG Activity: ISPAM_PRGFRM_STAMM
S_KK4_74001959	IMG Activity: ISPAM_FRM_DEF
S_KK4_74001960	IMG Activity: ISPSD_AKONTZTABELLE
S_KK4_74001961	IMG Activity: ISPSD_AKONTZZUGRFOLG
S_KK4_74001962	IMG Activity: ISPSD_AKONTZSCHEMATA
S_KK4_74001963	IMG Activity: ISPSD_AKONTZSCHLUESS
S_KK4_74001964	IMG Activity: ISPSD_AKONTZSACHKTZU
S_KK4_74001965	IMG Activity: ISPSD_AKONTTABELLE
S_KK4_74001966	IMG Activity: ISPSD_AKONTGRPVSG
S_KK4_74001967	IMG Activity: ISPSD_VUGESCHBEREICH
S_KK4_74001968	IMG Activity: ISPAM_BEDINGUNGENNST
S_KK4_74001969	IMG Activity: ISPAM_TJHPRINT
S_KK4_74001970	IMG Activity: ISPSD_VUBUKRS
S_KK4_74001971	IMG Activity: ISPAM_PARTNERSCHEMA
S_KK4_74001972	IMG Activity: ISM_KKBER_MAINTAIN
S_KK4_74001973	IMG Activity: ISPAM_STAMMNACHRART
S_KK4_74001974	IMG Activity: ISPAM_STAMMZUGRFOLG
S_KK4_74001975	IMG Activity: ISPAM_STAMMNACHRSCHE
S_KK4_74001976	IMG Activity: ISPSD_VUVERKGRP
S_KK4_74001977	IMG Activity: ISPSD_VUVERKBUERO
S_KK4_74001978	IMG Activity: ISPAM_STAMMNACHR_PAR
S_KK4_74001979	IMG Activity: ISPSD_VULAGERORT
S_KK4_74001980	IMG Activity: ISPAM_FKTNACHRSCHE
S_KK4_74001981	IMG Activity: ISPAM_FKTNACHR_PAR
S_KK4_74001982	IMG Activity: ISPAM_FKTKOND

S_KK4_74001983	IMG Activity: ISPSD_VUEKORG
S_KK4_74001984	IMG Activity: ISPAM_STAMMFELDKTLG
S_KK4_74001985	IMG Activity: ISPAM_STAMMKONDTAB
S_KK4_74001986	IMG Activity: ISPAM_KONZUGRFOLG
S_KK4_74001987	IMG Activity: ISPAM_KONNACHRSCHE
S_KK4_74001988	IMG Activity: ISPAM_KONNACHR_PAR
S_KK4_74001989	IMG Activity: ISPAM_KONKOND
S_KK4_74001990	IMG Activity: ISPAM_JJVTVKK
S_KK4_74001991	IMG Activity: ISPAM_NACHRADRESS
S_KK4_74001992	IMG Activity: ISPSD_VUVERKORG
S_KK4_74001993	IMG Activity: ISPAM_STAMMKOND
S_KK4_74001994	IMG Activity: ISPSD_VUVERTRIEBSWEG
S_KK4_74001995	IMG Activity: ISPAM_HIERAEND_DLI
S_KK4_74001996	IMG Activity: ISPAM_KONFELDKTLG
S_KK4_74001997	IMG Activity: ISPAM_KONKONDTAB
S_KK4_74001998	IMG Activity: ISPAM_KONNACHRART
S_KK4_74001999	IMG Activity: ISPAM_PROV_PRICE_2
S_KK4_74002000	IMG Activity: ISMAM_COND_FORSALVOL
S_KK4_74002001	IMG Activity: ISPAM_TJ183
S_KK4_74002002	IMG Activity: ISPSD_DYNBILDSCHMOD
S_KK4_74002003	IMG Activity: ISPSD_VARIABLTVARV
S_KK4_74002004	IMG Activity: ISMAM_BEZCOND_KOAR_Z
S_KK4_74002005	IMG Activity: ISPAM_DYN_MENU_KONPF
S_KK4_74002006	IMG Activity: ISPAM_ORDER_PRICE_KL
S_KK4_74002007	IMG Activity: ISPAM_ORDER_BEZKO_3
S_KK4_74002008	IMG Activity: ISPAM_ORDER_BEZKO_2
S_KK4_74002009	IMG Activity: ISPAM_ORDER_BEZKO_4
S_KK4_74002010	IMG Activity: ISPAM_ORDER_BEZKO_5
S_KK4_74002011	IMG Activity: ISPAM_ABS_COND14
S_KK4_74002012	IMG Activity: ISPAM_CONDIDX_JD
S_KK4_74002013	IMG Activity: ISPAM_COND_COPY_JD
S_KK4_74002014	IMG Activity: ISPAM_ABSCHL_PRICE_2
S_KK4_74002015	IMG Activity: ISPAM_ABS_COND13
S_KK4_74002016	IMG Activity: ISMAM_OUTBK_COND_EX
S_KK4_74002017	IMG Activity: ISPSD_GRUNDSYNPSDPAM
S_KK4_74002018	IMG Activity: ISM_GRUNDMNDPAEND
S_KK4_74002019	IMG Activity: ISPAM_ABS_COND11
S_KK4_74002020	IMG Activity: ISPAM_ABS_COND12
S_KK4_74002021	IMG Activity: ISP_GP_NRKRS_GP
S_KK4_74002022	IMG Activity: ISP_KTOGRP
S_KK4_74002023	IMG Activity: ISPAM_ORDER_PRICE_1
S_KK4_74002024	IMG Activity: ISPAM_ORDER_PRICE_2
S_KK4_74002025	IMG Activity: ISPAM_ORDER_PRICE_3
S_KK4_74002026	IMG Activity: ISP_GP_VORLFELD
S_KK4_74002027	IMG Activity: ISPSD_PABRPOLISTKOND
S_KK4_74002028	IMG Activity: ISPSD_PABRBEDING
S_KK4_74002029	IMG Activity: ISPSD_PABRFORMELN
S_KK4_74002030	IMG Activity: ISP_SDGP_EINRICHT
S_KK4_74002031	IMG Activity: ISP_DIFFUNIT
S_KK4_74002032	IMG Activity: ISPAM_COND_COPY_ORD
S_KK4_74002033	IMG Activity: ISPAM_CND_IDX_OVERF1
S_KK4_74002034	IMG Activity: ISPAM_ORDER_PRICE_9
S_KK4_74002035	IMG Activity: ISP_NRKRVERWEND
S_KK4_74002036	IMG Activity: ISPAM_ORDER_PRICE_4

S_KK4_74002037	IMG Activity: ISP_PARTNERROLLEN
S_KK4_74002038	IMG Activity: ISPAM_ORDER_PRICE_5
S_KK4_74002039	IMG Activity: ISPAM_ORDER_PRICE_11
S_KK4_74002040	IMG Activity: ISPAM_CONDIDX_ORDER
S_KK4_74002041	IMG Activity: ISPAM_PROV_PRICE_1_2
S_KK4_74002042	IMG Activity: ISPSD_VUKONSISTVERTR
S_KK4_74002043	IMG Activity: ISPAM_PROV_PRICE_1_1
S_KK4_74002044	IMG Activity: ISM_AKTLANDVERSION
S_KK4_74002045	IMG Activity: ISPSD_VUREGELNVTBER
S_KK4_74002046	IMG Activity: ISPSD_VUGBJEVTBER
S_KK4_74002047	IMG Activity: ISPAM_CND_IDX_OVERF2
S_KK4_74002048	IMG Activity: ISPSD_KONSISTEKORG
S_KK4_74002049	IMG Activity: ISPAM_CONDIDX_PROV
S_KK4_74002050	IMG Activity: ISPAM_PROV_PRICE_1_3
S_KK4_74002051	IMG Activity: ISPAM_PROV_PRICE_1_4
S_KK4_74002052	IMG Activity: ISPAM_PROV_PRICE_1_7
S_KK4_74002053	IMG Activity: ISPAM_COND_COPY_PROV
S_KK4_74002054	IMG Activity: ISPAM_VABR_BEZKON2
S_KK4_74002055	IMG Activity: ISPAM_CONTRACT_DISC
S_KK4_74002056	IMG Activity: ISP_ALLGSTEUPARAISP
S_KK4_74002057	IMG Activity: ISPAM_VABR_BEZKON1
S_KK4_74002058	IMG Activity: ISPAM_PROV_PRICE_1_6
S_KK4_74002059	IMG Activity: ISPSD_VUGBWERKSPART
S_KK4_74002060	IMG Activity: ISPAM_ORDER_PR_KL_P
S_KK4_74002061	IMG Activity: ISM_USEREXPROD
S_KK4_74002062	IMG Activity: ISPSD_USEXGP
S_KK4_74002063	IMG Activity: ISMAM_USEREXTECH
S_KK4_74002064	IMG Activity: ISMAM_USEREXABRECH
S_KK4_74002065	IMG Activity: ISPSD_USEXABRECHNUNG
S_KK4_74002066	IMG Activity: ISMAM_USEREXFAKT
S_KK4_74002067	IMG Activity: ISPSD_USEXFAKT
S_KK4_74002068	IMG Activity: ISM_WERKZUSEXVERS
S_KK4_74002069	IMG Activity: ISMAM_USEREXVERK
S_KK4_74002070	IMG Activity: ISPSD_USEXAUFTRAG
S_KK4_74002071	IMG Activity: ISPSD_USEXVERBREIT
S_KK4_74002072	IMG Activity: ISPSD_FAKTUBERLGJVAR
S_KK4_74002073	IMG Activity: ISP_GRUNDMASSKAL
S_KK4_74002074	IMG Activity: ISPAM_SELECTION_BLKS
S_KK4_74002075	IMG Activity: ISP_IS_BSTA_EINST_LA
S_KK4_74002076	IMG Activity: ISP_IS_BSTA_EINST_DA
S_KK4_74002077	IMG Activity: ISPAM_ERLV_KSCHL_UMS
S_KK4_74002078	IMG Activity: ISPSD_VERSPAPFONTS
S_KK4_74002079	IMG Activity: ISPSD_ABRUBERGJVAR
S_KK4_74002080	IMG Activity: ISM_USEXNACHRICHTEN
S_KK4_74002081	IMG Activity: ISP_IS_LDWDB_FELDKTI
S_KK4_74002082	IMG Activity: ISPSD_WERKZADRSYNCHR
S_KK4_74002083	IMG Activity: ISP_IS_LDWDB_WERKZ2
S_KK4_74002084	IMG Activity: ISPSD_BESCHSTEUERKZ
S_KK4_74002085	IMG Activity: ISP_IS_LDWDB_WERKZ31
S_KK4_74002086	IMG Activity: ISP_KLASSENSYSTEM
S_KK4_74002087	IMG Activity: _FICABTPYPR
S_KK4_74002088	IMG Activity: _FICABTPYPC_FQZX
S_KK4_74002089	IMG Activity: _FICABTPYPC_FQZV
S_KK4_74002090	IMG Activity: _ISISFICA_TKKVMZAHL

S_KK4_74002091	IMG Activity: _ISISFICA_TKKVNFAEL
S_KK4_74002092	IMG Activity: _ISISFICA_TKKVTXB
S_KK4_74002093	IMG Activity: _FICABTIC_VC_TFK056
S_KK4_74002094	IMG Activity: _FICABTIC_VC_T056GJI
S_KK4_74002095	IMG Activity: _FICABTIC_V_T056P
S_KK4_74002096	IMG Activity: _FICABTIC_V_T056R
S_KK4_74002097	IMG Activity: _FICABTPY_FPAC03
S_KK4_74002098	IMG Activity: _FICABTPY_FPARZ1
S_KK4_74002099	IMG Activity: _FICABTPY_VC_TFK042E
S_KK4_74002100	IMG Activity: _FICABTPY_VC_TFK042Z
S_KK4_74002101	IMG Activity: _FICA_BTPY_TFK042M
S_KK4_74002102	IMG Activity: _FICABTPY_FQP5
S_KK4_74002103	IMG Activity: _ISISFICA_V_TFK005A2
S_KK4_74002104	IMG Activity: _ISISFICA_VC_TKKV_RE
S_KK4_74002105	IMG Activity: _ISISFICA_TKKVZAFRQ
S_KK4_74002106	IMG Activity: _ISISFICA_VYZ10
S_KK4_74002107	IMG Activity: _FICABTPY_TFKPKC
S_KK4_74002108	IMG Activity: _FICABTPY_V_TFK008
S_KK4_74002109	IMG Activity: _FICABTPY_TFK001S
S_KK4_74002110	IMG Activity: _FICABTPY_FQZL
S_KK4_74002111	IMG Activity: _ISISFICA_TKKVMVARI
S_KK4_74002112	IMG Activity: _FICABTDU_VC_TFK047A
S_KK4_74002113	IMG Activity: _FICABTDU_V_TFK047L
S_KK4_74002114	IMG Activity: _ISISFICA_TKKVBAKT1
S_KK4_74002115	IMG Activity: _ISISFICA_VY6N(2)
S_KK4_74002116	IMG Activity: _ISUFICABTDU_000100
S_KK4_74002117	IMG Activity: _ISISFICA_V_TFK005A
S_KK4_74002118	IMG Activity: _FICABTDU_FQZ06
S_KK4_74002119	IMG Activity: _FICABTDU_TFK046A
S_KK4_74002120	IMG Activity: _FICABTDU_V_TFK047S
S_KK4_74002121	IMG Activity: _FICABTDU_V_TFK047F
S_KK4_74002122	IMG Activity: _ISISFICA_TKKVMAHNV
S_KK4_74002123	IMG Activity: _ISISFICA_VY7I
S_KK4_74002124	IMG Activity: _FICABTIC_FQI6
S_KK4_74002125	IMG Activity: _FICABTIC_TFK056C
S_KK4_74002126	IMG Activity: _FICABTIC_FQI4
S_KK4_74002127	IMG Activity: _FICABTIC_TFK056S
S_KK4_74002128	IMG Activity: _FICABTIC_TFK057
S_KK4_74002129	IMG Activity: _FICABTDU_FQI8
S_KK4_74002130	IMG Activity: _FICABTDU_VC_TFK047E
S_KK4_74002131	IMG Activity: _FICABTDU_FQZY
S_KK4_74002132	IMG Activity: _FICABTDU_V_TFK047H
S_KK4_74002133	IMG Activity: _FICABTDU_V_TFK047G
S_KK4_74002134	IMG Activity: _FICABTDU_V_TFK047J
S_KK4_74002135	IMG Activity: _FICABTPY_SWLD1
S_KK4_74002136	IMG Activity: _FICABTSE_V_ESECS
S_KK4_74002137	IMG Activity: _FICABTSE_V_ESECR
S_KK4_74002138	IMG Activity: _FICABTSE_FQSEC
S_KK4_74002139	IMG Activity: _FICABTSE_ESECU
S_KK4_74002140	IMG Activity: _FICABTSE_ENSE
S_KK4_74002141	IMG Activity: _ISISFICA_VVKKCSTR
S_KK4_74002142	IMG Activity: _ISUFICABTSE_000097
S_KK4_74002143	IMG Activity: _ISUFICABTSE_000096
S_KK4_74002144	IMG Activity: _FICABTSE_SE75

S_KK4_74002145	IMG Activity: _FICABTSE_TFK_SEC_RE
S_KK4_74002146	IMG Activity: _FICABTSE_FQI5
S_KK4_74002147	IMG Activity: _FICABTSE_V_ESECT
S_KK4_74002148	IMG Activity: _ISISFICA_VSC03
S_KK4_74002149	IMG Activity: _ISISFICA_V_TVS030A
S_KK4_74002150	IMG Activity: _ISISFICA_VSC02
S_KK4_74002151	IMG Activity: _ISISFICA_VSC01
S_KK4_74002152	IMG Activity: _ISISFICA_VC_TVSC
S_KK4_74002153	IMG Activity: _ISISFICA_VC_TVSC_PP
S_KK4_74002154	IMG Activity: _ISISFICA_TKKVVERD
S_KK4_74002155	IMG Activity: _ISISFICA_VYFS
S_KK4_74002156	IMG Activity: _ISISFICA_V_TFK080R2
S_KK4_74002157	IMG Activity: _ISISFICA_VC_TKKVPOV
S_KK4_74002158	IMG Activity: _ISISFICA_VC_TKKVPOG
S_KK4_74002159	IMG Activity: _ISISFICA_VVSCNUM
S_KK4_74002160	IMG Activity: _FICABTPYPP_V_TFK028
S_KK4_74002161	IMG Activity: _FICABTPY_TFK012
S_KK4_74002162	IMG Activity: _FICABTPYPP_FPN3
S_KK4_74002163	IMG Activity: _FICABTPY_FQZN
S_KK4_74002164	IMG Activity: _FICABPTY_TFK020K
S_KK4_74002165	IMG Activity: _FICABTPY_FQZJ
S_KK4_74002166	IMG Activity: _FICABTPY_SWLD
S_KK4_74002167	IMG Activity: _ISISFICA_TKKVBLERM
S_KK4_74002168	IMG Activity: _FICABTPY_V_T001FFK
S_KK4_74002169	IMG Activity: _FICABTPY_FQZT
S_KK4_74002170	IMG Activity: _ISISFICA_VY6P
S_KK4_74002171	IMG Activity: _FICAABTPY_VC_TFK006
S_KK4_74002172	IMG Activity: _ISISFICA_VYAF1
S_KK4_74002173	IMG Activity: _ISISFICA_V_TFK005A3
S_KK4_74002174	IMG Activity: _ISISFICA_V_TFK080R1
S_KK4_74002175	IMG Activity: _ISISFICA_TKKVBAKT
S_KK4_74002176	IMG Activity: _ISISFICA_TKKVFAART
S_KK4_74002177	IMG Activity: _FICABTSE_FQI7
S_KK4_74002178	IMG Activity: _FICABTPY_FQZI
S_KK4_74002179	IMG Activity: _FICABTPY_FQZ6
S_KK4_74002180	IMG Activity: _ISUFICABTPY_000101
S_KK4_74002181	IMG Activity: _ISTFICABTPY_000006
S_KK4_74002184	IMG Activity: _FICABTDCSV_FQZ07
S_KK4_74002185	IMG Activity: _FICABTDRP_FQZ10
S_KK4_74002186	IMG Activity: _ISUFICAINCO_000087
S_KK4_74002187	IMG Activity: _ISISFICA_TKKVCOPA
S_KK4_74002188	IMG Activity: _ISISFICA_TKKVBASIC
S_KK4_74002189	IMG Activity: _FICAINCM_V_TFK036V
S_KK4_74002190	IMG Activity: _FICA_TS_TFK000D
S_KK4_74002191	IMG Activity: _FICA_TS_1
S_KK4_74002192	IMG Activity: _FICAIS_V_TFK001REP
S_KK4_74002193	IMG Activity: _FICACLRE_FPU1
S_KK4_74002194	IMG Activity: _FICACLFC_V_TFK044A
S_KK4_74002195	IMG Activity: _FICACLFC_V_TFK030H
S_KK4_74002196	IMG Activity: _ISISFICA_VYAS21
S_KK4_74002197	IMG Activity: _ISISFICA_VVKK_BRCOL
S_KK4_74002198	IMG Activity: _ISISFICA_SE75
S_KK4_74002199	IMG Activity: _ISISFICA_IBR10
S_KK4_74002200	IMG Activity: _ISISFICA_IBR31

S_KK4_74002201	IMG Activity: _ISISFICA_IBR27
S_KK4_74002202	IMG Activity: _FICAINCM_V_TFK036S
S_KK4_74002203	IMG Activity: _FICAINGL_V_TFK020A
S_KK4_74002204	IMG Activity: _FICAINGL_FQZE
S_KK4_74002205	IMG Activity: _FICAINSD_FQC1210
S_KK4_74002206	IMG Activity: _FICAINSD_FQC1200
S_KK4_74002207	IMG Activity: _FICAINSD_TFK077DV
S_KK4_74002208	IMG Activity: _FICAEURO_FPO1(1)
S_KK4_74002209	IMG Activity: _FICAEURO_FPEW1
S_KK4_74002210	IMG Activity: _FICAEURO_FPEW2
S_KK4_74002211	IMG Activity: _FICAEURO_FPO2(1)
S_KK4_74002212	IMG Activity: _FICAEURO_FPMS
S_KK4_74002213	IMG Activity: _FICAEURO_FQC900
S_KK4_74002214	IMG Activity: _FICAEURO_FPO2(2)
S_KK4_74002215	IMG Activity: _FICAEURO_FPEW5
S_KK4_74002216	IMG Activity: _FICAEURO_FPEW8
S_KK4_74002217	IMG Activity: _FICAEURO_FPEW7
S_KK4_74002218	IMG Activity: _FICAEURO_FPEW6
S_KK4_74002219	IMG Activity: _FICAEURO_FPO1(2)
S_KK4_74002220	IMG Activity: _FICA_TFKFBC
S_KK4_74002221	IMG Activity: _FICA_FICAAOLA
S_KK4_74002222	IMG Activity: _FICA_FQMASS
S_KK4_74002223	IMG Activity: _FICA_TS_VC_TFK090
S_KK4_74002224	IMG Activity: _FICA_FQD2
S_KK4_74002225	IMG Activity: _FICA_TS_TFK000D2
S_KK4_74002226	IMG Activity: _FICAEURO_FPO1
S_KK4_74002227	IMG Activity: _FICAEURO_FPW1
S_KK4_74002228	IMG Activity: _FICAEURO_FPO2
S_KK4_74002229	IMG Activity: _FICAEURO_FPG1
S_KK4_74002230	IMG Activity: _FICAPE_FQP2
S_KK4_74002231	IMG Activity: _FICABTPY_VC_TFK042F
S_KK4_74002232	IMG Activity: _ISISFICA_VTIBRDEFAU
S_KK4_74002233	IMG Activity: _FICABTDI_FQZU
S_KK4_74002234	IMG Activity: _FICABTDI_TFK060A
S_KK4_74002235	IMG Activity: _FICABTDI_FQ06
S_KK4_74002236	IMG Activity: _FICABTDI_FQZQ
S_KK4_74002237	IMG Activity: _FICABTRE_FPAC04
S_KK4_74002238	IMG Activity: _FICABTRE_FPARR0
S_KK4_74002239	IMG Activity: _ISUFICABTDI_000065
S_KK4_74002240	IMG Activity: _ISUFICABTDI_000089
S_KK4_74002241	IMG Activity: _FICABTDI_FQ05
S_KK4_74002242	IMG Activity: _ISUFICABTDI_000092
S_KK4_74002243	IMG Activity: _ISUFICABTDI_000091
S_KK4_74002244	IMG Activity: _FICABTDI_FQZZ
S_KK4_74002245	IMG Activity: _FICABTRE_FQZS
S_KK4_74002246	IMG Activity: _FICABTRE_FQZF
S_KK4_74002247	IMG Activity: _FICABTRE_TFK012
S_KK4_74002248	IMG Activity: _FICABTRE_TFK045D
S_KK4_74002249	IMG Activity: _FICABTRE_VC_TFK045A
S_KK4_74002250	IMG Activity: _ISISFICA_VYAS22
S_KK4_74002251	IMG Activity: _FICABTRE_FPARR2
S_KK4_74002252	IMG Activity: _ISUFICABTRE_000074
S_KK4_74002253	IMG Activity: _FICABTRE_TFK046A
S_KK4_74002254	IMG Activity: _FICABTRE_V_TFK028G

S_KK4_74002255	IMG Activity: _FICABTRE_FP09FS
S_KK4_74002257	IMG Activity: _FICABT_V_TFK080E
S_KK4_74002258	IMG Activity: _FICABTDCSV_FQZ11
S_KK4_74002259	IMG Activity: _FICABTDCSV_FQZ08
S_KK4_74002260	IMG Activity: _FICABTDCSV_FQZ14
S_KK4_74002261	IMG Activity: _FICABTDCSV_FQZ13
S_KK4_74002262	IMG Activity: _FICABTDRP_FQZ09
S_KK4_74002263	IMG Activity: _ISISFICA_IBR15
S_KK4_74002264	IMG Activity: _ISISFICA_IBR24
S_KK4_74002265	IMG Activity: _ISISFICA_IBR23
S_KK4_74002266	IMG Activity: _ISISFICA_VCTIBRCLAR
S_KK4_74002267	IMG Activity: _ISISFICA_TIBRACTIVI
S_KK4_74002268	IMG Activity: _ISISFICA_V_TKKVHVTV
S_KK4_74002269	IMG Activity: _FICABTWO_TFK048C
S_KK4_74002270	IMG Activity: _FICABTWO_FQZ04
S_KK4_74002271	IMG Activity: _FICABTWO_FQZ03
S_KK4_74002272	IMG Activity: _FICABTWO_FQZ02
S_KK4_74002273	IMG Activity: _FICABTWO_V_TFK048A
S_KK4_74002274	IMG Activity: _FICABTCP_TFK_CRPO
S_KK4_74002275	IMG Activity: _FICABTRV_FQC1091
S_KK4_74002276	IMG Activity: _FICABFDP_FQZK
S_KK4_74002277	IMG Activity: _FICABTRV_FQZ01
S_KK4_74002278	IMG Activity: _FICABTIN_1054
S_KK4_74002279	IMG Activity: _FICABTIN_V_TFK050A
S_KK4_74002280	IMG Activity: _FICABTIN_TFK050B
S_KK4_74002281	IMG Activity: _ISISFICA_V_TVS030C
S_KK4_74002282	IMG Activity: _FICABFDP_TFK022C
S_KK4_74002283	IMG Activity: _ISUFICABFDP_000055
S_KK4_74002284	IMG Activity: _ISUFICABFDP_000066
S_KK4_74002285	IMG Activity: _ISTFICABFDP_000005
S_KK4_74002286	IMG Activity: _ISUFICABFDP_000053
S_KK4_74002287	IMG Activity: _FICABFCA_BULJ
S_KK4_74002288	IMG Activity: _FICABFDP_VTFK021KC
S_KK4_74002289	IMG Activity: _FICABFCA_BU0P
S_KK4_74002290	IMG Activity: _FICABFDP_TFK022D
S_KK4_74002291	IMG Activity: _FICABFDP_TFK022A
S_KK4_74002292	IMG Activity: _ISTFICABFDP_000004
S_KK4_74002293	IMG Activity: _FICABFDP_TFK000C
S_KK4_74002294	IMG Activity: _FICABFDP_FQH0
S_KK4_74002295	IMG Activity: _FICABFDP_FQC40
S_KK4_74002296	IMG Activity: _FICABFDP_FQZC
S_KK4_74002297	IMG Activity: _FICABFDP_FQZD
S_KK4_74002298	IMG Activity: _ISUFICABFDP_000052
S_KK4_74002299	IMG Activity: _ISISFICA_VY6I
S_KK4_74002300	IMG Activity: _ISISFICA_VY6H
S_KK4_74002303	IMG Activity: _FICABFDP_TFK021PC
S_KK4_74002304	IMG Activity: _FICABFDP_FPAC02
S_KK4_74002305	IMG Activity: _FICABFCA_V_TFK002F
S_KK4_74002306	IMG Activity: _FICABFDP_TFK003
S_KK4_74002307	IMG Activity: _FICABFDP_FQK8
S_KK4_74002308	IMG Activity: _FICABFDP_FQK6
S_KK4_74002309	IMG Activity: _FICABFOI_FQZ05
S_KK4_74002310	IMG Activity: _FICABFOI_FQZH
S_KK4_74002311	IMG Activity: _FICABTPY_TFK004B

S_KK4_74002312	IMG Activity: _FICABFOI_FQZ2
S_KK4_74002313	IMG Activity: _FICAPST_FQD1
S_KK4_74002314	IMG Activity: _FICABFDP_FQZ3
S_KK4_74002315	IMG Activity: _FICABFCA_BULL
S_KK4_74002316	IMG Activity: _FICABFDP_FQZM
S_KK4_74002317	IMG Activity: _FICABFCA_BULK
S_KK4_74002318	IMG Activity: _FICABFDP_FQZ5
S_KK4_74002319	IMG Activity: _FICABFDP_FQZ4
S_KK4_74002320	IMG Activity: _FICABFCA_SE75
S_KK4_74002321	IMG Activity: _FICABFDP_TG_TFK043U
S_KK4_74002322	IMG Activity: _FICABFDP_TG_TFK043V
S_KK4_74002323	IMG Activity: _FICABFDP_TFK001U
S_KK4_74002324	IMG Activity: _FICABFDP_V_TFK001C_
S_KK4_74002325	IMG Activity: _FICABFDP_FQZB
S_KK4_74002326	IMG Activity: _ISUFICABFDP_000009
S_KK4_74002327	IMG Activity: _ISUFICABFDP_000008
S_KK4_74002328	IMG Activity: _ISUFICABFDP_000007
S_KK4_74002329	IMG Activity: _ISUFICABFDP_000006
S_KK4_74002330	IMG Activity: _ISISFICA_V_TKKVFOAR
S_KK4_74002331	IMG Activity: _ISUFICABFDP_000012
S_KK4_74002332	IMG Activity: _ISUFICABFDP_000011
S_KK4_74002333	IMG Activity: _FICABFDP_TFK003A
S_KK4_74002334	IMG Activity: _ISUFICABFDP_000102
S_KK4_74002335	IMG Activity: _ISUFICABFDP_000010
S_KK4_74002336	IMG Activity: _FICABFDP_V_TFKTVO
S_KK4_74002337	IMG Activity: _ISUFICABFDP_000003
S_KK4_74002338	IMG Activity: _ISUFICABFDP_000001
S_KK4_74002339	IMG Activity: _ISUFICABFDP_000002
S_KK4_74002340	IMG Activity: _ISTFICABFDP_000008
S_KK4_74002341	IMG Activity: _ISUFICABFDP_000081
S_KK4_74002342	IMG Activity: _FICABFDP_V_TFKHVO
S_KK4_74002343	IMG Activity: _ISUFICABFDP_000004
S_KK4_74002344	IMG Activity: _ISUFICABFDP_000094
S_KK4_74002345	IMG Activity: _ISISFICA_TKKVBLART
S_KK4_74002346	IMG Activity: _ISUFICABFDP_000070
S_KK4_74002347	IMG Activity: _ISUFICABFDP_000013
S_KK4_74002348	IMG Activity: _FICABFDP_FQZG
S_KK4_74002349	IMG Activity: _FICABFDP_TFK000S
S_KK4_74002350	IMG Activity: _ISISFICA_TKKVPRGRP
S_KK4_74002351	IMG Activity: _ISISFICA_TKKVBUGRD
S_KK4_74002352	IMG Activity: _ISISFICA_TKKVRBART
S_KK4_74002353	IMG Activity: _FICABFDP_FQZA
S_KK4_74002354	IMG Activity: _FICABFDP_FQZ9
S_KK4_74002355	IMG Activity: _FICABFDP_FQZ8
S_KK4_74002356	IMG Activity: _FICABFDP_V_TFK000U
S_KK4_74002357	IMG Activity: _FICABFDP_FPN1
S_KK4_74002358	IMG Activity: _FICABFDP_SE75
S_KK4_74002359	IMG Activity: _ISUFICABFDP_000016
S_KK4_74002360	IMG Activity: _ISTFICABFDP_000001
S_KK4_74002361	IMG Activity: _ISUFICABFDP_000015
S_KK4_74002362	IMG Activity: _ISUFICABFDP_000014
S_KK4_74002363	IMG Activity: _ISUFICABFDP_000082
S_KK4_74002364	IMG Activity: _FICABFDP_TFK001P
S_KK4_74002365	IMG Activity: _FICABFDP_TFK001R

S_KK4_74002366	IMG Activity: _ISISFICA_VTKKVIVV
S_KK4_74002367	IMG Activity: _ISISFICA_VCTKKVEVOR
S_KK4_74002368	IMG Activity: _ISUFICABFDP_000099
S_KK4_74002369	IMG Activity: _FICABFTX_TFK007B
S_KK4_74002370	IMG Activity: _FICABFTX_TFK007M
S_KK4_74002371	IMG Activity: _FICABFTX_TFK007E
S_KK4_74002372	IMG Activity: _FICABFTX_TFK007U
S_KK4_74002373	IMG Activity: _FICABFTX_TFK048B
S_KK4_74002374	IMG Activity: _ISUUTPW_000008
S_KK4_74002375	IMG Activity: _FICAISAD_FQK3
S_KK4_74002376	IMG Activity: _FICAISAD_FQK2
S_KK4_74002377	IMG Activity: _FICAISAD_FQK1
S_KK4_74002378	IMG Activity: _FICAISAD_TFK021U
S_KK4_74002379	IMG Activity: _FICAISAD_V_TFK021SV
S_KK4_74002380	IMG Activity: _FICABFTX_V_TAXNUMTY
S_KK4_74002381	IMG Activity: _FICABFCA_FPN2
S_KK4_74002382	IMG Activity: _ISTFICABFAD_000007
S_KK4_74002383	IMG Activity: _ISUFICABFAD_000080
S_KK4_74002384	IMG Activity: _FICAISAD_FQK5
S_KK4_74002385	IMG Activity: _ISUUTPW_000005
S_KK4_74002386	IMG Activity: _FICABFCR_FPN4
S_KK4_74002387	IMG Activity: _ISTCA_T100
S_KK4_74002388	IMG Activity: _ISUFICABFCR_000093
S_KK4_74002389	IMG Activity: _FICABFAM_PFCG
S_KK4_74002390	IMG Activity: _FICA_TFK001B
S_KK4_74002391	IMG Activity: _FICAABFAC_TFK000
S_KK4_74002392	IMG Activity: _ISUFICABF_000057
S_KK4_74002393	IMG Activity: _ISUUTPW_000007
S_KK4_74002394	IMG Activity: _ISUUTPW_000006
S_KK4_74002395	IMG Activity: _ISUFICABF_000079
S_KK4_74002396	IMG Activity: _FICAISAD_FQZ1
S_KK4_74002397	IMG Activity: _ISISFICA_TKKVUVFRI
S_KK4_74002398	IMG Activity: _ISISFICA_TKKVUVORD
S_KK4_74002399	IMG Activity: _ISISFICA_TKKVUVSRT
S_KK4_74002400	IMG Activity: _ISISFICA_TKKVUVVAR
S_KK4_74002401	IMG Activity: _FICABFOI_FQZP
S_KK4_74002402	IMG Activity: _ISISFICA_TKKVKONTO
S_KK4_74002403	IMG Activity: _ISUFICABFOI_000095
S_KK4_74002404	IMG Activity: _ISISFICA_VY6J
S_KK4_74002405	IMG Activity: _FICABFCA_CACH
S_KK4_74002406	IMG Activity: _FICABFCA_CACT
S_KK4_74002407	IMG Activity: _ISISFICA_TKKVSLART
S_KK4_74002408	IMG Activity: _FICABFOI_TFK004A
S_KK4_74002409	IMG Activity: _FICABFOI_TFK043
S_KK4_74002410	IMG Activity: _ISISFICA_TKKVPNTYP
S_KK4_74002411	IMG Activity: _ISISFICA_TKKVBL2TP
S_KK4_74002412	IMG Activity: _ISISFICA_V_TFK002AV
S_KK4_74002413	IMG Activity: _ISUFICABFOI_000059
S_KK4_74002414	IMG Activity: _ISUFICABFOI_000060
S_KK4_74002415	IMG Activity: _ISUFICABFOI_000069
S_KK4_74002416	IMG Activity: _ISUFICABFOI_000103
S_KK4_74002417	IMG Activity: _FICABFOI_FQZO
S_KK4_74002418	IMG Activity: _ISUFICABFOI_000067
S_KK4_74002419	IMG Activity: _FICAISAD_V_TFK021L

S_KK4_74002420	IMG Activity: _FICABFCA_TFK002A
S_KK4_74002421	IMG Activity: _ISUFICABFOI_000072
S_KK4_74002422	IMG Activity: _FICAEURO_NACHBERCUS
S_KK4_74002423	IMG Activity: _FICAEURO_PERIOD_ASW
S_KK4_74002424	IMG Activity: _ISUFICAEURO_000001
S_KK4_74002425	IMG Activity: _FICAIS_DEVPAY
S_KK4_74002426	IMG Activity: _FICAEURO_BEWGEWINNE
S_KK4_74002427	IMG Activity: _FICA_V2_V3
S_KK4_74002428	IMG Activity: _FICAEURO_ARCHIV
S_KK4_74002429	IMG Activity: _FICABTPY_PRECOND
S_KK4_74002430	IMG Activity: _FICAEURO_HB
S_KK4_74002431	IMG Activity: _FICAEURO_UMSETZUNG
S_KK4_74002432	IMG Activity: _FICAEURO_FPE3
S_KK4_74002437	IMG Activity: IST_OM_OP_PRICING
S_KK4_74002438	IMG Activity: IST_OM_OP_ADDDATA
S_KK4_74002443	IMG Activity: IST_OM_OP_BUSEVENT
S_KK4_74002444	IMG Activity: IST_EMIGALL
S_KK4_74002447	IMG Activity: IST_CUST_MALF_EXIT
S_KK4_74002449	IMG Activity: IST_CUST_MAL_FAW
S_KK4_74002451	IMG Activity: IST_EQUIEXTGEN
S_KK4_74002452	IMG Activity: IST_MREXFIELDASSIGNM
S_KK4_74002454	IMG Activity: _ISTBDBP_000008
S_KK4_74002455	IMG Activity: SIMG_IST_KONTOKLASSE
S_KK4_74002456	IMG Activity: IST_CMODEQUI
S_KK4_74002467	Activation of Planned Change Docmnt
S_KK4_74002478	Belgium:BLIW-IBLC:Open Items Foreign
S_KK4_74002563	IMG Activity: _ISPSFICA_FMCADERIVE
S_KK4_74002581	IMG Activity: ISPSCA_IN_FIFMFIELDS
S_KK4_74002582	IMG Activity: ISPSCA_FMCADERIVE
S_KK4_74002613	IMG Activity: _FICABTPY_V_TFK126MA
S_KK4_74002614	IMG Activity: _FICABTPY_V_TFK125MA
S_KK4_74002615	IMG Activity: _FICABTPY_V_TFK122MA
S_KK4_74002616	IMG Activity: _FICABTPY_V_TFK123MA
S_KK4_74002617	IMG Activity: _FICACUSPOR_FISPLOGC
S_KK4_74002618	IMG Activity: _FICACUSPOR_V_TFIS01
S_KK4_74002619	IMG Activity: _FICABTIN_TFK050D
S_KK4_74002620	IMG Activity: _FICABTIN_FQZ22
S_KK4_74002621	IMG Activity: _FICABTPY_TFK020R
S_KK4_74002624	IMG Activity: _FICABTPY_TFK012DCV
S_KK4_74002625	IMG Activity: _FICABFTAXR_TFK020R1
S_KK4_74002629	IMG Activity: _FICABFOI_FQ0090
S_KK4_74002630	IMG Activity: _ISMCAIN_ISMCA05
S_KK4_74002631	IMG Activity: _ISMCAIN_ISMCA06
S_KK4_74002632	IMG Activity: _ISMCAIN_ISMCA07
S_KK4_74002633	IMG Activity: _FICABFDP_FQZ01
S_KK4_74002634	IMG Activity: _FICABTDCSV_FQZ2A
S_KK4_74002635	IMG Activity: _FICABFTX_FQ2101
S_KK4_74002636	IMG Activity: _FICABFTX_FQ2102
S_KK4_74002637	IMG Activity: _FICABTIC_FQI4Z
S_KK4_74002638	IMG Activity: _FICABFTX_FQZ04T
S_KK4_74002639	IMG Activity: _FICAIDOC_FKKEBSTOIS
S_KK4_74002640	IMG Activity: _FICAIDOC_FKKEBSTOIC
S_KK4_74002641	IMG Activity: _FICAIDOC_FQC1400
S_KK4_74002642	IMG Activity: _FICAIDOC_FQC1405

S_KK4_74002643	IMG Activity: _FICAIDOC_FKKEBSARSY
S_KK4_74002644	IMG Activity: _FICAIDOC_FKKEBSAROB
S_KK4_74002645	IMG Activity: _FICAIDOC_FQC1410
S_KK4_74002646	IMG Activity: _FICAIDOC_FKKEBSPOIS
S_KK4_74002647	IMG Activity: _FICA_TS_FKKEBSPOISY
S_KK4_82000014	List of Operands
S_KK4_82000015	List of Prices
S_KK4_82000016	Print Schema Steps
S_KK4_82000018	Customer Contacts
S_KK4_82000019	Analyze Insts, Devices, and Regs
S_KK4_82000020	MR Status of Devices: View
S_KK4_82000021	ALV List: Implausible MR Result
S_KK4_82000022	List of Installations
S_KK4_82000025	List of Billing Documents
S_KK4_82000027	REAGASDATE Program
S_KK4_82000079	IMG Activity: _ISPSFICA_OFMCA_PD05
S_KK4_82000080	IMG Activity: _ISPSFICA_V_TFKIVV
S_KK4_82000081	IMG Activity: _ISPSFICA_OFMCA_P000
S_KK4_82000082	IMG Activity: _ISPSFICA_OFMCA_P001
S_KK4_82000102	IS-H EDI: Evaluate Messsage Dispatch
S_KK4_82000118	IS-H*MED: Evaluation for Services,
S_KK4_82000213	SAPLS_CUS_IMG_ACTIVITY
S_KK4_82000319	IMG Activity: _ISPSFICA_PSOBNUM
S_KK4_82000320	IMG Activity: _ISPSFICA_V_TPSOB001
S_KK4_82000321	IMG Activity: _ISPSFICA_PSOB0100
S_KK4_82000322	IMG Activity: _ISPSFICA_B001FSTAT
S_KK4_82000323	IMG Activity: ISPSCA_PSOB0104
S_KK4_82000324	IMG Activity: _ISPSFICA_KCLL
S_KK4_82000326	IMG Activity: _ISPSFICA_KCLJ
S_KK4_82000327	IMG Activity: _ISPSFICA_KCLP
S_KK4_82000328	IMG Activity: _ISPSFICA_KC7R
S_KK4_82000333	IMG Activity: _ISPSFICA_V_TFMCA001
S_KK4_82000334	IMG Activity: _ISPSFICA_TFMCA002
S_KK4_82000335	IMG Activity: _ISPSFICA_V_TFMCA004
S_KK4_82000336	IMG Activity: _ISPSFICA_V_TFMCA003
S_KK4_82000337	IMG Activity: _ISPSFICA_V_TFK080R1
S_KK4_82000339	IS-M/AM: Order Update Worklist
S_KK4_82000403	IMG Activity: _ISPSFICA_TPSOB002
S_KK4_82000424	IMG Activity: _ISUBIBDRS_000069
S_KK4_82000435	IMG Activity: _ISPSFICA_OFMCA_P010
S_KK4_82000474	M/AM: Quantity Unit for Height
S_KK4_82000485	IS-M/SD Maint.View for Packing Chars
S_KK4_82000556	IMG Activity: _ISPSCA_V_TFK071_PS_
S_KK4_82000602	IMG Activity CM_XX_304
S_KK4_82000606	M/AM: Characteristic Assgmt (Online)
S_KK4_82000687	IMG Activity CM_XX_930
S_KK4_82000689	IMG Activity: ISPSCA_AUTH_CONTROBJ
S_KK4_82000690	IMG Activity: ISPSCA_V_TFMCA004004
S_KK4_82000705	IMG Activity: ISPSCA_V_TFK070P
S_KK4_82000744	IMG Activity: ISPSCA_V_TBD001
S_KK4_82000745	IMG Activity: ISPSCA_V_TBC001
S_KK4_82000754	IS-M/SD: Quantity Planning Versions
S_KK4_82000755	IS-M/SD Field Attribs - Maint. View
S_KK4_82000756	IS-M/SD Quantity Change - FMods

S_KK4_82000768	Create and Settle Settlement Doc.
S_KK4_82000769	Start Settlement Run
S_KK4_82000771	IMG Activity: ISMSD_SCS_REMERF
S_KK4_82000816	IMG Activity: ISPSCA_V_TFICA_DEF
S_KK4_82000860	IMG Activity (Docu, Attribute, Act.)
S_KK4_82000861	IMG Activity (Docu, Attribute, Act.)
S_KK4_82000863	IMG Activity: _ISPSCA_TFMCA006
S_KK4_82000864	IMG Activity: CM_XX_REGW02
S_KK4_82000865	IMG Activity: _ISPSCA_OFMCA_P020
S_KK4_82000866	IMG Activity: ISM_AM_COAEXT_BAPI
S_KK4_82000867	IMG Activity: ISM_AM_COA_BAPI
S_KK4_82000868	IMG Activity: ISM_AM_ORDER_BAPI
S_KK4_82000869	IMG Activity: ISM_AM_ORDEREXT_BAPI
S_KK4_82000870	IMG Activity: ISM_BP_BAPI
S_KK4_82000871	IMG Activity: ISM_BPEXT_BAPI
S_KK4_82000872	IMG Activity: ISU_CIC_ENV
S_KK4_82000873	IMG Activity: ISM_CIC_BP_SEARCH
S_KK4_82000874	IMG Activity: ISM_BP_TELNR_SPLITT
S_KK4_82000875	IMG Activity: _ISUCSFO_21
S_KK4_82000876	IMG Activity: ISPSCA_BFAD_000111
S_KK4_82000877	IMG Activity: ISM_PURCHASENR
S_KK4_82000878	IMG Activity: ISM_ORDER
S_KK4_82000879	IMG Activity: ISM_PRIORITY
S_KK4_82000880	IMG Activity: ISM_PARTNER
S_KK4_82000881	IMG Activity: ISM_SELLPRODUCTWWW
S_KK4_82000882	IMG Activity: ISM_UNSOLD
S_KK4_82000883	IMG Activity: ISM_UNSOLDQUANTITY
S_KK4_82000884	IMG Activity: ISM_INVOICE
S_KK4_82000885	IMG Activity: ISPSCA_FMCA_EHVD
S_KK4_82000886	IMG Activity: ISM_CONTRACT_NAVI
S_KK4_82000887	IMG Activity: ISM_CHECK_REQUEST
S_KK4_82000888	IMG Activity: ISM_MEDIA_MIX
S_KK4_82000889	IMG Activity: ISM_BADI_PROD_MASTER
S_KK4_82000890	IMG Activity: _ISUCSFO_0000
S_KK4_82000891	IMG Activity: ISMSD_MV_COLLNM
S_KK4_82000892	IMG Activity: _ISUBIBDRS_000070
S_KK4_82000893	IMG Activity: CM_XX_PROG01
S_KK4_82000894	IMG Activity: CM_XX_PROG02
S_KK4_82000895	IMG Activity: CM_XX_PROG03
S_KK4_82000896	IMG Activity: CM_XX_PIND01
S_KK4_82000897	IMG Activity: CM_XX_PIND02
S_KK4_82000898	IMG Activity: CM_XX_PIND03
S_KK4_82000899	IMG Activity: CM_XX_PIND04
S_KK4_82000900	IMG Activity: CM_XX_PIND05
S_KK4_82000901	IMG Activity: CM_XX_PIND06
S_KK4_82000902	IMG Activity: CM_XX_APPR_TYP
S_KK4_82000903	IMG Activity: CM_XX_APPR_ELEM
S_KK4_82000904	IMG Activity: CM_XX_APPR_TYP_ELEM
S_KK4_82000905	IMG Activity: CM_XX_APPR_TEMPL
S_KK4_82000906	IMG Activity: CM_XX_APPR_TEMPL_ASG
S_KK4_82000907	IMG Activity: CM_XX_APPR_BADI_SYM
S_KK4_82000908	IMG Activity: CM_XX_APPR_BADI_FUP
S_KK4_82000909	IMG Activity: CM_XX_APPR_BADI_ADM
S_KK4_82000910	IMG Activity: ISM_AM_BILLDOC_BAPI

S_KK4_82000911	IMG Activity: CM_XX_APPR_SW_TEMPL
S_KK4_82000912	IMG Activity: CM_XX_APPR_SW_ELEM
S_KK4_82000913	IMG Activity: CM_XX_STUD_USER
S_KK4_82000914	IMG Activity: CM_XX_STUD_REFUSER
S_KK4_82000915	IMG Activity: CM_AS_XX_602
S_KK4_82000916	IMG Activity: CM_AS_XX_603
S_KK4_82000917	IMG Activity: CM_AS_XX_605
S_KK4_82000918	IMG Activity: CM_XX_MOBU10
S_KK4_82000922	IMG Activity: CM_XX_GPST05
S_KK4_82000923	IMG Activity: CM_XX_GPST06
S_KK4_82000924	IMG Activity: CM_AS_XX_609
S_KK4_82000925	IMG Activity: ISMSD_SCS_REASONCODE
S_KK4_82000926	IMG Activity: CM_XX_STAT16
S_KK4_82000927	IMG Activity: CM_XX_FLEXDE02
S_KK4_82000928	IMG Activity: CM_XX_FLEXDE03
S_KK4_82000929	IMG Activity: CM_XX_FLEXDE04
S_KK4_82000930	IMG Activity: CM_XX_FLEXDE05
S_KK4_82000931	IMG Activity: CM_XX_APPR_STATUS
S_KK4_82000932	IMG Activity: _ISUFICA_IF000002
S_KK4_82000936	IMG Activity: _ISUFICA_FI000008
S_KK4_82000939	IMG Activity: SIMG_ISPSCA_FKKORDNR
S_KK4_82000940	IMG Activity: SIMG_FKKORDERRANG
S_KK4_82000941	IMG Activity: SIMG_ISPSCA_FQORD1
S_KK4_82000942	IMG Activity: ISPSCA_V_TBD002
S_KK4_82000943	IMG Activity: ISPSCA_V_TBC002
S_KK4_82000944	IMG Activity: ISPSCA_V_TBDC002
S_KK4_82000945	IMG Activity: ISPSCA_INTEGR_BP
S_KK4_82000946	IMG Activity: CM_XX_STUD16
S_KK4_82000947	IMG Activity: CM_AS_XX_611
S_KK4_82000948	IMG Activity: _ISMFICAJSDCA_001
S_KK4_82000949	IMG activity: BWISUISST_SALES_0010
S_KK4_82000950	IMG Activity: CM_XX_APPR_BADI_PERS
S_KK4_82000951	IMG Activity: _ISPSCA_OFMCA_P200
S_KK4_82000952	IMG Activity: _ISPSCA_OFMCA_P201
S_KK4_82000953	IMG Activity: _ISPSCA_OFMCA_P203
S_KK4_82000955	IMG Activity: ISM_AM_REVOBJ
S_KK4_82000956	IMG Activity: ISM_PLM_JPC1
S_KK4_82000957	IMG Activity: ISM_PLM_JPC4
S_KK4_82000958	IMG Activity: _ISMCAIN_ISMCA08
S_KK4_82000959	IMG Activity: ISM_AM_VOUCHER
S_KK4_82000960	IMG Activity: ISMSD_TRANSFER_RESTE
S_KK4_82000961	IMG Activity: CM_XX_1232
S_KK4_82000968	IMG Activity: ISMAM_FAKT_INDEX
S_KK4_82000969	IMG Activity: CM_XX_SELM04
S_KK4_82000970	IMG Activity: CM_XX_STUD02
S_KK4_82000971	IMG Activity: ISPSCA_FPN4
S_KK4_82000972	IMG Activity: ISM_MP_VERTR_STATUS
S_KK4_82000973	IMG Activity: ISM_ANNAHMESCHLUSS
S_KK4_82000974	IMG Activity: ISM_COA_REQ_DYN
S_KK4_82000976	IMG Activity: ISPSCA_V_TFMCA_COV_
S_KK4_82000977	IMG Activity: ISPSCA_VC_FMCA_COV_1
S_KK4_82000978	IMG Activity: ISPAM_COND_MFGR
S_KK4_82001005	IMG Activity: CM_XX_AUDIT02
S_KK4_82001078	IMG Activity: ISM_TLM_BDC_UNDO

S_KK4_82001179	IMG Activity: ISM_AM_INHK_KLEV1
S_KK4_82001190	IMG Activity: CM_XX_REGI09
S_KK4_82001193	IMG Activity: _ISUUTDE_000064
S_KK4_82001194	IMG Activity: _ISUUTDE_000065
S_KK4_82001327	IMG Activity: ISM_ADDR_SYNC
S_KK4_82001328	IMG Activity: CM_US_VETERANS_01
S_KK4_82001337	IMG Activity: CM_XX_AUDIT35
S_KK4_82001358	IMG Activity: ISMAM_TJHGR_REL_STAT
S_KK4_82001372	IMG Activity: ISMSD_VKRENADDPAYM
S_KK4_82001514	IMG Activity: _ISUUTDE_000079
S_KK4_82001521	IMG Activity: _ISUUTDE_000010
S_KK4_82001527	IMG Activity: JHVMSTZ_EOB
S_KK4_82001528	IMG Activity: CM_XX_AKST16
S_KK4_95000001	IMG Activity: _FICAXBFDP_FSCQS001
S_KK4_95000002	IMG Activity: _FICAXBFDP_FSCQS000
S_KK4_95000003	IMG Activity: _FICAXBFCR_FSCQS100
S_KK4_95000005	IMG Activity: _FICAXBFCA_TFSCKTOKL
S_KK4_95000006	IMG Activity: _FICAXBFCA_TFSC01
S_KK4_95000007	IMG Activity: _FICAXVORG_VTFSCHVTV
S_KK4_95000008	IMG Activity: _FICAXVORG_V_TFKIVV
S_KK4_96000001	IS-H: List Organizational Units
S_KK4_96000002	IS-H: Overview of Org. Hierarchy
S_KK4_96000003	IS-H: List Building Units
S_KK4_96000004	IS-H: Transport Org. Units
S_KK4_96000005	IS-H: Transport Building Units
S_KK4_96000006	IS-H: "Diagosis Required" for InsPrv
S_KK4_96000007	IS-H: "Diagosis Required" for InsPrv
S_KK4_96000008	IS-H: Set Head Office for Ins. Prov
S_KK4_96000009	IS-H: Edit IPs w/o FI Customer
S_KK4_96000010	IS-H: Edit IS-H Customers w/o RF/FI
S_KK4_96000012	IS-H: Set "Single/Cllct Invoice" for
S_KK4_96000013	IS-H: Set "Single/Cllct. Invoice" fo
S_KK4_96000014	IS-H: Adjust Controlling Indicator
S_KK4_96000015	IS-H: Transport Svce Master Data
S_KK4_96000016	IS-H: Import ICD-9 ZI Catalog
S_KK4_96000017	IS-H: Import ICD-10 ZI Catalog
S_KK4_96000018	IS-H: Copy Diagnosis Coding Catalog
S_KK4_96000019	IS-H: Merge Patients
S_KK4_96000020	IS-H: Patient Status Extract
S_KK4_96000021	IS-H: Defaults for Physician in P
S_KK4_96000022	IS-H: List Merge Patients
S_KK4_96000023	IS-H: Find Similar Patients
S_KK4_96000024	IS-H: Admission List
S_KK4_96000025	IS-H: Transfers to
S_KK4_96000026	IS-H: Admissions and Transfers to
S_KK4_96000027	IS-H: Companions
S_KK4_96000028	IS-H: From External Hospital
S_KK4_96000029	IS-H: Newborns
S_KK4_96000030	IS-H: Discharges
S_KK4_96000031	IS-H: Transfers from
S_KK4_96000032	IS-H: Discharges and Transfers to
S_KK4_96000033	IS-H: Deceased Patients
S_KK4_96000034	IS-H: Discharged to External Hospita
S_KK4_96000035	IS-H: Transfers

S_KK4_96000036	IS-H: Absence Times
S_KK4_96000037	IS-H: Quick Admissions
S_KK4_96000038	IS-H: Emergency Admissions
S_KK4_96000039	IS-H: Inpatient Waiting List
S_KK4_96000040	IS-H: Inpatient Emergency Cases
S_KK4_96000041	IS-H: Case Monitor
S_KK4_96000042	IS-H: List Inpatient Birthdays
S_KK4_96000043	IS-H: Evaluation of Outpat. Visits
S_KK4_96000044	IS-H: Outpatient Visits
S_KK4_96000045	IS-H: Quick Admissions
S_KK4_96000046	IS-H: Emergency Admissions
S_KK4_96000047	IS-H: Outpatient Waiting List
S_KK4_96000048	IS-H: Inpatient Emergency Cases
S_KK4_96000049	IS-H: Evaluate Treatment Certificate
S_KK4_96000050	IS-H: Case Monitor
S_KK4_96000051	IS-H: Outpatient Visits (with Phys.)
S_KK4_96000052	IS-H: Missing Outpat. Treatm.Certif.
S_KK4_96000053	IS-H: Treatment End for Outpat. Case
S_KK4_96000054	IS-H: Movement Lists
S_KK4_96000055	IS-H: Evaluation Report for Assigned
S_KK4_96000056	IS-H: Evaluation Report for Case
S_KK4_96000057	IS-H: Religious List
S_KK4_96000058	IS-H: Public List Dialog
S_KK4_96000059	IS-H: Public List
S_KK4_96000060	IS-H: Case Monitor
S_KK4_96000061	IS-H: List of Newborn Deliveries
S_KK4_96000062	IS-H: List Inpatient Birthdays
S_KK4_96000063	IS-H: List Referring/Post-Dschg.Phys
S_KK4_96000064	IS-H: Enhanced Waiting List
S_KK4_96000065	IS-H: Patient Traffic List
S_KK4_96000066	RNUAPP01
S_KK4_96000067	IS-H: Reorganize Provisional Appts
S_KK4_96000068	IS-H: Outpat.Clinic Mgmt: Appt List
S_KK4_96000069	IS-H: List Planning Objects
S_KK4_96000070	IS-H: Eval. Report for Diagnoses
S_KK4_96000071	IS-H: Evaluation Report for Diagnos
S_KK4_96000072	IS-H: Evaluations acc to FRH
S_KK4_96000073	IS-H: Case List By Ins. Provider
S_KK4_96000074	IS-H: Service List
S_KK4_96000075	IS-H: Case/Svce Evaluaton for DayPat
S_KK4_96000076	IS-H: Case/Service Evaluation for
S_KK4_96000077	IS-H: Adjust Services for Absence
S_KK4_96000086	IS-H: Service and Billing Statistics
S_KK4_96000088	IS-H: Extended Service with AltScvce
S_KK4_96000089	IS-H: Determine Data for Quality
S_KK4_96000090	IS-H: Discharges to Ext. Hospital
S_KK4_96000091	IS-H: Print IV Requests
S_KK4_96000092	IS-H: Print IV Requests
S_KK4_96000093	IS-H: Create IV Request Reminder
S_KK4_96000094	IS-H: Extend IV Request
S_KK4_96000095	IS-H: IV Status Tracking
S_KK4_96000096	IS-H: Monitor Insurance Verification
S_KK4_96000097	IS-H: Generate IV Request
S_KK4_96000098	IS-H: Generate IV Request

S_KK4_96000099	IS-H: Generate Copayment Request
S_KK4_96000100	IS-H: Post Back Dunned Copayment
S_KK4_96000101	IS-H: Dunned Copayment Request
S_KK4_96000102	IS-H: Repost Copayment to Ins.Prov.
S_KK4_96000103	IS-H: Display Copayment Request
S_KK4_96000104	IS-H: Down Payments Final Blld Cases
S_KK4_96000106	IS-H: Evaluation Mat./Admin.Costs
S_KK4_96000107	IS-H: Evaluation Cost Reimbursement
S_KK4_96000108	IS-H: Evaluation Report Dept OU/Svce
S_KK4_96000109	IS-H: Check Charges
S_KK4_96000110	IS-H: Propose Charges
S_KK4_96000111	IS-H: Case Monitor
S_KK4_96000112	IS-H: Patient Billing
S_KK4_96000113	IS-H: Bill. Doc. Mass Print Program
S_KK4_96000114	IS-H: Billing - Process Messages
S_KK4_96000115	IS-H: Billing - Case Selection
S_KK4_96000116	IS-H: Case Selection via Patient Nam
S_KK4_96000117	IS-H: Billing: Case Selection
S_KK4_96000118	IS-H: Billing: Case Selection
S_KK4_96000119	IS-H: Billing - Case Selection
S_KK4_96000120	IS-K: Billing - Copy Case Selection
S_KK4_96000121	IS-H: Cancel Bill. Document for
S_KK4_96000122	IS-H: Cancel Bill. Document for
S_KK4_96000123	IS-H: Cancel Invoice Items per
S_KK4_96000124	IS-H: Invoice Overview
S_KK4_96000125	IS-H: Invoice Stats for Blld Svces
S_KK4_96000126	IS-H: Invoice Statistics Billed
S_KK4_96000127	IS-H: Billing Indicator for a Case
S_KK4_96000128	IS-H: Billing Status Inpatient
S_KK4_96000129	IS-H: Case-Related Invoice Overview
S_KK4_96000130	IS-H: Cases w/o Billable Services
S_KK4_96000131	IS-H: Billing Block via Conditions
S_KK4_96000132	IS-H: Billing Block via Conditions
S_KK4_96000133	IS-H: Determine Cost Portions when
S_KK4_96000134	IS-H: Outpatient Cases w/o Services
S_KK4_96000135	IS-H: Revenue Accounts and Conditio
S_KK4_96000136	IS-H: Cancel Provisional Invoice
S_KK4_96000137	IS-H: Adjust Services with End Date
S_KK4_96000138	IS-H: Set Main Code Automatically
S_KK4_96000139	IS-H: Set 'Relevant for
S_KK4_96000140	IS-H: Delete NLKZ for Canceled NK
S_KK4_96000141	IS-H: Retroactive Price Change
S_KK4_96000142	IS-H: Copy Utility for NLAZ Maint.
S_KK4_96000143	IS-HCO: Transfer Services to
S_KK4_96000144	IS-H: Delete Cncld Non-Trnsfd Svces
S_KK4_96000145	IS-HCO Calculate & Transfer Inpat.
S_KK4_96000146	IS-HCO Calculate & Transfer Inpat.
S_KK4_96000147	IS-HCO Calculate & Transfer Inpat.
S_KK4_96000148	IS-HCO: Overview Svce to Be Transfrd
S_KK4_96000149	IS-H: Evaluate Transfer Information
S_KK4_96000152	IS-HCO: Create Orders
S_KK4_96000153	IS-HCO: Track Order Status
S_KK4_96000154	IS-HCO: Prel. Costing for Case Order
S_KK4_96000155	IS-HCO: Classify Case-Based Orders

S_KK4_96000156	IS-HCO: Transfer Services to
S_KK4_96000157	IS-H: Delete Cncld Non-Trnsfd Svces
S_KK4_96000158	IS-H: Evaluate Transfer Information
S_KK4_96000159	IS-HCO: Overview Svce to Be Transfrd
S_KK4_96000161	IS-H: BPflV 1995 L 1- Occupancy Data
S_KK4_96000162	IS-H: BPflV 1995 L 3 - Occup. Data
S_KK4_96000163	IS-H: BPflV 1995 L4 - Diagnosis Stat
S_KK4_96000164	IS-H: BPflV 1995 L 5- Surg. Stats
S_KK4_96000167	IS-H: KHStatV SA 91 -
S_KK4_96000168	IS-H: KHStatV SA 10
S_KK4_96000169	IS-H: KHStatV SA 11
S_KK4_96000170	IS-H: KHStatV SA 12
S_KK4_96000171	IS-H: KHStatV SA 13 - Stat. Beds
S_KK4_96000172	IS-H: KHStatV SA 20 - Sick Beds;
S_KK4_96000173	IS-H: KHStatV SA 40 - Dschgd DayPats
S_KK4_96000174	IS-H: KHStatV SA 50 - Deliveries
S_KK4_96000175	IS-H ES: CMBD and CMA Statistics
S_KK4_96000176	IS-H: Midnight Census Statistics
S_KK4_96000177	IS-H: Midnight Census Stats- Row Vrs
S_KK4_96000178	IS-H: Midnight Census Stats - Indiv.
S_KK4_96000179	IS-H: Geographical Area Statistics
S_KK4_96000180	IS-H: Service Statistics
S_KK4_96000189	IS-H: Service and Billing Statistics
S_KK4_96000190	IS-H: Org. Unit Occupancy Data
S_KK4_96000191	IS-H: Org. Unit Occupancy Data
S_KK4_96000192	IS-H: Evaluate ICPM/ICD Combination
S_KK4_96000193	IS-H: List Material Requested
S_KK4_96000194	IS-HCM: Format Messages
S_KK4_96000195	IS-HCM: Generate all S* Messages
S_KK4_96000196	IS-HCM: Generate all CUSTOMER Msgs
S_KK4_96000197	IS-HCM: Get Case-Related Services
S_KK4_96000198	IS-HCM: Get Diagnoses from Part.Syst
S_KK4_96000199	IS-HCM: Get Surgical Data from Part
S_KK4_96000200	IS-HCM: Get Med. Service Data from
S_KK4_96000201	IS-HCM: Selective Message Dispatch
S_KK4_96000202	IS-HCM: Display Report for Status
S_KK4_96000203	IS-HCM: System Monitoring
S_KK4_96000204	IS-HCM: Delete all old Status Msgs
S_KK4_96000205	IS-HCM: Part.Syst. Installation Chk
S_KK4_96000206	IS-HCM List Parameter System Setting
S_KK4_96000207	IS-HCM Message Standards
S_KK4_96000208	IS-HCM Message Types (Composition)
S_KK4_96000209	IS-HCM Message Segments (Compostion)
S_KK4_96000210	IS-HCM: Message Fields
S_KK4_96000211	IS-HCM Display Msgs Ready to Send
S_KK4_96000212	IS-HCM: Create a Message Type Copy
S_KK4_96000213	IS-HCM Create a Segment Copy
S_KK4_96000214	IS-HCM: Display Dispatch Logs
S_KK4_96000215	IS-HCM: Delete Dispatch Logs
S_KK4_96000216	IS-HCM Test Program: Simulate CM-r
S_KK4_96000217	IS-HCM Select Customer Msg Parts
S_KK4_96000218	IS-HCM: Simulate and Send Adm.Rcrd
S_KK4_96000219	IS-HCM Display Inbound Messages
S_KK4_96000220	IS-HCM: Delete Receipt Logs

S_KK4_96000221	IS-HCM Errored Inbound Messages
S_KK4_96000222	IS-HCM Errored Inbound Messages
S_KK4_96000223	IS-HCM Evaluations for Hosp.Communic
S_KK4_96000224	IS-HCM Messages from Log File
S_KK4_96000225	IS-HCM: Create HCM Partner System
S_KK4_96000226	IS-HCM: Delete Partner System
S_KK4_96000227	IS-HCM NC02 SAP-HCM Mssge Fieldwise
S_KK4_96000228	IS-HCM: All HCM Trace Entries in
S_KK4_96000229	IS-HCM: All Entries in Table
S_KK4_96000230	IS-HCM: All Entries in Table
S_KK4_96000231	IS-H EDI Overview of Partner Systems
S_KK4_96000232	IS-H EDI: Message Structure Tree
S_KK4_96000233	IS-HCM: Get OU-Related Services
S_KK4_96000234	IS-HCM: Communic. Acknow. Handling
S_KK4_96000235	IS-HCM: Check File Usability
S_KK4_96000236	IS-HCM: Copy IS-H Report Control
S_KK4_96000237	IS-H EDI: Order Processing
S_KK4_96000238	IS-H EDI: Create Message File
S_KK4_96000239	IS-H EDI Create File, Single Process
S_KK4_96000240	IS-H SG: EDI Trans.Pgrm for Express
S_KK4_96000241	IS-H EDI Import Program (File on
S_KK4_96000242	IS-H EDI Message Receipt. Automatic
S_KK4_96000243	IS-H EDI Message Receipt, Manual
S_KK4_96000244	IS-H EDI: Message Structure Tree
S_KK4_96000245	IS-H: EDI Assign Data Cllct Point to
S_KK4_96000246	IS-H EDI: Evaluate Messsage Dispatch
S_KK4_96000247	IS-H EDI: File Overview
S_KK4_96000248	IS-H EDI Display Msg Field by Field
S_KK4_96000249	IS-H EDI Seq. Number of DCP
S_KK4_96000250	IS-H EDI File/Message Processing
S_KK4_96000251	IS-H EDI Transfer System Files
S_KK4_96000252	IS-H EDI: List all Cases w/o EDI Msg
S_KK4_96000253	IS-H EDI Edit Individual Messages
S_KK4_96000254	IS-H EDI Delete Tab. NC30 Manually
S_KK4_96000255	IS-H EDI Assign New Data Cllct.Point
S_KK4_96000256	IS-H EDI: Case Analysis
S_KK4_96000257	IS-H D: EDI Compare Data Cllct Point
S_KK4_96000258	IS-H EDI Basics of Procedure Custom
S_KK4_96000259	IS-H: List all Setting for Work Org
S_KK4_96000260	IS-H: Delete of Change Entries
S_KK4_96000261	IS-H: Cllctv. Print of Admiss/Dschg
S_KK4_96000262	IS-H: Program for Deleting Form Logs
S_KK4_96000263	IS-H: Utility for Converting
S_KK4_96000268	IS-H: Trans. Data to Create Customer
S_KK4_96000269	IS-H: Trans. Data Quick Svce Entry
S_KK4_96000270	IS-H: Maintain Svce by Svce Pair
S_KK4_96000272	IS-H: Trans. Data to Create ISHCust
S_KK4_96000273	IS-H: Trans. Data to Create Bus.Part
S_KK4_96000274	IS-H: Trans. Data to Create Ins.Prov
S_KK4_96000275	IS-H: Trans. Data to Create Hospital
S_KK4_96000276	IS-H: Trans. Data to Create Services
S_KK4_96000277	IS-H: Trans. Data Pat. Insurance
S_KK4_96000278	IS-H: Trans.Data to Create Employee
S_KK4_96000279	IS-H: Delete Canceled Movements

S_KK4_96000280	IS-H: Delete Building Units
S_KK4_96000281	IS-H: Delete Canceled Services
S_KK4_96000286	IS-H*MED: Time Stamp Statistics
S_KK4_96000304	Document Archiving
S_KK4_96000309	IS-H: Severity of Illness for DRG
S_KK4_96000310	IS-H: Risk of Mortality for DRG
S_KK4_96000320	RAD Default Table
S_KK4_96000321	RAD: CT Default Table
S_KK4_96000322	RAD X-Ray Default Table
S_KK4_96000323	RAD MRT Preassignment Table
S_KK4_96000324	RAD Nuclear Med. Preassignment Table
S_KK4_96000325	RAD Sonography Preassignment Table
S_KK4_96000326	User ID - Employee Assignment
S_KK4_96000327	RAD ID Rel. DICOM-AETitle Source
S_KK4_96000328	IS-H*MED: Maintain System Parameters
S_KK4_96000333	IS-H: Pick List
S_KK4_96000334	IS-H IMG
S_KK4_96000337	IS-H: Public List
S_KK4_96000347	EDI Temporary Storage
S_KK4_96000365	IMG Activity: SIMG_ISH_BADI_DCOD
S_KK4_96000369	IS-H IMG
S_KK4_96000372	S_KK4_96000372
S_KK4_96000379	IS-H: Cost Reimb. - Direct Pat.Bill.
S_KK4_96000380	IMG Transaction
S_KK4_96000383	Change IMG Service
S_KK4_96000385	IMG Study Document
S_KK4_96000386	IMG RAD Findings Document
S_KK4_96000387	IMG
S_KK4_96000388	IMG
S_KK4_96000389	IMG
S_KK4_96000390	IMG RAD WL Filter etc.
S_KK4_96000391	IMG RAD Request
S_KK4_96000392	IMG RAD Examination
S_KK4_96000393	IMG AE Title
S_KK4_96000394	IMG
S_KK4_96000395	IMG
S_KK4_96000396	IMG
S_KK4_96000397	IMG
S_KK4_96000398	IMG
S_KK4_96000399	IMG
S_KK4_96000400	IMG MSI
S_KK4_96000401	IMG ADT
S_KK4_96000402	IMG RAD Report
S_KK4_96000404	IMG
S_KK4_96000405	IMG
S_KK4_96000406	IMG RIS-PACS Attribute Assignments
S_KK4_96000410	IS-H: Update Co-/Down Payments From
S_KK4_96000411	IMG RAD Attribute Conversion
S_KK4_96000415	IS-H: Key Figures for Diagnoses and
S_KK4_96000429	IMG LTE
S_KK4_96000442	P301
S_KK4_96000464	IS-H: Cancel Service Transfer
S_KK4_96000465	IMG Activity: ISH_ENHANCEMT_OVERVW
S_KK4_96000466	IMG Activity: BADI: ISH_FILL_RNF01

S_KK4_96000467	IMG Activity: BADI: ISH_FILL_RNF02
S_KK4_96000468	IMG Activity: BADI: ISH_FILL_RNF03
S_KK4_96000469	IMG Activity: BADI: ISH_FILL_RNF04
S_KK4_96000470	IMG Activity: BADI: ISH_FILL_RNF05
S_KK4_96000471	IMG Activity: BADI: ISH_FILL_RNF06
S_KK4_96000472	IMG Activity: BADI: ISH_FILL_RNF07
S_KK4_96000473	IMG Activity: BADI: ISH_FILL_RNF08
S_KK4_96000474	IMG Activity: BADI: ISH_FILL_RNF09
S_KK4_96000475	IMG Activity: BADI: ISH_FILL_RNF10
S_KK4_96000476	IMG Activity: BADI: ISH_FILL_RNF11
S_KK4_96000477	IMG Activity: BADI: ISH_FILL_RNF12
S_KK4_96000478	IMG Activity: BADI: ISH_FILL_RNF13
S_KK4_96000479	IMG Activity: BADI: ISH_FILL_RNF14
S_KK4_96000480	IMG Activity: BADI: ISH_FILL_RNF15
S_KK4_96000481	IMG Activity: BADI: ISH_FILL_RNF16
S_KK4_96000482	IMG Activity: BADI: ISH_FILL_RNF17
S_KK4_96000483	IMG Activity: BADI: ISH_FILL_RNF18
S_KK4_96000484	IMG Activity: BADI: ISH_FILL_RNF30
S_KK4_96000485	IMG Activity: BADI: ISH_FILL_RNF34
S_KK4_96000486	IMG Activity: BADI: ISH_FILL_RNF35
S_KK4_96000487	IMG Activity: BADI: ISH_FILL_RNF36
S_KK4_96000488	IMG Activity: BADI: ISH_FILL_RNF37
S_KK4_96000489	IMG Activity: BADI: ISH_FILL_RNF38
S_KK4_96000490	IMG Activity: BADI: ISH_FILL_RNF40
S_KK4_96000491	IMG Activity: BADI: ISH_FILL_RNF41
S_KK4_96000492	IMG Activity: BADI: ISH_FILL_RNF44
S_KK4_96000493	IMG Activity: BADI: ISH_FILL_RNF47
S_KK4_96000494	IMG Activity: BADI: ISH_FILL_RNF48
S_KK4_96000495	IMG Activity: BADI: ISH_FILL_RNF49
S_KK4_96000496	IMG Activity: BADI: ISH_FILL_RNF54
S_KK4_96000497	IMG Activity: BADI: ISH_FILL_RNF55
S_KK4_96000498	IMG Activity: BADI: ISH_FILL_RNF56
S_KK4_96000499	IMG Activity: BADI: ISH_FILL_RNF57
S_KK4_96000500	IMG Activity: BADI: ISH_FILL_RNF58
S_KK4_96000501	IMG Activity: BADI: ISH_FILL_RNF59
S_KK4_96000502	IMG Activity: BADI: ISH_FILL_RNF60
S_KK4_96000503	IMG Activity: BADI: ISH_FILL_RNF61
S_KK4_96000504	IMG Activity: BADI: ISH_FILL_RNF67
S_KK4_96000505	IMG Activity: BADI: ISH_FILL_RNF68
S_KK4_96000506	IMG Activity: BADI: ISH_FILL_RNFKS
S_KK4_96000507	IMG Activity: BADI: ISH_FILL_RNFP2
S_KK4_96000508	IMG Activity: BADI: ISH_PRINT_INVO
S_KK4_96000509	IMG Activity: BADI: ISH_PRINT_OPEN
S_KK4_96000510	IMG-Activity: BADI: ISH_DIAGNOSIS_
S_KK4_96000511	IMG Activity: BADI: ISH_GET_DIAGNO
S_KK4_96000512	IMG Activity: BADI: ISH_INIT_MD_ST
S_KK4_96000513	IMG Activity: BADI: ISH_NONSP_DIAG
S_KK4_96000514	IMG Activity: BADI: ISH_NONSP_PROC
S_KK4_96000515	IMG Activity: BADI: ISH_PROCEDURE_
S_KK4_96000516	IMG Activity: BADI: ISH_SPECIALCOD
S_KK4_96000517	IMG Activity: BADI: ISH_DOP_DEDUCT
S_KK4_96000518	IMG Activity: BADI: ISH_RNZUZBI1_S
S_KK4_96000519	IMG Activity: BADI ISH_REV_ASSIGNM
S_KK4_96000520	IMG Activity: BADI ISH_SERVICEFORM

S_KK4_96000521	IMG Activity: BADI ISH_PRICING_FIE
S_KK4_96000522	IMG Activity: BADI ISH_INV_CANCEL1
S_KK4_96000523	IMG Activity: BADI ISH_COPAY_REPAY
S_KK4_96000524	IMG Activity: BADI ISH_COPAY_TRANS
S_KK4_96000525	IMG Activity: BADI ISH_PICKLIST_01
S_KK4_96000526	IMG Activity: BADI ISH_PICKLIST_02
S_KK4_96000527	IMG Activity: BADI ISH_DE_DRG_SC_F
S_KK4_96000532	IMG-Activity: SIMG_ISHMED_VD_01
S_KK4_96000537	IMG Activity: BADI ISH_CONTRACT_MA
S_KK4_96000538	IMG Activity: BADI ISH_APPT_EXT
S_KK4_96000539	IMG Activity: BADI N_WP_MEDCONTROL
S_KK4_96000540	IMG Activity: BADI N1_WP_LSTAMB
S_KK4_96000541	IMG Activity: ISH_EXTPATID
S_KK4_96000542	IMG-Activity: SIMG_ISHMED_WORD01
S_KK4_96000543	IMG-Activity: SIMG_ISHMED_WORD02
S_KK4_96000545	IMG Activity: SIMG_ISHMED_TR_SUPP
S_KK4_96000546	IMG Activity: SIMG_ISHMED_ANFTYP
S_KK4_96000547	IMG Activity: ISHMED_PROC_ENCODING
S_KK4_96000548	IMG Activity: ISH_TN21L
S_KK4_96000549	IMG Activity: SIMG_ISHMED_RAD_BA07
S_KK4_96000550	IMG Activity: SIMG_ISHMED_RAD_BA08
S_KK4_96000551	IMG Activity: SIMG_ISHMED_RAD_BA09
S_KK4_96000552	IMG Activity: ISH_WL_ABSENCE
S_KK4_96000557	IMG Activity: SIMG_OCC_CHARACT
S_KK4_96000558	IMG Activity: ISHMED_CDOKU_CALL
S_KK4_96000559	IMG Activity: ISHMED_PROC_DIA_ENCD
S_KK4_96000560	IMG Activity: ISH_TNSTA0
S_KK4_96000561	IMG Activity: ISH_BS02
S_KK4_96000562	IMG Activity: ISH_BS52
S_KK4_96000563	IMG Activity: ISH_PAYMENT_TYPES
S_KK4_96000564	IMG Activity: ISHMED_PRO_VERSION
S_KK4_96000565	IMG Activity: ISHMED_DIA_VERSION
S_KK4_96000566	IMG Activity: ISH_CASH_DESK
S_KK4_96000567	IMG Activity: SIMG_ISHMED_NCXTY
S_KK4_96000568	IMG Activity: SIMG_ISHMED_NOCTY
S_KK4_96000570	IMG Activity: ISH_SERVICE_DPD
S_KK4_96000571	IMG Activity: ISH_SERVICE_MOVEMENT
S_KK4_96000572	IMG Activity: ISH_SERVICE_ENTRY
S_KK4_96000574	IMG Activity: SIMG_ISHMED_NCXTY_PR
S_KK4_96000575	IMG Activity: SIMG_ISHMED_NOCTY_PR
S_KK4_96000581	IMG Activity: SIMG_ISHMED_VD_00
S_KK4_96000582	IMG Activity: SIMG_ISH_PRGNR
S_KK4_96000583	IMG Activity: ISHMED_WAITLIST_TYPE
S_KK4_96000584	IMG Activity: ISHMED_WAITLIST_RSN
S_KK4_96000585	IMG Activity: ISHMED_PRG_KONTEXT
S_KK4_96000586	IMG Activity: ISH_WP_VIEW_TITLE
S_KK4_96000590	IMG Activity: ISH_MM_MEDCAT
S_KK4_96000591	IMG Activity: ISH_MM_AGENT
S_KK4_96000592	IMG Activity: ISH_OMT3B
S_KK4_96000593	IMG Activity: ISH_OMT3Z
S_KK4_96000594	IMG Activity: ISH_OMT3R
S_KK4_96000595	IMG Activity: ISH_OMT3E
S_KK4_96000596	IMG Activity: ISH_OMT3U
S_KK4_96000597	IMG Activity: ISH_OMSH

S_KK4_96000598	IMG Activity: ISH_MM_OMT2
S_KK4_96000599	IMG Activity: ISH_MM_OMSH
S_KK4_96000600	IMG Activity: ISH_MM_SXDA
S_KK4_96000601	IMG Activity: ISH_MM_OMSM
S_KK4_96000602	IMG Activity: SIMG_ISHMED_NRKR_VP
S_KK4_96000603	IMG Activity: SIMG_ISHMED_VS_STGR
S_KK4_96000604	IMG Activity: SIMG_ISHMED_N2DGAIST
S_KK4_96000605	IMG Activity: SIMG_ISHMED_N2DGAIUM
S_KK4_96000606	IMG Activity: SIMG_ISHMED_BAPIS
S_KK4_96000607	IMG Activity: ISH_PRG_BADI_STAT
S_KK4_96000609	IMG Activity: ISH_NWPLACE_DTM
S_KK4_96000610	IMG Activity: ISH_PREREG_CONTEXT
S_KK4_96000611	IMG Activity: SIMG_CFMENTNREL
S_KK4_96000612	IMG Activity: SIMG_ISHMED_RN2DGAIS
S_KK4_96000613	IMG Activity: ISH_EXP_WL_STATUS
S_KK4_96000614	IMG Activity: SIMG_ISHMED_DGAIEIN
S_KK4_96000615	IMG Activity: ISH_WP_PREREG_VIEW
S_KK4_96000616	IMG Activity: SIMG_ISHMED_RAD_BA10
S_KK4_96000617	IMG Activity: SIMG_ISHMED_VKGSTOID
S_KK4_96000618	IMG Activity: SIMG_ISHMED_RAD_BA11
S_KK4_96000619	IMG Activity: ISHMED_PRG_TN14H
S_KK4_96000620	IMG Activity: ISH_INVOICE_CHECK
S_KK4_96000621	IMG Activity: ISHMED_RAD_IC10
S_KK4_96000622	IMG Activity: ISHMED_RAD_IC11
S_KK4_96000623	IMG Activity: SIMG_ISHMED_ASPEKTE
S_KK4_96000624	IMG Activity: SIMG_ISHMED_SORT
S_KK4_96000625	IMG Activity: SIMG_ISHMED_AMBU
S_KK4_96000626	IMG Activity: ISHMED_NR19_BADI
S_KK4_96000627	IMG Activity: ISHMED_FALLZUO_BADI
S_KK4_96000628	IMG Activity: BADI: ISH_SURGERY_DRG
S_KK4_96000629	IMG Activity: BADI: ISH_ERROR_DRG
S_KK4_96000630	IMG Activity: BADI: ISH_UPGRADE_DRG
S_KK4_96000631	IMG Activity: ISH_MM_KAT_DEF_SINGL
S_KK4_96000632	IMG Activity: SIMG_ISHMED_WPTITLE
S_KK4_96000635	IMG Activity: ISHMED_PRG_BADI_SUBS
S_KK4_96000636	IMG Activity: SIMG_ISHMED_PERI004
S_KK4_96000637	IMG Activity: ISH_PRG_SRV_STAT
S_KK4_96000638	IMG Activity: SIMG_ISHMED_PERI005
S_KK4_96000639	IMG Activity: SIMG_ISHMED_PERI006
S_KK4_96000649	IMG Activity: ISHMED_CDOKU_SAVE
S_KK4_96000651	IMG Activity: ISHMED_CDOKU_RELEASE
S_KK4_96000652	IS-H: Materials List
S_KK4_96000653	Ad Hoc Purchas. and Consump.Analysis
S_KK4_96000654	IS-H: Mass Maint. of Mat. Catalogs
S_KK4_96000655	IMG Activity: ISH_NV2000_PBO
S_KK4_96000656	IMG Activity: ISH_NV2000_PAI_COMPL
S_KK4_96000657	IMG Activity: ISH_NV2000_PAI
S_KK4_98000054	IMG Activity: ISH_MD_FAS_BADI
S_KK4_98000118	IS-H*MED: Medication - Import Extern
S_KK4_98000119	IS-H*MED: Medication - Import Extern
S_KL1_11000037	Authorized/Actual Comparison of MPO
S_KL1_11000038	Scheduled Material Planning Objects
S_KL1_11000039	Remove Material Planning Objects
S_KM5_93000002	IMG Activity: SIMGMPWMM_OMILL_MMCL

S_KM5_93000003	IMG Activity: SIMGMPWSD_MILL_OOCU
S_KM5_93000004	IMG Activity: SIMGMPWSD_MILL_T160
S_KM5_93000005	IMG Activity: SIMGMPWSD_OMILL_VS
S_KP6_83000037	Hedging Relationship Settlement
S_KP7_36000001	IMG Activity: HR_LSO_M1C1D2A2
S_KP7_36000002	IMG Activity: HR_LSO_M1C6D3A1
S_KP7_36000003	IMG Activity: HR_LSO_M1C6D3A2
S_KP7_36000004	IMG Activity: HR_LSO_M2A5
S_KP7_36000005	IMG Activity: HR_LSO_M2A6
S_KP7_36000006	IMG Activity: HR_LSO_INFO
S_KP7_36000008	IMG Activity: HR_LSO_M1C3A7
S_KPE_16000003	IMG Activity: KPE_OPPE07
S_KPE_53000019	IMG Activity: KPE_V_CPPE_VSI_FORM
S_KPH_31000001	IMG activity: OHACN_TI370
S_KPH_31000002	IMG activity: OHACN_AB001
S_KPH_31000003	IMG activity: OHACN_AB002
S_KPH_31000004	IMG activity: OHACN_AB003
S_KPH_31000005	IMG activity: OHACN_AB004
S_KPH_31000006	IMG activity: OHACN_TI364
S_KPH_31000007	IMG activity: OHACN_TI340
S_KPH_31000008	IMG activity: SIMG_OHACN_463
S_KPH_31000009	IMG activity: OHACN_TI361
S_KPH_31000010	IMG activity: OHACN_TI363
S_KPH_31000011	IMG activity: OHACN_TI362
S_KPH_31000012	IMG activity: OHACN_AB200
S_KPH_31000013	IMG activity: OHACN_QUOTACOMP00
S_KPH_31000014	IMG activity: OHACN_QUOTACOMP01
S_KPH_31000015	IMG activity: SIMG_OHACN_457
S_KPH_31000016	IMG activity: SIMG_OHACN_431
S_KPH_31000017	IMG activity: OHACN_AB010
S_KPH_31000018	IMG activity: OHACN_AB005
S_KPH_31000019	IMG activity: SIMG_OHACN_451
S_KPH_31000020	IMG activity: OHACN_AB011
S_KPH_31000021	IMG activity: OHACN_AB009
S_KPH_31000022	IMG activity: OHACN_AB012
S_KPH_31000023	IMG activity: OHACN_UM101
S_KPH_31000024	IMG activity: OHACN_UM102
S_KPH_31000025	IMG activity: OHACN_UM103
S_KPH_31000026	IMG activity: SIMG_OHACN_615
S_KPH_31000027	IMG activity: OHACN_TI110
S_KPH_31000028	IMG activity: OHACN_UM105
S_KPH_31000029	IMG activity: OHACN_UM010
S_KPH_31000030	IMG activity: OHACN_EI000
S_KPH_31000031	IMG activity: OHACN_UM022
S_KPH_31000032	IMG activity: OHACN_UM023
S_KPH_31000033	IMG activity: OHACN_UM104
S_KPH_31000034	IMG activity: OHACN_TI321
S_KPH_31000035	IMG activity: OHACN_TI322
S_KPH_31000036	IMG activity: OHACN_TI323
S_KPH_31000037	IMG activity: OHACN_TI324
S_KPH_31000038	IMG activity: SIMG_OHACN_464
S_KPH_31000039	IMG activity: OHACN_TI325
S_KPH_31000040	IMG activity: OHACN_TI120
S_KPH_31000041	IMG activity: OHACN_TI130

S_KPH_31000042	IMG activity: OHACN_TI210
S_KPH_31000043	IMG activity: OHACN_TI310
S_KPH_31000044	IMG activity: SIMG_OHACN_471
S_KPH_31000045	IMG activity: OHACN_BW004
S_KPH_31000046	IMG activity: OHACN_DL022
S_KPH_31000047	IMG activity: OHACN_DL023
S_KPH_31000048	IMG activity: OHACN_JW000
S_KPH_31000049	IMG activity: SIMG_OHACN_515
S_KPH_31000050	IMG activity: OHACN_0902
S_KPH_31000051	IMG activity: OHACN_DL021
S_KPH_31000052	IMG activity: OHACN_DV001
S_KPH_31000053	IMG activity: SIMG_OHACN_506
S_KPH_31000054	IMG activity: OHACN_DL031
S_KPH_31000055	IMG activity: OHACN_DL032
S_KPH_31000056	IMG activity: OHACN_DL034
S_KPH_31000057	IMG activity: OHACN_TX202
S_KPH_31000058	IMG activity: OHACN_MZ001
S_KPH_31000059	IMG activity: OHACN_DT002
S_KPH_31000060	IMG activity: OHACN_DT003
S_KPH_31000061	IMG activity: OHACN_DT004
S_KPH_31000062	IMG activity: OHACN_TX201
S_KPH_31000063	IMG activity: OHACN_0911
S_KPH_31000064	IMG activity: OHACN_0912
S_KPH_31000065	IMG activity: OHACN_0913
S_KPH_31000066	IMG activity: OHACN_0903
S_KPH_31000067	IMG activity: SIMG_OHACN_416
S_KPH_31000068	IMG activity: OHACN_AV_P
S_KPH_31000069	IMG activity: SIMG_OHACN_814
S_KPH_31000070	IMG activity: OHACN_BW21
S_KPH_31000071	IMG activity: OHACN_BW22
S_KPH_31000072	IMG activity: SIMG_OHACN_518
S_KPH_31000073	IMG activity: OHACN_AV_ABCR
S_KPH_31000074	IMG activity: OHACN_BW005
S_KPH_31000075	IMG activity: OHACN_BW006
S_KPH_31000076	IMG activity: OHACN_BW019
S_KPH_31000077	IMG activity: SIMG_OHACN_530
S_KPH_31000078	IMG activity: OHACN_AV_2W
S_KPH_31000079	IMG activity: OHACN_SL003
S_KPH_31000080	IMG activity: SIMG_OHACN_507
S_KPH_31000081	IMG activity: OHACN_OCR001
S_KPH_31000082	IMG activity: OHACN_OCV001
S_KPH_31000083	IMG activity: OHACN_CPK001
S_KPH_31000084	IMG activity: OHACN_SL002
S_KPH_31000085	IMG activity: OHACN_PART
S_KPH_31000086	IMG activity: OHACN_KF001
S_KPH_31000087	IMG activity: OHACN_KF002
S_KPH_31000088	IMG activity: OHACN_KL000
S_KPH_31000089	IMG activity: OHACN_SL001
S_KPH_31000090	IMG activity: OHACN_PAI003
S_KPH_31000091	IMG activity: OHACN_PAI004
S_KPH_31000092	IMG activity: OHACN_PAI007
S_KPH_31000093	IMG activity: OHACN_GAI001
S_KPH_31000094	IMG activity: OHACN_GAI002
S_KPH_31000095	IMG activity: OHACN_RI061

S_KPH_31000096	IMG activity: OHACN_PAI001
S_KPH_31000097	IMG activity: OHACN_PAI002
S_KPH_31000098	IMG activity: OHACN_RI062
S_KPH_31000099	IMG activity: OHACN_PAI005
S_KPH_31000100	IMG activity: OHACN_PAI006
S_KPH_31000101	IMG activity: OHACN_RI055
S_KPH_31000102	IMG activity: OHACN_PHF009
S_KPH_31000103	IMG activity: OHACN_PHF003
S_KPH_31000104	IMG activity: OHACN_RI056
S_KPH_31000105	IMG activity: OHACN_PHF004
S_KPH_31000106	IMG activity: OHACN_PHF0011
S_KPH_31000107	IMG activity: OHACN_PHF002
S_KPH_31000108	IMG activity: OHACN_AFD001
S_KPH_31000109	IMG activity: OHACN_AFD002
S_KPH_31000110	IMG activity: OHACN_AFD003
S_KPH_31000111	IMG activity: OHACN_RI054
S_KPH_31000112	IMG activity: OHACN_RI053
S_KPH_31000113	IMG activity: OHACN_RI063
S_KPH_31000114	IMG activity: OHACN_PDS005
S_KPH_31000115	IMG activity: OHACN_PDS006
S_KPH_31000116	IMG activity: OHACN_PDS007
S_KPH_31000117	IMG activity: OHACN_PDS008
S_KPH_31000118	IMG activity: OHACN_RI081
S_KPH_31000119	IMG activity: OHACN_PDS004
S_KPH_31000120	IMG activity: OHACN_UM002
S_KPH_31000121	IMG activity: OHACN_RI090
S_KPH_31000122	IMG activity: OHACN_PDS001
S_KPH_31000123	IMG activity: OHACN_PDS002
S_KPH_31000124	IMG activity: OHACN_PDS003
S_KPH_31000125	IMG activity: OHACN_PDS009
S_KPH_31000126	IMG activity: OHACN_PF001
S_KPH_31000127	IMG activity: OHACN_PF002
S_KPH_31000128	IMG activity: OHACN_PF003
S_KPH_31000129	IMG activity: OHACN_PF004
S_KPH_31000130	IMG activity: OHACN_RI070
S_KPH_31000131	IMG activity: OHACN_RI071
S_KPH_31000132	IMG activity: OHACN_PDS0011
S_KPH_31000133	IMG activity: OHACN_RI080
S_KPH_31000134	IMG activity: OHACN_PC001
S_KPH_31000135	IMG activity: OHACN_PC002
S_KPH_31000136	IMG activity: OHACN_PC003
S_KPH_31000137	IMG activity: OHACN_SI0015
S_KPH_31000138	IMG activity: OHACN_RI042
S_KPH_31000139	IMG activity: OHACN_TX101
S_KPH_31000140	IMG activity: OHACN_TX107
S_KPH_31000141	IMG activity: OHACN_TX102
S_KPH_31000142	IMG activity: OHACN_SI0019
S_KPH_31000143	IMG activity: OHACN_SI001
S_KPH_31000144	IMG activity: OHACN_SI0013
S_KPH_31000145	IMG activity: OHACN_SI0014
S_KPH_31000146	IMG activity: OHACN_SI0017
S_KPH_31000147	IMG activity: OHACN_SI0016
S_KPH_31000148	IMG activity: OHACN_UM014
S_KPH_31000149	IMG activity: OHACN_UM006

S_KPH_31000150	IMG activity: OHACN_UM008
S_KPH_31000151	IMG activity: OHACN_UM010B
S_KPH_31000152	IMG activity: OHACN_UM013
S_KPH_31000153	IMG activity: OHACN_UM012
S_KPH_31000154	IMG activity: OHACN_TX103
S_KPH_31000155	IMG activity: OHACN_TX104
S_KPH_31000156	IMG activity: OHACN_TX105
S_KPH_31000157	IMG activity: OHACN_TX106
S_KPH_31000158	IMG activity: OHACN_RI015
S_KPH_31000159	IMG activity: OHACN_SI006
S_KPH_31000160	IMG activity: OHACN_SI003
S_KPH_31000161	IMG activity: OHACN_RI051
S_KPH_31000162	IMG activity: OHACN_PHF007
S_KPH_31000163	IMG activity: OHACN_PHF0010
S_KPH_31000164	IMG activity: OHACN_PHF008
S_KPH_31000165	IMG activity: OHACN_RI052
S_KPH_31000166	IMG activity: OHACN_PHF006
S_KPH_31000167	IMG activity: OHACN_PHF005
S_KPH_31000168	IMG activity: OHACN_PHF001
S_KPH_31000169	IMG activity: OHACN_SI002
S_KPH_31000170	IMG activity: OHACN_SI0018
S_KPH_31000171	IMG activity: OHACN_SI004
S_KPH_31000172	IMG activity: OHACN_SI005
S_KPH_31000173	IMG activity: OHACN_RI031
S_KPH_31000174	IMG activity: SIMG_OHACN_508
S_KPH_31000175	IMG activity: SIMG_OHACN_454
S_KPH_31000176	IMG activity: SIMG_OHACN_465
S_KPH_31000177	IMG activity: SIMG_OHACN_509
S_KPH_31000178	IMG activity: SIMG_OHACN_510
S_KPH_31000179	IMG activity: SIMG_OHACN_455
S_KPH_31000180	IMG activity: SIMG_OHACN_512
S_KPH_31000181	IMG activity: SIMG_OHACN_439
S_KPH_31000182	IMG activity: SIMG_OHACN_450
S_KPH_31000183	IMG activity: SIMG_OHACN_453
S_KPH_31000184	IMG activity: OHACN_AV_1
S_KPH_31000185	IMG activity: SIMG_OHACN_501
S_KPH_31000186	IMG activity: SIMG_OHACN_502
S_KPH_31000187	IMG activity: OHACN_TI330
S_KPH_31000188	IMG activity: SIMG_OHACN_614
S_KPH_31000189	IMG activity: SIMG_OHACN_613
S_KPH_31000190	IMG activity: SIMG_OHACN_612
S_KPH_31000191	IMG activity: SIMG_OHACN_611
S_KPH_31000192	IMG activity: SIMG_OHACN_456
S_KPH_31000193	IMG activity: SIMG_OHACN_521
S_KPH_31000194	IMG activity: SIMG_OHACN_522
S_KPH_31000195	IMG activity: SIMG_OHACN_523
S_KPH_31000196	IMG activity: SIMG_OHACN_524
S_KPH_31000197	IMG activity: SIMG_OHACN_513
S_KPH_31000198	IMG activity: SIMG_OHACN_514
S_KPH_31000199	IMG activity: OHACN_AL01
S_KPH_31000200	IMG activity: SIMG_OHACN_516
S_KPH_31000201	IMG activity: SIMG_OHACN_517
S_KPH_31000202	IMG activity: OHACN_RI012
S_KPH_31000203	IMG activity: OHACN_RI011

S_KPH_31000204	IMG activity: SIMG_OHACN_466
S_KPH_31000205	IMG activity: SIMG_OHACN_520
S_KPH_31000206	IMG activity: OHAKR_TX210
S_KPH_31000207	IMG activity: OHAKR_DT002
S_KPH_31000208	IMG activity: OHAKR_DT003
S_KPH_31000209	IMG activity: OHAKR_DT004
S_KPH_31000210	IMG activity: OHAKR_MZ001
S_KPH_31000211	IMG activity: SIMG_OHAKR_416
S_KPH_31000212	IMG activity: SIMG_OHAKR_515
S_KPH_31000213	IMG activity: OHAKR_SP900
S_KPH_31000214	IMG activity: OHAKR_SI110
S_KPH_31000215	IMG activity: OHAKR_SI310
S_KPH_31000216	IMG activity: OHAKR_SI320
S_KPH_31000217	IMG activity: OHAKR_TX020
S_KPH_31000218	IMG activity: OHAKR_TX040
S_KPH_31000219	IMG activity: OHAKR_TX110
S_KPH_31000220	IMG activity: SIMG_OHAKR_405
S_KPH_31000221	IMG activity: SIMG_OHAKR_406
S_KPH_31000222	IMG activity: SIMG_OHAKR_408
S_KPH_31000223	IMG activity: SIMG_OHAKR_527
S_KPH_31000224	IMG activity: SIMG_OHAKR_528
S_KPH_31000225	IMG activity: SIMG_OHAKR_529
S_KPH_31000226	IMG activity: SIMG_OHAKR_409
S_KPH_31000227	IMG activity: SIMG_OHAKR_506
S_KPH_31000228	IMG activity: SIMG_OHAKR_507
S_KPH_31000229	IMG activity: SIMG_OHAKR_518
S_KPH_31000230	IMG activity: SIMG_OHAKR_530
S_KPH_31000231	IMG activity: SIMG_OHAKR_525
S_KPH_31000232	IMG activity: SIMG_OHAKR_402
S_KPH_31000233	IMG activity: SIMG_OHAKR_403
S_KPH_31000234	IMG activity: OHAKR_BEN002
S_KPH_31000235	IMG activity: OHAKR_BEN003
S_KPH_31000236	IMG activity: OHAKR_BEN310
S_KPH_31000237	IMG activity: OHAKR_BEN004
S_KPH_31000238	IMG activity: OHAKR_BEN005
S_KPH_31000239	IMG activity: OHAKR_DV001
S_KPH_31000240	IMG activity: OHAKR_JW000
S_KPH_31000241	IMG activity: OHAKR_FAM100
S_KPH_31000242	IMG activity: OHAKR_FAM110
S_KPH_31000243	IMG activity: OHAKR_FAM300
S_KPH_31000244	IMG activity: OHAKR_FAM120
S_KPH_31000245	IMG activity: OHAKR_SER100
S_KPH_31000246	IMG activity: OHAKR_SER110
S_KPH_31000247	IMG activity: OHAKR_BEN001
S_KPH_31000248	IMG activity: OHAKR_SP202
S_KPH_31000249	IMG activity: OHAKR_SP302
S_KPH_31000250	IMG activity: OHAKR_SP130
S_KPH_31000251	IMG activity: OHAKR_SP400
S_KPH_31000252	IMG activity: OHAKR_SP500
S_KPH_31000253	IMG activity: OHAKR_SP600
S_KPH_31000254	IMG activity: OHAKR_SP802
S_KPH_31000255	IMG activity: OHAKR_0902
S_KPH_31000256	IMG activity: OHAKR_0911
S_KPH_31000257	IMG activity: OHAKR_0912

S_KPH_31000258	IMG activity: OHAKR_0913
S_KPH_31000259	IMG activity: OHAKR_0903
S_KPH_31000260	IMG activity: OHAKR_SP102
S_KPH_31000261	IMG activity: OHAKR_SP201
S_KPH_31000262	IMG activity: SIMG_OHAKR_470
S_KPH_31000263	IMG activity: SIMG_OHAKR_615
S_KPH_31000264	IMG activity: OHAKR_RI015
S_KPH_31000265	IMG activity: OHAKR_RI042
S_KPH_31000266	IMG activity: OHAKR_RI031
S_KPH_31000267	IMG activity: OHAKR_RI051
S_KPH_31000268	IMG activity: OHAKR_RI052
S_KPH_31000269	IMG activity: SIMG_OHAKR_459
S_KPH_31000270	IMG activity: SIMG_OHAKR_438
S_KPH_31000271	IMG activity: SIMG_OHAKR_461
S_KPH_31000272	IMG activity: SIMG_OHAKR_429
S_KPH_31000273	IMG activity: SIMG_OHAKR_427
S_KPH_31000274	IMG activity: SIMG_OHAKR_424
S_KPH_31000275	IMG activity: SIMG_OHAKR_467
S_KPH_31000276	IMG activity: OHAKR_RI070
S_KPH_31000277	IMG activity: OHAKR_RI071
S_KPH_31000278	IMG activity: OHAKR_RI080
S_KPH_31000279	IMG activity: OHAKR_RI081
S_KPH_31000280	IMG activity: OHAKR_RI090
S_KPH_31000281	IMG activity: OHAKR_UM002
S_KPH_31000282	IMG activity: OHAKR_UM003
S_KPH_31000283	IMG activity: OHAKR_RI056
S_KPH_31000284	IMG activity: OHAKR_RI053
S_KPH_31000285	IMG activity: OHAKR_RI054
S_KPH_31000286	IMG activity: OHAKR_RI055
S_KPH_31000287	IMG activity: OHAKR_RI061
S_KPH_31000288	IMG activity: OHAKR_RI062
S_KPH_31000289	IMG activity: OHAKR_RI063
S_KPH_31000290	IMG activity: SIMG_OHAKR_814
S_KPH_31000291	IMG activity: SIMG_OHAKR_415
S_KPH_31000292	IMG activity: SIMG_OHAKR_418
S_KPH_31000293	IMG activity: SIMG_OHAKR_419
S_KPH_31000294	IMG activity: SIMG_OHAKR_483
S_KPH_31000295	IMG activity: SIMG_OHAKR_484
S_KPH_31000296	IMG activity: OHAKR_EDTINTERNET
S_KPH_31000297	IMG activity: SIMG_OHAKR_407
S_KPH_31000298	IMG activity: SIMG_OHAKR_482
S_KPH_31000299	IMG activity: SIMG_OHAKR_410
S_KPH_31000300	IMG activity: SIMG_OHAKR_417
S_KPH_31000301	IMG activity: SIMG_OHAKR_413
S_KPH_31000302	IMG activity: SIMG_OHAKR_480
S_KPH_31000303	IMG activity: SIMG_OHAKR_414
S_KPH_31000304	IMG activity: SIMG_OHAKR_422
S_KPH_31000305	IMG activity: SIMG_OHAKR_423
S_KPH_31000306	IMG activity: SIMG_OHAKR_425
S_KPH_31000307	IMG activity: SIMG_OHAKR_437
S_KPH_31000308	IMG activity: SIMG_OHAKR_432
S_KPH_31000309	IMG activity: SIMG_OHAKR_426
S_KPH_31000310	IMG activity: SIMG_OHAKR_428
S_KPH_31000311	IMG activity: SIMG_OHAKR_431

S_KPH_31000312	IMG activity: SIMG_OHAKR_457
S_KPH_31000313	IMG activity: SIMG_OHAKR_451
S_KPH_31000314	IMG activity: SIMG_OHAKR_463
S_KPH_31000315	IMG activity: SIMG_OHAKR_464
S_KPH_31000316	IMG activity: SIMG_OHAKR_471
S_KPH_31000317	IMG activity: SIMG_OHAKR_435
S_KPH_31000318	IMG activity: OHAKR_DE1046
S_KPH_31000319	IMG activity: OHAKR_QUOTACOMP02
S_KPH_31000320	IMG activity: OHAKR_UM103
S_KPH_31000321	IMG activity: OHAKR_UM102
S_KPH_31000322	IMG activity: OHAKR_UM101
S_KPH_31000323	IMG activity: OHAKR_UM105
S_KPH_31000324	IMG activity: OHAKR_QUOTACOMP01
S_KPH_31000325	IMG activity: OHAKR_TI310
S_KPH_31000326	IMG activity: OHAKR_TI210
S_KPH_31000327	IMG activity: OHAKR_TI130
S_KPH_31000328	IMG activity: OHAKR_TI120
S_KPH_31000329	IMG activity: OHAKR_TI110
S_KPH_31000330	IMG activity: OHAKR_BW019
S_KPH_31000331	IMG activity: OHAKR_AV_2W
S_KPH_31000332	IMG activity: OHAKR_UM010
S_KPH_31000333	IMG activity: OHAKR_AV_ABCR
S_KPH_31000334	IMG activity: OHAKR_AV_P
S_KPH_31000335	IMG activity: OHAKR_BW006
S_KPH_31000336	IMG activity: OHAKR_UM104
S_KPH_31000337	IMG activity: OHAKR_UM023
S_KPH_31000338	IMG activity: OHAKR_UM022
S_KPH_31000339	IMG activity: OHAKR_BW004
S_KPH_31000340	IMG activity: OHAKR_BW005
S_KPH_31000341	IMG activity: OHAKR_QUOTACOMP00
S_KPH_31000342	IMG activity: OHAKR_AB004
S_KPH_31000343	IMG activity: OHAKR_AB005
S_KPH_31000344	IMG activity: OHAKR_TI363
S_KPH_31000345	IMG activity: OHAKR_AB011
S_KPH_31000346	IMG activity: OHAKR_TI361
S_KPH_31000347	IMG activity: OHAKR_AB003
S_KPH_31000348	IMG activity: OHAKR_TI370
S_KPH_31000349	IMG activity: OHAKR_AB001
S_KPH_31000350	IMG activity: OHAKR_AB002
S_KPH_31000351	IMG activity: OHAKR_TI364
S_KPH_31000352	IMG activity: OHAKR_TI362
S_KPH_31000353	IMG activity: OHAKR_TI324
S_KPH_31000354	IMG activity: OHAKR_TI323
S_KPH_31000355	IMG activity: OHAKR_TI322
S_KPH_31000356	IMG activity: OHAKR_TI321
S_KPH_31000357	IMG activity: OHAKR_TI325
S_KPH_31000358	IMG activity: OHAKR_TI340
S_KPH_31000359	IMG activity: OHAKR_AB009
S_KPH_31000360	IMG activity: OHAKR_AB012
S_KPH_31000361	IMG activity: OHAKR_AB010
S_KPH_31000362	IMG activity: OHAKR_AB200
S_KPH_31000363	IMG activity: OHAKR_QUOTAGEN00
S_KPH_31000364	IMG activity: OHAKR_DP112
S_KPH_31000365	IMG activity: OHAKR_UM014

S_KPH_31000366	IMG activity: OHAKR_ESS002
S_KPH_31000367	IMG activity: OHAKR_DP111
S_KPH_31000368	IMG activity: OHAKR_UM006
S_KPH_31000369	IMG activity: OHAKR_SL001
S_KPH_31000370	IMG activity: OHAKR_UM008
S_KPH_31000371	IMG activity: OHAKR_OCR001
S_KPH_31000372	IMG activity: OHAKR_DP102
S_KPH_31000373	IMG activity: OHAKR_KL000
S_KPH_31000374	IMG activity: OHAKR_ESS001
S_KPH_31000375	IMG activity: OHAKR_ESS004
S_KPH_31000376	IMG activity: OHAKR_DP200
S_KPH_31000377	IMG activity: OHAKR_DP103
S_KPH_31000378	IMG activity: OHAKR_PART
S_KPH_31000379	IMG activity: OHAKR_ESS003
S_KPH_31000380	IMG activity: OHAKR_KF001
S_KPH_31000381	IMG activity: OHAKR_KF002
S_KPH_31000382	IMG activity: OHAKR_UM012
S_KPH_31000383	IMG activity: OHAKR_UM010B
S_KPH_31000384	IMG activity: OHAKR_DE1040B
S_KPH_31000385	IMG activity: OHAKR_UM013
S_KPH_31000386	IMG activity: OHAKR_DE1048
S_KPH_31000387	IMG activity: OHAKR_BW22
S_KPH_31000388	IMG activity: OHAKR_BW21
S_KPH_31000389	IMG activity: OHAKR_DE1041
S_KPH_31000390	IMG activity: OHAKR_DE1044
S_KPH_31000391	IMG activity: OHAKR_SL002
S_KPH_31000392	IMG activity: OHAKR_SL003
S_KPH_31000393	IMG activity: OHAKR_DP101
S_KPH_31000394	IMG activity: OHAKR_TX030
S_KPH_31000395	IMG activity: OHAKR_DP100
S_KPH_31000396	IMG activity: OHAKR_DE1043
S_KPH_31000397	IMG activity: OHAKR_SP301
S_KPH_31000398	IMG activity: SIMG_OHAKR_520
S_KPH_31000399	IMG activity: SIMG_OHAKR_439
S_KPH_31000400	IMG activity: SIMG_OHAKR_450
S_KPH_31000401	IMG activity: SIMG_OHAKR_519
S_KPH_31000402	IMG activity: SIMG_OHAKR_453
S_KPH_31000403	IMG activity: OHAKR_SP801
S_KPH_31000404	IMG activity: OHAKR_RI012
S_KPH_31000405	IMG activity: SIMG_OHAKR_481
S_KPH_31000406	IMG activity: SIMG_OHAKR_401
S_KPH_31000407	IMG activity: OHAKR_TI330
S_KPH_31000408	IMG activity: OHAKR_AL01
S_KPH_31000409	IMG activity: SIMG_OHAKR_524
S_KPH_31000410	IMG activity: OHAKR_SP101
S_KPH_31000411	IMG activity: SIMG_OHAKR_523
S_KPH_31000412	IMG activity: SIMG_OHAKR_522
S_KPH_31000413	IMG activity: SIMG_OHAKR_521
S_KPH_31000414	IMG activity: OHAKR_RI011
S_KPH_31000415	IMG activity: SIMG_OHAKR_421
S_KPH_31000416	IMG activity: SIMG_OHAKR_513
S_KPH_31000417	IMG activity: SIMG_OHAKR_514
S_KPH_31000418	IMG activity: SIMG_OHAKR_456
S_KPH_31000419	IMG activity: SIMG_OHAKR_466

S_KPH_31000420	IMG activity: SIMG_OHAKR_455
S_KPH_31000421	IMG activity: SIMG_OHAKR_502
S_KPH_31000422	IMG activity: SIMG_OHAKR_501
S_KPH_31000423	IMG activity: SIMG_OHAKR_508
S_KPH_31000424	IMG activity: SIMG_OHAKR_509
S_KPH_31000425	IMG activity: SIMG_OHAKR_510
S_KPH_31000426	IMG activity: SIMG_OHAKR_512
S_KPH_31000427	IMG activity: OHAKR_AV_1
S_KPH_31000428	IMG activity: SIMG_OHAKR_841
S_KPH_31000429	IMG activity: SIMG_OHAKR_842
S_KPH_31000430	IMG activity: SIMG_OHAKR_843
S_KPH_31000431	IMG activity: SIMG_OHAKR_844
S_KPH_31000432	IMG activity: SIMG_OHAKR_516
S_KPH_31000433	IMG activity: SIMG_OHAKR_517
S_KPH_31000434	IMG activity: SIMG_OHAKR_454
S_KPH_31000435	IMG activity: SIMG_OHAKR_465
S_KPH_31000436	IMG activity: SIMG_OHAKR_611
S_KPH_31000437	IMG activity: SIMG_OHAKR_612
S_KPH_31000438	IMG activity: SIMG_OHAKR_613
S_KPH_31000439	IMG activity: SIMG_OHAKR_614
S_KPH_31000440	IMG activity: PAD_KR_MIL_210
S_KPH_31000441	IMG activity: PAD_KR_MIL_130
S_KPH_31000442	IMG activity: PAD_KR_MIL_120
S_KPH_31000443	IMG activity: PAD_KR_MIL_110
S_KPH_31000444	IMG activity: PAD_KR_DIS_100
S_KPH_31000445	IMG activity: PAD_KR_AWD_120
S_KPH_31000446	IMG activity: PAD_KR_AWD_110
S_KPH_31000447	IMG activity: PAD_KR_AWD_073
S_KPH_31000448	IMG activity: PAD_KR_AWD_072
S_KPH_31000449	IMG activity: PAD_KR_TAX_030
S_KPH_31000450	IMG activity: PAD_KR_SI_420
S_KPH_31000451	IMG activity: PAD_KR_SI_410
S_KPH_31000452	IMG activity: PAD_KR_SI_230
S_KPH_31000453	IMG activity: PAD_KR_SI_220
S_KPH_31000454	IMG activity: PAD_KR_SI_210
S_KPH_31000455	IMG activity: PAD_KR_SI_130
S_KPH_31000456	IMG activity: PAD_KR_SI_110
S_KPH_31000457	IMG activity: PAD_KR_AWD_071
S_KPH_31000458	IMG activity: PAD_KR_AWD_051
S_KPH_31000459	IMG activity: PAD_KR_ADR_011
S_KPH_31000460	IMG activity: PAD_KR_CHA_110
S_KPH_31000461	IMG activity: PAD_KR_NAT_110
S_KPH_31000462	IMG activity: PAD_KR_NAT_130
S_KPH_31000463	IMG activity: PAD_KR_NAT_120
S_KPH_31000464	IMG activity: PAD_KR_FAM_121
S_KPH_31000465	IMG activity: PAD_KR_AWD_061
S_KPH_31000466	IMG activity: PAD_KR_AWD_062
S_KPH_31000467	IMG activity: PAD_KR_AWD_063
S_KPH_31000468	IMG activity: PAD_KR_AWD_052
S_KPH_31000486	Remuneration Statements
S_KPH_31000487	Payroll Accounts
S_KPH_31000488	Payroll Journal --- International
S_KPH_31000489	Remuneration Statements
S_KPH_31000490	Payroll Accounts

S_KPH_31000492	Payroll Journal --- International
S_KPH_31000613	The payment certificate of earned in
S_L4H_49000475	IMG Activity
S_L4H_49000882	Report for INAIL SelfSettl Extract.
S_L4H_49000900	Customizing Activity: OHADKU230
S_L4H_49001275	Generate DMA TemSe Files Report
S_L4H_60400001	Information of Employee-Related Data
S_L4H_61015807	Pay Scale Reclassification
S_L6B_69000027	IMG Activity: OHPKFI001
S_L6B_69000102	IMG Activity: PAY_IN_LWF_400
S_L6B_69000188	VETS : US Legal Compliance Report fo
S_L6B_69000217	HR-PT: Generic Statistical Report
S_L6B_69000218	HR-PT: Structured Employment Survey
S_L6B_69000430	IMG Activity: OHALDL038
S_L6B_69000435	IMG Activity: OHARDL038
S_L6B_69000505	IMG Activity: PAY_IN_ROR_100
S_L6B_69000541	IMG Activity: OHPSUS1042S042
S_L6B_69000742	IMG activity: OHANBNI05
S_L6D_84000012	IMG Activity: OHIJ0181
S_L7D_24000172	IMG activity: OHPSMXISSSTE26
S_L7D_24000214	IMG activity: SIMGOHAIT_DM065
S_L7D_24000234	IMG Activity: OHAVAREM_009
S_L7D_24000235	IMG activity: OHAFOVERLAPPING01
S_L7D_24000236	IMG activity: OHAFIJSS01
S_L7D_24000239	IMG activity: OHAFRREINPSSAN
S_L7D_24000240	IMG activity: OHAFREIN01
S_L7D_24000241	IMG activity: OHAFREIN02
S_L7D_24000242	IMG activity: OHAFPAIEDECAL00
S_L7D_24000243	IMG activity: OHAFPAIEDECAL01
S_L7D_24000244	IMG activity: OHAFPAIEDECAL02
S_L7D_24000276	IMG Activity: PBS_NO_REP_SPK_500
S_L7D_24000579	IMG Activity
S_L7D_24000581	IMG Activity
S_L7D_24001045	IMG activity
S_L7D_24001071	Completeness Check for Payt Results
S_L7D_24001215	IMG Activity
S_L7D_24001239	Calculation of Basic Pay for Public
S_L7D_24001240	Public Administration Human Resource
S_L7D_24001241	Calculation of Seniority
S_L7D_24001342	IMG Activity
S_L7D_24001479	IMG Activity
S_L7D_24001522	Account Statement for Company Loans
S_L7D_24001545	Update Superannuation -NZ (IT0310)
S_L7D_24001880	Report RPCSCOG0
S_L7D_24002166	Define Perc. Single-Parent Benefit
S_L9C_94000001	Define PC Activity for ADHOC Query
S_L9C_94000002	S_L9C_94000002
S_L9C_94000003	S_L9C_94000003
S_L9C_94000004	S_L9C_94000004
S_L9C_94000025	Ad Hoc Query
S_L9C_94000066	S_L9C_94000066
S_L9C_94000067	S_L9C_94000067
S_L9C_94000068	S_L9C_94000068
S_L9C_94000069	S_L9C_94000069

S_L9C_94000070	S_L9C_94000070
S_L9C_94000071	S_L9C_94000071
S_L9C_94000072	S_L9C_94000072
S_L9C_94000080	S_L9C_94000080
S_L9C_94000081	S_L9C_94000081
S_L9C_94000082	S_L9C_94000082
S_L9C_94000095	Headcount Changes
S_L9C_94000137	SAPLS_CUS_IMG_ACTIVITY
S_L9C_94000152	SAPLS_CUS_IMG_ACTIVITY
S_L9C_94000420	S_L9C_94000420
S_L9C_94000421	S_L9C_94000421
S_L9C_94000422	S_L9C_94000422
S_L9C_94000471	Payroll schema
S_L9C_94000516	IMG activity: SIMGOHAXDL023
S_L9C_94000550	S_L9C_94000550
S_L9C_94000551	S_L9C_94000551
S_L9C_94000552	S_L9C_94000552
S_L9C_94000553	S_L9C_94000553
S_L9C_94000554	S_L9C_94000554
S_L9C_94000555	S_L9C_94000555
S_L9C_94000556	S_L9C_94000556
S_L9C_94000557	S_L9C_94000557
S_L9C_94000607	S_L9C_94000607
S_L9C_94000611	S_L9C_94000611
S_L9C_94000612	S_L9C_94000612
S_L9C_94000613	S_L9C_94000613
S_L9C_94000614	S_L9C_94000614
S_L9C_94000615	S_L9C_94000615
S_L9C_94000616	S_L9C_94000616
S_L9C_94000629	S_L9C_94000629
S_L9C_94000703	s_l9c_94000703
S_L9C_94000704	s_l9c_94000704
S_L9C_94000705	S_L9C_94000705
S_L9C_94000706	S_L9C_94000706
S_L9C_94000707	S_L9C_94000707
S_L9C_94000708	S_L9C_94000708
S_L9C_94000709	S_L9C_94000709
S_L9C_94000710	S_L9C_94000710
S_L9C_94000711	S_L9C_94000711
S_L9C_94000712	S_L9C_94000712
S_L9C_94000713	S_L9C_94000713
S_L9C_94000714	S_L9C_94000714
S_L9C_94000715	S_L9C_94000715
S_L9C_94000797	IMG activity: OHAZA_SOC01
S_L9C_94000798	IMG activity: OHAZA_SOC02
S_L9C_94000799	IMG activity: OHAZA_SOC03
S_L9C_94000800	IMG activity: OHAZA_WSP01
S_L9C_94000846	IMG activity: SIMGOHAIT_F24020
S_L9C_94000847	IMG activity: SIMGOHAIT_F24015
S_L9C_94000854	IMG activity: PAY_BR_DIV_010
S_L9C_94000855	IMG Activity: OHADBAV3010
S_L9C_94000856	IMG Activity: OHADBAV3020
S_L9C_94000857	IMG activity: PAY_BR_DIV_020
S_L9C_94000858	IMG Activity: OHADBAV3030

S_L9C_94000859	IMG activity: PAY_BR_DIV_030
S_L9C_94000860	IMG activity: PAY_BR_DIV_040
S_L9C_94000861	IMG activity: PAY_BR_DIV_050
S_L9C_94000862	IMG activity: PAY_BR_DIV_060
S_L9C_94000873	IMG activity: PAD_KR_JOBTY_01
S_L9C_94000874	IMG activity: PAD_KR_JOBTY_02
S_L9C_94000875	IMG activity: PAD_KR_REMEE_01
S_L9C_94000876	IMG activity: PAD_KR_REMEE_02
S_L9C_94000877	IMG activity: PAD_KR_DEVNI
S_L9C_94000878	IMG activity: PAD_KR_DEVSR
S_L9C_94000879	IMG activity: PAD_KR_DEVSD
S_L9C_94000885	IMG activity: OHA_KR_EDUBD01
S_L9C_94000886	IMG activity: OHA_KR_EDUBD02
S_L9C_94000892	IMG Activity: PAY_XX_AB_305
S_L9C_94000903	IMG Activity: PAY_XX_AB_306
S_L9C_94000927	IMG activity: PAY_BR_AU020
S_L9C_94000931	IMG activity: PAY_BR_AU019
S_L9C_94000932	IMG activity: PAY_BR_AU021
S_L9C_94000936	IMG activity: PAY_BR_TERC001
S_L9C_94000937	IMG activity: PAY_BR_TERC002
S_L9C_94000938	IMG activity: PAY_BR_TERC003
S_L9C_94000939	IMG activity: PAY_BR_TERC004
S_L9C_94000954	IMG activity OHAIAB0006
S_L9C_94000955	IMG activity OHAICT01
S_L9C_94000956	IMG activity OHAICT02
S_L9C_94000957	IMG activity OHAICT03
S_L9C_94000958	IMG activity OHAICA01
S_L9C_94000959	IMG activity OHAICD01
S_L9C_94000960	IMG activity OHAICD02
S_L9C_94000961	IMG activity OHAICD03
S_L9C_94000962	IMG activity OHAISP01
S_L9C_94000963	IMG activity OHAISP02
S_L9C_94000964	IMG activity OHAISP03
S_L9C_94000965	IMG activity OHAINR01
S_L9C_94000966	IMG activity OHAINR02
S_L9C_94000967	IMG activity: PAY_BR_PROV_001
S_L9C_94000968	IMG activity: PAY_BR_PROV_002
S_L9C_94000969	IMG activity: PAY_BR_PROV_003
S_L9C_94000970	IMG activity: PAY_BR_PROV_004
S_L9C_94000971	IMG activity: PAY_BR_PROV_005
S_L9C_94000972	IMG activity: PAY_BR_PROV006
S_L9C_94000973	IMG activity: PAY_BR_PROV_006
S_L9C_94000975	IMG activity: PAY_BR_RT019
S_L9C_94000976	IMG activity: PAY_BR_RT020
S_L9C_94001038	IMG activity: PAY_SG_EMPTXT_000
S_L9C_94001068	IMG activity: PBS_SG_PEN_001
S_L9C_94001069	IMG activity: PBS_SG_PEN_010
S_L9C_94001070	IMG activity: PBS_SG_PEN_020
S_L9C_94001071	IMG activity: PBS_SG_PEN_030
S_L9C_94001072	IMG activity: PBS_SG_PEN_040
S_L9C_94001073	IMG activity: PBS_SG_PEN_050
S_L9C_94001074	IMG activity: PBS_SG_PEN_060
S_L9C_94001143	IMG activity: PBS_SG_PAD_HDB_001
S_L9C_94001144	IMG activity: PBS_SG_PAD_HDB_002

S_L9C_94001145	IMG activity: PBS_SG_PAD_DEC_001
S_L9C_94001146	IMG activity: PBS_SG_PAD_DEL_001
S_L9C_94001147	IMG activity: PBS_SG_PAD_DEL_002
S_L9C_94001148	IMG activity: PBS_SG_PAD_DEL_003
S_L9C_94001149	IMG activity: PBS_SG_PAD_DEL_004
S_L9C_94001150	IMG activity: PBS_SG_DIS_01_001
S_L9C_94001151	IMG activity: PBS_SG_DIS_001
S_L9C_94001152	IMG activity: PBS_SG_DIS_002
S_L9C_94001153	IMG activity: PBS_SG_DIS_003
S_L9C_94001154	IMG activity: PBS_SG_DIS_004
S_L9C_94001155	IMG activity: PBS_SG_DIS_005
S_L9C_94001156	IMG activity: PBS_SG_DIS_006
S_L9C_94001157	IMG activity: PBS_SG_DIS_007
S_L9C_94001158	IMG activity: PBS_SG_BLA_001
S_L9C_94001159	IMG activity: PBS_SG_BLA_002
S_L9C_94001160	IMG activity: PBS_SG_BLA_003
S_L9C_94001161	IMG activity: PBS_SG_BLA_004
S_L9C_94001162	IMG activity: PBS_SG_PAD_DES_001
S_L9C_94001163	IMG activity: PBS_SG_PAD_DES_002
S_L9C_94001164	IMG activity: PBS_SG_PAD_DES_003
S_L9C_94001165	IMG activity: PBS_SG_PAD_DES_004
S_L9C_94001166	IMG activity: PBS_SG_PAD_DEB_001
S_L9C_94001167	IMG activity: PBS_SG_PAD_DEB_002
S_L9C_94001168	IMG activity: PBS_SG_PAD_DEB_003
S_L9C_94001169	IMG activity: PBS_SG_PAD_DEB_004
S_L9C_94001170	IMG activity: PBS_SG_PAD_DEN_001
S_L9C_94001171	IMG activity: PBS_SG_PAD_DEN_002
S_L9C_94001172	IMG activity: PBS_SG_PAD_DEN_003
S_L9C_94001218	IMG activity: PBS_SG_BLA_005
S_L9C_94001274	IMG activity: PBS_SG_PEN_070
S_L9C_94001275	IMG activity: PBS_SG_PEN_080
S_L9C_94001276	IMG activity: PBS_SG_PEN_090
S_L9C_94001277	IMG activity: PBS_SG_PEN_100
S_L9C_94001278	IMG activity: PBS_SG_PEN_110
S_L9C_94001279	IMG activity: PBS_SG_PEN_120
S_L9C_94001280	IMG activity: PBS_SG_PEN_085
S_L9C_94001357	IMG activity SIMG OHAISP02
S_L9C_94001358	IMG activity SIMG OHAISP03
S_L9C_94001359	IMG activity SIMG OHAISP04
S_L9C_94001360	IMG activity SIMG OHAISP05
S_L9C_94001361	IMG activity SIMG OHAICT02
S_L9C_94001362	IMG activity SIMG OHAICT03
S_L9C_94001363	IMG activity SIMGOHAICA02
S_L9C_94001364	IMG activity SIMG OHAICA03
S_L9C_94001365	IMG activity SIMGOHAICA04
S_L9C_94001371	IMG activity SIMGOHAINOR00
S_L9C_94001372	IMG activity SIMGOHAINOR01
S_L9C_94001424	IMG activity: PBS_SG_PEN_035
S_L9C_94001425	IMG activity: PBS_SG_PEN_130
S_L9C_94001426	IMG activity: PBS_SG_PEN_140
S_L9C_94001427	IMG activity: PBS_SG_PEN_150
S_L9C_94001428	IMG activity: PBS_SG_PEN_200
S_L9C_94001429	IMG activity: PBS_SG_PEN_210
S_L9C_94001430	IMG activity: PBS_SG_PEN_220

S_L9C_94001431	IMG activity: PBS_SG_PEN_230
S_L9C_94001432	IMG activity: PBS_SG_PEN_240
S_L9C_94001433	IMG activity: PBS_SG_PEN_300
S_L9C_94001434	IMG activity: PBS_SG_PEN_310
S_L9C_94001435	IMG activity: PBS_SG_PEN_320
S_L9C_94001436	IMG activity: PBS_SG_PEN_400
S_L9C_94001437	IMG activity: PBS_SG_PEN_410
S_L9C_94001438	IMG activity: PBS_SG_PEN_420
S_L9C_94001439	IMG activity: PBS_SG_PEN_430
S_L9C_94001440	IMG activity: PBS_SG_PEN_250
S_L9C_94001487	IMG activity SIMGOHAIT_CIG07
S_L9C_94001491	IMG activity SIMGOHAIAPR05
S_L9C_94001818	IMG activity: PAY_SG_GPML_000
S_L9C_94001819	IMG activity: PAY_SG_GPML_001
S_L9C_94001820	IMG activity: PAY_SG_GPML_002
S_L9C_94001821	IMG activity: PAY_SG_GPML_003
S_L9C_94001833	IMG-Aktivität: OHABSI60A
S_L9C_94001834	IMG-Aktivität: OHABSI61A
S_L9C_94001835	IMG-Aktivität: OHABSI62A
S_L9C_94001836	IMG-Aktivität: OHABSI62A
S_L9C_94001837	IMG-Aktivität: OHABSI65A
S_L9C_94001838	IMG-Aktivität: OHABSI66A
S_L9C_94001839	IMG-Aktivität: OHABSI67A
S_L9C_94002005	IMG activity: OHAVAREM_001
S_L9C_94002006	IMG activity: OHAVAREM_002
S_L9C_94002007	IMG activity: OHAVAREM_003
S_L9C_94002008	IMG activity: OHAVAREM_004
S_L9C_94002009	IMG activity: OHAVAREM_005
S_L9C_94002010	IMG activity: OHAVAREM_006
S_L9C_94002011	IMG activity: OHAVAREM_007
S_L9C_94002012	IMG activity: OHAVAREM_008
S_L9C_94002046	IMG activity: OHAVAREM_0035
S_L9C_94002048	IMG activity: OHAVAREM_0025
S_L9C_94002357	IMG activity: SIMGOHAIT_FIP00
S_L9C_94002358	IMG activity: OHAIT_FIP04
S_MEMORY_INSPECTOR	Memory Inspector
S_MID_66000001	IMG
S_NWDEMO_BP_SNRO	Number range maintenance: SDEMO_BP
S_NWDEMO_DG	Execute data generator for NW demo
S_NWDEMO_PO_SNRO	Number range maintenance: SDEMO_PO
S_NWDEMO_SO_SNRO	Number range maintenance: SDEMO_SO
S_P00_07000003	Display Directly Assigned Costs
S_P00_07000008	Display of Bank Changes
S_P00_07000050	Comparison of Currency Trans Keys
S_P00_07000056	Distribution of the bank master data
S_P00_07000057	Distribution of the bank master data
S_P00_07000064	Usage Level for Tax Exemption
S_P00_07000065	Anal.GR/IR Clrg Accts and Dis.Acq.Tx
S_P00_07000074	IMG Activity: SIMG_CFMENUOFTCOFD7
S_P00_07000077	TH01
S_P00_07000078	TH02
S_P00_07000079	Orders: Settlement Statement
S_P00_07000095	IMG Activity: House Banks
S_P00_07000106	INTRASTAT: File Creation

SAP Transaction Codes – Volume Two

S_P00_07000111	Advance Return for Tax on Sales/Pur.
S_P00_07000112	Advance Return for Tax on Sales/Pur.
S_P00_07000113	Addit. List for Advance Tax Return
S_P00_07000114	Assign Open Items from OI Management
S_P00_07000115	Tax Information (Country)
S_P00_07000116	Tax Information (Country)
S_P00_07000117	Annual Tax Return
S_P00_07000119	Tax Transfer Posting
S_P00_07000134	Generic Withholding Tax Reporting
S_P00_07000136	Transfer Deferred Tax
S_P00_07000152	Customizing
S_P00_07000163	Input Tax from Parked Documents
S_P00_07000217	Printout of Receipts After Payment
S_P00_07000218	Printout of Receipts Before Payment
S_P00_07000219	Change Status of Official Receipts
S_P00_07000220	Vendor Payment History
S_P00_07000221	EC Sales List in DME Format
S_P00_07000233	IMG Activity: SIMG_CFMENUOLSDNF06
S_P00_07000256	IMG Activity: W_WLFA_0005
S_P00_07000285	Vendor Operation
S_P00_07000329	Financial Statements
S_P00_07000330	Apportionment of (Payment) Document
S_P00_99000048	Sales/Sales Revenues/Discount
S_P00_99000049	Target Achievement
S_P00_99000050	Price History
S_P00_99000051	Development of Customer Sales
S_P00_99000052	Analysis of Operating Profit
S_P00_99000053	Analysis of Incoming Orders
S_P00_99000054	Analysis CM II
S_P00_99000128	SAP Standard Variant
S_P0D_25000029	WB2B_EXPENSE
S_P0D_25000043	Assoc. Management: Qty Overview
S_P0D_25000044	Association Management: Association
S_P0D_25000048	List for Add-On Data
S_P0D_25000049	Documents with Errors for Step
S_P0D_25000050	Archive Trading Documents
S_P0D_25000051	Read Trading Documents from Archive
S_P0D_25000052	Archived Trading Documents from DB
S_P0D_25000053	Archived Trading Documents from Arch
S_P0K_92000001	Portfolio List for Responsibility
S_P0K_92000002	Program RWB2PO01
S_P1H_12000001	Determine persons to be financed
S_P1H_12000003	Delete admin. data for cmmt
S_P1H_12000008	Personnel Cost Savings from Vacancy
S_P1H_12000011	Posting to Accounting: Posting
S_P1H_12000027	Maintain Completed Indicator
S_P1H_12000028	Commt Run for All Changed Objects
S_P1H_12000029	Create Cmmt
S_P2H_60000008	IMG Activity: HR_ECM_00_JP_004
S_P2U_59000008	IMG Activity: SIMG_PSMFG_ABP
S_P3H_97000003	IMG Activity: OHFBNPI06
S_P4I_82001735	IMG Activity
S_P6B_12000018	Cash Flow: Hungary
S_P6B_12000019	RFIDUS99C

SAP Transaction Codes – Volume Two

S_P6B_12000021	Maintain SWWs
S_P6B_12000025	Transfer Revaluation Fund (Turkey)
S_P6B_12000028	IN86: Cadastros, Files and Tabelas
S_P6B_12000029	Vendor Line Items (Poland)
S_P6B_12000038	Material Subledger (Poland)
S_P6B_12000089	Comparision Consolidat. Units/Groups
S_P6B_12000092	Goodwill Development
S_P6B_12000103	Stockholders' Equity Development
S_P6B_12000111	Check Balance Carryforward
S_P6B_12000112	Database List of Totals Records
S_P6B_12000113	Database List of Journal Entries
S_P6B_12000115	RFCJ10
S_P6B_12000118	Cash Journal
S_P6B_12000119	Cash Journal: Deleted Documents
S_P6B_12000123	F/S for Special Purpose Ledger
S_P6B_12000124	Actual/Actual Comparison for Year
S_P6B_12000127	Changes in Stockholders' Equity
S_P6B_12000128	Development of Goodwill
S_P6B_12000129	Check Balance Carryforward
S_P6B_12000131	AIS Profit Center Accounting
S_P6B_12000133	List of Vendors: Purchasing
S_P6B_12000135	List of GR/IR Balances
S_P6B_12000136	MM/FI Balance Comparison
S_P6B_12000137	Display Consignment Stocks
S_P6B_12000138	Display Change Documents
S_P6B_12000139	Display Change Documents
S_P6B_12000142	Change Documents for Conditions
S_P6B_12000143	Display Change Documents
S_P6B_12000144	Display Change Documents
S_P6B_12000145	Display Change Documents
S_P6B_12000148	Data Procurement
S_P6B_12000149	AIS Private Folder List of OIs
S_P6B_12000150	AIS Special Purpose Ledger
S_P6B_12000151	AIS, Private Folder (G/L)
S_P6B_12000152	AIS, Private Folder (C)
S_P6B_12000153	AIS, Private Folder (V)
S_P6B_12000154	AIS, Interactive List (G/L)
S_P6B_12000155	AIS, Interactive List (C)
S_P6B_12000156	AIS, Interactive List (V)
S_P6B_12000157	IN86: Foreign Trade File
S_P6B_12000158	IN86: Tabelas (4.9.2-4.9.7)
S_P6B_12000159	IN86: Cadastros (File 4.9.1)
S_P6B_12000160	IN86: Asset Accounting File
S_P6B_12000161	IN86: Bill of Material File
S_P6B_12000162	IN86: Material Inventory File
S_P6B_12000163	IN86: Material Movements File
S_P6B_12000164	IN86: Nota Fiscal Files
S_P6B_12000165	IN86: Vendor/Customer Data File
S_P6B_12000166	IN86: Accounting File
S_P6B_12000167	IN86: Accounting File
S_P6B_12000168	Physical Inventory Overview (Brazil)
S_P6B_12000172	Correction Report MAP + Trsfr Price
S_P6B_12000179	Post Memos for Exch. Rate Diffs
S_P6B_12000182	Comparison

S_P6B_12000186	Export G/L Account Balances
S_P6B_12000301	RFCNGAIS
S_P6B_12000331	IMG Activity: J_1BTAXSITPISV
S_P6D_40000025	Read view query log (extract splitte
S_P6D_40000026	DART: Associated data detector
S_P6D_40000027	DART: Associated data detector
S_P7C_98000279	IMG Activity: ISH_NV200_REN_TABPG
S_P7C_98000301	IMG Activity
S_P7C_98000334	IMG Activity
S_P7C_98000337	IMG Activity
S_P7C_98000338	IMG Activity
S_P7C_98000339	IMG Activity
S_P7C_98000340	IMG Activity
S_P7C_98000363	IMG Activity
S_P7C_98000374	IMG Activity
S_P7D_67000016	Transfer List w. Acct Assgmt Objects
S_P7D_67000036	IMG Activity: Translation Table
S_P7D_67000040	IMG Activity: V_IDT007RA
S_P7D_67000041	Audit
S_P7D_67000042	G/L Account List
S_P7D_67000043	Account Master
S_P7D_67000044	G/L Acct Dir. New Acquisits
S_P7D_67000045	Accounts with Deletion Flag
S_P7D_67000046	Audit Information System (AIS)
S_P7D_67000047	Audit Information System (AIS)
S_P7D_67000048	Audit Information System (AIS)
S_P7D_67000053	IMG Activity: WLF_TMIDTV
S_P7D_67000059	Audit Information System (AIS)
S_P7D_67000090	RFIDITSR12
S_P7D_67000154	IMG Activity
S_P7D_67000163	SAP AIS Tax Audit
S_P7E_63000022	IMG Activity: EHSW_EN_CHECK
S_P7F_76000010	IMG Activity: VV_T100C_IHC_XIXML
S_P7H_77000039	IMG Activity: OHFBNTL10
S_P7H_77000053	IMG Activity: HRAS_XI_ASSGNPROCGRP
S_P7H_77000087	Price Information Rail Connections
S_P7I_08000874	IMG Activity: SIMG_M_TICL085_ASG
S_P7I_60000005	PRA Tax History Archiving
S_P7I_60000021	IMG Activity: OIR_ARC_VAL
S_P7I_60000029	IMG Activity
S_P7I_82001625	IMG Activity: CM_XX_COHORT06
S_P7I_82001632	IMG Activity: CM_XX_2003
S_P7I_82001633	IMG Activity: CM_XX_2004
S_P7R_06000011	IMG Activity: WRF_PRC_SCD_BADI_05
S_P7U_18000004	IMG Activity: SIMG_GM_MM_TO_GM
S_P99_41000009	/1SDBF12L/RV14AK20
S_P99_41000018	Order Selection
S_P99_41000029	Reporting Rental Units
S_P99_41000033	Asset Report Data Retr. (Portugal)
S_P99_41000034	Asset Report Print Prog. (Portugal)
S_P99_41000051	IMG Activity: W_ZF_VK_0301
S_P99_41000062	Materials List: Prices and Inventory
S_P99_41000073	CO Data for Lease-In
S_P99_41000074	Actual Individual Items Lease-ins

S_P99_41000076	Statistical Key Figures
S_P99_41000093	List of VAT Invoices Issued (China)
S_P99_41000094	Monthly Invoice Report (China)
S_P99_41000095	Gen. Report for Ext. Withholding Tax
S_P99_41000096	Withholding Tax Report (Chile)
S_P99_41000097	Stamp Tax Ledger (Chile)
S_P99_41000098	COA Report (Peru)
S_P99_41000099	Payment List
S_P99_41000100	Reporting: LO - Conditions
S_P99_41000101	Check Register
S_P99_41000102	Check Lots
S_P99_41000102_10	Check Number Intervals
S_P99_41000103	Analyze Lease-Out Notices
S_P99_41000111	List of Existing Mat. Cost Estimates
S_P99_41000112	IMG Activity: W_ZF_VK_0312
S_P99_41000113	IMG Activity: SIMG_CFMENUOLSDOVA7
S_P99_41000114	IMG Activity: SIMG_CFMENUOLSDOVAK
S_P99_41000117	PrCtr Actual Data: Transfer to EIS
S_P99_41000118	PrCtr Plan Data: Transfer to EIS
S_P99_41000125	Create Logistics Calendar Agency Bsn
S_P99_41000147	RFFMRE10
S_P99_41000166	Bank directory
S_P99_41000182	Define limit types
S_P99_41000192	SAP Standard Variant
S_P99_41000199	Stamp Tax Ledger (Chile)
S_P99_41000205	Variant Objectives
S_P99_41000212	Formal Validation of Bank Data
S_P99_41000220	Standard Analysis for Info Struc. S2
S_P99_41000221	Merchandise Planning Variants
S_P99_41000225	IMG-Aktivität: POI_PARAMETERS
S_P99_41000247	IMG Activity: SIMG_HUMIDEANSCODE
S_P99_41000248	IMG Activity: SIMG_HUMIDEANETSCODE
S_P99_41000249	IMG Activity: SIMG_HUMIDTVSHP
S_P99_41000250	IMG Activity: SIMG_HUMIDHUEX
S_P99_41000251	IMG Activity: SIMG_HUMIDEANSSCCNOB
S_P99_41000252	IMG Activity: SIMG_HUMIDEANSSCCNWL
S_P99_41000253	IMG Activity: SIMG_HUMGLLFLAF
S_P99_41000254	IMG Activity: SIMG_HUMGLLFTAWE
S_P99_41000255	IMG Activity: SIMG_HUMGLPPPVHUP
S_P99_41000256	IMG Activity: PPPI_PD_510
S_P99_41000257	IMG Activity: PPPI_PD_520
S_P99_41000258	IMG Activity: PPPI_PD_530
S_P99_41000259	IMG Activity: HUMGLQM-TQHU1
S_P99_41000260	IMG Activity: SIMG_HUMIDEANSSCCNL
S_P99_41000261	IMG Activity: SIMG_HUMIDEANETPRO
S_P99_41000262	IMG Activity: SIMG_HUMIDTVTYNR
S_P99_41000263	IMG Activity: SIMG_CMMENUOSD6OPIN
S_P99_41000264	IMG Activity: SIMG_CFMENUOPI0OVHU0
S_P99_41000265	IMG Activity: SIMG_CFMENUOPI0OFP8
S_P99_41000266	IMG Activity: SIMG_CFMENUOPI0OFP2
S_P99_41000267	IMG Activity: SIMG_CFMENUOPI0OFP3
S_P99_41000268	IMG Activity: SIMG_CFMENUOPI0OFP4
S_P99_41000269	IMG Activity: SIMG_HUMGLTHUBEW2
S_P99_41000270	IMG Activity: SIMG_HUMGLTHUBEW3

S_P99_41000271	IMG Activity: SIMG_MMIM_V_156Q_VC
S_P99_41000272	IMG Activity: SIMG_MMIM_MB_DELIV
S_P99_41000273	IMG Activity: SIMG_XXMENUOLMLHU03
S_P99_41000274	IMG Activity: SIMG_XXMENUOLMLHU04
S_P99_41000275	IMG Activity: SIMG_HUMGLTECHIND
S_P99_41000277	IMG Activity: SIMG_XXMENUOLMLHU02
S_P99_41000278	IMG Activity: SIMG_XXMENUOLMLHU01
S_P99_41000281	Tenant Account Sheet: Screen List
S_P99_41000290	Rental Unit Use in Settlement
S_P99_41000294	Structured Account Balances
S_P99_41000301	Cost of Sales Statement
S_P99_41000303	Structured Account Balances
S_P99_41000307	Expense Account Balances
S_P99_41000308	G/L Account Balances
S_P99_41000311	IMG-Activity: SIMG_CFMENUOLSDFP4
S_P99_41000355	IMG Activity: SIMG_CFMENUOLSDOVK6
S_P99_41000375	IMG Activity: SIMG_CFMENUOFTC_OFDH
S_P99_41000404	Flow Types for Valuation
S_P9C_18000015	IMG Activity: SIMG_CFMENUOPI0OVHU3
S_P9C_18000044	Annual Sales Ret. to Tax Office (PT)
S_P9C_18000054	IMG Activity: EURO_FIFM_VOR_REV
S_P9C_18000152	Audit
S_P9C_18000153	Audit
S_P9C_18000154	Count Document Headers
S_PAD_19000003	Program RPCALCSTART00
S_PAD_19000004	Report for the payroll part of the m
S_PAD_19000006	Simulation
S_PAD_19000007	Payroll driver (UN)
S_PAD_19000008	Remuneration Statements
S_PAD_19000009	Posting to Accounting: Search for pa
S_PAD_19000011	H99_DISPLAY_PAYRESULT
S_PCO_36000218	Receivables: Segment
S_PCO_36000219	Payables: Segment
S_PCO_36000293	Person income tax (1-NDFL and 2-NDFL
S_PCO_36000354	Report of Sick people to the Swedish
S_PCO_36000374	IMG Activity: BBPC_RFC_DEST
S_PCO_36000456	IMG Activity: SIMG_CFMENUOLSDECT
S_PCO_36000457	IMG Activity: SIMG_CFMENUOLSDOVBC
S_PEN_05000095	Overview of Rail Connections by Loc.
S_PEN_05000096	Other Services by Type
S_PEN_05000138	IMG Activity: _ISPSFM_VV_FMISPS_3
S_PEN_05000310	IMG Activity: TDLOS_INS_BP
S_PH0_48000009	AL0K028900
S_PH0_48000029	IMG Activity
S_PH0_48000030	IMG Activity
S_PH0_48000032	IMG
S_PH0_48000040	AL0K028900
S_PH0_48000067	Standard Text Names
S_PH0_48000080	IMG activity: OHAWDL024
S_PH0_48000081	AL0K028900
S_PH0_48000082	AL0K028900
S_PH0_48000084	Pos. Generation for Quota Planning
S_PH0_48000085	Freezing the Planned Quota
S_PH0_48000086	Copying Current Required Positions

S_PH0_48000087	Copy Quota Plng into Anoth. PlngType
S_PH0_48000088	Delete Unoccupied Pos. on Key Date
S_PH0_48000096	Instructor Information
S_PH0_48000097	Instructor Information
S_PH0_48000098	Attendees (Organizational Units)
S_PH0_48000105	Delete Applicant Data
S_PH0_48000106	Complete Deletion of Pers. Numbers
S_PH0_48000107	Compare Fields Using Org. Assignment
S_PH0_48000108	Generate Features
S_PH0_48000109	User Master Data Reconciliation
S_PH0_48000110	Regeneration INDX for Struct.Auth.
S_PH0_48000111	Compare INDX and T77UU
S_PH0_48000112	Check and Compare T77UU
S_PH0_48000113	Installation Check
S_PH0_48000114	Check Database Consistency
S_PH0_48000115	Display/Settings Relationships with
S_PH0_48000116	Consistency Check PD-Database Table
S_PH0_48000117	Deleting Relatshps w/o existing Objs
S_PH0_48000118	Disp./Reconstr. Missg Oper.Proc.Recs
S_PH0_48000119	Display/Create Missing Inv.Relatshps
S_PH0_48000120	Personnel Planning Database Stats.
S_PH0_48000121	DB Statistics: No. Objects in PLOGI
S_PH0_48000122	DB Statistics: Notes Usage
S_PH0_48000123	DB Statistics: Usage of an Infotype
S_PH0_48000124	DB Statistics:Usage of all Infotypes
S_PH0_48000125	Transfer org. assignment (PA>PD)
S_PH0_48000126	Prepare Integration (PD with PA)
S_PH0_48000127	Org. Assgmt in Batch Input Session
S_PH0_48000128	Consistence Ck for OM-PA Integration
S_PH0_48000129	Transport of Pers. Planning Records
S_PH0_48000130	Manual Transport Link
S_PH0_48000131	Sequential PD Dataset
S_PH0_48000132	Transporting Objects via Obj. Lock
S_PH0_48000133	Further Transport of Planning Objs
S_PH0_48000134	Replace Persons in PD Data Records
S_PH0_48000135	Replace User in Holder Relationship
S_PH0_48000136	Merge Infotype Records
S_PH0_48000137	Display Personnel Planning Database
S_PH0_48000138	Table Fields from Data Dictionary
S_PH0_48000139	Display/Maintain PLOGI Object Index
S_PH0_48000140	Data Records from Personnel Planning
S_PH0_48000141	Delete Personnel Planning records
S_PH0_48000142	Check Infotypes in T777D/T77ID
S_PH0_48000143	Relate Objects
S_PH0_48000144	Related or Unrelated Objects
S_PH0_48000145	Create Multiple Object Copies
S_PH0_48000146	Activate Non-Activated Task
S_PH0_48000147	Program RHCTIMCO
S_PH0_48000148	Object Description: Main Program
S_PH0_48000149	RHDELIMOBS
S_PH0_48000150	Status Overview per Object Type
S_PH0_48000151	Maintain log
S_PH0_48000194	SAPLS_CUS_IMG_ACTIVITY
S_PH0_48000195	SAPLS_CUS_IMG_ACTIVITY

S_PH0_48000196	SAPLS_CUS_IMG_ACTIVITY
S_PH0_48000213	AL0K028900
S_PH0_48000214	Mass Planning
S_PH0_48000229	IMG Activity
S_PH0_48000309	Inbound Processing of IDocs Ready fo
S_PH0_48000327	Import Per Diems/Flat Rates
S_PH0_48000343	S_PH0_48000343
S_PH0_48000347	Export
S_PH0_48000348	RPCEMDX0_CALL
S_PH0_48000349	RPCEMDX0_COMBINED_CALL
S_PH0_48000350	RPCEPYX0_COMBINED_CALL
S_PH0_48000351	Payroll driver (international)
S_PH0_48000352	S_PH0_48000352
S_PH0_48000354	S_PH0_48000354
S_PH0_48000355	S_PH0_48000355
S_PH0_48000356	S_PH0_48000356
S_PH0_48000357	S_PH0_48000357
S_PH0_48000359	S_PH0_48000359
S_PH0_48000360	S_PH0_48000360
S_PH0_48000361	S_PH0_48000361
S_PH0_48000362	S_PH0_48000362
S_PH0_48000363	S_PH0_48000363
S_PH0_48000364	S_PH0_48000364
S_PH0_48000368	InfoSet Query: Compensation
S_PH0_48000369	AL0K028900
S_PH0_48000370	AL0K028900
S_PH0_48000371	AL0K028900
S_PH0_48000372	InfoSet Query: Personnel Development
S_PH0_48000373	AL0K028900
S_PH0_48000374	AL0K028900
S_PH0_48000375	AL0K028900
S_PH0_48000380	Transfer Remaining Leave from IT0005
S_PH0_48000381	Generate Absence Quotas
S_PH0_48000383	AL0K028900
S_PH0_48000384	AL0K028900
S_PH0_48000385	AL0K028900
S_PH0_48000407	IMG Activity
S_PH0_48000411	InfoSet Query: Administration
S_PH0_48000412	Links for Travel Manager
S_PH0_48000416	InfoSet Query: Administration
S_PH0_48000427	Constr. Ind.: Trainee Remuneration
S_PH0_48000433	InfoSet Query: Recruitment
S_PH0_48000441	IMG Activity
S_PH0_48000447	InfoSet Query: Administration
S_PH0_48000450	Date Monitoring
S_PH0_48000452	InfoSet Query: Recruitment
S_PH0_48000453	InfoSet Query: Administration
S_PH0_48000465	InfoSet Query: Administration
S_PH0_48000467	AL0K028900
S_PH0_48000468	SAPLS_CUS_IMG_ACTIVITY
S_PH0_48000469	SAPLS_CUS_IMG_ACTIVITY
S_PH0_48000471	AL0K028900
S_PH0_48000476	Business Event Information
S_PH0_48000525	InfoSet Query: Benefits

SAP Transaction Codes – Volume Two

S_PH0_48000527	AL0K028900
S_PH0_48000530	AL0K028900
S_PH0_48000535	Ad Hoc Query
S_PH0_48000542	Mini Master Export
S_PH0_48000543	Combined Payroll Export
S_PH0_48000544	Combined Payroll Export
S_PH0_48000545	Mini Master Export
S_PH9_13000019	Execution of off-cycle payroll run
S_PH9_13000020	Recalculation annual interest by e
S_PH9_13000021	Issue of Leave Notice
S_PH9_46000016	Qualifications Overview
S_PH9_46000017	Succession Overview
S_PH9_46000018	Objects with Unrated Qualifications
S_PH9_46000019	Objects w/o Qualis or Requirements
S_PH9_46000022	List of Alternative Qualifications
S_PH9_46000024	AL0K028900
S_PH9_46000025	AL0K028900
S_PH9_46000062	AL0K028900
S_PH9_46000064	AL0K028900
S_PH9_46000117	Wage Ledger (Japan)
S_PH9_46000118	Creation of payment order for benefi
S_PH9_46000122	History of Personnel Appraisals
S_PH9_46000123	Employee Action List
S_PH9_46000124	Personnel Record (Japan)
S_PH9_46000125	HR-J :Retire List
S_PH9_46000128	Leagal application form list for Emp
S_PH9_46000156	Bankverbindungen
S_PH9_46000172	Wage Type Reporter
S_PH9_46000205	Transfer Program for RPLRZBD0 and RP
S_PH9_46000206	Process Data Medium Records INL for
S_PH9_46000208	Default List for Advancement of Case
S_PH9_46000209	Non-Rec. Payt for Std Pay Increase
S_PH9_46000210	Display Directory for Deferrals
S_PH9_46000216	Service Anniversaries
S_PH9_46000217	Statistic: Gender by Service Age
S_PH9_46000218	Statistics: Gender Sorted By Age
S_PH9_46000219	Headcount Changes
S_PH9_46000220	Vehicle Search List
S_PH9_46000221	Birthday List
S_PH9_46000222	Family Members
S_PH9_46000223	EEs Who Entered And/Or Left Company
S_PH9_46000224	Education and Training
S_PH9_46000225	Powers of Attorney
S_PH9_46000227	Hay PayNet: Data Extraction
S_PH9_46000228	Data Extraction for Salary Survey
S_PH9_46000232	Tip income and allocated tips report
S_PH9_46000233	Pensionable Earnings and Hours Repor
S_PH9_46000255	Flight Availability Settings
S_PH9_46000330	file format for food vouchers
S_PH9_46000349	AL0K028900
S_PH9_46000354	Employer's return of remuneration an
S_PH9_46000355	Notification by an ER of an EE who c
S_PH9_46000356	Notification by an ER of an EE who i
S_PH9_46000357	Notification by an ER of an EE who i

S_PH9_46000358	Payroll results check tool
S_PH9_46000360	Exemption Expiration Report
S_PH9_46000361	W-4 Withholding Allowance Report
S_PH9_46000409	AL0K028900
S_PH9_46000410	AL0K028900
S_PH9_46000411	AL0K028900
S_PH9_46000412	AL0K028900
S_PH9_46000423	Budget Comparison
S_PH9_46000424	Cancellations per Business Event
S_PH9_46000425	Attendance and Sales Statistics
S_PH9_46000426	Attendees for Rebooking
S_PH9_46000427	Prebookings per Business Event Type
S_PH9_46000428	Prerequisites Matchup
S_PH9_46000429	Attendee's Qualifications
S_PH9_46000430	Attendance Prerequisites
S_PH9_46000431	Attendee's Training History
S_PH9_46000432	Employee List
S_PH9_46000433	Attendance List
S_PH9_46000434	Attendee List
S_PH9_46000435	Material Requirements per Event
S_PH9_46000436	Unassigned Resources per Event
S_PH9_46000437	Resource List per Event
S_PH9_46000438	Business Event Schedule
S_PH9_46000439	Unassigned Resources per Res. Type
S_PH9_46000440	Resource Reservation Statistics
S_PH9_46000441	Graphical Resource Reservation
S_PH9_46000451	Business Event Appraisals
S_PH9_46000452	Attendee Appraisals
S_PH9_46000520	Travel Expenses Clerk
S_PH9_46000529	IMG
S_PH9_46000588	Time Evaluation Messages Display
S_PH9_46000618	AL0K028900
S_PH9_46000826	Financing Overview
S_PH9_46000827	Overfinancing/Underfinancing
S_PH9_46000828	Overfinancing/Underfinancing
S_PH9_46000837	Display Carryforward Logs
S_PH9_46000838	Carry/Fwd Log by Responsibility
S_PH9_46000839	Display Carryforward Logs
S_PH9_46000840	Carry/Fwd Log by Responsibility
S_PH9_46000851	Check Carry Forward
S_PH9_46000852	Work List Log by Responsibility
S_PH9_46000859	Financing from BS Element Budgets
S_PH9_46000860	Available Budget Per BS Element
S_PH9_46000867	Different Service Type/Service Cat.
S_PH9_46000918	Financing Overview
S_PH9_46001026	IMG Activity: OHACHPBSAM1
S_PH9_46001027	IMG Activity: OHACHPBSOZ8
S_PH9_46001028	IMG Activity: OHACHPBSOZ5
S_PH9_46001029	IMG Activity: OHACHPBSOZ4
S_PH9_46001030	IMG Activity: OHACHPBSOZ3
S_PH9_46001031	IMG Activity: OHACHPBSOZ7
S_PH9_46001032	IMG Activity: OHACHPBSOZ1
S_PH9_46001124	Specify TMW Profile
S_PI6_40000223	Check occupational categories

S_PI6_40000224	Map Job Keys to Occup. Categories
S_PL0_09000018	IMG Activity: OHIGBPBSDRLDWN02
S_PL0_09000028	IMG Activity: OHIGBPBSBAR01
S_PL0_09000029	IMG Activity: OHIGBPBSBAR02
S_PL0_09000120	IMG Activity: OHIGBPBSDRLDWN03
S_PL0_09000127	Print Program: Spanish Invoice
S_PL0_09000158	Annual Operations Report (Spain)
S_PL0_09000159	RFUSVX11
S_PL0_09000175	IMG Activity: OHPSUSSBP002
S_PL0_09000240	NC-9901 Report: Generate Importable
S_PL0_09000241	IMG Activity: OHA_CN_BADI00
S_PL0_09000314	RFW1099M
S_PL0_09000315	Belgian Withholding Tax Report
S_PL0_09000347	IMG Activity: OCHA_BIC_ACT
S_PL0_09000349	IMG Activity: OCHA_BIC_SEL_ENH
S_PL0_09000350	IMG Activity: OCHA_BIC_SEL_ENHUSER
S_PL0_09000353	IMG Activity: OCHA_BIC_ACT_USER
S_PL0_09000447	Withholding Tax Report for Vendor
S_PL0_09000465	IMG Activity: OHPSUSNOA006
S_PL0_09000467	DME Engine: Convert Incoming File
S_PL0_09000485	IMG Activity: OHPSUSRIF001
S_PL0_86000007	IN359 - Magnetic File
S_PL0_86000027	RFUVXX00
S_PL0_86000028	Fin. Statements: Act/Act Comparison
S_PL0_86000029	Fin. Statement: Plan/Act. Comparison
S_PL0_86000030	G/L Account - Balances
S_PL0_86000031	Transaction Figures: Account Balance
S_PL0_86000032	SAP Structured Balance List
S_PL7_36000034	IMG Activity: TPM52
S_PL7_36000038	IMG Activity: CFM_MC_HM
S_PL9_08000041	Export Settings
S_PL9_08000042	Export Relevance
S_PL9_08000043	Change Relevance
S_PL9_08000044	Start Export
S_PL9_08000045	Overview of Change Pointers
S_PL9_08000046	Export Relevance:Customizing: Header
S_PLC_83000129	IMG Activity: CRM_BSP_DEB_CONCEPT
S_PLC_83000130	IMG Activity: CRM_BSP_DEB_CONCEPT
S_PLC_83000131	IMG Activity: CRM_BSP_DEB_CONCEPT
S_PLC_83000132	IMG Activity: CRM_BSP_DEB_CONCEPT
S_PLC_83000133	IMG Activity: CRM_BSP_DEB_GUIDELIN
S_PLC_83000134	IMG Activity: CRM_BSP_DEB_FAQ
S_PLN_06000113	Reconcile Accrual Engine w/ Finance
S_PLN_06000349	Inflow / Outflow List in Pos. Crcy
S_PLN_06000350	Inflow / Outflow List in Local Crcy
S_PLN_06000351	CMS-Batch Collateral coverage gap mo
S_PLN_06000352	Collateral coverage gap display
S_PLN_06000353	Deletion of coverage gap results
S_PLN_06000427	Account Clearing per Individual Item
S_PLN_06000428	Evaluation Provision Expiry Date
S_PLN_16000010	IMG Activity: _ISPSFM_N_DISTR_KEY
S_PLN_16000038	IMG Activity: COOPC110
S_PLN_16000039	IMG Activity: COOPC120
S_PLN_16000052	Document Journal

S_PLN_16000226	Determination of requirements
S_PLN_16000227	Query: Loan Position - Assets
S_PLN_16000228	Query: Loan Position - Liabilities
S_PLN_16000230	Query: Borrower's Note Loan Position
S_PLN_16000231	Query: NPV Borrower's Note Loan
S_PLN_16000232	Query:Commitment in Display Currency
S_PLN_16000233	Query: Commitment in Position Crcy
S_PLN_16000235	Query: Balanace List in Display Crcy
S_PLN_16000236	Query: Balance List in Position Crcy
S_PLN_16000237	Query: Revenue Analysis Loans
S_PLN_16000256	Reconstruction of commitment docs
S_PLN_16000269	Grants Management: Line Item Display
S_PLN_16000292	Revenue Forecast
S_PLN_16000293	Total commitment
S_PLN_16000303	IMG Activity: TIM_00_CE_030
S_PLN_16000376	IMG Activity: PAY_00_GP_004
S_PLN_16000398	Inflow/Outflow List
S_PLN_16000399	Sec. Info.: Display Sec. Acct Pos.
S_PLN_16000426	Customizing Activity
S_PLN_62000168	Deletion of Change History
S_PLN_62000182	Retrieve Auto-ID Information
S_PLN_62000224	Badi: Funct.Location from RE Object
S_PLN_62000386	S_PLN_62000386
S_PLN_62000387	S_PLN_62000387
S_PLN_62000388	S_PLN_62000388
S_PLN_62000389	S_PLN_62000389
S_PLN_62000390	S_PLN_62000390
S_PLN_62000391	S_PLN_62000391
S_PLN_62000392	IMG-Aktivität: HR_PAY_JP_FO_001
S_PLN_62000393	IMG-Aktivität: HR_PAY_JP_FO_004
S_PLN_62000394	IMG-Aktivität: HR_PAY_JP_FO_008
S_PLN_62000395	IMG-Aktivität: HR_PAY_JP_FO_007
S_PLN_62000396	IMG-Aktivität: HR_PAY_JP_FO_002
S_PLN_62000397	IMG-Aktivität: HR_PAY_JP_FO_003
S_PLN_62000398	IMG Activity: HR_PAY_CA_FO_001
S_PLN_62000402	IMG Activity: HR_PAY_CA_FO_004
S_PLN_62000403	IMG Activity: HR_PAY_CA_FO_008
S_PLN_62000404	IMG Activity: HR_PAY_CA_FO_007
S_PLN_62000405	IMG Activity: HR_PAY_CA_FO_002
S_PLN_62000406	IMG Activity: HR_PAY_CA_FO_003
S_PLN_62000476	IMG Activity: SIMG_CFMENUFBICRC010
S_PLN_62000622	Reasons for Escrow Account
S_PLN_62000646	IMG: Billing Parameters
S_PNI_82001579	IMG Activity: CM_XX_EXAM17
S_PNI_87000008	Upload lease tax and volume data
S_PNI_96000001	IS-H: Evaluation Report for Assigned
S_PR0_40000	Form T-60
S_PR0_40000026	Status of Payments for Cross-Payment
S_PR0_40000038	Program RCPE_MM_IMG
S_PR0_40000149	Form 4-FSS
S_PR0_40000150	Form T-60
S_PR0_40000151	Form T-61
S_PR0_40000152	Sickness Certificates Register
S_PTH_77000045	Fare Information f. Rail Connections

S_R99_53000009	Tenant Account Sheet: Screen List
S_RFIDPTAAV	Pro-Rata Asset Acquisition Value
S_RFIDPTDCAD	Pro-Rata DPR adjustment documents
S_RFIDPTDPR	Definitive Pro-Rata coefficient
S_RFIDPTPCAD	Pro-Rata periodic PPR documents
S_RFIDPTPOSTAG	Pro-Rata posting aggregation key
S_RFID_PTVPRADPRC00	Pro-Rata adjustments - Calculation
S_RFID_PTVPRADPRV00	Pro-Rata adjustments - Variation
S_S6D_98000009	IMG Activity: COM_PRD_ID_HANDLING
S_S7B_68000047	IMG Activity: COM_PROD_DX_JOB
S_S7B_68000056	IMG Activity: SIMG_GKFM_KF_SOURCE
S_S7B_68000059	IMG Activity: SIMG_BRF_BADIEXPRESS
S_SE3_50000099	Deletion of Batch Input Sessions
S_SE3_50000100	Creation of Batch Input Sessions
S_SE3_50000101	Sending Cost Events
S_SE3_50000102	Deletion of Processed Cost Events
S_SE3_50000103	Display Cost Events
S_SE3_50000104	Transfer Cost Event Files
S_SE3_50000266	Master Data List
S_SE3_50000279	Reorganization of Worklists
S_SE3_62000043	Shows Changes to Watchdog Setting
S_SE4_70000002	Administration: Selective Deletion
S_SE5_71000002	IMG Activity
S_SH1_20000001	IMG Activity: CBRC_SDCONDTAB
S_SH1_20000002	IMG Activity: CBRC_ERRORMAIL
S_SH1_20000003	IMG Activity: CBRC_USEREXITS
S_SH1_20000004	IMG Activity: CBRC_LIMITS
S_SH1_20000006	IMG Activity: CBRC_TRACK_SCENARIOS
S_SH1_20000007	IMG Activity: CBRC_CHECK_PREREQUIS
S_SH1_20000008	IMG Activity: CBRC_SELECT_CRITERIA
S_SH1_20000009	IMG Activity: CBRC_PERIODS
S_SH1_20000010	IMG Activity: CBRC_ERR_MESSAGES
S_SH1_20000011	IMG Activity: CBRC_MONITORING
S_SH1_20000012	IMG Activity: CBRC_JOB_VOL_TRACKNG
S_SH1_20000013	IMG Activity: CBRC_ONLINE_CHECKS
S_SH1_20000014	IMG Activity: CBRC_DATA_TRANSFER
S_SH8_22000003	IMG Activity: EHS_DDS_100_10_11
S_SH8_22000310	IMG Activity: WA_EA_SV_002
S_SH8_22000311	IMG Activity: WA_EA_SV_004
S_SH8_22000312	IMG Activity: WA_EA_INT_MM_002
S_SH8_22000313	IMG Activity: WA_EA_INT_PROC_002
S_SH8_22000314	IMG Activity: WA_EA_INT_CO_001
S_SH8_22000315	IMG Activity: WA_MD_009
S_SH8_22000316	IMG Activity: WA_EA_BS_003
S_SH8_22000317	IMG Activity: WA_EA_BS_004
S_SH8_22000318	IMG Activity: WA_EA_BS_001
S_SH8_22000319	IMG Activity: WA_EA_BS_002
S_SH8_22000320	IMG Activity: WA_EA_INT_CO_002
S_SH8_22000321	IMG Activity: WA_MN_MD_003
S_SH8_22000322	IMG Activity: WA_MN_MD_006
S_SH8_22000323	IMG Activity: WA_MN_SV_002
S_SH8_22000324	IMG Activity: WA_REPORTS_001
S_SH8_22000325	IMG Activity: WA_MD_AUTH_001
S_SH8_22000326	IMG Activity: CORA_22

S_SH8_22000327	IMG Activity: IHS_RA_002
S_SH8_22000328	IMG Activity: WA_MN_MD_000
S_SH8_22000329	IMG Activity: IHS_WA_010_02
S_SH8_22000330	IMG Activity: WA_MN_MD_001
S_SH8_22000331	IMG Activity: IHS_WA_010_01
S_SH8_22000332	IMG Activity: WA_MN_MD_004
S_SH8_22000333	IMG Activity: IHS_WA_05_04
S_SH8_22000334	IMG Activity: WA_MN_MD_005
S_SH8_22000335	IMG Activity: IHS_WAR_010_01
S_SH8_22000336	IMG Activity: IHS_WA_05_01
S_SH8_22000337	IMG Activity: WA_MN_MD_002
S_SH8_22000338	IMG Activity: IHS_AGT_010
S_SH8_22000339	IMG Activity: IHS_MD_100_04
S_SH8_22000340	IMG Activity: WA_MD_008A
S_SH8_22000341	IMG Activity: IHS_RA_008
S_SH8_22000342	IMG Activity: IHS_RA_005
S_SH8_22000343	IMG Activity: IHS_AC_005
S_SH8_22000344	IMG Activity: WA_MD_004A_02
S_SH8_22000345	IMG Activity: IHS_AC_010_07
S_SH8_22000346	IMG Activity: IHS_CORA_003
S_SH8_22000347	IMG Activity: WA_MD_004A_03
S_SH8_22000348	IMG Activity: AGT_34
S_SH8_22000349	IMG Activity: IHS_ACT_010_05
S_SH8_22000350	IMG Activity: WA_MD_004
S_SH8_22000351	IMG Activity: IHS_MD_100_02
S_SH8_22000352	IMG Activity: IHS_NEU_010
S_SH8_22000353	IMG Activity: IHS_MD_05
S_SH8_22000354	IMG Activity: WA_MD_003
S_SH8_22000355	IMG Activity: IHS_MD_00
S_SH8_22000356	IMG Activity: IHS_ACT_010_10
S_SH8_22000357	IMG Activity: WA_MD_004A_01
S_SH8_22000358	IMG Activity: IHS_IS_01
S_SH8_22000359	IMG Activity: IHS_MD_011_01
S_SH8_22000360	IMG Activity: WA_MD_005
S_SH8_22000361	IMG Activity: IHS_ACT_010_20
S_SH8_22000362	IMG Activity: IHS_ACT_010_30
S_SH8_22000363	IMG Activity: WA_MD_004B
S_SH8_22000364	IMG Activity: IHS_ACT_010_04
S_SH8_22000365	IMG Activity: IHS_ACT_010_33
S_SH8_22000366	IMG Activity: IHS_MD_100_05
S_SH8_22000367	IMG Activity: WA_MD_008
S_SH8_22000368	IMG Activity: IHS_MD_100_11
S_SH8_22000369	IMG Activity: IHS_MD_INFO
S_SH8_22000370	IMG Activity: WA_BS_004
S_SH8_22000371	IMG Activity: IHS_PS_000
S_SH8_22000372	IMG Activity: IHS_RA_004
S_SH8_22000373	IMG Activity: IHS_ACT_010_01
S_SH8_22000374	IMG Activity: IHS_QUEST_000
S_SH8_22000375	IMG Activity: IHS_PM_000
S_SH8_22000376	IMG Activity: WA_MD_007
S_SH8_22000377	IMG Activity: IHS_TM_000
S_SH8_22000378	IMG Activity: IHS_OM_000
S_SH8_22000379	IMG Activity: WA_MD_006
S_SH8_22000380	IMG Activity: WA_MD_004C

S_SH8_22000381	IMG Activity: WA_MD_003A
S_SH8_22000382	IMG Activity: WA_MD_001
S_SH8_22000383	IMG Activity: WA_EA_INT_MM_001
S_SH8_22000384	IMG Activity: WA_EA_INT_WM_001
S_SH8_22000385	IMG Activity: WA_EA_INT_PROC_001
S_SH8_22000386	IMG Activity: WA_MD_002
S_SH8_22000387	IMG Activity: WA_BS_002
S_SH8_22000804	IMG Activity: AGT_34
S_SH8_22000805	IMG Activity: IHS_AC_010_07
S_SH8_22000806	IMG Activity: IHS_RA_005
S_SH8_22000807	IMG Activity: IHS_RA_008
S_SH8_22000808	IMG Activity: IHS_AC_005
S_SH8_22000809	IMG Activity: IHS_AGT_010
S_SH8_22000810	IMG Activity: IHS_WA_05_04
S_SH8_22000811	IMG Activity: IHS_WA_010_01
S_SH8_22000812	IMG Activity: IHS_WA_010_02
S_SH8_22000813	IMG Activity: IHS_RA_002
S_SH8_22000814	IMG Activity: IHS_WAM_002
S_SH8_22000815	IMG Activity: IHS_ACT_010_04
S_SH8_22000816	IMG Activity: IHS_ACT_010_33
S_SH8_22000817	IMG Activity: IHS_ACT_010_10
S_SH8_22000818	IMG Activity: IHS_IS_01
S_SH8_22000819	IMG Activity: IHS_MD_011_01
S_SH8_22000820	IMG Activity: IHS_ACT_010_30
S_SH8_22000821	IMG Activity: IHS_CORA_004
S_SH8_22000822	IMG Activity: IHS_CORA_003
S_SH8_22000823	IMG Activity: SIMGCORA_22
S_SH8_22000824	IMG Activity: IHS_ACT_010_05
S_SH8_22000825	IMG Activity: IHS_ACT_010_20
S_SH8_22000826	IMG Activity: IHS_MD_100_05
S_SH8_22000827	IMG Activity: IHS_MD_100_11
S_SH8_22000828	IMG Activity: IHS_MD_100_02
S_SH8_22000829	IMG Activity: IHS_MD_100_23
S_SH8_22000830	IMG Activity: IHS_NEU_010
S_SH8_22000831	IMG Activity: IHS_MD_05
S_SH8_22000832	IMG Activity: IHS_MD_00
S_SH8_22000833	IMG Activity: IHS_MD_06
S_SH8_22000834	IMG Activity: IHS_WA_05_01
S_SH8_22000835	IMG Activity: IHS_WAM_001
S_SH8_22000836	IMG Activity: IHS_WAR_010_01
S_SH8_22000837	IMG Activity: IHS_PS_000
S_SH8_22000838	IMG Activity: IHS_RA_004
S_SH8_22000839	IMG Activity: IHS_OM_000
S_SH8_22000840	IMG Activity: IHS_QUEST_000
S_SH8_22000841	IMG Activity: IHS_ACT_010_01
S_SH8_22000842	IMG Activity: IHS_PM_000
S_SH8_22000843	IMG Activity: IHS_TM_000
S_SH8_22000844	IMG Activity: IHS_MD_INFO
S_SH8_72000001	Protocols > Exposure Groups
S_SH8_72000002	Persons > Assigned Protocols
S_SH8_72000004	Exposure Group > Persons
S_SH8_72000010	Persons > Examination Dates
S_SH8_72000011	Persons > Tasks
S_SH8_72000013	Persons > Protocols

S_SH8_72000014	Persons > Exposure Groups
S_SH8_72000015	Persons > Diagnoses
S_SH8_72000017	Persons > Objects
S_SH8_72000018	Persons > Tests > Physical Tests
S_SH8_72000020	Persons > Tests > Pulmonary Tests
S_SH8_72000021	Persons > Tests > Audiograms
S_SH8_72000023	Statistics on Protocols
S_SH8_72000024	Waste Approval Call-Off
S_SH8_72000025	Waste life-cycle analysis
S_SH8_72000026	Disposal Documents List Display
S_SH8_72000027	Disposal Documents List Display
S_SH8_72000028	Disposal Documents List Display
S_SH8_72000029	Check If Time and Quantity Exceeded
S_SH8_72000032	Partners in Entry Documents
S_SH8_72000033	Evaluation of Completed Questionn.
S_SH8_72000275	IMG Activity: OHSXX_40_01_01
S_SH8_72000276	IMG Activity: OHSXX_40_01_06
S_SH8_72000277	IMG Activity: HEA_SRV_001_08
S_SH8_72000278	IMG Activity: OHSXX_SHED_01
S_SH8_72000279	IMG Activity: OHSXX_SHED_02
S_SH8_72000280	IMG Activity: HEA_SRV_001_06
S_SH8_72000281	IMG Activity: HEA_SRV_001_07
S_SH8_72000282	IMG Activity: OHSXX_40_02_01
S_SH8_72000283	IMG Activity: OHSXX_40_02_02
S_SH8_72000284	IMG Activity: HEA_SRV_007_01
S_SH8_72000285	IMG Activity: OHSXX_40_04_04
S_SH8_72000286	IMG Activity: OHSXX_40_03_01
S_SH8_72000287	IMG Activity: OHSXX_40_01_05
S_SH8_72000288	IMG Activity: OHSXX_40_01_02
S_SH8_72000289	IMG Activity: HEA_SRV_001_02
S_SH8_72000290	IMG Activity: HEA_SRV_002_03
S_SH8_72000291	IMG Activity: HEA_SRV_002_04
S_SH8_72000292	IMG Activity: HEA_SRV_004_01
S_SH8_72000293	IMG Activity: HEA_SRV_003_03
S_SH8_72000294	IMG Activity: HEA_SRV_003_04
S_SH8_72000295	IMG Activity: HEA_SRV_003_05
S_SH8_72000296	IMG Activity: HEA_SRV_003_06
S_SH8_72000297	IMG Activity: HEA_SRV_001_03
S_SH8_72000298	IMG Activity: HEA_SRV_001_04
S_SH8_72000299	IMG Activity: HEA_SRV_001_05
S_SH8_72000300	IMG Activity: HEA_SRV_001_10
S_SH8_72000301	IMG Activity: HEA_SRV_001_11
S_SH8_72000302	IMG Activity: HEA_SRV_002_01
S_SH8_72000303	IMG Activity: HEA_SRV_002_02
S_SH8_72000304	IMG Activity: OHSXX_40_01_03
S_SH8_72000305	IMG Activity: OHSXX_055
S_SH8_72000306	IMG Activity: OHSXX_065
S_SH8_72000307	IMG Activity: HEA_FAL_010_04
S_SH8_72000308	IMG Activity: HEA_FAL_010_06
S_SH8_72000309	IMG Activity: HEA_FAL_010_05
S_SH8_72000310	IMG Activity: OHSXX_135
S_SH8_72000311	IMG Activity: OHSXX_136
S_SH8_72000312	IMG Activity: OHSXX_137
S_SH8_72000313	IMG Activity: HEA_FAL_010_03

S_SH8_72000314	IMG Activity: HEA_FAL_010_02
S_SH8_72000315	IMG Activity: HEA_MD_300_01
S_SH8_72000316	IMG Activity: OHSXX_40_01_04
S_SH8_72000317	IMG Activity: HEA_MD_400_01
S_SH8_72000318	IMG Activity: HEA_FAL_010_01
S_SH8_72000319	IMG Activity: HEA_FAL_010_16
S_SH8_72000320	IMG Activity: OHSXX_080
S_SH8_72000321	IMG Activity: HEA_FAL_010_09
S_SH8_72000322	IMG Activity: HEA_BAS_001_02
S_SH8_72000323	IMG Activity: HEA_BAS_001_03
S_SH8_72000324	IMG Activity: HEA_BAS_001_05
S_SH8_72000325	IMG Activity: HEA_BAS_001_04
S_SH8_72000326	IMG Activity: HEA_FAL_010_15
S_SH8_72000327	IMG Activity: OHSXX_40_01_08
S_SH8_72000328	IMG Activity: OHSXX_020
S_SH8_72000329	IMG Activity: OHSXX_245
S_SH8_72000330	IMG Activity: OHSXX_250
S_SH8_72000331	IMG Activity: HEA_BAS_001_01
S_SH8_72000332	IMG Activity: HEA_FAL_010_08
S_SH8_72000732	IMG Activity: WA_EA_SV_004
S_SH8_72000733	IMG Activity: WA_EA_INT_MM_002
S_SH8_72000734	IMG Activity: WA_EA_INT_PROC_002
S_SH8_72000735	IMG Activity: WA_EA_INT_CO_001
S_SH8_72000736	IMG Activity: WA_EA_INT_CO_002
S_SH8_72000737	IMG Activity: WA_EA_SV_002
S_SH8_72000738	IMG Activity: WA_MD_010
S_SH8_72000739	IMG Activity: WA_EA_BS_003
S_SH8_72000740	IMG Activity: WA_EA_BS_004
S_SH8_72000741	IMG Activity: WA_EA_BS_001
S_SH8_72000742	IMG Activity: WA_EA_BS_002
S_SH8_72000743	IMG Activity: WA_EA_INT_CO_003
S_SH8_72000744	IMG Activity: WA_MN_MD_003
S_SH8_72000745	IMG Activity: WA_MN_MD_006
S_SH8_72000746	IMG Activity: WA_MN_SV_002
S_SH8_72000747	IMG Activity: WA_REPORTS_001
S_SH8_72000748	IMG Activity: WA_MD_AUTH_001
S_SH8_72000749	IMG Activity: WA_MN_MD_002
S_SH8_72000750	IMG Activity: WA_MN_MD_000
S_SH8_72000751	IMG Activity: WA_MN_MD_001
S_SH8_72000752	IMG Activity: WA_MN_MD_004A
S_SH8_72000753	IMG Activity: WA_MN_MD_004
S_SH8_72000754	IMG Activity: WA_MN_MD_005
S_SH8_72000755	IMG Activity: WA_MD_009
S_SH8_72000756	IMG Activity: WA_MD_004A_02
S_SH8_72000757	IMG Activity: WA_MD_004A_03
S_SH8_72000758	IMG Activity: WA_MD_004A_01
S_SH8_72000759	IMG Activity: WA_MD_004B
S_SH8_72000760	IMG Activity: WA_MD_005
S_SH8_72000761	IMG Activity: WA_MD_003
S_SH8_72000762	IMG Activity: WA_MD_004
S_SH8_72000763	IMG Activity: WA_BS_005
S_SH8_72000764	IMG Activity: WA_BS_004
S_SH8_72000765	IMG Activity: WA_MD_003A
S_SH8_72000766	IMG Activity: WA_MD_006

S_SH8_72000767	IMG Activity: WA_MD_007
S_SH8_72000768	IMG Activity: WA_MD_008
S_SH8_72000769	IMG Activity: WA_MD_008A
S_SH8_72000770	IMG Activity: WA_MD_004C
S_SH8_72000771	IMG Activity: WA_EA_INT_PROC_001
S_SH8_72000772	IMG Activity: WA_EA_INT_WM_001
S_SH8_72000773	IMG Activity: WA_MD_001
S_SH8_72000774	IMG Activity: WA_BS_002
S_SH8_72000775	IMG Activity: WA_MD_002
S_SH8_72000776	IMG Activity: WA_EA_INT_MM_001
S_SH8_72000789	Check If Time and Quantity Exceeded
S_SH8_72000790	Entry Document List
S_SH8_72000831	Existing Exposure Groups
S_SH8_72000832	Exposure Groups > Protocols
S_SH8_72000833	Exposure Group > Persons > Protocols
S_SH8_72000834	Health Center > Persons
S_SH8_72000835	Persons > restrictions
S_SH8_72000836	Persons > Medical Service
S_SH8_72000837	Persons > Examinations
S_SH8_72000838	Persons > Agents
S_SH8_72000839	Persons > Tests > Laboratory Tests
S_SH8_72000840	Download Completed Questionnaires
S_SH8_72000841	IMG Activity: EHS_SD_100_10_10
S_SH8_72000842	IMG Activity: EHS_DDS_100_10_10
S_SH8_72000843	IMG Activity: EHS_DDS_100_10_20
S_SH8_72000844	IMG Activity: EHS_DDS_100_10_07
S_SH8_72000845	IMG Activity: EHS_DDS_100_10_50
S_SH8_72000846	IMG Activity: EHS_DDS_100_10_60
S_SH8_72000847	IMG Activity: EHS_DDS_100_10_26
S_SH8_72000848	IMG Activity: EHS_DDS_100_10_611
S_SH8_72000849	IMG Activity: EHS_DDS_100_10_30
S_SH8_72000850	IMG Activity: EHS_DDS_100_10_22
S_SH8_72000851	IMG Activity: EHS_SD_100_10_013_20
S_SH8_72000852	IMG Activity: EHS_SD_100_20_013_20
S_SH8_72000853	IMG Activity: EHS_SD_100_20_013_10
S_SH8_72000854	IMG Activity: EHS_SD_100_20_013_15
S_SH8_72000855	IMG Activity: EHS_SD_100_20_013_30
S_SH8_72000856	IMG Activity: EHS_SD_100_20_013_40
S_SH8_72000857	IMG Activity: EHS_SD_100_10_013_10
S_SH8_72000858	IMG Activity: EHS_SD_100_10_013_15
S_SH8_72000859	IMG Activity: EHS_SD_100_10_013_30
S_SH8_72000860	IMG Activity: EHS_SD_100_10_013_40
S_SH8_72000861	IMG Activity: EHS_SD_100_10_023
S_SH8_72000862	IMG Activity: EHS_DDS_100_10_29
S_SH8_72000863	IMG Activity: EHS_SR_230_10_5
S_SH8_72000864	IMG Activity: EHS_SR_230_10_6
S_SH8_72000865	IMG Activity: EHS_SR_230_10_7
S_SH8_72000866	IMG Activity: EHS_SR_230_10_8
S_SH8_72000867	IMG Activity: EHS_MD_120_30_3B
S_SH8_72000868	IMG Activity: EHS_SR_225_40
S_SH8_72000869	IMG Activity: EHS_SR_225_50
S_SH8_72000870	IMG Activity: EHS_SR_225_51
S_SH8_72000871	IMG Activity: EHS_SR_230_10_1
S_SH8_72000872	IMG Activity: EHS_SR_230_10_4

S_SH8_72000873	IMG Activity: EHS_SR_250_22
S_SH8_72000874	IMG Activity: EHS_SR_100_30
S_SH8_72000875	IMG Activity: EHS_DDS_100_10_03
S_SH8_72000876	IMG Activity: EHS_DDS_100_10_05
S_SH8_72000877	IMG Activity: EHS_DDS_100_10_27
S_SH8_72000878	IMG Activity: EHS_DDS_100_10_28
S_SH8_72000879	IMG Activity: EHS_SR_250_23
S_SH8_72000880	IMG Activity: EHS_SR_250_02
S_SH8_72000881	IMG Activity: EHS_SR_250_01
S_SH8_72000882	IMG Activity: EHS_SR_250_04
S_SH8_72000883	IMG Activity: EHS_SR_100_20
S_SH8_72000884	IMG Activity: EHS_SD_100_20_023
S_SH8_72000885	IMG Activity: EHS_BOMBOS_06
S_SH8_72000886	IMG Activity: EHS_BOMBOS_07
S_SH8_72000887	IMG Activity: EHS_MD_120_40_10
S_SH8_72000888	IMG Activity: EHS_MD_120_40_20
S_SH8_72000889	IMG Activity: EHS_MD_120_40_30
S_SH8_72000890	IMG Activity: EHS_SRE_IMP_70
S_SH8_72000891	IMG Activity: EHS_MD_100_6
S_SH8_72000892	IMG Activity: EHS_BOMBOS_02
S_SH8_72000893	IMG Activity: EHS_BOMBOS_01
S_SH8_72000894	IMG Activity: EHS_BOMBOS_05
S_SH8_72000895	IMG Activity: EHS_MD_140_40_01
S_SH8_72000896	IMG Activity: EHS_SR_60_50
S_SH8_72000897	IMG Activity: EHS_MD_120_50_01
S_SH8_72000898	IMG Activity: EHS_MD_120_50_02
S_SH8_72000899	IMG Activity: EHS_QM_100
S_SH8_72000900	IMG Activity: EHS_MD_150_01_1
S_SH8_72000901	IMG Activity: EHS_MD_140_40_02
S_SH8_72000902	IMG Activity: EHS_SR_60_10
S_SH8_72000903	IMG Activity: EHS_SR_60_20
S_SH8_72000904	IMG Activity: EHS_SR_60_30
S_SH8_72000905	IMG Activity: EHS_SR_60_40
S_SH8_72000906	IMG Activity: EHS_MD_110_02_1
S_SH8_72000907	IMG Activity: EHS_SD_100_20_20
S_SH8_72000908	IMG Activity: EHS_SD_100_20_30
S_SH8_72000909	IMG Activity: EHS_SD_100_20_40
S_SH8_72000910	IMG Activity: EHS_SD_200_10_10
S_SH8_72000911	IMG Activity: EHS_SD_200_10_20
S_SH8_72000912	IMG Activity: EHS_SD_100_40_16
S_SH8_72000913	IMG Activity: EHS_SD_100_40_17
S_SH8_72000914	IMG Activity: EHS_SD_100_10_15
S_SH8_72000915	IMG Activity: EHS_MD_130_20_2B
S_SH8_72000916	IMG Activity: EHS_SD_100_20_10
S_SH8_72000917	IMG Activity: EHS_SD_200_10_01
S_SH8_72000918	IMG Activity: EHS_MD_160_10
S_SH8_72000919	IMG Activity: EHS_MD_160_30
S_SH8_72000920	IMG Activity: EHS_MD_160_40
S_SH8_72000921	IMG Activity: EHS_MD_160_70
S_SH8_72000922	IMG Activity: EHS_MD_160_80
S_SH8_72000923	IMG Activity: EHS_SD_200_10_02
S_SH8_72000924	IMG Activity: EHS_SD_200_10_03
S_SH8_72000925	IMG Activity: EHS_SD_200_10_04
S_SH8_72000926	IMG Activity: EHS_SD_200_10_05

S_SH8_72000927	IMG Activity: EHS_SD_300_30
S_SH8_72000928	IMG Activity: EHS_MD_110_06
S_SH8_72000929	IMG Activity: EHS_MD_140_01_1
S_SH8_72000930	IMG Activity: EHS_MD_120_30_5
S_SH8_72000931	IMG Activity: EHS_MD_130_20_3
S_SH8_72000932	IMG Activity: EHS_MD_130_20_2
S_SH8_72000933	IMG Activity: EHS_MD_130_20_5
S_SH8_72000934	IMG Activity: EHS_MD_120_30_4
S_SH8_72000935	IMG Activity: EHS_MD_140_20
S_SH8_72000936	IMG Activity: EHS_MD_110_12_2
S_SH8_72000937	IMG Activity: EHS_MD_140_05_2
S_SH8_72000938	IMG Activity: EHS_MD_110_12_9
S_SH8_72000939	IMG Activity: EHS_MD_140_05_1
S_SH8_72000940	IMG Activity: EHS_MD_140_01_3
S_SH8_72000941	IMG Activity: EHS_MD_130_20_1
S_SH8_72000942	IMG Activity: EHS_MD_120_60_2
S_SH8_72000943	IMG Activity: EHS_MD_110_05_4
S_SH8_72000944	IMG Activity: EHS_MD_120_60_1
S_SH8_72000945	IMG Activity: EHS_MD_130_30_1
S_SH8_72000946	IMG Activity: EHS_MD_120_10_10_0
S_SH8_72000947	IMG Activity: EHS_MD_120_10_10_1
S_SH8_72000948	IMG Activity: EHS_MD_110_12_3
S_SH8_72000949	IMG Activity: EHS_MD_110_07
S_SH8_72000950	IMG Activity: EHS_MD_130_15
S_SH8_72000951	IMG Activity: EHS_MD_130_10_1
S_SH8_72000952	IMG Activity: EHS_MD_130_05_1
S_SH8_72000953	IMG Activity: EHS_MD_130_01_2
S_SH8_72000954	IMG Activity: EHS_MD_130_01_0
S_SH8_72000955	IMG Activity: EHS_MD_110_05_2
S_SH8_72000956	IMG Activity: EHS_MD_120_30_00
S_SH8_72000957	IMG Activity: EHS_MD_120_30_01
S_SH8_72000958	IMG Activity: EHS_MD_110_05_11
S_SH8_72000959	IMG Activity: EHS_MD_110_05_12
S_SH8_72000960	IMG Activity: EHS_MD_110_05_1
S_SH8_72000961	IMG Activity: EHS_MD_110_01_1
S_SH8_72000962	IMG Activity: EHS_MD_110_05_6
S_SH8_72000963	IMG Activity: EHS_MD_110_05_9
S_SH8_72000964	IMG Activity: EHS_MD_110_05_15
S_SH8_72000965	IMG Activity: EHS_MD_110_05_20
S_SH8_72000966	IMG Activity: EHS_MD_110_05_5
S_SH8_72000967	IMG Activity: EHS_MD_110_05_3
S_SH8_72000968	IMG Activity: EHS_MD_110_05_10
S_SH8_72000969	IMG Activity: EHS_MD_120_30_3
S_SH8_72000970	IMG Activity: EHS_MD_100_3
S_SH8_72000971	IMG Activity: EHS_MD_120_10_10_5
S_SH8_72000972	IMG Activity: EHS_MD_140_30
S_SH8_72000973	IMG Activity: EHS_MD_110_12_1
S_SH8_72000974	IMG Activity: EHS_MD_110_05_32
S_SH8_72000975	IMG Activity: EHS_SR_210_30_01
S_SH8_72000976	IMG Activity: EHS_SR_210_10_10
S_SH8_72000977	IMG Activity: EHS_MD_100_5
S_SH8_72000978	IMG Activity: EHS_MD_100_4
S_SH8_72000979	IMG Activity: EHS_MD_140_40_04
S_SH8_72000980	IMG Activity: EHS_MD_135_06

S_SH8_72000981	IMG Activity: EHS_MD_135_07
S_SH8_72000982	IMG Activity: EHS_MD_120_50_04
S_SH8_72000983	IMG Activity: EHS_MD_150_40_01
S_SH8_72000984	IMG Activity: EHS_MD_110_05_7
S_SH8_72000985	IMG Activity: EHS_MD_120_40_02
S_SH8_72000986	IMG Activity: EHS_MD_200_22
S_SH8_72000987	IMG Activity: EHS_MD_120_50_03
S_SH8_72000988	IMG Activity: EHS_MD_135_01
S_SH8_72000989	IMG Activity: EHS_MD_135_02
S_SH8_72000990	IMG Activity: EHS_MD_135_03
S_SH8_72000991	IMG Activity: EHS_MD_135_04
S_SH8_72000992	IMG Activity: EHS_MD_135_05
S_SH8_72000993	IMG Activity: EHS_MD_110_05_8
S_SH8_72000994	IMG Activity: EHS_SR_210_20_40
S_SH8_72000995	IMG Activity: EHS_SR_230_10_2
S_SH8_72000996	IMG Activity: EHS_SR_220_01
S_SH8_72000997	IMG Activity: EHS_SRE_IMP_90
S_SH8_72000998	IMG Activity: EHS_SR_250_21
S_SH8_72000999	IMG Activity: EHS_DDS_100_10_40
S_SH8_72001000	IMG Activity: EHS_SD_100_10_013_50
S_SH8_72001001	IMG Activity: EHS_SD_100_10_005
S_SH8_72001002	IMG Activity: EHS_SD_100_10_033
S_SH8_72001003	IMG Activity: EHS_SR_220_11
S_SH8_72001004	IMG Activity: EHS_SR_225_10
S_SH8_72001005	IMG Activity: EHS_SR_220_30
S_SH8_72001006	IMG Activity: EHS_SR_220_40
S_SH8_72001007	IMG Activity: EHS_SR_225_20
S_SH8_72001008	IMG Activity: EHS_SR_220_10
S_SH8_72001009	IMG Activity: EHS_SR_220_08
S_SH8_72001010	IMG Activity: EHS_SR_220_08_01
S_SH8_72001011	IMG Activity: EHS_SR_225_60
S_SH8_72001012	IMG Activity: EHS_SR_225_70
S_SH8_72001013	IMG Activity: EHS_MD_120_30_1
S_SH8_72001014	IMG Activity: EHS_SD_100_40_25
S_SH8_72001015	IMG Activity: EHS_SD_100_10_20
S_SH8_72001016	IMG Activity: EHS_MD_160_20
S_SH8_72001017	IMG Activity: EHS_MD_160_90
S_SH8_72001018	IMG Activity: EHS_MD_110_05_13
S_SH8_72001019	IMG Activity: EHS_SRE_IMP_80
S_SH8_72001020	IMG Activity: EHS_SRE_IMP_100_01
S_SH8_72001021	IMG Activity: EHS_SRE_IMP_120
S_SH8_72001022	IMG Activity: EHS_BOMBOS_08
S_SH8_72001023	IMG Activity: EHS_SD_100_40_20
S_SH8_72001024	IMG Activity: EHS_MD_120_30_2
S_SH8_72001025	IMG Activity: EHS_SD_100_20_013_50
S_SH8_72001026	IMG Activity: EHS_MD_120_20_40_2
S_SH8_72001027	IMG Activity: EHS_SD_100_40_05
S_SH8_72001028	IMG Activity: EHS_SD_100_40_06
S_SH8_72001029	IMG Activity: EHS_SD_100_40_10
S_SH8_72001030	IMG Activity: EHS_SD_100_40_15
S_SH8_72001031	IMG Activity: EHS_MD_120_10_20_1
S_SH8_72001032	IMG Activity: EHS_MD_120_10_20_5
S_SH8_84000001	EHS: Risk Assessment Overview
S_SH8_84000002	EHS: Hazardous Substance Inventory

S_SH8_84000003	EHS: 1000-Employee Quota
S_SH8_84000004	EHS: 1,000,000-Hour Quota
S_SH8_84000005	EHS: Read Reportable Accidents
S_SH8_84000006	EHS: Check and Correct Absences
S_SH8_84000007	EHS: Overview of Defined Statuses
S_SH8_84000008	EHS: Return Completed Tasks
S_SH8_84000009	EHS: Overview of IHS Measures
S_SH8_84000305	IMG Activity: GGA_300_140
S_SH8_84000306	IMG Activity: GGA_300_100
S_SH8_84000307	IMG Activity: GGA_100_320
S_SH8_84000308	IMG Activity: GGA_100_310
S_SH8_84000309	IMG Activity: GGA_100_290
S_SH8_84000310	IMG Activity: GGA_300_180
S_SH8_84000311	IMG Activity: GGA_300_170_300
S_SH8_84000312	IMG Activity: GGA_300_170_200
S_SH8_84000313	IMG Activity: GGA_300_170_100
S_SH8_84000314	IMG Activity: GGA_300_160
S_SH8_84000315	IMG Activity: GGA_100_430
S_SH8_84000316	IMG Activity: GGA_100_270
S_SH8_84000317	IMG Activity: GGA_100_250
S_SH8_84000318	IMG Activity: GGA_100_200
S_SH8_84000319	IMG Activity: GGA_100_150
S_SH8_84000320	IMG Activity: GGA_100_100
S_SH8_84000321	IMG Activity: GGA_100_420
S_SH8_84000322	IMG Activity: GGA_100_280
S_SH8_84000323	IMG Activity: GGA_100_240
S_SH8_84000324	IMG Activity: GGA_100_440
S_SH8_84000325	IMG Activity: GGA_100_410
S_SH8_84000326	IMG Activity: GGA_300_190_300
S_SH8_84000327	IMG Activity: GGA_300_190_200
S_SH8_84000328	IMG Activity: GGA_300_190_100
S_SH8_84000329	IMG Activity: GGA_300_480
S_SH8_84000330	IMG Activity: GGA_300_470
S_SH8_84000331	IMG Activity: GGA_400_200
S_SH8_84000332	IMG Activity: GGA_400_180
S_SH8_84000333	IMG Activity: GGA_400_120
S_SH8_84000334	IMG Activity: GGA_400_100
S_SH8_84000335	IMG Activity: GGA_400_050
S_SH8_84000336	IMG Activity: GGA_300_440
S_SH8_84000337	IMG Activity: GGA_300_112
S_SH8_84000338	IMG Activity: GGA_300_120
S_SH8_84000339	IMG Activity: GGA_300_202
S_SH8_84000340	IMG Activity: GGA_300_200
S_SH8_84000341	IMG Activity: GGA_200_204
S_SH8_84000342	IMG Activity: GGA_300_450
S_SH8_84000343	IMG Activity: GGA_300_460
S_SH8_84000344	IMG Activity: GGA_300_420
S_SH8_84000345	IMG Activity: GGA_300_430
S_SH8_84000346	IMG Activity: GGA_300_410
S_SH8_84000347	IMG Activity: GGA_800_200
S_SH8_84000348	IMG Activity: EHS_MD_130_30
S_SH8_84000349	IMG Activity: GGA_200_100_145
S_SH8_84000350	IMG Activity: GGA_200_300_220
S_SH8_84000351	IMG Activity: GGA_200_300_160

S_SH8_84000352	IMG Activity: GGA_200_300_140
S_SH8_84000353	IMG Activity: GGA_200_200_100
S_SH8_84000354	IMG Activity: GGA_200_300_120
S_SH8_84000355	IMG Activity: GGA_200_300_170
S_SH8_84000356	IMG Activity: GGA_200_100_180
S_SH8_84000357	IMG Activity: GGA_200_100_155
S_SH8_84000358	IMG Activity: GGA_200_100_140
S_SH8_84000359	IMG Activity: GGA_200_100_170
S_SH8_84000360	IMG Activity: GGA_100_300
S_SH8_84000361	IMG Activity: GGA_100_350
S_SH8_84000362	IMG Activity: GGA_500_100
S_SH8_84000363	IMG Activity: GGA_200_300_110
S_SH8_84000364	IMG Activity: GGA_200_300_100
S_SH8_84000365	IMG Activity: GGA_200_100_150
S_SH8_84000366	IMG Activity: GGA_200_300_200
S_SH8_84000367	IMG Activity: GGA_200_100_130
S_SH8_84000368	IMG Activity: GGA_200_200_110
S_SH8_84000369	IMG Activity: GGA_200_200_200
S_SH8_84000370	IMG Activity: GGA_700_100
S_SH8_84000371	IMG Activity: GGA_810_050_100
S_SH8_84000372	IMG Activity: GGA_810_050_200
S_SH8_84000373	IMG Activity: GGA_810_050_300
S_SH8_84000374	IMG Activity: GGA_800_120
S_SH8_84000375	IMG Activity: GGA_200_200_120
S_SH8_84000376	IMG Activity: GGA_200_300_150
S_SH8_84000377	IMG Activity: GGA_200_300_180
S_SH8_84000378	IMG Activity: GGA_400_250
S_SH8_84000379	IMG Activity: GGA_200_100_165
S_SH8_84000380	IMG Activity: GGA_800_060
S_SH8_84000381	IMG Activity: GGA_800_150
S_SH8_84000385	EHS: Label Sizes
S_SH8_84000386	EHS: Label Categories
S_SH8_84000387	EHS: Labeling Scenarios
S_SH8_84000388	EHS: Plant-Spec. Definition EPA
S_SH8_84000391	EHS: Change Transport Symbol Groups
S_SH8_84000392	EHS: Logistics RFC Connections
S_SH8_84000393	EHS: Size of Label Stock
S_SH8_84000394	EHS: Label Printer Management
S_SH8_84000395	EHS: Packaging Unit
S_SH8_84000396	EHS: Definition of Serial Numbers
S_SH8_84000397	EHS: Determination Method
S_SH8_84000398	EHS: Transfer GLM Printers
S_SH8_84000399	EHS: Reorg./Printout of Aud.Tr. Data
S_SH8_84000410	xxxx
S_SH8_84000412	EHS: Generation Server for Labeling
S_SH8_84000413	EHS: Printing Program for Labeling
S_SHV_87000003	IMG: Copy Settings
S_SK4_11000003	IMG Activity:
S_SK4_11000019	IMG Activity:
S_SK4_11000020	x
S_SK4_11000021	S_SK4_11000021
S_SK4_11000030	S_SK4_11000030
S_SK4_11000031	S_SK4_11000031
S_SK4_11000032	IMG Activity:

S_SK4_11000033	IMG Activity:
S_SK4_11000034	IMG Activity:
S_SK4_11000036	IMG Activity:
S_SK4_11000038	Facts Capture Application
S_SK4_11000040	IMG Activity:
S_SK4_11000051	IMG Activity:
S_SK4_11000053	IMG Activity:
S_SK4_49000001	Transact. for SAPLS_CUS_IMG_ACTIVITY
S_SK4_53000004	IMG Activity: ISMAM_TJHGRSALESAREA
S_SK4_82000475	IMG Activity: CM_XX_340
S_SK4_83000020	IMG Activity ISM_BP_PLM
S_SK4_84000020	IMG Activity: _FICABFDP_TEEXTDOCBR
S_SK4_84000021	IMG Activity: _FICABFDP_EK_EXT_BR
S_SK4_84000022	IMG Activity: _FICABTPY_TFK012DCV
S_SK4_84000023	IMG Activity: _FICABFTAXR_TFK020R1
S_SLN_44000017	Recursive Consistency Check for DDIC
S_SLN_44000018	Dictionary Check Tool: Schedule. On
S_SO5_65000001	IMG activity: SIMG_EURO_ROIHEW11
S_SO5_65000002	IMG activity: SIMG_EURO_ROIHEW21
S_SO5_65000003	IMG activity: SIMG_EURO_ROIHEW31
S_SO5_65000004	IMG activity: SIMG_EURO_ROIHEW22
S_SO5_65000005	IMG activity: SIMG_EURO_ROIHEW32
S_SO5_65000006	IMG activity: SIMG_EURO_ROIAEW10
S_SO5_65000007	IMG activity: SIMG_EURO_ROIAEW20
S_SO5_65000008	IMG activity: SIMG_EURO_ROIHEW10
S_SO5_65000009	IMG activity: SIMG_EURO_ROIHEW20
S_SO5_65000010	IMG activity: SIMG_EURO_ROIHEW30
S_SO5_65000011	IMG activity: SIMG_EXG_0020
S_SO5_65000012	IMG activity: SIMG_EXG_0021
S_SO5_65000014	IMG activity: SIMG_EXG_0023
S_SO5_65000015	IMG activity: SIMG_EXG_0024
S_SO5_65000016	IMG activity: SIMG_EXG_0025
S_SO5_65000017	IMG activity: SIMG_EXG_0029
S_SO5_65000018	IMG activity: SIMG_EXG_0030
S_SO5_65000019	IMG activity: SIMG_EXG_0053
S_SO5_65000021	IMG activity: SIMG_EXG_0054
S_SO5_65000022	IMG activity: SIMG_EXG_0015
S_SO5_65000023	IMG activity: SIMG_EXG_0016
S_SO5_65000024	IMG activity: SIMG_EXG_0017
S_SO5_65000025	IMG activity: SIMG_EXG_0018
S_SO5_65000026	IMG activity: SIMG_EXG_0019
S_SO5_65000027	IMG activity: SIMG_EXG_0031
S_SO5_65000028	IMG activity: SIMG_EXG_0045
S_SO5_65000029	IMG activity: SIMG_EXG_0046
S_SO5_65000030	IMG activity: SIMG_EXG_0047
S_SO5_65000031	IMG activity: SIMG_EXG_0048
S_SO5_65000032	IMG activity: SIMG_EXG_0049
S_SO5_65000033	IMG activity: SIMG_EXG_0050
S_SO5_65000034	IMG activity: SIMG_EXG_0032
S_SO5_65000035	IMG activity: SIMG_EXG_0033
S_SO5_65000036	IMG activity: SIMG_EXG_0026
S_SO5_65000037	IMG activity: SIMG_EXG_0027
S_SO5_65000038	IMG activity: SIMG_EXG_0028
S_SO5_65000039	IMG activity: SIMG_EXG_0041

S_SO5_65000040	IMG activity: SIMG_EXG_0051
S_SO5_65000041	IMG activity: SIMG_EXG_0056
S_SO5_65000042	IMG activity: SIMG_EXG_0043
S_SO5_65000043	IMG activity: SIMG_EXG_0044
S_SO5_65000044	IMG activity: SIMG_EXG_0052
S_SO5_65000045	IMG activity: SIMG_EXG_0005
S_SO5_65000047	IMG activity: SIMG_EXG_0006
S_SO5_65000048	IMG activity: SIMG_EXG_0007
S_SO5_65000049	IMG activity: SIMG_EXG_0008
S_SO5_65000050	IMG activity: SIMG_EXG_0009
S_SO5_65000051	IMG activity: SIMG_EXG_0010
S_SO5_65000052	IMG activity: SIMG_EXG_0001
S_SO5_65000053	IMG activity: SIMG_EXG_0035
S_SO5_65000054	IMG activity: SIMG_EXG_0002
S_SO5_65000055	IMG activity: SIMG_EXG_0003
S_SO5_65000056	IMG activity: SIMG_EXG_0034
S_SO5_65000057	IMG activity: SIMG_EXG_0042
S_SO5_65000058	IMG activity: SIMG_EXG_0004
S_SO5_65000059	IMG activity: SIMG_EXG_0011
S_SO5_65000060	IMG activity: SIMG_EXG_0012
S_SO5_65000061	IMG activity: SIMG_EXG_0039
S_SO5_65000062	IMG activity: SIMG_EXG_0058
S_SO5_65000063	IMG activity: SIMG_EXG_0040
S_SO5_65000064	IMG activity: SIMG_EXG_0036
S_SO5_65000065	IMG activity: SIMG_EXG_0014
S_SO5_65000066	IMG activity: SIMG_EXG_0037
S_SO5_65000067	IMG activity: SIMG_HPM_0004
S_SO5_65000068	IMG activity: SIMG_HPM_0005
S_SO5_65000069	IMG activity: SIMG_HPM_0006
S_SO5_65000070	IMG activity: SIMG_HPM_0007
S_SO5_65000071	IMG activity: SIMG_TDP_0020
S_SO5_65000072	IMG activity: SIMG_TDP_0021
S_SO5_65000073	IMG activity: SIMG_TDP_0022
S_SO5_65000074	IMG activity: SIMG_HPM_0001
S_SO5_65000075	IMG activity: SIMG_HPM_0002
S_SO5_65000076	IMG activity: SIMG_HPM_0003
S_SO5_65000077	IMG activity: SIMG_HPM_0008
S_SO5_65000078	IMG activity: SIMG_MAP_0019
S_SO5_65000079	IMG activity: SIMG_MAP_0018
S_SO5_65000080	IMG activity: SIMG_MAP_0017
S_SO5_65000081	IMG activity: SIMG_MAP_0016
S_SO5_65000082	IMG activity: SIMG_MAP_0015
S_SO5_65000083	IMG activity: SIMG_MAP_0021
S_SO5_65000084	IMG activity: SIMG_MAP_0025
S_SO5_65000085	IMG activity: SIMG_MAP_0024
S_SO5_65000086	IMG activity: SIMG_MAP_0023
S_SO5_65000087	IMG activity: SIMG_MAP_0001
S_SO5_65000088	IMG activity: SIMG_MAP_0002
S_SO5_65000089	IMG activity: SIMG_MAP_0003
S_SO5_65000090	IMG activity: SIMG_MAP_0004
S_SO5_65000091	IMG activity: SIMG_MAP_0006
S_SO5_65000092	IMG activity: SIMG_MCOE_0002
S_SO5_65000093	IMG activity: SIMG_MCOE_0003
S_SO5_65000094	IMG activity: SIMG_MCOE_0001

S_SO5_65000095	IMG activity: SIMG_MCOE_0004
S_SO5_65000096	IMG activity: SIMG_MCOE_0005
S_SO5_65000097	IMG activity: SIMG_MRN_0010
S_SO5_65000098	IMG activity: SIMG_MRN_0003
S_SO5_65000099	IMG activity: SIMG_MRN_0004
S_SO5_65000100	IMG activity: SIMG_MRN_0014
S_SO5_65000101	IMG activity: SIMG_MRN_0013
S_SO5_65000102	IMG activity: SIMG_MRN_0009
S_SO5_65000103	IMG activity: SIMG_MRN_0020
S_SO5_65000104	IMG activity: SIMG_MRN_0017
S_SO5_65000105	IMG activity: SIMG_MRN_0005
S_SO5_65000106	IMG activity: SIMG_MRN_0016
S_SO5_65000107	IMG activity: SIMG_MRN_0015
S_SO5_65000108	IMG activity: SIMG_MRN_0018
S_SO5_65000109	IMG activity: SIMG_MRN_0012
S_SO5_65000110	IMG activity: SIMG_MRN_0019
S_SO5_65000111	IMG activity: SIMG_MRN_0001
S_SO5_65000112	IMG activity: SIMG_MRN_0011
S_SO5_65000113	IMG activity: SIMG_MRN_0007
S_SO5_65000114	IMG activity: SIMG_MRN_0002
S_SO5_65000122	IMG activity: SIMG_TD_0063
S_SO5_65000124	IMG activity: SIMG_TD_0039
S_SO5_65000132	IMG activity: SIMG_TD_0020
S_SO5_65000133	IMG activity: SIMG_TD_0030
S_SO5_65000134	IMG activity: SIMG_TD_0031
S_SO5_65000135	IMG activity: SIMG_TD_0032
S_SO5_65000136	IMG activity: SIMG_TD_0033
S_SO5_65000137	IMG activity: SIMG_TD_0034
S_SO5_65000138	IMG activity: SIMG_TD_0035
S_SO5_65000139	IMG activity: SIMG_TD_0036
S_SO5_65000140	IMG activity: SIMG_TD_0037
S_SO5_65000141	IMG activity: SIMG_TD_0029
S_SO5_65000142	IMG activity: SIMG_TD_0021
S_SO5_65000143	IMG activity: SIMG_TD_0022
S_SO5_65000144	IMG activity: SIMG_TD_0023
S_SO5_65000145	IMG activity: SIMG_TD_0024
S_SO5_65000146	IMG activity: SIMG_TD_0025
S_SO5_65000147	IMG activity: SIMG_TD_0026
S_SO5_65000148	IMG activity: SIMG_TD_0027
S_SO5_65000149	IMG activity: SIMG_TD_0028
S_SO5_65000150	IMG activity: SIMG_TD_0009
S_SO5_65000151	IMG activity: SIMG_TD_0010
S_SO5_65000152	IMG activity: SIMG_TD_0011
S_SO5_65000156	IMG activity: SIMG_TD_0012
S_SO5_65000157	IMG activity: SIMG_TD_0038
S_SO5_65000158	IMG activity: SIMG_TD_0008
S_SO5_65000159	IMG activity: SIMG_TD_0001
S_SO5_65000160	IMG activity: SIMG_TD_0002
S_SO5_65000161	IMG activity: SIMG_TD_0003
S_SO5_65000162	IMG activity: SIMG_TD_0004
S_SO5_65000163	IMG activity: SIMG_TD_0005
S_SO5_65000164	IMG activity: SIMG_TD_0006
S_SO5_65000165	IMG activity: SIMG_TD_0064
S_SO5_65000166	IMG activity: SIMG_TD_0007

S_SO5_65000167	IMG activity: SIMG_TD_0013
S_SO5_65000168	IMG activity: SIMG_TD_0015
S_SO5_65000169	IMG activity: SIMG_TD_0014
S_SO5_65000170	IMG activity: SIMG_TD_0016
S_SO5_65000171	IMG activity: SIMG_TD_0017
S_SO5_65000172	IMG activity: SIMG_TD_0019
S_SO5_65000173	IMG activity: SIMG_TD_0018
S_SO5_65000174	IMG activity: SIMG_TD_0042
S_SO5_65000175	IMG activity: SIMG_TD_0041
S_SO5_65000176	IMG activity: SIMG_TD_0040
S_SO5_65000177	IMG activity: SIMG_TDP_0018
S_SO5_65000178	IMG activity: SIMG_TDP_BRAZIL_0001
S_SO5_65000179	IMG activity: SIMG_TDP_BRAZIL_0002
S_SO5_65000180	IMG activity: SIMG_TDP_BRAZIL_0003
S_SO5_65000181	IMG activity: SIMG_TDP_BRAZIL_0007
S_SO5_65000182	IMG activity: SIMG_TDP_BRAZIL_0008
S_SO5_65000183	IMG activity: SIMG_TDP_BRAZIL_0009
S_SO5_65000184	IMG activity: SIMG_TDP_0017
S_SO5_65000185	IMG activity: SIMG_TDP_0001
S_SO5_65000189	IMG activity: SIMG_TDP_0023
S_SO5_65000190	IMG activity: SIMG_TDP_0015
S_SO5_65000191	IMG activity: SIMG_TDP_0016
S_SO5_65000192	IMG activity: SIMG_TDP_BRAZIL_0010
S_SO5_65000193	IMG activity: SIMG_TDP_BRAZIL_0004
S_SO5_65000194	IMG activity: SIMG_TDP_BRAZIL_0005
S_SO5_65000195	IMG activity: SIMG_TDP_BRAZIL_0015
S_SO5_65000196	IMG activity: SIMG_TDP_BRAZIL_0014
S_SO5_65000197	IMG activity: SIMG_TDP_BRAZIL_0006
S_SO5_65000198	IMG activity: SIMG_TDP_BRAZIL_0016
S_SO5_65000199	IMG activity: SIMG_TDP_BRAZIL_0022
S_SO5_65000200	IMG activity: SIMG_TDP_BRAZIL_0021
S_SO5_65000201	IMG activity: SIMG_TDP_BRAZIL_0011
S_SO5_65000202	IMG activity: SIMG_TDP_BRAZIL_0012
S_SO5_65000203	IMG activity: SIMG_TDP_BRAZIL_0013
S_SO5_65000204	IMG activity: SIMG_TDP_BRAZIL_0020
S_SO5_65000205	IMG activity: SIMG_TDP_BRAZIL_0017
S_SO5_65000206	IMG activity: SIMG_TDP_BRAZIL_0018
S_SO5_65000208	IMG activity: SIMG_TDP_0024
S_SO5_65000209	IMG activity: SIMG_TDP_0013
S_SO5_65000210	IMG activity: SIMG_TDP_0014
S_SO5_65000211	IMG activity: SIMG_TDP_0028
S_SO5_65000212	IMG activity: SIMG_TDP_0029
S_SO5_65000213	IMG activity: SIMG_TDP_0030
S_SO5_65000214	IMG activity: SIMG_TDP_0027
S_SO5_65000215	IMG activity: SIMG_TDP_0006
S_SO5_65000216	IMG activity: SIMG_TDP_0007
S_SO5_65000217	IMG activity: SIMG_TDP_0008
S_SO5_65000218	IMG activity: SIMG_TDP_0009
S_SO5_65000219	IMG activity: SIMG_TDP_0010
S_SO5_65000220	IMG activity: SIMG_TDP_0011
S_SO5_65000221	IMG activity: SIMG_TDP_0012
S_SO5_65000224	IMG activity: SIMG_TDP_0032
S_SO5_65000225	IMG activity: SIMG_TDP_0005
S_SO5_65000226	IMG activity: SIMG_TDP_0026

S_SO5_65000227	IMG activity: SIMG_TDP_0031
S_SO5_65000228	IMG activity: SIMG_BDRP_0003
S_SO5_65000229	IMG activity: SIMG_BDRP_0004
S_SO5_65000231	IMG activity: SIMG_BDRP_0006
S_SO5_65000232	IMG activity: SIMG_BDRP_0009
S_SO5_65000233	IMG activity: SIMG_BDRP_0010
S_SO5_65000234	IMG activity: SIMG_BDRP_0011
S_SO5_65000235	IMG activity: SIMG_BDRP_0012
S_SO5_65000236	IMG activity: SIMG_BDRP_0007
S_SO5_65000237	IMG activity: SIMG_BDRP_0001
S_SO5_65000238	IMG activity: SIMG_BDRP_0002
S_SO5_65000240	IMG activity: SIMG_TSW_0008
S_SO5_65000241	IMG activity: SIMG_TSW_0007
S_SO5_65000242	IMG activity: SIMG_TSW_0016
S_SO5_65000244	IMG activity: SIMG_TSW_0022
S_SO5_65000245	IMG activity: SIMG_TSW_0009
S_SO5_65000246	IMG activity: SIMG_TSW_0014
S_SO5_65000247	IMG activity: SIMG_TSW_0013
S_SO5_65000248	IMG activity: SIMG_TSW_0012
S_SO5_65000249	IMG activity: SIMG_TSW_0010
S_SO5_65000250	IMG activity: SIMG_TSW_0015
S_SO5_65000251	IMG activity: SIMG_TSW_0017
S_SO5_65000253	IMG activity: SIMG_TSW_0001
S_SO5_65000254	IMG activity: SIMG_TSW_0019
S_SO5_65000255	IMG activity: SIMG_TSW_0023
S_SO5_65000256	IMG activity: SIMG_TSW_0020
S_SO5_65000257	IMG activity: SIMG_TSW_0021
S_SO5_65000258	IMG activity: SIMG_TSW_0018
S_SO5_65000259	IMG activity: SIMG_TSW_0005
S_SO5_65000260	IMG activity: SIMG_TSW_0004
S_SO5_65000261	IMG activity: SIMG_TSW_0003
S_SO5_65000262	IMG activity: SIMG_TD_TAS_0004
S_SO5_65000263	IMG activity: SIMG_TD_TAS_0005
S_SO5_65000264	IMG activity: SIMG_TD_TAS_0006
S_SO5_65000265	IMG activity: SIMG_TD_TAS_0007
S_SO5_65000266	IMG activity: SIMG_TD_TAS_0008
S_SO5_65000267	IMG activity: SIMG_TD_TAS_0003
S_SO5_65000268	IMG activity: SIMG_TD_TAS_0009
S_SO5_65000269	IMG activity: SIMG_TD_TAS_0001
S_SO5_65000270	IMG activity: SIMG_TD_TAS_0002
S_SO5_65000271	IMG activity: SIMG_TD_TPI_0006
S_SO5_65000272	IMG activity: SIMG_TD_TPI_0005
S_SO5_65000273	IMG activity: SIMG_TD_TPI_0004
S_SO5_65000274	IMG activity: SIMG_TD_TPI_0003
S_SO5_65000275	IMG activity: SIMG_TD_TPI_0002
S_SO5_65000276	IMG activity: SIMG_TD_TPI_0008
S_SO5_65000277	IMG activity: SIMG_TD_TPI_0009
S_SO5_65000278	IMG activity: SIMG_TD_TPI_0001
S_SO5_65000279	IMG activity: SIMG_TD_TPI_0007
S_SO5_65000604	IMG activity: SIMG_SSR_0033
S_SO5_65000605	IMG activity: SIMG_SSR_0034
S_SO5_65000675	Create location list on general leve
S_SO5_65000676	Create location list with business t
S_SO5_65000677	Create location list on business typ

S_SO5_65000678	Program ROIREDTF
S_SO5_65000685	QCI BAdI Navigation from Customizing
S_SO5_65000686	Customizing Message Handling QCI
S_SO6_65000725	Transfer of business location master
S_SO6_65000728	Transfer of business location materi
S_SO6_65000731	SSR Stocks - Material movements
S_SO6_65000776	Comparison of 2 DDIC structures and
S_SO6_65000778	Display glossary entries/terminology
S_SO6_65000779	Choose/display application log
S_SO6_65000789	Excise duty inventory check report
S_SO6_65000790	List of stock values: Balances
S_SO6_65000791	Follow-on docs comparison check prog
S_SO6_65000792	Test report to simulate Qty schedule
S_SO6_65000793	List netting cycle header(selection)
S_SO6_65000794	TD check shipment costing rel. tbles
S_SO6_65000795	TD-F repair report for SCDs
S_SO6_65000796	Check for data conflicts
S_SO6_65000797	Reapir from TD mass goods transports
S_SO6_65000798	Delete/emergency repair of mass good
S_SO6_65000800	IS-Oil shipment fill IDoc
S_SO6_65000801	ADRV-APPL_KEY setting for
S_SO6_65000802	Report on handling performs
S_SO6_65000803	Report on changing entries in
S_SO6_65000804	Business location archiving - archiv
S_SO6_65000805	Business loc archiving - del. prog
S_SO6_65000806	Business loc archiving - reload prog
S_SO6_65000807	Report for filling out oifsmcaddr
S_SO6_65000808	Conversion of int. name fields in
S_SO6_65000809	Conversion of "OIFOPBLT" setting
S_SO6_65000810	Report on creating status management
S_SO6_65000874	Program ROIRA_DELETE_APPL_LOG
S_SO6_65000875	Set the initial status for business
S_SO6_65000876	OIL-TSW: Remove expired entries from
S_SO6_65000879	OIL-TSW: Generate production/sales f
S_SO6_65000880	OIL-TSW: Generate rack issue actuals
S_SO6_65000881	IBU OIL & GAS - TSW - Delete inconsi
S_SO6_65000882	Post the goods issue for deliveries
S_SO6_65000883	LID assignment
S_SO6_65000884	Select rack meters from change point
S_SO6_65000885	Send location master data using chan
S_SO6_65000886	Select Vehicles from change pointers
S_SO6_65000887	Send driver idocs from change pointe
S_SO6_65000888	Check TPI document creation
S_SO6_65000891	Call customizing IMG directly (e.g.
S_SO6_65000897	Analysis of consistency between core
S_SO6_65000902	Generated Text
S_SO6_65000905	Margin Analysis report
S_SO6_65000908	PC Statistics: Yearly Overview
S_SO6_65000909	PC Statistics: Annual differences
S_SO6_65000910	PC Statistics: Monthly Overview
S_SO6_65000938	Generated Text
S_SO6_65000939	Generated Text
S_SO6_65000941	Generated Text
S_SO6_65000942	Generated Text

S_SO6_65000943	Generated Text
S_SO6_65000960	Generated Text
S_SO6_65000961	Generated Text
S_SO6_65000970	Generated Text
S_SO6_65000971	Generated Text
S_SO6_65000978	Generated Text
S_SO6_65000980	BAdI Navigation from Customizing
S_SO6_65000981	QCI BAdI Navigation from Customizing
S_SO6_65000982	QCI BAdI Navigation from Customizing
S_SO6_65000983	Generated Text
S_SO6_65000993	Generated Text
S_SO6_65000994	Generated Text
S_SO7_65000978	QCI BAdI Navigation from Customizing
S_SO7_65001010	Common Table Maintenance
S_SO7_65001019	Generated Text
S_SO7_65001025	Generated Text
S_SO7_65001026	Generated Text
S_SO7_65001027	Generated Text
S_SO7_65001070	Generated Text
S_SO7_65001074	Generated Text
S_SO7_65001075	Generated Text
S_SO7_65001076	Generated Text
S_SO7_65001077	Generated Text
S_SO7_65001078	Generated Text
S_SO7_65001080	Generated Text
S_SO7_65001081	Generated Text
S_SO7_65001095	Generated Text
S_SO7_65001096	Generated Text
S_SO7_65001097	Generated Text
S_SO7_65001098	Generated Text
S_SO7_65001099	Generated Text
S_SO7_65001102	Generated Text
S_SO7_65001103	Generated Text
S_SO7_65001105	Generated Text
S_SO7_65001107	Generated Text
S_SO7_65001114	Generated Text
S_SO7_65001116	Generated Text
S_SO7_65001122	Generated Text
S_SO7_65001124	Generated Text
S_SO7_65001125	Generated Text
S_SO7_65001131	Generated Text
S_SO7_65001132	Generated Text
S_SO7_65001133	Generated Text
S_SO7_65001134	Generated Text
S_SO7_65001135	Generated Text
S_SO7_65001139	Generated Text
S_SO7_65001141	Generated Text
S_SO7_65001142	Generated Text
S_SO7_65001143	Generated Text
S_SO7_65001144	Generated Text
S_SO7_65001152	Generated Text
S_SO7_65001186	Generated Text
S_SO7_65001197	Generated Text
S_SO7_65001202	Generated Text

S_SO7_65001205	Generated Text
S_SO7_65001230	Generated Text
S_SO7_65001231	Generated Text
S_SO7_65001232	Generated Text
S_SO7_65001251	QCI Default determination
S_SO7_65001253	Generated Text
S_SO7_65001254	Generated Text
S_SO7_65001256	BAdI Customizing
S_SO7_65001260	Generated Text
S_SO7_65001264	Generated Text
S_SO7_65001265	IMG activity: SIMG_SSR_0220
S_SO7_65001266	IMG activity: SIMG_OIO_RT_EVENT
S_SO7_65001267	IMG activity: SIMG_OIJ_TSW_038
S_SO7_65001268	IMG activity: SIMG_OIJ_TSW_039
S_SO7_65001269	IMG activity: SIMG_OIJ_TSW_040
S_SO7_65001270	IMG activity: SIMG_OIJ_TSW_041
S_SO7_65001271	IMG activity: SIMG_OIJ_TSW_042
S_SO7_65001272	IMG activity: SIMG_OIJ_TSW_043
S_SO7_65001273	IMG activity: SIMG_OIJ_TSW_044
S_SO7_65001274	IMG activity: OIO_SY_OBJTY
S_SO7_65001275	IMG activity: OIO_SY_APP
S_SO7_65001277	IMG activity: OIO_FS_SGP_C1
S_SO7_65001278	IMG activity: SIMG_OIJ_TSW_045
S_SO7_65001279	IMG activity: SIMG_OIJ_TSW_046
S_SO7_65001280	IMG activity: SIMG_OIJ_TSW_047
S_SO7_65001281	IMG activity: SIMG_OIJ_TSW_048
S_SO7_65001282	IMG activity: OIO_RT_FLDST
S_SO7_65001283	IMG activity: OIO_VG_FLDST
S_SO7_65001284	IMG activity: OIO_RT_FSGRP
S_SO7_65001285	IMG activity: OIO_CM_OBJGP
S_SO7_65001286	IMG activity: SIMG_OIJ_TD_048
S_SO7_65001287	IMG activity: OIUX1_ACT_MIGR
S_SO7_65001288	IMG activity: OIUX1_AGY_DEFN
S_SO7_65001289	IMG activity: OIUX1_RPT_SGRP
S_SO7_65001290	IMG activity: OIUX1_TXCD_XREF
S_SO7_65001291	IMG activity: OIUX1_EXEC_COMB
S_SO7_65001293	IMG activity: OIO_VG_FLDST_ASS
S_SO7_65001294	IMG activity: OIO_C1_FLDST
S_SO7_65001296	IMG activity: SIMG_OIJ_TSW_049
S_SO7_65001297	IMG activity: SIMG_OIJ_TSW_050
S_SO7_65001298	IMG activity: SIMG_OIJ_TSW_051
S_SO7_65001299	IMG activity: SIMG_OIJ_TSW_052
S_SO7_65001300	IMG activity: SIMG_OIJ_TSW_053
S_SO7_65001304	Program ROIUX1_TAX_PUID_MIGR
S_SO7_65001305	Program ROIUX1_TAX_MSTR_MIGRATION
S_SO7_65001307	Master table migration from old to g
S_SO7_65001308	History table migration from old to
S_SO7_65001309	royalty report
S_SO7_65001310	royalty report
S_SO7_65001311	IMG activity: SIMG_OIJ_TSW_055
S_SO7_65001312	IMG activity: SIMG_OIJ_TSW_056
S_SO7_65001314	IMG activity: SIMG_OIJ_TSW_057
S_SO7_65001315	IMG activity: SIMG_OIJ_TSW_058
S_SO7_65001316	IMG activity: OIO_RN_SVCAT

S_SO7_65001317	IMG activity: OIO_SP_DFLDA
S_SO7_65001318	IMG activity: OIUCW_CHECKLOT
S_SO7_65001319	IMG activity: OIUCW_CHECKNUMBERS
S_SO7_65001320	IMG activity: SIMG_OIJ_TSW_059
S_SO7_65001321	IMG activity: SIMG_OIJ_TSW_060
S_SO7_65001322	IMG activity: SIMG_OIJ_TSW_061
S_SO7_65001323	IMG activity: SIMG_OIJ_TSW_062
S_SO7_65001324	IMG activity: SIMG_OIJ_TSW_063
S_SO7_65001325	Exception report for GL/TPSL entries
S_SO7_65001326	IMG activity: SIMG_OIJ_TSW_064
S_SO7_65001327	IMG activity: SIMG_OIJ_TSW_065
S_SO7_65001332	IMG activity: SIMG_OIH_ETAX_0001
S_SO7_65001333	IMG activity: SIMG_OIH_ETAX_0002
S_SO7_65001334	IMG activity: SIMG_OIH_ETAX_0003
S_SO7_65001335	IMG activity: SIMG_OIH_ETAX_0004
S_SO7_65001336	IMG activity: SIMG_OIH_ETAX_0005
S_SOG_81000016	Generated Text
S_SOG_81000017	Generated Text
S_SOG_81000021	Generated Text
S_SOG_81000023	Generated Text
S_SOG_81000024	IMG activity: SIMG_OIUH_CM_STATE
S_SOG_81000025	IMG activity: SIMG_SB_MKT_TAX_DES
S_SOG_81000026	IMG activity: OIUREP_2014_CONFIG
S_SOG_81000027	IMG activity: OIUREP_ADJCD_XRF
S_SOG_81000028	IMG activity: OIUCM_BA_ADDRESS_TY
S_SOG_81000029	IMG activity: SIMG_OIUREP_013
S_SOG_81000030	IMG activity: OIUH_PREMAS_NR
S_SOG_81000032	IMG activity: OIUBL01_CONFIG
S_SOG_81000033	IMG activity: OIUBL01_NRIV
S_SOG_81000034	IMG activity: OIUBL_V_T100C
S_SOG_81000040	IMG activity: SIMG_SB_CTTYPGRP
S_SOG_81000043	IMG activity: OIUPR_MPVL_MR
S_SOG_81000044	IMG activity: OIUPR_MPMTD
S_SOG_81000045	IMG activity: OIUCM_PPARSN
S_SOG_81000047	IMG activity: OIURV_CTX
S_SOG_81000048	IMG activity: OIUCA_MAINTAIN_NRIV
S_SOG_81000049	IMG activity: OIUREP_MAINTAIN_NRIV
S_SOG_81000050	IMG activity: OIUCM_MAINTAIN_NRIV
S_SOG_81000051	IMG activity: OIUPR_MAINTAIN_PRES
S_SOG_81000052	IMG activity: OIUCM_COMB_PD_CD
S_SOG_81000053	IMG activity: OIUREP_SALES_TYPE
S_SOG_81000055	IMG activity: SIMG_OIJ_TSW_070
S_SOG_81000056	IMG activity: SIMG_OIJ_TSW_071
S_SOG_81000057	IMG activity: SIMG_OIJ_TSW_072
S_SOG_81000058	IMG activity: SIMG_OIJ_TSW_073
S_SOG_81000059	IMG activity: SIMG_OIJ_TSW_074
S_SOG_81000060	IMG activity: SIMG_OIJ_TSW_075
S_SOG_81000061	IMG activity: SIMG_OIJ_TSW_076
S_SOG_81000062	IMG activity: SIMG_OIJ_TSW_077
S_SOG_81000063	IMG activity: SIMG_OIJ_TSW_078
S_SOG_81000064	IMG activity: SIMG_OIJ_TSW_079
S_SOG_81000065	IMG activity: SIMG_OIJ_TSW_080
S_SOG_81000066	IMG activity: SIMG_SSR_0222
S_SOG_81000068	IMG activity: SIMG_OIJ_TSW_0013

S_SOG_81000069	IMG activity: SIMG_OIJ_TSW_0016
S_SOG_81000070	IMG activity: SIMG_OIJ_TSW_0017
S_SOG_81000071	IMG activity: SIMG_OIJ_TSW_0012
S_SOG_81000072	IMG activity: SIMG_OIJ_TSW_0010
S_SOG_81000073	IMG activity: SIMG_OIJ_TSW_0011
S_SOG_81000074	IMG activity: SIMG_OIJ_TSW_13
S_SOG_81000075	IMG activity: SIMG_OIJ_TSW_0006
S_SOG_81000076	IMG activity: SIMG_OIJ_TSW_0007
S_SOG_81000077	IMG activity: SIMG_OIJ_TSW_0008
S_SOG_81000078	IMG activity: SIMG_OIJ_TSW_0009
S_SOG_81000079	IMG activity: SIMG_OIJ_TSW_0003
S_SOG_81000080	IMG activity: SIMG_OIJ_TSW_0001
S_SOG_81000081	IMG activity: SIMG_OIJ_TSW_0002
S_SOG_81000082	IMG activity: SIMG_OIJ_TSW_0004
S_SOG_81000083	IMG activity: SIMG_OIJ_TSW_0005
S_SOG_81000084	IMG activity: SIMG_OIJ_TSW_0014
S_SOG_81000085	IMG activity: SIMG_OIJ_TSW_100
S_SOG_81000086	IMG activity: SIMG_OIJ_TSW_101
S_SOG_81000087	IMG activity: SIMG_OIJ_TSW_102
S_SOG_81000088	IMG activity: SIMG_OIJ_TSW_103
S_SOG_81000089	IMG activity: SIMG_OIJ_TSW_104
S_SOG_81000090	IMG activity: SIMG_OIJ_TSW_105
S_SOG_81000092	IMG activity: SIMG_OIJ_TSW_107
S_SOG_81000093	IMG activity: OIO_SH_VGCUS
S_SOG_81000094	IMG activity: OIUREP_2014_UOM
S_SOG_81000095	IMG activity: OIUPR_ASSIGN_SRV_GRP
S_SOG_81000096	IMG activity: OIUPR_CREATE_SRV_GRP
S_SOG_81000097	IMG activity: OIUCA_CREATE_SRV_GRP
S_SOG_81000098	IMG activity: OIUCA_ASSIGN_SRV_GRP
S_SOG_81000099	IMG activity: SIMG_OIJ_TSW_108
S_SOG_81000100	IMG activity: OIO_RT_DLPRC
S_SOG_81000101	IMG activity: SIMG_OIH_ETAX_0007
S_SOG_81000102	IMG activity: SIMG_OIH_ETAX_0006
S_SOG_81000103	IMG activity: SIMG_SSR_0223
S_SOG_81000104	IMG activity: OIO_RT_MAIN
S_SOG_81000105	IMG activity: SIMG_CROSS_OIL_010
S_SOG_81000106	IMG activity: SIMG_OIJ_TSW_109
S_SOG_81000107	IMG activity: SIMG_OIJ_TSW_1110
S_SOG_81000108	IMG activity: SIMG_OIJ_TSW_111
S_SOG_81000110	IMG activity: OIO_VGNUM
S_SOG_81000111	IMG activity: SIMG_OIJ_TSW_113
S_SOG_81000112	IMG activity: SIMG_OIJ_TSW_1114
S_SOG_81000113	IMG activity: SIMG_OIJ_TSW_1115
S_SOG_81000114	IMG activity: SIMG_OIJ_TSW_1116
S_SOG_81000115	IMG activity: SIMG_OIJ_TSW_1117
S_SOG_81000116	IMG activity: SIMG_OIJ_TSW_1118
S_SOG_81000117	IMG activity: SIMG_OIO_BADI_VG
S_SOG_81000119	IMG activity: SIMG_SB_REV_AR
S_SOG_81000120	IMG activity: OIUH_LEGEND_CODE
S_SOG_81000121	IMG activity: OIUH_ACTION_TAKEN
S_SOG_81000122	IMG activity: OIUH_LA_PARISH
S_SOG_81000123	IMG activity: SIMG_OIUREP_SUBMIT
S_SOG_81000124	IMG activity: OIUREP_MMS_2014_BADI
S_SOG_81000125	IMG activity: OIURV_CREATE_SRV_GRP

SAP Transaction Codes – Volume Two

S_SOG_81000126	IMG activity: OIURV_ASSIGN_SRV_GRP
S_SOG_81000127	IMG activity: SIMG_PRA_UOMBADI
S_SOG_81000129	IMG activity: OIUREP_MMS_2014_MESS
S_SOG_81000166	IMG activity: OIUX3_CONF
S_SOG_81000167	IMG activity: OIUX3_SN_NR_COMMON
S_SOG_81000168	IMG activity: OIUX3_RPT_COMP
S_SOG_81000169	IMG activity: OIUX3_RPT_COMPX
S_SOG_81000170	IMG activity: OIUX3_EDIT_SRV_GRP
S_SOG_81000171	IMG activity: OIUX3_CONF_PP
S_SOG_81000172	IMG activity: OIUX3_RPT_GRPPX
S_SOG_81000173	IMG activity: OIUX3_SN_NR_TX
S_SOG_81000174	IMG activity: OIUX3_TX_COMXRF
S_SOG_81000175	IMG activity: OIUX3_TX_TXCLEX
S_SOG_81000176	IMG activity: V_OIUX3_TX_REJ
S_SOG_81000177	IMG activity: V_OIUX3_TX_REJC
S_SOG_81000178	IMG activity: V_OIUX3_RPT_CFG
S_SOG_81000179	IMG activity: V_OIUX3_RPTCFGD
S_SOG_81000180	IMG activity: OIUX3_RPT_GRP
S_SOG_81000181	IMG activity: OIUX3_RPT
S_SOG_81000182	IMG activity: OIUX3_RPT_STEP
S_SOG_81000183	IMG activity: OIUX3_RPT_STEPX
S_SOG_81000184	IMG activity: OIUX3_STEPX_ST
S_SOG_81000185	IMG activity: OIUX3_MIG_GRP
S_SOG_81000186	IMG activity: OIUX3_MIG_GRPRX
S_SOG_81000187	IMG activity: OIUX3_MIG_ITEM
S_SOG_81000188	IMG activity: OIUX3_ITEM_ST
S_SOG_81000190	IMG activity: OIUX4_SN_NR
S_SOG_81000191	IMG activity: OIUX4_BAL_CTG
S_SOG_81000192	IMG activity: OIUX3_TX_RP_EDT1
S_SOG_81000193	IMG activity: OIUX3_TX_RP_EDT2
S_SOG_81000194	IMG activity: OIUX3_TX_RP_EDT2_2
S_SRM_25000001	Generation Rules from Client 000
S_VA6_57000005	IMG activity: GRCAC_MAINT_PARAM
S_VA6_57000006	IMG activity: GRCAC_MAINT_CODES
S_WP_CACHE_RELOAD	Load Workplace Runtime Data
S_WP_LOGSYS_ON_OFF	WP Systems: Configure Availability
S_WP_USERCOUNTRY_GET	Country for Users from HR System
S_XAH_05000014	RFID_PTVPRADPRC00
S_XAH_05000015	RFID_PTVPRADPRV00
S_XB3_95000001	IMG Activity: _ISUBDBP_000016
S_XB3_95000002	IMG Activity: _ISUCSPPM_000002
S_XB3_95000003	IMG Activity: _ISUINBB_000022
S_XB3_95000004	IMG Activity: _ISUINBB_000023
S_XB3_95000005	IMG Activity: _ISUINBB_000024
S_XB3_95000006	IMG Activity: _ISUINBB_000025
S_XB3_95000007	IMG Activity: _ISUINBB_000026
S_XB4_60000039	Dates
S_XB4_60000040	Calendar Use - Date Shift
S_XB4_60000041	Assign. Transfer Date - Incoterm
S_XB4_60000064	Date Calculation
S_XB4_60000065	Calculation and Change of Intervals
S_XB4_60000066	Semi-Automatic Date Shift
S_XB7_96000001	Application Components ACE
S_XB7_96000003	Accrual Methods

S_XB7_96000010	Accounting Principles
S_XB7_96000045	IMG
S_XB7_96000046	IMG
S_XB7_96000047	Validation ACE
S_XB7_96000048	Activation Validation ACE
S_XB7_96000049	Cust
S_XB7_96000050	Cust
S_XB7_96000052	IMG
S_XB7_96000056	IMG
S_XB7_96000057	IMG
S_XB7_96000059	Calc. Formula for Derived Accrl Type
S_XB7_96000060	Accrual Types
S_XB7_96000061	Customer Settings for Component
S_XB7_96000062	Accrual Types
S_XB7_96000063	Cust
S_XB7_96000065	Function Modules for ACE
S_XB7_96000069	Operators
S_XB7_96000070	Legacy Data Transfer
S_XB7_96000071	Derived Accrual Types
S_XB7_96000072	Alternative Data Elements
S_XB7_96000073	Component-Specific Programs
S_XB7_96000093	IMG
S_XB7_96000094	Customizing View
S_XB7_96000095	IMG Activity: V_TACEPSRULE
S_XB7_96000096	CoCode/Acctng Principle Combination
S_XB7_96000108	Start Periodic Accrual Run
S_XB7_96000109	Reverse Accrual Run
S_XB7_96000110	Unreasonable Accounting IRR
S_XB7_96000111	Accrual Engine - Balnce Carryforward
S_XB7_96000112	Cust
S_XB7_96000113	Cust
S_XB7_96000114	Cust
S_XB7_96000115	Percentage Rates
S_XB7_96000116	System Events in ACE
S_XB7_96000167	IMG
S_XB7_96000168	IMG
S_XB7_96000195	S_XB7_96000195
S_XB7_96000199	S_XB7_96000199
S_XB7_96000238	IMG
S_XB7_96000239	Disp.Unreasonable Int.Rate of Return
S_XB7_96000240	Contracts with Errors
S_XB7_96000241	Contracts with Errors
S_XB7_96000248	Display Calculated Accruals
S_XB7_96000249	Display Posted Accruals
S_XB7_96000274	IMG Activity: 0FIOTP_DOC_ADJUST
S_XBA_46000001	IMG Activity, RMS_FRM
S_XBA_46000002	IMG Activity, RMS_FRM
S_XBA_46000003	IMG Activity, RMS_FRM
S_XBA_46000004	IMG Activity, RMS_FRM
S_XBA_46000006	IMG Activity, RMS_FRM
S_XBA_46000007	IMG Activity, RMS_FRM
S_XBA_46000008	IMG Activity: RMS_FRM_50
S_XBA_46000009	IMG Activity, RMS_FRM
S_XBA_46000011	IMG Activity, CPPERCP

S_XBA_46000013	IMG Activity, CPPERCP
S_XBA_46000014	IMG Activity, CPPERCP
S_XBA_46000021	IMG Activity CPPERCP
S_XBA_46000022	IMG Activity CPPERCP
S_XBA_46000023	IMG Activity CPPERCP
S_XBA_46000024	IMG Activity CPPERCP
S_XBA_46000025	IMG Activity CPPERCP
S_XBA_46000028	IMG Activity CPPERCP
S_XBA_46000029	IMG Activity CPPERCP
S_XBA_46000030	IMG Activity CPPERCP
S_XBA_46000031	IMG Activity CPPERCP
S_XBA_46000032	IMG Activity CPPERCP
S_XBA_46000033	IMG Activity RMS_FRM
S_XBA_46000034	IMG Activity CPPERCP
S_XBG_76000001	IMG
S_XBG_76000002	IMG
S_XBG_76000003	IMG
S_XBG_76000004	IMG
S_XBG_76000005	IMG
S_XBG_76000006	IMG
S_XBG_76000007	IMG
S_XBG_76000008	IMG
S_XBG_76000009	IMG
S_XBG_76000010	IMG
S_XBG_76000011	IMG
S_XBG_76000012	IMG
S_XBG_76000013	IMG
S_XBG_76000014	IMG
S_XBG_76000015	IMG
S_XBG_76000016	IMG
S_XBG_76000017	IMG
S_XBG_76000018	IMG
S_XBG_76000019	IMG
S_XBI_19000067	IMG Activity: DOCUMENT_OBJ
S_XBK_47000059	IMG Activity: RMX_0027
S_XBO_33000001	IMG Activity: RMS_MRTRS_0100
S_XBO_33000002	IMG Activity: RMS_MRTRS_0200
S_XBO_45000001	IMG Activity: CMPC_0001
S_XBO_45000002	IMG Activity: CMPC_0002
S_XBO_45000003	IMG Activity: CMPC_0003
S_XBO_45000004	IMG Activity: CMPC_0004
S_XBO_45000005	IMG Activity: CMPC_0005
S_XBO_45000006	IMG Activity: CMPC_0006
S_XBO_45000007	IMG Activity: CMPC_0007
S_XML_CONFIG	Settings for XML Connection
S_Y9D_04000048	IMG Activity: WP_START_ARG2
T$GS	Number range maintenance: T_TEST
T108	Change tactical standard planning
T109	Change tactical spring/summer plng
T110	Change tactical fall/winter planning
T111	Change operational standard planning
T112	Change oper. spring/summer planning
T113	Change operational fall/winter plng
T114	Change OTB

SAP Transaction Codes – Volume Two

T115	Promotion planning
T123	Number Range Maintenance: TT123
TAANA	Table Analysis
TAANA_AV	Table Analysis: Analysis Variants
TAANA_VF	Table Analysis: Virtual Fields
TABLE_SCANNER	Search Several Tables
TABR	Settle
TAC1	Number range maintenance: FTA_GSART
TAC2	Number range maintenance: FTA_KLAMMR
TAC3	Number range maintenance: FTR_REFNR
TAC4	Number Range Maintenance: FTA_MAID
TAC5	Number Range Maintenance: FTA_AWKEY
TACD	Trader: Change Documents
TAISC0	Company Code Customizing
TAISC1	Product Type Customizing
TAISC2	Transaction Types Customizing
TAISC3	Acct Assignment Reference Customizg
TAISC5	Update Type Customizing
TAISC6	Valuation Class Customizing
TAISC7	Valuation Class Customizing
TAISC8	Valuation Class Customizing
TANMDCR	Define Structure Chart for MDCRS
TANMDCR_DS	Maintain Market Data Change Rate Set
TAV1	Fix Average Rate
TAV2	Reset Average Rate Fixing
TA_FITV_IMG_VIEWSAVE	Transaction Called to Save View Data
TB.5	FC valuation of hedged documents
TB01	Create forex hedge
TB02	Change forex hedge
TB03	Display forex hedge
TB04	Delete forex hedge
TB0A	TR: Maintenance view swap rates
TB10	Process hedge requests
TB11	Create Object Hedge
TB12	Change object hedge
TB13	Display object hedge
TB14	Reverse object hedge
TB18	Hedged underlyings
TB19	Forex Hedges - Collective Processing
TB20	Unallocated forex transactions
TB21	Allocated forex transactions
TB30	List of open items FI
TB35	Reconciliation of cleared items
TB60	List of processed hedge requests
TBA1	TR:Maint. Change trans. category
TBA2	TR:Maint. Change processing cat.
TBA3	TR: Maint. Change TCODES Menu TIMN
TBA4	TR:Maint. Change processing cat.
TBA5	TR:Maint.Chnge Alloc.Proc.cat/act.ct
TBA6	TR: Maint. Change flow/cond. cat.
TBA7	TR:Maint.ChngeAlloc.App./Flw.CondCat
TBA8	TR: Maint. Change act.proc/def.
TBB1	Execute postings
TBB1_LC	Flag Flows as Posted

SAP Transaction Codes – Volume Two

TBB1_LC_OP_ONLY		Flag flows as posted (before migr.)
TBB1_OP_ONLY		Perform postings (before migration)
TBB2	Reverse postings	
TBB2_OP_ONLY		Reverse postings
TBB3	Flag Flows as Reversed	
TBB3_OP_ONLY		Flag flows as reversed (before migr)
TBB4	Accrual/deferral	
TBB5	Reverse accrual/deferral	
TBC0	TR: Maintain manual reversal type	
TBC1	Datafeed: Define variants	
TBC2	Datafeed: adjust workflow	
TBC3	Define standard role	
TBC5	Responsibilities for Agent Assgnment	
TBC6	Transaction Release: Adjust Workflow	
TBCA	Index Definition	
TBCB	Maintain Index Rate Type	
TBCC	Exchanges	
TBCD	Treasury: Change Docs Transactions	
TBCF	Exchange rate volatilities	
TBCI	View Master data G/L account	
TBCJ	Maint.Planning Types for Trans.Types	
TBCK	Check account determination	
TBCL	Maintenance View Hedge-Relev. Curr.	
TBCM	Maintenance View Unit Types	
TBCN	Maintenance: Note for Transaction	
TBCO	Security price type	
TBCP	Retransfer of activity transition	
TBCQ	Alloc. ValuationFlowTypes-Transactn	
TBCR	TR: Maintain fixing attributes FX	
TBCS	Automatic fixing processing	
TBCU	Check Account Determination: Forex	
TBCV	Check Acct Determination: Money Mkt	
TBCW	Check Acct Determination:Derivatives	
TBCX	Maintain Acct Determination: Forex	
TBCY	Maintain Acct Determination: MM	
TBCZ	Maintain Acct Determination: DE	
TBD0	Datafeed: Adminster Archives	
TBD1	Datafeed: Table structure VTB_DFCU	
TBD2	Datafeed: Datafeed Customizing	
TBD3	Datafeed: Market data administration	
TBD4	Datafeed: Updated market data	
TBD5	Datafeed: Import market data file	
TBD6	Datafeed: Log file administration	
TBD7	Datafeed: Check Customizing	
TBD8	Datafeed: Archive	
TBD9	Datafeed: Reload archives	
TBDA	Datafeed: Real-Time Initialization	
TBDB	Datafeed: Read archives	
TBDC	Datafeed: Real-Time monitor	
TBDD	Datafeed: Feed/Mode/Destination	
TBDE	Datafeed:Text tables operating modes	
TBDF	Datafeed: View permitted feeds	
TBDG	Datafeed: Text table feeds	
TBDH	Datafeed: Text table instr.classes	

SAP Transaction Codes – Volume Two

TBDI	Datafeed: View Classes Allowed
TBDJ	Datafeed: Historical Market Data
TBDK	Datafeed: Code Conversion Program
TBDM	Market Data File Interface INPUT
TBDN	Market Data File Interface - OUTPUT
TBDO	Market Data File: Code Conversion
TBEX	Spreadsheet for Market Data
TBI1	Standg instrns Maintain pmnt details
TBI1D	Display SI Payment Details
TBI2	Standing instns Alloc. pmnt details
TBI5	Maintain Correspondence SI
TBI5D	Display SI Correspondence
TBI5_COPY	Copy Standing Instruct. for Corresp.
TBI5_DELE	Delete Standing Instr. for Corresp.
TBI6	Authorization - maintain SI
TBI6D	Authorization - display SI
TBI6_COPY	Copy SI for Transaction Authorizat.
TBI6_DELE	Delete SI for Trans. Authorization
TBI7	SI Maintain Derived Flows
TBI7D	Display SI Derived Flows
TBI7_COPY	Copy SI for Derived Flows
TBI7_DELE	Delete SI for Derived Flows
TBI8	Standing Instructions: Evaluations
TBIR	Mass Release of Interim Limits
TBK1	TR: Cust. loan acct assignment ref.
TBK2	TR: Cust. Acc.Ass.Ref. Securities
TBK4	TR: Cust. Acc.Ass.Ref. Forex
TBK5	TR: Cust. Acc.Ass.Ref. Money Market
TBK6	TR: Cust. Acc.Ass.Ref. Derivatives
TBL1	Limits: Change/Display
TBL10	Treasury: Delete Limits
TBL2	Limits: Change Documents
TBL3	Limits: Overview
TBL4	Limit Utilization: Overview
TBL6	Limit Utilization: Delete
TBL7	Limit Type: Delete Data
TBL8	Reorganize STC Logs
TBL9	Display STC Logs
TBLA	TR: Limit Maintenance for VC_ATLA
TBLARC	Archiving: Limits and Utilizations
TBLA_BANKING	TR: Limit Maint. VC_ATLA_BANKING
TBLA_CFM	TR: Limit Maint. VC_ATLA_CFM
TBLB	Limit Utilization: Overview
TBLC	Lock/Unlock Limits
TBLC01	Check of Determination Procedure
TBLD	Lock/Unlock Countries
TBLE	Limit Management: Lock Entries
TBLM	Flow List
TBLPECC	Change Posting Deadline
TBLP_CANC	Cancel Transfer/Loan
TBLP_COST	Cost Transfer/Loan
TBLP_CUST	Customizing Transfer/Borrow/Loan
TBLP_INFO	Transfer/Loan/Payback Info-Report
TBLP_M2M	Create Mat. to Mat. Group Transfer

SAP Transaction Codes – Volume Two

TBLP_PBCK	Pay Back Loan
TBLP_TRLO	Create Transfer/Loan
TBLR	Release Limits
TBLT01	Limit: Generate Table for Lim. Types
TBLT02	Limit: Move Data to Generated Table
TBLT03	Limit: Delete Generated Table
TBLT04	Limit: Reorganiz. of Analysis Char.
TBLT05	Limit: Check Analysis Characterist.
TBLT06	Check/Correct Consist. of Gen.Tables
TBLW1	Review: Send
TBLW2	Review: Change Review Recipient
TBM1	Treasury: Create Mast.Agreement
TBM2	Treasury: Chg. Mast. Agreement
TBM3	Treasury: Displ. Mast. Agreement
TBM4	Treasury: Master Agreement Changes
TBM5	Treasury: Assign Mast. Agreement
TBM6	Treasury: Vol. Check for Master Agr.
TBM7	Master Agreement: Maintain Memo IDs
TBMN	Currency Hedges
TBR0	Posting journal
TBR1	Treasury: Create netting
TBR2	Treasury: Change netting
TBR3	Treasury: Display netting
TBR4	Treasury: Reverse netting
TBR5	Treasury: Netting proposal list
TBR6	Treasury: Create reference
TBR7	Treasury: Change reference
TBR8	Treasury: Display reference
TBR9	Treasury: Reverse Reference
TBRL	Treasury: Coll. proc. references
TBRULESET_CD	FTR Rule Management: Change Documnts
TBSI_TOOLS	Tools for Standing Instructions
TBT1	Transaction Authorizat. for Traders
TBT1D	Display Trans. Auth. for Traders
TBX2	Conversion of SEC Corresp. Customiz.
TBZ1	Output Correspondence
TBZ11	Correspondence Monitor
TBZ12	Overview of Reset Counterconfirmatn
TBZ13	Printer Override Function
TBZ14	Exception Processing IDoc (Inbound)
TBZ15	Status Monitor - IDoc Confirmations
TBZ16	Maintain IDoc FTRCON Postprocessor
TBZ17	SWIFT Code -> Partner - Assignment
TBZ2	Incoming Confirmations Forex
TBZ3	Money Market: Incoming Confirmations
TBZ3A	Money Market: Incoming Confirmations
TBZ4	Incoming Confirmations Forex Options
TBZ5	List of Days Overdue Counterconf.
TBZ6	Match Incoming SWIFT Confirmation
TBZ7	Delete corr. planned records
TBZ8	Correspondence - Overview
TC02	Number range maint.: FTI_UGSART
TCL1	Define Lines of Credit
TCL2	Display Lines of Credit

SAP Transaction Codes – Volume Two

TCLSVERS	Default Values Logistic Switch
TCMK	Funds Management
TCMN	Funds Management
TCO	Start a TR in Parameter TCX
TCOM	Evaluate offers
TCURMNT	Maintain Exchange Rates
TDMN	Cash management
TDMN_DIST	Distribution of TR Cash Mgt Data
TEM1	Master Data Exposure Plng Profile
TEM10	Display and Maint. of Raw Exposures
TEM11	Display Raw Exposures
TEM15	Generate Version
TEM19	Versions Display
TEM20	Exposure Analysis
TEM30	Delete Last Version
TEMN_EXPOS	Number Range Maintenance: TEMN_EXPOS
TER1	SAPterm: Changing Status of Terms
TEST0002	Test 0002
TEST6999	Number range maintenance: TEST38
TEST999	Test 9999
TEST_ALEXANDER	Number Range Maintenance: Test
TEST_CLEAR	Test API Data Cleansing
TEST_SOFT_MOD	Test "Soft" Modifications
TEST_TEXTEDIT	Test for TextEdit Wrapper
TEST_TEXTEDITOR	Test Program for TextEditor
TF00	Collective Processing for Repos
TF01	Create Forward Security Transaction
TF02	Change Forward Securities Transactn
TF03	Display Forward Securities Transactn
TF04	Settle Forward Securities Transactn
TF05	Deliver Forward Securities Transactn
TF06	Reverse Forward Securities Transactn
TF07	Roll Over Forward Securities Trans.
TF08	History of Forward Securities Trans.
TF09	FST: Advance Maturity
TF10	FST: Display Activity
TF11	FST: Dividend Adjustment
TFBWD	Customizing Table TFBWD
TFBWE	Customizing Table TFBWE
TFCP	Coll. Processing: Forward Sec.Trans.
TFMN	Cash Flow
TFSCD_ACTIVATE_OPORD	Classification Key and Direct Input
TFWB	Maintain Mini-Templates
TF_01	Create Forward
TF_02	Change Forward
TF_03	Display Forward
TF_04	Reverse Forward
TF_05	Settle Forward
TF_06	Fixing Forward
TF_07	Fixing Settle Forward
TF_08	Terminate Forward
TF_09	Settle Termination Forward
TF_10	History Forward
TF_10H	History Forward

SAP Transaction Codes – Volume Two

TF_15	Settle Contract Forward
TF_76	Forward - History
TF_WS453012160001	Query About a Flight Booking
TF_WS700004380001	AbsenceRequestCreate
TF_WS770001350001	Leave request
TGANL	Create Separation Allowance
TGANZ	Display Separation Allowance Event
TGMOD	Change Separation Allowance
TGPER	Edit Separation Allowance
THIPAA	For checking past certificates
THM10	Exposure Expiration
THM11	Reverse Exposure Expiration
THM12	Hedge Plan Expiration
THM14	Hedging Relationship Dedesignation
THM15	Reverse HR dedesignations
THM30	Define NPVs on Inception Date
THM35	Adjustment of the interest rates
THM50	Transfer Prospect. Effect.Assessment
THM51	Reverse Trans. Prospect.Eff.Assess.
THM52	Retrospective Assessment
THM53	Reverse Retrospective Eff. Ass.
THM54	Manual OCI Reclassification
THM55	Reverse Manual OCI Reclassification
THM56	Fair value changes to be posted
THM57	Reverse FV Changes to be Posted
THM58	Automatic EC Reclassification
THM59	Reversal of Automatic EC Reclass.
THM80	Effectiveness test
THM81	OCI per hedging relationship
THM82	Hedge plan overview
THM83	Hedging Relationships per Derivative
THM84	Prematurely Reclassified OCI
THM85	Change documents for Hedge Managemnt
THM86	Hedge Relationship Documentation
THM87	Reverse Regression Assessment
THMEX	Hedge Management: Application
THMFLOWT_DER	FX_Flowtypes Hedge Management
THMFLOWT_FX	DER_Flowtypes Hedge Management
THMMM	Exposure Upload from Money Market
THMR1	Reverse single HR dedesignation
THMR2	Reverse single HR dissolve
THMRO	Exposure Upload From External Source
THMST	Hedging Relationship Status Overview
THM_COCO_SETTING	Number range for hedges
THM_COCO_SETTING1	Number range for hedging rel.ships
THM_COCO_SETTING2	Comp.-code settings for hedge mgmt
THM_NR_HEDGE	Define number ranges for hedges
THM_NR_HR	Define number ranges for HR
THM_NR_PLAN	Number range maintenance: THM_PLAN
THM_NR_TRANS	Number range maintenance: THM_TRANS
TI-3	Display Currency Option
TI00	Collective Processing for Futures
TI10	Create Interest Rate Adjustment
TI11	Change Interest Rate Adjustment

TI12	Display Interest Rate Adjustment
TI35	Collect.Processing: Listed Options
TI37	Reverse Interest Rate Adjustment
TI40	Currency Option Fast Entry
TI49	Change Currency Option
TI4A	Forex Fast Entry
TI4B	Currency Option Entry - Spread
TI55	Create Future Master Record
TI56	Chg.Futures Master
TI57	Displ.Futures Master
TI5AN	Options/Futures: Create Transaction
TI5BN	Options/Futures: Change Transaction
TI5CN	Options/Futures: Display Transaction
TI5DN	Options/Futures: Execute Order
TI5EN	Options/Futures: Order Expiration
TI5FN	Options/Futures: Settle Contract
TI5GN	Options/Futures: Reverse
TI5HN	Options/Futures: Display History
TI5W	Display Option Master
TI5X	Create Option Master
TI5Y	Change Option Master
TI70	Create Order
TI71	Create OTC Option
TI72	Change Transaction
TI73	Display Transaction
TI74	Reverse Contract
TI75	Settle Contract
TI76	OTC Transaction: History
TI77	Terminate Transaction
TI78	Execute Own Offer
TI79	Settle Termination
TI7A	Order Expiration
TI7B	Display Interest Settlements
TI80	Create OTC Option
TI81	Change OTC Option
TI82	OTC option: Display
TI83	OTC Option: Create Contract
TI84	OTC Option: Execute Offer
TI85	OTC Option: Settle Contract
TI86	Exercise OTC Option
TI87	OTC Option: Settle Exercise
TI88	OTC Option: Expired
TI89	OTC Option: Settle Expiration
TI8A	OTC Option: Reverse Activity
TI8B	OTC Option: Order Expiry
TI8C	OTC Option: Display Activity
TI8D	Terminate OTC Option
TI8E	OTC Option: Settle Termination
TI8F	OTC Option Knock-In
TI8G	OTC Option Knock-Out
TI8H	Settle OTC Knock-Out Option
TI8I	Settle OTC Knock-In Option
TI90	Posting Release
TI91	Collective Processing OTC Options

SAP Transaction Codes – Volume Two

TI91_MS	OTC Options
TI92	Collect.Processing-Int.Rate Instrum.
TI93	Manual Posting Block
TI94	Collective Monitoring of Options
TIC1	Number Range Maintenance: FTI_OPTFUT
TIDX1	Simulate Price Index
TIMECUST	Profile for Time Functions
TIMECUSTEV	Symbolic Names for Dates
TIMEPROF	Profile for Time Functions
TIMN	
TIS1	Overview - Positions
TIS10	Currency Analysis
TIS11	Simulated Valuation
TIS12	Total Commitment
TIS20	Analysis: Int.-Bearing Instruments
TIS5	Country Analysis
TIS50	Issue Position
TIS_IFRS7_1	Foreign Exchange Risk Reporting
TIS_IFRS7_2	Interest Rate Risk Report
TIS_IFRS7_3	Interest Rate Sensitivity Report
TIS_IFRS7_4	Changes in Fair Value Reports
TIS_IFRS7_5	Changes in Fair Value of Instruments
TIS_IFRS7_6	Changes in Fair value of Fin Instr
TIS_IFRS7_7	Risk Return Analysis
TIS_IFRS7_D1	FX Risk Reporting (Detailed)
TIS_IFRS7_D2	Int. Rate Risk Reporting (Detail)
TIS_IFRS7_D3	Int. Rate Sensitivity Report(Detail)
TIS_IFRS7_D4	Changes in Fair Value Reports
TIS_IFRS7_D5	Changes in Fair Value of Inst.(Detl)
TIS_IFRS7_D6	Changes in Fair Value of Inst.(Detl)
TIS_IFRS7_D7	Risk Return Analysis (Detailed)
TJ01	Journal of transactions
TJ02	Collective editing of options
TJ04	Payment Plan
TJ05	Automatic Interest Rate Adjustment
TJ05_REV	Reverse Automatic Int. Rate Adjust.
TJ06	Option Expiration
TJ07	Interest Rate Adjustment Schedule
TJ08	Transaction Release: Work Item List
TJ09	Update Planned Records
TJ10	Summary Journal Fin. Transctions
TJ11	Display Single Transaction
TJ12	Journal: Transactions w. Cash Flows
TK11	Create condition (shipment costs)
TK12	Change condition (shipment costs)
TK13	Display condition (shipment costs)
TK14	Create condition with ref.
TKCS	Start transaction sender programs
TKLFZ01MD	Facilities: Master Data Reporting
TKLFZDT01	Detail Reporting for Facilities
TL3M	List of curr. supported field names
TL3P	Maintain Variant Group
TL3Q	Maintain Variants
TL3R	Schedule Variant Groups

SAP Transaction Codes – Volume Two

TL3S	Define Variant Groups
TLL1	Limit: Create Limit Transfer
TLL2	Limit: Change Limit Transfer
TLL3	Limit: Display Limit Transfer
TLL4	Limit Transfer: Change Documents
TLL5	Limit Transfer: Collective Process.
TLM0	Execute Report
TLM1	Create Report
TLM2	Change Report
TLM3	Display Report
TLM4	Create Form
TLM5	Change Form
TLM6	Display Form
TLM7	Maintain authorization obj. present.
TLM8	Display authorization obj.presentatn
TLMA	Access Report Tree
TLMB	Maintain Batch Variants
TLMC	Limit Management: Manage Comments
TLMD	Split Report
TLMG	Limit Management: Character. Groups
TLMH	Maintain hierarchy
TLMJ	Maintain Hierarchy Nodes
TLMK	Maintain Key Figures
TLMM	Limit Mgmt: Drilldown Test Monitor
TLMO	Transport Reports
TLMP	Transport Forms
TLMQ	Import Reports from Client 000
TLMR	Import Forms from Client 000
TLMS	Display Structure
TLMT	Translation Tool - Drilldown Report.
TLMU	Convert drilldown reports
TLMV	Maintain Global Variable
TLMW	Maintain Crcy Translation Type TLM
TLMX	Reorganize Drilldown Reports
TLMY	Reorganize Report Data
TLMZ	Reorganize Forms
TLR1	Limit: Create Reservation
TLR2	Limit: Change Reservation
TLR3	Limit: Display Reservation
TLR4	Reservations: Mass Processing
TLR5	Reservations: Change Documents
TLR6	Reservations: Reorganization
TLR7	Limit: Copy Reservation
TLTA	Access Report Tree
TM00	Money Market: Collective processing
TM01	Create Fixed-Term Deposit
TM02	Change Fixed-Term Deposit
TM03	Display Fixed-Term Deposit
TM04	Roll Over Fixed-Term Deposit
TM06	Settle Fixed-Term Deposit
TM07	Reverse Fixed-Term Deposit
TM09	Fixed-Term Deposit History
TM0F	Fxd Term Dep. Fast Entry
TM11	Create Deposit at Notice

SAP Transaction Codes – Volume Two

TM12	Change Deposit at Notice
TM13	Display Deposit at Notice
TM14	Roll Over Deposit at Notice
TM15	Give Notice on Deposit at Notice
TM16	Settle Deposit at Notice
TM17	Reverse Deposit at Notice
TM19	Deposit at Notice History
TM1F	Deposit at Notice Fast Entry
TM20	Money Market: Collective Processing
TM21	Deposit at Notice Cash Flow Update
TM22	Check Dates against Calendar
TM30	Commercial Paper: NPV Calculator
TM31	Create Commercial Paper
TM32	Change Commercial Paper
TM33	Display Commercial Paper
TM35	Give Notice on Commercial Paper
TM36	Settle Commercial Paper
TM37	Reverse Commercial Paper
TM39	Commercial Paper History
TM3F	Commercial Paper Fast Entry
TM41	Create Cash Flow Transaction
TM42	Change Cash Flow Transaction
TM43	Display Cash Flow Transaction
TM46	Settle Cash Flow Transaction
TM47	Reverse Cash Flow Transaction
TM49	Cash Flow Transaction History
TMA5	Edit characteristics
TMA6	Edit Value Fields
TMB1	Premium reserve fund lists
TMB2	Statements
TMBA	BAV Information
TMBU	BAV Transfers
TMCA	Create fixed-term deposit offer
TMCB	Execute fixed-term deposit offer
TMCC	Display fixed-term deposit offer
TMDFX	IMG activity: SIMG_CFMENUORFBOB08
TMDIDX	IMG Activity: INDEX_INPUT
TMDNPV	IMG Activity: BARWERT_OTC
TMDSE	Maintain Security Price
TMEZ	Money Market: Effective Int. Calc.
TMFM	Money Market: Generate Cash Flow
TMMN	Money Market
TMR0	Money Market: Position list
TMR1	Money Market: Flexible Position List
TMRMB	Reporting Tree for MRM
TMSA	Create fixed-term deposit simulation
TMSB	Change/execute fixed-term dep.simuln
TMSC	Display fixed-term deposit simulatn
TMSD	Delete fixed-term deposit simulation
TMS_IACOR_EDIT	TMS IACOR Destination Maintenance
TMS_IACOR_SHOW	TMS IACOR Destination Maintenance
TMV1	IMG Activity: STOCK_PRICES_INPUT
TMV11	IMG: Change Price Index Values
TMV2	IMG activity: SIMG_CFMENUORFBOB08

TMV3	IMG Activity: SWAP_RATE_INPUT
TMV4	IMG activity: BARWERT_OTC
TMV5	IMG Activity: BETAFAK_PFLEGEN
TMV6	IMG Activity: INDEX_INPUT
TMV7	IMG: Change Price Index Values
TMV9	IMG Activity: SIMG_ZINSWERTE
TM_51	Create Interest Rate Instrument
TM_52	Change Interest Rate Instrument
TM_53	Display Interest Rate Instrument
TM_54	Settle Interest Rate Instrument
TM_55	Reverse Interest Rate Instrument
TM_59	History of Interest Rate Instrument
TM_60	Line of Credit and Utilization
TM_60A	Lines of Credit, Drawings, Fees
TM_61	Create Facility
TM_62	Change Facility
TM_63	Display Facility
TM_64	Settle Facility
TM_65	Reverse Facility
TM_69	History of Facility
TO01	Create OTC Interest Rate Instrument
TO02	Change OTC Interest Rate Instrument
TO03	Display OTC Interest Rate Instrument
TO04	Settle OTC Interest Rate Instrument
TO05	Reverse OTC Interest Rate Instrument
TO06	Give Notice on OTC Int. Rate Instr.
TO07	OTC Int. Rate Inst.: Display History
TO08	Execute OTC Int.Rate Instr. Order
TOK8	Condition exclusion proc. assig. F
TOM0	Clearing
TOOL10	Transaction for TTOOL01
TOOL11	Call VC_FAKNEU
TP00	Travel Management: Travel Planning
TP01	Planning Manager
TP02	Travel Planning (End User)
TP02_EWT	Travel Planning (End User)
TP03	Planning Manager (Expert)
TP04	Travel Request (End User)
TP04_EWT	Travel Request (End User)
TP10	Travel Plan Synchronization (AIR)
TP12	Travel Plan Synchronization (Manual)
TP14	Travel Plan Synchronization (Queue)
TP20	Create Travel Plan
TP30	Display Travel Planning report tree
TP31	Queries for Travel Planning
TP40	Maintain Routings
TP41	Initial Screen via IMG
TP50	Global flight availability
TP60	Synchronization of Hotel Catalog
TPC2	User for Authorization Check
TPC4	Programs for Authorization Check
TPC6	Periods for Authorization Check
TPCP	Travel Planning Customizing
TPCT	Current settings

SAP Transaction Codes – Volume Two

TPDA_CALL_EDITOR	Start Editor	
TPDA_SE37_TEST	TPDA: SE37 Test Framework Init	
TPDA_START	Start Master of TPDA Debugger	
TPDA_START_VERI	Start the TPDA Debugger (VeriMode)	
TPED	Maintain HR Master Data (ESS)	
TPES	Display HR Master Data (ESS)	
TPLOG	Short cut for TPLOG	
TPLP	Create/Change LPs for SABRE	
TPM1	Execute Valuation	
TPM10	Fix. post or reverse transactions	
TPM100	Transaction for Hedge Management	
TPM100_DISPLAY	Transaction to display Hedging Rel.	
TPM101	Classification	
TPM102	Reverse Classification	
TPM103	Postprocess Business Transactions	
TPM11	Post Reversal/Recalculation	
TPM110	Execute Effectiveness Test	
TPM112	Ineffective Hedge Relationships	
TPM12	Treasury Ledger: Position List	
TPM13	Treasury Ledger: Flow List	
TPM14	Update Types - Valn Class Transfer	
TPM15	Valuation Class Transfer	
TPM15M	Valuation Class Transfer	
TPM16	Reversal Valuation Class Transfer	
TPM16M	Reversal of Valuation Class Transfer	
TPM17	Define Securites Account Groups	
TPM18	Fix/Post Derived Business Transact.	
TPM19	Status Change TRL Bus. Transactions	
TPM2	Reverse Valuation	
TPM20	Posting Journal	
TPM21	Create Nominal Adjustment	
TPM22	Display Nominal Adjustment	
TPM23	Reverse Nominal Adjustment	
TPM24	Update Margin Flows	
TPM25	Post Margin Flows	
TPM26	Display quantity ledger positions	
TPM27	Generate Derived Flows	
TPM28	Transfer Acct Assignment Reference	
TPM29	Reverse Acct Assignm. Ref. Transfer	
TPM3	Account Asst Reference Allocations	
TPM30	Def. Determ. of Acct Assgmt Ref.	
TPM31	Def. Determ. of Acct Assgmt Ref.	
TPM32	Def. Determ. of Acct Assgmt Ref.	
TPM33	Account Determination Overview	
TPM35	Manual posting	
TPM4	Futures Account	
TPM40	Display Class Cash Flow for SecAcct	
TPM40A	Display SecAcct Class Position List	
TPM41	Display Sec. Account Position List	
TPM42	Display Class List	
TPM43	Process Restraints On Drawing	
TPM44	Fin.Products Profit Accrual/Deferral	
TPM45	Reverse Accrual/Deferral of Income	
TPM5	Create Class Pos. in Futures Account	

TPM50	Change Position Mgmt Procedure
TPM51	Periodic TRL Reporting
TPM52	Maintain Update Type Reconciliation
TPM53	Create Totals Records
TPM54	Delete Totals Records
TPM55A	Generate Position ID (Securities)
TPM55B	Generate Position ID (Loans)
TPM55C	Create Position Indicator (OTC)
TPM55D	Generate Pos.ID (Listed Derivatives)
TPM56A	Change Position ID (Securities)
TPM56B	Change Position ID (Loans)
TPM56C	Change PositionID (OTC Transactions)
TPM56D	Change Pos. ID (Listed Derivatives)
TPM57A	Display Position ID (Securities)
TPM57B	Display Position ID (Loans)
TPM57C	Display Pos. ID (OTC Transactions)
TPM57D	Display Pos. ID (Listed Derivatives)
TPM58A	Delete Position ID (Securities)
TPM58B	Delete Position ID (Loans)
TPM58D	Delete Pos. ID (Listed Derivatives)
TPM59	Exchange per Company Code/Class
TPM6	Change Class Pos. in Futures Account
TPM60	Save NPVs
TPM61	Execute Data Transfer Positions
TPM61A	Position Information: Securities
TPM62	Reverse Data Transfer Positions
TPM63	Execute Data Transfer
TPM63A	Val. Area-Independ. Data: Securities
TPM63B	Val. Area-Dependent Data: Securities
TPM63C	Val.Area-Dep. Data: MM, FX, OTC Der.
TPM63D	Val. Area-Dependent Data: Futures
TPM64	Reverse Data Transfer
TPM65	HM (FAM): Execute Data Transfer
TPM65A	Data for Securities w. Subpositions
TPM65B	Data for OTC with Subpositions
TPM65C	Data for Futures with Subpositions
TPM66	HM (FAM): Cancel Data Transfer
TPM7	Display Class Pos. in Futures Acct
TPM70	Record or Clear Impairment
TPM71	Reverse Impairment
TPM72	Maint. View Special Sec. Valuation
TPM73	Special security valn
TPM74	Enter Values for Manual Valuation
TPM75	Reference Report for Impairment
TPM8	Display Futures Account Cash Flow
TPM80	Fund Transfer
TPM81	Reversal of Fund Transfer
TPM82	Portfolio Transfer
TPM83	Reversal of Portfolio Transfer
TPM85	Inv.Pool Participants: Edit Add.Data
TPM85A	Inv.Pool Participants: Disp.Add.Data
TPM86	Generate Trans. f. Pool Participants
TPM87	Reverse Inv. Pool Participant Trans.
TPM88	Overview:Inv.Pool Participant Trans.

TPM89	Edit Investment Pool Master Data
TPM89A	Display Investment Pool Master Data
TPM9	Pos. List-Class Pos. in Futures Acct
TPM90	Edit Investments
TPM90A	Display Investments
TPM91	Matching for Futures/Options
TPM92	Matching Overview w. Reversal Funct.
TPMD	Maintain HR Master Data
TPMM	Personnel Actions
TPMN_TRAC1	Number Range Maint.: TPMN_TRAC1
TPMN_TRAC2	Number Range Maintenance: TPMN_TRAC2
TPMN_TRPR	Number Range Maintenance: TPMN_TRPR
TPMN_TRS	Number Range Maint.: TPMN_TRS
TPMO	Translation Performance Monitor
TPMS	Display HR Master Data
TPM_CTY11	Commodity Overview
TPM_CTY_MASTER	Maintain commodity master data
TPM_HR_GROUP1	Maintain HR Grouping 1
TPM_HR_GROUP2	Maintain HR Grouping 2
TPM_INITIALIZE	Initialization of Parallel Val.Areas
TPM_INIT_HREL	Initialization Hedging Relationship
TPM_INIT_HREL_OTC	Init.Hedging Relationship:Subpos.OTC
TPM_INIT_HREL_REV	Reverse Initialization Hedging Rel.
TPM_INIT_HREL_SEC	Init.Hedging Rel.: Sec.Subpositions
TPM_MIGRATION	Conversion to ERP2007
TPM_MIGRATION_CAT	Conversion Type
TPM_MIGRATION_FUTURE	Conversion of Futures from Rel. 4.6
TPM_MIGRATION_PMP	Conversion: PosManProc. No.Assgmt
TPM_NR_HINST	Number range maintenance: TPMN_HINST
TPM_NR_HITEM	Number range maintenance: TPMN_HITEM
TPM_NR_HREL	Number range maintenance: TPMN_HREL
TPM_PAY_ASSIGN	Generation Payment Indicator
TPM_PL_ASSIGN	Generate Profit/Loss Indicators
TPM_POSTAUTREV	Reverse Automatic Debit Position Run
TPM_TRM_HMD_REL01	Customizing for Docum. Release
TPM_TRM_HM_REL01	Customizing for Bus.Tr. Release
TPPF_D	Display Entry V_TA23PF by Key
TPPR	Travel Profile Display
TPQ0	Quicktrip Manager
TP_LOG	Log: Calls of GDS Functions
TR02	Change strategic planning
TR3M	List of curr. supported field names
TR3P	Maintain variant groups
TR3Q	Maintain Variants
TR3R	Schedule Variant Group
TR3S	Define Variant Group
TR3T	Reorganization of variant groups
TRACE	Program Trace
TRANSFER	Transfer/Borrow-Loan-Payback Menu
TRBS	Automatic Postings Loans: Activities
TRC0	Client Copy Customizing
TRC1	Client Copy Customizing
TRC2	Client Copy Customizing
TRC3	Client Copy Customizing

SAP Transaction Codes – Volume Two

TRC4	Client Copy Customizing
TRC5	Client Copy Customizing
TRC6	Client Copy Customizing
TRC7	Client Copy Customizing
TRC8	Client Copy Customizing
TRC9	Client Copy Customizing
TRCA	Client Copy Customizing
TRCB	Client Copy Customizing
TRCC	Client Copy Customizing
TRCD	C FI Maintain Table TBKSP
TRCE	Client Copy Customizing
TRCMB	Report Tree: Cash Management
TRCV_UPDATE_TYPE	Update Type
TRD1	Run Data Mining Report
TRD2	Create Data Mining Report
TRD3	Change Data Mining Report
TRD4	Display Data Mining Report
TRD5	Data Mining: Create Form
TRD6	Data Mining: Change Form
TRD7	Data Mining: Display Form
TRD8	Display Results of Data Mining
TRDEB	Report Tree: Derivatives
TRED	Treasury: Curr. Settings Derivatives
TREXADMIN	TREX Administration Tool
TRFMB	Report Tree: Cash Budget Management
TRFXB	Report Tree: Foreign Exchange
TRF_CLASSPOS_NR	Number Range Maintenance: FTR_TRF_CL
TRF_REV	Reverse Margin Flows
TRIG_IGT	Tcode for IGT processing
TRIP	Travel Manager
TRIP_EWT	Travel Manager
TRISB	Report Tree: Information System
TRLCCHK	TRL Customizing Check
TRLM	Treasury Management Basic Functions
TRLOB	Report Tree: Loans
TRLO_KORRES_VERWTBST	Where-Used for CML Texts
TRLO_TBSCOPY	Copy Texts Between Clients
TRM0	Execute Report
TRM0_NEW	Execute Report (CFM)
TRM1	Create Report
TRM1_NEW	Create Report (CFM)
TRM2	Change Report
TRM2_NEW	Change Report (CFM)
TRM3	Display Report
TRM3_NEW	Display Report (CFM)
TRM4	Create Form
TRM4_NEW	Create Form
TRM5	Change Form
TRM5_NEW	Change Form
TRM6	Display Form
TRM6_NEW	Display Form
TRM7	Maintain Auth.Object Presentation
TRM8	Display Auth.Object Presentation
TRMA	Access Report Tree

SAP Transaction Codes – Volume Two

TRMB	Maintain Batch Variants
TRMC	Comments Management: Treasury
TRMD	Distribute Report
TRME	Create Report
TRMF_FLDS_DEACTIVATE	Deactivate Fields (For All Users)
TRMF_USER_D_MAINTAIN	Maintain Dependencies: Cust. Char.
TRMF_USER_K_MAINTAIN	Maintain Fld Catalog: Cust.Key.Fig.
TRMF_USER_M_MAINTAIN	Maintain Field Catalog: Cust. Char.
TRMG	Characteristic Groups for TR Reports
TRMG_KFG_CREATE	Create Key Figure Group
TRMG_KFG_MAINTAIN	Maintain Key Figure Group
TRMH	Maintain hierarchy
TRMJ	Maintain Hierarchy Nodes
TRMK	Maintain Key Figures
TRMM	Treasury Drill Down Rptng Testmonit.
TRMMB	Report Tree: Money Market
TRMO	Transport reports
TRMP	Transport forms
TRMP_PERFORMANCE_BP	Reorganize Business Partner Texts
TRMP_PERFORMANCE_MV	Reorganize Risk Key Figures
TRMP_PERFORMANCE_MVT	Reorganize Risk Key Figures
TRMP_PERFORMANCE_ST	Set Buffer Table Parameters
TRMQ	Import reports from client 000
TRMR	Import forms from client 000
TRMS	Display Structure
TRMS_ALL	Display Structures
TRMS_DEACTIVATE	Deactivate Structures
TRMS_EXTENDED	Display Structure
TRMS_SINGLE	Display Structures
TRMS_USER_DEACTIVATE	Deactivate Structures: User-Depend.
TRMT	Translation Tool - Drilldown Report.
TRMT_TEXTS_GENERATE	Generates the Text Reader
TRMU	Convert drilldown reports
TRMU_FLDS_DEACTIVATE	Deactivate Fields: User-Dependent
TRMV	Maintain Global Variable
TRMW	Maintain currency exchange type TRM
TRMX	Reorganize Drilldown Reports
TRMY	Reorganize report data
TRMZ	Reorganize Forms
TRM_GENERATE	Generates Dependent Programs
TRN0	Number range: Land register no.
TRN1	N.Range: FVVD_BO Business Operation
TRN2	No. Range: FVVD_KINT Loans Inquiry
TRN3	No.range: FVV_OBJNR(address obj.no.)
TRN7	Number range: FVVD_KOBJ Object key
TRN8	Number range: Loan collateral no.
TRN9	No. range: FVVD_RBLNR coll.value no.
TRNA	No.range: FVVD_KSON special arrangmt
TRNB	Number range: FVVD_BEKI doc. number
TRNC	No.range: FVVD_RPNSP Gen.daybook no.
TRND	No.Range: FVV_VORG Release Procedure
TRN_REG_APPL	Settings of Application
TRN_REG_REQUESTS	Administration of Transport Requests
TRN_REG_REQ_BCS	Manage Transport Requests

TRP01	Create Repo Contract
TRP02	Change Repo Contract
TRP03	Display Repo Contract
TRP04	Settle Repo
TRP06	Reverse Repo Contract
TRP08	History
TRP10	Display Repo Contract
TRR_RDB_TEST	Test Program for TRR Reporting
TRSA	S-API Debugger
TRSEB	Report Tree: Securities
TRSR	Single Financial Object Calculation
TRS_NOMCORR_NR	Number Range Maintenance: FTR_TRS_NC
TRS_SEC_ACC	Securities account master data
TRTC	Access Report Tree
TRTD	Access Report Tree
TRTG	Access Report Tree
TRTK	Access Report Tree
TRTM	Access Report Tree
TRTM_CHECK_CORR	Check Correspondence Customizing
TRTM_CHECK_CORR_DE	Check Corr. Customizing Derivatives
TRTM_CHECK_CORR_FX	Check Correspond. Customizing Forex
TRTM_CHECK_CORR_MM	Check Corr. Customizing Money Market
TRTM_CHECK_CORR_SE	Check Corr. Customizing Securities
TRTM_CHECK_CORR_SI	Check Standing Instr. Correspondence
TRTM_TBSCOPY	Copy text module confirmations
TRTM_TBSTRAN	Transport Standard Texts
TRTM_TBSWRK	Standard Text Maintenance CFM
TRTR	Access Report Tree
TRTV	Access Report Tree
TRTW	Access Report Tree
TS00	Collective Processing
TS01	Create Securities Transaction
TS02	Change Securities Transaction
TS03	Execute Securities Order
TS04	Settle Securities Contract
TS05	Sec. Transaction: Order Expiration
TS06	Display Securities Transaction
TS07	Reverse Securities Transaction
TS08	Securities Transaction: History
TS09	Default Value Securities Account
TS10	Display Securities Transaction
TSCUST	Table Search: Customizing
TSE39	Old version of splitscreen editor
TSL00	Securities Lending: Coll. Processing
TSL01	Create Securities Lending
TSL02	Change Securities Lending
TSL03	Display Securities Lending
TSL04	Roll Over Securities Lending
TSL05	Give Notice on Securities Lending
TSL06	Settle Securities Lending
TSL07	Reverse Securities Lending
TSL09	Securities Lending History
TSL10	Sec. Lending, Collateral, Revenues
TSL21	Securities Lending Cash Flow Update

SAP Transaction Codes – Volume Two

TSMN	Internal SAP IMG for Treasury
TSRUN	Table Search: Start Screen
TST_RELEASE_TOOL	Test Appl. for the Release Tool
TSW1	SWIFT Generation MT300
TSW2	SWIFT Generation MT320
TS_CONVERT	Securities Transaction: Conversion
TS_TS20000256H	Transaction for task TS20000256
TS_TS20000780H	Transaction for Task TS20000780
TS_WS01200170H	ESS Notification of Marriage
TS_WS20000102H	Transaction for task WS20000102
TS_WS200001040100	Transaction to Task WS20000104
TS_WS200003771000	Transaction for Task WS20000377
TS_WS401000051000	Transaction for Task WS40100005
TS_WS456000041000	Transaction for Task WS45600004
TTEC_BUSPRTYP	Maintain Business Process Type
TTEC_CACS	Pricing / TTE: Access Sequences
TTEC_CNTY	TTE Maintain Tax Location [obsolete]
TTEC_COMMUNITY	Maintain Community
TTEC_COND	Maintain Tax Rates and Exemptions
TTEC_COND_WT	Withholding Tax Rates
TTEC_CPRP	Pricing / TTE: Calculation Procedure
TTEC_CTCT	Pricing / TTE: Condition Tables
TTEC_CTFC	Pricing / TTE: Field Catalog
TTEC_CTYP	Pricing / TTE: Condition Types
TTEC_CUST_PRICING	Generic call of pricing customizing
TTEC_DCTR	Decision Tree Maintenance
TTEC_DEDREAS	Maintain Deductability Reason
TTEC_DT	Decision Tree for Tax Determination
TTEC_DT_FISCO	Decision Tree for Tax Determination
TTEC_EXCC	Condition Exclusion Group
TTEC_EXCL_PROC	Generic call of pricing customizing
TTEC_EXCP	Condition Exclusion: Procedure assig
TTEC_EXCZ	Condition Exclusion: Procedure assig
TTEC_EXPIND	Maintain Export Indicator
TTEC_FISCCODE	Maintain Fiscal Code
TTEC_INCOTERMS	Maintain Tax Incoterms
TTEC_ORIGIN	Maintain Origin
TTEC_PATXGRP	Maintain Partner Taxability Group
TTEC_PATXTYP	Maintain Partner Taxability Type
TTEC_PRC_TAX_MAP	Maintain Mapping bet. Proc. and Tax
TTEC_PROCED	Tax Procedure
TTEC_PROCEDURE	Maintain Pricing Procedure
TTEC_PROCMODE	Maintain Process Mode
TTEC_ROLE	Maintain Partner Role
TTEC_TAXCAT	Maintain Tax Category
TTEC_TAXCOMP	Maintain Tax Component
TTEC_TAXTYP	Maintain Tax Type
TTEC_TAX_REG	maintain Tax Region
TTEC_TAX_TCODE	Maintain Tax Tariff Code
TTEC_THRSHIND	Maintain Threshold Indicator
TTEC_TRACEMOD	Maintain Trace Mode
TTEC_TRACE_STAT	Maintain Trace Status
TTEC_USAGE	Maintain Usage
TTE_CLIENT_COPY	Copy TTE customizing across clients

SAP Transaction Codes – Volume Two

TTE_COPY_COUNTRY	Copy all country specific settings
TTE_CUST_CHECK	Check Customizing
TTE_CUST_IMPORT_FROM	Import Customizing
TTE_CUS_IMPORT_FROM	Customizing Import from
TTE_DELETE_COUNTRY	Delete country specific settings
TTE_DT_COUNTRY_COPY	Copy decision tree to other country
TTE_REFRESH	Immediate Refresh Customizing
TTE_SIMULATION	Transaction Tax Engine Simulation
TTE_WT_CUST_CHECK	Check Customizing
TU02	Parameter changes
TUTT	Workbench Tutorial
TV20	Create Scenario
TV21	Change Scenario
TV22	Display Scenario
TV24	Conditions: V_T681F for A F
TV25	V-T681F: Index Field Catalog
TV28	Scenario Progression
TV35	Effective Rate/NPV Underlying
TV36	Currency exposure
TV38	Position Evaluation
TV39	Global Evaluation of Cash Flow
TV40	Effective Rate Evaluation FX General
TV42	Interest exposure
TV43	Global IRR
TV44	P/L Evaluation
TV45	Matrix Evaluations
TV46	Bond price calc.
TV48	Historical Simulation
TV49	Variance/Covariance
TV50	Save OTC NPVs
TVDT	Import DTB Derivatives Prices
TVM1	Market Risk and Analysis
TVMD	Transfer Mkt Data
TVS1	Statistics calculator
TWADMIN	Start Watcher
TX-2	Maturity schedule for fwd exch.trans
TX-3	Posting overview
TX-5	Settle forex transaction
TX.1	Forex fast entry - spot
TX.3	Display Forex Transaction
TX.5	Execute forex order
TX/5	Forex order expiry
TX01	Spot/Forward Transaction Entry
TX02	Change Forex Transaction
TX03	Display Forex Transaction
TX04	Reverse Activity
TX05	Spot/Forward Trans.: Add Activity
TX06	Forex: Collective processing
TX10	Create Forex Swap
TX11	Rollover on previous basis
TX12	Premature Settlement
TX13	Create Foreign Exchange Offer
TX14	Execute foreign exchange offer
TX21	Create Forex Transaction

TX22	Display foreign exchange offer
TX23	Create foreign exchange simulation
TX24	Change foreign exchange simulation
TX25	Display foreign exchange simulation
TX26	Delete foreign exchange simulation
TX30	Int. FX Transactions: Rate Overview
TX31	Create Internal Forex Transaction
TX32	Internal Forex Transactions Reserved
TX33	Internal Forex Transactions Reserved
TX34	Internal Forex Transactions Reserved
TX35	Internal Forex Transactions Reserved
TX39	Internal Forex Transactions Reserved
TX76	Forex Transaction History
TX78	Execute order - Forex
TXA5	Forex Order Processing
TXAK	Calculation of option premiums
TXBA	Text Module Maintenance
TXF5	Execute Fixing Order
TXMN	
TXV5	Execute Fixing Transaction
TXZI	Interest calculator
TYMN	Treasury Information System (TIS)
TZ10	Dialog Programming: Data Transport
TZ20	Dialog Programming: F Code Proc.
TZ30	Dialog Programming: Input Check
TZ31	Dialog Programming: Input Check
TZ40	Dialog Programming: Screen Control
TZ50	Dialog Programming: Screen Modif.
TZ60	Dialog Programming: Tables TC
TZ61	Dialog Programming: Tables SL
TZ70	Dialog Programming: Tables SL
TZ80	Dialog Programming: Authorizations
TZ90	Dialog Programming: Locking
TZA0	Dialog Programming: Asynch.Updates
TZB0	Dialog Programming: Doc. and Help
T_03	Cond.tab: Create (shipment costs)
T_04	CondTab: Change (shipment costs)
T_05	CondTab: Display (shipment costs)
T_06	Cond.types: Pricing shipment
T_07	Maintain access (shipment costs)
T_08	Conditions: Proc. for A F
T_09	Condition table: Change Index
T_31	Maintain excl. group shipment
T_32	Maintain CondTypes for ExclusionGrp
T_53	Assign purchasing data
T_54	Shipment cost relevance shipments
T_56	Shipment cost types and item cats
T_57	Shipment cost types and relevance
T_60	Date determination: Define rules
T_70	Maintain service agent group
T_71	Maintain document procedure group
T_72	Maintain shipping type group
T_73	Maintain pricing procedure
T_74	Maintain tariff zones

SAP Transaction Codes – Volume Two

T_75	Maintain tariff zone assignments
T_76	Tariff zones and assignments
T_80	Shipment Cost Information Profile
T_B2	Upper and lower condition limits
T_I1	Activation of Condition Index
T_I2	Reorganize condition indexes
T_LA	Create Pricing Report
T_LB	Change pricing report
T_LC	Display pricing report
T_LD	Execute pricing report
T_RSDOKU03	Where-used List for Hypertext Docu.
T_SLS_CHAN_USER_STAT	Change User Status
T_SLS_CREATE_SDOC	Transaction to create a sales doc.
T_SLS_CREATE_W_REF	Create with Reference
T_SLS_DISP_INC_LOG	Display Incompletion Log
T_SLS_EDIT_TEXTS	Edit Text Notes
T_SLS_LO_OIF_CONFIG	Start LO OIF UI Configuration View
T_VB	Copying Rules for Conditions
T_VC	Copying Rule for Condition Types
T_VD	Conditions: Overviews (freight)
T_VE	Conditions: View seq. A, F, prices
UAAT	Change Log
UAATR	Reorganize Change Log
UABATIMP	Create Batch Import Variant for PDCE
UACGS1	Assignment Price Type and Variant
UACGS2	Additional Business Transaction Cat.
UACGS3	Assignment Derivations CO-PA
UACOCOMAP	Mapping Fields: Remote <-->SEM
UACOCOMAPOTYP	Assignment ObjectTypes: Remote<->SEM
UACOCORFC	RFC Destinations Concurrent Costing
UACR100	CRun: Report 100 (Import)
UACR200	CRun: Report 200 (Calculate)
UACRM	Costing Run: Master Data
UAC_CONTROL_TEST	Assignment Control Test Program
UAGC	Group Costing
UAIPPE1	Import iPPE: Assignment Types
UAIPPE2	Import iPPE: Assignment Type Fields
UAIPPE3	Import iPPE: Assignment Links
UAIPPE4	Import iPPE: Assignment Link Fields
UAMO	Product Design Cost Estimate
UAMO_REPORTING	UAMO Reporting
UASE16N	Table Display
UAST	Costing Solutions: Structure Maint.
UAST_SE11	Parameter Transaction to SE11 Call
UAUPLCMD	Control R/3 Upload in Costing Engine
UAUPLMAP	Mapping R/3 Upload in Costing Engine
UAUPLTYPE	Create Upload Types
UAVMR	Registering Evaluation Methods
UAVNA	Value Network Analyzer
UAVPA	Activation of Planned Price Release
UAVPL	Maintain Price Type and Control
UAVPR	Settings of Planned Price Release
UAVSD	Maintain Strategy Derivation
UAVSM	Valuation Strategy Maintenance

UA_ABGRIR_C1	Activate Transaction-Based GR/IR
UA_ALV_REPORT	Display Costing Data
UA_BATIMP	Create Batch Import Variant, PDCE
UA_CE_REPORT	Costing Engine Analysis
UA_DATABASIS	Define Data Basis
UA_DERI_CC	Derivation Characteristics CCS
UA_DERI_CCS	Determination Characteristics CCS
UA_DERI_CC_OBJ	Derivation Charas CCS Object
UA_DERI_FORMULA	Derivation Rules in Formulas
UA_DERI_PERCENTAGE	Derivation Rules for Overhead Rates
UA_DERI_QUANTITY	Derivation Rules for Quantity Rates
UA_FUNC_GENERATE	Generate Appl. Library Functions
UA_IMG	IMG for Costing
UA_NO	Number Range Maintenance: UAELEMENT2
UA_QUERY_GENERATE	Generate BW Query Connection
UA_STRUC_MAINT1	Costing Solutions: Structure Maint.
UBC1	Customizing UBC_CSP
UBC2	Customizing UBC_CSP
UBC3	Import Bill
UBC4	Create Batch Input Sessions
UBC5	Communication - Service Billing
UBC8	Delete Batch Input Sessions
UBC_BI	Mapping for Batch Input
UBC_BI_NUM	Number Range Maintenance: UBC_SAPFI
UBC_INV_NUM	Number Range Maintenance: UBC_INVOIC
UBDC	Business Domain Lib: Remote Systems
UBDH	Business Domain Lib: BD Hierarchy a
UBDS	Business Domain Lib: Log onto BD
UBD_BW_GEN_CLASS	BD Lib: Class Gen. for BW Objects
UBD_LIGHT	BD Lib Light: Register Methods
UBIW0	Information System
UC00	SEM-BCS: Configuration Menu
UC01	BP: Convert Forms of Address
UC03	BP: Convert Marital Stat. TP03 TBO27
UC08	BP: Convert Legal Forms
UC09	BP: Conversion of Legal Entities
UC14	BP: Conversion of Address TP14 tb009
UC15	BP: Conversion of Functions
UC16	BP: Conversion of Department
UC17	BP: Convert industry T016 tB023
UC17A	Convert industries
UCBPUM	Select tables to be converted
UCBPUM_DEVC	Select tables to be converted
UCBPUM_DOM	Selection of domains to be encoded
UCBPUM_E	Sel. of tables not to be converted
UCBPUM_FUN	Selection of modules to be revised
UCBPUM_FUNC	Selection of modules to be revised
UCBPUM_ROL	Sel.of data elements to be converted
UCBPUM_TAB	Selection of old tables
UCC0	Initialize Control Tables
UCC1	BP conversion: Initial CBP Customiz.
UCC2	BP conversion: Cutomizing
UCCC0	SAP Cons: Customizing Comparison
UCCC1	SAP Cons: Display Cust.Comparison

UCCHECK	Unicode Syntax Check
UCCP0	Copy Cons Area
UCD01	Custom Data Types
UCD02	List of All Generated Models
UCD1	Delete converted partners
UCD3	Delete matched partner
UCDL0	Delete Cons Area-dependent Settings
UCDMODELTYPE	Display Data Types of Model
UCF01	Applications
UCF02	Method Categories
UCF03	List of Method Settings/Cons
UCF04	List of Method Settings/Plan
UCF05	Flexible Upload: Method Categories
UCF06	Currency Translation Keys
UCF07	Currency Translation Timeframes
UCF08	Currency Translation Procedure
UCF09	Exchange Rate Periods Used
UCF10	Procedure for E/R Determination
UCF6ANSEQ	Sort Activities
UCGEN	Select tables to be converted
UCH01	Integr.of References in Cust. Tables
UCH02	List Customizing Settings
UCH1	Display logs
UCH2_1	Determine data elements
UCH2_2	Determine tables
UCH2_3	Usage of Fields to be Converted
UCL21	Log Types
UCM01	Data Basis: Change RFC Destination
UCMON	Consolidation Monitor
UCMP0	Set Cons Area in Perm. Parameters
UCMP2	Change Cons Area for Multiple Users
UCMP3	Change Perm.Paras for Multiple Users
UCNOTA	BP: Convert general memos
UCNOTR	BP: Convert role category-dep. memos
UCNOTZ	BP: Conversion of Role-Dep. Memos
UCNUM1	Maintain Number Range Intervals
UCON0	Contact Management
UCON1	Administration of Distribution Lists
UCP1	Convert TR Partner to CBP
UCP11	General code conversion
UCP2	Convert Relationships
UCP2_3	Conversion FI fields to relat'ships
UCP3	Match: Selection without partner
UCP3_2	Match selected partners
UCP4	Structure partner-obj. relationship
UCP6	Convert Memos
UCP7	Display log
UCP8	Conversion of partner-object rel.
UCP9	Generate Coding
UCPP	Change Permanent Parameters
UCRLST	List of Totals Records
UCRRFC	Virtual Cubes: Destination BW->SEM
UCS01	Task Categories
UCSSG0	Generate Selection Screen

SAP Transaction Codes – Volume Two

UCSTC	Correct Task Status
UCSTI	Information for Status Management
UCU1	Conversion: Project definition
UCU2	Conversion: Module > Time period
UCU3	Conversion: Definition time period
UCU4	Conversion: Control
UCU5	Conversion: Sequence definition
UCU6	Conversion: Def. fields for conv.
UCUS0	Customizing
UCUST	BP: Business partner - applic.Cust.
UCWB	Consolidation Workbench
UCWB01	SAP Cons: Data Basis
UCWB02	SAP Cons: Consolidation Area
UCWB_FLD	Master Data Maintenance
UCWB_INT	Master data maintenance
UCWD_INT	Start Monitor from WebDynpro
UCWD_INT2	Start Monitor from WebDynpro
UCXI000	SEM-BCS Inbound: SMT Mapping
UCZ11	BP: Conversion of relationship type
UCZ12	BP: Conversion of applications
UCZ2	BP: Convert grouping TPZ2 TB001
UCZ3	BP: Conversion of role categories
UCZ7	BP: Conv. of relationship categories
UC_AREA_GENERATE	Generate Objects for Cons Area
UC_AREA_GEN_LIST	Display Gen. Objects for Cons Area
UC_DISPLAY_HIERARCHY	Display Hierarchies with Attributes
UC_MAINTAIN_UCM0000	Mapping Info Object <-> Field Name
UC_STAT0	SEM-BCS: Performance Statistics
UC_WATCHDOG_PROTOCOL	List of Transaction Data Log
UD96	Revenues Increasing Budget
UDM_AUTOWRITEOFF	Automatic Write-Off of Dispute Cases
UDM_BP	Collections Mgt Business Partner
UDM_BP_GRP	Change Business Partner Segment Data
UDM_BP_PROF	Assign/Change BP Collection Profile
UDM_BP_SPEC	Replace Collection Specialist
UDM_CASE_CREATE	Create Dispute Case
UDM_CASE_DETAIL	Details of Dispute Case
UDM_CASE_PROCESSOR	Dispute Case Regular Processor
UDM_CUSTOMIZING	Dispute Management Customizing
UDM_DISPUTE	Dispute Management
UDM_GENWL	Create Worklist
UDM_GENWL_BP	Recreate Business Partner Items
UDM_GROUP	Definition of Groups and Assignment
UDM_GROUP2SGMT	Assignment of Groups to Segments
UDM_GROUP_SPECIALIST	Assign Processors of Collection Grp
UDM_GROUP_SUBSTITUTE	Assign Substitutes
UDM_PRDIST	Distribute Worklist Items
UDM_PRMON	Monitor for Parallel Runs
UDM_RSM_DELETE	Delete Completed Resubmissions
UDM_SPECIALIST	Collection Specialist Worklist
UDM_STRATEGY	Collection Strategies
UDM_SUPERVISOR	Collection Manager Worklist
UDM_SYNCATTR	Maintain Attributes for Synchroniztn
UDM_WD_BOR_DISP	Display of a Linked Object

SAP Transaction Codes – Volume Two

UDOC0	Document Management
UG01	FIN Master Data: Settings
UGAREA_CHANGE_RFC	Changing of AREAID RFC Destination
UGB0	RFC Destination-dep. Gen. Classes
UGB1	Mapping Info Object <-> Field Name
UGCM_CAT	DMS: System Customizing
UGMD_CUST	Customizing of BDT Object UGMD
UGMD_DB_LOG_DISPLAY	Display of Database Log
UGMD_DEL_BUFFER	Delete Buffered Field Information
UGMD_DYN_REGEN	Containers for BDT Subscreen, Gener.
UGMD_FYV	Field Name: Leading FY Variant
UGMD_GEN_AREAID	Generate Application Area
UGMD_GEN_CATALOG	List of Generated Objects
UGMD_GEN_LIST	Display of Generated Objects
UGMD_ROLE_TEXT	Role ID
UGMW0001	BDT: Applications
UGMW0002	BDT: Field Groups
UGMW0003	BDT: Views
UGMW0004	BDT: Sections
UGMW0005	BDT: Screens
UGMW0006	BDT: Screen Sequences
UGMW0007	BDT: Events
UGMW0008	BDT: GUI Standard Functions
UGMW0009	BDT: GUI Additional Functions
UGMW0011	BDT: Assign Screen Field->DB Field
UGMW0012	BDT: Field Grouping Criteria
UGMW0013	BDT: Master Data Roles
UGMW0014	BDT: Master Data Role Groupings
UGMW0015	BDT: Application Transactions
UGMW0016	BDT: Tables
UGMW0017	BDT: Non-SAP Applications
UGMW0018	BDT: Activities
UGMW0019	Control: FMod. Activity (Ctrl)
UGMW0020	BDT: Search Help
UGMW0021	BDT: Assign DI Field->DB Field
UGMW0022	Master Data: Structure Used
UGMW0023	Master Data: Data Sets
UGMW0024	Master Data: Define Used View
UGMW0025	Master Data: Used Process - View
UGMW0026	BDT: Assign BAPI Field to Field Grp
UGMW0100	Master Data: Field Grouping Activity
UGMW0101	Master Data: Field Grouping Role
UGMW0102	Master Data: Authorization Types
UGMW0103	Master Data: Field Groups f. Author.
UGMW0104	Master Data: Screen Configuration
UGMW0105	Master Data: Field Grouping Non-SAP
UGMW0106	Master Data: Notes for Roles
UGMW0107	Master Data: Where-Used List
UGMW0108	Master Data: Field Grpg Appl. Object
UGMW0200	Master Data: Change Doc. Lists
UGMW3001	Assign. GUI Cl. <-> Field Group
UGMW3002	Assign. ScrNo.<->GUI Cl.
UGR31004_MAINTAIN	Maintain UGR31004 (V_UGR31004)
UGR31005_MAINTAIN	Maintain UGR31005 (V_UGR31005)

SAP Transaction Codes – Volume Two

UGR31006_MAINTAIN	Maintain UGR31006 (V_UGR31006)
UGR31007_MAINTAIN	Maintain UGR31007 (V_UGR31007)
UGWBCM	Data Model Synchronizer
UGWBGC	MDF Garbage Collector
UGWB_INT	FIN Master Data: Maintenance
UGWB_WITH_FIELD	FIN Master Data: Maintenance
UGXCM0	Data Model Synchronizer
UGXDB1	XBRL: Generation Data Basis
UGX_INSTDOC_MAIL_UI	SENDING MAIL SAPGUI
UGX_TRANSPORT_VAR	XBRL: Transport Variants
UG_BW_PFCG	Maintain Roles
UG_BW_RRC1	Create Currency Translation Type
UG_BW_RRC2	Edit Currency Translation Type
UG_BW_RRC3	Display Currency Translation Type
UG_BW_RRMX	Analyzer
UG_BW_RSA1	Admin Workbench: Modeling
UG_BW_RSBBS	Maintain BW Senders/Receivers
UG_BW_RSD1	Edit InfoObject
UG_BW_RSDCUBE	InfoCube
UG_BW_RSDMD	Master Data
UG_BW_RSDMPROM	MultiProvider
UG_BW_RSDMWB	Data Mining Workbench
UG_BW_RSDODSD	ODS Object
UG_BW_RSH1	Hierarchies
UG_BW_RSIC	InfoCatalog
UG_BW_RSISET	InfoSet
UG_BW_RSKC	Maintain Permitted Extra Characters
UG_BW_RSMO	Monitor
UG_BW_RSMON	Admin Workbench: Monitoring
UG_BW_RSORBCT	Admin Workbench: Business Content
UG_BW_RSORMDR	Admin Workbench: Metadata Repository
UG_BW_RSPC	Process Chains
UG_BW_RSPR	Print Jobs
UG_BW_RSPRCONF	Print Settings
UG_BW_RSQ02	Maintain InfoSets
UG_BW_RSQ10	SAP Query: Role Administration
UG_BW_RSQ11	InfoSet Query: Web Reporting
UG_BW_RSRCACHE	OLAP: Cache Monitor
UG_BW_RSRT1	Query Monitor
UG_BW_RSRTRACE	Trace Tool
UG_BW_RSRV	Analysis Tool
UG_BW_RSSM	Authorizations for Reporting
UG_BW_RSZC	Copy Queries Between InfoCubes
UG_BW_RSZDELETE	Delete Query Objects
UG_BW_RSZV	Maintain Variables
UG_BW_SMICM	ICM Monitor
UG_BW_SPRO	Customizing
UG_HR_PPOCE	Create Organization and Staffing
UG_HR_PPOME	Change Organization and Staffing
UG_HR_PPOSE	Display Organization and Staffing
UG_MD_APPL	Maintain Application
UG_MD_BASE_FIELD	Fieldname Base Field
UG_MD_FIELDNM_RENAME	Rename Field Name
UG_MD_GEN_LOG	Display of Generation Log

UG_MD_GEN_LOG_1	Display of Generation Log
UG_MD_GEN_SETTINGS	Settings of DDIC Generator
UG_MD_GEN_TYPE	Generic Types
UG_MD_INFOBJ_ROLE	Standard Role for InfoObject
UG_MD_INTERVAL	Assign Role - Ranges
UG_MD_LIST_BACKUP	Display Saved System Tables
UG_MD_LIST_HRY_SID	Hierarchy: Display SID
UG_MD_LIST_SID	SID List
UG_MD_LOCAL_ROLES	Local Role Maintenance
UG_MD_LOCAL_ROLESHRY	Local Role Maintenance (Hierarchies)
UG_MD_REPTEXT	Default Heading Texts, Remote-Fldnam
UG_MD_RFCPING	Settings for RFC Pings
UG_MD_ROLES	Role Maintenance
UG_MD_ROLE_ADDON	Role Maintenance - Add-ons
UG_MD_ROLE_HRY	Role Maintenance (External Hiers)
UG_MD_ROLE_REM_ATTR	Default Maps f. Role Attr.- Remote
UG_MD_ROLE_RENAME	Rename Role
UG_MD_ROLE_WU	Role - Where-Used List
UG_MD_TRANS	Settings for Transport
UG_MD_TRANS_CLASS	Transport Settings
UG_MD_TR_SYNC	Replication in BW During Import
UG_SEM_BEX	Business Explorer Analyzer
UG_SEM_NAV	Business Explorer Browser
UG_SHM	MDF: Shared Memory Settings
UHCA1	Monitor Collection Cases
UHC_CUSTOMIZING	Customizing Collection Case
UIBW	Maintain comment facility for chars
UIEWB	SEM-BIC: Editorial Workbench
UISPB	SEM-BIC: Source Profile Builder
UKM_ADDINFOS_DISPLAY	Additional Info in Credit Management
UKM_BLACK_WHITE	Simple Black + White Lists
UKM_BL_REASON	Lock Reasons
UKM_BOL_COMMS	Display Credit Exposure
UKM_BP	Credit Management Business Partner
UKM_BP_BP021	Display Bus. Partner Finance Data
UKM_BP_DISPLAY	Master Data List
UKM_BP_PROFILE	Display BP Credit Profile
UKM_BP_SEGMENT	Block/Unblock Customer Credit Acct
UKM_CASE_DETAIL	Display Details of Cr. Limit Request
UKM_CHECK_PARA	Field Groups for Check Parameters
UKM_CHECK_RULE	Events/Follow-On Processes
UKM_CHECK_SIMU	Simulation of Credit Check
UKM_COMMITMENTS	Credit Exposure
UKM_COMM_TYPES	Liability Categories
UKM_CREDIT_SGMT	Credit Segment
UKM_CUST_GRP	Credit Group
UKM_EVENT	Events/Follow-On Processes
UKM_FORMULAS	Formula Maintenance
UKM_INFOCAT	Info Categories
UKM_LIMIT_RULE	Scoring/Credit Limit Calc. Rules
UKM_LOGS_DISPLAY	Display Logs
UKM_MALUS_DSP	List of Credit Limit Utilization
UKM_MASS_DSP1	Credit Mgt: Display Credit Data
UKM_MASS_DSP2	Credit Mgt: Display BP Credit Data

SAP Transaction Codes – Volume Two

UKM_MASS_SHOW	Credit Management - Display Extracts
UKM_MASS_UPD1	Credit Mgt: Mass Change to Ext. Ratg
UKM_MASS_UPD2	Credit Mgt: Mass Change to Score
UKM_MASS_UPD3	Credit Mgt: Mass Change to Cr. Limit
UKM_MASS_UPD4	Credit Mgt: Mass Change to Rule
UKM_MONITOR	Update Entries for Ext. Credit Info.
UKM_RATING_PROC	Rating Procedure
UKM_RISK_CLASS	Maintain Risk Class
UKM_SEARCH_ID	ID Search at Information Provider
UKM_SEGMENT	Credit Segment for Control Area
UKM_TRANSFER_ITEMS	Liability Update
UKM_TRANSFER_VECTOR	Update FI Summaries
UKM_VECTORS	Payment Behavior Summary
UKVC	Number range maintenance: IDWTVC
UK_BCS_CXBCS20	Consolidation (EC-CS)
UMB_ADMIN	Balanced Scorecard Monitor
UMB_ADMIN1	Balanced Scorecard Monitor
UMB_AH	Scorecard Aggregation Hierarchy
UMB_BC_OB	Objective (Objective Template)
UMB_BC_PE	Perspective (Strategy Template)
UMB_BC_ST_NAV	Delivered Strategies
UMB_BSC_BWUPDT	Update BW Master Data
UMB_CM	Performance Overview
UMB_CO100	Common Objectives
UMB_CUST	Scorecard Design
UMB_CUST_WEB	Balanced Scorecard Wizard
UMB_EBB	Briefing Book Designer
UMB_GS100	Value Fields
UMB_GS105	Status & Score
UMB_LAUNCHPAD_WEB	Balanced Scorecard Launchpad
UMB_MM	Mass Maintenance
UMB_OB	Objective
UMB_OFL	Balanced Scorecard Download
UMB_PE	Perspective
UMB_PRES	My Balanced Scorecard
UMB_PRES1	Balanced Scorecard
UMB_PRES_WD	Balanced Scorecard
UMB_PRES_WEB	Balanced Scorecard
UMB_PRINT	Balanced Scorecard Reports
UMB_PTTRANS	Transport of Templates
UMB_SC	Scorecard Design
UMB_ST104	Strategy Categories
UMB_ST_MAP	Strategy Map
UMB_ST_NAV	Strategies
UMB_ST_VIEW	Strategy Template
UMB_ST_VIEW_CLIENT	Strategy Template: Current Client
UMB_UP100	Substitute
UMB_XML_UP	XML Scorecard Upload
UMC_CPM_CHECK	Check CPM Applications
UMC_CPM_MEAS	Performance Measurement Design
UMC_CPM_STRAT	Strategy Management Design
UMC_DFTRFC	Maintenance of the Default BW System
UMC_DSP_DFTRFC	Display default BW system
UMC_NOTIF	Ending Notifications

SAP Transaction Codes – Volume Two

UMC_PROXY_CUST   HTTP Connections - Proxy Details
UMC_TM   Periodization and Time Variables
UMIG_MONITOR   Incremental Migration to Unicode
UMK_BMK_XDL   Export Benchmark Values
UMK_BMK_XUP   Load Benchmark Values
UMK_KF   Measures & Benchmarks
UMK_MB   Measures & Benchmarks
UMK_MB400   Benchmark Selections
UMK_MB_BC   SAP Measures & Benchmarks
UMK_MB_BWHUPDT   Update BW Hierarchy
UMK_MB_BWUPDT   Update BW Master Data
UMK_MB_DISP   Display Measures & Benchmarks
UMK_MB_DISP_PARA   Call up Measure Builder
UMK_MB_MHUPDT   Update BW Hierarchy
UMK_MB_PROV   Maintenance of Provider Measure
UMK_MB_SAPBKIC   Benchmark Selections (SAP use only)
UMK_MB_TRANSL   Translation of measures
UMK_MB_TRANSP   Transport
UMK_MB_UPLOAD   Measures Upload
UMK_MB_XUP   Get Latest Provider Measures
UMK_V_MB400   Benchmark Selections
UMM_ADMIN   Management Cockpit Monitor
UMM_CUST   Management Cockpit Design
UMM_CUST_20B   Management Cockpit Design
UMM_HIER   Management Cockpit Hier. Maintenance
UMM_PRES   Management Cockpit Presentation
UMM_PRES_WEB   Management Cockpit Presentation
UMM_SH   Style Sheets
UMM_TRANS   Management Cockpit Transport
UMM_VA100   Variables
UMM_VAM   CPM Variable Maintenance
UMR_CUST   Risk Design
UMR_LOAD   Load Risk Estimation Data from BW
UMR_RB   Risk Builder
UMV_CUST   Value Driver Tree Design
UMV_PRES   Value Driver Tree Presentation
UNKR   Number range main.:W_AKTION
UPART   Business Partner: Conversion to CBP
UPART02   Business Partner: Conversion Phase 2
UPA_EXP   Profit Planning
UPBA   B/S Planning: Set Planning Area
UPBFW   Framework Settings
UPBPL   Execute Balance Sheet Plng Folders
UPBPM   Edit Balance Sheet Planning Folders
UPBPMD   Display Balance Sheet Plng Folders
UPBX   Direct Start of B/S planning Folders
UPB_APPL_IMPORT   Import SEM Planning Applications
UPB_CALL_LIQUID   Liquidity Planning
UPB_CALL_PERSON   Personnel Planning
UPB_CCP   SEM Cost Center Planning
UPB_CMI_CUST   Capital Market Interpreter: Design
UPB_CW   Customizing Wizard, Cost Center Plng
UPB_DATA_EXPORT   Export SEM-BPS Data
UPB_DATA_IMPORT   Import SEM-BPS Data

SAP Transaction Codes – Volume Two

UPB_DATA_TRANSPORT	Transport SEM-BPS Data
UPB_PERSPLAN_START	Execute Personnel Planning
UPB_PM_SETTINGS	Planning Folders: Techn. Settings
UPB_PROF	Profit Planning
UPB_RES	Resource Planning
UPB_RULE	Planning: Transfer Rules
UPB_STRUCT	Plng: Maint. of a Sender Structure
UPB_SY_GEN_CLASS	Connection Web Survey -> SEM-BPS
UPC_BW_DESTINATION	BW Installation
UPDA	Foreign Trade: Mater data transfer
UPIA	Set Investment Planning Area
UPIFW	Framework Settings
UPIPL	Execute Investment Planning Folders
UPIPM	Edit Investment Planning Folders
UPIPMD	Display Investment Planning Folders
UPIX	Direct Start of Investment Folders
UPPPL	Execute Personnel Planning Folders
UPPPM	Edit Personnel Planning Folders
UPPPMD	Display Personnel Planning Folders
UPPX	Direct Start: Personnel Plng Folders
UPS	ALE Distribution Units (UPS)
UPS01	Create ALE Distribution Unit
UPS02	Change ALE Distribution Unit
UPS03	Display ALE Distribution Unit
UPS04	Copy ALE Distribution Unit
UPSC00	ALE Distribution Unit: Setting
UPSC01	ALE Distribution Unit: Object Types
UPSC01S	Generation Object Type Serialization
UPSC02	ALE Distribution Unit: Packet Types
UPSC03	Scenario and Recipient for Pack.Type
UPSC07	ALE Distribution Unit: Middleware
UPSMAS	Post UPSMAS-IDocs
UPSPL	Execute Generic Planning Folder
UPSPM	Edit Generic Planning Folder
UPSPMD	Display Generic Planning Folders
UPSRCP	Replication Table: Organization
UPSREP01_CM	Create Repl. Table from Baselines
UPSREP02	Replication Table: Contents
UPSREP05	Post UPSRCP IDocs
UPSSETUP	Set Up UPS Automatically
UPSX	Direct Start of Generic Folders
UPXA	Select Planning Area
UPXPM	Edit Sales Planning Folders
UPX_CUST	Settings for Planning Services
UPX_CUST_NEW	Settings for Planning Services
UPX_EXEC	Execute Planning
UPX_EXEC_SSP	Execute Service Planning
UPX_MNTN	Settings for Planning Services
UPX_MNTN1	UPX: Data Sources Maintenance
UPX_XLA	Execute Planning with Excel
UPY_PM_START_ADM	Planning Folder Administrator PSM
UPY_PM_START_BA	Planning Folder for Bdgt Dprtmnt PSM
UPY_PM_START_FA	PSM Planning Folder
UPY_PM_START_VC	PSM Manager of Planning Folder

SAP Transaction Codes – Volume Two

URL_DEFINITION   Create Global URLs
URL_EXIT_DEFINITION   Maintain Table URL_EXITS
UR_ADMIN   Administration of Realignments
UR_DERIVATION   Derivation Realigner
UR_EXECUTE   Realignment Run Execution
UR_MAINTAIN   Realignment Request Maintenance
USMDA4_MAINTAIN_VC   Maintain Processor Assignment CR Pro
USMD_ACTIVE_DATAMOD   Display Active Data Model
USMD_DIS_PACKAGE   Maintain Master Data Packages
USMD_DIS_SERVICE   Maintain Distribution Services
USMD_DIS_SYSTEMS   Assign Systems to MD Packages
USMD_RULE   Validations and Derivations
USMD_TCT_FIN_MDM_ACC   Display Financial MDM Test Catalog
USMM   Customer measurement
USRM1   Total of All Company Shares
USRM2   Share Types
USRM3   Market Values
USS_BW_BATCH   Batch for writing data from SRm into
USS_CUST_TABLE   Updating of SRM Data in BW System
USS_CUST_TABLE1   SRM Customizing Table for Shares
USS_DFTRFC   Maintenance of the Default BW System
USS_FAS   File Upload to Application Server
USS_FDPROT   Logs for Stakeholder Transfer
USS_FDREGEL   EDT: Maintain Transfer Rules
USS_FDSEND   EDT: Generate Sender Structure
USS_FDUE   EDT: Start Transfer for Stakeholders
USS_XML2   Import From XML Files
USTH0   Stakeholder Management
USUR0   Web Survey: Edit Survey
USUR1   Web Survey: Select Recipients
UWLC   LDAP Variant Settings
UWS_BW_APPL   Maintain Form Services BW Applctn
UXB_APPL   Maintain Applications
UXP_APPL_PERS   KW Persistence of Applications
UXSA   Maintain Attribute URIs
UXS_XML_T   Maintain Form Services Translation
UXS_XSLT_T   Translation XSLT Program
UY6O   Cust. posting area V100
UY7O   Cust. posting area 1110
UYM8   Display Transfer Doc Data (new)
U_P_S   UPS : Area Menu
V   Quickstart RKCOWUSL
V+01   Create Sales Call
V+02   Create Telephone Call
V+03   Create Sales Letter
V+11   Create Direct Mailing
V+21   Create Sales Prospect
V+22   Create Competitor
V+23   Create Business Partner
V-01   Create Sales Order
V-02   Create Quotation
V-03   Create ordering party (Sales)
V-04   Create invoice recipient (Sales)
V-05   Create payer (Sales)

V-06	Create consignee (Sales)
V-07	Create one-time customer (Sales)
V-08	Create payer (Centrally)
V-09	Create ordering party (Centrally)
V-11	Create carrier
V-12	Create Customer Hierarchy Nodes
V-31	Create Freight 1
V-32	Create Freight 1 with Reference
V-33	Change Freight 1
V-34	Create Freight 1
V-35	Create Freight 1
V-36	Create Freight 1 with Reference
V-37	Change Freight 2
V-38	Display Freight 2
V-40	Display Taxes (Export)
V-41	Create Material Price
V-42	Create Material Price w/ref.
V-43	Change Material Price
V-44	Display Material Price
V-45	Create Price List
V-46	Create Price List w/ref.
V-47	Change Price List
V-48	Display Price List
V-49	Create Customer-Specific Price
V-50	Create Customer-spec. Price w/ref.
V-51	Change Cust.price
V-52	Display Cust.price
V-61	Create Cust.disc./surcharge
V-62	Create Customer Disc/Surch. w/ref
V-63	Change Cust.Disc/Surcharge
V-64	Display Cust.Disc/Surcharge
V-65	Create Mat.Disc/Surcharge
V-66	Create w/ref.Material Disc/Surcharge
V-67	Change Mat.Disc/Surcharge
V-68	Display Mat.Disc/Surcharge
V-69	Create Price grp Disc/Surch.
V-70	Create w/ref.Price Group Disc/Surch.
V-71	Change Price grp Disc/Surch.
V-72	Display Price grp Disc/Surch.
V-73	Create Mat.pr.grp Disc/Surch
V-74	Create w/ref.Mat.pr.grp Disc/Surch
V-75	Change Mat.pr.grp Disc/Surch
V-76	Display Mat.pr.grp Disc/Surch
V-77	Create Cust/MatPrGrp Disc/Su
V-78	Create w/ref.Cust/MatPrGrp Disc/Surc
V-79	Change Cust/MatPrGrp Disc/Su
V-80	Display Cust/MatPrGrp Disc/Su
V-81	Create Cust/mat.Disc/Surch.
V-82	Create w/ref.Cust/Mat.Disc/Surcharge
V-83	Change Cust/mat.Disc/Surch.
V-84	Display Cust/mat.Disc/Surch.
V-85	Create PGrp/MPrGrp Disc/Surc
V-86	Create w/ref.PrGrp/MatPrGrp Disc/Sur
V-87	Change PGrp/MPrGrp Disc/Surc

V-88	Display	PGrp/MPrGrp Disc/Surc
V-89	Create	PGrp/MPrGrp Disc/Surc
V-90	Create w/ref.PrGrp/Mat Disc/Surch.	
V-91	Change	PGrp/mat Disc/Surch.
V-92	Display	PGrp/mat.Disc/Surch.
V-93	Create Domestic Taxes	
V-94	Create Domestic Taxes w/Reference	
V-95	Change Domestic Taxes	
V-96	Display Domestic Taxes	
V-97	Create Cross-border Taxes	
V-98	Create Cross-border Taxes	
V-99	Change Cross-border Taxes	
V.00	List of Incomplete Documents	
V.01	Sales Order Error Log	
V.02	List of Incomplete Sales Orders	
V.03	List of Incomplete Inquiries	
V.04	List of Incomplete Quotations	
V.05	List of Incomplete Sched.Agreements	
V.06	List of Incomplete Contracts	
V.07	Periodic billing	
V.14	Sales Orders Blocked for Delivery	
V.15	Display Backorders	
V.20	Display Collective Delivery Process.	
V.21	Log of Collective Run	
V.22	Display Collective Runs	
V.23	Release Orders for Billing	
V.24	Display Work List for Invoice Lists	
V.25	Release Customer Expected Price	
V.26	Selection by Object Status	
V/03	Create Condition Table (SD Price)	
V/04	Change Condition Table (Sales pr.)	
V/05	Display Condition Table: (Sales Pr.)	
V/06	Condition Categories: SD Pricing	
V/07	Maintain Access (Sales Price)	
V/08	Conditions: Procedure for A V	
V/09	Condition Types: Account Determin.	
V/10	Account Determination: Access Seqnc	
V/11	Conditions: Account Determin.Proced.	
V/12	Account Determination: Create Table	
V/13	Account Determination: Change Table	
V/14	Account Determination: Display Table	
V/21	View V_TVSA_NAC	
V/22	View V_TVTY_NAC	
V/23	View V_TVST_KOM	
V/24	View V_TVTK_NAC	
V/25	View V_TVFK_NAC	
V/26	View V_TVKK_NAC	
V/27	Conditions for Output Determination	
V/30	Output Types (Sales Document)	
V/31	View V_TNAPN Appl V3	
V/32	Sales Doc Output Determtn Procedure	
V/33	View V_TNAPN Appl V7	
V/34	Maintain Condition Type Appl V2	
V/35	Customizing for Output Determination	

V/36	Delivery Output Determination Procdr
V/37	Assign Customer
V/38	Maintain Condition Type Appl V4
V/39	View V_TNAPR Appl V6
V/40	Maintain Condition Type Appl V3
V/41	View V_TVST_NAC
V/42	Output Detrmntn Procdr (Billing Doc)
V/43	View V_TVAK_NAC
V/44	Maintain Condition Type Appl DB
V/45	View V_TNAPN Appl K1
V/46	Output Determination Procdr Customer
V/47	View V_TNAPN Appl V1
V/48	Access Sequences (Sales Document)
V/49	View V_TNAPN Appl. V2
V/50	Access Sequence (Delivery)
V/51	View V_TNAPN Appl. V6
V/52	Access Sequences Appl. V3
V/53	View V_TNAPR Appl. V4
V/54	Access Sequence (Billing Document)
V/55	View V_TVBUR_NA
V/56	Output: Cond.Table - Create Orders
V/57	Output - Cond.Table - Change Order
V/58	Output - Cond.Table - Display Order
V/59	Output - Cond.Table - Create Dlv.
V/60	Output - Cond.Table - Change Dlv.
V/61	Output - Cond.Table - Display Dlv.
V/62	Output - Cond.Table - Create BillDoc
V/63	Output - Cond.Table - Change BillDoc
V/64	Output - Cond.Table - Display BillDc
V/65	Output CondTable/Create SalesSupport
V/66	Output CondTab./Change Sales Support
V/67	Output CondTab/Display Sales Support
V/68	Maintain Access Seqnc (Sales Actvty)
V/69	View V_TVAP_NAC
V/70	Maintain Condition Type Appl K1
V/71	View V_TVLK_NAC
V/72	Output Determination Procedure (CAS)
V/73	View V_TVLP_NAC
V/76	Maintain Product Hierarchy
V/77	Output -ConditTable- Create Transprt
V/78	Output -CondTable- Change Transport
V/79	Output -CondTable- Display Transport
V/80	Access Sequence (Transport)
V/81	View V_TNAPR Appl V7
V/82	Maintain condition type Appl. V7
V/83	View V_TNAPR Appl V3
V/84	Output Determination Transport
V/85	View V_TVKO_NAC
V/86	Conditions: V_T681F for B V1
V/87	Conitions: V_T681F for B V2
V/88	Conditions: V_T681F for B V3
V/89	Conditions: V_T681F for B V5
V/90	Conditions: V_T681F for B V6
V/91	Conditions: V_T681F for B V7

V/92	Conditions: V_T681F for B K1
V/93	Output -CondTable- Create Packaging
V/94	Output -CondTable- Change Packaging
V/95	Output -CondTable- Display Packaging
V/96	Access Sequence (Packaging)
V/97	Output Type Packaging
V/99	Output Determntn Procedure Packaging
V/C1	Strategy Types: Batch Determin.SD
V/C2	Access: Maintain Batch Determin. SD
V/C3	Batch Determin.: Procedure for SD
V/C4	Search Types: Optimize Access
V/C5	SD Tab. T683C "Search Proced.Det.
V/C6	Conditions: V_T681F for H V
V/C7	CondTable: Create (Batches, SD)
V/C8	CondTable: Change (Batch, SD)
V/C9	CondTable: Display (Batches, SD)
V/CA	Automatic Batch Determin.in SlsOrder
V/CL	Automatic Batch Determin.in Delivery
V/G1	Output CondTab/Create Group
V/G2	Output CondTab Change Group
V/G3	Output CondTab/Display Group
V/G4	Access Sequence (Groups)
V/G5	View V_TNAPR Appl K1
V/G6	Maintain Condition Type Appl V5
V/G7	View V_TNAPR Appl V1
V/G8	Output Determinatn Procedure Groups
V/G9	View VN_TNAPR Appl V2
V/I1	Activation of Condition Index
V/I2	Set up condition indices
V/I3	Conditions: Pricing SD - Index
V/I4	Conditions: Pricing SD - Index
V/I5	Condit: Pricing SD - Index in Backgr
V/I6	Display conditions using index
V/LA	Create Pricing Report
V/LB	Change Pricing Report
V/LC	Display Pricing Report
V/LD	Execute pricing report
V/LE	Generate pricing reports
V/N1	Maintain accesses (free goods - sls)
V/N2	Create free goods table
V/N3	Display free goods table (SD)
V/N4	Free goods types - Sales
V/N5	Free goods: Procedure for SD
V/N6	Free goods procedure determ. SD
V/T1	Maintain profile
V/T2	Network Types
V/T3	Deadlines:Assign NetwProf.to DlvType
V/T4	Maintain Deadline Functions
V/T5	Maintain Deviation Reasons
V/T6	Maintain assignment to plant
V/T7	Assign Shipping Deadlines to Shipmnt
V/T8	Shipping Deadlines-Graphics Settings
V070	ASSIGNMENT INT. KEY SUB-TRANSACS.
V101	Initial Sales Menu

SAP Transaction Codes – Volume Two

V12L3V_A	Create Pricing Report for Camp. Det.
V12L3V_B	Change Pricing Report for Camp. Det.
V12L3V_C	Display Pricing Report for Camp.Det.
V12L3V_D	Execute Pricing Report for Camp.Det.
V12LCA	Create Pricing Report
V12LCB	Change Pricing Report
V12LDVG_A	Create Condition List GTIN Mapping
V12LDVG_B	Change Condition List GTIN Mapping
V12LDVG_C	Display Condition List GTIN Mapping
V12LDVG_D	Execute Condition List GTIN Mapping
V12LDV_A	Create Pricing Report
V12LDV_B	Change Pricing Report
V12LDV_C	Display Pricing Report
V12LDV_D	Execute Pricing Report
V12LEV_A	Create Pricing Report (Rebate)
V12LEV_B	Change Pricing Report (Rebate)
V12LEV_C	Display Transactions (Rebate)
V12LEV_D	Execute Pricing Report (Rebate)
V12L_A	Create Pricing Report
V12L_B	Change Pricing Report
V12L_C	Display Pricing Report
V12L_D	Execute Pricing Report
V23	Sales Documents Blocked for Billing
V633	Customer Conversion Dec.Shipping
VA00	Initial Sales Menu
VA01	Create Sales Order
VA02	Change Sales Order
VA03	Display Sales Order
VA05	List of Sales Orders
VA05N	List of Sales Orders
VA07	Compare Sales - Purchasing (Order)
VA08	Compare Sales - Purchasing (Org.Dt.)
VA11	Create Inquiry
VA12	Change Inquiry
VA13	Display Inquiry
VA14L	Sales Documents Blocked for Delivery
VA15	Inquiries List
VA15N	Inquiries List
VA21	Create Quotation
VA22	Change Quotation
VA23	Display Quotation
VA25	Quotations List
VA25N	List of quotations
VA26	Collective Processing for Quotations
VA31	Create Scheduling Agreement
VA32	Change Scheduling Agreement
VA33	Display Scheduling Agreement
VA35	List of Scheduling Agreements
VA35N	List of Scheduling Agreements
VA41	Create Contract
VA42	Change Contract
VA42W	Workflow for master contract
VA43	Display Contract
VA44	Actual Overhead: Sales Order

SAP Transaction Codes – Volume Two

VA45	List of Contracts
VA45N	List of Contracts
VA46	Coll.Subseq.Processing f.Contracts
VA51	Create Item Proposal
VA52	Change Item Proposal
VA53	Display Item Proposal
VA55	List of Item Proposals
VA88	Actual Settlement: Sales Orders
VA94	Load Commodity Codes for Japan
VA94X	Load Commodity Codes for Japan
VA95	Merge Commodity Code/Import Code No.
VACB	Adv. Order Processing and Billing
VACF	Commit. carried forwrd: Sales orders
VAH1	Display Invoicing Items
VAKC	Items in Sales Order Configuration
VAKP	Configuration: Maintain T180
VALU	Valuation Analysis
VAM4	Merge: Japan - Commodity Code
VAN1	Actual Reval.: Sales Order
VAP1	Create Contact Person
VAP2	Change Contact Person
VAP3	Display Contact Person
VARA	Archiving
VARC	SD: User Guide to Archiving
VARCH	Change report variant
VARD	Display report variant
VARK	Archiving
VARR	Archiving
VASK	Deleting Groups
VAUGL_INFO	Forward Clearing Information
VAUN	Reload
VAZE	Credit Splitting (Multiple Payts)
VB(1	Rebate number ranges
VB(2	Rebate Agreement Type Maintenance
VB(3	Condition Type Groups Overview
VB(4	Condition Types in ConditType Groups
VB(5	Assignment Condition -> CondTypeGrp
VB(6	Rebate Group Maintenance
VB(7	Rebate Agreement Settlement
VB(8	List Rebate Agreements
VB(9	Maintain Sales Deal Types
VB(A	Promotion Type Maintenance
VB(B	Copying Control Maintenance
VB(C	Maintain Copying Control
VB(D	Rebate Agreement Settlement
VB01	Create Material Listing/Exclusion
VB02	Change Material Listing/Exclusion
VB03	Display Material Listing/Exclusion
VB04	Reference Material Listing/Exclusion
VB11	Create Material Substitution
VB12	Change Material Substitution
VB13	Display Material Substitution
VB14	Reference Material Substitution
VB21	Create Sales Deal

VB22	Change Sales Deal
VB23	Display Sales Promotion
VB25	List of Sales Deals
VB31	Create Promotion
VB32	Change Promotion
VB33	Display Promotion
VB35	Promotions List
VB41	Create cross-selling
VB42	Change cross-selling
VB43	Display cross-selling
VB44	Copy cross-selling
VBBLOCK	Documents Blocked for Billing
VBELN_SET_GENERATE	Generate Sales Order Set
VBG1	Create Material Grouping
VBG2	Change Material Grouping
VBG3	Display Material Grouping
VBK0	Bonus Buy Selection
VBK1	Create Bonus Buy
VBK2	Change Bonus Buy
VBK3	Display Bonus Buy
VBK6	Delete Bonus Buy
VBKA	Bonus Buy: Access Sequences
VBKB	Bonus Buy: Create Condition Table
VBKC	Bonus Buy: Display Condition Table
VBKD	Bonus Buy: Condition Types
VBKE	Bonus Buy: Calculation Schema
VBKF	Bonus Buy: Schema Determination
VBKG	Bonus Buy: Field Catalog
VBN1	Free goods - Create (SD)
VBN2	Free goods - Change (SD)
VBN3	Free goods - Display (SD)
VBO1	Create Rebate Agreement
VBO2	Change Rebate Agreement
VBO3	Display Rebate Agreement
VBOE	Currency conversion rebate agreemnts
VBOF	Rebate: Update Billing Documents
VBSY	Billing Plan Synchronization
VC/1	List of Customers
VC/2	Customer Master Data Sheet
VC/A	Sales Activity Description 01
VC/B	Sales Activity Description 02
VC/C	Sales Activity Description 03
VC/D	Sales Activity Description 04
VC/E	Sales Activity Description 05
VC/F	Sales Activity Description 06
VC/G	Sales Activity Description 07
VC/H	Sales Activity Description 08
VC/I	Sales Activity Description 09
VC/J	Sales Activity Description 10
VC00	Sales Support
VC01	Create Sales Activity
VC010102	Only Follow-up Activities
VC010103	Do not Delete Mail. Camp.+Addresses
VC010104	Internet mailing

SAP Transaction Codes – Volume Two

VC01N	Edit Sales Activity
VC01N_DRAG_KONTAKT	Edit Sales Activity
VC01N_DRAG_MAILING	Edit Sales Activity
VC01N_M	Edit Mailing
VC02	Change Sales Activity
VC03	Display Sales Activity
VC05	Sales support monitor
VC06	Parallel Processing for Address List
VC10	Report Tree - Select Addresses
VC10_BMENU	Area Menu for VC10
VC15	Crossmatching
VCAR	Archiving
VCC1	Payment Cards: Worklist
VCFCL	Clarif.Processing: Money Laundering
VCH1	Create Batch Search Strategy
VCH2	Change Batch Search Strategy
VCH3	Display Batch Search Strategy
VCHECKBONUS	Customizing Checks for Rebate
VCHECKT683	Customizing Check Pricing Procedure
VCHECKT685A	Customizing Check Condition Types
VCHECKTVCPF	Customizing Check Copying Control
VCHECKVOFA	Customizing Check Billing Types
VCHP	C SD Table TVLP Deliveries: Items
VCOMP	Completed SD Documents
VCPE_CRM_CUS	Commodity Pricing Customizing for SD
VCPE_CUS	Commodity Pricing Customizing for SD
VCPE_DOC	Commodity Pricing in SD Documents
VCPE_FA_ACC_SEQ	Access Sequence for Formula Assembly
VCPE_FA_COND_TYPE	Condition Types for Formula Assembly
VCPE_FA_CT	Cond. Tables for Formula Assembly
VCPE_FA_DET_PROC	Det. Procedure for Formula Assembly
VCPE_FA_FC	SD Field Catalog
VCPE_FA_GCM	Formula Master Data Maintenance
VCPE_MD	Commodity Pricing Master Data for SD
VCPE_WB	CPE Formula Workbench for SD
VCPH1	Perform Policyholder Change
VCPH2	Delete Data for PH Change
VCPH3	PH Change: Transfer Posting Specs
VCR1	Competitive products
VCTP	Maintain Allocation Structure
VCU3	Display Incompletion Log
VCUAC	Display Anti-dumping - Qty-dependent
VCUAE	Display Anti-dumping - Weight-depend
VCUDC	Display 3rd Country - Qty-dependent
VCUDE	Display 3rd Country - Weight-depend.
VCUN	Reload
VCUP1	Display Preference - Qty-dependent
VCUP2	Display Preference - Weight-depend.
VCUPC	Display Pharma.Prod. - Qty-dependent
VCUPF	Display Pharma.Prod. - Weight-depen.
VCUST	Customer List
VCUZ1	Display Ceiling - Quantity-dependent
VCUZ2	Display Ceiling - Weight-dependent
VCUZC	Display Quota - Quantity-dependent

SAP Transaction Codes – Volume Two

VCUZE	Display Quota - Weight-dependent
VCUZP	Display Ceilings - Percentage
VC_2	Customer Fact Sheet PDF Version
VC_ADSPCIPSTAT	SPEC2000: User Status Maintainence
VD01	Create Customer (Sales)
VD02	Change Customer (Sales)
VD03	Display Customer (Sales)
VD04	Customer Changes (SD)
VD05	Block customer (sales)
VD06	Mark customer for deletion (sales)
VD07	Ref. doc. det. for ref. customer
VD51	Maintain Customer-Material Info
VD52	Maintain Cust-Mat.Info w/Select.Scrn
VD53	Display Customer-Material Info
VD54	Display Customer-Material Info
VD59	List customer-material-info
VDBLOCK	Documents Blocked for Delivery
VDDI	EMU currency conversion cust. master
VDF1	Display Format Date Type/Period
VDH1	Customer Hierarchy Maintenance (SD)
VDH1N	Display/Maintain Customer Hierarchy
VDH2	Display Customer Hierarchy
VDH2N	Display customer hierarchy
VE01	INTRASTAT: Selection Dispatch to EU
VE02	INTRASTAT: Create Form - Germany
VE03	INTRASTAT: Create File - Germany
VE04	EXTRASTAT: Data selection for export
VE05	EXTRASTAT: Create File - Germany
VE06	INTRASTAT: Paper Form - Belgien
VE07	Create INTRASTAT Form for France
VE08	Create INTRASTAT File for Italy
VE09	Create INTRASTAT file for Belgium
VE10	Create INTRASTAT file for Holland
VE11	Create INTRASTAT file for Spain
VE12	Create INTRASTAT form for Holland
VE13	KOBRA data selection: export Germany
VE14	Create KOBRA file for Germany
VE15	Create disk - INTRA/EXTRA/KOBRA/VAR
VE16	Create INTRASTAT form for Austria
VE17	Create INTRASTAT form for Sweden
VE18	SED data selection for USA exporters
VE19	Create SED form for USA
VE20	Create AERP file for USA
VE21	VAR: Selection of bill. docs Switz.
VE22	Create VAR form for Switzerland
VE23	V.A.R.: File - Switzerland
VE24	Comm. Code Number Information (old)
VE24X	Commodity Code Information
VE25	SED: Selection: USA Carriers
VE26	Number of CAP Products List
VE27	HMF: Selection - USA
VE28	Name of Market Organization
VE29	Assigned Documents for Each License
VE30	Existing licenses

VE31	Blocked SD Documents
VE32	INTRASTAT: Paper Form - Ireland
VE33	INTRASTAT: Paper Form - U.K.
VE34	INTRASTAT: Paper Form - Belgien
VE35	Number of Market Organization
VE36	Group for CAP Products
VE37	INTRASTAT: File - France
VE38	INTRASTAT: Selection Simulation - EU
VE39	EXTRASTAT: Selection Simulation
VE40	KOBRA: Selection Simulation
VE41	VAR: Selection of bill. docs Switz.
VE42	INTRASTAT: File - Denmark
VE43	SED: Selection Exp. USA Simulation
VE44	SED: Select Carrier USA Simulation
VE45	INTRASTAT: Paper Form - Greece
VE46	INTRASTAT: File - Finland
VE47	PRODCOM No.
VE48	Customs Quota Code
VE49	Code for Pharmaceutical Products
VE50	Legal Regulation
VE51	Legal Regulation/License Type
VE52	Country/Legal Regulations
VE53	Export Situation for a Country
VE54	Preference Determination: Collective
VE55	Preference Determination: Individual
VE56	Check Export Control for Consistency
VE57	Country Classification
VE58	Product Classification
VE59	Legal Regulations/Country Grouping
VE60	Exp.Ctrl Class Accord.to Legal Reg.
VE61	Legal Regulations/Embargo Group
VE62	Material Group accord.to Legal Reg.
VE63	Customs Areas
VE64	Commodity Code/Customs Areas
VE65	Preference Reg./Percentage Rates
VE66	Preference Procedure
VE67	Aggregate Vendor Declarations
VE68	Request Vendor Declarations
VE69	Incompletion log
VE70	Place of manufacture
VE71	Preference: Determine Customs Area
VE72	Export - Billing Documents
VE73	Goods Catalog: Create Document
VE74	Goods Catalog: Create Diskette
VE75	Preference Code
VE76	Anti-dumping Code
VE77	Preference: Tariff Alternation
VE78	Plant Parameters for Vendor Decl.
VE79	Quota Code Determination
VE80	Assign Chapter to Section
VE81	Check Report: General FT Data
VE81X	Incompleteness: FT Material Data
VE82	Check Report: Export Control Data
VE82X	Incompleteness: Export Control Data

VE83	Check Report: Preference Data
VE83X	Incompleteness: Preference Material
VE84	Monitoring: Purchasing Info Records
VE85	Change Statistical Value - Import
VE86	Display Statistical Value - Import
VE87	Change Stat.Value - Subcontracting
VE88	Change Statistical Value - Export
VE89	Display Statistical Value - Export
VE90	Change preference values
VE91	Display Preference Values
VE92	Create INTRASTAT tape Luxembourg
VE93	EDI-CUSTEC Austria
VE94	Load Commodity Code for EU Countries
VE94X	Load Commodity Code for EU Countries
VE95	Create INTRASTAT papers: Portugal
VE96	EXTRASTAT Data Select.: Init. Screen
VE97	Create EXTRASTAT tape: Netherlands
VE98	Sales Invoice Values per Period
VE99	Create Document - Austria
VEA1	FT - Create commodity code import
VEA2	FT: Create commodity code export
VEA3	EXTRASTAT: File Version France
VEA4	EXTRASTAT: File Version France
VEA5	EXTRASTAT: File Version France
VEB1	Period-end Closings: Control
VEB2	DtA: Special Rule Countries/Regions
VEB5	Calculate Assemblies Individually
VEB6	Calculate Assemblies Collectively
VEB9	Customer Exits: Print Control
VECN	Profitability and Sales Accounting
VECS	Legal Control: Special Char. Code
VECZ	INTRASTAT: File - Czech Republic
VED1	Print Parameters for Export Docs
VED2	Form Data Control
VEFU	Foreign Trade: Add INTRASTAT Data
VEFUX	FT-GOV: Change transaction INTRASTAT
VEG1	Handling Unit Group 1
VEG2	Handling Unit Group 2
VEG3	Handling Unit Group 3
VEG4	Handling Unit 4
VEG5	Handling Unit Group 5
VEGK	FT: Comb. Bus Trans.Type - Procedure
VEGR	Material Group: Packaging Materials
VEHU	INTRASTAT: File - Hungary
VEI0	Create INTRASTAT CUSDEC EDI IE
VEI1	Display IDoc Import
VEI2	Display IDoc Export
VEI3	Display Stat.Value - Subcontracting
VEI4	Merge: Remaining Commodity Codes
VEI5	Create value limit subcontracting
VEI6	EDI: IDoc List - Import Basis
VEI7	Create INTRASTAT CUSDEC EDI GB
VEI8	Create INTRASTAT CUSDEC EDI AT
VEI9	Create INTRASTAT CUSDEC EDI ES

SAP Transaction Codes – Volume Two

VEIA	Create INTRASTAT CUSDEC EDI SE
VEIAE	EXTRASTAT Archiving
VEIAI	INTRASTAT Archiving
VEIB	Create INTRASTAT CUSDEC EDI PT
VEIC	Create INTRASTAT CUSDEC EDI FI
VEID	Create INTRASTAT CUSDEC EDI LU
VEIE	SAPMSED8: Call EXPINV02
VEII	SAPMSED8: Call IMPINV01
VEIV	Foreign Trade: Add EXTRASTAT Data
VEIW	Create file INTRA/EXTRA/KOBRA
VEIX	Create file INTRA/EXTRA/KOBRA
VEIY	Create file INTRA/EXTRA/KOBRA
VEIZ	Create file INTRA/EXTRA/KOBRA
VEKAB	Exp.Cont.(KOBRA)Data Maint.B Records
VEKAC	Exp.Cont.(KOBRA)Data Maint.C Records
VEKU	For. Trade: Change KOBRA Documents
VELC0	Vehicle Locator
VELO	Vehicle Manager
VELOARDI	Display Archived Vehicles
VELOARSL	Set/Delete Archiving Indicator
VELOAS	Assign Sales Docs to Vehicles
VELOB	Execute Actions in Batch
VELOBWC	Assign Class Char. to BW Char.
VELOC	Define Sales Campaign
VELOCM	Configuration mapping
VELOE	Emergency Monitoring
VELOK	Define Message Condition Records
VELOM	Status Monitor for Vehicle IDoc
VELOMCS	Mapping of models to calc. sheet
VELOMMAP	Mapping of Models to Config Charact.
VELOMNR	Models with Custom Number Ranges
VELONR	Number range maintenance: VMS_VHL
VELOOBJC	Include Obj. Char. in Configuration
VELOP	Define Configuration Change Profile
VELOP01	Log: Status Monitoring
VELOP02	Log: Reservation
VELOP03	Log: Action Execution
VELOPR	Evaluate Configuration Profiles
VELOR	Update Reservation Queue
VELORM	Assign Vehicle Model to VMS Roles
VELORO	Assign Org. Data to VMS Roles
VELORU	Assign VMS Roles to Users
VELOS	Define Action Control Determination
VELOUM	Define Used Vehicle Models
VELOV	Action Execution Job Variant
VELO_LCCONTENT	Maintain LiveCache Filter
VELO_LCINIT	Fill LiveCache with Vehicles
VELO_LCSTATUS	Activate/deactivate liveCache
VELO_SA	Control Table for Vehicle Attributes
VELO_SC	Control Table for Search
VEM4	Merge: EU - Commodity Code
VEPL	Create INTRASTAT CUSDEC EDI PL
VEPR	Customs log
VEREM	Deletion of Evaluation Results

639

SAP Transaction Codes – Volume Two

VESK	Create INTRASTAT CUSDEC EDI SK
VESUB	Subsequent Evaluation
VEU4	Load Commodity Code-Other Countries
VEU4X	Load Commodity Code-Other Countries
VEXP	Expiring SD Documents
VEXU	Foreign Trade: Add EXTRASTAT Data
VEXUX	FT-GOV: Change transaction EXTRASTAT
VF00	9Sales organization & is not defined
VF01	Create Billing Document
VF02	Change Billing Document
VF03	Display Billing Document
VF04	Maintain Billing Due List
VF04_AIS	VF04_AIS
VF05	List Billing Documents
VF05N	List of Billing Documents
VF06	Batch billing
VF07	Display bill. document from archive
VF08	Billing for ext. delivery
VF11	Cancel Billing Document
VF21	Create Invoice List
VF22	Change invoice list
VF23	Display Invoice List
VF24	Edit Work List for Invoice Lists
VF25	List of Invoice Lists
VF26	Cancellation invoice list
VF27	Display invoice list from archive
VF31	Output from Billing Documents
VF42	Update Sales Documents
VF43	Revenue Recognition: Posting Doc.
VF44	Revenue Recognition: Worklist
VF45	Revenue recognition: Revenue report
VF46	Revenue Recognition: Cancellation
VF47	Revenue Recognition:ConsistencyCheck
VF48	Revenue Recognition: Compare Report
VFAE	Archive EXTRASTAT Documents
VFAI	Archive INTRASTAT Documents
VFBS	Next screen control
VFBV	Reorganization of discount-rel. data
VFBWG	Bulkiness and minimum weights
VFBZ	Scale Basis for Pricing
VFLI	Log tax exemption
VFP1	Set Billing Date
VFRB	Retro-billing
VFS3	Adjusting info structure S060
VFSN	Reorganization info structure S060
VFUN	Reload
VFX2	Display Blocked Billing Documents
VFX3	List Blocked Billing Documents
VG01	Create Group
VG02	Change Group
VG03	Display Group
VGK1	Create Group for Delivery
VGK2	Change Group for Delivery
VGK3	Display Group for Delivery

SAP Transaction Codes – Volume Two

VGL1	Create Group for Delivery
VGL2	Change Group for Delivery
VGL3	Display Group for Delivery
VGM1	Create Group for Freight List
VGM2	Change Group for Freight List
VGM3	Display Group for Freight List
VGW1	Create Picking Wave
VGW2	Change Picking Waves
VGW3	Display Picking Waves
VHAR	Maintain/Create Packaging Matl Types
VHZU	Allowed Packaging Material Types
VI00	Shipment costs
VI01	Create shipment costs
VI02	Change shipment costs
VI03	Display shipment costs
VI04	Create shipment cost worklist
VI05	Change shipment cost worklist
VI06	Collective run in background
VI07	Collective run in background
VI08	Display FT data in purchasing doc.
VI08X	Display FT data in purchasing doc.
VI09	Change FT Data in Purchasing Doc.
VI09X	Change FT Data in Purchasing Doc.
VI10	Display FT Data in Billing Document
VI10X	Display FT Data in Billing Document
VI11	List shipment costs: Calculation
VI12	List shipment costs: Settlement
VI14	Change FT Data in Billing Document
VI14X	Change FT Data in Billing Document
VI15	Display logs (appl. log)
VI16	Logs for worklist shipment
VI17	Display FT Data in Inbound Delivery
VI17X	Display FT Data in Inbound Delivery
VI18	Display Anti-dumping
VI19	Display Third-country Customs Duties
VI20	Display Customs Quota
VI21	Display Pharmaceutical Products
VI22	Display Customs Exemption
VI23	Display Preferential Customs Duties
VI24	Code Number Information - Import
VI24X	Import Code No. Information
VI25	Display Gross Price - Customs
VI26	Display Surcharge/Discount - Customs
VI27	Display Freight - Customs
VI28	EDI: Customs ID Number - Vendor
VI29	Incompletion - Foreign Trade Data
VI30	Declara. to Authorities: Exclusion
VI31	Code Determin. - Pharmaceut.Products
VI32	Code Determination - Anti-dumping
VI33	Customs Exemption
VI34	Preferential Customs Duty Rate
VI35	Third-country Customs Duty Rate
VI36	CAS Number
VI37	Import Simulation Control

SAP Transaction Codes – Volume Two

VI38	Determination of Verification Docs
VI39	Authority for Verification Docs
VI40	Preference Type
VI41	Verification Document Type
VI42	Document Type (Export/Import)
VI43	Definition of Section
VI44	Assign Chapter to Section
VI45	Export --> Import Conversion
VI46	Conversion: Mode of Transport
VI47	Conversion of Business Transact.Type
VI48	Conversion of Customs Offices
VI49	Foreign Trade Data Control in Doc.
VI50	Conversion: Import/Export Procedure
VI51	Define Payment Guarantee Procedure
VI52	Define Form of Payment Guarantee
VI53	Change FT Data in Inbound Delivery
VI53X	Change FT Data in Inbound Delivery
VI54	Customs Approval Numbers
VI55	Approval Number per Plant
VI56	EDI: Customs ID Number - Customer
VI57	Legal Control - Order Header
VI58	Legal Control - Order Item
VI59	Legal Control - Delivery Header
VI60	Legal Control - Delivery Item
VI61	Conversion - Reference Country
VI62	Conversion - Reference Country
VI63	Assign Delivery Item Categories
VI64	Display FT Data in Outbound Delivery
VI64X	Display FT Data in Outbound Delivery
VI65	Maintain Market Organizations
VI66	Maintain No. of Market Organization
VI67	Maintain CAP Products List Nos
VI68	Control Commodity Code/Code Number
VI69	Maintain CAP Products Group
VI70	Default Values - Stock Transp. Order
VI71	Change Preference Values
VI72	Display Insurance - Customs
VI73	Maintain Vendor Declaration
VI73N	Maintain Vendor Declaration
VI74	Display Vendor Declaration
VI74N	Display Vendor Declaration
VI75	Vendor Declarations - Dunning notice
VI76	Mode of Transport - Office of Exit
VI77	Change FT Data in Outbound Delivery
VI77X	Change FT Data in Outbound Delivery
VI78	Foreign Trade: Country Data
VI79	Display FT Data in Goods Receipt
VI79X	Display FT Data in Goods Receipt
VI80	Change FT Data in Goods Receipt
VI80X	Change FT Data in Goods Receipt
VI81	Check Report: CAP Products
VI81X	Check Report: CAP Products
VI82	Check General Customer Master Data
VI82X	Incompleteness: FT Customer Data

VI83	Check Customer Master/Legal Control
VI83X	Incompleteness:Customer Control Data
VI84	Doc.Payments: Check Customer Master
VI84X	Billing Doc.Incompleteness Customer
VI85	Incompleteness: Foreign Trade Vendor
VI86	Incompleteness: Cross-plant
VI87	Foreign Trade: Header Data Proposal
VI88	Input Table for Preference Determin.
VI89	Customs Law Description
VI90	Fill Foreign Components in BOMs
VI91	Display Foreign Components in BOMs
VI92	Preference: Alternative Comm. Code
VI93	Foreign Trade: Import Control
VI94	Load Import Code Nos - EU Countries
VI94X	Load Import Code Nos - EU Countries
VI95	Def.Val.f.Foreign Trade Header Data
VI96	Customer Exits: Default Values
VI97	Define Control Codes
VI98	Receipt-Basis for Intercomp.Billing
VI99	Returns and Credit Memos
VIAR	Archive Shipment Costs
VIB1	Send IDoc Output
VIB2	Call Print Program From VI10/VI14
VIB3	Foreign Trade Output Status
VIB4	Print Transaction: Initial Procg
VIB5	Print Transaction: Repeat Procg
VIB6	Print Transaction: Error in Procg
VIB7	Send IDoc Output - Initial Procg
VIB8	Send IDoc Output - Repeat Procg
VIB9	Send IDoc Output - Error in Procg
VIBA	Send IDoc Output-AES-Initial Procg
VIBB	Send IDoc Output-AES-Repeat Procg
VIBC	Send IDoc Output-AES-Error in Procg
VIBD	Printing: Analysis form data audit
VIBN	Monitor messages
VIC00	Consistency Check IMG ShpmtCostCalc.
VICC	Convert format currency field
VICI	Call shipment info via CALL TRANS
VICZ	Create INTRASTAT CUSDEC EDI CZ
VIE4	Incompleteness Periodic Declarations
VIEX	FT: Journal Export Actual
VIFBW	Reorg: Shipment Costs in BW
VII4	Merge: Rest - Import Code Number
VII5	Import control in the material doc.
VIIE	Create INTRASTAT XML IE
VIIM	FT: Op. Cockpit: Purchase order
VIJ1	Journal Import
VIJ2	Journal Export
VILG	FT: Country Group Definition
VILI	FT: Export Deliveries Journal
VIM4	Merge: EU - Import Code Number
VIM6	Customer Exits: Data Selection
VIMM	Decl. Recpts/Disptch Min. Oil Prod.
VIMU	Foreign Trade: Comparison of codes

SAP Transaction Codes – Volume Two

VINC	List of Incomplete SD Documents
VINFO1	Forward Information
VINK	Import Processing: Quota Number
VINP	Import Processing: Ceiling Numbers
VINTEG1	Insurance Components Active?
VINTEG2	Define Information Origin
VINTEG3	Define Information Category
VINTEG4	Define Communication Type
VINTEG50	Process Information Container
VIPL	Display Customs Duty for Ceiling
VIR1	Import Reorg. - Incompleteness
VIR2	Export Reorg. - Incompleteness
VIRL	Reload shipments
VIS3	Check program: Cross-plant
VISW	Service: Information: Keywords
VITATAX	Correction Run for Italian Taxes
VIU4	Load Import Code No.-Other Countries
VIU4X	Load Import Code No.-Other Countries
VIUC	FT Upload: Convert cust.duty types
VIUL	Foreign Trade: Data Upload
VIWAX	Display FT Data in Goods Issue
VIWBX	Change FT Data in Goods Issue
VIWE	FT: Op. Cockpit: Goods Receipt
VIZB	Import Proc: Means of Transport
VIZN	Import Proc: Type of Goods ID Seal
VIZP	Import Processing: Package Type
VJ01	In-Force Bus. Groups Pension Funds
VJ02	Insurance Type
VJ03	Customer type
VJ04	In-Force Business Type
VJ05	Underwriting type
VJ06	Claim Type
VJ07	Risk type
VJ08	Functional area
VJ09	Organizational area
VJ10	Insurance Class
VJ11	Insurance Class: Reporting
VJ12	Reporting Transact. Type
VJ13	Insurance Type Reporting
VJ14	Business Transaction Type
VJ15	Country Where Risks are Situated
VJ16	In-Force Bus. Type Reporting
VJ17	Reporting Risk Type
VJ18	In-Force Bus. Group Reporting
VJ19	Reporting-Origin of Ins. Transactn
VK+C	Condition master data check
VK01	Conditions: Dialog Box for CondElem.
VK03	Create Condition Table
VK04	Change Condition Table
VK05	Display Condition Table
VK11	Create Condition
VK12	Change Condition
VK13	Display Condition
VK14	Create Condition with Reference

SAP Transaction Codes – Volume Two

VK15	Create Condition
VK16	Create Condition with Reference
VK17	Change condition
VK18	Display condition
VK19	Change Condition Without Menu
VK20	Display Condition Without Menu
VK30	Maintain Variant Conditions
VK31	Condition Maintenance: Create
VK32	Condition Maintenance: Change
VK33	Condition Maintenance: Display
VK34	Condition Maint.: Create with Refer.
VKA1	Archiving conditions
VKA2	Deleting conditions
VKA3	Reloading conditions
VKA4	Archiving agreements
VKA5	Deleting agreements
VKA6	Reloading agreements
VKAR	Read Archive File
VKAW	Generate Archive File
VKC1	Create General Strategy
VKC2	Change General Strategy
VKC3	Display General Strategy
VKDV	Number range maintenance: RV_SNKOM
VKK1	IS-IS/PP Ins. Solution Customizing
VKKM	Contract A/R + A/P
VKKMNEW	Contract A/R + A/P
VKKMOLD	FS-CD Area Menu
VKM1	Blocked SD Documents
VKM2	Released SD Documents
VKM3	Sales Documents
VKM4	SD Documents
VKM5	Deliveries
VKOA	Accnt Determination
VKOE	
VKP0	Sales Price Calculation
VKP1	Sales price calculation
VKP2	Display POS Conditions
VKP3	Pricing document for material
VKP4	Pricing document for org. structure
VKP5	Create Calculation
VKP6	Change pricing document
VKP7	Display pricing document
VKP8	Display Price Calculation
VKP9	Currency conversion in price calc.
VKPA	Archiving
VKPB	Sales price calc. in background run
VKPR	Read archive file
VKTT	Test Partners DI/RFC
VKU1	Report: Reval at Rtl for Rtl Pr.Chng
VKU10	Correction of Valuation at Retail
VKU11	Delete Count Document Items
VKU2	Total Revaluation at Retail
VKU3	Partial Revaluation at Retail
VKU4	Rtl Revaluation Docs for Material

SAP Transaction Codes – Volume Two

VKU5	Display Retail Revaluation Document
VKU6	Report: List Crtn for Rtl Pr. Change
VKU7	Report: Total Reval. for Rtl Pr. Chn
VKU8	Test Transaction BAPI Count List
VKU9	Rtl Reval. Correction: List Display
VKUN	Reload
VKVE	WFMC:
VKVF	Conditions: Dialog Box for CondElem.
VKVG	Maintain Condition Elements
VKVI	General View Maintenance - W.Qualif.
VKVN	WFMC:
VKXX	Create Test for RKA
VKYY	Change Test for RKA
VKZZ	Test for RKS-Surcharge Conditions
VL00	Shipping
VL01	Create Delivery
VL01N	Create Outbound Dlv. with Order Ref.
VL01NO	Create Outbound Dlv. w/o Order Ref.
VL02	Change Outbound Delivery
VL02N	Change Outbound Delivery
VL03	Display Outbound Delivery
VL03N	Display Outbound Delivery
VL04	Process Delivery Due List
VL06	Delivery Monitor
VL06C	List Outbound Dlvs for Confirmation
VL06D	Outbound Deliveries for Distribution
VL06F	General delivery list - Outb.deliv.
VL06G	List of Oubound Dlvs for Goods Issue
VL06I	Inbound Delivery Monitor
VL06IC	Confirmation of putaway inb. deliv.
VL06ID	Inbound Deliveries for Distribution
VL06IF	Selection inbound deliveries
VL06IG	Inbound deliveries for goods receipt
VL06IP	Inbound deliveries for putaway
VL06L	Outbound Deliveries to be Loaded
VL06O	Outbound Delivery Monitor
VL06P	List of Outbound Dlvs for Picking
VL06T	List Outbound Dlvs (Trans. Planning)
VL06U	List of Uncheckd Outbound Deliveries
VL08	Confirmation of Picking Request
VL09	Cancel Goods Issue for Delivery Note
VL10	Edit User-specific Delivery List
VL10A	Sales Orders Due for Delivery
VL10B	Purchase Orders Due for Delivery
VL10BATCH	VL10 Background planning
VL10BATCH_A	Background Planning VL10 (0 Tbstrps)
VL10BATCH_B	Background Planning VL10 (3 Tbstrps)
VL10C	Order Items Due for Delivery
VL10CU	Delivery Scenarios
VL10CUA	User Roles (List Profiles)
VL10CUC	Create Profile - Delivery
VL10CUE	Exclude Function Code Profile
VL10CUF	F Code VL10 Profile
VL10CUV	Delivery Scenarios

SAP Transaction Codes – Volume Two

VL10CU_ALL	User Roles (List Profiles)
VL10D	Purch. Order Items due for Delivery
VL10E	Order Schedule Lines due for Deliv.
VL10F	PurchOrd Schedule Lines due for Dlv.
VL10G	Documents due for Delivery
VL10H	Items Due for Delivery
VL10HU	Sales Orders Due for Dely With HUs
VL10I	Schedule Lines due for Delivery
VL10U	Cross-System Deliveries
VL10UC	Check / combine unchecked deliveries
VL10X	VL10 (technical)
VL12	Delivery creation in background
VL21	Post goods issue in background
VL21A	Post goods receipt as batch
VL22	Display Delivery Change Documents
VL22N	Display Delivery Change Documents
VL23	Goods Issue (Background Processing)
VL23N	Goods Issue (Background Processing)
VL30	Shipping
VL31	Create Inbound Delivery
VL31N	Create Inbound Delivery
VL31W	Create Inbnd Dlv. Notification (WEB)
VL32	Change Inbound Delivery
VL32N	Change Inbound Delivery
VL32W	Change Inbnd Dlv. Notification (WEB)
VL33	Display Inbound Delivery
VL33N	Display Inbound Delivery
VL34	Worklist Inbound Deliveries
VL35	Create Wave Picks: Delivery/Time
VL35_S	Create Wave Picks: Shipment
VL35_ST	Create Wave Picks: Shipment/Time
VL36	Change Picking Waves
VL37	Wave Pick Monitor
VL38	Groups Created: Wave Picks
VL39	Billing Documents for Wave Picks
VL41	Create Rough GR
VL42	Change Rough GR
VL43	Display Rough GR
VL51	Create Route Schedule: Initial Scr.
VL51A	Create Schedule
VL52	Change Route Schedule: Initial Scr.
VL52A	Change Schedule
VL53	Display Route Schedule: Initial Scr.
VL53A	Change Schedule
VL54A	Create Shipment From Schedule
VL60	Extended Inbound Delivery Processing
VL60C	Clearing
VL60P	Posting
VL60P1	Maintenance Profiles for GR Dialog
VL60P2	Maintenance of User Groups
VL60PM1	Maintenance of Function Profile
VL60PM2	Maintenance of Object Profiles
VL60PM3	Maintenance of Selection Profiles
VL60PM4	Maintain Column Profiles

647

SAP Transaction Codes – Volume Two

VL60PM5	Maintenance of Filter Profiles
VL60PM6	Maintenance of Config. Profiles
VL60V	Edit Document
VL64	Worklist Inbound Deliveries
VL65	Inbound Delivery Purge Report
VL66	Inbound Delivery Delete Report
VL70	Output From Picking Lists
VL71	Output from Outbound Deliveries
VL72	Output from Groups of Deliveries
VL73	Confirmation of Decentr.Deliveries
VL74	Output from Handling Units
VL75	Shipping Notification Output
VL76	Output from Rough Goods Receipt
VLAL	Archive Deliveries
VLBT	Plan Delivery Creation as a Job
VLE1	Picking with Picking Waves
VLK1	Picking with Picking Waves
VLK2	Picking with Picking Waves
VLK3	Picking with Picking Waves
VLLA	RWE: Picking/Goods Issue Analysis
VLLC	RWE: Archive Data
VLLD	Rough Workload Forecast: Delete Log
VLLE	RWE: Goods Receipt/Putaway Analysis
VLLF	Picking Waves: Archive Data
VLLG	RWE: Analyze Complete Overview
VLLP	Rough Workload Forecast: Display Log
VLLQ	RWE: Returns to Vendor Analysis
VLLR	RWE: Customer/Store Return Analysis
VLLS	Var. Stand. Analyses Setting App 42
VLLV	W&S: Control RWE/Picking Waves
VLMOVE	HU Goods Movements
VLPOD	POD - Change Outbound Delivery
VLPODA	POD - Display Outbound Delivery
VLPODF	Worklist: POD Subsequent Processing
VLPODL	Worklist: POD Deliveries
VLPODQ	Automatic PoD Confirmation
VLPODW1	Proof of Delivery (Communicator)
VLPODW2	Proof of Delivery via WEB
VLPP	Packing Req. for Item Categories
VLRL	Reload Delivery
VLSP	Subsequent Outbound-Delivery Split
VLSPS	Outbound Delivery Split via HU Scan
VLUNIV	Change Delivery (General)
VL_COMPLETE	Completion of Deliveries
VM01	Create Hazardous Material
VM02	Change Hazardous Material
VM03	Display Hazardous Material
VM04	Filling Haz. Substance Table MGEF
VMCJDB	VM Container Mini Debugger
VMG1	Create Material Group 1
VMG2	Create Material Group 2
VMG3	Create Material Group 3
VMG4	Create Material Group 4
VMG5	Create Material Group 5

SAP Transaction Codes – Volume Two

VN01	Number Assignment for SD Documents
VN03	Number Assignment for Doc.Conditions
VN04	Number Assignment for Master Conds.
VN05	No.Assignment for Address List(SSup)
VN06	Create No.Interval-Sales Activities
VN07	Maintain number range for shipments
VN08	Number range for shipment costs
VN09	Number range for proc. shipment cost
VN10	Number range maintenance: SD_SCALE
VNE1	Output: Create Cond.Tbl-Ship.Notif.
VNE2	Output-Cond.Table-Change Ship.Notif.
VNE4	Access Sequences (Ship.Notification)
VNE5	View V_TNAPN Appl. E1
VNE6	Output Determ.Procedure-Ship.Notif.
VNE7	View V_TVLK_NLA (Ship.Notification)
VNE8	View V_TVLK_NGW (Rough GI)
VNE9	Conditions: V_T681F for B E1
VNEA	Output: Create Cond.Table - Rough GR
VNEB	Output-Cond.Table-Change Ship.Notif.
VNEC	Output Types (Rough Goods Receipt)
VNED	Access Sequences (Rough GR)
VNEE	View V_TNAPN Appl. M1
VNEF	Output Determin.Proced. - Rough GR
VNEG	Conditions: V_T681F for B M1
VNEH	View V_TNAPR Appl. E1
VNEI	View V_TNAPR Appl. M1
VNKP	Number Range Maintenance: RV_VEKP
VNOP	C SD-VN Maintain TVAK
VNPU	Partner Conversion
VN_TP02	Salutation
VN_TP04	Marital property regime
VN_TP05	Employee Group
VN_TP06	Rating
VN_TP07	Credit Rating Institute
VN_TP10	Loan to manager
VN_TP11	Employment Status
VN_TP12	German Banking Act Credit Info.
VN_TP13	Target Group
VN_TP18	Undesirable Customer
VOA0	Order Information Configuration
VOA01	User exit lists sales
VOA1	Inquiry Information Configuration
VOA2	Quotation Information Configuration
VOA3	Configuration of Sched.Agreemt Info
VOA4	Contract Information Configuration
VOA5	Product Proposal Info. Configuration
VOB3	Comparison: Bill. Docs and Stats
VOBO	Config.for Backorder Processing
VOC0	Contract List Configuration
VOC1	Customizing for List of Addresses
VOD5	Configuration Cust.Indeped.Reqs.Info
VOE1	Maintain EDPST
VOE2	SD EDI Customer/Vendor
VOE3	SD EDI Partner Functions

SAP Transaction Codes – Volume Two

VOE4	SD EDI Conversion
VOEX	Incompleteness: Billing Document
VOF0	Configuration of Billing Information
VOF01	User exit lists sales
VOF02	User exit lists sales
VOF1	Configuration: Collective Billing
VOF2	Configuration Invoice List Info
VOF3	Edit Work List for Invoice Lists
VOFA	Billing Doc: Document Type
VOFC	Billing: Document Types
VOFM	Configuration for Reqs, Formulae
VOFN	Call Up Transaction VOFM
VOFS	Billing: Document Types
VOGL	Deliveries (Gen. and From Coll.proc)
VOIM	Incompleteness: Purchase Order
VOK0	Conditions: Pricing in Customizing
VOK1	Account Determination: Customizing
VOK2	Output Determination
VOK3	Message Determination: Purchasing
VOK4	Output Determination: Inventory Mgmt
VOK8	Condition Exclusion Assign Procdr V
VOKF	Configuration Release of CustPrice
VOKR	Configuration of Credit Release
VOL0	Delivery Information Configuration
VOL01	User exit lists sales
VOL1	Configuration: Collective Dlv.Proc.
VOL6	Configure information on
VOL7	Settings for Packing
VOLI	Incompleteness: Delivery
VONC	Output Form for each Group
VOP2	Configuration: Partner
VOP2_OLD	Configuration: Partner
VOPA	Configuration: Partner
VOPAN	Customizing Partners
VOR1	Joint Master Data: Distr. Channel
VOR2	Joint Master Data: Division
VORA	Archiving Control for Sales Doc.
VORB	Group Reference Sales Document Types
VORD	Route definition (to R/3 vers. 3.1)
VORF	Route Definition (Up To Rel. 4.0B)
VORI	Archiving Control Shipment Costs
VORK	Archiving Control for Sales Activity
VORL	Archiving Control for Delivery
VORN	Central Archiving Control
VORP	Repairs procedure:Short texts trans.
VORR	Archiving Control for Billing Docs
VORS	Group Reference Procedures
VORT	Archiving Control for Shipments
VORV	Repair procedure
VOTX	Configuration: Texts
VOTXN	Maintain Text Customizing
VOV4	Table TVEPZ Assign Sched.Line Cat.
VOV5	Table TVEPZ Assign Sched.Line Cat.
VOV6	Maintain Schedule Line Categories

SAP Transaction Codes – Volume Two

VOV7	Maintain Item Categories
VOV8	Document Type Maintenance
VOVA	Default Values for Material
VOVB	Screen Sequence Group Maintenance
VOVC	Item Field Selec.Group Maintenance
VOVD	Header Field Selection Group
VOVF	Variant matching procedure
VOVG	Define Characteristic Overview
VOVL	Cancellation Rules
VOVM	Cancellation Procedures
VOVN	Assignment Rules/Cancellation Proc.
VOVO	Val.period.category
VOVP	Rule Table for Date Determination
VOVQ	Cancellation Reasons
VOVR	Default Values for Contract
VOVS	Define Status in Overview Screen
VOW1	User assignment GRUKO_WF
VOWE	Incompleteness: Goods Receipt
VOZP	Planng dlv. sched.instr./split rule
VP01	Maintain Print Parameters
VP01SHP	Print parameter maintenance shipping
VP01SHPV	Print parameter maintenance shipping
VP01TRA	Print parameter maintenance transp.
VP01TRAV	Print parameter maintenance transp.
VP01_AG	Print parameter maint. agency bus.
VP01_NA	Print Parameter Maint. Subs. Sett.
VP01_PAG	Maintain print parameters
VP01_PNA	Maintain print parameters
VP01_PTC	Maintain print parameters
VP01_SD	Maintain Print Parameters SD
VP01_TC	Print Parameter Maint. Trading Cntr
VP94	Load Import Code No. for Japan
VP94X	Load Import Code No. for Japan
VPAR	Archiving Preference Logs
VPBD	Requirement for Packing in Delivery
VPE1	Create sales representative
VPE2	Change sales representative
VPE3	Display sales representative
VPM4	Merge: Japan - Import Code Number
VPN1	Number Range for Contact Person
VPNR	View of the active PNR in 1A
VPRE	PRICAT manual creation
VPRICAT	Maintain and Create Price Catalog
VPS2	Maintain Partn.Det.Proc.f.eachActTyp
VPSK	DisplPartnDetProc.f.each Activ.Type
VPVA	Dunning Proposal Insurance
VPVB	Dunning Activities
VPVC	Activities End Dunning Procedure
VPVE	Individual Dunning Notice
VPW1	Portal Workset Administration
VPWL	Portal Target Administration
VRAA	Maintain Coinsurer Specifications
VRAB	Transactions Postings Coins. Shares
VRCN	Posting Coinsurance Shares

651

VRCNHIST	Coinsurance History
VRLI	FT: Reorg. T609S Delivery
VRRE	Returns Delivery for RMA Order
VRWE	FT: Reorg. T609S Goods Receipt
VS00	SD Main Menu for Customer
VS01	Create Scale
VS02	Change Scale
VS03	Display Scale
VS04	Create Scale with Reference
VS05	List Scales
VS06	List Scales for Shipment Costs
VS36	Create Customer Conditions
VS37	Change Customer Conditions
VS38	Display Customer Conditions
VS39	Create Customer Conditions
VS40	Change Customer Conditions
VS41	Display Customer Conditions
VS42	Create Service Conditions
VS43	Change Service Conditions
VS44	Display Service Conditions
VS45	Create Conditions
VS46	Change Conditions
VS47	Display Conditions
VS48	Create Conditions
VS49	Change Conditions
VS50	Display Conditions
VSAN	Number Range Maintenance: RV_SAMMG
VSB1	SB Proc. Inbound Monitor - Old
VSB1N	Self-Billing Proc. Inbound Monitor
VSBA	Archiving for Self-Billing
VSBSMS	SBWAP Reporting
VSC01	Define Specifications for Reversal
VSC02	Define Specs for Scheduling Charges
VSC03	Define Specs for Payt Plan Change
VSC04	Define Specifications for Reversal
VSC05	Tax Specifications
VSC06	Early revenue posting
VSC07	HVORG/TVORG
VSC08	Define Specifications for Reversal
VSC09	Payment Plans: Cash Mgmt Duration
VSC10	Transactions Early Ending
VSC11	Transactions Early Ending (Charge)
VSCAN	Configuration of Virus Scan Servers
VSCANGROUP	Configuration of Virus Scan Groups
VSCANPROFILE	Configuration of Virus Scan Profiles
VSCANTEST	Test for Virus Scan Interface
VSCANTRACE	Memory Trace for Virus Scan Servers
VSIP	Contract Selection
VSK1	Condition Type: Services (Sales)
VSK2	Access: Maintain (Services Price)
VSK3	Cond. Determ. Procedure f. Services
VSK4	Valid Services Fields
VSK5	Create Conditions Table (Services)
VSK6	Change Conditions Table (Services)

SAP Transaction Codes – Volume Two

VSK7	Display Conditions Table (Services)
VSK8	SD Services: Exclusion
VSM0	Software Maintenance Process
VSM4	Assign rejection codes to SMP doc.
VSTK	Picking Confirmation
VT00	Transportation
VT01	Old: Create Shipment
VT01N	Create Shipment
VT02	Old: Change Shipment
VT02N	Change Shipment
VT02_MEM	Change Shipment (from Memory)
VT03	Old: Display Shipment
VT03N	Display Shipment
VT04	Transportation Worklist
VT05	Worklist Shipping: Logs
VT06	Select Shipments: Materials Planning
VT07	Collective run in background
VT09	Number Ranges for Log VT04
VT10	Select shipments: Start
VT11	Select Shipments: Materials Planning
VT12	Select Shipments: Transpt Processing
VT13	F4-Help Shipment Number
VT14	Select Shipments: Utilization
VT15	Select Shipments: Free Capacity
VT16	Select Shipments: Check In
VT17	Extended Help (F4) Shipment Number
VT18	Start F4 Help Shipping
VT19	Shipment Tendering Status Monitor
VT20	Overall Shipment Process Monitor
VT22	Display Change-Document Shipment
VT30	Initial internet tran for shipment
VT30N	Tendering Events for Carriers
VT31	Shipment tendering
VT31N	Selection Variants for Fwdg Agents
VT32	Shipment Status list
VT33	Ship.Planning for Carriers
VT34	Event Reports for Carriers via HTML
VT34M	Event Reports for Carriers via WML
VT60	Transfer Location Master Data to TPS
VT61	Ext. transport. planning deliveries
VT62	Send Deliveries to Forwarding Agent
VT63	Freight Plng Status from Deliveries
VT68	Deallocate delivery from TPS
VT69	Plan Deliveries from Freight Plng
VT70	Output for Shipments
VTAA	Order to order copying control
VTAF	Bill. doc. to order copying control
VTAR	Archive shipments
VTBT	Report for Definition of Batch Run
VTBW	Reorg.: Shipment Data in BW
VTCM	List of Continuous Moves
VTCU	Customizing Version types
VTCU_AKT	Customizing Version types
VTCU_SAKT	Customizing Version types

653

SAP Transaction Codes – Volume Two

VTDB	Assignment screen name - field name
VTDOCU	Tech. documentation transportation
VTFA	Order to bill copying control
VTFAKT	Bill Deliveries
VTFF	Bill to bill copying control
VTFG	Field groups material versions
VTFL	Delivery to bill copying control
VTLA	Order to delivery copying control
VTR1	XSI: Master Data: Service Codes
VTR2	XSI: Master Data: Routing Info
VTRC	XSI Cockpit
VTRC_VVTR0011	Delivery Tracking - Collective Reqst
VTRK	Tracking
VTRL	Reload shipments
VTRT	XSI: Carrier
VTWABU	Post goods issue
VTZB0AN_TRAN	Flow Types
VUA2	Maintain Doc.Type Incompletion Proc.
VUA3	Display Doc.Type Incompletion Proc.
VUA4	Assignm. Deliv. Type Incompl.Proced.
VUA5	Disp. Assignm.Del.Type to Incom.Proc
VUC2	Maintain Incompletion Log
VUE2	Maintain Sched.Line Incompletion Pr.
VUE3	Display Sched.Line Incompletion Proc
VULI	Unilife Incoming Payment
VUP2	Maintain Item Incompletion Procedure
VUP3	Display Item Incompletion Procedure
VUP4	Assignm. Deliv.Items to Incom.Proc.
VUP5	Display Assignm. Del.Items IncomProc
VUPA	Display Partner Incompletion Proc.
VV11	Create Output: Sales
VV12	Change output: Sales
VV13	Display Output: Sales
VV21	Create Output: Shipping
VV22	Change output: Shipping
VV23	Display Output: Shipping
VV31	Create Output : Billing
VV32	Change output: Billing
VV33	Display Output: Billing
VV51	Create Output for Sales Activity
VV52	Change Output: Sales Activity
VV53	Display Output: Sales Activity
VV61	Create Output: Handling Units
VV62	Change Output: Handling Unit
VV63	Display Output: Handling Unit
VV71	Create Output: Transportation
VV72	Change Output: Transportation
VV73	Display Output: Transportation
VVCB	Maintain Activity Authorization
VVG1	Create Output: Group
VVG2	Change output: Groups
VVG3	Display Output: Group
VVKK_CLEARING_CHECK	Activate Test: Money Laundering Law
VVO1	Manage Contracts With AcctBalIntCalc

VVOC	Create Ins. Obj. Int. Bal. Letter
VVOH	Bal. Int. Calc. History Ins. Obj.
VVOSUM	Summarization for Bal. Int. Calc.
VVOSUMA	Bal. Int. Calc.: Summarization
VVOZ	Balance Interest Calc. Ins. Object
VVOZACT	AcctBalIntCalcCurrChange: Activities
VVOZACTDEF	Currency Change: Define Activities
VVOZCURR	Permitted Currency Change
VVOZCURRSW	CurrChangeContractsAcctBalIntCalc.
VVSC	Scheduling
VVSCACT	Scheduling: Customizing Payt Opt Act
VVSCBEC	Scheduling: Customiz. Pmnt Opt Cond.
VVSCCACT	Scheduling: Customiz. Chng SchedItem
VVSCEACT	Scheduling: Customizing Payt Pl Act
VVSCERN	Scheduling: Customiz. Pmnt Plan Amt
VVSCHS1	SLV List for Payment Plan Change
VVSCHS2	List for Scheduling Item Change
VVSCIUB	Scheduling: Customiz. Payt Plan Over
VVSCNUM	Maintain Number Ranges Payment Plans
VVSCNUM1	Number Range Maintenance: VSC_ITEM
VVSCNUMITEM	Number Range Payment Plan Items
VVSCNUMPOS	Number Range Payment Plan Items
VVSCPO	Scheduling: Payment Option
VVSCPOGRU	Scheduling: Debit Entry: Item Groupg
VVSCPOVER	Scheduling: Debit Entry: Item Summrz
VVSCPOVEROPK	Schedulimg: Debit Entry: Summ. OI
VVSCPP	Scheduling: Payment Plan
VVSCSORT	Scheduling: ULIFE: Item Sort
VVSCSTOR1	Business Case Reversal
VVSCSTOR2	Payment Plan Reversal
VVSCSTOR3	Payment Plan Item Reversal
VVSCSTOR4	Business Case Reversal
VVSCSTOR5	Business Case Reversal
VVSCSTOR6	Business Case Reversal
VVSCSTORNO	Payment Plan Reversal
VVSCULIVECFC	Cust.-Init. Payment Clarification
VVSCVBE	Scheduling: Customiz. End Pmnt Plan
VVSCVERULI	Universal Life Clearing Control
VVSCZAE	Scheduling: Customiz. Pmnt Plan Amt
VVSCZOP	Scheduling: Customizing Payment Opt
VVSCZOPZPL	Scheduling: Assgt PmntOpt<->PmntPlan
VVSCZPL	Scheduling: Customizing Payment Plan
VVSC_PP_FS	Payment Plans Field Status
VVVORG	Customize Transactions
VW01	SD Scenario 'Incoming Orders'
VW02	SD Scenario 'Freedom to Shop'
VW10	SD Scenario 'Order Status'
VX00	Export Control
VX01	Create license (old)
VX01N	Create license
VX01X	Create control record (new)
VX02	Change license (old)
VX02N	Change license
VX02X	Change control record (new)

VX03	Display license (old)
VX03N	Display license
VX03X	Display control record (new)
VX04N	Maintain license
VX05	Customers for License
VX06	Export Control Classes for License
VX07	Simulation: License Check
VX08	Simulation: Boycott List Check
VX09	Simulation: Embargo Check
VX0C	Foreign Trade: Customizing Menu
VX10	Countries of Destination for License
VX11	Create Financial Document
VX11N	Create financial document
VX11X	Create Financial Document
VX12	Change Financial Document
VX12N	Change Financial Document
VX12X	Change Financial Document
VX13	Display Financial Document
VX13N	Display financial document
VX13X	Display Financial Document
VX14N	Maintain financial documents
VX16	BAFA diskette: Selection
VX17	Create BAFA diskette
VX22	Change license data (old)
VX22N	Change License Data
VX23	Display license data (old)
VX23N	Display license data
VX24N	Maintain control data
VX30	Legal Control: Export Ctrl Class
VX49	Doc.Paym.Guarantee: Fin.Doc.Types
VX50	Doc.Paym.Guarantee: Fin.Doc.Types
VX51	Doc.Paym.Guarantee: Bank Function
VX52	Doc.Paym.Guarantee: Field Ctrl ID
VX53	Doc.Paym.Guarantee: Fin.Doc.Type ID
VX54	Doc.Paym.Guar.: Fld Ctrl-Bank Funct.
VX55	Doc.Paym.Guar.: Export/Import Docs
VX56	Doc. Payment Guarantee: Bank IDs
VX57	Doc.Paym.Guar.: Export Docs Def.
VX58	Doc.Paym.Guar.: Export Docs Assignm.
VX70	Sanctioned Party List: Legal Regul.
VX71	Sanctioned Party List:Departure Ctry
VX72	Sanctioned Party List:Scope of Check
VX73	Sanctioned Party List: Aliases
VX74	Sanctioned Party List: Exclus.Texts
VX75	Sanctioned Party List: List Types
VX76	Sanctioned Party List: References
VX77	Sanctioned Party List: Delimiter
VX78	Sanctioned Party L.: Normalization
VX79	Sanctioned Party List: Phon. Check
VX80	CAP: CAP products list number
VX81	CAP: CAP products group
VX83	CAP: Components Leading Good
VX84	CAP: CAP material components
VX85	CAP: CAP Bill of Material

VX86	Maintain Market Organizations
VX87	Maintain No. of Market Organization
VX94	Declarations to Authorities: Check
VX98	Displ.FT Data in Purch.Doc.-INTERNET
VX99	FT/Customs: General overview
VXA1	Docs Assigned to Financial Documents
VXA2	Existing Financial Documents
VXA3	Financial Documents: Blocked Docs
VXA4	Financial Documents: Simulation
VXA5	Document. Payments: Print Monitoring
VXA7	Documentary Payments: Simulation
VXBC	SLS: List of Blocked Customers
VXC1	Activation of Future Changes
VXCZ	INTRASTAT: Form - Czech Republic
VXDA	SLS: Audit Trail - Customer Master
VXDG	Export Control
VXDP	Declarations to the Authorities
VXDV	List of Expiring SLS Records
VXF1	Retransfer Posting Data
VXGK	Export Control
VXH1	Transfer to general ledger
VXHU	INTRASTAT: Form - Hungary
VXIE	Maintain Foreign Trade Data
VXJ0	Foreign Trade: MITI Decl. - Japan
VXJ1	MITI Declarations
VXJ2	Declaration of ImportBill.Docs Japan
VXJ3	Foreign Trade: Import Decl. Japan
VXKA	SLS: Audit Trail: Vendor Master
VXKD	Declarations to the Authorities
VXKP	Configuration: Maintain Tables T180*
VXL1	Legal Control: SLS - Scenario 1
VXL2	Legal Control: SLS - Scenario 2
VXL3	Legal Control: SLS - Scenario 3
VXL4	Legal Control: SLS - Scenario 4
VXL5	Legal Control: SLS - Scenario 5
VXL6	Legal Control: SLS: Sim.: Customer
VXL7	Legal Control: SLS: Search Terms
VXL8	Legal Control: SLS: Change History
VXL9	Legal Control: SLS: Sim.: Vendor
VXLA	Legal Control: SLS - Audit Trail
VXLB	Legal Control: SLS: Sim.: Address
VXLC	SLS: Vendor Check - Scenario 3
VXLD	Legal Control: SLS - List Display
VXLE	SLS: Scenario 5 - Vendor Master
VXLP	Legal Control: SLS: Keyword: Address
VXLU	Legal Control: SLS - Data Service
VXLX	Legal Control: SLS: Sim. Customer
VXLY	Legal Control: SLS: Sim. Deliv.
VXLZ	Sanctioned Party List Screen
VXME	Declarations to the Authorities
VXMO	Common Agricultural Policy
VXPL	INTRASTAT: Form - Poland
VXPR	Export Control
VXS1	Legal Control: SLS: Create Entry

VXS2	Ges. Kontrolle: SLS: Change Entry
VXS3	Legal Control: SLS: Display Entry
VXSE	Declarations to the Authorities
VXSIM	Simulate Import
VXSK	INTRASTAT: Form - Slovakia
VXSL	Foreign Trade: Area Menu SLS
VXSW	Mass change material commodity code
VY01	Maintain account function modules
VY04	Start Excel with test data
VY05	List documents
VY08	String search in source code
VY13	DME processing
VY21	List RFC errors
VY22	Maintain account function modules
VY23	Maintain account function modules
VY40	Delete contract data
VY41	Delete dunning history w/VVKKMHIST
VY6A	Clearing Customiz.: Deadline variant
VY6B	Clearing Customizing: Ordinality
VY6C	Clearing Customizing: Sort. variants
VY6D	Clearing Customiz: Min amt variants
VY6E	Clearing Customizing: Variants
VY6F	Clearing Customizing: Item cats
VY6G	Clearing Customiz: DocType->ItmCat
VY6H	Acct Det. Reconc. Acct
VY6I	Revenue acct: acct determination
VY6J	Adv. pyt post reasons: acct determ.
VY6K	Acct Det. Reconc. Acct
VY6M	Acct det: Automatic clearing
VY6N	Cust. posting area V100
VY6O	Cust. posting area 1110
VY6P	Cust. Bank Clrg / Clarif. Acct - DME
VY6Q	Acct Determination: Coll. Invoices
VY6S	Transactions For Simulated Items
VY6T	Assign Transactions To Interest Keys
VY6U	Parameters for Currency Change
VY6V	G/L Accounts for Currency Change
VY6W	Parameters for Transfer Postings
VY6X	Closing Parameters
VY6Y	Customizing Acct Default Vals
VY7C	Customizing: Dunning amt limits
VY7D	Customizing: Dunning charges
VY7F	Customizing: Dunning grouping
VY7G	Dunning proc. det. posting area:V201
VY7H	Det DP Post Area V200 (old in V2.2)
VY7I	Det. Posting Area Dep Acct Interest
VY7J	Det. Dunning Proc. Postg Area V500
VY7K	Acct Det.: Revenue/Contract Acct
VY7L	CD Customizing Basic Settings
VY7M	Parameters for Open Account Clearing
VY7S	Customizing: Dunning block reasons
VY7T	Dunn. Determ. Posting Area: V202
VY8A	Account Determination
VYAAS	Doc. Type for Clearing Oldest Debt

SAP Transaction Codes – Volume Two

VYAC0	Bill Scheduling Archiving
VYAC1	Maintain General Scheduling Runtime
VYAC2	Archiving Business Case Reversal PP
VYAC21	Coinsurance Reporting Archiv.
VYAC22	Maintain General Coins. Runtime
VYAC23	Activate AS for Coinsurance
VYAC3	Durations Bus. Case Reversal PP
VYAC4	Activate AS for Bill Scheduling
VYAC5	Activate AS Bus. Case Reversal PPlan
VYAF	Invoicing History Archiving
VYAF0	Define General Invoicing Runtime
VYAF1	Define Runtime for Invoicing Types
VYAG0	Archiving Money Laundering Laws
VYAG1	Maintain Money Laundering Runtime
VYAITAG0	Archiving Agency Collections
VYAITAG1	Duration Agency Collections
VYAITAG2	AS Activate Agency Collections
VYAM0	Archiving of Broker Reports
VYAM1	Maintain Gen. Broker Report Runtime
VYAR	FS-CD: Posting Data Archiving
VYAS01	Display ISCD Broker Report Info Str.
VYAS21	Activate AS for Broker Report Arch.
VYAS31	Activate AS for invoicing history
VYAS41	Bal. Int. Calc. Hist. Archive
VYAS42	Maintain Gen. AcctBalIntCalcRuntime
VYAS43	Activate AS for Acct Bal. Int. Calc.
VYAUG	Clrg Restrictions for Transactions
VYAV0	Archiving Insurance Integration
VYAV2	AS Insurance Integration Active
VYBEZ	Item Is Regarded as Cleared, if:
VYBT	Field Status Setting for Doc Cat.
VYCA	Customizing: Cancel. Reason
VYCB	Customizing: Posting reasons
VYCC	Customizing: Document type
VYCD	Bank Acct Customizing
VYCE	Customizing Selection for Clearing
VYCF	Customizing: Invoice Types
VYCG	Customizing: TKKVABGRB
VYCH	Customizing: Notes to the Clerk
VYCM	Customizing: Doc Dunning Procedure
VYCO	Posting Specs for Coins. Shares
VYCOV004	Create Insurance Invoices
VYCOV008	Create Insurance Quotations
VYCOV018	Create Tax Office Certificates
VYCOV032	Create Balanced Contract Statements
VYCOV033	Create Ins. Balance Notifications
VYCQ	Customizing: Doc Type Deter.
VYCR	Customizing: Returns Reasons
VYCS	Customizing: Line Table TKKVSPAR
VYCU	Customizing for Sublines of Bus.
VYCV	Customizing: Summarization
VYCW	Customizing - Money Laundering Rptg
VYCX	Maintain Customer LR Enhancements
VYEV	Define External Transactions

SAP Transaction Codes – Volume Two

VYFS	Cust Structures for Post Data Transf
VYIE	Assign External Transactions
VYIV	Define Internal Transactions
VYKO	Open Item Accounting Carryforward
VYM10	Contract Dun. Status
VYM7	FI-CA Dunning History Archvg
VYM9	Define Dunning Archiving Runtime
VYSA	Reconcil. Progr. for Posting Run
VYSP	Parallelized Debit Entry
VYSPA	Insurance Debit Entry
VYT1	Note to Clerk from Clearing
VYTAX01	Doc. Evaluation for Ins. Tax. Reptg
VYTAX02	List Creation for Tax Report
VYTAX1	Insurance Tax Schedule Specs
VYTAX2	Transaction-Relevant Tax Code
VYTAX3	Main/Subtransaction for Payt on Acct
VYZ0	Customizing: Bank Clearing Accts
VYZ1	Customizing: Payment Frequency
VYZ10	Customizing POKEN -> Payt lock rsn
VYZ2	Customizing: Automatic Payments
VYZ3	Customizing: FMs for Due Dates
VYZ6	Customizing Act. Commission
VYZ9	Start Workflows for Clarif. Cases
VY_TT_1	Transaction for TKKV_T1
VY_V011	Cust. Receivables/Payables
VY_V021	Cust. Revenues/Expenses
VY_V050	Customizing Posting Area V050
VY_V131	Transaction-Relevant Tax Code
VY_V132	Activity Code/Distribution Type Arg.
VY_V133	Classification Determination (Taxes)
V_ATVO66	Assign Commodity ID
V_AUGL_AS	Clearing for Oldest Debt
V_BPID003_E	Identification Number Categories
V_BPUM_CTL	BP: Activate Parallel Maintenance
V_FMAC	Table maintenance for FMAC
V_FMITPOC1	View Maintenance V_FMITPOC1
V_FMITPOC2	View Maintenance V_FMITPOC2
V_FMITPOC3	View Maintenance V_FMITPOC3
V_FMITPOC4	View Maintenance V_FMITPOC4
V_FMPY	Table maintenance for FMPY
V_I7	Condit: Pricing SD - Index in Backgr
V_I8	Conditions: Pricing SD - Index
V_MACO	Manual Completion Sales Documents
V_NL	Edit net price list
V_R1	List of Backorders
V_R2	Display List of Backorders
V_RA	Backorder Processing: Selection List
V_SA	Collective Proc. Analysis (Deliv.)
V_TBC001	Business Partner: Grpng to Acct Grp
V_TBD001	Business Partner: Grpng to Acct Grp
V_TBPID	Characteristics of ID Numbers Cat.s
V_TD05_AT_FS	OeNB Target Groups
V_TP019	Values Table Group Category Fields
V_TP19	BP: Maintain Acquisn. Add.Data Types

SAP Transaction Codes – Volume Two

V_TP23	Maintain Diff. Type Criterion
V_TP23S	Control Diff. Type Criterion
V_TP24	Define Grouping Characteristic
V_TPR1	Assignment Categories
V_TPR2	BP: Assignment Category- Application
V_TPR4	BP: Assign modules to time periods
V_TPR5	BP: Role categories - application
V_TPR6	BP: Role categories - application
V_TPR9	BPR: Role for Grouping/Address Type
V_TPZ18	Category of Additional Data Fields
V_TPZ20	Set Information Category
V_TPZ6_N	Role Types
V_UC	Incomplete SD Documents
V_UC_7	Incomplete SD Documents
V_UKMCOMM_TYPES_PI	Credit Exposure Categories
V_V1	Updating Unconfirmed Sales Documents
V_V2	Updating Sales Documents by Material
W10E	SAP Retail: Goods Receipt
W10F	Store retailing
W10M	SAP Retail
W10T	SAP Retail main menu replcng S000
W3CUSX	Customizing Parameters for MiniApps
W3DEVMINI	Device Assignment for MiniApps
W3DEVTRAN	Device Assignment for Transactions
W3WEBAPP	MiniApp Maintenance
W3_SEARCH	Search in Internet Service Objects
W4E5	Maintain No. Ranges 5-Fig. Wt EANs
W4EM	Maintain No. Ranges for Weight EANs
W4EN	Maintain Number Ranges for EANs
W4EO	SAN Maintenance
W4EQ	Maintain EAN Prefixes
W4ES	Maintain Number Range Categories
WA/1	Create Mess. Cond. Tbl, Alloc Notif.
WA/2	Ch. Mess. Cond. Tbl, Alloc. Notif.
WA/3	Displ. Mess. Cond. Tbl, Alloc Notif.
WA/4	Maint. Access Seq. (Mess.) Alloc Tbl
WA/6	Maintain Mess. Schema, Alloc Tbl
WA/7	Assign Doc. Type/Schema, Alloc Tbl
WA/8	Ass. Mess. Type/Proc. Log, Alloc Tbl
WA/9	Requirements for Messages, Alloc Tbl
WA/A	Mess.Deter., Alloc Tbl: Creat.Cond.R
WA/B	Mess.Deter.,Alloc Tbl: Chng Cond.Rec
WA/C	Mess.Deter.Alloc Tbl: Displ Cond.Rec
WA/E	Ass. Mess.Type/Proc.Log Alloc Tbl Gr
WA00	Allocation Main Menu
WA01	Create Allocation Table
WA02	Change Allocation Table
WA03	Display Allocation Table
WA04	Alloc Tbl Processing: Plant Reply
WA05	Alloc Tbl FDG: Generate POs
WA06	Alloc Tbl FDG: Generate Deliveries
WA07	Alloc Tbl FDG: Generate Wrhse Orders
WA08	Generate Alloc. Table Follow-On Docs
WA09	Deletion of Allocation Tables

SAP Transaction Codes – Volume Two

WA09H	Allocation Table Emergency Deletion
WA10	Generation for PO and OAPAC
WA11	Message Bundling, Allocation Table
WA12	Create Reminders/Accept Plnd Qties
WA14	Reply, Plant
WA15A	Mess.Deter., Alloc Tbl: Creat.Cond.R
WA15B	Mess.Deter.,Alloc Tbl: Chng Cond.Rec
WA15C	Mess.Deter.Alloc Tbl: Displ Cond.Rec
WA21	Create Allocation Rule
WA22	Change Allocation Rule
WA23	Display Allocation Rule
WA30	Allocation Tables for Objects
WA31	Allocation Table List
WA35	Allocation Instruction
WA40	Adjust Alloc Tbl After Entering GR
WA50	Generate Allocation Rule
WA51	Reassign Gen. Alloc Rules/Plant
WA52	Alloc Rule Lists
WA53	Create Selection Variants
WA54	Generate Alloc Rule / Test RIS-L
WA56	Generate Allocation Rule (SAP BW)
WA60	Create Selection Variant for PO
WA61	Create Sel. Var. for Del. Generation
WAA01	WA Create (Auth-Apprvd Waste Genrtr)
WAA02	WA Change (Auth-Apprvd Waste Genrtr)
WAA03	WA Display (Auth-Apprvd Waste Gnrtr)
WAA04	WA Extend (Auth.-Appr. Waste Gener.)
WAA10	WA Create (Auth-Apprvd Waste Dispsr)
WAA11	WA Change (Auth-Apprvd Waste Dispsr)
WAA12	WA Display (AuthApprvd Waste Dispsr)
WAA13	WA Extend (Auth.-Appr. Wst Disposer)
WAA19	WA Create (AuthApprvd Waste Transp.)
WAA20	WA Change (AuthApprvd Waste Transp.)
WAA21	WA Display (AuthApprvd Waste Trnsp.)
WAA22	WA Extend (Auth.-Appr. Wst Transp.)
WAA23	WA Create (Authority)
WAA24	WA Change (Authority)
WAA25	WA Display (Authority)
WAA26	WA Extend (Authority)
WAAP	Number Range Maintenance: EWA_APPROV
WABCM1	Reconstruction of Credit Mgmt Data
WAB_CANCEL	Cancel Agency Documents
WAB_CLOSE	Complete Agency Documents
WAB_RELEASE	Release Agency Documents
WAB_REOPEN	Reopen Agency Documents
WACB01	Define Document Types
WACBA	Archive Posting Lists
WACBL	Restore Posting Lists
WACBLR	Delete Posting Lists from Archive
WACCIA	Archive Customer Settlements
WACCIR	Delete Archived Customer Settlements
WACLA	Archive Remuneration List
WACLF	Restore Vendor Billing Documents
WACLFA	Archive Vendor Billing Documents

WACLFR	Delete Billing Documents frm Archive
WACLR	Restore Remuneration Lists
WACLRR	Delete Remuner. Lists from Archive
WACM01	Define Doc. Types: Disp. Processing
WACM02	Define Doc. Cats for Follow-On Fctns
WACM03	Define Operation Types
WACM04	Define Follow-On Functions
WACM10	Material Type/Inventory Mgmt Active
WACM30	Parameters for Purchasing Management
WACO02	Waste Workbench
WACO02OLD	EHS: Edit Waste Code
WACO03OLD	EHS: Display Waste Code
WACO04OLD	EHS: Waste Code - Subs. Info. System
WACRL	Restore Settlement Request Lists
WACRLA	Archive Settlement Request Lists
WACRLR	Delete Settle. Req.Lists frm Archive
WACS1	Partner Type Customizing
WACS2	License Type Customizing
WACS3	Condition Type Customizing
WACS4	Proof Type Customizing
WACS6	Define Object Types for Integration
WACSIA	Activate Expense Settlements
WACSIR	Delete Archived Expense Settlements
WACZR	Restore Settlement Request
WACZRA	Archive Settlement Requests
WACZRR	Delete Settlem. Request from Archive
WADC	Number Range Maintenance: EWA_DISWAY
WADI	Number Range Maintenance: EWA_WAA130
WAE01	Create Entry Document
WAE02	Change Entry Document
WAE03	Display Entry Document
WAE10	Easy Entry
WAEA	Number Range Maintenance: EWA_ENTNAM
WAFS	Send Merchandise Category to AFS
WAGE	Number Range Maintenance: EWA_WAA100
WAHD1	Load Alternative Historical Data
WAHD2	Change Alternative Historical Data
WAHD3	Display Alternative Historical Data
WAHD4	Delete Alternative Historical Data
WAHDC	AHD/PDF Customizing
WAK0	Promotion management
WAK1	Create promotion
WAK10	Send reply f. promo. for each plant
WAK11	Display promotion for each plant
WAK12	Maintain promotion items
WAK13	Promotion Change Documents
WAK14	Report RWAKT310 (Promo for mat.)
WAK15	Report RWAKT320 (promos for plant)
WAK16	Price activation in background
WAK17	Batch Allocation Table Generation
WAK18	Batch Promotion Listing
WAK19	Batch Promotion Announcement
WAK2	Change promotion
WAK20	Batch Supply Source Determination

SAP Transaction Codes – Volume Two

WAK3	Display promotion
WAK4	Delete promotion
WAK5	Initial screen - Subseq. processing
WAK6	Initial scr.: overv. prices margins
WAK7	List promotion materials for plant
WAK8	Plant - materials in promotion
WAKC	Maintain promotion themes
WAKN	Output bundling promotions
WAKT_ARCHR	Read Promotion Archive
WAKT_SARA	Promotion archiving
WAKV	Promotion announcement preview
WAM01	Create Disposal Documents
WAM02	Edit Disposal Documents
WAM03	Display Disposal Documents
WAM04	Find Disposal Documents
WAM05	Disposal Documents List Display
WAMC	Number Range Maintenance: EWA_MNANOC
WAMI	Number Range Maintenance: EWA_MNINO
WAMR	Number Range Maintenance: EWA_MNANOR
WANP	Number Range Maintenance: W_PARTNER
WAO_QA32WP	QA32 -Call from Workplace/MiniApp
WAO_QM10WP	QM10 - Call from Workplace/MiniApp
WAO_QM13WP	QM13 - Call from Workplace/MiniApp
WAO_QPQA32	QM iView Selection Variant Insp.Lot
WAO_QPQM10	QM iView Selection Variant Notificat
WAO_QPQM13	QM iView Selection Variant Task
WAP1	Edit Appointments Worklist
WAP2	Change Appointments
WAP3	Display Appointments
WAP4	Appointments: Overview
WAP5	Appointment, Departure
WAP6	Change Appointment(Indiv. Maintnce)
WAP7	Appointments: Plnd/Actual Comparison
WAPRL	Settlement Request List - ApplStatus
WAPZR	Payment Docs for Application Status
WAR	Worklist for Manual Corrections
WAREP001	Update Report for Quantity Update
WAREPL	Material Replacement
WASM100	WA: Create Generator
WASM101	WA: Change Generator
WASM102	WA: Display Generator
WASM109	WA: Extend Generator
WASS100	WA Control: Applications
WASS101	WA Control: Field Groups
WASS102	WA Control: Views
WASS103	WA Control: Sections
WASS104	WA Control: Screens
WASS105	WA Control: Screen Sequences
WASS106	WA Control: Events
WASS107	WA Control: GUI Standard Functions
WASS108	WA Control: GUI Additional Functions
WASS110	WA Control: Matchcodes
WASS111	WA Control: Assgnmt Scrn Fld->DB Fld
WASS112	WA Control: Field Grouping Criteria

WASS113	WA Control: Role Categories
WASS114	WA Control: Role Category Groupings
WASS115	WA Control: Application Transactions
WASS116	WA Control: Tables
WASS117	WA Cust: Field Grouping - Activity
WASS118	WA Cust: Field Grouping - Role Cat.
WASS119	WA Cust: Authorization Types
WASS120	WA Cust: Field Groups for Authorizn
WASS121	WA Cust: Screen Configuration
WASS122	WA Control: Activities
WASS123	Field Control
WASS124	WA Control: Data Sets
WAST	Copied to CBWABDT (Copy BP Config
WATR	Number Range Maintenance: EWA_WAA160
WATREE	Call Master Data
WB/0	Assignment partner / mess. promotion
WB/1	Sub. cond.,cr. tab, promo announ.
WB/2	Sub.cond.,change tbl, promo ann.
WB/3	Sub. cond., disp. tab, promo ann.
WB/4	Maintain sequence (mes.) promotion
WB/5	Maintain message types,promotion
WB/6	Maintain Message Deter.Schema,Promo.
WB/7	Assignment promotion type / schema
WB/8	Ass. mess.type/pr.proc. promotions
WB/9	Message requirements, promotion
WB/A	Message deter. promo:create cond.rec
WB/B	Mess.deter.Promo: chng conditon rec
WB/C	Mess.deter.promo: display cond. rec.
WB/D	Maintain output types promotion grp
WB/E	Assmnt mess.type/progr.group promo.
WB00	Subsequent settlement
WB01	Create plant
WB02	Change plant
WB03	Display plant
WB06	Archiving flag, plant
WB07	Change plant/customer assignment
WB08	Change plant/vendor assignment
WB20	Global Trade
WB21	Trading contract: Create
WB22	Trading contract: Change
WB23	Trading contract: Display
WB24	Trading contract: Coll. status proc.
WB25	Trad. contract list: Contracts lists
WB25_COMP	Trad. Contract List: Contracts Lists
WB26	Trading Contract: Document Flow
WB27	Trading contract: Standard analysis
WB28	Trading contract: Change history
WB29_OPEN	Trading Contract: Open Control
WB29_PROFIT	Trading Contract: Profit Simulation
WB2B_CUS	Customizing Global Trade
WB2B_MOD	Customizing Global Trade
WB2B_NETUSER	Create User For TradingContract@Net
WB2C	Messages - Target Group: Customer
WB2GTS1	Export: Blocked Trading Contracts

SAP Transaction Codes – Volume Two

WB2GTS2	Import: Blocked Trading Contracts
WB2GTS3	Incorrectly Transferred Documents
WB2GTS4	Transfer Documents Again
WB2L	Long Short Analysis
WB2M	Messages for Management
WB2R	Global Trade General Control
WB2SEL_AB	Agency Document Selection (seltool)
WB2SEL_AB_LST	Agency List Selection (seltool)
WB2SEL_AC	Accounting Document Selection
WB2SEL_IV	Inbound Invoice Selection
WB2SEL_MD	Material Doc. Selection (seltool)
WB2SEL_OD	Delivery Selection (for seltool)
WB2SEL_PO	Purchasing Document Selection
WB2SEL_SI	Customer Billing Document Selection
WB2SEL_SI_LST	Customer Billing Doc. List Selection
WB2SEL_SO	Sales Order Selection (for seltool)
WB2SEL_TC	Tr. Contract Selection (for seltool)
WB2SEL_Z1	Selection for Add-On z1
WB2SEL_Z2	Selection for Add-On z2
WB2SEL_Z3	Selection for Add-On z3
WB2TEW_FULL	Dummy for ALV Variants (Fullscreen)
WB2TEW_HEAD	Dummy for ALV Variants Header
WB2TEW_ITEM	Dummy for ALV Variants Item
WB2V	Messages for Vendor
WB2_ARCHIVE_PREP	Archiving Preparation
WB30	Mass maintenance MG to plant
WB31	Trading Contract: Fincl Documents
WB35	Layout overview
WB40	List analysis for classes
WB50	Plant group, create alloc tbl
WB51	Plant group, change alloc tbl
WB52	Plant group, display alloc table
WB53	Plant group, delete alloc tbl
WB54	PG Maintain allocTbl, plant to class
WB55	PG AllocTbl, maintain class to class
WB56	PG AllTbl, maintain plants in class
WB57	PG AllocTbl display plants in class
WB58	PG Alloc tbl display class to class
WB59	PG AllocTbl display plants in class
WB5N	Stock in Transit (Consignment)
WB60	Plant group, create promotions
WB61	Plant group, change promotions
WB62	Plant group, display promotions
WB63	Plant group, delete promotions
WB64	PG Promotion, maint. plants to class
WB65	PG Promotion, maint. class to class
WB66	PG Promotion, maint. plants to class
WB67	PG Promotion, maint. plants to class
WB68	PG Promotion, displ. class to class
WB69	PG Promotion, displ. plants in class
WB70	Create assortment class
WB71	Change assortment class
WB72	Display assortment class
WB73	Delete assortment class

WB74	Maintain assortments to classes
WB75	Maintain classes to classes
WB76	Maintain assortments in class
WB77	Display assortments to classes
WB78	Display Class for Classes
WB79	Display assortments in class
WB80	Create plant group Other
WB81	Change plant group Other
WB82	Display plant group Other
WB83	Delete plant group Other
WB84	PG Other, maint. plant to classes
WB85	PG Other, maint. class to classes
WB86	PG Other, maint. plant in class
WB87	PG Other, displ.plant to classes
WB88	PG Other, class to class
WB89	PG Other, displ. plants in class
WBB0	Assortment list applicatiom menu
WBBA	Assortment List: Analyze Dates
WBBR	Reorganize Assort. List Versions
WBBS	Display Assortment List Versions
WBBS_ALV	Display Assort. List Versions
WBBV_HPR	Assortment List: Version Management
WBBV_HPR_ALV	Assortment List: Version Management
WBDEMO	Workbench Demo: Template Interface
WBF1	IS-R: Stock Overview, Empties
WBF2	Display GI/GR Diff. for Stck Trans.
WBG1	Maintenance
WBGT_SLG2_INDEX	Delete Log Global Trade Management
WBL1	Create posting list manually
WBL2	Change posting list
WBL3	Display posting list
WBL4	Release blocked posting lists
WBLFDETSIM	VBD Determination Simulation
WBLMC	Mass Change to Posting Lists
WBLR	Create posting lists using report
WBLRB	Posting Lists for Remuner. List
WBLS	Posting List Cancellation
WBOLI	Condition Overview
WBST	SAP Retail: Inventory Management
WBSXPD	Progress Tracking:WBS
WBTE	Export plant data (file transfer)
WBTI	Import plants (file transfer)
WBUDG01	Activate Budget Type
WBUDG02	Transport Budget Type
WBUDG03	Reorganize Budget Type
WBVK	Subsequent settlement
WBWF	Trading Contract: Workflw Workbench
WB_NEW_WINDOW	Workbench: Open new window
WC01	Edit Characteristic
WC02	Number Range for SP Calculation
WC03	Number range, allocation rule
WC04	Number ranges, Promotions
WC05	Number ranges, allocation table
WC06	Number Ranges Status Tracking

SAP Transaction Codes – Volume Two

WC07	Number ranges for free goods
WC08	Number ranges layout promo/plant
WC10	Batch Worklist for Pricing
WC11	Batch Changes, Assortments
WC12	Batch Settlement for Arrangements
WC13	Batch List Output for Arrangements
WC14	Batch Vendor Bus. Volume for Arrngmt
WC15	Batch Detailed Stmnt for Arrangement
WC16	Batch Extension Val. Period/Arrngmnt
WC17	Batch Update Vendor Business Volume
WC18	Batch Check Open GR Qty for Arrngmnt
WC19	Batch Stat. Recomp. Vendor Bus. Vol.
WC20	Batch Stat. Recom. on Individ. Lev.
WC21	Batch Reorg Data in LIS
WC22	Batch List Rtl Changes for Material
WC23	Batch IV, Immediate Cyclic Check
WC24	Batch POS Outbound
WC25	Batch Assortment List/Shelf-Edge Lab
WC26	Batch Forecast
WC27	Batch Requirements Planning per Plnt
WC28	Batch Set Central Block
WC29	Batch, Alloc Tbl Message Bundling
WC30	Batch, Promotion Message Bundling
WC31	Batch Preparation of Adv. Tax Return
WC32	Batch POS Outb. Ini
WC33	Assortment List: Initial. & FullVers
WC34	Batch repeat terminated upload
WC35	Batch repeat incorrect upload
WC36	Number range for revaluation
WC37	Number ranges, group message
WC38	Number ranges, document flow
WC40	Number range markdown planning
WC41	Batch worklist for doc. index
WC50	Matchcodes for Assortments
WC60	Number ranges, layout
WC61	Number Ranges for Replenishment Run
WC62	Market-Basket Pr. Calc. Numbr Ranges
WC63	Number Range for SP Calculation
WC64	Catalog code number ranges
WCA1	Output control by customer
WCAA	WCM: Archiving: WCM_WAPI
WCAE	WCM: Archiving: WCM_WAP
WCAY	WCM: Archiving: WCM_WCD
WCBDELWORKLIST	Delete Billing Worklist
WCBDISPLOG	Display Log Subsequent Billing
WCBINDEX	Subsequent Billing
WCB_SLG2_CC	Delete Condition Contract Log
WCB_SLG2_INDEX	Delete Subsequent Billing Log
WCB_SPPFP	Selection/Processing of Actions
WCC	Technical SAP Customizing
WCC1	Maintain Conflict Rules
WCC2	Assistant for Model Selection
WCC3	Generate Basic Settings
WCC4	WCM: No. Range Maintenance: WCNWAP

WCC5	WCM: No. Range Maintenance: WCNWAPI
WCC6	WCM: No. Range Maintenance: WCNWCDOC
WCC7	WCM: No. Range Maintenance: WCNTGNR
WCC8	Assign Technical Objects
WCC9	Assign Operational Conditions
WCCA	Generate Print Settings
WCCB	Create/Delete Applications
WCCD	WCM: Change Mode-Dependent Tagging
WCCE	WCM: Display Mode-Dependent Tagging
WCCF	WCM: Number Range Maint.: WCNLINEUP
WCFA	WCM: WCA (Field Selection)
WCFE	WCM: WAP (Field Selection)
WCFI	WCM: Application (Field Selection)
WCFV	WCM: Lineup (Field Selection)
WCFY	WCM: WCD Header Data (Field Sel.)
WCFZ	WCM: WCD Items (Field Selection)
WCF_LTX	Transaction Launcher integration
WCHAIN1	Create Transportation Chain
WCHAIN2	Change Transportation Chain
WCHAIN3	Display Transportation Chain
WCI1	WCM: Check - WCCO
WCI2	WCM: Check - WCCOR
WCI3	WCM: Check - WCCO <-> WCCOR
WCI4	WCM: Check - WCCA
WCL1	WCM: WCD Template (List Editing)
WCL2	WCM: WCD Template (List Editing)
WCL3	WCM: Op. WCD (List Editing)
WCL4	WCM: Op. WCD (List Editing)
WCL5	WCM: WCA (List Editing)
WCL6	WCM: WCA (List Editing)
WCL7	WCM: WAPI (List Editing)
WCL8	WCM: WAPI (List Editing)
WCL9	WCM: WAP (List Editing)
WCLA	WCM: WAP (List Editing)
WCLB	WCM: (Multi-Level List Editing)
WCLC	WCM: WCD (List Editing)
WCLD	WCM: WCD (List Editing)
WCLE	WCM: (Multi-Level List Editing)
WCLF	WCM: Operational Log
WCLG	WCM: Change Operational Lists
WCLH	WCM: Display Operational Lists
WCLI	WCM: Lineup Template
WCLJ	WCM: Lineup Template
WCLK	WCM: Operational Lineup
WCLL	WCM: Operational Lineup
WCLM	WCM: Change Lineup
WCLN	WCM: Display Lineup
WCM	Work Clearance Management
WCM1	Define CM area of responsibility
WCM2	Display worksheet for CM
WCM3	Display CM area of responsibility
WCM4	Delete CM area of responsibility?
WCMA	RIS: OTB - Selection
WCMB	RIS: OTB - Selection

SAP Transaction Codes – Volume Two

WCMC	RIS: OTB - Selection
WCMCP	Category Manager Workbench - Example
WCMD	RIS: OTB - Selection
WCME	RIS: STRPS/Mvmts + Stock - Selection
WCMP_MASS	Mass Complaints Processing
WCMP_PROCESSING	Complaints Processing
WCMP_RESULT	Results Log Mass Complaints Proc.
WCM_ROP	Start SMP from MAP
WCM_TEST_2	Test program for KW document bridge
WCOC	Contract Monitoring
WCOCO	Process Condition Contract
WCOCOAGBU	Chargeback Overview
WCOCOALL	Condition Contracts
WCOCS	Contract Monitoring (Doc. Display)
WCOLI	Condition Overview
WCPC	Customizing Internet product catalog
WCR1	WCM: Create WCD Template for WCD
WCR2	WCM: Create WCD Template for WAPI
WCR3	WCM: Create Op. WCD for WAPI
WCR4	WCM: Create Op. WCD for WCD
WCR5	WCM: Create WCA for Order
WCR6	WCM: Create WCA for WAP
WCR7	WCM: Create WCA for WCD
WCR8	WCM: Create WAP for Order
WCR9	WCM: Create WAP for WAPI
WCRA	WCM: Create WAP for WAP
WCRB	WCM: Create WCD Template for WAP
WCRC	WCM: Create Op. WCD for WAP
WCRD	WCM: Create WCA for WAPI
WCRF	WCM: Create WAP for WCD
WCRG	WCM: Create Op. WCD for Order
WCRH	WCM: Create WCD Template with Order
WCRJ	WCM: Create WAPI for Order
WCRK	WCM: Create WAPI for WAP
WCRM	WCM: Create WAPI for WAPI
WCRN	WCM: Create Lineup Template
WCRO	WCM: Create Operational Plan
WCSO	SAP Retail Store: Consumer Order
WCSOC	Change Order
WCSOD	Deliver Sales Order
WCSOS	SAP Retail Store: Cons. Order Status
WCSO_ENTRY	SAP Retail Store Sales Order
WCT1	WCM: Create WCD Template
WCT2	WCM: Change WCD Template
WCT3	WCM: Display WCD Template
WCT6	WCM: Create Operational WCD
WCT7	WCM: Change Operational WCD
WCT8	WCM: Display Operational WCD
WCTA	WCM: Create WAP
WCTB	WCM: Change WAP
WCTC	WCM: Display WAP
WCTH	WCM: Create WAPI
WCTI	WCM: Change WAPI
WCTJ	WCM: Display WAPI

WCTK	WCM: Create WCA
WCTL	WCM: Change WCA
WCTM	WCM: Display WCA
WCTP	WCM: Assignment of WAP
WCTQ	WCM: Assignment of WCA
WCTR	WCM: Assignment of Operational WCD
WCTS	WCM: Assignment of WAPI
WCTU	WCM: Assignment of Order
WCU1	Maintain customer
WCU2	SAP Retail Store: Customer Mainten.
WCUM	Maintain customer
WCV1	WCM: Create Operational Plan
WCV2	WCM: Change Operational Plan
WCV3	WCM: Display Operational Plan
WCV4	WCM: Create Lineup Template
WCV5	WCM: Change Lineup Template
WCV6	WCM: Display Lineup Template
WCW1	WCM: 'DLFL' Status Conversion
WCWB01	Process Complaints for Agency Docs
WCWB02	Process Complaints
WCWB03	Complaints for Agency Documents
WCWB04	List Complaints Data
WCWBNR	Number Range Maintenance: W_CWB
WDBI	Assort. List: Full Vers. and Init.
WDBI_ALV	Assort. List: Full Vers. and Init.
WDBI_HPR	Full Version and Initial: HPR
WDBI_HPR_ALV	Full Version and Initial: HPR
WDBM	Assortment List: Manual Request
WDBM_ALV	Assort. List.: Manual Request
WDBM_HPR	Manual Request HPR
WDBM_HPR_ALV	Manual Request HPR
WDBR_HPR	Assortment List: Restart Package
WDBU	Assortment List: Change Message
WDBU_ALV	Assortment List: Change Message
WDBU_HPR	Change Version: HPR
WDBU_HPR_ALV	Change Version: HPR
WDFR	Create Perishables Planning
WDFR2	Change Perishables Planning
WDFR3	Display Perishables Planning
WDH1	Maintain plant hierarchy (SD)
WDH2	Display customer hierarchy (SD)
WDIS	Materials Planning for SAP Retail
WDKQ_ACTION_REG	WDKQ InfoSet POWL type action maint.
WDKQ_DEREGISTER	Deregister InfoSet Query @ POWL
WDKQ_MAIN	Maintain Reporting POWL
WDKQ_REGISTER	Register InfoSet Query @ POWL
WDKQ_SELCRIT	Maintain selection critieria
WDKR	Create customers from vendors
WDK_APPL_REG	WDK application registration
WDK_APPNAV	Define application navigation
WDK_APPNAV_CHECK	Check ext. appl. navigation custom.
WDK_EASY_SCRIPT	WDK easy script creation
WDK_T_SE91	Variant Transaction for SE91
WDLS	Delete Error Messages

SAP Transaction Codes – Volume Two

WDL_COPY	IDoc Copy Management
WDL_COPY_FILL	IDoc Copy Management Customizing
WDRD1	Determine Delivery Relationship
WDRD2	Change Delivery Relationship
WDRD3	Display Delivery Relationship
WDRD4	Delete Delivery Relationship
WDR_ACF_WLIST	Administration ACF Sicherheitsliste
WDR_REC_PLUGIN	Web Dynpro: Recording Plug-In
WDR_REC_PLUGIN_COND	Web Dynpro: Recording Plug-In Cond.
WDSR	Reorg of download status tracking
WDTS	Delete Status Information
WDYID	Display Web Dynpro Application
WD_TRACE_TOOL	Web Dynpro Trace Tool
WE02	Display IDoc
WE05	IDoc Lists
WE06	Active IDoc monitoring
WE07	IDoc statistics
WE08	Status File Interface
WE09	Search for IDocs by Content
WE10	Search for IDocs by Content
WE11	Delete IDocs
WE12	Test Modified Inbound File
WE14	Test Outbound Processing
WE15	Test Outbound Processing from MC
WE16	Test Inbound File
WE17	Test Status File
WE18	Generate Status File
WE19	Test tool
WE20	Partner Profiles
WE21	Port definition
WE23	Verification of IDoc processing
WE24	DefaultValuesForOutboundParameters
WE27	DefaultValues for Inbound Parameters
WE30	IDoc Type Development
WE31	Development IDoc Segment
WE32	Development IDoc View
WE34	Object for Display of XML IDocs
WE40	IDoc Administration
WE41	Process codes, outbound
WE42	Process codes, inbound
WE43	Funct.module: Status record display
WE44	Partner Types and Checks
WE45	Forward (inbound) (V3, EDILOGADR)
WE46	Error and Status Processing
WE47	Status Maintenance
WE50	System process codes: Texts
WE51	System process codes: Change texts
WE54	FMs for changing file names
WE55	Function Module for Path Names
WE56	IDoc Administration
WE57	Assignment Messages for Appl. Objs
WE58	Status process codes: Texts
WE59	Change status process codes
WE60	Documentation for IDoc types

SAP Transaction Codes – Volume Two

WE61	Documentation for IDoc record types
WE62	Documentation for segments
WE63	Documentation
WE64	Documentation message types
WE70	Conversion: Basic types
WE71	Conversion: Extensions
WE72	Conversion: IDoc types
WE73	Conversion: Logical messages
WE81	Logical message types
WE82	Assign Messages for IDoc Type
WE84	Assignment of IDoc and appl. fields
WE85	Create Rule Names
WE86	Assignment Segm.Type and Lang.Field
WE87	Load MDMP Information
WEADM	ALE Debugging Control
WEBU	Printing Labels via Assortment List
WEB_EVALS_CREATED	Created Evaluations
WEB_EVALS_RECEIVED	Received Evaluations
WEB_EVALS_TODOLIST	Evaluations to Be Edited
WEB_EVAL_CREATE	Create Evaluation
WEB_PRICAT	Pricat on web
WECO	System Process Codes
WECP	Status CPIC Interface
WECRYPTDISPLAY	Fields for Encrypted Display
WEDI	EDI Basis
WEINBQUEUE	IDoc Inbound Queue
WEKF	Purchase order SAP Retail
WEL0	Forward (inbound) (EDILOGADR)
WEL1	EDI: Interface Invoice for EDILOGADR
WELI	Maintain Status Groups
WENA	Messages on Basis of Changes
WENOLINKS	Deactivate Link
WEOUTQUEUE	IDoc Outbound Queue
WER_RULE_CONFIG	Rule Configuration Application
WER_RULE_PROC_TEST	Test program for processing rules
WESO	Special Request for Labels
WEST	Labeling: Control Data
WETI	IS-R Labeling
WEV1	Create planned retail markup
WEV2	Change planned retail markup
WEV3	Display planned retail markup
WEV5	Create pl.retail markup (price list)
WEV6	Change pl.retail markup (price list)
WEV7	Disp. pl. retail markup (price list)
WEWU	EMU conversions in retail
WF00	Workflow: Choose Processes
WF01	Workflow: Process
WF02	Workflow: Rule Editor
WF03	Workflow: Display Process
WF04	Workflow: Process in Background
WF05	Workflow: Queue
WF06	Workflow: Process Type Categories
WF07	Workflow: Link Roles
WF08	Workflow: Function Module Parameters

SAP Transaction Codes – Volume Two

WF09	Number range: Processes
WF10	Collective Purchase Order
WF10A	Collective PO Without Tabstrips
WF20	Change Distribution
WF30	Merchandise Distribution: Monitor
WF40	Delete Distribution
WF50	Adjust Distribution
WF50A	Adjust Distribution
WF51	Modify Distribution (in Background)
WF60	Create Outbound Deliveries
WF61	Create Outbound Deliveries (Bkgd)
WF70	Create Distribution Orders
WF80	Merchandise Distribution Log
WF80_DEL	Display Delivery Generation Logs
WF90	Delete Merch. Distrib. Applic. Log
WF90_DEL	Delete Delivery Generation Logs
WFCS01	Run Sales Forecast
WFCS02	Delete Sales Forecast
WFCS03	Display Data for Sales Forecast
WFCS04	Sales Forecast: Consumption from MRP
WFCSL01	Sales Forecast: Display Logs
WFCSL02	Delete Sales Forecast Logs
WFDHR_RANGE	Number range maintenance: HRWFD
WFIL	Store Order for SAP Retail
WFL1	Document flow, vendor billing docs
WFL2	Document flow, posting lists
WFL3	Document Flow, Remuneration Lists
WFL4	Document flow, settlement requests
WFL5	Document Flow, Request Lists
WFMCVSTART	WFMC: Call View and View Cluster
WFRE	Distribution of Returns
WFWS	Maintain WebFlow Services (WSDL)
WF_CNT_MAINTENANCE	Diagnosis + Comparison of Container
WF_CPL	WebFlow Service Task Linkages
WF_EXTSRV	Maintain WebFlow Services
WF_HANDCUST	Customizing for Service Handler
WF_NEW_MAN	Customizing for WS01200136
WF_START	Start Workflow
WF_START_EWT	Start Workflow (EWT)
WG21	Create material groups
WG22	Change material groups
WG23	Delete material groups
WG24	Display material groups
WG26	Create assignments
WG27	Change assignment
WG28	Delete Assignments
WG29	Display assignments
WGCL	Classification system, Retail
WGRC1	Vendor Assignment
WGRC2	Resources
WGRC3	Occupation Plan
WGRC4	Postprocessing Monitor
WGRC5	Inactive Vendors
WGRC6	Delete

SAP Transaction Codes – Volume Two

WGRT	Transport of classifiable objects
WGSE	Sending material group hierarchy
WGUS	Where-used list MG hierarchy
WI00	Physical Inventory for SAP Retail
WIND_CUS	IMG Document Index Update
WIZ_DEFINE	Define a Wizard
WIZ_DEFINE_SHOW	Define a Wizard - Display
WIZ_MODUL	Wizard Module
WIZ_MODUL_SHOW	Wizard Module - Display
WI_BCE_56183338	Wizard WIZARDS_DEFINITION
WI_EXECUTE	Execute Work Item
WI_EXECUTE_EWT	Execute Work Item (EWT)
WI_EXE_STARTER	Start Work Item Execution
WJB3	Test: Import Assortment List IDoc
WJB5	Display Assortment List
WK00	Subsequent settlement
WKA01	Change paym. block and paym. method
WKA02	Document flow of purchase orders
WKA03	Check Expiry Dates of Certificates
WKK1	Create Market-Basket Price Calc.
WKK2	Change Market-Basket Price Calc.
WKK3	Display Market-Basket Price Calc.
WKK4	MB Price Calc. Price Activation
WKON	Conditions/Arrangements SAP Retail
WKUN	Customer
WKX1	Execute Object Method (SWOOBJID)
WL00	Vendor Master
WLA1	Read Remuneration Lists from Archive
WLA2	Read posting lists from the archive
WLA3	Read settlm req. lists from archive
WLA4	Read settlement req. from archive
WLA5	Archived Remuneration List Items
WLA6	Archived payment document items
WLA7	Archived settlement req. list items
WLA8	Archived posting list items
WLACI	Read Customer Settlements From AS
WLACII	Read Customer Settlements From AS
WLAM	Layout Maintenance
WLAMN	Layout Maintenance
WLAN	Listing Conditions for Layout Module
WLASI	Read Expense Settlement From Archive
WLASII	Read Expense Settlement From Archive
WLAY	Space Management: Display Layout
WLB1	Investment Buying Reqrmnt Determntn
WLB13	Automatic Load Building
WLB2	Investment buying analysis
WLB3	Autom. opt. PO-based load building
WLB4	Results List for Load Building
WLB5	Manual Load Building
WLB6	Investment Buying Simulation
WLB7	Vendor Service Level Analysis
WLB8	Simulation for Quantity Optimizing
WLBA	Config. Check for Load Building
WLBA_CUS	Cstmzng Analysis for Load Building

WLBB	Vendor Service Level
WLBC	Reorganization of Condition Pointers
WLBC1	Number ranges for collective numbers
WLBC2	Number ranges for log
WLCH	Communicating Layout Changes
WLCM	Delete LayoutListConds. for Assort.
WLCN	Delete Listing Conditions from LM
WLCPAR	External Parallel Processing
WLCPARC	Settings f. Ext. Parallel Processing
WLF1	Create vendor billing document
WLF1D	Create Expenses Settlement
WLF1K	Create Customer Settlements
WLF1L	Create Vendor Settlements
WLF2	Change vendor billing document
WLF2D	Change Expenses Settlement
WLF2K	Change Customer Settlement
WLF2L	Change Vendor Settlement
WLF2V	Change Vendor Billing Document
WLF3	Display vendor billing document
WLF3D	Display Expenses Settlement
WLF3K	Display Customer Settlement
WLF3L	Display Vendor Settlement
WLF3V	Display Vendor Billing Document
WLF4	Cancel vendor billing document
WLF4D	Cancel Expense Settlement
WLF4K	Cancel Customer Settlement
WLF4L	Reverse Vendor Settlement
WLF4V	Cancel Vendor Billing Document
WLF5	Reopen Vendor Billing Documents
WLF5D	Reopen Expenses Settlement
WLF5V	Reopen Vendor Billing Document
WLFA	IMG Agency Business
WLFB	List header data billing document
WLFC	List billing documents
WLFCOL	Collective Document Creation
WLFCOLD	Collective Document Creation
WLFD	List Remuneration List Header Data
WLFE	Display Remuneration List Data
WLFF	Mass release payment documents
WLFG	Display payment header data
WLFH	Display payment documents with items
WLFI	Cancellation of payment documents
WLFJ	Mass reversal of vendor billing docs
WLFK	Mass release vendor billing docs
WLFL	Mass Release Remuneration List
WLFLK	Mass release remunertn list customer
WLFM	Create Remuner. List from Bill. Docs
WLFM30	Conditn Change f. Vendor Bill. Doc.
WLFM31	Condition Change f. Expense Docs
WLFM40	Payment Document Condition Change
WLFM60	Customer Settlement Condition Change
WLFMC	Mass Change to Vendor Billing Docs
WLFMCD	Mass Change to Expenses Settlement
WLFMCK	Mass Change to Customer Settlement

WLFN	Create Rem. Lists from Payment Docs
WLFO	List of payment list header data
WLFP	List of payment list data
WLFQ	List of posting list header data
WLFR	List of posting list data
WLFS	Read archived vendor billing docs
WLFT	Archived billing docs with items
WLFU	Document flow information
WLFV	Create RemunLists from Posting Lists
WLFW	Complete Settlement Request Lists
WLI1	List Output Single Documents
WLI2	List Output Agency Documents
WLI3	List Output List Documents
WLI4	List of Listing Documents for Items
WLM	Worklist Monitor
WLMCO_OM_OPA	Worklist Monitor for CO-OM
WLMCO_PC_OBJ	Worklist Monitor for COC
WLMCO_PC_OBJ_COSTOBJ	WL Monitor - Cost Objects
WLMCO_PC_OBJ_MTO	WL Monitor for Sales Order Item
WLMCO_PC_OBJ_PRODORD	WL Monitor - Mfg Orders & PCC
WLMF	Fixture Maintenance
WLMM	Layout Module Maintenance
WLMMN	Layout Module Maintenance
WLMON	Worklist Monitor - Direct Selection
WLMPS	Worklist Monitor for Project System
WLMV	Maintenance of Layout Module Version
WLMVC	Conversion of Layout Module Versions
WLMVN	Maintenance of Layout Module Version
WLN1	Messages from vendor billing docs
WLN10	Messages Customer Settlement
WLN11	Messages Expenses Settlement
WLN12	Mess. Remun. List Customer Settlmnt
WLN13	Message Remuneration List Cost Settl
WLN14	Message Output Agency Documents
WLN15	Message Output for List Documents
WLN2	Messages from posting lists
WLN3	Messages Remuner.Lists, Vend.BillDoc
WLN4	Messages from settlement requests
WLN5	Messages from settlem. request list
WLN6	Messages Rem. List Settlement Req.
WLOR	Reorganization of Layout Objects
WLP1	Profit simulation single requests
WLP2	Profit Simulation Request Lists
WLR1	Create Remuneration List
WLR2	Change Remuneration List
WLR3	Display Remuneration List
WLRA	Rel. payment docs for Remuner. lists
WLRB	Rel. Invoices for Remuneration Lists
WLRMC	Mass Change to Remuneration Lists
WLRS	Cancellation of Remuneration Lists
WLS1	Go to vendor billing docs archive
WLS2	Go to posting list archive
WLS3	Go to Remuneration List Archive
WLS4	Go to settlement request archive

WLS5	Go to settlem. request list archive
WLS6	Goto AS for Customer Settlement
WLS7	Goto AS for Expense Settlement
WLSE	Direct Sending: Layout Module
WLWB	Layout Workbench
WLWBN	Layout Workbench
WM00	Material
WMATGRP01	Create Article Hierarchy
WMATGRP02	Change Article Hierarchy
WMATGRP03	Display Article Hierarchy
WMATGRP04	Delete Article Hierarchy
WMATGRP05	Activate Article Hierarchy
WMATGRP06	Copy Article Hierarchy
WMATGRP07	Deactivate Article Hierarchy
WMATGRP08	Simulate Article Hierarchy Copy
WMATGRP10	Reorganize Article Hierarchy
WMATGRP11	Export Article Hierarchy
WMB1	Create Competitor Price Entry
WMB2	Change Competitor Price Entry
WMB3	Display Competitor Price Entry
WMB4	Create Competitor Price Entry w/ Ref
WMBE	Stock Overview: Value-only Material
WMF0	Season management menu
WMF1	Create Markdown Plan
WMF2	Change Markdown Plan
WMF3	Display Markdown Plan
WMF4	Delete Markdown Plan
WMF5	Price Activation Markdown Plan
WMF6	Markdown Plan Price Calculation Test
WMF7	Markdown Plan Evaluation
WMF_ARCHR	Markdown Plan - Read Archive
WMF_SARA	Markdown Plan Archiving
WMN1	Aggregation and Sorting Sequence
WMN2	Maintain usage (sort, summarization)
WMN5	Maintain, Assign User Groups
WMN9	Subsequent Settlement Control
WMNB	Create Worklist (Subseq. Settlement)
WMNE	Process Worklist
WMNM	Object Usages for Object Category
WMNO	Define Object Types
WMNV	Object Usages for Object Category
WMPA	Markdown Profile Assignment
WMPA_REORG	Reorganize Profile Assignments
WMR1	Create Markdown Rule
WMR2	Change Markdown Rule
WMR3	Display Markdown Rule
WMR4	Delete Markdown Rule
WMSBA	Material Where-Used List
WOB0	Store
WOB1	Plant profiles
WOC1	Screen layout Plant profile
WOC2	Screen struc. Pl.fnc
WOC3	Call view blocking reasons
WOC4	Call view Copy rule

WOC5	Call view Define copy rule
WOC6	Transact-dep. screen selection Plant
WOF0	Store
WOG2	Maintain groups
WOG3	Plant groups
WOL1	Call view layout
WOL2	Maintain Layout Module
WOL5	View sales area
WOL6	Maintain area shares
WOL7	Layout Module Maintenance
WOM_CALL_MB5T	Prepare the parameters to call MB5T
WON1	General Settings for Replenishment
WOO1	Layout Number Ranges for ALE Inbound
WOPD	Assortment List: Display Log
WOPS	Partner Schema Assignment, Vendor
WORKINGAREA	Administrtation using work areas
WORO1	Call Shelf Management Profile View
WOS1	Call view layout display
WOS2	Display Layout Modules
WOS5	View sales area display
WOS6	Display area shares
WOS7	Display Layout Modules
WOSCR01	Cash Balancing - Account Grouping
WOSCR02	Expense Invoice - Group of Accounts
WOSCR_CBL	SAP Retail Store: Cash Balancing
WOSCR_EXI	Create Expense Invoice
WOSCR_SLOGIN	Silent Login Retail Store
WOSZ_MAT_SHOW	Material Details View
WOSZ_PRINTER	SAP Retail Store Assign Printer
WOTB1	WB: OTB Procurement
WOTB2	OTB Monitor
WOTB3	OTB Transfer
WOTB4	OTB: Reorganize Budgets
WOTB6	OTB Procurement: Special Release
WP00	Sales and Operations Planning
WP3R	Follow-Up Processes for Portal Roles
WPC1	Prepare product catalog IDocs
WPC2	Prepare item IDocs
WPC3	Prepare catalog change IDocs
WPC4	Prepare item change IDocs
WPC5	Convert product catalog
WPCA	Carry out settlement run
WPCC	Prepare prod. catalog change IDocs
WPCD	Delete settlement logs
WPCI	Prepare product catalog IDocs
WPCJ	Prepare product catalog IDocs
WPCP	Settlement log - Payment cards
WPCTRA	WB: PO Controlling Acting
WPCTRD	Delete Completed Items
WPCTRQ	Handling of Remaining Quantities
WPCTRR	WB: PO Controlling Reacting
WPCW	Repeat settlement run
WPDC	SRS - PDC Processing
WPDTC	Planned Delivery Time Calculation

WPED	Sales Audit Editor
WPER	POS interface monitor
WPER2	POS: Analysis/Auxiliary Reports
WPHF	Analysis report
WPI	Workplace Implementation Guide
WPIA	Repeat upload POS IDOCs
WPIE	Inbound modified IDocs
WPLG	Space Management
WPLGN	Space Management
WPMA	POS Download: Manual Request
WPMI	POS download: initialization
WPMU	POS download: change message
WPO1	Close Back Orders
WPOHF1	WB: PO Manager
WPOHF2C	Create Order List Item
WPOHF2D	Display Order List Item
WPOHF2DS	Display Order List Item
WPOHF2X	Change Order List Item
WPOHF2XS	Change Order List Item
WPOHF3C	Create Grouped PO Document
WPOHF3D	Display Grouped PO Document
WPOHF3DS	Display Grouped PO Document
WPOHF3X	Change Grouped PO Document
WPOHF3XS	Change Grouped PO Document
WPOHF4C	Create Purchase Order
WPOHF4D	Display Purchase Order
WPOHF4DS	Display Purchase Order
WPOHF4X	Change Purchase Order
WPOHF4XS	Change Purchase Order
WPOHF7	Generation of STOs Seasonal Proc.
WPOHF8	Doc. Creation Seasonal Procurement
WPOHF9	Number Range Order List Item
WPOHFIMG	Call IMG Seasonal Procurement
WPOS	POS Interface SAP Retail
WPOS_MASTER	POS inbound master data
WPPERS_CALL	Edit User Settings
WPPERS_TEST	Test User Settings
WPRI	PRICAT on the Internet
WPRI6	Templ.for Non-R/3 Fields at CatItem
WPRI7	Templ. for Non-R/3 Fields at QtyItem
WPS1	Revision Planning
WPS2	Create Order as Report
WPSRL1	Realloc.: Maintain Conversion rules
WPSRL2	Realloc.: Display Conversion rules
WPST	Start Downloads
WPSTLH1	Task List Hierarchy: Create
WPSTLH2	Task List Hierarchy: Change
WPSTLH3	Task List Hierarchy:Display
WPUF	Simulation inb. proc. FI/CO document
WPUK	POS simulation
WPUS	Simulation: Inbound Processing
WPUW	Goods movements simulation
WP_N203	IS-H*MED: Report Start N203
WP_NA30N	Report Start NA30N

SAP Transaction Codes – Volume Two

WP_NA40	Report Start NA40
WP_NG09	Work Station: Display Ins.Providers
WP_NK01	Report Start NK01
WP_NK06	Report Start NK06
WP_NP03	Report Start NP03
WP_NP10	Report Start NP10
WP_NP61	Report Start NP61
WQ00	Value and Quota Scales Appl. Menu
WQ01	Create Value Scale
WQ02	Change Value Scale
WQ03	Display Value Scale
WQ04	Delete Value Scale
WQ05	Reconcile with Characteristic
WQ11	Create Quota Scale
WQ12	Change Quota Scale
WQ13	Display Quota Scale
WQ14	Delete quota scale
WQ15	Matching quota scl f. plant/mat. cl.
WQ21	Automatically Generate Quota Scales
WR30	Replenishment: Generate wghtng prof.
WR31	Replen: Create frcst wghtng profiles
WR60	Replenishment: Parameter Overview
WR94	Replenishment: Change planning
WR95	Replenishment: Create planning
WRA1	Delete Reclassification Version
WRA2	Display Reclassification Version
WRA3	Change Reclassification Version
WRA4	Create Reclassification Version
WRAV	Update Reclassification Version
WRBDL	Detailed Stock List
WRBDL2	Detailed Stock List
WRC1	Delete MG reclassification
WRC2	Display MG reclassification
WRC3	Change MG reclassification
WRC4	Create MG reclassification
WRCK	Store Replenishment: Check Program
WRCR	Retail Reclassification
WRCV	Update MG reclassification
WRC_MACROS	Recording of System Macros
WRC_USER_MACROS	Recording of User Macros
WRDL	Replenishment run reorganization
WREGION	Regions
WRFAPC01	Operational APC: Create
WRFAPC02	Operational APC: Change
WRFAPC03	Operational APC: Display
WRFAPC11	Release Planned Materials
WRFAPC12	Release Purchasing List Items
WRFAPC14	Delete Purchasing Lists
WRFAPC15	Materials in Purchasing Lists
WRFAPC16	Display Application Log
WRFAPC17	Display Put Away Quantity Distrib.
WRFAPC21	Article Hierarchy Level OAPC
WRFAPC22	Active Key Figures OAPC
WRFAPC23	Sequence of Characteristics (OAPC)

SAP Transaction Codes – Volume Two

WRFAPC24	Attribute Fields in Purchasing List
WRFAPC25	Hide Tab Pages (OAPC)
WRFAPC26	Quota Scales per Hier. Node/Char
WRFAPC30	OAPC - Synchronisation report
WRFCATEGORYSHOP	Shop/Category Assignment
WRFCHVAL	Edit Characteristic Values
WRFCHVALGRP	Maintain Characteristic Value Groups
WRFCHVALTYPE	Maintain Characteristic Type Data
WRFCLOSESHOPS	Lock and Close Shops
WRFDELIVERYSITESHOPS	Change Supply Relationsh. for Shops
WRFDEP01	Create New Department Store
WRFE	Store Replen.: Preprocessing Program
WRFFUART	Maintain Succ./Subst. Article Name
WRFFUCD	Change Documents WRF_FOLUP_TYP_A
WRFFUREORG	Reorganize Succ./Subst. Articles
WRFGHPARAM	Edit Hierarchy Parameters
WRFGHTREE	Edit Hierarchy Tree
WRFMASSMAT	Integrated Mass Change
WRFMATBODY	Edit Material Core Master Data
WRFMATCHARVAL	Char. Value Change to Variants
WRFMATCOPY	Copy Material
WRFMATMON	Material Monitor
WRFMGROUP	Maintenance Group Management
WRFREGIONSHOPS	Change Delivery Regions for Shops
WRFSHOP01	Create New Shop
WRFSHOPCAT	Create Shops with Initial Category
WRFSHOPDEP	Create Shops w/Initial Dept. Store
WRFT_AT620	Maintian Extens. Alloc. Table Types
WRF_AL	Material Lists
WRF_AL_REORG	Reorg. Program for Material List
WRF_ARC_DEPSHOP	Archive Department Store/Shop
WRF_DIS_MON	Seas. Proc. Discontinuation Monitor
WRF_DIS_SEL	Seas. Proc. Material Discontinuation
WRF_MATGRP_INIT_DLD	Article Hierarchy Initial Download
WRF_MATGRP_REQ_DLD	Article Hierarchy Direct Download
WRF_PBAS_CUST_MESS	Customizable Messages
WRF_PPW01	Price Planning Workbench
WRF_PPW02	Price Plan: Approve
WRF_PPW03	Price Plans: Create Conditions
WRF_PPW04	Price Plans: Activate
WRF_PPW09	Price Plans: Reorganize
WRF_PPW10	Budget: Assign Price Planner Group
WRF_PPW11	Budget: Update Values
WRF_PPW12	Budget: Price Planner to Planning Gr
WRF_PPW13	Budgets: Reorganize
WRF_PPW14	Edit Price Planner Group
WRF_PPW15	Correct Promotion Budgets
WRF_PPW16	Delete Price Plans Without Check
WRF_PPW17	Assign Processor to Layout Group
WRF_PPW18	Edit Layout User Group
WRF_PPW20	Worklist: Enhance
WRF_PPW29	Delete Markdown Proposals
WRF_PPWNO	Number Range: Price Planning Workb.
WRF_PPW_LAY	Layout Definitions for PPW

SAP Transaction Codes – Volume Two

WRF_PPW_SLG1	Application Log for Price Planning
WRF_PRGRP01	Creation of Price Level Groups
WRF_PRGRP02	Changing of Price Level Groups
WRF_PRGRP03	Display of Price Level Groups
WRF_PRGRP04	Change Documents Price Level Groups
WRF_PRGRP05	Assignment of Price Group to Mat.Grp
WRF_PRGRP06	Reorganization of Price Level Groups
WRF_PRICAT_LOG1	Log for Price Catalog
WRF_REF	Ref. for Materials Without History
WRF_REF01	Create Reference Assignment
WRF_REF02	Change Reference Assignment
WRF_REF03	Display Reference Assignment
WRF_REF06	Delete Reference Assignment
WRF_REF_AUTO	Automatic Assignment of References
WRF_REF_MOD_NR	Maintain No. Range for Ref. Modules
WRF_WSM4	Reorg. Assortment Deletion Tables
WRF_WSM5	Deletion of Listing Cond. for DC
WRF_WSOA1	Create Assortments
WRF_WSOA2	Change Assortments
WRF_WSOA3	Display Assortments
WRF_WSOA4	Delete Assortment
WRF_WTAD_CA	Additionals: Price Changes
WRF_WTAD_CA1	Additionals: Create Work Data
WRF_WTAD_CA2	Additionals: Process Work Data
WRF_WTAD_CA3	Additionals: Analysis of Prc Changes
WRF_WTR3	Request Additionals IDoc for Doc.
WRL1	Create payment list document
WRL2	Create payment list request
WRL3	Display payment list request
WRL4	Mass release of settlem. req. lists
WRLI	Issue Inbnd IDoc List StlmntRqstList
WRLK	Correct. Workbench for StlmntRqstLst
WRLMC	Mass Change to Remuneration Lists
WRLS	Cancel: Settlement Request List
WRLV	Parked Settlement Request List
WRLVN	Create Using Report (New)
WRMA_1	Revaluation Run RMA
WRMA_C1	RMA settings valid for the client
WRMA_DIAG_R3	Diagnosis Support On/Off
WRMA_M1	RMA: Maintenance of plant parameter
WRMA_M2	RMA: Maint. of value-only art. assgt
WRMD	Data Export for RRM Interface
WRMO	Replenishment monitor
WRN1	Number range maintenance: WFWFACTORS
WROUTE	Maintain Move Times
WRP0	Replenishment
WRP1	Replenishment: Procurement
WRPFMM	Replenishment: Forecast (MM-IM)
WRPFSOP	Replenishment: Forecast (Replen.-IM)
WRSO	Store Replen.: Follow-On Doc. Gener.
WRSR	Store Replen.: Requirem. Calculation
WRST	Transfer Master Data for Matl Maint.
WRSTA	Materials Listing
WS-1	Call: price band cat. maintenance

SAP Transaction Codes – Volume Two

WS-2	Price point groups	
WS00	Assortment	
WS01000045	Employment and Salary Verification	
WS01000060	Leave of Absence Request	
WS01000090	W-2 Reprint	
WS01000109	Cancel Leave Request	
WS01000109M	Dummy for Authorization for Canc. WF	
WS04200009	Leave Request	
WS04200009M	Approve Leave Request	
WS11	Send assortment modules	
WS12	Send listing conditions	
WS12400005	Cancel Leave Request	
WS12400005M	Dummy for Authorization for Canc. WF	
WS13	Send assortments	
WS20000081	Leave Request	
WS20000081M	Approve Leave Request	
WSAD	Space Management: No of Error Logs	
WSADMIN	Web Service Administration	
WSAF001	SAF Configuration Maintenance	
WSAF002	DSX File Maintenance	
WSAF003	Calender Effects Maintenance	
WSAF004	Promo. Cat. Maintenance for Predict.	
WSAFR01	Data Transfer R/3 - SAF	
WSAFR02	SAF Configuration Generation	
WSAK	SAP Retail Store: Promotions	
WSAM_ENTRY	SAP Retail Store AM Entry	
WSAO_CYCLE	Attachments of Ordering Cycles	
WSAO_LKPLC	Assignment of Planning Calendars	
WSAU	SAP Retail Store: Allocation Table	
WSC1	Customizing season codes	
WSC2	Customizing annual season	
WSC3	Customizing markdown types	
WSC4	Maintain data variants	
WSCLASS	Web Service Classification	
WSCLASS_MAP_FIELDS	fields maping for import classficat.	
WSCM	Category Manager Workbench - Example	
WSCONFIG	Release Web Services	
WSDOCU_SERVER	Maintain documentation server for ER	
WSD_CBP	Close-By Plants Application	
WSD_KEYWORD	Keyword maintenance	
WSD_KW_NRANGE	Number range maintenance: WSD_KW	
WSD_REFMAT	Definition reference materials	
WSE1	Group-Wide Discontinuation	
WSE2	Vendor/material discontinuation	
WSE3	Material Discontinuation (Dist. Ch.)	
WSE4	Material/Plant Discontinuation	
WSE5	Error log, discontinuation	
WSE6	Mat. Discontinuation for Assortment	
WSE8	Display discontinuation status	
WSGM	SAP Retail Store: Full Menu	
WSHOPMIGR	Migration: Store to Shop	
WSHT	SAP Retail Store: Time Recording	
WSICF_PREFIX	Path Prefix in ICF for WSDs	
WSIDPADMIN	Idempotent Service Administration	

SAP Transaction Codes – Volume Two

WSII_ENTRY	SAP Retail Store II: Entry
WSIN	Initialize Selection Variant
WSINTCHECK	Get/Check WS Configurations
WSIS	Information system
WSI_OCI_GUI	Example Program for OCI with GUI
WSI_OCI_ITS	Example Program for OCI with ITS
WSK1	Assortments IS-R, copy store astmts
WSK2	Delete store assortments IS-R
WSK3	Assortment copy, batch input
WSK4	Delete Batch Input Assortment
WSL0	Consistency check for reference mat.
WSL1	Assortments, selection lists
WSL10	Materials in Assortment
WSL11	WSL11
WSL2	Check listing rules
WSL3	Material listed in plant before?
WSL4	Analyze material in module
WSL5	Modules in plant
WSL6	Assortment structure, Plants
WSL7	Vendor material list
WSL8	Assortment grade info
WSL9	Listing conditions coming to an end
WSLA	Assortment Users per Assortment
WSLB	Assortment per Assortment User
WSLC	Display of causes of listing
WSLDEST	Maintain logical destination
WSLF	Material per customer
WSLG	Compare promotion POs - sales orders
WSLH	Assortment modules for material
WSLI	Display change doc. listing cond.
WSLOG_CONFIG	Log viewer for srt configuration
WSLOG_PUBLICATION	WS Publication Log Report
WSM3	Recompil. of Listing acc. Material
WSM4	Relist after ch. plant/ mat. grp mas
WSM4A	Relist After Changes to Assortments
WSM4B	Relist After Changes to Plants
WSM4L	Automatic Relisting of Layout Data
WSM6	Delete Individual Listing, Material
WSM7	Delete Individual Listing, Material
WSM8	Setup assrt.owner assortment as WRF6
WSM9	Delete Expired Listing Conditions
WSM9A	Delete Change Docs WLK1 and ASMODULE
WSMP	merchandise planning menu - first so
WSN1	Number range main.: WSORT
WSN2	Number range maintenance: WSORTIMENT
WSO1	IS-R Listing Create Module
WSO2	Assortments IS-R, maintain module
WSO3	Assortments IS-R, display module
WSO4	Assortments IS-R, delete module
WSO5	Astmts IS-R, maint. module-> store
WSO7	IS-R Astmts, Display module-> store
WSOA1	Create assortments
WSOA2	Change assortments
WSOA3	Display assortments

685

SAP Transaction Codes – Volume Two

WSOA4	Delete assortment
WSOA5	Assign assortment to customer
WSOA6	Assortment Maintenance Tool
WSOA7	Mass Maintenance of Table WRS6
WSOD	Create assortment class
WSOE	Assign material groups
WSOF	Change assortment class
WSOG	Display assortment class
WSOH	Assortment to class assignment
WSOI	Class to assortment assignment
WSOJ	Assortment class -> assortment class
WSOK	Display assortment for class
WSOL	Display class for assortment
WSOM	Display assort. class/assort. class
WSOSDISPLAY	Display Possible Sources of Supply
WSP3	Delete individual listing
WSP4	Create indiv. listing, mat. - plant
WSP5	Change ind. listing, mat. - plant
WSP6	Delete ind. listing, mat. - plant
WSP7	Mat. grp mat. listing in plant
WSPARAM	Enterprise Registry Parameters(New)
WSPK	Complete missing mat. segments log
WSPL	Missing material master segments
WSPO_ENTRY	SAP Retail Store PO Entry Point
WSPUBLISH	Publish Web services
WSR1	Archiving worklist for assortments
WSR2	Deletion assortment and listing
WSR3	Reset assortment and listing
WSR4	Archiving Assortments
WSRESTRICT	Restrctions for services publication
WSRS_PLANT_COSTC	Mainten. of Cost Centers for Plants
WSS1	General settings for Assortments
WSSPROFILE	Edit Web Services Security Profile
WSSS	Set Stock Situation
WSSW	SAP Retail Store: Display Plant
WSTA	SAP Retail Store: Orders
WSTASKCHECK	Get/Check WS Configurations
WSTA_R_PDC_DATA	MRP Data - Outbound
WSTA_R_PDC_STRUCT	Structural Data - Outbound
WSTE	SAP Retail Store: Goods Receipt
WSTED	SAP Retail Store: Display open GR
WSTE_NEW	SAP Retail Store: Goods Receipt
WSTE_R_PDC_CUSTOMIZ	Customizing Data - Download
WSTE_R_PDC_DOCUMENT	Reference Document - Download
WSTE_R_PDC_GR	SRS: Auto Posting GR from PDC
WSTI	SAP Retail Store: Physical Inventory
WSTI_DOC	Retail Store Inv.: Doc. Creation
WSTI_MON	Retail Store Inventory: PDC Monitor
WSTI_R_PDC_PI	PDC Transactions Reorg. in Phys. Inv
WSTI_R_PI_CALC	Calc. Book Inventory for Count Time
WSTI_R_PI_POS	POS Transactions PI Reorganization
WSTI_R_PI_SHOW	List of Calc. of Book Inventory
WSTL	SAP Retail Store Labeling
WSTN11	Maintain prepack allocation planning

SAP Transaction Codes – Volume Two

WSTN13	Display prepack allocation planning
WSTN14	Process prepack allocation manually
WSTN15	Delete Alloc. Table (PP Alloc Plan)
WSTP	Retail Store Sales Prices
WSTSA	SAP Retail Store: Assortment List
WSTU	SAP Retail Store: Revaluation
WSTV	SAP Retail Store: Goods Movements
WSTV_R_PDC_CUST	Business Transaction - Download
WSTV_R_PDC_DATA	Vendors and Stores - Download
WSTV_R_PDC_MATDATA	Article Data - Download
WSUBST_CONTAB	Edit Substitution Assignments
WSUBST_SWITCH_REORG	Reorganization of Switchover Info
WSUBST_WORKLIST	Edit Substitution Worklist
WSUP	Space Management Using Plan Data
WSUP1	No. of Duplicate Listing Conditions
WSUP2	WSOF Migration Tool
WSUPDATECHECK	Get/Check WS DT-RT Changes
WSV1	SD listing/exclusion per order type
WSV2	Create value contract module
WSVD_ENTRY	SRS Vendor Master: Entry
WSVD_SAPGUI	Maintenance Auth. for Local Vendors
WSVD_VNDR_WLIST	Worklist for Local Vendors
WTAD	Additionals
WTAD_ADDI_AL	Analysis of Procedure for Additional
WTAD_APPL_LOG	Application Log for Additionals
WTAD_ARCHR	Read Archived Additionals
WTAD_FMCU_CHANGE	Proc. for Add./Customer Maintenance
WTAD_FMCU_DISP	Display Proc. for Additionals/Cust.
WTAD_IDOC_AL	Analysis of Procedure for Additional
WTAD_SARA	Archive Additionals Documents
WTAD_SRS	Obsolete - do not use
WTAD_STWB	Obsolete - do not use
WTAD_SUP_FM_CHANGE	Maintain Proc. for Adds./Vendors
WTAD_SUP_FM_DISP	Display Proc. for Adds./Vendors
WTAD_VKHM_DISPLAY	Display Materials/Additionals
WTAD_VKHM_MAINTAIN	Mass Maintenance Materials/Adds.
WTAM	Additionals Monitor
WTAOC	Generate POs for Additionals
WTCA	Change Analysis for Additionals
WTEW	Trading Execution Workbench
WTEW_CATT	Trading Execution Workbench for CATT
WTMG	Conversion of Withholding Tax Data
WTNR	w/tax certificate number range
WTOG	define output group
WTR1	Request for Additionals IDoc
WTR2	Request Additionals IDoc for Promo
WTRA1	Maintain Runtime Customizing Table
WTRA2	Runtime Measurement: Delete Logs
WTRA3	Runtime Measurement: Display Logs
WTY	Warranty Claim
WTYAP	Action profile maintenance
WTYAUT	Authorization
WTYCL	Create Credit Memo Lists
WTYDBSHOW	Warranty Claim: Table Display

SAP Transaction Codes – Volume Two

WTYMP	Mass Change Warranty Claim
WTYMP_A	Mass Change Warranty Claim Admin.
WTYNK	Number Range Warranty Claim
WTYOQ	Worklist Warranty
WTYOR	Execute Report
WTYRCL	Maintain Recall
WTYRP	Warranty: Part to Be Returned
WTYSC_WWB	Warranty workbench
WTYSE	Search Claim
WTY_ARCHIV	Display Archived Warranty Claim
WTY_SARA	Archive Warranty Claim
WTY_UPROF	Assign User Profiles (Warranty)
WTY_VSR_ACTIVE	Activate Validation/Substitution
WUFWUF	Customizing Transformation Workbench
WUSL	Where-Used List
WUSLTABL	Table Display
WV31	Create PhysDocs (Unrstrctd-Use Stck)
WVA1	Create planned mark-up
WVA2	Change planned mark-up
WVA3	Display planned mark-up
WVA5	Create planned markup (price list)
WVA6	Change planned markup (price list)
WVA7	Display planned markup (price list)
WVAL	Send Value Scale
WVB0	Recompile doc. index (pricing docs)
WVEB	Valuation SAP Retail
WVER	Shipping for SAP Retail
WVFB	Inbound store order processing
WVFD	Process phys. inventory doc. further
WVFI	Simulation: Store Physical Inventory
WVKF	Sales Order (extended copy)
WVM0	Replenishment
WVM1	Execute customer replenishment
WVM2	Transfer stock/sales figures
WVM3	Display material data transferred
WVM4	Display PROACT data received
WVM6	Customer replen.: Parameter overview
WVM7	Assignment of PO Data to Vendor
WVN0	Generate pricing worklist
WVN1	Pricing worklist for material
WVN2	Pricing worklist for organization
WVTU	Sales Support for SAP Retail
WW10	IAC product catalog
WW20	IAC Online Store
WW30	SD part for IAC MM-SD link
WW31	IAC Product Catalog for EBP
WWCD	Product catalog:Display change docs.
WWFL	Agency Business:Workflow Workbench
WWG1	Main Material Group Hierarchy Menu
WWG2	Main Material Group Menu
WWM1	Create product catalog
WWM2	Change product catalog
WWM3	Display product catalog
WWM4	Copy product catalog

SAP Transaction Codes – Volume Two

WWM5	Delete product catalog
WWMI	Product catalog area menu
WWN1	Create cond.table Subs.Sett-SettlRun
WWN2	Chng Cond Table. Subs.Settl-SettlRun
WWN3	Displ.Cond.Table Subs.Settl.-SettRun
WWN4	Mssg Access Seq. Subs.Sett. SettlRun
WWN6	Message Schema (Sub.Settl. -SettRun)
WWN9	Mssg Procc.Progr. Subs.Settl.SettRun
WWNA	Subs.Settl. -SettRun: Create Cond.S.
WWNB	Subs. Settl.-Sett.Run: ChangeCond.S.
WWNC	Subs. Settl. SettRun: DisplayCond.S.
WWND	Output Partner Arrngmt - Setlmt Run
WWNZ	Subs.Settlem. SetRun - Allowed Field
WWP1	Online Planning in the Planning WB
WWP2	Settings for Planning Workbench
WWP3	Order Cancelation in Planning WB
WWR1	Create cond. tab. messages Agen.Bus.
WWR2	Change cond.tab. messages Agency Bus
WWR3	Display cond.tab. messages AgencyBus
WWR4	Message access sequence Agency Busi.
WWR5	Message types, Agency Business
WWR6	Message schema (Agency Business)
WWR9	Message proc. program Agency Busines
WWRA	Agen.Bus. messages: Create cond. s.
WWRB	Ag. Bus. messages: Change cond. sch.
WWRC	Ag. Bus. messages: Display cond. sch
WWRD	Output partner, Agency Business
WWRZ	Ag. Bus. messages - allowed fields
WWS1	Create CondTab. Subseq.Settlement
WWS2	Change CondTab. Subseq. Settlement
WWS3	Display CondTab Subseq. Settlement
WWS4	Mssg AccessSeq. Subseq. Settlement
WWS6	Message Schema (Subseq. Settlement)
WWS9	Message Proc. Progr.Subseq.Settlemnt
WWSA	Subseq.Settle.: Create Cond. Records
WWSB	Subseq.Settle.:Change Cond. Records
WWSC	Subseq.Settle.: Display Cond.Records
WWSD	Output Partners, Arrangements
WWSZ	Subseq. Settle. - Allowed Field
WWT1	Message Cond.Tab. Create Trading
WWT2	Message Cond.Tab. Change Trading
WWT3	Message Cond. Tab. Display Trading
WWT5	Trading Contract Message Types
WWTA	Messages Trading: Create CondRecord
WWTB	Messages Trading: Change CondRecords
WWTC	Messages Trading: Display CondRecs
WWVT	Merchandise Distribution
WWY1	Web Transaction Tutorial 1
WWY2	Web Transaction Tutorial 2
WWY3	Web Transaction Tutorial 3
WWY4	Web Transaction Tutorial 4
WWY5	Web Transaction Tutorial 5
WWY6	Web Transaction Tutorial 6
WWY7	Web Transaction Tutorial 7

SAP Transaction Codes – Volume Two

WWY8	Web Transaction Tutorial 8
WXP0	Retail Planning
WXP01	Retail Planning Current Settings
WXP02	Create/Change Manual Planning
WXP03	Display Manual Planning
WXP04	Create Retail Planning Layout (Lib)
WXP05	Change Retail Planning Layout (Lib)
WXP06	Display Retail Planning Layout (Lib)
WXP07	Maintain Planning Scenario
WXP08	Display Planning Scenario
WXP09	Maintain Links
WXP1	Create Time-Based Distribution Key
WXP10	Display Links
WXP11	Execute Link
WXP12	Change Planning Hierarchy
WXP13	Display Planning Hierarchy
WXP14	Maintain Planning Hierachy Version
WXP15	Display Planning Hierarchy Version
WXP16	Maintain Automatic Planning
WXP17	Display Automatic Planning
WXP18	Execute Automatic Planning
WXP19	PlHierarchy: TransData Auto Setup
WXP2	Enter Time-Based Distribution Key
WXP20	PlHierarchy: Master Data Auto Setup
WXP21	Copy Planning Hierarchy Version
WXP22	Maintain Links
WXP23	Display Links
WXP24	Display Links
WXP25	Maintain Assignment for Add. KeyFigs
WXP26	Display Assignment for Add. KeyFigs
WXP27	Maintain Key Figure Parameters
WXP28	Display Key Figure Parameters
WXP29	Maintain Menu Status/Title
WXP3	Disply Time-Based Distribution Key
WXP30	Display Menu Status/Title
WXP31	Maintain Menu Functions
WXP32	Display Menu Functions
WXP33	Maintain Assignment Periods/Seasons
WXP34	Display Assignment Periods/Seasons
WXP35	Maintain Texts for CharAttributes
WXP36	Display Texts for CharAttributes
WXP37	Delete Planning Hierarchy Versions
WXP38	Change PlStep for Programs/Transact.
WXP39	Maintain Manual Planning Variants
WXP4	Delete Time-Based Distribution Key
WXP40	Display Manual Planning Variants
WXP41	Maintain Formula Groups
WXP42	Display Formula Groups
WXP43	Maintain Assignment Layout/FormulGrp
WXP44	Display Assignment Layout/FormulaGrp
WXP45	Display PlStep for Program/Transact.
WXP46	Execute Program/Transaction
WXP47	Transport Time-Bsed Ditribution Key
WXP48	Transport Planning Layouts

WXP48_OLD	Layouts w/o manual planning variants
WXP49	Import Planning Layouts
WXP5	Retail Plng: Maintain Plan Versions
WXP51	Maintain Store Groups
WXP52	Display Store Groups
WXP53	Maintain Store Group Assignment
WXP54	Display Store Group Assignment
WXP55	Maintain Planned Materials
WXP56	Display Planned Materials
WXP57	Manual Planning With Workflow
WXP58	Cross-Scenario Settings
WXP6	Plan Version Maintenance: InitScreen
WXP60	Maintain Promotion Interfaces
WXP61	Display Promotion Interfaces
WXP62	Maintain Grouping Break-Downs
WXP63	Display Grouping Break-Downs
WXP64	Maintain Allocation Table Interfaces
WXP65	Display Allocation Table Interfaces
WXP66	Promotion Interface Logs
WXP67	Allocation Table Interface Logs
WXP68	Maintain User Settings for Network
WXP69	Assignment of Interfaces to Layouts
WXP7	Display Plan Version: Initial Screen
WXP70	Delete File Names
WXP74	Maintain Assortment Assignment
WXP75	Display Assortment Assignment
WXP8	Retail Plng: Display Plan Versions
WXPA	Create Retail Planning Layout
WXPB	Change Retail Planning Layout
WXPC	Display Retail Planning Layout
WXPD	Delete Retail Planning Layout
WXPE	InitScreen Gen Layout Maintenance
WXPF	Retail: Maintain Report Tree
WXPG	Retail: Report Selection
WXPH	Maintain Manual Planning Variants
WXPI	Maintain Formula Groups
WXPJ	Maintain Assig. of Layout to FormGrp
WXPN1	Plan Network Planning Scenario
WXPN2	Design Network Planning Scenario
WXP_IMG	IMG Merchandise & Assortment Plng
WYC1	Price Marking Agreement
WYL2	Generate vert. model master + addr.
WYN1	Create Message: Warranty
WYN2	Change Message: Warranty
WYN3	Display Message: Warranty
WYP1	Create Condition
WYP2	Change Condition
WYP3	Display Condition
WYRL	Vendor for returns
WZFT01	FT: Wizard - Declara. to Auth. (MM)
WZFT02	FT: Wizard - Declara. to Auth. (SD)
WZFT03	FT Wizard: Data Service - Upload
WZFT04	FT: Data Service Wizard - Distribute
WZR0	Vendor Billing

SAP Transaction Codes – Volume Two

WZR1	Create settlement request
WZR2	Change settlement request
WZR3	Display settlement request
WZR4	Cancel settlement request
WZR5	Reopen Payment Document
WZRI	Issue Inbnd IDoc List of Pymt Docs
WZRMC	Mass Change to Payment Documents
WZRN	Number Range Maintenance: W_LFAKTURA
W_FRM_CUST_MAT	Display Material Settings
W_FRM_CUST_PLANT	Display Plant Settings
W_PARA	Maintain Variants f. Paral. Process.
W_PRICAT_ART_BACKGR	Automatic Copy
W_PRICAT_ASSIGN_001	Assignment ILN Vendor Pur. Group
W_PRICAT_ASSIGN_002	Assignment ILN Mat.Gr. SAP Mat. Gr.
W_PRICAT_ASSIGN_003	Assignment SAP Mat. Gr. - Purch.Gr.
W_PRICAT_DELETE	Delete Inbound Price Catalogs
W_PRICAT_DELPOS	Delete PRICAT Items
W_PRICAT_MAINTAIN	Maintain Price Catalog
W_PRICAT_PRE1	Field Catalog
W_PRICAT_PRE2	Field Catalog - Material Group
W_PRICAT_PRE3	Field Catalog - Mat.Group/Vendor
W_PRICAT_PROFILE	Maintain PRICAT Dialog Profiles
W_PRICAT_SEL_CREATE	Maintain Price Catalog
W_PRICAT_TERMINATION	Scheduled Data Creation
W_RHPE_SKILLSPROFILE	Skills Database
W_RHPE_WWW_START	W_RHPE_WWW_DEMO
W_SLS_PROFILES_MAINT	SLS - Maintain Profiles
XAAM	Number range maintenance: FR_DRU_AM
XAEU	Number range maintenance: FT_DRU_EUR
XAKK	Maintain Number Range: RV_AKKRED
XATD	Number range maintenance: FT_DRU_T
XATR	Number range maintenance: FT_DRU_ATR
XAUS	Number range maintenance: RV_EXPORT
XD01	Create Customer (Centrally)
XD02	Change Customer (Centrally)
XD03	Display Customer (Centrally)
XD04	Customer Changes (Centrally)
XD05	Block customer (centrally)
XD06	Mark customer for deletion (centr.)
XD07	Change Customer Account Group
XD99	Customer master mass maintenance
XDN1	Maintain Number Ranges (Customer)
XEIP	Number range maintenance: EXPIMP
XK01	Create Vendor (Centrally)
XK02	Change vendor (centrally)
XK03	Display vendor (centrally)
XK04	Vendor Changes (Centrally)
XK05	Block Vendor (Centrally)
XK06	Mark vendor for deletion (centrally)
XK07	Change vendor account group
XK11	Create Condition
XK12	Change Condition
XK13	Display Condition
XK14	Create with cond. ref. (cond. list)

SAP Transaction Codes – Volume Two

XK15	Create Conditions (background job)
XK99	Mass maintenance, vendor master
XKN1	Display Number Ranges (Vendor)
XLOC	Check Report for Sch.Agmnt/Sales Odr
XLOR	Stock in Transit Display - Recipient
XLOS	Stock in Transit Display - Supplier
XMSPKSTATCNF	Configuration of Package Statistics
XMSPKSTATMON	Monitoring of Package Statistics
XMS_SARA	Parameter Transaction for TA SARA
XSLS	Maintain Number Ranges: RV_SANCPL
XSLT	XSLT tester
XSLT_TOOL	Start XSLT Tool
XXTH	Test

www.ingramcontent.com/pod-product-compliance
Lightning Source LLC
LaVergne TN
LVHW022258060326
832902LV00020B/3147